THE OXFORD HANDBOOK OF

EVOLUTION, BIOLOGY, AND SOCIETY

THE OXFORD HANDBOOK OF

EVOLUTION, BIOLOGY, AND SOCIETY

Edited by

ROSEMARY L. HOPCROFT

OXFORD

UNIVERSITY PRESS

OXFORD
UNIVERSITY PRESS

Oxford University Press is a department of the University of Oxford. It furthers
the University's objective of excellence in research, scholarship, and education
by publishing worldwide. Oxford is a registered trade mark of Oxford University
Press in the UK and certain other countries.

Published in the United States of America by Oxford University Press
198 Madison Avenue, New York, NY 10016, United States of America.

Library of Congress Cataloging-in-Publication Data
Names: Hopcroft, Rosemary L. (Rosemary Lynn), 1962– editor.
Title: The Oxford handbook of evolution, biology, and society /
[edited by] Rosemary L. Hopcroft.
Other titles: Evolution, biology, and society
Description: New York : Oxford University Press, [2018] |
Includes bibliographical references.
Identifiers: LCCN 2017030134 | ISBN 9780190299323 (hardcover)
Subjects: LCSH: Sociobiology—Handbooks, manuals, etc.
Classification: LCC HM628 .O94 2018 | DDC 304.5—dc23
LC record available at https://lccn.loc.gov/2017030134

1 3 5 7 9 8 6 4 2

Printed by Sheridan Books, Inc., United States of America

CONTENTS

PART V SOCIOCULTURAL EVOLUTION

PART VI CONCLUSION

About the Editor

Rosemary L. Hopcroft is Professor of Sociology at the University of North Carolina at Charlotte. She has published widely in the areas of evolutionary sociology and comparative and historical sociology in journals that include the *American Sociological Review, American Journal of Sociology, Social Forces, Evolution and Human Behavior,* and *Human Nature.* She is the author of *Evolution and Gender: Why It Matters for Contemporary Life* (Routledge, 2016).

ABOUT THE CONTRIBUTORS

Daniel E. Adkins is Assistant Professor of Sociology, Human Genetics, and Psychiatry at the University of Utah. His research, broadly quantitative and interdisciplinary, integrates social inequality perspectives on stress with genomic big data to map how social disadvantage becomes epigenetically encoded, influencing downstream gene expression, health, and behavior. He has published over 50 peer-reviewed articles in high-impact sociology, psychiatry, and genetics journals. In addition to pursuing his own eclectic research interests and teaching statistics, he serves as statistical consultant to the Utah Consortium for Families and Health Research.

Kevin M. Beaver is Judith Rich Harris Professor of Criminology and Criminal Justice at Florida State University and visiting Distinguished Research Professor in the Center for Social and Humanities Research at King Abdulaziz University. His research examines the causes of antisocial behavior.

Marion Blute is Professor Emeritus of Sociology at the University of Toronto. Her theoretical interests are in selection processes of all sorts, and her empirical interests are in the sociology of science/scholarship and genders. She is a member of the editorial advisory board of *Biological Theory*, of the editorial board of *Spontaneous Generations: A Journal for the History and Philosophy of Science*, and an associate of *Behavioral and Brain Sciences*. She is past Chair of the Evolution, Biology and Society section of the American Sociological Association and a past member of the nominations and of the Marjorie Grene and Werner Callebaut Prize Committees of the International Society for the History, Philosophy and Social Studies of Biology. Her monograph, *Darwinian Sociocultural Evolution: Solutions to Dilemmas in Cultural and Social Theory*, was published by Cambridge University Press in 2010.

Eric J. Connolly is Assistant Professor in the Department of Criminal Justice and Criminology at Sam Houston State University. His research interests include biosocial criminology, criminological theory, developmental/life course criminology, and victimology. His work focuses on examining the genetic and environmental contributions to individual differences in antisocial behavior at different stages of the life course.

Timothy Crippen is Professor of Sociology at the University of Mary Washington. He has specialized expertise in the evolution of various aspects of human social behavior and in sociological theory. He is co-author (with Joseph Lopreato) of *Crisis in Sociology: The Need for Darwin* (Routledge, 2001). His work has been published in *Social*

Forces, *Human Nature*, and *Sociological Perspectives*, among other academic journals, and he has contributed chapters to various edited scholarly volumes.

Kristen Damron is a graduate student in sociology at California State University, Long Beach. Her work focuses on the impact of stressful social conditions on health. She plans to pursue research on positive psychology in the near future.

Jeff Davis is Professor at California State University in the Departments of Sociology and Human Development. He has published in the areas of neurosociology, human behavioral ecology, and social inequality. His research focuses on the harmful effects of structural inequalities on neurobiological functioning and social behaviors.

Anna R. Docherty is Assistant Professor of Psychiatry at the University of Utah and the Virginia Commonwealth University. Her research integrates dimensional phenotypic assessment and genomic data to predict risk for severe psychopathology. She explores strategies for genetic subtyping and risk analysis, and also the influences of comorbid conditions on psychiatric trajectories.

Lee Ellis is a semi-retired former Professor of Sociology at Minot State University and Visiting Professor in Anthropology and Sociology at the University of Malaya. His main areas of research are sex differences in behavior, social stratification, criminality, and religion.

Martin Fieder is Associate Professor of Evolutionary Demography in the Department of Anthropology at the University of Vienna. He has studied evolutionary anthropology, behavioral biology, and informatics. His main research areas are human reproduction and social status, homogamy, evolution of religions, and behavioral genetics.

David D. Franks has focused on the subject of neurosociology during the past decade. His book, *Neurosociology: The Nexus Between Neuroscience and Social Psychology* (Springer, 2010), received an award from the Evolution, Biology and Society section of the American Sociological Association (ASA). His book, *Neurosociology: Fundamentals and Current Findings*, will be published in 2018 by Springer. In 1977, he came from the University of Denver to chair the Department of Sociology at Virginia Commonwealth University. He retired as Professor Emeritus in 1999. In 2015, he was awarded a Lifetime Achievement Award from the Sociology of Emotions Section of the ASA. He was also elected Chair of the Evolution, Biology and Society Section of the ASA in 2014–2015.

Douglas A. Granger, PhD, is a psychoneuroendocrinology researcher who is well known for his development of methods related to saliva collection and analysis and the theoretical and statistical integration of salivary measures into developmental research. He is Chancellor's Professor of Psychology, Public Health, and Pediatrics at the University of California, Irvine, and has created and leads The Institute for Interdisciplinary Salivary Bioscience Research. He holds adjunct appointments in the School of Nursing, Bloomberg School of Public Health, and School of Medicine at Johns Hopkins University.

Michael Hammond is a retired Professor of Sociology at the University of Toronto. He currently lives in San Francisco, California (michaelhammond@rogers.com). His most recent project is titled "Fool's Gold: Repetition Allowances and Contrast Effects in Modern Economies."

Peter K. Hatemi is Distinguished Professor of Political Science, Microbiology and Biochemistry at The Pennsylvania State University. His research focuses on explicating individual differences in preferences, decision-making, and social behaviors on a wide range of topics, including political behaviors and attitudes, addiction, violence and terrorism, public health, gender identification, religion, mate selection, and the nature of interpersonal relationships.

Susanne Huber is Senior Research Fellow in the Department of Anthropology at the University of Vienna. She has studied behavioral biology. Her current research interests involve evolutionary explanations of human behavior, effects of the early environment, and epigenetic mechanisms underlying early life factor effects.

Fiona M. Jordan is Professor of Anthropology at the University of Bristol, where she leads a research group on explaining cultural diversity. Her work uses comparative phylogenetic methods to answer questions about cultural evolution across human populations, with a particular focus on kinship, language, and the Austronesian-speaking societies of the Pacific. Her integrative research draws on a multidisciplinary background in anthropology, evolutionary biology, psychology, and language sciences.

Cody Jorgensen is Assistant Professor in the Department of Criminal Justice at Boise State University. He earned his PhD in criminology from the University of Texas at Dallas in 2014. His areas of interest include biosocial criminology, criminological theory, statistics, policing, and forensics.

Satoshi Kanazawa is an evolutionary psychologist and intelligence researcher; Reader in Management at the London School of Economics and Political Science; and Honorary Research Associate in the Department of Clinical, Educational and Health Psychology at University College London. He is Fellow of the Society of Experimental Social Psychology, and serves as Associate Editor of the American Psychological Association journal *Evolutionary Behavioral Sciences*. He has written over 120 peer-reviewed scientific articles and book chapters in all of the social sciences (psychology, sociology, political science, economics, and anthropology), as well as in biology, medicine, epidemiology, gerontology, demography, and criminology. His article "Why Liberals and Atheists Are More Intelligent," published in the March 2010 issue of *Social Psychology Quarterly*, was widely reported in the media throughout the world, with the combined viewership of 400 million people worldwide (estimated by Meltware News). He is the author of *The Intelligence Paradox: Why the Intelligent Choice Isn't Always the Smart One* (Wiley, 2012) and coauthor (with Alan S. Miller) of *Why Beautiful People Have More Daughters* (Penguin, 2007). His LSE home page is http://personal.lse.ac.uk/Kanazawa.

Olga Kornienko, PhD, is Assistant Professor of Applied Developmental Psychology at George Mason University. Her research focuses on understanding how peer networks promote and constrain psychological adaptation, development, and health across the lifespan, particularly during adolescence. She approaches her research from an inter-disciplinary perspective, drawing on theories and methods from developmental and social psychology, sociology, network science, and psychoneuroendocrinology. Her research has been funded by National Institutes of Health and been published in *Child Development, Developmental Psychology, Social Neuroscience, Hormones and Behavior, Social Networks*, and other outlets.

Norman P. Li, MBA, PhD is Lee Kong Chian Fellow and Associate Professor of Psychology at Singapore Management University, and Associate Editor at the journal *Personality and Social Psychology Bulletin*. He adopts a multidisciplinary approach to the study of human behavior, integrating economic concepts and tools, evolutionary theory, and social psychological experimental methodology. His research focuses on human mating as well as problems at the individual, organizational, and societal levels caused by the mismatch between people's evolved psychological mechanisms and modern environments.

Adam Lockyer is a Senior Lecturer in Security Studies at Macquarie University. He was also the 2015 Fulbright Scholar in US–Australian alliance studies. His research focuses on US foreign policy, political strategy, political attitudes, and evolutionary theory.

Richard Machalek is Professor Emeritus of Sociology at the University of Wyoming. He studies and writes about the evolution of social behavior among both humans and nonhuman species. He is especially interested in the distribution of basic forms of social organization and interaction across species lines.

Douglas A. Marshall is Associate Professor of Sociology and Director of Honors Education at the University of South Alabama. His research lies at the intersection of sociological theory, social psychology, and evolutionary biosociology, particularly as applied to the sociology of rationality and to the sociology of religion, in which section he was awarded the ASA outstanding paper award in 2011. His current projects include *The Moral Origins of God*, a book integrating his work on ritual, the sacred, and theogenesis into a comprehensive evolutionary theory of religion, and *Sociology Distilled: Science, Force, and Structure*, a supplemental text for introductory sociology courses.

Alexandra Maryanski is Professor of Sociology at the University of California, Riverside. She has authored or co-authored six books as well as coedited a large *Handbook on Evolution and Society* (Paradigm, 2015), in addition to authoring dozens of research articles. Her primary scholarly interests revolve around bringing data on pri-mates, biological methods and models, network analysis, and neurology to the social sciences. She was one of the founders of contemporary evolutionary sociology as well as an early proponent of neurosociology. Her latest book, *Emile Durkheim and the Birth of* *the Gods* (Routledge, forthcoming) brings the accumulated data on primates, methods from biology and network analysis, comparative neurology, and evolutionary theory to an assessment of Emile Durkheim's theory on the origin and operation of religion in societies, as outlined in Durkheim's essays after 1895 and in his monumental book in 1912, *The Elementary Forms of Religious Life*.

Allan Mazur, a sociologist and engineer, is Professor of Public Affairs in the Maxwell School of Syracuse University. He is author or co-author of 10 books and nearly 200 academic articles, many on biological aspects of social behavior. He also studies the sociology of science, technology, and environment. Mazur is a Fellow of the American Association for the Advancement of Science. His most recent book is *Technical Disputes Over Public Policy: From Fluoridation to Fracking and Climate Change* (Routledge, 2017).

Rose McDermott is David and Mariana Fisher University Professor of International Relations at Brown University and Fellow in the American Academy of Arts and Sciences. She received her PhD in political science from Stanford University and has taught at Cornell University, University of California, Santa Barbara, and Harvard University. She has held fellowships at the Radcliffe Institute for Advanced Study, the Olin Institute for Strategic Studies, and the Women and Public Policy Program, all at Harvard University. She has been a Fellow at the Stanford Center for Advanced Studies in the Behavioral Sciences twice. She is the author of four books, a co-editor of two additional volumes, and author of more than 200 academic articles across a wide variety of disciplines encompassing topics such as experimentation, emotion and decision-making, and the biological and genetic bases of political behavior.

Colter Mitchell is Research Assistant Professor of Family Demography at the Institute for Social Research and Faculty Associate at the Population Studies Center, University of Michigan. His broad research interests include exploring biosocial mechanisms and interactions for health and well-being across the life-course with a focus on integrating genetic, epigenetic, and social factors. He also investigates new methods for collecting and analyzing biological and social data.

Joseph L. Nedelec is Assistant Professor in the School of Criminal Justice at the University of Cincinnati. His primary research interests lie within biosocial criminology, evolutionary psychology, behavioral genetics, and cybercrime. He is co-founder and Vice President of the Biosocial Criminology Association (https://www.biosocial-crim.org).

François Nielsen received a BA in sociology from Université Libre de Bruxelles and a PhD from Stanford University. He has been on the faculty at McGill University and University of Chicago and is currently Professor of Sociology at the University of North Carolina at Chapel Hill. From 2007 to 2010, he was editor of the journal *Social Forces*. His research and teaching center on social stratification and mobility, behavior genetics, sociobiology, sociocultural evolution, quantitative methodology, and the work of Vilfredo Pareto. He has published articles in journals including *American Journal of*

Sociology, American Sociological Review, European Sociological Review, Social Forces, and *Sociological Theory.*

Kelli M. Rasmussen is a doctoral student in the Population Health Sciences program at the University of Utah School of Medicine. She recently received her MS in sociology with an emphasis in population health sciences from the University of Utah. She is currently Senior Research Analyst for the VERITAS program within the Division of Epidemiology at the University of Utah School of Medicine. Her current research interests include biodemography, oncology, health systems research, environmental exposures and health outcomes, aging, and bioinformatics.

Kristin Liv Rauch received her PhD in anthropology from the University of California, Davis, where she studied human behavioral ecology. She teaches evolutionary anthropology at the California State University, Sacramento. Her research takes a biocultural perspective on social institutions and human evolution, especially regarding mating and life history strategies in complex societies.

Anna Rotkirch is Research Professor and Director of the Population Research Institute at Väestöliitto, the Finnish Family Federation in Helsinki. She has pioneered evolutionary studies in family sociology in Europe and currently studies childbearing and family relations in contemporary societies. Her research interests include sibling relations, grandparenting, friendship, and the impact of "baby fever" on fertility behavior. Her book on evolutionary family sociology, *Yhdessä* (*Together*), was published in Swedish (S&S) and Finnish (WSOY) in 2014, and her latest co-edited book, *Grandfathers: Global Perspectives*, was published by Palgrave MacMillan in 2016.

Frank Salter is a graduate of Sydney and Griffith Universities, Australia. He researched political ethology with the Max Planck Society in Andechs, Germany, from 1991 to 2011 and has lectured on ethnicity, nationalism, and other social science subjects in the United States and several European countries. Much of his research on ethnicity has examined the social impacts of diversity and their causes (e.g., see his edited volume *Welfare, Ethnicity and Altruism: New Findings and Evolutionary Theory;* Cass, 2004). Together with geneticist Henry Harpending, he provided the first estimate of ethnic kinship, finding it to be higher than previously assumed. His book, *On Genetic Interests: Family, Ethnicity, and Humanity in an Age of Mass Migration* (Transaction, 2003), explored the politics and morality of ethnic solidarity from a neo-Darwinian perspective. Now based in Sydney, Australia, he consults on academic, political, and management issues.

Stephen K. Sanderson taught for 31 years at Indiana University of Pennsylvania and for 8 years was Visiting Professor at the University of California, Riverside. He specializes in comparative–historical sociology, sociological and anthropological theory, and evolution and human behavior. He is the author or editor of 14 books in 21 editions, and he has published several dozen articles in professional journals, edited collections, and handbooks. His most recent books are *Rethinking Sociological Theory: Introducing and*

Explaining a Scientific Theoretical Sociology (Paradigm, 2012) and *Human Nature and the Evolution of Society* (Westview, 2014).

Joseph A. Schwartz is Assistant Professor in the School of Criminology and Criminal Justice at the University of Nebraska Omaha. His research interests include behavior genetics, developmental/life course criminology, and additional factors involved in the etiology of criminal behavior. He is also a cofounder and the current Treasurer/Secretary of the Biosocial Criminology Association (https://www.biosocialcrim.org).

Jonathan H. Turner is Research Professor at the University of California, Santa Barbara, and University Professor of the University of California system, as well as Distinguished Professor of Sociology, Emeritus, University of California, Riverside. He is primarily a general sociological theorist but has interests in many substantive areas of inquiry, including evolutionary sociology, neurosociology, and religion. He is the author of 41 books and more than 200 articles in theory and additional substantive areas, such as the sociology of emotions, stratification, ethnicity, and interpersonal behavior.

Anthony Walsh received his PhD in criminology from Bowling Green University. He is currently Professor at Boise State University, where he teaches biocriminology, statistics, and law. He has field experiences in both law enforcement and corrections, and he has published 38 books and approximately 150 journal articles and book chapters.

Joseph M. Whitmeyer is Professor of Sociology at the University of North Carolina at Charlotte. He has published extensively on group process research, particularly on exchange and status processes. He has also co-written a book (with Saul Brenner) on the processes that occur in one empirically important small group, the US Supreme Court.

PART I

INTRODUCTION

CHAPTER 1

INTRODUCTION

Evolution, Biology, and Society

ROSEMARY L. HOPCROFT

WHAT is evolution, biology, and society? First, it is a catch-all phrase encompassing any scholarly work that utilizes evolutionary theory and/or biological or behavioral genetic methods in the study of the human social group. Second, it is the name of a section of the American Sociological Association, formed in 2005, that is home to scholars who do this kind of work within sociology. The primary purpose of this volume is to showcase this body of work for sociologists who may be interested in the field but who may know little about it. The book contains an overview of the different types of research currently being done by sociologists and other social scientists in the area, as well as the methodologies employed by them. The book examines a wide variety of issues of interest to most sociologists, including the origins of social solidarity; religious beliefs; sex differences; gender inequality; the determinants of human happiness; the nature of social stratification and inequality and its effects; identity, status, and other group processes; race, ethnicity and race discrimination; fertility and family processes; crime and deviance; and cultural and social change. As an introduction to the field, it would also be of use to teaching upper level or graduate students in sociology or a related social science.

The scholars whose work is presented in this volume come from a variety of disciplines in addition to sociology and include psychologists, political scientists, and criminologists. In many ways, sociologists are late to the table in the business of using theory and methods from biology, the reasons for which are discussed in some of the chapters in this volume. Yet as the essays in this volume demonstrate, the potential of theory and methods from biology for illuminating social phenomena is apparent, and sociologists stand to gain from learning more about them and using them in their own work. The theory is of course the theory of evolution by natural selection, the primary paradigm of the biological sciences, whereas the methods include the statistical analyses with which sociologists are familiar, as well as other methods with which they may not be familiar, such as behavioral genetic methods, methods for including genetic factors in statistical analyses, gene-wide association studies, candidate gene studies, and methods for testing levels of hormones and other biochemicals in blood and saliva and including these factors in analyses.

The book is organized as follows. The first part discusses the history of the use of method and theory from biology in the social sciences and its often unfortunate results. In Chapter 2, Richard Machalek describes the different ways that sociologists and evolutionary biologists answer the following questions: Why do societies exist? And How do individuals become social? He particularly notes that sociologists rarely consider the fitness consequences of any behavior, whereas evolutionary biologists always do so. Sociologists focus on the proximate explanations for social behavior (the mechanism by which something happens) rather than the ultimate explanations (why a predisposition for a social behavior likely evolved). He further notes that sociologists do not consider that individuals are predisposed to any behaviors other than a few in-born reflexes but, rather, assume individuals are capable of learning an infinite range of behaviors. Evolutionary biologists consider rather that humans, like all species, have a set of species-specific evolved predispositions that bias learning in certain ways. Machalek also discusses whether evolutionary biology is on the verge of consilience with sociology. He discusses signs of the incorporation of methods and theories from evolutionary biology into sociology, and he notes how both disciplines can benefit from this cross-fertilization.

In Chapter 3, Douglas A. Marshall notes how the initial founders of the discipline of sociology, including Durkheim, were accepting of a role for a human nature based on a universal biology in the new discipline of sociology. However, the use of impoverished versions of "evolutionary" theory to fuel ideological causes—Herbert Spencer's social Darwinism, the eugenics movement, and Hitler's (and others') subsequent adoption of these ideas—meant that the use of biology in sociology fell radically out of favor by the middle of the 20th century. Marshall notes that the distaste for any use of biology or biological theory within sociology continues to this day. Yet he argues that sociology will never be able to fully explain human social behavior and the social forces, institutions, and structures that shape it without understanding the evolved human organism with its biologically imposed capacities, limitations, and imperatives. He, as does Machalek, notes there are signs of a possible consilience between sociology and evolutionary biology.

With regard to the history of the use of biology in the social sciences, Stephen K. Sanderson's essay on Edward Westermarck is the story of the road not taken by sociology. Unlike his better known contemporaries Emile Durkheim and Herbert Spencer, Westermarck utilized the idea of an evolved human actor in his examination of sociological topics, including marriage and the family and human morality. Yet for political and other reasons, including popular support for the ideas of Herbert Spencer, the work of this great Finnish sociologist is today largely unknown outside of Finland. As a result, except for the Westermarck hypothesis—the hypothesis that individuals who spend their early years together as children do not tend to find each other sexually attractive as adults—Westermarck's contributions have largely been forgotten. Sanderson suggests that as new interest has emerged in evolutionary ideas and their application within the social sciences, Westermarck should be restored as one of the founding fathers of sociology.

Part II of this handbook examines work using evolutionary approaches to social psychology, the area of sociology that focuses on the individual and the small group. In Chapter 5, Jonathan H. Turner outlines his theory of how *Homo sapiens* evolved to become the most social of the great apes, a long-standing question in evolutionary biology. He notes that most apes are relatively solitary with the exception of mother–child pairs, and they are absent even a pair bond between males and females. He relies on cladistic analysis of primates to show that the last common ancestor of humans and apes was most likely a relatively solitary primate. So how did humans become social enough to create complex societies and cultures? Turner argues that in humans, unlike other apes, expansion of the emotion centers in the brain made possible greater in-group solidarity, increased group sizes, and greater intelligence, in turn making the development of large, complex, human societies possible.

In Chapter 6, Alexandra Maryanski and Jonathan H. Turner follow up from the previous chapter to give an evolutionary theory for the origin of religiosity and religious beliefs, which are universal across human societies. They suggest that early hominoids' expanded emotional capacity, increased intelligence, and capacity for language were the cognitive basis on which religiosity could build. Religion is of course an important buttress of social solidarity in populations worldwide. They note that this argument cannot explain why or how religion became institutionalized in the first human societies, and a full story of human religion and religiosity requires an examination of the development of religion within specific sociocultural systems. In Chapter 7, Michael Hammond details how evolved characteristics of the human brain are not only the basis of religion but also can account for the human liking for transient novelty and the human attraction to status distinctions. He suggests that the transient novelty that modern capitalist societies can generate may have a much deeper and lasting appeal than postmodern critics suggest.

As Turner and Maryanski note, the evolution of human cognitive abilities was a major factor differentiating humans from all other primate species. Although human brains are all more alike than they are different, in Chapter 8 David D. Franks reviews sex differences in the brain that are likely a result of the different biological roles of males and females in the process at the heart of biological evolution: reproduction. Franks notes that there are consistent average sex differences in the brain that likely have implications for the social behavior of men and women. Debate rages about how much of these sex differences in the brain are due to socialization and how much to biology—although Franks notes that both socialization and biology play a role.

Since Durkheim's landmark book, *Suicide*, sociologists have been interested in what helps account for differences in levels of human happiness and misery across and within human societies. In Chapter 9, Satoshi Kanazawa and Norman P. Li present the savanna theory of happiness. They theorize that if individuals have evolved psychological mechanisms that predispose them to certain preferences and behaviors, such as preferences for ethnically homogeneous settings, lower population densities, and social interactions with friends, circumstances in the contemporary world that help them meet those preferences and/or promote those behaviors are likely to make individuals happier. They further predict that more intelligent individuals, who are presumably better able to comprehend and deal with the evolutionary novel circumstances of modern societies, will be better able to deal with situations that do not correspond to those evolved preferences for ethnic homogeneity, low population density, and social interactions with friends and therefore will be made less unhappy by such situations compared to less intelligent people. They test their predictions using US data from the Add Health survey (in which the average age of respondents is 22 years) on the effects of the ethnic composition of environment, population density, and socializing with friends on individual life satisfaction. As predicted, the negative effects on happiness of ethnic heterogeneity, high population density, and less socializing with friends are weaker among more intelligent individuals than among less intelligent individuals.

The mechanisms by which small groups operate and the forces that keep them together and split them apart are studied by group processes researchers within sociology. In Chapter 10, Joseph M. Whitmeyer discusses how research in the areas of social exchange, identity, and status processes could benefit from incorporating insights about individuals from evolutionary theory. He notes that evolutionary psychological reasoning suggests that we likely have evolved predispositions that facilitate exchange processes in the small group and that help ensure that public goods are provided for the group because these things would have been beneficial for individuals and their genetic relatives in the evolutionary environment. In particular, Whitmeyer suggests we have evolved traits that promote reciprocal and general exchange in the small group, including emotional responses to being rewarded or punished, sensitivity to unfairness, and attention to reputation. He provides a list of predictions for research on exchange processes implied by this reasoning. He notes identity processes motivate behaviors that indicate to others that the person is a reliable exchange partner and are thus ways of facilitating exchange within the group. Given the advantages of exchange within the group for individuals over evolutionary time, he suggests we also have evolved predispositions regarding individual identity processes. Based on this reasoning he provides another list of predictions for research on identity processes. Last, he notes that we likely have predispositions regarding status processes and the awarding of status within the group. It is likely that we evolved the predisposition to grant status to individuals who solved nonrival public goods problems for our group because this helped ensure that those problems would be solved to our and our relatives' benefit. This reasoning implies another list of predictions for research on status processes, including the prediction that the conferral of status is always accompanied by performance expectations.

The third part of the handbook examines research on the interaction of genes (and other biochemicals such as hormones) and environmental contexts on a variety of outcomes of sociological interest, including political behavior, status attainment, and individual responses to social stress. This area of research is often referred to as "biosociology."

In introducing studies examining genetic influences on social behavior, in Chapter 11, Colter Mitchell gives an overview of the methods and measures used to find the genetic correlates of social behaviors in genome-wide association studies (GWAS) and some of the findings of these GWAS with regard to health behaviors and social, economic, and political behaviors. Genetic correlates have been found that predict smoking behavior, alcohol use and dependence, risk-taking, impulsivity, aggression, educational attainment, intelligence, and political preferences. He also describes the limitations of this research and its promise for the future. In Chapter 12, Rose McDermott and Peter K. Hatemi explode the myth that biosocial explanations are somehow deterministic, and they use case studies of a variety of very different individuals to show how the same genetic endowment can result in very different consequences for different people depending on their social context and other environmental factors.

In Chapter 13, Kevin M. Beaver et al. review the research examining the genetic and genomic foundations of aggression, violence, and antisocial behavior. Again, the evidence indicates that genetic propensities interact with the environment of the individual to promote or inhibit antisocial behavior. They note the finding that antisocial behavior has a genetic component is not a cause for pessimism because findings on the interaction between genes and environment may be used to help design better interventions due to the fact that they demonstrate which environments promote prosocial behavior among individuals with genes for the opposite.

Chapter 14, by Adam Lockyer and Peter K. Hatemi, provides an overview of research on genetic influences on political behavior, including research using evolutionary theory, behavioral genetics research, GWAS, and candidate gene research. These authors note that this research can be grouped into answering why, what, and how questions about political behavior: Why do people have the political leanings they do? How much of the cause of political behavior is genetic? and What genes predispose individuals to what kinds of political behavior?

In Chapter 15, François Nielsen notes how there is evidence that genetic endowments influence status attainment outcomes such as educational and occupational attainment. For those who fear that any inheritance of traits such as cognitive ability will promote a rigidly stratified society, as the elite bequeaths its abilities to its offspring so those offspring in turn become the new elite, he notes that this does not necessarily follow. Genetic endowments differ from generation to generation, and on any trait there is typically regression to the mean from one generation to the next. This process prevents an elite from being formed and maintained across generations. He argues that incorporating individual genetic endowments into standard models of status attainment allows for better understanding and measurement of mobility and opportunity in a given society.

In Chapter 16, Olga Kornienko and Douglas A. Granger advocate investigating the relationship between social network characteristics and stress on individuals and its implications for physical and mental health. They note that most previous research has examined only ego-centered personal network data on individual stress responses and not how the entire network and its dynamics affect the individual. There are reasons to believe that the ego-centered approach may not always lead to a full understanding of the effects of social position on social stress, and an understanding of the characteristics of the entire social network in which an individual is embedded can better illuminate the causes of social stress.

In Chapter 17, Jeff Davis and Kristen Damron describe human and animal research on evolved stress responses in individuals and how environmental stresses can have long-term influences on the individual and affect that person's behavior for years after the experiences are over. They present a model of stress hormone actions and how they fluctuate depending on the agent's ability to maintain adaptive predictive control in his or her relationship with the environment.

In Chapter 18, Daniel E. Adkins, Kelli M. Rasmussen, and Anna R. Docherty further discuss the epigenetic mechanisms by which adversity "gets under the skin." These mechanisms modify gene activity with long-term consequences for the individual's health and behavior. They note how these mechanisms can help account for the long-term adverse effects of events such as prenatal deprivation, childhood trauma, and addiction. They argue that sociological theories and models of outcomes such as poor mental health and health disparities between groups should incorporate these findings and include biosocial factors to create complete explanations for these outcomes.

Small group researchers have long been interested in how status is allocated in the small group. In the last chapter in Part III on biosociology, Chapter 19, Allan Mazur describes the physiology of competition for status in the small group. He shows how individual hormone profiles change in response to competition and to winning and losing such competitions, and he discusses the consequences of these hormonal changes on consequent social interaction and status allocation processes.

Part IV of the handbook provides an overview of research that applies evolutionary theory to other traditional concerns of sociologists, including study of the family, fertility, sex and gender, religion, crime, and race and ethnic relations. Evolutionary theory is based on the concept of an evolved actor—that the individuals who make up sociological groups and societies are a product of evolution by natural selection and have evolved physical and psychological predispositions that interact with the totality of the individuals' environment, including its culture, in shaping behavior. Evolved predispositions include predispositions toward behaviors highly relevant to sociology, including sexual behavior and partner preferences, behaviors that favor kin (especially close kin), and status-seeking behavior.

In Chapter 20, Timothy Crippen describes the essentials of the evolutionary approach and many of the misunderstandings sociologists have of evolutionary theory, including unwarranted fears of biological determinism and reductionism. Crippen notes that evolutionary theory is a theory of how individual organisms, not groups, evolve and thus has implications for individual behavior only. The dynamics of the group, and the interaction of the individual's characteristics with the characteristics of the group, remain as the sociological domain of study. Crippen also highlights what he describes as the troubling resurrection of group selectionist ideas among evolutionists. Group selection is the idea in evolutionary biology that the unit of selection in the evolutionary process is not the gene or the individual but, rather, the entire group. That is, individuals have characteristics that were selected for over the course of evolution not because they helped each individual and his or her genes survive and reproduce but, rather, because they helped the group of which each individual is a member (e.g., the species) survive and reproduce. A common misunderstanding of evolutionary theory held by sociologists is that it necessarily implies group selectionism, and so individual traits are present because in the evolutionary past they helped the "species" or the "group" survive. Although the majority of biologists reject group selectionism as a major force in biological evolution, recently it has witnessed something of a revival. Crippen notes it was erroneous ideas of group selection—that some groups are successful because they have emerged from this process of group selection and are somehow fitter or better adapted than other groups—that was behind the abuses of biology in social Darwinism.

Evolutionary theory has as its heart differential reproduction and survival of individuals and their genes, and so it is not surprising that it is relevant to the study of the reproductive unit among humans—the family. In Chapter 21, Anna Rotkirch describes research in the field of evolutionary family sociology. She presents the evolutionary approach to the family, particularly how genetic relationship shapes the pattern of family ties. She notes that evolutionary approaches are complementary to traditional sociological approaches that do not refer to evolutionary theory at all. She then examines two broad areas of research within the area of evolutionary family sociology: (a) research on parenting, mating, and family systems; and (b) research focusing on grandparenting, particularly intergenerational transfers and proximity to offspring. Like many of the research areas described in this volume, this is an area in its infancy and many important questions have yet to be addressed.

In Chapter 22, Martin Fieder and Susanne Huber provide an overview of studies in the area of evolution and reproduction. They examine the relationship between sex, status, income, wealth, and fertility in contemporary societies; the relationship between genetic, educational, and religious homogamy and fertility; the relationship between father's age and genetic mutations in offspring; and the role of early life factors and epigenetics in fertility. They note that evolutionary theory can explain many of these associations. They also raise the intriguing idea that many behaviors, such as educational and religious homogamy and the pursuit of status by men, likely continue to be adaptive in terms of increasing individual genetic fitness even in contemporary, modern environments.

Again, the different biological roles of males and females in reproduction, a process at the heart of evolution, have implications for sex differences in behaviors particularly with regard to reproduction and parenting. In Chapter 23, Lee Ellis reviews the considerable evidence of universal average cognitive and behavioral differences between the sexes. He examines evolutionary and sex role explanations for these differences, and he introduces a new theoretical explanation he calls evolutionary neuroandrogenic theory, which stipulates that androgens have evolved as the main biochemicals responsible for masculinizing/defeminizing the brain of an otherwise female mammal. Ellis notes that sex role explanations of sex differences have difficulty accounting for the fact that many cognitive and behavioral differences between men and women are wider in societies that are more gender equitable. He suggests this is also a conundrum for evolutionary theories, including his own, possibly because more egalitarian societies that give individuals more freedom to express themselves actually promote the expression of sex-typed behaviors. He also suggests the intriguing possibility that freedom in choosing marriage partners in more egalitarian societies may actually promote the expression of genes for particular sex-typed behaviors.

In Chapter 24, Anthony Walsh and Cody Jorgensen argue that evolutionary psychology or evolutionary theory applied to understanding psychology can organize the theories and findings of criminology and hence unify a fragmentary field. They note that evolutionary psychology can help explain why some people victimize others while simultaneously explaining why most of us do not. They also argue that it can therefore reconcile the tension between the two major criminological traditions whose assumptions about criminal behavior are radically at odds—social learning theory (which assumes that most people are law abiding until taught otherwise) and social control theory (which assumes the reverse). Evolutionary theory suggests that all individuals have the potential to commit crime to a greater or lesser extent, and therefore crime is likely when circumstances favorable to criminal activity, such as a breakdown in social cohesion and order, occur.

Frank Salter, in Chapter 25, reviews literature from ethology, sociobiology, evolutionary psychology, and sociology on the biosocial study of ethnicity. He defines an "ethny" as a population with a collective proper name, a common myth of descent, a shared history, a distinctive shared culture, a connection to a known territory, and some degree of solidarity. He defines ethnicity as behavior contingent on membership of such a population. He notes that biology is a likely factor in any social phenomenon affected by descent, and he presents evolutionary explanations of ethnicity that rely on both individual and group selection arguments. He further notes that there are likely fitness benefits of pro-ethnic behavior because members of the same ethnic group likely share more genes than do members of different ethnic groups. Last, he argues that the full incorporation of insights from the biosocial literature would be advantageous for the study of race and ethnicity.

In Chapter 26, Kristin Liv Rauch and Rosemary L. Hopcroft present a sociosexual theory of racial discrimination, building on the subordinate male target hypothesis of Sidanius and co-authors. Sidanius and colleagues note that sexually selected predispositions for the targeting of out-group males (more so than out-group females) are likely to have evolved and continue to operate. This is because out-group males are competitors for mates, whereas out-group females are possible mates. However, Rauch and Hopcroft go beyond this work by noting that dominant group members often form coalitions to target out-group males and enlist support from cultural scripts and/or unconscious biases. The result of such targeting continues to have fitness consequences for dominant group males at the expense of subordinate group males in that it enhances mating opportunities for dominant group males and diminishes them for subordinate group males.

The last part of the book presents two chapters on cultural evolution. Cultural evolution is unlike biological evolution in that cultural evolution does not depend on the competition between living organisms for survival and reproduction because cultures and cultural products are not living organisms. Nevertheless, cultural evolution may be considered analogous to biological evolution in some respects (see Chapter 28, this volume). Furthermore, in sociology, comparative–historical cultural evolutionists such as Gerhard Lenski and Stephen K. Sanderson have long argued that it is necessary to have a conception of a universal evolved actor in the comparative study of societies, given that there are patterned universals across human societies and social factors that differ in predicable ways given different ecological and technological constraints.

In Chapter 27 on comparative–historical religious change, Stephen K. Sanderson presents a new theory for the rise of the religions of the "Axial age" from approximately 600 BCE to 1 CE (Judaism, Christianity, Hinduism, Buddhism, Confucianism, and Daoism). Sanderson reviews cognitive and evolutionary psychological theories of religiosity, which he groups into by-product theories (religiosity exists because it uses parts of the brain evolved for other purposes) and adaptationist theories (religiosity exists because it was adaptive in its own right). He takes an adaptationist view of religion—that is, he argues that religiosity is an evolved, universal human trait that likely evolved because of the adaptive advantages it gave to individuals. This meshes with his theory of the rise of the religions of the axial age because he argues that these new religions helped individuals deal with the insecurities and problems they were facing due to increases in urbanization and warfare at the time. He notes that the gods of these new religions, unlike the pagan gods, were transcendent or above the world and could help provide comfort to those who were suffering. This can account for the increasing abandonment of pagan religions and rise of the new Axial religions.

In Chapter 28, Marion Blute and Fiona M. Jordan provide an overview of scholarly work that uses phylogenetic methods from evolutionary biology to examine sociocultural evolution through history. They discuss evolutionary tree-building and phylogenetic comparative methods and how they can be used to answer a variety of questions about the evolution of languages, as well as the evolution of social, political, cultural, and economic organizations and artifacts. These methods can be used to answer questions such as the following: Where and when did a language originate? How fast is a language changing? What was the ancestral state of a particular sociocultural feature? How do sociocultural traits change together? and Is there a trend in the direction in which traits change?

The research discussed in this volume does not include all the ongoing research in the area of evolution, biology, and society nor all the topics covered by this research. It is hoped that the discussed research is enough to give a newcomer to the area an idea of what kinds of work is being done and to demonstrate the promise of this line of research for sociology. As many of these chapters argue, considering evolved, biological factors and including them in sociological theories and empirical research has the potential to both unify the discipline and help us create better explanations and achieve better understanding of social phenomena, a point I return to in Chapter 29.

CHAPTER 2

DIVERGENCE AND POSSIBLE CONSILIENCE BETWEEN EVOLUTIONARY BIOLOGY AND SOCIOLOGY

RICHARD MACHALEK

SCIENTISTS who study social life on earth are at no loss for available subjects. To date, biologists have identified at least 20,000 highly social species (Hölldobler & Wilson, 2009, p. xvi). Behavioral biologists routinely take full advantage of this abundance by focusing on multiple species in their studies of social behavior. Very few social and behavioral scientists, however, venture beyond *Homo sapiens* in their analyses of societies and social behaviors. Nevertheless, a number of sociology's founding thinkers, most notably Herbert Spencer and Emile Durkheim, approached the study of human societies from an evolutionary perspective. However, by the middle of the 20th century, biological thinking in general and evolutionary analyses in particular were rapidly disappearing from the social and behavioral science literature (Degler, 1991). During the last quarter of the 20th century, this began to change—a development due in large part to the work of Edward O. Wilson, a prominent biologist who studies ants (Wilson, 1971, 1975; see also Hölldobler & Wilson, 1990).

The book that had a major influence on the recent resurgence of interest in evolutionary thinking in the social and behavioral sciences is *Sociobiology: The New Synthesis* (Wilson, 1975). Although met initially with great skepticism and even overt hostility by many social scientists (Segerstråle, 2000), in time, sociobiology and the closely related discipline of behavioral ecology contributed to the development of "neo-Darwinian" (the integration of Darwinian evolutionary theory with Mendelian genetics) approaches to the study of human social behavior in the social and behavioral sciences. These efforts are now being consolidated under labels such as evolutionary psychology, evolutionary anthropology, evolutionary economics, and even evolutionary sociology. However, convergence between evolutionary biology and the social sciences has developed slowly and often against considerable resistance. Points of convergence and divergence between evolutionary biology and sociology are reviewed in this chapter by posing three questions: Why do societies exist? How do individuals become social? and Is sociology on the threshold of consilience with evolutionary biology?

Sociology is chosen as the discipline to represent the social sciences in the following discussion, although much of what is presented is applicable to most of the other social sciences as well.

Why Do Societies Exist?

Although thousands of social species almost certainly remain to be discovered, most organisms are not social. As an evolved attribute, sociality is distributed variably among taxa. Among large animals (those capable of being seen by humans with the unassisted eye), the most highly social species comprising motile individuals are the eusocial insects (ants, bees, wasps, and termites) followed, although at some distance, by humans. However, sociality in various forms and to different degrees also occurs among vertebrates, including fish, reptiles, amphibians, birds, and, of course, mammals. Given their almost exclusive devotion to the study of only one species, most sociologists conduct their work on the basis of a default assumption that humans are "social by nature," but they rarely try to explain why. Among evolutionary biologists, however, the question of why a particular species is social rather than solitary is fundamental to their inquiries.

Because sociality is not a trait that varies among humans to the degree that it varies among all other social species, it is understandable that few social scientists express much interest in why sociality exists at all. When sociologists conduct "comparative analysis," for example, they almost always focus only on variation among human societies, in contrast to biologists, for whom comparative analysis typically entails comparisons across species lines. Despite the empirical variation found among the cultures and structures of human societies, all humans exhibit the same basic social capabilities, regardless of whether they exist in foraging bands with populations numbering from as few as 30–50 individuals or in complex nation-states whose populations can exceed 1 billion members. Consequently, by not having their attention drawn consistently to a wide range of species among which sociality ranges from being nonexistent to extensive and complex (the ants are nonhuman exemplars of societal size and complexity), there is little occasion for most social scientists to find themselves puzzled about the existence of sociality among humans. Instead, sociologists are more likely to view their time as better spent trying to understand human social behavior in contemporary context, within the past 10,000 years or so.

The vantage point from which evolutionary biologists view sociality is starkly different. For evolutionary biologists, sociality is of interest primarily as an evolved *adaptation*. Adaptations are heritable traits that contribute to an organism's *fitness*, meaning its prospects of survival and reproductive success (Williams, 1966). Among some species, establishing patterns of cooperative interaction can enable individuals to be more suc-cessful in activities such as foraging, mating, caring for offspring, defense, shaping their habitat and constructing residences (e.g., ant nests, beehives, bird nests, and beaver lodges and ponds), acquiring information, and other activities pertaining to survival and reproduction (Alcock, 2001, 2013). Even simple aggregations such as bird flocks, fish schools, or ungulate herds can confer survival and reproductive benefits to individuals that belong to such collectivities. For example, such aggregations can provide defense against predators by "mobbing" actions or simply increase the chances that a predator will be detected before it can attack its prey. Although large aggregations of individuals can increase the likelihood of attracting predators, membership in such aggregations can also reduce the probability that any particular individual will be singled out as a tar-get by a predator—a phenomenon that biologist W. D. Hamilton (1971) called the "selfish herd effect."

Unlike most sociologists, who regard as self-evident the multiple and highly variable benefits of social life, evolutionary biologists make explicit efforts not only to determine why a given species is social rather than solitary but also to systematically link specific forms of sociality to specific fitness benefits they might confer. Stated simply, the first question an evolutionary biologist is almost certain to pose about any pattern of social behavior is the following: Is the behavior under consideration the product of evolved adaptations that confer fitness benefits to its executors and, if so, what are those spe-cific benefits? For example, upon observing coalitions among primates, an evolutionary biologist will ask if membership and participation in a coalition are likely to increase the ability of its members to survive, increase their ability to forage more successfully, increase their chances of mating and producing offspring, improve their ability to defend against threats such as predation, increase their chances of competing effectively for resources, and so on (de Waal, 2007). Any or all of these outcomes are likely to be fit-ness enhancing and thus intelligible in evolutionary terms.

At first consideration, it might appear that the basic approach taken by sociologists to studying such behaviors is not all that different. A first principle embraced (although often unreflectively) by almost any professional sociologist is that asocial human beings do not exist. To be human is to be social. Generations of sociology students have been taught that absent opportunities for nurturing social interaction early in life, children suffer developmental deficits, some of which are irreversible. In almost parable-like fashion, students are introduced to the classic work of Harry Harlow, who demon-strated that young monkeys exhibit strong preferences for intimate contact over food, even when the provider of intimate contact is nothing more than a towel-wrapped metal frame that substitutes for a mother. The preference for intimate contact illustrates the necessity for nurturance and close interpersonal contact to ensure normal develop-ment. Similarly, cases such as the "wild boy of Aveyron" or children such as Genie and Isabell are often discussed by sociologists to show how severe neglect and social isola-tion result in serious developmental deficits and failure to develop normal behavioral competences. In the vernacular of biologists, human sociality is an obligate, not facul-tative, trait. This means that for humans, being social is not a choice; it is an imperative.

Thus, although it can be said that the thinking of sociologists and evolutionary biologists converges on the key premise that *H. sapiens* is a social animal, practitioners of these two disciplines diverge in terms of conceptualizing how and why humans are adapted for social living. Most sociologists view human sociality as a highly generalized adaptation that is enabled by human powers of symbolization, language, learning, and the "capacity for culture." These generalized capabilities, in turn, enable humans to construct an almost limitless range of social strategies for living. However, the thinking of sociologists and evolutionary biologists begins to diverge with regard to two fundamental issues pertaining to human social behavior: (a) Sociologists rarely use the concept "adaptation" to mean the same thing as do evolutionary biologists; and (b) evolutionary biologists expect humans, like all other social species, to have evolved specialized forms of sociality that constitute evolved adaptations for coping with problems pertaining to survival and prospects for reproduction.

More often than not, when sociologists describe humans as "adapting" to various sorts of circumstances, they typically mean only that humans find ways of adjusting their behavioral responses in accordance with changing conditions. Thus, humans can "adapt" to challenges posed by food shortage by developing new innovations for harvesting game (developing more efficient hunting technologies), growing plants (inventing gardening and, later, plow-based agriculture), or harnessing more effective and efficient energy sources (exploiting fossil fuels to replace domesticated animals with machines such as tractors) (Lenski, 2005). The sociological literature on topics such as social change is replete with almost inexhaustible examples of such "adaptations" to new environmental circumstances created by the introduction of novelty, in almost any form, to a human society.

In evolutionary biology, however, the concept of an adaptation is more narrowly and specifically construed. When viewed at the level of an individual organism, an evolved trait is an adaptation only if it has the effect of increasing that individual's chances of both survival and reproduction. Alternatively, when viewed at the level of the individual's genotype, a trait is an adaptation when it increases the likelihood that the genes responsible for producing that trait are replicated and transmitted to the individual's descendants or the descendants of that individual's close kin. Simply stated, an adaptation is any trait (morphological, physiological, or behavioral) that increases an individual's ability to transmit copies of its genes to its descendants. Because individuals share varying proportions of their genes with biological kin, any trait possessed by an individual that enables him or her to assist his or her close kin in transmitting copies of a shared gene into subsequent generations is also viewed as an adaptation. In the terminology of evolutionary biology, organisms achieve *individual* (or Darwinian) fitness by producing descendants, and they achieve *inclusive* fitness by contributing to the Darwinian fitness of their close biological kin. These two processes are called, respectively, individual (or Darwinian) selection and kin selection (Wilson, 1975, pp. 117–121).

The difference in the way that evolutionary biologists and sociologists conceptualize a trait as adaptive has far-reaching consequences for how these two disciplines analyze and try to explain social behavior. When sociologists characterize behaviors as adaptations or as being adaptive, they almost never refer to the fitness consequences of behavior. Evolutionary biologists, however, interpret social behavior and society itself as evolved adaptations that exist because they enhance the inclusive fitness of organisms that express them. Furthermore, social behaviors are viewed as evolved adaptations for solving specific "Darwinian problems," such as securing mates, caring for offspring, forming alliances, achieving status, defending against predators, constructing nests and other habitations, and foraging for food, as well as other challenges pertaining to survival and reproductive success. Fifty years of research in *sociobiology* and *behavioral ecology* has adduced evidence that within each of these categories of Darwinian problems, even more specific adaptations can evolve. Behavioral ecology is the study of environmental influences on behavior, including social behavior, and sociobiology is the study of the biological basis of social behavior in humans and other animals (Alcock, 2013; Wilson, 1975). Regarding mating and reproduction, for example, sociobiologists have identified adaptations for modifying sex ratios of newborns, competing successfully to be selected as a reproductive partner by a member of the opposite sex, competing successfully with members of the same sex for reproductive partners, assessing the fitness value of a potential reproductive partner, determining how much or little a parent should invest in the care of offspring, deciding whether to nurture newborn offspring or kill them, and other behavioral strategies bearing on an organism's prospects for reproductive success.

Like evolutionary biologists, sociologists explore the manner in which humans approach these various dimensions of mating and reproduction. Unlike evolutionary biologists, sociologists rarely begin their research with the assumption that the human brain/mind may be equipped with specialized, evolved, neurocomputational programs for coping with these and other Darwinian problems (Tooby & Cosmides, 2016, pp. 3–8). Instead, they assume only that humans, by possessing a highly evolved general learning capacity and the "capacity for culture," will acquire behavioral strategies for coping with the various challenges presented by group life. Under the influence of Karl Marx and the "materialists" in sociological thought, sociologists have prioritized the study of how material (typically economic) interests shape human social life. Biologists routinely distinguish between "somatic" interests (health, nutrition, safety, etc.) and "reproductive interests" (producing offspring). Whereas evolutionary biologists typically analyze somatic interests in relation to reproductive interests, most sociologists rarely extend their analyses to include a consideration of reproductive interests, or fitness. Instead, their analyses are "materialist" only with regard to the somatic, not the reproductive, interests of the organism.

In short, evolutionary biologists approach their inquiries with the default assumption that humans may possess specialized, evolved social adaptations that enable them to cope with specific Darwinian problems, whereas sociologists pursue their craft with an emphasis on the general learning capabilities of humans and the equipotentiality of the human brain to enable humans to develop a behavioral repertoire that is called for by whatever historical, cultural, and general environmental conditions might prevail.

How Do Individuals Become Social?

Viewing the human brain as densely packed with specialized evolved cognitive adaptations versus viewing it as a tabula rasa, all-purpose, general information processing machine represents a significant point of divergence between evolutionary biologists and sociologists. Although both view humans as "social by nature," they disagree about how nature somehow *makes humans social*. In the view of most sociologists, newborn humans are regarded as innately endowed with the capacity to develop social behaviors, but a full ensemble of social behaviors can be acquired only by individual experience and socialization. From a traditional sociological viewpoint, a human without a biography could never become social and thus never fully human. Inasmuch as a baby begins life with only a prenatal biography, its sociality is, at best, nascent and will develop only as the infant accumulates social experience. In contrast, evolutionary scientists contend that the human brain is equipped, at birth, with an extensive suite of evolved cognitive adaptations for engaging in social behavior (Buss, 2016) and that, in the words of William Hamilton, the "*tabula* of human nature was never *rasa*, and it is now being read" (as quoted in Kanazawa, 2015, p. 142).

Even today, however, most contemporary sociological thought is based on some variant of the tabula rasa assumption (Pinker, 2002). The tabula rasa assumption is the core component of what has been called the standard social science model (SSSM) of human nature and human social behavior (Tooby & Cosmides, 1992, 2016). The SSSM comprises a number of key assumptions about human nature and behavior, basic among which are (a) human behaviors are learned, not innate; (b) the human brain influences social behavior only by the operation of general-purpose, content-independent, and equipotential learning mechanisms; (c) culture, not biology, explains most behavioral variation within and among human societies; and (e) patterns of social interaction and social organization are emergent realities and cannot be reduced to psychological or biological variables (Pinker, 2002; Tooby & Cosmides, 1992).

At most, the SSSM view of human nature allows for the existence of only a limited number of inborn "reflexes," such as rooting and suckling, swallowing, the Moro (startle) reflex, the Palmar grasp (grasping an object placed in the palm of the hand), and the Babinski reflex (extension of the big toe and fanning of other toes). Beyond this minimal inventory of innate behavioral predispositions, it is rare to find in contemporary sociology a view of the human brain and mind as instantiated, at birth, with an extensive suite of innate behavioral predispositions for producing complex behaviors, including social behaviors. Rather, the brain is typically viewed as a powerful, all-purpose, equipotential and complex information processing machine that captures, stores, organizes, and expresses information that is acquired almost exclusively by personal experience or cultural transmission. Accordingly, the human brain/mind is regarded as an evolved adaptation only in the broad sense that it equips humans with general learning capabilities and, most important, the capacity to produce and use symbols, the most important instantiation of which is culture. Consequently, the human mind is viewed as capable of developing an almost infinite range of social behaviors but, simultaneously, predisposed toward almost none.

An evolutionary account of human nature and the development of social behavior sharply repudiates the tabula rasa model of human nature. The "adapted mind" view of human nature sees the human brain as richly supplied with specialized cognitive mechanisms that are products of natural selection and constitute specialized computational algorithms for coping with adaptive challenges (Barkow, Cosmides, & Tooby, 1992; Buss, 2016; Tooby & Cosmides, 2016). These cognitive mechanisms are labeled variously as "evolved psychological (mental, cognitive) programs, neurocomputational programs, behavior-regulatory programs, adaptive specializations, 'modules,' information processing mechanisms" (Tooby & Cosmides, 2016), "neural subassemblies" (Turner, 2015), "behavioral predispositions" (Lopreato, 1984), and so on. The full suite of evolved neural programs shared by all humans for solving adaptive problems constitutes, in the view of evolutionary behavioral and social scientists, a "universal human nature" (Tooby & Cosmides, 2016, p. 3). Proponents of the adapted mind conception of human nature contend that the social worlds in which ancestral humans lived comprised arrays of selection forces that led to the evolution of specialized mental adaptations that enabled archaic hominins to cope with recurrent challenges and opportunities presented by group living. For example, one of the earliest of such claims is found in the work of Cosmides and Tooby (1992, 2005, 2016), which supports the hypothesis that humans possess an innate "cheating detection mechanism" that alerts individuals to the threat of nonreciprocity in relations of social exchange. Consistent with a vast body of sociological literature that documents the centrality of relations of reciprocity and exchange in human social life, Cosmides and Tooby contend that nonreciprocity in such relations posed a sufficiently significant threat to ancestral humans. As a consequence, they argue that natural selection installed computational machinery that equips humans with a specialized "aptitude" for detecting instances of nonreciprocity ("cheating"), which in turn enables individuals to defend themselves against being exploited by others in social contract relations. Although experience is required to *activate* such a mechanism, the propensity for humans to detect and respond appropriately to this adaptive challenge is innate and does not depend on a generalized learning capability or culture.

For most sociologists, claims about the existence of evolved, specialized mental mechanisms for navigating social life are not well-received because they are viewed as perilously close to long-discredited "instinct" theories of human social behavior. Also, as innumerable students of introductory sociology have been told, instincts are "fixed and inalterable" patterns of behavior, the existence of which has been refuted by a characterization of human social behavior as almost infinitely plastic and subject only to constraints of individual experience and the power of culture (Machalek & Martin, 2004). Evolutionary thinkers have long since abandoned such a conception of instincts, human nature, and behavior. Instead, as is true of many evolved traits, social behaviors are viewed as exhibiting variable "norms of reaction," a concept that acknowledges the influence of environments (including social and cultural environments) on the expression of genes. The norm of reaction of a gene or group of genes that produces a trait refers to "the total variation in the trait in all the survivable environments" (Wilson, 1998, p. 137). Thus, for example, although all humans are in possession of evolved mental mechanisms for the development of language, what Steven Pinker (1994) calls a "language instinct," the norm of reaction for the acquisition of a *specific language* is very broad and does not predispose the development of, for example, Finnish over French. As is true of all evolved, genetically prescribed traits, social behaviors develop by means of the process of *epigenesis*, which refers to the production of a trait under the influence of both genes and their environments (Francis, 2011). Some traits are more sensitive to variability in the environments in which they develop (e.g., the *specific* language that a person acquires) than are other traits, which can be almost totally impervious to environmental variation (e.g., the universal *ability to acquire* a spoken language).

Until recent developments in evolutionary biology and related fields of the behavioral sciences challenged the tabula rasa model of human nature, the social and behavioral sciences were dominated by a view of human behavior that placed primary emphasis on individual experience (biography), general learning mechanisms that are content-free, and cultural processes, all of which were said to constitute the basic causes of social behavior in humans. Although more than a half-century old, but still largely undisturbed by knowledge of recent research in the evolutionary behavioral sciences, many sociologists continue to subscribe to C. Wright Mills' tripartite conception of human social behavior as the product of "biography, history, and social structure" (Mills, 1959). Interpreted in evolutionary terms, Mills' view of human nature and behavior would mean that the determinants of human behavior are ecological (history and social structure) and psychological (biography) but that the *phylogenetic history* of the human brain is irrelevant to the production of specific social behaviors. What Mills calls "biography" depends on the experience of individuals, but it ignores the fact that experience is always processed by an evolved human nature. Thus, individual experience in the context of history and social structure is always acting on a universal, species-typical behavioral nature that is the product of evolution by natural selection (Tooby & Cosmides, 2016, pp. 3–8). In the flawed view of the social constructionists, all human capabilities for social behavior are said to be acquired during an individual's lifetime (biography) either *directly* by means of individual experience or, vicariously, by means of the *communication* of the experiences of predecessors, contemporaries, and/ or consociates (Schutz, 1967)—that is, by means of social interactions that are guided by culture. In contrast, from an evolutionary perspective, history, social structure, and biography all contribute to the production of human behavior, including social behavior, but their contributions are realized only by virtue of their influences on an evolved human nature.

An evolutionary perspective introduces the possibility of another way of viewing human nature and behavior as socially constructed. By conventional sociological reasoning, human nature and behavior are viewed as *historical contexts*. Furthermore, biographical and historical forces are viewed as acting on a brain that is virtually empty of behavioral content acquired during its phylogeny. An *adapted mind*, however, is instantiated with a rich supply of "neurocomputational programs" that comprise the machinery that drives the development of behavioral (including social) adaptations for coping with survival and reproductive challenges confronted by an entire lineage. Thus, an evolutionary update of Mills' tripartite "biography, history, and social structure" scheme for mapping out the causes of human social behavior would add a fourth component, and it would thus become "*phylogeny*, biography, history, and social structure." One might characterize this entailing the "Paleo-construction" of human society and social behavior. Consequently, sociology's traditional "actor" would thus be re-envisioned as Hopcroft's (2009b) "*evolved* actor," an actor supplied with specialized neurocomputational programs that generate adaptive social behaviors.

Is Sociology on the Threshold of Consilience with Evolutionary Biology?

In the first chapter of *Sociobiology: The New Synthesis*, Wilson (1975) notes that sociology differs from sociobiology in terms of its "largely structuralist and nongenetic approach" and that "sociology and the other social sciences . . . are the last branches of biology waiting to be included in the Modern Synthesis" (p. 4). In Wilson's view, the rightful place of the social sciences is alongside sociobiology and behavioral ecology, under the expansive umbrella of biology. This, however, was not the sentiment among many, perhaps even most, social scientists. Rather, many viewed Wilson's position as blatantly imperialistic and as signaling nothing less than an attempt at a hostile intellectual takeover of the social sciences (and even humanities) by biology, a move that needed to be resisted at all costs. Among sociologists, old fears of "biological reductionism," "genetic determinism," and the odious ideology of social Darwinism resurfaced. Among biologists and evolutionary-minded behavioral scientists, puzzlement about the hostility of many social scientists, including sociologists, toward sociobiology inspired the coining of a new term, "biophobia" (Daly & Wilson, 1988, pp. 152–156).

Eventually, however, a small core of sociologists began to explore the applicability of sociobiology and behavioral ecology to the study of human social behavior, and by 1998, a nascent "evolutionary sociology" had emerged (Maryanski, 1998). The remainder of this chapter explores the prospects for convergence between evolutionary biology and sociology in their respective quests for a scientific understanding of human social behavior and society. As discussed previously, the concept of adaptation is central to an evolutionary approach to the study of social behavior, but the *biological* versus *sociological* meanings of the term rarely coincide. This, in turn, has inhibited the full integration of the social sciences into the Modern Synthesis, the integration of Darwinian evolutionary theory and Mendelian population genetics.

THE IDEA OF ADAPTATION
IN EVOLUTIONARY BIOLOGY VERSUS
SOCIOLOGY

The concept of adaptation is, of course, central to thinking in evolutionary biology, and it has been prominent in various strains of sociological thought as well. However, the concept rarely has the same meaning when used by practitioners of these two fields.

In evolutionary biology, the traits of all living things are interpreted primarily in relation to their effects on the transmission of the genes that produced them. Again, traits that contribute to the survival and reproductive success of the individuals that bear them constitute adaptations, and at the level of genes, adaptations are essentially devices for gene replication and transmission. Adaptations comprise three basic types of traits: morphological traits (e.g., the anatomy of an organ such as the heart), physiological traits (e.g., digestion and respiration), and behavioral traits (e.g., seasonal migration). Thus, patterns of social behavior, and society itself, are of interest to evolutionary biologists as but one type of adaptation, and the relevance of social behavior to evolutionary analysis depends on the contributions that it makes toward enhancing either individual or inclusive fitness. Absent the prospect of investigating sociality as an evolved adaptation, there is little reason for evolutionary biologists to study social phenomena (Alcock, 2001).

Pursuing an inquiry into a pattern of behavior such as male sexual jealousy and possessiveness as a possible evolved adaptation represents a significantly different point of departure from that typically adopted by sociologists. Evolutionary biologists would be likely to approach such a phenomenon by asking if it might be an expression of "mate guarding," a behavioral strategy adopted by males in order to cope with the threat of being cuckolded by a competitor (Thornhill & Palmer, 2000). Among sexually reproducing species, the threat of "paternity uncertainty" confronting males can be expected to have given rise to such behaviors. Again, evolutionary biologists would devote effort to studying such behavior in the hope of determining its possible relevance to the fitness prospects of males engaged in mate guarding. In contrast, although sociologists might be no less interested in male sexual jealously and possessiveness, it would be highly unusual to find them puzzling about the possible fitness consequences of such behavior, much less attempting to determine if either males or females possessed evolved adaptations for coping with social situations in which conflicts of reproductive interests are at play. Instead, one could expect with greater confidence that a sociological inquiry into male sexual jealously and possessiveness would be framed in terms of notions of patriarchy and general sociocultural processes that subordinate females to males in most, if not all, spheres of human social life. Any ruminations about possible "fitness consequences" of such dynamics would likely be viewed by most sociologists as odd at best and, more likely, doomed at the outset as an ill-fated and futile manifestation of a deeply flawed and indefensible "essentialism."

As discussed previously, the use of the concept of adaptation in sociology rarely refers to the fitness consequences of behavior. For example, the prominent sociological theorist Talcott Parsons (1966), framing his work in evolutionary terms, wrote about the ability of social systems to undergo "adaptive upgrading" as they responded to increasing population size and structural differentiation. Similarly, Gerhard Lenski (2005), in his "ecological–evolutionary" theory of societies and social change, used the term adaptation to refer not to biological fitness but, rather, to the ability of a society to cope with environmental forces by adopting various technological innovations and inventions. Relatively recently, Jonathan Turner (2015), in developing a strain of evolutionary sociological theory that more closely resembles Darwinian theory, contends that the "only definition of fitness for a sociocultural system would be either the length of time that it exists in its environment or its ability to persist in a variety of environments" (p. 95).

In summary, evolutionary biology's interpretation of human social behaviors as possible evolved adaptations is sufficiently alien to the SSSM view of human nature and social behavior so as to make neo-Darwinian evolutionary thinking seem irrelevant, if not overtly objectionable, to many mainstream sociologists.

ULTIMATE AND PROXIMATE CAUSATION

Another way of understanding the divergence between evolutionary biology and sociology regarding their basic approaches to social behavior is to consider the distinction between "ultimate" and "proximate" causes of behavior (Alcock, 2001, 2013; Alcock & Sherman, 1994). A distinction made routinely in evolutionary biology, discussions of ultimate versus proximate causation are rarely found in sociology. As evolutionary biologists use the term, "proximate" causes are the "immediate" factors that contribute to the genetically based development of a behavior as well as the neuronal–hormonal processes that activate the behavior. The "ultimate" causes of a behavior refer to its phylogenetic (evolutionary) history as well as to the adaptive value of the behavior itself— the (genetic, not sociocultural) fitness benefits that are produced by that behavior (Alcock, 2013, p. 294). Thus, for example, prairie voles, unlike some other vole species, are often monogamous (Alcock, 2013, pp. 296–298). What causes monogamy among prairie voles? For the evolutionary biologist, a complete answer requires the identification of both proximate and ultimate causes that are at play in producing monogamy. The adaptive benefits, or ultimate causes, of monogamy for male prairie voles include higher paternity "confidence" because remaining with female mates reduces the threat of being cuckolded. For female voles, monogamous male mates can provide paternal care of offspring, thereby contributing to females' fitness. At the proximate level of causation, what is responsible for monogamy among prairie voles? Researchers have identified both physiological and possible genetic causes (Pitkow et al., 2001; Young & Wang, 2004). The hormone vasopressin appears to have an effect on receptor proteins in a specific part of the brain, the ventral pallidum, which makes mating with the same female rewarding for a male prairie vole. Furthermore, a specific gene (*avpr1a*) appears to be implicated in producing effects that strengthen the social bond between male and female prairie voles. This research on prairie voles illustrates how a particular type of social relationship, monogamy, is the product of two types of causes, ultimate and proximate, that are complimentary in their effects. Proximate causes are not restricted to the level of genes, hormones, or brain morphology. Rather, extrasomatic forces in the environment, including demographic and social environments, also constitute proximate forces that can contribute to producing a pattern of social behavior.

Alcock (2013) discusses human communication by means of language and speech as a behavioral complex that enables social behavior and derives from both ultimate and proximate causes (p. 431). Research on the genetic and neurological foundations of human speech reveals two sets of proximate causes that contribute to the development and use of speech by humans. Genetic research has led to the discovery of a gene, *FOXP2*, that is implicated in language ability (pp. 425–426). *FOXP2* contributes to the production of proteins that influence other genes and the proteins that they produce, which in turn eventually help produce the neural circuits on the basis of which speech is produced. Other genes influenced by *FOXP2* contribute to the production of specific parts of the brain that produce speech (Broca's area) and enable speech to be comprehended (Wernicke's area). Thus, specific genes and their morphological products are clearly proximate causes of spoken language and the social behavior that it enables. The ultimate causes of spoken language refer to its adaptive value. The contribution of spoken language to the development of complex forms of cooperation that constitute so much of human social life is a fitness-enhancing adaptation that is obvious even to those uniformed by evolutionary theory. However, Alcock reports that language confers other adaptive benefits as well, including a mechanism by means of which individuals can distinguish in-group from out-group members. Language also constitutes a mechanism by means of which men can display verbal competence that serves to attract prospective mates (pp. 430–431). As such, language competence may be a trait that females favor in prospective mates and thus becomes part of the broader repertoire of qualities that men advertise during the process of sexual selection (Miller, 2000).

The social sciences, including sociology, are largely indifferent to explanations of social behavior featuring analyses of ultimate causes. Consider, for example, the existence of stratification systems in human societies, especially class systems. Neither sociobiologists nor other evolutionary life scientists are likely to contend that a stratification system itself is a phenotype, the expression of a genotype. Instead, like virtually all sociologists, evolutionary biologists are likely to view stratification systems as emergent phenomena that are not reducible to a specific genotype that can be said to produce them. However, evolutionary-minded thinkers, including even some sociologists, have proposed the idea that humans may possess evolved cognitive adaptations for behaviors such as status-striving that, when expressed in the context of social interaction, are likely to be implicated in the development of *emergent* social phenomena such as stratification systems (Sanderson, 2014, pp. 245–263). This is not the same, however, as claiming that genotypes exist for the production of stratification systems themselves or that emergent phenomena such as social class systems can be interpreted as evolved adaptations that are fitness-enhancing in the genetic sense. Thus, although humans may very well possess evolved adaptations that support their efforts in status-striving, this does not mean that stratification systems themselves are to be interpreted as evolved adaptations and the product of ultimate causation.

Accordingly, the task of analyzing and interpreting the emergent processes by means of which societal institutions and complex patterns of social organization develop should not be left to evolutionary biologists, including sociobiologists, or evolutionary psychologists alone. Rather, the efforts of conventional, mainstream sociologists must be enlisted in any project dedicated to explaining emergent patterns of social organization and societal institutions (Machalek, 1999). Simply stated, whereas complex patterns of social organization and behavior such as class systems are the product of the behaviors of individuals equipped with evolved cognitive adaptations, the class systems themselves are emergent phenomena and not reducible to the forces of evolved, individual cognitive adaptations alone.

CULTURE AND SOCIAL BEHAVIOR

Differences between evolutionary biologists and sociologists in terms of the way they conceptualize an adaptation as well as differences in how they view causal processes lie at the root of many other differences in the way practitioners of these two fields approach the study of human social behavior. Not surprisingly, both evolutionary biologists and sociologists attribute fundamental behavioral significance to a species-definitive trait of humans—the capacity to produce and use symbols, especially language and its product, human culture. Contrary to an early misconception about sociobiology, the sociobiologist E. O. Wilson (1998) has stated unequivocally that

> we know that virtually all of human behavior is transmitted by culture. We also know that biology has an important effect on the origin of culture and its transmission. The question remaining is how biology and culture interact, and in particular how they interact across all societies to create the commonalities of human nature. (p. 126)

Furthermore, consider Wilson's comment about an important way in which humans differ from all other animals: "Culture allows a rapid adjustment to changes in the environment through finely tuned adaptations invented and transmitted without correspondingly precise genetic prescription. In this respect human beings *differ fundamentally from all other animal species* [emphasis added]" (p. 128). Wilson's declaration of the centrality of culture to an understanding of human behavior is in direct contrast to claims made by sociologists who write textbooks for educating students about sociology when they assert that sociology and sociobiology are diametrically opposed systems of explanation that pit "social learning" against "instinct" and that sociobiology not only neglects culture but also fails even to consider the role of "the uniquely human mind" in producing social behavior (Machalek & Martin, 2004, 2010).

These sorts of declaration are particularly bewildering in that they were made more than 15 years after Charles Lumsden and E. O. Wilson published *Genes, Mind and Culture: The Coevolutionary Process* (1981). In fact, more than a few sociobiologically minded thinkers, including Robert Boyd, Peter J. Richerson, Mark W. Feldman, L. Luca Cavalli-Sforza, and William H. Durham, are among a growing corps of scientists and scholars who have long been devoted to an evolutionary understanding of culture and its role in human social behavior. Sociobiologists, evolutionary psychologists, and evolutionary social scientists all acknowledge the primacy of culture in human social life. What remains at issue, however, is the way that evolutionary scientists versus sociologists think about culture in relation to human social behavior and society.

Having evolved a capacity for culture, humans are regarded by SSSM adherents as almost entirely exempt from biological influences on their social behaviors (Kanazawa, 2015, pp. 136–137). This assumption constitutes the foundation of a perspective on human behavior that regards humans as the *exception* to the forces of natural selection that design and install innate natures in all other species (Alcock, 2001; Kanazawa, 2015, p. 137). Only by means of individual experience enabled by general learning mechanisms and by cultural transmission are humans said to be able to develop patterns of social behavior. Accordingly, evolutionary thinkers such as sociobiologists are faulted (incorrectly) by SSSM thinkers for misattributing to biology behaviors that can be explained only by culture.

The claim that sociobiologists ignore culture as a determinant of human social behavior is closely linked to another misconception—the belief that sociobiologists attribute human behavior to instinct and disavow the role of learning in human social life. Those suffering this misconception could be freed of their misunderstanding by acquiring even minimal familiarity with the way that evolutionary scientists construe human nature. In contrast to the SSSM view of the human mind, the adapted mind model incorporates what psychologists call "prepared" or "biased" learning (Garcia & Koelling, 1966; Seligman, 1971; Seligman & Hager, 1972). In this view, the human brain is equipped with an extensive array of learning biases that enable humans to learn more quickly, easily, and reliably from experiences that are adaptively relevant—that is, experiences that have a significant bearing on an individual's survival and reproductive prospects. In contrast to the tabula rasa view of the human mind, the adapted mind conception characterizes the human brain as a complex and powerful information processing machine that is packed with a large array of "neurocomputational programs" for coping with adaptive challenges presented by environments (Tooby & Cosmides, 2016, pp. 3–8). A simple example is provided by Wilson (1998), who contends that the human mind is likely to possess a special learning bias that makes humans highly vigilant about snakes, an archaic and near-universal threat to humans in environments throughout the world (p. 79). An innate propensity to be particularly alert for serpentine forms and a behavioral inclination to behave very cautiously when they are detected represent a highly adaptive learning bias from which ancestral (as well as many contemporary) humans have benefitted. Also, as discussed previously, an example of learning biases that are directly related to human social behavior is the set of neurocomputational adaptations that enable humans to reason effectively about social contracts and relations of social exchange (Cosmides & Tooby, 1992, 2005, 2016). Thus, far from avowing that instincts rather than learning and culture shape human social behaviors, sociobiologists and evolutionary psychologists attribute to symbolic communication, learning, and culture an explanatory status no less significant for understanding human social behavior than is pheromone communication for understanding social behavior among ants and other social insects (Hölldobler & Wilson, 2009).

The efforts of neo-Darwinian social and behavioral scientists have yielded new ways of thinking about culture and the manner in which it shapes human social behavior. For example, evolutionary thinkers have proposed a conceptual distinction between two types of culture: "evoked" culture versus "transmitted" culture (Tooby & Cosmides, 1992; Walsh, 2014, pp. 108–114). The notion of transmitted culture refers to processes by means of which information (and the practices it enables) is transferred, by communication or imitation, from one mind to another (Tooby & Cosmides, 1992). It is the form of cultural diffusion familiar to SSSM thinkers. Evoked culture, on the other hand, refers to information (and the practices it enables) that is activated in some groups (populations) more than others because of different environmental conditions to which those groups are exposed (Tooby & Cosmides, 1992). The incidence of both types of culture, however, depends on the existence of evolved psychological mechanisms in order to become instantiated in minds and produce behavior that is informed and guided by the cultural elements so acquired (Buss, 2015). Thus, adopting an evolutionary approach to the study of social behavior in humans does not permit the indefensible notion that genes somehow replace culture as forces guiding human social behavior. Instead, evolutionary thinking raises new questions for theoretical inquiry and empirical research about the complex behavior manifested by a culture-bearing species.

Conclusion: What Are the Prospects for the Development of an Evolutionary Sociology?

Although Wilson's (1975) prediction that sociobiology might "reformulate the foundations of the social sciences in a way that draws these subjects into the Modern Synthesis" (p. 4) has yet to be realized, developments in both evolutionary biology and the social and behavioral sciences during the past 40 years provide clear evidence of movement toward consilience in these fields (see also Wilson, 1998). As increasingly more sociologists, as well as other social and behavioral scientists, become better informed about evolutionary sciences such as sociobiology, behavioral ecology, and evolutionary neuroscience, misconceptions that have inhibited the integration of evolutionary thinking into sociological inquiry will continue to dissipate.

For example, the growing body of literature in the newly emerging discipline of evolutionary sociology provides clear evidence that drawing upon theoretical ideas and empirical findings from sociobiology, behavioral ecology, and other evolutionary sciences does not mean having to succumb to "rigid genetic determinism" (Wilson, 1998, p. 30), reductionism in the absence of holism (Wilson, 1998, pp. 66–95), or naive instinct explanations of complex social behaviors (Machalek & Martin, 2004, 2012). Instead, an increasing number of sociologists (including some contributors to this volume) are bringing an evolutionary perspective to bear on topics of long-standing interest to sociologists, including sociocultural evolution (Blute, 2010; Lenski, 2005; Turner, 2010), gender relations (Hopcroft, 2009a, 2009b; Huber, 2007), mating and pair bonding (Crippen, 2015; Sanderson, 2001; Turner & Maryanski, 2015), emotions and social behavior (Turner, 2000), religion (Abrutyn, 2015a, 2015b; Machalek & Martin, 2010), crime (Kanazawa & Still, 2000; Savage & Kanazawa, 2002; Walsh, 2014), ethnicity (Salter, 2001; van den Berghe, 1981; Whitmeyer, 1997), dominance and deference (Mazur, 2005), intergroup aggression (Holmes, 2015), group formation (Dunn, 2015), and incest (Turner & Maryanski, 2005).

Nevertheless, it is likely that the efforts of most sociologists will remain focused on proximate rather than ultimate causes of human social behavior. As noted previously, the norms of reaction governing most categories of human social behavior are broad, and the ranges of environmentally induced variation among these behavioral categories are more than enough to capture and hold the attention of most sociologists. For example, although a growing body of evidence supports the idea that evolved cognitive mechanisms support and are implicated in status-striving and competition among humans, especially males, social stratification systems are emergent structures, the specific properties of which are unlikely to be predictable from a knowledge of evolved cognitive adaptations alone. Furthermore, although such cognitive mechanisms may very well have evolved because of the fitness-enhancing advantages that they conferred in the ancestral environments in which they evolved, few contemporary sociologists are likely to be concerned about the fitness consequences of patterns of social behaviors manifested in stratification systems. Accordingly, they are likely to continue pursuing their sociological inquiries into phenomena such as class stratification absent any interest in evolutionary dimensions of such phenomena.

As is commonly acknowledged by evolutionary scientists, social behaviors are tractable to explanation at either (or both) the proximate level or the ultimate level. Explaining a social behavior at the proximate level involves searching for "immediate" causes, such as environmental stimuli, that "trigger" or activate a behavior or behavioral complex, regardless of the possible adaptive value of the behavior (Alcock, 2013, pp. 319–321). In effect, sociology's almost exclusive focus on explanations framed in proximate causal terms versus sociobiology's primary focus on explanations in search of ultimate causes can be understood as a manifestation of a long-standing division of labor between these two disciplines. There is no reason not to expect that practitioners of these two fields can continue to work largely sequestered from each other and each other's explanatory efforts. Alternatively, however, any progress achieved toward greater consilience between sociology and the evolutionary life sciences, including sociobiology, offers hope for the emergence of a more complete understanding of human sociality, societies, and the human condition (Turner & Maryanski, 2008).

REFERENCES

Abrutyn, S. (2015a). Pollution-purification rituals, collective memory, and the evolution of religion: How cultural trauma shaped ancient Israel. *American Journal of Cultural Sociology*, 3(1), 123–155.

Abrutyn, S. (2015b). The institutional evolution of religion: Innovation and entrepreneurship in ancient Israel. *Religion*, 45(4), 505–531.

Alcock, J. (2001). *The triumph of sociobiology*. New York, NY: Oxford University Press.

Alcock, J. (2013). *Animal behavior* (10th ed.). Sunderland, MA: Sinauer.

Alcock, J., & Sherman, P. W. (1994). On the utility of the proximate–ultimate dichotomy in biology. *Ethology*, 96, 58–62.

Barkow, J. H., Cosmides, L., & Tooby, J. (Eds.). (1992). *The adapted mind: Evolutionary psychology and the generation of culture*. New York, NY: Oxford University Press.

Blute, M. (2010). *Darwinian sociocultural evolution: Solutions to dilemmas in cultural and social theory*. New York, NY: Cambridge University Press.

Buss, D. M. (2015). *Evolutionary psychology: The new science of the mind*. New York, NY: Routledge.

Buss, D. M. (Ed.). (2016). *The handbook of evolutionary psychology* (Vols. 1 & 2). Hoboken, NJ: Wiley.

Cosmides, L., & Tooby, J. (1992). Cognitive adaptations for social exchange. In J. H. Barkow, L. Cosmides, & J. Tooby (Eds.), *The adapted mind: Evolutionary psychology and the generation of culture* (pp. 162–228). New York, NY: Oxford University Press.

Cosmides, L., & Tooby, J. (2005). Social exchange: The evolutionary design of a neurocognitive system. In M. S. Gazzaniga (Ed.), *The new cognitive neurosciences, III* (pp. 1295–1308). Cambridge, MA: MIT Press.

Cosmides, L., & Tooby, J. (2016). The theoretical foundations of evolutionary psychology. In D. M. Buss (Ed.), *The handbook of evolutionary psychology: Volume 1. Foundations* (pp. 3–87). Hoboken, NJ: Wiley.

Crippen, T. (2015). The evolution of tenuous pair bonding in humans: A plausible pathway and indicators of design. In J. H. Turner, R. Machalek, & A. Maryanski (Eds.), *Handbook on evolution and society: Toward an evolutionary social science* (pp. 402–421). Boulder, CO: Paradigm.

Daly, M., & Wilson, M. (1988). *Homicide*. Hawthorne, NY: de Gruyter.

de Waal, F. (2007). *Chimpanzee politics: Power and sex among apes*. Baltimore, MD: Johns Hopkins University Press.

Degler, C. N. (1991). *In search of human nature: The decline and revival of Darwinism in American social thought*. New York, NY: Oxford University Press.

Dunn, M. B. (2015). Evolutionary transitions in individuality and selection in social evolution. In J. H. Turner, R. Machalek, & A. Maryanski (Eds.), *Handbook on evolution and society: Toward an evolutionary social science* (pp. 76–91). Boulder, CO: Paradigm.

Francis, R. C. (2011). *Epigenetics: The ultimate mystery of inheritance*. New York, NY: Norton.

Garcia, J., & Koelling, R. (1966). Relation of cue to consequence in avoidance learning. *Psychonomic Science, 4*, 123–124.

Hamilton, W. D. (1971). Geometry for the selfish herd. *Journal of Theoretical Biology, 31*(2), 295–311.

Hölldobler, B., & Wilson, E. O. (1990). *The ants*. Cambridge, MA: Belknap.

Hölldobler, B., & Wilson, E. O. (2009). *The superorganism: The beauty, elegance, and strangeness of insect societies*. New York, NY: Norton.

Holmes, M. H. (2015). Intergroup threat and extralegal police aggression: An evolutionary interpretation. In J. H. Turner, R. Machalek, & A. Maryanski (Eds.), *Handbook on evolution and society: Toward an evolutionary social science* (pp. 474–511). Boulder, CO: Paradigm.

Hopcroft, R. (2009a). Gender inequality interaction: An evolutionary account. *Social Forces, 87*(4), 1845–1872.

Hopcroft, R. (2009b). The evolved actor in sociology. *Sociological Theory, 27*(4), 390–406.

Huber, J. (2007). *On the origins of gender inequality*. Boulder, CO: Paradigm.

Kanazawa, S. (2015). Evolutionary psychology and its relevance to the social sciences. In J. H. Turner, R. Machalek, & A. Maryanski (Eds.), *Handbook on evolution and society: Toward an evolutionary social science* (pp. 136–156). Boulder, CO: Paradigm.

Kanazawa, S., & Still, M. (2000). Why men commit crimes (and why they desist). *Sociological Theory, 18*(3), 434–447.

Lenski, G. (2005). *Ecological-evolutionary theory: Principles and applications*. Boulder, CO: Paradigm.

Lopreato, J. (1984). *Human nature and biocultural evolution*. Winchester, MA: Allen & Unwin.

Lumsden, C. J., & Wilson, E. O. (1981). *Genes, mind and culture: The coevolutionary process*. Cambridge, MA: Harvard University Press.

Machalek, R. (1999). Elementary social facts: Emergence in nonhuman societies. *Advances in Human Ecology, 8*, 33–64.

Machalek, R., & Martin, M. W. (2004). Sociology and the second Darwinian revolution: A metatheoretical analysis. *Sociological Theory, 22*, 455–476.

Machalek, R., & Martin, M. W. (2010). Evolution, biology and society: A conversation for the 21st century sociology classroom. *Teaching Sociology, 38*(1), 34–45.

Machalek, R., & Martin, M. W. (2012). Sacrifice, gratitude, and obligation: Serial reciprocity in early Christianity. In W. Kalkhoff, S. Thye, & E. Lawler (Eds.), *Advances in group processes: Biosociology and neurosociology* (pp. 39–75). Bingley, UK: Emerald.

Maryanski, A. (1998). Evolutionary sociology. *Advances in Human Ecology, 7*, 1–56.

Mazur, A. (2005). *Biosociology of dominance and deference*. New York, NY: Rowman & Littlefield.

Miller, G. F. (2000). *The mating mind: How sexual choice shaped the evolution of human nature*. New York, NY: Doubleday.

Mills, C. W. (1959). *The sociological imagination*. New York, NY: Oxford University Press.

Parsons, T. (1966). *Societies: Evolutionary and comparative perspectives*. Englewood Cliffs, NJ: Prentice-Hall.

Pinker, S. (1994). *The language instinct*. New York, NY: HarperCollins.

Pinker, S. (2002). *The blank slate: The modern denial of human nature*. New York, NY: Penguin.

Pitkow, L. J., Sharer, C. A., Ren, X. L., Insel, T. R., Terwilliger, E. F., & Young, L. J. (2001). Facilitation of affiliation and pair-bond formation by vasopressin receptor gene transfer into the ventral forebrain of a monogamous vole. *Neuroscience, 21*, 7392–7396.

Salter, F. K. (2001). A defense and an extension of Pierre van den Berghe's theory of ethnic nepotism. In P. James & Goetze (Eds.), *Evolutionary theory and ethnic conflict.* Westport, CT: Praeger.

Sanderson, S. K. (2001). Explaining monogamy and polygyny in human societies. *Social Forces, 80,* 329–336.

Sanderson, S. K. (2014). *Human nature and the evolution of society.* Boulder, CO: Westview.

Savage, J., & Kanazawa, S. (2002). Social capital, crime, and human nature. *Journal of Contemporary Criminal Justice, 18,* 188–211.

Schutz, A. (1967). *The phenomenology of the social world.* Evanston, IL: Northwestern University Press.

Segerstråle, U. (2000). *Defenders of the truth: The battle for science in the sociobiology debate and beyond.* Oxford, UK: Oxford University Press.

Seligman, M. E. P. (1971). Preparedness and phobias. *Behavior Therapy, 2,* 307–320.

Seligman, M. E. P., & Hager, J. L. (1972). *Biological boundaries of learning.* New York, NY: Meredith.

Thornhill, R., & Palmer, C. T. (2000). *A natural history of rape: Biological bases of sexual coercion.* Cambridge, MA: Harvard University Press.

Tooby, J., & Cosmides, L. (1992). The psychological foundations of culture. In J. H. Barkow, L. Cosmides, & J. Tooby (Eds.), *The adapted mind: Evolutionary psychology and the generation of culture* (pp. 19–136). New York, NY: Oxford University Press.

Tooby, J., & Cosmides, L. (2016). The theoretical foundations of evolutionary psychology. In D. M. Buss (Ed.), *The handbook of evolutionary psychology: Volume 1. Foundations* (pp. 3–87). Hoboken, NJ: Wiley.

Turner, J. H. (2000). *On the origins of human emotions: A sociological inquiry into the evolution of human affect.* Stanford, CA: Stanford University Press.

Turner, J. H. (2010). *Theoretical principles of sociology: Volume 1. Macrodynamics.* New York, NY: Springer.

Turner, J. H. (2015). The evolution of the social mind: The limits of evolutionary psychology. In J. H. Turner, R. Machalek, & A. Maryanski (Eds.), *Handbook on evolution and society: Toward an evolutionary social science* (pp. 177–191). Boulder, CO: Paradigm.

Turner, J. H., & Maryanski, A. (2005). *Incest: Origins of the taboo.* Boulder, CO: Paradigm.

Turner, J. H., & Maryanski, A. (2008). *On the origin of the societies by natural selection.* Boulder, CO: Paradigm.

Turner, J. H., & Maryanski, A. (2015). Evolutionary sociology: A cross-species strategy for discovering human nature. In J. H. Turner, R. Machalek, & A. Maryanski (Eds.), *Handbook on evolution and society: Toward an evolutionary social science* (pp. 546–571). Boulder, CO: Paradigm.

van den Berghe, P. (1981). *The ethnic phenomenon.* New York, NY: Elsevier.

Walsh. A. (2014). *Biosociology: Bridging the biology–sociology divide.* London, UK: Transaction Publishers.

Whitmeyer, J. M. (1997). Endogamy as a basis for ethnic behavior. *Sociological Theory, 15*(2), 162–178.

Williams, G. C. (1966). *Adaptation and natural selection.* Princeton, NJ: Princeton University Press.

Wilson, E. O. (1971). *The insect societies.* Cambridge, MA: Belknap.

Wilson, E. O. (1975). *Sociobiology: The new synthesis.* Cambridge, MA: Belknap.

Wilson, E. O. (1998). *Consilience: The unity of knowledge.* New York, NY: Knopf.

Young, L. J., & Wang, Z. (2004). The neurobiology of pair bonding. *Nature Neuroscience, 7,* 1948–1954.

CHAPTER 3

SOCIOLOGY'S CONTENTIOUS COURTSHIP WITH BIOLOGY
A Ballad

DOUGLAS A. MARSHALL

As Meloni (2014) observes, biological and evolutionary themes run like a karst river through the history of sociology—sometimes overground, sometimes underground, and sometimes changing direction—but never completely absent. Indeed, although the newcomer could be forgiven for disbelieving it, sociology started out hand-in-hand with biology,[1] and despite the "ignorance, indifference, and hostility" that has characterized sociology's attitude toward biology for most of the last century (van den Berghe, 1990, p. 778), their relationship remains one of essential and multifaceted unity (Marshall, 2018).

If, as she herself frames it, Segerstrale's (2000) magisterial analysis of the "sociobiology wars" is an opera, then this chapter, which traces the trajectory of sociology's relationship with biology over a longer period but in more modest detail, is a ballad. As such, it aims to condense a complex history into five verses that, for all of their simplifications,[2] are of at least some interest and/or use to those of us who teach and write and research about society from a the biological perspective.

VERSE I: INFATUATION

Similarity is high among the primary determinants of human attraction (Berscheid & Reis, 1998). To the extent that this holds analogously true for entities other than human beings, it bears noting a priori that biology and sociology have a lot in common: Both emerged at roughly the same point in time, as manifestations of much the same enlightenment impulse to reform their nonscientific antecedents by shifting their respective field of study onto more empirical footings. Furthermore, both were, in a sense, historical sciences, in that their initially defining referents—species and societies—presented themselves as *fait accompli*, the products of long-term processes to which there were no living witnesses. Most important for our tale, the mysterious origins of the differences among species and among societies were both becoming acutely salient to Europeans in the late 18th and early 19th centuries as voyages (like that of the Beagle) brought specimens of new species, and stories of new societies, home at an unprecedented rate.

Within biology, the effort to make sense of such diversity begins well before Darwin, including efforts by his own grandfather, Erasmus, to devise workable theories of speciation via descent. The crucial figure at this point in the story is Jean-Baptiste Lamarck, whose widely influential model proposed that speciation occurs when changes in the environment alter an organism's biological structure, creating greater internal differentiation and complexity—changes subsequently inherited by the organism's offspring, who were themselves further altered by *their* environment, and so on until the accumulated changes produced a new (and, importantly, putatively better) species (Lamarck, 1809/2012).

Given the parallels between the problem of explaining the diversity of species and that of explaining the diversity of societies, it is unsurprising that Lamarck's model was soon transposed onto the social realm. The first to do so was proto-sociologist August Comte, who was proposing a Lamarckian vision of progressive social evolutionism as early as 1822 (Bourdeau, 2010) and who, although he famously described sociology as a kind of "social physics," was careful to "set [its] feet upon the soil of biology" (Tisdale, 1939, p. 29). However, the person most responsible for importing Lamarckianism into the social realm—and thus the real "matchmaker" in this affair—was another founding figure of the discipline: proto-sociologist, -psychologist, and -political scientist Herbert Spencer.

Starting from his conviction that human beings were part of nature rather than outside of it, and that thereby so were human society and culture, Spencer argued that the development of both paralleled that of species. Embracing the progressivist impulse inherent in Lamarck's theory, Spencer's model conceptualized different societies as representing different stages of advancement toward an ideal form, the closest approximation of which just happened to be Spencer's own. Just as species could be arrayed along a spectrum from lesser to greater differentiation and complexity (and thus sophistication) in Lamarck's system, so could societies in Spencer's system (Carniero, 2015).

Among the many admirers of Spencer's work was Charles Darwin, with whom our story will resume shortly, but it is worth pausing here to underscore Lamarck's own significance to our tale. As every student of biology knows, Lamarck's model would soon be replaced by that of Darwin, disproved by Weissman, and (mostly) discarded by biology. Nevertheless, the Lamarckian moment matters to the history of biology in sociology because its mistaken equation of "evolution" with "progress" fostered at least two fundamental errors that have done lasting damage to the relationship between the two disciplines.

At the time, Lamarck's "evolution" benefitted greatly from its ordination of differentiation and complexity as the defining indices of progress because it thereby provided "scientific" justification for the extant, and heretofore biblically legiti-mated, conceit that human beings represent the ultimate manifestation of life on earth. Spencer's transplanting of this model into the sociocultural realm further flat-tered European society by legitimating their conviction that, as the most complex and differentiated of known societies, theirs was likewise the most exalted manifes-tation thereof.

Despite Darwin's subsequent contraction of the term to designate one particular, directionless, mechanism of change, and its use within biology to mean only that ever since, Lamarck's identification of evolution with improvement has been stubbornly enduring. In popular culture, including, unfortunately, the minds of many sociologists, "evolution" is to this day commonly misunderstood to imply an inherently progressive directionality. Thus, the Lamarckian legacy ensures that conversations about biosoci-ology between critics possessed of such misconceptions and advocates versed in the narrower, more precise use of the term perpetually frustrate both parties, as the critics interpret its every evocation as a valorization of the speaker's own culture, society, or ethnicity at the expense of others, while advocates are dumbfounded as to how a mere mechanism of change could inspire such hostility.

More subtly, but just as injuriously, Lamarck's model not only told a story of past prog-ress but also provided a prescription for its propagation. His hypothesization of acquired characteristics was a boon to the Victorian pursuit of the perfectibility of humankind, suggesting that desirable changes to human nature could be induced by judicious alter-ations to human beings' environment—improvements that would be passed along to their offspring and thence retained by the species into perpetuity. As such, it fostered a false hope that evolution proffered a quick and effective means of improving humanity and its lot—a dream the death of which will itself prove highly damaging to sociology's relationship with biology.

To resume again where we left off, Darwin was less the instigator of the evolutionary movement than its culmination, in that his signal contribution was to correctly identify the mechanism (random variation/deselection)[3] by which biological speciation occurs (Degler, 1991). Although both his question and the answer he provided were strictly biological, Darwin is emblematic of the close early relationship between biology and sociology (again broadly defined) in several ways. First, there is the extent to which his theorizing was influenced by the proto-social science of his day. Most famous is the cata-lyzing role that Darwin's reading of Malthus' (1798/1983) essay on population played in inspiring his model of natural selection, but we must also acknowledge Spencer's influ-ence on its development. Darwin's reading of Spencer while he worked on *The Origin of Species* reinvigorated his determination to complete the project (Carneiro, 2015), and he seems to have adopted the very word "evolution" from Spencer (who first used the term in 1852), as well as (later and more reluctantly) the phrase "survival of the fittest" as a heuristic encapsulation of the theory. Finally, there is Darwin's own growing convic-tion over the ensuing years that behaviors, including such social behaviors as altruism and nonverbal communication, were, at least in part, evolved traits of human beings (Darwin, 1871/2004, 1872/2009).

Between them, Lamarck, Spencer, and Darwin ignited an "evolutionary century," ensuring the thorough biologicization of what would become sociology, well into the early 20th century—a period during which most social scientists were on record as to their great admiration for, and the inspiration they drew from, Darwin's work (Lopreato, 2001; van den Berghe, 1990). Witness Karl Marx, who upon reading *Origin* soon after its publication saw in it a validation for his own variety of materialism and a natural basis for the class struggle in history, reportedly holding forth on the topic for months afterwards, and eventually sending Darwin an (unsolicited and, alas, apparently unread) inscribed copy of *Das Capital* (Sanderson, 2015).

Durkheim's Darwinism is more subtle, but given his frequent invocation as the decisive justification for modern sociology's disregard for biology, it is worth at least pointing out that his most compelling rationale for the autonomy of sociology—the emergence of the living cell from nonliving molecules (Durkheim, 1895/1982)—is an explicitly biological analogy. Elsewhere, *The Division of Labor in Society* (Durkheim, 1895/1984) depends on a rather clearly natural selectionist model to instigate the transition from mechanical to organic solidarity (Lopreato & Crippen, 1999; Sanderson, 2015), and subsequently, the motivating question behind *Elementary Forms* (Durkheim, 1912/2001)—and arguably the rest of his life's work—was that of whether and how an organism that was naturally suited (read: evolved) for life in a high-moral-density social milieu could possibly survive in the new low-moral-density society that was just then coming to predominate.

Nor was biologicism lacking from sociology in the American context. In the form of ecology—particularly parallels between human and plant communities—it suffused the Chicago school at the time, including the work of such luminaries as Park, Burgess, and Small (Degler, 1991; Irwin, 2015). And of course, Lester Frank Ward, first president of the then unfortunately-named American Sociological Society, was himself originally a botanist who began his career in sociology by elaborating on the profound parallels he perceived between the two fields (Degler, 1991; Plotkin, 2004).

Thus, sociology and biology were off to a cracking good start. However, as Simmel (1908/1971) warns, love and hate are not in fact opposites but, rather, a unity, each providing the grounds for the other, so that they slide easily into one another. In the immortal words of B. B. King—"The way I used to love you baby, that's the way I hate you now" (King & Josea, 1961). Although "hate" is, one hopes, too strong a word for what was to come, sociology's attitude toward biology was about to undergo a radical reversal—with even Lester Ward ultimately advocating for their severance as he, like many others, became disenchanted with the first fruits of their union (Degler, 1991).

Verse II: Disillusionment

During the early 20th century, the once-auspicious liaison between biology and this new science of "sociology" began to unravel. That this relationship would be tumultuous, the site of sometimes heated conflict, and prone to dissolution was probably inevitable, given the singular pertinence of the intersection of the biological and social domains to both human civilization and human life. Consider the litany of foundational philosophical dilemmas commonly invoked in debates between proponents and critics of biosociology: monism versus dualism, materialism versus idealism, free will versus determinism, and continuity versus discontinuity between human and nonhuman, not to mention evolution's profound implications for epistemology itself (Campbell, 1987). These dilemmas are fixtures of the biosociology debate because such pre-theoretical commitments and ideologies are, as often as not, what is actually at stake for the "defenders of the truth" (Segerstrale, 2000) on both sides.

That biology also profoundly impinges upon the most salient ideologies, identities, and issues of human social life only makes strife all the more inevitable. To take just one example, the fact that the ultimate virtue in evolutionary biology is "fitness"—an organism's ability to produce viable carriers of its genes—and that, as a sexually reproducing species, our fitness is inextricable from our sexualities, our family structures, and our very bifurcation into male and female—means that biology unavoidably touches upon the most important and intimate aspects of our lives.

Thus, the *sturm und drang* surrounding biosociology is in no small part a function of its singular relevance both to our collective intellectual strivings and to our individual biographies. In this sense, the vigor of the quarrel is a testament to the significance of both the field and the fight. Ultimately, therefore, biosociology is contentious because it should be: Informed and robust critique is the lifeblood of science, especially when the questions at hand are of such broad and deep importance.[4]

But complete explanations for any phenomenon—including sociology's disillusionment with biology—must invoke not only ultimate causes but also proximate ones. However inevitable the conflict might have been at the ultimate level, in practice, it actually happened when and how it did for particular reasons and in response to particular events. This verse thus seeks to address the more specific sources of sociology's disillusionment with biology.

The soundtrack at this point in the tale is less B. B. King than Cole Porter, in that the relationship between sociology and biology at the turn of the century was indeed "too hot not to cool down" (Porter, 1935). In the wake of initial infatuation, overinflated expectations about one's partner can prove lethal to relationships. Sociologists and biologists of the late 19th century had been only too ready to view biology as the salve to many a real or perceived social problem of the day. As a result, oversimplified, underspecified, overreaching, and empirically unsupported models multiplied and thrived in this period—models that were, at best, untenable analogies or mistaken metaphors and, at worst, brash attempts to conscript biology into the service of assorted political and ideological interests (Degler, 1991; Runciman, 2015; Walsh, 2014). However easily ridiculed the former were, it was the latter that inflicted (and continue to inflict) the most lasting damage on sociology's view of biology, with three bearing particular responsibility:

Social Darwinism

"Social Darwinism" is an ironic misnomer having little to do with either Darwin's theory or his ideology but everything to do with those of Herbert Spencer. Spencer sought to map laissez-faire capitalism onto evolution so as to not only naturalize and legitimate its outcomes but to also associate it with the advancement of the species and of society via the economic triumph of superior individuals and (more insidiously) groups over inferior ones, as per Lamarck. It is telling that even as a Lamarckian (for whom competition should be of minor concern), and a full 8 years before Darwin would publish his selection-based alternative to Lamark's model, Spencer was already promoting a "fitness"-based formulation of evolution (Degler, 1991). When Darwin's model appeared on the scene, its manifest suitability for Spencer's purposes made its expropriation irresistible. Rechristening his ideology "social Darwinism," foisting his "survival of the fittest" catchphrase upon Darwin's mechanism, and glossing over the differences between his group-selectionist and Darwin's more individual-selectionist model did the trick. By thus associating "evolution," and Darwin's name and reputation in particular, with advocacy for a particularly rapacious variety of capitalism during its heyday, Spencer effectively turned many previously or potentially keen biosociologists (including Lester Ward [Degler, 1991; Walsh 2014]) away from evolutionary and biological approaches for good. The regularity with which his name and the "social Darwinism" pseudonym continue to be invoked in modern critiques of biosociology suggests that Darwinism's Spencerian makeover remains a potent obstacle to its acceptance.

Eugenics

The term "natural selection" has at least a more authentically Darwinian pedigree than does "social Darwinism." Darwin came to regret eschewing the more accurate "natural preservation" terminology in favor of "natural selection" (Lopreato, 2001), but our current interest lies with the first, and more settled, "natural" part of the phrase, which distinguishes his mechanism from the "artificial" selection that had by Darwin's day already been routine in animal husbandry for generations. Darwin had acknowledged the potential extension of artificial selection to human beings, but came down firmly against its practice, unlike his cousin Francis Galton, who was a major proponent of ameliorating human life and human societies by "improving" the human stock itself (Degler, 1991). Before this project—that is, eugenics—had run its course, forced sterilizations of the genetically "unfit" would be undertaken as a matter of government policy in multiple countries and in most of the United States, continuing in some places well into the second half of the 20th century.

Although commonly cited in the same breath as social Darwinism by opponents of biosociology, it bears noting that the two movements had only limited overlap at the time. Indeed, they represent sharply contrasting applications of evolutionism: Where social Darwinism militates for letting nature take its course without interference, eugenics prescribes active intervention to prevent nature from taking its course. Where social Darwinism was basically conservative in the sense of justifying the existing order and its inequalities, eugenics appeals to the contradictory idea that humanity's status quo can and, more importantly, should, be improved upon. These ideas are not necessarily exclusive in practice, but just as social Darwinism represents an attempt to conscript evolution to the preservation and justification of existing status and power hierarchies, eugenics represents in part an attempt to conscript it to the more traditionally progressive goals of social "improvement" (Degler, 1991; Plotkin, 2004; Walsh, 2014).

Recall that Lamarck's model had raised the prospect that biology could provide a simple and effective means by which humankind as a whole could be improved or even, as per Victorian ambitions, perfected. Its eclipse by Darwin's more "pessimistic" mechanism, whereby such durable alterations could come about only via the slow, bloody, and precarious process of deselecting "undesirable" alternatives, did not curtail the dream of, semi-permanent improvement. Rather, it was reinterpreted by disillusioned contemporaries to mean that progress was going to require the more draconian interventions of eugenics (Degler, 1991). Thus, although its critics are eager to cast it as such, the moral stain of eugenics is by no means Darwinism's alone. The chasm between Darwinism's implication that human nature *could be* artificially selected for and eugenics' insistence that it *should be* artificially selected for was not bridged by anything inherent to Darwinism itself but, rather, by larger and ostensibly prosocial cultural currents.

Ironically enough, although the Victorian vision of human perfectibility that helped bridge that gap is now but an artifact of intellectual history, echoes of it can still be heard, and they continue to undermine biology's relationship with sociology. To wit, one of the most consistent critiques leveled at biosociology is the charge that by uncovering the biological (i.e., "natural") foundations of social pathologies, it normalizes them and effectively surrenders the goal of combatting them, *a la* the naturalistic fallacy. However, apart from the patently fallacious equation of explanation with justification—understanding the Zika virus in no way diminishes the desire to spare as many families as possible from its heartbreaking consequences, and indeed, the former is well-nigh indispensable to accomplishing the latter—the idea that humans are helpless in the face of, "the natural" is absurd. Our history as a species is one long story of being so offended by our natural inability to keep warm at night, to fly, to regenerate failing organs, to travel beyond our atmosphere, to see individual cells and distant planets, to provide for the elderly, and to share our every waking thought with hundreds, thousands, or even millions of "followers" instantaneously, that we defied "nature" to do all these things and much more.

What I suspect is actually so offensive to opponents of biosociology is not the idea that the natural bases of social behavior means that we cannot ameliorate our social pathologies to significantly improve human life, for we quite obviously can and have (albeit, admittedly, unequally). Rather, it threatens the dream, descended from the Victorian vision of perfectibility, that these pathologies can be eliminated once and for all—that enduring solutions to the problems before us, once identified and implemented, will allow us to move ever closer to one or another version of a perfected, utopian, society. To the extent that the desire for a perfectible society does contribute to sociology's animus toward the biological dimension of social behavior, it fulfills a venerable truism: The perfect is the enemy of the good.

The moral lesson of biosociology is not that we cannot overcome collective violence, discrimination, inequality, criminality, or exploitation, but that doing so, like keeping fit, is something that is never "done." As behaviors that, if not inherent in, evidently have an affinity with human nature, the potential for them will always be present. Maintaining, much less extending, whatever progress we have made against them means that we, and in time our children and in turn their children, will have to go out and defend it every day, refighting battles that were believed to be behind us against foes we wrongly believed had already been vanquished. Which brings us to a third reverberating attempt at conscripting evolution to political purposes.

Intergroup Differences

Recall that the original problem that evolution was set to solve is that of accounting for the diversity of species, and that its original appeal to social science was its supposed parallel applicability to observed differences between social groups and peoples. In that, its application to such salient intergroup differences as race and gender is hardly surprising. Thus, for a good half-century after Darwin, evolutionary (and other) biological accounts of race and gender abounded—usually in the service of propping up extant inequalities with invidious comparisons between the sexes and among ethnicities. It was this enthusiastic application of biology to the reification of race and sex differences, and thereby the legitimation of extant racial stereotypes and gender roles, that drove the final wedge between social science and biology—leading many social scientists to turn away in dismay.

The legacy of this early focus on intergroup differences, and continued misunderstandings about their place in modern biosociology, remains a decisive contributor to the unfriendly reception that biosociological approaches receive from mainstream sociologists. Horowitz, Yaworsky, and Kickham (2014), for instance, find that attitudes towards the idea of innate gender differences remain a singularly strong predictor of overall attitudes toward evolutionary explanations among sociological theorists. In the same vein, Hanson (2010) points triumphantly to the finding that "99.9% of human genes are identical" to support "the 'sociological assumption' that at birth our similarities outweigh our differences" (p. 53), apparently unaware that biosociologists believe in, and rely on, such uniformity as much or more than do any other category of sociologists.

Indeed, the promise and project of biosociology is effectively antithetical to the search for intergroup genetic differences. For it is this very uniformity that makes the inclusion of genetic and biological factors imperative to our efforts to explain social behavior: The thing that unites the disparate phenomena we sociologists study across all the different times and places that we study them into one coherent discipline is that these social forces, structures, institutions, and behaviors arise from the same substrate—human organisms.[5] As such, it is only their shared, evolved, and biologically imposed capacities, limitations, imperatives, and disposition that give us any real hope of ever explaining (rather than just describing and categorizing) such phenomena in toto. In short, modern biosociology is about identifying and elaborating the universal underpinnings of social behavior. It is about understanding and explaining—down to their neurophysiological and neuropharmacological constituents and back to their evolutionary origins—the means by which sociality is possible in order to construct realistic models of just how those universal elements interact with variable social, cultural, and material environments and histories to produce the particular social phenomena, social behaviors, and social outcomes observed in the real world of human sociality.

This is not to say that intergroup differences have no role to play in that quest, but it is a small one, and for such purposes—mostly gauging the magnitude of heredity's influence in a given domain—behavioral geneticists are unlikely to look at anything so mundane as ethnicity since, thanks to modern technology, they can as easily, and far more fruitfully, compare groups assembled on the basis of the actual alleles they carry rather than a handful of salient but likely tangential phenotypes. Otherwise, whatever genetic intergroup differences may exist among humans are much more a source of noise obscuring the signals of human sociality that we are actually looking for than a goal in themselves.

One partial exception to this general disinterest in gene-based differences among biosociologists concerns that most unavoidable of sociological concerns—gender. To be absolutely clear, gender differences are qualitatively different from ethnic or other group differences, in that because males and females are everywhere and always reproductively dependent on one another, they decidedly do not constitute different genetic groups. Rather, they are alternate expressions of a polymorphic genotype that is differentially organized and activated by hormonal activity both before and after birth. The resulting differences in morphology are self-evident and uncontestable, as are the complementary, but simultaneously competing, reproductive strategies embodied in and necessitated by those morphological differences (Lopreato & Crippen, 1999). Biosociology simply takes up the obvious follow-up question: How, and to what extent, do these morphological differences in turn manifest themselves in behavioral dispositions, social structures, behaviors, and institutions? The answers that biosociology provides to this question are diverse and enlightening (Hopcroft, 2016; Hrdy, 2000; Huber, 2007), but in all cases, the purpose is not to reify or validate any such differences but, rather, to understand the implications of such differences for social life by pushing beyond such pseudo-explanatory constructs as "patriarchy."

A Wider Perspective on Biology's Ideological Associations

We have seen that social science's disillusionment with biology was largely a reaction to the latter's overenthusiastic adoption in support of some deplorable ideological causes and to its perceived responsibility for the consequences of these misapplications. Although these historical associations between biology and social Darwinism, eugenics, and invidious theories of gender and race superiority are real enough, other factors need to be taken into account before we deem such associations lethal to current and future applications of biology to sociology.

Anytime a new and powerful idea or technology emerges, existing groups of all stripes have strong incentives to conscript it to their cause. When Darwinian evolution arrived on the scene, such interested parties included capitalists, eugenicists, racists, and sexists, but it also attracted the efforts of feminists such as Eliza Burt Gamble, Charlotte Perkins Gilman, and Lester Frank Ward to draft it into the service of their movement (Degler, 1991), as well as of communists, including Marx, to enlist it in theirs.

That some such expropriations commanded more attention than others and/or had a greater impact on policy and culture than others says more about the institutions and ideologies prevailing at the time than it does about the inherent ideological affinities of biosociology per se. Had a different set of ideologies or institutions been ascendant at the time, we might today be discussing the legacy of "Darwinian socialism" or "equigenics." If, on the other hand, the exciting scientific breakthrough of the day had been the identification of a powerful new mechanism of cultural determinism, it, too, would have been conscripted into the service of the prevailing powers and we might today be discussing the violent culling of the carriers of undesirable cultural capitals (i.e., "memocide")[6] or, as per Pinker (2002), contemplating *tabula rasa's* role in the rise of American totalitarian ideology.

Likewise, it is naive to imagine, as some critics seem to, that racism or sexism or classism or predatory capitalism were unknown before Darwin. When evolutionary theory arrived in the middle of the 19th century, most white European males were already fully convinced that they constituted the supreme race, society, and gender. What the evolutionists did provide, with varying degrees of intentionality, were new legitimations that possessors of these existing pathologies seized upon in an attempt to maintain their relevance in the then newly emerging scientific era.

But in proposing scientific bases for ancient prejudices, advocates did not so much extend the life of these ideas as put them on the path to dissipation. Once one has dragged one's prescientific assumptions onto the ground of science, they must stand or fall there on the basis of empirical evidence. History shows that science proved to be hostile territory for racists' and sexists' and classists' assumptions. Scientists who started out believing in—and set out to demonstrate—racial or gender differences as often as not ended up revising and reversing their positions in light of their own data (Degler, 1991). Thus, it is not too great a leap to argue that ultimately, biosociology, in addition to whatever responsibility it bears for promulgating socially deleterious ideologies, also played a crucial role in, and deserves some credit for, rendering them unsustainable.

Between social Darwinism, eugenics, and the attempted legitimation of extant hierarchies of race and gender, by the early 20th century, many social scientists became convinced that the earlier dalliance with biology had been a youthful mistake from which they should and would now walk away. Thus began sociology's anti-evolutionary reaction (Ellis, 1996; Sanderson, 2001) and search for a different grounding for their discipline—one as far away from biology as possible.

Verse III: Estrangement

It is always easier to walk away from one relationship when doing so in the direction of another. In this case, as sociology was turning away from evolutionary explanations, it was being drawn toward the alternative explanatory apparatus of environmental causation. This approach assumed different guises in different quarters of social science: Watsonian Behaviorism, Boasian Culturalism, and a reified Durkheimian "Social"; but all contributed to the migration of sociologists' affections from one to the other.

Watsonian Behaviorism

Behaviorism originated as a reaction to the considerable theoretical and methodological shortcomings of its direct psychological antecedents, instinct theory and introspectionism. Its main proponent, John Watson, was originally trained in ethology and shared Darwin's belief that human and nonhuman behaviors have a common explanation. But whereas for Darwin that was because both were equipped with homologously evolved capacities and dispositions, their common thread in Watson's view was the complete absence of such dispositions. For him, behavior on the part of any organism was nothing more than a manifestation of a very basic set of reflexes and emotions elaborated via an individual history of environmental reinforcement. If human behavior appeared more complicated than that of other species, it was only because humans' capacity for conditioning extended into the domain of language, and thereby, "thought." Thus, for Watson, biology mattered only up to the point that it established the conditionability of the organism.[7] Otherwise, behavior was to be explained with only the most proximate manifestations of "cause" and "effect" and strictly as a function of the individual organism's reinforcement history. Behaviorism thus amounts to a rather deterministic environmentalism.

Despite its decades of hegemony within psychology, likely few sociologists view behaviorism as having had much influence on their own discipline, but it left its mark there, too, in ways pertinent to understanding sociology's long hiatus from biology. The major channel of its influence runs through George Herbert Mead, whose most seminal contribution to the discipline proclaims his behaviorist identity right in its subtitle—*From the Standpoint of a Social Behaviorist* (Mead, 1967).[8] This is no idle declaration, as the text's organizing principle is his effort to render three concepts (mind, self, society) that might appear anathema to behaviorism compatible with it.[9]

Mead's behaviorism impacts the biosociology debate in at least three ways. It is apparent, first, in Mead's insistence, following Watson, that thought amounts to language, and that it is primarily (or only) through language that mind, self, and even society can be rendered "social." In modern sociology, this feeds the false assumption that human social behavior can be understood, almost exclusively, as a function of symbolic manipulation, thereby ostensibly transcending biology.

The influence of behaviorism is also apparent in the causal myopia of much mainstream sociology. Watson was, in effect, an anti-theorist, having little use for constructs beyond the immediately observable stimulus, the immediately observable response, and the reinforcement history of the organism. Although Mead did not strictly adhere to that blinkered precedent (e.g., evoking such unobservable constructs as the "I" and the "Me"), he nevertheless maintains the ideal (e.g., defining "meaning" strictly in terms of observable gestures, responses, and consequences). Similarly, at least in their critiques of biosociology, sociologists still regularly evince a decided aversion to "remote" causes (Lopreato, 2001), confining their curiosity to only the most proximate, "social" level of causation, effectively giving up on the provision of complete explanations.

Last, behaviorism's influence can be discerned in the absolutist stance of critics who, like Watson, seem to believe that environment and biology are mutually exclusive causal mechanisms such that the demonstration of any causal role for the environment is tantamount to a refutation of all biological influence. A common tactic of biosociology's critics is to point to (perfectly valid) correlations between culture and a phenomena as though the latter's ability to account for some portion of the observed variance leaves no room for other, biological, factors to account for any other such variance. However, this argument relies on the straw-man assumption that biosociologists hew to the same absolutist, main-effects-only model of biological influence that theses critics apparently do. At least since the "Modern Synthesis" of the 1920s, evolutionary biology has revolved around the "interaction principle" that *any* observed phenotype, whether morphological or behavioral, is everywhere and always a function of the interaction of the organism's biological constitution (genotype) with its environment, including its culture (Machalek & Martin, 2010). Given that biology has long hewn to such interaction effects models for even the most basic morphological traits (e.g., height), it is high time that sociology—a field that prides itself on demonstrating the often subtle causal influence of the social—availed itself of a similar level of sophistication.

Boasian Culturalism

By their own accounts, Franz Boas is the pivotal figure in many social scientists' rejection of biology and subsequent embrace of the explanatory power of culture (Degler, 1991). Unlike Watson, his motivation for promoting an alternative to evolutionary explanations was indeed rooted in the moral and ideological excesses of early biosociology, particularly the idea that mental differences between ethnic groups were genetically determined.

Convinced that all human groups possessed the same cognitive and moral endowments, and that observed differences between them were therefore of cultural rather than genetic origin, Boas set out to demonstrate the power of the environment empirically, examining both its influence on morphology (head shape among immigrant children) and its influence on cognition (individuals' inability to discern similar but different sounds in the languages of other groups while being fully able to discern those relevant to one's own) (Boas, 1889, 1912).

Although Boas maintained a cultural and historical particularism that paralleled the individual particularism of Watson (Sanderson, 2001), his approach as a whole is surprisingly compatible with modern biosociology, certainly more so than was behaviorism. To wit, he never denied that human capacities and dispositions had a biological component that differentiated people at an individual level, but he (rightly) believed that such individual differences washed out when summed across the group. Indeed, he insisted that "all the essential traits of man are due primarily to heredity" (as quoted in Degler, 1991, p. 81), and his work on "alternating sounds" is an exemplary model of the ways that biology and culture interact to produce different outcomes (Boas, 1889).[10]

It is, rather, Boas' students—Margaret Mead, Ruth Benedict, and Alfred Kroeber, among others—who aggrandized his argument, popularizing and bequeathing to social science the somewhat stronger variety of cultural determinism that became a defining trait for latter-20th-century sociology.

The Durkheimian "Social"

Watsonian behaviorism and Boasian culturalism helped legitimate environmentalist alternatives for sociologists seeking to get past social science's earlier episodes of biological overreach, but sociologists already had a homegrown version of environmentalism, in the form of a prevailing (mis)reading of Durkheim, to fall back upon.

Apart from providing many of the discipline's key theoretical constructs, Durkheim's exalted position in sociology derives from his assertion of a unique domain of scientific inquiry and his corollary justification of the new discipline against rival competitors. Although originally intended to repel encroachments from both psychology and philosophy,[11] his "dictum" (Chagnon & Macfarlan, 2015) that "anytime a social fact is reduced to and explained in terms of a psychological fact, you can be certain the explanation is false (Durkheim 1895/1982, p. 129) has done double duty as a cornerstone in sociology's wall against both biological and psychological[12] intrusion throughout the years.

The troubling irony is that invoking Durkheim to this effect requires a very selective reading of his work on several counts. First, it ignores context, in that his primary goal was to establish and legitimate a new discipline in the face of more established contenders for its territory, a mission that naturally invites a certain degree of hyperbole and the foregrounding of distinctions over continuities. More important, it ignores the much more inclusive thrust of the totality of his writings on the topic. Consider, for example, the following caveat from *Rules* (Durkheim, 1895/1982), a description that equally well captures sociology's proper relationship to biosociology:

> This is not to say, of course, that the study of psychological facts is not indispensable to the sociologist. If collective life does not derive from individual life, the two are

nevertheless directly related; if the latter cannot explain the former . . . it can at least aid in the explanation. Psychological training . . . constitutes, then, a necessary preparation for the sociologist. (pp. 109–111)

Third, it ignores the evidence of his own example—not just that of his aforementioned uses of biological analogies and evolutionary mechanisms in *Division* (Durkheim, 1895/1984), but of, every major theoretical mechanism he posits, since each has its roots sunk deep into human nature. Mary Douglas (1978) observes, for example, that, "Durkheim proposed to speak only about social facts, but he based his whole theory of the sacred on two psychological factors" (p. xv).

Last and most important, it relies on a thorough misunderstanding of the key concept of "emergence." As Durkheim correctly observes, water is different from both of its constituents, hydrogen and oxygen, just as the social is different from the biological creatures that constitute it. But emergence is not magic. Although they are not the same, the properties of the whole (water) are nevertheless utterly dependent upon those of the constituents (hydrogen and oxygen). Replace the oxygen atom and one hydrogen atom with chlorine and one gets a liquid much more treacherous than water; replace both hydrogen atoms with a pair of nitrogen atoms and the result is a gas of somewhat greater medical (or recreational) value. Likewise, as per the previous quote, Durkheim understands the social as different from its constituents but nevertheless dependent on them. The lesson of his emergence argument is that the whole is indeed different from the sum of its parts, but it is so only because, and only in the ways that, the parts make it so. Thus, knowledge of such parts is necessary but not sufficient to the complete explanation of the whole.

Think of it this way: Knowing the first number of a combination lock will not by itself allow one to open the lock, nor will knowing the key in which a piece of music is written by itself allow one to play it, but knowing each renders their respective tasks immensely more tractable. In the same way, understanding the psychology and/or biology of social behavior will not by itself explain most social phenomena, but it does render the otherwise daunting, or even impossible task of doing so much more feasible.

The Long Rebound

Together, these three manifestations of environmental causal primacy made up what would come to be dubbed the "standard social science model" or SSSM (Cosmides & Tooby, 1992; Pinker, 2002), which proved to be sociology's more or less constant consort for most of the 20th century. Hitler's midcentury revival of eugenics and associated assumptions of invidious racial differences made sociology's desire to renounce its old flame all the more fervent. But memories of sociology's biological fling never completely faded away, and slightly more than a decade after the end of World War II, the first pieces of a reunion between the two began to fall into place.

VERSE IV: A STORMY REUNION

Just as it had for pseudo-biological legitimations of racism and sexism, empirical reality eventually intruded on sociology's idealized view of environmental explanation, and for much the same reason: Motivated more by ideology than by empirical evidence, sociology's use of the environment as a stand-alone explanatory device was as riddled with empirically unsubstantiated overstatement as had been its earlier misapplications of biology, to wit, Kuo's (1924) insistence that the only unacquired behavior in the entire animal kingdom was the sperm's fertilization of the egg.

Serious doubts about the *tabula rasa* foundations of the environmentalist edifice first emerged in a field seemingly far removed from sociology—ethology. Scientists who spent their days closely observing other species in the wild had never found the idea that all behavior is acquired completely plausible, but eventually, even true believers in the power of the environment began finding explanatory recourse to something that looked a lot like "instinct"[13] unavoidable (Breland & Breland, 1961). To them, it had become clear that although organisms can and do acquire many behaviors from their environment, they also come into the world pre-equipped with a suite of species-specific dispositions and action patterns that were not so much learned from the environment as evoked by it. The obvious adaptive utility of most such predisposed behaviors led the ethologists to further conclude that these behavioral dispositions were very likely of evolutionary origin (Tinbergen, 1951).

Meanwhile, the *tabula rasa* assumption was also taking a beating at the hands of psychological research[14] demonstrating that contra its core assumptions, some associations (e.g., between taste and nausea) were learned much faster than others (Garcia & Koelling, 1966), Neither could it adequately account for such salient phenomena as the human proclivity for language acquisition (Chomsky, 1965), nor even for infant attachment (Harlow, 1958) or problem-solving (Kohler, 1925) in nonhuman primates. Such findings converged with ethologists' aforementioned conviction that organisms were born with "innate schoolmarms" (Lorenz, 1965/1989)—an idea the psychologists rechristened "prepared learning" (Seligman, 1971).

The upshot of all this was that organisms, explicitly including human beings, were decidedly not, as per the culturalist assumption, "all-purpose clay" (Laland & Brown, 2011). Between such empirical refutations of *tabula rasa* and the growing awareness of the evidentiary problems plaguing some of its canonical works (e.g., the methodological and source reliability issues attending Margaret Mead's fieldwork [Freeman, 1983]), it became possible to publicly question whether or not the environment really could suffice as sociology's sole explanatory tool (Homans, 1964; Wrong, 1961), opening the door once again to biological/evolutionary explanations of human social behavior.

From the mid-1960s on, erstwhile anthropologists (Ardrey, 1961), actual anthropologists (Carniero, 1974; Tiger & Fox, 1971), political scientists (Masters, 1976; Somit, 1968; Thorson, 1970), and even sociologists (Alland, 1967; Doby, 1970; Eckland, 1967;

Lenski, 1966; Mazur & Robertson, 1972) began explicitly incorporating biology and/or evolution into their models of human social behavior. The watershed moment arrived when E. O. Wilson reciprocated these overtures on behalf of biology by publishing *Sociobiology: The New Synthesis* in 1975.

Wilson's ostensible goal was to compile and synthesize exciting new work on a topic that had vexed evolutionary thinkers since (and including) Darwin—the behavior of social insects. William Hamilton (1964) had deciphered the evolutionary origins of insect eusociality by changing the level of analysis to a gene's-eye view, and Wilson sought to garner it the attention this revolutionary approach deserved (Plotkin, 2004; Segerstrale, 2000) by augmenting Hamilton's insight with elements of game theory and behavioral ecology, testing the theory against detailed case studies, extending its implications beyond insects, and making the best possible case for this "new synthesis."

That it would indeed receive ample attention was guaranteed by the fact that Wilson bookended what would otherwise have been a pretty straightforward work on evolutionary entymological ethology between an introductory chapter in which he advocates relocating the study of ethics from philosophy to biology and announces the coming assimilation of social science to biology, and a concluding chapter that speculatively extends the gene's-eye perspective to the analysis of human social behavior.

The critical response to Wilson's work was swift and strident. In short order, an oppositional organization—"The Sociobiology Study Group"—had been formed, and it had published (over the signatures of, among others, two of Wilson's Harvard colleagues) a biting denunciation of his book in the *New York Review of Books* (Allen et al., 1975). This was but the first trickle of a torrent of published criticism that was soon to follow (Chorover, 1979; Lewontin, Rose, & Kamin, 1984; Sahlins, 1976), and Wilson was publicly assaulted—doused with cold water by assailants charging him with genocide—as he presented his work at the 1978 meeting of the American Association for the Advancement of Science (Segerstrale, 2000).

The vehemence of this response is itself so striking as to demand explanation. Painstakingly piecing together the evidence, including interviews with the principals, Segerstrale (2000) has provided what will long stand as the definitive sociological account of this chapter in intellectual history. As she demonstrates, the debate was shaped in part by personal dynamics among Wilson, his allies, and his critics; by tactical posturing on both sides; and by simple misunderstandings all around. But as the title of her book makes clear, the kernel of the conflict was essentially moral, in that members of each side viewed themselves as the "defenders of the truth"—but, crucially, of two different truths.

As Segerstrale (2000) describes the situation, critics of sociobiology were committed to a "moral reading" of the theory—one in which associations with the earlier ideological (mis)applications of the approach (see Verse II) were compounded with the (often incorrectly) imputed political goals of sociobiologists and with fears of future evils yet to be committed in its name so as to render sociobiology simply too dangerous to be considered as one would any other theoretical paradigm. This moral reading has been the primary lens through which a plurality of sociologists have viewed biological and evolutionary approaches for most of the past 40 years. The cost of this misreading, and of the subsequent rejection of biological approaches to the field, has been almost a half century of disciplinary fragmentation, intellectual stagnation, and a lack of cumulative progress (Ellis, 1996; Lopreato & Crippen, 1999) as the discipline, paralyzed by its own insecurities in the face of the phantom menace of reductionism, has occupied itself with speculative philosophy and identity politics rather than pursuing the comprehensive and unified explanations for the pressing social phenomena of the modernizing world that the embrace of biology would have enabled. As human civilization enters new waters of unprecedented technological power and exceptional political upheaval and uncertainty, this is a cost too dear to continue paying.

VERSE V: RECONCILIATION

If the goal of anti-sociobiology forces was to derail the rapprochement between sociology and biology heralded by the advent of sociobiology, they are, today, likely disappointed. Despite its opponents' considerable success at delaying that reunion (and, in the process, alienating large swathes of both disciplines from one another), a cadre of dedicated biosociologists continued to develop and promote the approach in the ensuing decades, and it is fair to say that a reconciliation between sociology and biology is now well underway. This reunion has already produced viable intellectual offspring across the social science spectrum. In addition to sociobiology, they can claim human behavioral ecology (Winterhalder & Smith, 1992), evolutionary anthropology (Cronk, 1991), evolutionary psychology (Barkow, Cosmides, & Tooby, 1992), and organizational ecology (Hannan & Freeman, 1989) among their progeny. However, most significant for present purposes is the emergence (datable, for convenience, from the 2005 establishment of the Evolution, Behavior, and Society section of the American Sociological Association [ASA]) of a distinct field of "biosociology" and the advent of what Machalek and Martin (2010) herald as "a new species of social scientist"—the "evolutionary sociologist."

As it approaches adolescence, this new subdiscipline appears healthy and vital: Mainstream journals, including such stalwarts as *American Sociological Review, American Journal of Sociology*, and *Social Forces*, publish biosociological articles on a semiregular basis and have even built special issues around the topic; a dedicated journal, *Frontiers in Sociology: Evolutionary Sociology and Biosociology*, has been launched; and of late, there is enough interest to warrant the publication of multiple handbooks on the topic (Turner, Machalek, & Maryanski, 2015; see also Chapters 2, 5, and 6, this volume) and of at least one explicitly bio-themed introductory sociology text (Hopcroft, 2010). A recent survey of sociological theorists even suggests significant increases in the nominal acceptability of biosociological approaches over previous such surveys (Horowitz et al., 2014).

Yet the same survey also reveals continuing widespread resistance to biosociology in many quarters and a dearth of theorists who are actively using the approach in their work (Horowitz et al., 2014). Meanwhile, mainstream introductory texts continue to effectively deny any role for human nature in sociology (Leahy, 2012), and history has shown that calls for consilience, even from the bully pulpit of the ASA presidency, have had but limited impact on the biophobic attitudes of most sociologists. Indeed, anyone who has, even recently, sought to publish on biosociology in mainstream sociological journals has tales to tell of readers' reports and decision letters brimming with the same misconceptions that have bedeviled the field for the past four decades.

To the extent that they are not looking backwards, critics of biosociology have even begun to seize on so-called "post-genomic biology"—for example, molecular epigenetics, evolutionary development, niche construction, and developmental systems theory—as new vindications of their long-standing insistence on the irrelevance of biosociology for understanding social behavior (Ingold & Palsson, 2013; Meloni, 2014; Oyama, 2000).

Taken together, these conflicting indicators, not to mention the perpetual salience and significance of the intersection of biology and sociology as discussed in Verse I, suggest that the relationship between biology and sociology will likely continue to vacillate. However, there are reasons to hope that sometime in the near future, the pendulum of their relationship will come to make less extreme orbits around a point somewhat closer to the biophillic end of its arc than is currently the case. Such optimism is driven by developments within both sociology and biology, as well as by an appreciation of the essential historical, ontological, continuous, analogous, and topical unities between the two disciplines.

Within Sociology

Within sociology, again broadly defined, at least three factors augur well for its nascent reconciliation with biology. The first of these is that proponents of the biosocial approach have a remarkable history of not only answering the critiques leveled at it but also incorporating the best of these into their own theoretical armamentarium. For instance, Gould's (1978) early critiques of sociobiology's predilection for Panglossian adaptationism led he and Lewontin (1979) to identify, empirically establish, and elaborate a number of non-optimizing evolutionary mechanisms, including "exaptation," in which some phenotypes may not themselves be adaptive but have nevertheless evolved as a necessary by-product of other traits that are adaptive. Such "spandrelist" models have since been widely incorporated into new and better theories of biosocial causation, most notably with regard to the evolutionary underpinnings of religion (Atran, 2002; Boyer, 2002; Dawkins, 2006; Marshall, 2016). Likewise, by taking seriously the refrains of critics who argued that biological approaches neglected the degree of culture's influence, proponents of biosociology have developed and applied sophisticated models of gene/culture co-evolution to many and diverse domains (Baumeister, Maner, & DeWall, 2006; Blute, 2006; Laland, Odling-Smee, & Myles, 2010; Mrazek, Chiao, Blizinsky, Lun, & Gelfand, 2013; Richerson & Boyd, 2005; Walsh, 2014). To the extent that "post-genomic" biology warrants a reconsideration of evolution as a whole—and there is much yet to understand before we can ascertain its net significance—this history suggests that it will prove less the end of biosociology than a basis of newer and still more fecund biosocial theories.

The second auspicious development is a shift in the zeitgeist of the field, specifically a sense that the various post-ist deconstructionisms have just about run their course and that social scientists are again searching for a reality beyond that of texts (Meloni, 2014). Taking assumptions and institutions apart to reveal that nothing is quite what it seems, thereby undermining the authority of said institutions, is heady stuff, and it at least feels empowering. But eventually, one runs out of constructs to disassemble, while the project's intellectual nihilism leaves one with little else to do, and has left one with no solid footing from which to make meaningful claims anyway. We can only hope that reflection upon their role in paving the path to post-truth politics will further curb sociologists' appetite for this self-destructive species of "social theory." The empirically tractable and embodied sociality represented by biosociology proffers the most obvious and promising foundation upon which to construct a new, more durable, wing of sociological theory.

Third, the import of biology to sociality in the form of human nature has heretofore been partially masked by the fact that being social, and doing so in the ways that we do, is exactly what we have evolved to do. In short, human sociality comes "naturally" (read: invisibly) to humans. As we in the near future interact increasingly more with nonhuman social actors such as organizations and artificial intelligences, differences between their natures and ours will become ever more pointed, occasioning an overdue re-emphasis on just what human nature is, in contrast to the machine natures and organization natures with which we interact. For our biologically constituted human nature puts us at a distinct disadvantage in such interactions: Human sociality evolved in a context in which other interactants were possessed of essentially the same capacities for empathy, and drives for reciprocity, as oneself. But machines, are constitutionally incapable of actually experiencing any such regulatory emotions—to the extent that they evince them, it is but a simulacrum, one potentially deployable in the service of further manipulating human beings. Likewise, although composed of human beings, organizations systematically dilute the natural social dispositions of their constituent individuals—even while concentrating their (naturally limited) capacities for rationality (Marshall, 2003).

Within Biology

Likely more important to their future relationship is the fact that biology is lately transforming itself in ways that render it much more palatable to sociologists. Stated simply, biology is becoming more social (Meloni, 2014), and it is doing so on at least two fronts. The first of these is an overdue shedding of some antiquated pre-theoretical assumptions. When biology first emerged, extant cultural beliefs about human nature got grafted onto it, just as racism and sexism were. In particular, Hobbesian ideas of life in the state of nature as "nasty, brutish, and short" and the Tennysonian image of "nature red in tooth and claw" accorded well with the individualistic and competitive dimensions of Darwin's mechanism, creating the impression that evolutionary accounts of human nature inevitably painted it in harsh colors of unremitting selfishness—pessimistic tints evident in sociobiological accounts that too often and too earnestly rendered love, generosity, and indeed everything noble about human beings, as but camouflaged varieties of selfishness.

But that picture of human nature is contrary not only to casual observation[15] (e.g., the ubiquity of social living and prosocial, even altruistic, behavior across the animal kingdom) but also to empirical evidence that the fitness of individual organisms—and of human organisms in particular—is intimately tied up with that of their coalitional conspecifics and even heterospecific members of their microbiome. Although it would be naive to deny that individual fitness remains the fundamental focus of selective pressure, and that there is thus an innately self-interested dimension to human nature, it would be equally misguided to ignore the fact that, properly understood, individual fitness is a non-zero-sum interaction with that of other individuals such that genuine prosociality is not only possible but also pervasive in our species. We are, in short, "hypersocial" "supercooperators" (Bowles & Gintis, 2011; Hrdy, 2009; Lieberman, 2014; Nowak, 2011; Warneken & Tomasello, 2006), whose sociality is built into our very anatomy and physiology at every level, including a suite of moral capacities (de Waal, 1996; Haidt, 2001; Hauser, 2006; Joyce, 2006) that are every bit as natural and real and influential as are the a- or antisocial tendencies of our natures.

The appeal that this view of human nature holds for sociology extends beyond its provision of a more flattering and optimistic perspective and includes the fact that it also bears close affinities with long-held but heretofore undersubstantiated sociological tenets. At the most abstract level, it makes it clear that, as per sociological convention, the very idea of the isolated presocial human individual always has been total fiction in that we were social long before we were human. Likewise, by positing the significance of units of analysis that are simultaneously below and above the individual (a gene is both one element of an individual's larger chromosome and shared across many individuals, as per inclusive fitness), biology decenters the individual organism as a singular unit of analysis, much as sociology has long sought to do.

At a more concrete level, the physiology of mirror neurons (Rinzolatti & Craighero, 2004) furnishes a means by which practices are routinely transmitted without knowledge of their reasons, as per Berger and Luckmann's (1967) model of reification. Likewise, work on the neuropharmacology of positive social interaction (Moll et al., 2006) dovetails well with Collins' (1993) hypostatization of "emotional energy," and Lieberman's (2014) work on the neural correlates of selfhood leads him to the sociological conclusion that the self is, perhaps above all else, a powerful means of social control.

More examples of biology–sociology convergence could be appended to this list. But before we get too self-congratulatory, note that not every sociological construct fares so well in the search for biological or evolutionary underpinnings. Even those that do may require significant alteration to better accord with what is empirically substantiable—wherein lies one of the most important advantages of incorporating biological (and, by extension, psychological) approaches into the discipline: By furnishing a sound basis for separating the wheat from the chaff of sociological theory, it allows us to dismiss less corroborated theories so as to concentrate more closely on those with more secure foundations.[16]

Even as it presents a more sociologically congenial image of human nature, thereby opening the door to greater consilience between the two disciplines, the social turn in biology has also revealed an acute irony about sociology that cannot be glossed over. Despite the considerable effort that sociologists have expended throughout the years promoting an omnipotent if amorphous view of "the social" as the only causal construct that sociology requires, it turns out to be mainstream sociology that has egregiously underestimated the profound sociality of human nature—and it is biology that has best demonstrated it. As noted in Verse II, Mead's project, or rather the understanding of it for which he is revered within sociology, was to demonstrate the ultimately social nature of such ostensibly psychological constructs as mind, self, and society—a challenge he addressed by constructing models of each that are ultimately dependent on human beings' quantitatively singular capacity for language. In his wake, generations of sociologists have erected a now-massive edifice of "the Social" upon these same narrow linguistic foundations.

This impoverished view of the social has severely and unnecessarily constricted the scope of sociology. For human sociality is in fact much older, more fundamental, and more extensive than mere language (Lieberman, 2014; Maryanski & Turner, 2015). Indeed, our capacity for cognition and language was likely possible only because we were an already intensely social species, and it was selected for primarily by the demands of social living (Dunbar, 1998). The component elements of this foundational sociality span from the morphological and perceptual (e.g., the singular emotional expressivity of our faces and our complementary ability to interpret the meanings of such expressions [Ekman, Frisen, & Ancoli, 1980], our highly visible sclera and our complementary ability to use it to follow one another's gaze [Tomasello, Hare, Lehmann, & Call, 2007], and our ability to detect and recognize faces above all other stimuli [Kanwisher & Yovel, 2006]) to the neuroanatomical (e.g., the default network of social cognition [Spunt, Meyer, & Lieberman, 2015], the exaptation of the physical pain system for social pain [Panskepp, 2003], and the aforementioned mirror neurons, enabling emotional entrainment, and thereby intersubjectivity [Hatfield, Cacioppo, & Rapson, 1994], and facilitating cultural transmission [Rinzolatti & Craighero 2004]), the neuropharmacology of oxytocin and vasopressin (Pedersen, Jirikowski, Caldwell, & Insel, 1992), and heightened emotionality, along with tools for controlling it (Turner, 2010).

The upshot of this far-from-complete itemization is that human social behavior is utterly dependent on an immense biological infrastructure of evolutionary origin, all of which is much older, and more fundamental, than is the human capacity for language. By heretofore excluding such elements from our theories in favor of language and symbol, sociology has missed most of what is most social about social behavior and social phenomena, underestimating and undermining the scope and power of sociological analysis and abdicating its duty to actually explain social behavior and phenomena. More positively (and more to the point of this section), sociology's neglect of so much of "the social" up to now means that its most productive days may yet lie in the future.

Finally, biology is not only becoming more congenial to sociology but also is in fact becoming more sociological. Although, as discussed previously, humans are unusually social, sociality is a recurrent feature of the entire history of life on earth in that biological evolution itself is a deeply social process. As Nowak (2011) argues, sociality amounts to evolution's "third leg" alongside variation and selection, and it is the primary means by which evolution increases complexity in the natural world. The literature on "major transitions" (Maynard-Smith & Szathmáry, 1995; Nowak, 2011) makes it clear that the crucial and oft-repeated pattern in the history of life on earth is that by which originally independent genes became collectivized into chromosomes; by which prokaryotic cells became consolidated into eukaryotic cells; by which single-celled creatures were combined into multicellular organisms; and by which individual organisms entered into an array of symbiotic conglomerations, including micro-biomes, copses, colonies, herds, flocks, schools, families, tribes, organizations, and nations. In each case, the breakthrough occurred when biological entities evolved capacities for suppressing competition among each other enough to combine themselves into new and collectively more fit entities. From this perspective, every organism embodies a prodigious feat of social cooperation at multiple levels and is, in turn, potentially a component of even larger entities.

The upshot of all this is that the arguably central question of sociology—How is social order possible?—turns out to be of universal applicability and consequence, extending all the way down to the simplest forms of life and all the way up to the suprahuman level of organizations, nations, and other potential superorganisms (Holldobbler & Wilson, 2009). Accordingly, at least some elements of social control, recur at multiple levels—for instance, the policing that occurs within clonal raider ant colonies as particular individuals are tasked with to hunting down and dismembering unauthorized ovulators (Trible & Kronauer, 2017). The takeaway here is that the scope of "sociology" has just become much larger than our founding figures ever imagined. Let us hope that sociology is able to collectively reconcile itself to its once and future alliance with biology in time to benefit from (and, more important, contribute to) this newly sociologicized view of life.

The Unity of Biology and Sociology

By far the most compelling reason to believe in sociology's bright future with biology is—to stretch the romantic conceit of our approach here just a wee bit further—that they belong together. By this I mean, as has been developed elsewhere (Marshall, 2018), that the relationship between sociology and biology is ultimately one of essential and multifaceted unity.[17] Rosenberg (2015) gets right to the core of the matter when he says that the "slam-dunk" argument for biosociology is the self-evident fact that "*Homo sapiens* is a biological species" so there is simply no way that anything we could be, do, or create can ever truly transcend biology (p. 31). Social behavior is enacted only by living entities, via mechanisms that are indubitably biological, the origins of which are undeniably products of evolution through a process that we can now be certain is inherently social. From this *ontological* unity spring several others: the *historical* unity outlined in Verse I; the *continuous* unity through which biology (originating via evolutionary mechanisms and actuated via psychological mechanisms) determines the limitations, capacities, imperatives, and dispositions through which the social becomes manifest; the *analogous* unity by which the variation/deselection mechanism first identified by Darwin in the biological realm is extensible as well to cultural, institutional, and other forms of social change; and the *topical* unity exemplified, on the one hand, by the universalization of the problem of social order through biology as described previously and, on the other hand, by the fact that it is biological developments—artificial life, genetic manipulation, life extension, and population growth—that will likely set the sociological *problematique* for the next generation of sociologists.

CONCLUSION

This brief review of the history of sociology's relationship with biology has shown it to be marked by misunderstandings, overreaching, justified and unjustified recriminations, and radical reversals. In that, it is not unlike the early stages of many human relationships. In light of this contentious history, and of the continued singular pertinence of their shared domain to issues of grave importance to human life and culture, it would be naive to imagine that they will now live happily ever after. However, although tensions between the two disciplines may be inevitable, the obstacles to their happy congress, some identified herein, are not insurmountable. In reviews such as this, it is usual for biosociologists to include a warning to their biophobic colleagues that their continued disavowal of biological mechanisms, concepts, and approaches—and thereby the unifying foundation that only they can provide—threatens the discipline's relevance, legitimacy, vitality, and very raison d'etre, which is all true enough. But let us close this chapter on a more positive note: If mainstream sociology can bring itself to shake off its reflexive disdain toward biology in all of its physiological, psychological, and evolutionary manifestations and actually engage with it in a serious (not to say uncritical) manner, the discipline's best days may yet lie ahead.

NOTES

1. Although "biology" and "evolution" are mutually integral, such that, as per Dobzhansky, the former only makes sense in the light of the latter, they are not perfectly coextensive. One can both talk about biological influences on social behavior at a proximate level (i.e.,

physiology) without explicit reference to evolution, and talk about evolutionary processes beyond the strictly biological realm (e.g., social and cultural evolution). Nevertheless, except where the text specifically parses them out, "biology" should herein be understood to include both concepts.

2. For more detailed accounts of this history, see Plotkin (2004), Segerstrale (2000), and of course Degler (1991), all of whom I have relied on throughout.

3. Although the usual shorthand for Darwin's model is "variation/selection," and that formulation also appears herein, note that this "deselection" formulation more accurately locates the action in the *removal of* alternative phenotypes rather than in any kind of active *selection for* the surviving version, as reflected in Darwin's eventual preference for the term "natural preservation" over "natural selection" (Lopreato, 2001).

4. The problem, of course, is that the critique of biosociology has thus far been somewhat less "informed" than "robust"—a problem the solution to which is unfortunately beyond the scope of this chapter.

5. I look forward to the day when sociology gets beyond is parochial anthropocentrism to realize that "the social" is much bigger than one species and that the discipline can only benefit from widening our purview to embrace a truly comparative (i.e., interspecies) sociology—in which case, the unifying substrate will be, for instance, mammalian nature, or chordate nature.

6. Stated bluntly, the concept of genes is not a necessary prerequisite to genocide. Pogroms against assorted out-groups preceded Darwin (and Mendel) by millennia, and the eradication of these "others" proceeded apace in the complete absence of genetic or evolutionary thought. Indeed, even the Nazi project was in no small part an attack on the cultural traits of modernity and cosmopolitanism, which were projected upon a group defined as much by cultural (religion) as by genetic factors (Buruma & Margalit, 2004; Herf, 1984; Smith, 1996). Because both genes and culture ultimately depend on individuals for their continuation and transmission, and because the extermination of those carriers is thereby equally lethal to both, it is foolish to think that biological thought has some unique affinity with intergroup violence or that cultural theories cannot equally be conscripted to genocidal causes.

7. Ironically, from a biosociological perspective, not only is such conditionability itself an evolved adaptation but also its mechanism is an example of Darwinism beyond biology— of "universal Darwinism" (Dawkins, 1983)—in that it depends on an organism emitting random behaviors (variation), some of which evoke a positive reinforcement (selection), on which basis only those behaviors will be repeated in the future (reproduction).

8. Because this work was compiled by his students, he did not exactly choose the title himself, but obviously his behaviorism had been clearly enough conveyed that they believed it integral to the title.

9. The extent to which self-proclaimed "Meadian" sociologists manage to elide the explicit and permeating behaviorism of his project, and the rather thorough determinism it represents, never fails to astound.

10. In that, as Boas recognized, although one's language community membership determines which sets of sounds one will and will not ultimately be capable of discerning the disposition to selectively attend to those distinctions that are relevant to one's own language community at the expense of those that are not seems to not only be an evolved aid to language learning but also one that operates via the fundamentally Darwinian mechanism of cognitive pruning in which the young brain's thicket of randomly varied connections is

selectively pruned via functional validation, whereby neurons that get used are retained and connected, whereas those that go unused are eliminated (Edelman, 1987).

11. Although Durkheim's (1982) vision of sociology was of a discipline also "independent of all philosophy" (p. 159), and despite the fact that he devotes as much effort in *Rules* to distinguishing sociology from philosophy as to distinguishing it from psychology, sociologists seldom get as indignant about philosophy's myriad encroachments into the discipline as they do about biology's and psychology's encroachments.

12. "Human nature" is the most proximate manifestation of biology to sociology and hence the form in which most sociologists will encounter it.

13. To be clear, what the ethologists proposed was decidedly not a disinterring of McDougall's "instinct theory" (1908/2001), which had overextended the concept of instinct to the point of absurdity.

14. It continues to do so, as methodological advances have made it possible to demonstrate just how very un-*rasa* the *tabula* actually is. Human infants exhibit a surprisingly sophisticated understanding of basic physics (Leslie & Keeble, 1987), mathematics (Wynn, 1992), and even rules of social evaluation (Hamlin, Wynn, & Bloom, 2007) (among other things), from what is obviously much too early an age for these abilities to have been acquired from the environment.

15. Likely the most compelling evidence of human sociality is the unconscious provenance of our social signaling mechanisms, in that our conscious control over crying, blushing, yawning, laughter, and other "given off" signs (Goffman, 1959) is limited, making it notoriously difficult to fully conceal our inner states and thoughts from others. In a truly Hobbesian world, such transparency would prove deadly and thereby be strongly selected against. That it has not been suggests an enduring social context in which honest signaling of our inner states had adaptive value over and above the costs of betraying them and that such revelations were, on balance, likely to elicit more assistance than exploitation, at least within our primary groups.

16. Other important advantages include tying the surviving theories to larger and more disparate literatures, expanding their scope and fecundity, achieving higher resolution, and reducing system noise so as to better detect the sociological signal.

17. Although not, to be clear, identity. The claim is not that the two are indistinguishable but, rather, that they are neighboring and overlapping aspects of the same entity.

References

Alland, A. (1967). *Evolution and human behavior.* Garden City, NY: Natural History Press.

Allen, E., Beckwith, B., Beckwith, J. et al. (1975). Against sociobiology. *The New York Review of Books, 13*(182), 184–186.

Ardrey, R. (1961). *African genesis: A personal investigation into the animal origins and nature of man.* New York, NY: Bantam.

Atran, S. (2002). *In gods we trust: The evolutionary landscape of religion.* New York, NY: Oxford University Press.

Barkow, J., Cosmides, L., & Tooby, J. (1992). *The adapted mind: Evolutionary psychology and the generation of culture.* New York, NY: Oxford University Press.

Baumeister, R., Maner, J., & DeWall, N. (2006). Evoked culture and evoked nature: Coevolution and the emergence of cultural animals. *Psychological Inquiry, 17,* 128–130.

Berger, P., & Luckmann, T. (1967). *The social construction of reality: A treatise in the sociology of knowledge*. Garden City, NY: Anchor.

Berscheid, E., & Reis, H. (1998). Interpersonal attraction and close relationships. In S. Fiske, D. Gilbert, G. Lindzey, & E. Aronson (Eds.), *Handbook of social psychology* (Vol. 2, pp. 193–281). New York, NY: Random House.

Blute, M. (2006). Gene–culture coevolutionary games. *Social Forces*, 85(1), 151–166.

Boas, F. (1889). On alternating sounds. *American Anthropologist*, A2(1), 47–54.

Boas, F. (1912). *Changes in bodily form of descendants of immigrants*. New York, NY: Columbia University Press.

Bourdeau, M. (2010). *Comte's Lamarckian heritage*. https://halshs.archivesouvertes.fr/halshs-00596702

Bowles, S., & Gintis, H. (2011). *A cooperative species: Human reciprocity and its evolution*. Princeton, NJ: Princeton University Press.

Boyer, P. (2002). *Religion explained: The evolutionary origins of religious thought*. New York, NY: Basic Books.

Breland, K., & Breland, M. (1961). The misbehavior of organisms. *American Psychologist*, 16, 681–684.

Buruma, I., & Margalit, A. (2004). *Occidentalism: The West in the eyes of its enemies*. New York, NY: Penguin.

Campbell, D. T. (1987). Evolutionary epistemology. In G. Radnitzky & W. Bartley (Eds.), *Evolutionary epistemology, rationality, and the sociology of knowledge* (pp. 47–90). LaSalle, IL: Open Court.

Carniero, R. (1974). The four faces of evolution. In J. J. Honigmann (Ed.), *Handbook of social and cultural anthropology* (pp. 89–110). Chicago, IL: Rand McNally.

Carniero, R. (2015). Spencer's conception of evolution and its application to the political development of societies. In J. H. Turner, R. Machalek, & A. Maryanski (Eds.), *Handbook of evolution and society: Toward an evolutionary social science* (pp. 215–227). London, UK: Routledge.

Chagnon, N., & Macfarlan, S. (2015). Yanomamo: The sociobiology people. In J. H. Turner, R. Machalek, & A. Maryanski (Eds.), *Handbook of evolution and society: Toward an evolutionary social science* (pp. 114–121). London, UK: Routledge.

Chomsky, N. (1965). *Aspects of the theory of syntax*. Cambridge, MA: MIT Press.

Chorover, S. (1979). *From Genesis to genocide: The meaning of human nature and the power of behavior control*. Cambridge, MA: MIT Press.

Collins, R. (1993). Emotional energy as the common denominator of rational action. *Rationality and Society*, 5(2), 203–230.

Cosmides, L., & Tooby, J. (1992). Cognitive adaptations for social exchange. In J. Barkow, L. Cosmides, & J. Tooby (Eds.), *The adapted mind: Evolutionary psychology and the generation of culture* (pp. 163–228). New York, NY: Oxford University Press.

Cronk, L. (1991). Human behavioral ecology. *Annual Review of Anthropology*, 20, 25–53.

Darwin, C. (2004). *The descent of man and selection in relation to sex*. New York, NY: Penguin Classics. (Original work published 1871)

Darwin, C. (2009). *The expression of emotion and man and animals*. Oxford, UK: Oxford University Press. (Original work published 1872)

Dawkins, R. (1983). Universal Darwinism. In D. S. Bendall (Ed.), *Evolution from molecules to man* (pp. 403–428). Cambridge, UK: Cambridge University Press.

Dawkins, R. (2006). *The god delusion*. Boston MA: Houghton Mifflin Harcourt.

de Waal, F. (1996). *Good natured: The origins of right and wrong in humans and other animals*. Cambridge, MA: Harvard University Press.

Degler, C. (1991). *In search of human nature: The decline and revival of Darwinism in American social thought*. New York, NY: Oxford University Press.

Doby, J. T. (1970). Man the species and the individual: A sociological perspective. *Social Forces, 49*(1), 1–15.

Douglas, M. (1978). *Cultural bias* (Occasional Paper No. 35). London, UK: Royal Anthropological Institute of Great Britain and Ireland.

Dunbar, R. I. (1998). The social brain hypothesis. *Evolutionary Anthropology, 6*(5), 178–190.

Durkheim, E. (1982). *The rules of the sociological method, and selected texts on sociology and its method*. New York, NY: Free Press. (Original work published 1895)

Durkheim, E. (1984). *The division of labor in society*. London, UK: Palgrave Macmillan. (Original work published 1895)

Durkheim, E. (2001). *The elementary forms of religious life*. New York, NY: Oxford University Press. (Original work published 1912)

Eckland, B. E. (1967). Genetics and sociology: A reconsideration. *American Sociological Review, 32*(2), 173–194.

Edelman, G. M. (1987). *Neural Darwinism: The theory of neuronal group selection*. New York, NY: Basic Books.

Ekman, P., Frisen, W., & Ancoli, S. (1980). Facial signs of emotional experience. *Journal of Personality and Social Psychology, 39*(6), 1125–1134.

Ellis, L. (1996). A discipline in peril: Sociology's future hinges on curing its biophobia. *American Sociologist, 27*(2), 21–41.

Freeman, D. (1983). *Margaret Mead and Samoa*. Cambridge, MA: Harvard University Press.

Garcia, J., & Koelling, R. (1966). Relation of cue to consequence in avoidance learning. *Psychonomic Science, 4*(3), 123–124.

Goffman, E. (1959). *The presentation of self in everyday life*. New York, NY: Anchor.

Gould, S. J. (1978). Sociobiology and human nature: A post-Panglossian vision. In A. Montagu (Ed.), *Sociobiology examined* (pp. 283–290). New York, NY: Oxford University Press.

Gould, S. J., & Lewontin, R. (1979). The spandrels of San Marco and the Panglossian paradigm: A critique of the adaptationist programme. *Proceedings of the Royal Society of London, Series B: Biological Sciences, 205*, 581–598.

Haidt, J. (2001). The emotional dog and its rational tail: A social intuitionist approach to moral judgment. *Psychological Review, 108*(4), 814–834.

Hamilton, W. D. (1964). The genetical theory of social behavior I and II. *Journal of Theoretical Biology, 7*, 1–32.

Hamlin, J. K., Wynn, K., & Bloom, P. (2007). Social evaluation by preverbal infants. *Nature, 450*, 557–559. doi:10.1038/nature06288

Hannan, M. T., & Freeman, J. (1989). *Organizational ecology*. Cambridge, MA: Harvard University Press.

Hanson, C. (2010). Teach softly and debunk with a big stick: A response to "Evolution, biology, and society: A conversation for the 21st-century sociology classroom." *Teaching Sociology, 38*(1), 50–53.

Harlow, H. F. (1958). The nature of love. *American Psychologist, 13*, 673–685.

Hatfield, E., Cacioppo, J. T., & Rapson, R. R. (1994). *Emotional contagion*. Cambridge, UK: Cambridge University Press.

Hauser, M. (2006). *Moral minds: How nature designed our universal sense of right and wrong*. New York, NY: HarperCollins.

Herf, J. (1984). *Reactionary modernism: Technology, culture, and politics in Weimar and the Third Reich*. Cambridge, UK: Cambridge University Press.

Holldobbler, B., & Wilson, E. O. (2009). *The superorganism: The beauty, elegance, and strangeness of insect societies*. New York, NY: Norton.

Homans, G. (1964). Bringing men back in. *American Sociological Review*, 29(5), 809–818.

Hopcroft, R. (2010). *Sociology: A biosocial introduction*. Boulder, CO: Paradigm.

Hopcroft, R. (2016). *Evolution and gender: Why it matters for contemporary life*. New York, NY: Routledge.

Horowitz, M., Yaworsky, W., & Kickham, K. (2014). Whither the blank slate? A report on the reception of evolutionary biological ideas among sociological theorists. *Sociological Spectrum*, 34(6), 489–509.

Hrdy, S. B. (2000). *Mother nature: Maternal instincts and how they shape the human species*. New York, NY: Ballantine.

Hrdy, S. B. (2009). *Mothers and others: The evolutionary origins of mutual understanding*. Cambridge, MA: Belknap.

Huber, J. (2007). *On the origins of gender inequality*. Boulder, CO: Paradigm.

Ingold, T., & Palsson, G. (2013). *Biosocial becomings: Integrating social and biological anthropology*. Cambridge, UK: Cambridge University Press.

Irwin, M. D. (2015). Evolving communities: Evolutionary analysis in classical and neoclassical human ecology. In J. H. Turner, R. Machalek, & A. Maryanski (Eds.), *Handbook of evolution and society: Toward an evolutionary social science* (pp. 316–332). London, UK: Routledge.

Joyce, R. (2006). *The evolution of morality*. Cambridge, MA: MIT Press.

Kanwisher, N., & Yovel, G. (2006). The fusiform face area: A cortical region specialized for the perception of faces. *Philosophical Transactions B, Biological Sciences*, 361(1476), 2109–2128.

King, B. B., & Josea, J. (1961). You done lost your good thing now. *My kind of blues*. EMI Records.

Kohler, W. (1925). *The mentality of apes*. London, UK: Kegan Paul.

Kuo, Z. Y. (1924). A psychology without heredity. *Psychological Review*, 31, 435–446.

Laland, K. N., & Brown, G. (2011). *Sense and nonsense: Evolutionary perspectives on human behavior*. Oxford, UK: Oxford University Press.

Laland, K. N., Odling-Smee, J., & Myles, S. (2010). How culture shaped the human genome: Bringing genetics and the human sciences together. *Nature Reviews Genetics*, 11, 137–148. doi:10.1038/nrg2734

Lamarck, J. (2012). *Zoological philosophy: An exposition with regard to the natural history of animals*. London, UK: Forgotten Books. (Original work published 1809)

Leahy, T. (2012). The elephant in the room: Human nature and the sociology textbooks. *Current Sociology*, 60(6), 806–823.

Lenski, G. (1966). *Power and privilege: A theory of social stratification*. Charlotte, NC: University of North Carolina Press.

Leslie, A. M., & Keeble, S. (1987). Do six-month-old infants perceive causality? *Cognition*, 25, 265–288.

Lewontin, R., Rose, S., & Kamin, L. (1984). *Not in our genes*. New York, NY: Penguin.

Lieberman, M. (2014). *Social: Why our brains are wired to connect*. New York, NY: Crown.

Lopreato, J. (2001). Sociobiological theorizing: Evolutionary sociology. In J. H. Turner (Ed.), *Handbook of sociological theory* (pp. 405–433). New York, NY: Kluwer.

Lopreato, J., & Crippen, T. A. (1999). *Crisis in sociology: The need for Darwin*. New Brunswick, NJ: Transaction Publishers.

Lorenz, K. (1986). *Evolution and modification of behavior*. Chicago, IL: University of Chicago Press. (Original work published 1965)

Machalek, R., & Martin, M. (2010). Evolution, biology, and society: A conversation for the 21st-century classroom. *Teaching Sociology*, 38(1), 35–45.

Malthus, T. R. (1983). *An essay on the principle of population and a summary view of the principle of population.* London, UK: Penguin Classics. (Original work published 1798)

Marshall, D. A. (2003). *Beyond a rational choice sociology: A sociology of rationality* Doctoral dissertation. Retrieved from Proquest Dissertation Publishing. http://libproxy2.usouthal.edu/login?url=http://search.proquest.com/docview/305302240?accountid=14672

Marshall, D. A. (2016, August 31). The moral origins of god: Darwin, Durkheim, and the *Homo duplex* theory of theogenesis. *Frontiers in Sociology.* https://doi.org/10.3389/fsoc.2016.00013

Marshall, D. A. (2018). Unity(s) within conflict: Mapping biology's relevance to sociological theory. In P Kivisto (Ed.), *Cambridge handbook of social theory.* Cambridge, UK: Cambridge University Press.

Maryanski, A., & Turner, J. H. (2015). Evolutionary sociology: A cross-species strategy for discovering human nature. In J. H. Turner, R. Machalek, & A. Maryanski (Eds.), *Handbook of evolution and society: Toward an evolutionary social science* (pp. 316–332). London, UK: Routledge.

Masters, R. (1976). The impact of ethology on political science. In A. Somit (Ed.), *Biology and politics: Recent explorations* (pp. 266–288). The Hague, the Netherlands: Mouton de Gruyter.

Maynard-Smith, J., & Szathmáry, E. (1995). *The major transitions in evolution.* Oxford, UK: Oxford University Press.

Mazur, A., & Robertson, L. S. (1972). *Biology and social behavior.* New York, NY: Free Press.

McDougall, W. (2001). *An introduction to social psychology.* London, UK: Methuen. (Original work published 1908)

Mead, G. H. (1967). *Mind, self, and society: From the standpoint of a social behaviorist.* Chicago, IL: University of Chicago Press.

Meloni, M. (2014). How biology became social, and what it means for social theory. *Sociological Review,* 62(3), 593–614.

Moll, J., Kreuger, F., Zahn, R., Pardini, M., Oliveria-Souza, R., & Grafman, J. (2006). Human fronto-mesolimbic networks guide decisions about charitable donation. *Proceedings of the National Academy of Sciences of the USA,* 103(42), 15623–15628.

Mrazek, A., Chiao, J., Blizinsky, K., Lun, J., & Gelfand, M. (2013). The role of culture–gene coevolution in morality judgment: Examining the interplay between tightness–looseness and allelic variation of the serotonin transporter gene. *Culture and Brain,* 1, 100–117. doi:10.1007/s40167-013-0009-x

Nowak, M. A. (2011). *Supercooperators: Altruism, evolution, and why we need each other to succeed.* New York, NY: Free Press.

Oyama, S. (2000). *The ontogeny of information: Developmental systems and evolution.* Durham, NC: Duke University Press.

Panskepp, J. (2003). Feeling the pain of social loss. *Science,* 302(5643), 237–239. doi:10.1126/science.1091062

Pedersen, C. A., Jirikowski, G. F., Caldwell, J. D., & Insel, T. R. (1992). *Oxytocin in sexual, maternal, and social behaviors.* New York, NY: New York Academy of Sciences.

Pinker, S. (2002). *The blank slate: The modern denial of human nature.* New York, NY: Penguin.

Plotkin, H. (2004). *Evolutionary thought in psychology: A brief history.* Hoboken, NJ: Wiley-Blackwell.

Porter, C. (1935). Just one of those things. *Jubilee* [Musical].

Richerson, P., & Boyd, R. (2005). *Not by genes alone: How culture transformed human evolution.* Chicago IL: University of Chicago Press.

Rinzolatti, G., & Craighero, L. (2004). The mirror-neuron system. *Annual Review of Neuroscience,* 27(1), 169–192.

Rosenberg, A. (2015). The biological character of social theory. In J. H. Turner, R. Machalek, & A. Maryanski (Eds.), *Handbook of evolution and society: Toward an evolutionary social science* (pp. 31–58). London, UK: Routledge.

Runciman, W. G. (2015). Evolutionary sociology. In J. H. Turner, R. Machalek, & A. Maryanski (Eds.), *Handbook of evolution and society: Toward an evolutionary social science* (pp. 194–214). London, UK: Routledge.

Sahlins, M. (1976). *The use and abuse of biology: An anthropological critique of sociobiology.* Ann Arbor, MI: University of Michigan Press.

Sanderson, S. (2001). *The evolution of human sociality: A Darwinian conflict perspective.* Lanham, MD: Rowman & Littlefield.

Sanderson, S. (2015). Darwinian conflict theory: A unified evolutionary research program. In J. H. Turner, R. Machalek, & A. Maryanski (Eds.), *Handbook of evolution and society: Toward an evolutionary social science* (pp. 228–266). London, UK: Routledge.

Segerstrale, U. (2000). *Defenders of the truth.* Oxford, UK: Oxford University Press.

Seligman, M. (1971). Phobias and preparedness. *Behavior Therapy, 2,* 307–320.

Simmel, G. (1971). Conflict. In D. Levine (Ed.), *On individuality and social forms: Selected writings* (pp. 70–95). Chicago, IL: University of Chicago Press. (Original work published 1908)

Smith, D. N. (1996). The social construction of enemies: Jews and the representation of evil. *Sociological Theory, 14*(3), 203–240.

Somit, A. (1968). Toward a more biologically-oriented political science: Ethology and psychopharmacology. *Midwest Journal of Political Science, 12,* 550–567.

Spunt, R. P., Meyer, M. L., & Lieberman, M. D. (2015). The default mode of human brain function primes the intentional stance. *Journal of Cognitive Neuroscience, 27*(6), 1116–1124.

Thorson, T. L. (1970). *Biopolitics.* New York, NY: Holt, Rhinehart & Winston.

Tiger, L., & Fox, R. (1971). *The imperial animal.* New York, NY: Holt, Rinehart & Winston.

Tinbergen, N. (1951). *The study of instinct.* New York, NY: Oxford University Press.

Tisdale, H. (1939). Biology in sociology. *Social Forces, 18*(1), 29–40.

Tomasello, M., Hare, B., Lehmann, H., & Call, J. (2007). Reliance on head versus eyes in the gaze following of great apes and human infants: The cooperative eye hypothesis. *Journal of Human Evolution, 52,* 314–320.

Trible, W., & Kronauer, D. J. (2017). Caste development and evolution in ants: It's all about size. *Journal of Experimental Biology, 220,* 53–62. doi:10.1242/jeb.145292

Turner, J. (2000). *On the origin of human emotion: A sociological inquiry into the evolution of human affect.* Stanford, CA: Stanford University Press.

Turner, J. H., Machalek, R., & Maryanski, A. (2015). *Handbook on evolution and society: Toward an evolutionary social science.* Boulder, CO: Paradigm.

van den Berghe, P. (1990). Why most sociologists don't (and won't) think evolutionarily. *Sociological Forum, 5*(2), 173–185.

Walsh, A. (2014). *Biosociology: Bridging the biology-sociology divide.* New Brunswick, NJ: Transaction Publishers.

Warneken, F., & Tomasello, M. (2006). Altruistic helping in human infants and young chimpanzees. *Science, 311,* 1301–1303. doi:10.1126/science.1121448

Wilson, E. O. (1975). *Sociobiology: The new synthesis.* Cambridge MA: Harvard University Press.

Wilson, E. O. (1998). *Consilience: The unity of knowledge.* New York, NY: Alfred A. Knopf.

Winterhalder, B., & Smith, E. A. (1992). *Evolutionary ecology and human behavior.* Piscataway, NJ: Aldine Transaction.

Wrong, D. (1961). The oversocialized conception of man in modern sociology. *American Sociological Review, 26*(2), 183–193.

Wynn, K. (1992). Addition and subtraction by human infants. *Nature, 358,* 749–750.

CHAPTER 4

....

EDWARD WESTERMARCK

The First Sociobiologist

....

STEPHEN K. SANDERSON

THE field known as sociobiology was officially launched in 1975 when the Harvard zoologist Edward O. Wilson published his almost instantly famous (or infamous) book, *Sociobiology: The New Synthesis*. The field (probably better identified as a theoretical approach or research program) was grounded in the Darwinian theory of biological evolution by natural selection and was defined by Wilson as the study of the biological basis of all social behavior, in both nonhuman animals and humans. In his book, Wilson concentrated mostly on nonhuman animals, but in the final chapter he sketched a set of ideas for understanding the biological basis of human social behavior. Marking a major intellectual revolution, it quickly attracted the attention of anthropologists and psychologists (and a handful of sociologists), but it also proved hugely controversial and was widely attacked (for an excellent history of the controversy, see Segerstråle, 2001). The name sociobiology seemed to have become toxic, and for this reason and several others, a number of psychologists and anthropologists changed the name to evolutionary psychology (Barkow, Cosmides, and Tooby, 1992). Whether the two approaches are the same thing with different names or something different is a matter of dispute, but it is clear that at the very least they are very close cousins, and in any event that debate is beyond the bounds of this chapter. (I prefer the term sociobiology and will use it here.). But Wilson and those who followed were actually not the first sociobiologists or evolutionary psychologists. This honor goes to Edward Westermarck.

Westermarck (1862–1939) was a sociologist who was part of the Swedish-speaking elite in Finland and took his doctorate at Imperial Alexander University, which is now the University of Helsinki. He was greatly influenced by Darwin, and in fact the bulk of his theoretical ideas owe to Darwin. He deserves to be called the first sociobiologist or evolutionary psychologist because he was applying Darwinian natural selectionist thinking in much the same way as modern-day practitioners of these approaches. Other sociologists who used Darwinian thinking at the time, such as Herbert Spencer, William Graham Sumner, and Albert G. Keller, used it to develop theories of *social* selection, not *natural* selection. (Natural selection is the environmental retention of favorable or adaptive genetic variants and the elimination of unfavorable or maladaptive genetic variations, whereas social selection is the retention of those ideas and institutions that prove most favorable to human survival and well-being in particular environments.) They were not seeking a deep Darwinian understanding of human nature that they could apply to understand social life, but that is exactly what Westermarck was doing. He was a thinker nearly a century ahead of his time.

Westermarck's best-known work was derived from his doctoral dissertation, which was a massive study of human marriage and family practices throughout the world. Written in English and completed in 1889, it was later published in 1891 as *The History of Human Marriage* (*HHM*). Westermarck revised and substantially updated *HHM* several times, with a greatly expanded fifth edition appearing in three volumes in 1922. Westermarck also had a keen interest in human morality, which led to his other major work, *The Origin and Development of the Moral Ideas* (*ODMI*), published in two volumes in 1906 (Vol. 1) and 1908 (Vol. 2). It is less well known than *HHM*, but it is an extremely important work. Both *HHM* and *ODMI* were written from a Darwinian evolutionary perspective.

A COMPARATIVE HISTORY
OF HUMAN MARRIAGE

Much of the first volume of *HHM* was devoted to a critique of the celebrated argument developed by several prominent social evolutionists of the day that the earliest humans lived in a state of sexual promiscuity. Westermarck exhaustively reviewed the evidence that its proponents used to justify this argument, and he found that on close examination, it utterly failed to garner any support. Regarding the statements that had been made of cases of primitive promiscuity, Westermarck said,

> It would be difficult to find a more untrustworthy collection of statements. Some of them are simply misrepresentations of theorists in which sexual laxity, frequency of separation, polyandry, group-marriage or something like it . . . is confounded with promiscuity. Others are based upon indefinite evidence which may be interpreted in one way or another, or on information proved to be inaccurate. And not a single statement can be said to be authoritative. (1922a:124)

Westermarck also observed that there were very good reasons for doubting that sexual promiscuity could ever have been a general pattern among humans. One reason was the emotion of sexual jealousy, which Westermarck thought to be extremely widespread and possibly universal. In this regard, he listed dozens of cases of the occurrence of sexual jealousy from many different types of societies from all over the world and also of the intensity and consequences of this jealousy. One consequence was the harsh condemnation and often severe punishment of the parties to adultery. Because jealousy was such an important human emotion everywhere, it was inconceivable to Westermarck that early humans could ever have tolerated widespread promiscuity.

Early humans, Westermarck contended, practiced marriage and lived in organized families. He viewed marriage and the family as both reproductive and economic institutions, it being the main role of the mother to nurture the children and of the father to provide economic support and protection. In classical Darwinian style, Westermarck sought the origins of the human family in humankind's hominoid ancestry:

> I think we have reason to believe that the family, implying marital and paternal care, was hardly less indispensable for primitive man than it is for the gorilla and chimpanzee. If this was the case, the family may have been an inheritance from the parent species out of which the Anthropoids and the Hominides . . . gradually developed. (1922a:69)

In the second volume of *HHM*, Westermarck developed the hypothesis on the origin of incest avoidance and exogamy for which he is today most famous, the "familiarity breeds aversion" theory. Westermarck thought that the tendency to avoid incestuous sexual relations with close kin sprang from a deep human emotion that had evolved by natural selection. He expressed the matter as follows:

> Generally speaking, there is a remarkable absence of erotic feelings between persons living very closely together from childhood. Nay more, in this, as in many other cases, sexual aversion when the act is thought of. This I take to be the fundamental cause of the exogamous prohibitions. (1922b:192)

Westermarck acknowledged that he was not the first to have thought of this, for he located similar ideas in the writings of Montesquieu, the sociologist William Isaac Thomas, Havelock Ellis, and even Plato. In good Darwinian fashion, Westermarck noted that not only is incest avoidance a human universal but also that it is the common practice in many species of animals, even birds and honeybees.

What is universal in the incest rules is the prohibition of sexual relations among members of the nuclear family. Having an almost encyclopedic knowledge of ethnographic practices, Westermarck well knew that there was considerable variation beyond the nuclear family, with many societies extending the prohibition to certain categories of cousins but not to others, and yet other societies prohibiting all first and even many second cousins. He accounted for these exogamous practices in the same way. Lineages or clans that practiced exogamy were often territorialized units in which cousins grew up in close contact. Where there was a prohibition on the marriage of clanmates who grew up at considerable distance from each other, Westermarck theorized that these separated clans had in the recent past once been territorial:

> The exogamous rules, though in the first place associated with kinship because near relatives normally live together, have come to include relatives who do not live

together—just as social rights and duties connected with kinship, although ultimately depending upon close living together, have a strong tendency to last after the
local tie is broken. (1922b:214)

But why did this disinclination to mate with agemates with whom one was in close
contact in early childhood evolve? How was it adaptive? Westermarck's answer is that
it evolved to prevent the damaging genetic consequences of close inbreeding. He even
cited statistical data from a number of studies of modern populations on the consequences of first-cousin marriages to support this claim, as well as observations of the
effects of cousin marriages in preliterate societies (Westermarck, 1922b:226–232).

Westermarck concluded his discussion of incest avoidance and exogamy by stating
that his theory "explains a world-wide institution by a mental characteristic which may
be presumed to be common to all races of men" and that the theory

co-ordinates three parallel groups of facts which seem intrinsically to belong
together: the exogamous rules, the aversion to sexual intercourse between persons
living together from childhood, and the injurious consequences of in-breeding. And
it finds the same general law governing analogous phenomena in the two great king-
doms of the organic world: the cross-fertilisation of plants, the various arrangements
to prevent in-breeding among animals, and the exogamy in mankind. (1922b:239)

Seldom has a sociologist, living or dead, held such a sophisticated conception of the
aim of science—parsimonious explanation of as much as possible with as little as possible and backed by as much evidence as possible—and demonstrated an equal ability to
practice it.

Nevertheless, Westermarck's theory, although highly regarded at the time, fell into
disrepute in later years and yielded to explanations that focused on the contribution
made by incest avoidance (and exogamy rules) to social cohesion (see, for example,
Davis, 1949; Lévi-Strauss, 1969). The theory was totally dismissed by almost all sociologists and anthropologists as a simple-minded notion that was of mere historical interest.
But the theory was revived in the 1970s when certain striking empirical data came to
light (Shepher, 1971, 1983; McCabe, 1983; Wolf, 1995; Sanderson, 2001:215–220, 238–239;
Turner and Maryanski, 2005:30–32; Wolf and Durham, 2005). Joseph Shepher (1971)
examined nearly 3,000 marriages undertaken between members of several Israeli kib-
butzim. Incredibly, he found that only 13 of these marriages occurred between children
who had grown up in the same communal nursery. This overwhelming preference of
young kibbutzniks to marry outside of their own childhood groups occurred despite the
absence of any norm against marrying nursery mates; indeed, kibbutzniks were generally encouraged to marry their nursery mates. When Shepher asked these kibbutz youth
about their failure to marry childhood associates, they often said such things as "we feel
like siblings" or "we have no attraction to each other."

Research by Arthur Wolf (1970, 1995) on Taiwanese marriage practices is also highly
consistent with Westermarck's theory. In the early 20th century, two contrasting marriage patterns were found in Taiwan, which Wolf called "major marriages" and "minor

marriages," the latter known locally as *sim-pua* marriage. In a major marriage, the bride and groom were individuals who did not know each other in childhood, often not even meeting until the day of the wedding. In the *sim-pua* marriages, the bride was a woman who had been adopted into her future husband's household as an infant or young child and brought up in close association with this boy. Wolf predicted that persons who married in *sim-pua* fashion would show much higher levels of marital dissatisfaction compared to persons who were involved in major marriages, and this is what he found. He determined that 24% of the *sim-pua* marriages ended in divorce or separation compared to only 1% of the major marriages. Moreover, 33% of the women in *sim-pua* marriages had committed adultery compared to only 11% of the women in the major marriages. Wolf also found that *sim-pua* marriages produced fewer offspring than did major marriages, which he interpreted to mean that intercourse was considerably less frequent in the *sim-pua* marriages.

Justine McCabe (1983) obtained results similar to those of Wolf in her research on Lebanese marriage practices. Some Lebanese groups have practiced what is known as patrilateral parallel-cousin marriage, which involves the marriage of cousins who belong to the same patrilineal descent group and who grew up together (a boy marries his father's brother's daughter). In most societies, this practice has been regarded as incestuous, and it is found almost exclusively in Arab societies in the Middle East and North Africa. McCabe found that compared to all other Lebanese marriages, parallel-cousin marriages were more than four times as likely to end in divorce and produced approximately 23% fewer children.

Relatively recently, Daniel Fessler discovered a fourth case, the Karo Batak of Indonesia (Fessler, 2007; Kushnick and Fessler, 2011). Among these people, the ideal form of marriage is one in which a boy marries a cousin who is his father's sister's daughter (from the girl's perspective, her husband would be her mother's brother's son). Despite parental encouragement of such marriages, the cousins, known locally as *impal*, seldom marry. The cousins say they do not marry because they are not sexually or romantically attracted and "feel like siblings." And, as the reader may already have concluded, the majority of *impal* grow up in close contact from early childhood.

The Westermarck theory also receives support from patterns of inbreeding avoidance among other animals. Incest avoidance is widespread (although not universal) among primates and other mammals, and it is also common in birds. Chimpanzees, for example, avoid close inbreeding by virtue of the fact that females from one community transfer to another community after sexual maturity and mate only with that community's males. Another very strong line of evidence derives from studies of inbreeding depression, which is the genetic defects and premature deaths that occur in the offspring of closely related individuals. Contemporary studies consistently show inbreeding depression in the offspring of related individuals and that the level of inbreeding depression increases, often dramatically, as genetic relatedness increases (Seemanova, 1971; other studies reviewed in Ember, 1983; Shepher 1983; Durham, 1991; Scheidel, 1996). In one of the most recent studies, Saggar and Bittles (2008), analyzing several different populations, estimated the likelihood that offspring of individuals related by one-fourth or one-half of their genes would carry two copies of a deleterious recessive gene. Their estimates were 8–10% for the offspring of uncle–niece and half-sibling matings (related by one-fourth of their genes) and a much larger 30% for parent–child or brother–sister matings (related by one-half). These are very large numbers. With numbers this high, inbreeding depression will be substantial in both instances, especially in the offspring related by one-half of their genes. The logical conclusion seems to be that incestuous mating is fitness reducing and has been strongly selected against in human evolutionary history.

Westermarck began the third volume of *HHM* (1922c) with a discussion of monogamy and polygyny, although he spent most of his time on the latter. Westermarck reviewed numerous ethnographic cases of polygyny, after which he focused on its causes. He argued that an excess of women was one cause, although it was not the only cause and, in fact, only an indirect cause. He contended that the direct cause was the male desire for more than one wife. Sex with a single wife is usually restricted by such things as her menstrual period, pregnancy, and postpartum sex taboos. A polygynously married man can then have sex with another wife who is at that time not subject to these conditions. There is also the importance of female youth and beauty, highly desired by men everywhere. As a first wife ages and loses her beauty, a young and still attractive woman can be taken on as a second wife. And when she eventually loses her attractiveness, yet another wife can be added. Men also have a strong desire for sexual variety; as Westermarck noted, the "sexual instinct is dulled by long familiarity and stimulated by novelty" (p. 74). In addition, men normally desire numerous offspring and thus can produce more offspring with several wives than with one. Polygyny also increases a man's material comfort in small-scale agricultural societies in which women do much of the cultivation and perform other economic tasks (e.g., milling, cooking, and carrying wood). Because several wives can produce more economic surplus than one, polygyny increases a man's wealth and thereby his status. The number of polygynous societies has tended to increase with social evolution, Westermarck contended, because more advanced societies have greater inequalities of wealth, and it is the wealthy who have the means to support several wives.

Westermarck said surprisingly little about monogamy. He noted that in the most advanced civilizations it became increasingly the norm. He thought this was because in the most advanced civilizations the desire for a large family had become less intense; because women's role as laborers declined; because women's feelings came to be held in higher regard; and because of an increase in the importance of romantic love. Numerous contemporary theories of monogamy have been proposed, but there is no consensus (Alexander, 1987; MacDonald, 1990; Posner, 1992). Perhaps the most promising current explanation of monogamy is that proposed by Richard Posner, which is similar to that of Westermarck. Posner proposes that polygyny is incompatible with companionate marriage, a type of marriage in which husbands and wives are intimate partners and vow to remain romantically and sexually exclusive for a lifetime. Because all modern industrial societies are based on companionate marriage, they must forbid polygyny. Posner's argument is boosted by the cases of Greece and Rome, the only ancient civilizations to prescribe monogamy. Women had a higher status in Rome than in virtually all other agrarian societies. When a woman took property into a marriage in the form of a dowry, her husband claimed control of it, but the wife was entitled to a considerable inheritance upon his death. For an agrarian society, Rome also gave an unusual amount of emphasis to the husband–wife unit, and in fact Rome may have had a kind of precursor of modern companionate marriage (Goody, 1990).

Concerning polyandry, Westermarck (1922c) devoted two chapters to describing and trying to explain it. He discussed numerous ethnographic cases, most of them found in Tibet and India and most of them fraternal (a woman marries two or more brothers). Westermarck suggested that polyandry could stem from an excess of men, but he devoted much more attention to a particular explanation suggested by numerous travelers and ethnographers in the 19th century and even as far back as the early 18th century. This explanation focused on the difficulty of making a living on lands that were relatively sterile. Low productivity, combined with high population density, made family plots small. An inheritance practice that divided the land among the sons would leave none of them with the means to survive. Therefore, brothers inherited the land collectively and brought in a single wife. Westermarck quoted a certain Rockhill (*Land of the Lamas*):

> If at the death of the head of the family the property was divided among the sons, there would not be enough to supply the wants of all of them if each had a wife and family.... [T]he only solution of the problem in this case was for the sons of a family to take one wife among them, by which means their ancestral estate remained undivided. (1922c:187)

Westermarck quoted a number of other early authorities to the same effect.

This explanation was revived by Stanford University anthropologist William Durham in 1991, who called it the "hypothesis of family property conservation." But Durham added to this explanation in a way that Westermarck, as a Darwinian, would very likely have appreciated. Durham asked whether polyandry could actually have reproductive advantages over monogamy under the circumstances in which polyandrous societies usually live. At first glance, the answer would seem to be a clear "no" because brothers can only inseminate a single woman. But Durham carried out computer simulations in which he calculated levels of reproductive success over several generations. He found that monogamy led to greater reproductive success for one or two generations but that polyandry was superior after three generations. Moreover, monogamy generally led to reproductive disaster after several generations, with entire family lines becoming extinct.

One of the ways in which Westermarck disagreed with Darwin was with respect to his concept of sexual selection. Natural selection is selection for the ability to survive and prosper, whereas sexual selection is selection for the ability to find mates. Darwin indicated two forms of sexual selection, male combat and female choice. Under the former, males fight for access to females. Here we see such traits as the antlers of moose and elk and the tusks and extremely large body size, relative to females, of sea lions and walruses. Dominant male sea lions and walruses are able to defeat their competitors, usually injuring and often killing them, and as a result they are able to monopolize the vast majority of the females. Female choice involves choosing males that have, for example, the brightest colors or the most rhythmical and harmonious sounds. The classic example of female choice is the large and beautiful tails of peacocks. During the mating season, peacocks parade in front of observing peahens, which choose the peacocks with the most impressive tails. (For details and citations, see Sanderson, 2014:115–119.)

Westermarck's objection to Darwin's concept of sexual selection was based largely on his observation that such a form of selection often works against natural selection. Westermarck stated that "far from cooperating with each other, these two kinds of selection seem even to work in opposite directions. Sexual selection, as described by Darwin, produces effects disadvantageous to the species" (1922a:478). He added that

> if we accept Darwin's theory of sexual selection, we are compelled to suppose that that inexplicable aesthetic sense of the females has been developed in the way most dangerous to the species. Conspicuous colours are admired by the females of those animals which, by means of such colours, are most easily discovered by their enemies, and sounds and odours are appreciated exactly in those species to which they are most perilous. (1922a:486)

It is indeed true that sexual selection can work against natural selection. A male bird with a brilliant hue is made more visible to predators. Because the hue is dangerous, Westermarck argued that natural selection has had to see to it that brilliant colors (or a euphonious song) would have a specific function, and this function Westermarck thought was to make it easier for the sexes to find each other during the mating season. He noted that "the sexual colours, scents, and sounds in the animal kingdom are complementary to each other *in the way that is best suited to make the animals easily discoverable*" (1922a:486, emphasis in original). He pointed out that bright colors are found almost entirely in species that are diurnal, which means that the colors will be easily visible. Nocturnal animals seldom have such colors because they would be difficult to detect at night.

Unfortunately, Westermarck makes several errors here. Although natural and sexual selection can work against each other, it is now recognized that evolution has worked out a compromise so that one does not swamp the other. Both can exist together as long as the reproductive benefits of one are at least equal to the reproductive benefits of the other. For example, peacocks' elaborate tails do indeed make them vulnerable to predators, but if they mate with enough peahens—peafowl are unusual among birds in being polygynous—their reproductive success can counterbalance the reproductive loss of their elimination through predation. Moreover, we now know that the peahens' choice is not arbitrary, as Sir Ronald Fisher thought many years ago. The most impressive peacocks are in fact fitter than their less impressive conspecifics—that is, they have better genes because it takes good genes and good health to grow an elaborate tail. In choosing these peacocks, peahens are in fact getting fitter offspring. (For details, see Sanderson 2014:115–119.)

In addition, Westermarck does not seem to realize that his own explanation is in fact one based on sexual rather than natural selection. It is just a different kind of sexual selection theory from that of Darwin. If sexual colors, scents, and sounds function to make it easier for the sexes to find each other, then this is sexual selection *tout court.* (And an incorrect theory, it must be added.) Moreover, the concept of sexual selection is now widely accepted by evolutionary biologists and plays a critical role in contemporary sociobiology and evolutionary psychology. (See Sanderson, 2014, Chap. 5.) Rejecting it was one of Westermarck's blunders.

Finally, Westermarck repeatedly invokes, both here and throughout his work, a trait's usefulness to the *species.* Certainly many traits are useful to the species. The sharp teeth and great speed of cheetahs are useful to all of them in chasing down and devouring gazelles. But there is, as Darwin stressed, always individual variation. Not all cheetahs are created equal. Those that are faster will feed more often than those that are slower. Nor are all peacocks created equal. Peacocks are competing with each other for mates, and those with the most impressive tails will acquire more mates and thus leave more offspring compared to those whose tails are less impressive. Having the most impressive tail benefits the peacock that has it, not the species as a whole. Indeed, it works to the disadvantage of those peacocks with poor tails because they mate less frequently or not at all.[1]

Most of the scholars who have followed up on Westermarck's work or have continued the overall evolutionary approach he used have been anthropologists. Few sociologists have appreciated Westermarck, but there are some. The first was perhaps Pierre van den Berghe. Van den Berghe wrote an entire book, *Human Family Systems: An Evolutionary View* (1979), in which he examined many aspects of family and marriage using evolutionary theory. He accepts Westermarck's theory of incest avoidance, but unlike Westermarck, who thought that it was the basis for exogamous marriage prescriptions, van den Berghe relies on Lévi-Strauss' (1969) famous alliance theory to explain exogamy. Incest avoidance is about sex, he contends, whereas exogamy is about marriage. He also discusses, inter alia, pair bonding; kin selection and inclusive fitness; male and female reproductive strategies; parental investment; cross-cultural models of marital residence and descent; and monogamy, polygyny, and polyandry.

Jonathan Turner and Alexandra Maryanski (2005) have written the most comprehensive book on incest avoidance and the incest taboo by sociologists. They make the very important point that despite avoidance and the taboo, some incest occurs in every society, but its extent varies by family dyad. Father–daughter incest is the most common, mother–son incest the least common (actually quite rare), and brother–sister incest somewhere in between. They accept Westermarck's explanation for brother–sister avoidance, but they argue that father–daughter and mother–son incest have to be explained in terms of traditional sociological theories. There is no hardwired aversion between fathers and daughters or between mothers and sons, and therefore societies have had to impose a cultural taboo in order to maintain family solidarity and avoid the costs of inbreeding depression. Their explanation is ultimately co-evolutionary: Incest avoidance and the incest taboo resulted from the coevolution of both biological and cultural forces. (For an assessment of the authors' overall argument, see Sanderson, 2005.)

THE EVOLUTION OF THE MORAL SENSE

Westermarck was also keenly interested in the source of moral concepts and judgments, and their evolution, which was the subject of his *ODMI*. Again we find Darwinian natural selectionist reasoning at work. Westermarck was a staunch critic of approaches to morality and moral philosophy that relied on intellect and reason, especially those of Hegel, Kant, and their followers. Early in his student days, Westermarck read Hegel, whose ideas he found distasteful (Pipping, 1984). As for Kant, Westermarck strongly objected to his famous categorical imperative to treat persons only as ends, never as means. According to Ihanus (1999:271–272), "Westermarck wrote that as a student he had become exhausted with Kant's style and his almost empty moral law. Westermarck's comments on Kant were usually polemically critical or ironic."

It was Westermarck's view that morality and ethics are not products of moral reasoning but, rather, products of moral *emotions*. Moral concepts are generalizations or objectifications of moral emotions involving either indignation or approval, and the moral emotions are actually part of a larger class of emotions that Westermarck called *retributive emotions*. Moral disapproval is a type of resentment closely related to anger and the desire for revenge, whereas moral approval is a type of kindly emotion very similar to gratitude. The retributive emotions themselves

> have been acquired by means of natural selection in the struggle for existence; both resentment and retributive kindly emotion are states of mind which have a tendency to promote the interests of the individuals who feel them. This explanation also applies to the moral emotions in so far as they are retributive: *It accounts for the hostile attitude of moral disapproval towards the cause of pain, and for the friendly attitude of moral approval towards the cause of pleasure.* Our retributive emotions are always reactions against pain or pleasure felt by ourselves; this holds true of the moral emotions as well as of revenge and gratitude. (1908:739, emphasis added)

Westermarck went on to analyze the nature of the principal moral concepts in these terms, holding that the concepts of vice, wrong, ought and duty, right and rights, and justice and injustice are rooted in moral disapproval, whereas the concepts of good, virtue, and merit are rooted in moral approval. It is easy to understand why good, virtue, and merit are grounded in moral approval, and vice and wrong in moral disapproval, but it is somewhat more difficult to understand how ought and duty, right and rights, and justice and injustice are grounded in moral disapproval. The basic idea is that the fulfillment of these prescriptions is no cause for any particular moral approval. One is expected to live up to these things without expecting moral praise for doing so. It is the *failure* to live up to them that generates moral disapproval. Concerning ought and duty, Westermarck states that the

> ideas of "ought" and "duty" thus spring from the same source as the ideas of "right" and "wrong." To say that a man ought to do a thing is, so far as the morality of his action is concerned, the very same thing as to say that it is bad, or wrong, of him not to do it—in other words, that the not-doing of it has a tendency to call forth moral disapproval. (1906:137)

With regard to right (as an adjective), the implication is that doing the opposite is wrong and thus calls forth moral disapproval. A right (as a noun) means that it should not be hindered, such hindrance being disapproved. And because justice is a type of rightness, injustice is a type of wrongness.

For Westermarck, the critical distinction between moral emotions and those that are nonmoral is that the former have the quality of *disinterestedness*. They extend beyond any individual to an entire community and thus are public in nature. Thus, individuals feel indignation when a neighbor is hurt by the culpable action of another, and they morally condemn the action. Likewise, they feel pleasure and moral approval when an individual receives a benefit from another member of the community. Westermarck states,

> The first moral judgments expressed not the private emotions of isolated individuals but emotions which were felt by the community at large. Public indignation is the prototype of moral disapproval and public approval the prototype of moral approbation. And these public emotions are characterized by generality, individual disinterestedness, and apparent impartiality. (1908:740)

Westermarck noted that there are both universal and variable moral judgments. The universal features of morality spring from a "general uniformity of human nature," whereas moral variations are due to "different external conditions." In terms of the former, both primitive and modern societies, for example, regard charity as a duty and generosity as a virtue. As examples of the latter, Westermarck states that economic hardship may lead to infanticide or the abandoning of the old and that "necessity and the force of habit may deprive these actions of the stigma which would otherwise be attached to them" (1908:742). Similarly, economic conditions have had an impact on moral ideas concerning such things as slavery. For Westermarck, there is no such thing as general moral truths or an absolute morality. This is because moral judgments, being dependent on emotions, are inherently subjective rather than objective and also because the concept of truth is a scientific rather than a moral one. Westermarck was a kind of ethical relativist; indeed, he wrote an entire book outlining his relativist perspective (Westermarck, 1932).

Westermarck was much concerned with the evolution of morality in overall societal evolution. He noted that in the course of moral evolution, there has been a strong tendency to condemn direct retaliation for wrongs and emphasize forgiveness as a moral duty. This shift was particularly apparent in the development of the major world religions, and it was part of an even more encompassing shift in the direction of greater altruism and sympathy toward a wider range of persons. Westermarck regarded this as a process of "moral enlightenment," and he noted that at its higher stages, morality was based more on reason and reflection than on emotion. Enlightened minds see that retaliation as a result of resentment is not impartial—that is, springs from entirely personal motives—and that such retaliation may often be directed against not only wrongdoers but also other innocent parties associated with them, such as lineage or clan mates. This heightened moral consciousness "condemns any retributive infliction of pain which it regards as undeserved; and it seems to be in the first place with a view to preventing such injustice that teachers of morality have enjoined upon men to love their enemies" (Westermarck, 1906:78–79).

At the same time, Westermarck noted that the aggressive nature of moral disapproval does not disappear in moral evolution. Instead, it becomes more disguised and expresses itself in new and different ways. Because the desire for retribution is so deeply imbedded in human nature, it cannot be abolished but merely transformed and redirected:

> Resentment is directed against the cause of the offence. . . . Deliberate and discriminating resentment is therefore apt to turn against the will rather than against the willer; as we have seen, it is desirous to inflict pain on the offender chiefly as a means of removing the cause of pain suffered, i.e., the existence of the bad will. (1906:91)

However, Westermarck noted that this conceptual distinction between will and willer, or between sin and sinner, is extremely difficult for humans to maintain in actual practice because "it may be fairly doubted whether [maintaining this distinction] is within the capacity of ordinary human nature" (1906:92).[2]

Just as Westermarck was ahead of his time with respect to a Darwinian understanding of marriage and family life, he was ahead of his time in terms of a Darwinian understanding of human morality. A number of modern scholars have begun to examine morality in a Darwinian light (Alexander, 1987; de Waal, 1996, 2006; Arnhart, 1998, 2005; Krebs, 2005). The evolutionary biologist Richard Alexander (1987) starts from the basic principle that each individual has been designed by natural selection to maximize the survival of his or her genes through reproduction and nepotism. This leads him to the nature of exchanges between individuals—"giving" and "taking." He proposes five basic strategies concerned with giving:

1. Give when the benefit goes to a genetic relative and its return to the giver via the improved reproduction of the relative is likely to be greater than the expense of the act multiplied by the fractional relationship of the recipient to the giver. Giving of this type is investment in direct or indirect nepotism.
2. Give when the recipient is likely to give back more than he or she receives. This is investment in direct reciprocity.

3. Give when not doing so is likely to cause others to impose costs on the giver greater than the expense of the giver's beneficence.
4. Give when giving is likely to cause a sufficient number of appropriate people to regard the act of giving as an indication of a significant probability that the giver will give back more than is received in future interactions. This shows that the giver is a reliable person in whom others can invest, and it is investment in indirect reciprocity.
5. In all other situations, be a taker rather than a giver.

These strategies come to be codified as rules and thus establish a moral system. The strategies are in a sense rudimentary, but they are nonetheless fundamental. Alexander summarizes his position thus:

> My view of moral systems in the real world . . . is that they are systems in which costs and benefits of specific actions are manipulated so as to produce reasonably harmonious associations in which everyone nevertheless pursues his own (in evolutionary terms) self-interest. (1987:191)

Because Alexander views morality as rooted in self-interest, he is skeptical that true altruistic behavior can apply to more than a tiny handful of people. True altruism in an evolutionary sense involves genetic self-sacrifice and is, Alexander claims, an "evolutionary mistake"; it is exceedingly unlikely, therefore, that any society could be built on true altruism.[3]

Larry Arnhart, a political philosopher, uses a Darwinian theory of morality to formulate a political and moral philosophy (Arnhart, 1998, 2005). He calls his formulation "Darwinian natural right," basing his terminology on Aristotle (minus the "Darwinian"). Darwinian natural right's most fundamental principle is "the good is the desirable." This means that a morally proper society is one that allows humans the freedom to satisfy the basic desires that make up their nature. Arnhart lists 20 such desires:

1. *A complete life*: Humans generally desire life, and a complete or long life, and can only be fully happy if they live out their full lifespan.
2. *Parental care*: Humans generally desire to care for their children, and children desire the care of adults. Despite the burdens of child care, parents are normally highly motivated to provide it.
3. *Sexual identity*: Sex is the most important dimension of personal identity, and humans strongly desire to categorize themselves as male or female. Women tend to be more nurturant than men, and men are more inclined than women to attain dominance and seek high-status positions.
4. *Sexual mating*: Humans strongly desire sexual coupling, and every society displays intense interest in sexuality. Men generally prefer to mate with young, attractive women, whereas women seek to mate with men who have high status and economic resources.

5. *Familial bonding*: Humans generally desire to live within families, the core of which is a mother with her children. All societies provide some arrangement for marriage, and kin relations are among the most important relations in every society, if not the most important.

6. *Friendship*: Humans generally seek social relationships based on mutual affection and shared interests, and humans can have enduring friendships with only a few people.

7. *Social ranking*: Humans generally seek social recognition through ranking in comparison with others, and they attain status by way of gaining prestige, honor, and fame.

8. *Justice as reciprocity*: Humans have a natural sense that justice requires returning benefit for benefit and injury for injury. Humans are inclined to feel the emotions of gratitude, love, and benevolence in response to the benefits conferred on them by others.

9. *Political rule*: Humans are political animals by nature; they have a natural tendency to struggle for power and control.

10. *War*: Humans generally desire to engage in war when such a course of action will advance their interests.

11. *Health*: Humans generally desire to live lives that provide adequately for their bodily needs. Much of social life is devoted to satisfying the desires that are fundamental to a healthy life.

12. *Beauty*: Humans generally desire beauty in the human body, and they esteem the bodily signs of health and vigor. They adorn their bodies for pleasing display, and men generally prefer women whose bodies show signs of youth and nubility.

13. *Wealth*: Humans generally desire the economic goods necessary for a healthy and flourishing life.

14. *Speech*: Humans generally desire to communicate about themselves and their world, and children are naturally adapted to learn the language of their group or society.

15. *Practical habituation*: Humans are creatures of habit, and it is through this that they seek to manage their appetites and passions.

16. *Practical reasoning*: Humans seek to deliberate in a rational manner about what a good life is and to organize their actions to conform to their notion of a good life.

17. *Practical arts*: Humans generally desire craftsmanship.

18. *Aesthetic pleasure*: Humans desire and receive pleasure from their own artistic creations and the natural environments in which they live. Humans take pleasure in such activities as singing, dancing, playing musical instruments, painting, and decorating objects. They also take pleasure in the natural landscapes that resemble the environments in which they first evolved.

19. *Religious understanding*: Humans generally desire to understand the world by means of postulating the actions of supernatural powers.

20. *Intellectual understanding*: Humans generally desire to understand the world through the use of the intellect in ways quite apart from religious understanding.

Arnhart claims that these 20 categories of desire

> are universally found in all human societies, that they have evolved by natural selec-
> tion over four million years of human evolutionary history to become components
> of the species-specific nature of human beings, that they are based in the physiolog-
> ical mechanisms of the brain, and that they direct and limit the social variability of
> human beings as adapted to diverse ecological circumstances. (1998:36)

Arnhart's work is both empirical and normative. Darwinian natural right for him translates into a conservative political philosophy that he calls *Darwinian conservatism*. Arnhart gives special attention to liberty, which for conservatives arises from spontaneous order, or order based on the mutual adjustment of people to each other rather than from centralized authority. He puts forth five principles of liberty that he believes flow from a Darwinian view of humans. Arnhart (2005) contends that Darwinism supports the following:

1. The conservative view of ordered liberty as rooted in natural desires, customary traditions, and prudential judgments
2. The conservative view of the moral sense as fundamental for the moral order of liberty
3. The conservative view of sexual differences, family life, and parental care as fundamental for the social order of liberty
4. The conservative view of property as fundamental for the economic order of liberty
5. The conservative view of limited government as fundamental for the political order of liberty

Arnhart even cites Westermarck twice, once with respect to family life and another time with regard to property rights. Concerning the former, he states,

> Westermarck employed Darwinian reasoning applied to the anthropological evi-
> dence to conclude that marriage and the family were universal throughout history
> because they were rooted in some biological instincts of human nature. He argued
> that because human offspring cannot survive and flourish without intensive and pro-
> longed parental care, natural selection would favor an instinct for parental care, par-
> ticularly in mothers. (2005:49)

Regarding property rights, he states,

> The universal condemnation of theft shows that some notion of the right of property
> arises in all human societies. . . . This arises from a natural human desire—shared
> with some nonhuman animals—to keep whatever one has appropriated. By sym-
> pathy with the feelings of others, Westermarck reasoned, human beings recognize
> this natural propensity to appropriate and feel resentment towards those who violate

someone's claim to property. This moral sentiment is then generalized into a social rule of respecting property rights and punishing theft. (2005:62)

Arnhart's grand conclusion is that Darwinian theory confirms scientifically what is already known to conservatives through common sense: Even though our moral judgments vary according to different circumstances, basic standards of right and wrong are rooted in human nature.[4]

WESTERMARCK AND DURKHEIM

Like all great thinkers, Westermarck had his rivals, and these rivals were themselves great thinkers of enormous influence. His main rival was the early sociologist Emile Durkheim, and although he outlived Durkheim by more than 20 years, they were born only 4 years apart and thus were contemporaries. In 1895, when *HHM* appeared in a French translation, Durkheim was quick to read and respond to it. He published a lengthy critique in *Revue philosophique*, "Origine du mariage dans l'espèce humaine d'après Westermarck" ["Origin of marriage in the human species according to Westermarck"]. Durkheim was highly critical of Westermarck for his reliance on Darwinism, which to Durkheim meant that explanations of social facts would then rest on a simple unproven and even untested hypothesis: "Faire réposer la sociologie sur le Darwinisme, c'est asseoir sur une hypothese, ce qui est au contraire à toute bonne méthode" ["To rest sociology on Darwinism is to situate it on a mere hypothesis, which is contrary to all good method"].

Westermarck replied to this critique in his article "Méthode de la récherche des institutions prehistoriques à propos d'un ouvrage du professeur Kohler" ["Method of researching prehistoric institutions with regard to a work of professor Kohler"], published in the *Revue internationale de sociologie* in 1897. He states the following (Westermarck, 1897:452; as quoted in Ihanus, 1999:141):

M. Durkheim s'oppose à l'importance que j'ai attachée à l'ethnographie et à la psychologie comme sources d'information concernant les institutions sociales. . . . M. Durkheim me réproche aussi d'avoir base mes récherches sur une hypothèse non prouvée. . . . Cette objection doit résonner étrangement aux oreilles de quiconque est un peu au courant des immenses progrès que la biologie a faits sur la base du darwinisme. Et je dois avouer qu'il m'est difficile d'entrer en controverse avec un auteur qui considère comme "contraire à toute bonne methode" l'hypothèse qui fait descendre l'homme d'une éspèce animale inferieur.

[Mr. Durkheim is opposed to the importance that I have attached to ethnography and to psychology as sources of information concerning social institutions. . . . Mr. Durkheim criticizes me as well for having based my research on an unproved hypothesis. . . . This objection must sound strange to the ears of anyone who is even slightly aware of the immense progress that biology has made on the basis of Darwinism. And I must declare that it is difficult for me to engage in debate with an author who considers as "contrary to all good method" the hypothesis which regards man as having descended from a lower animal species.]

Durkheim also criticized Westermarck's conceptualization of the family, especially his view that it was a natural phenomenon that had links to similar phenomena in nonhuman primates and other mammals. Durkheim insisted that the family was a human invention that appeared only after humans had invented *rules* and *sanctions*. For Durkheim, marriage was a social institution and could not rest simply on human emotional inclinations, as Westermarck seemed to be indicating. Durkheim went so far as to say, "Des amants qui restent unis toute leur vie ne sont pas pour cela des époux" ["Lovers who remain together their entire life are not by that simple fact spouses"). Another major point insisted upon by Durkheim was that the family, because it was a rule-based institution, varied far more widely than Westermarck acknowledged. Because the family took such diverse forms, a theory such as Westermarck's could never hope to succeed. Diverse family forms had to be explained by diverse social facts (Roos, 2008).

Just as he rejected Westermarck's theories of marriage and the family, so Durkheim rejected Westermarck's theory of incest avoidance, and for essentially the same kinds of reasons. Durkheim proposed his own theory, one that linked it to totemism. In the fifth edition of *HHM*, Westermarck summarized it thus:

> Professor Durkheim derives exogamy from a religious sentiment which is due to certain magical virtues attributed to blood, especially the menstrual blood of women, and the religious awe for blood is traced by him to totemism. Nay, totemism is the ultimate source not only of clan exogamy but of all other prohibitions against incest as well; the rule of clan exogamy, he maintains, has been extended to near relatives belonging to different clans because they are in no less intimate contact with each other than are the members of the same clan. And when totemism and at the same time clan relationships disappeared, the rule of clan exogamy was entirely transformed into a prohibition of marriage between near relatives, which in the course of evolution narrowed down to a prohibition of marriage between ascendants and descendants and between brothers and sisters only. (1922b:183)

Westermarck was highly critical of this theory, pointing out that Durkheim was trying to explain a universal phenomenon by means of a phenomenon that has appeared only among some societies. Exogamous clans, he pointed out, are not universal, and even where such clans are found, they are not always based on totems. But even if we could assume, for argument's sake, that totemic clan organization was in fact universal, Durkheim does not really explain the mechanism by which it leads to exogamy. Westermarck then referred to supporters of Durkheim's theory and to other somewhat similar theories and heaped scorn upon them all. It is at this point that Westermarck went on to present his own now famous theory.

The same year that Westermarck published the first volume of *ODMI*, Durkheim read it and reviewed it quite critically in *l'Année sociologique* (Durkheim, 1907). Unsurprisingly, the main argument of the review was that Westermarck failed to understand that moral ideas are essentially social. He contended that Westermarck illegitimately derived collective moral emotions from individual ones and that his effort to try to find the origins of morality was doomed to failure because such origins could never be found. And just as he did in his critique of *HHM*, Durkheim chastised Westermarck for failing to take rules and sanctions into account. However, Westermarck did not ignore rules and sanctions but actually considered them to be of fundamental importance. Where he differed from Durkheim was in refusing to make them the sine qua non of moral ideas and moral behavior (as well as marital and family behavior).

Durkheim was also critical of Westermarck on methodological grounds, stating, "Il est preoccupé avant tout d'accumuler les faits, non les choisir solides et demonstratifs" ["he is concerned above all with accumulating facts rather than choosing trustworthy and representative ones"] (Roos, 2008). Durkheim extended this methodological criticism more generally. He was highly critical of Westermarck for his use of the comparative method. He thought that this method ripped social traits out of their total social context and thus destroyed our ability to see societies as single functioning wholes. However, Westermarck was well aware of the limitations of the comparative method and said so directly, but he thought it was superior to Durkheim's own method. For example, in his *The Elementary Forms of the Religious Life*, Durkheim (1912/2008) relied on a single society, the Arunta of Australia, as a basis for generalizing to all religions in all societies. Moreover, Durkheim never set foot in Australia, instead relying on the ethnography produced by Sir Baldwin Spencer and F. J. Gillen (1899). Such a method would appear to have much more severe limitations than the comparative method of which Durkheim was so critical.

DECLINE INTO INVISIBILITY

As a major sociologist in the first third of the 20th century, Westermarck was even better known and more widely read than Durkheim (Roos, 2008). Indeed, Timothy Stroup states,

> When he was active as a writer (during the five decades from 1889 to 1939), Westermarck was almost universally respected, even by his occasional opponents, as a researcher of massive erudition who expounded important and innovative doctrines which demanded serious attention. (1984:575)

In addition, Morris Ginsberg, a student of Westermarck's close colleague at the London School of Economics, L. T. Hobhouse, states that Westermarck's work on morality was "carried out with an erudition, lucidity, and balance still unsurpassed" (1982:17). Ginsberg goes on to say of *HHM*, "When it first appeared it was hailed everywhere as a scientific work of the highest importance" (1982:17). Ginsberg then notes that the leading specialist on human sexuality of the day, Havelock Ellis, called it a monumental achievement unrivaled in the magnitude of its importance.

I have found in Westermarck's works a display of erudition and a mastery of detail rivaled only by the encyclopedic knowledge of Max Weber, and his ethnographic knowledge is vastly superior not only to that of Weber but also to that of every sociologist who has ever lived. And his ideas turn out to be astonishingly prescient and modern, and yet "he is scarcely even accorded his rightful place in the histories of philosophy and the social sciences, and the actual substance of his writings is little known or appreciated" (Stroup, 1984:575). He has subsided into an ignominious insignificance. His name does not even appear in the indexes of textbooks on the history of sociological theory. As Ronald Fletcher (1982:195) notes, "Most nineteenth-century sociologists are much talked about and little read. Westermarck is not even talked about." Only 9 years after his death, C. Wright Mills (1948) wrote a caustic appraisal of Westermarck, characterizing him as little more than some sort of "sociological stamp collector" who was not guided by any overall theory. (Of course, this is not even remotely accurate; indeed, the very opposite is true, as this chapter has amply demonstrated.) Stroup states, "When he is remembered at all, it is usually for his alleged errors of method: He is variously viewed as a simplistic analyzer of moral language, an inconsistent relativist, an armchair comparativist, a naive evolutionist, and a biological reductionist" (1984:575).

Why did his influence subside and his reputation collapse? It was, of course, because he was a Darwinian evolutionist confronted with the rising tide of social environmentalism that began to sweep through the social sciences in the 1930s. Under the circumstances, poor Westermarck did not have a chance. Westermarck's academic and intellectual struggle with Durkheim was won by Durkheim hands down. Durkheim was reportedly a master academic politician who could be quite ruthless. As Roos notes, Durkheim "was an empire builder who gathered followers, fought for academic power, tried to annihilate his enemies and competitors, whereas Westermarck lived many years in isolation in Morocco and shared his time between England, Finland, and Morocco" (2008:135). And Durkheim's ideas, of course, resonated much more with environmentalism and social determinism. As Durkheim's star rose, Westermarck's sank, and it sank virtually out of sight. Durkheim's basic sociological approach—explain social facts only in terms of other social facts—has continued to guide most sociological thinking, in very general terms at least, to the present day.

There are a few sociologists who are aware of Westermarck and regard him as an important early sociologist. But even then they are usually tepid. In Turner and Maryanski's (2005) book on the incest taboo discussed previously, for example, although they view Westermarck's theory favorably, they deny that it can apply to family dyads other than the brother–sister dyad. In personal conversation with the author, Maryanski has gone so far as to claim that even though the Westermarck effect is real, it is a "weak force," when in fact the evidence strongly suggests otherwise. Also, Turner and Maryanski show no interest in any other aspect of his work, either on the family and marriage or on the moral emotions (and despite the fact that Turner is a specialist in the subfield of sociology known as the sociology of emotions). In American social science today, Westermarck is best known to evolutionary anthropologists and psychologists, but they are mostly interested in his theory of incest avoidance.

Knut Pipping (1984), Timothy Stroup (1984), and Juhani Ihanus (1999) are aware of the full range and scope of Westermarck's work, and they have tried to resuscitate his reputation as a great thinker. But Ihanus is a Finn whose book on Westermarck was originally published in Finnish, and Westermarck is a legend in Finland. He is a national intellectual hero, just as Weber is in Germany and Durkheim and Bourdieu are in France. Pipping is also a Finn and, in fact, one of Westermarck's grandnephews. J. P. Roos and Anna Rotkirch are two other Finnish sociologists who have great admiration for Westermarck and indeed are part of a group of Finnish Westermarck scholars at the University of Helsinki. Stroup, although an American, is a moral philosopher rather than a sociologist and interested primarily in that aspect of Westermarck's work.

Conclusion

Pipping (1984) concludes that *HHM* and *ODMI* are today primarily of historical interest and that his ethnographies of Morocco and, perhaps, his work on ethical relativity represent his enduring contributions. I would reverse this conclusion. *HHM* and *ODMI* are masterpieces, both theoretically and empirically, and have never been surpassed in their brilliance even by that most erudite member of sociology's holy trinity, Max Weber. We have seen that his theories of incest avoidance and the moral emotions continue to be relevant and built on today. And there is much in these works that can still be mined. One is hard-pressed today, for example, to find research on tattooing, scarification, and body piercing, but Westermarck was already conducting research on these matters a century ago, with both ethnographic cases and a theoretical explanation.

It is said that history is written by the victors, and that is no less true of the history of academic disciplines than of history more generally. It is certainly true in sociology. Sociologists decided by the early 1970s that there were three great classical theorists—Marx, Durkheim, and Weber—who were worth most of our attention. Then there were some other more minor classical figures, such as Sumner, Simmel, Park, Cooley, Mead, Pareto, Thomas and Znaniecki, Mannheim, and of course Comte and Spencer (who on earth would study Comte today for reasons other than historical curiosity?). But in most textbooks on classical sociological theory or the history of sociology, Westermarck is conspicuously absent, and he has been absent for many decades (come to think of it, was he ever actually *in* a textbook on the history of sociological theory?). Students being introduced to classical theory through these textbooks come away from their courses not even knowing there was a man named Westermarck. It is time for this to change and for this prodigious scholar of great brilliance and erudition to be restored to his rightful place as one of the great masters. Will it happen? Certainly not soon, given the continuing hostility to biological explanations of human social life by most sociologists. Someday perhaps. Hope springs eternal.

NOTES

1. By the time the three volumes of the fifth edition appeared, *HHM* totaled a massive 1,753 pages. It is impossible to discuss in the space allotted here all of the topics Westermarck took up. In addition to the ones discussed previously, these include the following: Volume I: the frequency of marriage and the marriage age, celibacy, sexual modesty, courtship, female coyness, and primitive means of attraction; Volume II: endogamy, marriage by capture, consent as a condition of marriage, bride price and dowry, and marriage rites; and Volume III: group marriage and the duration of marriage and the right to dissolve it.

2. *ODMI* is a huge work of 1,568 pages, and the ideas discussed here take up little more than the first 200. However, they are the theoretical foundation on which the whole work rests. The remainder is mostly application to a wide range of moral issues and subjects, and the majority of Westermarck's discussion is descriptive. There is no space to discuss any of these issues; it may suffice to list them. Volume I: customs and laws as expressions of moral ideas; the general nature of the subjects of enlightened moral judgments; moral agents under intellectual disability; motives; forbearances and carelessness; conduct and character; homicide; the killing of parents, sick persons, and children; the killing of women and slaves; human sacrifice; blood revenge and compensation; dueling; bodily injuries; charity and generosity; hospitality; the subjection of children; the subjection of wives; slavery. Volume II: the right of property; the regard for truth and good faith; the respect for other men's honor and pride; regard for other persons' happiness; altruism; suicide; self-regarding duties and virtues; dietary prohibitions; cleanliness and uncleanliness; marriage; celibacy; free love; homosexual love; regard for the lower animals; regard for the dead; cannibalism; the belief in supernatural beings; duties to gods; gods as guardians of morality.

3. To be fair, it should be noted that a number of Darwinians, David Sloan Wilson most prominent among them, contend that altruism can evolve by group selection. For example, a group composed of 20% altruists could, because of its enhanced cooperation and thus superior organizational advantage, defeat a group with only 5% altruists. This may well be true, but Wilson and others do not explain how any group could consist of 20% altruists in the first place. See Sober and Wilson (1998).

4. I do not intend to be presenting Arnhart's conservative political philosophy, as represented in the previously presented five principles, as "correct." I simply offer it as a leading example of an attempt to ground a moral philosophy in Darwinian theoretical principles. As one might imagine, nearly all those on the political Left are anti-Darwinian with respect to moral and political philosophy. There is the occasional exception, however (e.g., Peter Singer's book *A Darwinian Left* [1999]). Westermarck himself was a liberal.

REFERENCES

Alexander, Richard. 1987. *The Biology of Moral Systems*. New York: Aldine de Gruyter.

Arnhart, Larry. 1998. *Darwinian Natural Right: The Biological Ethics of Human Nature*. Albany: State University of New York Press.

Arnhart, Larry. 2005. *Darwinian Conservatism*. Exeter, UK: Imprint Academic.

Barkow, Jerome H., Leda Cosmides, and John Tooby, eds. 1992. *The Adapted Mind: Evolutionary Psychology and the Generation of Culture*. New York: Oxford University Press.

Davis, Kingsley. 1949. *Human Society*. New York: Macmillan.

de Waal, Frans. 1996. *Good Natured: The Origins of Right and Wrong in Humans and Other Animals*. Cambridge, MA: Harvard University Press.

de Waal, Frans. 2006. *Primates and Philosophers: How Morality Evolved*. Princeton, NJ: Princeton University Press.

Durham, William H. 1991. *Coevolution: Genes, Culture, and Human Diversity*. Stanford, CA: Stanford University Press.

Durkheim, Emile. 1895. "Origine du mariage dans l'éspèce humaine d'après Westermarck." *Revue philosophique* 40: 606–623.

Durkheim, Emile. 1907. "Sur l'évolution générale des idées morales (Revue de Westermarck, *On the Origin and Development of the Moral Ideas*, Vol. I)." *L'Année sociologique* 10: 383–395.

Ember, Melvin. 1983. "On the Origin and Extension of the Incest Taboo." Pp. 65–108 in *Marriage, Family, and Kinship*, edited by Melvin Ember and Carol R. Ember. New Haven, CT: HRAF Press.

Fessler, Daniel M. T. 2007. "Neglected Natural Experiments Germane to the Westermarck Hypothesis: The Karo Batak and the Oneida Community." *Human Nature* 18: 355–364.

Fletcher, Ronald. 1982. "On the Contribution of Edward Westermarck. The Process of Institutionalization: A General Theory." Pp. 195–217 in *Edward Westermarck: His Life and Works* (Volume 34 of *Acta Philosophica Fennica*, Helsinki), edited by Timothy Stroup. Helsinki: Philosophical Society of Finland.

Ginsberg, Morris. 1982. "The Life and Work of Edward Westermarck." Pp. 1–23 in *Edward Westermarck: His Life and Works* (Volume 34 of *Acta Philosophica Fennica*, Helsinki), edited by Timothy Stroup. Helsinki: Philosophical Society of Finland.

Goody, Jack. 1990. *The Oriental, the Ancient, and the Primitive: Systems of Marriage and the Family in the Pre-industrial Societies of Eurasia*. Cambridge, UK: Cambridge University Press.

Ihanus, Juhani. 1999. *Multiple Origins: Edward Westermarck in Search of Mankind*. Translated by Juhani Ihanus and Maarika Toivonen. (Volume 6 of European Studies in the History of Science and Ideas.) Frankfurt am Main: Peter Lang.

Krebs, Dennis. 2005. "An Evolutionary Reconceptualization of Kohlberg's Model of Moral Development." Pp. 243–274 in *Evolutionary Perspectives on Human Development*, edited by Robert L. Burgess and Kevin MacDonald. 2nd ed. Thousand Oaks, CA: Sage.

Kushnick, Geoff, and Daniel M. T. Fessler. 2011. "Karo Batak Cousin Marriage, Cosocialization, and the Westermarck Hypothesis." *Current Anthropology* 52: 443–448.

Lévi-Strauss, Claude. 1969. *The Elementary Structures of Kinship*. Translated by James Harle Bell, John Richard von Sturmer, and Rodney Needham. Boston: Beacon Press. (Original French edition 1949)

MacDonald, Kevin. 1990. "Mechanisms of Sexual Egalitarianism in Western Europe." *Ethology and Sociobiology* 11: 195–238.

McCabe, Justine. 1983. "FBD Marriage: Further Support for the Westermarck Hypothesis of the Incest Taboo?" *American Anthropologist* 85: 50–69.

Mills, C. Wright. 1948. "Edward Alexander Westermarck and the Application of Ethnographic Methods to Marriage and Morals." Pp. 654–667 in *An Introduction to the History of Sociology*, edited by Harry Elmer Barnes. Chicago: University of Chicago Press.

Pipping, Knut. 1984. "Who Reads Westermarck Today?" *British Journal of Sociology* 35: 315–332.

Posner, Richard A. 1992. *Sex and Reason*. Cambridge, MA: Harvard University Press.

Roos, J. P. 2008. "Emile Durkheim Versus Edward Westermarck: An Uneven Match." Pp. 135–146 in *The New Evolutionary Social Science: Human Nature, Society, and Social Change*, edited by Tamas Meleghy, Peter Meyer, and Heinz-Juergen Niedenzu. Boulder, CO: Paradigm.

Saggar, Anand K., and Alan H. Bittles. 2008. "Consanguinity and Child Health." *Paedatrics and Child Health* 18: 244–249.

Sanderson, Stephen K. 2001. *The Evolution of Human Sociality: A Darwinian Conflict Perspective*. Boulder, CO: Rowman & Littlefield.

Sanderson, Stephen K. 2005. "The Incest Taboo: Biological Evolution, Cultural Evolution, or Coevolution?" *Evolution and Sociology Newsletter* 2(1): 6–10.

Sanderson, Stephen K. 2014. *Human Nature and the Evolution of Society*. Boulder, CO: Westview.

Scheidel, Walter. 1996. "Brother–Sister and Parent–Child Marriage Outside Royal Families in Ancient Egypt and Iran: A Challenge to the Sociobiological View of Incest Avoidance." *Ethology and Sociobiology* 17: 319–340.

Seemanova, Eva. 1971. "A Study of Children of Incestuous Matings." *Human Heredity* 21: 108–128.

Segerstråle, Ullica. 2001. *Defenders of the Truth: The Battle for Science in the Sociobiology Debate and Beyond*. Oxford, UK: Oxford University Press.

Shepher, Joseph. 1971. *Self-Imposed Incest Avoidance and Exogamy in Second-Generation Kibbutz Adults*. Xerox Monograph Series No. 72–871. Ann Arbor, MI: University Microfilms.

Shepher, Joseph. 1983. *Incest: A Biosocial View*. New York: Academic Press.

Singer, Peter. 1999. *A Darwinian Left: Politics, Evolution, and Cooperation*. New Haven, CT: Yale University Press.

Sober, Elliott, and David Sloan Wilson. 1998. *Unto Others: The Evolution and Psychology of Unselfish Behavior*. Cambridge, MA: Harvard University Press.

Spencer, Sir Baldwin, and F. J. Gillen. 1899. *The Native Tribes of Central Australia*. London: Macmillan.

Stroup, Timothy. 1984. "Edward Westermarck: A Reappraisal." *Man (N.S.)* 19: 575–592.

Turner, Jonathan H., and Alexandra Maryanski. 2005. *Incest: Origins of the Taboo*. Boulder, CO: Paradigm.

van den Berghe, Pierre L. 1979. *Human Family Systems: An Evolutionary View*. New York: Elsevier.

Westermarck, Edward. 1897. "Méthode de la récherche des institutions prehistoriques à propos d'un ouvrage du professeur Kohler." *Revue internationale de sociologie* 5: 444–457.

Westermarck, Edward. 1906. *The Origin and Development of the Moral Ideas*. Vol. 1. London: Macmillan.

Westermarck, Edward. 1908. *The Origin and Development of the Moral Ideas*. Vol. 2. London: Macmillan.

Westermarck, Edward. 1922a. *The History of Human Marriage*. Vol. 1. 5th ed. New York: Allerton.

Westermarck, Edward. 1922b. *The History of Human Marriage*. Vol. 2. 5th ed. New York: Allerton.

Westermarck, Edward. 1922c. *The History of Human Marriage*. Vol. 3. 5th ed. New York: Allerton.

Westermarck, Edward. 1932. *Ethical Relativity*. London: Routledge & Kegan Paul.

Wilson, Edward O. 1975. *Sociobiology: The New Synthesis*. Cambridge, MA: Harvard University Press.

Wolf, Arthur P. 1970. "Childhood Association and Sexual Attraction: A Further Test of the Westermarck Hypothesis." *American Anthropologist* 72: 503–515.

Wolf, Arthur P. 1995. *Sexual Attraction and Childhood Association: A Chinese Brief for Edward Westermarck*. Stanford, CA: Stanford University Press.

Wolf, Arthur P., and William H. Durham, eds. 2005. *Inbreeding, Incest, and the Incest Taboo: The State of Knowledge at the Turn of the Century*. Stanford, CA: Stanford University Press.

PART II

SOCIAL PSYCHOLOGICAL APPROACHES

CHAPTER 5

DISCOVERING HUMAN NATURE THROUGH CROSS-SPECIES ANALYSIS

JONATHAN H. TURNER

MUCH evolutionary analysis in the social sciences is directed at understanding and explaining the biological basis of human behaviors. Whether sociobiologists, evolutionary psychologists, evolutionary sociologists, or neurosociologists, the goal is to explain universal behavioral capacities and propensities that evolved during primate and then human evolution. Such an approach today can allow biologists and social scientists to offer a more precise and less speculative view of what has been rather loosely termed "human nature" or the propensity of humans to exhibit certain universal behaviors. From a sociological perspective, these universal behavioral propensities drive interpersonal interaction, the formation of social relations, and the construction of social structures and their attendant cultures. Thus, for sociologists, the ultimate goal is to understand how behavioral propensities help explain *the emergence of sociocultural formations* from which all societies are built.

One approach to realizing this goal has been comparative analysis of primates and humans, but early work in this area was often highly speculative. Fortunately, there is a methodology used in biology—cladistic analysis—that can provide a much firmer footing in making comparisons between primates and humans. This chapter outlines a program of research that I and Alexandra Maryanski have carried out for well over two decades that uses cladistic analysis to take us back to the last common ancestor (LCA) to both the hominin/human and the great ape clades (Maryanski & Turner, 1992; Turner & Maryanski, 2005, 2008, 2015).

Because humans share such a high percentage of their genes with the great apes— 99% with common and bonobo chimpanzees, 98% with lowland and highland gorillas, and 97% with orangutans—understanding the behavioral capacities and propensities of great apes along with their patterns of social organization can be used to give us real insight into what the distant ancestors of humans and present-day great apes were like millions of years ago. Cladistic analysis works much like the Hubble telescope and allows social scientists to see back in time to the very beginnings of hominin evolution that eventually led to *Homo sapiens*. In being able to go so far back in time, we can examine the selection pressures on hominins as evolving great apes and gain further insight into how natural selection reworked great ape neuroanatomy to give humans their basic nature. This nature is, in essence, great ape nature, but a nature that was subject to intense selection as the hominin ancestors of humans had to leave the forests, in which all great apes had evolved, and increasingly adapt to more open-country conditions on or near the African savanna. Only one ape can now live on the African savanna—*H. sapiens*—but many hundreds and perhaps thousands of species of apes tried to do the same thing but perished on the savanna or earlier in the forest habitats bordering the savanna. Thus, the story of human nature is how the basic behavioral capacities and propensities of great apes were modified by Darwinian natural selection as it worked on great ape neuroanatomy to accommodate the demands of the savanna habitat and, eventually, to produce *H. sapiens*.

I use Maryanski's (1986, 1987, 1992, 1993, 1995) extensive review of the published literature on great ape and monkey behaviors as they lead to the formation of social structures as a starting point for cladistic analysis, which in turn will provide a much more robust and less speculative view of human nature. Let me begin with a comparison of differences between ape and monkey societies, which will serve as the data for a reconstruction by the logic of cladistic analysis of humans' last common ancestor, or LCA, to extant great apes and contemporary humans.

THE SOCIAL STRUCTURE OF APE AND MONKEY SOCIETIES

Studies on the behaviors of primates, particularly those in the field, can yield data about their organizational structures—which is, after all, what sociology is all about. Alexandra Maryanski's groundbreaking use of accumulated data—mostly on behaviors rather than social structures—led to the construction of the network structures of great ape and monkey societies, and these data still provide new insights for the analysis of human nature. Many of these insights go against the presumed "sociality" of primates and humans, and this is why they are so important. Her construction of the social ties of conspecifics in ape and monkey societies reveals that great apes and monkeys have almost the reverse patterns of social organization, which is why apes perished on the savanna while monkeys flourished.

Social Structure Among Great Apes

Among great apes, the only strong ties are among (a) mothers and young offspring, which maintain strong ties (a virtual universal among mammals) until the offspring reach puberty, when both male and female gorillas and orangutans leave their natal community, never to return, whereas among chimpanzees, only females leave their natal community at puberty (males remain in the community and visit their mothers occasionally but do not form permanent groupings with them); and (b) occasional friendships among adult male chimpanzees with, at times, chimpanzee brothers forming moderate-to-strong ties. All other potential ties among great apes are nonexistent or weak. The result is a social structure in which there are no permanent groups and no intergenerational groups. Instead, all great apes are oriented to the larger regional community, which can be 10 square miles or even larger, with individuals moving about in the community alone or in proximity to others. Groups form for a short time, but then they disband. There are no moderate or strong adult male-adult females ties because all great apes are highly promiscuous, with the result that paternity is never known; hence, there are also no father-offspring ties. Occasionally, friendships sometimes develop among a particular male and female, but they never form a long-term conjugal group. Moreover, among gorillas, a female will join a lead silverback male when she is with young children, often using him as a babysitter while she wanders off to sexual liaisons with other males aggregating at the edge of the lead silverback's fluctuating group. There are no strong adult female–adult female ties among any of the great apes because all females are immigrants to the community from other communities (as they leave their natal community at puberty) and, unless they came from the same community, are strangers to each other. At best, there can be weak ties, but mostly females sit in proximity to let their offspring play but do not themselves form even moderate ties with each other.

As is evident, then, there are virtually *no ties* with which to build up social structures in great-ape societies. Great apes appear to be biologically programmed to recon their larger community, assessing who belongs and who does not and, at times, patrolling the perimeter of the community in temporary groups to kill any males who try to enter (females, however, are allowed to enter in order to replace all females who, at puberty, have left their natal community). There are no permanent groups, although, as noted previously, lead silverback males will often lead a group but its membership is constantly changing, and females that have temporarily used the lead silverback as a babysitter will leave once offspring are older (and the offspring will leave the community forever at puberty). Thus, humans are descendants of animals that are not highly social and that do not form any permanent groups. They do not reckon kinship beyond mother-younger offspring ties, and even that tie is broken at puberty. Thus, kin selection as portrayed by sociobiologists (Mitani, Merriwether, & Zhang, 2000) is not as powerful a force as it is among mammals for which larger sets and networks of kin remain in proximity for their lifetimes. As I emphasize later, the major adaptive problem for great apes near or on open-country savanna was to overcome the absence of kin selection to produce cohesive groups that would prove adaptive, as was the case for monkeys. For great apes, however, with male–female promiscuity, with no permanent relations among males and females (except the temporary one among gorillas), and with no intergenerational continuity across generates because of the transfer of males and females at puberty from

their natal communities (except for chimpanzee males), kinship did not provide a powerful organizational force, which is the reason why most great apes trying to adapt to
open-country conditions, filled with predators, went extinct. There are some friendship
ties among great apes, mostly among non-kin male chimpanzees and nondominant
gorillas, but these do not lead to permanent groupings, only temporary gatherings and
visitations. Thus, natural selection had by chance to find an alternative to kin selection if
hominins were ever to evolve into humans.

Here, I emphasize a critical point regarding research studies on contemporary primates, namely: Many of these studies have not been conducted in the larger community structures that were once common among all great apes, perhaps even bonobo
chimpanzees. This lack of research on great apes in their once natural habitat is obvious in studies of apes in zoos and other kinds of confined habitats. However, even at
such important sites as that of Jane Goodall's at Gombe, once feeding of chimpanzees
began, the habitat was disrupted and, in many ways, constricted as its members increasingly gathered near feeding sources. In other cases, such as the highland and, to a lesser
extent, lowland gorillas, human incursions have compressed their once expansive
habitats that allowed for larger home ranges. The result of these compressions has been
increased competition for resources and hierarchy formation that, much like prison
populations of humans, generate much more dominance and hierarchy than are typical of humans. The result is that studies often report more hierarchy than would normally exist, and hierarchy and increased dominance lead to more control of access to
females than existed in the natural habitats of both gorillas and chimpanzees. Less is
known about orangutans, but their habitats also have been under pressure. Thus, I think
that recent studies of great apes, especially of their reproductive and mating patterns,
reflect compression more than the original behavioral tendencies among apes. It is the
case that gorillas reveal hierarchy with the lead silverback and some group formation,
but not the harem pattern of mating that is often assumed, especially in Schaller's (1963,
1964) early study of highland gorillas in their more fully natural, uncompressed habitat.
It is also true that chimpanzees evidence some loss of episodic hierarchies, but in early
field studies (including those by Goodall at Gombe before feeding began), hierarchies
were not universal nor even constant, and they do not affect differential mating as much
as some hypothesize. What typifies great apes in their natural habitats is dispersion and
constant movement of individuals. At times, short-lived groups form within the larger
community, which may be as large as 10 square miles for chimpanzees, but individual
members can go without seeing each other for some time, whereas any groups that form
are soon disbanded, allowing individuals to go their own way. It would be most difficult
for hierarchies to form across such large communities and even more difficult for any
given male or set of males to dominate mating among such dispersed conspecifics.

This rather unusual organizational pattern stems from the adaptations of apes in their
competition with monkeys in the arboreal habitats of Africa. Apes lost out in this competition, with monkeys controlling the core areas of trees where there is more room,
more structural support by thicker branches, and more food to support larger and more
stable groupings. Apes were forced to the terminal feeding area of the forest habitat,

high in the trees, where structural supports are weak, there is less room, and there is certainly less food. Thus, bioprogrammers for strong kin relations that apes may have once had or for group formation more generally were selected out of the ape genome (a rather unusual event), setting up the pattern of offspring transfer away from their parental community, weak social ties among most conspecifics, and no permanent groups— all of which would keep densities low and, thereby, not tax the limited space, structural support, and food supply of any given location high in the trees. The transfer patterns of males and females at puberty would, in turn, ensure genetic mixing, whereas the generational movement of offspring away from their natal communities would sustain low densities as well as weak social ties and low levels of even transitory group formation.

Social Structure Among Monkeys

In contrast to great apes, monkeys evidence tight-knit group structures but do not demonstrate the larger community structure evident among great apes. Females never leave their natal group; in fact, they form dense networks of matrilines among generational and collateral female kin, sometimes with female leadership. Males transfer from their natal community at puberty and seek out other groups in which they may begin to enter the competition with other male migrants for leadership of their adopted groups. Males will generally form a dominance hierarchy in their adopted groups, often with the dominant male trying to horde females in matrilines as a kind of harem (often with little success). Thus, unlike great apes, monkeys exhibit a set of stronger ties, particularly among females, who form the stable grouping of monkey societies, whereas males form dominance hierarchies, with cliques of males at different places in the hierarchy sometimes emerging. Monkeys are oriented only to the group, and the female matrilines in the group constitute a strong-tie system of relations among females, thereby creating generational ties that do no form among great apes. These group structures can become quite large because monkeys dominate the more verdant portions of the arboreal habitat that can support more permanent and larger gatherings and grouping of conspecifics.

CLADISTIC ANALYSIS OF PRIMATE SOCIAL STRUCTURES

The Social Structure, or Lack Thereof, of the Last Common Ancestor

In Table 5.1, I have recapitulated Maryanski's cladistic analysis in abbreviated form. Key relations among age and sex classes for the three great apes are reported, and in the far-right column, the reconstruction of the social structures of the LCA to great apes and

Table 5.1 Strength of Social Ties Among Extant Species of Great Apes[a]

Social Ties	Species of Apes: Gorillas (*Gorilla*)	Chimpanzees (*Pan*)	Orangutans (*Pongo*)	Last Common Ancestor
Adult-to-adult ties				
Male–male	0	0/+	0	0*
Female–female	0	0	0	0*
Male–female	0/+	0	0	0*
Adult-to-adult offspring procreation ties				
Mother–daughter	0	0	0	0*
Father–daughter	0	0	0	0*
Mother–son	0	+	0	0*
Father–son	0	0	0	0*
Adult-to-preadolescent offspring ties				
Mother–daughter	+	+	+	+*
Father–daughter	0	0	0	0*
Mother–son	+	+	+	+*
Father–son	0	0	0	0*

[a]An asterisk denotes a reconstructed social structure—in this case, the likely structure of the last common ancestor to humans and extant great apes. As is evident, this structure is most like that of contemporary orangutans.

0, no or very weak ties; 0/+, weak to moderate ties; +, strong ties.

humans is listed. Cladistic analysis is very much like historical reconstruction in finding the root, ancestral language of a set of languages that are presumed to be related; those features that are common to all derived languages can be assumed to have been part of the root language. Because great apes share such a high percentage of genes with each other and with humans (albeit on an extra chromosomal pair compared to humans), we can be sure that the reconstruction is close to the social structure of the LCA. Cladistic analysis is based on two hypotheses: (a) the *relatedness hypothesis*, which assumes that any similarities found in a class of observations, such as social tie and network formation, are not due to chance but, rather, are the outcome of descent from a common ancestor; and (b) the *regularity hypothesis*, which assumes that modifications from the ancestral form to descendant forms are not randomly acquired but, rather, show a clear systemic bias that links these descendants to each other and to their LCA (Andrews & Martin, 1987; Jeffers & Lehiste, 1979; Platnick & Cameron, 1977).

Often, a control group of another set of related species is used to assess whether or not the pattern in the subject species is indeed distinctive and unique. Comparing monkey and great ape social structures clearly shows that ape societies are very unlike those organizing monkeys, with whom they share a very distant ancestor, and that this pattern of weak social ties, non-group formations, and reckoning of only community as the stable social unit of organization is indeed only along the great ape line and, as noted previously, is almost the exact opposite of the social structure evident among monkeys. Thus, we can be sure that the unusual pattern of organization among the great apes is unique to them.

Although orangutans are the most distant genetically to humans, sharing "only" 97% of their genes with humans, they are probably the closest living approximation of the LCA that have virtually no strong social ties and no group formations beyond the mother–offspring group that is destroyed when both males and females leave their natal community at puberty. Otherwise, orangutans are virtually solitary, with males hooking up with females for a short period of sexual contact and then leaving the females to raise any offspring alone. There are no other strong ties among orangutans beyond mother–offspring. Thus, the implication is clear: At their great ape core, humans are not as "naturally" social as much of sociology and social philosophy assume. Still, humans are more social than any of the great apes, and therein lies much of the story of human nature. How did natural selection work on great ape phenotype, including cognitive, emotional, and behavioral capacities and proclivities, to make humans more social and more capable of forming groups? And why was it necessary to make hominins and then humans more social?

The Changing Habitats of Africa

Approximately 10 million years ago, Africa began to cool, with the consequence that many of the great forests of Africa began to recede and the vast savannas began to expand. Many formerly arboreal species of primates would increasingly have to leave the now crowded forests and begin to adapt to the open-country, predator-ridden African savanna. This new habitat would place a premium on tight-knit group formations for collective defense against predation and foraging for resources. However, great apes were not well suited to this new habitat because they do not have bioprogrammers for strong social ties, do not form kinship groups beyond mother-offspring dyads, do not form permanent groups of any sort; instead, great apes would primarily orient themselves to the larger community in a new habitat where forming stable groups would be the key to survival. In contrast, monkeys were well suited to this habitat and, compared to apes, were able to survive to the present day on African savanna. All species of apes that sought to live on the savanna are now extinct except humans, and all extant great apes still live in the forests. The result is that today, apes represent only a handful of all species of primates, and all except one—humans—must still live in the forests, although a few common chimpanzees today can be observed in Senegal, West Africa, trying to survive in more open country (Baldwin, 1979; Baldwin, McGrew, & Tutin, 1982; McGrew, 1981, 1983, 1992, 2010; McGrew, Baldwin, & Tutin, 1981; Tutin, McGrew, & Baldwin, 1982).

Hence, the major obstacle to the evolution of the hominin/human clade was getting low-sociality, ape-like animals to be more social and more group oriented. Indeed, the lack of a tight-knit social morphology was compounded by other problems that a primate such as a great ape would have on the savanna, including the following: (a) Apes are slow and built to be mobile in a three-dimensional environment and, hence, cannot outrun potential predators; (b) apes cannot smell as well as most savanna-dwelling mammals because they became visually dominant in the arboreal niches and thus must rely on vision to see predators (which can hide) rather than chemical inputs to a large olfactory bulb; and (c) apes are highly individualistic and emotional, and when confronted with danger, they make a great deal of noise and run about in confusion, thus making them easier targets of predation. Thus, it is not surprising that with the exception of humans (and the verdict is still out on *H. sapiens*), apes represent a great evolutionary failure. Monkeys are far more successful than apes in the sense of being reproductively successful.

How, then, did great apes along the hominin line become more social and group oriented, given the lack of bioprogrammers for kin selection and group formation more generally? Cladistic analysis can again provide part of the answer, although it must be remembered that most species of apes, except hominins on the human clade, did not become sufficiently organized to survive on the savanna. However, the logic of cladistic analysis allows us to get a more detailed picture of what natural selection had to work on if selection was to make hominins more social and group oriented. As I outline later, great apes have a surprisingly large repertoire of behaviors that would seem to lend themselves to apes becoming more social and group oriented but for some reason did not for most species of great apes, except hominins on the human clade. Because all great apes share these traits that potentially could make hominins and eventually humans more social, we can be sure that the LCA also possessed these traits and, hence, that they were available for selection to work on, if by random chance selection took this route. Thus, part of the story of human nature is to understand the characteristics of apes that might, if selected upon or enhanced in some way, allow them to become better organized so as to survive in open-country savanna conditions.

APE NATURE AND THE LAST COMMON ANCESTOR

We can group the bundles of cognitive, emotional, and behavioral capacities of great apes and the LCA under the following rubrics: (a) *preadaptations* or capacities that were installed by natural selection as a by-product of selection working to install other capacities and that could, at a subsequent time, be selected upon if they promoted fitness; and (b) *behavioral capacities* that were installed in all great apes and, in some cases, all primates and mammals as well. Let me begin with preadaptations. In general, the history of hominin evolution since the LCA revolved around increasing hominin's capacity for sociality and stable group formations, which would be fitness enhancing for apes trying to adapt to open-country savanna conditions.

Preadaptations Among Great Apes Today and the Last Common Ancestor

As Darwinian natural selection works on variations of phenotypes, it often produces additional traits that, at some point in the future, may also be selected upon. Often, these additional traits have no effects on fitness for a long time or forever, but as environments change, they may have effects—thus activating selection on these traits. Next, I review those preadaptations that would increase sociality and capacities to form more stable groups among great ape-like hominins.

Language

When the first small, rodent-like mammals climbed or clawed their way into the arboreal habitat to initiate the primate order approximately 63 million years ago, selection immediately began to work to increase their ability to move about more safely in a three-dimensional environment in which one misstep meant death by gravity. Most mammals are olfactory dominate, and so, almost immediately, selection began to convert primates from olfactory to visual dominance by rotating the eye sockets forward to create stereoscopic vision for improved depth perception and, later, for color vision as well. In this conversion, a critical preadaptation was wired into the association cortices around the inferior parietal lobe where the temporal (auditory), parietal (haptic), and occipital (visual) lobes meet. In increasing the association cortices to convert an olfactory-dominant to a visual-dominant animal, the basic capacity for language was, by chance, also installed, but this capacity would not manifest itself unless a threshold of intelligence was passed (Geschwind, 1965a, 1965b; Geschwind & Damasio, 1984). Around the inferior parietal lobe are a series of association cortices where this transition to visual over olfactory dominance was accomplished. Furthermore, in this same area is Wernicke's area, which functions in great apes as it does in humans—to upload perceptions of the environment, including auditory calls and other information, into the brain's way of thinking. In contrast, human's Broca's area for downloading thinking into sequences of speech is more anterior to Wernicke's area and, thus, had to undergo considerable selection from what is at times called Broca's "cap" for great apes. Thus, this combination of association cortices around the inferior parietal lobe and a fully in place Wernicke's area for uploading symbolic meanings gave great apes the basic capacity to learn and understand human language, but without a full Broca's area and, more significantly, without the physiological structures in lips, tongue, larynx, vocal track, and muscles to generate precise auditory sounds in finely articulated speech, great apes cannot talk. However, through their dominant visual modality, they can communicate via the sign language of the deaf or via pictograms typed out in sentences on a computer. Great apes, and particularly chimpanzees, can make calls that are under voluntary control and that communicate common meanings among conspecifics. Also, many of these calls are constructed and hence can be viewed as quasi-cultural. Thus, the transition to fully blown human speech was not as large of a transition neurologically as is often supposed. The neurology was in place, and once the neocortex began to grow in late hominin evolution, selection began to select on Broca's area and on the physiology structures necessary for finely articulated speech.

All great apes would pass this threshold of intelligent for language facility, whereas lesser apes, such as gibbons and siamangs, and all monkeys do not possess the requisite intelligence to unleash what would eventually become a dominant trait among late hominins and humans. All great apes can thus learn human languages naturally by exposure to the auditory sounds because they possess Wernicke's area to upload symbols into the brain's means for processing information, and all great apes can "speak" in sentences using phonemes, morphemes, and syntax if allowed to use their visual and haptic sense modality—whether by hand signals of the deaf or pictograms on computers (Rumbaugh, 2013, 2015). As I argue later, this remarkable language capacity did not sit there for millions of years waiting for a larger neocortex; it was being used to make hominins more social and better organized. Eventually, of course, it would become the basis for culture among *H. sapiens*.

Emotionality

Great apes (and, hence, the LCA of humans and apes) are (were) highly emotional, and this trait probably worked against the survival of most apes on the savanna. However, somehow, natural selection allowed hominins to gain more neocortical control over subcortical emotion centers, and once this control was achieved, the wiring for expansion of the range of emotional valences was in place. Neurological control was critical for two reasons. One is that without full control over emotionally charged auditory outbursts, something that great apes can do until emotionally overloaded, emotional outbursts in open-country habitats would attract predators. Second, more fundamental to expanding the emotional palate, control of emotions generates, I hypothesize, the neurological capacity to differentiate emotions, at first new variations on primary emotions (e.g., anger, fear, sadness, happiness, and perhaps others such as disgust). Once this differentiation occurs and increases social bonds and hence fitness among low-sociality animals, new and more complex emotions are created by combining in various ways the expanded palette of emotions, including such important emotions as shame and guilt that chimpanzees and other great apes do not experience. Indeed, intelligence, culture, and language were not nearly as important to the survival of hominins as was increasing the flow of positive emotions among conspecifics that would need to spend ever-more

time in the open-country, predatory-ridden savanna habitat. The key to hominin survival and ultimately to human organization was the dramatic expansion of the capacity
for emitting more nuanced and complex emotions, thereby increasing sociality, attachment behaviors, commitments to conspecifics, and, most important, commitments to
group formations. Most other apes perished on the savanna because natural selection
did not randomly hit upon this "solution" to the low-sociality problem of an ape trying
to adapt to the savanna.

I have argued further that as this capacity for emotions expanded, the preadaptation for language was attached to emotional phonemes and morphemes and ordered
by a grammar to become a "language of emotions" (Turner, 2000, 2008). This language
evolved millions of years before anything like spoken language emerged among late
hominins or, perhaps, only with early *H. sapiens* (Enard et al., 2002a, 2002b). Indeed,
the language of emotions was not only more primal than spoken language for most of
hominin evolution over 10 million years but also is still more primary when humans
engage in attachment behaviors. They do so by reading emotions, and emotions reveal
phonemes, morphemes, and syntax along the dominant visual sense modality. Talk is
generally more instrumental, whereas emotions are read visually. One indicator of the
early evolution of emotions can be found in human infant development: A human infant
can imitate primary emotions emitted by caretakers within 2 weeks of birth, whereas it
takes 2 years of babbling to unleash auditory-based language capacities. Here, as is often
the case, a developmental sequence documents the likely evolutionary sequence in the
emergence of key behavioral traits. If great apes and the LCA had not already possessed
an enhanced emotional palette of emotions as a preadaptation (installed in most higher
mammals), the language of emotions (or body language in today's vocabulary) would
never have emerged, and all great apes forced to live on the African savanna would have
gone extinct.

Enhancing emotions was, as I will continue to outline, the key to enhancing the many
prosocial behavioral capacities and other preadaptations of great apes (and the LCA).
Without the emotional enhancements, the surprisingly large number of interpersonal
mechanisms of ape and human interactions would not have had the bonding effects
that they do when laced with emotions presented to others during the give and take
of normal human interactions. Thus, something extra was needed to make hominins
more social and group oriented, and that something was the language of emotions that
evolved many millions of years before spoken language.

Mother–Infant Bonding

Virtually all mammals evidence mother–infant bonds through the juvenile phase of
development; these are hardwired in the anterior cingulate gyrus. Great apes (and the
LCA) are (and were) no exception. Indeed, this is the only strong tie among gorillas and
orangutans, as well as most chimpanzees (except when males become close friends).
Thus, this bond was available for selection but, more important, given the promiscuity among great apes, selection had to find a means for attaching males to females with
infant offspring and, secondarily, to infants (whether or not the males were the actual

fathers) in order for the nuclear family to emerge. Indeed, nuclear families are a most unnatural unit for promiscuous great apes and, no doubt, for the LCA. Therefore, without bioprogrammers beyond mother–infant bonding, kin selection was not a very powerful force in great ape societies, and the same was true in hominin (and maybe even human) societies. Perhaps some additional hooks could be selected upon to pull males into mother–offspring relations, but probably far more critical was selection on subcortical emotion centers as a substitute for more direct bioprogrammers for kin selection evident among many mammals.

Non-harem Mating

Another related and critical preadaptation for the LCA was the nonharem mating pattern of great apes, with only the lead silverback gorilla having some tendencies in this direction. In contrast, dominant males among monkeys seek to use the female matrilines as an exclusive preserve for sexual partners, typically with only modest success. However, although promiscuity is not conducive to the nuclear family, which was the core structure for the first hunting and gathering bands, the existence of a harem pattern of mating would have prohibited the evolution of nuclear families. Selection clearly worked on subcortical areas of the great ape brain after the split with the LCA because all the subcortical emotion centers of the human brain are twice as large, controlling for body size, as they are in other apes (for references to the literature, see Turner, 2000, pp. 89–95). Of particular interest is the septum, which is responsible for the pleasure associated with sex in all mammals; among humans, it is well over twice as large as it is in any of the great apes, including chimpanzees, which are highly sexual and promiscuous. Because chimpanzees enjoy sex with multiple partners—"casual sex" was not invented by humans—it is curious that the septum of humans is twice as large as that among chimpanzees. This enlarging of the septum is perhaps "the smoking gun" of what natural selection was doing to pull males and pregnant females together. By enhancing the pleasure of not only the sexual act *per se* but also other positive emotions attached to sexual relationships—perhaps emotions such as "love"—blind and random natural selection hit upon a strategy that increased the likelihood that males and females would bond and begin to form the nuclear family. Without this key structural unit (the nuclear family), the hunting and gathering band would lack its structural base, and the mode of adaptation for *H. sapiens* (and perhaps late *Homo erectus*)—that is, bands of hunter-gathers composed of several nuclear families—could not have evolved and hominins would have gone the way of all extinct apes that could not adapt to the savanna habitat. Thus, the lack of a harem pattern opened the door to this route of using emotions—in the case of the nuclear family, positive emotions above and beyond the sexual act—to forge stronger bonds and to form more stable group structures. Genetically controlled bioprogrammers for harem mating patterns would have precluded this strategy; and once selection began to go down the path of enhancing emotions to forge bonds by rewiring the subcortical areas of the brain, it was perhaps inevitable that selection would hit upon the septum and begin installing the capacity to experience the emotions that led to evolution of the nuclear family.

Life History Characteristics

In addition to their organizational patterns, another difference between apes and monkeys is their "life history characteristics" (Turner & Maryanski, 2008, pp. 33–37). Apes live longer than monkeys, and they space their offspring further apart than do monkeys. Also, at every phase of the life cycle—gestation, nursing, infancy, and juvenile phases—they take longer to develop, and dramatically so. For instance, a large monkey such as a baboon will be in gestation for 175 days, whereas a chimpanzee male will remain in the womb for 228 days; the baboon will nurse for 420 days, whereas the chimpanzee will nurse for 1,460 days; and the baboon will be an infant for 1.6 years, whereas the chimpanzee will be an infant for 3.0 years. Overall, male baboons will be in nursing, infancy, and juvenile phases for 4.4 years, whereas male chimpanzees will be in these phases for 7.0 years.

These differences can be seen as a preadaptation for what eventually began to occur: the enlargement of the hominin brain. The brain of hominins did not grow dramatically for many millions of years after the split with the LCA, increasing in size compared to a chimpanzee brain of approximately 400 cc to slightly larger than 500 cc. Also, during the evolution of *H. erectus* and perhaps *Homo naledi* as well, the brain began to grow rapidly during the past 1.0 to 0.5 million years of hominin evolution to the lower end of the human range at slightly more than 1,000 cc. Without this preadaptation for life history features that keep the offspring in the womb and then, when out of the womb, care for them for more than 7 years, the brain could not have grown because a larger brain requires early exit from the womb when the brain is still small enough to pass through the female cervix and, as a result, is not well developed and must be protected while it continues growing in the first years of life. Monkey brains cannot become larger because the necessary life history characteristics are not programmed in monkeys' genomes, whereas great apes have hardwired life history patterns that would allow for less mature infants (with fragile growing brains) to be born and cared for. Thus, once selection began to enlarge the neocortex late in hominin evolution, life history characteristics did not shut off this route of evolution but, in fact, made it possible.

Moreover, prolonged infant care demands a nuclear family or at least stable groupings to protect the vulnerable infant. At the same time, the interpersonal emotions generated by kissing, licking, hugging, and other mammalian sigs of endearment, coupled with juvenile play and role-taking with adults, represented one more set of hooks pulling males into more conjugal relations with females, thereby further cementing in the nuclear family (Eibl-Eibesfeldt, 1996). However, the nuclear family of humans is not so much built from kin-selection bioprogrammers as by emotions of love and other positive sentiments. Although it could be argued that emotions are the mechanism by which kin selection operates, this argument ignores the fact that lack of kin-based groupings was the downfall of virtually all great apes that ever sought to adapt to open-country conditions. A mammal with strong bioprogrammers for kin selection would have been able to immediately form stronger groups, much like those among monkeys that have no problems surviving on the savanna, but great apes in the open country did not do so.

Play

Young mammals play, another activity stimulated by the anterior cingulate gyrus. Play involves a great many critical activities essential to human interaction and ultimately formation of strong social bonds (Burghardt, 2005). Play involves assuming and switching roles, role-taking, role-making, moving in and out of various faux states of aggression, reversing roles, and constant shifts in the roles that the young play out. This kind of activity is practice for adult roles among humans, in which individuals learn to read each other's gestures, interpret their meaning, and assess likely emotional dispositions and courses of action of others in order to select a line of conduct that promotes cooperation—as George Herbert Mead (1934) argued in his conception of the transition from the "play" to "game" stage of child maturation. Play is actually quite complex, as is human interaction in general, although this property of interpersonal behavior is not emphasized by most sociologists, who tend to emphasize one or two of the many mechanisms actually operating in interpersonal encounters (Turner, 2002, 2010). In a species without bioprogrammers for extensive kin selection and without programmers for social bonding per se, social bonds must be actively constructed. The extensive play activities of great apes can be seen as a preadaptation on which natural selection could go to work to expand *H. sapiens*' and perhaps late *H. erectus*' and *H. naledi*'s interpersonal skills to form stronger social bonds through role-taking and other interpersonal mechanisms discussed later.

Low Levels of Grooming and Cognitive Mapping

Robin Dunbar's (1996) well-known argument that language represented a kind of verbal grooming once groups became too large to physically groom all members of ape societies is probably not quite correct for two reasons: (a) Great apes do not often groom because they are low-sociality animals, and (b) great apes already reckon who belongs and does not belong in their community without either extensive grooming or language (Watts & Mitani 2001). Thus, unlike monkeys, which are constantly grooming, apes remain aware of who is present and who belongs because they constantly monitor the boundaries of their community and cognitively map the demography of who is in the community. Also, they occasionally engage in collective rituals among larger sets of conspecifics, much like human festivals with heightened emotions and a great deal of noise. Language, I argue, was not usurped to engage in verbal grooming; rather, language was used much earlier in hominin evolution to create the language of emotions that encourages stronger bonds with others. Moreover, the language of emotions leads to more physical grooming (handshakes, taps on part of the body, hugs, etc.) than most apes ever engage in; thus, emotions increase grooming behaviors. Emotion-arousing interaction rituals, with handshakes, pats on the back, active role-taking, and other emotional gestures, became hominins' first language, and it is still the primal and primary language for humans when they engage in social relations. We watch emotions in face and body more than we listen to talk, unless inflections of talk reveal emotions.

Another feature of cognitive mapping of community members is that this propensity probably served as a preadaptation for macro societies among such large animals as humans. Virtually all macro societies are among insects (Machalek, 1992), but large-bodied animals such as humans can create and sustain societies of millions, if not billions, of inhabitants. A monkey is oriented to the local, immediate group; thus, earth could never be a "planet of the monkeys," even though monkeys are far more successful than apes (save for humans). Big-brained primates such as humans that are not as oriented to groups as are monkeys, at least in their genetic programming, can create and sustain highly flexible bonds and groups through interpersonal mechanisms, but they can also reckon the larger social universe beyond the local group because the regional community, which can become as large as 10 square miles, is the primary unit of orientation to all great apes and hence the LCA. This cognitive capacity and indeed propensity was not needed for all of hominin evolution and for most of human evolution, but it allowed humans to do something that no other larger animal has ever done—create macro societies rivaling those of insects. Very few animals of any kind can do what humans can do—shift between kin and non-kin relations, generate and change friendships, forge groups and then leave them, move from group to group within organizations and communities, and forge emotionally charged intimacy with individuals and powerful emotional sentiments of commitment to macrostructures.

Behavioral Propensities of Great Apes and the Last Common Ancestor

As noted previously, great apes (and hence the LCA) reveal (and revealed) a large repertoire of interpersonal mechanisms for forging social bonds and group attachments. Indeed, interaction among humans is complex, and so it is among great apes, even though they do not forge strong bonds or group solidarities. However, they do have the capacity to read each other's minds and to respond with surprising empathy and sympathy, and this may be part of what is necessary if an animal lives in a larger community or home range and must reckon who belongs and engage in constantly changing weak-tie interactions with members of the larger community. It is clear that despite the rather long list of interpersonal mechanisms for forging ties that is presented next, these alone were not enough to prevent the extinction of species of apes that sought to survive on the African savanna. Something more was needed to super- or turbocharge these interpersonal mechanism so that they could be used to forge strong bonds and more stable groups. This "something" was enhancing emotions and creating a primal language of emotions that humans still use as they navigate between personal and impersonal situations in macro societies.

Individualism and Mobility

All great apes reveal high levels of individualism, often moving about their larger communities alone or in temporary groupings that form and then disband. These behavioral propensities in the LCA were not only a preadaptation for the macro societies that humans would eventually create but also enable humans to form relations of choice rather than relations imposed by bioprogrammers revolving around kin selection or rigid male-dominance hierarchies. In great ape societies, friendships form, particularly among chimpanzee males, more than kin relations among males (Mitani et al., 2000). Without being pushed by bioprogrammers to build ties around kinship, great apes can wander around their communities, hook up (to use human terminology), and then go their own way. This is all that a great ape community requires, but as selection pressures favored more tight-knit groups among hominins trying to adapt to the savanna, these same propensities would not necessarily lead to strong and more permanent bonds per se. They would need to be charged up a bit more, and particularly so if the nuclear family was to form and be the backbone of hunting and gathering bands. Individualism thus requires skills in engaging in interpersonal behaviors when meeting conspecifics because conspecifics are not constantly together in troops, packs, and kin units regulated by bioprogrammers; thus, each meeting among conspecifics in a larger community system requires a larger repertoire of interpersonal skills that, counterintuitively, is necessary to sustain weak ties rather than strong ties (which are generally sustained by genetically based bioprogrammers). Upon further reflection, then, it is not surprising that animals lacking the bioprogrammers of most mammals for kin selection and troop, pack, pod, herd, pride, and other group formations would actually have to be more skilled during interpersonal encounters with conspecifics. Furthermore, it should not be surprising that these skills for maintaining weak ties within a larger community would not lead to more intimate, permanent, and stable bonds and groupings without the enhancements that emotions can provide.

Reading Face and Eyes

Great apes are disposed to read the gestures of face and eyes of conspecifics (Menzel, 1971; Mitani & Watts, 2004; Osgood, 1966; Stanford, 1999); moreover, they will follow gaze and eye movements to ascertain what others are looking at and what they are thinking (Baizer, Baker, Haas, & Lima, 2007; Call & Tomasello, 2008; Hare, Call, & Tomasello, 2001, 2006; Itakura, 1996; Okamoto et al., 2002; Povinelli, 2000; Povinelli & Eddy, 1997; Tomasello & Call, 1997; Tomasello, Hare, & Fogleman, 2001). Because emotions are most apparent in the face and eyes, this propensity could be usurped and enhanced as the language of emotions of evolving hominins. Also, among humans today, reading eyes is critical to assessing others' emotional states.

Imitation of Facial Gestures Revealing Emotions

Great apes (and the LCA) learn the meanings of facial and body gestures very early, long before they learn the meaning of words (Ekman, 1984; Emde, 1969; Gergely & Csibra, 2006; Horowitz, 2003; Sherwood, Subiaul, & Zawidzki, 2008; Subiaul, 2007; Tomonaga, 1999). As noted previously, infants can imitate primary emotions of caretakers within 2 weeks of birth. Thus, literally as human infants leave the womb, they are behaviorally disposed to read emotions signaled by eyes, face, and body.

Role-Taking and Empathy

The previously discussed capacities make possible role-taking and empathy among great apes; thus, contrary to G. H. Mead's (1934) views (but not those of Darwin in *The Descent of Man* [1871/1875]), role-taking is not unique to humans but, in fact, comes to humans as a consequence of their great ape ancestry. As de Waal (1996, 2009) has documented, apes can read gestures of body and face (in addition to vocal cues) and achieve a sense of empathy with conspecifics. Thus, what Mead thought was a behavior unique to humans has always existed along the great ape and hominin line.

Rhythmic Synchronization, Mimicry, and Ritual

The discovery of mirror neurons (Rizzolatti, Fadiga, Fogassi, & Gallese, 2002; Rizzolatti & Sinigaglia, 2008) in monkeys and then apes and humans explained the neurology behind imitation, role-taking, and empathy enumerated previously. However, mirror neurons are also responsible for other behavioral propensities, including falling into rhythmic synchronization of voice and bodies during interaction, collective emotional contagion, and rituals among assembled apes engaged in carnival.

These processes all heighten emotions and allow both great apes and humans to become emotionally entrained (and certainly the LCA as well). Mirror neurons also encourage mimesis, which is the basic underpinning of rhythmic synchronization and "musilanguage" or a proto-language revolving around singing and rhythm (Mithen, 2005) that late hominins and certainly early humans used to generate solidarities as mirror neurons activated brain systems, thus generating prosocial neurotransmitters and neuroactive peptides in the primate brain. These brain systems are also responsible for ritual acts in which chimpanzees often engage during carnival, such as collective jumping around in unison, banging with sticks, and other acts that are ritual-like and highly rhythmic. It is but a short step from these behaviors to human ritual activities.

Emotional Effervescence

The carnival among assembled chimpanzees is very much like the collective effervescence reported in Emile Durkheim's (1912/1995) description of Aranda Aborigines assembling in the Todd River in Alice Springs, Australia (originally described by Spencer and Gillin [1899/1938]). Durkheim viewed these collective rituals as directed by symbols denoting the group structure and culture of the Aranda, and it was from Durkheim's secondary descriptions that Erving Goffman (1967) and, later, Randall Collins (1975, 2004) developed their respective theories of ritual. Interaction among humans is always ritualized, from greetings and departing rituals to more intense emotional entrainments. All rituals increase group solidarity; thus, if chimpanzees can celebrate in a ritual-like manner their collective community, it is not a large step neurologically to the rituals among described by Durkheim, Goffman, and Collins. There was clearly an already built-in behavioral propensity to engage in rhythmic actions to intensity emotions directed at the collective whole; thus, with more selection on this propensity, coupled with more emotions from subcortical areas of the brain and more cognitions from the expanded neocortex, rituals in the human measure could evolve. More important, however, as the capacity to engage in ritual-arousing emotions increased and was refined in late hominin evolution with enlargement of the neocortex to the lower end of the human distribution, there was from the very beginning of hominin evolution a solidarity-generating capacity programmed in the genome of the LCA.

Reciprocity

All higher primates and most advanced mammals engage in reciprocity for favors performed by conspecifics (Cosmides, 1989; de Waal, 1989, 1991, 1996; de Waal & Brosnan, 2006). Reciprocity reinforces existing exchanges while promoting social bonds, and reciprocal exchanges in which one favor is followed by a counter-favor are the most likely to promote social bonds. Because this capacity existed, it was always available for natural selection to enhance. Moreover, in a species without strong programmers for kin selection, what Trivers (1971, 2005) termed "reciprocal altruism" was an available substitute for the hardwired programmers that most mammals, but not great apes, reveal for forming groups. Also, as emotional capacities developed among hominins and, eventually, cognitive capacities from a larger neocortex also began to evolve, reciprocal altruism could be become, as it is today among humans, a powerful force for forging stronger ties and group solidarities. Again, it is not a giant step neurologically from what great apes with comparatively small brains (375–400 cc) can do to what humans do today.

Calculations of Justice and Fairness

Capuchin monkeys will stop emitting conditioned behaviors for food provided by a trainer when they observe a conspecific getting more food for the same behavior (Brosnan, Schiff, & de Waal, 2005). Similarly, in studies of chimpanzees, a chimp will cease exchanging with a trainer when it discovers that a relative is not receiving as much in its exchanges with trainers (Brosnan & de Waal, 2003). Thus, it is clear that higher primates can make complex calculations—comparing rate of exchange of self with another, experiencing a negative emotion, and ceasing to exchange until equity is restored. These calculations and the emotional reactions that they arouse can only be seen as moral, or at least proto-moral. Thus, long before hominins could have culture even close to the human measure, the LCA and its descendants had the capacity to experience injustice and unfairness and, moreover, to do something about it. Therefore, language is not a key ingredient in morality; rather, expectations for receipt of resources are a key ingredient, and when these expectations are not realized, higher mammals experience injustice and a lack of fairness. Human morality, then, is not such a giant leap as might be supposed, although it can be codified by humans into systems of moral codes and thus be used to regulate a wide range of conduct. However, long before culture in the human measure evolved, hominins were exchanging resources that would increase bonds and solidarity while monitoring and sanctioning those who did not exchange fairly. Solidarity is always based on exchanges and the implicit threat that cheaters and free-riders should and will be sanctioned negatively.

Seeing Self as an Object

Mead (1934) believed that only humans could see themselves as an object in their environment, but clearly he was wrong on this score. All great apes can recognize that the reflection that they see in a mirror is an image of themselves (Gallup, 1970, 1979, 1982), and so they have the basic cognitive capacity to see self. Currently, it is known that dolphins, elephants, and, most likely, whales can recognize themselves in a mirror (Whitehead & Rendell, 2015). Seeing oneself in a mirror is not the same as having identities that guide conduct and self-evaluations of persons, but it is not very far from it. For example, when seeing themselves in a mirror, chimpanzees and dolphins move about, looking and evaluating themselves as they record their movements in the mirror. They will smile or frown and thus are very close to recognizing the image of what they look like, but clearly their smaller brains and more limited emotional repertoire limit their ability to recognize themselves, and hence, their ability at identity formation. However, with expanded emotions and a larger neocortex, self-reflection and identity formation probably are inevitable among animals that orient to communities and that already possess a large palette of interpersonal techniques, such as role-taking and empathy, that allow them to see themselves from the perspective of others—especially as they read the emotions of others toward self. Therefore, at some point in hominin evolution, the threshold to full self-awareness and to conceptions of self that must be maintained emerged, perhaps only with late hominins but possibly earlier. Thus, self and self-evaluations are not a dramatic leap from what great apes today, and hence the LCA to apes and hominins, can (and could) do. Also, with a larger palette of emotions, self, role-taking, and empathy would mutually reinforce one another and enable conspecifics to form stronger bonds.

When self can be evaluated, a powerful mechanism of social control is unleashed: An animal can evaluate itself from the perspective of others, evaluate itself, and adjust conduct so as to affirm or reaffirm a conception of self. Because great apes can role-take, they are not far from having this powerful mechanism of social control. Moreover, new emotions that great apes and hence the LCA do (and did) not have the capacity to experience can evolve because they would enhance social control at the group level. Shame and guilt are only possible when an animal actively evaluates self not only from the perspective of others but also from moral codes. Emotions such as shame arise when a person feels that expectations of others have not be met, whereas emotions such as guilt at having violated a moral code can begin to exert their power to control people because they are so painful (Scheff, 1988; Turner, 2007). Because great apes (and the LCA) can role-take, can have a sense of morality or at least fairness in exchange, and can see themselves as an object, much of the necessary wiring was already in place as hominins evolved. At some point, emotions such as shame and guilt began to emerge as the emotional repertoire continued to evolve and as the neocortex began its spurt of growth with late *H. erectus*. If shame and guilt promoted social control in emerging group structures, they would be enhancing fitness. Thus, although the evolution of the capacity to experience shame and guilt appears to have been a major step, the other elements in hominin neurology for self-appraisal and self-control were already in place to make this a short but significant step toward increasing hominins' or perhaps only humans' capacity for self-control through self-sanctioning.

CONCLUSION

I have left many details out of this chapter to conform to the length requirements of the volume, but I have presented versions of this argument in a number of publications (e.g., Turner & Machalek, 2018; Turner & Maryanski, 2015). The key point is that there are alternative ways of examining basic and fundamental behavioral propensities that can supplement the insights of sociobiology and evolutionary psychology. The approach that I advocate does not study behavior per se but, rather, behavior as it is instantiated in interaction among individuals and how such interactions create, sustain, and change culture and social structures. Of course, it is critical to begin the sociological agenda by knowing something about behavior and how and why particular behavioral propensities evolved.

Primates can tell us a great deal about human origins, and by employing cladistic analysis on our closet primate cousins, the great apes, we can look back in time and get a sense of the behavioral and organizational patterns of the common ancestor for our great ape cousins and ourselves. Indeed, chimpanzees and probably gorillas as well, if not all the great apes, belong in the genus *Homo* to emphasize how closely related humans are genetically to chimpanzees, gorillas, and orangutans. Humans are little more than evolved great ape. Then, if we engage in neurosociology by comparing the brains of extant great apes and humans, we can begin to understand how the brain got rewired to convert a low-sociality, non-group-forming animal into an animal that can construct all kinds of sociocultural formations to the point of being the only large animal to ever form macro societies in the history of earth. However, it is important to recognize that humans are a blend of selection pressures that made great apes weak-tie, low-sociality animals and then, due to intense selection pressures on hominins, made humans into emotionally- charged, interpersonally-complex animals able to form and live in groups and even larger sociocultural formations. We are still great apes at our core, with emotional overlays made possible by the enlargement of subcortical areas of the brain and with cultural overlays made possible by the enlargement of the neocortex, which, it must be re-emphasized, was only possible with the prior enlargement of emotion centers. Without the ability to tag complex cognitions with complex emotional valences, there would be no fitness-enhancing reason for selection to enlarge the neocortex. Humans can develop culture, make complex decisions, and remember so much because they have a large palette with which to tag cognitions (Damasio, 1994), and with this expanded palette, enlarging the brain would be fitness enhancing. Still, none of what makes humans unique—capacities for spoken language, for complex thinking, for complex and rapid decision-making, for storing vast stores of information, and for innovations along many fronts—would have been possible without the prior rewiring of the hominin brain to make, in the end, humans the most emotional animals on earth. Emotions were the key to overcoming a lack of bioprogrammers for kinship, for group formation, and for stronger social ties; without emotions, hominins would have died on the savanna like all other apes that sought to live there. In addition, emotions are the key to the evolution of human intelligence and to the interaction processes that led to stronger social ties and commitments to social relations and whole societies. Thus, in closing, we should reorient evolutionary sociology to studying emotions first and then to explaining what emotions made possible for hominins and then humans. Ultimately, all human social relations and all human sociocultural formations are built from emotions as much as from spoken language, culture, or large brains. Humans' core "nature," then, resides in what was inherited from the LCA to all the great apes, including humans as an evolved great ape.

REFERENCES

Andrews, P., & Martin, L. (1987). Cladistic relationships of extant and fossil hominoids. *Journal of Human Evolution, 16,* 101–118.

Baizer, J. S., Baker, J. F., Haas, K., & Lima, R. (2007). Neurochemical organization of the nucleus paramedinaus dorsalis in the human brain. *Brain Research, 1176,* 45–52.

Baldwin, P. J. (1979). *The natural history of the chimpanzee (Pan troglodytes verus) at Mt. Assirik, Senegal.* PhD thesis, University of Stirling, Stirling, Scotland.

Baldwin, P. J., McGrew, W. C., & Tutin, C. E. G. (1982). Wide-ranging chimpanzees at Mt. Assirik, Senegal. *International Journal of Primatology, 3,* 367–385.

Brosnan, S. F., & de Waal, F. B. M. (2003). Animal behaviour: Fair refusal by capuchin oo6Donkeys. *Nature, 428,* 128–140.

Brosnan, S. F., Schiff, H. C., & de Waal, F. B. M. (2005). Tolerance for inequity may increase with social closeness in chimpanzees. *Proceedings of the Royal Society of London, 272,* 253–258.

Burghardt, G. M. (2005). *The genesis of animal play: Testing the limits.* Cambridge, MA: MIT Press.

Call, J., & Tomasello, M. (2008). Do chimpanzees have a theory of mind: 30 years later. *Trends in Cognitive Science, 12,* 187–192.

Collins, R. (1975). *Conflict theory: Toward an explanatory social science.* San Diego, CA: Academic Press.

Collins, R. (2004). *Interaction ritual chains.* Princeton, NJ: Princeton University Press.

Cosmides, L. (1989). The logic of social exchange: Has natural selection shaped how humans reason? *Cognition, 31,* 187–276.

Damasio, A. (1994). *Descarte's error: Emotion, reason, and the human brain.* New York, NY: Crosset/Putman.

Darwin, C. (1875). *The descent of man and selection in relation to sex.* New York, NY: Appleton. (Original work published 1871)

de Waal, F. B. M. (1989). Food sharing and reciprocal obligations among chimpanzees. *Journal of Human Evolution, 18,* 433–459.

de Waal, F. B. M. (1991). The sense of social regularity and its relation to the human sense of justice. *American Behavioral Scientist, 34,* 335–349.

de Waal, F. B. M. (1996). *Good natured: The origins of right and wrong in humans and other animals.* Cambridge, MA: Harvard University Press.

de Waal, F. B. M. (2009). *The age of empathy: Nature's lessons for a kinder society*. New York, NY: Three Rivers Press.

de Waal, F. B. M., & Brosnan, S. F. (2006). Simple and complex reciprocity in primates. In P. Kappeler & C. P. van Schaik (Eds.), *Cooperation in primates and humans: Mechanisms and evolution* (pp. 85–106). Berlin, Germany: Springer-Verlag.

Dunbar, R. (1996). *Grooming, gossip and the evolution of language*. London, UK: Faber & Faber.

Durkheim, E. (1995). *The elementary forms of the religious life*. New York: Free Press. (Original work published 1912)

Eibl-Eibesfeldt, I. (1996). *Love and hate: The natural history of behavior patterns*. New York: Aldine de Gruyter.

Ekman, P. (1984). Expression and the nature of emotion. In K. Scherer & P. Ekman (Eds.), *Approaches to emotion* (pp. 319–343). Hillsdale, NJ: Erlbaum.

Emde, R. N. (1969). Level of meaning for infant emotions: A biosocial view. In W. A. Collins (Ed.), *Development of cognition, affect, and social relations* (pp. 1–37). Hillsdale, NJ: Erlbaum.

Enard, W., Khaitovich, P., Klose, J., Zollner, S., Heissig, F., Giavalisco, P., . . . Paabo, S. (2002a). Intra- and interspecific variation in primate gene expression patterns. *Science, 296*, 340–342.

Enard, W., Przeworski, M., Fisher, S. E., Lai, C. S. L., Wiebe, V., Kitano, T., . . . Paabo, S. (2002b). Molecular evolution of *FOXP2*, a gene involved in speech and language. *Nature, 418*, 869–872.

Gallup, G. G., Jr. (1970). Chimpanzees: Self-recognition. *Science, 167*, 86–87.

Gallup, G. G., Jr. (1979). *Self-recognition in chimpanzees and man: A developmental and comparative perspective*. New York, NY: Plenum.

Gallup, G. G., Jr. (1982). Self-awareness and the emergence of mind in primates. *American Journal of Primatology, 2*, 237–248.

Gergely, G., & Csibra, G. (2006). Sylvia's recipe: The role of imitation and pedagogy. In N. J. Enfield & S. C. Levinson (Eds.), *The transmission of cultural knowledge* (pp. 229–255). Oxford, UK: Berg Press.

Geschwind, N. (1965a). Disconnection syndromes in animals and man: Part I. *Brain, 88*, 237–294.

Geschwind, N. (1965b). Disconnection syndromes in animals and man: Part II. *Brain, 88*, 585–644.

Geschwind, N., & Damasio, A. (1984). The neural basis of language. *Annual Review of Neuroscience, 7*, 127–147.

Goffman, E. (1967). *Interaction ritual*. Garden City, NY: Anchor.

Hare, B., Call, J., & Tomasello, M. (2001). Do chimpanzees know what conspecifics know? *Animal Behavior, 61*, 139–151.

Hare, B. Call, J., & Tomasello, M. (2006). Chimpanzees deceive a human competitor by hiding. *Cognition, 101*, 495–514.

Horowitz, A. C. (2003). Do humans ape? Or do apes human? Imitation and intention in humans (*Homo sapiens*) and other animals. *Journal of Comparative Psychology, 117*, 325–336.

Itakura, S. (1996). An exploratory study of gaze-monitoring in non-human primates. *Japanese Psychological Research, 38*, 174–180.

Jeffers, R., & Lehiste, I. (1979). *Principles and methods for historical linguistics*. Cambridge MA: MIT Press.

Machalek, R. (1992). Why are large societies so rare? *Advances in Human Ecology, 1*, 33–64.

Maryanski, A. (1986). *African ape social structure: A comparative analysis*. PhD dissertation, University of California, Irvine.

Maryanski, A. (1987). African ape social structure: Is there strength in weak ties? *Social Networks*, 9, 191–215.

Maryanski, A. (1992). The last ancestor: An ecological–network model on the origins of human sociality. *Advances in Human Ecology*, 2, 1–32.

Maryanski, A. (1993). The elementary forms of the first proto-human society: An ecological/social network approach. *Advances in Human Evolution*, 2, 215–41.

Maryanski, A. (1995). African ape social networks: A blueprint for reconstructing early hominid social structure. In J. Steele & S. Shennan (Eds.), *Archaeology of human ancestry* (pp. 67–90). London, UK: Routledge.

Maryanski, A., & Turner, J. H. (1992). *The social cage: Human nature and the evolution of society*. Stanford, CA: Stanford University Press.

McGrew, W. C. (1981). The female chimpanzee as a human evolutionary prototype. In F. Dahlberg (Ed.), *Woman the gatherer* (pp. 35–73). New Haven, CT: Yale University Press.

McGrew, W. C. (1983). Animal foods in the diets of wild chimpanzees (*Pan troglodytes*): Why cross cultural variation? *Journal of Ethology*, 1, 46–61.

McGrew, W. C. (1992). *Chimpanzee material culture: Implications for human evolution.* Cambridge, UK: Cambridge University Press.

McGrew, W. C. (2010). In search of the last common ancestor: New findings on wild chimpanzees. *Philosophical Transaction of the Royal Society of London*, 365, 3265–3267.

McGrew, W. C., Baldwin, P. J., & Tutin, G. E. G. (1981). Chimpanzees in hot, dry, and open habitat: Mt. Assirik, Senegal, West Africa. *Journal of Human Evolution*, 10, 227–244.

Mead, G. H. (1934). *Mind, self, and society*. Chicago, IL: University of Chicago Press.

Menzel, E. W. (1971). Communication about the environment in a group of young chimpanzees. *Folia Primatologica*, 15, 220–232.

Mitani, J. C., Merriwether, D. A., & Zhang, C. (2000). Male affiliation, cooperation and kinship in wild chimpanzees. *Animal Behavior*, 59, 885–893.

Mitani, J. C., & Watts, D. P. (2004). Why do chimpanzees eat meat? *Animal Behavior*, 61, 915–924.

Mithen, Steven J. (2005). The singing Neantherthas: The origins of music, language, mind, and body, London: Weidenfeld and Nicholson.

Osgood, Charles E. (1966). Dimensionality of the semantic space for communications via facial expressions. *Scandinavian Journal of Psychology*, 7, 1–30.

Pinker, S. (2012). *The false allure of group selection*. Retrieved from https://www.edge.org/conversation/steven_pinker-the-false-allure-of-group-selection

Platnick, N., & Cameron, H. D. (1977). Cladistic methods in textual, linguistic and phylogenetic analysis. *Systematic Zoology*, 26, 380–385.

Povinelli, D. J. (2000). *Folk physics for apes: The chimpanzee theory of how the world works.* Oxford: Oxford University Press.

Povinelli, D. J., & Eddy. T J. (1997). Specificity of gaze-following in young chimpanzees. *British Journal of Developmental Psychology*, 15, 213–222.

Premack, D., & Woodruff, G. (1978). Does the chimpanzee have a theory of mind? *Behavior and Brain Science*, 1, 515–526.

Rizzolatti, G., Fadiga, L., Fogassi, L., & Gallese, V. (2002). From mirror neurons to imitation: Facts and speculations. In W. Prinz & A. N. Meltzoff (Eds.), *The imitative mind: Development, evolution and brain bases* (pp. 247–266). Cambridge, UK: Cambridge University Press.

Rizzolatti, G., & Sinigaglia, C. (2008). *Mirrors in the brain: How our minds share actions, emotions and experience.* Oxford: Oxford University Press.

Rumbaugh, M. D. (2013). *With apes in mind: Emergents, communication and competence.* Distributed by Amazon.com.

Rumbaugh, M. D. (2015). A salience theory of learning and behavior and rights of apes. In J. H. Turner, R. Machalek, & A. Maryanski (Eds.), *Handbook on evolution and society: Toward an evolutionary social science* (pp. 514–536). Boulder, CO: Paradigm.

Schaller, G. B. (1963). *The mountain gorilla—Ecology and behavior.* Chicago, IL: University of Chicago Press.

Schaller, G. B. (1964). *The year of the gorilla.* Chicago, IL: University of Chicago Press.

Scheff, T. (1988). Shame and conformity: The deference-emotion system. *American sociological review, 53,* 395–406.

Sherwood, C. C., Subiaul, F., & Zawidzki, T. W. (2008). A natural history of the human mind: Tracing evolutionary changes in brain and cognition. *Journal of Anatomy, 212,* 426–454.

Spencer, B., & Gillin, F. (1938). *The native tribes of central Australia.* (Original work published 1899)

Stanford, C. B. (1999). *The hunting apes: Meat eating and the origins of human behavior.* Princeton NJ: Princeton University Press.

Subiaul, F. (2007). The imitation faculty in monkeys: Evaluating its features, distribution, and evolution. *Journal of Anthropological Science, 85,* 35–62.

Tomasello, M., & Call, J. (1997). *Primate cognition.* Oxford, UK: Oxford University Press.

Tomasello, M., Hare, B., & Fogleman, T. (2001). The ontogeny of gaze following in chimpanzees, *Pan troglodytes,* and rhesus macaques, *Macaca mulatta. Animal Behavior, 61,* 335–343.

Tomonaga, M. (1999). Attending to others' attention in Macaques' joint attention or not? *Primate Research, 15,* 425.

Trivers, R. L. (1971). The evolution of reciprocal altruism. *Quarterly Review of Biology, 46,* 35–57.

Trivers, R. L. (2005). Reciprocal altruism: 30 years later. In P. M. Kappeler & C. P. van Schaik, (Eds.), *Cooperation in primates and humans: Mechanisms of evolution* (pp. 67–84). New York, NY: Springer.

Turner, J. H. (2000). *On the origins of human emotions: A sociological inquiry into the evolution of human affect.* Stanford, CA: Stanford University Press.

Turner, J. H. (2002). *Face to face: Toward a theory of interpersonal behavior.* Palo Alto, CA: Stanford University Press.

Turner, J. H. (2007). *Human emotions: A sociological theory.* Oxford, UK: Routledge.

Turner, J. H. (2010). *Theoretical principles of sociology, Volume 2: Microdynamics.* New York, NY: Springer.

Turner, J. H., & Maryanski, A. (2005). *Incest: Origins of the taboo.* Boulder, CO: Paradigm.

Turner, J. H., & Maryanski, A. (2008). *On the origins of societies by natural selection.* Boulder, CO: Paradigm.

Turner, J. H., & Maryanski, A. (2015). Evolutionary sociology: A cross-species strategy for discovering human nature. In J. H. Turner, R. Machalek, & A. R. Maryanski (Eds.), *Handbook of evolution and society: Toward an evolutionary social science* (pp. 546–571). Boulder, CO: Paradigm.

Turner, J. H., & Machalek, R. (2018). *The new evolutionary sociology: New and Revitalized Methodological and Theoretical Approaches.* New York and London: Routledge.

Tutin, W., McGrew, W. C., & Baldwin, P. J. (1982). Responses of wild chimpanzees to potential predators. In B. Chiarelli & R. Corruccini (Eds.), *Primate behavior and sociobiology* (pp. 136–141). Berlin, Germany: Springer-Verlag.

Watts, D. P., & Mitani, J. C. (2001). Boundary patrols and intergroup encounters in wild chimpanzees. *Behaviour, 138,* 299–327.

Whitehead, H., & Rendell, L. (2015). *The cultural lives of whales and dolphins.* Chicago IL: University of Chicago Press.

CHAPTER 6

THE NEUROLOGY OF RELIGION

An Explanation from Evolutionary Sociology

ALEXANDRA MARYANSKI AND
JONATHAN H. TURNER

In recent years, there has been an unfortunate tendency to view religion as the outcome of rather simple neurological forces. For example, Dean Hammer (2005) announced that there is a "God gene" (*VMAT2*) that hardwires the neurological propensity for faith. As another example, Pascal Boyer (2001) has "explained religion" with reference to cognitive "modules" in the brain underlying "agent detection processes," including the gods as agents. What these and other scholars argue may indeed be part of the story about humans' capacity for religion, but what their arguments ignore is the evolution of human neurology and the cognitive and emotional dynamics involved in a capacity for religion. From a sociological perspective, religion is more than a propensity to behave in a religious manner. It is at least the following: (a) forming *communities of individuals* revolving around shared *beliefs in a sacred and supernatural realm* inhabited *by forces and beings* with *powers* to intervene in the mundane world; (b) engaging *in emotional-arousing rituals* directed to these forces and beings; and (c) *organizing rituals within cult (social) structures* among communities of fellow worshipers, often led by religious specialists and practitioners. Religion is then, at one and the same time, a neurological, behavioral, and organizational process, and it would be rather amazing if any cognitive module, to say nothing of a particular "God gene" (Hammer, 2005), regulating vesicular monoamine levels of serotonin, dopamine, and norepinephrine represented the sole set of driving forces of human religiosity in its behavioral and organization forms.

As we argue in this chapter, religion evolved as a consequence of natural selection on both subcortical and neocortical divisions of the brain during hominin evolution on the human clade. However, selection was not working on a facility for religion *per se* but, rather, on the hominin brain to increase sociality and capacities for group formation among humans' ancestors. The neocortical and subcortical areas of the brain are both involved in the human capacity to perceive and conceive of a supernatural realm and to organize rituals directed at beings and forces in this realm. Thus, it is the way in which the brain became reorganized and the set of cognitive, emotional, and behavioral propensities that evolved during hominoid and hominin evolution that are responsible for religious behavior and organization. There is no modular "smoking gun" or "God gene" in this or that structure of the brain but, instead, an evolutionary enhancement of the brain to generate a more complex and passion-hued emotionality rooted in earlier adaptations. Only after Darwinian selection for such an encompassing emotionality was installed in subcortical areas of the brain did selection begin expanding the size of the neocortex during the past 1 million years of hominin evolution. Indeed, although much early evolutionary psychology (EP) was flawed in its views on how this neurology evolved, with its emphasis on new adaptive modules in the brain during the late Pleistocene (Cosmides & Tooby, 1992), early EP was nonetheless correct in its negative assessment of the "standard social science model" that emphasizes the large human neocortex as it generates capacities for spoken language and culture as the key to the uniqueness of humans.

As we outline, early hominin survival rested initially more on enhancements in the subcortical than in neocortical portions of the brain. Thus, the rewiring of the subcortex was essential for early hominin well-being, and it was a necessary prerequisite for the later evolution of spoken language and culture in the human measure. Indeed, spoken language emerged late in hominin evolution and, in all likelihood, only with the emergence of *Homo sapiens* approximately 200,000 years ago (Disotell, 2012; Enard et al., 2002a, 2002b; Lambert & Tishkoff, 2009).

In this chapter, we trace the evolution of the hominin brain under selection pressures working on earlier adaptations and hardwired behavioral propensities of the last common ancestor (LCA) to humans and present-day great apes in order to understand why humans became disposed to engage in religious behaviors. This analysis is Darwinian in that we focus on selection forces working on the neuroanatomy of hominins over millions of years. However, the propensity for religious behaviors is, we argue, a secondary product of selection working to make low-sociality and non-group-forming hominins, as descendants of their common ancestor with extant great apes, more social (Maryanski & Turner, 1992; Turner & Maryanski, 2008; Turner & Maryanski, 2015). For, in contrast to most social mammals, cladistic analysis of great ape ties reveals that present-day great apes and their common ancestor with humans had few, if any, direct neurological bioprogrammers (i.e., heritability components for social and behavioral traits) for high levels of sociality, kin selection, and group formation (see Chapter 5, this volume).

Let us begin by reviewing the "nature" of the hominin ancestors of humans, drawing from the material outlined in detail in Chapter 5. The origins of religious behaviors, then, are to be explained by why and how natural selection made hominins and then humans more social and group oriented. Our analysis is part of a larger project in evolutionary sociology and one of its recent subfields, neurosociology (Franks, 2010; Franks & Turner, 2013; Maryanski, 2013).

SELECTION PRESSURES ON HOMININS

The Weak-Tie and Non-Group Patterns of Social Relations

In Chapter 5, Maryanski's (1986, 1987, 1992, 1993, 1995) cladistic analysis of great ape social relations and network structures was reviewed. The foremost conclusion from this analysis (the details of which do not need to be repeated here) is that present-day great apes, with whom humans share from 97% to 99% of their DNA, are not highly social (compared to monkeys), nor do they sustain permanent group structures over intergenerational time. For chimpanzees (*Pan*) and orangutans (*Pongo*), the only lasting structure and point of orientation is at the regional population level. Chimpanzees are organized into a rare "fission–fusion" social formation that Jane Goodall (1986) called a community because it is composed of a stable population of 40–150 fancy-free nomads who actively move about alone or join a variety of momentary gatherings or "parties" (that form and disband constantly) within a bounded community that can range anywhere from 8 to 80 square miles. Gorillas (*Gorilla*) are organized into more stable band-level structures that average approximately 15 residents, with several bands sharing a regional home range; however, band membership over time is in flux because residents, whether male or female (aside from the leader silverback), can depart a band at any time (Bradley et al., 2005; Harcourt & Stewart, 2007).

One reason why apes have such a loose-knit sociality (compared to monkeys) is that all adolescent ape females depart their natal unit at puberty, usually forever, to be replaced by immigrating females that are generally strangers to each other and thus have only weak/neutral ties. Adolescent males also leave their natal unit after puberty in both orangutan and gorilla societies as well. Thus, in ape societies, it is only chimpanzee males that stay home for a lifetime in their natal community. However, given the combination of chimpanzee females departing their natal community after puberty, thus ruling out matrilineal ties, and a chimpanzee mating pattern of promiscuity, ruling out patrilineal ties (because paternity is unknown), blood-tied kinship networks are not a powerful integrating force for any great ape society. In fact, for chimpanzees, it plays at best "an ancillary role in structuring patterns of wild chimpanzee behaviour within social groups" (Mitani, Merriwether, & Zhang, 2000, p. 885; see also Goldberg & Wrangham, 1997).

Whereas primate behaviors are shaped by an interplay between genes and the environment, great ape populations appear to lack bioprogrammers (or heritability components) for permanent groupings. Instead, their defining organizational features are a shifting collection of individuals within a regional space of at least several square miles, fusion–fission patterns of mobility, female and male transfer at puberty (except for male chimpanzees), and overall mostly weak ties among conspecifics (for discussions of hominoid lifeways, see Bradley et al., 2005; Fleagle, 2013; Harcourt & Stewart, 2007;

Maryanski, 1987, 1992, 1995; Mitani, Call, Kappeler, Palombit, & Silk, 2012; Mitani et al., 2012). By studying these ape evolutionary novelties, which are rare among Old World monkeys and mammals in general, it becomes possible to make reasonable inferences about the social nature of the LCA and its living hominoid representatives and, in turn, to reflect on the consequences of these social affinities in human evolution. For as Hans Kummer, the legendary primatologist, concluded in 1971,

> the adaptive potential of a species is limited by phylogenetic dispositions. New behavioral adaptations are possible only if the necessary dispositions are within the scope of the behavioral heritage, and if they can be accommodated within the existing social system. (p. 129)

Thus, by traversing uncharted evolutionary boundaries, our intent is to show that the roots of religion lie deep in humans' phyletic heritage.

Cladistics: A Mirror to the Distant Past

Maryanski's cladistic analysis of great ape social relations and structures was outlined in Chapter 5 of this volume (for general reviews of the methodology of cladistic analysis, see Andrews & Martin, 1987; Jeffers & Lehiste, 1979; Platnick & Cameron 1977). This long-established procedure makes possible a reconstruction of the behavioral and organizational patterns of the LCA of great apes and humans. This LCA was an ancestral population of hominoids estimated to have lived approximately 16 million years ago (Bradley 2008; Chatterjee, Ho, Barnes, & Groves, 2009). The logic of cladistics is the same as that used in historical linguistics, textual criticism or, relatively recently, biogeography. For example, to reconstruct an ancestral stem language, the procedure starts with a related set of languages to assess the words shared by these descendent languages and, with qualifications outlined in Chapter 5, assuming that these entities are *cognates* derived from the mother language. Because this methodology can be used to reconstruct any comparative information for any set of related (or homologous) entities, it can be used to assemble the social structure of the last hominoid ancestor to great apes and humans by accessing the social network ties held in common by present-day orangutans, gorillas, and chimpanzees. What becomes evident from this analysis (Maryanski & Turner, 1992; Turner & Maryanski, 2008) and dramatically evident in the right column of Table 6.1 is that this ancestral lineage had *few or no* strong ties, except for that of mothers and young offspring, and this maternal tie is severed when both male and female offspring disperse after puberty.

Present-day orangutans are the best representative of this LCA social formation because the red apes are semi-solitary, lacking stable groupings and no strong ties beyond the mother–dependent offspring bond (as both sexes disperse from the mother at puberty). What all great apes reveal, however, is an orientation to a macro-level unit of

Table 6.1 Relative Size of Brain Components of Apes and Humans Compared to Tenrecinae[a]

Brain Component	Apes (Pongids)	Humans (*Homo*)
Neocortex	61.88	196.41
Diencephalon	8.57	14.76
Thalamus		
Hypothalamus		
Amygdala	1.85	4.48
Centromedial	1.06	2.52
Basolateral	2.45	6.02
Septum	2.16	5.48
Hippocampus	2.99	4.87
Transition cortices	2.38	4.43

[a]Numbers represent how many times larger each area of the brain is compared to those of Tenrecinae, with Tenrecinae representing a base of 1.

Source: Data from Stephan (1983), Stephan and Andy (1969, 1977), and Eccles (1989), Stephan, Baron, and Frahm 1988, Stephan, Frahm, and Baron (1981).

the larger regional population. Indeed, despite their reclusive ways, it is now speculated that orangutan locals are co-residents of a widely dispersed but bounded fission–fusion community by virtue of their sporadic participation in small brief gatherings and their joint ownership of a regional locality. As discussed previously, chimpanzees are also organized into well-studied communities in which all the residents are rarely, if ever, in propinquity. Instead, they episodically gather into small but fleeting "parties" within a bounded geographical/spatial area. However, despite a lack of close proximity in stable groups (as is the case for monkeys), residents are seemingly integrated by cognitive unity and emotional connections resting on a "sense of belonging" to a larger social whole—or as Goodall (1986, 1990) stated, chimpanzees share "a sense of community." Even among gorillas, it has long been speculated that gorilla bands are not wholly discrete units but, rather, segments of a local "big band community." For example, Goodall and Groves (1977) discovered that the gorilla bands that interacted with each other also shared a regional ranging area, with weak ties linking a number of bands and lone males together. These data on apes point to the strong possibility that a larger scale basis of organization is an adaptive hominoid (i.e., ape and human) character derived from the last common ancestral population (for reviews, see Campbell, Fuentes, Mackinnon, Bearder, & Stump, 2011; Fleagle, 2013; Watts, 2012; see also McGrew [1981, 1992, 2010], who has also employed cladistic analysis using primates).

The Consequences of a Marginal Habitat: An Overview

Early hominoids (i.e., the precursors of apes and humans) evolved in the heavily forested zones of Africa in the Miocene Epoch (24 to 5 million years ago) during a time of rising global temperatures. The Early Miocene was the "golden age" of apes, a "milk and honey" time when monkey species were extremely rare and apes dominated the forest scene, filling up most of the arboreal niches occupied by Old World monkeys today. However, by the Middle Miocene, as the earth began to cool, it shrank the African forests and expanded the open woodlands and savannas, leading to a dramatic decline in ape species. Fortunately, early ape species got a reprieve when the cooling temperatures caused a buildup of ocean waters in the expanding Antarctic ice caps that in turn opened up a land bridge between Eurasia and Africa, making possible an ape migration to warmer climates in Asia and Europe (Andrews & Kelley, 2007). This immigration, beginning approximately 16 million years ago, led to an ape population explosion in Eurasia, resulting in such a diversity of ape genera that some even took up a semi-terrestrial lifestyle in woodlands and marshes. For example, *Gigantopithecus*, a resident of Asia, was so enormous that based on its jaws and teeth, this ape is conjectured to have weighed more than 600 pounds and to have been 9 feet tall (Andrews & Kelley, 2007; Conroy & Pontzer, 2012; Meldrum, 2006; Potts, 2004).

However, by the Late Miocene, the ill-winds of change returned (approximately 11 million years ago), ushering in a global cooling trend that concentrated the wet forests and expanded the dryer woodlands and bushlands. This climatic shift is associated with a massive extinction of ape species in both Eurasia and Africa. A reduction in forest zones is one factor responsible for the great ape die-off, but the picture is far more complicated. Most ape species perished, and oddly enough, the once rare Miocene monkeys not only survived but also thrived and moved into the vacated niches of dead apes. Today, monkey families dominate the forests of Africa and Asia, whereas only a handful of species represent the hominoid family (i.e., apes and humans), and except for humans, all apes live in restricted and specialized niches.

Why would selection favor monkeys over apes? A reduction in habitat and food would certainly give monkeys a competitive edge. Monkeys are small-bodied (most apes are large-bodied), monkey dietary habits are generalized (apes rely mostly on ripe fruits), and monkey life history characteristics (e.g., maturity and reproduction rates) are much faster (apes mature slowly and have fewer offspring). A second long-standing hypothesis is that Miocene monkeys evolved a capacity to digest unripe fruits, thereby usurping the dietary staple of apes (Andrews, 1989; Kay & Ungar, 1997; Temerin & Cant, 1983). What makes this hypothesis plausible is that some present-day monkeys, the colobines (*Colobinae*) that inhabit the rainforests of both Africa and Asia, have multichambered stomachs that can effectively neutralize the toxic compounds found in certain plants, seeds, and unripe fruits that are poisonous for apes.

Did Miocene monkeys evolve stomachs to detoxify and digest raw fruits? If so, it would sound the death knell for apes that must wait for fruits to ripen before consumption. Soft tissue rarely fossilizes, but the timing fits this hypothesis because both the molecular clock and the fossil record are in agreement that colobine monkeys first appeared in the Middle Miocene between 16.2 and 14.7 million years ago, with a split between Eurasian and African colobines in the Late Miocene approximately 11.5 million years ago (for discussion, see Fashing, 2011; Raaum et al., 2005; Sterck, 2012).

Lending support to the unripe fruit hypothesis is why the few remaining ape lineages lived on, despite the odds against survival. We need to briefly sketch why selection would "cherry-pick" some ape lineages for survival because this event not only altered the course of hominoid evolution but also laid the foundation blocks for the origin of religion.

In brief, on the basis of skeletal elements, Early Miocene apes can be sorted into two types: (a) *Proconsulidae* or *Proconsul* and (b) *Mortopithecus*. The *Proconsul* apes represent the prototype of early apes because they reproduced in vast numbers and inhabited the central zones of the forest canopy, reigning supreme in the African forests for millions of years. In characters, *Proconsul* had distinctive ape dentition and some contemporary ape postcranial characteristics, but strangely, their fossilized limb bones evidence a pronograde posture for a type of locomotion that uses the hands and feet. That is, *Proconsul* lacked distinctive skeletal features shared by living apes and humans and, instead, had an anatomy much like that of present-day monkeys, with both forelimbs and hindlimbs adapted to traveling about on the tops of tree limbs.

In comparison, *Morotopithecus*, a rare ape, had a postcranial skeleton corresponding more to present-day apes and humans. That is, *Morotopithecus* had limb bones adapted for suspension by using the arms for hanging and a more orthograde posture for vertical climbing. Using only the arms and shoulders for hanging or to propel the body through space is unique among mammals, requiring major evolutionary changes in skeletal and neurological features (e.g., in shoulders, finger bones, wrist joint stability, feet, and neurological cross-modal associations for hand–eye coordination features), especially compared to the rather stereotyped movement of the four-footed *Proconsul*. These novelties signal that *Morotopithecus* did not occupy the conventional early ape niche but, rather, one that required to some degree an under-the-branch foraging strategy. Because limb bones in primates reflect their mode of locomotion, *Proconsul* limb bones point to an adaptation dependent on a quadrupedal progression with emphasis on the hindlimbs for propulsion, whereas *Morotopithecus* bones point to a dependence on limbs that can act independently by using the forelimbs for support and for propulsion of the body through space (for discussions, see Conroy & Pontzer, 2012; Gebo, Maclatchy, & Kityo, 1997; Maclatchy, 2004).

We can use the skeletal features that distinguish *Proconsul* and *Morotopithecus* for insights into the cataclysmic extinction of most Miocene ape species. The losses were catastrophic because selection targeted the prolific *Proconsul*-type ape for extinction, leaving the rare *Morotopithecus*-type ape swinging on the hominoid family tree. Why *Proconsul*? The answer takes us back to the unripe fruit hypothesis. A four-footed *Proconsul* foraging for ripe fruits travels step by step on the tops of sturdy tree limbs—just as monkeys do today. If Miocene monkeys evolved a specialized digestive tract for consuming unripe fruits, the *Proconsul* apes would lose out in the competition for fruits concentrated in the central zones of the forest canopy. However, neither monkeys nor *Proconsul* could step out onto the slender swaying branches at the terminal ends of the forest canopy. Only *Morotopithecus* could master this gymnastic feat by using its prehensile hands and feet differentially, spreading each limb widely apart and using multiple branches for support or using one hand for hanging from a higher branch while deploying the other to grab a soft, ripe fruit.[1]

We can take for granted that the LCA of apes and humans inherited these suspensory habits because they are embodied in all present-day apes and humans. Now, if we consider the LCA social structure (see Chapter 5, this volume), a weakly tied social structure must have promoted survival and reproductive success or great apes and humans would not be here today. But why would weak ties rather than strong ties be beneficial for *Morotopithecus*-type apes?

The answer lies, we believe, in the particulars of a foraging area at the marginal endpoints of the Miocene hominoid habitat. The rare suspensory capacities of *Morotopithecus* clearly reflect an adaptation to a narrow and specialized niche. Here we come to our main point: Primate locomotor patterns interface with organizational and social network patterns in complex and reciprocal interdependencies that are not only reflected in ape physiology but also, in the case of *Morotopithecus*, indicative of *an atypical form of social organization* for a primate.

All Old World monkey societies are known as female-bonded societies because up to four generations of blood-tied females socialize in tight-knit cliques. Matrilines are the main source of integration for most primates (and mammals in general) because they provide a reliable source of social support, obligation, and group cohesion by keeping individuals embedded in a matrix of strong and lifelong kinship ties.

In contrast, a social structure of mostly weak ties is intuitively viewed as tenuous and easily broken. However, there is a positive aspect to a weakly-tied social structure: It fosters independence by placing few constraints or obligations on individuals because they are not locked into strong-tie cliques. In the case of the LCA of apes and humans, weak ties would have promoted the self-reliance needed for foraging alone; for how many large-bodied apes can forage in proximity for scattered and seasonal fruits at the terminal ends of branches? To minimize competition, an ape community would need a means for easily dispersing members in light of the limited resources in the marginal niches of the arboreal extremes. We cannot know when a weakly tied social structure originally evolved. However, the handiwork of selection is still evident in present-day ape societies, and along with the fossil record and molecular data, we do know how the weak-tie system of organization was accomplished.

The fossil and molecular data tell us that the *first* monkeys and apes branched away from their LCA population during the Late Oligocene approximately 30 to 28 million years ago (Glazko & Nei, 2003; Zalmout et al., 2010). Given that species typically build on the social structure that they inherit, early monkey and ape lineages both likely started out with female matrilines and with male dispersal at puberty because these traits are found in all Old World monkeys (and most social mammals). Natural selection is parsimonious, so the easiest and most efficient pathway to dampen competition in a marginal zone would be to circumvent the formation of strong, blood-tied female cliques by dispersing not just adolescent males but also adolescent females at sexual maturity.

Thus, when reproductive success is optimized by tightly knit relational formations (as in monkey societies), strong ties are best, whereas when reproductive success is optimized by loosely knit relational formations, weaker ties are best because they generate an open-ended flexibility that is difficult to achieve with strong-tie formations. In the case of great apes, a social structure of mostly weak ties allows individuals the freedom to forage with others or alone, depending on available resources. Moreover, because individuals can maintain many more weak ties on average than strong ties, community members can interact with a greater number of members within a scattered fission–fusion population. The end result is an alternative type of structural integrity organized on some kinship ties but mostly voluntary non-kinship ties.

Thus, in Chapter 5 (see Table 5.1), cladistic analysis revealed that the LCA to apes and humans handed down a weak-tie social structure to its descendants. However, as descendants branched away from the LCA and adapted over generations to new ecologies, strengthening of ties was seemingly needed for survival and reproductive success. Selection can only act, however, on traits present in a species' repertoire. Random mutations do occur, but as the "principle of conservation" states, following Stebbins (1969),

> Once a unit of action has been assembled at a lower level of the hierarchy of organization . . . mutations that might interfere with the activity of this unit are so strongly disadvantaged that they are rejected at the cellular level and never appear in the adult individual in which they occur. (p. 105)

Thus, the probability of a favorable large mutation at this late stage of hominoid evolution is remote. Fortunately for apes and humans, the LCA also bequeathed to its descendants a suite of neurological preadaptations (or exaptations) that were seemingly entailed to a weak-tie social structure (for this cladistic analysis, see Maryanski, 2013). But once in place, these preadaptations would be available for selection to work on, even though they originally had nothing to do with a future adaptation. Next, our focus is on those preadaptations that enabled humans to become religious and especially on how emotions worked to forge stronger bonds and then, with a later enlargement of the neocortex shaped by natural selection, to begin conceptualizing a sacred universe beyond the profane and mundane activities of social life.

THE NEUROLOGICAL BASIS OF RELIGIOUS BEHAVIORS

Comparative Neuroanatomy

One approach to neurosociology focuses on the hominoid brain (i.e., ape and human) in order to explain human behavioral and organization patterns. Hominoid brains began to expand approximately 20 million years ago, starting with the Miocene apes *Proconsul* and *Morotopithecus*, which had brain volumes of approximately 150 cc (approximately the size of the largest monkey brains today). By the Late Miocene, ape brain volume had expanded to approximately 350 cc, which is in the range of the brain volume of great apes today. Although both humans and apes are the end products of equally long ancestral lineages, apes never left the forest zones during the past 20 million years; thus, their neuroanatomy has not undergone the extensive changes of hominins that had to adapt to open-country ecologies. The great ape brain, then, offers a rather good approximation of the brain of the LCA to humans and present-day great apes (Sherwood, Subiaul, & Zawidzki, 2008).

The logic of cladistic analysis (see Chapter 5, this volume) enables us to be confident that differences between great ape and human brains reflect the footprints of natural selection as it went to work to rewire hominins to be more social and group oriented. Thus, although apes and humans have similar brain structures, two basic differences stand out. First, the human brain is much larger—approximately three times the size of the great ape brain—particularly the neocortex, controlling for body size, which is roughly correlated with brain size among mammals. The neocortex gets most of the press in commentaries on this difference, but subcortical areas of the brain are also much larger—approximately two times as large in humans as among great apes, again controlling for body size.[2] The second major difference between great ape and human brains is an increase in the convoluted surface of the human brain, with dramatically more connectivity within and between subcortical and neocortical areas of the brain.

Enhancing what is already present makes a great deal of evolutionary sense, especially in brains in which large mutations would almost always be harmful.

As R. A. Fisher (1930) in *The Genetical Theory of Natural Selection* highlighted long ago, "*favorable mutations* must . . . be generally exceedingly minute in their somatic effects" (p. 83). Thus, the early assertion of evolutionary psychology that the hominin brain was altered by the creation of new modules makes little evolutionary sense because such a process would be slow (because it would rely on random mutations, genetic drift, and gene flow). Also, in the case of mutations creating new brain modules, they would surely be harmful and maladaptive, especially given the great complexity of a brain that had already been subjected to 20 million years of hominoid evolution. Again, as Fisher (as quoted in Stebbins, 1969) made crystal clear, "the probability that individual mutations will contribute to evolution is in inverse correlation to the intensity of their effect on the developing phenotype" (p. 10).

A much more parsimonious way to rewire brain structures is for selection to work on existing tails of trait distributions. And this is just what appears to have occurred: Selection increased the size of key structures by selecting on the tail ends of the distributions arraying variations in relative size and the tail ends of distributions where variations in connectivity among existing structures or modules were high. The result was that no new modules were created but, rather, alterations to existing ancestral modules occurred as selection acted to increase their size and connectivity as well as usurp existing structures, enhancing and often expanding their functions for the

operation of the brain as an organic system. Thus, the result is that the basic organizational structure of great ape and human brains is much the same, but new assemblages,
enriched neuron densities, and more dense network circuit connections among larger
brain structures are now what distinguish these closely related descendants of an LCA.
This description paints a very different imagery than that originally offered by Cosmides
and Tooby (1992); fortunately, this portion of their approach appears to have receded in
recent work within this theoretical perspective (Turner & Machalek, 2017).

An important consideration in comparative paleoneurology is the sequencing of
changes in the brain after hominins diverged from their LCA with chimpanzees between
5 and 7 million years ago. In the Early Pliocene (approximately 4.2 million years ago),
both chimpanzees and the early hominin *Austrapithecus* had a similar physical appearance and a similar small brain—Austrapithecine brains ranged from 340 to 450 cc, which
is within the chimpanzee range. What distinguished Austrapiths from chimpanzees was
not an increase in brain size but, rather, small canine teeth and, above all, an adaptive
modification in some postcranial features for an upright walking gait—that is, habitual
bipedalism.[3] This revolutionary shift in moving about signals that the Austrapiths, like
the early ape *Mortopithecus*, were occupying an innovative adaptive zone. Moreover,
because locomotor patterns are interlaced with behavioral and organizational patterns
(as discussed previously), these innovations surely involved selection pressures for neurophysiological changes as well. However, no leap occurred in brain size or neocortical
expansion. As Conroy and Pontzer (2012) stated, "Adaptations to bipedalism occurred
before any significant brain expansion. . . . In a metaphorical sense, then, humans
evolved like a breech delivery—feet first" (p. 270). In fact, the Australopithecine line
survived in the African forest/woodland ecology with few changes in brain size from
4 million to 1 million years ago (Conroy & Pontzer, 2012; Stanford, Allen, & Antón 2013).
Then, approximately 2 million years ago, early *Homo* genera appeared on the African
scene, with a mosaic of Australopithecine and *Homo*-like features and with an uptick in
the average cranial capacity of approximately 650 cc.

This unfolding trend in "homininzation" involved far more than "feet first," habitual
upright walking. Selection during those millions of years was also working on changes
to the subcortical areas of the brain. Lower cortex structures would not have been as
visible in endocasts from the fossil record as would neocortical growth because limbic structures are much lower in the cranial encasement, but selection on subcortical
areas was very significant because the subcortex is where most of the key centers for
emotional arousal and initial memory formation are located. Figure 6.1 outlines the
basic structures of the human brain, emphasizing the divide between the subcortex and
neocortex, which is mediated in humans by the cingulate ring, the anterior portions of
which are responsible for typical mammalian behaviors such as female attachment to
offspring, infant and juvenile play, and the separation cry of both offspring and mothers. The anterior is also part of the emotional processing system of primates and, hence,
humans as well (Gothard & Hoffman, 2010, pp. 298–300).

Looking at the subcortical portions of Figure 6.1, the structures highlighted in Table
6.1 are all involved in the production of emotions: The amygdala is an ancient area for

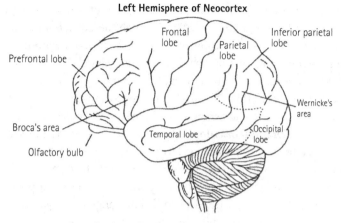

Left Hemisphere of Neocortex

Frontal lobe

Prefrontal lobe

Parietal lobe

Inferior parietal lobe

Wernicke's area

Broca's area

Temporal lobe

Occipital lobe

Olfactory bulb

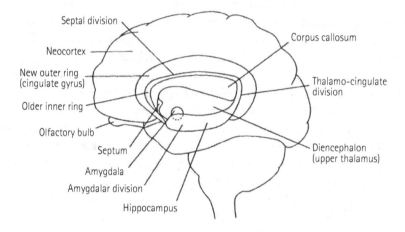

Cross-Sectional Outline of Paleomammalian Complex
(and components of limbic system)

Septal division

Neocortex

New outer ring (cingulate gyrus)

Older inner ring

Olfactory bulb

Septum

Amygdala

Amygdalar division

Hippocampus

Corpus callosum

Thalamo-cingulate division

Diencephalon (upper thalamus)

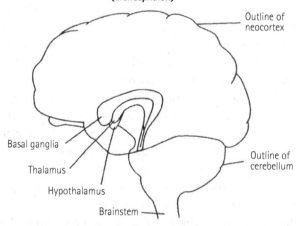

Cross-Sectional Outline of Reptilian Complex
(diencephalon)

Outline of neocortex

Basal ganglia

Thalamus

Hypothalamus

Brainstem

Outline of cerebellum

FIGURE 6.1 Key areas of the human brain and the basis for religion.

fear responses and defensive aggression when cornered; neurotransmitters and neuro-active peptides are generated by the structures of the diencephalon—brainstem, thalamus, hypothalamus, and pituitary gland. Also, the hippocampus and attached transition cortices are responsible for holding cognitions for short-term memory and then for tagging cognitions with emotions for their storage before eventually (after 2 years) being transferred to the frontal lobe for longer term storage and memory.

One reason for the initial growth of subcortical areas of the brain resides in empirical findings obtained during the past half-century indicating that rational deliberations and memory are only possible when the cognitions involved are tagged with emotional valences (Damasio, 1994). Thus, the old philosophical distinction between emotionality and rationality is wrong. Rationality is impossible without emotional tags on the various alternatives being considered, as Damasio (1994) and others have documented in empirical studies. Brains on earth, then, are structured so that intelligence depends on the range of emotions a species can generate to provide nuanced tags for complex cognitions. This is why the most intelligent birds are also the most emotional; the same is true even with reptiles that, in general, are not highly intelligent. With regard to humans, one of the most significant features of their brains is the large size of their emotion centers relative to the size of those in great apes. Table 6.1 presents some very old but carefully performed measurements of the relative size, controlling for body size, of subcortical structures, with the differences between the respective size of the neocortex for humans and great apes also reported (see Note 2 for more recent data). These measurements were not made for our specific argument, but they do suggest one very important facet of hominin brain evolution: Selection was rewiring hominin brains to equip them with a far greater range of emotions than is evident in any other primates. Selection was doing so by increasing the size of subcortical structures relative to those among great apes, and selection was also increasing connectivity among emotion centers and between emotion centers and the neocortex, particularly the prefrontal cortex, in which decision-making occurs in mammals. Indeed, there is a significant increase in the number and size of the neurons connecting the prefrontal cortex to emotions centers.

Some of the increases in size are suggestive. For example, the amygdala—the ancient area for the production of fear and anger—is twice the size in humans as in great apes. Why would this be so? The answer is revealing: Most of the increase is in the lateral portions where areas for happiness and pleasure have been grafted on but also, more significantly, where the reading of emotions in others is made possible (Barger, Stefanacci, & Semendeferi, 2006; Barger et al., 2012; Bienvenu et al., 2011). Furthermore, the amygdala has been usurped (beyond that of other primates) as a kind of switching station for neuronets moving across emotion centers and most particularly between the prefrontal cortex in the neocortex and the subcortical hippocampus where cognitions are tagged with emotions and stored for a year or two and, if reactivated with the emotional tags during that time period, will then be transferred the frontal lobe for storage as long-term memory.

Thus, as emotions were being enhanced, new neuronets were also developing to connect emotions to cognitions and, then, to the prefrontal cortex and ultimately the front lobe. These neural networks would make even a smaller brained animal more intelligent, but growing the neocortex without a capacity for filling it with a large repertoire of more complex memories would not be fitness enhancing because a large brain consumes an enormous amount of energy and thus requires large amounts of protein to sustain itself. Thus, a larger neocortex standing empty would represent an enormous energy cost to an animal and not enhance fitness. The neocortex would not grow, then, until a point was reached where emotional tags were nuanced and diverse. Therefore, intelligence in hominins could only have come about with the *prior enhancement of emotions* during the millions of years of early hominin evolution.

Other subcortical structures also offer telltale signs of how natural selection was acting to enhance emotions, social bonding, and group formation. For example, the septum is the area in mammals that generates the pleasure associated with sex—obviously a center critical to reproductive success. Great apes and, in particular, humans' closest chimpanzee relatives are promiscuous and highly sexed. They enjoy a great deal of sexual pleasure with many partners, and they reveal no tendencies to hook up in more permanent pairings. Paternity for chimpanzees is never known (except with a DNA analysis) because females solicit sexual intercourse with many different males. Why, then, would the septum need to be well over twice as large in humans as in chimpanzees, which are already wired to be highly sexual? The answer must lie in the addition of some new emotions with this enlargement—perhaps "love sentiments" and other attachment emotions—that would be necessary if the nuclear family was ever to be formed during late *Homo erectus* or perhaps only during early human evolution.

Whereas a mother and her dependent offspring comprise the natural and elementary family for all primate species (and mammals), the nuclear family of mother, father, and their dependent offspring is a very unnatural structure for great apes; thus, it is intriguing that this unnatural structure eventually became the structural core for all early human societies. Without bioprogrammers for extended families (and intergenerational continuity), how was something like nuclear families, the building block of human kinship systems, to be constructed among promiscuous, low-sociality, and non-group-forming hominins? The answer was surely a palate of new emotions with a range of affective responses that could be used to forge stronger social bonds among conspecifics, especially between mated pairs. In the end, these new emotion-driven bonds enabled later hominins to form more stable and cohesive groupings and, most important, something like a nuclear family that could, in turn, be the building blocks for the first bands of hunter–gatherers. The clues revealed by simple measurements are tantalizing, but we need to place them into a broader view of what natural selection was doing to the hominin line if we are to understand the forces creating religious behaviors in humans.

Selection for Increased Sociality and Group-Oriented Behaviors

The line of argument being developed here is that selection hit upon a fitness-enhancing strategy by selecting on tail ends of the bell curves arraying variations in the size of key brain structures and their connectivity. The first push of selection was to increase hominin emotional capacities that, in turn, provided the platform that would make later selection on the size of the neocortex fitness enhancing. This combination of dramatically enhanced emotionality, coupled with the subsequent enlargement of the neocortex, also made culture and spoken language possible. However, long before culture and spoken language in the human measure could evolve, the challenge of selection forces was to increase hominin sociality and group formation so that hominins could survive outside forest zones.

By the Late Pliocene (approximately 2 million years ago), another global cooling phase was taking hold. As the ice caps began to form, the forests in Africa began to shrink, expanding the woodlands, bushlands, and open savanna habitats. Nothing less than intensifying emotions could forge stronger and more permanent bonds among hominins and, in turn, create and sustain groups in Africa's open country. In so doing, selection dramatically increased the existing interpersonal, cognitive, and emotional capacities already inherent in great apes. Thus, it is not emotions per se that made the difference but, rather, the power and diversity of emotions to enhance a long set of great ape capacities that, at first glance, would seem sufficient by themselves to forge stronger bonds. However, it takes only a glance at the hominoid family tree to see that after the large-scale die-off in the Miocene, apes never recovered in species or numbers (except for humans), with all apes today living in narrow and restricted forest niches. Indeed, extant great apes are the least successful of all the primates (again, not counting humans), whether measured in numbers of individuals, number of species, or range of locations.

In contrast, the tightly knit female-bonded Old World monkeys dominate the primate scene, whether in species, numbers, or range of locations. Monkey organizational skills are so extraordinary that today they inhabit forests, woodlands, snow-covered mountain habitats, and the semi-deserts of Saudi Arabia, and they are unwelcome visitors stealing food in rural villages in Asia and in urban areas. Clearly, the great apes' already hardwired interpersonal abilities are not sufficient, by themselves, to forge stronger group formations typical of monkey societies. These interpersonal characteristics are reviewed in more detail in Chapter 5, and so here, we simply list them in Table 6.2.

However, the potential was there for these ape proclivities to be built upon for foraging stronger bonds and, it would seem, more stable groupings as well. In particular, by the logic of cladistics, the behavioral propensities of present-day apes and the LCA would naturally be inherited by early hominins as well; thus, most of the key interpersonal practices used in human relations today are simply extensions of those that all great apes have today and, hence, the LCA had millions of years ago. No new modules or major mutational changes in the brain were necessary for humans to acquire a larger repertoire of interpersonal skills and behavioral propensities. Chimpanzees, for example, engage naturally in (a) mutual reading of eyes and face to read emotions, (b) role-taking (Mead, 1934) or what is often called theory of mind (Hare, Call, & Tomasello, 2001), (c) empathizing, (d) reciprocal exchanging of resources, (e) calculating justice and fairness in exchanges, (f) seeing self as an object of potential evaluation, (g) participating in rituals as well as mutual synchronizing of body and voice, and (h) self-agency. As Tomasello and Herrmann (2010) concluded,

> Great apes operate on their cognitive worlds in ways very similar to humans.... Apes not only perceive and understand things in the immediate here and now but they also recall things they have perceived in the past and anticipate or imagine things that might happen in the future. (pp. 3–4)

Thus, as listed in Table 6.2, there was a very extensive suite of hardwired capacities that selection would work on to forge strong bonds among weak-tie hominins in

---

Table 6.2 Hardwired Preadaptations and Behavioral Propensities of the Last Common Ancestor to Humans and Great Apes

Preadaptations

1. Neurological capacity to learn and communicate using human language
2. Strong ties between mothers and offspring
3. Promiscuous mating system with paternity never known
4. Life history characteristics: long gestation, infancy, and juvenile periods of development; larger average size of bodies compared to monkeys; and greater intelligence that all other primates except humans
5. Play activities among all young
6. Orientation to community rather than groups, with cognitive mapping of territory and who belongs and who does not belong inside the boundaries of the territory

Behavioral Propensities

1. High individualism and mobility around home range
2. Transfer of males and females at puberty from their natal community to another community, never to return (except chimpanzee males)
3. High levels of reading eyes and faces of conspecifics for meanings and dispositions to act
4. At birth, high rates of imitation of facial gestures signaling emotions
5. Rhythmic synchronization of bodies and voice, mimicry, and ritual when conspecifics assemble in larger numbers, mostly among chimpanzees
6. High levels of emotional effervescence during assemblies of conspecifics
7. Attention to reciprocity of others who have received resources
8. Calculations as to fairness and justice in exchanges of resources
9. Capacity of individuals to see themselves as objects in their environment, especially vis-à-vis others and the responses of others to self

open-country ecologies. If we add to these critical interpersonal skills the preadaptations listed at the top of Table 6.2—that is, (a) neurological capacity for linguistic-based
symbolic skills made possible by the association cortices around the inferior parietal
lobe, (b) greater intelligence than monkeys and most mammals, (c) large palate (for
a mammal) of emotions used in interaction with conspecifics, (d) innate capacity for
play involving mutual give and take of coordinated behaviors, (e) cognitive mapping
of who belongs in a community, and (f) orientation to community as the basic unit of
organization—then it is clear that hominins possessed a large suite of capacities that
could lead to strong bonds in more permanent groupings. Many of these capacities
are the neurological foundation of religious behaviors—language articulating a sacred
realm beyond the mundane world, emotion-arousing rituals and synchronization of
bodies and voice, emotional effervescence, moral codes revolving around reciprocity and justice, reckoning a larger and more inclusive community of worshipers, and
assuming the perspective of not just others (role-taking) but also potentially god-like
others and forces in the supernatural realm (for discussions of great ape interpersonal skills, see Gallup, 1970, 1982; Kaneko & Tomonaga, 2011; Karg, Schmelz, Call, &
Tomasello, 2015; Maclean & Hare, 2012; Maryanski, 2013; Sherwood et al., 2008).

However, this potential was only fully activated with very late *H. erectus* and perhaps
only with *H. sapiens*. As we have emphasized, the missing links are twofold: (a) a larger
palate of emotions that could enhance the power of these preadaptations and behavioral
propensities and (b) a larger neocortex that could conceive of another universe inhabited by sacred forces and beings with powers to influence mundane activities. The first
link—enhanced emotionality—is what gave the interpersonal behaviors their power to
overcome the lack of bioprogrammers for strong ties and groups. Once interpersonal
practices of all apes were supercharged with emotions with what Turner (2000) called
the "language of emotions," selection for the larger neocortex that would now allow
for the emergence of complex cultural systems and spoken language would be fitness
enhancing and, as a by-product, also allow humans to conceive of a sacred supernatural
realm inhabited by forces and beings to whom emotionally charged ritual appeals could
be directed.

Interpersonal Behaviors and the "Language of Emotions"

We begin with what appears to be a paradox: Why would low-sociality and non-group-
forming apes have such a large and complex suite of interpersonal skills? The answer
resides in the nature of great ape organization. Chimpanzees, for example, wander
around a large, inclusive community, often alone, or they stop to socialize in impromptu
gatherings with constantly changing sets of community members for a few moments,
a few hours, or a day. Animals without proclivities for extended kin affiliation (aside
from mother and her dependent offspring) and group formations (pods, herds, packs,
troops, prides, etc.) must actively work at forging even temporary episodes of interaction because face-to-face encounters are often between nodding acquaintances that are

not in proximity on a daily basis and when meeting up require spontaneously expressed "greeting rituals" (e.g., vocalizations, holding hands, and hugs) and other interpersonal mechanisms to manage these brief encounters. Not surprisingly, as Jane Goodall underscored (1986), "Many of the greeting gestures described for chimpanzees have striking parallels in the greeting behaviour of man" (p. 284). The result is that the mechanisms listed in Table 6.2 (and elaborated on in Chapter 5, this volume) evolved because they had fitness-enhancing value by giving individuals a cognizance of belonging to something greater than self or a "sense of community" in a weakly tied social formation while sustaining for individuals a certain level of individual autonomy and freedom to move about the community.

Humans also work at interpersonal episodes of interaction, often in contemporary societies with strangers or acquaintances. Unlike great apes, however, humans can have stronger ties and more stable groups because they can develop enhanced emotional attachments to others and groups. Using complex mechanisms for interaction, laced with more diverse and powerful emotions, makes interaction even more work because humans must now always monitor the emotional consequences of what they do and say during the course of interpersonal encounters. In this way, the lack of direct bio-programmers for attachments and group solidarity can be overcome, but at a cost of expending a great deal of emotional energy.

Thus, humans are just as unique for their capacities to create and sustain social relations and group solidarities by the complex set of behavioral propensities listed in Table 6.2 because they have a very large palette of emotions to supercharge the operation of these behavioral propensities in ways that create and sustain social ties—granted, at a cost. This new basis of social ties began millions of years ago under selection pressures to get early hominins better organized. Great apes have a comparatively large palate of emotions built from variants of such primary emotions as happiness, sadness, fear, anger, and perhaps a few other primary emotions, including disgust and surprise (for various schemes on primary emotions, see Turner & Stets, 2005, pp. 14–15), and by the logic of cladistic analysis, so did the LCA of great apes and hominins. Hence, there was an existing emotional capacity in the LCA's subcortex on which natural selection could go to work to increase the range of emotional responses among the LCA's hominin descendants.

We have outlined our views on how natural selection expanded the palate of emotions during hominin evolution (Turner, 2000, 2002, 2007, 2010; Turner & Maryanski, 2008). We believe the basic process was probably as follows: Once early hominins began to forage outside safe forest zones, the first priority would be to avoid being eaten by ground-living predators. However, hominins lacked projecting canines for mounting a defense like (*Papio*) baboons or speed for running away like (*Erythrocebus*) patas monkeys (which can run 35 miles per hour) or natural defensive weapons of any sort. Even worse, hominins are visually dominant for object recognition (and most spatial information), which is obviously a great advantage in a safe three-dimensional forest habitat, but on the ground it is disadvantageous because vision is often preoccupied; it is not self-altering, and it is useless after dark for detecting anything. Hominins are also such large-bodied primates that they would have to forage in small parties, vulnerable to predation.

For these reasons, all ground-dwelling mammals are olfactory dominant and equipped with two major self-alerting warning systems: a sophisticated auditory system to locate a sound and a dominant olfactory system that can detect both the immediate and the lingering smells of both predators and prey. If ever a mutation or module was needed to duck predators, this was the time. However, as Fisher (1930) noted, species do not sit idle waiting for a favorable mutation. They do not need to because "without the occurrence of further mutations all ordinary species must already possess within themselves the potentialities of the most varied evolutionary modifications" (p. 96).

So what modifications were possible for hominins in a predator-ridden, open-country habitat? We believe selection started by neurologically shifting the integration of the sensory modalities, especially with regard to the rewiring of the auditory cortex. In short, apes and humans have nearly the same sensory equipment, and in particular, they have an auditory cortex that is specialized for serving as a self-alerting warning "device" for detecting predators (or any sharp or abrupt sound). After perceiving a sound, the auditory system alerts the (non-self-alerting) dominant visual system to attend to the sound-emitting object in space. One key modification in hominin evolution was to upgrade the auditory system, and it is this modification that led to cardinal evolutionary changes.

Both apes and humans have full neocortical control over the *comprehension* of sounds. In other words, sound perception is flexible and open-ended because it is under voluntary control. An ape's vocal–auditory channel for sound *production*, however, is under subcortical (or limbic) control so that an ape's vocal responses are, with a few exceptions, mostly fixed and inflexible. Thus, apes have an open-ended auditory cortex for receiving and comprehending sounds, but in responding to these sounds, they emit mostly species-specific emotionally based vocalizations in specific social contexts. Selection acted on this dichotomy in human evolution by rewiring this arrangement and liberating the auditory/vocal channel from subcortical control and integrating it with the already cortically based haptic and visual modalities. This gave early hominins the revolutionary advantage of making voluntary and intentional judgments on how to respond and whether to respond or to stay silent. Once the vocal–auditory channel was under cortical control and the neuronal circuits that stamped a fixed emotion onto a fixed species-specific call in a fixed context were severed, the auditory cortex became functional for both comprehending and responding to environment stimuli. It also paved the way for selection to work on the mediation and augmentation of subcortical emotional states for open-ended and intentional vocal responses that are both symbolic and affective.

With this new wiring in the brain, it also became possible to expand the number and scope of variants of primary emotions. Later, combinations of two primary emotions could dramatically expand the emotional palette of hominins, and eventually, combinations of several primary emotions could expand even further. By blending important combinations among several primary emotions (e.g., sadness, fear, and anger), the ability to experience emotions such as shame and guilt would evolve (Turner, 2000). Such emotions are critical to self-control in groups and for building moral codes that can regulate conduct.

In turn, expanding the palate of emotions also led to stronger bonds by overcoming three significant roadblocks. First, most primary emotions are negative (e.g., fear, anger, sadness, and disgust) in the sense of not promoting solidarity, but combinations of these with the one positive primary emotion—happiness—would expand the palette of associative emotions. Second, the larger palette of emotions would allow more complex and nuanced responses of hominin conspecifics to each other. Third, this more nuanced and extensive palette of emotions could give power to all the interpersonal practices listed in Table 6.2 and discussed in more detail in Chapter 5 so that they could be used to forge stronger bonds and, eventually, allow for the formation of more stable groupings.

Turner (2000, 2007) has also argued that the preadaptation for symbolic-based gestural communication that all great apes possess via their visual/haptic modality did not "just sit there" in the brain for millions of years. Rather, it was used in conjunction with the expanding emotional palette discussed previously to create the first primal and still primary mode of human expression—the "language of emotions." All great apes today have a stock of symbolic gestures used for communication that are socially conditioned and familiar to all community members. Juveniles and adolescents, for example, even have some preferred vernacular gestures not used by adults (much like human teenagers do). Also, according to Jane Goodall (1986), chimpanzees simply "invent new gestural signals when needed." In noting the resemblance between chimpanzees and human gestures, Roberts, Vick, Roberts, Buchannan-Smith, and Zuberbühler (2012) even proposed that gestural communication "is likely to have also been pivotal in human language evolution" (p. 588; see also Call & Tomasello, 2007; Parr, Waller, & Fugate, 2005).

All great apes can also comprehend—and spontaneously learn—any human language by simply being exposed when young to a linguistic environment (because auditory perception, as with humans, is under voluntary control, as discussed previously). To comprehend human speech entails an inherent ability to isolate out phonemes, apply rules of grammar, and string morphemes together to understand meaningful sentences (Savage-Rumbaugh & Lewin, 1994). Lieberman (2006) concluded that the key finding in ape language research is that "apes have the biologic capacity to acquire and productively use human words and syntax at a reduced level equal to that of most three-year old children" (p. 45).

Apes cannot speak, of course, because their vocal–auditory channel for vocalizing is still under subcortical control, and they also lack the lips, tongue, larynx, and other evolved elements enabling them to modify sounds and to sequence phonemes to make rapid speech production. This capacity arrived very late in hominin evolution and, in all likelihood, only in early humans approximately 200,000 years ago (Enard et al., 2002a, 2002b). This dating, however, conflicts with recent reanalysis of older fossils that pushes the emergence of humans back to 300,000; and so it is possible that finely articulated speech was not evident among the first *Homo sapiens*. However, great apes can "speak" through the dominant sense modality of all primates—vision—by using their symbolic gestural–haptic system. Great apes can also utilize the words and phrases used in the gestural sign language of the deaf, or they can use a computer keyboard composed of arbitrary pictograms to construct sentences and respond to human vocalizations. Also, not surprisingly, young apes tend to employ the same utterances (albeit in simpler forms) of young human children by articulating requests, naming things, and referring to past events (Lyn, Greenfield, Savage-Rumbaugh, Gillespie-Lynch, & Hopkins, 2011, p. 73). Thus, even without finely articulated speech early *Homo sapiens* could "talk" in ways that would carry common meanings.

Given this already-in-place precursor in apes for language, Turner has argued that emotions, which are generally read visually, were easily organized along with symbolic gestures into an initial system of linguistic communication. Indeed, emotions can even be seen as organized by a syntax, and these are read visually. One can simply turn off the sound to a movie and still follow the story relatively easily because all humans can effortlessly understand the "language of emotions." Also, when humans seek to bond and forge stronger ties, they rely much more heavily on "body language" (face, eyes, and countenance) than on spoken language. With a palate of emotions, social relations can be built from mutual "conversations" of emotional states. Early hominins initiated this process, and it is still the dominate way that humans forge stronger bonds of solidarity with each other in groups.

We argue, then, that spoken language is built on the neurological platform provided by manual gestures and the syntax of emotions; and it is for this reason that keeping emotions out of talk is difficult, and it is the rare person who can exercise such complete expressive control. More significant for our purposes is that a more complex, nuanced, and larger palette of emotions could eventually serve as the preadaptation that would make growing the neocortex more fitness enhancing. Emotions offered a template for how a spoken language could become organized and laced with intonations, and a "language" of emotions also provided a more sophisticated way to tag cognitions with emotions so that they can be remembered and retrieved in deliberations. Thus, had not natural selection hit upon the solution of enhancing the palette of emotions among low-sociality hominins, humans would not be so intelligent because the neocortex could never have grown to its large proportions (relative to body size). Emotions thus served as a preadaptation for language production, human intelligence, and culture in the human sense. As a further consequence, religious behavior among human primates would never have evolved.

The Sudden Increase in the Size of the Hominin Neocortex

An animal that can store a great deal of information from past experience, almost instantaneously retrieve that information when needed, and use this information in either deliberations about how to act or even in reflexive actions without much deliberation is likely to be more fit in most environments. Importantly, if this information can be communicated to others by virtue of speech, individuals can engage in more complex and coordinated tasks, which further increases fitness. Also, if information can include cultural codes carrying moral overtones that produce guilt and shame when not adhered to, this animal can live in much larger social structures, regulated not so much by bioprogrammers as by interpersonal and intrapersonal mechanisms of social control and by cultural symbols organized into moral codes.

None of the previously mentioned processes, however, were possible without a major uptick in emotions because cognitions cannot be remembered if not tagged with emotions, and complex cognitions cannot even form without emotions to tag this complexity. Memory in all brains in all life forms on earth is only possible by emotional tags, and the more sophisticated the system of emotional tags, the more sophisticated cognitions of a species can become. Therefore, a dramatically expanded palette of emotions is necessary for a large brain, capable of storing and retrieving a large body of cultural information. Thus, it should not be surprising that the hominin neocortex did not grow dramatically for millions of years because emotions had to precede any growth in the cognitive capacities of hominins. The lack of growth of the neocortex among Australopithecines and then the modest increase with early *H. erectus* indicate that selection was not yet pushing neocortical growth. Then, rather suddenly (in evolutionary time), the neocortex began to grow under directional selection on the tail ends of distribution on the relative size of cranial capacity among hominins. This growth was clearly fitness enhancing because *H. erectus* was able to populate much of the world and live in dramatically different habitats and niches. We can only conclude that the threshold to support greater cognitive capacities had been reached, and once selection began to push in this direction, both emotional and cognitive dynamics in the lower and upper portions of the brain could be pushed simultaneously by natural selection in ways that are evident when looking at the increased connectivity within and between the (older) subcortex and (newer) neocortex. As this transformation occurred, the neocortex reached its current size of approximately three times that of chimpanzees. The size of the chimpanzee brain is 375–425 cc, whereas the human brain is 1150–1450 cc. The combination of a larger neocortex and emotionally charged behavioral propensities (see Table 6.2) is what ultimately produced religious behavior and what made humans receptive to participation in religious organizations.

Interpersonal Behavior and Religion

An animal that has to construct relations without strong bioprogrammers is, in many ways, freed of what can be a dysfunctional constraint. With a complex of interpersonal behaviors that can be used to reconstruct social relations, with a palette of emotions that can be aroused to reinforce these new constructions, and with emotions that can tag and order cognitions about social relations, there is increased complexity but with more flexibility than most mammals with powerful bioprogrammers reveal. Whereas higher primates such as Old World monkeys are quite flexible in their ability to adapt to diverse environments and changes in environment, human primates can change the very environments to which they must adapt. Of course, much can go wrong with such an emotional primate who is constantly having to construct and reproduce social relations through constant monitoring of self and others' respective actions and downloading the relevant information to keep on track with interpersonal behaviors.

The reliance on emotions, culture, and spoken language, coupled with all the interpersonal behavioral propensities listed in Table 6.2, also works to make humans religious, once they have the cognitive capacity to conceive of the sacred and supernatural. Humans are very disposed to give emotional significance to special situations, including their emotionally charged social relations. They also may have a cognitive bias to symbolize these relations with totems, as Emile Durkheim (1912/1995) emphasized, and to direct emotion-arousing rituals toward these totems or their symbolic representations (e.g., emblems, flags, and crests) (Maryanski, 2018).

A totem can be anything that serves to bring individuals together into a collective because it creates a special emotional relation with an object and its symbolic representation. For example, in contemporary societies, sport mascots (e.g., USC Trojans, North Alabama Lions, and Georgia Bulldogs) serve as a vehicle for identity and unity, with fans wearing their team logos on their person or putting them on their cars and coffee cups. Eager fans even paint their faces and bodies and engage in ceremonial rituals to their "sacred" totem (Serazio, 2013, p. 2). In human evolution, once these kinds of behaviors become part of fitness-enhancing social solidarities, it is but a short step to adopting and adapting them to interactions with the beings and forces of a sacred–supernatural realm. Prayers to the supernatural are very much like a conversation with others in mundane situations that have been loaded with symbolism requiring rituals and other responses. None of these interpersonal processes evolved to make humans religious; rather, they evolved to make stronger social bonds and more permanent groups in an animal without bioprogrammers to do so "naturally."

Rhythmic synchronization of bodies and mimicry in normal interactions are easily usurped for ritual appeals to the supernatural. Calculations of fairness and justice in exchanges are easily converted into moral codes articulated by the gods. Emotional effervescence at successful interpersonal rituals can readily be seen as something that the gods can bestow on persons who make the proper appeals to the supernatural. Role-taking and empathy can very easily become the means by which persons come to understand what the supernatural expects of them, reinforced by moral codes.

Most important, the capacity of seeing self as an object in the environment also means that persons come to assess themselves in terms of others' responses to their self-presentation. Such a capacity is critical to maintaining the flow of interaction and the formation of social bonds and group solidarities, but it is easily extended to seeing self in the eyes of the supernatural forces, evaluating self in terms of whether or not a person has abided by the expectations, as codified into moral codes, of supernatural forces and beings. An animal without a sense of self, or the capacity to see itself in the environment, especially the environment imposed by social relations and expectations of others, could not be religious and could not engage in self-evaluations and self-control in the same way as an animal with a sense of self.

An animal with self, and indeed a self that needs to be confirmed by others, will be very attuned to what others think and be ready to adjust conduct in order to cooperate. Only large-brained animals such as humans (and great apes, dolphins, elephants, and whales) have a sense of self, and perhaps only humans, with a very large neocortex (relative to their body size), can begin to adjust their conduct to the expectations of others in a special supernatural realm that they cannot see but feel. Indeed, given all the insecurities among animals that must constantly monitor "how they are doing" in the eyes of others, it may be a natural tendency for humans to construct a safer world in which interactions with supernatural beings and forces can affirm self, as long as one engages in the proper rituals and abides by the expectations of the supernatural as codified in moral codes.

One of the problems that humans confront in their neuroanatomy is that they experience very intense emotions, biased numerically to the negative side, and can remember what happened in the past, can ponder what is currently happening in the present, and can anticipate or worry about what may happen in the future. Interaction with the supernatural can often mitigate these problems built into a big-brained animal who is also the most emotional animal to evolve on earth.

CONCLUSION

Religious behavior can be explained by Darwinian natural selection as it worked on hominin neuroanatomy to make, in the end, humans more social and able to form stable groupings. Religion is the by-product of selection enhancing emotions to make the large suite of preadaptations and behavioral propensities of all great apes, and hence the LCA to apes and humans, more effective for forming stronger social ties among hominins and, then, among humans. This increase in the emotionality allowed humans' hominin ancestors to survive without significant increases in the size of the neocortex. However, as a complex array of emotions evolved, it became a preadaptation for growth in the neocortex of late hominins and eventually of early humans; this combination of an assortment of emotions, language, culture, and large set of interpersonal mechanisms also created a propensity for religious behavior among the first humans. However, this summary of a more complex and detailed argument (Turner et al., 2017) cannot explain why and how religion became institutionalized in the first human societies and why it has remained a part of human societies ever since. In this chapter, we have only examined the biological part of the story of religion, focusing on Darwinian natural selection on the neuroanatomy of ape-like hominins. A full story of religious evolution, of course, requires examining the developmental phrases of religion in sociocultural systems to understand how social selection dynamics operated to institutionalize religion in the first hunter–gather bands and, subsequently, to drive religious evolution during the past 5,000 years as societies have become larger and more complex (Turner & Abrutyn, 2016; Turner et al., 2017).

NOTES

1. A paper was presented at an American Anthropological Association meeting in 2015 in which the authors proposed an alternative hypothesis for the origin of the suspensory adaptation of the 20-million-year-old *Morotopithecus*. They suggested that it evolved so this ape could travel between gaps in a broken forest canopy. Although this contrasts with the long-standing unripe fruit hypothesis, the new explanation still depicts a marginal niche for *Morotopithecus*, and it remains supportive of the weak-tie hypothesis and its evolutionary consequences. The broken canopy explanation does not, however, help explain the massive wipeout of *Proconsul* apes (Maclatchy, Rossie, & Kingston, 2015).

2. More recent measurements of the relative size of subcortical portions of the brain do not record differences in this, but the methodologies of the early studies that we are relying on and those of more recent studies differ; thus, it is difficult to determine which set of data is more correct. Nonetheless, both studies report larger subcortical structures that would exceed expectations. Thus, in the end, they reached the same conclusions (Barger, Stefanacci, & Semendeferi, 2006; Barger et al., 2012).

3. All apes can walk upright for short periods. Walking habitually on two limbs involves some radical adaptations in skeletal locomotor anatomy and muscular elements, including changes in the pelvis area, the spine, and the foot. Normative bipedalism even changes a hominin's balance because it changes the normal ape's center of gravity.

REFERENCES

Andrews, P. (1989). Palaeoecology of Laetoli. *Journal of Human Evolution, 18*, 173–181.

Andrews, P., & Kelley, J. (2007). Species diversity and diet in monkeys and apes during the Miocene. In C. B. Stringer (Ed.), *Aspects of human evolution*. London: Taylor & Francis.

Andrews, P., & Martin, L. (1987). Cladistic relationships of extant and fossil hominoids. *Journal of Human Evolution, 16*, 101–118.

Barger, N., Stefanacci, L., Schumann, C. M., Sherwood, C. C., Anneses, J., Allman, J. M., . . . Semendeferi, K. (2012). Neuronal populations in the basolateral nuclei of the amygdala increase in humans compared to apes: A stereological study. *Journal of Comparative Neurology, 520*, 3035–3054.

Barger, N., Stefanacci, L., & Semendeferi, K. (2006). Comparative volumetric analysis of the amygdaloid complex and basolateral division of the human and ape brain. *American Journal of Physical Anthropology, 134*, 392–403.

Bienvenu, T., Guy, F., Coudyzer, W., Gilissen, E., Roualdes, G., Vignaud, P., & Brunet, M. (2011). Assessing endocranian variations in great apes and humans using 3D data from virtual endocasts. *American Journal of Physical Anthropology, 145*, 231–246.

Boyer, P. (2001). *Religion explained: The evolutionary origins of religious thought*. New York, NY: Basic Books.

Bradley, B. (2008). Reconstructing phylogenies and phenotypes: A molecular view of human evolution. *Journal of Anatomy, 212*, 337–353.

Bradley, B., Robbins, M., Williamson, E., Steklis, H., Steklis, N., Eckhardt, N., . . . Vigilant, L. (2005). Mountain gorilla tug-of-war: Silverbacks have limited control over reproduction in multimale groups. *Proceedings of the National Academy of Sciences of the USA, 102*, 9418–9423.

Call, J., & Tomasello, M. (2007). *The gestural communication of apes and monkeys.* Hillsdale, NJ: Erlbaum.

Campbell, C., Fuentes, A., Mackinnon, K., Bearder, S., & Stump, R. (2011). *Primates in perspective.* Oxford, UK: Oxford University Press.

Chatterjee, H., Ho, S., Barnes, I., & Groves, C. (2009). Estimating the phylogeny and divergence times of primates using a supermatrix approach. *BMC Evolutionary Biology, 9,* 259–278.

Conroy, G., & Pontzer, H. (2012). *Reconstructing human origins: A modern synthesis.* New York: W. W. Norton.

Cosmides, L., & Tooby, J. (1992). Cognitive adaptations for social exchange. In J. H. Barkow, L. Cosmides, & J. Tooby (Eds.), *The adapted mind: Evolutionary psychology and the generation of culture* (pp. 163–228). New York, NY: Oxford University Press.

Damasio, A. (1994). *Descartes' error: Emotion, reason, and the human brain.* New York, NY: Putman.

Disotell, T. (2012). Archaic human genomics. *Yearbook of Physical Anthropology, 5*(5), 24–39.

Durkheim, E. (1995). *The elementary forms of the religious life.* New York, NY: Free Press. (Original work published 1912)

Eccles, J. C. (1989). *Evolution of the brain: Creation of self.* London, UK: Routledge.

Enard, W., Khaitovich, P., Klose, J., Zollner, S., Heissig, F., Giavalisco, P., . . . Paabo, S. (2002a). Intra- and interspecific variation in primate gene expression patterns. *Science, 296,* 340–342.

Enard, W., Przeworski, M., Fisher, S. E., Lai, C. S. L., Wiebe, V., Kitano, T., . . . Paabo, S. (2002b). Molecular evolution of *FOXP2*, a gene involved in speech and language. *Nature, 418,* 869–872.

Fashing, P. (2011). African colobine monkeys. In C. Campbell, A. Fuentes, K. Mackinnon, S. Bearder, & R. Stumpf (Eds.), *Primates in perspective* (pp. 203–228). New York, NY: Oxford University Press.

Fisher, R. A. (1930). *The genetical theory of natural selection.* Oxford, UK: Clarendon.

Fleagle, J. (2013). *Primate adaptation and evolution:* New York, NY: Elsevier.

Franks, D. D. (2010). *Neurosociology: The nexus between neuroscience and social psychology.* New York, NY: Springer.

Franks, D. D., & Turner, J. H. (2013). *Handbook of neurosociology.* New York, NY: Springer.

Gallup, G. G., Jr. (1970). Chimpanzees: Self-recognition. *Science, 167,* 86–87.

Gallup, G. G., Jr. (1982). Self-awareness and the emergence of mind in primates. *American Journal of Primatology, 2,* 237–248.

Gebo, D. L., Maclatchy, L., & Kityo, R. (1997). A hominoid genus from the early Miocene of Uganda. *Science, 276,* 401–404.

Glazko, G. V., & Nei, M. (2003). Estimation of divergence times for major lineages of primate species. *Molecular Biology and Evolution, 20*(Suppl.), 424–434.

Goldberg, T., & Wrangham, R. (1997). Genetic correlates of social behavior in wild chimpanzees: Evidence from mitochondrial DNA. *Animal Behaviour, 54,* 559–570.

Goodall, A., & Groves, C. (1977). The conservation of eastern gorillas. In P. Rainier, III, & G. Bourn (Eds.), *Primate conservation* (pp. 559–637). New York, NY: Academic Press.

Goodall, J. (1986). *The chimpanzees of Gombe: Patterns of behavior.* Cambridge, MA: Harvard University Press.

Goodall, J. (1990). *Through a window: 30 Years observing the Gombe chimpanzee.* London: Weidenfeld and Nicolson.

Gothard, K. M., & Hoffman, K. L. (2010). Circuits of emotion in the human brain. In M. L. Platt & A. A. Ghazanfar (Eds.), *Primate neurology* (pp. 292–315). Oxford, UK: Oxford University Press.

Hammer, D. (2005). *The god gene: How faith is hardwired into our genes*. New York, NY: Doubleday.

Harcourt, A. H., & Stewart, K. J. (2007). Gorilla society: What we know and don't know. *Evolutionary Sociology, 16*, 147–158.

Hare, B., Call, J., & Tomasello, M. (2001). Do chimpanzees know what conspecifics know? *Animal Behavior, 61*, 139–151.

Jeffers, R., & Lehiste, I. (1979). *Principles and methods for historical linguistics*. Cambridge, MA: MIT Press.

Kaneko, T., & Tomonaga, M. (2011). The perception of self-agency in chimpanzees (*Pan troglodytes*). *Proceedings of the Royal Society of London, 278*, 3695–3701.

Karg, K., Schmelz, M., Call, J., & Tomasello, M. (2015). The goggles experiment: Can chimpanzees use self-experience to infer what a competitor can see? *Animal Behaviour, 105*, 211–221.

Kay, R., & Ungar, P. (1997). Dental evidence for diet in some Miocene catarrhines with comments on the effects of phylogeny on the interpretation of adaptation. In D. Begun, C. Ward, & M. Rose (Eds.), *Function, phylogeny, and fossils: Miocene hominoid evolution and adaptations* (pp. 131–151). New York, NY: Plenum.

Kummer, H. (1971). *Primate societies*. Chicago, IL: Aldine & Atherton.

Lambert, C. A., & Tishkoff, S. A. (2009). Genetic structure in African populations: Implications for human demographic history. *Cold Spring Harbor Symposia on Quantitative Biology, 74*, 395–402.

Lieberman, P. (2006). *Toward an evolutionary biology of language*. Cambridge, MA: Harvard University Press.

Lyn, H., Greenfield, P. M., Savage-Rumbaugh, S., Gillespie-Lynch, K., & Hopkins, W. D. (2011). Non-human primates do declare! A comparison of declarative symbol and gesture use in two children, two bonobos and a chimpanzee. *Language and Communication, 31*, 61–64.

Maclatchy, L. (2004). The oldest ape. *Evolutionary Anthropology, 13*, 90–103.

Maclatchy, L., Rossie, J., & Kingston, J. (2015). *The ecological niche of the Morotopithecus, with implications for hominoid evolution*. Paper presented at the 84th annual meeting of the American Association of Physical Anthropologist.

MacLean, E., & Hare, B. (2012). Bonobos and chimpanzees infer the target of another's attention. *Animal Behaviour, 83*(2), 345–353.

Maryanski, A. (1986). *African ape sociality: A comparative analysis*. PhD dissertation, University of California, Irvine.

Maryanski, A. (1987). African ape social structure: Is there strength in weak ties? *Social Networks, 9*, 191–215.

Maryanski, A. (1992). The last ancestor: An ecological-network model on the origins of human sociality. *Advances in Human Ecology, 2*, 1–32.

Maryanski, A. (1993). The elementary forms of the first proto-human society: An ecological/social network approach. *Advances in Human Evolution, 2*, 215–241.

Maryanski, A. (1995). African ape social networks: A blueprint for reconstructing early hominid social structure. In J. Steele & S. Shennan (Eds.), *Archaeology of human ancestry* (pp. 67–90). London, UK: Routledge.

Maryanski, A. (2013). The secret of the hominin mind: An evolutionary story. In D. Franks & J. Turner (Eds.), *Handbook of neurosociology* (pp. 257–287). New York, NY: Springer.

Maryanski, A. (2018). *Emile Durkheim and the birth of the gods*. New York and London: Routledge.

Maryanski, A., & Turner, J. H. (1992). *The social cage: Human nature and the evolution of society*. Stanford, CA: Stanford University Press.

McGrew, W. C. (1981). The female chimpanzee as a human evolutionary prototype. In F. Dahlberg (Ed.), *Woman the gatherer* (pp. 35–73). New Haven, CT: Yale University Press.

McGrew, W. C. (1992). *Chimpanzee material culture: Implications for human evolution.* Cambridge, UK: Cambridge University Press.

McGrew, W. C. (2010). In search of the last common ancestor: New findings on wild chimpanzees. *Philosophical Transaction of the Royal Society of London, 365,* 3265–3267.

Mead, G. H. (1934). *Mind, self, and society.* Chicago, IL: University of Chicago Press.

Meldrum, J. (2006). *Sasquatch: Legend meets science.* New York, NY: Forge.

Mitani, J., Call, J., Kappeler, P., Palombit, R., & Silk, J. (2012). *The evolution of primate societies.* Chicago, IL: University of Chicago Press.

Mitani, J., Merriwether, D. A., & Zhang, C. (2000). Male affiliation, cooperation and kinship in wild chimpanzees. *Animal Behaviour, 59,* 885–893.

Parr, L., Waller, B., & Fugate, J. (2005). Emotional communication in primates: Implications for neurobiology. *Current Opinion in Neurobiology, 15,* 716–720.

Platnick, N., & Cameron, H. D. (1977). Cladistic methods in textual, linguistic and phylogenetic analysis. *Systematic Zoology, 26,* 380–385.

Potts, R. (2004). Paleoenviornmental basis of cognitive evolution in great apes. *American Journal of Primatology, 62,* 209–228.

Raaum, R., Kirstin, L., Sterner, N., Noviello, C., Stewart, C., & Disotell, T. (2005). Catarrhine primate divergence dates estimated from complete mitochondrial genomes: Concordance with fossil and nuclear DNA evidence. *Journal of Human Evolution, 48,* 237–257.

Roberts, A., Vick, S. J., Roberts, S., Buchannan-Smith, H., & Zuberbühler, K. (2012). A structure-based repertoire of manual gestures in wild chimpanzees: Statistical analyses of a graded communication system. *Evolution and Human Behavior, 33,* 578–589.

Savage-Rumbaugh, S., & Lewin, R. (1994). *The ape at the brink of the human mind.* New York, NY: Wiley.

Serazio, M. (2013, January 29). Just how much is sports fandom like religion? *The Atlantic* (online), 1–6.

Sherwood, C. C., Subiaul, F., & Zawidzki, T. W. (2008). A natural history of the human mind: Tracing evolutionary changes in brain and cognition. *Journal of Anatomy, 212,* 426–454.

Stanford, C., Allen, J., & Antón, S. (2013). *Biological anthropology.* Boston, MA: Pearson.

Stebbins, G. L. (1969). *The basis of progressive evolution.* Chapel Hill, NC: University of North Carolina Press.

Stephan, H. (1983). Evolutionary trends in limbic structures. *Neuroscience and Biobehavioral Review, 7,* 367–374.

Stephan, H., & Andy, O. J. (1969). Quantitative comparative neuroanatomy of primates: An attempt at phylogenetic interpretation. *Annals of the New York Academy of Science, 167,* 370–387.

Stephan, H., & Andy, O. J. (1977). Quantitative comparison of the amygdala in insectivores and primates. *Acta Antomica, 98,* 130–153.

Stephan, H., Baron, G., & Frahm, F. (1988). Comparative size of brains and brain components. In H. Steklis & J. Erwin (Eds.), *Neurosciences* (Vol. 4) (1–38). New York, NY: Liss.

Stephan, H., Frahm, F., & Baron, B. (1981). New and revised data on volumes of brain structures in insectivores and primates. *Folia Primatologica, 35,* 1–29.

Sterck, E. (2012). The behavioral ecology of colobine monkeys. In J. Mitani, J. Call, P. Kappeler, R. Palomit, & J. Silk (Eds.), *The evolution of primate societies* (pp. 46–58). Chicago, IL: University of Chicago Press.

Temerin, A., & Cant, J. (1983). The evolutionary divergence of Old World monkeys and apes. *American Naturalist*, 122, 335–351.

Tomasello, M., & Herrmann, E. (2010). Ape and human cognition: What's the difference? *Current Directions in Psychological Science*, 19, 3–8.

Turner, J. H. (2000). *On the origins of human emotions: A sociological inquiry into the evolution of human affect.* Stanford, CA: Stanford University Press.

Turner, J. H. (2002). *Face to face: Toward a theory of interpersonal behavior.* Stanford, CA: Stanford University Press.

Turner, J. H. (2007). *Human emotions: A sociological theory.* Oxford, UK: Routledge.

Turner, J. H., & Abrutyn, S. (2016). Returning the "social" to sociocultural evolution: Reconsidering Spencer, Durkheim, and Marx's models of selection. *Sociological Perspectives*, 60(3), 529–566.

Turner, J. H., & Machalek, R. S. (2018). *The new evolutionary sociology: Recent and revitalized theoretical and methodological approaches.* New York and London: Routledge.

Turner, J. H., & Maryanski, A. (1992). *The social cage: Human nature and the evolution of society.* Stanford, CA: Stanford University Press

Turner, J. H., & Maryanski, A. (2008). *On the origins of societies by natural selection.* Boulder, CO: Paradigm.

Turner, J. H., & Maryanski, A. (2015). Evolutionary sociology: A cross-species strategy for discovering human nature. In J. H. Turner, R. Machalek, & A. R. Maryanski (Eds.), *Handbook of evolution and society: Toward an evolutionary social science* (pp. 546–571). New York, NY: Routledge/Paradigm.

Turner, J. H., Maryanski, A., Peterson, A. K., & Geertz, A. (2018). *On the origin and development of religions: By means of natural selection.* New York, NY: Routledge.

Turner, J. H., & Stets, Jan E. (2005). *The sociology of emotions.* Cambridge, UK: Cambridge University Press.

Watts, D. (2012). The apes: Taxonomy, biogeography, life histories, and behavioral ecology. In J. Mitani, J. Call, P. Kappeler, R. Palombit, & J. Silk (Eds.), *The evolution of primate societies.* Chicago, IL: University of Chicago Press.

Zalmout, L., Sanders, W., Maclatchy, L., Gunnell, G., Al-Mufarreh, Y., Ali, M., . . . Gingerich, P. (2010). New Oligocene primate from Saudi Arabia and the divergence of apes and Old World monkeys. *Nature*, 466, 360–364.

CHAPTER 7

REWARD ALLOWANCES AND CONTRAST EFFECTS IN SOCIAL EVOLUTION

A Challenge to Zygmunt Bauman's Liquid Modernity

MICHAEL HAMMOND

ALL interests that are part of our evolutionary heritage are not created equal. One way in which they are unequal is in terms of reward allowances. A reward allowance is an indicator of how many rewards from the body a stimulus can trigger over the long term and, by extension, how many resources should be devoted to the pursuit of these rewards. The range and evolutionary origins of these rewards in neurochemistry, positive emotions, and physical pleasures are described in Hammond (2013). The two most important allowances are for repetition and variety. A repetition reward allowance, hereafter referred to as a repetition allowance, indicates roughly how many rewards a repeated stimulus is likely to trigger over time. A variety reward allowance, referred to as a variety allowance, points to approximately how many rewards a variety of stimuli might trigger. A high allowance means there can be many rewards for repetition or variety in the long term and, therefore, that many resources should be devoted to such arousers. Because repetitive stimuli are normally less costly in terms of time and effort, a high repetition allowance is the gold standard of natural selection for reward release in terms of costs and benefits. A lower allowance means that there are fewer rewards for such stimuli. These allowances create windows for the emergence of social structures able to trigger additional rewards by taking advantage of the impact of contrast effects on our reward release rules.

As Ben Williams (1997) notes in his review of Charles Flaherty's (1996) classic book on contrast effects for rewards in humans and nonhumans, these effects are among the most Byzantine of behavioral phenomena. There is not yet a consistent set of underlying concepts about the evolutionary origins and various roles for these effects, and it appears that different types of contrast—such as successive, anticipatory, and behavioral contrast—reflect somewhat different processes (Williams, 1997, p. 140). However, it is clear that there is something about relative value, both positive and negative, that impacts behavior on a regular basis right down to the neural level (Montague & Berns, 2002; Montague, King-Casas, & Cohen, 2006). The recurring pattern is that the higher the contrast value, the greater the impact, and vice versa, the lesser the contrast effect, the lower the impact. Humans use these contrast effects to create social structures with high-contrast repetition, such as religion and inflated ascriptive inequality, and with high variety, such as the serial novelty of modern economies (Hammond, 2015a, 2015b). From this perspective, serial novelty is viewed as a possible substitute for much of the elevated ascriptive inequality that is so costly on a mass scale, especially when it is linked to religion. However, there are many who do not take such a cautiously optimistic view of this substitution (Hammond, 2015a). One of those theorists is Zygmunt Bauman.

Liquid Modernity

Like many postmodernist theorists, Bauman (2000) finds the transient and ever-changing quality of all things today to be the main obstacle in the way of fulfilling the promise of a new and better modern world that began in the Industrial Revolution. His term for this stage of development is *liquid modernity*. Like Ulrich Beck's (1992) "second modernity," it is part of a three-part model of social evolution. First, there is the solidity, or at least the goal of solidity, of the premodern, and now there is the growing liquidity of the postmodern world. In between, there is a transition period called modernity, marked by an attempt to replace one solid form with another. For Bauman, this interim condition is the world analyzed by classical theorists such as Marx, Durkheim, and Weber. They differ on many things, but they converge on the idea that a new solidity is emerging, be it in a socialist, organic, or bureaucratic form.

In examining the transitional stage, Bauman (2000) points to Durkheim's use of the term *solidarity*. There are two different kinds of solidarity—mechanical for the premodern world and organic for our world—but there is always the root concept of solidarity and a long-term movement toward solidarity when things become temporarily imbalanced. Durkheim's key assumption is that humans could not continue for long to do without some form of macro solidarity. It is an existential necessity (pp. 20, 183). Marx's model was similar in concept. A new modern solidity in a socialist or communist form would eventually emerge after the "melting of solids" in feudal and capitalist forms (p. 3). Weber believed that the iron cage of instrumental rationality and the pervasive bureaucratic model would provide the solidity for any large-scale modern world, be it capitalist or noncapitalist (p. 4). However, for Bauman, all these classical theorists erred in not seeing that the initial emergence of modernity was just a step in a wider civilizational shift.

This general model of contemporary fluidity is shared with other social scientists having a very different political agenda than Bauman (Hammond, 2015a). For instance,

Joseph Schumpeter's social evolutionary model of a mostly static "steel frame" in the premodern world and the more dynamic creative destruction of the capitalist world is very similar to Bauman's distinction between solid and fluid cultures. However, Schumpeter believed that the relentless and ever-shifting quality of creative destruction was unsustainable and eventually individuals would fall back on more solidarity heavy systems, such as socialism. Humans might experiment with systems of endless innovation, not just in economics but also in the arts and in their personal lives. However, this experiment in serial novelty was at its core unsustainable. The economic and, equally important, the existential difficulties of living in such a liquid world were just too great, and eventually we would move back to less fluid structures.

Bauman (2000) does not share this vision of a fluid world. His view is dystopian. Real resistance to inequality and a host of other problems in the premodern world was difficult enough during the transition to modernism. Now it appears even more hopeless in the face of challenging something that is constantly shifting around and away. Bauman sees clearly the dynamism of destructive creativity (p. 28). Schumpeter embraced this creative disruption, but he did not believe that it could persist. Bauman is appalled by it but does not see any way out of its diffusion throughout any specific culture and throughout the world.

In a world increasingly moving to a consumer capitalism of planned obsolescence in everything, the state is "no longer hoped, promising, or willing to act as the plenipotentiary of reason and the master-builder of the rational society" (Bauman, 2000, p. 48). As capital becomes increasingly more liquid, flowing across borders, so too does this liquidity come to mark other parts of the world, such as work, personal ties, and definitions of the self. In this process, the public is colonized by the private (p. 37). Bauman states that "in a world in which deliberately unstable things are the raw building material of identities that are by necessity unstable" (p. 85), there can only be

> musical chairs of various sizes and styles as well as of changing number and positions, which prompt men and women to be constantly on the move and promise no "fulfillment," no rest, and no satisfaction of "arriving," or reaching the final destination where one can disarm, relax, and stop worrying. (pp. 33–34)

In such a world, there is "no longer the measurable set of articulated needs," but instead there is "desire . . . a self-begotten and self-propelled motive that needs no other justification or cause" (p. 74). "Divided, we shop," and we can shop around for a vast range of new things, including our identities (pp. 87, 89). Where any sense of community remains, it is not defined by solidarity but, rather, by fear, gates, or other kinds of barriers (pp. 92–94). Weak ties are the new norm, and long-term commitments such as marriage suffer (pp. 148–149). For most, work has been redefined, made more precarious, and devalued (pp. 138–140). In the face of such troublesome developments, "signs of malaise are abundant and salient," but "they seek in vain a legitimate expression in the world of politics" (p. 214).

Bauman (2000) seems somewhat mystified by such a paradigmatic change toward "the unholy trinity of uncertainty, insecurity, and unsafety" (p. 181) in a world that originally promised so much of the opposite if only we would abandon the premodern and embrace the new enlightened world emerging from its ruins. This betrayal of the original promise of modernity is not a conspiracy of a few key individuals, and unlike Bentham and Foucault's image of the panopticon metaphor of control, there is no all-seeing elite group in charge, directly or indirectly, of the fluid world (pp. 10–11). Clearly, there is something more in play in such mass upheavals than theorists have generally considered, but Bauman is not sure what it is. He is hopeful that some groups, such as sociologists, might play an "engaged" role "aimed at disclosing the possibility of living together differently" (pp. 215–216), but that hope is largely buried in a shopping list of bad news.

So the questions remain: How could the serial novelty of the liquid world, so often superficial or even negative in its consequences, be so irresistible? And how could it be so irresistible after so many millennia of individuals embracing one or another form of more solid familiarity? One part of the answer to such questions can be found in our evolutionary origins and in the reward release rules that are a part of that heritage. Bauman's (2000) model points to two strategies to exploit our evolutionary heritage of preconscious triggers for reward release from the body. Both can provide additional rewards on a mass scale, and not just for the occasional individual or small group (Hammond, 2013). One bonus window emerges early and is predominant throughout most of our history. The second is the new kid on the block. Both have their origins in reward allowances and contrast effects.

Reward Allowances and Contrast Effects

Individuals of any species cannot respond to all stimuli equally. This would make no sense in terms of natural selection. Stimuli must be ranked in one way or another and responded to appropriately. One of the most common evolutionary ranking systems is in terms of reward allowances for different interests and, by extension, for the stimuli related to those interests. A stimulus that can tap a high repetition allowance is going to be very appealing because it is going to be very rewarding over the short term in successive repetition and over the long term in periodic repetition. Survival normally entails a great deal of repetitive behaviors; and without a high allowance, attention will soon fade as repetitions pile up. Natural selection repeatedly uses a high allowance to ensure the pursuit of certain repetitive actions. All core human interests have this allowance as part of their reward dynamics.

With so many rewards for repetition, there is going to be limited room for reward additions relying on contrast effects for more reward spikes or yet more rewarding repetitions. Otherwise, too many rewards could go to some stimuli and leave too few rewards for other arousers. However, what if there is not a natural high repetition allowance over the long term? What if there is a lower allowance with room for some short-term spikes and repetition surges? In this case, different stimuli with different contrast values can lead to very different reward totals. There is more potential room for additions in reward spikes and in repetitions still producing some rewards. Given our general behavioral flexibility and our outstanding cognitive skills, humans have the capacity to take advantage of preconscious contrast effects in order to trigger additional reward release over the long term where there is not a natural high repetition allowance.

Familiar arousers are the most common category of stimuli. With a high repetition allowance, these can be a major source of rewards even without high contrast values. Without such an allowance, there is a possible double bonus for high-contrast familiarity. Higher contrasts can gather more reward spikes and can slow the repetition suppression of rewards over time. This double bonus also means that individuals will pay extra costs in terms of time, effort, and risk in order to reap these rewards. However, these costs generally cannot be much greater than the rewards they bring in. Otherwise, individuals will look elsewhere for a better cost–benefit ratio. Social creations that can spread and even offset some of those costs while offering high-contrast arousers are going to be very appealing throughout a population.

Novelty presents another window for exploiting contrast effects with a double-reward bonus. Novelty is a contrast with short-term elevated rewards but also with a low repetition allowance over the long term. It can have a contrast impact producing more rewards per presentation than familiar stimuli in the same value category (Bunzeck, Doeller, Dolan, & Duzel, 2012; Bunzeck & Duzel, 2006; Kakade & Dayan, 2002). Such a bonus makes additional repetitions more attractive until familiarity sets in, and novelty rewards decrease and then disappear. Furthermore, in a halo effect, mixing novel arousers with more familiar ones reduces the repetition suppression rates for those familiar stimuli (Bunzeck et al., 2012). The evolutionary origin and selective impact of these novelty reward responses are tied to their occasional but important role in our early history (Hammond, 2013). Again, these responses leave a window of opportunity to extract additional rewards.

The disadvantage of using novelty to trigger additional rewards is that any specific set of rewards is self-extinguishing as familiarity sets in over time. However, because the decline of one set of novelty rewards sets the stage for a new set of rewards, there is a possibility to overcome this erosion problem by using serial novelty with a string of novel arousers stretched out over time in order to provide a long-term amplified reward total. The contrast effects in serial novelty provide a renewable resource. Indeed, it is useful to think of serial novelty as repeating novelty, a back-door repeating pattern having a high reward allowance. With sufficient serial novelty, the reward totals can potentially equal those of high-contrast familiar arousers. Again, these extra rewards mean that individuals will be willing to pay extra costs in order to access such reward packages and also that social creations offsetting or otherwise limiting some of these costs are going to be very appealing. It is only late in our history that serial novelty can be offered on a mass scale; however, when that possibility finally emerges, there is a radical impact.

In terms of these reward rules, long-term high-contrast serial novelty would be among the most effective reward triggers of all time. However, so far in our history, this option has only been available for a few individuals or small groups. No culture has yet found a vehicle to provide such arouser packages consistently to most or to all of a population, and it is this mass scale that is under consideration here. Instead, as discussed later, what have emerged on a mass basis are social creations having the renewable rewards of serial novelty with occasional high contrasts, many lesser contrasts, and limited repetitions per contrast. These stand as a possible substitute for other social creations marked by consistent high contrasts and high repetitions for a smaller number of special familiar arousers. The key is that the total contrast effects and the potential reward release totals of these two packages are quite similar in the long term.

In summary, for familiar arousers without a high repetition allowance, it is the consistent high-contrast window that is going to be most effective in piling up additional rewards in the long term. For novel arousers, serial novelty is going to be the most effective. This provides two alternatives: (a) Stress long-term high contrasts and high repetition in playing with our reward release rules; and (b) stress long-term serial novelty with on average lesser contrasts and fewer repetitions, but also with the novelty bonus. Of course, these two platforms can also be mixed and matched in different proportions. Historically, many cultures have offered a predominance of high-contrast familiar arousers, with only occasional novelty and rarely, if at all, with serial novelty. Contemporary capitalist cultures offer less regular high-contrast distinctions on a mass basis but do offer far more serial novelty. This often means a contest between high-contrast repetition and serial novelty as platforms for triggering the bonus reward release we all find so attractive. This contest can sometimes be friendly, but very often it will be antagonistic.

REWARD RULES AND THE EMERGENCE OF RELIGION

Different interests have different potentials for making use of one or another of these platforms to extend an interest through reward harvesting across a wide swath of the population. Because natural selection made a high repetition allowance so attractive, it is no wonder that humans would be interested in finding more high allowances to add to those provided by our biological evolution. What interests could be extended by social constructions offering these allowances?

As noted previously, all interests are not created equal by natural selection. Some are given a high repetition allowance. This means that over the long term, there can be many rewards for the repetition of a stimulus, and hence many resources can be fruitfully applied to the pursuit of such stimuli. Because attractive repetition is normally less costly in terms of time and effort than the pursuit of variety, a high repetition allowance will virtually guarantee that certain behaviors will occur. Metaphorically, this is just what natural selection is counting on in favoring the evolution of such a reward pattern. For example, different patterns of personal interaction have different repetition allowances and different contrast sensitivities (Fisher, Aron, Mashek, Li, & Brown, 2002). A prime example of a high repetition allowance is found in our interest in long-term strong attachments. These bonds evolved as a means to try to ensure that there is a central circle of strong, and hence more reliable, ties to provide all kinds of support for, comparatively speaking, an instinct-poor species. These bonds can have high rates of repetitive interaction and continue to generate rewards; thus, there is no necessity for high contrast values within any specific tie over the long term. Something like romantic infatuation might provide high contrast values in the short term (Aron et al., 2005), but this is not a permanent requirement for a high reward release total in these close ties. They are the gold standard of attachment rewards.

However, this part of our general attachment interest also has a low variety allowance. This allowance is a measure of how many rewards a variety of stimuli can trigger. A low allowance means that only a small variety can consistently generate rewards in the long term. This low variety allowance for strong attachments means that only a small number of ties can take advantage of the high repetition allowance in harvesting rewards. Some strong attachments are necessary in all circumstances, but they are costly in terms of time and effort. The selective logic in a low variety allowance is that any more variety could raise even further the already high costs of such ties, and this could interfere with efforts to meet the demands of other interests.

Of course, there is another part of our general attachment interest that has a lower repetition allowance linked to a higher variety allowance. This reward combination is the basis of our attraction to a larger number of less strong attachments. These ties have more occasional short-term reward spikes and lower reward totals compared to long-term strong bonds, but depending on circumstances, they are also more flexible in terms of numbers, relative strength, and costs. The selective logic is such an additional circle of ties is found in their role of providing a further and more flexible expansion of a social support network.

One possibility that emerges from this flexibility is that humans could use some of the wiring for less strong ties as a platform for adding high-contrast effects that could raise the long-term repetition allowance and thereby raise the reward totals for these bonds. The natural range of contrast values among individuals in a population is not normally going to have such a special impact. However, what about creating elevated contrast effects in beings that are more than human and then using these contrasts to trigger more reward release? Imaginary contrasts can be as powerful as real contrasts, and therefore, these extra-human gods and spirits would be very pleasing. Because they are fueled by piggybacking on already existent reward wiring, these imaginary creations would feel real for those who believe in them. The extra costs in terms of time and effort to create and maintain such elevated contrasts would be too great on an individual basis, but they would be possible to sustain on a collective basis. Having others engaged in the same pursuit of a third circle of supporting ties would also reinforce this reward extraction enterprise and provide a very useful macro platform for collective interaction.

Neuroscience research has pointed to an overlap between religious and attachment stimuli in terms of impact on certain areas of the brain, suggesting that attachment wiring is one source of rewards for religion (Granqvist, Mikulincer, & Shaver, 2010; Kirkpatrick & Granqvist, 2008; McNamara, 2009; Newberg, d'Aquili, & Rause, 2001). This piggybacking could be purely opportunistic. The window was there, humans learned early on how to use it, and they can continue to use it today. Another possibility is that after an opportunistic beginning, there were enough initial benefits from the creation of such elevated contrast effects that there were sufficient selective pressures to generate their own attachment wiring, not for gods per se but, rather, for some high-contrast additions to our other attachment circles. In our context of origin with micro populations and limited technologies, religious creations would be the most likely vehicle for such additions. Either possibility would provide one reward base for the social construction of religion. Either would have much the same long-term consequences. Furthermore, in another example of the piggybacking model as a source of rewards for religion, Pascal Boyer (2001) suggests that there are many rewards for such creations coming from their cognitive piggybacking and their "aggregate relevance" in the "successful activation of a whole variety of mental systems" (p. 298) that are rewarding because "religious concepts are parasitic upon other mental capacities" (p. 311).

What characteristics of these imaginary high-contrast arousers would be most effective in cementing their reward release possibilities? First, they would probably have some human qualities because these anthropomorphic aspects would make it much easier to piggyback on attachment wiring. However, they would also have more super-human attributes that give them the contrast values necessary for such piggybacking. For instance, they might not have to die, so they can be there generation after generation, consistently providing existential anchors. From their permanent elevated positions, they can be given powers over the many parts of the world where humans so often appear to be powerless unless they can influence these special beings. Occasional novelty in religion might have some attractive qualities, but in total, there would be only a limited appeal in comparison to the rewards from such eternal consistency and familiarity. Similarly, the even greater impermanence of serial novelty in religious beings is not going to be attractive to most believers most of the time, and this is especially true at the micro social scale of our early history. As a result, in Bauman's (2000) terms, cultures deeply embracing these high-contrast social creations are going to be more solid than fluid.

THE ELEVATION OF INEQUALITY

Our status interest is the second interest that historically is amplified by bonus windows framed with contrast effects. Although not as advanced as the study of the inner workings of attachment, status is a research area that neuroscientists are beginning to study increasingly more (Chiao et al., 2009; Izuma, Saito, & Sadato, 2008; Ly, Haynes, Barter, Weinberger, & Zink, 2011; Martinez et al., 2010; Saxe & Haushofer, 2008; Zink et al., 2008). In comparison to attachment wiring, status dynamics touch on some other areas of the brain (Hammond, 2013), but in terms of social emergence, the outcome is much the same because status wiring appears to also have a window for exploiting the reward release potential of contrast sensitivity. Again, the first social creations to use this reward window intensely are more static than dynamic.

A status interest is by definition contrast sensitive, but of course, among species, there are many ways to frame contrast effects (Hammond, 2015b). For instance, in both experimental and natural settings for nonhuman primates such as the chimpanzee, long-term elevated status distinctions appear even when there are only a small number of individuals. For this to regularly occur, there must be preconscious wiring with rewards for a high degree of repetition in terms of status interaction with any single individual. With even small natural differences among individuals, this high repetition allowance can bring high reward totals from using these personal differences in the pursuit of status. Status interactions between specific individuals can occur again and again, and reward harvesting continues for the dominant individuals. Thus, even with very small populations, there can be a major status expansion for a few members. The costs in terms of risk, time, and effort to occupy these positions are very great, and the dominance time of any specific individual is normally limited. However, the fall of a dominator is the rise of another, and elevated inequality persists in the long term.

The historical evidence from anthropology and paleoanthropology suggests that the human case is different. Because status distinctions, both individual and collective, seem to appear in all human populations, there was clearly some selective advantage to status differentiation in our context of origin. However, if the same basic rules for status reward release existed in humans as in some other primates such as the chimpanzee, these human populations should all have the same elevated status inequality of these other primates. Instead, it appears that although human micro populations such as those of our context of origin exhibit occasional short-term elevated status spikes, rarely are individuals or groups successful in making these distinctions permanent or in creating a line of such dominance over time. Any such attempts to produce inflated inequality are generally met with successful resistance in the long term (Boehm, 1999). Human status reward rules could be one key factor in this pattern, suggesting that humans do not have the same high repetition allowance for status interaction with any single individual that some other primate species have. Instead, it appears that there is a moderate repetition allowance guaranteeing that some status differentiation will appear in all human populations, and there is also room for an increase in this allowance given sufficient contrast effects. With a more limited repetition allowance, even if some individuals or groups try to use high contrasts to increase rewards over time, there would not be at this social scale enough variety of individuals consistently available to fuel an increase in the repetition allowance and thereby trigger the elevated reward totals necessary to compensate for the high costs of creating and defending high-status positions in the long term. There is no variety of individuals to offer the losers in one high contrast distinction an alternative elevated distinction of their own.

However, in these same cultures, there are also a number of occasional and temporary situations in which status escalation occurs. These appear in circumstances in which the variety of status arousers is increased, either in terms of circumstantial variety or numerical variety. For instance, there are periodic gatherings when normally dispersed populations come together for one reason or another, such as raiding or warfare, information and mate exchanges, and religious rituals (Johnson & Earle, 2000). Such temporary assemblies create special opportunities for status differentiation fueled by the contrast effects of additional variety of circumstances and individuals. The high contrast between these special situations and normal daily life would be one source of additional rewards, and this high contrast would also promote more rewarding repetitions. The extra variety of individuals available for reinforcing more elevated distinctions would be another source of extra rewards. The regular expansion of social differentiation in these special situations seems to indicate a selective advantage for status reward rules with this behavioral scaling. However, these special conditions are not sustainable. Over time, these groups break up and return to a smaller base and more repetitive behavior patterns, thereby dampening most opportunities to continue reaping the extra status rewards of the special situations. The same is true for other special circumstances, such as combat with other groups over access to resources, where there can be temporary but generally unsustainable spikes in both individual and collective inequality. Of course, this behavioral flexibility in scaling status reward release can have some messy qualities because it leaves open the possibility that some individuals or groups might make inappropriate responses to different conditions. Nonetheless, metaphorically speaking, natural selection is interested in what works and not necessarily in what is the cleanest or most elegant, and it is clear that this status flexibility had selective advantages in our context of origin.

With the exodus from our context of origin, larger population concentrations become a permanent part of the social landscape, and the variety contrast effects only available occasionally in earlier history now become the normal situation. The result is a reversal of fortune as the very rules that limit the growth of inequality in our context of origin become the fuel for the regular expansion of status distinctions. With expanded variety, there is less repetition of any specific arouser and, hence, more rewards. This means that individuals and groups will also bear more costs in the pursuit of those additional rewards. Furthermore, in order to take even more advantage of such expanded variety, some can seek out very special long-term high-contrast status distinctions that offer both higher reward spikes on average and more repetitions. These inflated distinctions can offer even greater reward totals. However, there normally are not natural differences among individuals great enough to sustain such elevated contrast values. Instead, there must be a magnification of natural differences among individuals or, like religion, a creation of high contrasts by simply fabricating inflated differences.

The advantages of inflated inequality to a select few at the top are clear, but is there a vehicle to facilitate mass access to such additional reward release through the status inflation of whole groups throughout a population? One problem in such a mass expansion is that there are even fewer natural differences between groups of individuals than there are among individuals, such that high-contrast natural differences are not going to be available for reward triggers in the pursuit of elevated distinctions on a mass scale. Where then to find such distinctions? The solution to this problem is again, as with religion, to use our cognitive skills to create elevated distinctions having little or no reality outside of a belief in them. One path is to use small or moderate natural performance differences between groups, such as differences in gender and physical strength, dramatically inflate these differences, and then attribute to them a host of other high-contrast distinctions. Another path is to take nonperformance differences such as skin color and attribute to such superficial differences all kinds of other high-contrast distinctions. Also, imaginary contrasts can trigger as much reward release as real contrasts, and that makes it possible to simply fabricate differences between groups based on culture or whatever and ascribe to these fabrications a host of other distinctions. Next, make these inflated attributions permanent so they can consistently offer high-contrast familiarity over the long term. One way to do this is to make these distinctions the work of the gods. Then, use these attributions to try to exclude others from any fair competition for access to even the small social resources that a group might control. These fixed elevated distinctions can lead to additional reward release, and as in the case of religion, they will feel real. Of course, being completely or largely imaginary, these high-contrast arousers can be made regularly available throughout a population. Similarly, as with religion, creating and maintaining such distinctions is monumentally costly for a specific individual, but a collective construction can offer a better deal. Thus, the exodus produces a permanent mass reward window that earlier had only been open on an occasional and temporary basis.

There are significant costs associated with these social status creations. Inflated inequality produces many categories of winners and losers, and the negative consequences of being in the loser category also escalate. The fact that so many individuals have borne so much of these costs for so long demonstrates just how addictive the additional reward release coming from mass elevated inequality can be. Even in the face of economic impoverishment, large numbers of individuals cling to their inflated ascriptive distinctions. Naturally, the best way to reinforce these distinctions is to deny their historicity and to make them in principle eternal and permanent divisions, such as by declaring them as god-given. Once again, throughout much of our history, it is in Bauman's (2000) terms the solid construction that is preferable in triggering these additional rewards, and it is no wonder that powerful statics such as religion and ascriptive inequality so often become entangled with one another and work together to handicap resistance to such status inflation over the long term.

Given the massive costs that such a pyramidal pattern creates for so many individuals, resistance to elite domination does not disappear, but cooperation and coordination by groups opposing this domination are severely handicapped, if not paralyzed, by the predominance of inflated ascriptive distinctions throughout the population. Generally, resistance either fails outright or, when successful in the short term, is transformed over time into another version of the very structures it originally opposed. Specific elites and constellations of mass ascriptive inequality rise and fall as these pyramidal constructions topple and re-emerge again and again, but the general pattern remains the same. It is high-contrast repetition in inflated status distinctions that spreads through a population and dominates despite its enormous social costs. Novelty in status rewards only occurs occasionally, and only for a small part of the population. This is even truer for serial novelty. After all, how could any such novelty compete on a mass basis with the emergent and ever-present post-exodus reward surge of fixed social creations such as elevated ascription?

Just as in the case of the emergence of religion, the expansion of reward release in such status inflations is not infinite for an individual. There are eventually physiological limitations for both basic interests and any expansion windows that are directly or indirectly a part of human biological evolution. Thus, as social scale grows, status pyramids become more elevated and elaborate, but this does not mean that the status interest itself is expanding. Instead, as scale expands, if there is a continuing commitment to a pyramidal pattern of status differentiation, groups must divide and subdivide in order to provide a growing range of variety and contrasts necessary to simply continue to take some long-term advantage of our status reward rules. Most have to make do with whatever status distinctions they can access, such as elevated ascription protecting even small amounts of a social resource, while being dominated by other distinctions controlled by other groups. This mass trade-off opens a window for a great substitution when a new reward-triggering opportunity begins to emerge.

THE SECOND EXODUS AND THE GREAT SUBSTITUTION

The basis of this new opportunity to play with our reward release rules comes from the gradual accumulation of technology over millennia. Eventually, this accumulation reaches a take-off point where continuing competition among still predominantly agrarian elite systems could begin to propel technology forward at an increasingly greater rate until it could fully emerge as a key part of the scaffolding for a new social system. Why is technology so important in terms of our reward release rules? First, with its mass production capacities, it can compete on a mass basis with the reward release power of high-contrast and high-repetition social creations such as ascriptive inequality. Second, it can compete while offering many individuals a better cost–benefit ratio in terms of the time and effort in the pursuit of these amplified rewards. This makes technology a very tempting vehicle to put to use in substituting one reward release package for another.

With technology's productivity surge, contrast effects can be tapped to offer additional reward release by reducing repetition through increased variety and, most important, through increased novelty in goods and services for a host of interests. This productivity offers regularly rewarding additions that are only available occasionally and temporarily earlier in history, and it can often make this offer without a parallel increase in costs for individuals. In particular, with technology's boost, novelty can be transformed from an occasional to a serial part of the lives of many individuals. Technology therefore does not have to rely as much on high contrasts for additional reward release. It can stress more short-term additions, but in a manner that can add up over time to a grand total equal to the alternative classic additions. Altogether, technology's full emergence and the social innovations it requires justify being labeled as the second exodus (Hammond, 2012).

Familiar ways of doing things mean that once something is learned, it can be returned to again and again. Familiarity also means that the costs are generally known for access- ing these arousers. As long as the rewards keep coming from such return visits and the costs are also familiar, it is often not easy to get individuals to look elsewhere for such rewards. Lessening repetition by increasing the distinct variety of attractive arousers is fine in itself, but there is always a potential cost problem lurking in this alternative: As noted previously, repetition is normally the most cost effective in terms of time and effort. How then to increase variety without incurring too many additional costs that make less appealing any additional rewards reaped from additional variety? This is an especially important question in the face of the declining marginal utility that normally accompanies the addition of variety for most all of our interests. For instance, if indi- viduals have some familiar foods that are attractive and readily available, they may be interested in some additional variety, but only if the costs are limited to access those additions. Each addition is likely to provide a lower marginal reward gain than the ear- lier additions. If the costs of accessing these food additions remain the same as with the first foods, then with rewards declining, the cost–benefit ratio for each addition is likely to be less appealing and eventually to discourage continued interest. However, if there are technological and social innovations that allow access to all the additional foods without an equivalent cost increase, or even at a lesser cost, then the cost–benefit ratio shifts dramatically. At least for a few centuries in the capitalist era, the productivity of multiple innovations has had the impact of controlling many of the individual costs for such increased variety and thereby making this new reward release platform more enticing.

The cost–benefit problem is even more acute in regard to novel arousers. After all, novelty rewards are self-extinguishing. Novelty can be very appealing in terms of both increasing reward spike averages and making short-term repetitions more desirable; however, if the costs are not known, very difficult to assess, or even continue after the rewards are gone, then novelty becomes less appealing. Serial novelty can be even more difficult in this regard because individuals now must assess costs and benefits over a longer time span in which novel arouser is followed by novel arouser. However, once again, if there are technological and social innovations limiting some or all of these potential costs, then serial novelty is that much more attractive. In fact, extensive variety and serial novelty in goods and services for a host of interests are extremely difficult to provide on a mass scale without such innovations. If this was not the case, then our ear- lier history should be marked by low technology culture after culture adding variety and novelty to their reward packages on a regular and long-term basis. The actual historical record shows the opposite. Without vast technological aids, adding much variety and novelty as reward releasers on a mass basis is almost impossible.

Of course, even major technological innovations are no guarantee that such additional variety and novelty will become available across a population. For instance, there are many important technological changes associated with the exodus from our context of origin, but most of these are soon overwhelmed by population growth. Population surges with the new technologies that make possible horticultural and agricultural societies, and the resultant changes in per capita income, are not all that great. This leaves little opportunity to provide a significant increase in the variety of arousers available to a wide range of individuals. For example, in regard to a food interest, neuroscientists have demonstrated that many primate species and all humans have elaborate reward architecture for responding to different foods (Berridge, Ho, Richard, & Feliceantonio, 2010; Rolls, Murzi, Yaxley, Thorpe, & Simpson, 1986). If the technological changes of the exodus could make available heightened variety and novelty in food availability, then there would be many rewards available; however, much the opposite actually occurs historically. More people are sustained, but with less food variety and often with less food quantity and quality. Of course, with a series of technological innovations, there would be a point at which such food provisioning is possible on a mass basis; long before that occurs, however, there emerge elevated inequality structures with little interest in such developments.

The focus of these pyramidal structures is to limit further changes and to resist possibilities that might alter the status quo. The result is that only elites are able to take full advantage of the post-exodus changes in food production in order to have a quantity and variety of food that could also provide bonus rewards from something like serial novelty. This same pattern occurs in regard to interest after interest for which increased variety and serial novelty could have been alternative sources of reward release. New technologies are resisted outright, or severely dampened in their impact by the demands to keep the powerful elite status quo going. In the face of such innovation dampening, it is no wonder that the possibilities of using technologies on a mass scale as an alternative reward release source only appear late in our history. Similarly, after the exodus, there are occasional cases of serial novelty in which an individual or small group rises from obscurity to fame and fortune. However, these surges are few and far between, and when they are successful, they most often become over time another form of elevated and fixed inequality.

Even in generally static cultures, technological innovations continue, particularly in regard to areas of competition between these pyramidal structures such as in military matters, but at a very slow rate on an occasional basis. However, after millennia of a gradual accumulation of technologies, there eventually emerges a point at which a new alternative mass source of bonus rewards would be available. Again, it is important to stress that this reward release option only appears late in our history. To compete with the reward release power of classic high-contrast and high-repetition social creations such as religion and ascriptive inequality, wave after wave of technological innovation would be required, and even to begin this competition requires a vast amount of time. Such a sea change also requires new elites to emerge as its champion, and the dominant long-term representative of these new elites has been the capitalist class. What sets them apart from previous elites is not inequality itself but, rather, the consistent commitment of a part of this new high-inequality group to a process of relentless innovation, no matter what the collateral damage might be.

Inflated ascription and the mass production of an expanding range of goods and services are not as compatible with one another in comparison to combining high-contrast packages such as religion and ascription. A religion-backed high-contrast ascription is based on trying to exclude whole groups as much as possible from access to key social resources, be it in terms of marriage partners, economic resources, political positions, or whatever. Without such exclusions, the contrast value of the status distinction decreases, and so does the reward release. However, a mass production economy requires mass consumption, and this in turn requires that many are not so excluded from access to the increased range of goods and services being produced. Mass production must be directed more to inclusion rather than exclusion. If such production is a small part of the total production of an economy, then high-contrast ascription can still thrive; however, as this production spreads, mass elevated ascription must more or less gradually give way as more individuals seek alternative vehicles for harvesting rewards. Ascription does not disappear completely, but at least it will have to take on a lighter imprint.

The potential for social organization and political cooperation in non-elites grows as these mass inflated ascriptive distinctions erode, and this has a major impact on long-term resistance to traditional elites. Of course, in the face of the continuing deep appeal of high-contrast arousers, it is not surprising that the new capitalist elite try to use their special positions in a mass production economy to continue to maximize inflated economic inequality and the many different rewards tied to it. However, once again, such positions are very costly to the economy as a whole, and only a limited number can be sustained even in a very rich society. Many more will have to substitute alternative reward packages, and many will have to embrace a more moderate inequality in adopting this substitution.

INEQUALITY IN A FLUID WORLD

In predominantly "solid" preindustrial cultures, much of the strength of classic elites comes from the fact that so many individuals across the population try to imitate more or less successfully the elite use of high-contrast differentiation. As noted previously, the widespread embrace of this high-contrast platform severely handicaps successful long-term resistance to such elites. However, the emerging mass production economy cannot rely as heavily on this imitation. Mass production requires mass consumption, and both require an erosion of elevated mass ascription. The long-term success of the new capitalist elite greatly depends on their new role in promoting an economic machine providing an increasingly greater variety and novelty of goods and services, and they face growing political and organizational pressure from non-elites seeking a share of this mass production sufficient to fuel a mass reward substitution. The new elite cannot ignore these substitution dynamics, and as the gradual shift to a fluid economic form gains momentum over time, the new deal between capitalists and consumers becomes increasingly more important and takes different forms in different circumstances.

A mass consumption culture is incredibly demanding on all aspects of a culture as the great substitution spreads across a population, and each change can be problematical with the struggle to deliver year after year and decade after decade the goods and services to fuel alternative reward-triggering packages. However, we should not let these problems obscure the basic civilizational shift that has occurred with the second exodus. Now, serial novelty has the same potential appeal that inflated ascriptive inequality had with the first exodus. No wonder such novelty is so pervasive. No wonder it seems irresistible, even to opponents such as Bauman. It has a set of contrast effects every bit as potent as the first great reward expansion into mass elevated inequality. It can be used in the economy, in the polity, in creating a self or many selves, in personal ties, and in remaking work. Theorists such as Bauman find all of this to be appalling. Such a pattern is bound to be highly superficial in many aspects in regard to real structural change, but that does not mean it is not deeply appealing. Contrast effects provide a renewable reward resource that can be used and exploited on a mass scale in a thousand different ways. There is risk in such shifting dynamics, but there are also rewards. This is all part of a deep structural shift in which inflated inequality on both an elite and a mass scale is replaced with serial novelty for many and elevated economic inequality for a few. The coexistence of these two groupings is difficult for theorists such as Bauman to accept, but it has its origins deep in our evolved reward release rules.

The coexistence does not imply that there are not widespread problems of one kind or another. The fluid culture form that Bauman describes is one of continual, grinding change requiring constant adjustment and adaptation at all levels of the society. The spread of serial novelty will alter not just consumption patterns but also the nature and appeal of jobs producing these goods and services, as well as the educational preparation for those jobs. Different individuals and groups are going to be more or less able or willing to make such relentless changes and to absorb the risks involved in such changes. Because the mass reward vehicles of inflated inequality and serial novelty are both emergent late in our history, there are always going to be controversies and conflicts within and between such different reward platforms. After all, in terms of our evolutionary origins, neither of the great post-exodus reward-triggering structures of high-contrast familiarity or serial novelty represents "true" human nature. Both bonus packages play with our ancient reward release rules in post-exodus conditions very different than our context of origin in which those rules were forged by natural selection. As a result, both have numerous problematical elements built into them.

On the one hand, if there is nothing inherently natural about static elevated inequality, there will always be conflict and struggles of one kind or another in creating and maintaining any specific social creation embracing such inequality. The collapse of one pyramid will set the stage for the rise of another, and this can go on century after century. As an elite fights within itself, or with other elites, or with non-elites, many will suffer grievously and die early in a dynamic that can never reach a definitive conclusion.

On the other hand, if there is nothing natural about long-term serial novelty, there will always be a host of difficulties based on the self-extinguishing qualities of the reward bonuses offered by such novelty. Many will feel like they are running increasingly harder just to keep up with the erosion of rewards not based on classic high-contrast familiarity. In such a race, liquid modernity will often appear as a glass half full and half empty at any time, making it difficult for many to judge exactly where they stand, thereby producing insecurity and even fear. As the fluid goes global, there will be even more unpredictable elements that can have a negative effect on any temporary success in one country or one part of the world with reward harvesting using this new platform. Furthermore, because so little persists over the long term in these new reward packages, there are bound to be some who look nostalgically for an alternative to the restlessness in such a self-extinguishing pattern. This quest will bring them into conflict, and sometimes violent conflict, with others who no longer embrace a belief in a more fixed package of reward release. Serial novelty is not a panacea that will sooner or later wash away most social problems. It is in many respects preferable to a mass bonus reward vehicle such as collective inflated ascription, but it is not a cure-all. It simply changes many outcomes that in turn create their own set of problems. Of course, one of those problems is that the collective costs of technology-driven serial novelty threaten the earth itself, along with a myriad of species inhabiting this world along with us.

The failure of the Great Recession to trigger much in the way of structural changes reducing economic inequality is one sign of how strong the new combination of reward release structures might be, and how much leeway such a combination might give to elites in accumulating yet more economic resources (Hammond, 2015a). So many who abhor the new fluidity had real hopes that such a severe and prolonged recession might mark the beginning in a shift in perceptions about the validity and sustainability of this fluid world of serial novelty and high inequality; those hopes, however, like earlier hopes about other crises in this new world, have come to little or nothing. So far at least, no other system has accepted so much disruption and, indeed, has so embraced serial disruption. No other system has offered such massively unequal economic rewards for this disruption. The combination is yet to be successfully challenged over the long term.

It is important to remember how persistent inflated inequality was with the first exodus, despite all kinds of problematical elements and massive collateral damage. Its capacity to use contrast effects to addict individuals to its structures in order to make it irresistible for individuals to use in reward triggering might be instructive in regard to the future of serial novelty. Once inflated inequality became available on a mass scale, few could resist, especially when it was linked to another contrast effects creation such as religion. A fluid world of serial novelty could have much the same deep appeal, entwining many interests all wired to be sensitive to these effects. The contrast effects of such novelty are just too appealing, and they come to many with lesser costs than the classic contrast vehicles of elevated inequality. Both are "unnatural" in the sense that they were not a part of our context of origin in which our reward release rules were shaped, but both rely on and manipulate those same rules for their strong appeal. Both are full of contradictions, but both can endure given their deep roots in our ancient reward release rules.

Conclusion

In an emerging fluid world, serial novelty for many can coexist with elevated economic inequality for a few, and this combines two of the most powerful reward windows for contrast effects. With a renewable reward resource such as serial novelty, a fluid culture could be very long-lasting, not in specific details but, rather, in overall longevity, just like the classic premodern cultures built on high-contrast familiarity. Given the impact of contrast effects on reward release, many will not just adapt to the new fluid world but also thrive, just as those who embraced elevated inequality in one form or another thrived with the exodus. Once again, we seem unable as a population to resist such reward vehicles. They create a trail across history, an emergent pattern rooted in our evolutionary heritage when reward release rules were forged so long ago.

References

Aron, A., Fisher, H., Mashek, D. J., Strong, G., Li, H., & Brown, L. L. (2005). Reward, motivation, and emotion systems associated with early-stage intense romantic love. *Journal of Neurophysiology, 94*, 327–337.

Bauman, Z. (2000). *Liquid modernity*. Oxford, UK: Blackwell.

Beck, U. (1992). *Risk society: Towards a new modernity*. London, UK: Sage.

Berridge, K. C., Ho, C. Y., Richard, J. M., & Feliceantonio, A. G. (2010). The tempted brain eats: Pleasure and desire circuits in obesity and eating disorders. *Brain Research, 1350*, 43–64.

Boehm, C. (1999). *Hierarchy in the forest: The evolution of egalitarian behavior*. Cambridge, MA: Harvard University Press.

Boyer, P. (2001). *Religion explained: The human instincts that fashion gods, spirits, and ancestors*. New York, NY: Basic Books.

Bunzeck, N., Doeller, C., Dolan, R., & Duzel, E. (2012). Contextual interaction between novelty and reward processing within the mesolimbic system. *Human Brain Mapping, 33*(6), 1309–1324.

Bunzeck, N., & Duzel, E. (2006). Absolute coding of stimulus novelty in the human substantia nigra/VTA. *Neuron, 51*(3), 369–379.

Chiao, J. Y., Harada, T., Oby, E., Li, Z., Parrish, T., & Bridge, D. (2009). Neural representations of social status hierarchy in human inferior parietal cortex. *Neuropsychologia, 47*, 354–363.

Fisher, H., Aron, A., Mashek, D. J., Li, H., & Brown, L. L. (2002). Defining the brain systems of lust, romantic attraction, and attachment. *Archives of Sexual Behavior, 31*(5), 413–419.

Flaherty, C. F. (1996). *Incentive relativity*. Cambridge, UK: Cambridge University Press.

Granqvist, P., Mikulincer, M., & Shaver, P. R. (2010). Religion as attachment. *Personality and Social Psychology Review, 14*(1), 49–59.

Hammond, M. F. (2012). *Back to the future: The partial reversal in social evolution theories*. Annual meeting of the American Sociological Association, Denver, CO.

Hammond, M. F. (2013). The neurosociology of reward release, repetition, and social emergence. In D. Franks & J. Turner (Eds.), *Handbook of neurosociology* (pp. 311–329). New York, NY: Springer.

Hammond, M. F. (2015a). Contrast effects in social evolution and Schumpeter's creative destruction. In J. Turner, R. Machalek, & A. Maryanski (Eds.), *Handbook of evolution and society: Toward an evolutionary social science* (pp. 609–628). Boulder, CO: Paradigm.

Hammond, M. F. (2015b). *Reward allowances and contrast effects in social evolution: A challenge to Bauman's liquid modernity*. Annual meeting of the American Sociological Association, Chicago, IL.

Izuma, K., Saito, D. N., & Sadato, N. (2008). Processing of social and monetary rewards in the human striatum. *Neuron, 58*(2), 284–294.

Johnson, A. W., & Earle, T. (2000). *The evolution of human societies*. Stanford, CA: Stanford University Press.

Kakade, S. M., & Dayan, P. (2002). Dopamine: Generalization and bonuses. *Neural Networks, 15,* 549–559.

Kirkpatrick, L. A., & Granqvist, P. (2008). Attachment and religious representations and behavior. In J. Cassidy & P. R. Shaver (Eds.), *Handbook of attachment* (pp. 906–933). New York, NY: Guilford.

Ly, M., Haynes, M. R., Barter, J. W., Weinberger, D. R., & Zink, C. F. (2011). Subjective socioeconomic status predicts human ventral striatal responses to social status information. *Current Biology, 21*(9), 794–797.

Martinez, D., Orlowska, D., Narendran, R., Slifstein, M., Liu, F., Kumar, D., . . . Kleber, H. D. (2010). Dopamine type 2/3 receptor availability in the striatum and social status in human volunteers. *Biological Psychiatry, 67*(3), 275–278.

McNamara, P. (2009). *The neuroscience of religious experience*. Cambridge, UK: Cambridge University Press.

Montague, P. R., & Berns, G. S. (2002). Neural economics and the biological substrates of valuation. *Neuron, 36*(2), 265–284.

Montague, P. R., King-Casas, B., & Cohen, J. D. (2006). Imaging valuation models in human choice. *Annual Review of Neuroscience, 29,* 417–448.

Newberg, A. B., d'Aquili, E., & Rause, V. (2001). *Why God won't go away: Brain science and the biology of belief*. New York, NY: Ballantine.

Rolls, E. T., Murzi, E., Yaxley, S., Thrope, S. J., & Simpson, S. J. (1986). Sensory specific satiety: Food-specific reduction in responsiveness of ventral forebrain neurons after feeding in the monkey. *Brain Research, 368,* 79–86.

Saxe, R., & Haushofer, J. (2008). For love or money: A common neural currency for social and monetary reward. *Neuron, 58*(2), 164–165.

Williams, B. A. (1997). Varieties of contrast: A review of incentive relativity by Charles F. Flaherty. *Journal of the Experimental Analysis of Behavior, 68*(1), 133–141.

Zink, C. F., Tong, Y., Chen, Q., Bassett, D. S., Stein, J. L., & Mayer-Lindenberg, A. (2008). Know your place: Neural processing of social hierarchy in humans. *Neuron, 58*(2), 273–283.

CHAPTER 8

....

SEX DIFFERENCES IN
THE HUMAN BRAIN

....

DAVID D. FRANKS

THE contents of this chapter[1] derive from the perspective of neurosociology. Many still view anything concerned with biology, including the human brain, as deterministic and reductionist, but this view reflects an unfamiliarity with the field. Even leading neurologists such as Damasio (1994) have long decried the kind of reductionism that does not give the social processes its due. It may still be useful to quote Damasio's aged and classic statement about this:

> I am not attempting to reduce social phenomena to biological phenomenon, but rather to discuss the powerful connection between them. It should be clear that although culture and civilization arise from the behavior of biological individuals, the behavior was generated by collectivities of behavior interaction in social environments. Culture and civilization could not have arisen from singular individuals and thus cannot be reduced to biological mechanisms, and even less, can they be reduced to a subset of genetic specifications. Their comprehension demand not just general biology and neurobiology but the methodologies of the social sciences.

Another Nobel Prize-winning neuroscientist, Gerald Edelman (1992), joins the chorus with Damasio:

> To reduce a theory of individual behavior to a theory of molecular reactions is simply silly, a point made clear when one considers how many different levels of physical, biological and social interaction must be put into place before high-level consciousness emerges.

Neurosociology is thus firmly rooted in social psychology's basic unit of analysis, which is at least two persons interacting with each other and very frequently changing each other's behavior (Franks, 2010, p. 10).

Just how social the human brain is can hardly be overstated. Mathew Lieberman (2013, p. 18) talks of our default network that comes on like a reflex when other tasks are completed and one is thought to be doing nothing. However, using positron emission tomography scans, Lieberman found that humans are literally always thinking of something, and that something is other people—"making sense of them and ourselves." Our default mechanism is both reflexive or automatic and social to the core. Lieberman and colleagues gave people math problems to solve with only seconds between them. Instead of getting ready for the next problem, people impulsively started thinking of others and their relations with them. According to Lieberman (2013), "Evolution made a big bet on using our social intelligence for the overall success of our species by focusing the brain's full time on it" (pp. 19–20).

One of the numerous pieces of evidence supporting Lieberman's (2013) statement has been supplied by Steve Cole(2016). He, along with John Cacioppo (Cacioppo & Patrick, 2008), has shown how loneliness places people at significantly greater risk for heart attacks, metastatic cancer, Alzheimer's disease, and other ills. Cole has even determined why this is so. It has to do with social isolation's strong tendency to turn up the activity of genes responsible for inflammation and turn down the activity of genes that produce antibodies to fight infection.

DIFFERENCES IN SEX AND GENDER

Here, we must ask the question, What is a chapter on sex differences doing in a handbook of evolution, biology and society? Much of the answer has to do with the differences between sex and gender. According to Tim Newmann (2016), in the recent past the terms have been used interchangeably, but currently the meaning of these words have become more distinct. Most often, *sex* means biologically set differences in females and males, whereas *gender* has to do with something more sociological—the social role of males and females in society. Transgendered persons, of course, possess either male or female sex differences, but they prefer acting like the role of the opposite sex identity. Thus, some men who have the identity of female may talk in ways considered unmanly, but many—perhaps most—do not. The more "objective" or scientific sex of a person is defined by the person's genetics. Females have 46 chromosomes (thread-like bodies that carry genes) plus two X's. Men have 46 chromosomes and an X and a Y. The Y chromosome is dominant and signals the embryo to grow testicles. Sex is often, or mostly, considered in a "one or the other," black or white manner, but there is in fact a significant amount of middle ground. Some believe it should be viewed as a continuum instead of in an "either–or" manner.

There was a time when some people argued that sex or gender differences in the human brain were nonexistent, but today the available data make such arguments very difficult. It is true that a small number of researchers say these differences are minimal, but there is much to say about the differences that do exist. For example, in *The Female Brain*, Louann Brizentine (2006) begins with an uncontested statement:

> More than 99% of male and female genetic coding is exactly the same. Out of the thirty thousand genes in the human genome, the less than one percent of the variation between the sexes influences every cell in our bodies—from the nerves that register pleasure and pain to the neurons and their synapsis that transmit information to perception, thoughts, feelings and emotions.

Male brains are larger by 9% even after correction for body size. In the 19th century, scientists took that to mean that women had less thought capacity than men. It is now known that women and men have the same number of brain cells. The cells are just packed more densely in women—cinched corset like into a smaller skull.

When dealing with sex differences in the brain, as in any other sociological endeavor, we need to remember that facts must be related to theories. It follows from this that the important question "So what?" is frequently not asked. Next, I highlight the problems and issues that address this question.

SOCIAL RELATIONSHIPS AND SEX DIFFERENCES

As many people know through personal experience, females are more adept at being attuned to other's emotions and simply human relationships in general. This should remind us of the overlap between the sexes in all these generalizations. There are always exceptions. This may well be partly due to the fact that the ventromedial prefrontal lobe of women's brains is larger than that of men. The reader might be aware of the famous case of Phineas Gage, who unwittingly drove a spike through his ventromedial prefrontal lobe, leaving him unable to control his temper, make decisions, and get along with others.

This same area is named the "straight gyrus" (SG) and runs through the middle of the bottom of the prefrontal cortex. After correcting for brain size, Wood and Eagly (2002) found that the SG was 10% larger in women than in men. The size of the SG correlated with tests of interpersonal capacities for both sexes. This correlation was even higher when specifically gender traits, such as choices in clothes, interests, hobbies, and careers, were considered. Remember that the human brain is plastic in the sense that long-term behavior can actually change it. We need to ask, then, whether the female's larger SG is the result of long-term socialization or is the cause of social sensitivity. Wood and co-authors next examined these differences from an evolutionary perspective. Here, the plasticity of the brain allowed for the likely possibility that the SG of women's brains grew larger because they had been caretakers of children for many thousands of years.

GRAY AND WHITE MATTER

In a sample of 7,934 brains, men had 9% larger gray matter compared to women. Herein are located the synapses that join and communicate with other neurons. This neuron-to-neuron communication supplies the driving force of the brain and literally makes it work. It is a dark, knobby tissue containing the core of nerve cells.

In a sample of 7,515 brains, white matter took up 13% more space in women than in men. This is because of myelin, which is a fatty substance that lubricates nerve fiber, making communications to other fibers faster. White matter consists of myelinated axons that provide communications between neurons or gray areas and connect with different regions. They regulate electric signals in the axons.

Another major study of sex differences in the human brain from 1990 to 2013 included brains from birth to 80 years old. In a sample of 14,000 brains, males on average had more intracranial space (12%) compared to women. The cortex covers the brain's surface, with convoluted ridges allowing it to fit inside the skull. The brain has been divided into four lobes: the frontal lobes, which enable cognition and thought; the parietal lobe, which is associated with movement and perception; the occipital lobe, which enables visualization; and the temporal lobe, which enables memory and speech. Gray matter was 9% larger in men compared to women in a sample of 7,934 brains.

Female brains have more neurons in certain areas because more estrogen bathes them during early development. In boys, this same "bath" is testosterone, which enhances other parts of the brain as early as 26 weeks of the mother's pregnancy. Thus, boys and girls have different tendencies as soon as they come into the world. These can then be worked on differently by the social environment. Wood et al. (2007) note that the corpus callosum connecting the right and left hemispheres of the brain is thicker in females than in males. Wood et al. (2007) read a novel to both sexes, with the result being that females had both hemispheres involved whereas males used only the cognitively oriented left brain to listen. This helps explain why females have stronger language skills compared to males.

In terms of language abilities, women are more accurate in identifying emotions as well as identifying facial changes and distinguishing between vocal intonations in contrasts. The brain circuits going from the prefrontal lobes to the amygdale, the seat of emotions, are larger in females than in males. However, both Wood et al. (2007) and Ruben Gur (Ingalhalikar et al., 2014) think that the brain variations between sexes that do exist are for the best, complimenting each other. According to Gur (Kogler et al., 2016), they help the whole species. However, there are exceptions. Cordelia Fine (2011) was one of the first to note that wiring differences are an effect of brain size, but this tells us nothing about sex differences in behavior.

Inattention is characteristic of girls, whereas boys have difficulty with impulse control. There are differences in researcher's opinions here, however. Gina Rippon (2015) insists that gender differences are the result of environmental factors rather than being innate or hardwired. Lisa Eliot (2009) joins Rippon against assuming that these differences are hardwired and inevitable. Many differences in our plastic brains are due to cultural socialization, and this too gives us brain differences that appear to be hardwired but are not.

Ruben Gur (Kogler et al., 2016) also worked in the area of male and female brain differences, but he failed to include data on "effect size." He also ignored gendered factors such as hobbies. In addition, he used stereotyped speculation on how such brain wiring could cause behavioral distinctions between the sexes. There is more disagreement about sex differences in the brain, but enough has been said previously for the reader to understand that many researchers think that sex differences in brain size are significant.

To make the issue more difficult, Kate Wheeling (2015) joins some others who insist that the brains of men and women are not very different—that is, brains do not fit neatly into male and female. She says that it is true that men "have a larger amygdala than women but the differences are small and sensitive to the environment." The brain is hardly hardwired in this view.

Wheeling (2015) is also among those who think brain differences are overdone. She states, "Our brains share a patchwork of forms: some that are more common in males, some that are more common in females and some that are common to both.

With the use of functional magnetic resonance imaging to obtain images of the brain, scientists could verify that men have a larger amygdala, the seat of emotions. In terms of gender roles, emotionality is supposed to be associated with females. The left hippocampus, which is involved with memory, is usually larger in men. However, each region has significant overlap between the sexes. This is interesting in light of the previous discussion about sex differences being placed on a continuum rather than being seen in an "either–or" manner. Wheeling (2015) reports that researchers created a continuum of maleness to femaleness for the entire brain. Then they scored every subject on where they fell on the continuum. The majority of brains were a mosaic of male and female structures. Between 23% and 53% of the brains revealed a mix of regions falling on the female and male ends of the continuum. Only a modicum of brains contained all male or all female structures—between 0% and 8%. The conclusion is that there is no one type of male or female brain.

This raises the question of why men and women act differently, which can only be answered by gender roles, or, says Joel Daphna (2015), "that too may be a myth." In a more practical vein, she says that the extreme variability of human brains undermines the justification for single-sex education. I qualify this position by adding that there are other reasons that justify single-sex schools.

Also, it is a well-known fact that females are 40–50% more likely than males to suffer from depression. This is an important finding that reflects why we should, indeed, study male and female brains. Also, instead of merely asking about sex differences that exist and how large they are, we need to ask how they function. In general, Daphna's (2015) call for us to stop assuming that sex differences matter may be going way too far.

Larry Cahill (2014) mounts a convincing argument that sex differences in the brain exist and they are important. He begins by citing the 2013 US Food and Drug

Administration's directive to cut the recommended dose of the well-known sleeping aid Ambien in half, but only for women. The explanation was that the biomedical community had long assumed that biological sex did not matter for the brain, but as of 2013, it knew better. Neuroscientists had known that the hypothalamus, a deep brain structure, controlled the production of hormones and affected sleep patterns. Where they erred was in studying only men, under the assumption that there were no brain differences between the sexes. Animal studies also were only performed on males for the same reason. A large study on both sexes, however, found differently. The brains of women revealed much stronger patterns of connectivity across brain hemispheres and other regions. This is due to females having more white matter so that neuron-to-neuron connections are more efficient in women compared to men. Again, we find that biology supersedes gender. The brain is plastic and amenable to change, but only within the limits set by biology. Cahill's summary statement is that brains across the sexes may be equal, but they are not the same.

SEX DIFFERENCES IN PATHOLOGY

Consistent with Cahill (2014), McCarthy et al. (2009) study of sex differences in the human brain has become recognized as important because of the light it sheds on neuropsychiatric disorders. Sex differences are involved in numerous disorders, including attention deficit hyperactivity disorder, autism, post-traumatic stress disorder, bulimia, anorexia, late-onset schizophrenia, depression, and anxiety. Multiple sclerosis is four times more frequent in women. It is vital to determine what in the brain causes these differences and how. Mong and Cusmano (2016) also take the position that aspects of sleep disorders may occur at different rates in women than in men. Insomnia is 40% more common in females. Sleep disorder is a risk factor in depression, which is also 40% more frequent in women. According to Eden and Grigorenko (2014), dyslexia is two or three times more prevalent in males than in females. Symptoms also differ. McCarthy et al. (2009) calls attention to the fact that the "exploratory power of comparing and contrasting males and females can not be overstated and will not go away any time soon." She reasonably concludes that sex differences in the brain are essential for understanding neuropathology. An important question here is the following: How much difference does it make to take a difference?

CONCLUSION

In a handbook on evolution, biology, and society, it can be argued including a chapter that considers the sex differences in the human brain is important, perhaps especially for those sociologists whose expertise and interests lie elsewhere. Certainly, as this chapter demonstrates, the days when some could state that there are no sex differences in the brain should be over, even if these differences are by no means large. There is clearly no one type of male and female brain. I have also drawn attention to the fact that the brain is plastic and can change itself. In addition to the differences that biologically exist in the brain, age after age of being the primary socializer of infants can change the brain's makeup. As Lieberman (2013) has argued effectively, our brains are hardwired to be extremely social. The field of neurosociology testifies to this (see especially the works of Franks, 2010; Kalkhoff, Thye, & Pollock, 2016). We have also seen that sex differences in the brain have a significant impact on various mental disorders, especially depression and schizophrenia. Although sex differences are important, a great deal of what happens is genetic and occurs in the womb.

NOTE

1. Much of the contents of this chapter were derived from Savic (2010).

REFERENCES

Brizentine, L. (2006). *The female brain*. New York, NY: Three Rivers Press.

Cacioppo, J., & Patrick, W. (2008). *Loneliness*. New York, NY: Norton.

Cahill, L. (2014). *Equal is not the same: Sex differences in the human brain*. New York, NY: The Dana Foundation.

Cole, S. (2016, March 21). What the health effects of loneliness say about illness and cell activity. *Medical and Research News*.

Damasio, A. (1994). *Descartes's error: Emotion, reason, and the human brain*. New York, NY: Avon.

Eden, J., & Grigorenko, E. (2014). *The dyslexia debate* (Cambridge Studies in Perceptual Development No. 14). New York, NY: Cambridge University Press.

Eliot, L. (2009). *Pink brain, blue brain: How small differences grow into troublesome gaps—and what we can do about them*. Boston, MA: Houghton Mifflin Harcourt.

Fine, C. (2011). *Delusions of gender: How our minds, society and neurosexism create differences*. New York, NY: Norton.

Franks, D. (2010). *Neurosociology: The nexus between neuroscience and social psychology*. New York, NY: Springer.

Ingalhalikar, M., Smith, A., Parker, D., Satterthwaite, T.D., Elliott, M.A., Ruparel, K., Hakonarson, H., Gur, R.E., Gur, R.C. & Verma, R. (2014). Sex differences in the structural connectome of the human brain. *Proceedings of the National Academy of Sciences, 111*(2), 823–828.

Joel, D., Berman, Z., Tavor, I., Wexler, N., Gaber, O., Stein, Y., Shefi, N., Pool, J., Urchs, S., Margulies, D.S. & Liem, F. (2015). Sex beyond the genitalia: The human brain mosaic. *Proceedings of the National Academy of Sciences, 112*(50), 15468–15473.

Kalkhoff, W., Thye, S. R., & Pollock, J. (2016). Developments in neurosociology. *Sociology Compass, 10*, 242–258.

Kogler, L., Müller, V. I., Seidel, E. M., Boubela, R., Kalcher, K., Moser, E., . . . Dernt, B. (2016). Sex differences in the functional connectivity of the amygdala Associated with cortisol. *Neuroimage, 134*, 410–423.

Lieberman, M. (2013). *Social: Why our brains are wired to connect*. New York, NY: Crown.

Lippa, R. (2009). Sex differences in sex drive, sociosexuality and height across 53 nations: Testing evolutionary and social structural theories. *Archives of Sexual Behavior, 38,* 631–651.

McCarthy, M. M., Auger, A. P., Bale, T. L., De Vries, G. J., Dunn, G. A., Forger, N. G., Murray, E.K., Nugent, B.M., Schwarz, J.M. and Wilson, M. E. (2009). The epigenetics of sex differences in the brain. *Journal of Neuroscience, 29*(41), 12815–12823.

McGaugh, J. L. (2013). Making lasting memories: Remembering the significant. *Proceedings of the National Academy of Sciences of the USA, 110,* 10402–10407.

Mong, J., & Cusmano, D. (2016, February 19). Sex differences in sleep impact of biological sex and sex steroids. *Philosophical Transactions of the Royal Society B Biological Sciences, 371*(1688).

Newman, T. (2016, March 24). Sex and gender: What is the difference? *Medical News Today.*

Rippon, G. (2015, November 30). A welcome blow to the myth of distinct male and female brains. *New Scientist, 30.*

Savic, J. (Ed.). (2010). *Progress in brain research* (Vol. 18). New York, NY: Elsevier.

Wheeling, K. (2015, November 30). The brains of men and women aren't really that different. *Science.*

Wood, W., & Eagly, A. (2002). A cross-cultural analysis of the behavior of women and men: Implications for the origin of sex differences. *Psychological Bulletin, 128,* 699–727.

Wood, J. L., Heitmiller, D., Andreasen, N. C. & Nopoulos, P., (2007). Morphology of the ventral frontal cortex: relationship to femininity and social cognition. *Cerebral Cortex, 18*(3), 534–540.

CHAPTER 9

THE SAVANNA THEORY
OF HAPPINESS

SATOSHI KANAZAWA AND NORMAN P. LI

HAPPINESS is a topic that has received significant attention in recent years, as researchers and governments alike have become increasingly interested (Diener, Oishi, & Lucas, 2015). For Americans, happiness has always been important, as evidenced by "happiness" appearing twice in the Declaration of Independence and even a third time in an earlier draft penned by Thomas Jefferson. More recently, Baker (2014) identified the pursuit of happiness as one of 10 core American values. Happiness, however, is not just an American or Western concept (Oishi, Graham, Kesebir, & Galinha, 2013). In Bhutan, for example, gross national happiness (GNH) has replaced gross domestic product (GDP) as the country's main development indicator (Biswas-Diener, Diener, & Lyubchik, 2015).

In the past few decades, positive psychologists have accumulated an impressive amount of knowledge on who is happier than whom, when, and how (Diener, 2012). Yet, despite all the attention and research, very little if anything is known about *why* some individuals are happier than others. In this chapter, we describe an evolutionary perspective called the *savanna theory of happiness* (Kanazawa & Li, 2015; Li & Kanazawa, 2016), which, along with various lines of associated empirical support, can potentially explain a great deal of *why* some individuals garner happiness more easily than others.

THE SAVANNA THEORY OF HAPPINESS

With a few exceptions (Diener, Kanazawa, Suh, & Oishi, 2015; Heintzelman & King, 2014), positive psychologists have not drawn on insights from evolutionary psychology, the branch of psychology that deals with ultimate causations of psychological phenomena (Buss, 1995; Cosmides & Tooby, 2013; Tooby & Cosmides, 1992). One of the fundamental observations in evolutionary psychology is that, just like any other organ of any other species, the human brain is designed for and adapted to the conditions of the ancestral environment, not necessarily the current environment, and is therefore pre-disposed to perceive and respond to the current environment as if it were the ances-tral environment (Tooby & Cosmides, 1990). Known variously as the *Savanna Principle* (Kanazawa, 2004b), the *evolutionary legacy hypothesis* (Burnham & Johnson, 2005), or the *mismatch hypothesis* (Hagen & Hammerstein, 2006; Li, Lim, Tsai, & O, 2015), this observation suggests that the human brain may have difficulty comprehending and dealing with entities and situations that did not exist in the ancestral environment, roughly the African savanna during the Pleistocene Epoch.

The Savanna Principle explains why some otherwise elegant scientific theories of human behavior, such as game theory, often fail empirically, because they posit enti-ties and situations that did not exist in the ancestral environment. For example, nearly half the players of one-shot prisoner's dilemma games make the theoretically irrational choice to cooperate with their partner (Sally, 1995). The Savanna Principle suggests that this may be because the human brain has difficulty comprehending completely anon-ymous social exchange and absolutely no possibility of knowing future interactions (which together make the game truly one-shot and defection the only rational choice) (Hagen & Hammerstein, 2006; Kanazawa, 2001). Neither of these situations existed in the ancestral environment, where all social exchanges were in person and poten-tially repeated; however, they are crucial for the game-theoretic prediction of universal defection.

Further, recent developments in evolutionary psychology indicate that general intel-ligence may have evolved to solve evolutionarily novel problems (Kanazawa, 2004a, 2010). *Evolutionarily novel* problems are those that our ancestors did not encounter routinely and repeatedly in the ancestral environment, whereas *evolutionarily famil-iar* problems are those that our ancestors encountered routinely and repeatedly in the ancestral environment. Psychological mechanisms evolved to solve adaptive problems that recurrently presented themselves in different domains of life throughout human evolutionary history, such as social exchange, infant care, and incest avoidance (Tooby & Cosmides, 1990). They are domain-specific and operate only within narrow domains of life, taking as input very specific types of information.

Recent theoretical developments suggest that general intelligence may also have evolved as such a domain-specific evolved psychological mechanism. It may have evolved to allow individuals to solve a wide variety of *non-recurrent* adaptive challenges that also directly or indirectly affected survival or reproduction. All such non-recurrent adaptive problems were *evolutionarily novel.* General intelligence may thus have evolved to solve evolutionarily novel problems, as a psychological adaptation for the domain of evolutionary novelty.

This suggests that the evolutionary constraints on the human brain—on the opera-tions of the evolved psychological mechanisms—proposed by the Savanna Principle may be stronger among less intelligent individuals than among more intelligent individ-uals. Even though all humans may have these evolutionary constraints on their brain, making it more difficult to comprehend and deal with evolutionarily novel entities and situations, such constraints may operate to a greater extent among less intelligent individuals than among more intelligent individuals. Less intelligent individuals may therefore have greater difficulty comprehending and dealing with such evolutionarily novel entities and situations than more intelligent people do. More intelligent individuals, who possess higher levels of general intelligence and thus greater ability to solve evolutionarily novel problems, may face less difficulty in comprehending and dealing with evolutionarily novel entities and situations than less intelligent individuals do.

Consistent with this reasoning, more intelligent individuals are more likely to make the theoretically rational choice to defect in one-shot prisoner's dilemma games (Kanazawa & Fontaine, 2013). This may be because more intelligent individuals are better able to comprehend the evolutionarily novel situations of complete anonymity and absolutely no possibility of knowing future interactions and make the rational decision to defect. In contrast, less intelligent individuals may have greater difficulty comprehending such evolutionarily novel situations, and, as a result, make the theoretically irrational (*albeit evolutionarily rational*) decision to cooperate.

The Savanna Principle in evolutionary psychology, applied to happiness, suggests that it may not be only the consequences of a given situation in the current environment that influence individuals' happiness but also what its consequences *would have been* in the ancestral environment. Having implicit difficulty comprehending and dealing with evolutionarily novel situations, the human brain may respond to the ancestral consequences of the current situation and individuals' happiness may fluctuate accordingly. Further, the effect of such ancestral consequences of current situations on happiness may be greater among less intelligent individuals, for whom the evolutionary constraints specified by the Savanna Principle are stronger, than among more intelligent individuals, for whom they are weaker.

The savanna theory of happiness therefore suggests that, having implicit difficulty comprehending and dealing with evolutionarily novel situations, the human brain may respond to the ancestral consequences of the current situation and individuals' happiness may fluctuate accordingly. Situations and circumstances that would have increased our ancestors' happiness in the ancestral environment may still increase our happiness today, and those that would have decreased their happiness then may still decrease ours today. The savanna theory further suggests that such effects of ancestral consequences on current happiness may be stronger among less intelligent individuals than among more intelligent individuals.

Positive psychologists have long debated the precise definition of happiness and related concepts, such as life satisfaction and subjective well-being (Miao, Koo, & Oishi, 2013; Oishi et al., 2013; Pavot & Diener, 2013). The savanna theory of happiness is not committed to any particular definition and is compatible with any reasonable conception of happiness, subjective well-being, and life satisfaction (cognitive vs. affective; hedonic vs. eudaimonic, etc.). The theory does, however, treat happiness as a state, rather than a trait; it cannot by itself explain the (partly genetically determined) "happiness set point" (Headey & Wearing, 1989), to which individuals tend to return after momentary and situational perturbations to their baseline levels of happiness. The theory instead explains such temporary and situational fluctuations from the happiness baseline as a function of the potential evolutionary consequences of the current situations and circumstances.

Available Evidence in Support of the Theory

Various lines of evidence have recently come to light with regard to the savanna theory of happiness. We describe below such empirical evidence in a variety of domains in life.

Ethnic Differences in Happiness

There are observable ethnic differences in happiness (Krause, 1993; Okazaki, 1997; Scollon, Diener, Oishi, & Biswas-Diener, 2004).[1] However, there currently exist no comprehensive explanations for such ethnic differences. The savanna theory of happiness provides one potential explanation.

Our ancestors lived their entire lives in ethnically homogeneous groups (Oppenheimer, 2003). A multiethnic society like the United States today is a very recent phenomenon in human evolutionary history. Perhaps the clearest evidence of the evolutionary novelty of ethnic diversity is the fact that, while humans appear to possess evolved psychological mechanisms to classify others automatically by sex and age, they do not possess a comparable mechanism to classify them by ethnicity (Kurzban, Tooby, & Cosmides, 2001). From the perspective of the Savanna Principle, this may be because individuals of varied sexes and ages existed in the ancestral environment and thus were evolutionarily familiar, whereas individuals of varied ethnicities did not exist in the ancestral environment and thus are evolutionarily novel.

In the ancestral environment, being among others who dressed, looked, spoke, and behaved differently from oneself usually meant that one was captured or abducted by a neighboring group or at the very least that one was living without the assistance and cooperation of one's genetic kin and allies. Even though people of different ethnicities can and do live together harmoniously in modern multiethnic societies, being an outgroup minority would have been precarious in the ancestral environment, as neighboring tribes were often unfriendly (Diamond, 2012).

Thus, despite the fact that living among others of different ethnicities today, especially in multiethnic societies like the United States, poses very few negative consequences that threaten survival and reproduction, the human brain, designed for and adapted to the ancestral environment, may nonetheless experience such situations as a potential threat, as it would have been in the ancestral environment. Individuals may consequently experience lower levels of happiness. For instance, in a recent study, using an ingenious within-subject design, Burrow and Hill (2013) showed that train passengers experienced increased distress and negative mood when they were surrounded by passengers of different ethnicities. The savanna theory of happiness therefore suggests that the human brain may implicitly experience being surrounded by others of different ethnicities and being an ethnic minority as a potential threat, and, accordingly, happiness may be lower in such circumstances.

The theory further suggests that such an effect of living as an ethnic minority among others of different ethnicities on happiness may be stronger among less intelligent individuals. More intelligent individuals may be better able to comprehend the evolutionarily novel situation of ethnic diversity and living as an ethnic minority for what it generally is today—benign and safe. In contrast, less intelligent individuals may have greater difficulty comprehending the same evolutionarily novel situation of ethnic diversity and living as an ethnic minority and may perceive it as if it were in the ancestral environment—potentially dangerous and threatening. Accordingly, less intelligent individuals' happiness may decrease to a greater degree than that of more intelligent individuals when faced with ethnic diversity and living as an ethnic minority. The theory would therefore suggest that ethnic diversity and intelligence may have a statistical interaction effect on happiness.

Specifically, the degree of ethnic *homogeneity*—the extent to which one lives among others of the same ethnicity—may have a positive effect on happiness and further that such an effect of ethnic homogeneity on happiness will be stronger among less intelligent individuals. In particular, it would lead us to predict that, in a society with a clear ethnic majority population like the United States, the majority—White Americans—will experience greater happiness than all other ethnic groups, but such ethnic differences in happiness will disappear once the ethnic composition of the immediate environment is controlled. It would also lead us to predict that the statistical effect of ethnic composition on happiness will interact significantly with individual's intelligence.

An analysis of the National Longitudinal Study of Adolescent Health (Add Health) confirmed both of these predictions (Kanazawa & Li, 2015). Relative to the reference category of White Americans, all ethnic minorities had significantly lower life satisfaction, even when we controlled for sex, age, education, and current marital status.[2] However, once we controlled for the proportion of the state population that was the same ethnicity as the respondent, African Americans and Native Americans no longer had lower life satisfaction than White Americans. While Asian Americans still had lower overall satisfaction than White Americans, this difference was significantly smaller in states with larger Asian populations. The state ethnic composition itself had a marginally significantly positive association with life satisfaction.

The results were the same if we controlled for the proportion of the county population that was the same ethnicity as the respondent. African Americans and Native Americans no longer had lower life satisfaction than White Americans, and, while Asian Americans were still less satisfied overall than White Americans, this difference was significantly smaller in counties in which the Asian population was larger. The county ethnic composition itself had a statistically significantly positive association with life satisfaction.

Figure 9.1 shows the statistical effect of county ethnic composition on ethnic differences in life satisfaction. The left panel shows that, in the full sample of Add Health respondents, White Americans had significantly higher life satisfaction (M = 4.19)

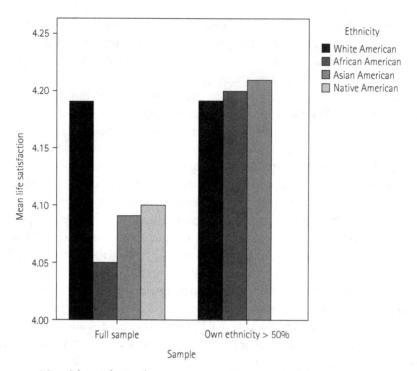

FIGURE 9.1 Mean life satisfaction by county proportion own ethnicity.

Source: Reprinted from *Journal of Research in Personality, 59*, Satoshi Kanazawa
and Norman P. Li, Happiness in modern society: Why intelligence and ethnic composition matter, 111–120,
Copyright (2015), with permission from Elsevier.

than African Americans (4.05), Asian Americans (4.09), and Native Americans (4.10) ($F(3, 14773) = 26.868, p < .001$). Among Add Health respondents who lived in counties that consisted of 50% or more of their own ethnicity (right panel), however, there were no ethnic differences in life satisfaction ($F(2, 9624) = .004, p = .996$). In fact, White Americans ($M = 4.19$) had very slightly (though nonsignificantly) *lower* life satisfaction than African Americans (4.20) and Asian Americans (4.21). (There were no Native American respondents in Add Health who lived in majority-Native American counties.)

Further statistical analyses showed that, consistent with the prediction, the association between ethnic composition and life satisfaction was significantly stronger among less intelligent individuals than among more intelligent individuals. The interaction term between intelligence and ethnic composition was significantly negative for both state and county. Figure 9.2 presents the statistical interaction effect graphically. Among less intelligent individuals (with a mean IQ of 81.39, one standard deviation below the mean), county ethnic composition had a relatively large association with life satisfaction. Those living in a county with a high (.9102) proportion of own ethnicity indicated greater life satisfaction ($M = 4.192$) than those living in a low (.2816) proportion did (4.071). In contrast, among more intelligent individuals (with a mean IQ of 115.57, one standard deviation above the mean), there was a much smaller difference in life satisfaction between those living in a high proportion of their own ethnicity (4.205) and those living in a low proportion (4.174).

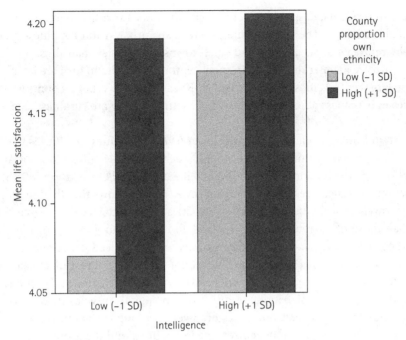

FIGURE 9.2 Interaction effect between intelligence and county ethnic composition on life satisfaction.

Source: Reprinted from *Journal of Research in Personality, 59*, Satoshi Kanazawa and Norman P. Li, Happiness in modern society: Why intelligence and ethnic composition matter, 111–120, Copyright (2015), with permission from Elsevier.

Wave III of Add Health measured other affective states besides life satisfaction, such as depression and self-esteem. However, the patterns of ethnic differences in depression and self-esteem were completely different from those in life satisfaction (Kanazawa & Li, 2015, p. 115). While Asian Americans had the lowest level of life satisfaction, they had the lowest level of depression. At the same time, while White Americans had the highest level of life satisfaction, they had the highest level of depression. And, consistent with previous studies (Graham, 1994; Tashakkori & Thompson, 1991), African Americans had a significantly higher mean level of self-esteem than any other ethnic group. It therefore appeared that the pattern of ethnic differences in life satisfaction that we documented above, where all ethnic minorities had significantly lower levels of life satisfaction than White Americans, and that we partially explained as a function of local ethnic composition, may be unique to life satisfaction and not shared by other affective states like depression and self-esteem.

Population Density

Ruralites in economically developed nations tend to be happier than their urbanite counterparts (Berry & Okulicz-Kozaryn, 2009; Easterlin, Angelescu, & Zweig, 2011).[3] Even in the still-developing China, rural residents report higher levels of happiness than urban residents, despite the fact that city dwellers are vastly wealthier (Knight & Gunatilaka, 2010). In the United States, there is an "urban–rural happiness gradient," whereby residents of rural areas and small towns are happier than those in suburbs, who in turn are happier than those in small central cities, who in turn are happier than those in large central cities (Berry & Okulicz-Kozaryn, 2011). What accounts for the differences in happiness across these residential settings? Why are ruralites happier than urbanites?

A current leading explanation for the lower level of happiness in cities is that urban life is accompanied by numerous "social ills," such as anomie, alienation, social disorganization, and depression (Berry & Okulicz-Kozaryn, 2011; Evans, 2009; Wirth, 1938). A functional magnetic resonance imaging (fMRI) study shows that the brains of current city dwellers and those who grew up in cities respond to stress with greater activities than those of current country dwellers and those who grew up in the country (Lederbogen et al., 2011). These studies, however, simply raise further questions: *Why* does the human brain perceive urban life, but not rural life, as stressful, alienating, and depressing? *Why* does urban life, but not rural life, induce alienation and depression?

The savanna theory of happiness offers one potential answer. There is converging evidence to suggest that our ancestors lived in groups of about 150 individuals. Comparative data on relative neocortex size in the brain and the group size among 38 genera of primates suggest that the natural size for human groups given its neocortex ratio is about 150 (Dunbar, 1992). Indeed, the mean band or village size of nine modern hunter-gatherer societies is 148.4 (Dunbar, 1993). Computer simulations of the evolution of risk aversion suggest that it can only evolve in small groups of about 150 individuals (Hintze, Olson, Adami, & Hertwig, 2013). The mean size of personal networks suggested by the number of annual Christmas cards sent is 153.5 (Hill & Dunbar, 2003). The mean size of social networks suggested by two "small world" experiments is 134 (Killworth, Bernard, & McCarty, 1984). The typical size of Neolithic villages in Mesopotamia was 150–200 (Oates, 1977); the mean size of Hutterite farming communities in Canada is 107 (Mange & Mange, 1980); and the mean size of Amish parishes in central Pennsylvania is 112.8 (Hurd, 1985). The typical size of military unit in the classical Roman army was 120–130, and the mean company size of armies in World War II was 180 (MacDonald, 1955). Gautney and Holliday (2015) estimate the population density in Africa and Eurasia during the Pleistocene Epoch to be between .03 and .12 individuals per square kilometer, about one-tenth of the population density of the least dense state in the United States (Alaska = .46 individuals/km^2) in 2010 but denser than the least dense counties in the United States (Yukon-Koyukuk Census Area, Alaska = .015; and Lake and Peninsula County, Alaska = .027).

When the number of individuals in a group exceeds 150–200, the group typically fissions into and forms two separate groups, because in larger groups social organization based on cooperation and reciprocity becomes exceedingly difficult (Chagnon, 1979). Because the major constraint on human group size is cognitive (Dunbar, 1992, 1993), it is possible that as the population density becomes too high, the human brain feels uneasy and uncomfortable, and such unease and discomfort may translate into reduced happiness. For example, job satisfaction is significantly negatively associated with organizational size (Indik, 1965; Porter & Lawler, 1965). The savanna theory of happiness may therefore suggest that group sizes and population densities much higher than were typical in the ancestral environment may decrease subjective well-being. It further suggests that such a negative effect of population density on happiness may interact with general intelligence, such that the negative effect is greater among less intelligent individuals than among more intelligent individuals.

The analysis of the Add Health data confirmed both of these predictions (Li & Kanazawa, 2016). Whether measured at the level of census block group (a subdivision of a census tract and the smallest geographic unit for which the Census Bureau tabulates aggregate data), census tract, county, or state, population density was significantly negatively associated with Add Health respondents' life satisfaction. This did not change at all when we controlled for sex, age, ethnicity, education, and current marital status. Consistent with the prediction derived from the savanna theory of happiness, the higher the population density of the immediate environment, the less satisfied with life Add Health respondents were.

Further analyses showed that, consistent with the prediction, the negative association between population density and life satisfaction was significantly stronger among less intelligent individuals than among more intelligent individuals. The interaction terms between population density and intelligence were statistically significantly positive for block group, census tract, county, and state.

Figure 9.3 presents the statistical interaction graphically. While county population density had a significantly negative association with life satisfaction among both less intelligent (with IQ of 81.39) and more intelligent (with IQ of 115.57) individuals, the negative association was greater among less intelligent individuals (M = 4.2617 vs. 4.1090) than among more intelligent individuals (M = 4.2161 vs. 4.1495). In other words, in a county with low population density (41 persons/km^2, one standard deviation below the mean), less intelligent individuals had higher mean life satisfaction than more intelligent individuals did. In contrast, in a county with high population density (937 persons/km^2, one standard deviation above the mean), more intelligent individuals had higher mean life satisfaction than less intelligent individuals did.

Given that our data are correlational and population density and life satisfaction were measured at the same time, we cannot rule out an opposite causal order to what we hypothesize in the savanna theory of happiness, where people who experience higher life satisfaction are more likely to move to rural areas. This does not appear to be the case. While life satisfaction at Wave III was significantly positively associated with the distance Add Health respondents moved between Waves I and III, the distance moved was more strongly positively associated with Wave III population density. In other words, longer-distance movers were more likely to move to urban areas, not rural areas, and they became more satisfied with their life *despite* their long-distance move (to urban areas), not because of it. As a result, controlling for the distance moved *strengthens* the negative association between population density and life satisfaction, not weakens or eliminates it, at all levels except for state, where the association remains unchanged.

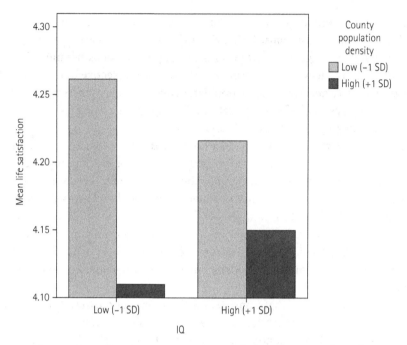

FIGURE 9.3 Interaction effect between county population density and intelligence on life satisfaction.

Source: Reprinted from *British Journal of Psychology, 107,* Norman P. Li and Satoshi Kanazawa, Country roads, take me home . . . to my friends: How intelligence, population density, and friendship affect modern happiness, 675–697, Copyright (2016), with permission from John Wiley and Sons.

Interestingly, Add Health respondents' intelligence was significantly *negatively* associated with the natural log of population density. It means that more intelligent individuals did *not* selectively migrate to urban areas, and less intelligent individuals did *not* selectively migrate to rural areas, in order to take advantage of their respective levels of intelligence to become more satisfied with life. We believe there are two potential (and non-mutually exclusive) reasons for this. First, individuals in general may not be (either consciously or unconsciously) aware of the negative effect of population density on happiness and its divergent effects by intelligence. Second, individuals may not have complete freedom to move where they want in order to pursue life satisfaction, especially at such a young age. They may be constrained by the requirements of their education, employment, and family.

Habitat Preference

Orians' (1980, 1986) savanna hypothesis—not to be confused with the Savanna Principle (Kanazawa, 2004b)—posits that humans have an innate preference for certain landscape and environment. They prefer open spaces with trees and rich vegetation, which can provide food resources and allow them to look out for potential predators without being seen by them. In other words, humans have a natural, evolutionarily given preference for savanna-like habitat.

Orians' savanna hypothesis has been widely supported by numerous studies and surveys with subjects and respondents from a wide variety of cultures and societies (Balling
& Falk, 1982; Orians & Heerwagen, 1992; Ulrich, 1986). For example, hospital patients
recover from surgery more quickly and with fewer complications if their hospital room
windows face natural habitat than if they face a brick wall (Ulrich, 1984). And a mere
presence of flowers—which in the African savanna signal the arrival of spring and more
abundant food supply—in a hospital room improves the patients' rate of recovery and
psychological mood (Watson & Burlingame, 1960).

Orians' savanna hypothesis is perfectly consistent with our savanna theory of happiness, and the human preference for savanna-like habitat follows equally from both
theories. In addition, the human preference for low population density and rural areas
discussed above may be one manifestation of the savanna hypothesis in the contemporary United States. Rural America affords more savanna-like landscapes than urban
America.

Friendships

One of the most important determinants of happiness is the quality of social relationships, particularly friendships (Diener & Seligman, 2004, pp. 18–20; Dolan, Peasgood, &
White, 2008, pp. 106–108). The more friends one has, and the more time one spends
with them, the happier one tends to be on average, although recent studies suggest that
the *quality* of friendships is more important for happiness than their *quantity* (Demir,
Orthel, & Andelin, 2013; Demir, Orthel-Clark, Özdemir, & Özdemir, 2015). The association between satisfaction with friendships and happiness is particularly stronger
in more individualistic cultures (Diener & Diener, 1995; Li & Cheng, 2015). While the
strong impact of friendships on subjective well-being may make intuitive sense, why are
friends important for happiness *theoretically*?

Perhaps the strong effect of friendships on life satisfaction is too obvious to explain;
to our knowledge, only one scholar has offered a systematic explanation for why
friendships increase happiness. Melikşah Demir and colleagues (Demir, 2015; Demir
& Davidson, 2013; Demir & Özdemir, 2010; Demir, Özen, Doğan, 2012; Demir, Özen,
Doğan, Bilyk, & Tyrell, 2011) argue that friendships increase happiness because they satisfy some basic psychological needs, such as relatedness, the knowledge that one matters
to others, and the desire to share and amplify good news and events (captured in the
Swedish proverb "Shared joy is a double joy, shared sorrow is half a sorrow"). Demir's
explanation, however, raises even more fundamental questions: *Why* do humans have
these basic psychological needs in the first place? And why can they be satisfied only (or
primarily) by friends?

The savanna theory of happiness can provide one potential answer to such fundamental questions. As noted above, our ancestors lived as hunter-gatherers in small bands
of about 150 individuals (Dunbar, 1992, 1993). In such settings, having frequent contact
with lifelong friends and allies was likely necessary for survival and reproduction for

both sexes, as evidenced by studies of both contemporary hunter-gatherers (Apicella, Marlowe, Fowler, & Christakis, 2012; Hruschka, 2010; Lewis, Al-Shawaf, Russell, & Buss, 2015) and our primate cousins (Smuts, 1985; de Waal, 1982). For instance, cooperative alliances may have allowed men to overcome critical challenges posed by hunting and warfare (Bowles, 2009; Geary, Byrd-Craven, Haord, Vigil, & Numtee, 2003), and close relationships among unrelated women may have facilitated joint childcare and allomothering (Hrdy, 2009). Likewise, reciprocal food-sharing among group members occurs commonly in modern-day hunter-gatherers and may have allowed our ancestors to survive despite success or failure in hunting and gathering on any given day (Hill & Hurtado, 1996).

The evolutionary significance of friendships and alliances is suggested by numerous studies indicating that ostracism is invariably painful and distressful across various contexts and sources (Williams, Forgas, & von Hippel, 2005). In one experiment, participants earned money to be excluded in a game and lost money to be included. Despite earning more money, those who were ostracized still experienced pain (van Beest & Williams, 2006). Indeed, fMRI studies show that being ostracized activates the same region of the brain that lights up when individuals experience physical pain (Eisenberger, Lieberman, & Williams, 2003). Given the available evidence, it is reasonable to assume that humans evolved to detect ostracism (Gruter & Masters, 1986) largely because friendship ties and alliances were very important for the survival and reproductive success of our ancestors (Lewis et al., 2015).

In contrast, survival and reproduction today depend increasingly more on one's ability to navigate myriad evolutionarily novel entities such as the internet, governments, banks, corporations, trusts, and the legal system. Instead of relying on reciprocal cooperation with friends and allies for basic needs, modern-day individuals deal with strangers or faceless entities and have no way of identifying those involved in the procurement and processing of necessities such as food (Pollan, 2006). It is entirely possible for individuals in modern society to survive and reproduce successfully without having any friends; friendships are not as critically necessary today for day-to-day living as they were in the ancestral environment. Hruschka (2010) notes, in a book entirely devoted to the importance of friendship, that "while friends make us happy and help us in small ways, it is not entirely clear that they are important in the high-stakes game of survival and reproduction" (p. 2). In 1998, 9% of respondents in the General Social Survey in a representative sample of noninstitutionalized American adults responded that they did not have any good friends to whom they felt close (Smith, Marsden, & Hout, 2015, p. 639).

The savanna theory of happiness therefore suggests that the human brain may have implicit difficulty comprehending and dealing with life without frequent contact with close friends and allies, and such difficulty may decrease individuals' happiness. Further, such an effect of friendships on happiness may be particularly stronger among less intelligent individuals, who are likely less able to adapt to evolutionarily novel circumstances such as a dearth of close friends. Thus, we expect friendships to have a positive effect on happiness and further (and more importantly) that such an effect will be stronger among less intelligent individuals.

The analysis of the Add Health data confirmed both of these predictions (Li & Kanazawa, 2016). Once current marital status was controlled, frequency of socialization with friends had a significantly positive association with life satisfaction, and this did not change even when we further controlled for age, sex, ethnicity, and education. Consistent with the prediction, the positive association between frequency of socialization with friends and life satisfaction was significantly stronger among less intelligent individuals than among more intelligent individuals. The interaction term between intelligence and frequency of socialization with friends was significantly negative.

Figure 9.4 presents the statistical interaction graphically. Among less intelligent individuals (with a mean IQ of 81.39), frequency of socialization with friends had a significantly positive effect on life satisfaction. Those who socialized with friends more frequently (6.71, nearly every day) had a significantly higher life satisfaction (M = 4.1586) than those who socialized with friends less frequently (1.95, less than twice a week) (M = 4.1163). In contrast, among more intelligent individuals (with a mean IQ of 115.57), those who socialized with friends more frequently were actually *less satisfied with life* (M = 4.1063) than those who socialized with friends less frequently (M = 4.1311). The statistical interaction was so strong that more intelligent individuals were actually *less* satisfied with life if they socialized with their friends more frequently.

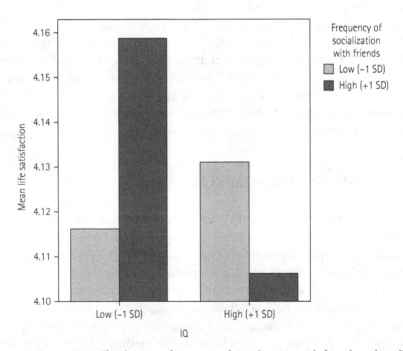

FIGURE 9.4 Interaction effect between frequency of socialization with friends and intelligence on life satisfaction.

Source: Reprinted from *British Journal of Psychology, 107,* Norman P. Li and Satoshi Kanazawa, Country roads, take me home . . . to my friends: How intelligence, population density, and friendship affect modern happiness, 675–697, Copyright (2016), with permission from John Wiley and Sons.

Given that our data are correlational and frequency of socialization with friends and life satisfaction were measured at the same time, we cannot rule out an opposite causal order to what we hypothesize, where happier people choose to socialize with their friends more frequently. We are sure there are some mutual influences between life satisfaction and frequency of socialization with friends, but there are a few considerations suggesting that the results largely reflect our hypothesized causality. For instance, Baker, Cahalin, Gerst, and Burr (2005) showed that the positive effect of seeing family and friends on subjective well-being remained even after controlling for the earlier level of life satisfaction in a previous wave of a longitudinal survey. Similarly, in our data, frequency of socialization with friends was still significantly associated with life satisfaction even after happiness at Waves I and II, in addition to current marital status, was controlled.

Interestingly, Add Health respondents' intelligence was significantly *positively* associated with the frequency of socialization with friends; more intelligent individuals socialized with their friends more frequently. The association between intelligence and frequency of socialization with friends was stronger among currently unmarried individuals than among currently married individuals. It means that more intelligent individuals did *not* voluntarily decrease their frequency of socialization with friends, and less intelligent individuals did *not* voluntarily increase it, in order to take advantage of their respective levels of intelligence to increase their life satisfaction. Once again, we believe there are two potential (and non-mutually exclusive) reasons for this. First, individuals in general may not be (either consciously or unconsciously) aware of the divergent effect of socialization with friends on happiness by intelligence. Second, individuals may not have complete control over how frequently to socialize with their friends (or how many friends to have). Friendship is a two-way street, and friends must mutually seek each other to establish friendship and socialize together—something that may be increasingly difficult to do in transient modern environments. More intelligent individuals may simply have more friends to begin with.

Seasonal Affective Disorder (SAD)

While there are some individual differences in the circadian rhythm, where some individuals are more nocturnal than others (Kanazawa & Perina, 2009), humans are basically a diurnal (as opposed to nocturnal) species. Humans rely very heavily on vision for navigation but, unlike genuinely nocturnal species, cannot see in the dark or under little lighting. Our ancestors did not have artificial means of illumination during the night until the domestication of fire; even then, it did not compare to sunlight in its power of illumination. Any human in the ancestral environment up and about during the night would have been at risk of predation by nocturnal predators. Ethnographic evidence uniformly suggests that our ancestors rose shortly before sunrise and went to sleep shortly after sunset, in order to avoid extended nocturnal activities that might jeopardize their safety (Chagnon, 1992; Cronk, 2004; Hill & Hurtado, 1996; Lee, 1979; Levinson, 1991–1995; Whitten, 1976).

Given the inherent danger that darkness presented during human evolutionary history, in contrast to the safety that bright daylight afforded a diurnal species that relied heavily on vision, it is reasonable to speculate that prolonged periods of darkness might have made our ancestors nervous, cautious, afraid, and therefore unhappy. This may be the evolutionary origin of the seasonal affective disorder (SAD). Medical researchers have known for three decades that a lack of daylight leads some individuals to experience chronic depression (Rosenthal et al., 1984). Individuals normally experience SAD during the winter months, when there are fewer daylight hours, especially in higher latitudes like Nordic countries, and, as a result, the most effective treatment of SAD is to expose the patients to many hours of artificial light (Partonen & Lönnqvist, 1998; Winkler, Pjrek, Iwaki, & Kasper, 2006). Such extended exposure to bright light simulates daylight, which signified relative safety to our ancestors, compared to the danger inherent in darkness. Positive evolutionary consequences of prolonged and abundant daylight provided in the light therapy apparently reduces chronic depression and SAD and restores higher levels of happiness.

The association between sunshine and happiness is apparent even in a representative (nonclinical) sample of Americans. Wave IV of Add Health measures the respondents' happiness with the question: "During the past seven days, how often did you feel happy?" As Figure 9.5 shows, there is a clear and monotonic association between happiness and the amount of sunshine individuals receive. Add Health respondents who are

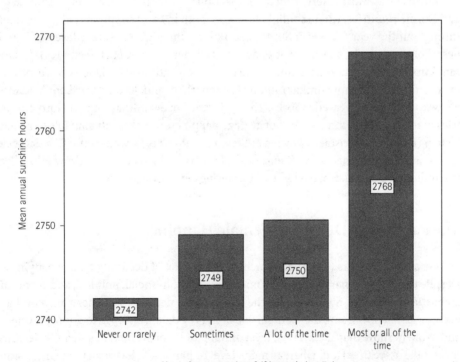

FIGURE 9.5 Association between happiness and annual sunshine hours.

"never or rarely" happy in the past seven days on average receive 2,742 hours of sunshine a year in their city of residence. Those who are "sometimes" happy in the past seven days receive 2,749 hours, those who are happy "a lot of the time" receive 2,750 hours, and those who are happy "most or all of the time" receive 2,768 hours ($F(3, 15621) = 3.263$, $p < .05$). Americans who live in sunnier locations do appear to be happy more frequently.

If the relative lack of daylight hours and implied danger of darkness during ancestral times are the reason that some individuals experience SAD, then the savanna theory of happiness would predict that less intelligent individuals are more likely to suffer from SAD than more intelligent individuals. This indeed appears to be the case. A couple of studies (Rajajärvi et al., 2010; Sullivan & Payne, 2007) show that individuals suffering from SAD score lower on standardized IQ tests than controls and unaffected relatives. The authors of both of these studies unquestioningly assume that SAD leads to cognitive impairment. However, because the data in both studies are correlational—SAD symptoms and IQ were measured at the same time—their findings are equally compatible with the interpretation that less intelligent individuals are more likely to suffer from SAD than more intelligent individuals. Only prospectively longitudinal studies and controlled experiments can adjudicate between these two causal explanations for the negative association between IQ and SAD.

Even though a relative lack of daylight may reduce happiness and increase depression and SAD, this component of happiness is unlikely to be a major determinant of global life satisfaction. Most international comparisons show that citizens of Scandinavian and Nordic countries, where sunlight hours are both in short supply and highly variable throughout the year (Pearce & Smith, 2000), have the highest average levels of happiness. For example, in one study of 55 nations (Diener, Diener, & Diener, 1995), Iceland ranks first, Sweden second, Denmark fourth, Norway 12th, and Finland 13th. Veehoven's data on 149 nations show similar ranking (Denmark second, Iceland third, Finland fifth, Norway seventh, and Sweden 10th). The high ranks of Scandinavian and Nordic countries in international comparisons of average happiness are likely attributable to genetic factors (De Neve, Christakis, Fowler, & Frey, 2012; Proto & Oswald, 2014; Rice & Steele, 2004) or ethnic homogeneity (Kanazawa & Li, 2015), which appear to drown the negative influence of the lack of daylight and resulting depression and SAD.

The Paradox of Declining Female Happiness

Stevenson and Wolfers (2009) document the "paradox of declining female happiness." Despite the extraordinary progress women have made in social, political, and economic arenas in the United States during the past several decades, American women have become less happy. Using the General Social Survey data from 1972 to 2006, Stevenson and Wolfers show that the average level of happiness for women has steadily declined during the 35-year period, whereas men's level of happiness has remained largely constant. As a result, even though American women have historically been happier than American men, now (in 2006) men are slightly happier than women in the United

States. What explains "the paradox of declining female happiness" in the past several decades in the face of enormous progress women have made socially, politically and economically?

While there may be many potential reasons for the declining levels of happiness among American women, such as the increasing divorce rates since 1972, the savanna theory of happiness can offer one potential explanation. One of the manifestations of the extraordinary progress that women have made is that many of them now have demanding careers and professions. While few married women with children had their own jobs and careers in the 1950s and 1960s, an increasing number of women have maintained their careers even after marriage and parenthood in the last half-century.

One of the necessary consequences of married women with children taking on demanding jobs and careers is that they can spend much less time with their children during the week. Throughout human evolutionary history and until the last half-century, childcare was almost exclusively a female task, and mothers spent their entire time with their children (Hrdy, 1999). While ancestral men with children went on long hunting trips that took them away from their band (and family and children) for days at a time, it was very rare for women with children to spend extended periods of time away from their children. Further, given human infants' high levels of defenselessness and dependence on constant maternal care, small children away from their mothers for hours would be in grave danger of predation, injury, or even death. In order to prevent this, human mothers are evolutionarily designed to be constantly mindful of where their children are, to make sure that they are safe, and to be alarmed and anxious if they were out of sight for an extended period of time (Savage & Kanazawa, 2004). At the same time, the savanna theory of happiness can also explain why children who have extensive exposure to daycare and other nonmaternal care tend to grow up to have emotional and behavioral problems, especially when their daycare experience begins during the first year of life (Belsky & Eggebeen, 1991). Given that mothers were the primary carers of children throughout human evolutionary history, men were far less likely to be worried when they were physically away from children for a long period of time.

Women's social, political, and economic advancement in the last half-century, which necessarily took them away from their children for most of the day, while their children were cared for by professional nannies and daycare center staff, is therefore expected to reduce women's happiness because of what such separation *would have meant* in the ancestral environment (the immediate possibility of injury and death for the children). In the current environment, children are usually perfectly safe when they are in the care of genetically unrelated paid carers. However, the evolutionary constraints on women's brains might implicitly perceive the situation as a potential danger to their children, and their psychological well-being may decrease as a result. Because ancestral men spent less time on childcare, men's brains would be less likely to perceive extended physical separation from their children as potential threat and danger to their children. This may be the evolutionary origins of the declining female happiness in the United States in the past half-century.

The savanna theory of happiness would further predict that more intelligent mothers are less likely to perceive routine separation from their children during the day as a threat and, as a result, may be more likely to delegate their childcare to paid professional staff. At the same time, more intelligent mothers, who typically have greater earnings and more flexible work schedule and environment, may depend on higher-quality daycare or on less daycare altogether. More intelligent mothers are therefore expected to experience less decline in their happiness by doing so than less intelligent mothers. This prediction awaits empirical confirmation. At any rate, the savanna theory of happiness can provide one potential explanation for the "paradox of declining female happiness" documented by Stevenson and Wolfers (2009).

CONCLUSION

In this chapter, we discussed a new evolutionary psychological theory of individual differences in happiness—why some individuals are happier than others. The savanna theory of happiness posits that because of the evolutionary constraints on the human brain, happiness is affected by not only the current consequences of what a given situation means now but also the ancestral consequences of what it *would have meant* during evolutionary history. The theory further posits that because general intelligence evolved to solve evolutionarily novel problems, the effect of such ancestral consequences on happiness is greater among less intelligent individuals than among more intelligent individuals.

Several pieces of evidence support the savanna theory of happiness. Being an ethnic minority, living in urban areas, and having few friends all negatively impact happiness at least in part because of what such conditions would have meant in the ancestral environment. Further, the savanna theory of happiness can offer a novel explanation for SAD and the paradox of declining female happiness in the United States in the past half-century.

As we mentioned elsewhere (Kanazawa & Li, 2015), the savanna theory of happiness is an explanatory theory in basic science, which aims to identify some of the causal factors in happiness and life satisfaction and account for some individual differences in them. It is emphatically *not* a prescription for life. As basic scientists, we do *not* give advice to people on how to live their lives or seek happiness. In particular, we are decidedly *not* advocating that individuals move to neighborhoods and cities where they are ethnic majorities or to countries and regions closer to the equator that have longer and more consistent hours of daylight. We are decidedly *not* encouraging less intelligent individuals to move to rural areas or socialize with their friends more. Nor are we encouraging more intelligent individuals to move to urban areas or socialize with their friends less. Nevertheless, the theory and findings discussed herein likely have various implications for improving happiness that applied researchers and practitioners may wish to take note and explore.

THE SAVANNA THEORY OF HAPPINESS   189

To our knowledge, the savanna theory of happiness is the first systematic theory (evolutionary or otherwise) that explains *why* some individuals are happier than others. We welcome other researchers to build on the emerging body of work that we have described above or to propose their own competing theories and empirically test them against ours. Scientific efforts to understand the evolutionary origins of, and individual differences in, happiness have just begun.

Notes

1. This section draws from Kanazawa and Li (2015).
2. Preliminary analysis showed that earnings had no association with life satisfaction among Add Health respondents, perhaps because of their relative youth (mean age = 22.0) and little variance in earnings. This was consistent with earlier studies, which showed that variance in earnings generally increased with age (Beach, Finnie, & Gray, 2010; Caswell & Kluge, 2015; Lam & Levison, 1992).
3. This and the following sections draw from Li and Kanazawa (2016).

References

Apicella, C. L., Marlowe, F. W., Fowler, J. H., & Christakis, N. A. (2012). Social networks and cooperation in hunter-gatherers. *Nature, 481,* 497–501.

Baker, L. A., Cahalin, L. P., Gerst, K., & Burr, J. A. (2005). Productive activities and subjective well-being among older adults: The influence of number of activities and time commitment. *Social Indicators Research, 73,* 431–458.

Baker, W. (2014). *United America: The surprising truth about American values, American identity and the 10 beliefs that a large majority of Americans hold dear.* Canton, MI: Read the Spirit Books.

Balling, J. D., & Falk, J. H. (1982). Development of visual preference for rural environments. *Environment and Behavior, 14,* 5–28.

Beach, C. M., Finnie, R., & Gray, D. (2010). Long-run inequality and short-run instability of men's and women's earnings in Canada. *Review of Income and Wealth, 56,* 572–596.

Belsky, J., & Eggebeen, D. (1991). Early and extensive maternal employment and young children's socioemotional development: Children of the National Longitudinal Survey of Youth. *Journal of Marriage and the Family, 53,* 1083–1110.

Berry, B. J. L., & Okulicz-Kozaryn, A. (2009). Dissatisfaction with city life: A new look at some old questions. *Cities, 26,* 117–124.

Berry, B. J. L., & Okulicz-Kozaryn, A. (2011). An urban–rural happiness gradient. *Urban Geography, 32,* 871–883.

Biswas-Diener, R., Diener, E., & Lyubchik, N. (2015). Wellbeing in Bhutan. *International Journal of Wellbeing, 5,* 1–13.

Bowles, S. (2009). Did warfare amongst ancestral hunter-gatherers affect the evolution of human social behaviors? *Science, 324,* 1293–1298.

Burnham, T. C., & Johnson, D. D. P. (2005). The biological and evolutionary logic of human cooperation. *Analyse & Kritik, 27,* 113–135.

Burrow, A. L., & Hill, P. L. (2013). Derailed by diversity? Purpose buffers the relationship between ethnic composition on trains and passenger negative mood. *Personality and Social Psychology Bulletin, 39*, 1610–1619.

Buss, D. M. (1995). Evolutionary psychology: A new paradigm for psychological science. *Psychological Inquiry, 6*, 1–30.

Caswell, H., & Kluge, F. A. (2015). Demography and the statistics of lifetime economic transfers under individual stochasticity. *Demographic Research, 32*, 536–588.

Chagnon, N. A. (1979). Mate competition, favoring close kin, and village fissioning among the Yanomamö Indians. In N. A. Chagnon & W. Irons (Eds.), *Evolutionary biology and human social behavior: An anthropological perspective* (pp. 86–131). North Scituate, MA: Duxbury.

Chagnon, N. A. (1992). *Yanomamö* (4th ed.). Fort Worth, TX: Harcourt Brace Jovanovich.

Cosmides, L., & Tooby, J. (2013). Evolutionary psychology: New perspectives on cognition and motivation. *Annual Review of Psychology, 64*, 201–229.

Cronk, L. (2004). *From Mukogodo to Maasai: Ethnicity and cultural change in Kenya.* Boulder, CO: Westview.

De Neve, J.-E., Christakis, N. A., Fowler, J. H., & Frey, B. S. (2012). Genes, economics, and happiness. *Journal of Neuroscience, Psychology, and Economics, 5*, 193–211.

Demir, M. (Ed.). (2015). *Friendship and happiness: Across life-span and cultures.* Dordrecht, the Netherlands: Springer.

Demir, M., & Davidson, I. (2013). Toward a better understanding of the relationship between friendship and happiness: Perceived responses to capitalization attempts, feelings of mattering, and satisfaction of basic psychological needs in same-sex best friendships as predictors of happiness. *Journal of Happiness Studies, 14*, 525–550.

Demir, M., Orthel, H., & Andelin, A. K. (2013). Friendship and happiness. In I. Boniwell, S. David, & A. C. Ayers (Eds.), *The Oxford handbook of happiness* (pp. 860–870). Oxford, UK: Oxford University Press.

Demir, M., Orthel-Clark, H., Özdemir, M., & Özdemir, S. B. (2015). Friendship and happiness among young adults. In M. Demir (Ed.), *Friendship and happiness: Across the life-span and cultures* (pp. 117–135). Dordrecht, the Netherlands: Springer.

Demir, M., & Özdemir, M. (2010). Friendship, need satisfaction and happiness. *Journal of Happiness Studies, 11*, 243–259.

Demir, M., Özen, A., & Doğan, A. (2012). Friendship, perceived mattering and happiness: A study of American and Turkish college students. *Journal of Social Psychology, 152*, 659–664.

Demir, M., Özen, A., Doğan, A., Bilyk, N. A., & Tyrell, F. A. (2011). I matter to my friend, therefore I am happy: Friendship, mattering, and happiness. *Journal of Happiness Studies, 12*, 983–1005.

Diamond, J. (2012). *The world until yesterday: What can we learn from traditional societies?* New York, NY: Viking.

Diener, E. (2012). New findings and future directions for subjective well-being research. *American Psychologist, 67*, 590–597.

Diener, E., & Diener, M. (1995). Cross-cultural correlates of life satisfaction and self-esteem. *Journal of Personality and Social Psychology, 68*, 653–663.

Diener, E., Diener, M., & Diener, C. (1995). Factors predicting the subjective well-being of nations. *Journal of Personality and Social Psychology, 69*, 851–864.

Diener, E., Kanazawa, S., Suh, E., & Oishi, S. (2015). Why people are in a generally good mood. *Personality and Social Psychology Review, 19*, 235–256.

Diener, E., Oishi, S., & Lucas, R. E. (2015). National accounts of subjective well-being. *American Psychologist, 70,* 234–242.

Diener, E., & Seligman, M. E. P. (2004). Beyond money: Toward an economy of well-being. *Psychological Science in the Public Interest, 5,* 1–31.

Dolan, P., Peasgood, T., & White, M. (2008). Do we really know what makes us happy? A review of the economic literature on the factors associated with subjective well-being. *Journal of Economic Psychology, 29,* 94–122.

Dunbar, R. I. M. (1992). Neocortex size as a constraint on group size in primates. *Journal of Human Evolution, 20,* 469–493.

Dunbar, R. I. M. (1993). Coevolution of neocortical size, group size and language in humans. *Behavioral and Brain Sciences, 16,* 681–735.

Easterlin, R. A., Angelescu, L., & Zweig, J. S. (2011). The impact of modern economic growth on urban–rural differences in subjective well-being. *World Development, 39,* 2187–2198.

Eisenberger, N. I., Lieberman, M. D., & Williams, K. D. (2003). Does rejection hurt? An fMRI study of social exclusion. *Science, 302,* 290–292.

Evans, R. J. (2009). A comparison of rural and urban older adults in Iowa on specific markers of successful aging. *Journal of Gerontological Social Work, 52,* 423–438.

Gautney, J. R., & Holliday, T. W. (2015). New estimations of habitable land area and human population size at the Last Glacial Maximum. *Journal of Archeological Science, 58,* 103–112.

Geary, D. C., Byrd-Craven, J., Haord, M. K., Vigil, J., & Numtee, C. (2003). Evolution and development of boys' social behavior. *Developmental Review, 23,* 444–470.

Graham, S. (1994). Motivation in African Americans. *Review of Educational Research, 64,* 55–117.

Gruter, M., & Masters, R. D. (1986). Ostracism as a social and biological phenomenon: An introduction. *Ethology and Sociobiology, 7,* 149–158.

Hagen, E. H., & Hammerstein, P. (2006). Game theory and human evolution: A critique of some recent interpretations of experimental games. *Theoretical Population Biology, 69,* 339–348.

Headey, B., & Wearing, A. (1989). Personality, life events, and subjective well-being: Toward a dynamic equilibrium model. *Journal of Personality and Social Psychology, 57,* 731–739.

Heintzelman, S. J., & King, L. A. (2014). Life is pretty meaningful. *American Psychologist, 69,* 561–574.

Hill, K., & Hurtado, A. M. (1996). *Ache life history.* New York, NY: Aldine.

Hill, R. A., & Dunbar, R. I. M. (2003). Social network size in humans. *Human Nature, 14,* 53–72.

Hintze, A., Olson, R. S., Adami, C., & Hertwig, R. (2013). *Risk aversion as an evolutionary adaptation.* Retrieved from https://pdfs.semanticscholar.org/0ac0/b777d7162fb-f09a0137689a696774fe3d1bd.pdf

Hrdy, S. B. (1999). *Mother nature: A history of mothers, infants, and natural selection.* New York, NY: Pantheon.

Hrdy, S. B. (2009). *Mothers and others: The evolutionary origins of mutual understanding.* Cambridge, MA: Harvard University Press.

Hruschka, D. J. (2010). *Friendship: Development, ecology, and evolution of a relationship.* Berkeley, CA: University of California Press.

Hurd, J. P. (1985). Sex differences in mate choice among the "Nebraska Amish of central Pennsylvania. *Ethology and Sociobiology, 6,* 49–57.

Indik, B. P. (1965). Organization size and member participation: Some empirical tests of alternative explanations. *Human Relations, 18,* 339–350.

Kanazawa, S. (2001). De gustibus *est* disputandum. *Social Forces, 79,* 1131–1163.

Kanazawa, S. (2004a). General intelligence as a domain-specific adaptation. *Psychological Review, 111,* 512–523.

Kanazawa, S. (2004b). The Savanna Principle. *Managerial and Decision Economics, 25,* 41–54.

Kanazawa, S. (2010). Evolutionary psychology and intelligence research. *American Psychologist, 65,* 279–289.

Kanazawa, S., & Fontaine, L. (2013). Intelligent people defect more in a one-shot prisoner's dilemma game. *Journal of Neuroscience, Psychology, and Economics, 6,* 201–213.

Kanazawa, S., & Li, N. P. (2015). Happiness in modern society: Why intelligence and ethnic composition matter. *Journal of Research in Personality, 59,* 111–120.

Kanazawa, S., & Perina, K. (2009). Why night owls are more intelligent. *Personality and Individual Differences, 47,* 685–690.

Killworth, P. D., Bernard, H. R., & McCarty, C. (1984). Measuring patterns of acquaintanceship. *Current Anthropology, 25,* 381–397.

Knight, J., & Gunatilaka, R. (2010). The rural–urban divide in China: Income but not happiness? *Journal of Development Studies, 46,* 506–534.

Krause, N. (1993). Race differences in life satisfaction among aged men and women. *Journal of Gerontology, 48,* S235–S244.

Kurzban, R., Tooby, J., & Cosmides, L. (2001). Can race be erased? Coalitional computation and social categorization. *Proceedings of the National Academy of Sciences of the USA, 98,* 15387–15392.

Lam, D., & Levison, D. (1992). Age, experience, and schooling: Decomposing earnings inequality in the United States and Brazil. *Sociological Inquiry, 62,* 220–245.

Lederbogen, F., Kirsch, P., Haddad, L., Streit, F., Tost H., Schuch, P., . . . Meyer-Lindenberg, A. (2011). City living and urban upbringing affect neural social stress processing in humans. *Nature, 474,* 498–501.

Lee, R. B. (1979). *The !Kung San: Men, women, and work in a foraging society.* Cambridge, UK: Cambridge University Press.

Levinson, D. (Editor-in-Chief.). (1991–1995). *Encyclopedia of world cultures* (10 vols.). Boston, MA: G. K. Hall.

Lewis, D. M. G., Al-Shawaf, L., Russell, E. M., & Buss, D. M. (2015). Friends and happiness: An evolutionary perspective on friendship. In M. Demir (Ed.), *Friendship and happiness: Across the life-span and cultures* (pp. 37–57). Dordrecht, the Netherlands: Springer.

Li, N. P., & Kanazawa, S. (2016). Country roads, take me home . . . to my friends: How intelligence, population density, and friendship affect modern happiness. *British Journal of Psychology, 107,* 675–697.

Li, N. P., Lim, A. J. Y., Tsai, M.-H., & O, J. (2015). Too materialistic to get married and have children? *PLoS One, 10,* e0126543.

Li, T., & Cheng, S.-T. (2015). Family, friends, and subjective well-being: A comparison between the West and Asia. In M. Demir (Ed.), *Friendship and happiness: Across the life-span and cultures* (pp. 235–251). New York, NY: Springer.

MacDonald, C. B. (1955). Company. *Encyclopedia Britannica* (14th ed.). London, UK: Encyclopedia Britannica Limited.

Mange, A. P., & Mange, E. J. (1980). *Genetics: Human aspects.* New York, NY: Saunders.

Miao, F. F., Koo, M., & Oishi, S. (2013). Subjective well-being. In I. Boniwell, S. A. David, & A. C. Ayers (Eds.), *The Oxford handbook of happiness* (pp. 174–184). Oxford, UK: Oxford University Press.

Oates, J. (1977). Mesopotamian social organisation: Archaeological and philological evidence. In J. Friedman & M. J. Rowlands (Eds.), *The evolution of social systems* (pp. 457–485). London, UK: Duckworth.

Oishi, S., Graham, J., Kesebir, S., & Galinha, I. C. (2013). Concepts of happiness across time and cultures. *Personality and Social Psychology Bulletin, 39,* 559–577.

Okazaki, S. (1997). Sources of ethnic differences between Asian American and White American college students on measures of depression and social anxiety. *Journal of Abnormal Psychology, 106,* 52–60.

Oppenheimer, S. (2003). *Out of Eden: The peopling of the world.* London, UK: Robinson.

Orians, G. (1980). Habitat selection: General theory and applications to human behavior. In J. S. Lockard (Ed.), *The evolution of human social behavior* (pp. 49–66). Chicago, IL: Elsevier.

Orians, G. (1986). An ecological and evolutionary approach to landscape aesthetics. In E. C. Penning-Rowsell & D. Lowenthal (Eds.), *Landscape meaning and values* (pp. 3–25). London, UK: Allen & Unwin.

Orians, G. H., & Heerwagen, J. H. (1992). Evolved responses to landscapes. In J. H. Barkow, L. Cosmides, & J. Tooby (Eds.), *The adapted mind: Evolutionary psychology and the generation of culture* (pp. 555–579). New York, NY: Oxford University Press.

Partonen, T., & Lönnqvist, J. (1998). Seasonal affective disorder. *Lancet, 352,* 1369–1374.

Pavot, W., & Diener, E. (2013). Happiness experienced: The science of subjective well-being. In I. Boniwell, S. A. David, & A. C. Ayers (Eds.), *The Oxford handbook of happiness* (pp. 134–151). Oxford, UK: Oxford University Press.

Pearce, E. A., & Smith, C. G. (2000). *The Hutchinson world weather guide* (5th ed.). Oxford, UK: Helicon.

Pollan, M. (2006). *The omnivore's dilemma: A natural history of four meals.* London, UK: Penguin.

Porter, L. W., & Lawler, E. E., III. (1965). Properties of organization structure in relation to job attitudes and job behavior. *Psychological Bulletin, 64,* 23–51.

Proto, E., & Oswald, A. J. (2014). *National happiness and genetic distance: A cautious exploration.* Department of Economics, University of Warwick, Coventry, UK.

Rajajärvi, E., Antila, M., Kieseppä, T., Lönnqvist, J., Tuulio-Henriksson, A., & Partonen, T. (2010). The effect of seasons and seasonal variation on neuropsychological test performance in patients with bipolar I disorder and their first-degree relatives. *Journal of Affective Disorders, 127,* 58–65.

Rice, T. W., & Steele, B. J. (2004). Subjective well-being and culture across time and space. *Journal of Cross-Cultural Psychology, 35,* 633–647.

Rosenthal, N., Sack, D. A., Gillin, J. C., Lewy, A. J., Goodwin, F. K., Davenport, Y., . . . Wehr, T. A. (1984). Seasonal affective disorder: A description of the syndrome and preliminary findings with light therapy. *Archives of General Psychiatry, 41,* 72–80.

Sally, D. (1995). Conversation and cooperation in social dilemmas: A meta-analysis of experiments from 1958 to 1992. *Rationality and Society, 7,* 58–92.

Savage, J., & Kanazawa, S. (2004). Social capital and the human psyche: Why is social life "capital"? *Sociological Theory, 22,* 504–524.

Scollon, C. N., Diener, E., Oishi, S., & Biswas-Diener, R. (2004). Emotions across cultures and methods. *Journal of Cross-Cultural Psychology, 35,* 304–326.

Smith, T. W., Marsden, P. V., & Hout, M. (2015). *General social surveys, 1972-2014: Cumulative codebook.* Chicago, IL: National Opinion Research Center.

Smuts, B. B. (1985). *Sex and friendship in baboons.* New York, NY: Aldine.

Stevenson, B., & Wolfers, J. (2009). The paradox of declining female happiness. *American Economic Journal: Economic Policy, 1*, 190–225.

Sullivan, B., & & Payne, T. W. (2007). Affective disorders and cognitive failures: A comparison of seasonal and nonseasonal depression. *American Journal of Psychiatry, 164*, 1663–1667.

Tashakkori, A., & Thompson, V. D. (1991). Race differences in self-perception and locus of control during adolescence and early adulthood. *Genetic, Social, and General Psychology Monographs, 117*, 133–152.

Tooby, J., & Cosmides, L. (1990). The past explains the present: Emotional adaptations and the structure of ancestral environments. *Ethology and Sociobiology, 11*, 375–424.

Tooby, J., & Cosmides, L. (1992). The psychological foundations of culture. In J. Barkow, L. Cosmides, & J. Tooby (Eds.), *The adapted mind: Evolutionary psychology and the generation of culture* (pp. 19–136). New York, NY: Oxford University Press.

Ulrich, R. S. (1984). View through a window may influence recovery from surgery. *Science, 224*, 420–421.

Ulrich, R. S. (1986). Human responses to vegetation and landscapes. *Landscape and Urban Planning, 13*, 29–44.

van Beest, I., & Williams, K. D. (2006). When inclusion costs and ostracism pays, ostracism still hurts. *Journal of Personality and Social Psychology, 91*, 918–928.

de Waal, F. B. M. (1982). *Chimpanzee politics: Power and sex among apes.* Baltimore, MD: Johns Hopkins University Press.

Watson, D., & Burlingame, A. W. (1960). *Therapy through horticulture.* New York, NY: Macmillan.

Whitten, N. E., Jr. (1976). *Sacha Runa: Ethnicity and adaptation of Ecuadorian jungle Quichua.* Urbana, IL: University of Illinois Press.

Williams, K. D., Forgas, J. P., & von Hippel, W. (Eds.). (2005). *The social outcast: Ostracism, social exclusion, rejection, and bullying.* New York, NY: Psychology Press.

Winkler, D., Pjrek, E., Iwaki, R., & Kasper, S. (2006). Treatment of seasonal affective disorder. *Expert Reviews in Neurotherapeutics, 6*, 1039–1048.

Wirth, L. (1938). Urbanism as a way of life. *American Journal of Sociology, 44*, 1–24.

CHAPTER 10

HOW EVOLUTIONARY PSYCHOLOGY CAN CONTRIBUTE TO GROUP PROCESS RESEARCH

JOSEPH M. WHITMEYER

SOME conception of human qualities or tendencies is fundamental to all group process theories—to the way they explain social processes in groups. Evolutionary psychology involves the use of evolutionary reasoning to construct hypotheses about human qualities and tendencies. Hence, it is a method for making our conception of those qualities and tendencies more accurate and, thus, should be useful to those who study and build theory concerning group processes. My purpose in this chapter is to suggest specifically how that can happen.

By "evolutionary reasoning," I mean reasoning logically what features and traits of an organism might have evolved and what features are not likely to have evolved. A feature or trait might have evolved if physiologically it *could* have arisen and if, once having arisen, it would have enhanced its own existence in the population, through enhancing the reproductive success of the organism that possessed it or her or his relatives. When applied to humans, evolutionary reasoning must pertain explicitly or implicitly to the human *evolutionary environment*. The evolutionary environment for humans is existence in foraging bands, groups of probably fewer than 100 individuals, that supported themselves through gathering food and hunting animals and moved about from place to place. Most members of the group were kin or, if not kin, "in-laws," so that they shared genetic interests in descendants. People generally spent long periods of time—many years—with more or less the same people, thus essentially in the same foraging band. However, there was occasional movement of individuals or small groups of people from one band to another. Bands were rather sparsely spread out (Binmore, 2001). Nevertheless, bands had relationships with other bands, possibly conflictual and violent, and possibly relationships of exchange, either peaceable or coercive, including exchange of mates.

This chapter focuses on three areas of group processes that are important now and are likely to have been important in the evolutionary environment as well: exchange, identity, and status. The procedure is simply to apply evolutionary reasoning to these processes, or to describe how others have applied it. This will suggest a number of ways evolutionary psychology can contribute to improving our theories of these processes.

The most general points concerning these three areas, elaborated in the remainder of the chapter, are as follows. In the area of exchange, in the evolutionary environment, it is likely that sustaining ongoing two-person relationships would be important as well as an individual's exchanges with the long-term group to which he or she belonged. We can expect, therefore, predispositions that would have tended to bring beneficial outcomes in these areas to have evolved and still be important. In the area of identity, evolutionary reasoning suggests that what is important is how identity matters affect behavior. Thus, predispositions concerning identity whether regarding ourselves or others should be oriented to producing the best outcomes for ourselves rather than, for example, toward being accurate. In the area of status, evolutionary reasoning suggests that our predispositions concerning status will stem from its close association with provision of goods to a long-term group. This produces predictions concerning, for example, when we will award status to others and when we will not.

In this chapter, I make a pair of assumptions that assist evolutionary reasoning. I assume that if a behavioral trait or predisposition is innate, it has evolved. This may not be inevitable, but it is likely and reasonably should be taken as the default assumption. In addition, I assume that if a behavior trait is universal—that is, found in all human societies—then a predisposition for that behavior or trait is innate and so, by the previous assumption, is evolved.

Exchange Processes

It is reasonable to suppose that humans may have evolved characteristics to facilitate exchange. The fact that in the evolutionary environment people tended to be in particular groups for long periods of time and that those groups were small, on the order of 50–80 people (Boehm, 1999; Maryanski & Turner, 1992), implies at least three characteristics of exchange processes in the evolutionary environment. First, reciprocal exchange, in which there is a time lag between giving and receiving (as opposed to negotiated exchange in which the giving and receiving are worked out concurrently; see Emerson, 1981), would have been quite common. Second, generalized exchange, in which a person gives and receives but there is no contingent relationship between the gift and the receipt (Ekeh, 1974; Yamagishi & Cook, 1993), would have been prevalent and probably crucial for survival. Third, exchanges often would have possessed a strong group orientation. Let us examine the implications of these characteristics.

Generalized Exchange

It is likely that in the evolutionary environment, it would have been advantageous for individuals to participate in generalized exchange (Kameda, Takezawa, Tindale, & Smith, 2002; Kelly, 1995) and, thus, that there would have been selection for predispositions that facilitated generalized exchange. Especially in that environment, help would have been critical for survival. Moreover, the small size of the group and the fact that most people remain with the group a long time would have enhanced the feasibility of generalized exchange. In addition, people frequently would have had common genetic interests with the person they were helping, so that even if they never were repaid, the help would not have been a complete loss.

One important feature of generalized exchange is that it is oriented to some group; let us call it the "generalized exchange group." Evolutionary reasoning suggests that when some exchange group of which a person is a member is important in producing consequences for that person, it should become important psychologically to that person. Generally, this will be the case when the group qua group produces something valuable for its members, often having had to get past some sort of free-rider problem to do so. Thus, evolutionary reasoning suggests that *the more group-oriented successful exchange processes are, the more rewarding identification and association with the group will be for its members.* This should be revealed in things such as positive emotions toward the group and in confirming group identity as a motivation for its members. These predispositions are likely to have evolved because being a part of successful groups would have been evolutionarily advantageous for individual humans.

Note that group orientation is a variable quality that can be strong with any type of exchange process. Generalized exchange, which occurs in the context of a generalized exchange group, clearly is likely to possess strong group orientation. However, even negotiated exchange may take on group orientation. Within generalized exchange, group orientation is likely to vary in strength. Indirect reciprocity or indirect exchange refers to a situation in which one person, for example, A, gives to another, B, who gives not back to A but, rather, to another, C, who gives to another, and so forth, but at some point someone gives back to A. A public goods problem is a situation in which there is some positive benefit that everyone in the group inevitably receives if it is produced and so all are tempted to let others produce it. Although both indirect reciprocity and solved public goods problems are forms of generalized exchange, the generalized exchange group for indirect reciprocity will tend to be less salient than for public goods problems. The group orientation of public goods problems, therefore, generally will be greater than for indirect reciprocity (Lawler, 2001). This implies that solved public goods problems will produce positive emotion connected with the group (Lawler, Thye, & Yoon, 2000), more so than indirect reciprocity does, as Lawler (2001) predicts. Indirect reciprocity also will be less valuable for confirming identification with the group.

Reciprocal exchange tends to be more group oriented compared to negotiated exchange, with the groups in both cases being the pair of people who are exchanging. Part of the reason for this is that the risk of cheating is greater in reciprocal exchange, making trust more crucial, and trust is more likely if the relationship is an ongoing relationship. This leads the partners to focus on whether or not they have an ongoing relationship—orienting the exchange toward the group—on the one hand; on the other hand, it means that successful reciprocal exchange actually confirms the ongoing nature of the relationship. Indeed, reciprocal exchange often is used as a means primarily of confirming the existence of an ongoing relationship to the partners rather than of increasing their material satisfaction. This suggests an advantage to attaching automatically a wider meaning concerning the exchanging pair to the process of reciprocal exchange. In other words, evolutionary reasoning suggests that reciprocal exchange should tend to produce greater emotional attachment to the group—that is, to the exchanging pair—than does negotiated exchange, as Molm, Peterson, and Takahashi (1999) found and contrary to Lawler's (2001) prediction.

Finally, note that it may be possible to manipulate the degree to which an exchange is oriented to a group. Thye, Lawler, and Yoon (2011), for example, show that group orientation increases with increasing inclusion in exchange and more structural equality. This may be done to increase the likelihood of exchange (Lawler & Yoon, 1996), creating a kind of positive feedback loop. We also can predict that if group orientation is increased, then successful exchange will produce more positive emotions toward the group and greater satisfaction from confirming group identity in the partners, and failed exchange will produce the opposite.

Cheating

The prevalence of opportunities for reciprocal exchange and generalized exchange and the benefits they offered make it likely that we evolved mechanisms for handling reciprocal and generalized exchange situations well. By this, I mean that we probably evolved specialized abilities and predispositions to deal with special problems posed by those situations (Cosmides & Tooby, 1992; Hoffman, McCabe, & Smith, 1996). The chief problems have to do with cheating, by others and by us. In reciprocal exchange, your partner may cheat you by taking more from you than he or she reciprocates. In generalized exchange, others in the group may free-ride and not contribute or undercontribute when it is their time to do so.

As for ourselves, we have the temptation to cheat in the short term, although it may hurt us in the long term. When our turn to give comes in reciprocal exchange, we can gain in the short term by refusing to give or by giving less than would be fair. In generalized exchange, we gain in the short term by refusing to help someone who could use help we could give, by contributing less than our fair share to the group project, or by doing a poor job when it is our turn to do something for the group. This cheating is likely to be costly to us in the long term because others will react in ways to stop or punish us.

A number of qualities would help prevent being cheated by others or help us resist the temptation to cheat disadvantageously in reciprocal or generalized exchange. Table 10.1 presents a list, organized according to whether the quality is a solution for others' cheating or a solution for our own. I discuss each in turn.

Table 10.1 Predispositions Suggested by Evolutionary Reasoning for Dealing with the Problem of Cheating by Others and by Ourselves

Solutions for Others	Solutions for Ourselves
Emotional responses to being rewarded or punished	Emotional responses to being rewarded or punished
Sensitivity to unfairness	Loyalty
Keeping balance sheet in reciprocal exchange relationship	Sensitivity to fairness
Identifying the generalized exchange group	Keeping balance sheet in reciprocal exchange relationship
Attention to others' exchange reputations	Attention to our own exchange reputation
Monitoring, reporting, and sanctioning others' exchange behavior	Social exchange heuristic
Using ostracism as negative sanction	Concern with our identity
Evaluation of others' worthiness	
Concern with others' identity	
Social intelligence	
Trust ability	
Risk aversion	

Emotions

Let us begin with emotional reactions to being cheated or being treated well. For this, we can go back to Homans (1974). One of his fundamental propositions states that if we are punished, especially unexpectedly, we become angry, and results of aggression become rewarding to us. If we are rewarded, especially unexpectedly, we become pleased, and results of approving behavior become rewarding to us. In other words, if punished unexpectedly, we enjoy being aggressive. If rewarded unexpectedly, we enjoy being nice. These emotions help lessen cheating by others because they drive behavior antagonistic to cheating others or that perpetuates cooperative relationships. We may also experience these emotions when we discover others being cheated or helped, with similar effects.

The emotional reactions to which Homans (1974) refers also work against our cheating of others. Namely, when we are rewarded, our happiness may override a more calculated assessment of potential gain in the situation, which in the short term at least might say we should keep our reward and not do anything in return. When we are punished, our anger may lead us to disregard the short-term cost of carrying out retaliation.

Specific behavioral tendencies that follow on from emotional reactions to being cheated or not being cheated also may have evolved to be innate predispositions. In the evolutionary environment, principal recourses to being cheated would have been direct confrontation, cutting off malefactors from future exchange, and telling others in the group what happened. Although we have additional recourses now, including through formal institutions such as the police, we still use the same informal ones a great deal.

Loyalty

Another quality with an emotional aspect is loyalty or commitment. Loyalty is a preference for maintaining a pre-existing reciprocal exchange relationship, which can outweigh the lure of gains to be made by switching to a more profitable relationship. Loyalty typically is accompanied by positive emotions (Lawler & Yoon, 1998), which again is an indication that loyalty is likely to be an inherited quality. The evolutionary advantage of loyalty is that it would tend to keep us as good long-term or reciprocal exchange partners, which would make sense in the evolutionary environment in which people had continued opportunities to exchange with the same people. There, opportunistic switching of exchange partners could well be a poor long-term strategy because it would curtail possibilities for long-term gains from reciprocal exchange relationships.

Sensitivity to Unfairness

Cheating, social unfairness, and social injustice may be essentially identical in how we mentally process their occurrence. Sensitivity to cheating or unfairness has two elements to it—ability to detect unfairness and an emotional reaction to unfairness. With experimental support, Cosmides and Tooby (1992) have suggested we have an evolved, innate ability to detect cheating—again, an ability to detect unfairness. We also experience emotion: anger when others are unfair and guilt when we are unfair (Jasso, 1993). This emotional aspect makes it likely that sensitivity to unfairness is an evolved trait, as others have suggested (Binmore, 2001; Cosmides, 1989; Fiske, 1991; Turner, 2002). Sensitivity to unfairness would have had advantages in the evolutionary environment— indeed, it does in our own—by tending to keep all types of exchanges (negotiated, reciprocal, and generalized) mutually beneficial. It would work to keep ourselves from cheating others, to keep others from cheating us, and to keep third parties transacting between each other from cheating each other.

The well-established finding that losses affect people more than gains (Tversky & Kahneman, 1981) may be due to the fact that in the evolutionary environment loss often would have been the result of being cheated in some way; thus, excessive aversion or reaction to loss would have helped prevent being cheated. Note that this asymmetric response should also apply to third-party situations. Thus, we can predict that third-party reactions will be stronger to seeing someone receive less than promised than to seeing someone receive more than promised. Moreover, we can predict this difference in reaction will be greater in a non-zero-sum situation, in which being overbenefited does not result in someone else's being underbenefited. In a zero-sum situation, third parties should be bothered also by someone's being overbenefited because it comes at someone else's expense. As a last point, whether or not a situation invokes our sensitivity to cheating may depend on the framing of that situation, as Cosmides and Tooby

(1992) found for detection of cheating and Tversky and Kahneman (1981) found for loss aversion.

Keeping the Balance Sheet of Exchange

Reciprocal exchange makes mental demands that negotiated exchange does not, in that both parties need to remember who owes whom and what. Obviously, the one who owes needs to remember, and the one who is owed is less likely to be cheated if she or he remembers as well. Evidence suggests that we keep a sophisticated account of the status of reciprocal exchanges, not necessarily explicitly or even fully consciously (Kollock, 1993). The fact that we do this monitoring and accounting along with its obvious benefits mean that it is likely to be an innate predisposition. Note that keeping the balance sheet of exchange works against cheating not only by others but also by ourselves. It lessens the chance that we will sabotage an exchange relationship mistakenly or damage our reputation with others.

Identifying the Generalized Exchange Group

In the evolutionary environment, knowing "us" and "them" would have been important, at times a life-or-death matter. "Us" means a generalized exchange group, a long-term group of cooperation, a group in which one can give help and expect that at some point one will be repaid somehow. Social psychologists have known for a while now that we are quick to classify people into "in-group" and "out-group" (Bruner, 1958; Devine, 1989) and that the classification affects subsequent perceptions and behaviors (Sherif, Harvey, White, Hood, & Sherif, 1961; Tajfel, 1982; Vine, 1992). Yamagishi (1998; see also Yamagishi, Jin, & Kiyonari, 1999) has emphasized that this classification is not just capricious, however, but in fact is aimed at locating ourselves in a generalized exchange group.

Attending to Exchange Reputation

"Exchange reputation," what others believe about the trustworthiness in exchange of a potential exchange partner, is important for exchange, as many scholars have noted (Klein, 1997; Milinski, Semmann, & Krambeck, 2002). Note that this is separate from what might be called someone's "asset reputation," what others believe about what a potential partner can bring to exchange, such as material goods or abilities. Attention to others' exchange reputation will help prevent being cheated by partners in exchange, especially reciprocal exchange, given the heightened vulnerability of whoever gives first. Simpson and Willer (2008) study people's interest in having a reputation for altruistic behavior, which can be viewed as an exaggerated version of exchange reputation.

If exchange reputation matters for exchange, then we should care about our own exchange reputation, and generally we do (Barclay, 2012). It is likely that attending to exchange reputation, both our own and that of others, is an evolved predisposition. Burt (2001) notes that in closed, smallish groups—which would have characterized the evolutionary environment—reputations have a tendency to become set without necessarily being accurate. Caring about exchange reputation would have at least as many advantages in the evolutionary environment as it does now, and those who attended to exchange reputation on the whole would have done better than those who did not (Barclay, 2012). The fact that attention to exchange reputation is so automatic with us, and that exchange reputation problems are accompanied by emotions (Frank, 1988; Trivers, 1971), suggests too that these concerns are innate.

Monitoring, Reporting, and Sanctioning Others' Exchange Behavior

Three behavioral predispositions that would facilitate exchange in small, long-term groups are (a) attending to people's prosocial behavior or lack thereof, (b) reporting on people's prosocial behavior or lack thereof to others, and (c) sanctioning people for prosocial behavior and especially for its lack. The first two suggest an evolved predisposition for gossip (Runciman, 2000). In the evolutionary and every other social environment, we benefit by wanting information about the trustworthiness of anyone who is a current or possible future exchange partner. Because any given person is likely to be neither party nor witness to many instances of prosocial behavior or its opposite, group members benefit by sharing this information with each (Burt & Knez, 1996; Klein, 1997).

Sanctioning others' prosocial—or not—behavior often is accompanied by emotions, a sign of evolutionary roots. As Heckathorn (1990, 1993) has shown, under some circumstances it may be profitable even in the short term to engage in the second-order cooperation such sanctioning often requires. However, other work suggests that these behaviors need not be calculated and may be oriented to the long term (Fehr & Gächter, 2002).

Using Ostracism as Negative Sanction

One particular negative sanction for failure to cooperate, ostracism, almost certainly was very important in the evolutionary environment both as a punishment and as a safeguard, a sort of inoculation, for the group (Boehm, 1999). It is likely, therefore, that we are predisposed to use ostracism and partial ostracism as a means of sanctioning. For example, Koudenburg, Postmes, and Gordijn (2013) argue that brief conversational silences in group discussion are essentially ostracism threats that bring those who want to be group members into greater conformity. The silence means "We don't want anything to do with what you're saying," which is threatening "We don't want anything to do with you." It is likely that we have a complementary predisposition to sanction negatively those who violate the ostracism or partial ostracism and cooperate inappropriately.

Social Exchange Heuristic

Kiyonari, Tanida, and Yamagishi (2000) suggest we have a predisposition to treat transactions that are not parts of ongoing exchange relationships as generalized exchange (see also Hoffman et al., 1996). They call this a "social exchange heuristic" and propose that it is innate. Consider the appearance of a generalized exchange situation. Either we are making an outright gift or at best it is a one-shot transaction with the potential for cheating such as a prisoner's dilemma in which both parties know there is only one interaction with the given partner. In the evolutionary environment, almost all helping or one-shot transactions with potential for cheating would have been generalized exchange decisions because the group was small and members tended to be with the group for an extended period of time. That is, you may not ever be helped or engage in a similar transaction with that person in the future, but still it is exchange because others in the group will have opportunity to help you or engage in one-shot transactions with you in the future, probably with knowledge of how you have behaved.

Evaluation of Others' Worthiness

In helping or cooperation situations, especially that are not simply negotiated or reciprocal exchange, we may have an innate tendency to evaluate whether the other person seems likely to be a member in good standing of the generalized exchange group and to help or cooperate or not on that basis. We can call this the person's "worthiness." The reason to evaluate worthiness is that if the person is a member of the group in good standing and likely to remain so, then cooperation makes sense because we are likely to get paid back by someone at some point, and if we do not cooperate, then we may suffer in the future. However, if the person is in fact not a member in good standing of the group, or not likely to remain a member, then we face an increased risk that no one will repay our cooperation. Evaluation of worthiness may affect reciprocal exchanges somewhat as well. If our partner is worthy—that is, a full-fledged member of some generalized exchange group of ours—then it is less likely that the partner will cheat us and that we will cheat the partner. That is because cheating by either person may damage the cheater's standing with the group.

Concern with Our Own and Others' Identity

Problems of cheating in the various types of exchange may have led to an evolved tendency to concern ourselves with identities, of others in the group and of ourselves. Psychologists have noted a basic human tendency that they call the fundamental attribution error—that we tend to overascribe behavior of others to personality and intrinsic qualities of the person (Nisbett & Ross, 1980). From an evolutionary standpoint, however, this may be a useful trait rather than an error. For this labeling of others may be in part a means of social control, especially as identity information gets passed along. The labels will have consequences for the person's future attempts to be involved in exchanges. Consequently, the person in all situations has incentive to get advantageous labels and avoid disadvantageous labels. Note that from the standpoint of our own self-interest, what matters is whether a person cooperates with us or not, regardless of extenuating circumstances. In other words, by labeling a person regardless of circumstances, that person is motivated to be cooperative, and so get advantageous labels, regardless of circumstances, which is precisely what will benefit us most. Hence, for purposes of getting cooperation, it is likely to be advantageous to attribute identity irrespective of circumstances.

Social Intelligence

This is a faculty identified and labeled by Toshio Yamagishi (see Yamagishi, Kikuchi, & Kosugi, 1999). Social intelligence is the ability to discern the intentions of others in exchange, namely whether or not they are likely to cheat us. Information about reputation will feed into this inference, as will information from monitoring a person's past exchange behavior with us. However, our social intelligence also is likely to process all sorts of cues about the prospective partner, as well as information about the situation. Yamagishi (1998) suggests that the more people have to gain from entering new exchange relationships, the more they will try to develop their social intelligence.

Trust Ability

Complementing our social intelligence is the ability to trust appropriately—call it "trust ability." Trust amounts to taking a chance on a partner in a reciprocal exchange situation. Being skillful at placing trust would be beneficial because trust pays off if the partner comes through but not if he or she does not. Supported by empirical results, Yamagishi (1998) has suggested that in identical situations, some people are more likely than others to place trust. His results also suggest that people who are more willing to place trust also tend to be higher in social intelligence (Yamagishi, Kikuchi, & Kosugi, 1999). Thus, high trust ability amounts to trusting to the amount appropriate for the situation and for our level of social intelligence—being cautious when we are not very good at detecting likely cheaters and so forth.

Implications for Research on Exchange Processes

The key contribution of evolutionary reasoning to theory and empirical research on exchange processes is a better, more accurate model of the actor (Kanazawa, 2001). Thus, to common assumptions and operationalizations that people are trying to obtain more resources (e.g., money; Molm, 1997) can be added motivations of status, reputation (in its manifold forms, including exchange, asset, and worthiness), identity, and so forth. This means also ensuring we investigate rich enough situations for people to use their full set of exchange-related attributes, including trust ability and social intelligence, and to pursue the wide range of exchange strategies, such as loyalty, gossip, reputation building, and ostracism threats. Box 10.1 presents some research suggestions and predictions produced by evolutionary reasoning in the area of exchange.

One specific implication, for example, concerns theories of effects of network structure on exchange outcomes. Most such research has concerned negotiated exchange in short-lived networks. In many natural situations, however, people's exchange networks involve reciprocal exchange and often are embedded in larger, long-term groups. Evolutionary reasoning suggests that the resultant generalized exchange and especially reciprocal exchange considerations will be important for people. Research should try to accommodate these considerations. For example, allowing people to choose network partners or even networks, along with more information or history on potential partners, would allow factors such as reputation, identity, social intelligence, and trusting ability to matter.

Box 10.1 Suggestions for Research and Predictions in the Area of Exchange

Exchange Suggestions

Research on exchange in networks
> Make not exchanging a viable option.
> Allow actors to choose or change networks.
> Analyze phenomena of loyalty, reputation, worthiness, impressing others, and hostility to rivals. Always monitor emotions.

Research on reciprocal and generalized exchange
> Allow network choice.
> Look at effects of reputation, identity, social intelligence, and trusting ability.

Research on social dilemmas
> Look at effects of preferences for material gain, prestige, impressing others, excluding rivals, reputation, identity, and risk.
> Find out what mechanisms of reputation people will create and use on their own, and the degree to which these are optimal.

Research on reputation systems
> Investigate circumstances under which people will develop formal reputation systems.
> Determine whether or not those systems are of optimal toughness.

Research on exchange systems generally
> Investigate the part identity (self-identification) plays in loyalty and in use of punishment.
> Investigate what affects these effects of identity.

Exchange Predictions

Reciprocal exchange will tend to produce greater emotional attachment to the group than negotiated exchange.

As group orientation is increased, successful exchange will produce more positive emotions toward the group and greater satisfaction from confirming group identity; failed exchange will produce the opposite.

In ultimatum game, when the payoff is earned, allocations will be more equal, and when they are unequal will arouse stronger anger than when the payoff is not earned.

Third parties will react more strongly to seeing someone receive less than promised than to seeing someone receive more than promised. This difference will be greater in a non-zero-sum situation.

IDENTITY PROCESSES

Identity concerns are the focus of a number of perspectives within social psychology and the study of group processes, including symbolic interactionism, identity theory, social identity theory, and affect control theory. These perspectives recognize that our perceptions of who others are, who we are ourselves, and who others perceive that we are matter to us.

Two of those perspectives, identity theory (Burke & Stets, 2009) and affect control theory (Heise, 1979, 2013; MacKinnon & Heise, 1993), are formalized control theories; their central mechanism is roughly as follows. Individuals have a certain standard—a conception of how the social situation they are in is in reality. They perceive what is happening in their social situation and try to fit it to the standard, taking action to do so if necessary. Thus, if something happens to deflect perceptions away from the standards, individuals will attempt to adjust things, to change the situation or change their perceptions, to restore a correspondence between the situation and their standards.

Evolutionary reasoning implies that if identity concerns and, possibly, related control mechanisms are characteristic of all human individuals, then they are innate, evolved. Moreover, the close link of these processes with emotions, explicitly laid out in affect control theory (Heise, 1979), reinforces that implication because much of the structure of emotions appears to be set genetically (LeDoux, 1996; Panksepp, 1998; Turner, 2000). If control processes are evolved, then we can apply evolutionary reasoning further to these processes, asking why they would have evolved and exactly what is likely to have evolved.

I suggest that identity concerns and associated mental mechanisms evolved to cope with exchange processes. Then, our concern with our own identity would be an evolved mechanism for being members in good standing of generalized exchange groups and for being desirable partners in reciprocal and negotiated exchange. Our concern with identities of others would have evolved to combat the problem of defection or cheating, especially in generalized and reciprocal exchange.

Concerning self-perception, one point is that members of generalized exchange groups should possess certain traits, and so we should too. These traits are likely to include honesty, truthfulness, kindness, generosity, and perhaps others more specific to the group, including group identity. Others' perceptions should be critical in this process because ultimately it is others' perceptions and not our own that decide whether or not we are in the generalized exchange group. Thus, "taking the role of the other" is key. The ultimate question is "Will they want me on their team?" and we want to be the kind of person who makes the answer "yes." It works similarly for reciprocal exchange. We are concerned with appearing equitable enough that others will want to continue reciprocal exchange relationships. For reciprocal and negotiated exchange especially, we also should want to appear valuable to others, as though we have something to offer. Note that it has been found that we, unsurprisingly, are distressed when others evaluate us lower than we perceive ourselves. However, we are pleased with a mild overevaluation, from our standpoint, and again distressed by a large overevaluation (Stets & Burke, 2014).

Control theories also describe how we deal with perceptions of our external social situation. It is likely that the mechanisms they describe evolved to keep tabs on our social environment so that we can deal with it effectively, again specifically in terms of generalized and reciprocal exchange. For example, notice that the three dimensions that affect control theory uses—evaluation (essentially goodness vs. badness), potency (powerfulness vs. powerlessness), and activity (being active vs. inactive)—all are highly relevant for partners in reciprocal or generalized exchange.

However, four important differences distinguish current control theories and evolutionary reasoning concerning these mechanisms. First, control theories suggest we have a perception of ourselves that is acquired and that we try to maintain. Evolutionary reasoning, on the other hand, suggests we do not so much have a self-identity as engage in a continual process of self-identification. Any evolutionary advantage must come from a feature affecting our behavior. Thus, there is no evolutionary advantage to simply having a belief about our identity. Self-identify can matter and could have mattered only if it affects behavior, in which case it is really a *process* of self-identification. Moreover, it is not a matter of affirming a self-identity that we possess. For a belief that needs to be affirmed is not a belief at all.

In this process, we may be motivated to perceive in ourselves traits that we do possess but also traits that may not in fact be true of us at all but would be advantageous for us to have (Whitmeyer, 1998). We try to perceive those qualities in ourselves, which involves control theory-like mechanisms of trying to confirm such qualities especially when they have been disconfirmed. The evolutionary advantage is that doing this in fact would tend to make us appear better partners for generalized and reciprocal exchange.

Evolutionary reasoning also suggests that our desires to perceive certain traits and not to perceive other traits in ourselves are weighed in the balance with our other motivations when we decide on behavior. We may have evolved the ability and predisposition to take identity matters into consideration, as described previously, but it would have been in light of our situation and other incentives present. Note that this view of identity reconciles Burke and Stets' (1999) and Lawler and Yoon's (1996, 1998) findings concerning commitment formation. Burke and Stets found that if partners confirmed each other's self-identity, then commitment to the relation increased. If wanting to have certain traits confirmed is a motivation or desire, then reciprocal confirmation of what the other wants to hear simply constitutes a positive exchange. This has the ultimate effect of increasing commitment, exactly the process Lawler and Yoon discussed. This also explains Carter's (2013) finding that in an ethically challenging situation, students behaved in accordance with their moral identity when the identity was activated.

The third difference concerns perceptions of others. Control theories state we have standards that we try to make our perceptions fit. Evolutionary reasoning suggests a different process. The greatest benefit to us should be for being accurate in our perceptions of social situations; thus, we should have evolved to be fairly accurate. However, perceptions can be very much in error. Most of us, at one time or another, have completely misconstrued a situation. For this reason, evolution probably would have favored a conservative approach to processing perceptions. If our perceptions of something social do not fit our preconceptions or standards, we initially infer that something is wrong in our perceptions, that there are other elements in the situation of which we were not aware, or something similar. However, over time, with increasing discrepant evidence, we become more likely to change fundamental understandings.

The fourth difference also concerns perceptions of others. The fact about others that is most important to us probably is whether or not they are worth having as exchange partners. In generalized exchange, almost everyone is *potentially* useful. Thus, the key questions are as follows. For negotiated and especially reciprocal exchange, we ask what the likelihood is that this person will cheat us. For generalized exchange, we ask if the person is a member in good standing of some generalized exchange group of ours. Largely, this is what was previously called *worthiness*: Is the person a member in good standing of the group (or likely to be so)?

Note that using evolutionary reasoning to develop theory about exchange processes and identity processes in fact points to an integrated theory that handles both types of processes. Taking exchange almost by definition to be the essence of social relationships, evolutionary reasoning puts identity processes and, as discussed later, status processes as well in the service of exchange. As the preceding discussion implies, identity processes are especially likely to be important in reciprocal and generalized exchange.

Let us consider what these modifications to theory concerning identity imply for research into group processes, first, incorporating concerns about *ourselves*—how we perceive ourselves and how others perceive us. Typically, we can incorporate self-identity matters into theoretical models by translating them into preferences or motives. In empirical research, this can be operationalized, for example, by attaching identity labels to behavior in exchange studies or linking exchange behavior or outcomes to justice. Many studies of exchange include reputation as a factor (Abell & Reyniers, 2000; Ensminger, 2001; Kollock, 1999). Explicit labels, however, can be introduced, for example, along the "cooperating" versus "cheating" dimension, an "exploitative" to "generous" dimension, and so forth. Transmission of information concerning exchange behavior can be varied, for example, by encouraging intermingling and conversation—gossip— or simply by allowing bystander observation.

Turning to concerns about *others'* identities, we can incorporate these more explicitly into the framework of generalized exchange. This means examining identity effects in the context of helping behavior, one-shot prisoner's dilemmas, and more formal generalized exchange structures. We know that in-group and out-group labels have effects (Tajfel, 1982; Yamagishi, Jin, & Kiyonari, 1999), but we can go far beyond this. We can examine the effects of perceived worthiness. We can study the process of collecting and transmitting information about identities. For example, when presented with a new, unfamiliar person in a generalized exchange situation, people should be willing to make efforts to ascertain the person's group membership, standing in the group, and exchange reputation. We can study ostracism. For example, we should be able to predict its likelihood depending on the situation and perceived behaviors and reasons for them. All these processes are likely to be implemented via emotions—for example, empathy, sympathy, and anger. This implementation deserves study as well, if only because emotions

---

Box 10.2 Suggestions for Research and Predictions in the Area of Identity

Identity Suggestions

In exchange studies, examine effects on exchange behavior of attaching identity labels to that behavior, such as "exploitative" or "generous." Examine effects of allowing gossip and of allowing bystander observation. Examine effects of these factors on evaluation of one's own exchange behavior.

Investigate the relationship of ostracism to exchange behaviors and to how the group labels a person, including in-group or out-group membership labels.

Investigate the role of emotions, such as empathy, sympathy, and anger, in the attaching of identity labels to people and their behavior.

Identity Predictions

The more exchange advantages possessing a particular trait appears to confer, the more likely people will be to claim that they possess that trait, including performance of behaviors demonstrating they possess that trait.

The more exchange advantages membership of a group appears to confer, the more likely people will be to claim they are members of that group, including performance of behaviors demonstrating they are members of that group.

People will treat evidence contradicting well-established attachment of traits to a person or especially a class of people more skeptically than evidence contradicting a recent attachment of traits.

As evidence contradicting well-established attachment of traits to a person or even a class of people increases, the attachment of traits itself becomes more likely to change.

When joined by an unfamiliar person in a generalized exchange situation, people will try to ascertain the person's group membership, standing in the group, and exchange reputation.

---

do not perfectly track costs and benefits in situations, including generalized exchange ones, and thus need to be included to have accurate explanations.

Box 10.2 summarizes the principal research suggestions and predictions produced by evolutionary reasoning in the area of identity that I have discussed.

STATUS PROCESSES

Status Characteristics

We know that in task-focused, collectively oriented groups, typically a hierarchy forms quickly and endures (Webster, 1975). Under certain conditions, such as a confining but yet unstructured social setting, a hierarchy is likely to form in a non-task-focused group as well (Gould, 2003; Martin, 2009). Given that status processes are rapid, practically automatic, and ubiquitous—not just among human groups but also among virtually all social animals (de Waal, 1996; Wilson, 1975)—it is likely that inherited qualities in humans play a specific role in their occurrence. Clarifying that role should help us improve our explanations.

In sociology, one body of research has built up theory and empirical evidence concerning *status characteristics*, which are attributes that, if group members differ on them and know that they do so, typically result in predictably different expectations for performance. An obvious question concerns the extent to which at what level predispositions concerning the association between the characteristic and the performance expectations are evolved and thus innate. As noted previously, inevitably at some level, they are innate, even if all that evolved was a general ability to acquire an association between a human characteristic and performance expectations. However, for some characteristics, the association may be less flexible. Applying evolutionary reasoning, educational degree, for example, which works as a diffuse status characteristic in modern American society (Berger, Fisek, Norman, & Zelditch, 1977), could not be innate because educational degrees were not conferred in the evolutionary environment. On the other hand, all past and present human societies of which we know not only make gender and age distinctions but also are stratified by gender and age to varying extents (Brown, 1991). In fact, this is a feature of ape societies generally. Thus, gender and age are good candidates for being status characteristics innately.

Hopcroft (2006) presents and gives experimental evidence for the hypothesis that the status implications of gender depend on age, the evolutionary reason being that for women past the age of childbearing, physical and physiological differences from men are less, as are psychological and behavioral differences resulting from those physical and physiological differences. Similar reasoning suggests other conditional or interaction effects for status characteristics. For example, status effects of height might be conditional on age or gender. Greater height would suggest greater physical strength and speed, which would have mattered more for what the young did. Height also tends to indicate the quality of background because children who are better nourished and whose mothers are better nourished will tend to be taller. However, this correlation would have tended to become less important as people distanced themselves in age from their background, as their parents and other senior relatives who might have helped them died. Thus, status effects of height may have evolved to diminish as age increases. As for an interaction between height and gender, both qualities signaled by height—physical strength and speed and quality of background—might have mattered more for men than for women. Thus, height might have evolved to be a status characteristic more for men than for women.

Hierarchy in Small Groups

The fact that in small groups that are task-focused and collectively oriented, a ranking process occurs quickly, automatically, and without explicit attention, and as far as we know, universally (Webster, 1975), suggests that group members have evolved predispositions that facilitate it happening. That assumption, if correct, is an aid to explaining the process theoretically because it puts a key constraint on the process: It has to be in people's interests to cooperate with the process, at least generally and in the long term.

Let us distinguish between four elements in the hierarchy formation process: leadership behavior, prestige or rank, performance expectations, and performance obligations. As anticipated by Homans (1974), Coleman (1990), and others, the requirement from evolutionary reasoning that the hierarchy formation process generally must be in everyone's interests suggests that the process in essence is exchange. Namely, group members confer *prestige* on certain group members, those for whom they have higher *performance expectations*, as an inducement and reward for *leadership behavior*. However, accompanying the conferral of prestige are *performance obligations*.

The evolutionary rationale for this explanation is that, on the one hand, leadership behaviors would have been costly, involving extra work or risks or both (see Lévi-Strauss' [1955] description of a foraging group). On the other hand, prestige is a strong human preference or reward, as emphasized more than a century ago by Veblen (1899/1918) and by many others since. It is almost certainly an innate preference because high prestige almost always has brought advantages, such as more power, more resources, and, the ultimate evolutionary coin, more or more valuable offspring (Ball & Eckel, 1996; Kaplan & Hill, 1985). The exchange, then, is that people will confer high prestige (e.g., leadership positions) on those for whom they hold high performance expectations with regard to leadership behaviors, contingent on corresponding performance obligations being met.

The one catch is the question of why a given individual should give the "leader" prestige and implicitly accept low rank him- or herself. The leader provides a benefit to the group, so let others in the group defer and provide the prestige. If this "free-rider" logic holds, it will hold for each group member and we will have a collective action problem. There will be, in general, no conferral of prestige and no evolution of such a tendency. Simulation studies suggest, however, that in such exchange situations, the free-rider logic will not hold if the public good provided is nonrival—that is, if the amount of the public good one person receives is not affected by the number of others also receiving the good (Whitmeyer, 2007). The public goods provided by many leaders—military direction, strategic guidance, political representation, and ideological inspiration—are, and in the evolutionary environment would have been, indeed nonrival. Thus, it is plausible that people would have evolved a predisposition to automatically award prestige to those whom they believe will deliver on the obligations of leadership.

We can investigate and test this reasoning further. One prediction is that in task-focused, collectively oriented groups, if high-prestige members fail to meet their performance obligations, low-ranking members will tend to withdraw their awarded prestige and to become angry and possibly aggressive toward the delinquent high-prestige members. Second, suppose in such a group there is good reason to believe that a person for whom high performance expectations have formed will not deliver on performance obligations. Then we can predict that other group members will award that person neither prestige nor material benefits. Correspondingly, they also will not form high reward expectations for that person—that is, they will not expect that person to receive a disproportionately high share of benefits. Third, all these considerations imply, at a more general level, that leadership reputation will matter to members of such a group. In other words, people should be willing to expend time and other resources finding out and communicating about leadership qualities of potential leaders, perhaps as a positive function of the benefits at stake.

Several predictions follow from the idea that prestige is a benefit, whereas performance of leadership behaviors is a cost. Increasing apparent prestige or rank of group members should increase their performance of leadership behaviors and even the quality of their contributions, whereas decreasing apparent prestige should have the opposite effect. Increasing anonymity of contributions should lower the performance of leadership behaviors by high-prestige members. Adding costs to being a leader, such as attaching some onerous task to the position, should decrease initial competition for that position. Adding benefits to being a leader, such as wider trumpeting of prestige or increased power in some areas, should increase that initial competition. All these predictions can be tested in the laboratory.

Similarly, we can predict effects of self-identity—or rather, as I suggested previously, self-identification—issues on prestige outcomes. Under some circumstances, people may take prestige outcomes or even aspects of group process as relevant for self-identification, which thereby adds another motivation, another cost–benefit component, to the mix of behavioral determinants. For example, if someone has been accused of being "weak" or "unassertive," she may try to refute that to herself by being especially active in discussion, with possible results for prestige outcomes. Likewise, heightening the perceived relevance of group participation or prestige outcomes to more general abilities or traits is likely to affect group participation and prestige outcomes in predictable ways.

Box 10.3 summarizes the principal research suggestions and predictions produced by evolutionary reasoning in the area of status processes that I have discussed.

Box 10.3 Suggestions for Research and Predictions in the Area of Status

Status Suggestions

Investigate possible innateness of certain status characteristics, such as age, beauty, disability, gender, height, and title.

Investigate possible interaction between status characteristics in their effects on performance expectations. Especially likely are interactions with age and with gender.

In task-oriented group, investigate formation of alliances of group members to limit power of leader.

Investigate relevance of prestige outcomes and other aspects of group process for self-identification and also how that affects individual behavior and group process.

(continued)

Box 10.3 Continued

Status Predictions

In the absence of *any* rewards for leadership behaviors—including recognition by others and self-identification with a desired trait—people will tend to choose to follow instead.

People will be more willing to provide prestige and its trappings to those who provide non-rival goods than to those who provide rival goods.

Suppose the high-prestige group member harms group performance. Other group members' performance expectations for the high-prestige person should decrease *more* if the high-prestige person is trying to meet performance obligations but failing than if the high-prestige person simply is shirking, is not trying.

The longer or the more a group leader delivers on performance, the more likely group members are to continue to award that leader prestige in the presence of a seemingly better alternative.

In a long-term group, group members will be more tolerant of occasional poor performance by the leader than will members in a short-term group.

Poor performance by a leader will lead to negative emotions. However, when the leader is illegitimate compared to legitimate, scorn is more likely and anger is less likely.

Excellent performance by an illegitimate leader will increase the leader's legitimacy—that is, the prestige group members award to the leader.

Suppose group members have formed high performance expectations for a group member. The less likely that person is to deliver on performance obligations, the less prestige and material benefits they will award that person, and the lower will be reward expectations they form for that person.

The greater the benefits to group members from high group performance, the more resources they will be willing to expend finding out about leadership qualities of high-status group members.

Increasing the apparent prestige or rank of group members will increase their performance of leadership behaviors and the quality of their contributions. Decreasing their apparent prestige will have opposite effect.

Increasing anonymity of contributions will lower the performance of leadership behaviors by high-prestige members.

Adding costs to being a leader, such as attaching some onerous task to the position, will decrease initial competition for leadership. Adding benefits to being a leader, such as wider trumpeting of prestige or increased power in some areas, will increase that initial competition.

The greater the perceived relevance of group participation or prestige outcomes to more general abilities or traits, the more self-identification and self-presentation motivations concerning those abilities and traits will affect group participation and prestige outcomes.

CONCLUSION

In this chapter, I have applied evolutionary reasoning within three principal areas of group process research to generate suggestions for future research and specific predictions to test. It is important to note that evolutionary reasoning, an application of evolutionary psychology, is neither competitor nor substitute for usual sociological theories and methods in group process research. Rather, it is a complementary tool, which can help advance theory and suggest new areas of empirical investigation. For example, current theories of effects of network structure on negotiated exchange outcomes make accurate predictions under the usual conditions. However, evolutionary reasoning suggests that reciprocal and generalized exchange considerations will be important for people in most situations. They can be included, for example, by allowing network choice, at which point factors such as reputation, identity, social intelligence, and trusting ability may become influential. In the area of status processes, evolutionary reasoning suggests that performance obligations are likely to be an important element and should be included more explicitly in theory and research.

Beyond the specific contributions that evolutionary psychology may be able to make in different areas, evolutionary reasoning may help bring about a unified group process theory—a comprehensive, logical coherent, appropriately parsimonious method of explanation and prediction for any and all group processes. For example, I have suggested in this chapter that concerns with both our own and others' identities exist primarily to help us in exchange processes. Likewise, I have suggested that status processes in task-focused and collectively oriented groups are operating implicitly in an exchange process, of prestige for leadership. This, in turn, implies that ultimately we may be able to put all these processes together under an exchange framework. At a more fundamental level, we should be able to take the different individual-level models at the heart of currently distinct group process theories and put them together into a single individual-level model that will be the basis for our unified group process theory. Indeed, from a different perspective, any person's behavior—both overt and internal—is produced by a fairly discrete system and therefore, at least in theory, must be capable of being modeled by a single model.

This returns again to the potential contribution of evolutionary psychology. As the word "psychology" suggests, any contribution evolutionary psychology can make will improve our conception of the individual. Doing so can improve group process theories and may even be able to bring them together.

REFERENCES

Abell, P., & Reyniers, D. (2000). Generalised reciprocity and reputation in the theory of cooperation: A framework. *Analyze & Kritik, 2000*, 3–18.

Ball, S. B., & Eckel, C. C. (1996). Buying status: Experimental evidence on status in negotiation. *Psychology and Marketing, 13*, 381–405.

Barclay, P. (2012). Harnessing the power of reputation: Strengths and limits for promoting cooperative behaviors. *Evolutionary Psychology, 10*, 868–883.

Berger, J., Fisek, M. H., Norman, R. Z., & Zelditch, M., Jr. (1977). *Status characteristics and social interaction: An expectation states approach.* New York, NY: Elsevier.

Binmore, K. (2001). The breakdown of social contracts. In S. N. Durlauf & H. P. Young (Eds.), *Social dynamics* (pp. 213–234). Washington, DC: Brookings Institution Press.

Boehm, C. (1999). *Hierarchy in the forest: The evolution of egalitarian behavior.* Cambridge, MA: Harvard University Press.

Brown, D. E. (1991). *Human universals.* Philadelphia, PA: Temple University Press.

Bruner, J. S. (1958). On perceptual readiness. *Psychological Review, 64*, 123–152.

Burke, P. J., & Stets, J. E. (1999). The link between identity and role performance. *Social Psychology Quarterly, 44*, 83–92.

Burke, P. J., & Stets, J. E. (2009). *Identity theory.* Oxford, UK: Oxford University Press.

Burt, R. S. (2001). Bandwidth and echo: Trust, information, and gossip in social networks. In A. Casella & J. E. Rauch (Eds.), *Networks and markets: Contributions from economics and sociology* (pp. 30–74). New York: Russell Sage Foundation.

Burt, R. S., & Knez, M. (1996). Trust and third-party gossip. In R. M. Kramer & T. R. Tyler (Eds.), *Trust in organizations: Frontiers of theory and research* (pp. 68–89). Thousand Oaks, CA: Sage.

Carter, M. J. (2013). Advancing identity theory: Examining the relationship between activated identities and behavior in different social contexts. *Social Psychology Quarterly, 76*, 203–223.

Coleman, J. S. (1990). *Foundations of social theory.* Cambridge, MA: Harvard University Press.

Cosmides, L. (1989). The logic of social exchange: Has natural selection shaped how humans season? *Cognition, 31*, 187–276.

Cosmides, L., & Tooby, J. (1992). Cognitive adaptations for social exchange. In J. H. Barkow, L. Cosmides, & J. Tooby (Eds.), *The adapted mind: Evolutionary psychology and the generation of culture* (pp. 163–228). New York, NY: Oxford University Press.

de Waal, F. (1996). *Good natured: The origins of right and wrong in humans and other animals.* Cambridge, MA: Harvard University Press.

Devine, P. G. (1989). Stereotypes and prejudice: Their automatic and controlled components. *Journal of Personality and Social Psychology, 56*, 5–18.

Ekeh, P. P. (1974). *Social exchange theory: The two traditions.* Cambridge, MA: Harvard University Press.

Emerson, R. M. (1981). Social exchange theory. In M. Rosenberg & R. Turner (Eds.), *Social psychology: Sociological perspectives* (pp. 30–65). New York, NY: Basic Books.

Ensminger, J. (2001). Reputations, trust, and the principal agent problem. In K. S. Cook (Ed.), *Trust in society* (pp. 185–201). New York, NY: Russell Sage Foundation.

Fehr, E., & Gächter, S. (2002). Altruistic punishment in humans. *Nature, 415*, 137–140.

Fiske, A. P. (1991). *Structures of social life: The four elementary forms of human relations.* New York, NY: Free Press.

Frank, R. H. (1988). *Passions within reason: The strategic role of the emotions.* New York, NY: Norton.

Gould, R. V. (2003). *Collision of wills: How ambiguity about social rank breeds conflict.* Chicago, IL: University of Chicago Press.

Heckathorn, D. D. (1990). Collective sanctions and compliance norms: A formal theory of group-mediated social control. *American Sociological Review, 55*, 366–384.

Heckathorn, D. D. (1993). Collective action and group heterogeneity: Voluntary provision versus selective incentives. *American Sociological Review, 58*, 329–350.

Heise, D. R. (1979). *Understanding events*. New York, NY: Cambridge University Press.

Heise, D. R. (2013). Modeling interactions in small groups. *Social Psychology Quarterly*, 76, 52–72.

Hoffman, E., McCabe, K., & Smith, V. L. (1996). Social distance and other-regarding behavior in dictator games. *American Economic Review*, 86, 653–660.

Homans, G. C. (1974). *Social behavior: Its elementary forms*. New York, NY: Harcourt Brace Jovanovich.

Hopcroft, R. L. (2006). Status characteristics among older individuals: The diminished significance of gender. *Sociological Quarterly*, 47, 361–374.

Jasso, G. (1993). Choice and emotion in comparison theory. *Rationality and Society*, 5, 231–274.

Kameda, T., Takezawa, M., Tindale, R. S., & Smith, C. M. (2002). Social sharing and risk reduction: Exploring a computational algorithm for the psychology of windfall gains. *Evolution and Human Behavior*, 23, 11–33.

Kanazawa, S. (2001). De gustibus est disputandum. *Social Forces*, 79, 1131–1162.

Kaplan, H., & Hill, K. (1985). Food sharing among ache foragers: Tests of explanatory hypotheses. *Current Anthropology*, 26, 233–245.

Kelly, R. L. (1995). *The foraging spectrum: Diversity in hunter–gatherer lifeways*. Washington, DC: Smithsonian Institution Press.

Kiyonari, T., Tanida, S., & Yamagishi, T. (2000). Social exchange and reciprocity: Confusion or a heuristic? *Evolution and Human Behavior*, 21, 411–427.

Klein, D. B. (1997). Promise keeping in the great society: A model of credit information sharing. In D. B. Klein (Ed.), *Reputation: Studies in the voluntary elicitation of good conduct* (pp. 267–287). Ann Arbor, MI: University of Michigan Press.

Kollock, P. (1993). An eye for an eye leaves everyone blind: Cooperation and accounting systems. *American Sociological Review*, 58, 768–786.

Kollock, P. (1999). The production of trust in online markets. In S. R. Thye, E. J. Lawler, M. W. Macy, & H. A. Walker (Eds.), *Advances in group processes* (Vol. 16, pp. 99–123). Stamford, CT: JAI.

Koudenburg, N., Postmes, T., & Gordijn, E. H. (2013). Resounding silences: Subtle norm regulation in everyday interactions. *Social Psychology Quarterly*, 76, 224–241.

Lawler, E. J. (2001). An affect theory of social exchange. *American Journal of Sociology*, 107, 321–352.

Lawler, E. J., Thye, S. R., & Yoon, J. (2000). Emotion and group cohesion in productive exchange. *American Journal of Sociology*, 106, 616–657.

Lawler, E. J., & Yoon, J. (1996). Commitment in exchange relations: Test of a theory of relational cohesion. *American Sociological Review*, 61, 89–108.

Lawler, E. J., & Yoon, J. (1998). Network structure and emotion in exchange relations. *American Sociological Review*, 63, 871–894.

LeDoux, J. (1996). *The emotional brain*. New York, NY: Simon & Schuster.

Lévi-Strauss, C. (1955). *Tristes tropiques*. Paris, France: Plon.

MacKinnon, N. J., & Heise, D. R. (1993). Affect control theory: Delineation and development. In J. Berger & M. Zelditch, Jr. (Eds.), *Theoretical research programs: Studies in the growth of theory* (pp. 64–103). Stanford, CA: Stanford University Press.

Martin, J. L. (2009). Formation and stabilization of vertical hierarchies among adolescents: Towards a quantitative ethology of dominance among humans. *Social Psychology Quarterly*, 72, 241–264.

Maryanski, A., & Turner, J. H. (1992). *The social cage: Human nature and the evolution of society*. Stanford, CA: Stanford University Press.

Milinski, M., Semmann, D., & Krambeck, H.-J. (2002). Reputation helps solve the "tragedy of the commons." *Nature, 415*, 424–426.

Molm, L. (1997). *Coercive power in social exchange*. Cambridge, UK: Cambridge University Press.

Molm, L., Peterson, G., & Takahashi, N. (1999). Power in negotiated and reciprocal exchange. *American Sociological Review, 64*, 876–890.

Nisbett, R., & Ross, L. (1980). *Human inference: Strategies and shortcomings of social judgment*. Englewood Cliffs, NJ: Prentice-Hall.

Panksepp, J. (1998). *Affective neuroscience: The foundations of human and animal emotions*. New York, NY: Oxford University Press.

Runciman, W. G. (2000). *The social animal*. Ann Arbor, MI: University of Michigan Press.

Sherif, M., Harvey, O. J., White, J., Hood, W., & Sherif, C. (1961). *Intergroup conflict and cooperation: The robber's cave experiment*. Norman, OK: University of Oklahoma, Institute of Intergroup Relations.

Simpson, B., & Willer, R. (2008). Altruism and indirect reciprocity: The interaction of person and situation in prosocial behavior. *Social Psychology Quarterly, 71*, 37–52.

Stets, J. E., & Burke, P. J. (2014). Emotions and identity nonverification. *Social Psychology Quarterly, 77*, 387–410.

Tajfel, H. (1982). *Social identity and intergroup relations*. Cambridge, UK: Cambridge University Press.

Thye, S. R., Lawler, E. J., & Yoon, J. (2011). The emergence of embedded relations and group formation in networks of competition. *Social Psychology Quarterly, 74*, 387–413.

Trivers, R. (1971). The evolution of reciprocal altruism. *Quarterly Review of Biology, 27*, 1–32.

Turner, J. H. (2000). *On the origins of human emotions: A sociological inquiry into the evolution of human affect*. Stanford, CA: Stanford University Press.

Turner, J. H. (2002). *Face to face: Toward a sociological theory of interpersonal behavior*. Stanford, CA: Stanford University Press.

Tversky, A., & Kahneman, D. (1981). The framing of decisions and the psychology of choice. *Science, 211*, 453–458.

Veblen, T. (1918). *The theory of the leisure class*. New York, NY: Viking. (Original work published 1899)

Vine, I. (1992). Altruism and human nature: Resolving the evolutionary paradox. In P. M. Oliner, S. P. Oliner, L. Baron, L. A. Blum, D. L. Krebs, & M. Z. Smolenska (Eds.), *Embracing the other: Philosophical, psychological, and historical perspectives on altruism* (pp. 73–103). New York, NY: New York University Press.

Webster, M., Jr. (1975). *Actions and actors*. New York, NY: Winthrop.

Whitmeyer, J. M. (1998). A human actor model for social science. *Journal for the Theory of Social Behaviour, 28*, 403–434.

Whitmeyer, J. M. (2007). Prestige from the provision of collective goods. *Social Forces, 85*, 1765–1786.

Wilson, E. O. (1975). *Sociobiology: The new synthesis*. Cambridge, MA: Belknap.

Yamagishi, T. (1998). *The structure of trust: The evolutionary games of mind and society*. Tokyo, Japan: Tokyo University Press.

Yamagishi, T., & Cook, K. S. (1993). Generalized exchange and social dilemmas. *Social Psychology Quarterly, 56*, 235–248.

Yamagishi, T., Jin, N., & Kiyonari, T. (1999). Bounded generalized reciprocity: Ingroup boasting and ingroup favoritism. In S. R. Thye, E. J. Lawler, M. W. Macy, & H. A. Walker (Eds.), *Advances in group processes* (Vol. 16, pp. 161–197). Stamford, CT: JAI.

Yamagishi, T., Kikuchi, M., & Kosugi, M.. (1999). Trust, gullibility, and social intelligence. *Asian Journal of Social Psychology, 2*, 145–161.

PART III

BIOSOCIOLOGICAL APPROACHES

CHAPTER 11

··

THE GENETICS OF HUMAN BEHAVIOR

A Hopeless Opus?

··

COLTER MITCHELL

HUMAN behaviors—especially health and social behavior—are important variables for scientists in a range of disciplines. For many fields, behavior is the culmination of layers of mechanisms and, possibly more important, is observable when many other aspects of human life are not. Also, frequently behaviors can be modified and thus interventions and policy can be created and enacted. Individual behaviors help us predict future social interactions, processes, and even structures. Thus, it is not surprising that behaviors often stand in the contested overlapping areas of research such as psychology, biology, health, sociology, economics, and demography. This chapter focuses on one aspect of this literature—the genetics of health and social behavior—with an emphasis on recent work linking genome-wide data to human behavior. This particular focus is interesting because despite the importance of these behaviors to sociologists, they have not generally participated in examination of the genetic basis of these behaviors. Nevertheless, there is much evidence for genetic effects on things social scientists care about—social behaviors such as delinquency, substance abuse, and educational attainment—and that evidence is likely to increase in the future, so it is important for sociologists to be aware of it and include it in their theories and empirical studies. Consequently, this chapter provides a primer for sociologists interested in understanding potential genetic contributions to well-examined health and social behaviors.

This chapter has two distinct sections. First is an overview and discussion of the methods and measures used in the genome-wide studies of the genetics of behavior. These methods provide an amazing—almost overwhelming—amount of information. However, they are also misunderstood and often misinterpreted. The second is a review of recent genome-wide association studies of some key health and social behaviors. After completing this chapter, readers should be more aware of the methods in the field, their strengths and limitations, and should have a sampling of the literature.

Heritability and the Excitement of Genetics

Long before researchers measured people's molecular genetic makeup (i.e., through DNA), they used twins to estimate the average influence of genetics in a population through comparisons between monozygotic and dizygotic twins. In short, twin studies rely on the fact that monozygotic (identical) twins share essentially 100% of their DNA, whereas dizygotic (fraternal) twins share the same amount as all full siblings do— 50%. Thus, outcome, or phenotype, differences between identical twins must occur as a result of differences in experiences (nutritional, social, physical, etc.) that only one twin experienced. Furthermore, comparing the correlation of any outcome of interest for same-sex dizygotic twins to the correlation of the same outcome for monozygotic twins provides an estimate of how much of an effect sharing twice as much of the genome has on the outcome. There are other important assumptions that, if violated, make the estimates biased, such as the equal environments assumption and the random mating assumption, but these are beyond the scope of this chapter (Freese, 2008; Freese & Powell, 2003; Turkheimer, 2012).

During approximately the past 50 years, a tremendous research effort using tens of millions of twins to study tens of thousands of traits has resulted in thousands of articles (Tucker-Drob & Bates, 2015; Turkheimer, 2012). Based on a recent meta-analysis of these studies (Tucker-Drob & Bates, 2015), some broad conclusions can be surmised: (a) The samples are nonrandom (US accounted for 34%, whereas Asia, Africa, and South America in total accounted for 1.2%); (b) the examined traits are nonrandom (of the >17,000 examined traits, more than half could be classified as psychiatric, cognitive, or metabolic); (c) with some variation, almost everything that has been examined thus far has a significant "genetic" component (on average, approximately 0.49 on a scale from 0 to 1); and (d) most traits have a small or almost no effect on the "shared environment" (the environment that affects the twins in the exact same way). It is the last two aspects that have excited some and frustrated other scientists (Freese, 2008; Freese & Powell, 2003; Turkheimer, 2012).

The assumptions and meanings of the results of twin models have long been debated in social science (Freese, 2008; Freese & Powell, 2003; Tucker-Drob & Bates, 2015). For example, the extent to which the genetic component measures direct genetic effects or more interactive genetic effects (i.e., gene–gene or gene–environment) is evident in many articles. Similarly, the unshared environment (the third component along with the genetic and shared environment component) is a large and ambiguous component of environmental influences that affect the twins differently (e.g., having two different exposures to violence even if they are raised in the same neighborhood). Regardless of the debate, twin studies have provided an estimate for which later scientists have attempted to either discredit or match (Freese, 2008; Freese & Powell, 2003; Tucker-Drob & Bates, 2015; Turkheimer, 2012).

If we give the benefit of the doubt and assume the twin studies are providing an accurate estimate of the heritability (a population-level estimate of the percentage of outcome variation accounted for by genetic variation), the heritability of most behavioral outcomes ranges from approximately 0.2 to 0.7, with most over 0.33 (Selzam et al., 2017; Tucker-Drob & Bates, 2015; Turkheimer, 2012). In other words, genetic variation would be expected in explain, on average, more than 33% of variation in any behavioral phenotype in a population. Interestingly, more research is showing that these estimates of genetic heritability are not constant across populations or subpopulations. For example, one of the most important social science phenotypes, education, shows approximately 40% heritability, 35% shared environment, and 25% non-shared environment (Tucker-Drob & Bates, 2015; Turkheimer, 2012). However, these proportions change by country, gender, and birth cohort (Tucker-Drob & Bates, 2015). For example, countries with fewer social welfare or social support programs report stronger genetic components, as do males and people born later in the 20th century. Thus, even broad genetic effects still have nontrivial interactions with the environment. Ultimately, however, results of twin research suggest that there is a sizable percentage of all behavior that is accountable by genes in some way. The specifics as to which genes and to what extent it is a result of gene–environment interactions or other mechanisms stem from the concept that there is, in fact, a genetic effect.

It was in the context of decades of twin research that in 2003 the Human Genome Project finalized the mapping of the human genome (Collins et al., 1998; Pritchard & Cox, 2002). Although clearly dedicated more to uncovering the genetics of human disease, human behavioral phenotypes followed closely behind. The advances in the availability of molecular genetic data quickly allowed more fine-grained analyses attempting to pinpoint the specific genetic loci involved in human behavior. The findings were both over- and underwhelming.

First, the human genome is enormous, composed of approximately 3 billion pairs of nucleotide molecules (the smallest unit is a single nucleotide base pair [BP]). The Human Genome Project identified and mapped each BP in the sequence (over the 23 chromosome pairs). The human genome has approximately 20,000–23,000 regional groupings of BPs that have been designated as genes (Collins et al., 1998; Pritchard & Cox, 2002). Each gene provides the instructions that are used for building RNA, amino acids, proteins, and ultimately all cells in the body. Second, despite its impressive size, there is a surprising lack of variation. Across 99.6% of the entire genome, there is virtually no variation in the nucleotides across individuals. Out of the 3 billion BPs in the human genome, only approximately 15–20 million have variation in more than 5% of the population. This was far less variation than scientists expected (and approximately one-fifth the number of genes they expected). Furthermore, only approximately one-fourth to one-third of the genome appears to be in the genes that can be detected—the rest is what was initially thought to be "junk DNA" but has since been shown to be extremely important (Pennisi, 2012).

With the relative lack of variation in the genome, with few genes, paired with a wide range of phenotypic variation and typically high genetic heritability, the "common-disease, common-variant" hypothesis was widely held (Freese & Shostak, 2009; Gibson, 2012). This hypothesis essentially suggested that a few common (i.e., available in more than 5% of the population) variants each explained a small (1–8%) variance in every outcome. Thus, if education was 40% heritable, it may take 8–12 genetic loci to explain most of the variation due to genetics. Within a few years, this hypothesis was generally disproven (Freese, Li, & Wade, 2003; Freese & Shostak, 2009; Gibson, 2012). That is, even with studies of hundreds of thousands of participants, with millions of genetic markers, we still only explain less than 10% (and often less than 1%) of the variance—far below the expected 30–50% estimated by twin research. Moreover, the loci implicated in these studies were not from 8–12 regions but, rather, from hundreds of regions across the genome (Allen et al., 2010). This general concept of the difference between expected heritability (from twin research) and estimated variance accounted for with measured genes is called the "missing heritability problem" (Manolio et al., 2009; Zuk, Hechter, Sunyaev, & Lander, 2012).

As researchers dispersed into different camps examining the underlying reasons for this missing heritability, fundamental differences in the methods used to detect the genetics of behavior emerged. One distinguishing factor of the different groups was the way in which they leaned toward narrow-sense heritability versus broad-sense heritability. The broad-sense heritability model posits that additive contributions of genetic variants are insufficient to explain the missing heritability. Proponents of this model point to a long history of detection of genotype-by-genotype interactions (GxG interactions, also known as epistasis) and genotype-by-environment interactions (GxE interactions) in model organism quantitative genetic research, and they note the increasing number of studies documenting epigenetic effects and inheritance of DNA methylation patterns (Miller, 2010; Richards, 2006). The notion here is that genetic studies measure only the average effects of alleles across thousands of individuals; they are incapable of capturing heterogeneity of effect sizes at the individual level that would be the hallmark of these broader components of the genetic architecture. The narrow-sense heritability group is primarily focused on main, additive effects of genes but can differ tremendously on the fundamentals of how those are manifest within the genetic architecture. This camp of researchers primarily focuses on finer grain measurement of the genome (including sequencing) on larger samples, with the assumption that larger samples will allow for more precise estimates of the hundreds or thousands of effects likely influencing any behavioral outcome.

Although beyond the scope of this chapter, which focuses on research related to narrow-sense heritability, broad-sense heritability has a large and diverse field. The first research in this camp primarily utilized "candidate" genes or regions (Belsky, Moffitt, & Caspi, 2013; Hewitt, 2012; Mitchell et al., 2013). This research has heavily relied on animal models to determine which genetic markers to examine, and there has been a preference for use of smaller, but often far more phenotypically rich, samples (Hewitt, 2012; Mitchell et al., 2013). This is the research most familiar to sociologists, psychologists, and economists. This is the research that is found in the top journals of these fields, such as the *American Journal of Sociology* (e.g., see the special issue 2008, Vol. 114 (S1)),

American Sociological Review, and *Child Development* (see special issue 2013. Vol. 84 (1)), and covers a wide range of human behavior studied in those fields. Also, although there has been tremendous promise and some limited successes, failure for results to replicate in this area across populations and even within studies has shown the complexity and difficulty of conducting this type of work (Belsky, Moffitt, & Caspi, 2013; Hewitt, 2012; Mitchell et al., 2013). Without focusing on one particular researcher or area for criticism, researchers within this area are working out their own methods for solidifying this research. To be fully transparent, this is where the majority of my early biosocial work currently exists. Possibly in the near future, a more thorough review of broad-sense heritability of social behaviors will be possible, but for now I point readers to a particularly well-done review for psychologists (Manuck & McCaffery, 2014), who have participated in this area far more than have sociologists.

THE AGE OF GENOME-WIDE ASSOCIATION STUDIES

For the purpose of this chapter, the primary focus is on research examining the additive main effects of genes. For clarity, it is important to understand how genome-wide association studies (GWAS) are conducted because that is the focus of the rest of the chapter (for more detailed information, see McCarthy et al., 2008; Pearson & Manolio, 2008)). GWAS is currently built on the smallest measures of the genome—a base pair. For the vast majority of base pair locations, there are only two possible nucleotides that occur (e.g., a cytosine or a thymine). The nucleotide that is more common in a population is called the "major allele," and the nucleotide that is less common is called the "minor allele." Thus, for each base pair locus, there are three possibilities: An individual has zero minor alleles and two major alleles, one minor and one major allele, or two minor alleles but no major alleles. If the minor allele is present in at least 5% of the population, it is called a single nucleotide polymorphism (SNP). It is the measurement of hundreds to now millions of SNPs that has constituted most of the GWAS era.

Once a study has collected a tissue (typically saliva or blood) for the purpose of measuring DNA (unlike other biomarkers, DNA is the same in all tissue types), the next step is to genotype the participants. Initially, this was done through very labor-intensive processes, but in the past decade, there has been a rapid increase in the use of genome-wide SNP microarrays (or SNP chips). Most commonly, these SNP chips are a selection of microscopic polystyrene beads, each with a specific probe that hybridizes DNA, which is then quantified luminescence. Due to the microscopic measurement, these chips, which are 2–3 × 3–4 inches in size, provide anywhere from a few thousand to, more commonly, millions of genotyped markers (i.e., SNPs). Algorithms are applied to the image from each probe to determine the genotype for that particular locus. This is the raw genotype data; some probes work well and are able to detect genotypes for everyone, whereas other probes are not as efficient, causing many participants to not have a genotype for specific SNPs. Determining the cut-off for genotyping quality is part of the quality control process, and it should be reported as part of the data release.

There are several different makes and models of DNA microarrays, which offer different counts of probes or foci for the targeted genotypes (e.g., for cancer or psychiatric work), but most of the chip is taken up with "tag SNPs." Tag SNPs attempt to create a sample of the whole genome—with little concern of the extent to which a particular SNP is responsible for creating a protein (i.e., functional) or predictive of any behavior. Instead, tag SNPs utilize the fact that SNPs are typically highly correlated ($r > 0.95$) with many SNPs in close proximity to a particular SNP (called linkage disequilibrium). Thus, even if a study genotypes only 1–5 million SNPs, using reference panels with sequenced genetic data (i.e., they genotyped 20+ million SNPs) and concept of linkage disequilibrium, the study can impute to tens of millions of SNPs (Pearson & Manolio, 2008). This imputation is not multiple imputation but, rather, uses information provided by the tag SNPs to find the closest matches in the reference panel and then takes the average genotype count from the reference panel. Some genotyped SNPs are also often imputed to test the imputation quality. For many populations, imputation quality is exceptionally high, and low imputation quality SNPs are removed in analysis. These data provide the basis for a GWAS.

Controlling for some basic ancestry measures (called population stratification adjustments; for further discussion, see Abdellaoui et al., 2013; Campbell et al., 2005; Hamer, 2000; Price et al., 2006) and typically one to three key control variables (sex, age, etc.), the phenotype or outcome of interest is regressed on each SNP individually—resulting in millions of regression models (with only a few coefficients in each model). Although these individual regressions could be done in any statistical package, specialized software such as PLINK (http://zzz.bwh.harvard.edu/plink/) has been created to handle the massive size of the millions of genetic variables. Results are typically constrained to report the effect size and p value of the individual loci (i.e., SNP). Although additional complexity can be added, this is a fundamental process for generating results for a GWAS.

However, at this point, it is important to note that early on, GWAS researchers recognized two important facts: (a) With so many tests, false positives were essentially guaranteed, and (b) unless effects were exceptionally large, much larger samples were needed to be powered to identify the weak genetic effects. The first problem resulted in the adjustment of the significance test from $p < 0.05$ to $p < 5 \times 10^{-8}$ and the requirement to replicate the finding in another, preferably independent, sample (Pearson & Manolio, 2008). The need for larger samples led to the formation of consortia of dozens to even hundreds of studies on a wide array of topics. These consortia included the Psychiatric Genetics Consortium (PGC), the Genetic Investigation of ANthropometric Traits (GIANT) consortium, and the Social Science Genetic Association Consortium (SSGAC). Consortia work with the collaborative member studies to harmonize phenotypes and analyses and then pool results into meta-analyses. Typically, one set of studies acts as a discovery sample, while another set acts as the replication sample. This has resulted in the discovery of thousands of genetic associations that pass the major hurdles to be accepted as validated associations (McCarthy et al., 2008; Okbay et al., 2016a; Pearson & Manolio, 2008).

Genome-wide approaches can also be used to estimate the heritability of outcomes in samples of individuals who are not related, thereby addressing some concerns about particular assumptions of twin models (J. Yang et al., 2010, 2012). Recall that among the 0.4% of DNA that is *not* shared identically among all humans, monozygotic twins share 100% of that 0.4%, whereas dizygotic twins, full siblings, and parent–child relationships share 50%; half-siblings and grandparent–grandchild relationships share 25%; first cousins share 12.5% and second cousins share 3.125%; and for most genetic studies, an unrelated individual shares less than 2.5% of that 0.4%. Thus, in the same way that twin studies contrast the 100% shared genes with the 50% shared genes, molecular studies use the small genetic correlation of unrelated individuals to examine phenotypic correlation (J. Yang et al., 2010, 2012). With a large enough sample size, the result, in theory, is a measure of narrow-sense genetic heritability (J. Yang et al., 2010, 2012).

LIMITATIONS OF THE METHODS AND DATA

As presented in the next section, the previously discussed methods and data are generating a large scientific literature. However, although the area has directly addressed many important limitations (multiple testing, population stratification, etc.), other limitations are seemingly ignored. Potentially the major concern for most social and behavioral scientists (and, recently, for some in the genetics community as well) is that most genome-wide studies have a tremendously skewed sample (David et al., 2012; Popejoy & Fullerton, 2016). In brief, higher socioeconomic status (SES) European ancestry is overrepresented by a substantial degree in this research compared to what might be expected in the world population (David et al., 2012; Popejoy & Fullerton, 2016). Although it is tempting to simply blame this lack of diversity in the sample on ethnocentrism and discrimination, the situation is more complex. For example, there are scientific justifications for why European ancestry populations are so prominently used. As described previously, there is concern about false relationships due to population stratification—the strong link between allele frequencies and ancestry—so most analyses stratify by race/ethnicity (Price et al., 2006). Similarly, the mixing of two or more distinct ancestries—population admixture—makes mixed populations very challenging to study. Add to that the fact that among major ancestral groups (East Asian, African, etc.), the European ancestry diaspora has the least amount of genetic variance, thus narrowing the analytic space tremendously. The combination of all these factors has resulted in a scientifically rational reason to have such unrepresentative samples. However, it is also important to note that until recently, most of the genetic research was completed in European ancestry countries; thus, samples are often draw from the home countries. Of course, as has been laid out elsewhere (Popejoy & Fullerton, 2016), there is also strong scientific and moral reasoning for why it is important to build a literature on more diverse and representative samples. Although there are far more complex (and more negative) explanations for the current data situation, the fact of the matter is that the current genetic literature is highly biased toward European ancestry samples; furthermore, it is not uncommon for genetic loci that work in one ancestry to fail to work in another ancestry (Ware et al., 2016).

Less discussed, but along a similar tangent, is the fact that like much of the rest of biosocial work, genetic studies often do not rely on population-based samples (Falk et al., 2013). Rather, they use clinic, hospital, community, or convenience samples. Depending on the design, these studies can provide reliable estimates, but that does not mean they are generalizable. There are population-based studies that have genome-wide data publically available (e.g., Health and Retirement Study, http://hrsonline.isr.umich.edu; The National Study of Adolescent Health, http://www.cpc.unc.edu/projects/addhealth; and Wisconsin Longitudinal Study, http://www.ssc.wisc.edu/wlsresearch), and some of those studies participate in the genetic consortia (for social scientists, the best consortia to follow is the Social Science Genetic Association Consortium, https://www.thessgac.org), but the vast majority of the consortia are not representative of any particular population and thus external validity may be weak. The degree to which sample size and the more recent small increase in sample/study diversity may overcome that bias has not fully been explored. The extent to which these genetic associations hold for different subpopulations is ultimately of critical importance in determining the generalizability of these models (Popejoy & Fullerton, 2016; Ware et al., 2016).

As described previously, the GWAS framework relies on independent examinations of millions of SNPs, conditional on only a handful of key covariates, such as measures of ancestry, gender, and age. Thus, the interpretation of a strong, reliable GWAS result is that of an SNP that is significant (5×10^{-8}) in a pooled meta-analysis of many studies, typically for one ancestral group, which has been replicated in samples not used in the discovery phase. If an SNP's association with a phenotype is strong enough in a number of studies, considering the great potential for uncontrolled environmental influences in the samples (i.e., some samples are clinical, whereas others are population based, etc.), it begs the question as to what the GWAS effects really might be. Another way to interpret a significant and replicated locus might be that it is an SNP that was able to penetrate a wide variety of environments and study designs and is significant in the "average" environmental context. This might suggest that if the effect of an SNP is highly responsive to the environment or other genetic loci, it may not be detectible, depending on the distribution of the environments and genomes found in the analytic data. Indeed, we may be finding the least interactive genetic loci using these methods.

Note that rarely are other SNPs included as covariates, nor are gene–gene or gene–environment interactions tested in such a rigorous and coordinated way. Thus, currently genetic research is the narrowest version of genetic effects (i.e., only additive). Although some geneticists suggest additive genetic effects are a generally safe assumption, others suggest this is not correct (Belsky, Moffitt, & Caspi, 2013; Boardman, Daw, & Freese, 2013; Mitchell et al., 2013; Pearson & Manolio, 2008). That is, even if most genes

operate in an additive manner, the largest effects may be nonlinear for a variety of reasons. Currently, these effects are not being explored in the same rigorous way as the
additive models. A major reason for that is because the assumption is that if genes have
very weak associations with behavior (as shown later), then interactions are expected
to be even more challenging to find (Boardman et al., 2013; Mitchell et al., 2013; Pearson
& Manolio, 2008). In addition, if phenotypes are challenging to harmonize, then har-
monizing both phenotypes and environments would appear to be exceptionally challenging. For the most part, every social science study has been funded to be at least
somewhat unique—either as a unique sample or a unique measure—and this complicates potential discovery and replication of gene–environment interactions.

Before moving to the literature review, it is important to mentioned that as genomic
data have become more widely available in behavioral studies of human populations, the
ability to estimate genetic scores for study participants that compactly represent individual genetic risk or susceptibility has become a valuable tool for integrating genetic
variation into models of social and behavioral processes (Belsky, Moffitt, & Caspi, 2013;
Belsky, Moffitt, Sugden, et al., 2013; Mitchell et al., 2013). One such type of analysis is the
polygenic score (PGS), which is sometimes called the genetic risk score. A PGS is created by summarizing the results of a large exploratory meta-analysis of genetics of a trait
into a single measure that presumably taps into the underlying individual-level genetic
propensity toward that outcome (Belsky, Moffitt, & Caspi, 2013). For example, a GWAS
of smoking cessation could be used to create a single measure for all individuals in a
study with genetic data for their genetic propensity to stop smoking. Although there are
actually hundreds of variations in the methods for PGS creation, the general concept is
to weight each SNP by the inverse of the p value or by the effect size (so weak effects are
essentially 0) and then sum them into one weighted score (Ware et al., 2016). Decisions
on which SNPs are used based on a p value cut-off or linkage disequilibrium, which
GWAS effects to use, which populations they can apply to, and so on have a major impact
on the explanatory power of these scores—although this is rarely formally tested (Ware
et al., 2016). Nevertheless, because they are single-measure summaries of the entire
genome, they are particularly exciting for researchers not trained in analyzing large
genetic data. PGS may potentially provide genetic controls for phenotypes not available
in the analyzing data and broader genetic measures in G×E research. For example, in a
study of cognition in healthy middle-aged adults, PGS of heart disease, Alzheimer's disease, longevity, or diabetes could be used to account for some unmeasured (or yet to be
revealed) disease propensities. Also, in an analysis of smoking treatments or policies, a
PGS of smoking could eliminate some of the variance due to genetics. Studies are beginning to produce these scores as a data product, but for now, the scores are created separately by team—which may lead to problems of replication if the score creation is not
fully documented (Ware et al., 2016). Nevertheless, the major assumption of these scores
is that the underlying GWAS model is correct.

What follows is a review of GWAS's for two broad areas of research on the genetics of behavior: health behaviors and social behaviors. The brief review is further filtered by attempting to limit articles to those with samples of more than 10,000 (with

a few exceptions). The main reason for this filter is that although there have been early GWAS studies of some of these behaviors, ultimately most have proven unreliable and underpowered.

Health Behaviors

Smoking

Smoking was one of the first major behavioral phenotypes examined because of the frequency with which it is asked about in many studies. Twin and family studies have shown that there is not one specific gene that determines who will develop a smoking addiction but, rather, several genes that cause an individual to become more susceptible to being addicted to nicotine (Davies & Soundy, 2009). An early meta-analysis of several smoking phenotypes was conducted within cohorts of the Tobacco and Genetics Consortium (N = 74,053) and then replicated in the European Network of Genetic and Genomic Epidemiology (ENGAGE) and Oxford–GlaxoSmithKline (Ox-GSK) consortia ($N >$ 140,000) (Tobacco and Genetics Consortium, 2010). Three loci associated with number of cigarettes smoked per day were identified: the nicotinic receptor gene *CHRNA3*, two 10q25 SNPs, and another locus in *EGLN2*. For smoking initiation, eight SNPs exceeded genome-wide significance, with the strongest association in *BDNF* on chromosome 11. Only one SNP located near *DBH* on chromosome 9 was significantly associated with smoking cessation (Tobacco and Genetics Consortium, 2010). One example of a non-White GWAS used the Study of Tobacco in Minority Populations Genetics Consortium (N = 32,389) to examine smoking behavior in African Americans. Researchers found a significant effect in the *CHRNA5* gene and effects that approached genome-wide significance at *PSMA4* and *CHRNA3* for smoking quantity, in addition to a signal represented by three SNPs in the *SPOCK2* gene on chromosome 10 (David et al., 2012). The association confirms that this region is an important susceptibility locus for smoking quantity in men and women of African ancestry (David et al., 2012). Interestingly, a number of European GWAS and subsequent candidate gene-based associated studies investigating the genetic variants associated with nicotine dependence and smoking-related phenotypes have shed more light on the *CHRNA5/A3/B4* gene cluster on chromosome 15, which encodes the α_5, α_3, and β_4 nAChR subunits, respectively—suggesting a robust and generalizable finding (Thorgeirsson et al., 2010; Wen, Jiang, Yuan, Cui, & Li, 2016).

Alcohol Use/Dependence

Alcohol use/dependence has received significant attention in the genome-wide research of health behaviors. In 2009, the first GWAS of an alcohol phenotype in Germany was performed that included 487 male inpatients with alcohol dependence and an age at onset younger than 28 years and 1,358 population-based control individuals (Treutlein et al., 2009). The follow-up study included 1,024 male inpatients and 996 age-matched male controls. In the combined analysis, two closely linked intergenic SNPs on chromosome 2 met genome-wide significance, and nine other SNPs (in *CDH13* and *ADH1C*) found in prior literature were replicated (Treutlein et al., 2009). Another study examined consumption but not dependence, and although no single SNP met genome-wide criteria for significance, several clusters of SNPs provided mutual support (Edenberg et al., 2010)—namely a cluster of genes on chromosome 11 (*SLC22A18*, *PHLDA2*, *NAP1L4*, *SNORA54*, *CARS*, and *OSBPL5*) with alcohol dependence (Edenberg et al., 2010). In addition, several SNPs nominated as candidates in earlier GWAS were replicated (*CPE*, *DNASE2B*, *SLC10A2*, *ARL6IP5*, *ID4*, *GATA4*, *SYNE1*, and *ADCY3*) (Edenberg et al., 2010). In a larger study among 12 population-based samples of European ancestry, comprising 26,316 individuals, with replication genotyping in an additional 21,185 individuals, an *autism susceptibility candidate 2* gene (*AUTS2*) was associated with alcohol consumption (Schumann et al., 2011). Yet another recent study reported a GWAS of alcohol dependence (AD) in European American (EA) and African American (AA) populations, with replication in independent samples of EAs, AAs, and Germans (Gelernter et al., 2014). The sample for discovery and replication was 16,087 subjects, the largest sample for AD GWAS to date. Numerous genome-wide significant (GWS) associations were identified, many of which were novel. Most associations were population specific, but in several cases there were GWS in EAs and AAs for different SNPs at the same locus, showing biological convergence across populations—notably *ADH1B*, *MTIF2*, *CCDC88A*, and *ADH1C* (in both AA and EA); *LOC100507053* and *METAP* (in AAs), and *PDLIM5* (in EAs)—and in AAs ($p = 3.35 \times 10^{-8}$) (Gelernter et al., 2014). In a recent study of measured heritability of 2,875 African Americans, including 1,719 AD cases and 1,156 controls, researchers found that 23.9% (standard error, 9.3%) of the phenotypic variance could be explained by using all of the common SNPs on the array (C. Yang et al., 2014) (for comparison, twin studies estimate AD is 64% heritability; Heath et al., 1997).

Risk-Taking/Impulsivity/Aggression

Measures of risk-taking are of great interest for genetic analyses, but in contrast to smoking or alcohol use, there are fewer harmonized measures of risk-taking—thereby reducing the sample sizes. Nevertheless, some GWAS exist. For example, using the Excitement-Seeking scale of the Revised NEO Personality Inventory, one study performed GWAS on six samples of European ancestry ($N = 7,860$) and identified a genome-wide significant association between the Excitement-Seeking scale the *catenin cadherin-associated protein, alpha 2* (*CTNNA2*) gene, which encodes for a brain-expressed α-catenin critical for synaptic contact. Despite the effect of the SNP being in the same direction in all six samples, it did not replicate in additional samples ($N = 5,105$) (Terracciano et al., 2011). In a large community-representative sample ($N = 7,188$), researchers examined the following measures of behavioral disinhibition: nicotine use/ dependence, alcohol consumption, alcohol dependence, and drug use. Using a subsample of twins ($n = 2,877$), they estimated heritability ranging from 0.42 to 0.58, whereas using measured genetic heritability (via the genome-wide data), the aggregated SNPs explained 10–30% of the variance in the traits (Vrieze, McGue, Miller, Hicks, & Iacono, 2013). These estimates were generally replicated in a Caucasian sample of similar size, suggesting that common variants genotyped on the GWAS array appear in aggregate to account for a sizable proportion of heritable effects in multiple indicators of behavioral disinhibition, yet at least half of the additive heritability remains "missing" (Vrieze, McGue, Miller, Hicks, & Iacono, 2013). A systematic review of candidate gene studies of aggression and violence found 1,331 potentially relevant investigations, 185 studies constituting 277 independent associations on 31 genes, but replication using larger genome-wide data did not support the use of such genes to predict dangerousness or as markers for therapeutic interventions (Vassos, Collier, & Fazel, 2014). However, another study analyzed data from 9 population-based studies ($N = 18,988$) and assessed aggressive behavior using well-validated parent-reported questionnaires. The meta-analysis of the total sample identified one region in chromosome 2 (2p12) and within *AVPR1A* (Pappa et al., 2016).

SOCIAL, ECONOMIC, AND POLITICAL BEHAVIORS

Educational Attainment

Potentially the most exciting and controversial social science GWAS analysis examined so far is on educational attainment. Education is one of the most powerful predictors in almost all health, behavioral, and ideational research. Furthermore, it is a primary mechanism for intervention. For these reasons, researchers are eager to examine the genetics of educational attainment and are similarly skeptical that the genetics of education will be interpreted correctly. It was with these concerns in mind that the SSGAC created a frequently asked questions (FAQs) website for their education papers (https://www.thessgac.org/faqs; Okbay et al., 2016b; Rietveld et al., 2013). These FAQs are well written and address many of the questions most social scientists and lay audience members have about this type of research. It is required reading for the area, and it would serve the area well to encourage these types of public interface for all biosocial work going forward. Nevertheless, the earliest GWAS of education was an Australian family sample of 9,538 individuals in which top hits were checked for replication in an independent sample of 968 individuals. The researchers identified a polymorphism on chromosome 11 weakly associated with educational attainment, suggesting a large polygenic architecture of educational attainment (Martin et al., 2011). This study led to the first SSGAC study in 2013, which was a GWAS of educational attainment in a discovery sample of 101,069 individuals and a replication sample of 25,490 (Rietveld et al., 2013). Three independent SNPs were genome-wide significant. Estimated effects sizes were small (coefficient of determination $R^2 \approx 0.02\%$), approximately 1 month of schooling per allele. Genes in the region of the loci have previously been associated with health, cognitive, and central nervous system phenotypes, and bioinformatics analyses from neurological and neuroscience work suggest the involvement of the anterior caudate nucleus. Between the publication of the two SSGAC papers was a third prominent paper that similarly found evidence for common, small genetic contributions to educational attainment but also emphasized the likely life-course nature of this genetic effect (Ward et al., 2014). Results here also, by an alternative route, suggest that existing methods for child examination are able to recognize early life variation likely related to ultimate educational attainment in the Avon Longitudinal Study of Parents and Children (Ward et al., 2014). Finally, the most recent of the education GWAS papers found that genetic factors account for at least 10% of the variation across individuals (Okbay et al., 2016b). Further expanding the GWAS discovery sample from 101,069 individuals to 293,723 individuals, in addition to a replication study in an independent sample of 111,349 individuals from the UK Biobank, helped identify 74 genome-wide significant loci associated with the number of years of schooling completed (Okbay et al., 2016b). SNPs associated with educational attainment are disproportionately found in genomic regions regulating gene expression in the fetal brain. In addition, genome-wide SNPs explain one-third of the variance of educational performance and one-half of the correlation between educational performance and family SES (Krapohl & Plomin, 2016). Finally, a UK research team conducted a GWAS on social deprivation and on household income using 112,151 participants of UK Biobank. They found that common SNPs explained 21% of the variation in social deprivation and 11% of household income. Two independent loci attained genome-wide significance for household income, with the most significant SNPs on chromosomes 2 and 19. Genes in the regions of these SNPs have been associated with intellectual disabilities, schizophrenia, and synaptic plasticity. These findings suggest that some SNPs associated with SES are involved in the brain and central nervous system. The genetic associations with SES obviously do not reflect direct causal effects and are probably mediated via other partly heritable variables, including cognitive ability, personality, and health (Hill et al., 2016).

Cognition/Intelligence

Although not a social behavior, it is commonly assumed that the genetic effects found in the educational attainment GWAS are in part a product of genes related to cognition, memory, or intelligence. For nearly a century, twin and adoption studies have yielded substantial estimates of heritability for cognitive abilities, and now using genome-wide data, estimates suggest that approximately 66% of the estimated heritability can be found in the GWAS if the sample is large enough (Plomin et al., 2013). One study reported the first GWAS on childhood intelligence (age range, 6–18 years) from 17,989 individuals in six discovery and three replication samples. Although no individual SNPs were detected with genome-wide significance, it was shown that the aggregate effects of common SNPs explain 22–46% of phenotypic variation in childhood intelligence in the three largest cohorts. *FNBP1L*, previously reported to be the most significantly associated gene for adult intelligence, was also significantly associated with childhood intelligence. Polygenic prediction analyses resulted in a significant correlation between predictor and outcome in all replication cohorts. The proportion of childhood intelligence explained by the predictor reached 1.2%, 3.5%, and 0.5% in three independent validation cohorts (Benyamin et al., 2014).

A larger study conducted a meta-analysis of GWAS of 31 cohorts ($N = 53{,}949$) of adults, in which the participants had undertaken multiple, diverse cognitive tests. A general cognitive function phenotype was tested for and created in each cohort by principal component analysis. The study reported 13 genome-wide significant SNP associations in three genomic regions: 6q16.1, 14q12, and 19q13.32 (*MIR2113, AKAP6*, and *APOE/TOMM40*, respectively). These genes have previously been associated with neuropsychiatric phenotypes. The proportion of phenotypic variation accounted for by all genotyped common SNPs was approximately 28%. In hypothesis-driven tests, there was significant association between general cognitive function and four genes previously associated with Alzheimer's disease: *TOMM40, APOE, ABCG1*, and *MEF2C* (Davies et al., 2015).

Politics and Preferences

The first GWAS on political ideology used data from three samples: a 1990 Australian sample involving 6,894 individuals from 3,516 families, a 2008 Australian sample of 1,160 related individuals from 635 families, and a 2010 Swedish sample involving 3,334 individuals from 2,607 families. No polymorphisms reached genome-wide significance in the meta-analysis. The results suggest that political ideology constitutes a fundamental aspect of one's genetically informed psychological disposition, but these genetic influences derive from thousands of small effects rather than a few larger one (Hatemi et al., 2014). Similarly, another study showed genome-wide significance for Openness to Experience near the *RASA1* gene on chromosome 5 (De Moor et al., 2012).

Hopeless Opus?

One could read to this point in the chapter and be disheartened. The GWAS method relies on data that are highly selective (although there is much of it). The models assume strong additive genetic effects that fundamentally do not square with the vast majority of social scientists' worldviews. Moreover, although there have been many validated and replicated findings, these effects are exceedingly small and often explain less than 5% of the variance. Nevertheless, there are several reasons why this is not hopeless. First, although the current methods are leading to finding increasingly smaller effects (which is not surprising because sample sizes are increasing), the data have been collected. This means that to some extent, we are just waiting for new and better methods to estimate broad-sense genetic effects (including GxG and GxE). Although the smaller scale genetic interaction literature is also complex and murky, it is not without merit. However, applying current GWAS methods is likely a foolish endeavor. It seems likely that an exploratory search of all potential SNP × environment or SNP × SNP associations with any given behavioral outcome is strictly an exercise in fruitless number crunching.

In the near short term, the GWAS community will continue to push what has worked well: increasingly larger samples and better and cheaper genotyping. However, there are signs that this cannot and will not be the only way forward. Already, signs of greater complexity in modeling are evident. Greater focus on phenotype construction and external validity is improving the methods and the data collected in the field. In the longer term, there will likely be a swing back toward more hypothesis-driven exploration of genetic research—this time with much more genetic data (i.e., hundreds of SNPs in a gene region instead of one or two SNPs) and a much larger expectation of replication (which will be aided by being part of consortia). It is hoped that the research community begins to also accept more well-constructed quasi-replications in order to build a literature of examinations of a finding in a variety of samples and using a variety of methods. With the exception of a few specific examples, such as 5-HTT child maltreatment and depression, few findings have been so thoroughly examined (Hewitt, 2012; Mitchell et al., 2013). Yet in those few we have learned where the replication fails and where it succeeds—which is the point of science. In addition, more information, such as epigenetic moderation of genetic effects, is likely to enter into the research literature (Miller, 2010).

CONCLUSION

Three aspects appear most important for social and behavioral scientists in terms of working in the area of the genetics of social behavior. First, social scientists are needed for improving the measurement of the phenotype. In part, because of the field's focus on genetic measurement and, more important, the drive to have the largest sample size possible, phenotypes used in GWAS analyses often more general measures of the phenotype, or consist of more variable measures of a phenotype than most behavioral experts would like. For example, in a GWAS of depression, studies may use several different scales of depression or depression-like outcomes depending on the primary purpose of the study. Thus, although the scales may be tapping into slightly different aspects of depression, in order to have a large enough sample size for a properly powered GWAS, a more harmonized but amorphous measure of depression is used. Indeed, there is a question regarding the point at which the measurement error induced by attempting to harmonize increasingly more studies counteracts the larger sample size generated by adding more studies. Therefore, social scientists are requisite for promoting better measurement of phenotypes, or at least providing more understanding of the the the potential biases will be tremendously important.

Second, the representativeness of the samples used for GWAS needs to be improved dramatically. Recent calls from within the genetic community and funders are likely to result in a rapid increase in data on populations for which few previously existed (Falk et al., 2013; Popejoy & Fullerton, 2016). Social scientists, especially population scientists, will be particularly helpful in providing more generalizable findings, as well as providing estimates of the potential bias of current results.

Third, social scientists need to have a better understanding of how these genetic findings will and will not inform policy or interventions. The science of genetics—their downstream effects—are of fundamental interest, but they also cannot be changed for a given individual. This makes policy or interventions using genetics as a basis challenging. For example, although it may be interesting to note that one segment of the population has an increased risk of initiation of smoking, it would be dangerous to craft policy to reduce access to cigarettes for that population when so many other mechanisms are likely to work even better. Of course, whereas smoking policy is a relatively tame example, far more challenging situations arise when considering outcomes such as educational attainment or as reported in the SSGAC FAQ "What policy lesson or practical advice do you draw from this study? None whatsoever. Any practical response—individual or policy-level—to this or similar research would be extremely premature" (https://www.thessgac.org/faqs). More important, some social scientists need to be better able to explain how this research provides more evidence that genes are not purely deterministic and that understanding the genetic aspects of human behavior will allow for better, more nuanced examinations of the social aspects of human behavior.

REFERENCES

Abdellaoui, A., Hottenga, J.-J., de Knijff, P., Nivard, M. G., Xiao, X., Scheet, P., . . . Davies, G. E. (2013). Population structure, migration, and diversifying selection in the Netherlands. *European Journal of Human Genetics, 21,* 1277–1285.

Allen, H. L., Estrada, K., Lettre, G., Berndt, S. I., Weedon, M. N., Rivadeneira, F., . . . Raychaudhuri, S. (2010). Hundreds of variants clustered in genomic loci and biological pathways affect human height. *Nature, 467,* 832–838.

Belsky, D. W., Moffitt, T. E., & Caspi, A. (2013). Genetics in population health science: Strategies and opportunities. *American Journal of Public Health, 103,* S73–S83.

Belsky, D. W., Moffitt, T. E., Sugden, K., Williams, B., Houts, R., McCarthy, J., & Caspi, A. (2013). Development and evaluation of a genetic risk score for obesity. *Biodemography and Social Biology, 59,* 85–100.

Benyamin, B., Pourcain, B., Davis, O. S., Davies, G., Hansell, N. K., Brion, M.-J., . . . Miller, M. B. (2014). Childhood intelligence is heritable, highly polygenic and associated with FNBP1L. *Molecular Psychiatry, 19,* 253–258.

Boardman, J. D., Daw, J., & Freese, J. (2013). Defining the environment in gene–environment research: Lessons from social epidemiology. *American Journal of Public Health*, *103*, S64–S72.

Campbell, C. D., Ogburn, E. L., Lunetta, K. L., Lyon, H. N., Freedman, M. L., Groop, L. C., . . . Hirschhorn, J. N. (2005). Demonstrating stratification in a European American population. *Nature Genetics*, *37*, 868–872.

Collins, F. S., Patrinos, A., Jordan, E., Chakravarti, A., Gesteland, R., & Walters, L. (1998). New goals for the US human genome project: 1998–2003. *Science*, *282*, 682–689.

David, S. P., Hamidovic, A., Chen, G. K., Bergen, A. W., Wessel, J., Kasberger, J. L., . . . Furberg, H. (2012). Genome-wide meta-analyses of smoking behaviors in African Americans. *Translational Psychiatry*, *2*, e119.

Davies, G., Armstrong, N., Bis, J. C., Bressler, J., Chouraki, V., Giddaluru, S., . . . Lahti, J. (2015). Genetic contributions to variation in general cognitive function: A meta-analysis of genome-wide association studies in the CHARGE consortium (*N* = 53,949). *Molecular Psychiatry*, *20*, 183–192.

Davies, G. E., & Soundy, T. J. (2009). The genetics of smoking and nicotine addiction. *South Dakota Medicine*, No. 43-9.

De Moor, M. H., Costa, P. T., Terracciano, A., Krueger, R. F., De Geus, E. J., Toshiko, T., . . . Derringer, J. (2012). Meta-analysis of genome-wide association studies for personality. *Molecular Psychiatry*, *17*, 337–349.

Edenberg, H. J., Koller, D. L., Xuei, X., Wetherill, L., McClintick, J. N., Almasy, L., . . . Aliev, F. (2010). Genome-wide association study of alcohol dependence implicates a region on chromosome 11. *Alcoholism: Clinical and Experimental Research*, *34*, 840–852.

Falk, E. B., Hyde, L. W., Mitchell, C., Faul, J., Gonzalez, R., Heitzeg, M. M., . . . Maslowsky, J. (2013). What is a representative brain? Neuroscience meets population science. *Proceedings of the National Academy of Sciences of the USA*, *110*, 17615–17622.

Freese, J. (2008). Genetics and the social science explanation of individual outcomes. *American Journal of Sociology*, *114*, S1–S35.

Freese, J., Li, J.-C. A., & Wade, L. D. (2003). The potential relevances of biology to social inquiry. *Annual Review of Sociology*, *29*, 233–256.

Freese, J., & Powell, B. (2003). Tilting at twindmills: Rethinking sociological responses to behavioral genetics. *Journal of Health and Social Behavior*, *44*(2), 130–135.

Freese, J., & Shostak, S. (2009). Genetics and social inquiry. *Annual Review of Sociology*, *35*, 107–128.

Gelernter, J., Kranzler, H. R., Sherva, R., Almasy, L., Koesterer, R., Smith, A. H., . . . Rujescu, D. (2014). Genome-wide association study of alcohol dependence: Significant findings in African- and European-Americans including novel risk loci. *Molecular Psychiatry*, *19*, 41–49.

Gibson, G. (2012). Rare and common variants: Twenty arguments. *Nature Reviews Genetics*, *13*, 135–145.

Hamer, D. H. (2000). Beware the chopsticks gene. *Molecular Psychiatry*, *5*, 11–13.

Hatemi, P. K., Medland, S. E., Klemmensen, R., Oskarsson, S., Littvay, L., Dawes, C. T., . . . Klofstad, C. A. (2014). Genetic influences on political ideologies: Twin analyses of 19 measures of political ideologies from five democracies and genome-wide findings from three populations. *Behavior Genetics*, *44*, 282–294.

Heath, A. C., Bucholz, K. K., Madden, P. A. F., Dinwiddie, S. H., Slutske, W. S., Bierut, L. J., . . . Martin, N. G. (1997). Genetic and environmental contributions to alcohol dependence risk in a national twin sample: Consistency of findings in women and men. *Psychological Medicine*, *27*, 1381–1396.

Hewitt, J. K. (2012). Editorial policy on candidate gene association and candidate gene-by-environment interaction studies of complex traits. *Behavior Genetics, 42*, 1–2.

Hill, W. D., Hagenaars, S. P., Marioni, R. E., Harris, S. E., Liewald, D. C., Davies, G., . . . Deary, I. J. (2016). Molecular genetic contributions to social deprivation and household income in UK Biobank. *Current Biology, 26*, 3083–3089.

Krapohl, E., & Plomin, R. (2016). Genetic link between family socioeconomic status and children's educational achievement estimated from genome-wide SNPs. *Molecular Psychiatry, 21*, 437–443.

Manolio, T. A., Collins, F. S., Cox, N. J., Goldstein, D. B., Hindorff, L. A., Hunter, D. J., . . . Chakravarti, A. (2009). Finding the missing heritability of complex diseases. *Nature, 461*, 747–753.

Manuck, S. B., & McCaffery, J. M. (2014). Gene–environment interaction. *Annual Review of Psychology, 65*, 41–70.

Martin, N. W., Medland, S. E., Verweij, K. J., Lee, S. H., Nyholt, D. R., Madden, P. A., . . . Martin, N. G. (2011). Educational attainment: A genome wide association study in 9538 Australians. *PLoS One, 6*, e20128.

McCarthy, M. I., Abecasis, G. R., Cardon, L. R., Goldstein, D. B., Little, J., Ioannidis, J. P., & Hirschhorn, J. N. (2008). Genome-wide association studies for complex traits: Consensus, uncertainty and challenges. *Nature Reviews Genetics, 9*, 356–369.

Miller, G. (2010). The seductive allure of behavioral epigenetics. *Science, 329*, 24–27.

Mitchell, C., McLanahan, S., Brooks-Gunn, J., Garfinkel, I., Hobcraft, J., & Notterman, D. (2013). Genetic differential sensitivity to social environments: Implications for research. *American Journal of Public Health, 103*, S102–S110.

Okbay, A., Baselmans, B. M., De Neve, J.-E., Turley, P., Nivard, M. G., Fontana, M. A., . . . Cesarini, D. (2016a). Genetic variants associated with subjective well-being, depressive symptoms, and neuroticism identified through genome-wide analyses. *Nature Genetics, 48*(6), 624–633.

Okbay, A., Beauchamp, J. P., Fontana, M. A., Lee, J. J., Pers, T. H., Rietveld, C. A., . . . Benjamin, D. J. (2016b). Genome-wide association study identifies 74 loci associated with educational attainment. *Nature, 533*(7604), 539–542. doi:10.1038/nature17671

Pappa, I., St. Pourcain, B., Benke, K., Cavadino, A., Hakulinen, C., Nivard, M. G., . . . Davies, G. E. (2016). A genome-wide approach to children's aggressive behavior: The EAGLE consortium. *American Journal of Medical Genetics Part B: Neuropsychiatric Genetics, 171*, 562–572.

Pearson, T. A., & Manolio, T. A. (2008). How to interpret a genome-wide association study. *JAMA, 299*, 1335–1344.

Pennisi, E. (2012). ENCODE project writes eulogy for junk DNA. *Science, 337*, 1159–1161.

Plomin, R., Haworth, C. M., Meaburn, E. L., Price, T. S., Davis, O. S., & Wellcome Trust Case Control Consortium. (2013). Common DNA markers can account for more than half of the genetic influence on cognitive abilities. *Psychological Science, 24*(4), 562–568.

Popejoy, A. B., & Fullerton, S. M. (2016). Genomics is failing on diversity. *Nature, 538*, 161.

Price, A. L., Patterson, N. J., Plenge, R. M., Weinblatt, M. E., Shadick, N. A., & Reich, D. (2006). Principal components analysis corrects for stratification in genome-wide association studies. *Nature Genetics, 38*, 904–909.

Pritchard, J. K., & Cox, N. J. (2002). The allelic architecture of human disease genes: Common disease–common variant . . . or not? *Human Molecular Genetics, 11*, 2417–2423.

Richards, E. J. (2006). Inherited epigenetic variation—Revisiting soft inheritance. *Nature Reviews Genetics, 7*, 395–401.

Rietveld, C. A., Medland, S. E., Derringer, J., Yang, J., Esko, T., Martin, N. W., . . . Agrawal, A. (2013). GWAS of 126,559 individuals identifies genetic variants associated with educational attainment. *Science, 340,* 1467–1471.

Schumann, G., Coin, L. J., Lourdusamy, A., Charoen, P., Berger, K. H., Stacey, D., . . . Amin, N. (2011). Genome-wide association and genetic functional studies identify autism susceptibility candidate 2 gene (AUTS2) in the regulation of alcohol consumption. *Proceedings of the National Academy of Sciences of the USA, 108,* 7119–7124.

Selzam, S., Krapohl, E., von Stumm, S., O'Reilly, P. F., Rimfeld, K., Kovas, Y., . . . Plomin, R. (2017). Predicting educational achievement from DNA. *Molecular Psychiatry, 22,* 267–272.

Terracciano, A., Esko, T., Sutin, A. R., De Moor, M. H. M., Meirelles, O., Zhu, G., . . . Realo, A. (2011). Meta-analysis of genome-wide association studies identifies common variants in CTNNA2 associated with excitement-seeking. *Translational Psychiatry, 1,* e49.

Thorgeirsson, T. E., Gudbjartsson, D. F., Surakka, I., Vink, J. M., Amin, N., Geller, F., . . . Walter, S. (2010). Sequence variants at CHRNB3–CHRNA6 and CYP2A6 affect smoking behavior. *Nature Genetics, 42,* 448–453.

Tobacco and Genetics Consortium. (2010). Genome-wide meta-analyses identify multiple loci associated with smoking behavior. *Nature Genetics, 42,* 441–447.

Treutlein, J., Cichon, S., Ridinger, M., Wodarz, N., Soyka, M., Zill, P., . . . Dahmen, N. (2009). Genome-wide association study of alcohol dependence. *Archives of General Psychiatry, 66,* 773–784.

Tucker-Drob, E. M., & Bates, T. C. (2015). Large cross-national differences in gene × socioeconomic status interaction on intelligence. *Psychological Science, 27*(2), 138–149.

Turkheimer, E. (2012). Genome wide association studies of behavior are social science. In K. S. Plaisance & T. A. C. Reydon (Eds.), *Philosophy of Behavioral Biology* (pp. 43–64): New York, NY: Springer.

Vassos, E., Collier, D. A., & Fazel, S. (2014). Systematic meta-analyses and field synopsis of genetic association studies of violence and aggression. *Molecular Psychiatry, 19,* 471–477.

Vrieze, S. I., McGue, M., Miller, M. B., Hicks, B. M., & Iacono, W. G. (2013). Three mutually informative ways to understand the genetic relationships among behavioral disinhibition, alcohol use, drug use, nicotine use/dependence, and their co-occurrence: Twin biometry, GCTA, and genome-wide scoring. *Behavior Genetics, 43,* 97–107.

Ward, M. E., McMahon, G., St. Pourcain, B., Evans, D. M., Rietveld, C. A., Benjamin, D. J., . . . Timpson, N. J. (2014). Genetic variation associated with differential educational attainment in adults has anticipated associations with school performance in children. *PLoS One, 9,* e100248.

Ware, E. B., Schmitz, L. L., Faul, J., Gard, A., Mitchell, C., Smith, J. A., . . . Kardia, S. L. (2016). *Heterogeneity in polygenic scores for common human traits.* Paper presented at the Integrating Genes and Social Sciences–2016 conference, Boulder, CO.

Wen, L., Jiang, K., Yuan, W., Cui, W., & Li, M. D. (2016). Contribution of variants in CHRNA5/A3/B4 gene cluster on chromosome 15 to tobacco smoking: From genetic association to mechanism. *Molecular Neurobiology, 53,* 472–484.

Yang, C., Li, C., Kranzler, H. R., Farrer, L. A., Zhao, H., & Gelernter, J. (2014). Exploring the genetic architecture of alcohol dependence in African-Americans via analysis of a genome-wide set of common variants. *Human Genetics, 133,* 617–624.

Yang, J., Benyamin, B., McEvoy, B. P., Gordon, S., Henders, A. K., Nyholt, D. R., . . . Montgomery, G. W. (2010). Common SNPs explain a large proportion of the heritability for human height. *Nature Genetics, 42,* 565–569.

Yang, J., Ferreira, T., Morris, A. P., Medland, S. E., Madden, P. A., Heath, A. C., . . . Loos, R. J. (2012). Conditional and joint multiple-SNP analysis of GWAS summary statistics identifies additional variants influencing complex traits. *Nature Genetics, 44,* 369–375.

Zuk, O., Hechter, E., Sunyaev, S. R., & Lander, E. S. (2012). The mystery of missing heritability: Genetic interactions create phantom heritability. *Proceedings of the National Academy of Sciences of the USA, 109,* 1193–1198.

CHAPTER 12

....

DNA IS NOT DESTINY

....

ROSE MCDERMOTT AND PETER K. HATEMI

GENETICS has become the meta-narrative of our time. Both popular culture and political elites often refer to things that exist within our "DNA." Lady Gaga establishing a
"Born This Way" foundation at the Harvard University Graduate School of Education
and Vice President Joe Biden's speech at the 2012 Democratic National Convention, in
which he stated "Barack and I see a future—It's in our DNA—where no one, no one is
forced to live in the shadows of intolerance," are a few prominent examples. Public and
scholarly interest in the use of DNA to understand and potentially ameliorate behavioral differences has catalyzed into virtual ubiquity; scholars, pundits, and citizens often
invoke genetics as both explanation and expiation for a wide variety of propensities,
proclivities, and failings, just as they often credit hard work, will, skill, and discipline for
notable successes. Unfortunately, despite well-articulated research that shows the opposite, the public's conception of genetics often assumes that such features of our biology
are more direct, immutable, entrenched, and deterministic than forces in the environment that also serve to shape us (Bearman 2008). As the notion of genetic influence
on outcomes and behaviors has captivated the public imagination, a misunderstanding
of what genetics can tell us has simultaneously permeated academic, public policy, and
legal discourse (Paul 2012; Sifferlin 2012).

Comprehensive surveys by the Genetics and Public Policy Center at the National
Human Genome Research Institute reveal widespread misunderstandings among the
public regarding genetic information (Bollinger et al. 2012; Javitt 2006; Kaufman et al.
2008; Murphy et al. 2008; Scott and Hudson 2005). The same misunderstanding is
found in decision makers, Aspinwall, Brown, and Tabery (2012), for example, find that
experienced US justices fall prey to a bias in their judgments based on a misunderstanding of genetics as well. In a study involving 181 US state court justices, the introduction
of a biological cause increased judges' consideration of mitigating factors in legal decisions from 29.7% to 47.8%, resulting in an average reduced sentence of more than 1 year.
Such confusion is exacerbated by media representations that portray genes as "causing"
some behavior, or extrapolating findings from aggregate data to sensationalize and predict a given individual's behavior. Provocative, but factually baseless, media claims and

misrepresentations of research such as "Researchers Find the Liberal Gene" (Kaplan 2010) are commonplace. Yet the overwhelming majority of credible genetics research argues that genes promote particular processes under certain environmental conditions, and no single genetic marker will regulate complex social or behavioral traits in a meaningful way (Hall and Morley 2003; Kendler 2006; Rodríguez-Paredes and Esteller 2011). Humans are not slaves to their environments or their genotypes; rather, behavior is shaped by both factors in circuitous and interactive ways.

Genotype plays some role in predisposing individuals toward a tendency to select into certain environments, be exposed to certain stimuli, affiliate with certain individuals, and respond to particular environments in a certain manner. Social forces provide at least the same and arguably, in many cases, greater opportunities and constraints. Genotype alone, or independently, cannot account for human choice, preclude personal responsibility, or restrict the ability to make conscious choices, even when powerful urges exist. For example, alcoholics, whose behaviors are partially influenced by genetic makeup, can decide not to drink, to achieve sobriety through Alcoholics Anonymous or other means, or choose to drive drunk. The same ecological fallacy that applies to social traits applies equally to genetic traits. It is the totality of the continual interaction between social forces, environmental stimuli, human agency, and thousands of genetic markers and their downstream biological processes that leads to different developmental trajectories and different outcomes, contributing to individual variance. Scientists model these processes to identify probabilities in terms of how certain behaviors are more or less likely under particular conditions or contingencies at any given moment in time. Differences in DNA correlate with differences in behavior, but these represent average effects, as might be generated by any social science method, and are in no way determinative of any given individual's behavior.

Much genetics research has proved beneficial, especially in the areas of public health and to a more limited degree in social policies promoting anti-discrimination, as for example in the case of gay rights (Wood and Bartkowski 2004). However, there is growing confusion about what genetic influences mean, what type of actions are warranted based on genetic findings, and how best to use genetic information for the public good (Berryessa and Cho 2013). This confusion has emerged most strikingly in the domain of legal decisions that have reduced or abnegated responsibility for individual action based on genetic liability. For example, recently, an Italian appeals court reduced the sentence for an individual who committed a violent crime due in part to the argument that the perpetrator had the low activity form of the monoamine oxidase A (MAOA) genotype. The defense argued that this characteristic precluded the person's ability to regulate his behavior to such an extent that he deserved some dispensation from personal responsibility for his actions. It appears this may have set a new legal precedent (Baum 2013; Church 2012; Farisco and Petrini 2012; Feresin 2009; Morse 2011; Petrini 2010; Stradella 2012). Bennett (2012) argues that "neurolaw evidence is already influencing jury trials in the United States and abroad."

This presents a critical problem because there is no scientific evidence that supports a view that *individual-level assessments* can accurately be made based on *population-level* studies. That is, probabilities derived from population-level data cannot be used to justify any one individual's actions. This dilemma occurs precisely because of translation problems between scientists, policymakers, and the public. DNA is embodied in an organism that can think and feel and interact and choose. Humans have agency. Genes constitute part of the basic architecture on which differences in cognitive and emotive processes are built, but no single genetic marker or group of genes can be said to determine complex behavior or preclude personal responsibility.

Genetic analyses provide important information regarding variation in behavior across a broad population. In this way, genetics is useful for helping understand why and how, on average, people differ in a population, especially under similar circumstances. Like any statistical approach, these analyses focus on generalizations and provide probabilities for the population; statistical relationships derived from large-N genotyping studies are meaningful and relevant for large-scale policymaking in areas such as public health. They can prove helpful in developing prevention and intervention programs for the public at large—for example, in such areas as smoking cessation or obesity reduction (Uhl et al. 2008). However, this kind of information cannot be properly used to reach conclusions about any one individual.

A critical message is often overlooked as a result of the way statistical estimates are conveyed. Genetic influences are not fixed or unmalleable. They are no more deterministic than social forces, and their expression can only properly be understood in an environmental context (Burt and Simons 2014; Conley and Bennett 2000). Thus, prior to making any individual assessment, it remains imperative to explicate exactly how genes operate within the context of any given individual life, not in a determinist manner but, rather, in a contingent, environmentally informed way that is profoundly affected by human agency and experience. Humans retain the ability to make choices that preclude or override inherent tendencies, even if this proves more difficult in some areas for certain individuals than for others. We cannot absolve any one individual with a low promoter form of MAOA (believed to have some role in why people differ in their proclivity toward aggression), for example, from legal or moral responsibility for violent actions any more than we can if the individual grew up in a bad neighborhood and thus suffered from environmental deprivations during childhood. Just as similarity in the social environment cannot explain why two children raised under the exact same conditions express different behaviors, neither can genetics explain why two individuals with the same genotype make different choices. Both environments and genotypes have some role, however direct or indirect, in creating, sustaining, and extinguishing complex social behaviors, and these respective contributions may differ depending on circumstances. Thus, large-scale population studies and individual interviews are not competing methods but instead offer different information for diverse purposes. However, if we wish to make comprehensive assessments about any one individual, as opposed to designing large-scale public policy based on population averages, we also need to incorporate information about individuals' social and environmental circumstances.

In this chapter, we illustrate the complex interaction between genotype and environment and why population-level findings cannot be applied to particular individuals by exploring the role of a genotype known to be linked to aggression, MAOA, in light of the deep contextual information about one's life. Rather than conduct a large population study to identify significant genotype–environment interactions, we recognize such interactions exist (for a meta-analysis, see Byrd and Manuck 2014) and extend this research by combining genotyping and personal interviews to undertake an in-depth exploration of the foundations of individual aggressive and peaceful behavior in different contexts. In so doing, we marry qualitative data with survey data, biometric modeling, and genetic techniques to achieve a more comprehensive understanding of the complexity of human aggressive behavior. Our approach here is consistent with other applications in the social sciences that seek to understand the contingencies involved in tracing the influence of various genetic factors (Molenaar 2004) without in any way abnegating responsibility.

The Case of MAOA and Violent Behavior

A substantial amount of research has implicated genes in the dopaminergic, serotonergic, and adrenergic systems in the expression of behavioral aggression and violence (Davidge et al. 2004; Olivier and van Oorschot 2005; Reif et al. 2007). One of the most widely noted findings is that a low-activity variant on the monoamine oxidase gene, MAOA, may play a role in the manifestation of physical aggression and violence, particularly under conditions of provocation or in the wake of traumatic life events (Frazzetto et al. 2007; Kim-Cohen et al. 2006; Widom and Brzustowicz 2006). This polymorphism occurs in approximately 35% of men in most populations; only the Maori of New Zealand have a higher prevalence, displaying approximately a two-thirds prevalence of this variant (Gilad et al. 2002).

In general, the MAOA system is believed to contribute to violent behavior under provocation by means of abnormal activation and dysregulation of emotion-related amygdala functions combined with reduced inhibition and cognitive control. There is evidence for several pathways by which this effect might occur. MAOA has some role in the degradation of serotonin, noradrenaline, and dopamine neurotransmitters; in human and animal studies, dysregulation of serotonin neurotransmitters has been associated with violence due to the reduction of inhibitory motivations (Buckholtz and Meyer-Lindenberg 2008). Other work has shown that the MAOA gene promoter contains glucocorticoid, a stress hormone linked to testosterone, which is a steroid hormone from the androgen group tied to aggression; such a biological precipitant can help accentuate the tendency toward violent response to provocation (Sjöberg et al. 2007). Using brain imaging techniques, researchers have also found that the low expression variant of MAOA is associated with brain regions linked to emotional processing; the functional connectivity between the ventromedial prefrontal cortex, a region implicated in impulse repression, and the amygdala, a region implicated in emotional salience, is increased in males with the low MAOA genotype (Buckholtz et al. 2008; Meyer-Lindenberg et al. 2006). In summary, lower promotion of MAOA correlates with greater aggression and violence.

It is critical to note, however, that the MAOA genetic marker accounts for less than a fraction of 1% of the variance in violent or aggressive behaviors. Indeed, studies that focus on a single genetic marker only represent a fraction of the genome and, at best, provide some hint as to the larger gene–environment pathway involved in the expression of any particular behavior (Duncan and Keller 2011). In every case, a trigger for action is required. Freese (2008, S17) provides an important framework to explicate the mechanisms involved that includes (a) genes–environment, (b) person–situation, and (c) agency–structure. The history of the person, his or her general psychological architecture developed across the life course, and current environmental contingencies contribute to gene expression; genetic architecture contributes to the psychological development of the person in different ways under different circumstances. The path from genotype to observable behavior is long and complex, and it involves multiple social and developmental pathways. Individuals who possess the low-activity form of MAOA may never engage in aggressive action. Similarly, people without the low-activity form of MAOA can and will engage in horrific crimes and acts of physical violence. It is the totality of one's genotype and life experiences that leads to particular behaviors, and any claim of determinism on the basis of any individual genetic marker, or even hundreds of markers, is unsupported by scientific evidence. DNA has a role in why and how individuals differ, yet DNA is not destiny.

Focusing on the Person, Not the Population

In this section, we demonstrate, through a combination of DNA analysis along with detailed investigation of individual life histories, that at an individual level, the influence of DNA can only be appreciated in combination with developmental and environmental factors. We obtained genetic results from 225 male individuals who belonged to one of several social groups identified as having a norm of engaging or not engaging in violence. These individuals volunteered their samples after answering an advertisement in a local newspaper in return for the possibility of being on a television program being filmed by National Geographic. Individuals were genotyped on MAOA by FamilyTreeDNA.com. Of these, 84 had the low-activity MAOA variant, and 141 had higher activity variants; the low-activity form is the variant previously found to be associated with a higher risk of violence. The percentage that possessed the low-activity variant, approximately 37%, is typical for a Western population sample (Gilad et al. 2002).

Of this original sample, we were able to conduct detailed and repeated interviews with 34 individuals. For our specific purposes, the number of interview cases remains on par with other studies based on detailed structural interviews. Note that this study is not focused on population-level statistical significance linking MAOA to violence. This has already been accomplished (Åslund et al. 2011; Forsman and Långström 2012; Weder et al. 2009). We undertook extensive interviews with everyone we were able to contact out of the original sample. Some people could not be contacted because they had given inaccurate contact information, and some did not return calls: Two Buddhist monks had had their numbers disconnected, and one gang member had been killed in the interim between genotyping and interviews. Each interview lasted several hours. Subjects chose their preferred method of interview: in person or by telephone. Some subsequent fact-checking questions were conducted by e-mail. Participants included those from Caucasian, African American, and Latino ancestry, whose ages ranged from 24 to 47 years; the larger sample of subjects for whom we had genotype information represented a wider age distribution and included some from Asian ancestry as well.

We administered questionnaires to, and conducted interviews with, individuals across various socioeconomic and religious groups. Within our interview group, we located six practicing Buddhist monks living in a celibate pacifist community; counterintuitively, all possessed the low-activity form of MAOA (the variant associated with violence). We interviewed five successful and active professional mixed martial arts (MMA) fighters from our population who make their living engaging in violence; remarkably, none of these individuals possessed the low-activity MAOA variant associated with violence. We obtained genotypes on six members of a well-known motorcycle club (i.e., a biker gang); half had the low-activity form of MAOA, and the other half possessed the high-activity form. We obtained genetic status on six former inner-city gang members, all of whom had served jail time for murder; four of them possessed the low-activity (higher aggression) form of the MAOA. In addition, we interviewed four chief executive operating officers (CEOs) of major multinational companies with earnings in the hundreds of millions of dollars annually; one had the low-activity form of the allele. None of the four professional prominent actors or producers we tested possessed the low-activity form of MAOA. Finally, three of the four academic professors did possess the low-activity form of MAOA. This diversity alone encourages further inquiry, investigation, and a tempering of any interpretation that the low-activity form of MAOA alone determines the propensity toward aggression and the form of violence favored by any given individual.

We created a detailed structured interview protocol (Robins et al. 1988) to address specifically those aspects of background and environment that the literature suggested might potentiate aggression among those who possess the MAOA genotype (Kim-Cohen et al. 2006; McDermott et al. 2009; Reif et al. 2007; Widom and Brzustowicz 2006). The general topics in the interview protocol are shown in Box 12.1. We divided the interviews into four groups, along the dimensions of MAO status (low or high) and whether or not the person had an aggressive occupation.

We based our specific questions on literature that pointed to the role of traumatic early life events and immediate provocations in particular. Specifically, we asked about family background, early physical fights, developmental history, educational experiences, deviance, trouble with the law, gang activity, neighborhood environment,

Box 12.1 Interview Topics

Baseline demographic topics:

1. Age
2. Ethnicity
3. Religion
4. Parents' social class and income
5. Number and sexes of siblings
6. Marital or relationship status and history
7. Number and sexes of children
8. Citizenship and ancestry
9. Political orientation and values

Substantive question topic areas: These questions only represent the initial question within a particular topic. Depending on the respondent answer, follow-up questions were administered.

1. What kind of a home did you grow up in? Did your parents fight a lot? Physically?
2. Can you tell me about the first time you got in a physical fight?
3. Did you get into a lot of fights at school?
4. How many times have you been in a physical fight?
5. Do you tend to win these physical fights?
6. How often did you witness, take part in, or experience physical violence?
7. What was your home environment like as a child?
8. How do you feel about physical altercations (do you like them, do you avoid them)?
9. Has this feeling changed over time?
10. Can you tell me about the first time you almost died?
11. When did you come into yourself and your own power?
12. How did you make your choices in life? Were they forced on you?
13. How did you get where you are now?
14. How do you handle conflicts? Do you have a short fuse?
15. Does it matter if the conflict is interpersonal in nature?
16. Are there certain triggers that are more likely to make you respond physically (disrespect, jealousy)?
17. Have you ever been arrested?
18. Do you enjoy extreme sports?

interpersonal relationships with family and peers, employment, income, life trajectories, and current circumstances. We examined and compared common themes in each area, and we explored whether and how the core genetic and environmental predictors of behavioral propensity toward aggression in the literature linked with real-life behavior across a diverse population of individuals in varying contexts. Thus, although we use genetics as well as social opportunities and constraints to illuminate part of our inquiry, the story we tell of these individual lives goes beyond biology or surveyed environmental measures to enlighten the developmental path by which people come to engage, or avoid, aggressive behavior.

Through the structured interviews, the participants, regardless of profession, educational level, or income, were thoughtful and articulate about the experiences that led them to their current place in life. Everyone we reached agreed to participate and gave informed consent. No one refused to answer any question, although some requested we anonymize their responses. All participants were guaranteed anonymity and confidentiality in return for their open and honest responses; thus, to ensure no identifying information will be offered in this report, we changed a few potentially identifying details of participant stories.

We propose that although genotypes clearly matter in the aggregate, as the literature suggests, individually, they do not independently preclude, prohibit, or potentiate complex behavior, criminal acts of aggression, and violence specifically on an individual level. The world is complex, and each human being manifests myriad forms of individual variance that erupt from the intersection of genotype, environment, society, and culture. The choices individuals make in their lives can mitigate or escalate the importance of any genetic proclivities they possess to determine whether they will be more or less violent in response to any threat, provocation, conflict, or opportunity.

SUMMARY OF INTERVIEWS

We divide our discussion into four groups based on MAO status and occupation. We provide representative quotes from our interviews that include responses to questions about family background and early life events, other developmental factors such as early fights, trouble with the law, and current life circumstances, although not every group has relevant experiences in each of these areas.

Low MAO (Higher Aggression Variant) and Aggressive Occupation

Perhaps surprisingly, among many of the participants who engage in violence regularly, only one claimed to have experienced serious violence directed against himself in the home as a child. This 37-year-old gang member, who had the low variant (high aggression) of MAO, said his father "would hit him but he didn't know why," whereas his mother would spank him but communicate what he did wrong. He said he appreciated that his mother would tell him what he did wrong. When he was 3 years old, his 16-year-old aunt "caved in" his head, whipping him with a microphone when he urinated on himself. He said he believed this event caused him to "weigh the consequences of actions meticulously."

Some respondents reported witnessing violence directed against others when they were children. For example, a 36-year-old former gang member, also with the low variant of MAO, reported witnessing extreme violence from an early age. He stated that when he was 3 years old, he watched his mother get hit in the face with a brick by his brother's father. His own father died of a heroin overdose when he was a few days old, and his mother was an addict.

Most participants with the low-activity form of MAOA conveyed dramatic stories of participating in numerous physical fights from a young age, unlike those with the high-activity form. One of the former gang members with the low-activity form of MAOA began fighting at age 5 or 6 years, often, he claimed, to protect his sister. He was expelled from multiple schools for this behavior. Another former gang member with the low-activity form of MAOA had a proclivity for fighting that got him expelled from two school districts. When this happened, he began selling drugs. He eventually became a competitive street fighter. Over time, he says he developed a spiritual outlook on fighting, which he likens to that he experiences while surfing, and he currently trains ex-prisoners in this spiritual approach to fighting.

Another former gang member with the low-activity MAOA variant said he was in more physical fights than he could count. He remembered getting into his first fight in second grade. He stated that one kid in his class walked in and said he knew karate and could beat anyone. Our subject immediately rushed him and then hit him in the face, telling him "Show me what you got!" He then grabbed the putative karate expert by the throat and threw him on the desk, laying on top of him and choking him. He remembers the kid struggling but then grabbing a sharp pencil on the desk and stabbing him in the arm. At this point, a teacher walked in and asked what was going on, and the future gang member stated that he did not say anything because there is a rule in the projects that you "never snitch."

This story is similar to that told by another participant with the low-activity form of MAOA who recalled a fat bully who bothered him in the third grade. This person said, "The rules are that if someone bugs you, you have to protect yourself." So when this bully started to bug him and prepared to hit him, he

> saw the blow coming and I hit him first. I was so pumped up with adrenaline after this. Fat Fred was shocked. Fat Fred never messed with me again. Protecting myself was a boost to myself. I learned that no matter how big they are, I should hit first. I remember thinking I am very proud of myself.

One gang member likened the experience to the time he took cocaine, whereas two others volunteered that the only thing it felt similar to was sex, reflecting studies in the extant literature (de Aguirre 2006; Malamuth, Check, and Briere 1986).

Two of the former gang members and one of the academics recounted significant developmental experiences that affected their future tendencies toward aggression. The first former gang member, who possessed the low-variant (higher aggression) form of MAO, starting lifting weights in the fifth or sixth grade in order to gain strength to be able to win physical fights. By the ninth grade, he could bench press 315 pounds, a significant amount of weight considering the average maximum bench press for a man in his 20s is 180 pounds. He said he had a very short fuse, but for him,

> it was more about survival. I knew that I had to be tougher than the next guy. Lifting weights gave me an edge. By 15 or 16 years old, I was fighting guys who came out of prison. This was a survival mechanism. I had to build a harder shell to protect the softness in my heart.

Evidence for this claim was emblazoned on his body, on which intricate and beautiful tattoos portrayed surprisingly sentimental images, including female family members, hearts, flowers, and animals. This person said that how people looked at him determined his level of aggressiveness. He said he "had to defend myself to show the opponent that I wasn't weak. I would confront a person right away if they looked at me funny. I felt I had to build a reputation so people wouldn't mess with me."

One of the former gang members noted that he often got into physical fights was because of his inability to eschew sexual pleasure. He said when he met someone he wanted to be with, he could

> only think about the pleasure and how good it would feel. I don't think about whatever man she has and then when he finds out, you got a fight on your hands. I don't want that fight, but I do want that pleasure, and I can't always think ahead to that possibility at the beginning.

His most recent stint in prison resulted from assault on the boyfriend of one of the women with whom he had been involved. When the boyfriend looked at him "funny" on the street, he asked him what his problem was and the boyfriend told him his problem was that he was "taking over" his girlfriend, after which our subject attacked him because "he deserved it for dissing me."

The threat posed by a provocative gaze found resonance in another gang member (Ellsworth and Carlsmith 1973). He said, "It's all about territory, not just the specific person. It's like the Arabs and Jews having conflicts for many years. You grow up knowing who your enemies are and you fight them." This former gang member said that the one thing that would have prevented his life in a gang was a job. He tried to join a "Clean and Green" social project designed to accomplish just that goal when he was 12 years old, but he was not allowed to participate because he was too young. After that, he said it was too late. He said he

> wanted to wear cool shoes, like Nikes. Otherwise, people would make fun of me and girls wouldn't be interested in me. The only other way to make money was to sell

drugs. I hung out with dealers, but was embarrassed to go up to the main dealers to ask if I could sell cause I didn't want to get rejected. When I asked, though, the dealer gave me a bottle and I made money the same day. Selling drugs is easy money. It makes you happy because you have money in your pocket and girls are attracted to you. And so you think "Fuck 'clean and green.'"

This participant offered an even more profound reflection on his experience growing up in the projects and how it not only affected his propensity for violence but also deeply shattered his sense of the future. His reflection deserves extensive quotation:

The way we grew up in the projects determined my choices. I grew up with 15 people in a three-bedroom house including aunts and uncles. I knew right from wrong. I knew how to go the right way: go to school; don't do drugs; listen to mom and grandma. It was a choice not to do those things. But growing up in the projects is different than growing up on the streets. Projects are like living with everyone. You watch each other grow up, know one another's strengths and weaknesses. When the majority of your friends in the projects are going in a certain direction, it's hard to make a different choice. If you choose to be a nerd, you'll get fucked with. What's education going to do when you know you're going to die by the time you're 18 anyway? In junior high, the counselor asked me, "Don't you want to be something?" When you actually think about this, you stop and think about it, and I realized I don't need an education. I know how to make money, I know how to survive, I'm going to die and don't think I'll see 18. If I'm not going to be around to use education, why would I go to school? At this point, I started being more hard-core. I stopped school after the 7th grade.

By age 19 years, he had been shot in the head, but he did not die; the bullet remains lodged there.

Just as with physical fights, most respondents claimed to have been arrested "more times than I can count." One former gang member with the low-variant form of MAO deliberately got himself arrested at age 13 years by selling drugs to a guy he knew was an undercover cop since the police officer used a 1970s word for the kind of drugs he wanted. The respondent wanted to join his twin brother in juvenile hall because he had never been separated from him before. His brother had been arrested and hog-tied by officers from the the Los Angeles Police Department for carjacking. Our subject started to run away from the cop "for the fuck of it, I needed to blow some adrenaline" and got away, but he let the cop find him by giving himself up. Within an hour of arriving in juvenile hall, he started a fight. Our young offender "unloaded everything" because it was his first fight inside and he considered it a rite of passage. He noted that inside "all you have is your fists and you have to defend yourself." This person has since been arrested multiple times, including for urban terrorism because, he says, a cop had a grudge against his brother. He was 25 years old when he went to prison, and he said this was good because all his close friends had died or were in prison for life by that point. He ended up serving 2½ years of a 4-year term. This person was the one whose brother could not be reached for interview because he had been killed.

One of the former gang members declared, "I know I have the 'warrior' gene, but I also feel I have a choice. Love will conquer everything." Yet our other participants often fell short of both work and luck but remained long on friends whose lifestyles dissuaded them from more propitious forms of education and employment. One of the former gang members with the low-activity variant of MAO defended the positive aspects of violence by saying, "In a way physical violence is good, you are physically active, and you learn about yourself, understand your power and how to use it. You learn to understand physical ability. But you can also hurt yourself physically." These comments reflect the scientific literature on the subject as well (Hawley and Vaughn 2003).

Low MAO (Higher Aggression Variant) and Low-Aggression Occupation

In contrast to the previous group of participants, other participants with the short version of MAO who ended up in less aggressive occupations reported no early exposure to violence. One of the academics with the low variant form, a 44-year-old male, had divorced parents but never witnessed physical violence toward himself or his parents growing up. One of the Buddhist monks reported that he believed he was the fifth generation of males in his family to possess the low-activity form of the MAOA genotype; he witnessed and participated in a great deal of verbal fighting in his household growing up, and he stated that he enjoyed the verbal sparring, experiencing a strong sense of victory when he dominated such contests. He went on to win numerous national debating contests in college, but he never saw or sustained physical violence in his youth, claiming a strong aversion to such actions, having been raised to seek resolution of conflicts through verbal debate.

One of the academics with the low-activity form of the MAOA genotype similarly recalled getting into his first fight at age 3 or 4 years when someone attacked his older brother. He ran outside, grabbed a rock, and threw it at the attacker. This person went on to note the importance of "setting a standard of how tough you are early on." This interviewee told the story of a fight he got into when he was 15 years old after having sex with a girl. He said he "didn't know if she had a boyfriend, didn't care, didn't ask." Indeed, the instigation for violence in pursuit of sexual activity posed a common theme in many of the interviews. It turned out the girl was attached to a gang member, and between 50 and 70 "friends" of the boyfriend, along with the boyfriend, came to teach him a lesson. He called his brother to back him up. In what he described as a "victory or death household, where it was known to be completely unacceptable to lose, where you don't quit, you don't give up," his brother told him that "if you don't win, I'll beat you worse when you get home." His brother drove to his location and proceeded to hit the biggest guy in the crowd with a roll of quarters, breaking his jaw and thus allowing for a fair fight between the subject and the angry boyfriend. Our subject emerged victorious, having learned a critical lesson: "Always take out the biggest and toughest guy first. If you take down the leader, most of the others will run away or not fight as hard."

This sentiment was echoed by one of the academics with the low-activity form of MAOA who said that he learned early to "hit his enemies first." He said that the key is "to know when violence will occur, and, if so, be the first one to commit it. It is not about whether it is right; if violence is going to happen, you have to attack first." This academic, who had also been in the military, attributes his victories in fighting less to his skill as a combatant and more to his ability to absorb an enormous amount of punishment. He said he never sought out a fight and "did not go looking for trouble." He said that he would only "instigate violence when there is a provocation where it is deserved," but he did notice that

> once I go off, there is no turning it off. It goes until it is done. Once the rage rises and sits under the skin, I become committed to it. Once that happens, there is no end. I feel stronger, warmer, I hear better and am more focused and have greater mental sense. It feels good.

Indeed, many of the respondents noted that they liked the physical feeling that both instigated and followed physical aggression, finding it intrinsically, internally rewarding in a direct, immediate somatic way.

Similarly, a second academic and one of the Buddhist monks, both with the low-activity form of MAOA, did not recall getting into many fights as children. Both claimed that they did not like such altercations and that they tried to avoid them whenever possible.

Another participant who also said he had been arrested "more times than I can count" explained that he did not resist if "they had me dead to right. If I can, I run away. But I would not allow myself to be arrested for anything serious." He claimed to have "no respect for the law" and considered the police to be a "criminal organization empowered by the state to do its bidding." Another participant, obviously sharing a similar belief, told the story of being unable to prevent himself from antagonizing a police officer who stopped him for a traffic violation, asking him if he did not have something better to do, "like find a sale at a donut shop." The subject quickly found himself surrounded by police cars on all sides. At this point, the large dog he had in the back seat of the car growled at the officer. The subject indicated he would not be able to control his dog if the officer touched him, which he knew to be a lie, taking pride in his complete control over the animal. The officer then backed away, clearly fearful of the animal but warning the subject that the dog needed to be leashed at all times when outside.

When we asked individuals how they got to where they are now, the answers varied by their life circumstances. One of the academics who had the low-activity form of MAOA and who claimed not to engage in extreme sports, for example, nonetheless noted the irony in that statement by stating,

> I would never intentionally jump out of a plane or bungee jump (I do not see the point) . . . but I have spent much of my life working in jungles, cities, traveling the world and experiencing what many folks might call "risk" in those contexts.

He went on to say that he got to where he is with "hard work, luck, friends, pretty much the same way anyone would get anywhere." This person says he never handles conflict with violence, although he will occasionally be aggressive to an inanimate object, like punching a wall.

One of the participants with the low-activity genotype elaborated on this theme eloquently when he stated that growing up in a bad neighborhood allowed him to develop skills he never could have mastered in a middle-class neighborhood, where he would have been simply a troublemaker:

> People tried to force choices on me, and tried to get me to acquiesce to the system, but I knew how to manipulate the system by junior high. I learned to size people up quickly, learned to handle firearms early, learned not to follow the herd. It became second nature. Tell people what they want to hear, they don't follow up and then you can do what you want. I used a combination of these same tools and ingenuity to be an entrepreneur, not to feel pressure or get stressed, to be able to slow things down in my own mind and look far ahead, and to know when you don't need to do certain things, and in that way, I was able to do things that kept me from folding under pressure. I get the job done no matter what. I learned to manipulate others, to get people to betray their friends without knowing it, and over 20 years I learned to thrive in new, novel environments, to hone my skills, to do whatever it took, to commit any heinous act necessary to further the ends deemed necessary.

However, this recognition also points to the role of choice among options. The recognition of choice was echoed by one of the Buddhist monks, who said,

> I choose not to be provoked. I feel the impulse rise, but I have spent a lifetime of practice learning to control and overcome that urge. It is a choice. I choose not to hurt any other sentient being, regardless of how they might hurt me, or how angry I might get initially. That is the only path to peace, both individually and for society. If we all retaliate, the violence will never end. We have to choose not to harm. It may be harder for some than for others, but it is a choice for everyone.

We consider that it may be the awareness of one's own violent impulses and tendencies that encouraged these individuals to become monks in the first place; they sought a life path that would limit their tendency to engage in actions they simultaneously felt drawn to but found abhorrent.

Interestingly, even those who may be genetically influenced to be more likely to resolve conflict with aggression note the importance of self-control in the process. One of the academics noted,

> I could control my rage. I show them it will cost too much and they do not want to get involved with anything. I regulate when I dole out punishment. I do not want to be goaded, manipulated, or used. I use measured aggression for a cool, long-term measured response.

Another participant, a professional dancer, said he considered gaining control over his anger and aggression to constitute a spiritual journey and practice:

As I came to be able to marshal my anger better, I could use it in my work, to motivate my movement. It is often hard, but I have come to see it as a kind of meditation. That control means I don't waste as much of my energy on things I cannot change, like obsessions about how I am going to get back at someone who dissed me. I know I have wasted years obsessing about how to get back against someone who it turned out never intended to hurt me. That has been a real learning curve for me. Now, with effort and attention, I can pour that energy into my art and it makes my movement much more authentic, cause the source of the feeling is real but it is put into artistic movement and not personal revenge.

Similarly, the CEO who possessed the low-activity form of MAOA declared,

Aggression comes in many forms, only some of which appear explicitly violent, but all of which can potentially be destructive. When I close a factory in a town that depends on those jobs to survive, is that any less aggressive than some nut job who takes a gun to a school? I can justify it because this is how capitalism works, and many others benefit from my choices, including our stockholders, but I am certain the guy who lost his job at 55 with only a high school degree, a sky high mortgage on a worthless house, and health problems because he smokes and drinks away the stress from having a fat bitchy wife who won't put out but sits at home and complains about what she can't afford to her lazy friends while not putting any work into making herself attractive, and two surly kids who would rather go to college than work at Wal-Mart, does not agree.

When this CEO was asked at the end of the interview if there was anything else he wanted to say, he paused and then blurted,

Well, since you asked, and since you are one, I gotta tell you. I've worked with a lot of people in a lot of different capacities doing a lot of different jobs, and the group of people who are most vicious and selfish, by far, are academics. Why? Because they are all completely aggressive and the only place they can direct it is toward each other 'cause nothing they do matters in the real world. It doesn't make money, it doesn't save lives, it doesn't make people happy and they resent that no one loves them, so they have to find a way to feel good about their worthless lives by pretending that it is somehow good to be smarter than anyone else. Street smart is essential for survival, but what did book smart ever get you? It sure as hell never got anyone laid and that, after all, is all any of us want anyway when it all comes right down to it.

High MAO (Lower Aggression Variant) and High-Aggression Occupation

Interestingly, one of the MMA fighters, who did not possess the low-activity form of MAOA genotype, in reflecting on why he became a professional fighter, said he was good at fighting from an early age and worked hard to improve his native skills and abilities. In contrast with those who did have the low-activity form of MAOA, this professional fighter did not report a similar sense of feeling good in his body before, during, and after fighting; rather, he indicated that he did it because it was one of the few legal avenues available to him to make a lot of money. When asked if he liked to fight, he paused and said, "Only when I win." When asked if he got into physical fights in his personal life, he physically pulled back, looked shocked, and said, "Never. It would endanger my job." He then went on to say that he believed his advantage in fighting was that he could control his emotions where others could not, and thus he had the ability to take his time and to think strategically about the best way to conduct and win each contest, as opposed to those whose emotions get the better of them in a contest. He said,

> I have fought a lot of guys a lot bigger and a lot better than me, but I have managed to win more of those fights than I should because I could stay calm where they lost their cool. You lose your cool in a fight, you lose. Rage makes you sloppy. I never take it personally. It is like playing a game you get paid for. I often try to piss off the guys who get angry easily in fights, 'cause then I know it is an easy win. He gets pissed, he gets sloppy, I win.

In this way, this fighter used rational violence as a means to the end of earning an easy paycheck, exploiting and leveraging the advantage provided to him by the weaknesses he found in his more impulsive opponents.

High MAO (Lower Aggression Variant) and Low-Aggression Occupation

The group within our population that possessed high MAO and worked in traditionally low-aggression jobs mostly comprised actors and producers. Because this sample was drawn from the larger Los Angeles area, several of these individuals were quite prominent in the industry. Most of these individuals had more typical, mostly unremarkable childhoods, growing up in stable, two-parent households. Often, the largest conflict these men had had with their parents was over their career choice, with the parents wanting them to choose more traditional or conservative occupations. Without exception, none of these people had any history of physical fights or trouble with the law. They commonly reported that when they got into conflicts with other kids growing up, they usually "entertained" their way out of the problem by cracking jokes, distracting observers, or otherwise endearing themselves to potential rivals through the conscious, if not exactly manipulative, use of their superior social skills.

One cinematographer had started his career filming pornography in the San Fernando Valley. When asked what that was like, he said, "boring." He explained that he had left that industry because it was such a feminist-oriented and -dominated industry that he came to believe it would be difficult for him to advance professionally, and so he switched to making documentaries for the military. He told of one experience in which he was shooting a simulated scene involving a terrorist attack and, after several rehearsals, the munitions were loaded with real gunpowder for what he described as "the money shot." The shoulder-launched missile being used was old and exploded, and one of the actors was seriously injured in his face. Because it happened so fast, he caught the whole event on camera, describing it as one of the most traumatic he had ever experienced. As he described it,

> It was completely disorienting. There was blood everywhere. If we had not been on a military base with medical personnel close by, I'm sure the actor would have been killed. The producer was furious, he ripped the entire logistics staff new assholes for not double checking the launcher, although apparently you can't always tell about these things until you use real explosive. He fired them all on the spot and went rampaging around until we heard the guy would live. The producer had me keep filming, I think mostly for cya purposes to show all the stuff we did to try to save the guy. Once it was over, I just broke down and cried once I got home.

One of the producers had moved to Los Angeles from England because he believed there were more opportunities in the United States. He said he liked working with actors and other creative people, and he never saw a reason to get mad in response to adversity:

> Look, sure I get mad but I never see a good reason to take it out on others, especially not violently. For me, only people who lack a strong creative outlet have to resort to such Neanderthal behavior. If you are smart and clever, there is always another way to let those feelings out in a constructive, creative manner which contributes to the social good, even if what you are doing is making an angry documentary about some injustice you see in the world.

One of the actors, who had been quite prominent as a child actor and then lost some of his fame, had devolved into drug abuse before going on to help others who had fallen prey to addiction problems. As he explained,

> I wasn't mad that I lost my fame so much as lost without work, lost without having a channel for all my energy. I just wanted to have fun but I didn't want to hurt anyone else. And so I ended up hurting myself until I realized I had to love myself if I was going to love anyone else, or if anyone else was going to love me. Actors want the same thing politicians do: to be loved by every random stranger, and lots of them.

He then added with an infectious smile: "We're just better at it than politicians."

DISCUSSION

We have sought to inform the nature of individual behavior on the basis of both genotype and individuated life history data and dispel incorrect notions that apply population-level findings to individual-level responsibility. The in-depth structured interviews undertaken here demonstrate how qualitative data can exponentially enhance our understanding of genetic information. This point remains critical in assessing personal responsibility and understanding the limits of making individual assessments on the basis of genotype. If someone with a particular genetic disposition chooses to kill someone, or gets into massive credit card debt, it does not mean that person should be absolved of responsibility for his or her actions. To argue the opposite would also require the logically consistent belief that growing up in a rough neighborhood makes people innocent of crimes they commit later in life or that abused children should be condemned because they have a higher probability of becoming abusers themselves. Rather, individuals make choices; their choices operate through a complex interplay of genotype and environmental precipitants. Personal responsibility cannot be abnegated simply by virtue of genotype.

As we describe in our life history interviews, developmental, environmental, cultural, and genetic factors all play a part in differentiating the life trajectories of those who resort to violence in the face of provocation from those who do not, even among those who share an identical genotype. Our interviews provide some novel insight, in that genotype may have a role in preferences and rewards, but it does not preclude reasoned decisions. Clearly, certain kinds of developmental, environmental, and cultural circumstances alter the expression of the MAOA genotype in ways that affect the behavioral variance we observe among its possessors. The low-activity form of MAOA may come to express itself more in contexts in which the environmental triggers signal danger and threat or one in which violence is environmentally rewarded. A developmental history of exposure to violence may serve to environmentally calibrate the upregulation of physical aggression in the face of threat in order to maximize prospects for survival in a threatening environment. On the other hand, a familial environment that encourages peaceful solutions may be able to mitigate such tendencies. This is encouraging news for those searching for strategies of social intervention to remediate avenues toward violence. That is, altering the environmental circumstances in which individuals, potentially "predisposed" or not, grow up appears to be the best avenue to lower one's risk for engaging in violence as adults.

This suggests individual variance in the literal experience of physical aggression. Just as some people can consume alcohol regularly and never become addicted or dependent, and some people feel physically good following exercise, whereas others do not, some individuals appear to have a different responsivity to the biological rewards of aggression (Ramírez, Bonniot-Cabanac, and Cabanac 2005). This raises the question of whether aggression, like other substances, requires increasing doses in order to achieve the same internal rewards or whether other, more social, incentives continue to reinforce and support such responses.

The only obvious and consistent difference between the low-activity form of MAOA monks, professors, and CEOs who led a life of peace and the gang members who led a life of violence was economic class. The monks came from wealthier backgrounds, had more formal education, and were more likely to emerge from intact homes largely devoid of physical aggression—precisely the kind of environmental factors that social science has previously identified as independent mitigating factors for violence regardless of genotype. Notably, the more pacific of the low-MAOA (linked to higher aggression) academics shared with the monks a more stable home environment growing up, and this may account for differences in outcome as well. Any serious investigation of the relationship between biology and culture needs to consider these complex genetic, social, developmental, economic, and cultural factors in seeking to mitigate the manifestation of aggression in society. Thus, in addition to identifying genotype, scholars might also strive to identify those salient individual-level developmental factors and environmental cues that ameliorate or potentiate violence in order to better unpack the complex mechanisms of personal choice.

These interviews indicate that the nature of a person's social networks reinforces particular patterns of behavior, and social values would need to shift in order to influence more than a few individuals to move outside established cultures of violence. Cultures of deprivation and poverty exist in reciprocal causal interaction with genetic predispositions. The gang members spoke eloquently of the importance of violence for survival in the context of their social and cultural milieu growing up. The interviews with the monks lend some hint as to possible prevention or intervention strategies for those with a greater proclivity toward violence, whether that arises in small part due to the low-activity form of MAOA or life circumstances; they provide less insight into what makes some people want to overcome such impulses, whereas others prefer to indulge them.

Some enjoyed violence, whereas others did not. This is very important because it suggests, and speaks to, the divergent inner life experience of those with high and low variants of MAO. Individuals may not have a choice in the endogenous cards they are dealt, but ultimately what matters is how each individual plays the cards he or she is dealt. Difference in background, lifestyle, and environment may result in individuals making divergent life choices, but this does not diminish the fact that the internal experience may be vastly different depending in part on genotype. Some people may simply not find aggression as attractive as others, making the achievements of the monks who have gone to such lengths to overcome their temptations much more impressive than a similar choice by someone whose endogenous reinforcement mechanisms may not provide the same kind of positive experience from engaging in violence. This might be similar, for example, to those who literally feel better from exercising physically, as opposed to those who simply feel morally sanctimonious for doing so, or those who derive genuine physiological calm from ingesting carbohydrates, whereas others can pass them up without a second thought. Alcohol provides an even more extreme comparison between alcoholics and those who can imbibe or demure with complete indifference. Understanding the mechanisms and pathways that establish and support these sources of rewards is an important next step in this research.

If any one thing can be taken from this study, it is that information about a single MAOA marker cannot be used to justify, excuse, or predict with accuracy whether any particular individual will commit any given act of violence. Overall, the relationship between MAOA, adverse events in childhood, provocation, and violence appears to exist in some of our interview data, just as has been shown in previous large-N studies. However, these expected relationships were not present in many individuals. Some individuals with the predisposing genotype, such as the monks, made a conscious choice to structure their lives to render the possibility of violence all but impossible. Others, including the professional MMA fighters, who did not have the MAOA genotype linked to violence, still manage to make their living engaging in violence. These professional fighters used violence as rational means for income, but they did not claim to enjoy it for its own sake. Still others who possess the genotype, most notably the former gang members, indulge in a life of violence both personal and professional, often at great cost, but also without any sense of viable alternative social or economic options. Interestingly, by contrast, many of those gang members with the low-activity form of MAOA did report finding aspects of aggression and violence enjoyable, whereas other gang members with the high-activity form did not, again suggesting different endogenous mechanisms of reinforcement for such behavior based at least in part on genotype. Thus, the meaning, function, utility, and experience of violence appear to shift across both individuals and environments. However, whereas a relationship between MAOA, traumatic early life events, provocation, and aggression exists on an aggregate level, the vast majority of difference among and between individuals occurs within the context of the individual choices people make based on background and social circumstances.

Our findings are consistent with recent findings from statistical approaches (Simons et al. 2011), but they are unique in the inclusion of deep contextual factors. Human choice encompasses a wide panoply of options that can involve becoming captured by or rejecting genetic liability to many complex social forces, including violence. Genotype, like environments, appears to indirectly predispose individuals to find some choices easier, more natural, or preferable than others. But human agency allows for the possibility that individuals can choose cooperation over conflict, compassion over vengeance, or generosity and gratitude over rigidity and resentment. Love may not always find a way, but sometimes it can vanquish hate, just as redemption can flourish in the light of forgiveness.

Acknowledgments

We thank Bennett Greenspan, President of FamilyTreeDNA.com, and his extremely accommodating staff for their help and support with this research. We thank Aidan Pickering of Edge West Productions for helping us recruit participants through a project sponsored by National Geographic. We thank Nicole Cerra for her tenacious help tracking down the participants. And we thank the participants for generously sharing their time and experience so fully and openly with us.

References

Åslund, C., N. Nordquist, E. Comasco, J. Leppert, L. Oreland, and K. W. Nilsson. 2011. "Maltreatment, MAOA, and Delinquency: Sex Differences in Gene–Environment

Interaction in a Large Population-Based Cohort of Adolescents." *Behavior Genetics* 41(2): 262–272.

Aspinwall, L. G., T. R. Brown, and J. Tabery. 2012. "The Double-Edged Sword: Does Biomechanism Increase or Decrease Judges' Sentencing of Psychopaths?" *Science* 337(6096): 846–849.

Baum, Matthew. 2013. "The Monoamine Oxidase A (MAOA) Genetic Predisposition to Impulsive Violence: Is It Relevant to Criminal Trials?" *Neuroethics* 6(2): 287–306.

Bearman, Peter. 2008. "Exploring Genetics and Social Structure." *American Journal of Sociology* 114(S1): i–vi.

Bennett, Alison. 2012. "Neurolaw: Trial Tips for Today and Game Changing Questions for the Future." *The Jury Expert* 24(5): 1–3.

Berryessa, Colleen M., and Mildred K. Cho. 2013. "Ethical, Legal, Social, and Policy Implications of Behavioral Genetics." *Annual Review of Genomics and Human Genetics* 14(1): 515–534.

Bollinger, J., J. Scott, R. Dvoskin, and D. Kaufman. 2012. "Public Preferences Regarding the Return of Individual Genetic Research Results: Findings from a Qualitative Focus Group Study." *Genetics in Medicine* 14(4): 451–457.

Buckholtz, J. W., J. H. Callicott, B. Kolachana, A. R. Hariri, T. E. Goldberg, M. Genderson, M. F. Egan, V. S. Mattay, D. R. Weinberger, and A. Meyer-Lindenberg. 2008. "Genetic Variation in MAOA Modulates Ventromedial Prefrontal Circuitry Mediating Individual Differences in Human Personality." *Molecular Psychiatry* 13(3): 313–324.

Buckholtz, Joshua W., and Andreas Meyer-Lindenberg. 2008. "MAOA and the Neurogenetic Architecture of Human Aggression." *Trends in Neurosciences* 31(3): 120–129.

Burt, Callie H., and Ronald L. Simons. 2014. "Pulling Back the Curtain on Heritability Studies: Biosocial Criminology in the Postgenomic Era." *Criminology* 52(2): 223–262.

Byrd, Amy L., and Stephen B. Manuck. 2014. "MAOA, Childhood Maltreatment, and Antisocial Behavior: Meta-Analysis of a Gene–Environment Interaction." *Biological Psychiatry* 75(1): 9–17.

Church, Dominique J. 2012. "Neuroscience in the Courtroom: An International Concern." *William and Mary Law Review* 53(5): 1825–1854.

Conley, Dalton, and Neil G. Bennett. 2000. "Is Biology Destiny? Birth Weight and Life Chances." *American Sociological Review* 65(3): 458–467.

Davidge, Kristen M., Leslie Atkinson, Lori Douglas, Vivien Lee, Solomon Shapiro, James L. Kennedy, and Joseph H. Beitchman. 2004. "Association of the Serotonin Transporter and 5HT1D[Beta] Receptor Genes with Extreme, Persistent and Pervasive Aggressive Behaviour in Children." *Psychiatric Genetics* 14(3): 143–146.

de Aguirre, María Inés. 2006. "Neurobiological Bases of Aggression, Violence, and Cruelty." *Behavioral and Brain Sciences* 29(3): 228–229.

Duncan, L. E., and M. C. Keller. 2011. "A Critical Review of the First 10 Years of Candidate Gene-by-Environment Interaction Research in Psychiatry." *American Journal of Psychiatry* 168(10): 1041–1049.

Ellsworth, Phoebe, and J. Merrill Carlsmith. 1973. "Eye Contact and Gaze Aversion in an Aggressive Encounter." *Journal of Personality and Social Psychology* 28(2): 280.

Farisco, M., and C. Petrini. 2012. "The Impact of Neuroscience and Genetics on the Law: A Recent Italian Case." *Neuroethics* 5(3): 317–319.

Feresin, Emiliano. 2009. "Lighter Sentence for Murderer with 'Bad Genes.'" *Nature.* doi:10.1038/news.2009.1050.

Forsman, M., and N. Långström. 2012. "Child Maltreatment and Adult Violent Offending: Population-Based Twin Study Addressing the 'Cycle of Violence' Hypothesis." *Psychological Medicine* 42(9): 1977–1983.

Frazzetto, G., G. Di Lorenzo, V. Carola, L. Proietti, E. Sokolowska, A. Siracusano, C. Gross, and A. Troisi. 2007. "Early Trauma and Increased Risk for Physical Aggression During Adulthood: The Moderating Role of MAOA Genotype." *PLoS One* 2(5): e486.

Freese, Jeremy. 2008. "Genetics and the Social Science Explanation of Individual Outcomes." *American Journal of Sociology* 114(S1): S1-S35.

Gilad, Yoav, Shai Rosenberg, Molly Przeworski, Doron Lancet, and Karl Skorecki. 2002. "Evidence for Positive Selection and Population Structure at the Human MAO-A Gene." *Proceedings of the National Academy of Sciences of the USA* 99(2): 862–867.

Hall, Wayne D., and Katherine I. Morley. 2003. *Is There a Genetic Susceptibility to Engage in Criminal Acts?* Australian Institute of Criminology, Canberra City, Australia.

Hawley, Patricia H., and Brian E. Vaughn, eds. 2003. "Aggression and Adaptive Functioning: The Bright Side to Bad Behavior." *Merrill-Palmer Quarterly* 49(3): 239–242.

Javitt, G. 2006. "Policy Implications of Genetic Testing: Not Just for Geneticists Anymore." *Advances in Chronic Kidney Disease* 13(2): 178–182.

Kaplan, Jeremy. 2010. "Researchers Find the Liberal Gene." *Fox News.* http://www.foxnews.com/scitech/2010/10/28/researchers-liberal-gene-genetics-politics

Kaufman, D., J. Murphy, J. Scott, and K. Hudson. 2008. "Subjects Matter: A Survey of Public Opinions About a Large Cohort Study." *Genetics in Medicine* 10: 831–839.

Kendler, Kenneth S. 2006. "'A Gene for . . .': The Nature of Gene Action in Psychiatric Disorders." *Focus* 4(3): 391–400.

Kim-Cohen, J., A. Caspi, A. Taylor, B. Williams, R. Newcombe, I. W. Craig, and T. E. Moffitt. 2006. "MAOA, Maltreatment, and Gene–Environment Interaction Predicting Children's Mental Health: New Evidence and a Meta-Analysis." *Molecular Psychiatry* 11(10): 903–913.

Malamuth, Neil M., James V. Check, and John Briere. 1986. "Sexual Arousal in Response to Aggression: Ideological, Aggressive, and Sexual Correlates." *Journal of Personality and Social Psychology* 50(2): 330.

McDermott, R., D. Tingley, J. Cowden, G. Frazzetto, and D. D. Johnson. 2009. "Monoamine Oxidase A Gene (MAOA) Predicts Behavioral Aggression Following Provocation." *Proceedings of the National Academy of Sciences of the USA* 106(7): 2118–2123.

Meyer-Lindenberg, A., J. W. Buckholtz, B. Kolachana, R. Hariri A., L. Pezawas, G. Blasi, A. Wabnitz, R. Honea, B. Verchinski, J. H. Callicott, M. Egan, V. Mattay, and D. R. Weinberger. 2006. "Neural Mechanisms of Genetic Risk for Impulsivity and Violence in Humans." *Proceedings of the National Academy of Sciences of the USA* 103(16): 6269-62674.

Molenaar, Peter C. M. 2004. "A Manifesto on Psychology as Idiographic Science: Bringing the Person Back into Scientific Psychology, This Time Forever." *Measurement* 2(4): 201–218.

Morse, Stephen J. 2011. "Genetics and Criminal Responsibility." *Trends in Cognitive Sciences* 15(9): 378–380.

Murphy, J., J. Scott, D. Kaufman, G. Geller, L. LeRoy, and K. Hudson. 2008. "Public Expectations for Return of Results from Large-Cohort Genetic Research." *American Journal of Bioethics* 8: 36–43.

Olivier, Berend, and Ruud van Oorschot. 2005. "5-HT1B Receptors and Aggression: A Review." *European Journal of Pharmacology* 526(1–3): 207–217.

Paul, Annie M. 2012. "Born to Be Bright: Is There a Gene for Learning? New Research Has Identified Genetic Markers Associated with Academic Achievement—and Failure." *Time Magazine.*

http://ideas.time.com/2012/07/18/born-to-be-bright-is-there-a-gene-for-learning/#ixzz26jkfx9Ko

Petrini, Carlo. 2010. "Ethical, Legal, and Social Implications of Behavioral Genetics." *AJOB Neuroscience* 1(4): 19.

Ramírez, J. Martin, Marie-Claude Bonniot-Cabanac, and Michel Cabanac. 2005. "Can Aggression Provide Pleasure?" *European Psychologist* 10(2): 136–145.

Reif, A., M. Rosler, C. M. Freitag, M. Schneider, A. Eujen, C. Kissling, D. Wenzler, C. P. Jacob, P. Retz-Junginger, J. Thome, K. P. Lesch, and W. Retz. 2007. "Nature and Nurture Predispose to Violent Behavior: Serotonergic Genes and Adverse Childhood Environment." *Neuropsychopharmacology* 32(11): 2375–2383.

Robins, L., J. Wing, H. Wittchen, J. E. Helzer, T. F. Babor, J. Burke, A. Farmer, A. Jablenski, R. Pickens, and D. A. Regier. 1988. "The Composite International Diagnostic Interview: An Epidemiologic Instrument Suitable for Use in Conjunction with Different Diagnostic Systems and in Different Cultures." *Archives of General Psychiatry* 45(12): 1069–1077.

Rodríguez-Paredes, Manuel, and Manel Esteller. 2011. "Cancer Epigenetics Reaches Mainstream Oncology." *Nature Medicine* 17(3): 330–339.

Scott, J., and K. Hudson. 2005. "Genetic Town Halls: Generating Informed Opinions About Reproductive Genetic Testing." *Professional Ethics Report* 18(1): 1–2.

Sifferlin, Alexandra. 2012, May 3. "Does Meat Gross You Out? It May Be Genetic." *Time Magazine*.

Simons, Ronald L., Man Kit Lei, Steven R. H. Beach, Gene H. Brody, Robert A. Philibert, and Frederick X. Gibbons. 2011. "Social Environment, Genes, and Aggression: Evidence Supporting the Differential Susceptibility Perspective." *American Sociological Review* 76(6): 883–912.

Sjöberg, Rickard L., Francesca Ducci, Christina S. Barr, Timothy K. Newman, Liliana Dell'Osso, Matti Virkkunen, and David Goldman. 2007. "A Non-Additive Interaction of a Functional MAO-A VNTR and Testosterone Predicts Antisocial Behavior." *Neuropsychopharmacology* 33(2): 425–430.

Stradella, Elettra. 2012. "Personal Liability and Human Free Will in the Background of Emerging Neuroethical Issues: Some Remarks Arising from Recent Case Law." *International Journal of Technoethics* 3(2): 30–41.

Uhl, George R., Qing-Rong Liu, Tomas Drgon, Catherine Johnson, Donna Walther, Jed E. Rose, Sean P. David, Ray Niaura, and Caryn Lerman. 2008. "Molecular Genetics of Successful Smoking Cessation: Convergent Genome-Wide Association Study Results." *Archives of General Psychiatry* 65(6): 683–693.

Weder, N., B. Z. Yang, H. Douglas-Palumberi, J. Massey, J. H. Krystal, J. Gelernter, and J. Kaufman. 2009. "MAOA Genotype, Maltreatment, and Aggressive Behavior: The Changing Impact of Genotype at Varying Levels of Trauma." *Biological Psychiatry* 65(5): 417–424.

Widom, Cathy Spatz, and Linda M. Brzustowicz. 2006. "MAOA and the 'Cycle of Violence': Childhood Abuse and Neglect, MAOA Genotype, and Risk for Violent and Antisocial Behavior." *Biological Psychiatry* 60(7): 684–689.

Wood, Peter B., and John P. Bartkowski. 2004. "Attribution Style and Public Policy Attitudes Toward Gay Rights." *Social Science Quarterly* 85(1): 58–74.

CHAPTER 13

....

ON THE GENETIC AND GENOMIC BASIS OF AGGRESSION, VIOLENCE, AND ANTISOCIAL BEHAVIOR

....

KEVIN M. BEAVER, ERIC J. CONNOLLY, JOSEPH L. NEDELEC, AND JOSEPH A. SCHWARTZ

INTEREST about the genetic basis to antisocial behavior has increased at a significant rate during the past two decades. Barely a week goes by without a new study reporting genetic influences on criminal, delinquent, or antisocial behavior. These reports are frequently picked up by the media and garner a substantial amount of public interest. Of all the research that is generated on the etiology of antisocial behaviors, studies examining genetic influences are most likely to produce the most controversy while at the same time resulting in the most confusion over their meaning (Beaver, 2013). Critics, for instance, argue that researchers who investigate the genetic basis to crime and delinquency are evil-minded and secretly harbor racist, fascist, or sexist beliefs. In a similar vein, there is a prevailing belief among many scholars, particularly criminologists, that should a genetic basis to crime be detected, the only policies that could emerge from such research would be oppressive and highly punitive, including the revitalization of a eugenics movement. Despite this outpouring of concern leveled by some in the academy and the public, never before has so much been written on the genetic basis of criminal behavior as there is today.

Against this backdrop, the goal of this chapter is to review the research examining the genetic and genomic foundations to aggression, violence, and antisocial behavior. Before proceeding, however, we must clarify what we mean by aggression, violence, and antisocial behavior. Unique definitions of aggression and violence as well as antisocial behaviors have been discussed in detail in previous publications (Beaver, 2009a), and we do not want to get bogged down in arguing for one definition or another. Rather, we take a relatively straightforward approach in the current chapter: When we use the terms *violence* and *aggression*, we are referring to behaviors for which victimization is personal and physical in nature; when we use the terms *delinquent* or *criminal involvement*, we are referring to behaviors that violate some type of legal statute; and when we use the term *antisocial behaviors*, we are referring to a wide range of behaviors that would be considered as violating conventional values or social norms in industrialized nations. This term is broad and encompasses violence, aggression, crime, delinquency, and any other behavior that violates widely accepted values and norms. For the most part, we use *antisocial behavior* when discussing broad themes and findings in the literature (because the literature employs many different outcomes [violence, crime, etc.]), but if we are speaking directly about findings that apply to just one type of behavior, then we use specific language (e.g., violent behavior or criminal involvement).

This chapter is divided into five sections. First, we present findings from the voluminous literature on the heritability of antisocial behaviors that provide us with a starting point on the extent to which genetic influences might matter for antisocial behaviors. Second, we transition into a discussion of the specific genetic polymorphisms that have been linked to various forms of antisocial behaviors. The third section focuses on contemporary cutting-edge research using genome-wide association techniques to explore the genetic basis to antisocial behaviors. Fourth, we review the literature estimating gene–environment interactions as they apply to the development of antisocial behavior. Last, we conclude by presenting some closing remarks, including how these findings might be used for intervention and areas where future research is needed.

HERITABILITY OF ANTISOCIAL BEHAVIOR

In order to provide a starting point for the role that genes might play in the etiology of antisocial behavior, it is first important to determine the relative influence of genetic and environmental effects. Heritability estimates are useful in this regard. Heritability estimates indicate the proportion of phenotypic variance in a group or population that is accounted for by genetic variance (Plomin, DeFries, Knopik, & Neiderhiser, 2013). The variance left unexplained by heritability is accounted for by environmental influences (and error). Should genetic influences have little or no influence on antisocial behaviors, then time, energy, and other resources should not be devoted to studying the role of genes in the genesis of antisocial behaviors. If, however, genes are found to be associated with antisocial behaviors, then it would be useful to explore the genetic basis to antisocial behaviors in much greater detail. A substantial amount of research has been devoted to addressing this issue by estimating the heritability of virtually every measureable source of antisocial behavior. Heritability estimates can be generated from a number of different research designs, but the most widely used methodology is the twin-based research design.

The twin-based methodology used to estimate heritability takes advantage of the naturally occurring phenomenon of twinning. With the twinning process, there are two types of twins: monozygotic (MZ) twins and dizygotic (DZ) twins. MZ twins share 100% of their DNA, whereas DZ twins share 50% of their distinguishing DNA. Both types of twins, however, are assumed to share environments that are approximately the same—an assumption known as the equal environments assumption (EEA). As long as the EEA is upheld—and there is strong mathematical research showing that it is (Barnes et al., 2014)—then accurate heritability estimates can be generated. Heritability estimates are largely a function of the phenotypic similarity of MZ versus DZ twins. The logic of this approach is that the only reason why MZ twins should be more similar to each other than DZ twins (on any phenotypic measure, including antisocial phenotypes) is because MZ twins share twice as much genetic material compared to DZ twins. As the similarity of MZ twins increases relative to the similarity of DZ twins, then heritability estimates increase as well.

Not all twin-based research compares the similarity of MZ twins to DZ twins; rather, some studies exploit the relatively rare situations in which MZ twins are separated at birth and reared in separate families without even knowing that they have a long-lost twin. It is only later in life that they discover that they have an MZ twin, and thus the contact between them is limited to only later in life. These cases present a rare opportunity to estimate genetic influences by comparing the similarity of the MZ twins. Any similarity between them would be attributable to genetic influences because their environments should be orthogonal. A team of researchers at the University of Minnesota led by Thomas Bouchard has provided systematic analyses of MZ twins who were separated at birth (Bouchard, Lykken, McGue, Segal, & Tellegen, 1990). By using this type of research design, it is possible to examine the robustness of heritability estimates across different types of twin-based analyses.

Twin-based methodologies are not the only research designs that can be used to examine the heritability of antisocial behaviors (Beaver, 2013). One alternative to twin research is the adoption-based research design (Beaver, 2011a). In adoption studies, the adopted-away child's behavior is compared to the behavior of the child's biological parents and to the behavior of the adoptive parents. If the adoptee was adopted early in life and had no contact with his or her biological parents, then the only reason the adoptee should be phenotypically similar to them is because of the genetic material the adoptee shares with his or her parents. Because the adoptee shares no genetic material with his or her adoptive parents, the only reason the adoptee should be phenotypically similar to them is because of environmental influences. Although the adoption-based research design is quite powerful, it is not used as widely as the twin-based research design largely because samples containing an adequate number of adoptees are rarer than samples of twin pairs.

Collectively, twin and adoption studies account for the vast majority of all research estimating the heritability of antisocial behaviors. Heritability estimates tend to vary, however, based on sample characteristics (e.g., age range of respondents), the precise measure of antisocial behavior being studied, and other study-specific factors. Four meta-analyses have been conducted (Ferguson, 2010; Mason & Frick, 1994; Miles & Carey, 1997; Rhee & Waldman, 2002), and a number of literature reviews have been completed (Beaver, 2013), in order to provide a summary of the findings across the hundreds of existing twin and adoption studies of antisocial behaviors. The results of these studies have been remarkably consistent in their conclusions, all of which indicate that approximately 50% of the variance in antisocial behaviors is accounted for by genetic factors (i.e., heritability estimates ≈ .50).

Although the meta-analytic results indicate that one-half of the variance in antisocial behavior is due to genetic influences, there is good reason to believe that when it comes to more extreme types of antisocial behaviors, heritability estimates might be significantly greater. For instance, one study estimated the heritability for different types of offenders, including those who were considered to be life-course persistent (LCP) offenders and those who were considered to be adolescence-limited (AL) offenders (Barnes, Beaver, & Boutwell, 2011). LCPs are typified as offending throughout their entire life, they engage in serious types of criminal and violent behaviors, and they account for the vast majority of all criminal offenses. ALs, in contrast, offend only during adolescence and engage in behaviors that are relatively age-appropriate (e.g., experimenting with minor forms of drug use). Heritability estimates were generated for both types of offenders, and the result revealed that as much as 70% of the variance in LCPs was accounted for by genetic influences, whereas only 35% of the variance in ALs was accounted for by genetic influences. Similar findings have been detected in other studies whereby genetic influences tend to increase as the types of antisocial behaviors being studied increase in seriousness (DiLalla & Gottesman, 1991).

Although these findings show the consistent and relatively strong influence of genes on individual differences in antisocial behaviors, they further reveal that the environment also influences variation in antisocial behaviors. Whatever variance is not accounted for by genetic influences must be accounted for by environmental influences (or error). Following this logic, the environment appears to account for approximately 50% of the variance in antisocial behaviors, although the effect will ebb and flow in response to heritability estimates (i.e., environmental influences decrease when heritability increases and vice versa). Findings from twin and adoption studies underscore the importance of two different types of environmental influences: shared environmental influences and nonshared environmental influences (Beaver, 2008). Shared environments are environments that are the same between siblings and that work in a way that makes them more similar to each other. Examples of shared environments are family-wide parenting practices, neighborhood characteristics, and the socioeconomic status of the family. Nonshared environments are environments that are unique to each sibling and that work to make them different from each other. Examples of nonshared environments are peer groups, child-specific parenting, and unique life experiences.

What is particularly interesting about shared and nonshared environmental influences is that they have very different effects on antisocial behaviors (Plomin et al., 2013; Turkheimer, 2000). Findings from twin-based research, for example, have shown consistently that the shared environment accounts for approximately 10–15% of the variance, depending on the specific measure of antisocial behavior examined. These same studies show that approximately 40% of the variance in antisocial behaviors is accounted for by nonshared environmental influences (and error). These strong differential effects for the two types of environments suggest that the nongenetic etiology of antisocial behaviors is most likely to be found in nonshared environments rather than shared environments.

Estimates of genetic and environmental influences from twin- and adoption-based research designs are latent, meaning that they only provide information about the extent to which they account for phenotypic variance; they do not provide any insight into the specific genetic polymorphisms (or the particular environments) that might be accounting for the variance. Therefore, other research designs are needed to examine the precise genes that might be involved in the development of antisocial behaviors. We next turn our attention to a discussion of these research designs and the findings flowing from them.

GENETIC POLYMORPHISMS LINKED TO ANTISOCIAL BEHAVIORS

Since the heritability of antisocial behaviors has been firmly established to be approximately .50, there has been a great deal of interest of trying to move past simply estimating heritability and identify the precise genes that are driving heritability estimates. These studies attempt to identify the alleles of genetic polymorphisms to determine whether they correlate with variation in measures of antisocial behavior. If a significant association is detected between certain alleles and the antisocial behavior of interest, then it can be concluded that the examined genetic polymorphism is involved, in some capacity, with the heritability of the examined behavior. The majority of research attempting to link alleles to antisocial behaviors has done so by conducting what are known as candidate gene association studies. In this work, usually only one gene (or, at most, a small handful of genes) is examined.

Scholars attempting to conduct candidate gene association studies have always been confronted with the same question: Where should they begin? The human genome is composed of tens of thousands of genes, and trying to select just one gene that is associated with antisocial behavior is akin to finding the proverbial needle in the genetic haystack. Most research has focused on genetic polymorphisms that are involved in neurotransmission because neurotransmitters and cognitive processes, in general, have been found to be linked to an assortment of antisocial behaviors. The reasoning, therefore, is that genetic polymorphisms would affect neurotransmission/cognition, and neurotransmission/cognition would, in turn, influence antisocial behaviors. When viewed in this way, genes do not code directly for antisocial phenotypes but, rather, operate through a chain of mediating variables (sometimes referred to as endophenotypes).

Candidate gene association studies have identified a number of genetic polymorphisms linked to a range of negative, maladaptive, and criminal outcomes. Although important exceptions exist, most of these studies have focused on three sets of genes: dopaminergic genes, serotonergic genes, and genes involved in metabolizing neurotransmitters. Dopaminergic genes, such as DAT1, DRD2/ANKK1, DRD3, DRD4, and DRD5, have been linked to drug use, gambling, alcoholism, adolescent victimization, and criminal involvement. Serotonergic genes, including 5HTTLPR, 5HTR2A, 5HTR1B, and 5HTR2C, have also been found to be associated with antisocial behaviors, such as impulsivity, gambling, conduct disorder, and criminal and delinquent involvement. The last system of genes—those that are involved in metabolizing neurotransmitters—includes polymorphisms such as monoamine oxidase A (MAOA) and catechol-O-methyltransferase (COMT), which have been linked to criminal and aggressive outcomes (for a review of the literature, see Beaver, 2013). MAOA, however, deserves particular attention given the substantial amount of research that has examined it.

Of all the genetic polymorphisms studied, MAOA has been most consistently associated with a wide range of antisocial behaviors. MAOA codes for the production of the MAOA enzyme, which is responsible for degrading neurotransmitters. Some of the earliest research linking MAOA to antisocial behaviors was performed by Brunner and associates (Brunner, Nelen, Breakefield, Ropers, & van Oost, 1993). Brunner's research team was made aware of a Dutch kindred in which certain males engaged in various forms of violent, criminal, and antisocial behavior. For example, some of the males had previously engaged in rape, arson, and also suffered from reduced neurobiological functioning. Females in the family, however, appeared to be relatively immune to this syndrome of behaviors. Brunner et al. hypothesized that these behaviors were the result of a genetic defect, and they further reasoned that the genetic defect was on the X chromosome, explaining why only males were inflicted with these behaviors. The results of genetic testing confirmed their suspicions: Males with this syndrome had inherited an MAOA gene (which is located on the X chromosome) that was defective and did not produce any MAOA. Without MAOA present, their neurotransmitter levels were unregulated and neurotransmission did not operate effectively.

Although the discovery of the mutant MAOA gene in this cohort spawned discussions about the discovery of the "crime gene," future research revealed that this mutation was not found in the general population. What this necessarily means is that this mutation could not account for crimes that were committed on an everyday basis. Research did reveal, however, that the MAOA gene was polymorphic, where two groups of alleles could be inherited: alleles that coded for the production of low-activity MAOA and alleles that coded for the production of high-activity MAOA. The low-activity alleles are considered risk alleles that confer an increased probability of engaging in antisocial behaviors. A line of research has provided relatively strong support for the link between the low-activity MAOA allele and antisocial behavior by showing a connection to delinquency, psychopathic personality traits, criminal involvement, weapon use, and gang membership (Beaver, Barnes, & Boutwell, 2014; Beaver, DeLisi, Vaughn, & Barnes, 2010; Beaver et al., 2013; Schwartz & Beaver, 2011). No other gene has been so consistently linked to antisocial behaviors as the MAOA gene.

Relatively recently, a "super" low-activity MAOA allele has been identified (known as the 2-repeat [2R] allele). This allele has been found to have an even lower level of activity compared with the other low-activity alleles (Guo, Ou, Roettger, & Shih, 2008). Only a few studies have examined the 2R allele of the MAOA gene, but the results have been striking: This allele has been shown to increase the risk for shooting someone, stabbing someone, being arrested, being incarcerated, engaging in crime over the life course, and engaging in a variety of serious and violent behaviors (Beaver et al., 2013, 2014; Guo et al., 2008). These findings should be interpreted with caution because only a few studies have examined the 2R allele, and all of the cited studies have analyzed the same sample.

These candidate gene association studies that focus on a single gene, although informative, are somewhat misguided. To understand why, it is first necessary to recognize how genotypic variance could ultimately produce phenotypic variance, including variance in antisocial behaviors. Regarding phenotypic variance, there are three key ways that genes could directly be responsible for producing such variance. First, one gene could be the sole cause of that phenotype. If a person possesses that gene, then he or she will develop the phenotype; if a person does not possess that gene, then he or she will not develop the phenotype. This mechanism is known as a monogenic effect or an OGOD (one gene, one disorder) effect. Although thousands of diseases and disorders are produced by monogenic processes, complex phenotypes, including antisocial phenotypes, are not produced by such a simple genetic transmission model.

The second way that genes could directly affect antisocial behaviors is through a process known as polygenic effects. With phenotypes that are produced by polygenic effects, there are hundreds or thousands of genes that each have a small influence on the phenotype. When aggregated, however, these small effects can account for a large proportion of phenotypic variance. Under a polygenic model, single genes are neither necessary nor sufficient for the phenotype to surface; rather, genes work in a probabilistic manner whereby the possession of a single allele increases (or decreases) the probability that the phenotype will emerge. The consensus appears to be that complex phenotypes, such as antisocial phenotypes, are the result of a polygenic model pattern of transmission. This means that most genes (although not all) will likely only have a very small influence on antisocial behaviors, but when these genes are all identified collectively, they should account for approximately 50% of the variance in antisocial behaviors.

The third way that genes can produce phenotypic variance is known as a pleotropic effect. In a pleotropic model, a single gene has effects on multiple phenotypes. The effects that these genes have can be quite small (or quite large), but typically they are assumed to be part of a larger polygenic effect on each particular phenotype. Although not explored as fully as polygenic effects, there is a solid body of research indicating that pleotropic effects have direct application to criminal, violent, and antisocial behaviors.

Relatively recent research has employed a more realistic approach and instead of focusing on just one genetic polymorphism, multiple genes are studied at the same time (Beaver, 2009b; Belsky & Beaver, 2011; Schwartz & Beaver, 2014). Perhaps even more important is that these genes are not always examined in isolation but, rather, are summed together to create a polygenic risk index that includes the effects of all the genes at the same time. Findings from this line of research have been enlightening by showing that polygenic risk scales are more consistently predictive of antisocial behaviors compared to single-gene studies and that they typically account for a larger proportion of phenotypic variance. These findings should not be too surprising, given that antisocial phenotypes are likely developed under a polygenic model, resulting in polygenic risk indexes, as opposed to single-gene studies, predicting a greater proportion of variance in such phenotypes.

FINDINGS FROM GENOME-WIDE ANALYSES

Although molecular genetic studies have provided some information about specific polymorphisms that might contribute to antisocial phenotypes, these studies have been hampered by a number of limitations, including the inability to replicate novel findings. Fortunately, other types of research designs are available that can overcome some of these limitations. Perhaps the most cutting-edge studies conducted by behavioral scientists in recent years to identify specific genetic markers for antisocial behavior are known as genome-wide association studies (GWAS). GWAS examine whether common genetic variants across different individuals are associated with a given phenotype. GWAS research primarily focuses on assessing links between single nucleotide polymorphisms (SNPs) and certain traits. Although GWAS designs have been commonly used by medical researchers to explore associations between SNPs and disease, this sophisticated methodology has recently begun to be used by behavioral scientists to replicate previous candidate gene findings and search for additional genes involved in the development of antisocial behavior. As discussed later, GWAS offer much promise for understanding the genetic origins of antisocial behavior.

Whereas most behavioral genetic research requires the use of sibling or twin data, GWAS relies on genome-wide data, where genotyping methods are used to provide information on the genomes of several thousand unrelated individuals. In contrast to candidate gene research that focuses on examining the association between specific genes and phenotypes, GWAS genotypes individuals for millions of SNPs and examines whether the allele frequency for a commonly known SNP is different in the group with a history of antisocial behavior compared to a control group that does not have a history of antisocial behavior. If differences in allele frequency are observed through this case–control method, then this finding is interpreted as support for a link between variation in a specific gene and antisocial behavior. Due to the taxing nature of searching for specific SNPs among millions of others SNPs, very large samples are required in order to have enough statistical power for SNPs to reach genome-wide significance (which is conventionally established as $p < 5 \times 10^{-8}$). Unfortunately, this standard has been difficult to achieve for many GWAS examining antisocial behavior.

A study conducted by Dick and colleagues (2011) used genome-wide data to explore the association between specific genetic markers and conduct disorder symptomology. The results from their analysis revealed a significant genome-wide association link between two SNPs located in the gene C1QTNF7 and conduct disorder. Although this study was the first to provide evidence of a specific gene associated with conduct disorder symptomology, much is unknown about the gene C1QTNF7 and how it is involved in the development of conduct disorder. Another GWA study used data on a community sample of 4,816 respondents who answered self-report questions about their involvement in antisocial behavior during adulthood (Tielbeek et al., 2012). No significant genome-wide associations were found between a host of genetic polymorphisms and adult antisocial behavior. However, the strongest association between a specific genetic polymorphism and adult antisocial behavior was found when examining DYRK1A, a gene that has been associated with abnormal brain development. The authors recognize, however, that their findings may reflect a lack of statistical power to detect genome-wide significant associations, and they encourage future researchers to use larger samples.

Tiihonen et al. (2015) used genome-wide data on two independent cohorts of prisoners in Finland and found strong associations between chromosome 16q23.3 in the CDH13 gene among extremely violent offenders who were in prison for 10 or more violent crimes. Interestingly, previous research has found significant associations between the CDH13 gene and other behavioral outcomes commonly related to antisocial behavior, including autism (Sizoo et al., 2010), attention deficit hyperactivity disorder (Arias-Vásquez et al., 2011), schizophrenia (Børglum et al., 2014), and bipolar disorder (Xu et al., 2014). Findings from this recent analysis shed new light on a specific genetic polymorphism that may play an important role in the development of severe antisocial behavior, and this analysis also demonstrates how GWA research can help uncover salient genetic markers for antisocial behaviors.

Despite the growth of GWAS of antisocial behavior in the past 5 years, the majority of studies find very few significant associations between genetic polymorphisms and antisocial behavior that reach genome-wide significance; when they do, findings are often different from those of other GWA research, suggesting an inherent problem with nonreplication. However, recent GWA research has found reliable genetic associations between individual SNPs and behavioral traits when analyzing large population cohorts that are well powered for GWAS (Rietveld et al., 2014). As such, the future and promise of GWAS for antisocial behavior rely on access to large samples with genomic data and indicators of antisocial behavior. GWAS has the ability to further unpack the black box of genetic markers intimately involved in the etiological development of antisocial behavior and may help intervention/prevention science create more targeted programming efforts to reduce the social burden produced by antisocial behaviors.

GENE–ENVIRONMENT INTERACTIONS

It might seem as though genetic influences operate in a vacuum and are orthogonal with environmental influences. In reality, however, this simply is not the case. Unlike the outdated nature versus nurture debate, which pitted environmental influences against genetic influences to determine which one had the greatest impact, today there is widespread recognition that genetic and environmental influences are highly interconnected. One way that genes and the environment are intertwined is through what are known as gene–environment interactions. Gene–environment interactions refer to the process by which the effect of genes is conditional on the presence of certain environmental stimuli or where the effect of environments is conditional on the presence of certain genes. To illustrate, consider that a certain gene may increase the likelihood of aggressive behavior, but only when that gene is paired with a rearing environment that is typified by low levels of love and affection and high levels of stress, abuse, and neglect. That same gene might have no influence on aggressive behavior when it is paired with a rearing environment that has high levels of warmth, love, and attachment and the absence of abuse and neglect. In short, the environment is moderating the influence of genetic effects on behavior. Keep in mind that the opposite process can also be at play. In this case, the environment may only have an effect on phenotypes for people who possess certain genotypes. Gene–environment interactions are quite useful in this regard because they provide an explanation for why the same environments can produce significant variation in how people respond.

A sizable amount of research has been devoted to empirically assessing the merits of gene–environment interactions as they relate to antisocial phenotypes. There are two key ways that this body of research has tested for gene–environment interactions. First, respondents can be grouped into different categories based on their exposure to environmental conditions, and then heritability estimates can be calculated for respondents in each of those categories. If heritability estimates vary between respondents who are differentially exposed to environments, then that is usually interpreted as evidence of a gene–environment interaction. For example, a sample could be divided into two groups—one group that experienced abuse in childhood and one group that did not. Heritability estimates could then be generated for both of these groups. If the heritability was greater for one group versus the other, then the most common interpretation would be that the environment is moderating the influence of genes. A number of studies have employed this approach to examine gene–environment interactions for antisocial behavior. Beaver (2011b) conducted perhaps the most exhaustive examination of gene–environment interactions on antisocial behavior using this method. He examined whether 13 different criminogenic environments, such as exposure to delinquent peers, family risk, and religiosity, moderated genetic influences on serious delinquency, violent delinquency, and victimization. The results of his analysis revealed broad support for gene–environment interactions on these antisocial phenotypes, with the effects of genes being more pronounced in the presence of criminogenic environments.

The second and more widely used approach to test for gene–environment interactions is by examining the effect of a single genetic polymorphism and a single environmental pathogen, usually within a regression-based framework. To test for a gene–environment interaction, the genetic polymorphism and the environmental pathogen are included in a regression model as a multiplicative interaction term. If that multiplicative interaction term is statistically significant, then that provides evidence of a gene–environment interaction. During approximately the past 10 years, there has been a proliferation of research testing for gene–environment interaction with this modeling strategy. The results of these studies have uncovered a great deal of gene–environment interactions on antisocial phenotypes. For example, dopaminergic polymorphisms have been found to interact with delinquent peers, family risk/adversity, and marital stability/status to predict variation in number of police contacts, number of criminal arrests, desistance from delinquency, and even early onset offending. Other interactions have been detected with other environments and with other systems of genes (e.g., those from the serotonergic system) to predict antisocial phenotypes.

Of all the gene–environment interactions examined, however, the gene–environment interaction between MAOA and childhood maltreatment has been the most scrutinized. The first study to show a gene–environment interaction between MAOA and child maltreatment was that of Caspi et al. (2002). In this study, they analyzed data from the Dunedin Multidisciplinary Health and Development Study. The results of their analysis revealed that MAOA did not have a statistically significant main effect on any measure of antisocial behavior. When they analyzed the effect of the MAOA gene in conjunction with childhood maltreatment, a very different pattern of results emerged. Specifically, they reported that males who carried a low-activity MAOA allele and who were maltreated during childhood accounted for only 12% of the entire sample, but they accounted for 44% of the antisocial behavior. Moreover, 85% of them were characterized as displaying some type of antisocial behavior or trait. This study provided the first evidence of a gene–environment interaction between a measured polymorphism, a measured environment, and a measured antisocial phenotype. Perhaps as a result, it has generated a considerable amount of interest and ignited a large number of replication studies.

The results of these replication studies have provided support in favor of this gene–environment interaction, but some studies have failed to confirm this interaction in independent samples (for an overview of these studies, see Byrd & Manuck, 2014). Two meta-analyses have been conducted to shed some additional light on the robustness of this gene–environment interaction. The results of both meta-analyses revealed significant support in favor of the gene–environment interaction for males (Byrd & Manuck, 2014; Kim-Cohen et al., 2006), and the most recent meta-analysis revealed a fail-safe N of 93 (Byrd & Manuck, 2014). This means that there has to be at least 93 unpublished studies showing no evidence of a gene–environment interaction for the results of the meta-analyses to be incorrect. Given this substantial amount of empirical support, there is good reason to believe that the gene–environment interaction between MAOA and childhood maltreatment is involved—at least in some capacity—in the production of variation in antisocial phenotypes.

Until relatively recently, the interpretation of the MAOA interaction, and all other gene–environment interactions, was quite straightforward and relied solely on the diathesis–stress model. According to the logic of the diathesis–stress model, variation in individual vulnerability to criminogenic influences was based on their genetic risk profiles for antisocial phenotypes. Genetic influences, in other words, set the parameters for behaviors, and environmental factors were responsible for allowing those parameters to be reached. Belsky (Belsky, 1997; Belsky & Pluess, 2009), however, has advanced a different explanation for the interpretation of gene–environment interactions, which he refers to as the differential susceptibility model. The logic of this model rests on the assumption that genetic polymorphisms should not be viewed as biological risk factors but, rather, as biomarkers of plasticity. The greater the number of plasticity alleles that an individual possesses, the more vulnerable the individual is to all environmental conditions. When viewed in this way, it is easy to understand that plasticity markers can prime an individual for antisocial phenotypes in the face of criminogenic environments and, at the same time, plasticity markers can prime an individual for prosocial phenotypes in the face of advantageous environments. In short, genes identify how plastic an individual is, and the environment to which the individual is exposed determines how he or she will develop. The differential susceptibility model captures this process with the slogan, "for better and for worse," which essentially means that those individuals with the greatest number of plasticity alleles will turn out the best when exposed to positive environments and the worst when exposed to negative environments (Belsky, Bakermans-Kranenburg, & Van IJzendoorn, 2007).

A good deal of research has been devoted to examining which explanation is better situated to explain gene–environment interactions for phenotypic outcomes, including antisocial outcomes. The results of these studies have not produced unequivocal results. Some studies have provided support for the diathesis–stress model, some studies have provided support for the differential susceptibility model, and some studies have provided support for both models (Belsky & Pluess, 2009). Given the importance of understanding how and why gene–environment interactions operate in the way that they do, there can be little doubt that even more research will examine the merits of these approaches in the upcoming years.

CONCLUSION

The past two decades have witnessed a tremendous increase in the amount of research examining the genetic foundations to virtually every measure of antisocial behavior. These findings have quickly revolutionized conventional wisdom about the etiology of antisocial phenotypes and the role that genetics plays in the development of such phenotypes. Although these findings have produced a solid knowledge base about the genetic foundation to antisocial phenotypes, this body of research remains in its infancy. As a result, there remain debates regarding the findings of many aspects of the genetic basis to antisocial behaviors (Beaver, Barnes, & Boutwell, 2015). Future research will be useful in clarifying points of disagreement and uncovering newer ways of thinking about the role that genes play in the genesis of crime, aggression, violence, and other antisocial phenotypes. As for now, and as our review has revealed, there are a number of highly robust findings that have been replicated so consistently that any objective, empirically guided scientist would have to believe. These include the following:

- The heritability of antisocial behavior is approximately .50. For more extreme types of antisocial behavior, the heritability is probably much greater, hovering around .70 to .80. Heritability estimates are highly robust and are built on assumptions that have been thoroughly vetted and substantiated (Barnes et al., 2014).
- Nonshared environmental influences—as opposed to shared environmental influences—account for the overwhelming majority of all environmental variance in antisocial behaviors.
- Although a significant amount of research has been devoted to examining the molecular genetic basis to antisocial behaviors, only a handful of polymorphisms have been consistently linked to antisocial behavior. Nonreplication of novel molecular genetic findings remains a problem.
- Genetic polymorphisms involved in neurotransmission have most frequently been connected to antisocial phenotypes.
- Genome-wide association studies suggest that genes involved in cognitive ability and the development of psychiatric disorders are commonly associated with various forms of antisocial behavior.
- Genetic and environmental influences frequently interact to predict variation in antisocial outcomes.
- Of all the gene–environment interactions detected, that between MAOA and childhood maltreatment has been the most consistent and the most widely replicated.

There can be little doubt that the amount of research devoted to the genetic basis to criminal behavior has only just begun and that there will continue to be an exponential growth in this line of research in the near future. As increasingly more research is accumulated, there will be questions regarding the manner in which findings flowing from this body of literature can be used by the criminal justice system. Although genetic research has not made any significant contributions to policies focused on the reduction of antisocial behavior in the past few decades, we offer two possibilities. First, criminological research examining the effectiveness of rehabilitation programs has shown that not all offenders are equally amenable to change (Smith, Gendreau, & Swartz, 2009). Rather, high-risk offenders are much more likely to reap the benefits of rehabilitation programs compared to low-risk offenders. Currently, a number of actuarial risk assessment tools are used to determine risk level. Findings from genetic research could easily be integrated into these tools, whereby offenders are genotyped for certain polymorphisms that might increase their risk level. Of course, the extent to which genetic research could help delineate offender risk will depend largely on future research being able to identify replicable results that link certain polymorphisms to criminal and antisocial behaviors.

The second way in which genetic findings might be able to guide policy is by providing more individualized treatment and rehabilitation services. There is now a solid pool of research showing variation in response to rehabilitation programs among individual offenders (Smith et al., 2009). Specifically, certain individual-level characteristics, such as age and gender, moderate program effectiveness. This pattern of findings has resulted in an attempt to match treatment to specific offender characteristics in order to increase program effectiveness. To date, there has not been any systematic approach to examine whether genotype might moderate success rates of rehabilitation programs. Even so, given that genes have been shown to moderate responses to environments in general (in the form of gene–environment interactions discussed previously), it would make logical and intuitive sense to believe that genes could also moderate rehabilitation program effectiveness. Only time will tell, but given the potential payoffs, including the payoff of increased public safety, research and resources should be devoted to the possibility that genes moderate the effectiveness of rehabilitation programs.

This is an exciting time to be examining the various ways in which genetic influences may contribute to the development of antisocial behaviors. Although much has been learned about the genetic etiology of antisocial phenotypes, numerous mysteries still remain. There can be little doubt, however, that as the amount of genetic research continues to accrue, many of these mysteries will be solved and the solutions used in a progressive way to promote a better, safer society.

References

Arias-Vásquez, A., Altink, M. E., Rommelse, N. N. J., Slaats-Willemse, D. I. E., Buschgens, C. J. M., Fliers, E. A., . . . Buitelaar, J. K. (2011). CDH13 is associated with working memory performance in attention deficit/hyperactivity disorder. *Genes, Brain and Behavior, 10*, 844–851.

Barnes, J. C., Beaver, K. M., & Boutwell, B. B. (2011). Examining the genetic underpinnings to Moffitt's developmental taxonomy: A behavioral genetic analysis. *Criminology, 49*, 923–954.

Barnes, J. C., Wright, J. P., Boutwell, B. B., Schwartz, J. A., Connolly, E. J., Nedelec, J. L., & Beaver, K. M. (2014). Demonstrating the validity of twin research in criminology. *Criminology, 52*, 588–626.

Beaver, K. M. (2008). Nonshared environmental influences on adolescent delinquent involvement and adult criminal behavior. *Criminology, 46*, 341–369.

Beaver, K. M. (2009a). Aggression and crime. In J. Michell Millder (Ed.), *21st century criminology: A reference handbook* (pp. 36–43). Thousand Oaks, CA: Sage.

Beaver, K. M. (2009b). The interaction between genetic risk and childhood sexual abuse in the prediction of adolescent violent behavior. *Sexual Abuse: A Journal of Research and Treatment, 20*, 426–443.

Beaver, K. M. (2011a). Genetic influences on being processed through the criminal justice system: Results from a sample of adoptees. *Biological Psychiatry, 69*, 282–287.

Beaver, K. M. (2011b). Environmental moderators of genetic influences on adolescence delinquent involvement and victimization. *Journal of Adolescent Research, 26*, 84–114.

Beaver, K. M. (2013). *Biosocial criminology: A primer* (2nd ed.). Dubuque, IA: Kendall/Hunt.

Beaver, K. M., Barnes, J. C., & Boutwell, B. B. (2014). The 2-repeat allele of the MAOA gene confers an increased risk for shooting and stabbing behaviors. *Psychiatric Quarterly, 85*, 257–265.

Beaver, K. M., Barnes, J. C., & Boutwell, B. B. (2015). *The nurture vs. biosocial debate in criminology: On the origins of criminal behavior and criminality.* Thousand Oaks, CA: Sage.

Beaver, K. M., DeLisi, M., Vaughn, M. G., & Barnes, J. C. (2010). Monoamine oxidase A genotype is associated with gang membership and weapon use. *Comprehensive Psychiatry, 51,* 130–134.

Beaver, K. M., Wright, J. P., Boutwell, B. B., Barnes, J. C., DeLisi, M., & Vaughn, M. G. (2013). Exploring the association between the 2-repeat allele of the MAOA gene promoter polymorphism and psychopathic personality traits, arrests, incarceration, and lifetime antisocial behavior. *Personality and Individual Differences, 54,* 164–168.

Belsky, J. (1997). Variation in susceptibility to rearing influence: An evolutionary argument. *Psychological Inquiry, 8*(3), 182–186.

Belsky, J., Bakermans-Kranenburg, M. J., & Van IJzendoorn, M. H. (2007). For better and for worse: Differential susceptibility to environmental influences. *Current Directions in Psychological Science, 16*(6), 300–304.

Belsky, J., & Beaver, K. M. (2011). Cumulative-genetic plasticity, parenting and adolescent self-regulation. *Journal of Child Psychology and Psychiatry, 52,* 619–626.

Belsky, J., & Pluess, M. (2009). Beyond diathesis stress: Differential susceptibility to environmental influences. *Psychological Bulletin, 135*(6), 885–908.

Børglum, A. D., Demontis, D., Grove, J., Pallesen, J., Hollegaard, M. V., Pedersen, C. B., . . . Mors, O. (2014). Genome-wide study of association and interaction with maternal cytomegalovirus infection suggests new schizophrenia loci. *Molecular Psychiatry, 19,* 325–333.

Bouchard, T. J., Lykken, D. T., McGue, M., Segal, N. L., & Tellegen, A. (1990). Sources of human psychological differences: The Minnesota Study of Twins Reared Apart. *Science, 250,* 223–228.

Brunner, H. G., Nelen, M., Breakefield, X. O., Ropers, H. H., & van Oost, B. A. (1993). Abnormal behavior associated with a point mutation in the structural gene for monoamine oxidase A. *Science, 262,* 578–580.

Byrd, A. L., & Manuck, S. B. (2014). MAOA, childhood maltreatment, and antisocial behaviors: Meta-analysis of a gene–environment interaction. *Biological Psychiatry, 75,* 9–17.

Caspi, A., McClay, J., Moffitt, T. E., Mill, J., Martin, J., Craig, I. W., . . . Poulton, R. (2002). Role of genotype in the cycle of violence in maltreated children. *Science, 297*(5582), 851–854.

Dick, D. M., Aliev, F., Krueger, R. F., Edwards, A., Agrawal, A., Lynskey, M., . . . Bierut, L. (2011). Genome-wide association study of conduct disorder symptomatology. *Molecular Psychiatry, 16,* 800–808.

DiLalla, L. F., & Gottesman, I. I. (1991). Biological and genetic contributors to violence: Widom's untold tale. *Psychological Bulletin, 109,* 125–129.

Ferguson, C. J. (2010). Genetic contributions to antisocial personality and behavior: A meta-analytic review from an evolutionary perspective. *Journal of Social Psychology, 150,* 160–180.

Guo, G., Ou, X.-M., Roettger, M., & Shih, J. C. (2008). The VNTR 2 repeat in MAOA and delinquent behavior in adolescence and young adulthood: Association and MAOA promoter activity. *European Journal of Human Genetics, 16,* 626–634.

Kim-Cohen, J., Caspi, A., Taylor, A., Williams, B., Newcombe, R., Craig, I. W., & Moffitt, T. E. (2006). MAOA, maltreatment, and gene–environment interaction predicting children's mental health: New evidence and a meta-analysis. *Molecular Psychiatry, 11,* 903–913.

Mason, D. A., & Frick, P. J. (1994). The heritability of antisocial behavior: A meta-analysis of twin and adoption studies. *Journal of Psychopathology and Behavioral Assessment, 16,* 301–323.

Miles, D. R., & Carey, G. (1997). Genetic and environmental architecture on human aggression. *Journal of Personality and Social Psychology*, 72, 207–217.

Plomin, R., DeFries, J. C., Knopik, V. S., & Neiderhiser, J. M. (2013). *Behavioral genetics* (6th ed.). New York, NY: Worth.

Rhee, S. H., & Waldman, I. D. (2002). Genetic and environmental influences on antisocial behavior: A meta-analysis of twin and adoption studies. *Psychological Bulletin*, 128, 490–529.

Rietveld, C. A., Conley, D., Eriksson, N., Esko, T., Medland, S. E., Vinkhuyzen, A. A., . . . Teumer, A. (2014). Replicability and robustness of genome-wide association studies for behavioral traits. *Psychological Science*, 25, 1975–1986.

Schwartz, J. A., & Beaver, K. M. (2011). Evidence of a gene × environment interaction between perceived prejudice and MAOA genotype in the prediction of criminal arrests. *Journal of Criminal Justice*, 39, 378–384.

Schwartz, J. A., & Beaver, K. M. (2014). Exploring whether genetic differences between siblings explain sibling differences in criminal justice outcomes. *Comprehensive Psychiatry*, 55, 90–103.

Sizoo, B., Van den Brink, W., Franke, B., Vasquez, A. A., van Wijngaarden-Cremers, P., & Van der Gaag, R. J. (2010). Do candidate genes discriminate patients with an autism spectrum disorder from those with attention deficit/hyperactivity disorder and is there an effect of lifetime substance use disorders? *World Journal of Biological Psychiatry*, 11, 699–708.

Smith, P., Gendreau, P., & Swartz, K. (2009). Validating the principles of effective intervention: A systematic review of the contributions of meta-analysis in the field of corrections. *Victims and Offenders*, 4, 148–169.

Tielbeek, J. J., Medland, S. E., Benyamin, B., Byrne, E. M., Heath, A. C., Madden, P. A., . . . Verweij, K. J. (2012). Unraveling the genetic etiology of adult antisocial behavior: A genome-wide association study. *PLoS One*, 7, e45086.

Tiihonen, J., Rautiainen, M. R., Ollila, H. M., Repo-Tiihonen, E., Virkkunen, M., Palotie, A., . . . Paunio, T. (2015). Genetic background of extreme violent behavior. *Molecular Psychiatry*, 20(6), 786–789.

Turkheimer, E. (2000). Three laws of behavior genetics and what they mean. *Current Directions in Psychological Science*, 9, 160–164.

Xu, W., Cohen-Woods, S., Chen, Q., Noor, A., Knight, J., Hosang, G., . . . Vincent, J. B. (2014). Genome-wide association study of bipolar disorder in Canadian and UK populations corroborates disease loci including SYNE1 and CSMD1. *BMC Medical Genetics*, 15, 2.

CHAPTER 14

....

GENETICS AND POLITICS

A Review for the Social Scientist

....

ADAM LOCKYER AND PETER K. HATEMI

NATURE, NURTURE, AND POLITICS

....

SINCE antiquity, philosophical debates have persisted as to whether it is nature or nurture that guides humanity. Today, we know, it is neither alone. Empirical findings across the natural and social sciences have provided compelling evidence that simplistic monocausal biological or environmental explanations for complex social traits are implausible. Instead, in order to have any true understanding of the origins and development of complex behaviors, we must focus on developmental processes that treat nature and nurture as interdependent (Lewkowicz, 2011).

Universal human traits and variance in such traits, including political values, are the product of the complex interaction between inherited physiology, socialization, and personal experiences. The process is not linear but, rather, recursive. Individuals' inherited biology and experiences influence how they interconnect with their social world, which in turn activates, represses, and conditions psychological and biological responses (McDermott & Hatemi, 2013; Ridley, 2003). These then, of course, condition, alter, and change one's experiences, including the environments people select into and the way people see, perceive, and interpret their social world, and thus how they react to it and how others react to them—creating an indefinite circle of development.

Not all are on board with this position. Indeed, remarkably, after thousands of years and overwhelming evidence to the contrary, the nature versus nurture dichotomy continues to doggedly persist in modern academic and public discourse (Eagly & Wood, 2013). Although it is difficult to find a scientist who believes any complex social trait or behavior is all nature, there are still social scientists who argue that it is all nurture (Charney, 2008a; Shultziner, 2013). Nevertheless, when it comes to the majority of the social sciences, the tide has turned. During the past 40 years, research has eroded the belief in such a dichotomy, and during the past 10 years in particular, this erosion appears to be leading to a complete collapse of the division (Hatemi & McDermott, 2012a).

Today, most social scientists are no longer asking whether genes influence political behavior. Instead, the discussion has moved on to asking why, what, when, and to what extent particular environments trigger or repress specific genetic processes (Benjamin et al., 2012; Hatemi, Byrne, & McDermott, 2012; Hatemi & McDermott, 2012a). A surging wave of energy has been directed at elucidating the influence of genetic factors on political attitudes and behaviors, including vote choice (Dawes & Fowler, 2009; Fowler, Baker, & Dawes, 2008; Fowler & Dawes, 2008; Hatemi, Medland, Morley, Heath, & Martin, 2007; Littvay, Weith, & Dawes, 2011), political ideologies (Alford, Funk, & Hibbing, 2005; Hatemi, Eaves, & McDermott, 2012), political attitudes (Alford et al., 2005; Cranmer & Dawes, 2012; Hatemi, Funk, et al., 2009; Hatemi & McDermott, 2016; Hatemi et al., 2010, 2014; Smith & Hatemi, 2013), party identification and identity (Dawes & Fowler, 2009; Fazekas & Littvay, 2012; Hatemi, Alford, Hibbing, Martin, & Eaves, 2009; Settle, Dawes, & Fowler, 2009; Weber, Johnson, & Arceneaux, 2011), political trust (Merolla, Burnett, Pyle, Ahmadi, & Zak, 2013; Ojeda, 2016; Oskarsson, Dawes, Johannesson, & Magnusson, 2012; Sturgis et al., 2010), political participation (Dawes et al., 2014; Fazekas & Hatemi, 2016; Fowler et al., 2008; Fowler, Dawes, & Settle, 2011; Klemmensen, Hatemi, Hobolt, Petersen, et al., 2012), sophistication and efficacy (Arceneaux, Johnson, & Maes, 2012; Klemmensen, Hatemi, Hobolt, Petersen, et al., 2012; Klemmensen, Hatemi, Hobolt, Skytthe, et al., 2012), and aggression and conflict (McDermott, Dawes, Prom-Wormley, Eaves, & Hatemi, 2013; McDermott & Hatemi, 2017; McDermott, Tingley, Cowden, Frazzetto, & Johnson, 2009; Stam, Von Hagen-Jamar, & Worthington, 2012). A number of reviews on evolutionary theory, genetic theory, and what genes are and how they operate, in addition to primers on advanced statistical and molecular genetics, are present in the social science literature (Barkow, Cosmides, & Tooby, 1992; Fowler & Schreiber, 2008; Hatemi, Byrne, et al., 2012; Hatemi & McDermott, 2011a, 2011b; Hibbing & Smith, 2007; Lopez, McDermott, & Petersen, 2011; Lumsden & Wilson, 1981; McDermott & Hatemi, 2013; Medland & Hatemi, 2009; Rushton, Littlefield, & Lumsden, 1986; Smith, Larimer, Littvay, & Hibbing, 2007; Verhulst & Hatemi, 2013). Also, funded workshops on genetic analyses are available annually through multiple mediums specifically tailored for social scientists.

The creation of the link between genetic inherence and social traits promises to be one of the most exciting and productive avenues of social science inquiry in the 21st century. It has not gone unnoticed that over the course of the 20th century, the natural sciences greatly outperformed the social sciences. King (2011) noted,

> Fifteen years ago, Science published predictions from each of 60 scientists about the future of their fields. The physical and natural scientists wrote about a succession of breathtaking discoveries to be made, inventions to be constructed, problems to be solved, and policies and engineering changes that might become possible. In sharp

contrast, the (smaller number of) social scientists did not mention a single problem they thought might be addressed, much less solved, or any inventions or discoveries on the horizon. Instead, they wrote about social science scholarship, how we once studied this and in the future we're going to be studying that. (p. 719)

Between 1900 and 2000, aerospace went from having never successfully flown an airplane to putting a man on the moon. Medical science extended the average human life expectancy by decades. Engineering went from steam engines to bullet trains, the Internet, and artificial intelligence. Even meteorologists, formerly the subject of jokes, now reliably and consistently forecast the weather. In contrast, the social sciences have made relatively little progress. Economists have been studying the causes of the Great Depression for almost 100 years but could not predict the 2007–2008 global financial crisis. Experts in international relations have been studying the causes of World War I but were totally blindsided by the fall of the Berlin Wall and modern Islamic terrorism. Others have been studiously researching American voting behavior for 100 years, but before late spring 2016, few believed, much less predicted, that Donald Trump would win the Republican nomination and the presidency.

We are, of course, being too hard on our discipline. The natural sciences have many advantages in comparison. One that we might be able to leverage, however, is a universal theory of behavior—evolution. In the natural sciences, contradictory theories tend not to survive long, even between different branches (e.g., chemistry and geology). They tend to be lightning rods for empirical researchers who rush to resolve the debate. The speed of publication, the focus on evidence, the willingness to let go of established wisdom, and the focus on innovation and discovery comprise the nature of the natural sciences. The same has not been true of the social sciences. Keynesian and Hayekian economic theories exist side by side, like realism and liberalism continue to coexist in international relations, and rational choice and structuralism in political science. The contending schools of thought in the social sciences more often speak past one another rather than to each other, which retards the advancement of disciplinary knowledge and often impedes interdisciplinary research.

Genetically informed social science research has the potential to cut through many existing cleavages. It may provide social scientists with a common foundation on which explanations of social behavior can be built. Empirical research in genetics demands replication, and it is in a constant and dynamic state of advancement, with new methods and approaches developed almost daily. Inclusion of genetics requires social scientists to move beyond all-encompassing and often conflicting paradigmatic worldviews and begin to have the same conversations the natural sciences were having throughout their hyperproductive 20th century. Already, genetically informed research is having an impact on many areas of political science research, including providing rational choice theories with some hint of where preferences originate, which has long puzzled the field (Benjamin et al., 2012; Camerer, Loewenstein, & Prelec, 2005; Cesarini, Dawes, Johannesson, Lichtenstein, & Wallace, 2009; Dawes et al., 2012; Hatemi & McDermott, 2011b; Hibbing, Smith, & Alford, 2013).

Considering the importance and promise of genetic approaches to the social sciences, this chapter offers a review for those new to the area. In so doing, an extensive list of references is provided to assist readers in delving deeper into the area.

The Why, What, and How of Genetics and Politics

Genetics offers a suite of methods to better explicate the pathways that lead to variation on traits of interest. That is, genetics provides tools to better understand why individuals differ and why people are also the same. They do not replace other methods but provide additional information. The rapidly expanding research on genetics and political science can be categorized a number of different ways. The most popular have been either by research method (e.g., classical twin studies vs. genome studies; see Hatemi, Dawes, Frost-Keller, Settle, & Verhulst, 2011) or by traits (e.g., political attitudes vs. vote choice; see Hatemi & McDermott, 2012a). In this chapter, we take a more functional approach by cataloging the recent literature on the topic and dividing it along lines of its overall "research objectives." Simply stated, we categorize the literature by studies that ask "Why?" "What?" or "How?"

A first avenue of research has asked "why" the human genome has evolved to exercise an influence on political traits. This research avenue has primarily been theoretical and deductive and has employed evolutionary reasoning and primate observations to deduce the origins of genetic influences on political attitudes (Lockyer & Hatemi, 2014; Lopez et al., 2011; Petersen, 2010; Proctor & Brosnan, 2011). Generally, this research agenda assumes that modern humans have evolved to display political traits; because these traits have been "selected in," then they must have served a purpose through human evolutionary history. This assumes that modern political interactions are reflections of tribal living. Hence, deductively reasoning as to "why" humans have evolved to have genetically influenced political traits may point empirical researchers toward why human systems are similar across diverse ecologies.

The second research grouping has attempted to determine "what" political traits (e.g., voting) are genetically influenced. This research is akin to identifying omitted independent variables on discrete political behaviors and more than the other research agenda has been responsible for showing that significant biological influences exist on political traits. Not only has it been extremely successful in identifying that genetic influences operate on a range of different political beliefs and behaviors but also, perhaps more important, this research agenda has encouraged the wider exploration of the effects of neurobiology, hormones, and other physiological characteristics on political traits (Hatemi & McDermott, 2011b, 2012a; Hibbing et al., 2013; McDermott & Hatemi, 2013; Mooney, 2012; Shenkman, 2016; Tuschman, 2013; Weeden & Kurzban, 2014).

Finally, there is a nascent stream of research that is inquiring into "how" and which genes influence specific political traits. This research is attempting to reveal the neurological and chemical pathways that link the genes and regions of the genome with the eventual political trait. Researchers have used advanced imaging technology and samples of people with brain damage or abnormalities to attempt to trace neurological and neurochemical pathways from DNA to the expressed political trait. This research is in its early stages and holds much promise of bringing true discovery back into the social sciences.

Why Do Our Genes Influence Political Traits?

Since the mapping of the human genome, there is a growing body of evidence supporting the thesis that certain inherited genetic markers are the product of human's evolutionary need to overcome problems related to group living (Lockyer & Hatemi, 2014; Lopez et al., 2011; Petersen, 2012, 2015). Long before empirical approaches became available to identify and quantify genetic influences, however, scholars approached the question of the relationship between genes and political traits by using deductive reasoning and evolutionary theory (Barkow et al., 1992; Cosmides & Tooby, 1997; Faulkner, Schaller, Park, & Duncan, 2004; Hammond & Axelrod, 2006; Hibbing & Smith, 2007; Kurzban & Leary, 2001; McDermott, 2004; Tooby & Cosmides, 1988, 2010; Wrangham, 1999). They sought to explain why political attitudes and behavior appear universally across human societies and why humans' DNA evolved to have such traits at all.

The empirical record shows that all human societies revolve around communal living. Communities provide many advantages to individuals, including greater security, safety, support, and a division of labor between rearing children and gathering food. Communal living, however, also creates problems that early humans would have needed to solve, such as ensuring that everyone has an opportunity to pass their genes on to the next generation and that communal resources are fairly distributed. There is no one universal solution to these problems. Humans have proven themselves to be immensely malleable and have organized communities ranging from strict hierarchical structures to more egalitarian pluralistic collectives. In an evolutionary sense, the specific political solutions were not universal: Hierarchical communities have been equally as successful as egalitarian ones, but everyone within the tribe must subscribe to the same solution.

This is the evolutionary reason why people have evolved to have such strong political attitudes. Political attitudes are different from attitudes in general. Political attitudes "are not just how an individual feels about something but how individuals believe others in society ought to feel and behave" (Lockyer & Hatemi, 2014, p. 552). A person may have an attitude toward ice cream or music without any expectation that other people ought to possess the same attitude. The same is not generally true regarding political issues, such as abortion, punishment for norms violators, marriage, immigration, or how resources are allocated.

Humans have been shown to have particularly strong political attitudes on the domains of sex and reproduction, child-rearing, in-group/out-group relations, defense, fairness, survival, cooperation, security, and affiliation (Apicella, Marlowe, Fowler, & Christakis, 2012; Barkow et al., 1992; Cosmides & Tooby, 1997; Fowler & Schreiber, 2008;

Hatemi & McDermott, 2011a; Hibbing & Smith, 2007; Kurzban & Leary, 2001; Lockyer & Hatemi, 2014; Lopez & McDermott, 2012; Lopez et al., 2011; McDermott & Hatemi, 2013; Miller, 2011; Petersen, 2012; Petersen & Aaroe, 2012; Petersen, Sell, Tooby, & Cosmides, 2012; Smith et al., 2007; Thayer, 2000; Tooby & Cosmides, 1988, 2010; Tuschman, 2013). People inherit the propensity to have political attitudes, but cultural and environmental factors will shape how these political attitudes are defined in an almost infinite number of ways. For instance, historically, immigration has been an emotionally charged political issue across time and between countries. The issue of "foreigners" was as politically charged in ancient Rome as it is in modern-day Britain. However, individuals can link immigration back to either the domain of "out-group" relations or "fairness." Either way, individuals are likely to feel particularly emotional about the political issue, but they may well fall on different sides of the debate. The context, labels, and policies will change between countries and across time, but the most politically charged debates will often be those that can be traced back to one of the domains people have evolved to be the most important to group living.

From an evolutionary perspective, observed preferences and behaviors are not simply the result of the current environment. Like the rest of the human anatomy, the brain is a product of evolution. Over the course of thousands of generations, the human brain has evolved certain universal structures and functions to overcome recurring social dilemmas. That is, the architecture of the human brain produces certain universal systems, including those of cognition, emotion, preference formation, and need for security. These evolutionary structures are different from instincts in that they are cognitive and emotional pathways for processing information. That is, instincts are evolved reactions to stimuli, such as the fight-or-flight response to being surprised. Human behavioral predispositions, on the other hand, are the product of the human brain having evolved to process information in particular ways. For example, humans have a strong predisposition to the in-group compared to the out-group. However, how these groups are defined is a social contract and is completely malleable between individuals and over time.

In this view, modern-day political choices are more complex versions of the basic problems that have surrounded group living since the inception of humanity. Modern national defense and foreign policy issues and decisions to use military force are only recent reflections of tribal decision to protect the in-group from outsiders. The political and technological context may be dramatically different; however, how people frame the decision and the thought process that goes into the decision-making are the product of thousands of years of evolution. Today's political attitudes surrounding child-rearing, sexual liberties, and marriage are the modern-day equivalent of the ancestral need to ensure access to mates and have offspring. The strong opinions on immigration reflect modern insecurities, but those insecurities are seated in the primitive need to balance protecting against unknown and unfamiliar others with the potential gains from diversity (e.g., genetic diversity[strengthening the mating pool], resource security, social norms differences, and pathogen protections). The economic issues of today (e.g., taxes and welfare) address the same core concerns of how to share resources in a community.

Certainly, the issues of today are more complex. Institutions, political parties, social groups, nation states and non-state actors, cultural and historical conflicts, elites, communication, transportation, technology, and globalism, among many other factors, make social interactions much more complicated than those our ancestors confronted. Also, the relative importance and nuances of political issues differ depending on different environmental conditions, social forces (e.g., social customs, traditions, and material constraints), local histories, and ecology. Nevertheless, the fundamental psychological processes used to make political choices today are not so different as they were in the Pleistocene. The labels and rhetoric of issues change across cultures, time periods, and countries; modern economic and political structures levy their own influence on the mass public's understanding and organization of political thoughts; and the channels through which preferences are conveyed in large modern societies are much less personal and direct than in the past; however, the underlying issues that are important, including family, reproduction, defense, and resources, remain the same. That is, when humans have to make decisions on how to manage societal life today, they are relying on the same cognitive and emotional mechanisms to address the same fundamental problems that their ancestors relied on.

Genetics has brought with it a unifying theory of human behavior—evolution. The natural, medical, and physical sciences have a variety of microtheories, but all behavioral studies rest on a theory of evolution. Whether or not evolutionary theory becomes the core theory of behavior in the social sciences remains to be seen; however, due to its capacity to lead to new discoveries, advances, and scientific progress, it may be the vehicle by which the social sciences catch up to the natural sciences.

Identifying Genetic Influences

A second research agenda emerged in conjunction with the first, albeit more slowly, and it is empirical in nature. This research approach has sought to reveal what political traits are genetically influenced. Utilizing a classical twin design (CTD), Lindon Eaves and Hans Eysenck (1974) performed the first study to find that political traits are genetically influenced. The CTD compares the co-twin correlations between monozygotic (MZ; identical) and dizygotic (DZ; fraternal) twins. MZ twins develop from a single fertilized egg and, thus, share their chromosomal sequence. DZ twins grow from two separate eggs, fertilized from two different sperm, and share approximately half their genetic inherence, similar to non-twin siblings. This combination of twin pairs provides researchers with the ability to control for comparable familial influence. The underlining assumption is that, on average, MZ and DZ co-twins grow up exposed to equivalent familial experiences, such as having the same meals, living in the same neighborhood and at the same time, attending the same schools, and having similar peer groups. This allows researchers the ability to partition out factors common to the twins (genes and familial factors) and unique to the twins (personal experiences).[1]

Heritability estimates focus on individual differences; that is, they do not explain the value of a trait but, rather, the difference of values within a population. Thus, when a heritability estimate of 0.35 is reported for sex attitudes, for example, it is not that genes explain 35% of sex attitudes; rather, it is that 0.35 of the variance, or individual differences in sex attitudes within the population, is accounted for by the aggregate of genetic influences. That is, heritability estimates provide a population estimate of how people differ. They are not an estimate of the percentage within any given individual that is accounted for by genetic factors. They are not to be interpreted to mean that for every person in the population, 0.35 of a person's attitudes are due to genes.

Eaves and Eysenck (1974) measured social and political attitudes on a wide range of different issues, including the death penalty, unions, unemployment, and abortion. Their pioneering study supported the proposition that individual differences in political attitudes were a function of both biology and environment. Despite their work being published in *Nature*, it was more than a decade before such findings received much attention. Indeed, the work most often credited as the foundational piece in the genetics of politics literature was published 12 years later in *Proceedings of the National Academy of Sciences*. Along with his advisor, Lindon Eaves, Martin et al. (1986) substantially extended the earlier work with much larger samples, a wider range of political orientations, and more complex analyses that included the role of assortative mating. This work found that differences in political orientations were genetically influenced to a larger extend that previously thought.

The first genetically informed research to make a serious impression on the social sciences, however, came much later, in 2005, when John Hibbing and John Alford (Alford, Funk, & Hibbing, 2005) republished results from Eaves and Martin's works (Eaves et al., 1997; Eaves & Eysenck, 1974; Eaves, Eysenck, & Martin, 1989; Eaves et al., 1999; Martin et al., 1986) in the *American Political Science Review.* Following Alford et al. (2005), twin studies emerged as the most popular methods for exploring genetic influences on political beliefs and social behaviors. Taking up the mantle from Eaves and Martin, Hatemi, Fowler, and Dawes have perhaps led the second wave of research to rediscover the usefulness of twin studies in the research on political traits (Cesarini et al., 2008, 2009; Cranmer & Dawes, 2012; Dawes et al., 2014; Dawes & Fowler, 2009; Fazekas & Hatemi, 2016; Fowler et al., 2008; Fowler & Dawes, 2008, 2013; Fowler et al., 2011; Hatemi, 2013; Hatemi, Alford, et al., 2009; Hatemi, Eaves, et al., 2012; Hatemi & McDermott, 2014; Hatemi, McDermott, Eaves, Kendler, & Neale, 2013; Hatemi, Medland, & Eaves, 2009; Hatemi et al., 2014; Hatemi & Verhulst, 2015; Klemmensen, Hatemi, Hobolt, Petersen, et al., 2012; Klemmensen, Hatemi, Hobolt, Skytthe, et al., 2012; Littvay et al., 2011; Loewen & Dawes, 2012; Loewen et al., 2013; McDermott et al., 2013; Oskarsson et al., 2012; Smith et al., 2012; Smith & Hatemi, 2013; Verhulst, Eaves, & Hatemi, 2012; Verhulst & Hatemi, 2013; Verhulst, Hatemi, & Eaves, 2012). Many critical discoveries have come from these works, summarized in several review articles (Hatemi, Dawes, et al., 2011; Hatemi & McDermott, 2012a, 2012b, 2016; Hibbing, Smith, Peterson, & Feher, 2014)

First, the heritability of political traits differed greatly within and across traits (Figure 14.1 provides a summary of results from published articles). On the higher end of the scale, roughly 50% or more of the variation in political knowledge, social trust, ideology, participation, and interest can be attributed to genetic influences, comparable to cognitive ability, perceptual accuracy, and prosociality (58–70%). More than 40% of the variation in attitudes on sex topics (e.g., gay rights), religious items (e.g., Bible truth), economic items (e.g., welfare), defense items, freedom and liberties, and efficacy can be attributed to genetic influences, whereas less than 30% of the variation regarding out-group and punishment attitudes can be attributed to genetic influences. On the low end are ethnocentrism (<20%), civic duty (<15%), and party identification (~5%). These findings have been replicated across multiple countries and decades. For example, Hatemi and colleagues (2014) included samples spanning from the 1970s through 2010 from Australia, Denmark, Sweden, and the United States and found that genetic influences on political attitudes and social, economic, and defense ideologies, in addition to author-itarianism, were similar across time and cultures, whereas social and environmental factors manifested themselves differently according to local ecologies and constraints. Second, genetic influences remained even when the most sophisticated modeling tech-niques were used, such as those that included all types of relatives; addressed the effects of assortative mating; included specific environmental or socialization factors, or used multivariate models, which included other psychological traits.

Assortative mating is important to consider because both heritability and social transmission approaches, for example, assume that mating is randomized. This is

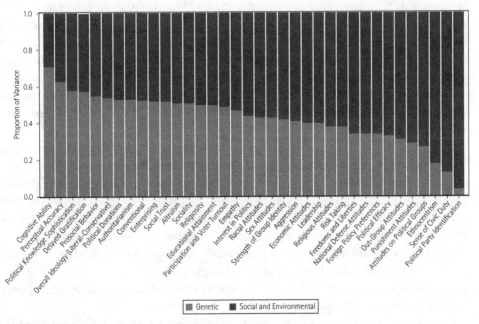

FIGURE 14.1 Sources of individual differences on political traits.

critical because studies have shown that one of the strongest correlates of long-term mates is political ideology (Alford, Hatemi, Hibbing, Martin, & Eaves, 2011; Eaves & Hatemi, 2008; Eaves, Hatemi, Heath, & Martin, 2011; Klofstad, McDermott, & Hatemi, 2012, 2013; Martin et al., 1986). That is, even controlling for ideological convergence and social homogamy, research has shown that people tend to select mates who share their positions on political orientations and issues (Luo & Klohnen, 2005; Luo & Zhang, 2009). If there is assortative mating on a trait of interest and that trait is genetically influenced, then the inherited genetic influences will be underestimated, while environmental and shared experiences will be overestimated. This is true because if parents assort on the trait of interest and the trait is genetically influenced, parents will be more genetically similar for that trait; when they produce offspring, the shuffling of genetic code produced by sexual reproduction will result in less genetic variation among DZ twins (or any full sibling types) than assumed. Thus, DZ genetic similarity will be on average greater than the 0.5 assumed in twin models, leaving MZ/DZ co-twin observed trait differences to be explained by a smaller amount of genetic differences. Such a circumstance would mean twin models underestimate genetic influences. Extrapolating this to a population, the higher the proportion of mates who share genes for a trait, the closer the DZ correlation will become to the MZ correlation and the more the genetic variance of this trait will be underestimated.

This means that the influence of genetic factors in determining the political attitudes of individuals begins even before fertilization. Hatemi and colleagues (Eaves & Hatemi, 2008; Eaves et al., 2011; Hatemi et al., 2010; Keller et al., 2009) addressed this issue by using extended kinship models based on data collected from twins' parents and twins' spouses. This technique resulted in genetic influences accounting for even more of the variance reported on political attitudes and ideologies. Assortative mating may well be the single most important factor in determining an individual's political attitudes because it precludes and determines genetic transmission, parent–child socialization, environment, and personal experiences (Eaves & Hatemi, 2008).

A number of studies have also explored the importance of specific environments. Littvay and Fazekas included twin-specific and shared environments and also election-specific factors, whereas Hatemi focused on critical life events (Fazekas & Hatemi, 2016; Fazekas & Littvay, 2015; Hatemi, 2013; Littvay, 2012). These researchers found that social factors have an important role in shifting the relative import of both genetic and environmental influences. When social forces (i.e., social and material constraints) are absent, genetic influences emerge as more important in how people differ. When personal life events or social forces are overwhelming or constraining, genetic influences become all but absent in explaining variation. For example, genetic influences on individual behavior will be visible in highly disciplined religious communities. Critically important, however, is that when the constraining crisis recedes, or social influences allow people to differ, individuals revert back to their initial disposition and genetic influence re-emerge as important.

One of the first substantive challenges to the research stream on what political traits are genetically influenced was the idea that the heritability of political orientations might simply be an artifact or spurious, deriving from some covariate, particularly personality. On the surface, this idea seemed plausible; individual differences in personality are an equal function of genes and environment. However, despite much discussion and the widespread belief that personality is strongly related to political traits, the empirical record shows otherwise. Most personality traits are neither consistently nor significantly related to political values. The major exceptions are that the personality trait of "openness to new experiences" is positively associated with socially liberal attitudes, whereas "conscientiousness" is positively associated with socially conservative attitudes. Even here, the correlations between the two are modest. Nevertheless, a series of multivariate genetic studies have found that the overwhelming majority of genetic influences on political traits are unique to the traits themselves and not accounted for by personality, morality, or other psychological constructs (Dawes et al., 2014; Hatemi & Verhulst, 2015; Oskarsson et al., 2015; Smith, Alford, Hibbing, Martin, & Hatemi, 2017; Verhulst, Eaves, et al., 2012; Verhulst, Hatemi, & Martin, 2010).

There are of course many challenges to the methods and assumptions of twin studies. We refer readers to published critiques and exchanges for greater details (Alford, Funk, & Hibbing, 2008a, 2008b; Charney, 2008a, 2008b, 2012; Fowler & Dawes, 2013; Hannagan & Hatemi, 2008; Hatemi et al., 2010; Hibbing et al., 2013; Littvay, 2012). We simplify the criticisms to one dimension here. The concern largely revolves around reductionism in some form or another. Some of the loudest critics argue that one cannot assume general similarity in environments, make on-average estimates, partition any trait variance into a discrete amount of genes or environments, and so on with or without bounds or confidence intervals. These criticisms, although they seem reasonable, are criticisms of science in general and are specious. In truth, no credible scientist actually challenges such concerns on a theoretical level. However, science is naturally reductionist. Until a better approach than empirical estimates come along, we are left with estimates with confidence intervals and other bounds to graph or display probabilities and possibilities.

The modern scientist knows that it is not valuable to simply ask if nature *or* nurture determines the form of a particular trait, or even how *much* each factor contributes to a trait. Although these are often portrayed by the methodologies available in quantitative behavioral genetics and molecular biology, science has progressed to the point that it is known that any dichotomy does not stand up to either empirical or conceptual scrutiny. Quantifying the extent to which nature or nurture contributes to a trait, however, provides a critical starting point because these two classes of factors are both always present. They are interactive and operate differentially during different developmental stages and life experiences. Therefore, the methods used are simply a first step to answer *how* our traits develop and how they are maintained over the life course—that is, how it is that genetic, social, and all other factors, including people and populations, interact to produce behavioral traits.

Unfortunately, there is no single method to model the complexities of life—that is, the "life" package in R does not yet exist to perfectly model development, nor do we have the data to do so. However, a number of extensions to classical twin approaches have begun this process. Longitudinal twin studies have the advantage of being able to track sources of variation across different life stages. These studies have found that the political attitudes of MZ and DZ co-twins were no different until they left home (Eaves et al., 1997; Hatemi, Funk, et al., 2009). That is, in childhood, there were no genetic influences present on political traits. Yet, when children left home, MZ co-twins continued to show strong correlations, whereas DZ co-twins' political attitudes diverged. This suggested that after leaving the parental home, DZ co-twins selected into or found themselves experiencing different environments and social influences at greater rates than did MZ co-twins. Thus, the home environment repressed individual differences, and genetic influences only emerged once children left home. These developmental studies have only begun, and there are few methodologies and data to fully explore the developmental trajectories of genetic and environmental influences.

How Do Genes Influence Political Traits?

Although twin studies provide valuable insights into the latent causal genetic pathways, they cannot identify the specific genetic and neurobiological markers and associated systems that operate on political traits. Thus, molecular genetics has become an emerging area of research that attempts to identify how genes influence traits through their neurological and neurochemical pathways. In contrast with the first empirical avenue of research that is largely focused on revealing if and to what extent latent genetic factors influence individual differences in political and social traits, this avenue of research is concerned with process tracking and identifying the specific genetic variants, how they work, and how social and environmental factors influence and are influenced by these traits, directly and indirectly. (For a detailed review on how genes operate with specific pathways for political traits, see Bergner & Hatemi, 2016; Hatemi, Byrne, et al., 2012).

This avenue of inquiry has only recently begun and thus there are only a handful of empirical studies. To date, two approaches have been used. The first method is an inductive empirical approach. This method involves scanning the entire genome for a genetic marker or chromosomal region that shows a correlation with the political trait of interest (Hirschhorn, 2009; Rietveld et al., 2013). Like most inductive studies, this method's strength lies in there being no prior assumptions made on the underlying causes. That is, no prior knowledge is assumed on the underlying biological pathways or causes of a political trait. This avenue is in fact one of true discovery because it identifies causal pathways that were previously unknown. Every region of the genome is tested, and strict statistical significance thresholds are maintained to allow for the multiple testing of the millions of genetic markers. Being genome-wide, this method is the most empirically rigorous of the two methods, and before any general conclusion can be reached, independent replication is required. For example, in the first genome-wide linkage study of political attitudes, Hatemi, Gillespie, et al. (2011) used a sample of 13,000 Australians and identified several regions containing methyl-D-aspartate, serotonin, glutamate, dopamine, olfactory, and G protein-coupled-related receptors that potentially corresponded to liberal and conservative political beliefs. However, two follow-up studies applied genome-wide association analyses and found no markers related to political ideologies or attitudes that reached a significance level of $5 \times 10^{-0.8}$ or better (Benjamin et al., 2012; Hatemi et al., 2014). That is, the markers were not replicated in independent samples.

The challenge of genome-wide analyses is that they require extremely large samples in order to obtain significant results. This is because the influence of any single genetic marker on a complex social or political trait, such as vote choice or ideology, is infinitesimal. Indeed, Rietveld et al. (2013) showed that for complex traits such as educational attainment, samples into the hundreds of thousands are required to identify individual genetic markers that are statistically significant. As such, although genome-wide analysis is a highly promising avenue of research, there is is currently an insufficient amount of data to accurately perform this analysis. Thus, technological and methodological advances and additional data in the future are bound to turn this avenue of research into one of the most important in the field.

A second gene mapping technique relies on a priori knowledge to identify likely candidate genes—that is, those genes that can be expected to be associated with specific political and social traits based on prior associations with similar or root traits. The "candidate marker approach" has proven to be more popular than genome-wide studies. This should not be surprising because it reduces costs, saves time, and exploits the greater availability of data. Fowler and Dawes (2008) relied on previous evidence that identified two genetic polymorphisms, monoamine oxidase A (MAOA) and 5HTT (serotonin), as being associated with prosocial and antisocial behavior. MAOA, for example, correlated with prosocial behavior, and a lack of MAOA appeared to be significant in antisocial behavior. Treating voter turnout as a prosocial behavior, they found that the "high" allele of MAOA and the "long" allele of 5HTT were related to higher voter turnout. However, these markers were only significant in specific socializing conditions, such as religious service attendance. That is, genetic markers previously associated with sociability required some additional social priming in order to operate on voter turnout. Several follow-up articles presented some evidence of replication for serotonin having a role in participation (Dawes & Fowler, 2009; Deppe, Stoltenberg, Smith, & Hibbing, 2013; Fowler & Dawes, 2008, 2013).

Although there have been some hints at novel pathways using candidate gene studies, most of these studies account for very small variance and few have stood up to replication (Duncan & Keller, 2011). At this early stage, no single genetic variant has been found to account for a significant portion of a discrete political trait with a strong degree of certainty. The lack of clear associations is partly a reflection of the fact that this area of genetic research remains in its infancy.

These findings, however, are only a first step. Research has begun to link differences in the gene sequence, genetic expression, hormones, and neurological function, which will lead to a better understanding of the full developmental and biobehavioral pathways to political preferences and actions. Endocrinological, psychopharmacological, and neurochemical studies have observed the role of hormones in regulating the release and modulation of peptides (e.g., vasopressin, serotonin, dopamine, and oxytocin), which in turn alter neurological function identified through event-related brain potentials. Functional magnetic resonance imagining and lesion studies show that activity in the brain is triggered by subcellular activity and specific genetic mechanisms under specific environmental conditions. This research has been conducted on a wide range of traits correlated with political traits, including emotion regulation and recognition (Canli & Lesch, 2007; Uzefovsky, Shalev, Israel, Knafo, & Ebstein, 2012), social affiliation (Walum et al., 2012), cognition (Meyer-Lindenberg et al., 2006), anxiety (Myers et al., 2014), moral judgments (Koenigs et al., 2007), power seeking (Madsen, 1985, 1987), stereotyping of out-groups and in-groups (Hart et al., 2000), trust (Kosfeld, Heinrichs, Zak, Fischbacher, & Fehr, 2005), self-awareness (Gusnard, 2005), empathy (Carr, Iacoboni, Dubeau, Mazziotta, & Lenzi, 2003), and decision-making (Sanfey, Rilling, Aronson, Nystrom, & Cohen, 2003).

WHAT HAVE WE LEARNED?

Perhaps the greatest challenges to the integration of genetics into the social sciences are dispelling myths and the need to find a common language. The vast majority of degree programs in the social sciences do not require basic science courses; thus, social and natural scientists start with large knowledge gaps. Most PhD graduates in social sciences have only a basic knowledge of how genes operate and, as such, many interpret genetic research as arguing that human social behavior is purely deterministic, which is absurd. On the other hand, those entirely focused on genetics or biology often miss the subtleties of the social constructs they seek to understand. For instance, neuroimaging, physiological, and other biological studies have often mistakenly treated party identification, ideology, attitudes, and vote choice as synonyms when, in fact, they are well known to be quite different constructs. Party identification, for example, is more often about identity than values, whereas discrete attitudes tend to reflect beliefs. So, for the social scientist unfamiliar with genetics, what are the takeaways? What have we learned in the past 40 years at the intersection of genetics and politics?

First, political traits are not simply the result of modern institutions, governments, economies, or circumstance. Rather, humans have evolved to be political in order to address the needs, constraints, and benefits that can be derived from communal living. Politics is a fundamental part of what it is to be human—not in a colloquial sense but in an evolutionary sense.

Second, traits result from the interaction of both genetic and environmental influences through developmental pathways. Genetic factors only operate in conjunction with environmental ones. There is no "gene for" any complex trait. That is, there is no "political" gene. No complex social trait will ever be only nature or nurture. Genetic influences on the predilection to exhibit any political or social trait will be indirect and result from the aggregate effects of the interaction of thousands of genes interacting with immeasurable immediate and long-term environmental conditions and experiences that change during the life course.

Third, genetics is as much about human universals as it is about individual differences. Understanding the cognitive and emotional mechanisms will allow researchers to map the basic architecture of how humans operate, such as universal brain function, the role of specific hormones, and the downstream cognitive and emotional processes humans use to make decisions and form preferences. At the same time, although all healthy people use the same neural architecture, people differ, even if so slightly in their genetic makeup, resulting in differences within those cognitive, emotive, and perceptual pathways, which will result in trait variation. People are different. We are different at the genetic level, and we are different socially. Environmental forces will not have the same impact on all individuals. Genetic differences will not have the same result across environments. For example, only some soldiers from the same unit who fight in the same battle develop post-traumatic stress disorder; others repress the experience, and still others write books and easily recount the battle's details. Even when raised in the exact same environments, there will be differences in individual responses to stimuli. The overwhelming majority of research on political traits treats people as the same (rational actors) and views socializing agents and experiences as the source of individual differences. This simply cannot continue under the weight of the evidence to the contrary. The hundreds of millions of combinations of polymorphic markers that differ between people in conjunction with social experiences lead to differences in perception, cognition, emotion, reasoning, preferences, and eventual behavior. In short, the one tenet that buttresses many of our core theories in social science, the blank slate, is no longer valid.

Fourth, although there are major individual differences within societies, there are scant differences across them. People are different. Peoples are the same. Less than 1% of DNA differs between individual humans (Redon et al., 2006), and more than 85% of those differences exist *within* populations (Jorde & Wooding, 2004). In other words, there are greater genetic differences door-to-door than continent-to-continent. Molecular genetic research affirms that we are mostly the same across ethnicities. This simple fact has arguably led to increases in tolerance and changes in policy. We can think of no better or more politically salient example than the issue of equal rights for lesbian, gay, bisexual, and transgender (LGBT) individuals in Western democracies. Since Hamer, Hu, Magnuson, Hu, and Pattatucci (1993) implicated genetic loci for homosexuality, the narrative changed from one of deviant behavior and choice to one of inherent disposition (Hatemi & McDermott, 2011c, 2012a). Subsequently, elite views, including state and US Supreme Court decisions, changed, which filtered down to the public's change in its view of sexual preference. Today, the trend is acceptance and increasing tolerance.

Fifth, identifying genetic systems and their related perceptual, physical, cognitive, and emotional processes has led to novel hypotheses regarding the nature and manifestation of political preferences and behavior. For example, we have learned that smell and pathogen avoidance, and their genetic mechanisms, have a significant role in determining why individuals differ in their attitudes about immigration (Hatemi et al., 2013; McDermott, Tingley, & Hatemi, 2014; Navarrete & Fessler, 2006). Such findings could not have been obtained using social- or environmental-only approaches to behavior.

Finally, in a world of both genes and environments, environments become more—not less—important. Genetic theory provides a vast new avenue to explore environmental influences. It is not that people are born liberal or conservative or any other political orientation. Nor are they simply socialized as so. Genes rarely, if ever, have a direct role in any complex trait. Rather, individuals with certain genetic profiles will be more or less likely to find themselves engaging in or seeking certain experiences and then perceiving and reacting to experiences in a certain way. The sum of those interactions alongside all the differences in constraints, opportunities, and people with whom they engage, among others, and simple happenstance will result in certain probabilities of, for example, joining the military, turning out to vote, being influenced by a candidate's speech, or even running for office (Fazekas & Hatemi, 2016). In this sense, sociology is even more important in explaining why people differ. Understanding what a gene is, which genes are activated or repressed, and how they inform behavior requires a greater, not lesser, understanding of the social environment. By including genetics, the environment represents much more than the observed stimuli humans experience. Rather, the concept of the "environment" expands beyond social experiences but includes the in utero environment, internal cellular environments, and all the experiences that occur across the lifespan. That is, environment includes everything inside and outside the body both before and after an individual is born. It also includes the environments of our ancestors. Differences in the individual's circumstances, such as war or having a child, can have effects on both the internal mechanisms and the person's overall behavior, but these experiences can trigger entirely different genetic mechanisms that may or may not work together or in opposition to one another. Environments trigger and restrict gene expression, and without these triggers, genetic influences are not realized. In short, without biology, we cannot fully explain why people differ under the same environmental conditions, and without the environment, we cannot explain why people with the same DNA differ in behavior outcomes. As such, we have much more to do to reinvest in understanding socialization, and life experiences, than ever before.

CONCLUSION

Now, perhaps more than at any point in the past 200 years, the social sciences are back in a time of discovery. King's (2011) observation of how we viewed our future 60 years ago does not have to be how we view our future today. We rarely have had the means of true discovery in the social sciences. Rather, social scientists have most often sought to empirically validate something already observed. Genetics identifies the unobserved. It provides a starting point to identify novel developmental pathways to preferences and behaviors. Understanding differences in the genome can help identify why people who experience the same social environment physically perceive it differently and react to it differently. It allows for the exploration of individual trajectories. This line of research has only begun, and we are excited to see genetic and other biological methods and approaches further incorporated into the study of political traits.

NOTE

1. In addition to the classical twin design, a number of studies have reported similar finding using twins reared apart and adoption studies (Abrahamson, Baker, & Caspi, 2002; Bouchard & Loehlin, 2001; Bouchard, Lykken, McGue, Segal, & Tellegen, 1990; Bouchard & McGue, 2003; Oskarsson et al., 2015; Tesser, 1993).

REFERENCES

Abrahamson, A. C., Baker, L. A., & Caspi, A. (2002). Rebellious teens? Genetic and environmental influences on the social attitudes of adolescents. *Journal of Personality and Social Psychology, 83*(6), 1392–1408.

Alford, J. R., Funk, C. L., & Hibbing, J. R. (2005). Are political orientations genetically transmitted? *American Political Science Review, 99*(2), 153–167.

Alford, J. R., Funk, C. L., & Hibbing, J. R. (2008a). Beyond liberals and conservatives to political genotypes and phenotypes. *Perspectives on Politics, 6*(2), 321–328.

Alford, J. R., Funk, C. L., & Hibbing, J. R. (2008b). Twin studies, molecular genetics, politics, and tolerance: A response to Beckwith and Morris. *Perspectives on Politics, 6*(4), 793–797.

Alford, J. R., Hatemi, P. K., Hibbing, J. R., Martin, N. G., & Eaves, L. J. (2011). The politics of mate choice. *Journal of Politics, 73*(2), 362–379.

Apicella, C. L., Marlowe, F. W., Fowler, J. H., & Christakis, N. A. (2012). Social networks and cooperation in hunter–gatherers. *Nature, 481*(7382), 497–501.

Arceneaux, K., Johnson, M., & Maes, H. H. (2012). The genetic basis of political sophistication. *Twin Research and Human Genetics, 15*(1), 34–41.

Barkow, J. H., Cosmides, L. E., & Tooby, J. E. (1992). *The adapted mind: Evolutionary psychology and the generation of culture.* New York, NY: Oxford University Press.

Benjamin, D. J., Cesarini, D., van der Loos, M. J., Dawes, C. T., Koellinger, P. D., Magnusson, P. K., . . . Visscher, P. M. (2012a). The genetic architecture of economic and political preferences. *Proceedings of the National Academy of Sciences of the USA, 109*(21), 8026–8031.

Bergner, C., & Hatemi, P. K. (2016). Integrating genetics into the study of electoral behavior. In K. Arzheimer, J. Evans & M. S. Lewis-Beck (Eds.), *The Sage handbook of electoral behaviour* (pp. 367–405). Thousand Oaks, CA: Sage.

Bouchard, T. J., & Loehlin, J. (2001). Genes, evolution, and personality. *Behavior Genetics, 31*(3), 243–273.

Bouchard, T. J., Lykken, D. T., McGue, M., Segal, N. L., & Tellegen, A. (1990). Sources of human psychological differences: The Minnesota Study of Twins Reared Apart. *Science, 250*(4978), 223–228.

Bouchard, T. J., & McGue, M. (2003). Genetic and environmental influences on human psychological differences. *Journal of Neurobiology, 54*(1), 4–45.

Camerer, C., Loewenstein, G., & Prelec, D. (2005). Neuroeconomics: How neuroscience can inform economics. *Journal of Economic Literature, 43*, 9–64.

Canli, T., & Lesch, K. P. (2007). Long story short: The serotonin transporter in emotion regulation and social cognition. *Nature Neuroscience, 10*(9), 1103–1109.

Carr, L., Iacoboni, M., Dubeau, M.-C., Mazziotta, J. C., & Lenzi, G. L. (2003). Neural mechanisms of empathy in humans: A relay from neural systems for imitation to limbic areas. *Proceedings of the National Academy of Sciences of the USA, 100*(9), 5497–5502.

Cesarini, D., Dawes, C. T., Fowler, J. H., Johannesson, M., Lichtenstein, P., & Wallace, B. (2008). Heritability of cooperative behavior in the trust game. *Proceedings of the National Academy of Sciences of the USA, 105*(10), 3721–3726.

Cesarini, D., Dawes, C. T., Johannesson, M., Lichtenstein, P., & Wallace, B. (2009). Genetic variation in preferences for giving and risk taking. *Quarterly Journal of Economics, 124*(2), 809–842.

Charney, E. (2008a). Genes and ideologies. *Perspectives on Politics, 6*(2), 299–319.

Charney, E. (2008b). Politics, genetics, and "greedy reductionism." *Perspectives on Politics, 6*(2), 337–343.

Charney, E. (2012). Behavior genetics and postgenomics. *Behavioral and Brain Sciences, 35,* 331–358.

Cosmides, L., & Tooby, J. (1997). *Evolutionary psychology: A primer.* Santa Barbara, CA: University of California at Santa Barbara.

Cranmer, S. J., & Dawes, C. T. (2012). The heritability of foreign policy preferences. *Twin Research and Human Genetics, 15*(1), 52–59.

Dawes, C. T., Cesarini, D., Fowler, J. H., Johannesson, M., Magnusson, P. K., & Oskarsson, S. (2014). The relationship between genes, psychological traits, and political participation. *American Journal of Political Science, 58*(4), 888–903.

Dawes, C. T., & Fowler, J. H. (2009). Partisanship, voting, and the dopamine D2 receptor gene. *Journal of Politics, 71*(3), 1157–1171.

Dawes, C. T., Loewen, P. J., Schreiber, D., Simmons, A. N., Flagan, T., McElreath, R., . . . Paulus, M. P. (2012). Neural basis of egalitarian behavior. *Proceedings of the National Academy of Science of the USA, 109*(17), 6479–6483.

Deppe, K. D., Stoltenberg, S. F., Smith, K. B., & Hibbing, J. R. (2013). Candidate genes and voter turnout: Further evidence on the role of 5-HTTLPR. *American Political Science Review, 107*(2), 375–381.

Duncan, L. E., & Keller, M. C. (2011). A critical review of the first 10 years of candidate gene-by-environment interaction research in psychiatry. *American Journal of Psychiatry, 168*(10), 1041–1049.

Eagly, A. H., & Wood, W. (2013). The nature–nurture debates: 25 years of challenges in understanding the psychology of gender. *Perspectives on Psychological Science, 8*(3), 340–357.

Eaves, L. J., & Eysenck, H. J. (1974). Genetics and the development of social attitudes. *Nature, 249*(454), 288–289.

Eaves, L. J., Eysenck, H. J., & Martin, N. G. (1989). *Genes, culture, and personality: An empirical approach.* London. UK: Academic Press.

Eaves, L. J., & Hatemi, P. K. (2008). Transmission of attitudes toward abortion and gay rights: Effects of genes, social learning and mate selection. *Behavior Genetics, 38*(3), 247–256.

Eaves, L. J., Hatemi, P. K., Heath, A. C., & Martin, N. G. (2011). Modeling biological and cultural inheritance. In P. K. Hatemi & R. McDermott (Eds.), *Man is by nature a political animal: Evolution, biology, and politics* (pp. 101–184). Chicago, IL: University of Chicago Press.

Eaves, L. J., Heath, A., Martin, N. G., Maes, H. H., Neale, M. C., Kendler, K., . . . Corey, L. (1999). Comparing the biological and cultural inheritance of personality and social attitudes in the Virginia 30,000 study of twins and their relatives. *Twin Research, 2*(2), 62–80.

Eaves, L. J., Martin, N., Heath, A., Schieken, R., Meyer, J., Silberg, J., . . . Corey, L. (1997). Age changes in the causes of individual differences in conservatism. *Behavior Genetics, 27*(2), 121–124.

Faulkner, J., Schaller, M., Park, J. H., & Duncan, L. A. (2004). Evolved disease-avoidance mechanisms and contemporary xenophobic attitudes. *Group Processes & Intergroup Relations, 7*(4), 333–353.

Fazekas, Z., & Hatemi, P. K. (2016) . Individual differences exist in individual characteristics: The role of disposition in "voice and equality." In C. A. Klofstad (Ed.), New Advances in the Study of Civic Voluntarism: Resources, Engagement, and Recruitment (pp. 196–224). Philadelphia, PA: Temple University Press. Available at https://www.amazon.com/New-Advances-Study-Civic-Voluntarism/dp/1439913250/ref=sr_1_2?ie=UTF8&qid=1513133096&sr=8-2&keywords=Klofstad

Fazekas, Z., & Littvay, L. (2012). Choosing sides: The genetics of why we go with the loudest. *Journal of Theoretical Politics, 24*(3), 389–408.

Fazekas, Z., & Littvay, L. (2015). The importance of context in the genetic transmission of US party identification. *Political Psychology, 36*(4), 361–377.

Fowler, J. H., Baker, L. A., & Dawes, C. T. (2008). Genetic variation in political participation. *American Political Science Review, 102*(2), 233–248.

Fowler, J. H., & Dawes, C. T. (2008). Two genes predict voter turnout. *Journal of Politics, 70*(3), 579–594.

Fowler, J. H., & Dawes, C. T. (2013). In defense of genopolitics. *American Political Science Review, 107*(2), 362–374.

Fowler, J. H., Dawes, C. T., & Settle, J. E. (2011). Genes, games, and political participation. In P. K. Hatemi & R. McDermott (Eds.), *Man is by nature and nurture a political animal: Evolution, Biology, and Politics* (pp. 207–223). Chicago, IL: University of Chicago Press.

Fowler, J. H., & Schreiber, D. (2008). Biology, politics, and the emerging science of human nature. *Science, 322*(5903), 912–914.

Gusnard, D. A. (2005). Being a self: Considerations from functional imaging. *Consciousness and Cognition, 14*(4), 679–697.

Hamer, D. H., Hu, S., Magnuson, V. L., Hu, N., & Pattatucci, A. M. (1993). A linkage between DNA markers on the X chromosome and male sexual orientation. *Science, 261*(5119), 321–327.

Hammond, R. A., & Axelrod, R. (2006). The evolution of ethnocentrism. *Journal of Conflict Resolution, 50*(6), 926–936.

Hannagan, R. J., & Hatemi, P. K. (2008). The threat of genes: A comment on Evan Charney's "Genes and Ideologies." *Perspectives on Politics, 6*(2), 329–335.

Hart, A. J., Whalen, P. J., Shin, L. M., McInerney, S. C., Fischer, H., & Rauch, S. L. (2000). Differential response in the human amygdala to racial outgroup vs. ingroup face stimuli. *Neuroreport, 11*(11), 2351–2354.

Hatemi, P. K. (2013). The influence of major life events on economic attitudes in a world of gene–environment interplay. *American Journal of Political Science, 57*(4), 987–1000.

Hatemi, P. K., Alford, J. R., Hibbing, J. R., Martin, N. G., & Eaves, L. J. (2009). Is there a "party" in your genes? *Political Research Quarterly, 62*(3), 584–600.

Hatemi, P. K., Byrne, E., & McDermott, R. (2012). Introduction: What is a "gene" and why does it matter for political science? *Journal of Theoretical Politics, 24*(3), 305–327.

Hatemi, P. K., Dawes, C. T., Frost-Keller, A., Settle, J. E., & Verhulst, B. (2011). Integrating social science and genetics: News from the political front. *Biodemography and Social Biology, 57*(1), 67–87.

Hatemi, P. K., Eaves, L., & McDermott, R. (2012). It's the end of ideology as we know it. *Journal of Theoretical Politics*, 24(3), 345–369.

Hatemi, P. K., Funk, C. L., Medland, S. E., Maes, H. M., Silberg, J. L., Martin, N. G., & Eaves, L. J. (2009). Genetic and environmental transmission of political attitudes over a life time. *Journal of Politics*, 71(3), 1141–1156.

Hatemi, P. K., Gillespie, N. A., Eaves, L. J., Maher, B. S., Webb, B. T., Heath, A. C., . . . Martin, N. G. (2011). A genome-wide analysis of liberal and conservative political attitudes. *Journal of Politics*, 73(1), 271–285.

Hatemi, P. K., Hibbing, J. R., Medland, S. E., Keller, M. C., Alford, J. R., Smith, K. B., . . . Eaves, L. J. (2010). Not by twins alone: Using the extended family design to investigate genetic influence on political beliefs. *American Journal of Political Science*, 54(3), 798–814.

Hatemi, P. K., & McDermott, R. (2011a). Evolution as a theory for political behavior. In P. K. Hatemi & R. McDermott (Eds.), *Man is by nature and nurture a political animal* (pp. 13–46). Chicago, IL: University of Chicago Press.

Hatemi, P. K., & McDermott, R. (Eds.). (2011b). *Man is by nature a political animal: Evolution, biology, and politics*. Chicago, IL: University of Chicago Press.

Hatemi, P. K., & McDermott, R. (2011c). The normative implications of biological research. *PS: Political Science & Politics*, 44(2), 325–329.

Hatemi, P. K., & McDermott, R. (2012a). The genetics of politics: Discovery, challenges, and progress. *Trends in Genetics*, 28(10), 525–533.

Hatemi, P. K., & McDermott, R. (2012b). The political psychology of biology, genetics, and behavior. *Political Psychology*, 33(3), 307–312.

Hatemi, P. K., & McDermott, R. (2014). The study of international politics in the neurobiological revolution: A review of leadership and political violence. *Millennium*, 43(1), 92–123.

Hatemi, P. K., & McDermott, R. (2016). Give me attitudes. *Annual Review of Political Science*, 19, 331–350.

Hatemi, P. K., McDermott, R., Eaves, L., Kendler, K., & Neale, M. C. (2013). Fear as a disposition and an emotional state: A genetic and environmental approach to out-group preferences. *American Journal of Political Science*, 57(2), 279–293.

Hatemi, P. K., Medland, S. E., & Eaves, L. J. (2009). Do genes contribute to the "gender gap"? *Journal of Politics*, 71(1), 262–276.

Hatemi, P. K., Medland, S. E., Klemmensen, R., Oskarsson, S., Littvay, L., Dawes, C. T., . . . Martin, N. G. (2014). Genetic influences on political ideologies: Twin analyses of 19 measures of political ideologies from five democracies and genome-wide findings from three populations. *Behavior Genetics*, 44(3), 282–294.

Hatemi, P. K., Medland, S. E., Morley, K. I., Heath, A. C., & Martin, N. G. (2007). The genetics of voting: An Australian twin study. *Behavior Genetics*, 37(3), 435–448.

Hatemi, P. K., & Verhulst, B. (2015). Political attitudes develop independently of personality traits. *PLoS One*, 10(3), e0118106.

Hibbing, J. R., & Smith, K. B. (2007). The biology of political behavior: An introduction. *Annals of the American Academy of Political and Social Science*, 614(1), 6–14.

Hibbing, J. R., Smith, K. B., & Alford, J. R. (2013). *Predisposed: Liberals, conservatives, and the biology of political differences*. New York, NY: Routledge.

Hibbing, J. R., Smith, K. B., Peterson, J. C., & Feher, B. (2014). The deeper sources of political conflict: Evidence from the psychological, cognitive, and neurosciences. *Trends in Cognitive Sciences*, 18(3), 111–113.

Hirschhorn, J. N. (2009). Genomewide association studies—Illuminating biologic pathways. *New England Journal of Medicine*, 360(17), 1699.

Jorde, L. B., & Wooding, S. P. (2004). Genetic variation, classification and "race." *Nature Genetics, 36*, S28–S33.

Keller, M. C., Medland, S. E., Duncan, L. E., Hatemi, P. K., Neale, M. C., Maes, H. H., & Eaves, L. J. (2009). Modeling extended twin family data I: Description of the Cascade model. *Twin Research and Human Genetics, 12*(1), 8–18.

King, G. (2011). Ensuring the data-rich future of the social sciences. *Science, 331*(6018), 719–721.

Klemmensen, R., Hatemi, P. K., Hobolt, S. B., Petersen, I., Skytthe, A., & Nørgaard, A. S. (2012). The genetics of political participation, civic duty, and political efficacy across cultures: Denmark and the United States. *Journal of Theoretical Politics, 24*(3), 409–427.

Klemmensen, R., Hatemi, P. K., Hobolt, S. B., Skytthe, A., & Nørgaard, A. S. (2012). Heritability in political interest and efficacy across cultures: Denmark and the United States. *Twin Research and Human Genetics, 15*(1), 15–20.

Klofstad, C. A., McDermott, R., & Hatemi, P. K. (2012). Do bedroom eyes wear political glasses? The role of politics in human mate attraction. *Evolution and Human Behavior, 33*(2), 100–108.

Klofstad, C. A., McDermott, R. I., & Hatemi, P. K. (2013). The dating preferences of liberals and conservatives. *Political Behavior, 35*(3), 519–538.

Koenigs, M., Young, L., Adolphs, R., Tranel, D., Cushman, F., Hauser, M., & Damasio, A. (2007). Damage to the prefrontal cortex increases utilitarian moral judgements. *Nature, 446*(7138), 908–911.

Kosfeld, M., Heinrichs, M., Zak, P. J., Fischbacher, U., & Fehr, E. (2005). Oxytocin increases trust in humans. *Nature, 435*(7042), 673–676.

Kurzban, R., & Leary, M. R. (2001). Evolutionary origins of stigmatization: The functions of social exclusion. *Psychological Bulletin, 127*(2), 187–208.

Lewkowicz, D. J. (2011). The biological implausibility of the nature–nurture dichotomy and what it means for the study of infancy. *Infancy, 16*(4), 331–367.

Littvay, L. (2012). Do heritability estimates of political phenotypes suffer from an equal environment assumption violation? Evidence from an empirical study. *Twin Research and Human Genetics, 15*(1), 6–14.

Littvay, L., Weith, P. T., & Dawes, C. T. (2011). Sense of control and voting: A genetically-driven relationship. *Social Science Quarterly, 92*(5), 1236–1252.

Lockyer, A., & Hatemi, P. K. (2014). Resolving the difference between evolutionary antecedents of political attitudes and sources of human variation. *Canadian Journal of Political Science, 47*(3), 549–568.

Loewen, P. J., & Dawes, C. T. (2012). The heritability of duty and voter turnout. *Political Psychology, 33*(3), 363–373.

Loewen, P. J., Dawes, C. T., Mazar, N., Johannesson, M., Koellinger, P., & Magnusson, P. (2013). The heritability of moral standards for everyday dishonesty. *Journal of Economic Behavior and Organization, 93*, 363–366.

Lopez, A. C., & McDermott, R. (2012). Adaptation, heritability, and the emergence of evolutionary political science. *Political Psychology, 33*(3), 343–362.

Lopez, A. C., McDermott, R., & Petersen, M. B. (2011). States in mind: Evolution, coalitional psychology, and international politics. *International Security, 36*(2), 48–83.

Lumsden, C. J., & Wilson, E. O. (1981). *Genes, mind, and culture: The coevolutionary process.* Cambridge, MA: Harvard University Press.

Luo, S., & Klohnen, E. C. (2005). Assortative mating and marital quality in newlyweds: A couple-centered approach. *Journal of Personality and Social Psychology, 88*(2), 304–326.

Luo, S., & Zhang, G. (2009). What leads to romantic attraction: Similarity, reciprocity, security, or beauty? Evidence from a speed-dating study. *Journal of Personality, 77*(4), 933–964.

Madsen, D. (1985). A biochemical property relating to power seeking in humans. *American Political Science Review, 79*(2), 448–457.

Madsen, D. (1987). Political self-efficacy tested. *American Political Science Review, 81*(2), 571–581.

Martin, N. G., Eaves, L. J., Heath, A. C., Jardine, R., Feingold, L. M., & Eysenck, H. J. (1986). Transmission of social attitudes. *Proceedings of the National Academy of Sciences of the USA, 83*(12), 4364–4368.

McDermott, R. (2004). The feeling of rationality: The meaning of neuroscientific advances for political science. *Perspectives on Politics, 2*(4), 691–706.

McDermott, R., Dawes, C. T., Prom-Wormley, E., Eaves, L., & Hatemi, P. K. (2013). MAOA and aggression: A gene–environment interaction in two populations. *Journal of Conflict Resolution, 57*(6), 1043–1064.

McDermott, R., & Hatemi, P. K. (2013). Political ecology: On the mutual formation of biology and culture. *Political Psychology, 35*, 111–127.

McDermott, R., & Hatemi, P. K. (2017). The relationship between physical aggression, foreign policy and moral choices: Phenotypic and genetic findings. *Aggressive Behavior, 43*(1), 37–46.

McDermott, R., Tingley, D., Cowden, J., Frazzetto, G., & Johnson, D. D. (2009). Monoamine oxidase A gene (MAOA) predicts behavioral aggression following provocation. *Proceedings of the National Academy of Sciences of the USA, 106*(7), 2118–2123.

McDermott, R., Tingley, D., & Hatemi, P. K. (2014). Assortative mating on ideology could operate through olfactory cues. *American Journal of Political Science, 58*(4), 997–1005.

Medland, S. E., & Hatemi, P. K. (2009). Political science, biometric theory, and twin studies: A methodological introduction. *Political Analysis, 17*(2), 191–214.

Merolla, J. L., Burnett, G., Pyle, K. V., Ahmadi, S., & Zak, P. J. (2013). Oxytocin and the biological basis for interpersonal and political trust. *Political Behavior, 35*(4), 753–776.

Meyer-Lindenberg, A., Buckholtz, J. W., Kolachana, B., Hariri A., R., Pezawas, L., Blasi, G., . . . Weinberger, D. R. (2006). Neural mechanisms of genetic risk for impulsivity and violence in humans. *Proceedings of the National Academy of Sciences of the USA, 103*(16), 6269–6274.

Miller, G. (2011). *The mating mind: How sexual choice shaped the evolution of human nature.* New York, NY: Anchor.

Mooney, C. (2012). *The Republican brain: The science of why they deny science—and reality:* New York, NY: Wiley.

Myers, A. J., Williams, L., Gatt, J. M., McAuley-Clark, E. Z., Dobson-Stone, C., Schofield, P. R., & Nemeroff, C. B. (2014). Variation in the oxytocin receptor gene is associated with increased risk for anxiety, stress and depression in individuals with a history of exposure to early life stress. *Journal of Psychiatric Research, 59*, 93–100.

Navarrete, C. D., & Fessler, D. M. T. (2006). Disease avoidance and ethnocentrism: The effects of disease vulnerability and disgust sensitivity on intergroup attitudes. *Evolution and Human Behavior, 27*(4), 270–282.

Ojeda, C. (2016). The effect of 9/11 on the heritability of political trust. *Political Psychology, 37*(1), 73–88.

Oskarsson, S., Cesarini, D., Dawes, C. T., Fowler, J. H., Johannesson, M., Magnusson, P. K., & Teorell, J. (2015). Linking genes and political orientations: Testing the cognitive ability as mediator hypothesis. *Political Psychology, 36*(6), 649–665.

Oskarsson, S., Dawes, C. T., Johannesson, M., & Magnusson, P. K. E. (2012). The genetic origins of the relationship between psychological traits and social trust. *Twin Research and Human Genetics, 15*(1), 21–33.

Petersen, M. B. (2010). Towards a folk psychology of security: Insights from evolutionary psychology. *H-Diplo/ISSF Roundtable Forums*, 1(1), 57–63.

Petersen, M. B. (2012). Social welfare as small-scale help: Evolutionary psychology and the deservingness heuristic. *American Journal of Political Science*, 56(1), 1–16.

Petersen, M. B. (2015). Evolutionary political psychology: On the origin and structure of heuristics and biases in politics. *Political Psychology*, 36, 45–78.

Petersen, M. B., & Aaroe, L. (2012). Is the political animal politically ignorant? Applying evolutionary psychology to the study of political attitudes. *Evolutionary Psychology*, 10(5), 802–817.

Petersen, M. B., Sell, A., Tooby, J., & Cosmides, L. (2012). To punish or repair? Evolutionary psychology and lay intuitions about modern criminal justice. *Evolution and Human Behavior*, 33(6), 682–695.

Proctor, D., & Brosnan, S. (2011). What other primates can tell us about the evolutionary roots of our own political behavior. In P. K. Hatemi & R. McDermott (Eds.), *Man is by nature a political animal: Evolution, biology, and politics* (pp. 47–71). Chicago, IL: Chicago University Press.

Redon, R., Ishikawa, S., Fitch, K. R., Feuk, L., Perry, G. H., Andrews, T. D., . . . Hurles, M. E. (2006). Global variation in copy number in the human genome. *Nature*, 444(7118), 444–454.

Ridley, M. (2003). *Nature via nurture: Genes, experience, and what makes us human*. New York, NY: HarperCollins.

Rietveld, C. A., Medland, S. E., Derringer, J., Yang, J., Esko, T., Martin, N. W., . . . Koellinger, P. D. (2013). GWAS of 126,559 individuals identifies genetic variants associated with educational attainment. *Science*, 340(6139), 1467–1471.

Rushton, J. P., Littlefield, C. H., & Lumsden, C. J. (1986). Gene–culture coevolution of complex social behavior: Human altruism and mate choice. *Proceedings of the National Academy of Sciences of the USA*, 83(19), 7340–7343.

Sanfey, A. G., Rilling, J. K., Aronson, J. A., Nystrom, L. E., & Cohen, J. D. (2003). The neural basis of economic decision-making in the Ultimatum Game. *Science*, 300(5626), 1755–1758.

Settle, J. E., Dawes, C. T., & Fowler, J. H. (2009). The heritability of partisan attachment. *Political Research Quarterly*, 62(3), 601–613.

Shenkman, R. (2016). *Political animals: How our Stone-Age brain gets in the way of smart politics*. New York, NY: Basic Books.

Shultziner, D. (2013). Genes and politics: A new explanation and evaluation of twin study results and association studies in political science. *Political Analysis*, 21(3), 350–367.

Smith, K. B., Alford, J. R., Hatemi, P. K., Eaves, L. J., Funk, C., & Hibbing, J. R. (2012). Biology, ideology, and epistemology: How do we know political attitudes are inherited and why should we care? *American Journal of Political Science*, 56(1), 17–33.

Smith, K. B., Alford, J. R., Hibbing, J. R., Martin, N. G., & Hatemi, P. K. (2017). Intuitive ethics and political orientations: Testing moral foundations as a theory of political ideology. *American Journal of Political Science*, 61(2), 424–437.

Smith, K. B., & Hatemi, P. K. (2013). OLS is AOK for ACE: A regression-based approach to synthesizing political science and behavioral genetics models. *Political Behavior*, 35(2), 383–408.

Smith, K. B., Larimer, C. W., Littvay, L., & Hibbing, J. R. (2007). Evolutionary theory and political leadership: Why certain people do not trust decision makers. *Journal of Politics*, 69(2), 285–299.

Stam, A. C., Von Hagen-Jamar, A., & Worthington, A. B. H. (2012). Fear and attitudes towards torture and preventive war. *Twin Research and Human Genetics*, 15(1), 60–70.

Sturgis, P., Read, S., Hatemi, P., Zhu, G., Trull, T., Wright, M., & Martin, N. (2010). A genetic basis for social trust? *Political Behavior, 32*(2), 205–230.

Tesser, A. (1993). The importance of heritability in psychological research: The case of attitudes. *Psychological Review, 100*(1), 129–142.

Thayer, B. A. (2000). Bringing in Darwin: Evolutionary theory, realism, and international politics. *International Security, 25*(2), 124–151.

Tooby, J., & Cosmides, L. (1988). *The evolution of war and its cognitive foundations.* Paper presented at the Evolution and Human Behavior annual meeting, Ann Arbor, MI.

Tooby, J., & Cosmides, L. (2010). Groups in mind: The coalitional roots of war and morality. In H. Hogh-Olesen (Ed.), *Human morality and sociality: Evolutionary and comparative perspectives* (pp. 91–234). New York, NY: Palgrave Macmillan.

Tuschman, A. (2013). *Our political nature: The evolutionary origins of what divides us.* Amherst, NY: Prometheus.

Uzefovsky, F., Shalev, I., Israel, S., Knafo, A., & Ebstein, R. P. (2012). Vasopressin selectively impairs emotion recognition in men. *Psychoneuroendocrinology, 37*(4), 576–580.

Verhulst, B., Eaves, L. J., & Hatemi, P. K. (2012). Correlation not causation: The relationship between personality traits and political ideologies. *American Journal of Political Science, 56*(1), 34–51.

Verhulst, B., & Hatemi, P. K. (2013). Gene–environment interplay in twin models. *Political Analysis, 21*(3), 368–389.

Verhulst, B., Hatemi, P. K., & Eaves, L. J. (2012). Disentangling the importance of psychological predispositions and social constructions in the organization of American political ideology. *Political Psychology, 33*(3), 375–393.

Verhulst, B., Hatemi, P. K., & Martin, N. G. (2010). The nature of the relationship between personality traits and political attitudes. *Personality and Individual Differences, 49*(4), 306–316.

Walum, H., Lichtenstein, P., Neiderhiser, J. M., Reiss, D., Ganiban, J. M., Spotts, E. L., . . . Westberg, L. (2012). Variation in the oxytocin receptor gene is associated with pair-bonding and social behavior. *Biological Psychiatry, 71*(5), 419–426.

Weber, C., Johnson, M., & Arceneaux, K. (2011). Genetics, personality, and group identity. *Social Science Quarterly, 92*(5), 1314–1337.

Weeden, J., & Kurzban, R. (2014). *The hidden agenda of the political mind: How self-interest shapes our opinions and why we won't admit it.* Princeton, NJ: Princeton University Press.

Wrangham, R. W. (1999). Evolution of coalitionary killing. *American Journal of Physical Anthropology,* Suppl. 29, 1–30.

CHAPTER 15

....

GENES AND STATUS
ACHIEVEMENT

....

FRANÇOIS NIELSEN

INTRODUCTION: THE STATUS
ACHIEVEMENT MODEL

....

SINCE the 1960s, the dominant paradigm in studies of social stratification by sociologists and economists has been the status achievement model first proposed by Blau and Duncan (1967). The model represents various status-related outcomes—completion of formal education, first occupation, current occupation, and income—as arrayed in roughly successive stages along the life course (Blau and Duncan 1967). Later outcomes are represented as caused by earlier ones, with the most distal predictors of status consisting of socioeconomic characteristics of the family of origin, such as father's education and occupation. The direct links among the various outcomes can be estimated from data as standardized regression coefficients. From the direct links, one can derive the indirect effect of a variable on a status outcome downstream in the causal flow. A typical status achievement model similar to that used by Blau and Duncan but estimated from more recent data is shown in Figure 15.1.

Blau and Duncan (1967) drew three major substantive conclusions from their empirical analysis. First, direct effects of father's occupation and father's education on son's occupation were small or nonsignificant, suggesting that there is little direct reproduction of social status. In Figure 15.1, for example, these effects are −.020 and .052, respectively, both nonsignificant. Second, there was a strong indirect effect of father's occupation and father's education on occupation through education, suggesting that education is a powerful mechanism of social reproduction. In Figure 15.1, the indirect effect of father's education on respondent's occupation was $.452 \times .520 = .235$. Third, a large part of the total association between education and occupation was due to the indirect effect of residual factors of education, which are (by construction) independent

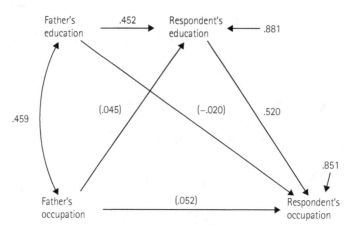

FIGURE 15.1 A simple status achievement model. Numbers along straight arrows are standardized regression coefficients; numbers along curved arrows are correlations; and coefficients in parentheses are nonsignificant ($p \geq .05$).

Source: Nielsen (2016).

of social origins, suggesting that achievement was influenced to a considerable extent by unmeasured personal motivations and abilities unrelated to parental socioeconomic status that could be conceptualized as *merit*. In Figure 15.1, the effect of residual factors on education is .881 (represented as the arrow pointing to respondent's education and calculated as the square root of $1 - R^2$ for the regression of education on background measures) and the effect of education on occupation is .520, so the indirect effect of education residuals on occupation is .881 × .520 = .458, a large proportion of the bivariate correlation of .524 between education and occupation.

The third empirical pattern was particularly meaningful to Blau and Duncan (1967) because it appeared to reflect a major role of merit independent of social origins, as opposed to ascription at birth, in the determination of occupational status in modern industrial society. In a later publication, Duncan (1968) was able to estimate an expanded model including measures of mental ability (IQ), a putative component of the education residuals. He found strong effects of IQ on status achievement, which he took as confirming an important role of merit on mobility chances.

Later research found that other psychological traits affected achievement independently of the measured socioeconomic status of the family of origin. Noncognitive behavioral traits associated with achievement outcomes include perseverance, dependability, and consistency (Bowles and Gintis 1976); leadership, study habits, industriousness, and perseverance (Jencks 1979); the Big Five personality traits, especially conscientiousness and emotional stability (Barrick, Mount, and Judge 2001; Judge, Higgins, Thoresen, and Barrick 1999); and self-esteem and locus of control (Heckman and Rubinstein 2001; Heckman, Stixrud, and Urzua 2006).

There is relatively strong evidence that similar cognitive skills and noncognitive behavioral traits are key determinants of both educational and occupational outcomes

(Farkas 2003). The considerable role of education residuals in occupational achievement had two implications that would slowly emerge in the literature. First, because unmeasured cognitive and noncognitive traits promoting educational attainment are also likely to enhance occupational success, residuals of these two outcomes are likely to be correlated. If this is the case, the estimated direct effect of education on occupation in the status achievement model is likely to be in part spurious (due to common causes) rather than causal. The causal language commonly used to interpret the associations among status-related outcomes as "effects" would then be misleading.

Second, the major role of individual psychological characteristics included in the education residuals, because they are unrelated by construction to measured family background, raises the question of the origin of these traits. They could be caused by other, unmeasured dimensions of the family environment. But they could also be a function of the individual's genetic heritage. Duncan (1968) was well aware of the possibility that intelligence (measured by IQ) has a genetic origin. He viewed, in fact, possible influences of genes on ability as strengthening an interpretation of the role of education residuals as indicative of opportunity in an achievement-oriented society. The next section outlines the development of this idea.

GALTON AND HIS LEGACY

Almost a century before Blau and Duncan (1967), polymath genius Francis Galton (1869) collected detailed genealogies of men who had attained "eminence" in a variety of fields. Galton's data included judges, statesmen, military commanders, scientists, artists, and even oarsmen and wrestlers. In an insightful analysis well worth reading today, Galton found that among relatives of an eminent man, the numbers of men who are also eminent decline with the degree of relatedness: There were more eminent fathers, sons, and brothers than grandfathers, and the numbers among cousins and more distant relatives were smaller still. This pattern, found in all the fields of eminence, strongly suggested to him that eminence is hereditary. Galton also found a large number of remarkable women in the genealogies, which suggested to him that eminence is transmitted through mothers as well as fathers. He found evidence of assortative mating (homophily, or the tendency of like marrying like), which moved him to impugn the common stereotype of his days that "clever men marry silly women" (p. 324).

Galton (1869) found that in some fields, such as sciences and the arts, there are considerably more eminent men among sons than among brothers or fathers. He attributed this pattern to a stronger environmental effect of the family through example and encouragement—what we would call today "role modeling"—in some fields of achievement than in others.

Galton's (1869) work predated current understanding of the laws of genetics, which emerged in the early 20th century from the combination of Gregor Mendel's laws of particulate inheritance governing hereditary transmission of discrete traits (e.g., yellow or green color of peas) with Darwin's theory of the evolution of continuous traits, that resulted in the modern evolutionary synthesis (Fisher 1918; Wright 1920).

The workhorse of the modern synthesis was the model proposed by Fisher (1918) for the determination of a continuous trait. The model assumes that the trait is polygenic— that is, determined by a large number of independent genetic and environmental causes, each of which has a small effect on the trait. The genetic causes of the trait sum up into an overall additive effect, commonly denoted as A.

In humans, who typically grow up in families, nongenetic influences on a trait such as height or IQ can be partitioned into environmental influences (called shared) that are common to all siblings, such as family socioeconomic status insofar as it affects nutrition levels and intellectual stimulation, and tend to make siblings similar on the trait, and environmental influences (called unshared) that are specific to an individual sibling, such as an accident or infectious disease that affects mental ability of one sibling and not others, and tend to make siblings different from each other. The combined effects of shared and unshared environmental causes are commonly denoted C and E, respectively. The unshared component E includes errors of measurement of the trait.

With this notation, the value y of a continuous trait can be written as $y = aA + cC + eE$, where the A, C, and E components are standardized (with mean 0 and standard deviation 1). When y is also standardized, and certain assumptions are satisfied, it can be shown that $\text{var}(y) = a^2 + c^2 + e^2 = 1$, where a^2, c^2, and e^2 denote the proportions of the variance in a trait due to additive effects of genes, the shared environment, and the unshared environment, respectively. (Purcell [2002] discusses the assumptions of the model and the consequences of violating them.)

The decomposition of y into the three components is called the ACE model. In humans, the variance components are estimated traditionally using so-called biometric methods based on designs involving relatives, most commonly pairs of identical and fraternal twins, or adopted children and their adoptive and biological parents. More recently developed molecular genetic methodologies provide alternative estimates of heritability using (sometimes very) large samples of unrelated individuals whose DNA has been sequenced (Chabris, Lee, Cesarini, Benjamin, and Laibson 2015). Heritability estimates are then derived from the associations between the presence of a genetic variant for a large number of genes and the measured value of the individual on the trait (Belsky and Israel 2014; Okbay et al. 2016). The classic twins design is based on a comparison of identical (monozygotic or MZ) and fraternal (dizygotic or DZ) twins raised together. MZ twins share all their genes, whereas DZ twins share only approximately half their genes (assuming random mating of parents). It can be shown that the correlations between twins on a trait are therefore $r_{MZ} = a^2 + c^2$ for MZ twins and $r_{DZ} = \frac{1}{2}a^2 + c^2$ for DZ twins, so the variance components can be estimated with Falconer's formulas as $a^2 = 2 \times (r_{MZ} - r_{DZ})$, $c^2 = 2 \times r_{DZ} - r_{MZ}$, and $e^2 = 1 - a^2 - c^2$ (Falconer and Mackay 1996).

For example, in a sample of young adult twins in the United States, correlations for occupational education (average education of incumbents of an occupation, a measure of occupational status) are .547 for MZ twins and .258 for DZ twins (data discussed in Roos and Nielsen 2015). Applying Falconer's formulas, $a^2 = 2 \times (.547 - .258) = .578$;

$c^2 = 2 \times .258 - .547 = -.031$; and $e^2 = 1 - .578 - (-.031) = .453$ (the small negative value for c^2 is not statistically different from zero). Thus, sources of influences on occupational education of young adults appear largely genetic (58%) and nonshared environmental (45%), with little contribution of shared family influences.

Components of the variance in a trait have important substantive meanings in the context of social stratification and mobility. The additive genetic component a^2 is called the *heritability* of the trait. It represents the proportion of the population variance in a trait that is contributed by all genetic sources of influence. As suggested by Duncan (1968), a larger role of genes in a trait measuring socioeconomic achievement indicates greater opportunity for individuals to achieve their native potential, high or low, and a lesser role of ascription based on status of the family of origin. Higher values of a^2 thus indicate a more achievement-oriented society (Guo and Stearns 2002; Heath et al. 1985; Nielsen 2006).

The *shared environment* c^2 represents the effects on a status-related outcome of all characteristics of the family or embedding social environment that tend to make siblings similar on the outcome; it includes effects of social class and of other factors such as ethnicity or the quality of local schools that tend to vary more between than within families. The shared environment component can be thought of as measuring the strength of ascription, or the degree to which status is socially reproduced (Conley 2008). From a policy-oriented viewpoint, c (the square root of c^2) measures the potential effect on the trait (expressed in standard deviation units) of raising the quality of the family environment by one standard deviation. c^2 thus reflects the extent of improvement on the trait achievable by an intervention modifying the environment *within the existing range of environmental variation* (Behrman and Taubman 1989; Rowe 1994; Taubman 1976). Highlighting in the previous sentence points to the fact that a low c^2 should not be interpreted as a limit on environmental malleability of an outcome, because c^2 does not include potential effects of environmental manipulations (e.g., effective but undiscovered or underutilized interventions) that are not currently contributing to population variation. In contrast with plant and animal breeding, where a^2 is crucial in predicting success of artificial selection and the environment is largely under experimental control, social scientists also have a major interest in the size of c^2, representing as it does a measure of social closure.

The unshared environment e^2 represents the effects of all environmental influences that tend to make siblings different from each other, such as an accident, disease, parental preference, or an encounter with an inspiring role model that affects one sibling but not the other(s). e^2 includes (but is not limited to) measurement error.

GENES AND ENVIRONMENTS
IN STATUS-RELATED TRAITS

I use the expression *status-related trait* or *outcome* to mean any measure, continuous or categorical, that either predicts or reflects status achievement of individuals. Over the life course, therefore, status-related outcomes range from measurement of IQ in child-hood, through high school graduation and completion of formal education, to occupa-tion, income, and subjective social status in adulthood.

Behavioral and social scientists have accumulated considerable research applying the ACE model to various human traits. Turkheimer (2000) summarized the results of that research with his "three laws of behavior genetics" (p. 160):

1. All human behavioral traits are heritable.
2. The effect of being raised in the same family is smaller than the effect of genes.
3. A substantial portion of the variation in complex human behavioral traits is not accounted for by the effects of genes or families.

In terms of the ACE decomposition, $a^2 \neq 0$, $c^2 < a^2$, and $e^2 \gg 0$ (see also Freese 2008). The three laws have been spectacularly confirmed in a massive meta-analysis of 2,748 twin studies of human traits published between 1958 and 2012 (Polderman et al. 2015).

Many status-related outcomes have been found to be affected by genes (Adkins and Guo 2008). Among predictors of educational and occupational achievements, intelli-gence (measured as IQ) has received the most attention. Abundant research based on twin or adoption studies has found substantial heritability of IQ. For example, the meta-analysis of a large number of studies by Devlin, Daniels, and Roeder (1997) found a^2s in the 47–68% range (see also Plomin and Spinath 2004). However, studies summarized by these authors are dominated by studies of children because it is much easier to recruit and test samples of school-aged twins than samples of adults. More recent studies using molecular genetic technology have yielded similarly strong estimates of heritability and confirmed that intelligence is a highly polygenic trait (Davies et al. 2011; Martin et al. 2011).

Studies have documented a systematic pattern of change in the relative importance of genes and the shared environment for IQ during development, with heritability being contingent on age. A typical pattern is that exhibited by samples of Dutch twins varying in age from 5 to 50 years. At age 5 years, genes account for 20% and the shared environment for 55% of the variance in IQ. There is then a steady increase in the role of genes and decline in the role of the shared environment so that by age 12 genes account for more than 80% of the variance and the role of the shared environment dwindles to zero. From then on, heritability of IQ remains high (Bouchard and McGue 2003). The age dependence of the heritability of IQ implies that estimates from older studies of IQ largely based on children, such as the ones summarized by Devlin et al. (1997), were biased toward zero.

Among noncognitive traits potentially related to socioeconomic achievement, per-sonality traits conscientiousness and emotional stability (absence of neuroticism) have shown consistent associations with job performance (Barrick et al. 2001). Bouchard and McGue (2003, p. 21, Table 5) report the average heritability in four recent studies to be 49% for conscientiousness and 48% for neuroticism. The role of the shared environ-ment for these traits is not significantly different from zero. Adkins and Guo (2008) cite literature suggesting that mental and physical health, both predictors of achievement, have a strong genetic substrate. For example, they report heritabilities on the order of 37% for depression, 81% for schizophrenia, and approximately 30% for overall longevity.

Among educational outcomes, educational attainment, measured as highest degree earned or years of completed schooling, has been studied most extensively due to ease of measurement and the view that it serves as a proxy for intelligence (although an imperfect one, as the education–IQ correlation of only .56 in Table 15.2 suggests). A meta-analysis of the international literature found that the mean contribution of genes to educational attainment in twin studies is 40% and that of the shared environment 36% (Branigan, McCallum, and Freese 2013), a pattern confirmed in the meta-analysis of all human traits by Polderman et al. (2015), who found similarly high effects of the shared environment, besides education, only for traits related to conduct disorders and religion and spirituality. The important role of the shared environment in educational attainment is therefore unusual and cannot be readily explained by the effect of cognitive and noncognitive abilities, which may be "ingredients" of educational attainment, because the latter traits themselves have near zero shared environmental variance in adults (Bouchard and McGue 2003). Nielsen and Roos (2015) find a similar pattern in a large US sample of variously related siblings, and they suggest that the large c^2 may be the result of a persistent role of family financial resources in educational attainment. Freese and Jao (2017) discuss alternative explanations of the phenomenon.

For income, Björklund, Jäntti, and Solon (2005) find moderate heritabilities in the range of 20–30% depending on the model, with shared environmental component typically less than 10%. These results suggest heritability of adult financial success is non-zero but low relative to other status-related outcomes.

Roos and Nielsen (2015) estimate the ACE model for 15 status-related outcomes over the life course for the same large sample of adolescent siblings first interviewed during adolescence and followed up until young adulthood (average age ~28 years). Results for outcomes roughly arranged in order of occurrence in the life course are shown in Table 15.1 and Figure 15.2. Estimated heritabilities range from small (9%) for home ownership to a high of 60% for college graduation. The shared environment is substantial for some outcomes, such as educational attainment (29%), college plans (23%), verbal IQ (22%), and some college (21%), but zero for personal earnings. In agreement with Turkheimer's (2000) second law, the effect of genes (a^2) is invariably higher than the effect of the family (c^2).

Some of the more salient findings pertain to status-related outcomes that are more rarely analyzed in a behavior genetic perspective. Heritability of personal earnings (34%) is at the high end for that outcome measured in a single year (compare with Björklund et al. 2005), and the absence of shared environment effect ($c^2 = 0$) may be surprising. Two measures of occupational prestige (occupational education and occupational wages) that are of special interest to sociologists show moderately high heritabilities (33% and 25%, respectively) but low effects of the shared environment (13% and 3%, respectively), especially in comparison with educational outcomes. The moderate heritability (31%) but low impact of the shared environment (2%) for subjective social

Table 15.1 Variance Components Decomposition of Status–Related Outcomes

Outcome	a^2	c^2	e^2	lcpos
Verbal IQ	0.462	0.315	0.223	1
GPA	0.464	0.179	0.357	2
College plans	0.318	0.255	0.427	3
HS graduation	0.249	0.158	0.593	4
Some college	0.291	0.212	0.497	5
College graduation	0.611	0.138	0.251	6
Graduate school	0.368	0.097	0.535	7
Educational attainment	0.355	0.286	0.359	8
Occupational education	0.349	0.134	0.517	9
Occupational wages	0.281	0.030	0.689	10
Personal earnings	0.362	0	0.638	11
Household income	0.266	0.198	0.536	12
Household assets	0.160	0.127	0.713	13
Home ownership	0.071	0.175	0.754	14
Subjective social status	0.317	0.028	0.655	15

HS, high school; lcpos, approximate life course position.

Source: Data from Roos and Nielsen (2015).

status may be surprising because one would expect any cultural mechanism of intergenerational transmission of status to affect this subjective dimension most strongly.

Roos and Nielsen (2015) found systematic patterns in the genetic architecture of successive status-related outcomes over the life course that affected the overall impact of the family of origin on the outcome, from both genetic and environmental sources. First, both a^2 and c^2 tended to decrease, and e^2 increase, with the position of an outcome later in the life course, resulting in a trend of declining family resemblance (which the authors measured as $\frac{1}{2}a^2 + c^2$, the resemblance between ordinary siblings predicted by the ACE model, which they call familiality). The trend suggests that as individuals grow older, status-related outcomes become less affected by family influences (both genetic and shared environmental) and increasingly reflect idiosyncratic (nonshared) individual characteristics.

Second, c^2 represented a significantly greater proportion of family resemblance for outcomes related to the household and shared with a spouse or household partner (household income, household assets, and home ownership)—although family resemblance is typically low for these outcomes—than for individually defined outcomes such

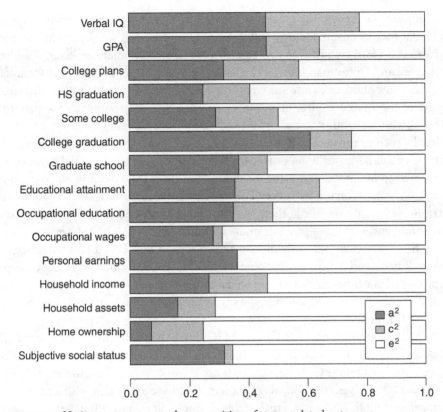

FIGURE 15.2 Variance components decomposition of status-related outcomes.

Source: Data from Roos and Nielsen (2015).

as personal earnings. This pattern may indicate a recrudescence of nongenetic shared influences of the family of origin on outcomes associated with (respondent's own) family formation. See Roos and Nielsen (2015) for further discussion.

GENE–ENVIRONMENT INTERACTIONS

Scarr-Salapatek (1971) conjectured that the relative roles of genetic and shared environmental sources of intelligence and academic achievement would vary according to socioeconomic status of the family. In advantaged environments, genetic potential can be fully expressed so that heritability of mental ability will be high and the effect of the shared environment low. In deprived environments, expression of genes will be inhibited so that heritability will be lower and the impact of the shared environment greater. The conjecture has been called the *Scarr–Rowe hypothesis* of gene × socioeconomic status (SES) interaction (Tucker-Drobs and Bates 2016). In general interactions between genes and environment of this type are called G×E (Shanahan and Hofer 2005).

Significant moderation of genetic expression as a function of environment quality for intelligence has been documented in US studies, such as those by Rowe, Jacobsen, and Van den Oord (1999); Guo and Stearns (2002); and Turkheimer, Haley, Waldron, D'Onofrio, and Gottesman (2003). The latter study, for example, finds that for intelligence in young children in low SES environments, heritability is only 10%, with a strong impact of the shared environment (58%). In high SES environments, the pattern is reversed, with heritability at 72% and the shared environment at 15%.

Results such as those of Turkheimer et al. (2003) have captured the imagination of social scientists because they appear to reaffirm a central role for the social environment as opposed to biological endowment (Nisbett 2009). In the case of intelligence, however, the systematic review by Tucker-Drob and Bates (2016) finds mixed support for the Scarr–Rowe hypothesis. The authors find that low SES was associated with attenuated genetic influences on intelligence in studies conducted in the United States, but that the interaction was not significantly different from zero in non-US studies (conducted in western Europe and Australia). Tucker-Drob and Bates believe that G×E may be higher in the United States because of a more inegalitarian access to economic resources in the society. Even in US studies, however, the size of the interaction is typically less than that found by Turkheimer et al.

The mixed support for G×E in the case of IQ should be related to the high heritability of IQ in adulthood, which ensures that there is little room for any environmental effect. It does not mean that the G×E mechanism is not at work for status-attainment outcomes other than IQ, such as educational attainment, that have a substantial shared environment component in adulthood. Further studies might illuminate this issue.

The Scarr–Rowe hypothesis assumes that heritability increases monotonically as a function of social status. The simplest model is that heritability increases linearly with SES. A variant model is that starting from the most deprived environment, heritability at first increases rapidly as conditions improve and then more slowly once environmental conditions are above a "humane threshold" bounding the normal species range (Scarr 1992). Sociological literature suggests alternative hypotheses to the Scarr–Rowe conjecture of monotonically increasing gene expression with environment quality. In his conception of social mobility and the circulation of elites, Pareto (1909/1971) conjectured that the effect of innate qualities on success traces an inverted-U shape with family SES: In the lowest stratum of SES, environmental conditions are so impoverished that individuals are held back irrespective of innate talent; in the highest SES stratum, resources are so readily available that even individuals with low levels of ability are protected from downward mobility. It is in the middle stratum of SES that the effect of innate qualities is strongest, as resources are sufficiently abundant to allow talented individuals to rise but not sufficient to prevent downward mobility of the less able. Pareto's model thus predicts that heritability is highest in the middle stratum and lower in both bottom and top strata, a curvilinear relationship of a^2 with environmental resources.

Still another hypothesis is implied by Saunders (2010), who found that in modern Great Britain the only deviation from perfect meritocratic mobility was a tendency for those born in the upper occupational classes to experience downward mobility at a lower rate than that expected in a fully meritocratic society. The rate of upward mobility from lower to upper classes, however, was consistent with the meritocratic hypothesis. Saunders' interpretation of the finding is that being born a member of the upper stratum has a greater effect on achieved status (in preventing downward mobility) than has being born to the working class (in preventing upward mobility). In terms of the ACE, this would imply that the shared environment c^2 increases monotonically with family SES and, conversely, that the effect (a^2) of genes on status achievement declines apace. Nielsen (2016) suggests that the predicted negative relationship between heritability of individual socioeconomic success and family SES might be called the *Saunders* or *reverse Scarr–Rowe* hypothesis. Studies of G×E for educational attainment would seem a promising strategy for future research because this adult outcome is characterized by a substantial shared environment component.

The theoretical significance of G×E has been greatly expanded in discussions by Adkins and Guo (2008) and Adkins and Vaisey (2009). These authors contend that parameters of the ACE models are macro-sociological concepts characterizing the nature of the stratification system in a society, with average heritability in a society measuring opportunity to reach one's potential and, conversely, the shared environment representing social ascription and social closure. They conjecture that more open and egalitarian societies will exhibit greater heritability and smaller effects of the shared environment.

Heath et al. (1985) illustrate the way the ACE decomposition of the variance in status provides macrosocial indicators of fluidity of the social structure of a society. The authors compared resemblances in educational attainment between DZ and MZ twins in a large Norwegian sample to estimate the components of the ACE model for different birth cohorts, separately by sex. Comparing older (born 1915–1939) and younger (born 1950–1960) cohorts, they found that, for males, the effect of genes on educational attainment increased (from 18% to 76%) and the role of the shared environment correspondingly decreased (from 68% to 9%). Heath et al. interpret these changes in the ACE parameters as resulting from liberal policy reforms in Norway that made access to education more open.

For females during the same period, the role of genes in schooling also increased (from 28% to 46%), and the role of the shared environment decreased (from 61% to 43%), but not as much as for males. Heath et al. (1985) conclude that equality of opportunity, measured as the relative size of the genetic component, did not improve to the same extent for females as for males so that the role of family privilege in educational attainment, measured as the shared environment component, remained correspondingly greater for females (see also Branigan et al. 2013). These interpretations are consistent with the theoretical discussions of Adkins and Guo (2008) and Adkins and Vaisey (2009).

INTERRELATIONSHIPS OF
STATUS-RELATED OUTCOMES

It has been known since at least the beginning of status achievement research that status-related outcomes over the life course are correlated with each other and with characteristics of the family background. Average correlations from a meta-analysis of a large number of independent studies by Strenze (2007, p. 412, Table 1, column p) are shown in Table 15.2. Average correlations of the three principal status outcomes in adulthood (measured after age 29 years) with intelligence (measured before age 19 years) are .56 for education, .45 for occupation, and .23 for income, suggesting that intelligence predicts income less well than it does education or occupation. A similar pattern holds for academic performance. Adult outcomes are explained almost equally well by background characteristics, especially when combined into an SES index, which is correlated .55 with education, .38 with occupation, and .09 with income. A general pattern is that income is more weakly associated with predictors than other outcomes.

The classic status achievement model interprets associations among status-related outcomes in a causal perspective. Rowe (1994) has noted that causal interpretations are likely to be spurious because successive outcomes (e.g., education and occupation) may be associated due to unmeasured common causes such as ability and ambition, including genetic ones, rather than causally (Eckland 1979). As an alternative account, Rowe (1994) proposed a multivariate extension of the ACE model in which associations among outcomes are due not to direct causal effects but, rather, to effects of latent (i.e., unmeasured) environmental and genetic sources that may themselves be correlated (see also Petrill and Wilkerson 2000). Structural equation modeling (SEM) methodology permits estimating the proportions of the zero-order association (correlation) between any two status-related outcomes that are due to genetic, shared-environmental and unshared-environmental sources, respectively.

Table 15.2 Correlations Between Three Principal Measures of
Status and Predictors[a]

	Measure of Status		
Predictor	Education	Occupation	Income
Intelligence (all studies)	.56	.43	.20
Intelligence (best studies)	.56	.45	.23
Father's education	.50	.31	.17
Mother's education	.48	.27	.13
Father's occupation	.42	.35	.19
Parental income	.39	.27	.20
SES index	.55	.38	.18
Academic performance	.53	.37	.09

[a]Correlations shown are sample size weighted averages corrected for unreliability and dichotomization.

Source: Data from Strenze (2007, p. 412, Table 1, column p).

Nielsen (2006, 2016) describes a multivariate ACE model of the interrelationships among verbal IQ (VIQ), high school grades (GPA), and college plans (CPL) estimated from a large sample of adolescent sibling pairs living in the same household and related to different degrees (MZ twins, DZ twins, full siblings, half siblings, cousins, and non-related siblings). SEM methodology was used to compare the fit of a variety of models and test hypotheses concerning the structure of latent factors responsible for the observed relationships. The analytical strategy consisted in initially fitting a maximal model with as many latent A, C, and E factors as there are outcomes. These latent factors were assumed uncorrelated among each other and linked to the observed outcomes in a triangular pattern called a Cholesky factorization. The original model was then simplified through successive steps testing structural hypotheses such as whether several outcomes can be explained by the same latent factor or whether factors corresponding to different outcomes are uncorrelated. The model was finally rotated so that each outcome is a function of only one A, C, and E factor, and factors for a given latent source may be correlated. Among the findings were the following:

1. Each of the outcomes was substantially affected by genes (a^2 was 53% for VIQ, 67% for GPA, and 59% for CPL).
2. Only VIQ was substantially affected by shared-environment sources (c^2 was 14% for VIQ, 0 for GPA, and 3% for CPL).
3. There were moderate correlations between genes affecting verbal IQ and GPA (.43) and GPA and college plans (.55); the correlation was lower for verbal IQ and college plans (.26), suggesting that genes affecting these two traits overlap only partially. The hypothesis that there is a single set of "ability genes" affecting all three outcomes was statistically rejected.
4. The hypothesis that there is a single "privilege" dimension of the shared environment affecting all three outcomes could not be rejected.
5. The associations among the three outcomes were largely the results of common genetic sources, as the proportion of the correlation due to genes was 70% for VIQ–CPL and 100% for both VIQ–GPA and GPA–CPL, with little contribution of either shared or nonshared environments.

Reports of large contributions of genetic sources to the association between status-related outcomes have become commonplace (Calvin et al. 2012; Marioni et al. 2014). Although much work remains to be done in that area, such findings contribute to the mounting evidence that the ostensibly "causal" links in the status achievement model are generated to a substantial extent by common genetic sources rather than environmental factors or direct causation. These findings suggest that much of career continuity (i.e., the tendency of most careers to trace a monotonic status trend, devoid of wild swings) has genetic origins.

One important limitation of the multivariate ACE is that it assumes associations among outcomes are entirely explained by latent factors. It is not possible to add direct causal links to the full ACE model (represented by its Cholesky factorization) because they would not be estimable. This is problematic in situations in which there are substantive reasons to expect a direct causal influence of one outcome on another. For example, in the model described previously, it would be reasonable to think that by providing the student with an external clue of his or her academic potential, GPA affects college plans directly and independently of abilities (which would perhaps disturbingly imply that deliberate manipulation of GPA by school officials might enhance or discourage college ambitions). As an important instance, much research in economics has focused on the effect of education on earnings because economists are interested in estimating the financial return to an additional year of education net of individual endowments (Ashenfelter and Krueger 1994; Behrman and Rosenzweig 1999; Miller, Mulvey, and Martin 2006).

Kohler, Behrman, and Schnittker (2011) have clarified the conditions under which causal effects of the type assumed in the classic status achievement model can be incorporated into the multivariate ACE. The authors show that a direct causal link can be estimated if sufficiently stringent assumptions are made. In the case of GPA $\rightarrow$ CPL, the most natural extra constraint would be that the unshared E components for GPA and CPL are uncorrelated—that is, idiosyncratic factors that affect the GPA of an individual sibling are uncorrelated with idiosyncratic factors affecting CPL for that sibling. If that assumption holds, the direct effect GPA $\rightarrow$ CPL can be estimated. Kohler et al. show convincing examples of application of the strategy, but the question whether it is plausible to assume uncorrelated unshared components for two status-related outcomes will likely arise in specific applications of the method.

MOBILITY IMPLICATIONS OF THE ROLE OF GENES

The preceding discussion suggests that the traits that enhance socioeconomic success, such as intelligence and personality traits, are strongly influenced by genes. Thus, in a society with any degree of openness, individuals with favorable genes for these traits will tend to gravitate toward high-status positions so that social class of destination is determined in part by genes. This is the gist of Herrnstein's (1973) syllogism, quoted by Rowe (1994, p. 141):

1. If differences in mental abilities are inherited, and
2. If success requires those abilities, and
3. If earnings and prestige depend on success,
4. Then social standing (which depends on earnings and prestige) will be based to some extent on inherited differences among people.

The syllogism can be extended in an obvious way from mental abilities to include the role of noncognitive traits that affect success.

The idea that social class might have a genetic basis generated strong negative reactions among the public and in academia. Herrnstein's (1973) syllogism, and its later formulation in Herrnstein and Murray (1994), seemed to predict a dismal future in which society would be partitioned into residentially segregated and quasi-hereditary castes based on genes, a social arrangement all the more detestable because it could conceivably be morally justified on meritocratic grounds. However, Herrnstein's scenario may have downplayed the potential role of a powerful mechanism of reproduction in preventing the hardening of social classes into ability-based hereditary castes: regression to the mean.

Human beings, as sexually reproducing organisms, do not produce clones of themselves. Instead, a couple produces offspring with whom parents each share a random 50% of their genes. For a continuous trait affected by many genes, each of which has a small effect (a "complex trait"), the parent–child correlation is $r_{PC} = \frac{1}{2}a^2 + c^2$—that is, half the heritability plus the shared environmental component—and the same correlation holds for other first-degree relatives such as ordinary (full) siblings. Thus, even for a perfectly heritable trait (with $a^2 = 1$ and $c^2 = 0$), the parent–child correlation due to genetic inheritance cannot be larger than .5.

The high heritabilities found for many traits may seem implausible or even scary because they seem to imply a strong, overwhelming genetic basis of "family resemblance." Sociologists, like most people, base their intuition of family resemblance on the similarity of parents and offspring, and the similarity of ordinary siblings, with respect to visible outcomes such as college graduation. They know from their personal experience that children from a given family tend to be alike in obtaining college degrees. It seems natural to interpret the similarity in outcomes as resulting from similar expectations for siblings and their exposure to similar resources, role models, and encouragements. Invocation of a strong role of genes in college completion seems unnecessary and difficult to believe.

However, the shared environment plays a greater role in family resemblance than may at first appear. This is because for first-degree relatives such as ordinary siblings, who are genetically related at only 50%, the correlation on the trait involves the full contribution of the shared environment c^2 but only half of the impact of genes denoted as a^2. Therefore, the resemblance between ordinary siblings reflects the full contribution of the shared environment to trait variance but only half of the contribution of genes.

A concrete example is provided by the meta-analytic estimates of $a^2 = .40$ and $c^2 = .36$ for the variance components of educational attainment found by Branigan et al. (2013). In a population characterized by these parameters, the predicted correlation between ordinary siblings is $r_{sibs} = \frac{1}{2} \times .40 + .36 = .56$. Thus, the shared environment plays the major role in the resemblance of ordinary siblings (.36/.56 = 64%), and genetic factors play a relatively minor one (.20/.56 = 36%). An alternative interpretation is that shared environmental characteristics of the family induce a correlation of .36 between the educational attainments of siblings, while genetic factors induce an added .20. The role of genes, viewed in this way, might seem more plausible (and relatively nonthreatening), even for a social scientist convinced of the predominant importance of environmental factors. Genetic sources of variation in a trait are fully reflected only in the resemblance of identical twins, which, of course, can be astonishing. Most people, however, do not know more than a few pairs of identical twins—too few to ground their intuition about family resemblance.

The imperfect correlation between parent and child in a trait produces the phenomenon of regression to the mean, another discovery of Francis Galton (1886). Taking height (a highly heritable trait) as an example, regression to the mean implies that the height of offspring of tall parents will exhibit considerable scatter, with a mean in between the average height of the parents and the average height of the population. Conversely, the offspring of short parents will be taller on average than the parents but shorter than the population average.

The extent to which the average trait in the parents regresses to the mean in the offspring is a function of the heritability of the trait. Specifically, the offspring average on the trait is equal to the population mean plus the deviation of the parental average (called the *midparent*) from the population mean times the heritability (Falconer and Mckay 1996).[1] Taking intelligence as an example, suppose an exceptionally intelligent couple has an average IQ of 130. Because IQ is distributed with mean 100 and standard deviation of 15, the midparent is 2 standard deviations above the mean, corresponding to the 98th percentile of the IQ scale. Assuming heritability is .6, the expected IQ of the offspring of the couple is $100 + .6 \times 30 = 118$, which corresponds to the 88th percentile of IQ, well above average but less exceptional than that of the parents. Actual IQ scores for the offspring will vary considerably around this expected value. Although highly successful couples with a disappointing child may discover regression to the mean with consternation, it is important to keep in mind that the phenomenon is symmetrical so that a below average couple will produce offspring with IQ higher than theirs on average.

If people chose their mate randomly, irrespective of the status-related traits of spouses, the average midparent over all couples would be equal to the population mean, and the average trait in the offspring would regress to the population mean in each generation. However, this does not happen due to assortative mating, or *homophily*, the tendency of spouses to choose partners similar to themselves. Homophily, measured as the correlation of the trait between spouses, tends to be high for status-related traits, such as intelligence (~.4) and education (~.6), in comparison with physical traits such as height and weight (~.2) (Plomin and Deary 2015). Assortative mating of parents on a trait results in an increase in the additive genetic variance of the trait in the offspring, relative to what it would be under random mating. The increase in variance occurs each generation until an asymptote is reached. For example, Jensen (1972, pp. 106–108), assuming heritability of .8 and spousal correlation of .6, calculates that without assortative mating, the standard deviation of IQ would decline from 15 to 12.9.

A crucial implication of the regression to the mean of a trait that promotes socioeconomic success is that biological inheritance by itself will produce considerable intergenerational mobility in the trait. Sexual reproduction ensures that there is a natural reshuffling of genes in each generation so that many individuals in the higher classes are born with abilities lower than those of their parents, and many in the lower classes are born with abilities higher than those of their parents. To the extent that socioeconomic achievement in a society is based on merit, biological inheritance will thus naturally induce a certain amount of social mobility, both downward and upward. Rowe (1994, p. 142) estimates that in industrialized societies, in each generation 30% of individuals move up from the class of their parents, 30% move down, and the rest remain in the class of origin. This conception corresponds to (with respect to political power) the "circulation of elites" of Pareto (1909/1971, 1917–1919/1965) and (with respect to intelligence and social status) approaches such as hinted at by Duncan (1968) and explicitly proposed by Burt (1961), Herrnstein (1973), Marks (2014), and Saunders (2010).

Ascriptive mechanisms can slow down the natural rate of intergenerational mobility caused by genetic regression to the mean. Although there is probably some degree of mobility in all societies, ascriptive mechanisms by which offspring of higher strata are protected from downward mobility while upward mobility of offspring of the lower strata is stunted can reduce overall mobility to near zero, as in extreme cases such as endogamous castes of traditional India or hereditary aristocracies of medieval Europe (Scarr-Salapatek 1971). The relative strength of ascriptive mechanisms related to unequal quality of rearing environments or deliberate social closure can be estimated at the societal level as the size of the shared environment component c^2 (Conley 2008; Nielsen 2006).

The observed association between parent and child on a status-related outcome such as occupation or income has traditionally been used in social mobility research as a measure of social closure, or inverse measure of social fluidity, with a strong association implying a closed social structure in which ascription plays a paramount role and a weak association implying an open structure with more opportunities for achievement (Ganzeboom, Luijkx, and Treiman 1989; Solon 2008).

The quantitative genetic decomposition of the parent–offspring correlation together with the substantial role of genes documented for many status-related outcomes imply that intergenerational associations of status-related traits are ambiguous because a strong association may be due to high heritability of the trait—in which case it actually reflects high opportunities for achievement in a more open society—or to a high value of the shared family environment—in which case it does indeed reflect greater social closure (Eckland 1967). This implies that variance components a^2 and c^2 from the ACE decomposition of the trait variance, considered separately, are better measures of the degrees of opportunity and ascription, respectively, than the overall intergenerational association (Heath et al. 1985; Jencks and Tach 2006; Nielsen 2006).

CONCLUSION

Genetic inheritance play a central role in all aspects of social stratification and mobility.

Most status-related outcomes—individual characteristics predicting or reflecting socioeconomic success—are substantially affected by genes. Some outcomes, notably educational attainment, are also appreciably affected by circumstances of the family of origin (shared environment). There is evidence that the extent to which genes affect an outcome depends on the social context, particularly the availability of resources (gene–environment interaction).

Genetic inheritance plays an important role in career continuity, the serial correlation of status outcomes at successive stages of the life course, reflected in findings that associations among outcomes are often predominantly or entirely explained by effects of common genes on the outcomes but only in smaller measure by shared environmental effects.

Because parents individually transmit only one-half of their genes to the offspring, the mechanism of genetic inheritance ensures that levels of status-relevant traits of parents and offspring are imperfectly correlated. There is a regression to the mean in which the expected offspring level of a trait is in between the average levels of parents and the population mean.

In a society in which status achievement is related to any appreciable extent to individual qualities ("merit"), genetic inheritance will thus produce a degree of intergenerational mobility as individuals with low qualities born to higher strata will tend to move downward in status, whereas individuals with high qualities born to lower strata will tend to move upward. These movements tend to generate (and restore) an association between status-related qualities and social strata.

Components of the variance in a status-related outcome representing the relative effects of genes (heritability) versus the family environment of origin (shared environment) are direct measures of, respectively, the degree of opportunity versus the weight of social ascription facing individuals in a society. These measures are to be preferred to measures of overall intergenerational association that are ambiguous because they confound the two components.

Research is ongoing on all these issues, and much remains to be learned.

NOTE

1. Technically, parent–offspring resemblance is a function of narrow-sense heritability, which is the proportion of trait variance due to the additive effects of genes, excluding variance due to interaction of genes due to mechanisms of dominance or epistasis (Falconer and MacKay 1996). It appears that resemblance between relatives for a majority of continuous human traits is due to additive effects exclusively (Polderman et al. 2015).

REFERENCES

Adkins, Daniel E. and Guang Guo. 2008. "Societal Development and the Shifting Influence of the Genome on Status Attainment." *Research in Social Stratification and Mobility* 26: 3 (September): 235–255.

Adkins, Daniel E. and Stephen Vaisey. 2009. "Toward a Unified Stratification Theory: Structure, Genome, and Status Across Human Societies." *Sociological Theory* 27: 2 (June): 99–121.

Ashenfelter, Orley and Alan Krueger. 1994. "Estimates of the Economic Return to Schooling from a New Sample of Twins." *American Economic Review* 84: 5: 1157–1173.

Barrick, Murray R., Michael K. Mount, and Timothy A. Judge. 2001. "Personality and Performance at the Beginning of the New Millennium: What Do We Know and Where Do We Go Next?" *Personality and Performance* 9: 1/2 (March–June): 9–30.

Behrman, Jere R. and M. R. Rosenzweig. 1999. "'Ability' Biases in Schooling Returns and Twins: A Test and New Estimates." *Economics of Education Review* 18: 2 (April): 159–167.

Behrman, Jere R. and Paul Taubman. 1989. "Is Schooling Mostly in the Genes? Nature–Nurture Decomposition Using Data on Relatives." *Journal of Political Economy* 97: 6: 1425–1446.

Belsky, Daniel W. and Salomon Israel. 2014. "Integrating Genetics and Social Science: Genetic Risk Scores." *Biodemography and Social Biology* 60: 2: 137–155.

Björklund, Anders, Markus Jäntti, and Gary Solon. 2005. "Influences of Nature and Nurture on Earnings Variation: Preliminary Results from a Study of Various Sibling Types in Sweden." Pp. 145–164 in *Unequal Chances: Family Background and Economic Success*, edited by Samuel Bowles, Herbert Gintis, and Melissa Osborne Groves. New York, NY: Russell Sage.

Blau, Peter M. and Otis Dudley Duncan. 1967. *The American Occupational Structure*. New York, NY: Wiley.

Bouchard, Thomas J., Jr. and Matt McGue. 2003. "Genetic and Environmental Influences on Human Psychological Differences." *Journal of Neurobiology* 54: 1 (January): 4–45.

Bowles, Samuel and Herbert Gintis. 1976. *Schooling in Capitalist America*. New York, NY: Basic Books.

Branigan, Amelia R., Kenneth J. McCallum, and Jeremy Freese. 2013. "Variation in the Heritability of Educational Attainment: An International Meta-Analysis." *Social Forces* 92: 1 (September): 109–140.

Burt, Cyril. 1961. "Intelligence and Social Mobility." *British Journal of Statistical Psychology* 14 (May): 3–24.

Calvin, Catherine M., Ian J. Deary, Dinand Webbink, Pauline Smith, Cres Fernandes, Sang Hong Lee, et al. 2012. "Multivariate Genetic Analyses of Cognition and Academic Achievement from Two Population Samples of 174,000 and 166,000 School Children." *Behavior Genetics* 42: 5 (September): 699–710.

Chabris, Christopher F., James J. Lee, David Cesarini, Daniel J. Benjamin, and David I. Laibson. 2015. "The Fourth Law of Behavior genetics." *Current Directions in Psychological Science* 44: 4 (August): 304–312.

Conley, Dalton. 2008. "What Do Low (or High) Sibling Correlations Tell Us About Social Ascription?" Pp. 596–609 in *Social Stratification* (3rd ed.), edited by David B. Grusky. Boulder, CO: Westview.

Davies, G., A. Tenesa, A. Payton, J. Yang, S. E. Harris, D. Liewald, et al. 2011. "Genome-Wide Association Studies Establish That Human Intelligence Is Highly Heritable and Polygenic." *Molecular Psychiatry* 16: 996–1005. doi:10.1038/mp.2011.85; published online 9 August 2011.

Devlin, B., Daniels, M., and Roeder, K. 1997. "The Heritability of IQ." *Nature* 388: 468–471.

Duncan, Otis Dudley. 1968. "Ability and Achievement." *Eugenics Quarterly* 15: 1: 1–11.

Eckland, Bruce K. 1967. "Genetics and Sociology: A Reconsideration." *American Sociological Review* 32: 2 (April): 173–194.

Eckland, Bruce K. 1979. "Genetic Variance in the SES-IQ Correlation." *Sociology of Education* 52: 3: 191–196.

Falconer, D. S. and Trudy F. C. Mackay. 1996. *Introduction to Quantitative Genetics* (4th ed.). Harlow, UK: Pearson.

Farkas, George. 2003. "Cognitive Skills and Noncognitive Traits and Behaviors in Stratification Processes." *Annual Review of Sociology* 29: 541–562.

Fisher, Ronald A. 1918. "The Correlation Between Relatives on the Supposition of Mendelian Inheritance." *Transactions of the Royal Society of Edinburgh* 52, Part 2: 399–433.

Freese, Jeremy. 2008. "Genetics and the Social Science Explanation of Individual Outcomes." *American Journal of Sociology* 114 Supplement: S1–S35.

Freese, Jeremy and Yu-Han Jao. 2017. "Shared Environment Estimates for Educational Attainment: A Puzzle and Possible Solutions." *Journal of Personality* 85: 1 (February): 79–89.

Galton, Francis. 1869. *Hereditary Genius*. London, UK: Macmillan.

Galton, Francis. 1886. "Regression Towards Mediocrity in Hereditary Stature." *Journal of the Anthropological Institute of Great Britain and Ireland* 15: 246–263.

Ganzeboom, H. B. G., Luijkx, R., and Treiman, D. J. 1989. "Intergenerational Class Mobility in Comparative Perspective." *Research in Social Stratification and Mobility* 8: 3–84.

Guo, Guang, and Elizabeth Stearns. 2002. "The Social Influences on the Realization of Genetic Potential for Intellectual Development." *Social Forces* 80: 881–910.

Heath, A. C., K. Berg, L. J. Eaves, M. H. Solaas, L. A. Corey, J. Sundet, et al. 1985. "Education Policy and the Heritability of Educational Attainment." *Nature* 314 (6013): 734–736.

Heckman, James J. and Yona Rubinstein. 2001. "The Importance of Noncognitive Skills: Lessons from the GED Testing Program." *American Economic Review* 91: 2 (May): 145–149.

Heckman, James J., Jora Stixrud, and Sergio Urzua. 2006. "The Effects of Cognitive and Noncognitive Abilities on Labor Market Outcomes and Social Behavior." *Journal of Labor Economics* 24: 3 (July): 411–482.

Herrnstein, Richard J. 1973. *I.Q. in the Meritocracy*. Boston, MA: Little, Brown.

Herrnstein, Richard J. and Charles Murray. 1994. *The Bell Curve: Intelligence and Class Structure in American Life*. New York, NY: Free Press.

Jencks, Christopher. 1979. *Who Gets Ahead? The Determinants of Economic Success in America*. New York, NY: Basic Books.

Jencks, Christopher and Laura Tach. 2006. "Would Equal Opportunity Mean More Mobility?" Pp. 23–58 in *Mobility and Inequality: Frontiers of Research from Sociology and Economics*, edited by Stephen Morgan, David Grusky, and Gary Fields. Stanford, CA: Stanford University Press.

Jensen, Arthur R. 1972. *Genetics and Education*. New York, NY: Harper & Row.

Judge, Timothy A., Chad A. Higgins, Carl J. Thoresen, and Murray R. Barrick. 1999. "The Big Five Personality Traits, General Mental Ability, and Career Success Across the Life Span." *Personnel Psychology* 52: 3 (September): 621–652.

Kohler, Hans-Peter, Jere R. Behrman, and Jason Schnittker. 2011. "Social Science Methods for Twins Data: Integrating Causality, Endowments, and Heritability." *Biodemography and Social Biology* 57: 1: 88–141.

Marioni, Riccardo E., Gail Davies, Caroline Hayward, Dave Liewald, Shona M. Kerr, Archie Campbell, et al. 2014. "Molecular Genetic Contributions to Socioeconomic Status and Intelligence." *Intelligence* 44: May–June: 26–32.

Marks, Gary N. 2014. *Education, Social Background and Cognitive Ability: The Decline of the Social*. New York, NY: Routledge.

Martin, Nicolas W., Sarah E. Medland, Karin J. H. Verweij, S. Hong Lee, Dale R. Nyholt, Pamela A. Madden, et al. 2011. "Educational Attainment: A Genome Wide Association Study in 9538 Australians." *PLoS One* 6: 6 (June): e20128.

Miller, Paul, Charles Mulvey, and Nick Martin. 2006. "The Return to Schooling: Estimates from a Sample of Young Australian Twins." *Labour Economics* 13: 5 (October): 571–587.

Nielsen, François. 2006. "Achievement and Ascription in Educational Attainment: Genetic and Environmental Influences on Adolescent Schooling." *Social Forces* 85: 1 (September): 193–216.

Nielsen, François. 2016. "The Status-Achievement Process: Insights from Genetics." *Frontiers in Sociology* 1: Article 9. doi:10.3389/fsoc.2016.00009

Nielsen, François and J. Micah Roos. 2015. "Genetics of Educational Attainment and the Persistence of Privilege at the Turn of the 21st Century." *Social Forces* 94: 2 (December): 535–561.

Nisbett, Richard E. 2009. *Intelligence and How to Get It: Why Schools and Cultures Count.* New York, NY: Norton.

Okbay, Aysu, Jonathan P. Beauchamp, Mark Alan Fontana, James J. Lee, Tune H. Pers, et al. 2016. "Genome-Wide Association Study Identifies 74 Loci Associated with Educational Attainment." *Nature* 533 (7604): 539–542.

Pareto, Vilfredo. [1909] 1971. *Manual of Political Economy.* Translated by A. S. Schwier, edited by A. S. Schwier and A. N. Page. New York, NY: A. M. Kelley.

Pareto, Vilfredo. [1917–1919, 1935] 1965. *Mind and Society: A Treatise on General Sociology.* Translated by A. Bongiorno and A. Livingston, edited by A. Livingston. New York, NY: Dover.

Petrill, Stephen A. and Bessie Wilkerson. 2000. "Intelligence and Achievement: A Behavioral Genetic Perspective." *Educational Psychology Review* 12: 2 (June): 185–199.

Plomin, R. and I. J. Deary. 2015. "Genetics and Intelligence Differences: Five Special Findings." *Molecular Psychiatry* 20: 98–108. doi:10.1038/mp.2014.105

Plomin, R. and F. M. Spinath. 2004. "Intelligence: Genetics, Genes, and Genomics." *Journal of Personality and Social Psychology* 86: 1 (January): 112–129.

Polderman, Tinca J. C., Beben Benyamin, Christiaan A de Leeuw, Patrick F. Sullivan, Arjen van Bochoven, Peter M. Visscher, and Danielle Posthuma. 2015. "Meta-Analysis of the Heritability of Human Traits Based on Fifty Years of Twin Studies." *Nature Genetics* 47: 7 (July): 702–709.

Purcell, Shaun. 2002. "Variance Components Models for Gene–Environment Interaction in Twin Analysis." *Twin Research* 5: 6: 554–571.

Roos, J. Micah and François Nielsen. 2015. "Genetic and Environmental Influences on Status-Related Outcomes in the Early Lifecourse." American Sociological Association annual meeting, Chicago, IL, August.

Rowe, David C. 1994. *The Limits of Family Influence: Genes, Experience, and Behavior.* New York, NY: Guilford.

Rowe, David C., Kristen C. Jacobson, and Edwin J. C. G. Van den Oord. 1999. "Genetic and Environmental Influences on Vocabulary IQ: Parental Education Level as Moderator." *Child Development* 70: 1151–1162.

Saunders, Peter. 2010. *Social Mobility Myths.* London, UK: Civitas.

Scarr, Sandra. 1992. "Developmental Theories for the 1990s: Development and Individual Differences." *Child Development* 63: 1 (February): 1–19.

Scarr-Salapatek, Sandra. 1971. "Unknowns in the IQ Equation." *Science* 174: 4015 (December 17): 1223–1228.

Shanahan, Michael J. and Scott H. Hofer. 2005. "Social Context in Gene–Environment Interactions: Retrospect and Prospect." *Journal of Gerontology Series B* 60B: Special Issue 1: 65–76.

Solon, Gary. 2008. "Intergenerational Income Mobility." Pp. 481–485 in *Social Stratification: Class, Race, and Gender in Sociological Perspective,* edited by David B. Grusky. Boulder, CO: Westview.

Strenze, Tarmo. 2007. "Intelligence and Socioeconomic Success: A Meta-Analytic Review of Longitudinal Research." *Intelligence* 35: 5 (September–October): 401–426.

Taubman, Paul. 1976. "The Determinants of Earnings: Genetics, Family and Other Environments; A Study of White Male Twins." *American Economic Review* 66: 5 (December): 858–870.

Tucker-Drob, Elliot and Timothy C. Bates. 2016. "Large Cross-National Differences in Gene × Socioeconomic Status Interaction on Intelligence." *Psychological Science* 27: 2 (February): 138–149.

Turkheimer, Eric. 2000. "Three Laws of Behavior Genetics and What They Mean." *Current Directions in Psychological Science* 9: 5 (October): 160–164.

Turkheimer, Eric, Andreana Haley, Mary Waldron, Brian D'Onofrio, and Irving I. Gottesman. 2003. "Socioeconomic Status Modifies Heritability of IQ in Young Children." *Psychological Science* 14: 623–628.

Wright, Sewall. 1920. "The Relative Importance of Heredity and Environment in Determining the Piebald Pattern of Guinea-Pigs." *Proceedings of the National Academy of Science of the USA* 6: 6 (June 1): 320–332.

CHAPTER 16

PEER NETWORKS, PSYCHOBIOLOGY OF STRESS RESPONSE, AND ADOLESCENT DEVELOPMENT

OLGA KORNIENKO AND DOUGLAS A. GRANGER

A consistent focus of psychobiology research has been on discovering how social relationships shape the activity of the stress response system (Eisenberger & Cole, 2012; Hostinar, Sullivan, & Gunnar, 2014) in an effort to advance our understanding of the effects of the social environment on human health and development (Chrousos & Gold, 1992; Weiner, 1992). The hypothalamic–pituitary–adrenal (HPA) axis is one of the major components of the psychobiology of the stress response, and its end product, hormone cortisol, is sensitive to social stressors involving social threat, uncertainty, ambiguity, and novelty (Denson, Spanovich, & Miller, 2009; Dickerson & Zoccola, 2013). Adolescence is a developmental period during which social relationships with peers are increasingly salient (Somerville, 2013) but also represent potent sources of interpersonal stress (Murray-Close, 2013). Developmental research has delineated how youths' experiences in the context of their peer relationships (e.g., aggression and rejection) are related to the physiological stress response system at the level of the individual. However, the depth of our understanding of the impact of the structure and dynamics of adolescents' peer networks on HPA axis activity in the normative context of adolescents' everyday social worlds remains uncharted. This is an important omission because peer social networks are a proximal context for youth development, and they depict a structure of social relationships among group members shaping the way in which developmental resources and social experiences are distributed. Thus, in this chapter, we integrate developmental perspective on peer relations, networks science perspective, and salivary bioscience to describe the need and future directions for research on the relationship between peer social networks and the psychobiology of stress response during adolescence.

The stress response system has evolved and develops in response to the local environment, and it closely monitors, responds to, and adapts to the degree of risk, unpredictability, and resources in that environment, which are critical for successful reproductive efforts and survival (Belsky, 2005; Boyce & Ellis, 2005; Del Giudice, Ellis, & Shirtcliff, 2011; Ellis & Boyce, 2008). During infancy and early childhood, the caregiver relationship provides social regulation of the child's stress response system (for reviews, see Feldman, 2015; Gunnar & Quevedo, 2007). Starting in middle childhood and especially in adolescence, social relationships with peers emerge as potent sources of social stressors, such as rejection, isolation, and aggression, that activate and continue to shape the stress response system (for a review, see Murray-Close, 2013). Interestingly, peer relationships also start to serve a buffering role in facilitating adolescent physiological recovery after experiencing social stressors (for a review, see Gunnar & Hostinar, 2015).

Contemporary developmental research conceptualizes peer relations to be both sources of interpersonal stress and protective against stressors. For instance, being a target of relational aggression (i.e., reputation-damaging comments) is a potent stressor for an adolescent girl, but if the target of such aggression has strong supportive ties with other youth, the detrimental effects of overactivation of physiological stress responses could be attenuated. Whereas decades of developmental research has considered such interactive social dynamics at the level of the individual (for a review, see Parker, Rubin, Erath, Wojslawowicz, & Buskirk, 2006), ethological (Hinde, 1976) and social network (Borgatti, Mehra, Brass, & Labianca, 2009) perspectives suggest that these interactional dynamics need to be considered at the level of the social group, in which supportive interactions do not occur in a vacuum from aggressive ones. We propose that considering the structure and dynamics of social relationships within a peer group could augment our understanding of the role of social ecology because multiple social experiences simultaneously transpire in networks, shaping the structure of social ties at the group level of analysis as well as network position and developmental outcomes, including the activity of the stress response system, considered at the individual level of analysis. Focusing on peer social networks enables a more nuanced description of the proximal social ecology that allows disentangling protective and detrimental influences of social networks on stress physiology. Consistent with modern psychobiology research (Granger et al., 2012), we view the relationships between the stress response system and the proximal context of peer networks as unfolding in a bidirectional manner such that physiological stress responses are likely to be influenced by the network position an individual occupies and vice versa.

Thus, in this chapter, we describe the tools that social network analysis (SNA) provides to capture the individual's position in the structure of peer relationships by considering the patterning of friendships and other types of social relationships (e.g., rejection and bullying). To illustrate the implications that network position has for stress response and development processes, we start by reviewing the psychobiology of the stress response. Next, we briefly note the developmental significance of social networks; introduce key

SNA concepts and levels of analysis from which a system of social ties can be considered; and then discuss implications of various indices of network position for capturing psychosocial processes, including interpersonal stressors and sources of social buffering, to delineate their role for stress physiology and adolescent development.

PSYCHOBIOLOGY OF STRESS RESPONSE: HYPOTHALAMIC–PITUITARY–ADRENAL AXIS

The HPA axis is one of the major components of the psychobiology of the stress response (Chrousos & Gold, 1992). Cortisol, a glucocorticoid, is the primary end product of activity of the HPA axis in humans. Its key functions are to increase blood sugar; suppress the immune system; and aid in the metabolism of fat, protein, and carbohydrates. In general, higher cortisol levels and cortisol reactivity are associated with distress and negative affect, social anxiety, and social evaluative threat (Weiner, 1992). Cortisol levels trend higher when individuals (a) appraise a situation to be challenging, uncertain, and intense; and (b) experience rumination and social status threat (Denson et al., 2009; Dickerson, 2008; Dickerson & Kemeny, 2004). Short-term elevation of cortisol is considered to be adaptive in novel or dynamic social environments (Sapolsky, Romero, & Munck, 2000), whereas prolonged activation of this component of the stress response has potential to translate into cumulative wear and tear on many biological systems, with downstream consequences for health (Danese & McEwen, 2012; McEwen & Gianaros, 2010; Miller, Chen, & Cole, 2009).

The evolutionary and developmental significance of the stress response system is that it closely tracks risk and unpredictability in the local ecology, and this is critical for successful survival and reproductive effort (Del Giudice et al., 2011). Developmental plasticity in the activity of the stress response system recalibrates its activation thresholds, reactivity, recovery, and regulation in response to the local early childhood environment (Del Giudice et al., 2011; Weiner, 1992). Significant changes in the child's ecology appear to recalibrate the stress response system. For instance, institutionalized Romanian children, who were initially raised in conditions of severe deprivation and neglect, demonstrated improvement in the regulation of physiological stress response upon being placed in high-quality foster care systems; however, these improvements only occurred for those who were removed from orphanages before 2 years of age (MacLaughlin et al., 2015). Adolescence appears to be another sensitive period during which recalibration of the stress response system due to puberty occurs (for reviews, see, Peper & Dahl, 2013; Romero, 2010; Susman & Dorn, 2009) and could lead to detrimental consequences for mental and physical health (for reviews, see Lupien, McEwen, Gunnar, & Heim, 2009; Rudolph, 2014). Social stressors emanating from peer relationships are prominently featured in the contemporary models of developmental psychopathology (Rudolph, Landsford, & Rodkin, 2016).

Adolescent Peer Relationships and Social Stress

Adolescents substantially increase the time they spend with peers (Larson, 2001). Research shows that peer rejection influences adolescents' self-evaluations (O'Brien & Bierman, 1988), underscoring the heightened motivational and affective salience of peer relationships during this developmental period (Crone & Dahl, 2012). Adolescents' peer affiliations, although ubiquitous and enjoyable, can be intense in their affective tone, transient, and require navigation of multidimensional and multilevel peer hierarchies (Brown & Larson, 2009). Peer groups can be challenging social landscapes for youth due to their social inexperience, the instability of relationships, chronic exposure to socio-evaluative threats, and hypervigilance of those threats (Somerville, 2013). Many of the experiential components of adolescents' social worlds are associated with stress and have been identified as triggers activating the psychobiology of the stress response (Del Giudice et al., 2011; Denson et al., 2009; Dickerson & Kemeny, 2004).

Links between stressful social experiences and cortisol in adolescence, in particular, have attracted empirical attention (for a review, see Murray-Close, 2013). Patterns of cortisol secretion are associated with a number of adverse social experiences, including victimization (Kliewer, 2006; Rudolph, Troop-Gordon, & Granger, 2010), social rejection and exclusion (Stroud et al., 2009), negative co-rumination (Byrd-Craven, Granger, & Auer, 2011), and inappropriate disclosures about others (Afifi, Granger, Denes, Joseph, & Aldeis, 2011). Another aspect of social group living that has been consistently related to elevated activity of the HPA axis among nonhuman primates is status in a dominance hierarchy (Sapolsky, 2005). Although low dominance status could be a source of stress, this association tends to be moderated by other characteristics of the social organization of a group, including stability of ranks, the presence of supportive relationships, and opportunities to avoid high-ranking individuals (Sapolsky, 2005). Experiences of social rejection in children (Gunnar, Sebanc, Tout, Donzella, & van Dulmen, 2003; Tarullo, Mliner, & Gunnar, 2011) and adolescents (Adam, 2006; Blackhart, Eckel, & Tice, 2007) have also been associated with elevated physiological stress responses. Social support, engagement, and higher quality of social relationships appear to be protective by attenuating activation of the stress response system and leading to salubrious effects (Gunnar & Hostinar, 2015; Hostinar et al., 2014).

Peer Relationships as Social Networks

Developmental scholars have long viewed social groups to which the developing individual belongs as providing a context for and constraints on development (Cairns, Xie, & Leung, 1998). Social ties within a group are not formed and dissolved randomly;

human behavior in a social system is driven by fundamental motivations to belong and affiliate (Baumeister & Leary, 1995) and to gain and maintain social status (Hawley, 1999). Social networks are relevant for individuals' development because, on the one hand, the pattern of network ties provides access to developmentally salient provisions such as social attention and admiration, information, and social support (Berkman, Glass, Brissette, & Seeman, 2000; Borgatti et al., 2009). These social provisions have been linked to social buffering or attenuation of activity of the physiological stress system (Gunnar & Hostinar, 2015). On the other hand, the landscape of networked social relationships within a bounded group (e.g., classroom or school) in which adolescents spend a lot of time provides numerous opportunities for potent interpersonal stressors of social evaluation, social rejection, ambiguity, uncertainty, and uncontrollability (Dickerson & Zoccola, 2013).

Network science provides conceptual and analytical (SNA) tools to link the social group structure and dynamics to the behavior of its constituent members (Pinter-Wollman et al., 2014). Social network *structure* is an emergent property of a social organization that is represented by enduring patterns of social *relationships*, which are, in turn, composed of a series of social *interactions* (Hinde, 1976). Multiple types of relationships exist in social networks across the animal kingdom, including friendships and enduring affiliative relationships (Brent, Semple, Dubuc, Heistermann, & MacLarnon, 2011); dominance relations in nonhuman primates (Sapolsky, 2005); and rejection, exclusion, victimization, or conflict relationships in human social systems (DeWall, 2013). Importantly, examining social networks is necessary for understanding the associations between group dynamics and an individual's functioning because psychosocial processes are associated with a position that individual occupies within a network, including social support provision, social status acquisition and maintenance, and strain and conflict, which in turn impact physiological stress processes (Berkman et al., 2000; Crosier, Webster, & Dillon, 2012; Kornienko, Clemans, Out, & Granger, 2013). In general, much less is known about the impact of the structure and dynamics of children's and adolescents' peer networks on the stress response system; nonetheless, social relationships organized into networks are viewed as influencing the activity of the stress response system (Sapolsky, 2005), and physiological stress responses are viewed as shaping the nature and quality of social connections of an individual.

DESCRIBING SOCIAL NETWORK POSITION

SNA describes network structures and dynamics that contribute to understanding the relationship between biological and behavioral systems within a specific social context (for reviews, see, O'Malley & Mardsen, 2008; Robins, 2013; Snijders, 2011). Measures of network position can be derived from peer nominations collected from both individuals (*egos* in SNA terminology) and their peers (*alters*) within a specified group (e.g., classroom, school, or organization). These data are known as complete or sociocenteric data (Wasserman & Faust, 1994; note that "complete" in this context refers to the multi-informant assessment of network ties and not to sample participation rates). Complete network data provide a nuanced description of the social structure compared to ego-centered, or personal, network data, which have dominated most of the research linking social networks to activity of biological systems (Pressman et al., 2005; Segerstrom, 2007). Complete network data provide two perspectives on the social structure in which the ego is embedded by focusing on *local* and *global networks* as the levels of analysis. Specifically, a local network is constructed from a perspective of an ego and all alters to whom ego is directly connected, and a global network is obtained from a system-level perspective and includes direct and indirect social ties (Valente, 2010). Another advantage of the complete networks approach is that it allows the consideration of directionality of relationships within a social system. Considering directed or asymmetrical relationships enables the examination of social networks from the perspective of a focal individual and from the perspective of his or her friends. Research shows that such friendship tie asymmetries are uniquely associated with health outcomes. For example, in a study using complete friendship networks to examine longitudinal effects of depression on adolescent friendship selection, depressive symptoms predicted fewer friendship nominations that an adolescent sent out (i.e., withdrawal from peers) but not fewer nominations that he or she received from peers (i.e., rejection by peers) or preference to affiliate with others who had similar levels of depressive symptoms (i.e., homophily) (Schaefer, Kornienko, & Fox, 2011). Using complete friendships network data allowed examination of several mechanisms linking depression to social ties, which would not be possible if only the ego-centered or personal networks approach was used.

The local, or ego-centered, network and a position that an individual occupies in it capture the most proximal and direct system of social relationships for that individual. *Degree* is a fundamental measure of network structure. *Indegree* describes incoming friendship nominations (i.e., nominations received), and it measures one's popularity or prestige among friends (Valente, 2010; Wasserman & Faust, 1994). *Outdegree* describes outgoing friendship nominations (i.e., nominations sent out), and it is a measure of social activity or gregariousness in a friendship network (Wasserman & Faust, 1994). Another fundamental characteristic of one's position in a network is the degree of interconnectedness or cohesion among the friends of the focal individual, which is described by network *density* (Valente, 2010). Thus, network density is a structural measure of social cohesion among one's friends. More densely connected networks are likely to be more efficient in delivering social support and resources to the focal individual under stress and, therefore, could be expected to have stress-buffering effects (Walker, Wasserman, & Wellman, 1993). Alternatively, highly interconnected networks could increase interpersonal stress if it is gossip or other relationally aggressive behaviors that are being transmitted among peers because dense structures would facilitate the faster spread of the reputation-damaging information.

Another level of analysis applicable to an individual's position in a complete network structure involves indices of position in a global network. An individual's *network centrality* is measured by outgoing ties and has implications for access to resources, which is likely to serve a buffering effect against social threat and stress. *Closeness centrality* describes how close each particular individual is to all other individuals in a network (Wasserman & Faust, 1994). *Bonacich centrality* is defined as centrality of a focal individual that is weighted by the centrality of his or her friends, capturing the idea that being connected to others who are highly connected increases one's centrality in a network (Wasserman & Faust, 1994). Individuals who occupy a central position in a network have a unique opportunity to transmit information and attitudes, which may have implications for stress coping processes and support provision processes among peers. Another index is *betweenness centrality*, which measures how often the ego lies on the shortest path between all possible pairs of people in a network (Wasserman & Faust, 1994). This index of network position captures the extent to which an individual's position in a network enables him or her to connect otherwise disconnected network members. Individuals who occupy positions of high betweenness centrality are thought of as brokers who are integral to connecting and integrating otherwise disconnected parts of the networks (Burt, Kilduff, & Tasselli, 2013). Although being a broker may be an advantageous position, brokerage may pose challenges to the individual's psychological well-being because of the tension arising from connecting disparate clusters. Indeed, adolescent girls with high levels of betweenness centrality reported increased social stress and decreased life satisfaction (Carboni & Gilman, 2012). An individual's *network prestige* is a weighted measure of incoming ties; thus, this measure has implications for how visible and prominent a person is in a network. The proximity prestige index (De Nooy, Mrvar, & Batagelj, 2005) quantifies the status of an individual by adding the number of direct and indirect friendship nominations that an individual receives, which is then weighted by (a) how close these friends are (direct incoming ties have greater weight than indirect ones) and (b) how popular/prestigious those friends are, as captured by the number of the incoming ties they receive themselves. In summary, SNA provides numerous indices for quantifying social network positions. Next, we describe how these indices of social network position, which represent the psychosocial processes relevant to interpersonal stress generation and social buffering effects, could be associated with physiological stress responses.

PEER NETWORKS AS SOURCES OF SOCIAL STRESS

As psychosocial processes related to status, rejection, and isolation transpire in social groups, they leave traces on the structure of social ties. Thus, the patterning of connections represents structural measures of social status, rejection, and isolation. Another important insight into social dynamics provided by the network perspective involves recognition of multiplexity of social ties underscoring that both positive (i.e., helpful and supportive) and negative (i.e., strained and conflicted) interpersonal exchanges occur among group members, leading to the emergence of positive and negative social ties (for a review, see Labianca & Brass, 2006). All of these psychosocial processes have been connected to physiological stress responses at the level of the individual, and here we describe how these research domains could be advanced using insights from social network theory and analytical applications.

Social Status

Social status encapsulates salient features of the social context and describes visibility and prominence of an individual within a social system (Pellegrini, Roseth, Van Ryzin, & Solberg, 2011). Social status provides benefits and poses costs to an individual. On the one hand, status provides opportunities for access to important psychosocial resources such as positive attention and regard (Hawley, 1999), as well as social capital, support, and opportunities for meaningful engagement (Berkman et al., 2000). These provisions of social status are associated with salubrious and stress-buffering properties (Berkman et al., 2000). On the other hand, social status may come at a cost when it confers psychosocial stress to individuals at the top of a social hierarchy. That is, adolescents, particularly girls, of high status are more likely to exclude others and use relational aggression toward their peers (Cillessen & Mayeux, 2004), who, in turn, consider these popular adolescents to be mean and snobby and resent them (Closson, 2008).

Biobehavioral research with nonhuman primates has shown that social status is related to stress response and the activity of the HPA axis (Sapolsky, 2005). Moreover, the nature of these associations is moderated by characteristics of individuals and the social structure in which they are embedded. Sapolsky suggests that, on the one hand, high-status individuals may experience higher stress levels if the nature of social interactions in the system is competitive and challenging, with low availability of social support and coping. In other words, high status can pose psychosocial stress because being at the top of the group hierarchy may require the capacity to detect and respond to potential threats to one's standing among conspecifics. Contemporary work on stress response and activation of the HPA axis in humans parallels this view and posits that rising cortisol for high-status individuals is instrumental in mobilization of coping resources to adapt to one's local environment and when individuals are increasingly sensitive to social cues and feedback (Del Giudice et al., 2011). Consequently, high-status positions that expose individuals to a high degree of psychosocial stress and socio-evaluative threat are expected to be positively associated with cortisol levels (Dickerson & Kemeny, 2004). On the other hand, Sapolsky proposes that high-status individuals may be less stressed when the group interactions are cooperative and supportive. Indeed, recent work with nonhuman primates supports the stress-buffering role of social status by demonstrating that high-status individuals in an affiliation network are buffered against prolonged HPA axis activation because they derive social capital support and also support from their social relationships (Brent et al., 2011). Thus, occupying positions of high status is expected to be inversely associated with cortisol levels under conditions in which social status confers greater access to social support and engagement.

SNA provides useful methods for describing one's social status focusing on an individual's social standing because (a) they describe an individual's position within a system of social relationships by focusing on direct and indirect (i.e., a friend of a friend) ties, and (b) they consider the directionality of these ties. Because SNA methods use both direct and indirect ties, they yield a nuanced view of an individual's position in a network. In this view, social status emerges from the pattern of dyadic ties that, in aggregate, connect all individuals within a specified ecology. Importantly, this patterning of ties is not random; rather, it is driven by individuals' preferences to affiliate with those of higher status (Gould, 2002; Rivera, Soderstrom, & Uzzi, 2010). These local preferences accumulate and jointly make central individuals even more central. Such preferences create status differentials and patterns of connectivity that are not easily detectable with individual-level data. Furthermore, from the SNA perspective, the directionality of ties has a particular meaning, such that ties sent out by an individual (i.e., outgoing ties) reflect an individual's activity and gregariousness within a network, whereas incoming ties capture the peer network's perspective on the focal individual and thus provide a more objective view (i.e., as a function of ties) of network status (Borgatti et al., 2009; Valente, 2010; Walker et al., 1993).

Occupying a position of high closeness centrality implies that an individual is linked via direct and indirect outgoing ties to many others in the network through a relatively small number of intermediate relations. These individuals benefit from greater connections with other peers (i.e., they require relatively few intermediate actors to reach another network member) and thus have more efficient access to distant members of a network (O'Malley & Mardsen, 2008). High social centrality may buffer individuals against adverse effects of stress because they have higher perceived social capital and support (e.g., if I think of myself as your friend, I am more likely to approach you for help or other resources; Berkman et al., 2000; Hostinar et al., 2014). It is expected that network centrality could be inversely associated with cortisol levels.

Considering a structural measure of status derived from incoming ties, individuals with high scores on network prestige may also have access to much social capital within the network, but network prestige is perceived by other network members, not necessarily by the individual him- or herself. Because many other people think of the individual as their friend, they may be more likely to approach that individual to ask for resources, increasing that individual's social stress. In addition, this network position is associated with demands and challenges related to being highly visible in an extensive network of friends, such as jealousy and negative stereotypes from less prestigious peers (Closson, 2008). Thus, whereas network centrality may be associated with reduced psychosocial stress, high levels of network prestige—especially if not accompanied by accordingly high centrality—may actually be associated with higher psychosocial stress. For prestigious youth, cortisol activity may serve an adaptive function, increasing awareness to social threat and helping individuals cope with psychosocial challenges associated with this network position (Dickerson, 2008). Thus, occupying positions of higher status based on incoming ties is hypothesized to be positively related to cortisol levels.

Social Rejection

Being rejected from a social group is one of the most potent social stressors because human beings have a fundamental need to belong to social groups (Baumeister & Leary, 1995). Although individual differences exist in the strength of belongingness needs, this fundamental desire to maintain positive relationships with a group is a powerful motivator for our social activity and relationships that we create. Research shows that children (Gunnar et al., 2003; Peters, Riksen-Walraven, Cillessen, & Weerth, 2011; Tarullo et al., 2011) and adolescents (Adam, 2006; Blackhart et al., 2007) who are rejected by their peers exhibit elevated physiological stress responses. Cortisol has been posited to be one of the components of the social self-preservation system, which monitors "the potential for a loss of social acceptance, esteem, and status" (Dickerson & Zoccola, 2013, p. 143). This model has received empirical support in experimental settings simulating intense experiences of social rejection, exclusion, and evaluation (Dickerson, 2008; Dickerson & Kemeny, 2004). Given that the landscape of networked social ties in a classroom or school in which adolescents spend a substantial amount of time (Larson, 2001) provides numerous opportunities for operation of these potent social stressors of rejection and evaluation, which are highly salient for adolescents (Somerville, 2013), SNA methods could be useful for examining the dynamics associated with the formation of rejected or antipathy networks among youth (Berger & Dijkstra, 2013; Rambaran, Dijkstra, Munniksma, & Cillessen, 2015). Social networks composed of rejection or dislike ties represent negative social relations, and a more prominent network position within such a social setting is expected to be positively related to the physiological stress response system. In addition, because balance theory suggests positive and negative types of relationships are inversely related (Heider, 1958), individuals who receive a small number of friendship ties would be considered rejected within a group of friends because incoming ties provide a measure of a peer group's perspective on their ties with the focal youth. Having a low number of incoming friendship ties is expected to be positively associated with activation of the HPA axis.

Social Isolation

Another potent stressor of social living is social isolation, also known as feelings of *loneliness*. Evolutionary perspective suggests that loneliness signals to an individual that he or she needs to seek and develop satisfactory social connections because in ancestral landscapes being isolated from one's group increased the risk of death from others and predators (Cacioppo, Capitanio, & Cacioppo, 2014). Being isolated from the social group is a major stressor, and neuroendocrine and physiological systems related to self-preservation become amplified. Indeed, research has documented associations between loneliness and heightened activity of the HPA axis (Adam, Hawkley, Kudielka, & Cacioppo, 2006; Doane & Adam, 2010; Pressman et al., 2005; Steptoe, Owen, Kunz-Ebrecht, & Brydon, 2004). Loneliness is usually measured by self-report measures, but indices of social network position could also be used to quantify youth who are underintegrated in the context of their friendship or affiliation ties (Cacioppo, Fowler, & Christakis, 2009). Specifically, sending a small number of friendship ties would be reflective of being socially isolated within a group of friends because outgoing ties provide a measure of a focal individual's social activity. Because loneliness is also thought of as perceived social isolation and emotional state signaling a suboptimal state of one's social connections (Hawkley & Cacioppo, 2010), it is likely that lonely individuals would also report lower quality social ties. Thus, considering social tie characteristics (e.g., closeness and satisfaction) would also augment our understanding of the social world of lonely individuals and its impact for the stress response system. In summary, it is expected that individuals with lower numbers and quality of outgoing friendship ties will exhibit increased cortisol levels.

The Negative Side of Peer Networks: Bullying and Victimization

Whereas the vast majority of research has focused on networks of positive relationships, such as friendships and affiliations, there is also a negative side to social relationships in a peer group. Developmental research has shown that forms of dominance striving such as bullying and victimization are prevalent patterns of social interaction during adolescence with significant consequences for health and well-being (Hawley, 2015; Hong & Espelage, 2012). Indeed, empirical evidence suggests that negativity and aversive interactions within close relationships are significant stressors (Rook, 2001) and have detrimental health effects (Kiecolt-Glaser & Newton, 2001). At the individual level of analysis, previous research has shown that being victimized and bullied is associated with increased activation of the HPA axis (Calhoun et al., 2014; Carney, Hazler, Oh, Hibel, & Granger, 2010; Rudolph et al., 2010; Vaillancourt et al., 2008). However, we know surprisingly little about the consequences of being embedded in bullying–victimization networks for activation of stress responses during adolescence, despite the fact that these are fundamentally social experiences (Espelage & Holt, 2001). Emerging research has begun to document how bullying and friendship networks change over time and reciprocally influence one another (Huitsing et al., 2012; Huitsing, Snijders van Duijn, & Veenstra, 2014), with a potential for social buffering. This research could be augmented by incorporating salivary measurement of cortisol to capture the activity of the HPA axis when youth are embedded in the naturalistic ecology of their peer networks. It is expected that receiving a higher number of incoming ties in a network of bullying relations will be positively related to cortisol levels.

Peer Networks as Sources
of Social Buffering

Decades of research has documented that the presence and nature of social relationships has an impact on physical health (Cohen, 2004; Holt-Lunstad, Smith, & Layton, 2010; House, Landis, & Umberson, 1988). This research has shown that social networks play a protective role against deleterious effects of environmental stressors and promote effective coping (Berkman et al., 2000; House et al., 1988). The *social buffering hypothesis* posits that social support derived from one's social relationships serves protective effects by attenuating the physiological stress response (Carter, 1998; Gunnar & Hostinar, 2015; Hostinar et al., 2014). This hypothesis has received consistent support within the context of caregiver–offspring relationships during early childhood (for reviews, see Feldman, 2015; Gunnar & Quevedo, 2007). Interestingly, emerging research suggests that parental support is no longer effective in promoting recovery of the HPA axis after a public speaking task during adolescence, whereas friend support has a protective effect on physiological stress responses during adolescence (Hostinar, Johnson, & Gunnar, 2015). Furthermore, the presence of a friend appears to have dampening effects on the reactivity of the HPA axis to negative social experiences assessed in naturalistic ecology (Adams, Santo, & Bukowski, 2011) and the laboratory (Calhoun et al., 2014). Finally, friends were found to partially reduce the physiological stress associated with social exclusion during middle childhood (Peters et al., 2011).

As protective effects of friends have been documented at the individual level of analysis, we suggest that this work could be augmented by considering indices of position in a social network that are consequential for social integration, engagement, and social support (Berkman et al., 2000). Because patterns of network ties are instrumental in channeling the flow of social support in the networks, certain network positions have been identified to be more conducive to support provision (Walker et al., 1993). Specifically, being embedded in social networks characterized by higher levels of density, or degree of interconnectedness, could be associated with an attenuated stress reactivity profile because such network structure optimizes the delivery of supportive resources. Furthermore, having a large number of outgoing ties and occupying positions of high network centrality could also buffer against stressors within naturalistic ecologies of peer groups because such positions provide individuals with access to social capital that promotes effective coping processes (Brent et al., 2011). It is expected that occupying such network positions will be associated with decreased cortisol levels.

Social Networks and Cortisol

Although research in behavioral endocrinology has revealed that the expression of hormone–behavior associations is socially regulated, this research has paid little attention to their role in social networks (with the exception of research on nonhuman primate dominance hierarchies; Sapolsky, 2005). Through a combination of SNA and salivary bioscience methods, investigators began exploring how activity of neuroendocrine systems related to stress is associated with social networks. Emerging studies of nonhuman and human primates suggest that hormones are associated with social network structure. Specifically, high-ranking free-ranging female macaques were shown to have lower glucocorticoid levels when their association networks were smaller and more focused, as indexed by a lower number of outgoing connections (Brent et al., 2011). Among female nursing students (Kornienko et al., 2013; Kornienko, Clemans, Out, & Granger, 2014) and male rugby players (Ponzi, Zilioli, Mehta, Maslov, & Watson, 2016), salivary cortisol levels were also inversely associated with gregariousness levels; these findings are in line with prior research documenting the impact of social isolation and loneliness on HPA axis activity.

Building on this work, another investigation explored the role of cortisol levels in predicting friendship tie maintenance and creation over time in a social network of late adolescent members of a collegiate marching band (Kornienko, Schaefer, Weren, Hill, & Granger, 2016). The findings revealed that over time, individuals with lower cortisol levels were more likely to maintain friendships, and those with higher cortisol levels were more likely to create new ties. To fully understand the role of hormones in network selection dynamics requires considering the patterns of association in conjunction with the effects relating hormone levels to receiving friendship nominations and befriending others who are similar. The results of Kornienko et al. (2016) indicated that the major predictor of friend selection was the hormone level of the individual sending the friendship tie (Figure 16.1).

Kornienko and colleagues (2016) found that friendships were most durable when egos with the lowest levels of cortisol befriended others of similarly low cortisol levels, suggesting that there is a homophily, or a preference for a similar other, at the low levels of cortisol (Figure 16.1a). New friendships were more likely when egos with higher cortisol levels befriended alters with low cortisol (Figure 16.1b), suggesting that there is heterophily, or a preference for a different other, on cortisol levels among new friends. This pattern underscores that homophily at the lowest levels of cortisol was associated with increased likelihood of friendship maintenance, and heterophily on cortisol was associated with increased likelihood of new friendship creation. These observations extend the existing evidence on synchronization or attunement on cortisol levels in social relationships (Granger et al., 1998; Waters et al., 2014). These findings suggest that activity of the HPA axis, which is responsive to social stress and evaluation within a context of social relationships, may be a signal for a change in lower quality friendships. Taken together, this research expands models of environmental sensitivity and biobehavioral reactivity by documenting that individual differences in the activity of these biological systems are not only reactive to the social environment but also have the potential to influence the construction and composition of one's social ecology.

CONCLUSION

The nature and quality of social relationships have both protective and detrimental roles in adolescent development. Accumulating evidence suggests that these effects may be

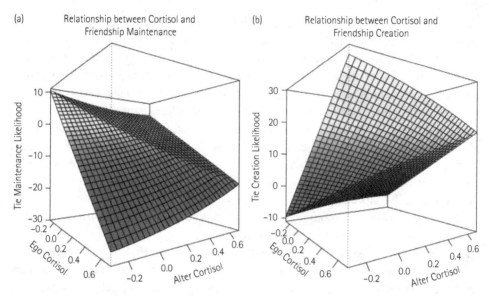

FIGURE 16.1 Likelihood of friendship maintenance and creation by ego and alter hormone levels. To provide an integrative representation of how cortisol contributes to network selection, parameter estimates were used to calculate the predicted likelihood of tie creation and maintenance conditioned on ego's and alter's hormone levels. The three-dimensional plots represent these likelihoods of ties: ego's hormone levels on the y-axis, alter's hormone levels on the x-axis, and the z-axis represents the likelihood of friendship maintenance or creation. The color palette (dark to light) on the plane of z-axis represents the range of values for likelihood of ties such that lighter color depicts increased likelihood of ties and darker color depicts decreased likelihood of ties. Individuals are more likely to maintain their friendship ties when they have lower levels of cortisol (a), and they are more likely to create ties when they have higher levels of cortisol (b).

Source: Reprinted from *Hormones and Behavior*, Volume 80, Olga Kornienko, David R. Schaefer, Serena Weren, Gary W. Hill, Douglas A. Granger, Cortisol and testosterone associations with social network dynamics, pp. 92–102, Copyright 2016, with permission from Elsevier.

moderated by the influence of the social context on the HPA axis and related environmentally sensitive biological systems. Considerable theoretical interest and research have focused on the concept of individual differences in biological sensitivity to context (Boyce & Ellis, 2005; Ellis & Boyce, 2008) and differential susceptibility to context (Belsky, 2005; Belsky & Pluess, 2009). We posited that because peer relationships represent an increasingly salient context for youth and they are actively creating their peer networks, our understanding of the impact that the social world has on youth development and stress physiology is limited without considering how these processes transpire within and are mediated by the structure and dynamics of peer networks. Drawing on existing developmental research, we identified how several psychosocial processes representing potent social stressors (i.e., social status, rejection, isolation, bullying, and victimization) could be examined via an integration of developmental, social network analysis, and salivary bioscience methods. Because starting in adolescence peer relationships also serve a protective or buffering role in facilitating physiological recovery after experiencing social stressors (Gunnar & Hostinar, 2015), we also outlined how future research could employ social network approaches to examine social buffering in the context of peer networks. We described how SNA approaches inform future research efforts directed at disentangling the complex and bidirectional associations between indices of social network position and physiological stress responses to elucidate the role of social ecology for adolescent development and adaptation.

DISCLAIMER

In the interest of full disclosure, Douglas A. Granger is founder and Chief Scientific and Strategy Advisor at Salimetrics LLC, and this relationship is managed by the policies of the committees on conflict of interest at Johns Hopkins University School of Medicine and Office of Research Integrity and Adherence at Arizona State University. Granger and the Institute for Interdisciplinary Salivary Bioscience Research are in the process of transitioning to University of California, Irvine, where similar oversight will be established. Olga Kornienko has no information to disclose.

REFERENCES

Adam, E. K. (2006). Transactions among adolescent trait and state emotion and diurnal and momentary cortisol activity in naturalistic settings. *Psychoneuroendocrinology*, *31*, 664–679. doi:10.1016/j.psyneuen.2006.01.010

Adam, E. K., Hawkley, L. C., Kudielka, B. M., & Cacioppo, J. T. (2006). Day-to-day dynamics of experience–cortisol associations in a population-based sample of older adults. *Proceedings of the National Academy of Sciences of the USA*, *103*, 17058–17063.

Adams, R. E., Santo, J. B., & Bukowski, W. M. (2011). The presence of a best friend buffers the effects of negative experiences. *Developmental Psychology*, *47*, 1786–1791. doi:10.1080/03637751.2011.589460

Afifi, T. D., Granger, D. A., Denes, A., Joseph, A., & Aldeis, D. (2011). Parents' communication skills and adolescents' salivary α-amylase and cortisol response patterns. *Communication Monographs*, *78*, 273–295.

Baumeister, R. F., & Leary, M. R. (1995). The need to belong: Desire for interpersonal attachments as a fundamental human motivation. *Psychological Bulletin*, *117*, 497–529. http://dx.doi.org/10.1037/0033-2909.117.3.497

Belsky, J. (2005). Differential susceptibility to rearing influences: An evolutionary hypothesis and some evidence. In B. Ellis & D. Bjorklund (Eds.), *Origins of the social mind: Evolutionary psychology and child development* (pp. 139–163). New York, NY: Guildford.

Belsky, J., & Pluess, M. (2009). Beyond diathesis stress: Differential susceptibility to environmental influences. *Psychological Bulletin*, *135*, 885–908. http://dx.doi.org/10.1037/a0017376

Berger, C., & Dijkstra, J. K. (2013). Competition, envy, or snobbism? How popularity and friendships shape antipathy networks of adolescents. *Journal of Research on Adolescence*, *23*, 586–595. doi:10.1111/jora.12048

Berkman, L. F., Glass, T., Brissette, I., & Seeman, T. E. (2000). From social integration to health: Durkheim in the new millennium. *Social Science & Medicine, 51*, 843–857.

Blackhart, G. C., Eckel, L. A., & Tice, D. M. (2007). Salivary cortisol in response to acute social rejection and acceptance by peers. *Biological Psychology, 75*, 267–276. doi:10.1016/j.biopsycho.2007.03.005

Borgatti, S. P., Mehra, A., Brass, D. J., & Labianca, G. (2009). Network analysis in the social sciences. *Science, 323*, 892–895. doi:10.1126/science.1165821

Boyce, W. T., & Ellis, B. J. (2005). Biological sensitivity to context: I. An evolutionary-developmental theory of the origins and functions of stress reactivity. *Development & Psychopathology, 17*, 271–301. doi:10.1017/S0954579405050145

Brent, L. J. N., Semple, S., Dubuc, C., Heistermann, M., & MacLarnon, A. (2011). Social capital and physiological stress levels in free-ranging adult female rhesus macaques. *Physiology & Behavior, 102*, 76–83. doi:10.1016/j.physbeh.2010.09.022

Brown, B. B., & Larson, J. (2009). Peer relationships in adolescence. In R. M. Lerner & L. D. Steinberg (Eds.), *Handbook of adolescent psychology* (3rd ed., pp. 74–103). Hoboken, NJ: Wiley.

Burt, R. S., Kilduff, M., & Tasselli, S. (2013). Social network analysis: Foundations and frontiers on advantage. *Annual Review of Psychology, 64*, 527–547. doi:10.1146/annurev-psych-113011-143828

Byrd-Craven, J., Granger, D. A., & Auer, B. J. (2011). Stress reactivity to co-rumination in young women's friendships: Cortisol, alpha-amylase, and negative affect focus. *Journal of Social and Personal Relationships, 28*, 469–487. doi:10.1177/0265407510382319

Cacioppo, J. T., Fowler, J. H., & Christakis, N. A. (2009). Alone in the crowd: The structure and spread of loneliness in a large social network. *Journal of Personality and Social Psychology, 97*, 977–991. http://dx.doi.org/10.1037/a0016076

Cacioppo, S., Capitanio, J. P., & Cacioppo, J. T. (2014). Toward a neurology of loneliness. *Psychological Bulletin, 140*, 1464–1504. http://dx.doi.org/10.1037/a0037618

Cairns, R., Xie, H., & Leung, M. C. (1998). The popularity of friendship and the neglect of social networks: Toward a new balance. *New Directions for Child and Adolescent Development, 109*, 25–54. doi:10.1002/cd.23219988104

Calhoun, C. D., Helms, S. W., Heilbron, N., Rudolph, K. D., Hastings, P. D., & Prinstein, M. J. (2014). Relational victimization, friendship, and adolescents' hypothalamic–pituitary–adrenal axis responses to an in vivo social stressor. *Development and Psychopathology, 26*, 605–618. http://dx.doi.org/10.1017/S0954579414000261

Carboni, I., & Gilman, R. (2012). Brokers at risk: Gender differences in the effects of structural position on social stress and life satisfaction. *Group Dynamics: Theory, Research, and Practice, 16*, 218–230. doi:10.1037/a0028753

Carney, J. V., Hazler, R. J., Oh, I., Hibel, L. C., & Granger, D. A. (2010). The relations between bullying exposures in middle childhood, anxiety, and adrenocortical activity. *Journal of School Violence, 9*, 194–211. doi:10.1080/15388220903479602.

Carter, C. S. (1998). Neuroendocrine perspective on social attachment and love. *Psychoneuroendocrinology, 23*, 779–818.

Chrousos, G. P., & Gold, P. W. (1992). The concepts of stress and stress system disorders: Overview of physical and behavioral homeostasis. *Journal of American Medical Association, 267*, 1244–1252. doi:10.1001/jama.1992.03480090092034

Cillessen, A. H. N., & Mayeux, L. (2004). From censure to reinforcement: Developmental changes in the association between aggression and social status. *Child Development, 75*, 147–163. doi:10.1111/j.1467-8624.2004.00660.x

Closson, L. M. (2008). Status and gender differences in early adolescents' descriptions of popularity. *Social Development, 18*, 412–426. doi:10.1111/j.1467-9507.2008.00459.x

Cohen, S. (2004). Social relationships and health. *American Psychologist, 59*, 676–684. doi:10.1037/0003-066X.59.8.676

Crone, E. A., & Dahl, R. E. (2012). Understanding adolescence as a period of social-affective engagement and goal flexibility. *Nature Reviews Neuroscience, 13*, 636–650. doi:10.1038/nrn3313

Crosier, B. S., Webster, G. D., & Dillon, H. M. (2012). Wired to connect: Evolutionary psychology and social networks. *Review of General Psychology, 16*, 230–239. doi:10.1037/a0027919

Danese, A., & McEwen, B. S. (2012). Adverse childhood experiences, allostasis, allostatic load, and age-related disease. *Physiology & Behavior, 106*, 29–39. doi:10.1016/j.physbeh.2011.08.019

de Nooy, W., Mrvar, A., & Batagelj, V. (2005). *Exploratory social network analysis with Pajek.* New York, NY: Cambridge University Press.

Del Giudice, M., Ellis, B. J., & Shirtcliff, E. A. (2011). The adaptive calibration model of stress responsivity. *Neuroscience & Biobehavioral Reviews, 35*, 1562–1592. doi:10.1016/j.neubiorev.2010.11.007

Denson, T. F., Spanovich, M., & Miller, N. (2009). Cognitive appraisals and emotions predict cortisol and immune responses: A meta-analysis of acute laboratory social stressors and emotion inductions. *Psychological Bulletin, 135*, 823–853. doi:10.1037/a0016909

DeWall, C. N. (Ed.). (2013). *The Oxford handbook of social exclusion.* New York, NY: Oxford University Press. doi:10.1093/oxfordhb/9780195398700.001.0001

Dickerson, S. S. (2008). Emotional and physiological responses to social-evaluative threat. *Social and Personality Psychology Compass, 2/3*, 1362–1378. doi:10.1111/j.1751-9004.2008.00095.x

Dickerson, S. S., & Kemeny, M. E. (2004). Acute stressors and cortisol responses: A theoretical integration and synthesis of laboratory research. *Psychological Bulletin, 130*, 355–391. doi:10.1037/0033-2909.130.3.355

Dickerson, S. S., & Zoccola, P. M. (2013). Cortisol responses to social exclusion. In C. N. DeWall (Ed.), *Oxford handbook of social exclusion* (pp. 143–151). New York, NY: Oxford University Press.

Doane, L. D., & Adam, E. K. (2010). Loneliness and cortisol: Momentary, day-to-day, and trait associations. *Psychoneuroendocrinology, 35*, 430–441. doi:10.1016/j.psyneuen.2009.08.005

Eisenberger, N. I., & Cole, S. W. (2012). Social neuroscience and health: Neurophysiological mechanisms linking social ties with physical health. *Nature Neuroscience, 15*, 669–674. doi:10.1038/nn.3086

Ellis, B. J., & Boyce, W. T. (2008). Biological sensitivity to context. *Current Directions in Psychological Science, 17*, 183–187. doi:10.1111/j.1467-8721.2008.00571.x

Espelage, D. L., & Holt, M. K. (2001). Bullying and victimization during early adolescence: Peer influences and psychosocial correlates. *Journal of Emotional Abuse, 2*, 123–142.

Feldman, R. (2015). The neurobiology of mammalian parenting and the biosocial context of human caregiving. *Hormones and Behavior, 77*, 3–17. http://dx.doi.org/10.1016/j.yhbeh.2015.10.001

Gould, R. V. (2002). The origins of status hierarchies: A formal theory and empirical test. *American Journal of Sociology, 107*, 1143–1178. doi:10.1086/341744

Granger, D. A., Fortunato, C. K., Beltzer, E. B., Virag, M., Bright, M., & Out, D. (2012). Salivary bioscience and research on adolescence: an integrated perspective. *Journal of Adolescence, 32*, 1081–1095. doi: 10.1016/j.adolescence.2012.01.005

Granger, D. A., Serbin, L. A., Schwartzman, A. E., Lehoux, P., Cooperman, J., & Ikeda, S. (1998). Children's salivary cortisol, internalizing behavior problems, and family environment: Results from the Concordia Longitudinal Risk Project. *International Journal of Behavioral Development, 22*, 707–728. doi: 10.1080/016502598384135

Gunnar, M. R., & Hostinar, C. E. (2015). The social buffering of the hypothalamic–pituitary–adrenocortical axis in humans: Developmental and experiential determinants. *Social Neuroscience, 10*, 479–488. doi:10.1080/17470919.2015.1070747

Gunnar, M. R., & Quevedo, K. (2007). The neurobiology of stress and development. *Annual Review of Psychology, 58*, 145–173. doi:10.1146/annurev.psych.58.110405.085605

Gunnar, M. R., Sebanc, A. M., Tout, K., Donzella, B., & van Dulmen, M. M. H. (2003). Peer rejection, temperament, and cortisol activity in preschoolers. *Developmental Psychobiology, 43*, 346–368. doi:10.1002/dev.10144

Hawkley, L. C., & Cacioppo, J. T. (2010). Loneliness matters: A theoretical and empirical review of consequences and mechanisms. *Annals of Behavioral Medicine, 40*, 218–227. doi:10.1007/s12160-010-9210-8

Hawley, P. H. (1999). The ontogenesis of social dominance: A strategy-based evolutionary perspective. *Developmental Review, 19*, 97–132. doi:10.1006/drev.1998.0470

Hawley, P. H. (2015). Social dominance in childhood and its evolutionary underpinnings: Why it matters and what we can do. *Pediatrics, 135*, S31–S41. doi:10.1542/peds.2014-3549D

Heider, F. (1958). *The psychology of interpersonal relations.* New York, NY: Wiley.

Hinde, R. A. (1976). Interactions, relationships and social structure. *Man, 11*, 1–17.

Holt-Lunstad, J., Smith, T. B., & Layton, J. B. (2010). Social relationships and mortality risk: A meta-analytic review. *PLoS Medicine, 7*, e1000316.

Hong, J. S., & Espelage, D. L. (2012). A review of research on bullying and peer victimization in school: An ecological system analysis. *Aggression and Violent Behavior, 17*, 311–322.

Hostinar, C. E., Johnson, A. E., & Gunnar, M. R. (2015). Parent support is less effective in buffering cortisol stress reactivity for adolescents compared to children. *Developmental Science, 18*, 281–297. doi: 10.1111/desc.12195

Hostinar, C. E., Sullivan, R. M., & Gunnar, M. R. (2014). Psychobiological mechanisms underlying the social buffering of the hypothalamic–pituitary–adrenocortical axis: A review of animal models and human studies across development. *Psychological Bulletin, 140*, 256–282. doi:10.1037/a0032671

House, J. S., Landis, K. R., & Umberson, D. (1988). Social relationships and health. *Science, 241*, 540–545.

Huitsing, G., Snijders, T. A. B., van Duijn, M. A. J., & Veenstra, R. (2014). Victims, bullies, and their defenders: A longitudinal study of the coevolution of positive and negative networks. *Development and Psychopathology, 26*(3), 645–659. http://dx.doi.org/10.1017/S0954579414000297

Huitsing, G., van Duijn, M. A. J., Snijders, T. A. B., Wang, P., Sainio, M., Salmivalli, C., & Veenstra, R. (2012). Univariate and multivariate models of positive and negative networks: Liking, disliking, and bully–victim relationships. *Social Networks, 34*, 645–657. doi:10.1016/j.socnet.2012.08.001

Kiecolt-Glaser, J. K., & Newton, T. L. (2001). Marriage and health: His and hers. *Psychological Bulletin, 127*, 472–503. http://dx.doi.org/10.1037/0033-2909.127.4.472

Kliewer, W. (2006). Violence exposure and cortisol responses in urban youth. *International Journal of Behavioral Medicine, 13*, 109–120. doi:10.1207/s15327558ijbm1302_2

Kornienko, O., Clemans, K., Out, D., & Granger, D. A. (2013). Friendship network position and salivary cortisol levels. *Social Neuroscience, 8*, 385–396. doi:10.1080/17470919.2013.795500

Kornienko, O., Clemans, K. H., Out, D., & Granger, D. A. (2014). Hormones, behavior, and social network analysis: Exploring associations between cortisol, testosterone, and network structure. *Hormones & Behavior, 66*, 534–544. doi:10.1016/j.yhbeh.2014.07.009

Kornienko, O., Schaefer, D. R., Weren, S., Hill, G. W., & Granger, D. A. (2016). Cortisol and testosterone associations with social network dynamics. *Hormones and Behavior, 80*, 92–102. doi:10.1016/j.yhbeh.2016.01.013

Labianca, G., & Brass, D. J. (2006). Exploring the social ledger: Negative relationships and negative asymmetry in social networks in organizations. *Academy of Management, 31*, 596–614. doi:10.5465/AMR.2006.21318920

Larson, R. W. (2001). How U.S. children and adolescents spend time: What it does (and doesn't) tell us about their development. *Current Directions in Psychological Science, 10*, 160–164. doi:10.1111/1467-8721.00139

MacLaughlin, K. A., Sheridan, M. A., Tibu, F., Fox, N. A., Zeanah, C. H., & Nelson, C. A. (2015). Causal effects of the early caregiving environment on development of stress response systems in children. *Proceedings of the National Academy of Sciences of the USA, 112*, 5637–5642. doi:10.1073/pnas.1423363112

McEwen, B. S., & Gianaros, P. J. (2010). Central role of the brain in stress and adaptation: Links to socioeconomic status, health, and disease. *Annals of the New York Academy of Sciences, 1186*, 190–222. doi:10.1111/j.1749-6632.2009.05331.x

Miller, G., Chen, E., & Cole, S. W. (2009). Health psychology: Developing biologically plausible models linking the social world to physical health. *Annual Review of Psychology, 60*, 501–524.

Murray-Close, D. (2013). Psychophysiology of adolescent peer relations I: Theory and research findings. *Journal of Research on Adolescence, 23*, 236–259. doi:10.1111/j.1532-7795.2012.00828.x

O'Brien, S. F., & Bierman, K. L. (1988). Conceptions and perceived influence of peer groups: Interviews with preadolescents and adolescents. *Child Development, 59*, 1360–1365.

Parker, J. G., Rubin, K. H., Erath, S. A., Wojslawowicz, J. C., & Buskirk, A. A. (2006). Peer relationships, child development, and adjustment: A developmental psychopathology perspective. In D. Cicchetti & D. J. Cohen (Eds.), *Developmental psychopathology: Vol. 1. Theory and methods* (2nd ed., pp. 419–493). New York, NY: Wiley.

Pellegrini, A. D., Roseth, C. J., Van Ryzin, M. J., & Solberg, D. W. (2011). Popularity as form of social dominance: An evolutional perspective. In A. H. N. Cillessen, D. Schwartz, & L. Mayeux (Eds.), *Popularity in the peer system* (pp. 123–140). New York, NY: Guilford.

Peper, J. S., & Dahl, R. E. (2013). Surging hormones: Brain–behavior interactions during puberty. *Current Directions of Psychological Science, 22*, 134–139. doi:10.1177/0963721412473755

Peters, E., Riksen-Walraven, J. M., Cillessen, A. H., & de Weerth, C. (2011). Peer rejection and HPA activity in middle childhood: Friendship makes a difference. *Child Development, 82*, 1906–1920.

Pinter-Wollman, N., Hobson, E. A., Smith, J. E., Edelman, A. J., Shizuka, D., de Silva, S., . . . McDonald, D. (2014). The dynamics of animal social networks: Analytical, conceptual, and theoretical advances. *Behavioral Ecology, 25*, 242–255. doi:10.1093/beheco/art047

Ponzi, D., Zilioli, S., Mehta, P. H., Maslov, A., & Watson, N. V. (2016). Social network centrality and hormones: The interaction of testosterone and cortisol. *Psychoneuroendocrinology, 68*, 6–13. doi:10.1016/j.psyneuen.2016.02.014

Pressman, S. D., Cohen, S., Miller, G. E., Barkin, A., Rabin, B. S., & Treanor, J. (2005). Loneliness, social network size, and immune response to influenza vaccination in college freshmen. *Health Psychology, 24*, 297–306. doi:10.1037/0278-6133.24.3.297

Rambaran, J. A., Dijkstra, J. K., Munniksma, A., & Cillessen, A. H. N. (2015). The development of adolescents' friendships and antipathies: A longitudinal multivariate network test of balance theory. *Social Networks, 43*, 162–176. doi:10.1016/j.socnet.2015.05.003

Rivera, M. T., Soderstrom, S. B., & Uzzi, B. (2010). Dynamics of dyads in social networks: Assortative, relational, and proximity mechanisms. *Annual Review of Sociology, 36*, 91–115. doi:10.1146/annurev.soc.34.040507.134743

Robins, G. (2013). A tutorial on methods for the modeling and analysis of social network data. *Journal of Mathematical Psychology, 57*, 261–274.

Romero, R. D. (2010). Adolescence: A central event in shaping stress reactivity. *Developmental Psychobiology, 52*, 244–253. doi:10.1002/dev.20437

Rook, K. S., (2001). Emotional health and positive versus negative social exchanges: A daily diary analysis. *Applied Developmental Science, 5*, 86–97. doi:10.1207/S1532480XADS0502_4

Rudolph, K. D. (2014). Puberty as a developmental context of risk for psychopathology. In M. Lewis & K. D. Rudolph (Eds.), *Handbook of developmental psychopathology* (pp. 331–355). New York, NY: Plenum.

Rudolph, K. D., Landsford, J. E., & Rodkin, P. C. (2016). Interpersonal theories of developmental psychopathology. In D. Cicchetti (Ed.), *Developmental psychopathology* (3rd ed.). Hoboken, NJ: Wiley.

Rudolph, K. D., Troop-Gordon, W., & Granger, D. A. (2010). Peer victimization and aggression: Moderation by individual differences in salivary cortisol and alpha-amylase. *Journal of Abnormal Child Psychology, 38*, 843–856. doi:10.1007/s10802-010-9412-3

Sapolsky, R. M. (2005). The influence of social hierarchy on primate health. *Science, 308*, 648–652. doi:10.1126/science.1106477

Sapolsky, R. M., Romero, L. M., & Munck, A. U. (2000). How do glucocorticoids influence stress responses? Integrating permissive, suppressive, stimulatory, and preparative actions. *Endocrine Reviews, 21*, 55–89. doi:10.1210/edrv.21.1.0389

Schaefer, D. R., Kornienko, O., & Fox, A. M. (2011). Misery does not love company: Network selection mechanisms and depression homophily. *American Sociological Review, 76*, 764–785. doi:10.1177/0003122411420813

Segerstrom, S. C. (2007). Stress, energy, and immunity: An ecological view. *Current Directions in Psychological Science, 16*, 326–330. doi:10.1111/j.1467-8721.2007.00522.x

Snijders, T. A. B. (2011). Statistical models for social networks. *Annual Review of Sociology, 37*, 131–153. doi:10.1146/annurev.soc.012809.102709

Somerville, L. H. (2013). The teenage brain: Sensitivity to social evaluation. *Current Directions in Psychological Science, 22*, 121–127. doi:10.1177/0963721413476512

Steptoe, A., Owen, N., Kunz-Ebrecht, S. R., & Brydon, L., (2004). Loneliness and neuroendocrine, cardiovascular, and inflammatory stress responses in middle-aged men and women. *Psychoneuroendocrinology, 29*, 593–611. doi:10.1016/S0306-4530(03)00086-6

Stroud, L. R., Foster, E., Papandonatos, G. D., Handwerger, K., Granger, D. A., Kivlighan, K. T., & Niaura, K. (2009). Stress response and the adolescent transition: Performance versus peer rejection stressors. *Development and Psychopathology, 21*, 47–68. doi:10.1017/S0954579409000042

Susman, E. J., & Dorn, L. D. (2009). Puberty: Its role in development. In R. M. Lerner & L. Steinberg (Eds.), *Handbook of adolescent psychology* (pp. 116–151). Hoboken, NJ: Wiley.

Tarullo, A. R., Mliner, S., & Gunnar, M. R. (2011). Inhibition and exuberance in preschool classrooms: Associations with peer social experiences and changes in cortisol across the preschool year. *Developmental Psychology, 47*, 1374–1388. http://dx.doi.org/10.1037/a0024093

Vaillancourt, T., Duku, E., Decatanzaro, D., Macmillan, H., Muir, C., & Schmidt, L. A. (2008). Variation in hypothalamic–pituitary–adrenal axis activity among bullied and non-bullied children. *Aggressive Behavior, 34*, 294–305. doi:10.1002/ab.20240

Valente, T. W. (2010). *Social networks and health: Models, methods, and applications.* New York, NY: Oxford University Press.

Walker, M. E., Wasserman, S., & Wellman, B. (1993). Statistical models for social support networks. *Sociological Methods Research, 22*, 71–98. doi:10.1177/0049124193022001004

Wasserman, S., & Faust, K. (1994). *Social network analysis: Methods and applications.* Cambridge, UK: Cambridge University Press.

Weiner, H. (1992). *Perturbing the organism: The biology of stressful experience.* Chicago, IL: University of Chicago Press.

CHAPTER 17

....

STRESS AND STRESS HORMONES

....

JEFF DAVIS AND KRISTEN DAMRON

ENVIRONMENTALLY induced stress is a highly influential factor in evolution by natural selection. It impacts all levels of biological organization—from the population to molecular processes (Badyaev, 2005; Hoffmann & Parsons, 1991; Wingfield, 2009). Our first goal for this chapter is to give the reader an overview of research on stress and stress hormones from the perspective of evolutionary biology. We review the mechanics and evolution of hormones, followed by a discussion of hormonal signaling processes and the physiology of stress pathways. Most attention is placed on the actions of steroid hormones. We discuss the commonly studied structures (e.g., the limbic system) and the commonly studied pathways (e.g., the hypothalamic–pituitary–adrenal axis). Many details are purposefully omitted, but the reader should have a solid basis for exploring the literature much further. We end this section with a review of two major theoretical perspectives on stress—homeostasis and allostasis models.

Our second goal is to present a model of stress for evolutionary sociology. The sociological relevance of stress research has long been known (Barchas, 1976). In a wealth of studies, researchers have demonstrated that dynamic changes in social position within a status hierarchy precede changes in circulating levels of stress hormones (Mazur, 2005). Our model proposes that stress hormones facilitate actions toward adaptive predictive control—a condition in which the individual can accurately predict future changes in an environment and bring about future environmental changes favorable to the individual's fitness preferences. Individuals can "feel" their progress toward adaptive predictive control because stress hormone levels vary with positive and negative prediction outcomes. We discuss how social structure enables and disrupts efforts to achieve adaptive predictive control. Last, we put forth general typology of the relationship between adaptive predictive control and stress hormone processes.

Environmental Stressors

In evolutionary biology, stress is any significant reduction in survivability and reproductive chances (i.e., fitness) over a period of time (Hoffmann & Parsons, 1991). Ultimately, fitness depends on the performance of an individual in a given environment, where performance includes the acquisition and allocation of energy to growth, maturation, survival, and reproduction (Stearns, 1992). Fitness increases with the degree of optimality of performance. In turn, performance is a function of how well an individual can predict outcomes of actions and exert control over key environmental dimensions (Wingfield, 2009). Hence, stressors are typically measured on two general axes: predictability and controllability of fitness-relevant environmental conditions (Wingfield, 2009).

Wingfield's (2009) model of the interactions between environment and hormones exemplifies the general approach to stress in evolutionary biology. He posits three major environmental factors that shape an individual's performance: predictive information, labile perturbations, and synchronizing and integrating information. Predictive information includes long-term and short-term information. Both consist of cues an individual can use to anticipate large-scale changes in the *physical* environment. Long-term cues vary predictably and include events such as long-term seasonal rhythms and annual photoperiods, which are significantly linked to reproductive behaviors and immune functioning (Walton, Weil, & Nelson, 2011). Short-term cues are used to adjust performance within a local spatiotemporal context. These cues include events such as sudden severe storms, landslides, excess rain, dry spells, and heat waves (Wingfield, 2009).

Labile perturbations are chief environmental sources of unpredictable environmental stressors. As named, these stressors are temporary. Some, such as an encounter with a predator, may last only seconds. Other events, such as viral or bacterial infections, can persist for days or weeks. Labile perturbation events are significant because they trigger "emergency life history strategies" in the individual. The definition of "life history" approximates the definition of "life course" in the social sciences. Theories of life history are primarily concerned with the timing of developmental events such as sexual maturation and senescence (Stearns, 1992). In response to labile perturbations, developmental timing accelerates. Events, such as first childbirth, occur sooner than average. The effects have been observed in studies of reproductive timing among nonhumans and humans. In summary, recent studies report moderate, inverse associations between increased exposure to mortality-related environmental cues and individual-level differences in the timing of fertility. In areas with higher exposure, the timing of sexual maturation occurs sooner in the life course. The association is overall moderate but consistent across numerous studies (Brumbach, Figueredo, & Ellis, 2009; Davis, 2012; Ellis, Figueredo, Brumbach, & Schlomer, 2009; Nettle, 2011; Uggla & Mace, 2016; Wilson & Daly, 1997).

Synchronizing and integrating information comes from biological relatives and unrelated conspecifics sharing the same environment. This information essentially "tunes" the individual—physiologically, psychologically, and sociologically—in anticipation of changes in environmental conditions (Wingfield, 2009). Various experiences comprise synchronizing and integrating information. One major tuning influence is referred to as maternal effects. The definition of maternal effect varies somewhat in the literature but generally refers to the nongenetically transmitted, causal influence of the mother's phenotype on offspring development (Bjorklund, 2006; Wolf & Wade, 2009). Recent research has found compelling evidence of maternal effects on offspring in utero. The phenomenon is referred to as fetal programming. Studies suggest that the mother's exposure to social stressors ramps up her circulating levels of stress hormones. The information is transmitted to the fetus via the umbilical cord. In response, circulating levels of stress hormones increase in the fetus. The end result is a developmental trajectory of the offspring marked by increased sensitivity to stress (Drake & Walker, 2004). Agonistic social interactions also comprise synchronizing and integrating information in the forms of social competition and conflict over positions within a hierarchy (Barchas, 1976; Kemper, 1990; Mazur, 2005; Sapolsky, 2004).

Stress Hormones

Hormones are the major mechanisms that determine the totality of the behavioral response to environmental stressors—from signal transduction to allocation of energetic resources (Adkins-Regan, 2005). They are literally the first messengers to report environmental conditions to the nervous system (Cole et al., 2007; Gomperts, Kramer, & Tatham, 2003). In this section, we present current knowledge of types of stress hormones, with emphasis on their effects on nervous system structures. Studies conducted on nonhuman vertebrates and mammals are included in our review. Nonhuman species, such as the common house mouse, are model systems—animals bred to allow investigation into a variety of biological processes. Hormonal processes in model systems closely resemble those found in humans (Adkins-Regan, 2005). Some hormones have an identical effect in human and nonhuman model systems (Adkins-Regan, 2005).

Hormones are synthesized in and secreted from gland nuclei and into the bloodstream (Adkins-Regan, 2005). In humans, the glands most associated with stress responsivity are the pituitary gland in the brain located near the hypothalamus and adrenal glands located atop each kidney (Adkins-Regan, 2005). There are three types of hormones differentiated by molecular size and function (Adkins-Regan, 2005). Peptide and protein hormones are composed of large molecular structures compared to steroid hormones. A peptide is a chemical compound consisting of amino acids, which are the building blocks of all known life forms. Peptide hormones are water-soluble and perform their roles outside the cell membrane. After contacting a cell, peptide hormones trigger the release of second messengers within the cell, which in turn interact with the cell nucleus to generate a specific action (Gomperts et al., 2003). Protein hormones have similar cellular interactions but are composed of longer chains of amino acids (Adkins-Regan, 2005). Steroid hormones consist of long chains of peptides (or polymers). Unlike peptide and protein hormones, steroid hormones can pass through the cell membrane and directly impact the cell activity by influencing gene expression or by nongenomic effects (Evanson, Herman, Sakai, & Krause, 2010). Their properties make steroid hormones especially relevant in research on stress and stress responses.

Figure 17.1 illustrates the genomic and nongenomic actions of a steroid hormone on a cell. Numerous elements are not shown for the sake of simplicity. In the genomic pathway, the steroid hormone crosses the cell membrane with the aid of a membrane receptor. Receptors are proteins that respond to electrical and chemical stimuli external to the cell (Adkins-Regan, 2005). These stimuli have either excitatory or inhibitory effects on the activity of receptors (Adkins-Regan, 2005). A steroid hormone excites the cell surface and, in turn, opens a channel, allowing access to cytoplasm. It maintains its connection to the receptor and is transported into the cell nucleus. There, it interacts with the gene to influence the expression of proteins that dictate cell behavior. They have been observed influencing the transcription phase of gene expression, which produces messenger RNA, and the translation phase, in which the protein is synthesized (Cole, 2008, 2013).

Through the genomic pathway, the effect of a steroid hormone on cellular action can require relatively long time periods to manifest. In some cases, it takes several minutes; in others cases, it takes hours (Wingfield et al., 1998). The nongenomic route results in a much faster response to environmental stressors on the order of seconds. Through this pathway, a steroid or nonsteroid hormone does not cross the cell membrane nor does it directly interact with DNA in the cell nucleus. Rather, the hormone excites the serial release of enzymes crucially involved in intracellular signaling. In the first phase, the hormone excites the cell membrane to activate adenylyl cyclase (AC), an enzyme found

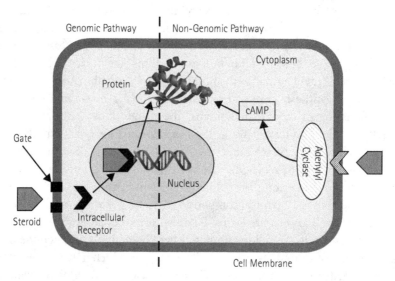

FIGURE 17.1 Steroid hormone actions.

Source: Adapted from Lösel and Wehling (2003, p. 53).

in all cells. In simple terms, the primary function of AC is to carry out chemical processes that allow the steroid hormone to access the cell membrane (Evanson et al., 2010). In turn, it activates a group of "second messengers" such as cyclic adenosine monophosphate (cAMP). cAMP directly instructs the nongenomic production of proteins (Lösel & Wehling, 2003). Second messengers such as cAMP initiate a cascade of activity within the cytoplasm, including cell growth or cell death (Gomperts et al., 2003).

Glucocorticoids and Glucocorticoid Receptors

Glucocorticoids (GCs) are, arguably, the most thoroughly studied class of stress hormones. They include some well-known hormones such as cortisol and corticosterone. GCs belong to a class of steroid hormones called corticosteroids, which are involved in an extensive range of physiological processes—stress response, immune response, inflammatory responses at the cellular level, and some of the most vital metabolic activities (Adkins-Regan, 2005). GCs are synthesized and released from the adrenal glands in direct response to exposure to stressful environmental stimuli, including stressful experiences in competition over social status (Knight & Mehta, 2014). GCs have many targets in the brain that are identified by the presence of receptor sites on cell membranes (Malven, 2000). GCs influence cell activity through genomic and nongenomic mechanisms. Through genomic pathways, GCs pass through the cell membrane and interact with intracellular glucocorticoid receptors (GRs). Once GCs bind, GRs can escort GCs into critical areas of genomic activity, such as the mitochondria or the cell nucleus (Haller, Mikics, & Makara, 2008; Mikics, Kruk, & Haller, 2004). Low doses of GCs have beneficial effects on cell functioning. However, persistently high levels of GCs can cause harm by inducing oxidative stress within the cell (Epel, 2009). This is a condition in which the cell's ability to maintain functional levels of oxygen molecules is compromised. GCs can elevate oxygen levels above the cell's ability to eliminate excess oxygen with sufficient speed. Multiple harmful outcomes are possible, including cell death (apoptosis) (Groeneweg, Karst, de Kloet, & Joëls, 2011).

Glucocorticoids have some remarkable effects on adaptive outcomes. For instance, a large number of studies have found compelling evidence of maternal effects of GCs on stress responsivity in children. GC levels in mothers living in stressful environmental conditions (e.g. war, disease, poverty) essentially transmit information about the environment to the developing embryo (Weaver et al., 2004). GCs have tuning effects on the development of the embryo's hypothalamic–pituitary–adrenal (HPA) axis. Exposure to high levels of GC upregulates the activity of the HPA, causing the embryo to become overly sensitive to environmental stressors (Kapoor, Dunn, Kostaki, Andrews, & Matthews, 2006). Maternal GC effects are found in a wide range of placental species (Wolf & Wade, 2009).

A few evolutionary perspectives propose that increased sensitivity to stressors has some adaptive benefits because the process essentially "prepares" offspring for life in a stressful environment (Burgess & Marshall, 2014; Love, Chin, Wynne-Edwards, &

Williams, 2005). However, there is a trade-off. Higher GC levels increase offspring susceptibility to accelerated erosion of telomeres (Haussmann & Marchetto, 2010). Telomeres are protein "caps" at the end of a chromosome that maintain its structural integrity. Telomere length shortens naturally with age due to gene replication, which is necessary to preserve cell functions. Persistent exposure to environmental stressors and subsequent increases in glucocorticoid receptor activity accelerate telomere shortening via oxidative stress on cells (Monaghan, 2014). Thus, stress literally causes faster aging. As another instance, GC effects may underlie observations of racial disparities in telomere length. Recent chromosomal analyses of women and men living in the United States found significantly shorter telomere lengths in Blacks in comparison to Whites. The overall racial difference suggested Blacks were on average 10 years older genetically than Whites. In comparison to all other groups, Black women had significantly higher levels of stress hormones such as C-Reactive Protein and, thus, were aging faster (Geronimus et al., 2010).

Interneuron Signaling

The workhorse throughout hormonal processes is the neuron. Neurons are specialized cells in the nervous system that receive and send electrical and chemical information from and to various tissues (e.g., organs and muscle). There are three major classes of neurons: sensory neurons, motor neurons, and interneurons (Levitan & Kaczmarek, 1997a). Names imply functions. Sensory neurons act in concert with sensory receptor fields located in the eyes, on the surface of the skin, on the tongue, and elsewhere to transmit information to respective regions of the brain. Motor neurons coordinate fine and gross motor movements. These neurons have been at the center of a hotly contested debate about the ways humans establish a fundamental social connection with each other. So-called mirror neurons allow an individual to recognize others with shared physical traits via imitation of motor movements (Rizzolatti & Sinigaglia, 2008). The presence of mirror neurons has been firmly verified in nonhuman primate species but not yet in humans (Franks & Davis, 2012). Interneurons are the intermediary linkages between the brain and neurons involved in the detection of stimuli (Levitan & Kaczmarek, 1997a). One chief role is the tight regulation of the level of excitability of neurons in the central and peripheral nervous systems (Rossignol, 2011; Spruston, 2008).

Neurons have many different shapes, which can indicate their function or location in the nervous system. Spindle neurons (or von Economo neurons), for example, have a shape very distinct from those of other neurons and are found in only two locations in the cerebral cortex: the frontal insular cortex and the anterior cingulate cortex (Allman, Tetreault, Hakeem, & Park, 2011). Spindle neurons have received a great deal of attention from neuroscientists because there is evidence and some speculation that spindle neurons contribute significantly to the development of social cognitive abilities in several mammalian species, including humans. They may play a significant role in the cultural transmission of information in some nonhuman mammals. Furthermore, they may shed light on the evolution of big-brained animals such as humans, whales, and elephants (Allman, Hakeem, & Watson, 2002).

Figure 17.2 shows the basic anatomy of a neuron. Only some of the major parts are labeled. The overall length and width of a neuron varies considerably. Compared to the width of a human hair, a neuron can be approximately 100 times smaller (Levitan & Kaczmarek, 1997a). The soma (or cell body) contains the cytoplasm and nucleus of the neuron. Electrical and chemical signals are received through the dendrites from the terminal buttons of another neuron. The incoming signal excites the neuron to synthesize a neurotransmitter—sometimes a hormone—which will reach its eventual target location. The axon hillock serves a threshold function. An electrical current must reach a critical value before the axon hillock will allow the signal to proceed to the axon and to the terminals. The axon shown in Figure 17.2 is myelinated. Myelin is a coating of cells wrapped around the axon and serves two major functions: (a) insulating the neuron from ambient electrical and chemical activity and (b) acceleration of incoming information to the axon terminals (Bercury & Macklin, 2015; El Waly, Macchi, Cayre, & Durbec, 2014). The incoming signal "skips" along the axon by leaping between the nodes of Ranvier (Levitan & Kaczmarek, 1997b). Each myelin sheath contains Schwann cells responsible for supplying nutrients (e.g., sugars) and neurogenesis (Kempermann, 2011).

Figure 17.3 illustrates activity at the point of communication between neurons called the synapse. The synaptic cleft is the physical space between the neurons. The larger circles in the presynaptic neuron are vesicles containing neurotransmitters (Adkins-Regan, 2005). These are chemical instructions for the activation of the postsynaptic neuron. An action potential releases the neurotransmitters from the vesicles into the synaptic cleft. The receptors of the postsynaptic neuron are voltage-gated. The electrical pulse from the presynaptic neuron stimulates the activity of receptors for the neurotransmitter located on the membrane of the postsynaptic neuron. When gates are effectively opened, the neurotransmitter can pass into the postsynaptic neuron. The signaling process continues until a target cell is reached. Typically, the target cell is an

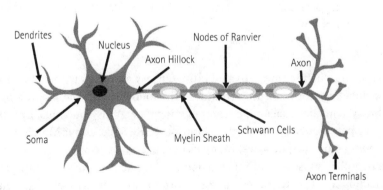

FIGURE 17.2 Neuron anatomy.

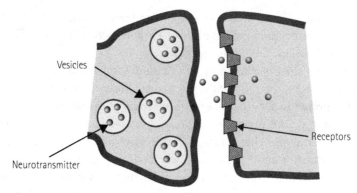

Vesicles

Neurotransmitter

Receptors

Pre-synaptic Neuron Dendrite   Post-synaptic Neuron Dendrite

FIGURE 17.3 Synapse and synaptic cleft.

astrocyte (glial cell) that allows neurotransmitter or hormone to cross the blood–brain barrier (Adkins-Regan, 2005).

Integrated Systems of the Stress Response

Figure 17.4 schematically illustrates the basic stress response. The multiple lines connecting each component indicate that there are multiple connections to different subparts of a component. An environmental stimulus is detected by sensory receptor fields located in various parts of the body (e.g., eyes, hands, nose, and tongue). This information is then routed to respective regions on the cerebral cortex. For example, visual information is routed to the primary visual cortex in the posterior region of the brain (Franks, 2010). Smells are detected and assigned values in the olfactory bulb posterior to the nasal cavities (Adkins-Regan, 2005). All of the incoming information about the stimulus is compiled in parts of the cerebral cortex known as association areas. The neural activities of association areas create meaningful recognition of the stimulus—friend or foe, harmful or pleasant, moving fast or moving slow (Franks, 2010). The outcome of encoding and processing in association areas largely determines the next cortical or subcortical destination of the input.

Limbic System

Limbic system structures are activated if the sensory and association area inputs indicate a challenging or threatening stimulus. The following are the major structures of the limbic system: amygdala, hippocampus, cingulate gyrus, thalamus, hypothalamus, fornix, and parahippocampal gyrus (Goodson & Kabelik, 2009; Morgane, Galler, & Mokler, 2005). For our purposes, we focus on the connections between the amygdala and the hypothalamus. Neural information communicated from the amygdala to the hypothalamus largely determines whether a stress response is activated. The amygdalae are almond-sized nuclei (group of cells) found in the right and left hemispheres. They

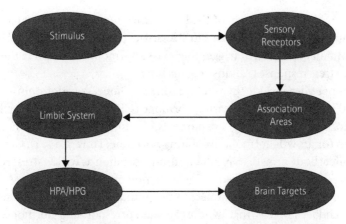

FIGURE 17.4 Components of the stress response. HPA, hypothalamic–pituitary–adrenal axis; HPG, hypothalamic–pituitary–gonadal axis.

are major hubs of activity in the stress response (Phelps, 2006; Vrtička, Andersson, Grandjean, Sander, & Vuilleumier, 2008; Whalen & Phelps, 2009). For example, when an individual perceives the face of another person, information about the face is routed from sensory cortices to the fusiform facial area—an association area located on the ventral side of the temporal lobe (Franks, 2010). If the face is recognizable or has a friendly expression, information bypasses the amygdala and goes to the thalamus and then to the ventral medial prefrontal cortex (Franks, 2010). If the face is unrecognizable or has an unfriendly expression, that information activates the amygdalae, specifically neurons that modulate the release of cortisol from other brain structures. This is a first stage in the fight-or-flight stress response (Whalen & Phelps, 2009).

The thalamus and hypothalamus lay in the general vicinity of the amygdalae. Like amygdalae, the thalamus and hypothalamus are lateralized structures. The thalamus is a crucial link between sensory fields and areas of the cerebral cortex. Connections from the amygdalae and other limbic structures arrive in the anterior nuclei of the thalamus. The hypothalamus consists of nuclei concentrated in the ventral posterior (i.e., front and low) of the thalamus (Vertes, Linley, & Hoover, 2015; Wolff, Alcaraz, Marchand, & Coutureau, 2015). In a crucial role, the thalamus modulates the strength of a stress signal coming from the amygdalae (Paydar et al., 2014; Penzo et al., 2015). Prolonged stress exposure, however, has detrimental effects on the size and function of the thalamus. Research on medical patients with post-traumatic stress disorder (PTSD) has found smaller than average thalamus sizes (Sussman, Pang, Jetly, Dunkley, & Taylor, 2016). Chronic stress such as PTSD physically alters the size of brain structures net of the effects of neurogenetic predispositions to stress (Sussman et al., 2016).

Hypothalamus–Pituitary Axes

Information from the limbic system outputs to two systems that influence a wide range of social behaviors: the HPA axis and the hypothalamic–pituitary–gonadal (HPG) axis. Both axes are the central routes by which stress-related hormones reach their target areas in the brain or other parts of the body. Once reached, hormonal activities pro-duce phenotypic changes in response to stress. The paraventricular nuclei in the hypo-thalamus contain peptides that trigger the release hormones involved in the crucial first stages of the stress response (Adkins-Regan, 2005).

The major peptides include thyroid-releasing hormone, gonadotropin-releasing hor-mone (GnRH), corticotropin-releasing hormone (CRH), dopamine, growth hormone-releasing hormone, luteinizing hormone (LH), follicle-stimulating hormone, and somatostatin (or growth hormone-inhibiting hormone) (Imura, 1994). Generally, these hormones affect body growth, reproduction, and lactation as well as stress responses. To varying degrees, many are involved in the regulation of social behaviors (Malven, 2000).

Neurons in the hypothalamus project to the pituitary gland, which contains the cor-responding endocrine cells that synthesize the corresponding hormone. It has two distinct sections: posterior and anterior (Kannan, 1987). The anterior pituitary houses stress-related hormones such as corticotropin and dopamine (Kannan, 1987; Malven, 2000). The posterior pituitary contains other hormones with known associations with rudimentary sociological behaviors such as social affiliation and defense of long-term pair bonds (Insel & Young, 2000; Young & Wang, 2004). From the pituitary gland, hor-mones enter the bloodstream. Neurons and neurotransmitters do not directly connect to veins (or hypophyseal veins) in the pituitary. They enter via astrocytes. In the case of the pituitary, these cells are called pituicytes (Imura, 1994). Astrocytes are wrapped around small capillary veins in the hypophyseal located just above the pituitary (Imura, 1994; Levitan & Kaczmarek, 1997a; Shepherd, 1998).

There are two main axes formed by the connections between the hypothalamus, pitu-itary, and glandular bodies outside the brain: the HPA axis and the HPG axis. The one most associated with stress responses is the HPA axis. The HPA axis is activated by the synthesis of CRH in the hypothalamus. After reception of the signal from hypothalamic neurons, the endocrine cells in the pituitary synthesize a substance called adrenocor-ticotropic hormone (ACTH) and release it into the bloodstream via the hypophyseal veins (Kannan, 1987; Malven, 2000). The target gland is the adrenal gland located on top of each kidney. The adrenal gland consists of an outer layer of tissue called the adre-nal cortex, which encloses the central structure called the adrenal medulla (Kannan, 1987; Malven, 2000). The adrenal cortex is where three major steroid hormones are synthesized: glucocorticoids, mineralocorticoids, and androgens (Malven, 2000). Glucocorticoids are generally involved in rapid metabolic responses and inflammatory responses to a variety of types of stressors (Cole, 2008; Djordjevic, Adzic, Djordjevic, & Radojcic, 2009; Furay, Bruestle, & Herman, 2008). Glucocorticoids are synthesized and enter the bloodstream at regular, hourly time intervals, but they can be upregulated based on the size of the dose of ACTH coming from the pituitary gland (Munhoz et al., 2006). In their interactions with other hormones, glucocorticoids serve as an inhibitor or catalyst. During stressful episodes, glucocorticoids suppress the actions of reproduc-tive hormones such as GnRH and LH. Thus, when the HPA axis is activated, the HPG axis decreases activity (Munhoz et al., 2006).

Effects of Stress Hormones on Specific Brain Targets

Hormones synthesized in the adrenal glands enter the bloodstream and have specific target sites in the brain. The effect of a hormone on a particular brain structure depends on the presence, density, and diversity of receptors on the structure's cellular membranes. Cells with glucocorticoid receptors are widely dispersed throughout the brain, including regions that exert direct control over social behaviors (Schulkin, Gold, & McEwen, 1998). The level and duration of receptor activity depends on the type and length of exposure to an environmental stressor. In some cases, relationships between hormones and their effects on adaptive performance have an inverted-U shape. An initial increase in receptor activity can have adaptive effects on physiological functioning; however, prolonged activity can degrade performance over time (Belanoff, Gross, Yager, & Schatzberg, 2001; Vyas et al., 2016).

Next, we review evidence of the relationship between glucocorticoid receptor activity and the functioning of various parts of the brain closely involved with the regulation of social behaviors. Note that most studies cited in the following sections (and those cited previously) are based on model organisms, not humans. Primates, rodents, and other mammalian species are model organisms for much biological and behavioral research for several reasons. Most important, they share vital brain structures and processes with humans (Goodson, 2005; Newman, 1999). Structures such as the amygdala and hypothalamus are homologous among mammalian species in shape, size, and function (Butler & Hodos, 2005). The same is true regarding stress hormones and pathways (Butler & Hodos, 2005). Homology in stress systems is the result of the strong conservation of neurophysiological traits throughout evolution (Jess et al., 2012; Yao, Stenzel-Poore, & Denver, 2007).

Medial Extended Amygdala

The medial extended amygdala (MEA) is a central structure in what is referred to as the mammalian social behavior network (Newman, 1999) and, relatively recently, the vertebrate social behavior network (Goodson, 2005). It controls rudimentary social behaviors such as male mating behavior, female sexual behavior, parenting behaviors, and aggressive defense of long-term pair bonds (Newman, 1999). Glucocorticoid receptors are densely concentrated in the MEA (Wang, Yan, Hofman, Swaab, & Zhou, 2010). The number of GRs activated in this area of the amygdala positively correlates with the intensity of the stress response (Geuze et al., 2012). One of the major causes of activation of GRs is stress resulting from loss of agonistic competitions with conspecifics (Fekete et al., 2009). Studies indicate that damage to the MEA causes hyper-anxiety in response to stressors, even mild stressors (Davis, 1992; Davis, Walker, & Lee, 1997).

Cingulate Gyrus and Prefrontal Cortex

These two areas of the brain play crucial roles in social decision-making processes (Fuster, 1997). The anterior cingulate gyrus, in a sense, controls how an individual weighs the costs and benefits of an action (Rushworth, Walton, Kennerley, & Bannerman, 2004). The prefrontal cortex is the locus of action planning and the prediction of likely outcomes of actions. The expression of GRs strongly influences how well both regions perform their respective functions. Under acute stress, the expression of GRs facilitates learning and predicting the relationships between actions and outcomes. GRs have an adaptive effect; however, in periods of chronic stress GRs have a maladaptive effect (Gourley et al., 2012; Olausson, Kiraly, Gourley, & Taylor, 2013). The effect causes neural network connections between the cingulate and prefrontal cortices to degrade over time (Swanson, Shapiro, Whyte, & Gourley, 2013). Specifically, GRs erode glial cells (e.g., Schwann cells, astrocytes, and oligodendrocytes), which maintain the viability of neurons. Once glial cells are compromised, the strength of signals passing between neurons weakens significantly (Jauregui-Huerta et al., 2010).

Orbitofrontal Cortex

The orbitofrontal cortex is one of the brain regions originally associated with the "social brain" (Brothers, 1997). It is a chief mechanism of control over impulsive behaviors and deliberation over social decisions (Wallis, 2007). It receives input from several structures in the limbic system, including the amygdala and the hypothalamus (Fuster, 1997; Morecraft & Van Hoesen, 1998). Neurons in the orbitofrontal cortex send output to midbrain structures, such as the ventral tegmentum, which are considered to be the reward center of the mammalian brain (Price, 2006; Thorpe, Rolls, & Maddison, 1983). Damage and dysfunction in the orbitofrontal cortex have been linked to violent antisocial behavior and the onset of other types of psychopathological behaviors (Blair, 2004). Crucially, the activity of GRs in the orbitofrontal cortex has been directly linked to severe forms of mental illness, including major depression and schizophrenia. Again, higher levels of GR activity are associated with a higher likelihood of the onset of mental illnesses (Sinclair, Webster, Fullerton, & Weickert, 2012).

MODELS OF THE INTERNAL REGULATION OF THE STRESS RESPONSE

The basic mechanics of the stress response are understood quite well, and there is not much debate surrounding the roles of hormones, proteins, and physiological systems. However, debates about how the stress response is regulated are vibrant. Early models of the stress response were based on the concept of homeostasis advanced by Claude Bernard and later by Hans Selye (Schulkin, 2003). The model assumes that physiological systems equilibrate at a singular, optimal point. When exposure to environmental stressors creates disequilibrium, physiological systems engage negative feedback mechanisms to return the systems to their optimal operating value.

The more recent view is the allostasis model (Schulkin, 2011; Sterling, 2012). Unlike the homeostasis model, the allostasis model begins from an evolutionary perspective

(Schulkin, 2011). It is based on the assumption that there is no set equilibrium point. Rather, natural selection has favored physiological systems that can adapt to a new point stasis. Determinants of the new stasis point include genetic and environmental factors. However, adaptive adjustments are energetically expensive to maintain. When the energy limit is reached, the system experiences allostatic load. This initiates a cascade of maladaptive actions at the cellular and genetic level (Schulkin, 2011). These include elevated levels of cortisol and C-reactive protein; above normal scores on the body mass index; and higher levels of dehydroepiadrenosterone (DHEAS), a hormone that triggers cell death (Glei, Goldman, Chuang, & Weinstein, 2007; McEwen & Seeman, 1999). Maladaptive effects comprise the "wear and tear" of stress on physiological systems (Schulkin, 2011).

The most significant distinction between the two models is the emphasis on feedforward regulation of the stress response (allostasis) versus the feedback regulation (homeostasis) (Sterling, 2012). In a feedforward process, a physiological system acts as if it is trying to "predict" the next level of energy demands and makes preadjustments. At the center of a feedforward system is the storage of information from previous interactions with environmental stimuli (Clark, 2015; Hohwy, 2014). This storage is sometimes referred to as an internal model—a key component in adaptive decision-making (Ito, 2008; Sutton & Barto, 1981). When a stressor is encountered, the physiological system can draw upon previous information to determine the hormonal response. Feedforward regulation is a faster and more energetically efficient regulatory mechanism for maintenance of viability in the environment (McEwen, 2004; Sterling, 2012).

There is some empirical evidence supporting the allostasis model. Most of it measures and tests the association between environmental conditions and biomarkers of allostatic load. The associations moderate in strength, but findings are compelling. Greater exposure to environmental stressors in the form of gender, racial, and class inequalities does appear to independently increase allostatic load (Geronimus et al., 2010; Gruenewald et al., 2012; Wallace et al., 2013; Zannas et al., 2015). A review of the literature did not yield any studies that conducted direct tests of feedforward mechanisms in the stress response. However, feedforward regulation in other physiological systems is common (Llinás, 2001).

EVOLUTIONARY SOCIOLOGY OF STRESS

Numerous books and review articles have been published on the sociological relevance of stress hormones. However, the literature is somewhat thin in terms of theoretical integrations. Here, we outline a model of stress hormone actions based squarely within the perspective of evolutionary sociology. The central concept in the model is adaptive predictive control (APC). APC is a relational concept; it represents a state in the relationship between the individual (agent) and the environment. It is the point at which the agent can accurately predict changes in the environment and those changes only arise from the agent's effects on the environment.

The model is based on four general premises. The first states that APC is a necessary antecedent to fitness maximization over the long term. There are various environmental cues to indicate ideal and/or threatening conditions for survival and reproduction. Traits evolve that co-vary with these cues, and these traits are commonly associated with control mechanisms (Geary, 2005). As discussed later, predictive learning is a major trait contributing to the agent's ability to anticipate and control environmental conditions. The second premise states that social structure evolved as a strategy to increase the probability of achieving APC far above the probability associated with acting alone. Social structure effectively and efficiently stabilizes environmental conditions. It allows agents to conserve time and energy. The third premise states that incumbency in the highest position in the organization grants an agent control of the "definition of situations," even from a distant temporal, spatial, or social location. The agent can affix present and future interactions to a predictable pattern favoring the agent's long-term fitness. The fourth premise states that hormones signal the agent's level of predictive control over the environment. Hormones allow agents to "feel" the environment and adjust behavior (Damasio, 1999; Gigerenzer, 2007; Miceli, Castelfranchi, & Ortony, 2015). Hormonal signaling systems (e.g., the stress system and the reward system) interact to motivate finer adjustments in behavior.

The Agent

The first principle for the model states that the agent's impulse to action is a consequence of thermodynamic inefficiencies in metabolic processes. Biological systems are dissipative structures—they are constantly in a thermodynamic state "far-from-equilibrium" (Nicolis & Prigogine, 1989). Only a portion of subsistence consumed by the agent is converted into usable energy; a larger portion is excreted as waste product or detritus (Nicolis & Prigogine, 1989; Odling-Smee, LaLand, & Feldman, 2003). Thermodynamic inefficiency requires the agent to spend much of its time foraging for additional subsistence in the local environment (Odling-Smee et al., 2003). Hence, the agent's overall fitness becomes closely tied to the available energy within a local environment. In turn, the agent's energetic dependency on the environment becomes the target of natural selection.

The agent's goal is to maximize fitness. Successful adaptation requires the agent to optimally allocate finite energy resources (and time) to various developmental tasks, such as growth, sexual maturation, relationship maintenance, and investing in the next generation of offspring through parenting or alloparenting (Stearns, 1992). The agent will face significant problems inherent in each task, such as choosing a mate, competing for reproductive opportunities, and defending the relationship against would-be rivals. The agent will also encounter other environmentally induced constraints during allocation decisions, social and otherwise. Levels of subsistence resources may fluctuate unpredictably due to natural processes (e.g., floods and droughts) (Wingfield, 2009). Under a social hierarchy, the agent may be barred from accessing high-quality subsistence resources (Betzig, 1986; Lee, 1994). To summarize the problem, innate thermodynamic limitations and environmental constraints may force the agent to make negative fitness trade-offs in allocation decisions. Investing time and energy in one task may enhance fitness in the short term but decrease fitness in the long term (Stearns, 1992).

Prediction, Prediction Error, and Stress Hormones

Thermodynamic inefficiencies and environmental constraints are believed to be the driving factors in the evolution of predictive learning. Predictive learning is the act of recognizing a temporal association between two or more events, storing that information into memory, and using it to modify behavior in the present or the future (Shettleworth, 1998). Prediction helps the agent plan allocations, consider possible outcomes under "mental simulations" (Barsalou, 2011) of environmental conditions, and identify a strategy for allocating resources that avoids negative fitness trade-offs. Predictive learning has been observed in primitive organisms with deep phylogenetic roots (Llinás, 2001)—an indication that the capacity for predictive learning has been highly conserved over evolutionary time (Tagkopoulos, Liu, & Tavazoie, 2008).

Theorists reason that predictive learning evolved due to a speed advantage in processing information about the relationship between the agent and its environment. The typical view of learning is based on the notion of a feedback effect. An agent carries out an action to achieve a goal, observes the consequences of the action, and adjusts the next behavior to move closer to that goal. Feedback learning requires the agent to wait for crucial information from sensory mechanisms before the next action can be taken. Predictive learning is based on a feedforward mechanism. Figure 17.5 sketches the prediction process applicable to humans and nonhumans with homologous brain functions.

An agent takes stored information about a goal and predicts the actions necessary to reach the goal. Information is stored in what is often referred to as an internal model (Sutton & Barto, 1981; Wolpert, Miall, & Kawato, 1998). It is a model of the agent–environment relationship built from three basic sources: evolved preferences such as the inherent value placed on higher social status and hierarchical group formation (Berger & Zelditch, 1997; Fiske, 1991; Huberman, Loch, & Önçüler, 2004; Levi Martin, 2009); personality factors such as trust and altruism (Reuter, Frenzel, Walter, Markett, & Montag, 2011); and social and cultural experiences that tune the internal model to the local environment. At the detection of a stimulus, information from the internal model is sent forward to the sensory mechanisms and compared. If the information matches incoming stimulus, then the agent continues with its current actions. If there is a mismatch (a prediction error), then sensory mechanisms send information about the error back to the internal model, which in turn sends another prediction forward.

Three interconnected brain regions are central to making and evaluating predictions: the cerebellum, the prefrontal cortex, and the ventral tegmental area. The cerebellum houses the internal model(s) of the environment. It processes and stores highly

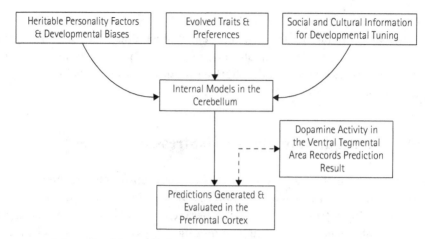

FIGURE 17.5 Schematic of the prediction process.

abstract information such as keeping track of time, learning intertemporal associations between events, and generating predictions about the consequences of physical movements through an environment (Ito, 2008; Koziol, Budding, & Chidekel, 2012; O'Reilly, Mesulam, & Nobre, 2008). Information from the internal model, via cerebellar neurons, is sent to the prefrontal cortex, which in turn generates predictions about incoming stimuli and evaluates the accuracy of a prediction. Comparisons between incoming stimuli and information received from the internal model are made in the prefrontal cortex (Middleton & Strick, 2001). The ventral tegmental area (VTA), located in the midbrain, registers whether a prediction is correct and initiates behavioral modifications accordingly (Fiorillo, Tobler, & Schultz, 2003; Schultz, Dayan, & Montague, 2002). Like the prefrontal cortex, it receives output from nuclei within the cerebellum (Watson, Becker, Apps, & Jones, 2014).

When a prediction about the association of two or more environmental conditions is correct, the activity of dopaminergic neurons in the VTA spikes to above-baseline levels. Consequently, the agent experiences a reward sensation (Schultz et al., 2002). When a prediction is incorrect, the error causes a decrease in the activity of dopaminergic neurons to a level below baseline (Fiorillo et al., 2003; Schultz et al., 2002). Neurons in the prefrontal cortex trigger the release of GCs into the VTA. In turn, higher levels of GCs suppress the activity of dopaminergic neurons in the VTA. Rather than a reward sensation, the agent experiences psychological distress. The level of GCs increases as additional prediction errors are recorded by dopamine neurons. Over time, the capacities of the prefrontal cortex to control cognition and behaviors become inhibited by persistently high levels of GCs (Arnsten, 2009).

Social Structure

Humans are one of a few species that have experienced a major evolutionary transition—the transition from ecological vulnerability to ecological dominance. The emergence of social structure rapidly drove this transition (Alexander, 1987, 1990; Flinn, 2009). Social structure allowed humans to impose a critical degree of order and predictability on the physical environment through various forms of niche engineering such as farming and the construction of infrastructures that kept vital physical resources (e.g., water) at optimal levels for the survival of members of the community (Lenski, 1984; Megarry, 1995). As a fitness strategy, social structure reduced time and energy constraints imposed by the physical environment and natural predators to minimal concerns. However, like all other adaptive innovations, social structure itself imposed significant constraints on fitness maximization, such as competitive, hierarchical social orders and concomitant structurally driven inequalities in the distribution of control over resources. Structural inequalities manifested in the concentration of wealth among higher positions in the social order. Incumbents of higher positions in the social order were also able to hoard opportunities for the accumulation of wealth. The intergenerational durability of structural inequalities increased with the emergence of wealth inheritance systems (Flannery & Marcus, 2012; Lenski, 1984).

In very real ways, social structure worsened the problem of environmental unpredictability, at least for some. Agents in lower social positions suffered most. They were still most vulnerable to the harsh, unpredictable conditions of the physical environment. In early societies, for example, lower social status relegated an agent to menial amounts of water and other subsistence resources; lower quality housing that provided weak protection from storms and floods; and disproportionate vulnerability to aggressive actions by out-groups, including conscription into military service. Contractions in the availability of subsistence resources would expose agents in lower statuses to intense competitions with neighbors, especially unrelated kin. Opportunities to learn valuable skills became more difficult to acquire. Competition exposed once-stable, cooperative relationships to risk of dissolution. Family and friends would have to migrate to other lands. An agent might have been unreasonably stigmatized, leading to social rejection and isolation (Flannery & Marcus, 2012).

Research on lives in contemporary societies shows that the experiences of agents in lower social positions have not changed much regarding exposure to environmental uncertainties. Quantitative and qualitative studies suggest that agents in lower social positions still experience stress-inducing negative fitness trade-offs. For example, additional time and energy devoted to work deplete time and energy needed to sufficiently maintain healthy family relationships (Glavin, Schieman, & Reid, 2011; Schieman, Whitestone, & Van Gundy, 2006). However, the full consequences of making a negative fitness trade-off become less predictable in lower social positions. Ethnographic studies of communities in poverty show that young adults commonly face a trade-off between additional work and additional schooling. However, the long-term outcomes of the trade-off decision are highly uncertain. Additional schooling might not lead to a future increase in standard of living. There are no or few signals coming from the environment that indicate otherwise. Many young adults conclude that time would be better invested in finding gainful employment in the local labor market. Unfortunately, gains from employment might soon stagnate, which increases uncertainties about the future (Anderson, 1978; MacLeod, 1995).

In contrast, agents in higher status positions have exercised much greater control over the physical and social environment in early and modern societies. Access to a disproportionate amount of subsistence resources creates a thick buffer against harmful fluctuations in natural resources. The social power of agents in higher positions is exemplified in the capacity to influence social interactions from far temporal and spatial distances via reputation and prestige enhancements. Perhaps the most powerful tool of social influence is embodied in myths that impart supernatural powers to the agent. (Think of the recent claim that "A vote against Trump is a vote against the will of God.") In some societies, an agent in a higher social status must demonstrate commitment to the community by engaging in acts of "costly signaling" (Bird & Smith, 2005; Smith & Bird, 2000). However, such acts ultimately solidified the reputation, prestige, and mythical characteristics of the agent (Bird & Smith, 2005).

Adaptive Predictive Control Hypothesis

Structurally induced fitness trade-offs force agents into uncertain situations in everyday life. Any effort to minimize fitness trade-offs must increase predictive control over situations. From a sociological perspective, the agent must be able to control the definition of the situation in social interactions with other agents. Definition of the situation consists of the norms, social roles, and relative statuses of agents engaged in interaction. An agent with higher social status in the interaction is in a better position to control the definition of the situation (Ball-Rokeach, 1973). Table 17.1 presents the three main levels of control, the predicted stress hormone profile for an agent in that condition, the predicted behavior in direct response to changes in stress hormone levels, and the trade-offs largely in terms of the maladaptive effects of stress hormones.

We treat APC as a Weberian ideal type condition. The agent exercises complete control over the definition of the situation and can maintain it efficiently due to the material and nonmaterial resources granted by formal social organization. The agent's sphere of control spans social and physical boundaries via reputation effects. APC allows the agent to maximize fitness over generational time. In any situation, the agent can discover the optimal fitness strategy through trial and error. The endocrinological profile of the agent would indicate fluctuations in levels of GCs and dopamine within ranges that enhance prefrontal cortex.

The most adaptive action would be positive niche construction, which is defined as constructing the local environment in a way that extends the agent's access to vital resources over spatial and temporal distances (Odling-Smee et al., 2003). Of course, stress levels among agents in the APC condition should be significantly lower compared to agents in less certain, less controllable situations. GC and dopamine levels will fluctuate within ranges that facilitate adaptive decision-making and behavior. However, when the relationship between the agent and the environment is in a state of "allostatic control," the agent can exercise limited control over the definition of the situation but control is still contingent upon external factors, including competitive pressures from other agents. The agent's movements through the environment resemble a random walk process. There is an observable path taken by the agent to increase control over the definition of the situation; however, the path is obscured by random deviations from the path.

Table 17.1 Levels of Predictive Control

	Adaptive Predictive Control	Allostatic Control	Ineffectual State
Definition	High level of control over the definition of the situations; Control spans social and physical spaces and intergenerational time	Narrow control over the definitions of the situations but considerable amount of ambiguity remains in social interactions	Complete absence of definitions of the situations
Agent State	Agent can predict future changes in social interactions and effect those changes using personal and organizational resources	Agent has a limited sphere of control in time and space; Experiences unpredicted shocks to control from external environmental factors (e.g. social competition)	Agent cannot produce anticipated effects on others or the physical environment; Socially disorganization situation
Hormone Actions	GC and dopamine levels remain within ranges which maintain PFC functions near basal levels	Increase in dopamine levels in the PFC; GC levels decline in cortical and subcortical structures	GCs inhibit the expression of dopamine in the PFC; Dopamine levels increase in subcortical structures such as the amygdala and VTA
Fitness Strategy	Best option for maximizing long-term fitness can be identified through trial-and-error testing	Time preference values the present and the values of future outcomes are discounted	Bet-hedging – Diversify strategic behaviors until a definition of the situation can be established; Wingfield's "Emergency Life History Stage"
Effects	Minimal effect of negative tradeoffs	Persistently high levels of dopamine and low levels of GCs raise the risk of addictive behaviors	GCs will degrade PFC functioning if they persist at high levels for extended periods of time. The agent suffers a loss of executive control over thoughts and behaviors

This situation might be found in working-class and middle-class households in which income is sufficient to maintain a stable family life but financial challenges may still arise unexpectedly. Sudden illness, auto repairs, and home repairs may strain the household budget (Morduch & Schneider, 2017). Allostatic control might also be observed among workers in the financial sector, in which an agent can see the immediate effects of decisions. However, uncertainty about the decisions of others will dictate many outcomes beyond the control of the agent (Pixley, 2012).

In a state of allostatic control, the APC model predicts the agent will resolve allostasis by focusing on his or her efforts to increase control over the definition of the immediate situation. The agent does not have the resources to extend his or her influence further in time or space. We predict the agent's time preferences will increase the value of immediate rewards for actions over delayed rewards. The chief biomarker of an agent in this condition will be higher levels of dopamine and lower levels of GCs in the prefrontal cortex. The increase in dopamine levels above baseline induces focused attention on the immediate circumstance. It also triggers a strong reward sensation that drives impulsive decision-making (Coates, Gurnell, & Sarnyai, 2010). However, if the condition persists over time, elevated dopamine levels combined with lower GC levels will increase the agent's vulnerability to addictive behavior (Yi, Mitchell, & Bickel, 2010).

An ineffectual state is the least desirable condition of existence for the agent. There is no identifiable definition of the situation the agent can draw upon. It has been aptly described as a condition of pervasive ambiguity (Ball-Rokeach, 1973). Information about social roles is completely absent; there are no visible connections between organizational elements of the social environment (e.g., family, school, and employment); and there is no observable starting point at which agents could collectively begin construction of a new definition of the situation (Ball-Rokeach, 1973). Attempts to effect predictive control are frustrated by the fact that ineffectuality can describe areas that have suffered decades of socioeconomic decline due to industrial transitions. The strengths of social institutions and local infrastructures rapidly decline.

Again, the main argument of the APC model states that the actions of stress hormones guide the agent through a stressful environment. Stress signals from change in glucocorticoid levels motivate the agent toward actions to increase control over the definition of the situation. Reward signals from a change in dopamine levels comprise a mechanism for evaluating actions. The interactions between GCs and dopamine should take on specific patterns given a particular level of predictive control.

Ineffectuality will induce higher levels of GCs in the prefrontal cortex. Dopamine levels will increase in subcortical structures such as the VTA and the amygdala. Higher levels of GCs in the prefrontal cortex inhibit cognitive control of behavior by suppressing the activity of dopamine neurons. However, GCs cause a flow of dopamine out of the prefrontal cortex and into subcortical regions (Butts, Weinberg, Young, & Phillips, 2011).

The interactions between GCs and dopamine have a behavioral effect known as "bet-hedging" (Seger & Brockmann, 1987; Wilbur & Rudolf, 2006). In the face of pervasive ambiguity, the agent pursues multiple strategies to reduce uncertainty as would a stock trader betting on the value of a stock in an uncertain market. Behaviorally, the evolved agent switches between long-term fitness strategies and short-term strategies (Grafen, 1999). Sociologically, the agent switches between two or more strategies designed to cope with the present and build a stable definition of the situation over the long term (Ball-Rokeach, 1973). If one strategy fails, another might succeed.

Studies show that interactions between GCs and other hormones, such as dopamine and testosterone, drive bet-hedging behavior. Levels of steroid hormones such as testosterone have a positive association with risk-taking; however, GCs modulate the association. Low levels of cortisol allow a high, positive correlation between testosterone and the propensity for risk-taking behavior in men. Higher levels of cortisol suppress the association (Mehta, Welker, Zilioli, & Carre, 2015). Thus, the switch between two or more strategies may be regulated by stress hormones.

If ineffectuality persists for long periods of time (months or years), the agent's fitness will decline as a direct result of the impact of GCs on cellular tissue. In some cases, the effect will depend on the age of the agent. For example, interleukin-6 (IL-6) is a promoter gene that controls pro-inflammatory and anti-inflammatory responses to social stress (Cole et al., 2011). However, its action depends on the developmental period of the agent. IL-6 releases anti-inflammatory proteins among youth exposed to social stress, boosting resilience. Among older adults, IL-6 increases vulnerability to social stress by releasing pro-inflammatory proteins into cells (Cole et al., 2011).

Another outcome of a persistent state of ineffectuality might be the nongenetic intergenerational transmission of stress hormone levels. During fetal development, genes are particularly responsive to conditions in the maternal environment (Burns et al., 2012; Sokolowski, 2010). Recent research on "fetal programming" has shown that pregnant mothers living in stressful circumstances tend to bear children with abnormal sensitivity to stress. Stress hormones in the mother seem to tune the child's default endocrinological profile. One result is that the child will have a higher risk of stress-related diseases in adulthood (Drake & Walker, 2004; Lupien, King, Meaney, & McEwen, 2000).

Conclusion

The major goal of this chapter is to present a semi-detailed review of hormones, their effects, and their evolutionary significance. The body of literature has an intense focus on the role of social forces in hormone evolution and functioning. Recent work on humans has demonstrated the hormonal and genetic mechanisms through which social inequalities and adversities "get under the skin." However, sociological processes are much more complex than issues covered thus far. There are still very important questions to be answered. For instance, can hormonal mechanisms operating in an endogenous role yield novel insights on the of structural inequality? Do hormones play an exogenous role in decisions among economic and political elites that lead to vast and rigidly oppressive hierarchies? Do collective efforts to resist structural inequality (and other environmental stressors) regulate hormonal mechanisms within the individual? We believe a model of stress as a function of prediction error has unique potential to deliver correct answers to these important questions. Previous ethnographic studies of communities in poverty, for example, suggest that mobility decisions are substantially impacted by predictions about future life chances and prediction errors. Recent research in behavioral economics and neuroscience proposes that the interplay between environment, agent, and hormones contributed directly to destructive decision-making among leaders on Wall Street (Coates et al., 2010; Pixley, 2012). Our future work will explore the adaptive predictive control model in a range of sociological contexts.

References

Adkins-Regan, E. (2005). *Hormones and animal social behavior*. Princeton, NJ: Princeton University Press.

Alexander, R. D. (1987). *The biology of moral systems*. Chicago, IL: Aldine de Gruyter.

Alexander, R. D. (1990). *How did humans evolve? Reflections on the uniquely unique species* (Vol. 1, pp. 1–38). Ann Arbor, MI: Museum of Zoology, University of Michigan.

Allman, J. M., Hakeem, A., & Watson, K. (2002). Two phylogenetic specializations in the human brain. *The Neuroscientist, 8*(4), 335.

Allman, J. M., Tetreault, N. A., Hakeem, A. Y., & Park, S. (2011). The von Economo neurons in apes and humans. *American Journal of Human Biology, 23*(1), 5–21.

Anderson, E. (1978). *A place on the corner*. Chicago, IL: University of Chicago.

Arnsten, A. F. T. (2009). Stress signalling pathways that impair prefrontal cortex structure and function. *Nature Reviews Neuroscience, 10*(6), 410–422.

Badyaev, A. V. (2005). Role of stress in evolution: From individual adaptability to evolutionary adaptation. In B. Hallgrímsson & B. K. Hall (Eds.), *Variation: A central concept in biology* (pp. 277–302). Amsterdam, the Netherlands: Elsevier.

Ball-Rokeach, S. J. (1973). From pervasive ambiguity to a definition of the situation. *Sociometry, 36*(3), 378–389.

Barchas, P. R. (1976). Physiological sociology: Interface of sociological and biological processes. *Annual Review of Sociology, 2*(1), 299–333.

Barsalou, L. W. (2011). Simulation, situated conceptualization, and prediction. In M. Bar (Ed.), *Predictions in the brain: Using our past to generate a future* (pp. 27–39). Oxford, UK: University of Oxford.

Belanoff, J. K., Gross, K., Yager, A., & Schatzberg, A. F. (2001). Corticosteroids and cognition. *Journal of psychiatric research, 35*(3), 127–145.

Bercury, K. K., & Macklin, W. B. (2015). Dynamics and mechanisms of CNS myelination. *Developmental Cell, 32*(4), 447–458.

Berger, J., & Zelditch, M. (1997). *Status, power and legitimacy: Strategies and theories*. New Brunswick, NJ: Transaction Publishers.

Betzig, L. L. (1986). *Despotism and differential reproduction: A Darwinian view of history*. New York, NY: Aldine.

Bird, R. L. B., & Smith, E. A. (2005). Signaling theory, strategic interaction and symbolic capital. *Current Anthropology, 46*(2), 221–248.

Bjorklund, D. F. (2006). Mother knows best: Epigenetic inheritance, maternal effects, and the evolution of human intelligence. *Developmental Review, 26*(2), 213–242.

Blair, R. J. (2004). The roles of orbital frontal cortex in the modulation of antisocial behavior. *Brain and Cognition, 55*(1), 198–208.

Brothers, L. (1997). *Friday's footprint: How society shapes the human mind*. Oxford, UK: Oxford University Press.

Brumbach, B., Figueredo, A., & Ellis, B. (2009). Effects of harsh and unpredictable environments in adolescence on development of life history strategies. *Human Nature, 20*(1), 25–51.

Burgess, S. C., & Marshall, D. J. (2014). Adaptive parental effects: The importance of estimating environmental predictability and offspring fitness appropriately. *Oikos, 123*(7), 769–776.

Burns, J. G., Svetec, N., Rowe, L., Mery, F., Dolan, M. J., Boyce, W. T., & Sokolowski, M. B. (2012). Gene–environment interplay in *Drosophila melanogaster*: Chronic food deprivation in early life affects adult exploratory and fitness traits. *Proceedings of the National Academy of Sciences of the USA, 109*(Suppl. 2), 17239–17244.

Butler, A. B., & Hodos, W. (2005). *Comparative vertebrate neuroanatomy: Evolution and adaptation* (2nd ed.). Hoboken, NJ: Wiley-Interscience.

Butts, K. A., Weinberg, J., Young, A. H., & Phillips, A. G. (2011). Glucocorticoid receptors in the prefrontal cortex regulate stress-evoked dopamine efflux and aspects of executive function. *Proceedings of the National Academy of Sciences of the USA, 108*(45), 18459–18464.

Clark, A. (2015). *Surfing uncertainty: Prediction, action, and the embodied mind.* Oxford, UK: Oxford University Press.

Coates, J. M., Gurnell, M., & Sarnyai, Z. (2010). From molecule to market: Steroid hormones and financial risk-taking. *Philosophical Transactions of the Royal Society B: Biological Sciences, 365*(1538), 331–343.

Cole, S. W. (2008). Social regulation of leukocyte homeostasis: The role of glucocorticoid sensitivity. *Brain, Behavior, and Immunity, 22*(7), 1049–1055.

Cole, S. W. (2013). Social regulation of human gene expression: Mechanisms and implications for public health. *American Journal of Public Health, 103*(Suppl. 1), S84-S92.

Cole, S. W., Arevalo, J. M., Manu, K., Telzer, E. H., Kiang, L., Bower, J. E., . . . Fuligni, A. J. (2011). Antagonistic pleiotropy at the human IL6 promoter confers genetic resilience to the proinflammatory effects of adverse social conditions in adolescence. *Developmental Psychology, 47*(4), 1173–1180.

Cole, S. W., Hawkley, L., Arevalo, J., Sung, C., Rose, R., & Cacioppo, J. (2007). Social regulation of gene expression in human leukocytes. *Genome Biology, 8*(9), R189.

Damasio, A. (1999). *The feeling of what happens: Body and emotion in the making of consciousness.* New York, NY: Harcourt Brace.

Davis, J. (2012). Perceived environmental threats as a factor in reproductive behavior: An examination of American youth. *Evolution and Human Behavior, 33*(6), 647–656.

Davis, M. (1992). The role of the amygdala in fear and anxiety. *Annual Review of Neuroscience, 15*(1), 353–375.

Davis, M., Walker, D. L., & Lee, Y. (1997). Amygdala and bed nucleus of the stria terminalis: Differential roles in fear and anxiety measured with the acoustic startle reflex. *Philosophical Transactions: Biological Sciences, 352*(1362), 1675–1687.

Djordjevic, A., Adzic, M., Djordjevic, J., & Radojcic, M. B. (2009). Stress type dependence of expression and cytoplasmic-nuclear partitioning of glucocorticoid receptor, Hsp90 and Hsp70 in Wistar rat brain. *Neuropsychobiology, 59*(4), 213–221.

Drake, A. J., & Walker, B. R. (2004). The intergenerational effects of fetal programming: Nongenomic mechanisms for the inheritance of low birth weight and cardiovascular risk. *Journal of Endocrinology, 180*(1), 1–16.

El Waly, B., Macchi, M., Cayre, M., & Durbec, P. (2014). Oligodendrogenesis in the normal and pathological central nervous system. *Frontiers in Neuroscience, 8*, 145. doi:10.3389/fnins.2014.00145

Ellis, B., Figueredo, A., Brumbach, B., & Schlomer, G. (2009). Fundamental dimensions of environmental risk. *Human Nature, 20*(2), 204–268.

Epel, E. S. (2009). Telomeres in a life-span perspective: A new "psychobiomarker"? *Current Directions in Psychological Science, 18*(1), 6–10.

Evanson, N. K., Herman, J. P., Sakai, R. R., & Krause, E. G. (2010). Nongenomic actions of adrenal steroids in the central nervous system. *Journal of Neuroendocrinology, 22*(8), 846–861.

Fekete, É. M., Zhao, Y., Li, C., Sabino, V., Vale, W. W., & Zorrilla, E. P. (2009). Social defeat stress activates medial amygdala cells that express type 2 corticotropin-releasing factor receptor mRNA. *Neuroscience, 162*(1), 5–13.

Fiorillo, C. D., Tobler, P. N., & Schultz, W. (2003). Discrete coding of reward probability and uncertainty by dopamine neurons. *Science*, *299*(5614), 1898–1902.

Fiske, A. P. (1991). *Structures of social life: The four elementary forms of human relations.* New York, NY: Free Press.

Flannery, K. V., & Marcus, J. (2012). *The creation of inequality: How our prehistoric ancestors set the stage for monarchy, slavery, and empire.* Cambridge, MA: Harvard University Press.

Flinn, M. V. (2009). Are cortisol profiles a stable trait during child development? *American Journal of Human Biology*, *21*(6), 769–771.

Franks, D. D. (2010). *Neurosociology: The nexus between neuroscience and social psychology.* New York, NY: Springer.

Franks, D. D., & Davis, J. (2012). Critique and refinement of the neurosociology of mirror neurons. In W. Kalkhoff, S. R. Thye, & E. J. Lawler (Eds.), *Biosociology and Neurosociology* (pp. 77–117). Bingley, UK: Emerald Group.

Furay, A. R., Bruestle, A. E., & Herman, J. P. (2008). The role of the forebrain glucocorticoid receptor in acute and chronic stress. *Endocrinology*, *149*(11), 5482–5490. doi:10.1210/en.2008-0642

Fuster, J. M. (1997). *The prefrontal cortex: Anatomy, physiology, and neuropsychology of the frontal lobe* (3rd ed.). Philadelphia, PA: Lippincott Williams & Wilkins.

Geary, D. C. (2005). *The origin of mind: Evolution of the brain, cognition, and general intelligence.* Washington, DC: American Psychological Association.

Geronimus, A., Hicken, M., Pearson, J., Seashols, S., Brown, K., & Cruz, T. (2010). Do US Black women experience stress-related accelerated biological aging? *Human Nature*, *21*(1), 19–38.

Geuze, E., van Wingen, G. A., van Zuiden, M., Rademaker, A. R., Vermetten, E., Kavelaars, A., . . . Heijnen, C. J. (2012). Glucocorticoid receptor number predicts increase in amygdala activity after severe stress. *Psychoneuroendocrinology*, *37*(11), 1837–1844.

Gigerenzer, G. (2007). *Gut feelings: The intelligence of the unconscious.* New York, NY: Viking Penguin.

Glavin, P., Schieman, S., & Reid, S. (2011). Boundary-spanning work demands and their consequences for guilt and psychological distress. *Journal of Health and Social Behavior*, *52*(1), 43–57.

Glei, D. A., Goldman, N., Chuang, Y. L., & Weinstein, M. (2007). Do chronic stressors lead to physiological dysregulation? Testing the theory of allostatic load. *Psychosomatic Medicine*, *69*(8), 769–776.

Gomperts, B. D., Kramer, I. M., & Tatham, P. E. R. (2003). *Signal transduction.* New York, NY: Academic Press.

Goodson, J. L. (2005). The vertebrate social behavior network: Evolutionary themes and variations. *Hormones and Behavior*, *48*(1), 11–22.

Goodson, J. L., & Kabelik, D. (2009). Dynamic limbic networks and social diversity in vertebrates: From neural context to neuromodulatory patterning. *Frontiers in Neuroendocrinology*, *30*(4), 429–441.

Gourley, S. L., Swanson, A. M., Jacobs, A. M., Howell, J. L., Mo, M., DiLeone, R. J., . . . Taylor, J. R. (2012). Action control is mediated by prefrontal BDNF and glucocorticoid receptor binding. *Proceedings of the National Academy of Sciences of the USA*, *109*(50), 20714–20719.

Grafen, A. (1999). Formal Darwinism, the individual-as-maximizing-agent analogy and bet-hedging. *Proceedings of the Royal Society of London, Biological Sciences*, *266*, 799–803.

Groeneweg, F. L., Karst, H., de Kloet, E. R., & Joëls, M. (2011). Rapid non-genomic effects of corticosteroids and their role in the central stress response. *Journal of Endocrinology*, *209*(2), 153–167.

Gruenewald, T. L., Karlamangla, A. S., Hu, P., Stein-Merkin, S., Crandall, C., Koretz, B., & Seeman, T. E. (2012). History of socioeconomic disadvantage and allostatic load in later life. *Social Science & Medicine*, 74(1), 75–83.

Haller, J., Mikics, E., & Makara, G. B. (2008). The effects of non-genomic glucocorticoid mechanisms on bodily functions and the central neural system: A critical evaluation of findings. *Frontiers in Neuroendocrinology*, 29(2), 273–291.

Haussmann, M. F., & Marchetto, N. M. (2010). Telomeres: Linking stress and survival, ecology and evolution. *Current Zoology*, 56(6), 714–727.

Hoffmann, A. A., & Parsons, P. A. (1991). *Evolutionary genetics and environmental stress*. Oxford, UK: Oxford University Press.

Hohwy, J. (2014). *The predictive mind*. Oxford, UK: Oxford University Press.

Huberman, B. A., Loch, C. H., & Önçüler, A. (2004). Status as a valued resource. *Social Psychology Quarterly*, 67(1), 103–114.

Imura, H. (1994). *The pituitary gland* (2nd ed.). New York, NY: Raven Press.

Insel, T. R., & Young, L. J. (2000). Neuropeptides and the evolution of social behavior. *Current Opinion in Neurobiology*, 10(6), 784–789.

Ito, M. (2008). Control of mental activities by internal models in the cerebellum. *Nature Reviews Neuroscience*, 9(4), 304–313.

Jauregui-Huerta, F., Ruvalcaba-Delgadillo, Y., Gonzalez-Castañeda, R., Garcia-Estrada, J., Gonzalez-Perez, O., & Luquin, S. (2010). Responses of glial cells to stress and glucocorticoids. *Current Immunology Reviews*, 6(3), 195–204.

Jess, N., Noboru, H. K., Andrew, M., Mandy, J., Douglas, H. B., David St., C., . . . Seth, G. N. G. (2012). Synaptic scaffold evolution generated components of vertebrate cognitive complexity. *Nature Neuroscience*, 16(1), 16–24.

Kannan, C. R. (1987). *The pituitary gland*. New York, NY: Plenum.

Kapoor, A., Dunn, E., Kostaki, A., Andrews, M. H., & Matthews, S. G. (2006). Fetal programming of hypothalamo-pituitary-adrenal function: Prenatal stress and glucocorticoids. *Journal of Physiology*, 572(Pt. 1), 31–44.

Kemper, T. D. (1990). *Social structure and testosterone: Explorations of the socio-bio-social chain*. New Brunswick, NJ: Rutgers University Press.

Kempermann, G. (2011). *Adult neurogenesis* (2nd ed.). New York, NY: Oxford University Press.

Knight, E. L., & Mehta, P. H. (2014). Hormones and hierarchies. In J. T. Cheng, J. L. Tracy, & C. Anderson (Eds.), *The psychology of social status* (pp. 269–301). New York, NY: Springer.

Koziol, L., Budding, D., & Chidekel, D. (2012). From movement to thought: Executive function, embodied cognition, and the cerebellum. *The Cerebellum*, 11(2), 505–525.

Lee, P. C. (1994). Social structure and evolution. In P. J. B. Slater & T. R. Halliday (Eds.), *Behaviour and evolution* (pp. 266–303). Cambridge, UK: Cambridge University Press.

Lenski, G. (1984). *Power and privilege: A theory of social stratification*. Chapel Hill, NC: University of North Carolina Press.

Levi Martin, J. (2009). Formation and stabilization of vertical hierarchies among adolescents: Towards a quantitative ethology of dominance among humans. *Social Psychology Quarterly*, 72(3), 241–264.

Levitan, I. B., & Kaczmarek, L. K. (1997a). *The neuron: Cell and molecular biology* (2nd ed., Vol. 1). New York, NY: Oxford University Press.

Levitan, I. B., & Kaczmarek, L. K. (1997b). *The neuron: Cell and molecular biology* (2nd ed., Vol. 2). New York, NY: Oxford University Press.

Llinás, R. R. (2001). *I of the vortex: From neurons to self*. Cambridge, MA: MIT Press.

Lösel, R., & Wehling, M. (2003). Nongenomic actions of steroid hormones. *Nature Reviews: Molecular and Cellular Biology, 4*(1), 46–55.

Love, O. P., Chin, E. H., Wynne-Edwards, K. E., & Williams, T. D. (2005). Stress hormones: A link between maternal condition and sex-biased reproductive investment. *American Naturalist, 166*(6), 751–766.

Lupien, S. J., King, S., Meaney, M. J., & McEwen, B. S. (2000). Child's stress hormone levels correlate with mother's socioeconomic status and depressive state. *Biological Psychiatry, 48*(10), 976–980.

MacLeod, J. (1995). *Ain't no makin' it: Leveled aspirations in a low income neighborhood.* Boulder, CO: Westview.

Malven, P. V. (2000). *Mammalian neuroendocrinology.* Boca Raton, FL: CRC Press.

Mazur, A. (2005). *Biosociology of dominance and deference.* Lanham, MD: Rowman & Littlefield.

McEwen, B. S. (2004). *The end of stress as we know it.* Washington, DC: Joseph Henry Press.

McEwen, B. S., & Seeman, T. (1999). Protective and damaging effects of mediators of stress: Elaborating and testing the concepts of allostasis and allostatic load. *Annals of the New York Academy of Sciences, 896*(1), 30–47.

Megarry, T. (1995). *Society in prehistory: The origins of human culture.* New York, NY: New York University Press.

Mehta, P. H., Welker, K. M., Zilioli, S., & Carre, J. M. (2015). Testosterone and cortisol jointly modulate risk-taking. *Psychoneuroendocrinology, 56,* 88–99.

Miceli, M., Castelfranchi, C., & Ortony, A. (2015). *Expectancy and emotion.* Oxford, UK: Oxford University Press.

Middleton, F. A., & Strick, P. L. (2001). Cerebellar projections to the prefrontal cortex of the primate. *Journal of Neuroscience, 21*(2), 700–712.

Mikics, E., Kruk, M. R., & Haller, J. (2004). Genomic and non-genomic effects of glucocorticoids on aggressive behavior in male rats. *Psychoneuroendocrinology, 29*(5), 618–635.

Monaghan, P. (2014). Organismal stress, telomeres and life histories. *Journal of Experimental Biology, 217*(1), 57–66.

Morduch, J., & Schneider, R. (2017). *The financial diaries: How American families cope in a world of uncertainty.* Princeton, NJ: Princeton University Press.

Morecraft, R. J., & Van Hoesen, G. W. (1998). Convergence of limbic input to the cingulate motor cortex in the rhesus monkey. *Brain Research Bulletin, 45*(2), 209–232.

Morgane, P. J., Galler, J. R., & Mokler, D. J. (2005). A review of systems and networks of the limbic forebrain/limbic midbrain. *Progress in Neurobiology, 75*(2), 143–160.

Munhoz, C. D., Lepsch, L. B., Kawamoto, E. M., Malta, M. B., Lima Lde, S., Avellar, M. C., . . . Scavone, C. (2006). Chronic unpredictable stress exacerbates lipopolysaccharide-induced activation of nuclear factor-kappaB in the frontal cortex and hippocampus via glucocorticoid secretion. *Journal of Neuroscience, 26*(14), 3813–3820.

Nettle, D. (2011). Flexibility in reproductive timing in human females: Integrating ultimate and proximate explanations. *Philosophical Transactions of the Royal Society of London B: Biological Sciences, 366*(1563), 357–365.

Newman, S. W. (1999). The medial extended amygdala in male reproductive behavior: A node in the mammalian social behavior network. *Annals of the New York Academy of Sciences, 877,* 242–257.

Nicolis, G., & Prigogine, I. (1989). *Exploring complexity: An introduction.* New York, NY: Freeman.

Odling-Smee, J. F., LaLand, K. N., & Feldman, M. W. (2003). *Niche construction: The neglected process in evolution*. Princeton, NJ: Princeton University Press.

Olausson, P., Kiraly, D. D., Gourley, S. L., & Taylor, J. R. (2013). Persistent effects of prior chronic exposure to corticosterone on reward-related learning and motivation in rodents. *Psychopharmacology (Berlin), 225*(3), 569–577.

O'Reilly, J. X., Mesulam, M. M., & Nobre, A. C. (2008). The cerebellum predicts the timing of perceptual events. *Journal of Neuroscience, 28*(9), 2252–2260.

Paydar, A., Lee, B., Gangadharan, G., Lee, S., Hwang, E. M., & Shin, H. S. (2014). Extrasynaptic GABAA receptors in mediodorsal thalamic nucleus modulate fear extinction learning. *Molecular Brain, 7*(1), 1–18.

Penzo, M. A., Robert, V., Tucciarone, J., De Bundel, D., Wang, M., Van Aelst, L., . . . Li, B. (2015). The paraventricular thalamus controls a central amygdala fear circuit. *Nature, 519*(7544), 455–459.

Phelps, E. A. (2006). Emotion and cognition: Insights from studies of the human amygdala. *Annual Review of Psychology, 57*(1), 27–53.

Pixley, J. (2012). *Emotions in finance: Booms, busts and uncertainty* (2nd ed.). New York, NY: Cambridge University Press.

Price, J. L. (2006). Connections of the orbital cortex. In D. H. Zald & S. Rauch (Eds.), *The orbitofrontal cortex* (pp. 39–56). Oxford, UK: Oxford University Press.

Reuter, M., Frenzel, C., Walter, N. T., Markett, S., & Montag, C. (2011). Investigating the genetic basis of altruism: The role of the COMT Val158Met polymorphism. *Social Cognitive and Affective Neuroscience, 6*(5), 662–668.

Rizzolatti, G., & Sinigaglia, C. (2008). *Mirrors in the brain: How our minds share actions and emotions*. New York, NY: Oxford University Press.

Rossignol, E. (2011). Genetics and function of neocortical GABAergic interneurons in neurodevelopmental disorders. *Neural Plasticity, 2011*, 25.

Rushworth, M. F., Walton, M. E., Kennerley, S. W., & Bannerman, D. M. (2004). Action sets and decisions in the medial frontal cortex. *Trends in Cognitive Science, 8*(9), 410–417.

Sapolsky, R. M. (2004). Social status and health in humans and other animals. *Annual Review of Anthropology, 33*, 393–418.

Schieman, S., Whitestone, Y. K., & Van Gundy, K. (2006). The nature of work and the stress of higher status. *Journal of Health and Social Behavior, 47*(3), 242–257.

Schulkin, J. (2003). *Rethinking homeostasis: Allostatic regulation in physiology and pathology*. Cambridge, MA: MIT Press.

Schulkin, J. (2011). *Adaptation and well-being: Social allostasis*. Cambridge, UK: Cambridge University Press.

Schulkin, J., Gold, W., & McEwen, S. (1998). Induction of corticotropin-releasing hormone gene expression by glucocorticoids: Implication for understanding states of fear and anxiety and allostatic load. *Psychoneuroendocrinology, 23*(3), 219–243.

Schultz, W., Dayan, P., & Montague, P. R. (2002). A neural substrate of prediction and reward. In J. Cacioppo, G. G. Berntson, R. Adolphs, C. S. Carter, R. J. Davidson, M. K. McClintock, . . . S. E. Taylor (Eds.), *Foundations in social neuroscience* (pp. 541–554). Cambridge, MA: MIT Press.

Seger, J., & Brockmann, H. J. (1987). What is bet-hedging? *Oxford Surveys in Evolutionary Biology, 4*, 182–211.

Shepherd, G. M. (1998). *The synaptic organization of the brain* (4th ed.). Oxford, UK: Oxford University Press.

Shettleworth, S. J. (1998). *Cognition, evolution, and behavior.* Oxford, UK: Oxford University Press.

Sinclair, D., Webster, M. J., Fullerton, J. M., & Weickert, C. S. (2012). Glucocorticoid receptor mRNA and protein isoform alterations in the orbitofrontal cortex in schizophrenia and bipolar disorder. *BMC Psychiatry, 12,* 84.

Smith, E. A., & Bird, R. L. B. (2000). Turtle hunting and tombstone opening: Public generosity as costly signaling. *Evolution and Human Behavior, 21,* 245–261.

Sokolowski, M. B. (2010). Social interactions in "simple" model systems. *Neuron, 65*(6), 780–794.

Spruston, N. (2008). Pyramidal neurons: Dendritic structure and synaptic integration. *Nature Reviews Neuroscience, 9*(3), 206–221.

Stearns, S. C. (1992). *The evolution of life histories.* Oxford, UK: Oxford University Press.

Sterling, P. (2012). Allostasis: A model of predictive regulation. *Physiology & Behavior, 106*(1), 5–15.

Sussman, D., Pang, E. W., Jetly, R., Dunkley, B. T., & Taylor, M. J. (2016). Neuroanatomical features in soldiers with post-traumatic stress disorder. *BMC Neuroscience, 17,* 1–11.

Sutton, R. S., & Barto, A. G. (1981). An adaptive network that constructs and uses an internal model of its world. *Cognition and Brain Theory, 4*(3), 217–246.

Swanson, A. M., Shapiro, L. P., Whyte, A. J., & Gourley, S. L. (2013). Glucocorticoid receptor regulation of action selection and prefrontal cortical dendritic spines. *Communicative & Integrative biology, 6*(6), e26068.

Tagkopoulos, I., Liu, Y. C., & Tavazoie, S. (2008). Predictive behavior within microbial genetic networks. *Science, 320*(5881), 1313–1317.

Thorpe, S. J., Rolls, E. T., & Maddison, S. (1983). The orbitofrontal cortex: Neuronal activity in the behaving monkey. *Experimental Brain Research, 49*(1), 93–115.

Uggla, C., & Mace, R. (2016). Local ecology influences reproductive timing in Northern Ireland independently of individual wealth. *Behavioral Ecology, 27*(1), 158–165.

Vertes, R. P., Linley, S. B., & Hoover, W. B. (2015). Limbic circuitry of the midline thalamus. *Neuroscience & Biobehavioral Reviews, 54,* 89–107.

Vrtička, P., Andersson, F., Grandjean, D., Sander, D., & Vuilleumier, P. (2008). Individual attachment style modulates human amygdala and striatum activation during social appraisal. *PLoS One, 3*(8), e2868.

Vyas, S., Rodrigues, A. J., Silva, J. M., Tronche, F., Almeida, O. F. X., Sousa, N., & Sotiropoulos, I. (2016). Chronic stress and glucocorticoids: From neuronal plasticity to neurodegeneration. *Neural Plasticity, 2016,* Article 6391686.

Wallace, M., Harville, E., Theall, K., Webber, L., Chen, W., & Berenson, G. (2013). Preconception biomarkers of allostatic load and racial disparities in adverse birth outcomes: The Bogalusa Heart Study. *Paediatric & Perinatal Epidemiology, 27*(6), 587–597.

Wallis, J. D. (2007). Orbitofrontal cortex and its contribution to decision-making. *Annual Review of Neuroscience, 30*(1), 31–56.

Walton, J. C., Weil, Z. M., & Nelson, R. J. (2011). Influence of photoperiod on hormones, behavior, and immune function. *Frontiers in Neuroendocrinology, 32*(3), 303–319.

Wang, S. S., Yan, X. B., Hofman, M. A., Swaab, D. F., & Zhou, J. N. (2010). Increased expression level of corticotropin-releasing hormone in the amygdala and in the hypothalamus in rats exposed to chronic unpredictable mild stress. *Neuroscience Bulletin, 26*(4), 297–303.

Watson, T. C., Becker, N., Apps, R., & Jones, M. W. (2014). Back to front: Cerebellar connections and interactions with the prefrontal cortex. *Frontiers in Systems Neuroscience, 8,* 4.

Weaver, I. C., Cervoni, N., Champagne, F. A., D'Alessio, A. C., Sharma, S., Seckl, J. R., . . . Meaney, M. J. (2004). Epigenetic programming by maternal behavior. *Nature Neuroscience*, *7*(8), 847–854. doi:10.1038/nn1276

Whalen, P. J., & Phelps, E. A. (2009). *The human amygdala*. New York, NY: Guilford.

Wilbur, H. M., & Rudolf, V. H. W. (2006). Life-history evolution in uncertain environments: Bet hedging in time. *American Naturalist*, *168*(3): 398–411.

Wilson, M., & Daly, M. (1997). Life expectancy, economic inequality, homicide, and reproductive timing in Chicago neighbourhoods. *British Medical Journal*, *314*, 1271–1282.

Wingfield, J. C. (2009). Hormone–behavior interrelationships in a changing environment. In P. T. Ellison & P. B. Gray (Eds.), *Endocrinology of social relationships* (pp. 74–94). Cambridge, MA: Harvard University Press.

Wingfield, J. C., Maney, D. L., Breuner, C. W., Jacobs, J. D., Lynn, S. H. A. R., Ramenofsky, M. A. R. I., & Richardson, R. D. (1998). Ecological bases of hormone–behavior interactions: The "emergency life history stage." *Integrative and Comparative Biology*, *38*(1), 191–206.

Wolf, J. B., & Wade, M. J. (2009). What are maternal effects (and what are they not)? *Philosophical Transactions of the Royal Society B: Biological Sciences*, *364*(1520), 1107–1115.

Wolff, M., Alcaraz, F., Marchand, A. R., & Coutureau, E. (2015). Functional heterogeneity of the limbic thalamus: From hippocampal to cortical functions. *Neuroscience & Biobehavioral Reviews*, *54*, 120–130.

Wolpert, D. M., Miall, R. C., & Kawato, M. (1998). Internal models in the cerebellum. *Trends in Cognitive Sciences*, *2*(9), 338–347.

Yao, M., Stenzel-Poore, M., & Denver, R. J. (2007). Structural and functional conservation of vertebrate corticotropin-releasing factor genes: Evidence for a critical role for a conserved cyclic AMP response element. *Endocrinology*, *148*(5), 2518–2531.

Yi, R., Mitchell, S. H., & Bickel, W. K. (2010). Delay discounting and substance abuse-dependence. In G. J. Madden & W. K. Bickel (Eds.), *Impulsivity: The behavioral and neurological science of discounting* (pp. 191–211). Washington, DC: American Psychological Association.

Young, L. J., & Wang, Z. (2004). The neurobiology of pair bonding. *Nature Neuroscience*, *7*(10), 1048–1054.

Zannas, A. S., Arloth, J., Carrillo-Roa, T., Iurato, S., Roh, S., Ressler, K. J., . . . Mehta, D. (2015). Lifetime stress accelerates epigenetic aging in an urban, African American cohort: Relevance of glucocorticoid signaling. *Genome Biology*, *16*, 266.

CHAPTER 18

SOCIAL EPIGENETICS OF HUMAN BEHAVIOR

DANIEL E. ADKINS, KELLI M. RASMUSSEN,
AND ANNA R. DOCHERTY

WHAT IS EPIGENETICS? WHAT IS ITS RELEVANCE TO THE SOCIAL SCIENCES?

EPIGENETICS is the study of molecular processes occurring on and around the genome that regulate gene activity without changing the underlying DNA sequence. The importance of epigenetics becomes immediately apparent if one considers that although virtually all cells in an organism share a single, identical genome, this single genome gives rise to all of the diverse cell types, tissues, and organs present in the organism. These differences in cellular structure and function are almost entirely due to epigenetic mediation, which functions by regulating how and when genes are expressed—silencing some and activating others.

Beyond its fundamental role in cellular differentiation and development, epigenetics is of primary concern to the social sciences as an empirically validated mechanism through which social environments biologically embed, causing changes in gene expression that influence downstream health and behavior (Weaver et al., 2004). Indeed, the potential to measure functionally relevant epigenetic marks left by environmental exposures has generated considerable interest among researchers investigating central social science concepts including stress diathesis, resilience and vulnerability, and gene–environment interaction (Adkins, Daw, McClay, & Van den Oord, 2012; Belsky & Pluess, 2009; Cicchetti & Rogosch, 2012; Heim & Binder, 2012). Furthermore, as elaborated below, epigenetics is of fundamental relevance to the social sciences in its complication of the nature–nurture dichotomy, as it demonstrates that environmental exposures can profoundly change the function of genes long after the resolution of the triggering exposure and that, contrary to orthodox evolutionary theory, such phenotypically relevant epigenetic changes can be transmitted across generations (Szyf, 2015).

In this chapter, we offer a primer on the biology of epigenetics and a summary of current knowledge regarding the role of epigenetics in social and behavioral processes. We review evidence showing that although epigenetics research is still in its infancy, robust case studies demonstrating its relevance to the social sciences have been established, as have the tools necessary to collect and integrate epigenetic data into behavioral research. In examining the topic and its relevance to the social and behavioral sciences, we begin with a discussion of epigenetic molecular biology. This section elaborates the foundational maxim of epigenetics—that through reversible microstructural changes, which do not alter the DNA's nucleotide sequence (e.g., attaching a small molecule to a specific region of DNA, as in *DNA methylation*, or coiling a stretch of DNA such that its contents become inaccessible and inactive, as in *histone modification*), epigenetics regulate gene expression, influencing downstream biological processes and, ultimately, health and behavior.

The next section details a canonical example of a social environmental factor, childhood maltreatment, causing specific epigenetic modifications at the *NR3C1* gene regulating stress hormone activity in the brain, which increases vulnerability to mental illness in adulthood (Turecki & Meaney, 2016; Weaver et al., 2004). Afterward, we discuss the importance of studying similar mechanisms for various social processes and behavioral outcomes, particularly those involving psychosocial stress. We then review recent scientific and technical developments that have, for the first time, allowed extensive investigation of behavioral epigenetics in humans. In this section, we discuss technologies capable of quantitatively assaying the entire human epigenome (i.e., the full complement of epigenetic phenomena present in a genome) and particularly promising research designs supporting strong causal inference. Finally, we detail the current state of empirical knowledge regarding the social epigenetics of human behavior, concluding with suggestions for future research.

MOLECULAR BIOLOGY OF EPIGENETICS

Epigenetic changes modify the expression of specific genes without changing the genetic sequence of DNA. Thus, epigenetics describe the microstructure of DNA and its associated proteins, which may be modified to induce activation or silencing of associated genes. Epigenetic mechanisms include three primary, closely related processes: DNA methylation, chromatin remodeling, and histone modification.

The first primary mechanism, DNA methylation, refers to the attachment of a small molecule (i.e., methyl group) to a specific DNA nucleotide locus. Although the full range of effects of this process are not completely understood, one major function of DNA methylation is to silence the expression of the associated gene by blocking the interaction of regulatory molecules to the methylated DNA (Bird, 2002). A second, related epigenetic mechanism is chromatin remodeling, which describes the process through which chromatin, which is the three-dimensional structure in which DNA is coiled around large scaffolding proteins, shifts to either expose or condense DNA. This can facilitate or block interaction between genes and the regulatory proteins that influence the rates at which genes are expressed. Thus, chromatin remodeling can physically collapse a gene, silencing its expression, or expose the DNA strand, increasing regulatory protein access and, consequently, gene expression. The principal driver of local chromatin remodeling is histone modification, in which histones, the main protein component of chromatin, are modified by the attachment/detachment of small molecules (e.g., methyl and acetyl groups). These changes alter the local covalent bonding patterns of the chromatin, causing it to shift, thus changing regulatory access and gene expression. As DNA methylation is currently the best understood molecular epigenetic mechanism, our review focuses on it, with secondary attention to histone modifications and other chromatin remodeling processes.

Genome-wide patterns of DNA methylation and chromatin structure are not static throughout life but, rather, undergo specific, coordinated changes across developmental stages. Thus, one essential function of epigenetic processes in multicellular organisms is orchestrating cell differentiation such that only the genes that are necessary for a given tissue and cell type are activated while the other genes remain repressed. Another feature of epigenetic modifications is that they are typically preserved during mitotic cell division during the lifespan of the organism. And although epigenetic modifications do not generally persist across generations of organisms, if they occur in a germline cell (e.g., sperm or egg) that becomes fertilized, these changes can be transferred to the next generation through a process referred to as transgenerational epigenetic inheritance. Although the full range of epigenetic function is currently unknown, several specific epigenetic processes are relatively well characterized, including, as discussed at length below, gene silencing (Prendergast & Ziff, 1991). Other well-studied epigenetic phenomena include X chromosome inactivation, the process through which one female X chromosome is deactivated to equalize gene products between males and females (Avner & Heard, 2001), and carcinogenesis, the process through which healthy cells transform into cancer (Baylin & Jones, 2011). For a comprehensive survey of the current state of epigenetic knowledge, see Allis (2015).

Regulatory Mechanics of Epigenetic Function

Although epigenetic phenomena are often delineated into primary types, including DNA methylation, histone modification, and chromatin remodeling, these distinctions conceal considerable overlap across categories, as well as divisions within them. DNA methylation is instructive in this regard as it comprises multiple closely related DNA modifications, including methylation, hydroxymethylation, and formylmethylation (Feng et al., 2015; McCarthy & Nugent, 2015). Although most research to date has focused on methylation, recent studies have also implicated hydroxymethylation

(Kriaucionis & Heintz, 2009), which is highly abundant in brain, in learning and memory, with initial studies suggesting a regulatory role in increasing the expression of associated genes (Feng et al., 2015; Szulwach et al., 2011). Furthermore, there are tentative indications that, like methylation, hydroxymethylation modifications in brain may mediate the effects of environmental insults on mood, cognition, and behavior (Feng et al., 2014).

In addition to methylation's well-known function of silencing genes by blocking the binding of transcription factors to their recognition elements (Prendergast & Ziff, 1991), it has also been shown to play a role in gene splicing. Gene splicing is the process through which an RNA transcript copy of the gene's DNA is edited, with some segments (i.e., introns) snipped out and the remaining segments (i.e., exons) combined to finalize the instructions for protein translation (Shukla et al., 2011). Methylation has been shown to have further, downstream gene expression effects via moderating concentrations of the non-protein-coding RNAs responsible for regulating complex gene networks. Although it is beyond the scope of this review to fully explore the complexity of these methylation-regulated gene expression networks, we direct interested readers to the primary literature for additional details (Maunakea et al., 2010; Thomson et al., 2010).

In mammalian cells, DNA methylation occurs primarily at cytosine nucleotides (i.e., the C's in the A, C, G, and T's that comprise the genome sequence) and is catalyzed by the DNA methyltransferase (DNMT) family of enzymes, which facilitate the transfer of a methyl group to DNA. DNMTs work inseparably with histone modifications to regulate gene transcription. As visualized in Figure 18.1, histone modifications refer to the transfer of small molecular groups, including methylation, acetylation, ubiquitination, and phosphorylation, to three specific amino acids on the histone tails. These modifications influence how DNA strands are packaged and, consequently, their transcriptional activity. Histone modifications that loosen DNA's association with histones generally provide a permissive environment for transcription, whereas histone modifications that tightly package DNA nucleosomes typically repress gene expression.

One major avenue of epigenetic crosstalk between DNA methylation and histone modification is the direct interaction of DNMTs with enzymes that regulate the histone modifications typically involved in gene repression. For instance, both DNMT1 and DNMT3b can bind to histone deacetylases that remove acetylation from histones, thus packing DNA more tightly and restricting access for transcription (Fuks, Burgers, Brehm, Hughes-Davies, & Kouzarides, 2000; Geiman et al., 2004). More generally, DNMTs cooperate with histone-modifying enzymes involved in adding and/or stripping histone markers in order to impose a repressive state on the associated gene region. This relationship is bidirectional because histone modifications also influence DNA methylation patterns. For instance, elevated histone acetylation can trigger DNA demethylation (Cervoni & Szyf, 2001; D'Alessio, Weaver, & Szyf, 2007). Methyl binding proteins are another well-established link between DNA methylation and histone modification because methyl-CpG binding domains (MBDs) and related proteins interact with methylated DNA and histones to enhance gene repression (Moore, Le, & Fan, 2012). Furthermore, methyl-CpG binding protein 2 (MeCP2) enhances the repressive chromatin state by recruiting histone

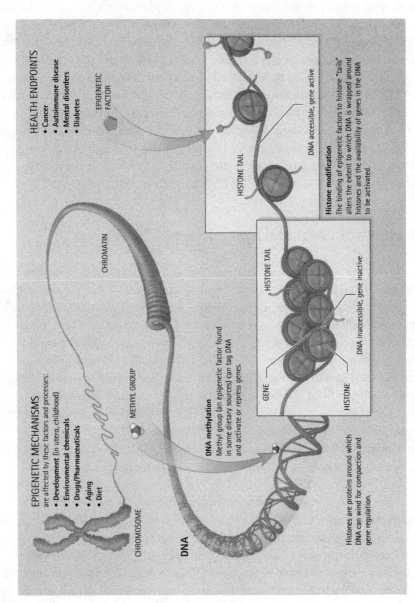

FIGURE 18.1 The molecular mechanics of DNA methylation and histone modification.

Source: National Institutes of Health, Common Fund.

methyltransferases that promote repressive histone methylation (Fuks et al., 2003). Thus, although current knowledge is limited, it is clear that DNA methylation and histone modifications interact extensively to regulate gene expression.

While social scientists are primarily interested in environmental causation of epigenetic phenomena, it is important to note that epigenetic phenomena are also under substantial genetic influence (Bell & Spector, 2012; Kaminsky et al., 2009). This observation has motivated studies aimed at identifying specific locations where DNA methylation is under genetic control, known as methylation quantitative trait loci (meQTLs). Several early reports focusing on candidate loci found instances of DNA methylation levels correlated with DNA sequence variants (Meaburn, Schalkwyk, & Mill, 2010). These studies of meQTLs found abundant local (i.e., spatially proximate) effects in all tissues analyzed. Furthermore, findings suggest that methylation sites under genetic influence are typically associated with single nucleotide polymorphisms (SNPs) in very close proximity, and these SNPs often determine the presence/absence of the CpG motif typically required for methylation to occur (McClay et al., 2015; Zhi et al., 2013).

Physical Environment and Epigenetics

An accumulation of evidence from animal research and a growing body of human studies have demonstrated that adverse environmental factors can result in persistent epigenetic changes with long-term phenotypic consequences. Diet, drugs, and toxins provide the most conceptually direct avenue through which the environment gets "under the skin" to interact with the epigenome. Accordingly, numerous studies have demonstrated such relationships in both animal model systems and humans. For instance, in aphids, the chemical signals related to predators, crowding, and other stresses induce a shift in the population from wingless animals to winged animals (Feil & Fraga, 2012). Additional examples include royal jelly-induced differentiation of genetically identical female honeybees into workers versus queens (Kamakura, 2011).

One particularly well-studied animal model is the agouti viable yellow allele in the mouse. This locus comprises a specific genomic sequence referred to as an *upstream intracisternal A-particle (IAP) retrotransposon*. When this transposon is unmethylated, the *agouti* gene is expressed, producing a distinctive yellow coat color paired with obesity and diabetes (Rakyan, Blewitt, Druker, Preis, & Whitelaw, 2002; Rosenfeld, 2010). During mouse gestation, dietary intake of folate together with other methionine-linked compounds affects offspring A^{vy} methylation and its phenotypic correlates, changes that are then heritable across multiple generations (Rakyan & Beck, 2006). Various other animal experiments have demonstrated the epigenetic relevance of gestational diet (Lim & Brunet, 2013), including an increased incidence of type 2 diabetes due to targeted methylation changes in pancreatic islets in the offspring of rat dams subjected to low-protein diets (Sandovici et al., 2011).

Similar findings highlighting the epigenetic sensitivity to perinatal (i.e., the period leading up to birth) nutrition have emerged from quasi-experimental human research studies. One particularly well-documented example is the Dutch famine of 1944, which resulted in an array of adverse metabolic and psychological phenotypes in individuals suffering periconceptional (i.e., the period leading up to conception) famine exposure (Painter et al., 2008). Epigenetic studies of this cohort have reported altered methylation in several imprinted genes, including insulin-like growth factor-2 (IGF-2) and insulin, as well as several loci implicated in metabolic disease and growth, such as interleukin-10, leptin, and ATP-binding cassette A1 (Heijmans et al., 2008; Tobi et al., 2009). A second study in this vein identified various genes exhibiting significant variation in methylation between individuals, and then tested whether periconceptional nutritional status affected these methylation marks by comparing rural Gambian children conceived during either the dry season or the rainy season (Waterland et al., 2010). Methylation at the epigenetic loci was elevated in individuals conceived during the nutritionally challenging rainy season, providing further evidence of persistent, systemic effects of periconceptional environment on the human epigenome.

TOWARD A ROBUST PROGRAM OF SOCIAL EPIGENETICS

Although genetic sequence variation clearly contributes to individual differences in behavior and mental health, frequent discordance among monozygotic twins demonstrates the importance of additional mechanisms. Social processes, including psychosocial stress and substance abuse, are robust examples here, as they have been shown to significantly influence behavior and mental health (Adkins, Wang, Dupre, van den Oord, & Elder, 2009; Clark, Gillespie, Adkins, Kendler, & Neale, 2016). Such social environmental exposures result in cascades of modification in gene expression, neural signaling pathways, cognition, and behavior. Mounting evidence suggests that these changes are substantially maintained by epigenetic modifications in brain (Sun, Kennedy, & Nestler, 2013). In recent years, the study of DNA methylation, in particular, has yielded several important insights into the etiology and molecular maintenance of behavioral dysfunction and mental illness. An exemplar in this regard is research demonstrating that childhood maltreatment increases methylation at a glucocorticoid receptor gene promoter in hippocampus, which in turn upregulates the hypothalamic–pituitary–adrenal (HPA) axis stress response and vulnerability to mood disorders in adulthood (Turecki & Meaney, 2016). Given the importance of this research topic as a foundational case study in social epigenetics, it is worth examining in some detail.

Social Adversity, Epigenetic Glucocorticoid Regulation, and Mood Disorder

The finding that epigenetic modifications to the glucocorticoid receptor gene (NR3C1) in brain mediate the stress–depression link has served as a model for behavioral epigenetic studies by focusing on a promising candidate gene and integrating findings across biological scales to provide a comprehensive account of psychopathology development. This multifaceted approach has yielded profound insights into the epigenetics of social adversity while also offering a robust analytical approach for future research. Research on the topic began with the observation of maternal effects on the development of individual differences in behavioral and HPA stress responses in rodents and nonhuman primates (Higley, Hasert, Suomi, & Linnoila, 1991; Meaney, 2001). Maternal treatment was then shown to influence HPA responses to stress in rat through tissue-specific effects on gene expression (Liu et al., 1997), including glucocorticoid receptor expression in brain, the activation of which inhibits HPA activity through negative feedback inhibition (De Kloet, Joëls, & Holsboer, 2005). Thus, selective knockdown of glucocorticoid receptor expression in the corticolimbic system in rodents is associated with increased HPA activity under both basal and stressful conditions (Boyle et al., 2005; Ridder et al., 2005). Conversely, glucocorticoid receptor overexpression is associated with a dampened HPA stress response (Reichardt, Tronche, Bauer, & Schütz, 2000).

These findings were further bolstered by evidence that familial dysfunction and childhood adversity are also linked to altered HPA stress responses in humans, which in turn are associated with increased risk to various types of psychopathology (De Bellis et al., 1994; Heim & Nemeroff, 2001; Pruessner, Champagne, Meaney, & Dagher, 2004). For instance, there is evidence for decreased hippocampal glucocorticoid receptor expression in several psychopathological conditions associated with suicide, including schizophrenia and mood disorders (Szyf, 2013). Thus, environmental events that associate with decreased hippocampal glucocorticoid receptor expression and increased HPA activity enhance general vulnerability to psychopathology across a range of mammalian species.

The molecular mechanism through which environmental exposures influenced hippocampal glucocorticoid receptor expression and HPA activity remained a black box until Michael Meaney's research group combined rodent models with emerging epigenetic technologies to show that the effects of maternal care on hippocampal glucocorticoid receptor expression, and therefore HPA responses to stress, in adult rodents are associated with an epigenetic modification of a neuron-specific exon 1_7 glucocorticoid receptor (NR3C1) promoter (Figure 18.2; Weaver et al., 2004; Zhang, Labonte, Wen, Turecki, & Meaney, 2013). That is, adult offspring of rats born to mothers with low rates of maternal care show increased methylation at a glucocorticoid receptor gene promoter in the hippocampus, which in turn upregulates HPA stress response in adulthood. Moreover, the pattern of increased methylation at the NR3C1 promoter and decreased nerve growth factor-inducible protein A (NGFI-A) binding has also been observed in human suicide victims (McGowan et al., 2009). In addition, there is a growing body of research showing its relevance to a variety of human outcomes related to psychosocial stress (Turecki & Meaney, 2016).

Although maltreatment-induced NR3C1 methylation is the best characterized example of epigenetic mediation of the effects of social environments on human behavior, targeted research on brain-derived neurotrophic factor (BDNF) has also been informative.

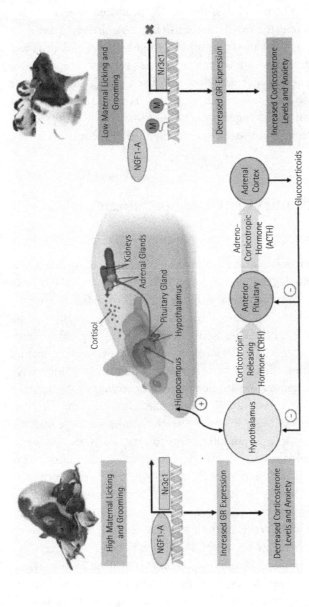

FIGURE 18.2 The effect of maternal care on epigenetic regulation of the glucocorticoid receptor gene (*NR3C1*) in hippocampus and its consequent effects on HPA dysregulation and mood dysfunction. The sides of the figure visualize the process through which maternal care of pups induces the expression of transcription factor NGFI-A and encourages its binding with the *NR3C1* gene promoter in hippocampus, by triggering demethylation within the NGFI-A binding region of the gene. This subsequently increases the ability of NGFI-A to activate *NR3C1* gene expression, resulting in decreased HPA axis activity and anxiety. The middle of the figure is a schematic of the HPA axis, the pivot of which is the biochemical cascade induced by corticotropin-releasing hormone (CRH) released from the hypothalamus, which stimulates adrenal glucocorticoid release. Glucocorticoids act on multiple brain regions, including the hippocampus, to inhibit the synthesis and release of CRH, which functions as negative feedback on adrenal gluco-corticoid release. The adult offspring of mothers that exhibit high maternal care show increased *NR3C1* expression in hippocampus, enhanced negative feedback sensitivity to glucocorticoids, and reduced HPA reactivity to stress, relative to low-maternal-care offspring.

This epigenetic research builds on work showing that depression patients have decreased circulating levels of *BDNF*, which normalize after chronic antidepressant treatment (Boulle et al., 2012; Molendijk et al., 2011), as well as studies demonstrating that *BDNF* gene expression is under epigenetic influence via the repressive effects of MeCP2 (Im, Hollander, Bali, & Kenny, 2010). Thus, *BDNF* has long been considered a high-priority candidate epigenetic mediator of mood dysfunction. And, indeed several studies in humans and rodents have supported this hypothesis (Baker-Andresen, Flavell, Li, & Bredy, 2013; Perroud et al., 2011). For instance, using a mouse model of depression, Onishchenko and colleagues (2008) have shown that a decrease in hippocampal BDNF mRNA levels is mediated by promoter hypermethylation. Other targeted, candidate gene investigations have reported associations between social adversity and related mental health outcomes and methylation marks at genes including *FKBP5*, *CFR*, *ADCYAP1R1*, and *ALS2* (Elliott, Ezra-Nevo, Regev, Neufeld-Cohen, & Chen, 2010; Klengel et al., 2013; Ressler et al., 2011).

From Candidate Gene Studies to Whole Epigenome Investigations

Although targeted behavioral epigenetic studies have met with some success, given limited understanding of the neurobiological mechanisms underlying behavioral dysfunction and psychological distress, comprehensive methods screening the full epigenome are needed. This is because it is not clear where the most relevant epigenetic sites are located, as they may occur far from the commonly assayed coding regions or transcriptional start sites. Also, the effects of social adversity are likely pervasive, affecting multiple biological systems beyond the HPA axis. A growing number of studies have used genome-wide methylation approaches in the context of mental health, typically using array-based methods, which are essentially standardized chips assaying a limited number of specific methylation loci (e.g., see https://www.illumina.com/techniques/microarrays/methylation-arrays.html). As an alternative to arrays, advances in next-generation sequencing have enabled large-scale assessment of methylation status across the entire methylome (i.e., the full complement of DNA methylation sites in a genome) (Laird, 2010; Rakyan, Down, Balding, & Beck, 2011). The most comprehensive method for ascertaining methylation, bisulfite sequencing (Li et al., 2010), is currently prohibitively expensive, requiring the sequencing of the complete genome, most of which (70–80%) does not contain methylation. However, sequencing costs are projected to decrease markedly in the near term; if so, bisulfite sequencing is likely to become widespread. Thus, although array-based technologies currently represent the most feasible approach to integrating epigenomic assays into behavioral research, if past trends hold, sequencing-based approaches will soon offer comprehensive coverage at a competitive price.

In considering strategies supporting a robust program of social epigenomics, it is worth noting the utility of experimental animal models as an adjunct to human studies.

That is because, although behavioral epigenomic studies in humans have obvious benefits, they are also characterized by various limitations, including expense, limited access to primary (central nervous system) tissue, and difficulty controlling confounders. One particularly difficult challenge in human epigenomic research is the threat to causal inference posed by confounding factors. This problem arises because there are many possible differences between subjects that affect the epigenome (e.g., race/ethnicity, gender, pharmacotherapy, diet, substance use/abuse, and comorbid health conditions). Because these confounding factors may correlate with both dependent (e.g., behavioral outcomes) and independent variables (epigenetic marks), they may cause spurious associations. If measured, such factors can be statistically adjusted for, but the list of potential confounders is long, only a subset is typically measured, and many confounders are simply unknown. Experimental animal models circumvent these limitations, cost-effectively providing primary tissue access and precise control of experimental exposures. Critically, the experimental control provided by model systems controls the risk of confounding in ways that are impossible in observational human studies (e.g., randomization). These advantages, paired with the extensive genomic annotations available (Blake et al., 2014), make animal model epigenomics a valuable complimentary research strategy to human studies for disorders with valid experimental models.

CURRENT KNOWLEDGE ON SOCIAL EPIGENETICS AND HUMAN BEHAVIOR

The past few years have seen rapid progress in behavioral epigenomics research, with recent studies implicating novel mechanisms in mood disorders, addiction, aging, and gender. Rapid technological and scientific developments, including the proliferation of epigenome-wide approaches, have generated an exponentially expanding body of knowledge detailing how social exposures become epigenetically embedded to affect health and behavior. Here, we provide a concise overview of current knowledge on how social processes influence, and are influenced by, epigenetic processes.

Mood Disorders

Mood disorders have been a primary focus of social epigenetics research to date. As noted previously, candidate gene research on *NR3C1* and *BDNF* has yielded foundational case studies of epigenetic encoding of social adversity and mediation of downstream effects on affect and behavior. Research is now moving beyond these case studies in both animal and human research. Regarding animal research, several studies have examined histone modifications and/or DNA methylation in various brain regions. For instance, chronic stress has been associated with increased methylation of glial cell-derived neurotrophic factor (*GDNF*) and *CRF* in mice (Sterrenburg et al., 2011; Uchida et al., 2011). Several major methylation advances have been made using the chronic social defeat stress model, a well-validated mouse model of trauma and depression, in which the test mouse is chronically exposed to a larger aggressive mouse, thus experiencing chronic violent bullying and displaying a range of depression-like behaviors (Golden, Covington, Berton, & Russo, 2011). Such findings include increased dimethylation of histone H3 at lysine-27 (*H3K27me2*), as well as both genome-wide (i.e., global) and specifically at *BDNF* (Tsankova et al., 2006; Wilkinson et al., 2009). Antidepressant use has been associated with distinct epigenetic modifications, and it has been shown to reverse the effects observed with chronic social defeat stress (Tsankova et al., 2006).

The vast majority of studies in humans exploring the link between depression development/treatment and epigenetic modifications have focused on DNA methylation. Methylation has been measured in various tissues, including peripheral tissues of blood, buccal tissue, and saliva, as well as several brain regions using postmortem samples. Although many studies have used candidate gene approaches, several whole epigenome studies, using a variety of different technologies and tissues and examining hundreds of thousands of genetic markers, have also been reported (Labonté et al., 2012, 2013; Nagy et al., 2015; Weder et al., 2014). For instance, a study of monozygotic twins discordant for depression, examining genome-wide methylation using the Infinium 450K array in white blood cells, found lower global methylation among depressed females, as well as higher variance in global methylation among depressed subjects (Byrne et al., 2013). Additional genome-wide epigenetic studies have implicated genetic networks clustering in distinct biological pathways involved in brain development, tryptophan/serotonin production, and also with psychopathology-associated genes (Uddin et al., 2011), with specific methylation markers occurring at *CPSF3, LASS2, PRIMA1, ZNF263, ID3, TPPP, GRIN1, STK32C,* and *ZBTB20* (Davies et al., 2014; Dempster et al., 2014; Weder et al., 2014).

Cumulatively, these advances have great promise to address current gaps in our knowledge of the sociology of mental health. For example, many theories of health sociology, including Pearlin's stress process and Link and Phelan's fundamental causes, aim to map the ways in which proximate and distal social environmental factors get under the skin to affect health outcomes (Link & Phelan, 1995; Pearlin, Menaghan, Lieberman, & Mullan, 1981). However, the most crucial aspect of these models has largely remained an enigma—that is, generations of social scientists have puzzled over the mystery of how intangible social exposures become biologically embedded in the tissues of an individual. Recent advances in epigenomics, and related breakthroughs in behavioral neuroscience, have begun to elucidate this process, opening the possibility for social scientists to systematically map the social impacts on health and behavior from macro social and cultural processes down to specific molecular modification and back again to human-scale outcomes.

Addiction

Addiction involves long-term behavioral dysfunction caused, in vulnerable individuals, by repeated exposure to a drug of abuse. The persistence of these behavioral changes suggests that durable alterations in gene expression within particular regions of the brain (e.g., the nucleus accumbens [Nac] and other components of the mesolimbic reward pathway) likely play an important role in the development and maintenance of addiction. This observation, combined with evidence of epigenetic mechanisms driving lasting changes in gene expression, has prompted research on the influence of epigenetics in mediating the long-term effects of drugs of abuse on the brain. This work has produced robust evidence that repeated exposure to drugs of abuse induces changes within the brain's reward regions in various modes of epigenetic regulation, including histone modifications and DNA methylation (Nestler, 2014). In several instances, it has been possible to directly demonstrate the contribution of such epigenetic changes to addiction-related behavioral abnormalities.

Drugs of abuse induce changes in histone modifications throughout the reward circuitry by altering histone-modifying enzymes, manipulation of which has revealed a role for histone modification in addiction-related behaviors. Research in this area has produced a substantial literature, with replicated evidence implicating histone-modifying proteins, including histone deacetylase (HDAC), sirtuin, and G9a, as well as ΔFosB, a transcriptional regulator of genes in the nucleus accumbens (Nestler, 2014; Sun et al., 2013). Moreover, HDAC inhibitors have been implicated as a potential treatment for cocaine addicts. HDACs are enzymes that can deacetylate histone tails, which can activate genes for transcription. Several experiments have shown that inhibiting HDACs involved in H3K9 deacetylation reduces drug-seeking behavior (Sun et al., 2013).

Given the hypothesized importance of DNA methylation in mediating sustained transcriptional change, it is unfortunate that there have been relatively few studies of this epigenetic mechanism in drug abuse models. However, several suggestive findings indicate the promise of this research direction. For instance, expression levels of DNMT3a in NAc are differentially altered by acute versus chronic cocaine exposure and during extended withdrawal (Nestler, 2014). In addition, NAc knockout of MeCP2 has been shown to enhance amphetamine reward (Deng et al., 2010). In contrast, chronic cocaine use increases MeCP2 expression in the dorsal striatum, in which local knockdown of the protein attenuates cocaine self-administration (Bork et al., 2010). These findings underscore the complexity of drug regulation of DNMTs and MeCP2, but they do not provide definitive evidence of a role for altered DNA methylation because these proteins may also serve other functions. Also, although a small number of studies have investigated DNA methylation changes at particular genes of interest, there has been little genome-wide mapping of such regulation, leaving this a priority area for future research.

Age and Health

The effects of aging on the genome include telomere attrition and accumulation of mutations (Sahin & DePinho, 2010). In addition, epigenetic factors are increasingly being recognized as centrally important to the aging process. Among epigenetic modifications, the most intensively studied is DNA methylation. Previous studies have shown that age-related hypermethylation occurs preferentially at CpG islands (Calvanese,

Lara, Kahn, & Fraga, 2009), around bivalent chromatin domain promoters associated with key developmental genes (Grönniger et al., 2010), and at Polycomb-group protein targets (Fraga, 2009). Although the epigenomic landscape varies markedly across tissue types and many age-related changes depend on tissue type, several recent studies have shown that age-dependent CpG signatures can be defined independently of cell type, sex, disease state, and methylation assay technique (Horvath, 2013; McClay et al., 2014).

Although replicable age-related epigenetic marks have been known for some time, these findings have recently been synthesized into an *epigenetic clock* through the work of Horvath (2013), who analyzed 8,000 samples from 82 Illumina DNA methylation array data sets, encompassing 51 healthy tissues as well as pathological cell types (e.g., various cancers) and samples from other primate species. Through this exercise, Horvath was able to identify a tissue-independent set of 393 CpG sites that could predict the age of subjects with a remarkable correlation of $r = 0.96$. This result has since held in numerous replications using a variety of different technologies (Breitling et al., 2016; Christiansen et al., 2016). The development of a robust, easy-to-implement index of epigenetic age is of significant potential utility to epidemiological researchers and social scientists. The measure could be used to empirically assess the degree to which social experiences, and consequent measures of morbidity, are associated with acceleration of the normative aging process. This provides a helpful instrument to test specific social science theories (e.g., the *weathering hypothesis* [Geronimus, 1992]), as well as more generally providing a novel, robust molecular indicator of health for sociological research examining the effects of social experiences on health and longevity. In fact, given the remarkable sensitivity of Horvath's epigenetic clock, one can imagine it becoming an essential tool in health disparities research, serving as a molecular indicator of cumulative disadvantage.

Sex and Gender

Methylation is associated with sex differentiation in fundamental ways. For instance, it has long been known that methylation is a key factor in X chromosome inactivation, through which one X chromosome is inactivated in all female mammalian cells to prevent female cells from having twice as many X chromosome gene products as males (Hellman & Chess, 2007; Venolia & Gartler, 1983). Recent human research has indicated further sex differences, including global hypomethylation among females relative to males (El-Maarri et al., 2007; Zhang et al., 2011), as well as various, replicated locus-specific sex differences (e.g., *SLC9A2, SPESP1, CRISP2,* and *NUPL1* [McCarthy et al., 2014]). Animal studies have also been informative, with sex-differentiated methylation patterns identified in a range of model organisms (D'Avila, Garcia, Panzera, & Valente, 2010; Nikoshkov et al., 2011). For example, multiple studies have shown sex differences in the methylation status of CpGs found in estrogen and progesterone receptor genes during rat neonatal development (Jessen & Auger, 2011; Kolodkin & Auger, 2011; Schwarz, Nugent, & McCarthy, 2010). This research dovetails with cell culture studies demonstrating dynamic cyclical methylation of promoters in the estrogen receptor *ESR1* regulating expression of that gene (Kangaspeska et al., 2008). Methylation has also been directly implicated in controlling the onset of puberty, with increasing methylation in the promoters of two genes (*EED* and *CBX7*) repressing gonadotropin-releasing hormone secretion nondissociably tied to initiation of female puberty in rats (Lomniczi et al., 2013).

The principal drivers of sex differences are steroid hormones, which differ profoundly in males and females at some times of life and very little at others. Early exposure to steroids has enduring effects, and most brain sex differences are established during a critical developmental window, although the timing of the window may vary for different endpoints as well as for masculinization versus feminization. During the critical period, circulating testosterone is markedly higher in males, and some portion of this gains access to the brain, where it is locally converted into estradiol. Relatively recently, studies have also demonstrated that the epigenetic profile of the brain is responsive to gonadal hormones during windows of dynamic hormonal change, including the perinatal window of brain masculinization, and during menopause (Morgan & Bale, 2011; Rao et al., 2013). In agreement with these studies, investigation of sex differences in microRNA expression patterns in a region of the prefrontal cortex undergoing sex-biased development during puberty has found remarkable sex-specific patterns of expression here. Clustering of the expression patterns of 249 of the most abundant microRNAs completely segregated male and female samples into distinct clusters (Morrison, Rodgers, Morgan, & Bale, 2014). These findings demonstrate the importance of epigenetic mediators in the sexually dimorphic development of the brain during the pubertal period.

Epigenetic regulation of sex differences is also important to processes not considered directly biological, such as cultural and social experiences in humans. Repeated sex-typic experiences or expectations could potentially impact the epigenome in a manner that further enhances or canalizes sex differences. Conversely, the malleability of epigenetics could contribute to discordance between biological sex and sexually differentiated endpoints such as gender identity or sexual preference. Thus, understanding the factors that regulate epigenetic changes in males and females and the impact these changes have on brain and behavior has wide-ranging implications to sociological perspectives on gender and sexuality, contradicting the more extreme variants of social constructionism while opening critically important new avenues for the study of socialization and cultural influence.

Transgenerational Epigenetic Inheritance

The idea that inherited genotypes define phenotypes is a cornerstone of the current evolutionary paradigm of modern biology. The question remains, however, whether stable phenotypes could also be inherited from parents independent of DNA sequence. Recent research has suggested that parental experiences can be transmitted behaviorally, through fetal exposure to the maternal environment, and through the germline.

The biological mechanisms underlying such transmission have been unclear, however. In the past decade, it has been proposed that epigenetic mechanisms may be a key component in multigenerational transmission of phenotypes and transgenerational inheritance. The prospect that ancestral experiences are encoded in our epigenome has significant implications for our understanding of human behavior and health.

Epidemiological evidence from multigenerational studies has demonstrated the potential of epigenetic modification to encode ancestral dietary distress in humans. For instance, examining harvest and vital records from the multigenerational Swedish Overkalix cohorts, Pembrey and colleagues found that variation in food supply during the early life of paternal grandparents was associated with variation in mortality rate in their grandchildren (Grossniklaus, Kelly, Ferguson-Smith, Pembrey, & Lindquist, 2013; Pembrey et al., 2006). There were notable sex-specific transmissions, such that food scarcity of the paternal grandfather was associated with the mortality rate of grandsons only, whereas food scarcity of the paternal grandmother was instead associated with the mortality rate of granddaughters (Grossniklaus et al., 2013; Pembrey et al., 2006). Interestingly, the effects were seen only when exposures occurred before puberty, supporting the hypothesis that reprogramming of gametes was involved. Given these patterns of transmission over three generations, some sort of transgenerational molecular memory is clearly at work. It is unclear, however, the degree to which this molecular memory is encoded by epigenetic phenomena versus some other, as yet undiscovered, molecular process, but epigenetics is currently the leading explanation.

Additional evidence derives from studies of children of mothers exposed to the Dutch famine of 1944. These studies have shown that maternal famine exposure during the last trimester of pregnancy and the first months of life was associated with less obese offspring than controls, whereas exposure in the first half of pregnancy resulted in higher obesity rates than in controls (Ravelli, Stein, & Susser, 1976). Famine exposure early in pregnancy was associated with hypermethylation of insulin-like growth factor 2 receptor gene (*IGF-2R*) 60 years later, further supporting DNA methylation involvement (Heijmans et al., 2008).

These findings, combined with a large body of supporting experimental animal studies (Szyf, 2015), raise provocative possibilities. For instance, might epigenetic mechanisms play a role in "rapid evolution" of traits in response to new environmental exposures at rates that are orders of magnitude faster than the stochastically arising genetic alterations posited by natural selection? This possibility has potential implications for the social sciences because it suggests that the intergenerational transmission of adversity and its consequent psychological and behavioral impacts may be conducted via a third major avenue in addition to direct genetic and environmental factors, which presents interesting complications to behavioral genetic analytical approaches (Neale & Cardon, 1992; Tan, Christiansen, von Bornemann Hjelmborg, & Christensen, 2015). Significantly, from a social science perspective, it also opens the possibility of mapping the intergenerational epigenetic transmission of traumatic historical events, including slavery/Jim Crow era deprivation in America, the Holocaust in Europe, and the long-standing conflicts in Iraq and Syria.

CONCLUSION

It is well established that social and economic adversity, particularly in childhood, negatively impact health, resulting in increased morbidity and mortality. Various theoretical efforts to map this process, including *stress process* and *fundamental causes* theories, have arrived at models positing that distal, fundamental causes, such as poverty, increase exposure to various forms of stress and deprivation that in turn act as proximate causes of psychological distress and physiological dysfunction (Adkins et al., 2009; Link & Phelan, 1995; Pearlin et al., 1981). Research has further indicated that the effects of social adversity can be long-lasting, leading to a host of negative health outcomes persisting decades after the resolution of the precipitating environmental insult. Although these epidemiological patterns are clear, the underlying mechanisms through which adversity becomes biologically embedded have been less obvious. Here, we summarized recent research investigating this process, showing that epigenetic mechanisms play an important role in mediating the effects of social adversity on gene expression and downstream biological and behavioral outcomes.

The molecular impacts of environmental factors can now readily be studied in social and behavioral research. This impressive scientific development is a result of decades of advances in molecular biology, biotechnology, statistical genetics, and bioinformatics. Through this work, it has been shown that epigenetic modifications facilitate phenotypic plasticity in response to environmental change through overlapping molecular processes, including DNA methylation, histone modification, and chromatin remodeling. DNA methylation, in particular, has yielded definitive examples demonstrating the importance of epigenetics as a mediator of social impacts on health, behavior, and cognition. Chief among these is the finding that childhood maltreatment increases methylation at a glucocorticoid receptor gene (*NR3C1*) promoter in the hippocampus, which then upregulates HPA stress response and vulnerability to mood disorders in adulthood (Szyf, 2013a; Weaver et al., 2004). But while such research has demonstrated the relevance of epigenetics to the social sciences, these findings still only explain a small portion of the variance in complex health outcomes. This is because the genome is vast and we simply do not know where most of the relevant regions for health and behavioral outcomes are located. Thus, it is the task of future research to use genome-wide approaches to consider the complex patterns of epigenetic regulation occurring as a result of social experiences that mediate, via altered gene expression, the development of behavioral and health outcomes.

In surveying the current state of research on the social epigenetics of human behavior, a few areas emerge as particularly promising for future study. First, although previous research has demonstrated that childhood maltreatment and acute traumatic stress cause functionally relevant epigenetic changes that influence later life health (Turecki & Meaney, 2016), the epigenetic effects of adult exposures and chronic stressful environments remain poorly understood. Thus, socioeconomic status represents a particularly high-impact topic (Hackman, Farah, & Meaney, 2010), and we encourage research into the ways in which epigenetic effects mediate and/or moderate the effects of poverty on consequent health disparities (Adkins & Guo, 2008; Adkins & Vaisey, 2009). In addition to socioeconomic status, several other chronic social adversities are particularly promising for epigenetic study, including social support/isolation, bullying, marital history, and family structure. It is also worth noting that the intense focus of epigenetic researchers on internalizing disorders has left the epigenetic mechanics of externalizing disorders less well characterized. However, there is good reason to suspect that adverse social environments also play a biological role in the development of aggression, antisocial behavior, and delinquency (e.g., via modifying amygdala reactivity) (Rosell & Siever, 2015). Thus, research on the epigenetics of externalizing behavior represents another promising direction, albeit one characterized by challenging ethical and legal implications.

Actualizing the promise of social epigenetics will be no simple task. Along with the opportunities discussed previously are serious analytical challenges. Most fundamentally, unlike genetic sequence, which provides a causal anchor via the central dogma of molecular biology (Crick, 1970), epigenetic variation can be both an effect and a cause of behavior. Substance use is an illustrative example because it has been demonstrated that repeated exposure to drugs of abuse can cause long-term changes to epigenetic mechanics in the brain's reward pathways, that then induce further drug craving/seeking (Nestler, 2014). This bidirectional property of epigenetic phenomena complicates causal inference, as does the fact that many epigenetic changes appear to be stochastic and without apparent functional significance (Landan et al., 2012). That is, many epigenetic responses to environmental cues do not meaningfully influence gene expression or exert any other regulatory influence. However, social scientists are well situated to address some of these limitations, particularly those related to causal inference, as they have developed extensive econometric and psychometric toolkits for addressing precisely these issues (Baltagi, 2013; Bollen, 1989). Indeed, several of the research designs and statistical methods developed by social scientists to strengthen causal inference in observational research will be of significant utility in the oncoming social epigenetics synthesis, including using longitudinal data to analyze within-subject change (Baltagi, 2013; Bjornsson et al., 2008) and leveraging structural equation models and family data to parse genetic and environmental effects of the epigenome (Neale & Cardon, 1992; Tan et al., 2015). Such methods will provide a useful human compliment to the strong causal inference provided by the experimental animal models favored by biologists.

Social and behavioral researchers now have an unprecedented opportunity to epigenetically map the ways in which deprivation, domination, and psychosocial stress biologically embed to undermine the health and well-being of disadvantaged groups. From the perspective of intellectual history, the emergence of social epigenetics is a notable turn of events in that genetics, which has traditionally been perceived as aligned with conservative ideological perspectives (Galton, 1869; Herrnstein, 1994), has given birth to a discipline capable of achieving a progressive holy grail—empirically demonstrating how structural inequality undermines the health of the disadvantaged by altering the function of genes at the most basic molecular level. By engaging this opportunity, social scientists can advance important humanistic insights while contributing to the development of more nuanced and comprehensive models of human behavior.

ACKNOWLEDGMENT

This research was supported by the National Institute of Mental Health (grants K01MH093731 and K01MH109765).

GLOSSARY

Agouti viable yellow allele: Canonical mouse model in which a mouse's coat color is determined by a specific epigenetic modification. This modification can be triggered by maternal dietary changes.

Amino acids: Organic molecules that serve as the building blocks of proteins.

Amygdala: Brain region, located in the basal ganglia, involved with the experiencing of emotions.

Bioinformatics: Research area at the intersection of computer science and molecular biology focused on the analysis of complex biological data such as genetic sequence.

Bisulfite sequencing: Genetic sequencing laboratory method using bisulfite treatment of DNA to determine patterns of methylation.

Brain-derived neurotrophic factor (BDNF): Protein that is encoded by the BDNF gene in humans. BDNF is a member of the neurotrophin family of growth factors, which are involved in neuronal growth and maintenance.

Carcinogenesis: The initiation of cancer formation.

Central dogma of molecular biology: The two-step process of transcription and translation by which the information in genes flows into proteins: DNA → RNA → protein.

Chromatin: The complex of DNA and structuring proteins of which chromosomes are composed. Chromatin plays a major role in epigenetics by determining how much genes are compressed/silent versus unpacked/active genes.

Chromatin remodeling: Dynamic modifications of chromatin architecture that moderate access of DNA to regulatory proteins, and thereby regulate gene expression.

Chronic social defeat stress: Chronic social defeat stress, a canonical animal model of depression and trauma, consists of a small male rodent being repeatedly introduced into the home cage of a larger, highly aggressive male rodent. After suffering repeated episodes of social defeat (i.e., violent bullying), the small rodent typically show depressive-like behavior and physiology, which can be remedied by antidepressant exposure.

CpG: A cytosine nucleotide occurring next to a guanine nucleotide in the linear genetic sequence of nucleotide bases. "CpG" is shorthand for "—C—phosphate—G—," cytosine and guanine bases linked by a phosphate connecter. DNA methylation primarily occurs at these locations.

CpG islands: CpG islands (or CG islands) are regions characterized by a high density of CpG sites. The usual formal definition of a CpG island is a region with at least 200 DNA nucleotides and a GC percentage that is greater than 50%. They commonly occur in gene promoter regions and are involved in moderating gene expression.

Cytosine nucleotide: A nucleotide base that forms a base pair with guanine. Most DNA methylation occurs at this nucleotide.

Deacetylation: The reverse of acetylation, where an acetyl group is removed from a histone protein.

DNA methylation: DNA methylation is a process by which small methyl group molecules are attached to the DNA. Methylation is a canonical epigenetic mechanism because it can change the activity of a DNA segment without changing the sequence. When located in a gene promoter, DNA methylation typically acts to repress gene transcription.

DNA methyltransferase: A family of enzymes that catalyze the transfer of a methyl group onto DNA.

DNA sequence: The precise order of nucleotides within a DNA molecule. It includes any order of the four bases—adenine, guanine, cytosine, and thymine—in a strand of DNA.

Dorsal striatum: Brain region involved in the limbic/reward system; also called the dorsal basal ganglia. Addiction and related substance dependence processes involve alterations to the structure and function of this brain region.

Epigenetics: The study of changes in organisms caused by modifications of gene expression that do not involve alteration of the genetic sequence itself.

Epigenome: The full complement of all epigenetic features occurring in a genome.

Exon: A DNA segment located within a gene containing information for producing a protein or peptide sequence.

Externalizing disorders: A broad class of psychiatric disorders that includes substance use disorders, conduct disorder, and oppositional defiant disorder.

Gene expression: The process through which information from a gene is transformed into RNA transcripts that then control the creation of protein products.

Gene repression: The process by which a DNA-binding repressor blocks the attachment of RNA polymerase to the promoter, thus preventing transcription of the genes into RNA.

Gene silencing: See "Gene repression."

Gene splicing: A post-transcriptional modification in which RNA from a single gene can be rearranged to produce multiple proteins.

Global methylation: The total level of DNA methylation across the entire genome.

Glucocorticoid receptor gene (*NR3C1*): Gene encoding the glucocorticoid receptor, which can function both as a transcription factor that binds to responsive genes to activate their transcription and as a regulator of other transcription factors. Expression regulates processes involved in HPA/stress reactivity and immune function.

Hippocampus: Region of the brain composed of elongated ridges on the floor of each lateral ventricle that is thought to be relevant to emotion, memory, and the autonomic nervous system.

Histone: Any of a group of basic proteins found in chromatin. Provides primary scaffolding for DNA.

Histone acetylation: Acetylation of histones alters accessibility of chromatin and allows DNA binding proteins to interact with exposed sites to activate gene transcription and downstream cellular functions.

Histone deacetylase: A class of enzymes that remove acetyl groups from an amino acid on a histone, allowing the histones to wrap the DNA more tightly.

Histone deacetylases (HDACs): A class of enzymes that remove acetyl groups on a histone, thus allowing histones to wrap the DNA more tightly.

Histone methyltransferases: Histone-modifying enzymes (e.g., histone-lysine *N*-methyltransferases and histone-arginine *N*-methyltransferases) that catalyze the transfer of methyl groups to lysine and arginine residues of histones.

Histone modification: A covalent molecular modification that can impact gene expression by altering local chromatin structure or recruiting histone modifiers.

Histone phosphorylation: A covalent post-translational modification to histone proteins.

Histone tail: Part of the histone that can be modified in addition to the histone core. Modifications to the histone tail are the principal mechanism for histone epigenetics. Combinations of modifications are thought to constitute a histone code.

Histone ubiquitination: The addition of ubiquitin to a histone that can affect proteins in many ways: signaling for degradation, altering cellular location, and promoting or preventing protein interactions.

HPA axis: The hypothalamic–pituitary–adrenal axis (HPA axis) is a complex set of feedback interactions among three endocrine glands: the hypothalamus, the pituitary gland, and the adrenal glands. The HPA axis is of key relevance for stress reactivity in mammals.

Human genome: The complete set of nucleic acid sequence for humans, encoded as DNA. Human genomes include both protein-coding DNA genes and noncoding DNA. It includes 23 sets of chromosomes in addition to a smaller mitochondrial DNA molecule.

Hydroxymethylation: Similar to methylation, hydroxymethylation replaces, at the C5 position in cytosine, the hydrogen atom by a hydroxymethyl group, as opposed to a methyl group in standard methylation. Hydroxymethylation is abundant in mammalian brain and appears relevant to behavioral phenotypes.

Intron: A segment of DNA/RNA, occurring within a gene, that does not code for proteins. Typically removed from RNA transcript prior to protein translation through the process of gene splicing.

Locus/loci : A genetic locus (plural loci) refers to the position of a genetic variant at a specific location on a chromosome.

Methyl-CpG binding domain (MBD): A domain that binds to DNA that contains one or more symmetrically methylated CpGs.

Methyl-CpG binding protein 2 (MECP2): The gene encoding the protein MECP2, which is essential for the normal function of nerve cells. MECP2 seems to be particularly important for mature nerve cells, in which it is present in high levels and is epigenetically functional.

Methylation arrays: Chip-based method for assaying methylation. Unlike sequencing methods that agnostically query the methylome, arrays target only the known methylated regions of the genome.

Methylation quantitative trait loci (meQTLs): DNA sites associated with methylation levels at specific locations. These DNA sites can influence the methylation pattern across an extended genomic region, but more frequently they show only local effects.

Methylome: The full complement of DNA methylation modifications in an organism's genome.

MicroRNA (miRNA): A small non-coding RNA molecule that functions in RNA silencing and post-transcriptional regulation of gene expression.

Mood disorders: A class of psychological disorders characterized by the disruption of a person's mood, such as depression, anxiety, and bipolar disorder.

Next-generation sequencing (NGS): Also known as high-throughput sequencing, the broad term is used to describe a number of different modern DNA sequencing methods.

NGFI-A: Nerve growth factor-inducible protein A, a transcription factor that binds to an exon within the hippocampus. NGFI-A is critically involved in the biological process through which psychosocial stress is epigenetically encoded at the glucocorticoid receptor gene.

Non-protein coding RNA (ncRNA): An RNA molecule that is not translated into a protein. It often functions as a gene expression regulator.

NR3C1 gene: See "Glucocorticoid receptor gene."

Nucleosome: A structural unit of a eukaryotic chromosome, consisting of a length of DNA coiled around a core of histones.

Nucleotide: A compound consisting of a nucleoside linked to a phosphate group. Nucleotides form the basic structural unit of nucleic acids such as DNA.

Nucleus accumbens: A region in the basal forebrain, reliant on dopamine and serotonin, that plays a central role in the limbic system and the experience of reward. It is involved in the development of addiction.

Phenotypic plasticity: The ability of an organism to moderate the expression of genotype to phenotype in response to changes in the environment.

Promoter: DNA region that forms the site at which the transcription of a gene starts.

Recognition element: DNA sequence found in the promoter region of most genes. Serves as a docking site for transcription factors and is thus involved in the initiation of transcription.

Regulatory proteins: Proteins that interact with DNA to influence gene expression, including transcription factors.

Retrotransposon: A transposon is a DNA sequence that can change position within a genome, sometimes creating or reversing mutations, whose sequence shows homology with that of a retrovirus.

Steroid hormones: A class of chemical compounds known as steroids and secreted by three "steroid glands": the adrenal cortex, the testes, and the ovaries. Cortisol, a primary steroid, is in the glucocorticoid class of hormones and is released in response to stress and low blood glucose concentration.

Transcription: The first step of gene expression, transcription is the process of making an RNA copy of a DNA gene sequence. This copy, called a messenger RNA (mRNA) molecule, leaves the cell nucleus and directs the synthesis of a protein.

Transcription factors: Proteins involved in the process of converting DNA into RNA. Transcription factors include a wide number of proteins that initiate and regulate the transcription of genes.

Transgenerational epigenetic inheritance: The process through which epigenetic marks can be acquired on the DNA of one generation and passed through the gametes to the next generation.

Translation: The process of translating the sequence of a messenger RNA molecule to a sequence of amino acids during protein synthesis.

Transposon: A DNA sequence that can change position within a genome, sometimes creating or reversing mutations.

X chromosome inactivation: A process by which one of the copies of the X chromosome present in female mammals is inactivated by being epigenetically packaged such that it has a transcriptionally inactive structure known as heterochromatin.

REFERENCES

Adkins, D. E., Daw, J. K., McClay, J. L., & Van den Oord, E. (2012). The influence of five monoamine genes on trajectories of depressive symptoms across adolescence and young adulthood. *Development and Psychopathology*, 24(1), 267–285. doi:10.1017/80954579411000824

Adkins, D. E., & Guo, G. (2008). Societal development and the shifting influence of the genome on status attainment. *Research in Social Stratification and Mobility*, 26(3), 235–255.

Adkins, D. E., & Vaisey, S. (2009). Toward a unified stratification theory: Structure, genome, and status across human societies. *Sociological Theory*, 27(2), 99–121. doi:10.1111/j.1467-9558.2009.01339.x

Adkins, D. E., Wang, V., Dupre, M. E., van den Oord, E., & Elder, G. H. (2009). Structure and stress: Trajectories of depressive symptoms across adolescence and young adulthood. *Social Forces*, 88(1), 31–60.

Allis, C. D. (2015). *Epigenetics*. Cold Spring Harbor, NY: Cold Spring Harbor Laboratory Press.

Avner, P., & Heard, E. (2001). X-chromosome inactivation: Counting, choice and initiation. *Nature Reviews Genetics*, 2(1), 59–67.

Baker-Andresen, D., Flavell, C. R., Li, X., & Bredy, T. W. (2013). Activation of BDNF signaling prevents the return of fear in female mice. *Learning & Memory*, 20(5), 237–240.

Baltagi, B. H. (2013). *Econometric analysis of panel data* (5th ed.). Chichester, UK: Wiley.

Baylin, S. B., & Jones, P. A. (2011). A decade of exploring the cancer epigenome—Biological and translational implications. *Nature Reviews Cancer*, 11(10), 726–734. doi:10.1038/nrc3130

Bell, J. T., & Spector, T. D. (2012). DNA methylation studies using twins: What are they telling us? *Genome Biology*, 13(10), 172.

Belsky, J., & Pluess, M. (2009). Beyond diathesis stress: Differential susceptibility to environmental influences. *Psychological Bulletin*, 135(6), 885.

Bird, A. (2002). DNA methylation patterns and epigenetic memory. *Genes & Development*, 16(1), 6–21.

Bjornsson, H. T., Sigurdsson, M. I., Fallin, M. D., Irizarry, R. A., Aspelund, T., Cui, H., . . . Harris, T. B. (2008). Intra-individual change over time in DNA methylation with familial clustering. *JAMA*, 299(24), 2877–2883.

Blake, J. A., Bult, C. J., Eppig, J. T., Kadin, J. A., Richardson, J. E.; Mouse Genome Database Group. (2014). The Mouse Genome Database: Integration of and access to knowledge about the laboratory mouse. *Nucleic Acids Research*, 42(D1), D810-D817. doi:10.1093/nar/gkt1225

Bollen, K. A. (1989). *Structural equations with latent variables*. New York, NY: Wiley.

Bork, S., Pfister, S., Witt, H., Horn, P., Korn, B., Ho, A. D., & Wagner, W. (2010). DNA methylation pattern changes upon long-term culture and aging of human mesenchymal stromal cells. *Aging Cell*, 9(1), 54–63.

Boulle, F., van den Hove, D. L., Jakob, S. B., Rutten, B. P., Hamon, M., van Os, J., . . . Kenis, G. (2012). Epigenetic regulation of the BDNF gene: Implications for psychiatric disorders. *Molecular Psychiatry*, 17(6), 584–596. doi:10.1038/mp.2011.107

Boyle, M. P., Brewer, J. A., Funatsu, M., Wozniak, D. F., Tsien, J. Z., Izumi, Y., & Muglia, L. J. (2005). Acquired deficit of forebrain glucocorticoid receptor produces depression-like changes in adrenal axis regulation and behavior. *Proceedings of the National Academy of Sciences of the USA*, 102(2), 473–478.

Breitling, L. P., Saum, K. U., Perna, L., Schottker, B., Holleczek, B., & Brenner, H. (2016). Frailty is associated with the epigenetic clock but not with telomere length in a German cohort. *Clinical Epigenetics*, 8, 21. doi:10.1186/s13148-016-0186-5

Byrne, E., Carrillo-Roa, T., Henders, A., Bowdler, L., McRae, A., Heath, A., . . . Wray, N. (2013). Monozygotic twins affected with major depressive disorder have greater variance in methylation than their unaffected co-twin. *Translational Psychiatry*, 3(6), e269.

Calvanese, V., Lara, E., Kahn, A., & Fraga, M. F. (2009). The role of epigenetics in aging and age-related diseases. *Ageing Research Reviews*, 8(4), 268–276.

Cervoni, N., & Szyf, M. (2001). Demethylase activity is directed by histone acetylation. *Journal of Biological Chemistry*, 276(44), 40778–40787.

Christiansen, L., Lenart, A., Tan, Q. H., Vaupel, J. W., Aviv, A., McGue, M., & Christensen, K. (2016). DNA methylation age is associated with mortality in a longitudinal Danish twin study. *Aging Cell*, 15(1), 149–154. doi:10.1111/acel.12421

Cicchetti, D., & Rogosch, F. A. (2012). Gene × environment interaction and resilience: Effects of child maltreatment and serotonin, corticotropin releasing hormone, dopamine, and oxytocin genes. *Development and Psychopathology*, 24(2), 411–427.

Clark, S. L., Gillespie, N. A., Adkins, D. E., Kendler, K. S., & Neale, M. C. (2016). Psychometric modeling of abuse and dependence symptoms across six illicit substances indicates novel dimensions of misuse. *Addictive Behaviors*, 53, 132–140.

Crick, F. (1970). Central dogma of molecular biology. *Nature*, 227(5258), 561–563.

D'Alessio, A. C., Weaver, I. C., & Szyf, M. (2007). Acetylation-induced transcription is required for active DNA demethylation in methylation-silenced genes. *Molecular and Cellular Biology*, 27(21), 7462–7474.

D'Avila, M. F., Garcia, R. N., Panzera, Y., & Valente, V. L. (2010). Sex-specific methylation in *Drosophila*: An investigation of the *Sophophora* subgenus. *Genetica*, 138(8), 907–913. doi:10.1007/s10709-010-9473-9

Davies, M. N., Krause, L., Bell, J. T., Gao, F., Ward, K. J., Wu, H., . . . Collier, D. A. (2014). Hypermethylation in the ZBTB20 gene is associated with major depressive disorder. *Genome Biology*, 15(4), R56.

De Bellis, M. D., Chrousos, G. P., Dorn, L. D., Burke, L., Helmers, K., Kling, M. A., . . . Putnam, F. W. (1994). Hypothalamic–pituitary–adrenal axis dysregulation in sexually abused girls. *Journal of Clinical Endocrinology & Metabolism*, 78(2), 249–255.

De Kloet, E. R., Joëls, M., & Holsboer, F. (2005). Stress and the brain: From adaptation to disease. *Nature Reviews Neuroscience*, 6(6), 463–475.

Dempster, E. L., Wong, C. C., Lester, K. J., Burrage, J., Gregory, A. M., Mill, J., & Eley, T. C. (2014). Genome-wide methylomic analysis of monozygotic twins discordant for adolescent depression. *Biological Psychiatry*, 76(12), 977–983.

Deng, J. V., Rodriguiz, R. M., Hutchinson, A. N., Kim, I.-H., Wetsel, W. C., & West, A. E. (2010). MeCP2 in the nucleus accumbens contributes to neural and behavioral responses to psychostimulants. *Nature Neuroscience*, 13(9), 1128–1136.

El-Maarri, O., Becker, T., Junen, J., Manzoor, S. S., Diaz-Lacava, A., Schwaab, R., . . . Oldenburg, J. (2007). Gender specific differences in levels of DNA methylation at selected loci from human total blood: A tendency toward higher methylation levels in males. *Human Genetics*, 122(5), 505–514. doi:10.1007/s00439-007-0430-3

Elliott, E., Ezra-Nevo, G., Regev, L., Neufeld-Cohen, A., & Chen, A. (2010). Resilience to social stress coincides with functional DNA methylation of the *Crf* gene in adult mice. *Nature Neuroscience*, 13(11), 1351–1353. doi:10.1038/nn.2642

Feil, R., & Fraga, M. F. (2012). Epigenetics and the environment: Emerging patterns and implications. *Nature Reviews Genetics*, 13(2), 97–109. doi:10.1038/nrg3142

Feng, J., Shao, N., Szulwach, K. E., Vialou, V., Huynh, J., Zhong, C., . . . Nestler, E. J. (2015). Role of Tet1 and 5-hydroxymethylcytosine in cocaine action. *Nature Neuroscience*, 18(4), 536–544. http://www.nature.com/neuro/journal/v18/n4/abs/nn.3976.html#supplementary-information

Feng, J., Wilkinson, M., Liu, X., Purushothaman, I., Ferguson, D., Vialou, V., . . . Shen, L. (2014). Chronic cocaine-regulated epigenomic changes in mouse nucleus accumbens. *Genome Biology*, 15(4). doi:R6510.1186/gb-2014-15-4-r65

Fraga, M. F. (2009). Genetic and epigenetic regulation of aging. *Current Opinion in Immunology*, 21(4), 446–453.

Fuks, F., Burgers, W. A., Brehm, A., Hughes-Davies, L., & Kouzarides, T. (2000). DNA methyltransferase Dnmt1 associates with histone deacetylase activity. *Nature Genetics*, 24(1), 88–91.

Fuks, F., Hurd, P. J., Wolf, D., Nan, X., Bird, A. P., & Kouzarides, T. (2003). The methyl-CpG-binding protein MeCP2 links DNA methylation to histone methylation. *Journal of Biological Chemistry*, 278(6), 4035–4040.

Galton, F. (1869). *Hereditary genius: An inquiry into its laws and consequences*. London, UK/New York, NY: Friedmann/St. Martin's.

Geiman, T. M., Sankpal, U. T., Robertson, A. K., Zhao, Y., Zhao, Y., & Robertson, K. D. (2004). DNMT3B interacts with hSNF2H chromatin remodeling enzyme, HDACs 1 and 2, and components of the histone methylation system. *Biochemical and Biophysical Research Communications*, 318(2), 544–555.

Geronimus, A. T. (1992). The weathering hypothesis and the health of African-American women and infants: Evidence and speculations. *Ethnicity & Disease*, 2(3), 207–221.

Golden, S. A., Covington, H. E., 3rd, Berton, O., & Russo, S. J. (2011). A standardized protocol for repeated social defeat stress in mice. *Nature Protocols*, 6(8), 1183–1191. doi:nprot.2011.361 [pii] 10.1038/nprot.2011.361

Grönniger, E., Weber, B., Heil, O., Peters, N., Stäb, F., Wenck, H., . . . Lyko, F. (2010). Aging and chronic sun exposure cause distinct epigenetic changes in human skin. *PLoS Genetics*, 6(5), e1000971.

Grossniklaus, U., Kelly, W. G., Ferguson-Smith, A. C., Pembrey, M., & Lindquist, S. (2013). Transgenerational epigenetic inheritance: How important is it? *Nature Reviews Genetics*, 14(3), 228–235.

Hackman, D. A., Farah, M. J., & Meaney, M. J. (2010). Socioeconomic status and the brain: Mechanistic insights from human and animal research. *Nature Reviews Neuroscience*, 11(9), 651–659.

Heijmans, B. T., Tobi, E. W., Stein, A. D., Putter, H., Blauw, G. J., Susser, E. S., . . . Lumey, L. H. (2008). Persistent epigenetic differences associated with prenatal exposure to famine in humans. *Proceedings of the National Academy of Sciences of the USA*, 105(44), 17046–17049. doi:10.1073/pnas.0806560105

Heim, C., & Binder, E. B. (2012). Current research trends in early life stress and depression: Review of human studies on sensitive periods, gene–environment interactions, and epigenetics. *Experimental Neurology*, 233(1), 102–111.

Heim, C., & Nemeroff, C. B. (2001). The role of childhood trauma in the neurobiology of mood and anxiety disorders: Preclinical and clinical studies. *Biological Psychiatry*, 49(12), 1023–1039.

Hellman, A., & Chess, A. (2007). Gene body-specific methylation on the active X chromosome. *Science*, 315(5815), 1141–1143. doi:10.1126/science.1136352

Herrnstein, R. J. (1994). *The bell curve: Intelligence and class structure in American life*. New York, NY: Free Press.

Higley, J., Hasert, M., Suomi, S., & Linnoila, M. (1991). Nonhuman primate model of alcohol abuse: Effects of early experience, personality, and stress on alcohol consumption. *Proceedings of the National Academy of Sciences of the USA*, 88(16), 7261–7265.

Horvath, S. (2013). DNA methylation age of human tissues and cell types. *Genome Biology*, 14(10), R115. doi:10.1186/gb-2013-14-10-r115

Im, H. I., Hollander, J. A., Bali, P., & Kenny, P. J. (2010). MeCP2 controls BDNF expression and cocaine intake through homeostatic interactions with microRNA-212. *Nature Neuroscience*, 13(9), 1120–1127. doi:nn.2615 [pii] 10.1038/nn.2615

Jessen, H. M., & Auger, A. P. (2011). Sex differences in epigenetic mechanisms may underlie risk and resilience for mental health disorders. *Epigenetics*, 6(7), 857–861. doi:16517

Kamakura, M. (2011). Royalactin induces queen differentiation in honeybees. *Nature*, 473(7348), 478–483.

Kaminsky, Z. A., Tang, T., Wang, S.-C., Ptak, C., Oh, G. H., Wong, A. H., . . . Tysk, C. (2009). DNA methylation profiles in monozygotic and dizygotic twins. *Nature Genetics*, 41(2), 240–245.

Kangaspeska, S., Stride, B., Metivier, R., Polycarpou-Schwarz, M., Ibberson, D., Carmouche, R. P., . . . Reid, G. (2008). Transient cyclical methylation of promoter DNA. *Nature*, 452(7183), 112–115.

Klengel, T., Mehta, D., Anacker, C., Rex-Haffner, M., Pruessner, J. C., Pariante, C. M., . . . Binder, E. B. (2013). Allele-specific FKBP5 DNA demethylation mediates gene–childhood trauma interactions. *Nature Neuroscience*, 16(1), 33–41. doi:10.1038/nn.3275

Kolodkin, M. H., & Auger, A. P. (2011). Sex difference in the expression of DNA methyltransferase 3a in the rat amygdala during development. *Journal of Neuroendocrinology*, 23(7), 577–583. doi:10.1111/j.1365-2826.2011.02147.x

Kriaucionis, S., & Heintz, N. (2009). The nuclear DNA base, 5-hydroxymethylcytosine, is present in brain and enriched in Purkinje neurons. *Science*, 324(5929), 929–930. doi:10.1126/science.1169786

Labonté, B., Suderman, M., Maussion, G., Lopez, J. P., Navarro-Sanchez, L., Yerko, V., . . . Turecki, G. (2013). Genome-wide methylation changes in the brains of suicide completers. *American Journal of Psychiatry*, 170(5), 511–520. doi:10.1176/appi.ajp.2012.12050627

Labonté, B., Suderman, M., Maussion, G., Navaro, L., Yerko, V., Mahar, I., . . . Meaney, M. J. (2012). Genome-wide epigenetic regulation by early-life trauma. *Archives of General Psychiatry*, 69(7), 722–731.

Laird, P. W. (2010). Principles and challenges of genomewide DNA methylation analysis. *Nature Reviews Genetics*, 11(3), 191–203. doi:10.1038/nrg2732

Landan, G., Cohen, N. M., Mukamel, Z., Bar, A., Molchadsky, A., Brosh, R., . . . Tanay, A. (2012). Epigenetic polymorphism and the stochastic formation of differentially methylated regions in normal and cancerous tissues. *Nature Genetics*, 44(11), 1207–1214. http://www.nature.com/ng/journal/v44/n11/abs/ng.2442.html#supplementary-information

Li, Y., Zhu, J., Tian, G., Li, N., Li, Q., Ye, M., . . . Zhang, X. (2010). The DNA methylome of human peripheral blood mononuclear cells. *PLoS Biology*, 8(11), e1000533. doi:10.1371/journal.pbio.1000533

Lim, J. P., & Brunet, A. (2013). Bridging the transgenerational gap with epigenetic memory. *Trends in Genetics*, 29(3), 176–186. doi:10.1016/j.tig.2012.12.008

Link, B. G., & Phelan, J. (1995). Social conditions as fundamental causes of disease. *Journal of Health and Social Behavior* (Extra issue), 80–94.

Liu, D., Diorio, J., Tannenbaum, B., Caldji, C., Francis, D., Freedman, A., . . . Meaney, M. J. (1997). Maternal care, hippocampal glucocorticoid receptors, and hypothalamic–pituitary–adrenal responses to stress. *Science*, 277(5332), 1659–1662.

Lomniczi, A., Loche, A., Castellano, J. M., Ronnekleiv, O. K., Bosch, M., Kaidar, G., . . . Ojeda, S. R. (2013). Epigenetic control of female puberty. *Nature Neuroscience*, 16(3), 281–289. doi:10.1038/nn.3319

Maunakea, A. K., Nagarajan, R. P., Bilenky, M., Ballinger, T. J., D'Souza, C., Fouse, S. D., . . . Zhao, Y. (2010). Conserved role of intragenic DNA methylation in regulating alternative promoters. *Nature*, 466(7303), 253–257.

McCarthy, M. M., & Nugent, B. M. (2015). At the frontier of epigenetics of brain sex differences. *Frontiers in Behavioral Neuroscience, 9*, 221. doi:10.3389/fnbeh.2015.00221

McCarthy, N. S., Melton, P. E., Cadby, G., Yazar, S., Franchina, M., Moses, E. K., . . . Hewitt, A. W. (2014). Meta-analysis of human methylation data for evidence of sex-specific autosomal patterns. *BMC Genomics, 15*(1), 981. doi:10.1186/1471-2164-15-981

McClay, J. L., Aberg, K. A., Clark, S. L., Nerella, S., Kumar, G., Xie, L. Y., . . . Van Den Oord, E. J. C. G. (2014). A methylome-wide study of aging using massively parallel sequencing of the methyl-CpG-enriched genomic fraction from blood in over 700 subjects. *Human Molecular Genetics, 23*(5), 1175–1185. doi:10.1093/hmg/ddt511

McClay, J. L., Shabalin, A. A., Dozmorov, M. G., Adkins, D. E., Kumar, G., Nerella, S., . . . Van Den Oord, E. J. C. G. (2015). High density methylation QTL analysis in human blood via next-generation sequencing of the methylated genomic DNA fraction. *Genome Biology, 16*, 291. doi:10.1186/s13059-015-0842-7

McGowan, P. O., Sasaki, A., D'Alessio, A. C., Dymov, S., Labonte, B., Szyf, M., . . . Meaney, M. J. (2009). Epigenetic regulation of the glucocorticoid receptor in human brain associates with childhood abuse. *Nature Neuroscience, 12*(3), 342–348. doi:10.1038/nn.2270

Meaburn, E. L., Schalkwyk, L. C., & Mill, J. (2010). Allele-specific methylation in the human genome: Implications for genetic studies of complex disease. *Epigenetics, 5*(7), 578–582.

Meaney, M. J. (2001). Maternal care, gene expression, and the transmission of individual differences in stress reactivity across generations. *Annual Review of Neuroscience, 24*(1), 1161–1192.

Molendijk, M. L., Bus, B. A., Spinhoven, P., Penninx, B. W., Kenis, G., Prickaerts, J., . . . Elzinga, B. M. (2011). Serum levels of brain-derived neurotrophic factor in major depressive disorder: State-trait issues, clinical features and pharmacological treatment. *Molecular Psychiatry, 16*(11), 1088–1095. doi:10.1038/mp.2010.98

Moore, L. D., Le, T., & Fan, G. (2012). DNA methylation and its basic function. *Neuropsychopharmacology, 38*(1), 23–38. doi:10.1038/npp.2012.112

Morrison, K. E., Rodgers, A. B., Morgan, C. P., & Bale, T. L. (2014). Epigenetic mechanisms in pubertal brain maturation. *Neuroscience, 264*, 17–24. doi:10.1016/j.neuroscience.2013.11.014

Nagy, C., Suderman, M., Yang, J., Szyf, M., Mechawar, N., Ernst, C., & Turecki, G. (2015). Astrocytic abnormalities and global DNA methylation patterns in depression and suicide. *Molecular Psychiatry, 20*(3), 320–328.

Neale, M., & Cardon, L. (1992). *Methodology for genetic studies of twins and families* (Vol. 67). New York, NY: Springer.

Nestler, E. J. (2014). Epigenetic mechanisms of drug addiction. *Neuropharmacology, 76*(Part B), 259–268. doi:10.1016/j.neuropharm.2013.04.004

Nikoshkov, A., Sunkari, V., Savu, O., Forsberg, E., Catrina, S. B., & Brismar, K. (2011). Epigenetic DNA methylation in the promoters of the IGF1 receptor and insulin receptor genes in db/db mice. *Epigenetics, 6*(4), 405–409.

Onishchenko, N., Karpova, N., Sabri, F., Castren, E., & Ceccatelli, S. (2008). Long-lasting depression-like behavior and epigenetic changes of BDNF gene expression induced by perinatal exposure to methylmercury. *Journal of Neurochemistry, 106*(3), 1378–1387. doi:10.1111/j.1471-4159.2008.05484.x

Painter, R. C., Osmond, C., Gluckman, P., Hanson, M., Phillips, D. I., & Roseboom, T. J. (2008). Transgenerational effects of prenatal exposure to the Dutch famine on neonatal adiposity and health in later life. *BJOG, 115*(10), 1243–1249. doi:10.1111/j.1471-0528.2008.01822.x

Pearlin, L. I., Menaghan, E. G., Lieberman, M. A., & Mullan, J. T. (1981). The stress process. *Journal of Health and Social Behavior, 22*(4), 337–356.

Pembrey, M. E., Bygren, L. O., Kaati, G., Edvinsson, S., Northstone, K., Sjöström, M., & Golding, J. (2006). Sex-specific, male-line transgenerational responses in humans. *European Journal of Human Genetics*, 14(2), 159–166.

Perroud, N., Paoloni-Giacobino, A., Prada, P., Olié, E., Salzmann, A., Nicastro, R., . . . Dieben, K. (2011). Increased methylation of glucocorticoid receptor gene (NR3C1) in adults with a history of childhood maltreatment: A link with the severity and type of trauma. *Translational Psychiatry*, 1(12), e59.

Prendergast, G. C., & Ziff, E. B. (1991). Methylation-sensitive sequence-specific DNA binding by the c-Myc basic region. *Science*, 251(4990), 186–189.

Pruessner, J. C., Champagne, F., Meaney, M. J., & Dagher, A. (2004). Dopamine release in response to a psychological stress in humans and its relationship to early life maternal care: A positron emission tomography study using [11C] raclopride. *Journal of Neuroscience*, 24(11), 2825–2831.

Rakyan, V. K., & Beck, S. (2006). Epigenetic variation and inheritance in mammals. *Current Opinion in Genetics & Development*, 16(6), 573–577. doi:10.1016/j.gde.2006.09.002

Rakyan, V. K., Blewitt, M. E., Druker, R., Preis, J. I., & Whitelaw, E. (2002). Metastable epialleles in mammals. *Trends in Genetics*, 18(7), 348–351.

Rakyan, V. K., Down, T. A., Balding, D. J., & Beck, S. (2011). Epigenome-wide association studies for common human diseases. *Nature Reviews Genetics*, 12(8), 529–541. doi:10.1038/nrg3000

Ravelli, G.-P., Stein, Z. A., & Susser, M. W. (1976). Obesity in young men after famine exposure in utero and early infancy. *New England Journal of Medicine*, 295(7), 349–353.

Rao, Y.S., Mott, N.N., Wang, Y., Chung, W.C.J., & Pak, T.R. (2013). MicroRNAs in the aging female brain: A putative mechanism for age-specific estrogen effects. *Endocrinology* Aug;154(8): 2795–2806.

Reichardt, H. M., Tronche, F., Bauer, A., & Schütz, G. (2000). Molecular genetic analysis of glu-cocorticoid signaling using the Cre/loxP system. *Biological Chemistry*, 381(9–10), 961–964.

Ressler, K. J., Mercer, K. B., Bradley, B., Jovanovic, T., Mahan, A., Kerley, K., . . . May, V. (2011). Post-traumatic stress disorder is associated with PACAP and the PAC1 receptor. *Nature*, 470(7335), 492–497. doi:10.1038/nature09856

Ridder, S., Chourbaji, S., Hellweg, R., Urani, A., Zacher, C., Schmid, W., . . . Henn, F. A. (2005). Mice with genetically altered glucocorticoid receptor expression show altered sensitivity for stress-induced depressive reactions. *Journal of Neuroscience*, 25(26), 6243–6250.

Rosell, D. R., & Siever, L. J. (2015). The neurobiology of aggression and violence. *CNS Spectrums*, 20(3), 254–279. doi:10.1017/s109285291500019x

Rosenfeld, C. S. (2010). Animal models to study environmental epigenetics. *Biology of Reproduction*, 82(3), 473–488.

Sahin, E., & DePinho, R. A. (2010). Linking functional decline of telomeres, mitochondria and stem cells during ageing. *Nature*, 464(7288), 520–528.

Sandovici, I., Smith, N. H., Nitert, M. D., Ackers-Johnson, M., Uribe-Lewis, S., Ito, Y., . . . Ozanne, S. E. (2011). Maternal diet and aging alter the epigenetic control of a promoter–enhancer interaction at the *Hnf4a* gene in rat pancreatic islets. *Proceedings of the National Academy of Sciences of the USA*, 108(13), 5449–5454. doi:10.1073/pnas.1019007108

Schwarz, J. M., Nugent, B. M., & McCarthy, M. M. (2010). Developmental and hormone-induced epigenetic changes to estrogen and progesterone receptor genes in brain are dynamic across the life span. *Endocrinology*, 151(10), 4871–4881. doi:10.1210/en.2010-0142

Shukla, S., Kavak, E., Gregory, M., Imashimizu, M., Shutinoski, B., Kashlev, M., . . . Oberdoerffer, S. (2011). CTCF-promoted RNA polymerase II pausing links DNA methyla-tion to splicing. *Nature*, 479(7371), 74–79.

Sterrenburg, L., Gaszner, B., Boerrigter, J., Santbergen, L., Bramini, M., Elliott, E., . . . Kozicz, T. (2011). Chronic stress induces sex-specific alterations in methylation and expression of corticotropin-releasing factor gene in the rat. *PLoS One, 6*(11), e28128.

Sun, H., Kennedy, P. J., & Nestler, E. J. (2013). Epigenetics of the depressed brain: Role of histone acetylation and methylation. *Neuropsychopharmacology, 38*(1), 124–137. doi:10.1038/npp.2012.73

Szulwach, K. E., Li, X., Li, Y., Song, C.-X., Wu, H., Dai, Q., . . . Jin, P. (2011). 5-hmC-mediated epigenetic dynamics during postnatal neurodevelopment and aging. *Nature Neuroscience, 14*(12), 1607–1616. http://www.nature.com/neuro/journal/v14/n12/abs/nn.2959.html#supplementary-information

Szyf, M. (2013a). DNA methylation, behavior and early life adversity. *Journal of Genetics and Genomics, 40*(7), 331–338. doi:10.1016/j.jgg.2013.06.004

Szyf, M. (2013b). How do environments talk to genes? *Nature Neuroscience, 16*(1), 2–4. doi:10.1038/nn.3286

Szyf, M. (2015). Nongenetic inheritance and transgenerational epigenetics. *Trends in Molecular Medicine, 21*(2), 134–144. doi:10.1016/j.molmed.2014.12.004

Tan, Q., Christiansen, L., von Bornemann Hjelmborg, J., & Christensen, K. (2015). Twin methodology in epigenetic studies. *Journal of Experimental Biology, 218*(1), 134–139. doi:10.1242/jeb.107151

Thomson, J. P., Skene, P. J., Selfridge, J., Clouaire, T., Guy, J., Webb, S., . . . James, K. D. (2010). CpG islands influence chromatin structure via the CpG-binding protein Cfp1. *Nature, 464*(7291), 1082–1086.

Tobi, E. W., Lumey, L. H., Talens, R. P., Kremer, D., Putter, H., Stein, A. D., . . . Heijmans, B. T. (2009). DNA methylation differences after exposure to prenatal famine are common and timing- and sex-specific. *Human Molecular Genetics, 18*(21), 4046–4053. doi:10.1093/hmg/ddp353

Tsankova, N. M., Berton, O., Renthal, W., Kumar, A., Neve, R. L., & Nestler, E. J. (2006). Sustained hippocampal chromatin regulation in a mouse model of depression and antidepressant action. *Nature Neuroscience, 9*(4), 519–525.

Turecki, G., & Meaney, M. J. (2016). Effects of the social environment and stress on glucocorticoid receptor gene methylation: A systematic review. *Biological Psychiatry, 79*(2), 87–96. doi:10.1016/j.biopsych.2014.11.022

Uchida, S., Hara, K., Kobayashi, A., Otsuki, K., Yamagata, H., Hobara, T., . . . Watanabe, Y. (2011). Epigenetic status of Gdnf in the ventral striatum determines susceptibility and adaptation to daily stressful events. *Neuron, 69*(2), 359–372.

Uddin, M., Koenen, K., Aiello, A., Wildman, D., de Los Santos, R., & Galea, S. (2011). Epigenetic and inflammatory marker profiles associated with depression in a community-based epidemiologic sample. *Psychological Medicine, 41*(5), 997–1007.

Venolia, L., & Gartler, S. M. (1983). Comparison of transformation efficiency of human active and inactive X-chromosomal DNA. *Nature, 302*(5903), 82–83.

Waterland, R. A., Kellermayer, R., Laritsky, E., Rayco-Solon, P., Harris, R. A., Travisano, M., . . . Prentice, A. M. (2010). Season of conception in rural Gambia affects DNA methylation at putative human metastable epialleles. *PLoS Genetics, 6*(12), e1001252.

Weaver, I. C., Cervoni, N., Champagne, F. A., D'Alessio, A. C., Sharma, S., Seckl, J. R., . . . Meaney, M. J. (2004). Epigenetic programming by maternal behavior. *Nature Neuroscience, 7*(8), 847–854. doi:10.1038/nn1276nn1276

Weder, N., Zhang, H., Jensen, K., Yang, B. Z., Simen, A., Jackowski, A., . . . Perepletchikova, F. (2014). Child abuse, depression, and methylation in genes involved with stress, neural plasticity, and brain circuitry. *Journal of the American Academy of Child & Adolescent Psychiatry, 53*(4), 417–424.

Wilkinson, M. B., Xiao, G., Kumar, A., LaPlant, Q., Renthal, W., Sikder, D., . . . Nestler, E. J. (2009). Imipramine treatment and resiliency exhibit similar chromatin regulation in the mouse nucleus accumbens in depression models. *Journal of Neuroscience, 29*(24), 7820–7832.

Zhang, F. F., Cardarelli, R., Carroll, J., Fulda, K. G., Kaur, M., Gonzalez, K., . . . Morabia, A. (2011). Significant differences in global genomic DNA methylation by gender and race/ethnicity in peripheral blood. *Epigenetics, 6*(5), 623–629.

Zhang, Y., Labonte, B., Wen, X. L., Turecki, G., & Meaney, M. J. (2013). Epigenetic mechanisms for the early environmental regulation of hippocampal glucocorticoid receptor gene expression in rodents and humans. *Neuropsychopharmacology, 38*(1), 111–123. doi:10.1038/npp.2012.149

Zhi, D., Aslibekyan, S., Irvin, M. R., Claas, S. A., Borecki, I. B., Ordovas, J. M., . . . Arnett, D. K. (2013). SNPs located at CpG sites modulate genome–epigenome interaction. *Epigenetics, 8*(8), 802–806.

....

CHAPTER 19

PHYSIOLOGY OF
FACE-TO-FACE COMPETITION

....

ALLAN MAZUR

WE have barely begun to integrate biology with sociology, forming falsifiable hypotheses about human behavior. Like the natural sciences of the 19th century, this research is mostly done by people freed of the full-time pursuit of wages, working with limited resources, often self-funded. Early natural science, despite many wrong turns, did lay the basis for modern knowledge. Perhaps the same will be true of biosociology, but currently nearly all we think we know in this area is tentative, awaiting more resources to enable stronger testing.

I focus on face-to-face competition for status, an active area of biosocial research that builds on the classical finding that previously unacquainted subjects, when formed into a group, sort themselves into a status hierarchy, differentiating leaders from followers. Usually this happens quickly, even when subjects have no overt status signs (or "diffuse status characteristics") that differentiate them at the outset (Fisek & Ofshe, 1970). Rankings may not be strictly linear or transitive, but they are reliably recognizable by amount of speech, ability to start or end a discussion topic, who is the focus of attention, nonverbal behaviors including body posture and facial expressions, and evaluations by other group members about quality of participation and leadership (Mast, 2002; Mazur, 2005).

Pre-biological theories of status and leadership in small groups, notably by Bales (1953), Homans (1961), and Berger, Cohen, and Zelditch (1972), presume that we humans allocate status ranks by using our uniquely high-functioning cognitive abilities—for example, by discerning who can best lead the group in performing a task. If our physical bodies are relevant at all, it is though biases about external appearance (e.g., race, size, gender, and age) or, as in Goffman (1967), by nonverbal gestures and postures of assertion or deference. A newer "biosocial model" emphasizes that status allocation in face-to-face human groups follows a general primate pattern and that, as in other primates, physiology is highly responsive during social interaction, affecting and being affected by status allocation.

The hormones testosterone (T) and cortisol (C) comprise a physiological substrate underlying serious face-to-face competition for status. Because it is now easy to assay these hormones in the saliva of experimental subjects, and because hormone measurements are increasingly included in publically available data sets with large samples, there has been a proliferation of research reports, often with one contradicting or failing to replicate another. The situation is complicated by journal editors' insistence on significant results for publication, and the pressure this places on researchers to find "significant" effects one way or another (Head, Holman, Lanfear, Kahn, & Jennions, 2015), encouraging the appearance of strange and probably nonreplicable findings in the literature. Another problem is that some researchers conflate status in a face-to-face group with socioeconomic status in a large society, although hormones are theoretically implicated only at the micro, not the macro, level (Mazur, 2005). One more complication, specifically for T, involves gender differences. Men produce far more T that do women, making it easier to assay accurately. In males, T is produced by different organs and targets different tissues than in women, and T functions differently in the development of the two sexes. Whether T is associated with dominant behavior only in men or in both sexes remains an open question.

Fortunately, there are occasional overviews of this messy literature (Archer, 2006; Hamilton, Carré, Mehta, Olmstead, & Whitaker, 2015; Mazur & Booth, 1998). Broadly speaking, high T is associated with dominance behaviors and potentially higher status (at least in males), whereas C tends to be associated with lower status and greater exposure to stressors; however, there are unexplained inconsistencies in the literature, perhaps due to erroneous findings that too often creep into the literature or to unrecognized mediators. Mehta and Josephs (2006) propose a promising "dual hormone" hypothesis whereby testosterone and cortisol jointly regulate dominance. They provide evidence that testosterone effects occur mostly when a person's cortisol is low. This hypothesis is intuitively appealing, suggesting that the people most likely to act dominantly, to break norms or otherwise scale stressful barriers, are those least bothered by the stressor and thus low in cortisol. For high-cortisol individuals, the barrier is too intimidating to challenge.

This chapter first places status processes in primary groups of humans into a broader primate pattern. Then, it sketches the physiological substrate of T, C, and α-amylase underlying status competition. It describes separately the physiology of stress, perhaps the central component of competition. Finally, it describes advances in real-time measurement of stress during conversation.

THE PRIMATE PATTERN

Features of status in small human groups, long recognized by social psychologists, have corollaries among the other primates, particularly African apes, suggesting common evolutionary roots. I give an extended treatment of these corollaries elsewhere (Mazur 1973, 2005). One is that low-ranked members of a primate group often appear

more nervous than higher ranked members, and high-ranked members can manipulate the stress experienced by—and thereby the performance of—low-ranked members.
In human groups or gangs, the cool confidence of leaders versus the timidity of lowest
ranked members has become a cliché.

Another commonality is that high-ranked members—particularly the leaders—
perform service and control functions for other members and for the group as a whole.
Leaders of baboon and macaque troops are in the forefront during intertroop combat or
in defense against a predator. When a dispute breaks out between troop members, the
leader may stop it with a threat, and the leader will protect a mother with an infant who
is threatened by another animal. High-ranking chimpanzees sometimes adopt a control role, breaking up fights or systematically protecting the weak against the strong (de
Waal, 2000).

Apes as well as humans usually establish and maintain their day-to-day status relationships without physical fights or aggressive threats. Displays of dominance must be
viewed within the broader context of communication. Monkeys and lower primates
(prosimians) are limited, repetitive, and stereotypic in their displays; higher primates
(apes and humans) are more flexible and capable of using diverse and novel forms of
expression. Of course, apes can make violent dominance displays, but these are relatively infrequent. During her pioneering years of studying chimps in the wild, Jane
Goodall found her subjects apparently so uncompetitive that she could not at first discern their dominance relationships: "However, when regular observations became possible on the interactions between the various individuals it gradually became evident
that the social status of each chimpanzee was fairly well defined in relation to each other
individual" (van Lawick-Goodall, 1968, p. 315).

Every individual has certain observable *signs* or *signals* that suggest his or her social
status is (or ought to be) high or low. Those displaying high-status signs are not guaranteed to hold correspondingly high rank in their group's status hierarchy, but if we know
an individual's signs, we can make a better than random guess about the individual's
actual status. Some status signs are limited to a particular species. Others are similar
across primate species; for example, large size, physical strength, vigor, good health,
age (i.e., adult vs. juvenile), being male (but not in lemurs), and (among the higher primates) having a high-ranked mother are all signs associated with high status, whereas
their opposites suggest low status. Apes with their protocultures are more flexible than
monkeys, and intrinsically cultural humans are most flexible of all (e.g., wearing expensive and fashionable clothing as a signal of high status). A beautiful wife, desirable to
other men, or one with a rich dowry gives prestige to her husband; a rich or powerful
husband or protector elevates a woman's rank.

A common feature of status signals, at least those that can be controlled by the actor,
is that they are capable of changing the level of stress in an interaction, making an
exchange more or less tense or relaxed. Stress sometimes makes actors uncomfortable
but at other times adds pleasurable excitement.

Status hierarchies, once set, are fairly stable. However, when a new group forms,
there must be an initial allocation of ranks, and in established groups some individuals

occasionally alter their positions. Allocation may occur *cooperatively*, by consensus of those involved, after each actor "reads" the other's status signs, which may clearly signal who is superior to whom, and the matter is thus settled without competition.

When there is disagreement regarding who should be superior, and actors opt to vie for high position rather than leave the field, ranking is settled by one or more episodes, often called "dominance contests." This would seem a situation for violence to arise, as indeed it routinely does among monkeys and lower primates, but among apes and humans physical attack is infrequent. More typically, their dominance contests are played out through an exchange of nonphysical stressors. During routine status interactions among humans, such episodes are often polite and friendly, with stress levels barely perceptible to those competing.

The Physiological Substrate: Testosterone, Cortisol, and α-Amylase

Two similar models associate T with dominant behavior. One, called the "biosocial model," was formulated for primates (Mazur, 1976, 1985); the other, the "challenge model," was applied to birds (Wingfield, Hegner, Dufty, & Ball, 1990). The biosocial model for primates presumes that high or rising T supports the expression of high-status signs, whereas low or declining T shifts signaling toward deferent signs.

The link between T and dominance is reciprocal. Not only does T affect dominance behavior but also changes in dominance behavior or in social status cause changes in T in competitions as varied as athletic events, laboratory tasks, market transactions, and elections. However, there are caveats: T effects are most often found among subjects who compete seriously, when a considerable reward or their reputation is at stake.

Cortisol, a product of the hypothalamus–pituitary axis, is often called the "stress hormone" because it usually elevates under physically or socially stressful conditions. Testosterone and C, individually or in combination, comprise a physiological substrate for status allocation (see Figure 19.1).

Acute stress during dominance contests can activate the hypothalamic–pituitary–adrenal (HPA) axis and sympathetic nervous system (SNS), producing elevations in the salivary enzyme α-amylase (AA)—another component of the physiological substrate—as well as in C and heart rate. Cortisol and AA might rise together in some stressful situations, but having different physiological bases, they need not act in concert. Cortisol is a hormone originating in an endocrine gland of the HPA axis, circulating in the blood; AA is not, being produced in the exocrine salivary glands of the SNS. The diurnal pattern of AA shows a steep decline within 30 minutes of waking, followed by gradute increase through the day, virtually the opposite of C's diurnal pattern (Nater, Rohleder, Scholtz, Ehlert, & Kirschbaum, 2007). Cortisol and AA are best considered alternate

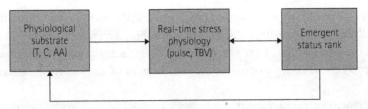

FIGURE 19.1 The biosocial model.

responses to stress (Chen, Raine, & Granger, 2015). All components of the physiological substrate—T, C, and AA—are conveniently measured through saliva.

Research on human subjects consistently shows a time lag (usually on the order of minutes) between the elevation of a hormone and its related behavior. In contrast, peripheral physiological measures, specifically pulse rate and thumb blood volume (TBV), respond almost instantly, permitting the monitoring of a subject's stress level in real time. The biosocial model takes advantage of these differently timed responses, placing the slower reacting substrate of hormones and AA temporally (and perhaps causally) prior to instantaneous (real-time) changes in pulse and TBV. The biosocial model is conceptualized in Figure 19.1, in which emergent status feeds back to both real-time physiology and the prior substrate.

STRESS

Stress is an organism's subjective-plus-physiological responses to threatening or demanding stimuli. Subjectively, this response is experienced as discomfort, whether as anxiety, fear, anger, annoyance, or depression. Physiologically, it involves a complex response of the neurohormonal system: release of adrenocorticotropin from the anterior pituitary, glucocorticoids from the adrenal cortex, epinephrine (adrenaline) from the adrenal medulla, and norepinephrine from the sympathetic nerves of the autonomic nervous system, all of which produce effects on other parts of the body. This total reaction is often called the "fight-or-flight response" because it admirably prepares the organism to flee or face the threat. The central nervous system is aroused; the body provides glucose for quick energy; skeletal muscle increases contractility and loses fatigue; heart output increases; blood is shunted from viscera and the periphery of the body to the heart, lungs, and large muscles; and there is increased ventilation. This is not a wholly stereotyped pattern, its different components coming more or less into play depending on the character of the threat and the previous experience of the organism.

The model assumes that during status contests, Ego's dominant actions heighten the stress of interaction with Alter. That this occurs during violent contests involving overt threats and attacks can hardly be doubted. The occurrence of milder stress responses during more subtle contests, such as staredowns, is less obvious although well supported by experimental evidence. Increases in pulse and decreases in TBV are convenient indicators of stress, showing increased heart beat and the shift of blood from the periphery of the body to the skeletal muscles. Human subjects engaged in a staredown report feelings of discomfort, and they experience a significantly greater decrease in TBV than do subjects in control conditions of no stare or of unreciprocated stare (Mazur et al., 1980).

With stress a central variable in the biosocial model, we can explain some of the corollary features of primate status hierarchies, described at the beginning of this chapter. In most species, the low-ranked members of a group show more stress symptoms than do higher ranked members during common interaction. Often, the low-ranked are described as "nervous, insecure," whereas those of high rank appear "relaxed, confident." We now see that the processes of rank allocation, especially dominance contests, encourage the upward movement of those group members most able to withstand stress and best equipped to impose stress on others, whereas those with the most difficulty handling stress, or the least interest in stressing others, move downward. Thus, there is a natural sorting that places individuals who are comfortable with stress near the top of the hierarchy and those who are "nervous" at the bottom.

Top-ranked individuals are well equipped with high-status signs and can easily impose stress on those down the hierarchy, enforcing compliance if it is not freely given. The imposition of stress is not only a powerful sanction on those below but also directly inhibits their performance. Although the stress response admirably equips the body for the gross actions of fight or flight, it also produces muscle tension and tremor that interfere with finer actions, such as those required for controlled accuracy in sports or weapons competition. By intimidating our opponent in a duel or tennis match, we degrade his body's usual level of skill, diminishing his chances of scoring against us. Extreme stress can enervate an organism and, if chronic, cause physical morbidity. It is difficult for one of low rank to act dominantly toward a higher ranked individual, for such an action is "presumptuous" (in human terms) and therefore may produce more stress on the low-status actor than on his or her higher status target.

The stress variable also explains why the leaders rather than the low-ranked members of the group are most likely to face external threats such as predators, strange intruders, or hostile conspecifics. Those who handle stress most comfortably have been sorted into the high ranks, so they, rather than the low-ranked nervous individuals, are least intimidated by external threat and therefore most likely to advance against it. In human groups, the individuals who best handle stress are not only prone to become leaders but also, depending on circumstances, may be the thrill-seekers and those most willing and able to violate laws or other norms.

MEASURING STRESS DURING CONVERSATION

An objection to applying a general primate model to human competition is that our language capability sets us far apart from other animals. Theorists have the choice of treating humans as unique, to be explained on our own terms, or of treating spoken language as simply one of several modes of signaling whereby primates communicate status-relevant information to conspecifics. I take the latter course, assuming that human speech works physiologically like other dominant and deferent signs, specifically in affecting the stress levels of interlocutors. Dominant or deferent signs may be communicated in what is said ("I came, I saw, I conquered" vs. "I am the dust beneath your feet"), in postures and gestures that accompany speech, in the amount of speaking time (i.e., holding or yielding the floor), in setting or accepting topics for discussion or otherwise directing the conversation, and in opening or closing the interaction (Mast, 2002; Mazur, 2005).

We now have the capability, while video recording conversations among subjects, to simultaneously measure pulse rate and TBV as indicators of stress and later play back these synchronized recordings for analysis in real time.

Figure 19.2 is an example, showing approximately 40 seconds of a waveform produced by an undergraduate male subject sitting across a table from me as we conversed. He is describing his participation in a campus organization, finishing his speech approximately 8 seconds in from the left, and saying "So, yah," a signal that it is my turn to speak. But I manipulate the conversation, remaining silent while looking at him—a violation of turn-taking that is a dominant signal. The student's waveform narrows, indicating his felt stress, and widens only after he resumes speaking, thus deferring to my lead. Here is the script (Mazur, 2015):

> STUDENT: "... bridging the gaps here in Syracuse [University] along with the ones in the city—the university and the city—they have to be a little more connected, in my opinion. So, yah.
> [Student signals the end of his turn by looking at the professor, who remains silent. Two seconds pass.]
> STUDENT: "And, um—anything else?"

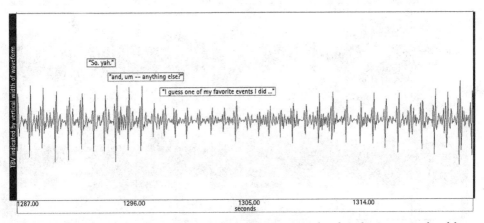

FIGURE 19.2 Waveform of a male student during 40 seconds when he is manipulated by a professor.

[Two more seconds of silence.]
STUDENT: "I guess, uh."
[Another 2 seconds pass. Then the student resumes speaking.]
STUDENT: "I guess one of my favorite events I did with that organization was ..."

Perhaps the simplest signaling of conversational dominance/deference is whether an individual is speaking—holding the floor—or listening. It is this difference that explains the generally reliable finding that those of high status speak more than those of low status (Mast, 2002; Mazur, 2005). This is illustrated with another lab setup in which two same-sex subjects, some unacquainted and some recruited as friends, sit side by side, across the table from me. I instruct one to talk about any topic of his or her choosing, sustaining the speech for at least 30 seconds. (Subjects usually speak longer, often interrupted by questions or interjections from the other subject or myself.) When that subject finishes, I make the same request of the other. This alternation is repeated twice, so each subject has three prolonged speaking turns and three listening turns. Figure 19.3 shows the waveforms of two male subjects across their six speaking-or-listening turns, covering a total of approximately 20 minutes. The top waveform is of the first speaker (in the left seat). His three speaking turns are accompanied by constriction of his waveform (i.e., higher stress), and his three listening turns are accompanied by widening of the waveform (relaxation). The bottom waveform is of the first listener (in the right seat), widening as the other subject talks, and narrowing during his own speaking turns. The overall picture is one of a "dance" between waveforms, with the speaker's narrowing while the listener's widens.

I have chosen a particularly neat run for illustration, not for confirmation. Occasional pairs—especially of female subjects—show waveforms not at all resembling Figure 19.3, for reasons I do not understand. Still, for 30 men run in this setup, the overall pattern is to be more stressed while speaking than while listening (mean speaking pulse = 79 beats

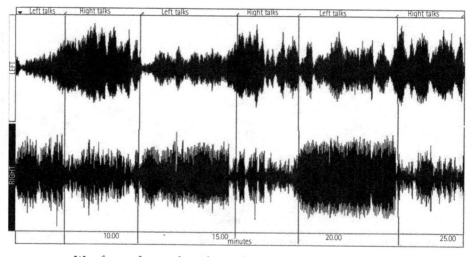

FIGURE 19.3 Waveforms of two male students taking turns talking to a professor.

per minute [bpm], mean listening pulse = 75 bpm, $p < .01$; mean speaking TBV [in normalized units] = 0.06, mean listening TBV = 0.09, $p < .01$).

These were casual conversations with no task to be solved or reward to be won, unlike most prior research on the biosocial model, which has used overtly competitive, strongly goal-oriented activities, including laboratory challenges and athletic contests. I wondered if the physiology diagramed in Figure 19.1 affects status allocation *in the absence of competition*, specifically in casual discussion groups with little or nothing at stake.

I sat three unacquainted male university students at a table, paid each $10 for their participation, placed sensors on their thumbs, and asked them to converse for 10 minutes about any topic of their choosing. I ran 10 triads in Study 1, taking saliva samples collected before and after the conversation for assays of T and C. Unfortunately, only as an afterthought did I include assays of AA, not previously used in studies of competition, so AA was obtained for only 5 triads in Study 1. I ran 5 additional triads in Study 2, intended to introduce competition by offering a $20 reward to the man afterward chosen as having led the conversation. Most results from the two studies are similar, suggesting that the $20 reward had little effect (Mazur, Welker, & Peng, 2015).

The 10-minute conversations were generally cordial and relaxed. Fully or partially transitive status hierarchies formed in 14 of the 15 triads. (The highest ranked man was scored 1, lowest 3, with ties allowed.) Playback of the videos allowed the marking of each man's speaking turns. If the stress of speaking is greater than the stress of listening, then the ratio of pulse-while-speaking to pulse-while-listening is >1, and the ratio of TBV-while-speaking to TBV-while-listening is <1. As expected, speaking was more stressful (i.e., higher pulse and lower TBV) than listening. Especially interesting is that talking was most stressful (relative to listening) for the lowest ranked men (Figure 19.4).

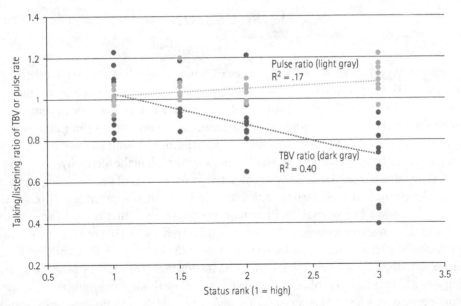

FIGURE 19.4 Talking is more stressful, relative to listening, for lower ranked men.

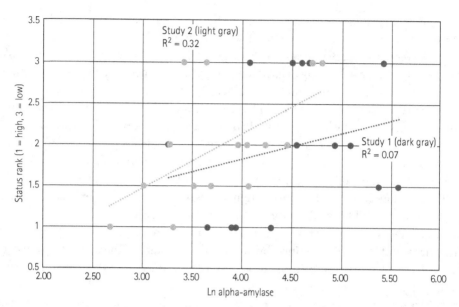

FIGURE 19.5 High α-amylase is associated with low status, especially in Study 2.

Testosterone, C, and AA barely changed from the beginning to the end of the sessions, apparently because there was little competitive stress, even with the $20 reward in Study 2. Testosterone and C, whether alone or in combination, had no effect on status rank. However, status was related to the stress enzyme, with low-ranked men having significantly higher AA in Study 2 (Figure 19.5).

DISCUSSION

The physiology underlying our behavior is, with new methods, becoming increasingly apparent. We may now watch conversations in real time, accompanied by fluctuating indicators of stress in the participants, making visible an otherwise hidden dimension of the interaction. These changes are instantaneous compared to the minutes-long response times of T, C, and AA. They are also perhaps more sensitive, enabling a "microscopic" view of bodily reactions as people compete for rank in the hierarchy.

Testosterone has for decades been central to considerations of the physiology underlying dominance, at least among males. Cortisol, commonly called the "stress hormone," became a nearly equal partner with the recognition that serious face-to-face competition for status among apes and humans is rarely violent but instead involves an exchange of stressors, until one individual reaches the outer limit of its comfort zone, either withdrawing or accepting the subordinate position. The recently proposed "dual hormone hypothesis" combines these two hormonal workhorses, arguing that T affects dominance only when C (i.e., stress) is low and not inhibiting (Mehta & Josephs, 2006).

Recently, the "stress enzyme" AA has been added to the physiological substrate underlying dominance behavior, and it too can be envisioned as working interactively with T. Possibly, as the stress of competition increases, first the sympathetic nervous system is activated, elevating AA, and only with further increase in seriousness does the HPA axis come online, elevating C. When stresses are very low, as when there is little or nothing to be gained by attaining high versus low rank, the entire array of T, C, and AA may remain inactive and not affect or be affected by status allocation.

We are still groping for specific biosocial mechanisms, a task burdened by a literature too inconsistent to inspire great confidence, including many "findings" that may be false positives (perhaps including the relationship between AA and status noted previously). A reality of research life is the constraint imposed by limited funding. Nineteenth-century natural scientists did manage with that, despite entering blind alleys and dead ends.

REFERENCES

Archer, J. (2006). Testosterone and human aggression: An evaluation of the challenge hypothesis. *Neuroscience and Biobehavioral Reviews, 20*, 319–345.

Bales, R. (1953). The equilibrium problem in small groups. In T. Parsons, R. Bales, & E. Shils (Eds.), *Working papers in the theory of action* (Chap. 4). New York, NY: Free Press.

Berger, J., Cohen, B., & Zelditch, M., Jr. (1972). Status characteristics and social interaction. *American Journal of Sociology, 37*, 209–219.

Chen, F., Raine, A., & Granger, D. (2015). Tactics for modeling multiple salivary analyte data in relations to behavior problems. *Psychoneuroendocrinology, 51*, 188–200.

Fisek, M., & Ofshe, R. (1970). The process of status evolution. *Sociometry, 33*, 327–346.

Hamilton, L., Carré, J., Mehta, P., Olmstead, N., & Whitaker, J. (2015). Social neuroendocrinology of status: A review and future directions. *Adaptive Human Behavior and Physiology, 1*, 202–230.

Head, M., Holman, L., Lanfear, R., Kahn, A., & Jennions, M. (2015). The extent and consequences of p-hacking in science. *PLoS Biology, 13*(3), e1002106. doi:10.1371/journal.pbio.1002106

Homans, G. (1961). *Social behavior: Its elementary forms.* New York, NY: Harcourt, Brace and World.

Goffman, E. (1967). *Interaction ritual.* Garden City, NY: Doubleday.

Mast, M. (2002). Dominance as expressed and inferred through speaking time: A meta-analysis. *Human Communication Research, 28*, 420–450.

Mazur, A. (1973). A cross-species comparison of status in small established groups. *American Sociological Review, 38*, 513–550.

Mazur, A. (1976). Effects of testosterone on status in primate groups. *Folia Primatologica, 26*, 214–226.

Mazur, A. (1985). A biosocial model of status in face-to-face primate groups. *Social Forces, 64*, 377–402.

Mazur, A. (2005). *Biosociology of dominance and deference.* New York, NY: Rowman & Littlefield.

Mazur, A. (2015). Biosociology of dominance and deference. In J. Turner, A. Maryanski, & R. Machalek (Eds.), *Handbook on evolution and society* (pp. 474–492). New York, NY: Paradigm.

Mazur, A., & Booth, A. (1998). Testosterone and dominance in men. *Behavioral and Brain Sciences, 21,* 353–363.

Mazur, A., Rosa, E., Faupel, M., Heller, J., Leen, R., & Thurman, B. (1980). Physiological aspects of communication via mutual gaze. *American Journal of Sociology, 90,* 125–150.

Mazur, A., Welker, K., & Peng, B. (2015). Does the biosocial model explain the emergence of status differences in conversations among unacquainted men? *PLoS One, 10*(11), e0142941. doi:10.1371/journal.pone.0142941

Mehta, P., & Josephs, R. (2006). Testosterone change after losing predicts the decision to compete again. *Hormones and Behavior, 50,* 684–692.

Nater, U., Rohleder, N., Scholtz, W., Ehlert, U., & Kirschbaum, C. (2007). Determinants of the diurnal course of salivary alpha-amylase. *Psychoneuroendocrinology, 32,* 392–401.

van Lawick-Goodall, J. (1968). A preliminary report on expressive movements and communications in the Gombe Stream chimpanzees. In P. Jay (Ed.), *Primates: Studies in adaptation and variability* (pp. 313–374). New York, NY: Holt, Rinehart & Winston.

de Waal, F. (2000). Primates: A natural heritage of conflict resolution. *Science, 289,* 586–590.

Wingfield, J., Hegner, R., Dufty, A., & Ball, G. (1990). The "challenge hypothesis": Theoretical implications for patterns of testosterone secretion, mating systems, and breeding strategies. *American Naturalist, 136,* 829–846.

PART IV

EVOLUTIONARY
APPROACHES

CHAPTER 20

....

EVOLUTIONARY BEHAVIORAL SCIENCE

*Core Principles, Common Misconceptions,
and a Troubling Tendency*

....

TIMOTHY CRIPPEN

GENUINELY evolutionary explanations of human social behavior are, at best, only dimly grasped by the vast majority of social and behavioral scientists. This state of affairs is unfortunate for many reasons. Chief among them is the manner in which familiarity with such explanations may enable social scientists to construct more nearly coherent theoretical statements about their subject matter. After all, it is plainly evident that we need some explanatory assistance. As many have remarked, over the course of the past century or two, social science theory has proliferated, but without much in the way of producing a cumulative body of knowledge (Lenski, 1988). Innumerable and often contradictory theories have been spun that strive to explain the social behavior of just one moderately sized mammal—humans. And, it goes without saying, not a single one of these theories has been able to unify the social sciences or has produced anything of lasting or genuine *scientific* significance (Lopreato and Crippen, 1999).

By contrast, in the wake of Darwin's (1859/1964, 1871/1981) revolutionary contributions, evolutionary biologists have succeeded in developing a small kit of theoretical tools that has proved to be remarkably productive. This small set of interrelated explanatory principles has enabled biologists to explain systematically the social behavior of a diverse range of animal organisms, including various avian, insect, fish, and mammalian species. In view of the fact that students of human social behavior have not been so successful in developing similarly satisfying explanations—despite the focus on just a single animal species—perhaps, as a colleague and I have argued elsewhere (Lopreato and Crippen, 1999), the time has come to borrow from the theoretical insights of evolutionary biology and to see how far they can take us.

That many social scientists remain resolutely ignorant of developments in behavioral ecology, evolutionary biology, the neurosciences, and population genetics that are directly relevant to the study of social behavior is a discouraging state of affairs. The situation is even more egregious when one considers that during the past few decades, a number of cultural anthropologists, psychologists, and, even sociologists have been gravitating in this direction and have published a considerable number of articles and books geared explicitly toward an audience of social scientists (e.g., in anthropology: Barkow, 1989, 2006; Betzig, 1986, 1988, 1992, 1993; Chagnon, 1979, 1980, 1988, 2000; Cronk, 1991, 2000; Hrdy, 1981, 1997, 1999, 2009; Irons, 1979, 2000; Konner 1982, 2010; Low, 2000; in psychology: Badcock, 1991; Barash, 1982; Buss, 1989, 1994; Pinker, 2002; and in sociology: Crippen, 1994a, 1994b, 2015; Hopcroft, 2005, 2006; Lopreato, 1984; Lopreato and Crippen, 1999; Machalek and Martin, 2004; Nielsen, 1994; Sanderson, 2001; Udry, 1994, 2000; van den Berghe, 1979, 1981). Thus, ignorance of these issues is no longer a defensible option. It is simply unacceptable for social scientists today merely to assert the irrelevance of these developments in evolutionary theory. Nor is it justifiable to offer "critiques" without engaging the available literature in a full and honest manner. There are, in short, no longer any excuses for what some have called the "bioilliteracy" that so aptly describes far too many social scientists today (for similar assessments, see Crippen, 2014; Machalek and Martin, 2004; van den Berghe, 1990).

The literature on these theoretical developments is rich and vibrant, although I do not intend to offer a thorough and detailed account (for more extended treatments, see Alexander, 1974; Lopreato and Crippen, 1999, Chapters 4 and 5; Nielsen, 1994). For those not so well acquainted with these topics, the citations provided herein may serve as guidance for further inquiry. Darwin's profound insight, of course, must be our starting point. We cannot escape our organic heritage and, thus, must recognize that the phenotypic characteristics of the human animal—all aspects of our anatomy, physiology, psychology, and behavior—are, at least to some degree, the product of evolution by means of natural selection.

CORE PRINCIPLES OF EVOLUTIONARY BEHAVIORAL SCIENCE

"Nothing in biology makes sense except in light of evolution." Dobzhansky's (1973) oft-quoted aphorism has great merit. Prior to Darwin (1859/1964), biology could hardly have been called a genuinely scientific enterprise. Instead, what was then commonly referred to as Natural History was a descriptive and classificatory project. Darwin's keen insight—what he called his theory of descent with modification and what we today more commonly call his theory of evolution by means of natural selection—provided, among other things, the theoretical basis for the emergence of a truly scientific biology.

Darwin, Social Behavior, and the Problem of Altruism

A fundamentally Malthusian premise underlies the logic of Darwinian theory. Organisms compete for access to resources crucial to their survival and reproductive success. Within a given population in a specific ecological niche, individuals compete for access to food, water, safe nesting sites, and protection from predation, among other things. Those who exhibit traits that allow them to be more successful in acquiring such resources are typically better able to survive in contrast to those less well-equipped. Such traits are said to be adaptive not merely because they better enable certain individuals to survive but also because, more crucially, the individuals so equipped are more likely to produce a larger number of surviving offspring (i.e., offspring who themselves survive to reproductive maturity) in contrast to those individuals whose traits are less well-adapted to the ecological exigencies. In short, the former are equipped with traits that yield a higher degree of "Darwinian fitness" (a measure of an organism's ability to produce surviving offspring) in contrast to the latter.

Better adapted, or more "fit," individuals thus are more successful in projecting replicas of their anatomical, physiological, and behavioral traits into succeeding generations. Over vast stretches of time, the trait profile of a population thereby transforms as more adaptive traits are retained and proliferate while less adaptive traits diminish proportionately or vanish. In this manner, the trait profile of a population may be said to evolve over time.

From a Darwinian perspective, therefore, at any given point in time organisms in a given population are expected to exhibit traits that are well-suited to the environmental pressures that weigh heavily on the ability of individuals to survive and reproduce (or, more properly, on their immediate ancestors' ability to survive and reproduce). In fact, when one examines the trait portfolio of millions and millions of distinct species of plants and animals, that is precisely what is found to be the case in nearly all instances. As Darwin along with countless of his followers have so ably documented, organisms appear to be exquisitely "designed" to cope with the stresses imposed by the environments they occupy. Without question, therefore, predictions derived from Darwin's theory have received enormous empirical verification.

The empirical evidence in support of Darwinian theory is equally persuasive when attention focuses specifically on the behavior of social animals. Sociality—the inclination to cooperate with conspecifics—is a rather rare trait in the animal kingdom. But it, too, has demonstrated itself to be tractable by reference to evolutionary theoretical principles. As is well known, however, some aspects of animal social behavior perplexed Darwin and his immediate followers. A full century of thoughtful inquiry after the appearance of Darwin's *Origin* was required before a more nearly complete account was developed.

The crucial issue here is the so-called problem of altruism. As noted previously, Darwin's theory predicts the emergence and persistence of traits that contribute to the organism's ability to survive and produce some number of surviving offspring. In this sense, it may be said that natural selection pressures give rise, over time, to anatomical, physiological, and behavioral traits that tend to serve the selfish reproductive interests of individuals in a population. And yet, as Darwin himself recognized, one aspect of animal social behavior—altruism or self-sacrificing behavior—poses a peculiar difficulty for the theory. If organisms are expected to behave in terms of their selfish reproductive interests, how to explain those instances in which social animals sometimes act in ways that benefit the reproductive interests of others while, at the same time, diminishing their own reproductive success (e.g., offering resources to other group members in the absence of return receipts, sacrifice of one's life in defense of other group members, and even the curious facts associated with caste sterility in some social insects)?

For several decades, and even after the forging of the modern synthesis in the 1930s (i.e., the unification of Mendelian genetics with Darwin's theory of evolution by means of natural selection, sometimes called neo-Darwinism), biologists struggled with this devilish problem. For many analysts, the facts of reproductive self-sacrifice were said to be accounted for to the extent that such behaviors contributed to the survival of the species, or at least to the survival of the group or population to which such altruists belonged. Wynne-Edwards's (1962) now discredited theory of "group selection" is perhaps the best known version of this line of thinking. However, in view of the fact that natural selection acts most proximately on the phenotypic traits of *individuals* (or, even more properly and ultimately, on the genetic information that underlies the expression of such phenotypic traits) within a given environment, the claim that self-sacrificing behaviors emerged and persisted in populations of social animals due to their contribution to *group* or *species* survival remained a largely unsatisfying "solution" (for convincing critiques of the group selection thesis, see Dawkins [1976] and Williams [1966]).

It was not until the 1960s that a more elegant solution, consistent with neo-Darwinian theory, to the problem of altruism was proposed, and it remains a cornerstone of contemporary behavioral biology. Hamilton's (1964) influential two-part article on "the genetical evolution of social behaviour" offered this remarkable achievement. Therein, he fundamentally altered the conception of "fitness" (proposing a more satisfying alternative to the notion of "Darwinian fitness") and outlined what has come to be called the theory of kin selection. Together, these developments represent a crucial lynchpin of modern evolutionary theory.

For Darwin, as previously discussed, the relative fitness of an individual's traits was measured in terms of their contribution to the production of some number of surviving offspring. Reproductive success (RS) was the long-standing measure of "fitness" following Darwin's remarkable contributions in the 19th century. Those individuals with higher levels of RS in a population were deemed to be more "fit" in contrast to those individuals with lower levels of RS. With the rediscovery of Mendel's pioneering experiments and his specification of the laws of segregation and independent assortment in 1900 and in the wake of the modern synthesis, however, biologists recognized that the fundamental unit of selection was not the individual or the phenotypic traits exhibited by individuals. Instead, they recognized that, ultimately, what differentially survives in populations across vast stretches of time is genetic information—the gene, as it were, is the fundamental unit of selection.

With that in mind, one of Hamilton's more significant contributions was to recognize that organisms may project copies of their genes into succeeding generations in two distinct ways. Obviously, they may do so directly through their own successful reproductive effort. The direct production of offspring represents one mechanism by which an organism may launch a predictable fraction of its genetic information into the next generation. But, in addition to this direct mechanism for transmitting genes intergenerationally (in a manner generally consistent with the long-standing measure of "Darwinian fitness"), an organism may indirectly project copies of its genes into succeeding generations by offering aid and resources to others with whom it is closely related—aid and resources that those others may be able to convert into units of their own reproductive success. Thereby a predictable fraction of the "helper's" genes are indirectly projected into the next generation through assistance given to the reproductive effort of its close kin.

Given these considerations, Hamilton recognized that the measure of "Darwinian fitness" was insufficient for correctly gauging the adaptiveness of traits. Instead, Hamilton reasoned that the more appropriate measure was what he called "inclusive fitness"—a measure of an organism's ability to project copies of its genes into succeeding generations either directly through its own reproductive effort or indirectly by offering assistance and resources that contribute to the reproductive success of closely related others. In short, he recognized that behaviors that diminish an organism's "Darwinian fitness" may nevertheless be selectively retained in a population to the extent that those same behaviors contributed to its "inclusive fitness."

The crucial upshot is that social behaviors that appear to be altruistic or self-sacrificing are behaviors that, to a very large extent, are consistent with the genetic self-interest of the "altruist." Somewhat more formally, Hamilton's theory of kin selection states that behaviors that are beneficial to the reproductive success of others, at the expense of the organism's reproductive success, may nevertheless emerge and persist in a population if, and only if, $rB > C$, where C is a measure of the reproductive costs incurred by the helper, and rB is a measure of the reproductive benefit to the recipient (B) discounted by the coefficient of genetic relatedness (r) between helper and recipient. This statement summarizes fairly the theoretical principle of kin selection.

The statement is also associated with a corollary principle that is commonly referred to as the maximization principle. The principle is a logical derivation of the theory of kin selection and has been formulated in various ways in the literature. For our purposes, it may be summarized as follows: *Organisms behave as if inclined to maximize their inclusive fitness.* This elegant analytic statement has demonstrated itself to have remarkable predictive power in studies of the biological bases of animal behavior, including human behavior. Nevertheless, it is perhaps worth emphasizing—especially for those not so well acquainted with this literature—that the statement is by no means intended to imply that organisms (human or otherwise) are consciously aware of the underlying motivation to enhance fitness. All that is being claimed is that, over the lengthy course of evolution, organisms enter this world equipped with deep-seated inclinations to behave in a manner consistent with their inclusive fitness interests (or, again more properly, inclinations to behave in a manner that served the inclusive fitness interests of their immediate and more distant ancestors).

The enormous significance of Hamilton's contribution is beyond dispute. The theory of kin selection (along with the associated maximization principle) represents the most elegant evolutionary solution to the problem of self-sacrifice proposed to date. It has done much to clarify and systematize the study of social behavior across a diverse range of animal species. Among other things, it helps us understand why social organisms are much more inclined to cooperate intensely with closely related others, in contrast to unrelated or not so closely related others. It further helps us comprehend the manner in which organisms may be encouraged, via manipulation of kin recognition mechanisms (e.g., adoption in humans or "slave-making" in various species of ants), to treat unrelated others as if they were close kin. And it helps us grasp why most of those organizational entities that we call animal societies, including human societies up until just a few thousand years ago when our ancestors began to abandon their ancient forager strategies of existence, are composed primarily of closely related individuals. It is no great exaggeration to state that animal societies are, to a very large extent, extended kin networks.

Group Selection Revisited: A Note on a Recent Controversy

Those well acquainted with the evolutionary literature know that, in recent years, a small number of analysts have tried to resuscitate some version or another of group selectionist reasoning. These scholars claim, among other things, that Hamilton's theory of kin selection cannot account fully for the extraordinary displays of cooperation and self-sacrifice in many animal species. Often framed as expressions of multilevel selection theory, the basic intent of these efforts is to explain instances of apparent individual self-sacrifice by reference to their contribution to enhanced group survival. Among the principal players in this attempt to revise evolutionary thinking are D. S. Wilson (1975, 1997), E. O. Wilson (Wilson and Hölldobler, 2005), and M. A. Nowak (Nowak with Highfield, 2011). A core assertion common to all these approaches is that "selfish individuals might out-compete altruists within groups, but internally altruistic groups out-compete selfish groups. This is the essential logic that has come to be known as multilevel selection theory" (Wilson and Wilson, 2007, p. 328).

Although proponents of multilevel selection argue vigorously on behalf of these presumed advances, their claims to have uncovered logical and empirical flaws in kin selection theory have met considerable resistance from the vast majority of evolutionary scholars. Consider, for example, an article published in *Nature* by Nowak, Tarnita, and Wilson (2010). Therein, the authors claim that the contributions of kin selection theory, especially as applied to the study of the eusocial insects, "must be considered meagre" and that whatever advances on the topic that have been made in recent decades have not "been stimulated or advanced by inclusive fitness theory, which has evolved into an abstract enterprise largely on its own" (p. 1058). Numerous critics pounced quickly on these claims. In a commentary signed by 137 evolutionary scientists (Abbot et al., 2011, p. E1), Nowak et al. are chided for their "misunderstanding of evolutionary theory and a misrepresentation of the empirical literature." Others (Boomsma et al., 2011, p. E4) scold them for crucial empirical omissions that render "the paper largely irrelevant for the understanding of eusociality." Still another comment (Strassmann et al., 2011, p. E5) reminds readers of the fact that Hamilton's insights have proven to be "extraordinarily productive for understanding the evolution of sociality." Similarly, Ferriere and Michod (2011, p. E6) insist that Nowak et al. "misrepresent the role that inclusive fitness theory has played in the theory of social evolution" and thereby "create a conceptual tension which . . . is unnecessary, and potentially dangerous for evolutionary biology." This series of critical comments ends with a brief note by Herre and Wcislo (2011, p. E7), who claim that "Nowak et al. fail to make their case for logical, theoretical, and empirical reasons."

As things currently stand with respect to this sometimes acrimonious debate, the vast majority of evolutionary scientists remain unconvinced of the merits associated with group selectionist reasoning, either in its earlier formulation (Wynne-Edwards, 1962) or in the more recent attempts to develop coherent models of multilevel selection. In fact, as noted by Bourke (2011, pp. 63–71), the alleged contrast between inclusive fitness models of the evolution of sociality and multilevel selection models is less than meets the eye and largely boils down to minor mathematical differences regarding how to partition units of fitness among individuals within and between populations. And, even more tellingly, Marshall (2015, pp. 55–56) demonstrates that predictions derived from inclusive fitness theory match those derived from multilevel selection models when viewed through the lens of the influential "Price equation" (Price, 1970). Thus, until such time that proponents of multilevel selection can make a more compelling case, the elegance and the demonstrated predictive power of the theory of kin selection (including the related maximization principle) testify to its explanatory centrality for studies of animal social behavior. I return to these and related matters toward the end of this chapter, where, as discussed, certain versions of logically questionable group selectionist reasoning continue to tantalize at least some social scientists in ways that are cause for some lingering concern. For now, however, I resume this brief sketch of the basic principles of the evolutionary behavioral sciences.

Reciprocity

The theory of kin selection and the associated maximization principle go a long way toward organizing and explaining observed social behavior in animals, including humans. But they do not tell the whole story. After all, there are times when organisms enter into stable cooperative relations with unrelated others. Often, these relationships endure for extended periods of time and, in the case of humans at least, are mediated by powerful emotional bonds of affection and affiliation. And in the animal kingdom more generally, such cooperative bonds may even involve mutualistic relations between individuals belonging to different species. Clearly, considerations of close genetic relatedness cannot explain the bases of such social bonds.

For such relationships to be grasped, we need to turn attention briefly to contributions to the theory of reciprocity. Among others, the work of Trivers (1971) is especially relevant. In a compelling manner, he explores the conditions necessary for the emergence and persistence of stable patterns of exchange among individuals otherwise expected to behave in terms of their proximate and ultimate selfish interests. In short, he wonders why self-interested organisms should be inclined to offer assistance, favors, or resources to others, especially to others with whom they are genetically unrelated.

The easy answer is that organisms are inclined to do so because, under the appropriate conditions, they may "expect" that such favors will be returned at a later date. On the basis of this initial consideration, it would seem that exchanges for mutual benefit clearly involve behaviors that are consistent with a fundamental evolutionary logic— such behaviors have every appearance of serving the selfish interests of participating organisms. In fact, however, one must probe a bit more deeply in order to grasp the general dynamics of relations built on the principle of exchange for mutual benefit. As Trivers (1971) (along with a host of other analysts, including economists and exchange and rational-choice theorists in other social sciences) points out, the "problem of reciprocity" is slightly more complicated. In a nutshell, the complication comes down to the possibility of cheating.

Although it is true that exchanges for mutual benefit serve the self-interest of each party, the fact remains that either party could benefit still more by striving to take advantage of the exchange partner. If, for example, you and I agree to exchange resources that we perceive to be of roughly comparable value, we both benefit by living up to the terms of the contract. But I could gain an even bigger advantage by accepting the resource that you offer without upholding my end of the bargain. I obtain the benefit of your generosity without incurring the costs associated with the giving in return. In a variety of areas in the social sciences, this is often referred to as the problem of the free-rider—of the party who is more than content to rely on resources provided by others without contributing his or her "fair share" to the well-being of those others.

It is with this consideration in mind—the possibility of cheating—that Trivers (1971) contributes mightily to our understanding of reciprocal relations. He assesses quite persuasively the conditions under which stable patterns of reciprocity may emerge and persist in populations of otherwise self-interested organisms, even with the ever-present threat of cheating. Among other things, such relationships may emerge when (a) individuals have many opportunities to enter into such exchange relations during the course of their lifetimes; (b) a given cooperator "repeatedly interacts with the same small set of individuals," and (c) cooperating individuals are of roughly comparable status and the resources exchanged are of roughly comparable value (p. 37).

Trivers' (1971) analysis of these conditions for the emergence of stable reciprocal relations has been demonstrated to be quite insightful, and it helped to set the stage for several additional advances in this line of inquiry in a manner consistent with the principles of neo-Darwinian theory (e.g., see Axelrod, 1984). And of course, these developments are especially relevant for students of human social behavior in view of the extraordinary changes in societal organization unleashed in the wake of the Neolithic revolution beginning approximately 10,000 years ago. Tremendous increases in societal population size/density and in organizational complexity that eventually accompanied the rise of agrarian states and empires and, even more recently, the emergence of modern industrial societies dramatically escalated the degree to which stable social relations in human societies depend extensively on reciprocal relations. As noted by any number of social scientists, the mechanisms undergirding these relationships typically involve some combination of behavioral surveillance, implicit or explicit coercive threats, bureaucratic rules, and written legal codes, among other regulatory devices, designed to encourage generally cooperative behavior among vast numbers of unrelated individuals otherwise expected to behave in a self-interested manner. My immediate task does not permit me the luxury of exploring these noteworthy contributions in any detail. Instead, I merely note that, among other things, they reveal a fundamental fact regarding all cooperative ties rooted in reciprocal obligations. However important such obligations may be for the participating parties, however much parties may mutually benefit from such exchange relations, and for however long such relationships have endured, always and everywhere such relationships remain vulnerable to the threat of cheating. In this manner, an evolutionary approach to the study of human social behavior sensitizes observers to the fact that social order is always precarious in situations in which obligations depend heavily on the principle of exchange for mutual benefit. Attentiveness to the extraordinary fragility of human social bonds—including relationships so central to the human condition such as the pair bond (Crippen, 2015)—is thereby keenly encouraged.

Sexual Selection and Parental Investment

A final aspect of the theoretical toolkit of evolutionary approaches to the study of social behavior involves aspects of mate competition. Again, we may return to Darwin, who was among the first to recognize and seriously consider this matter.

As much as his theory of natural selection contributed to the understanding of the evolution of anatomical, physiological, and behavioral traits in organisms, Darwin (1859/1964) remained somewhat puzzled by the persistence of traits that, at first glance, had no obvious benefit for or were even potentially detrimental to the reproductive success of their bearers. How to make sense, for example, of such curious traits, more commonly exhibited among males in sexually reproducing species, as "excessive" size, flashy coloration, specialized weaponry, and, perhaps most peculiar of all, the glorious tail feather display of the peacock?

After all, these traits are costly to produce, and the theory of natural selection implies a certain degree of economy in the evolutionary process. Hence, what could possibly be gained for the organism (usually a male) who must convert precious resources into the production of, for example, larger than average body size; cumbersome antlers that are shed and regrown on a seasonal basis; or special and potentially predator-attracting coloration of feathers, scales, or skin? Is this natural selection run amok, a wasteful expenditure of resources merely for the purpose of superficial display?

The answer is no. Darwin (tentatively [1859/1964], but much more fully [1871/1981]) reasoned that organisms compete for many resources in the struggle for existence. They compete for preferential access to food, water, safe nesting sites, and protection from predation, among other things. Those individuals better equipped to more efficiently acquire and utilize such resources are better able to survive the stresses of their environment and, more important, to produce a greater number of surviving offspring. In addition, in sexually reproducing species, yet another crucial dimension of resource competition is of capital significance—individuals compete for mates and mating opportunities. This consideration led Darwin to develop his theory of sexual selection as a corollary to his theory of evolution by means of natural selection.

For Darwin, there were two varieties of such sexual selection. One is commonly termed intrasexual selection and refers to the manner in which members of one sex compete among themselves for access to members of the opposite sex. He reasoned (correctly as it turned out) that competition among males for preferential access to females is a somewhat stronger selection pressure on the evolution of male traits (e.g., size and specialized weaponry) in contrast to competition among females for access to males as a selection pressure on female traits.

The second variety is commonly referred to as intersexual selection and concerns the manner in which the mating preferences of one sex serve as a selection pressure on the trait profile of the opposite sex. Again, Darwin reasoned correctly that what he called "female choice" is a stronger selection pressure on the emergence and persistence of male traits (e.g., flashy coloration, the ability to produce "songs," and the famous peacock's tail feather display) in contrast to the role of "male choice" on the evolution of female traits. In short, Darwin viewed mate competition as a potent selective pressure on the emergence and persistence of sex-differentiated traits in various species of sexually reproducing plants and animals.

More recently, and in the wake of the neo-Darwinian synthesis, evolutionary analysts have come to understand more fully why Darwin's reasoning along these lines was essentially correct. The crux of the matter is what has come to be called "relative parental investment" (Trivers, 1972) in sexually reproducing species.

Sex differences in parental investment fundamentally begin with the phenomenon of anisogamy—the basic difference in the characteristics of the gametes produced by the two sexes. Across sexually reproducing species, females are those organisms that produce a relatively small number of large, resource-rich gametes (e.g., eggs). By contrast, males are those organisms that produce vast quantities of minuscule, resource-poor gametes (e.g., sperm). A crucial upshot of this descriptive difference between the sexes is that at the very moment of conception, females have invested far more resources in a prospective offspring than have males. A single egg is more costly to produce and offers far more nutrient resources in contrast to a single male gamete.

In some species, and especially in mammals, anisogamy is merely the beginning of considerable differences in levels of parental investment by males and females. When, for instance, one considers the resources and risks that female mammals contribute via pregnancy, birthing, lactation, and offspring care, their investment relative to male mammals is vastly greater. Such differences in requisite levels of investment in offspring underlie crucial differences in the reproductive interests of males and females. As Trivers (1972) states so succinctly,

> Individuals of the sex investing less will compete among themselves to breed with members of the sex investing more, since an individual of the former can increase its reproductive success by investing successively in the offspring of several members of the limiting sex. (p. 140)

In addition, and in keeping with Trivers' reasoning, the key factor that constrains the reproductive success of females (generally the more heavily investing sex) is access to material resources. For example, among females in a population of a sexually reproducing species, those who enjoy preferential access to food resources generally produce more surviving offspring than do females who have less adequate access to food. By contrast, the principal limiting factor on the reproductive success of males (the sex that generally invests less heavily in offspring) is sexual access to females.

These factors give rise to any number of well-documented sex-differentiated traits that bear heavily on the mating tactics and strategies commonly observed in all sexually reproducing species. With specific reference to the human animal, in general, in contrast to men, women tend to adopt a somewhat more cautious approach to mating decisions and tend to be more attracted to men who exhibit signs of greater resource-holding potential (e.g., greater authority, higher status, and more wealth). Conversely, men tend to compete more keenly among themselves for sexual access to women and are generally more attracted to women who exhibit signs of good reproductive health as indicated, for example, by factors such as relative age and other aspects of physical appearance. The empirical evidence in support of these and several other sex-differentiated behavioral inclinations in humans is enormous (for an extended discussion and review of some of this extensive evidence, see Lopreato and Crippen, 1999, especially Chapters 6 and 7), and the theory of relative parental investment proves to be a useful tool for assessing the complementary and conflicting interests that motivate crucial aspects of the social behavior of men and women.

By Way of Brief Summation

One would be hard-pressed to exaggerate the manner in which these few theoretical statements—in particular, the theory of kin selection and the related maximization principle, the theory of reciprocity, and the theory of relative parental investment—have enabled analysts to make coherent sense of and to develop numerous novel hypotheses regarding all manner of animal social behavior (Alcock, 2001; Barkow, 2006). Moreover, these same theoretical statements are increasingly employed to develop more nearly complete explanations of a wide range of human social behavior in a variety of sociocultural settings. My immediate task does not afford me the space even to begin listing, let alone discussing, such studies (of course, many references included herein, and in several other chapters in this handbook, offer some guidance regarding this grow-ing body of research and scholarship). Nevertheless, readers may wish to consult the research findings routinely reported in journals such as *Evolution & Human Behavior, Evolutionary Behavioral Sciences, Frontiers in Evolutionary Sociology and Biosociology,* and *Human Nature*, among other outlets, to read about just how productive a genuinely evolutionary approach to the study of human social behavior is increasingly demon-strating itself to be.

Common Misconceptions

The preceding and admittedly brief review of the core principles of the evolutionary behavioral sciences was offered mainly for the uninitiated. The effort seems worth-while in view of the fact that, as noted at the outset of this chapter, too many students of human social behavior remain uninformed about these tools and their various pro-ductive uses. Even more distressing is the manner in which at least some such untu-tored souls, steadfast in their resistance to forging a closer alliance between evolutionary biology and the social sciences, presume to criticize that which they do not fully grasp. Here, I call attention to some of the misconceptions and misrepresentations of the evo-lutionary behavioral sciences commonly voiced by social scientists. In addressing these errors, I shall not cite specific scholars by name, but it may be noted that the literature is littered with such unfortunate assertions. Nevertheless, for those who wish to track down such unwarranted complaints, they are free to consult previous efforts to itemize and effectively dismiss these errors and other distortions (Alcock, 2015; Crippen, 1994b; Hopcroft, 2009; Lopreato and Crippen, 1999; Machalek and Martin, 2004; Pinker, 2002; Walsh, 2014).

Erroneous Claims Regarding a Resurgent Social Darwinism

The misuse of biological theory and biological analogies in the social sciences during the latter half of the 19th century and the first third of the 20th century is beyond dispute. Ill-conceived suggestions of innate superiority (or of the allegedly greater "fitness") of some individuals and groups in relation to others were not uncommon at a time when group selectionism dominated evolutionary thinking in the biological and social sciences. In part as a result of this unfortunate history, many sociologists today seem to fear that evo-lutionary behavioral science somehow may be used to justify patterns of exploitation, expropriation, and persistent inequality.

The concern is baseless, and it reveals a failure to grasp the nature of contemporary behavioral biology and how much it differs from the pernicious character of social Darwinism. Moreover, despite the historical misuses of biological theory, those past and now irrelevant sins are no excuse for failure to confront and engage the insights of neo-Darwinian theory by contemporary social scientists. For those who remain skeptical of this initiative, Degler's (1991) fascinating history of the role of biological theory in the social sciences persuasively refutes efforts to portray contemporary neo-Darwinian approaches to the study of human social behavior as veiled restatements of properly and thoroughly discredited versions of social Darwinism. Also, along these lines, it is worth recalling that what is commonly called social Darwinism is more appropriately labeled social Spencerism; thus, in reality, this vile viewpoint is more a part of the legacy of the nascent social sciences than of evolutionary biology (Degler, 1991; Lopreato and Crippen, 1999; Pinker, 2002).

Be that as it may, it is more important to emphasize that evolutionary behavioral analysts today are keenly attentive to the dangers inherent in the "naturalistic fallacy." No one claims, for example, that attempts to explain "what is" are to be taken as justifications for "what ought to be." Indeed, there is a curious irony embedded in these fears of a resurgent social Darwinism expressed by a number of analysts who are reluctant to engage the principles of evolutionary biology. The plain fact is that it is not terribly difficult to demonstrate that social scientists today are much more inclined to confound the descriptive/analytic dimensions of inquiry with the prescriptive/moralistic dimensions in various accounts of the human condition. Thus, if one wishes to fret about the manner in which ideological prejudices may impede dispassionate and reasoned analysis, attention should focus more properly on the social sciences, in which one more commonly observes such tendencies in sharp contrast to the literature in the evolutionary behavioral sciences.

Still, the facts of the human condition, unpleasant as they sometimes may be, must be confronted. Only those with the most constrained vision could deny that there are most assuredly many instances of exploitation, vicious and sometimes deadly conflicts, and sharply unequal access to valued resources among individuals and groups within and between human societies across time and space. That such facts represent unsavory features of the human experience do not make them any less real. And here it may be noted that the evolutionary perspective, perhaps even to a greater degree than that which can be found in conventional sociological theorizing, sensitizes observers to the manner in which human social relations, by their very nature, are teeming with complex conflicts of interests and to the deep-seated and fundamental motives that underlie them. Individuals compete with one another for access to all manner of scarce resources, and in doing so they frequently align themselves into contending coalitions (based on, among other things, kin ties, ethnicity, religion, class, and nation) in their efforts to secure one sort of advantage or another. In forging such coalitions and in attempting to gain a competitive edge, individuals commonly rely on mechanisms such as deception, self-deception, and coercion to better achieve their proximate aims (Lopreato and Crippen, 1999; Trivers, 2011; van den Berghe, 1981). The deep-seated motivations underlying such competition and the mechanisms employed by individuals to secure preferential access to scarce resources no doubt reflect, at least to some degree, behavioral dispositions rooted in our species' distant ancestry. But recognition of this fact by no means implies that those individuals or coalitions of individuals who, at any given time or in any given place, manage to accumulate more material and symbolic resources therefore may be considered to be somehow "superior" to those whose acquisitions are more modest. To claim otherwise is to fall victim to the "naturalistic fallacy."

Unfortunately, most social scientists today fail to recognize that few analytical tools are better equipped to describe and explain the forces underlying these competitive dynamics and their consequences than are the tools of the evolutionary behavioral sciences. Thus, far from serving as some sort of "justification" for these more unsettling features of the human condition, evolutionary reasoning helps to lay bare the conditions from which they arise, thereby informing analysts and commentators where to begin searching for potential means of mitigation. After all, for those who wish to minimize the adverse consequences associated with varied expressions of exploitation and inequality, where better to begin than with a clear understanding of the behavioral inclinations that give rise to such persistent patterns of human social behavior?

Erroneous Claims Regarding Determinism and Essentialism

To argue that aspects of human social and cultural behavior may be influenced, to any degree, by psychological, physiological, neurological, endocrinological, or even genetic factors is taken by some social and cultural scientists to be an expression of theoretical heresy. Here, I am referring to the alleged sins of "determinism" and "essentialism" that are frequently denounced in a knee-jerk manner by so many social scientists whenever they encounter even a faint whiff of biology in assessments of human social conduct. The concern is unwarranted inasmuch as the evolutionary behavioral sciences are grounded in an explicit interactionist assumption. This fundamental premise of evolutionary biology asserts that an organism's phenotypic traits—anatomical, physiological, and behavioral—are invariably the result of a complex interaction between the organism's genotype and various environmental influences. For this reason, in modern evolutionary behavioral science, there simply is no such thing as either "genetic" or "biological" determinism. No one argues, for example, that genes and genes alone give rise to any specific phenotypic trait, to any specific aspect of an organism's anatomy, physiology, or behavior. Instead, such traits always represent the product of a complex interaction between inherited genetic information and environmental influences—what has been dubbed the "interaction principle" (Lopreato and Crippen, 1999).

To be sure, when attention turns to the social behavior of the human animal, we do need to recognize that such behavior is proximately "brain based"—we are capable of behaving as we do only because we enter this world equipped with a particular type of brain, central nervous system, and endocrine system that are the undeniable products of our species' evolutionary history. Still, it must be emphasized that the characteristics of human neuroanatomy and neurophysiology are proximate phenotypic traits resulting from the complex interaction of the organism's genotype and its biophysical and sociocultural environment. For their part, the genetic instructions involved in the assembly of this neurological machinery operate more as a rather complex recipe than as an unalterable blueprint (Dawkins, 1976; see also Cronin, 1991, pp. 40–47). Thus, no evolutionary behavioral scientist argues that there exists anything like a "one-to-one" correspondence between specific information encoded in the human genome and any specific feature of the anatomy of the human central nervous system. Instead, evolutionary analysts are keenly mindful of the manner in which environmental influences (including especially for humans the influences of the social and cultural environment) shape and channel the development of the neuroanatomical and neurophysiological machinery that participates in the expression of human social behavior. Such shaping and channeling influences, of course, are not limitless—the human mind is not a "blank slate" (Pinker, 2002)—but they are nevertheless potent factors to which evolutionary analysts certainly pay heed.

Closely related to this misconceived concern about a nonexistent genetic or biological determinism is the erroneous notion, often asserted with unjustified authority, that traits rooted in an organism's biological heritage must therefore be fixed and immutable, incapable of or at the very least highly resistant to variation. Critics who make such claims seem to fear that recognition of any biological bases of human social behavior must necessarily go hand in hand with the foolish assertion that such behaviors are somehow inflexible, robotic expressions of an invariant "human essence." Such concerns, again, are without foundation. Evolutionary assessments of human behavioral dispositions—of a universal human nature, if you will—instead strive to specify universal *inclinations* that are observable, to some degree, among individuals in all human societies. Thus, the fundamental aspects of human nature are portrayed as average behavioral tendencies rather than as invariant properties (Brown, 1991; Count, 1958; Konner, 1982; Lopreato, 1984; Wilson, 1978). Nothing is claimed regarding an unalterable "essence" that expresses itself uniformly in all individuals across space and time.

Erroneous Grasp of the Maximization Principle

To some degree in connection with the erroneous claims regarding "determinism" and "essentialism," many ill-informed social scientists misconstrue the nature of and predictions derived from the maximization principle. Such critics are quick to point out that behaviors do not invariably yield fitness maximization and that, therefore, it is inappropriate to construe such behaviors as adaptations rooted in our species' evolutionary history. The complaint is based largely on a misunderstanding of what evolutionary analysts mean by expressions such as "fitness" or "adaptiveness" when assessing the phenotypic traits exhibited by organisms. The terms, as noted, certainly are not meant to suggest reference to some fixed, unalterable quality or consequences of any specific trait. This erroneous interpretation has been addressed forthrightly by, among others, Mills and Beatty (1984, p. 42; see also Smith and Winterhalder, 1992, pp. 26–28) in their discussion of the meaning of the term "fitness." Briefly, they argue that references to the fitness of any trait concern its "*propensity* to survive and reproduce in a particularly specified environment and population" (p. 42). The traits exhibited by an organism, therefore, may be more or less adaptive, largely depending on the environment inhabited by the organism. In general, anatomical, physiological, and behavioral traits are adaptive to the extent that organisms featuring them remain in something that closely resembles their "environment of evolutionary adaptedness" or EEA (Bowlby, 1969; see also Barkow, 1989; Nielsen, 1994; Symons, 1992; Tooby and Cosmides, 1989; van den Berghe, 1981). Thus, the assessment of the fitness of any particular trait is always a matter of probability and must consider explicitly the environmental conditions in which it is expressed.

Along these lines, a useful emendation that some refer to as the "discordance hypothesis" (Eaton, Shostak, and Konner, 1988) helps to clarify matters. Briefly, the hypothesis asserts that traits that emerge and persist because they contribute to an organism's fitness within a specific environment may very well be traits that eventually yield nonadaptive or even maladaptive consequences for the organism's descendants should features of the environment change. In the specific case of human behavioral dispositions, therefore, it is typically useful to consider them as adaptations to the sociocultural environments most commonly encountered by our distant forager ancestors. Such environments temporally dominated our species' existence, long predating the more recent environmental modifications associated with the earliest evidence of the domestication of plants and animals some 10,000 years ago or the even more recent changes stemming from industrialization. In this sense, today we are organisms inhabiting a decidedly "foreign" sociocultural landscape to which our fundamental behavioral inclinations may or may not be all that well-adapted. Attentiveness to such environmental transformations and to the manner in which they may affect the adaptive consequences of any phenotypic trait (including deep-seated behavioral inclinations) is integral to the neo-Darwinian perspective. Thus, those who assert that evolutionary analyses of human behavioral traits imply some necessary and invariably adaptive consequences are leveling a charge that falls far wide of its intended target.

Naive Claims Regarding Reductionism as a Theoretical Strategy

Many social scientists, and perhaps sociologists in particular, sometimes speak as if any explanatory concession to the evolutionary behavioral sciences represents an explicit threat to the integrity of their distinct disciplines. This lingering echo of Durkheim's famous, albeit narrow and erroneous, dictum that only "social facts" can explain other "social facts" is voiced all too readily by social scientists intent on defending their "sacred" turf. This chauvinistic inclination to invoke the charge of "reductionism" in order to erect a fortified barrier between the social sciences and evolutionary biology has every appearance of being a sort of verbal talisman designed to ward off some perceived "evil spirit." Such ritual chanting may rally the intellectual tribe; unfortunately, however, its only real effect is to forestall the development of a genuine social *science*.

Such fears are rooted in a profound misunderstanding of the productive role of reductionism as a strategy of scientific theory construction. To counter this unfortunate confusion, consider briefly Pinker's (2002, pp. 69–72) distinction between what he calls "greedy reductionism" and "hierarchical reductionism." The former refers to the most simplistic brand of the strategy and one that scientists routinely reject. Greedy reductionists, where they may exist, attempt "to explain a phenomenon in terms of its smallest and simplest constituents" (pp. 69–70). If, for example, one were to suggest that male aggression in mammals could be explained merely by reference to the presence of a Y chromosome, one would be making a "greedy reductionist" argument—not to mention an exceedingly foolish one. Hierarchical reductionism, by contrast, does not strive to replace explanation at one level of analysis by substituting explanation at another level. Instead, the goal is to integrate distinctive levels of analysis by logically subsuming theoretical statements regarding higher or more complex levels of analysis under principles initially developed to explain phenomena at lower or less complex levels of analysis. It is, simply stated, the logical strategy of connecting or unifying scientific explanation at distinctive layers of complexity—a strategy that Wilson (1998) refers to as "consilience" and that, recently, Weinberg (2015) labels "the grand reduction."

Hierarchical reductionism thus deepens our understanding of some specific subject matter; it renders prospective explanations more nearly complete and satisfying. As Pinker (2002) states,

> It is the difference between stamp collecting and detective work, between slinging around jargon and offering insight, between saying that something just is and explaining why it had to be that way as opposed to some other way it could have been. (p. 72)

And there can be little doubt that many avenues of inquiry in the social sciences have demonstrated themselves to be amenable to such productive linkages with genuine evolutionary theorizing, often resulting in the specification of novel hypotheses not derivable from more narrowly conceived and excessively environmental statements that frequently pass for theorizing in the social sciences (see again, e.g., the references to evolutionary approaches to the study of human social behavior in the fields of anthropology, psychology, and sociology cited at the beginning of this chapter). This development is hardly surprising inasmuch as hierarchical reductionism is the way of science—the scientific craft is, by its very nature, a reductionist enterprise. Thus, despite the resistance commonly expressed by many sociologists, a genuinely scientific sociology by necessity will be committed to the reductionist strategy (Crippen, 1994a; Lenski, 1988; Lopreato and Crippen, 1999; Machalek and Martin, 2004).

A TROUBLING TENDENCY

The misconceptions of and unwarranted concerns about evolutionary approaches to the study of human social behavior such as the ones briefly discussed in the preceding section are disturbing to any fair-minded observer. That those unacquainted with the basic premises of evolutionary behavioral science should presume to criticize them bespeaks a profound arrogance. Perhaps even more troubling, however, is the recent work of some social scientists who, on the one hand, claim sympathy with evolutionary approaches to the study of their subject matter, but who, on the other hand, seemingly do not have as clear a grasp of the basic principles as they may think. As a result, their efforts sometimes incorporate remarks that are occasionally awkward and, in some instances, unfortunately erroneous. There are a number of such statements available in the literature to which I could refer. For the sake of brevity, however, I focus my remarks on only one fairly representative example of this sort of reasoning. In a recent essay, Turner and Maryanski (2015) appear to argue on behalf of a closer alliance between evolutionary biology and sociology. However, by drawing attention to the alleged limitations of the former, they appear to be more intent on reinforcing the wall that separates these analytical spheres. I make no attempt to offer a detailed critique of their entire argument. Instead, my aim is to focus attention only on some troublesome aspects of it.

Misconceptions of Evolutionary Theorizing

In various places throughout their essay, Turner and Maryanski (2015) express statements that reveal an erroneous grasp of evolutionary theorizing. Early in their essay, for example, they strive to draw a distinction between biological evolution and what they (and others) choose to call sociocultural evolution. As discussed later, the very notion of sociocultural "evolution" is troublesome in its own right. But, in this specific aspect of their argument, they are striving to emphasize the teleological and Lamarckian qualities of sociocultural evolution in contrast to biological evolution. In doing so, they insist that biological evolution involves the "random selection of variants" (p. 95). The error here is an elementary one. To be sure, biological evolution is neither teleological nor Lamarckian. But, in contrast to their claim, it is a process that involves the *nonrandom selection of randomly occurring trait variations.*

Another curious aspect of their argument involves the occasional tendency to confuse the metaphor of "selfish genes" with some necessary expression of "selfish behavior" (Turner and Maryanski, 2015, p. 100). In doing so, they seemingly fail to recognize that the evolutionary behavioral sciences have been able to elucidate the manner in which "selfish genes" may contribute to the expression of various prosocial behavioral tendencies across a range of social animals, including humans. What must be emphasized in this regard is that genes are said to be "selfish" only to the extent that they encode information that helps build organisms that behave in ways that promote the transmission and long-term survival of their chemical replicas. At the level of the organism's phenotype, such behaviors may, in certain circumstances, have every appearance of being selfish. But it is also the case that, especially in social animals, intensely cooperative and even self-sacrificing behavioral tendencies may very well promote the survival of such "selfish genes." In short, "selfish genes" do not inevitably underlie necessarily selfish behavior in humans or any other social animal, and they certainly do not preclude their participation in the assembly of intensely cooperative creatures.

As just one final example of the manner in which Turner and Maryanski (2015) misconstrue genuine evolutionary theorizing in the behavioral sciences, they make various statements that appear to accuse evolutionary behavioral scientists of committing the sort of "greedy reductionism" briefly discussed in the preceding section. They seem to suggest that when appeal to the logical priority of the maximization principle is made in efforts to explain various aspects of complex human social behavior, such statements may be viewed as little more than dogmatic denials of the emergent qualities of human social organization (e.g., pp. 103–106, 109). This is a gross misunderstanding. No respectable evolutionary behavioral scientist suggests, as Turner and Maryanski seemingly claim, that insistence on the fact that selection ultimately operates at the level of the gene (or, more proximately, at the level of the individual organism) thereby requires analysts to dismiss the emergent character of group life in social animals, including humans. Instead, analysis of animal social behavior from an evolutionary perspective invokes the maximization principle for explanatory and heuristic purposes in ways that profoundly deepen our grasp of the subject matter. So, when, for example, Turner and Maryanski (p. 99) claim that the *distinctive* qualities of human social existence presumably demand *distinctive* theories to explain them, evolutionary behavioral scientists would not object. They merely would go on to insist that such distinctive sociological theories must be logically consistent with and ultimately reducible to the more general principles of neo-Darwinian theory. Such a claim, of course, is utterly uncontroversial within the realm of scientific inquiry. After all, hierarchical reductionism is the name of the scientific game. Thus, the aversion to explicating the logical linkages between the social sciences and evolutionary biology is counterproductive to the development of a truly scientific sociology.

Tendency Toward Reification

Closely related to the excessive insistence on the distinctive and emergent qualities of human group life is Turner and Maryanski's (2015) unfortunate tendency to reify aspects of group structure in the human condition. They even go so far as to suggest that such human groups "have a capacity for agency, they can change their structure at any time" (p. 94). This sort of language is, at best, sloppy. In what sense can it be said that a household, a village, a chiefdom, a state, a business enterprise, a marketplace, or any other manifestation of human groups have "agency"? In what sense are they "actors" with "emergent" intentions?

Although they do make some effort to clean up this conceptual mess (Turner and Maryanski, 2015, p. 96), their preferred language fails to emphasize that the "agentic" unit of analysis is always and everywhere real, flesh and blood humans who construct, reconstruct, and at times modify the structure of these organizational coalitions, largely in ways that serve the immediate self-interest of participating individuals. Indeed, when one encounters statements suggesting that human groups exhibit some sort of "agency," one cannot help but to be reminded of Homans' (1961) dismissive remarks about the tendency to reify human groups, often expressed by proponents of the functionalist school of sociological analysis:

> Institutions do not keep going just because they are enshrined in norms, and it seems extraordinary that anyone should ever talk as if they did. They keep going because they have pay-offs, ultimately pay-offs for individuals. Nor is society a perpetual-motion machine, supplying its own fuel. It cannot keep itself going by planting in the young a desire for those goods and only those goods that it happens to be in shape to provide. It must provide goods that men find rewarding not simply because they are sharers in a particular culture but because they are men. (p. 336)

In view of developments that have transpired since Homans voiced this concern, we may certainly take issue with his reliance on the excessively environmental and unproductive behaviorist principles of operant conditioning to underpin his version of exchange theory. Still, his work reveals a genuine grasp of the manner in which the structures of group life emerge from repetitive patterns of face-to-face encounters between real, living, breathing human beings, and his understanding that it is the latter who properly may be said to express "agency."

A Worrisome Brand of Group Selection

This tendency to reify distinctive levels of organizational units unfortunately opens the door to logically questionable versions of group selectionist reasoning discussed previously. For example, Turner and Maryanski (2015, pp. 103–106) insist that distinctive levels of human group organization may be viewed as "superorganisms" (itself a decidedly contestable claim) and then venture forward to assert the plausibility of models of multilevel selection. As noted previously, such efforts to revitalize some version of group selectionist reasoning have met with considerable skepticism by nearly all serious evolutionary biologists—concerns that seem to have great merit. More troubling still, they go on at times to describe some organizational forms or even some specific organizational entities as exhibiting higher levels of "fitness" in contrast to others. At its best, such language is imprecise. At its worst, and as cause for even greater concern, it potentially resuscitates the specter of social Darwinism that those committed to a genuinely evolutionary approach to the study of human social behavior have fought so valiantly to expunge from the intellectual landscape.

The crucial source of the error committed by Turner and Maryanski (2015) is located in their failure to focus precisely on the appropriate unit of selection. Consider, for example, the following claim:

> If social science can contribute anything to biology, it is this idea of group selection that breaks the dogma—indeed, the collective mantra—that selection works

on individuals but it is the population that evolves. . . . Group selection surely must count for something in this distribution [of traits], because herds, pods, flocks, troops, packs, swarms, hives, schools (of fish), prides, troops [*sic*], and other forms of group-level organization affect the fitness of their incumbents. (p. 106)

Perhaps the most useful way to address this logically awkward statement is to unravel the errors that emanate from this incorrect specification of the appropriate unit of selection. Evolutionary theory focuses attention on the gene (or, more precisely, on the allele—a variant of a particular gene) as the fundamental unit of selection, not on individuals as Turner and Maryanski (2015) incorrectly imply. In this regard, perhaps no one has done more to clarify the conceptual and theoretical issues at stake than has Dawkins (1982), who persuasively argues for the utility of distinguishing between "replicators" and "vehicles" in analyzing the evolution of all forms of organic life. Strictly speaking, natural selection acts only on replicators—on those entities that are capable of making copies of themselves with an extraordinary degree of fidelity, fecundity, and longevity. In the organic realm, only genetic information replicates in this fashion; individual organisms do not generate copies of themselves in such a manner, and the groups to which such organisms may belong certainly do not meet these criteria. As a result, when speaking of the evolution of any organic population, ultimately reference is being made to the long-term change in the frequency of specific alleles in that population. Genetic variants that contribute to the construction of individual organisms better equipped to survive and reproduce within a specific ecological niche tend to be selectively retained and proliferate in the population; those variants that contribute to the construction of organisms less well-equipped tend to diminish in frequency or to be eliminated from the population. This statement merely reiterates a conventional neo-Darwinian principle discussed in the main portion of this chapter.

Therefore, strictly speaking, individuals are not the unit of selection. Instead, individual organisms represent an assembly of phenotypic traits (anatomical, physiological, and behavioral traits) that, in Dawkins' (1982) colorful imagery, serve as the "survival machines" of the genetic information that ultimately provides the recipe for their construction. In this sense, individual organisms are vehicles that carry and differentially project copies of their replicators into succeeding generations.

To be sure, the selection pressures emanating from the environment that govern the relative fitness of gene variants in a population are encountered most directly at the level of their proximate bearers—at the level of individual organisms. And it is for this reason that we may usefully assess the relative adaptive significance of anatomical, physiological, and behavioral traits exhibited among individuals within a specific population embedded in a specific environment. But once we move beyond the level of these individual phenotypic traits and focus on the patterns of group living that emerge from the behavioral inclinations of social animals, including humans, it becomes increasingly tenuous to claim in any meaningful way that such emergent characteristics represent "adaptations" or exhibit some degree of relative "fitness." For this reason, among others, Dawkins' (1982) distinction between replicators and vehicles is enormously useful.

Of course, as Dawkins (1982) has freely admitted, his own contribution to the clarification of this matter owes a great debt to the work of Williams (1966), whose volume on *Adaptation and Natural Selection* is properly recognized as one of the more significant statements of evolutionary theorizing in the 20th century. His critique of group selection theory and his vigorous brief on behalf of Hamilton's (1964) contributions did much to lend logical coherence to the evolutionary understanding of social behavior and to the structure of modern evolutionary theory.

It is worth noting, of course, that Williams (1966) did not deny either the logical or the empirical possibility of individual traits emerging and persisting in populations by means of group selection. Instead, he argued that one needs to exercise great caution whenever such selection pressures are invoked:

> The basic issue . . . is whether organisms, by and large, are using strategies for genetic survival alone, or for both genetic and group survival. If both, then which seems to be the predominant consideration? If there are many adaptations of obvious group benefit which cannot be explained on the basis of genic selection [i.e., serving the inclusive fitness interest of the individual organism], it must be conceded that group selection has been operative and important. If there are no such adaptations, we must conclude that group selection has not been important, and that only genic selection—natural selection in its most austere form—need be recognized as the creative force in evolution. We must always bear in mind that group selection and biotic adaptation [i.e., for group or population traits] are more onerous principles than genic selection and organic [i.e., individual] adaptation. They should only be invoked when the simpler explanation is clearly inadequate. Our search must be specifically directed at finding adaptations that promote group survival but are clearly neutral or detrimental to individual reproductive survival in within-group competition. (pp. 123–124)

Much of the remainder of Williams' book is devoted to an examination and analysis of why, at best, group selection may be viewed as an extraordinarily weak (if not entirely nonexistent) evolutionary pressure in contrast to selection pressures at the level of the individual or, more properly, at the level of the gene.

The rejection of, or even agnosticism toward, the doctrine of group selection does not equate with the dismissal of group-level qualities and dynamics as potential and even critical selection pressures that, indeed, may contribute to the emergence and persistence of individual traits within a population. Competition between groups, for example, certainly exists and represents a crucial feature of the environment within which social organisms are embedded. As a result, such competition may engender the emergence of traits that better enable individuals to forge stronger and more effectively coordinated in-group coalitions as they do battle with various out-groups. Inclinations such as intense in-group loyalty and even self-sacrifice in defense of the in-group may emerge in individuals whose survival and reproductive success keenly depend on their affiliation with others in their group. A group selectionist argument, however, is not needed to explain such facts. As recently demonstrated in a clever experiment, the theory of kin selection rather effectively accounts for such outcomes (Waibel, Floreano, and Keller, 2011).

Thus, an emphasis on selection operating primarily at the individual or genic level is entirely consistent with recognition of the emergent traits of human groups to which such individuals belong. But—and this is the crucial point—in contrast to the traits exhibited by individual organisms, it makes very little sense to speak of such group-level characteristics as "adaptations" or as exhibiting relative levels of "fitness" in any genuinely evolutionary sense. Indeed, speaking in such a manner leaves a distinctive and extremely unpleasant social Darwinian taste in one's mouth. Instead, these emergent qualities are much more usefully conceived as aspects of the human "extended phenotype" (Dawkins, 1982), as products of the behavioral inclinations of individuals striving in various ways to satisfy their distinctive proximate needs and wants. In this sense, my understanding of the relationship between evolved human behavioral dispositions and the emergent social structures to which they give rise is analogous to Williams' (1966) assessment of the relationship between schooling behavior in fish and the schools themselves: The "schooling behavior (the individual activity) is adaptive, but a school (the statistical consequence) is not" (p. 215).

No one, of course, denies the various emergent qualities of animal, including human, social behavior. But, to reiterate, these properties are not viewed usefully as "units of selection," and they do not in any genuinely neo-Darwinian sense "evolve," at least not by means of natural selection. They certainly do change, develop, and transform over time. Thus, one properly may speak of organizational change, development, and transformation. But there is little reason to think that one may meaningfully speak of organizational "evolution," and it would behoove social scientists to avoid such slippery language. To be sure, dating at least to the 19th century, social scientists have employed evolutionary language in an analogous and not terribly precise manner. In this wide-ranging literature, one encounters an assortment of references to processes such as "sociocultural variation," "sociocultural selection," and the "stabilization or deletion of sociocultural traits." But it frankly is unwise to get carried away with such analogies and thereby confuse them with genuinely evolutionary theorizing, especially given how easily such language can veer analysts toward an unbecoming social Darwinian point of view (even when such is not the intent). To speak in such a manner does not promote a genuinely "evolutionary sociology." Instead, it speaks to a sociology of organizational change, development, or transformation. Such theorizing, to be sure, has a proper place, and one may hope that in the not too distant future it will achieve a much greater degree of analytic elegance. And yet, we must bear in mind that such statements, if they are to have any explanatory worth whatsoever, must be consistent with and reducible to the fundamental principles of evolutionary behavioral science. Absent such hierarchical reduction, sociological theory will never be genuinely scientific.

Conclusion

Some readers may surmise that the foregoing commentary reveals something like a profound pessimism on my part regarding the future of sociology, in particular, and of the social sciences, in general. Actually, such is not the case. And so I shall conclude this chapter with a few remarks that I hope will illustrate otherwise.

There can be little doubt that sociologists and other social scientists have discovered a great deal about human social behavior. Indeed, we have accumulated an enormous amount of descriptive details regarding our subject matter, and a reasonable portion of these data is quantitatively quite sophisticated. The achievement is no mean feat and deserves its proper recognition. Equally true, however, is the claim that we have yet to discover the tools that enable us to assemble this vast array of facts into anything resembling a coherent body of knowledge. We must bear in mind that science is neither merely an accumulation of facts and observations nor merely a conceptual or classificatory enterprise concerned with the description of such facts. Instead, science is an explanatory craft that seeks to discover those few, elegant, general laws that enable practitioners to explain (to predict) in a logically coherent manner various aspects of material existence. The history of science is the history of the discovery and specification of these general laws. Absent such discoveries, a genuinely scientific sociology, at least up to the present, remains unrealized and, unfortunately, leaves the discipline intellectually disorganized, fragmented, and unanchored (Lopreato and Crippen, 1999).

By and large, the quality of what generally passes for sociological theorizing is quite discouraging. Far more often than not, such "theories" rarely transcend the level of empirical generalizations, of statements that specify certain regularities of observed human social behavior. Such statements are not unimportant, but frankly they represent little more than additions to our accumulated factual knowledge. As such, statements of empirical generalizations are in need of scientific explanation as opposed to standing alone as explanations. Sadly, perhaps, this deficit of genuine explanatory statements may represent, to some degree, the legacy of the unproductive Mertonian suggestion to sociologists to focus their efforts on the development of "middle-range" theories.

But any science, including all of the social sciences, must go further. We must strive to discover the most abstract and general covering laws that can (a) logically subsume, in a coherent and satisfying manner, more specific statements of empirical regularities; and (b) provide the basis for generating additional, novel hypotheses that may extend knowledge of our subject matter. Sociologists have yet to discover independently even one such "law" or general principle that is widely agreed upon and that unifies our endeavor (Lopreato and Crippen, 1999). Thus, perhaps we would do well to lift a page from the history of our sister sciences and borrow from the general principles developed within the scientific discipline that is most closely aligned with our concerns, namely the principles of the evolutionary behavioral sciences reviewed in the main portion of this chapter. Movement along this pathway is increasingly evident in the various social sciences, perhaps most especially in the fields of anthropology and psychology. These advances are encouraging, and one hopes that more sociologists eventually will come to recognize the merits of such an interdisciplinary alliance.

Finally, in addition to the manner in which linkage with evolutionary biology may lend much needed logical coherence to the project of the social sciences, it also should be emphasized that the alliance buttresses a crucial substantive orientation to which many social scientists properly and wholeheartedly subscribe. Stated simply, and to an even greater degree than that which can be found in the conventional social sciences, the evolutionary perspective and the theoretical tools that inform it encourage an approach to the study of human social behavior that is deeply comparative and historical. As organisms, we enter this world equipped with bodies, brains, and central nervous and endocrine systems "designed" to promote behaviors that served the inclusive fitness of our immediate and more distant ancestors. As much as some may prefer to think otherwise, we cannot escape this legacy of our ancestral heritage that, to this day, reveals itself in our most fundamental behavioral inclinations. These propensities, of course, display themselves in variable ways, depending crucially on the sociocultural environments in which they are expressed. And yet, they linger as among the more profound impulses underlying the behavioral repertoire of the human social animal. As a fundamental orienting framework, therefore, the evolutionary behavioral sciences both broaden the scope of inquiry and encourage the development of deeper and more satisfying explanations of human social behavior. One can hardly imagine a more productive starting point for the construction of a genuine social science.

References

Abbot, P. et al. (2011). Inclusive fitness theory and eusociality. *Nature, 471*, E1–E4.

Alcock, J. (2001). *The triumph of sociobiology.* New York, NY: Oxford University Press.

Alcock, J. (2015). Where do we stand with respect to evolutionary studies of human behavior? In J. H. Turner, R. Machalek, and A. Maryanski (Eds.), *Handbook on evolution and society: Toward an evolutionary social science* (pp. 157–176). Boulder, CO: Paradigm.

Alexander, R. D. (1974). The evolution of social behavior. *Annual Review of Ecology and Systematics, 5*, 325–383.

Axelrod, R. (1984). *The evolution of cooperation.* New York, NY: Basic Books.

Badcock, C. (1991). *Evolution and individual behavior: An introduction to human sociobiology.* Oxford, UK: Basil Blackwell.

Barash, D. P. (1982). *Sociobiology and behavior*, 2nd ed. New York, NY: Elsevier.

Barkow, J. H. (1989). *Darwin, sex, and status: Biological approaches to mind and culture.* Toronto, Ontario, Canada: University of Toronto Press.

Barkow, J. H. (Ed.). (2006). *Missing the revolution: Darwinism for social scientists.* New York, NY: Oxford University Press.

Betzig, L. L. (1986). *Despotism and differential reproduction: A Darwinian view of history.* Hawthorne, NY: Aldine.

Betzig, L. L. (1988). Mating and parenting in Darwinian perspective. In L. Betzig, M. Borgerhoff, and P. Turke (Eds.), *Human reproductive behaviour* (pp. 3–20). New York, NY: Cambridge University Press.

Betzig, L. L. (1992). Roman polygyny. *Ethology and Sociobiology, 13*, 309–349.

Betzig, L .L. (1993). Sex, succession, and stratification in the first six civilizations: How powerful men reproduced, passed power on to their sons, and used power to defend their wealth, women, and children. In L. Ellis (Ed.), *Socioeconomic stratification and social inequality* (pp. 37–74). New York, NY: Praeger.

Boomsma, J. J., M. Beekman, C. K. Cornwallis, A. S. Griffin, L. Holman, W. O. H. Hughes, L. Keller, B. P. Oldroyd, and F. L. W. Ratnieks. (2011). Only full-sibling families evolved eusociality. *Nature, 471*, E4–E5.

Bourke, A. F. G. (2011). *Principles of social evolution*. Oxford, UK: Oxford University Press.

Bowlby, J. (1969). *Attachment and loss: Attachment* (Vol. 1). New York, NY: Basic Books.

Brown, D. E. (1991). *Human universals*. New York, NY: McGraw-Hill.

Buss, D. M. (1989). Sex differences in human mate preferences: Evolutionary hypotheses tested in 37 cultures (with commentaries). *Behavioral and Brain Sciences, 12*, 1–49.

Buss, D. M. (1994). *The evolution of desire: Strategies of human mating*. New York, NY: Basic Books.

Chagnon, N. A. (1979). Is reproductive success equal in egalitarian societies? In N. A. Chagnon and W. Irons (Eds.), *Evolutionary biology and human social behavior: An anthropological perspective* (pp. 373–401). North Scituate, MA: Duxbury.

Chagnon, N. A. (1980). Kin selection theory, kinship, marriage and fitness among the Yanomamö Indians. In G. Barlow and J. Silverberg (Eds.), *Sociobiology: Beyond nature/nurture* (pp. 545–571). Boulder, CO: Westview.

Chagnon, N. A. (1988). Life histories, blood revenge, and warfare in a tribal population. *Science, 239*, 985–992.

Chagnon, N. A. (2000). Manipulating kinship rules: A form of male Yanomamö reproductive competition. In L. Cronk, N. A. Chagnon, and W. Irons (Eds.), *Adaptation and human behavior: An anthropological perspective* (pp. 115–131). New York, NY: Aldine de Gruyter.

Count, E. (1958). The biological basis of human sociality. *American Anthropologist, 60*, 1049–1085.

Crippen, T. (1994a). Toward a neo-Darwinian sociology: Its nomological principles and some illustrative applications. *Sociological Perspectives, 37*, 309–335.

Crippen, T. (1994b). Neo-Darwinian approaches in the social sciences: Unwarranted concerns and misconceptions. *Sociological Perspectives, 37*, 391–401.

Crippen, T. (2014). Forward. In A. Walsh (Ed.), *Biosociology: Bridging the biology–sociology divide* (pp. ix–xi). New Brunswick, NJ: Transaction Publishers.

Crippen, T. (2015). The evolution of tenuous pair bonding in humans: A plausible pathway and indicators of design. In J. H. Turner, R. Machalek, and A. Maryanski (Eds.), *Handbook on evolution and society: Toward an evolutionary social science* (pp. 402–421). Boulder, CO: Paradigm.

Cronin, H. (1991). *The ant and the peacock*. New York, NY: Cambridge University Press.

Cronk, L. (1991). Wealth, status and reproductive success among the Mukogodo of Kenya. *American Anthropologist, 93*, 345–360.

Cronk, L. (2000). Female-biased parental investment and growth performance among the Mukogodo. In L. Cronk, N. Chagnon, and W. Irons (Eds.), *Adaptation and human behavior: An anthropological perspective* (pp. 203–221). New York, NY: Aldine de Gruyter.

Darwin, C. (1859/1964). *On the origin of species*. Cambridge, MA: Harvard University Press.

Darwin, C. (1871/1981). *The descent of man and selection in relation to sex*. Princeton, NJ: Princeton University Press.

Dawkins, R. (1976). *The selfish gene*. New York, NY: Oxford University Press.

Dawkins, R. (1982). *The extended phenotype*. New York, NY: Oxford University Press.

Degler, C. N. (1991). *In search of human nature*. New York, NY: Oxford University Press.

Dobzhansky, T. (1973). Nothing in biology makes sense except in light of evolution. *American Biology Teacher, 35*, 125–129.

Eaton, S. B., M. Shostak, and M. Konner. (1988). *The Paleolithic prescription*. New York, NY: Harper & Row.

Ferriere, R. and R. E. Michod. (2011). Inclusive fitness in evolution. *Nature, 471*, E6–E8.

Hamilton, W. D. (1964). The genetical evolution of social behaviour, I & II. *Journal of Theoretical Biology, 7*, 1–52.

Herre, E. A. and W. T. Wcislo. (2011). In defence of inclusive fitness theory. *Nature, 471*, E8–E9.

Homans, G. C. (1961). *Social behavior: Its elementary forms*. New York, NY: Harcourt, Brace and World.

Hopcroft, R. L. (2005). Parental status and differential investment in sons and daughters: Trivers–Willard revisited. *Social Forces, 83*, 1111–1136.

Hopcroft, R. L. (2006). Sex, status, and reproductive success in the contemporary United States. *Evolution and Human Behavior, 27*, 104–120.

Hopcroft, R. L. (2009). The evolved actor. *Sociological Theory, 27*, 390–406.

Hrdy, S. B. (1981). *The woman that never evolved*. Cambridge, MA: Harvard University Press.

Hrdy, S. B. (1997). Raising Darwin's consciousness: Female sexuality and the prehominid origins of patriarchy. *Human Nature, 8*, 1–49.

Hrdy, S. B. (1999). *Mother nature: Maternal instincts and how they shape the human species*. New York, NY: Ballantine.

Hrdy, S. B. (2009). *Mothers and others: The evolutionary origins of mutual understanding*. Cambridge, MA: Harvard University Press.

Irons, W. (1979). Cultural and biological success. In N. A. Chagnon and W. Irons (Eds.), *Evolutionary biology and human social behavior: An anthropological perspective* (pp. 257–272). North Scituate, MA: Duxbury.

Irons, W. (2000). Why do Yomut raise more sons than daughters? In L. Cronk, N. A. Chagnon, and W. Irons (Eds.), *Adaptation and human behavior: An anthropological perspective* (pp. 223–236). New York, NY: Aldine de Gruyter.

Konner, M. (1982). *The tangled wing: Biological constraints on the human spirit*. New York, NY: Holt.

Konner, M. (2010). *The evolution of childhood: Relationships, emotion, mind*. Cambridge, MA: Harvard University Press.

Lenski, G. (1988). Rethinking macrosociological theory. *American Sociological Review, 53*, 163–171.

Lopreato, J. (1984). *Human nature and biocultural evolution*. London, UK: Allen & Unwin.

Lopreato, J. and T. Crippen. (1999). *Crisis in sociology: The need for Darwin*. New Brunswick, NJ: Transaction.

Low, B. S. (2000). *Why sex matters: A Darwinian look at human behavior*. Princeton, NJ: Princeton University Press.

Machalek, R. and M. W. Martin. (2004). Sociology and the second Darwinian revolution: A metatheoretical analysis. *Sociological Theory, 22*, 455–476.

Marshall, J. A. R. (2015). *Social evolution and inclusive fitness theory: An introduction*. Princeton, NJ: Princeton University Press.

Mills, S. K. and J. H. Beatty. (1984). The propensity interpretation of fitness. In E. Sober (Ed.), *Conceptual issues in biology* (pp. 34–57). Cambridge, MA: MIT Press.

Nielsen, F. (1994). Sociobiology and sociology. *Annual Review of Sociology, 20*, 267–303.

Nowak, M. A. with R. Highfield. (2011). *Supercooperators: Altruism, evolution, and why we need each other to succeed*. New York, NY: Free Press.

Nowak, M. A., C. E. Tarnita, and E. O. Wilson. (2010). The evolution of eusociality. *Nature, 466*, 1057–1062.

Pinker, S. (2002). *The blank slate: The modern denial of human nature*. New York, NY: Viking.

Price, G. R. (1970). Selection and covariance. *Nature, 227*, 520–521.

Sanderson, S. K. (2001). *The evolution of human sociality: A Darwinian conflict perspective*. New York, NY: Rowman & Littlefield.

Smith, E. A. and B. Winterhalder. (1992). Natural selection and decision-making: Some fundamental principles. In E. A. Smith and B. Winterhalder (Eds.), *Evolutionary ecology and human behavior* (pp. 25–60). New York, NY: Aldine de Gruyter.

Strassmann, J. E., R. E. Page, Jr., G. E. Robinson, and T. D. Seeley. (2011). Kin selection and eusociality. *Nature, 471*, E5–E6.

Symons, D. (1992). On the use and misuse of Darwinism in the study of human behavior. In J. H. Barkow, L. Cosmides, and J. Tooby (Eds.), *The adapted mind: Evolutionary psychology and the generation of culture* (pp. 137–159). New York, NY: Oxford University Press.

Tooby, J. and L. Cosmides. (1989). Evolutionary psychology and the generation of culture: Part I. *Ethology and Sociobiology, 10*, 29–49.

Trivers, R. L. (1971). The evolution of reciprocal altruism. *Quarterly Review of Biology, 46*, 35–57.

Trivers, R. L. (1972). Parental investment and sexual selection. In B. H. Campbell (Ed.), *Sexual selection and the descent of man, 1871–1971* (pp. 126–179). Chicago, IL: Aldine.

Trivers, R. (2011). *The folly of fools: The logic of deceit and self-deception in human life*. New York, NY: Basic Books.

Turner, J. H. and A. Maryanski. (2015). The prospects and limitations of evolutionary theorizing in the social sciences. In J. H. Turner, R. Machalek, and A. Maryanski (Eds.), *Handbook on evolution and society: Toward an evolutionary social science* (pp. 92–111). Boulder, CO: Paradigm.

Udry, J. R. (1994). The nature of gender. *Demography, 31*, 561–573.

Udry, J. R. (2000). Biological limits of gender construction. *American Sociological Review, 65*, 443–457.

van den Berghe, P. (1979). *Human family systems*. New York, NY: Elsevier.

van den Berghe, P. (1981). *The ethnic phenomenon*. New York, NY: Elsevier.

van den Berghe, P. (1990). Why most sociologists don't (and won't) think evolutionarily. *Sociological Forum, 5*, 173–185.

Waibel, M., D. Floreano, and L. Keller. (2011). A quantitative test of Hamilton's rule for the evolution of altruism. *PLoS Biology, 9*(5): e1000615. doi:10:1371/journal.pbio.1000615

Walsh, A. (2014). *Biosociology: Bridging the biology–sociology divide*. New Brunswick, NJ: Transaction Publishers.

Weinberg, S. (2015). *To explain the world: The discovery of modern science*. New York, NY: HarperCollins.

Williams, G. C. (1966). *Adaptation and natural selection: A critique of some current evolutionary thought*. Princeton, NJ: Princeton University Press.

Wilson, D. S. (1975). A theory of group selection. *Proceedings of the National Academy of Sciences of the USA, 72*, 143–146.

Wilson, D. S. (1997). Altruism and organism: Disentangling the themes of multilevel selection theory. *American Naturalist, 150*(Suppl.), S122–S134.

Wilson, D. S. and E. O. Wilson. (2007). Rethinking the theoretical foundations of sociobiology. *Quarterly Review of Biology, 82*, 327–348.

Wilson, E. O. (1978). *On human nature*. Cambridge, MA: Harvard University Press.

Wilson, E. O. (1998). *Consilience: The unity of knowledge*. New York, NY: Knopf.

Wilson, E. O. and B. Hölldobler. (2005). Eusociality: Origin and consequences. *Proceedings of the National Academy of Sciences of the USA, 102*, 13367–13371.

Wynne-Edwards, V. C. (1962). *Animal dispersion in relation to social behaviour*. Edinburgh, UK: Oliver & Boyd.

CHAPTER 21

....

EVOLUTIONARY FAMILY SOCIOLOGY

....

ANNA ROTKIRCH

EVOLUTIONARY family sociology explores how evolved psychological predispositions and genetic relatedness shape the organization of reproduction and caring
within households and in society at large. Compared to mainstream family sociology,
this means a return to Edward Westermarck's ambition to explain the human family
with regard to the families of other species and the long history of hominid evolution.
Although Westermarck was a founding father of both sociology and evolutionary studies, during most of the 20th century, his approach was either forgotten or deplored, as
discussed in more detail in Chapter 4, this volume. Thus, many of his original insights—
most famously, the evolutionary roots of incest aversion (Westermarck, 1891)—had to
be rediscovered (Fox, 1962). When the sociobiological synthesis emerged in the 1960s
and 1970s in the United States, Westermarck's legacy was revived. By then, evolutionary
family sociology could also benefit from the rapid theoretical advances in evolutionary biology. Pierre van den Berghe's (1979) seminal book, *Human Family Systems: An
Evolutionary View*, featured an introductory quote by Westermarck and went on to discuss new developments in sexual selection and kin selection theory. He outlined the
evolutionary logic of sexual behavior, marital systems, and gender roles, the biological
roots of which had become taboo in mainstream family sociology (for a discussion of
the sociobiological science wars in the 1970s and 1980s, see Segerstråle, 2000).

The past few decades have witnessed astonishing further advances in studies of the
human family. A cross-disciplinary, new view of the human family has established itself
since the 1990s. This new synthesis—one dare even talk about a new paradigm in family studies—approaches humans as a species with cooperative breeding. The cooperative breeding paradigm is rooted in biological theory and thus able to situate human
families alongside those of other species. It aims to answer fundamental questions about
why, and in which socioecological conditions, certain family structures and behaviors are more prevalent than others. Evolutionary sociological theory offers ultimate
explanations alongside the mid-level explanations or descriptive findings that are more

common in non-evolutionary sociology. This is why evolutionary and other types of explanations are more often than not complementary: One focuses on "why" and the other on "how."

Crucially, the new family studies paradigm employs new theories, such as life history theory, kin selection theory, sexual selection theory, parent–offspring conflict theory, and sibling competition theory, and their concepts of parental investment, mate choice, intrasexual competition, alloparents, parent–offspring conflict, life history trade-offs, and so on. These concepts provide handy tools for any sociologist, including those outside the field of family studies. They tend to be more strictly defined than corresponding conventional sociological terms, and they are used to test specific hypotheses.

The new view of the human family was presented to the general public through the best-selling books by primatologist Sarah Hrdy, especially *Mother Nature* (1999) and *Mothers and Others* (2009). She popularized several decades of research on family systems in evolutionary biology (Hamilton, 1964; Trivers, 1972) and ecology (Emlen, 1995), as well as primate studies conducted by herself and others (Silk, 1983; van Schaik, van Noordwijk, & Nunn, 1999). These books were central in spreading the notion of humans as cooperative breeders, among whom many individuals can participate in rearing a child, ranging from the child's mother and father to their own parents and other children, more distant kin, and also individuals unrelated to the child. Hrdy stressed the difference between cooperatively breeding humans and our closest primate relatives, among whom only mothers provide care for offspring. She questioned not only some basic tenets of feminist and family sociology, such as the exclusively "social construction" of maternal love, but also male chauvinism within her own field, sociobiology. Positioning herself as a woman, mother, and feminist, it was more difficult for the academic left to dismiss Hrdy on political grounds or accuse her of sexism. This may partly explain why Hrdy's books became so influential in the social sciences and also in the humanities (Xu, 2014).

At the same time, around the millennium shift, a growing number of natural scientists dared to embark on the study of contemporary humans. Previously, a reluctance to study humans alongside other species had characterized not only sociology but also biology and ecology. This wall of caution became gradually dismantled. For instance, biologist Virpi Lummaa investigated grandparents in agrarian Finland (Lahdenperä, Lummaa, Helle, Tremblay, & Russell, 2004), evolutionary ecologist Ruth Mace (2008) explored the challenges of parenting in large cities, and primatologist Robin Dunbar studied relations between Dutch in-laws (Burton-Chellew & Dunbar, 2011). The evolutionary study of contemporary familes were further fuelled by many anthropologists, often from the United States and trained by the first generation of sociobiologists, who began reaping the fruits of prolonged fieldwork (Borgerhoff Mulder, 1987; Flinn & England, 1995; Strassmann, 1997). Furthermore, the newly established field of evolutionary psychology produced experimental and survey research related to family dynamics, predominantly about sexuality and mate choice but sometimes also about parenthood (Buss, 2017). This multidisciplinary progress in family studies is reflected in the collections *Oxford Handbook of Evolutionary Psychology* (Dunbar & Barrett, 2007), *Family*

Relationships (Salmon & Shackelford, 2008), *Oxford Handbook of Evolutionary Family Psychology* (Salmon & Shackelford, 2011), and *Applied Evolutionary Anthropology* (Gibson & Lawson, 2014).

Today, the evolutionary approach to understanding families is spreading, gradually if unevenly, within the discipline of sociology. Again, this development first took off in the United States, where books by sociologists Sanderson (2001; see also Sanderson, 2014a) and Hopcroft (2010) featured comprehensive sections on sexuality, gender, and kinship, and the terms "evolutionary sociology" and "biosociology" are being used in sociological conferences and overviews (Runciman, 2015; Walsh, 2014). Also in Europe, evolutionary theories became more accepted among social scientists. Human evolutionary theory remains rarely taught and often bypassed but is nevertheless not as vilified as in the past, paving the way for natural curiosity and much of the empirical research discussed later. (The notable exception here is gender studies, where the taboo against evolutionary approaches remains practically impenetrable and sexual selection theory is not taught or used, despite prolonged efforts by various individual feminist scholars.)

This chapter outlines recent advances in evolutionary family sociology. It is mostly limited to families in contemporary industrial societies. I present two broad research fields in which the sociological and biological research interests meet. First, studies on family systems investigate parenting and mating in different social and ecological contexts. This research field includes questions about the conditions for gender equality and involved fatherhood, the effects of divorce and family recomposition on individual well-being, and the effects of sex ratios on family dynamics. Second, grandparenting and cross-generational relations represent a field in which a fruitful integration and dialogue between Darwinian theory and traditional family sociology is already well underway. Questions of helping, conflicts, genetic relatedness, kin lineages, and the interactions between public and private transfers, are central to this field. Before discussing these two research strands, I outline the basics of the evolutionary theory of the family as they have crystallized in the past decades.

A Familial Species with Cooperative Breeding

Families are situated "between sex and power" (Therborn, 2004); they create bodies and minds and shape social life and population dynamics. In families, lives are by definition intertwined: We are born into families; put our greatest efforts into acquiring, keeping, and nurturing close family ties; and wish to die surrounded by family members.

Families are one way to organize the reproduction of a species. All sexually reproducing species have mating systems, and many of them have parents raising offspring. Familial relations need not be confined to mating and parenting, however. Evolutionary ecologist Steven Emlen (1995) interestingly defines the family as a kin group in which social relations continue after offspring have reached adulthood. But unlike the impression one gets from Disney animations, in which animals embark on a search for their long-lost parents, lasting family bonds are exceedingly rare in nature. Only in approximately 3% of bird and mammal species do adult individuals keep in touch with their parents or siblings. These familial species include humans, primates, elephants, dolphins, and some apes and birds (Emlen, 1995).

It is noteworthy that this evolutionary definition of the family rests on the quality of dyadic kin ties: the ability to recognize close kin and a preference for interacting with them. One should probably add, for pair-bonded species such as humans, the capacity for lasting attachment to a long-term romantic partner who is rarely close kin, "the spouse." Being a family is ultimately about long-term affiliation. This is something on which all family sociologists would agree, whatever their theoretical inclinations.

The rarity of "familial" species in nature means that there have to be specific and rarely met conditions in order for natural selection to have favored the emergence of family ties. In nature, it is much more common for species to secure reproduction through mating only (as many fish do) or through mating and parenting only until offspring reach sexual maturity (as many birds do). One condition that promotes the evolution of familial ties is dependent offspring. When offspring have to be fed and taken care of for an extended period of time, lasting attachment bonds are needed. Familial species are thereby typically cooperative breeders.

Attachment and Conflict

The evolution of close kin ties is explained by kin selection theory (Hamilton, 1964). The theory predicts that natural selection should favor helping among close kin if such assistance can increase inclusive fitness, defined as the number of genes an individual passes on to the next generation either through own reproduction or through the offspring of kin. In addition to helping each other, close kin often compete for the same resources, such as household resources and parental attention. In some situations, the strength of kin competition may even override that of kin altruism. Both conventional family sociology and evolutionary sociology are interested in these two sides of family relations: cooperation versus conflict and closeness versus ambivalence (Fingerman, Hay, & Birditt, 2004; Salmon & Shackelford, 2008).

Mammals have two main psychological mechanisms that shape kin behavior: emotional attachment and sexual aversion. Both of these develop spontaneously given the required species-typical conditions in early life. In tandem, they constitute the building blocks of the parent–child bond and of siblinghood, and probably also the ties between a grandparent and a grandchild, an aunt and a nephew, an uncle and a niece, and so on. The development of attachment and incest aversion is triggered through specific physiological and ecological cues. Incest aversion develops mainly through co-residence, when raising a child or when children are being raised together (Turner & Maryanski, 2005). Attachment develops in several interrelated ways. For instance, breast-feeding releases hormones aimed at strengthening the psychological bond between mother and child. In addition, the presence of the child's father in the household can lengthen the time a mother spends breast-feeding, further strengthening maternal attachment to the baby as well as his own ties to the mother and child (Quinlan & Quinlan, 2007). Attachment theory was developed within psychology and has not been largely contested within sociology. By contrast, incest aversion fuelled a century-long debate within the social sciences. It was first proposed to be an evolved emotion by Edward Westermarck, who criticized the purely cultural and psychological explanations proposed by anthropological and psychoanalytic schools of thought (Roos, 2008; see Chapter 4, this volume). Empirical research has confirmed and refined Westermarck's original assumptions (Antfolk, Karlsson, Bäckström, & Santtila, 2012; Turner & Maryanski, 2005).

Once the evolutionary roots of incest aversion were recognized, the door was open for a larger consideration of the effects of genetic relatedness on familial sentiment and behavior. However, incest aversion is a comparatively "easy" emotion, due to its universality and largely instinctual components. Attachment processes are usually more sensitive to individual and environmental conditions than is incest aversion (Bentley & Mace, 2012; del Giudice, 2009). When we consider other family characteristics, such as sibling competition, which vary with family type and also with gender, age, personality, and family size, the scope of ecological and cultural variation increases even further.

Genetic Relatedness in the Human Family

What are human families made of? The short answer is vertical and horizontal generational ties between genetic and affinal kin. Depending on the cultural and social context, other ties may be added, including "fictive kin ties" between godparents and godchildren or between employers and servants. Our species thus has a full card deck of potential "allomothers," an expression referring to all individuals who can help the biological mother in rearing offspring. Some major principles structure this variation, however. They were developed by zoologist Austin Hughes (1988) in his pioneering—if too little quoted—book *Evolution and Human Kinship*. Hughes appears to have been the first to systematically investigate how the human family structure with its involvement of three or more family generations, and two or more kin lineages, is likely to change given the logic of natural selection.

Hughes' (1988) starting point is the Darwinian assumption that the group structure of biological relatedness will affect how family members behave. Genetic relatedness among family members usually amounts to an average of either 50% shared genes, as between parent and offspring or between full siblings, or of 25% shared genes, as between grandparents and grandchildren, half siblings, or an aunt and her niece. First cousins share 12.5% of their genes, as do great-grandparents and their great-grandchildren (if they are related through only one parent, as is usually the case in larger populations). Spouses, step kin, and adoptive kin are likely to be unrelated in today's societies, although they would often have been at least distant kin in small-scale societies of the

Table 21.1 Genetic Relatedness and Family Generational Relations (*r*) Between Ego and Family Members

Generation	*r* = 1	*r* = 0.5	*r* = 0.25	*r* = 0.125	*r* = 0
Same family generation	Identical twins	Full siblings	Half-siblings	First cousins	Spouses Step-siblings
Different family generation		Parent–child	Grandparent–grandchild	Great-grandparent–great-grandchild	Step- or adoptive parent–child
			Aunt/uncle–nephew/niece		Step- or adoptive grandparent–child

past. Table 21.1 summarizes genetic kin relations between key family members of different family generations (as expanded from Schnettler & Steinbach, 2011, p. 126).

Spouses are marked as unrelated in Table 21.1; if they are genetically related, as in a cousin marriage, relatedness of other family members is consequently higher. Also note that the numbers are average estimates and that the actual relatedness between, for instance, full siblings may in real life vary from almost zero to greater than 90. The estimates also assume paternity certainty, or that the person thought to be a genetic father actually is the genetic father.

Kin recognition rests on psychological cues. This is why dividing kin into biological and nonbiological provides useful but insufficient knowledge (Coall, Hilbrand, & Hertwig, 2014). The crux of kin affiliation is in attachment, and individuals who are not genetic kin can be emotionally "made into kin" in several different ways. For instance, through adoption, an unrelated individual becomes an "own child" psychologically, if the relevant psychological processes, including attachment and incest aversion, are activated. A similar process can happen regarding paternity. If the actual genetic father is not the assumed genetic father—for example, due to an extramarital affair of the mother—family members can still become attached to each other just like he was indeed the genetic father. Another discrepancy between genetic and psychological attachment arises through assisted reproduction with gamete donations. The mother or father of the child born through assisted reproduction may not be the biological parent, and this fact may or may not be known to other family members. When secrecy is involved, the psychological incentives and cues for detecting nongenetic parenthood and the resulting social effects on family members will of course differ vastly from those cases when the lack of genetic relatedness is no secret.

A different way of turning unrelated others into "emotional kin" is through reproduction. Hughes (1988, p. 65) cleverly extended kin selection theory to include affinal kin. Through shared genetic relatedness with a child, he noted, maternal and paternal kin become indirectly related to each other. Even if not genetically related through a shared ancestor, they have a shared genetic interest in their "terminal descendant," a child or a grandchild. This is why spouses and affines are expected to treat each other almost like they treat their genetic relatives in, for instance, their willingness to help each other altruistically. Speeches at weddings about two families being joined are thereby not purely symbolic but true in their behavioral effects as well. Of course, in-laws do not always get along—indeed, in-laws are usually emotionally more distant from each other than are genetic kin. The point here is that in-laws become more "kin-like" compared to other unrelated individuals.

Hamilton's (1964) original prediction of kin altruism was relevant for close kin, the border value for which is likely to be approximately at least ⅛ of shared genes (see Table 21.1). Close psychological attachment in a family dyad appears to require at least ¼ or 25% of genetic relatedness, taking into account the caveats outlined earlier. Relations to a "parent," "child," or "sibling" (½ shared genes on average) as well as relations to a "grand-parent," "grandchild," "aunt," "uncle," "niece," or "nephew" (¼ shared genes on average) have their special emotional quality (Euler, Hoier, & Rohde, 2001). By contrast, the emotional flavor of the "cousin" or "great-grandparent" (⅛ shared genes) relation may be more like a diluted version of sibling or grandparental ties, respectively. This is mere speculation because research on the hormonal and psychological mechanisms underlying attachment outside the parent–child and sibling bond is largely lacking.

Parenting

A broad research field merging evolutionary and sociological interests concerns mating, parenting and family systems. It explores how marital arrangements and group living are organized in different societies and ecologies.

Evolutionary ecologists classify families through the number of breeding females. Following this logic, a unit with a single breeding female is called a simple family; a unit with two or more breeding females is called an extended family (Emlen, 1995). This definition starkly contrasts with that of conventional family sociology, in which the nuclear family and the male "head of the household" used to be the starting point. If we apply Emlen's definition to humans, a single mother family and a nuclear family would both be called simple families, whereas a household with several brothers and their wives, or a polygamous household with one man who has several wives, would both be called an extended family. As Emlen drily notes, "The presence of a breeding male is not essential to the definition of a family" (p. 8093) on a general biological level. The presence of reproducing men in the human family unit does, however, crucially affect the provision of paternal investment as well as the presence of other kin and the distribution of power between genders and generations. In all human societies, mothers and women invest most heavily in the care of small children, whereas the male contribution to parenting and alloparenting can vary substantially.

Monogamy and Paternal Care

Family systems are often divided into patrilocal, matrilocal, or neolocal households, depending on whether a young couple move to live with the husband's parents, the wife's parents, or live on their own (Fortunato, 2012; van den Berghe, 1979). Mating systems, or who can marry whom, include polygamy, strict monogamy and serial monogamy (in the latter, divorce and remarriage are allowed). Mating systems also vary with regard to whether same-sex marriages are possible. Among human societies, the most prevalent socially prescribed form has been patrilocal polygyny, in which men can have several wives. Not all men can afford to have several wives even under polygyny, however. That is why throughout history, children have often, maybe predominantly, been raised by a monogamous heterosexual couple and their kin (Chapais, 2013).

Recent centuries have witnessed a remarkable trend from patrilineal and patrilocal families, often polygamous and with strict control of female sexuality, toward neolocal and monogamous families with greater gender equality and freer sexuality. This trend, spearheaded by the northern European family system, is currently global if not always developing very smoothly. Sociologist Göran Therborn (2004) documented the steady demise of patriarchy in the world's five main family systems, which he identifies as the European, the East Asian, the West Asian, the Northern African, and the sub-Saharan African family systems.

Family systems regulate which kind of pair bonds are socially accepted; how couples are geographically and economically tied to their kin; how strictly sexual behavior, especially that of youth, females and sexual minorities, is controlled; and how fathers participate in family life (Marlowe, 2012; Therborn, 2004). Evolutionary studies have contributed to family systems theory by demonstrating how cultural practices can have biological roots as well as biological effects (Sanderson, 2014b). For instance, strict religious control of female sexuality is likely to stem from sexual selection and the possibility of paternity uncertainty, which have provided men with a psychological incentive to guard their wives from the sexual interests of other men (Scelza, 2011). Social control of female sexuality, in turn, affects marital behavior and fertility. Thus, the use of menstrual huts among the Dogon in Mali signals to the whole community whether and when a woman is menstruating (and, by implication, fertile and not pregnant). In the long turn, control of sexuality will also affect the structure of genetic relatedness in a population, by minimizing paternity uncertainty and strengthening male lineages (Strassmann & Kurapati, 2016). Among the Dogon, the use of menstrual huts is associated with higher paternity certainty on a genetic level compared to a neighboring community with no menstrual huts (Strassmann et al., 2012).

Evolutionary anthropologists have also investigated conditions for monogamy and paternal investment (Chapais, 2013; Fortunato & Archetti, 2010; Waynforth, 2013). In a cross-cultural historical comparison, Marlowe (2000) studied how modes of subsistence and male status hierarchies affect mating systems. Wealth accumulation and social stratification were associated with the emergence of patriarchal family systems, patrilocal residence, and a pronounced role of men as family providers. Marlowe also found that active fatherhood is directly related to monogamy: "All else equal, the greater the level of paternal investment, the more monogamous the society" (p. 58).

In evolutionary theory, the correlation between male paternal care and monogamy is conceptualized as a "trade-off" between parenting and mating. The term is used in life history theory, which posits that all living individuals face the choice of how to allocate limited supplies of energy and resources to different types of activities affecting reproduction (for its use in family studies, see ; Gillette & Gudmunson, 2014; Gorelik, Shackelford, & Salmon, 2010). These activities can generally be classified as efforts devoted to individual growth and maintenance, activities related to mating and mate guarding, and activities related to reproduction and parenting (Kaplan, 1996). A "trade-off" situation arises, for instance, when a focus on acquiring new mates detracts from a focus on parenting, or when parenting threatens individual well-being (and thus indirectly also the well-being of other parental offspring).

Solutions to specific trade-offs are reflected in different reproductive strategies, the ultimate evolutionary goal of which is to increase reproductive success (Gangestad & Simpson, 2000). Reproductive strategies can be distinguished on a population level as, for instance, the previously mentioned classification into societies with a focus on monogamy and male parental investment (Marlowe, 2000). Reproductive strategies may also differ between social groups within the same society. For instance, a parent can be expected to invest more in an offspring if the return per investment is higher, suggesting that fathers of higher socio-economic status should be more involved in child rearing (Kaplan & Lancaster, 2003). In line with this prediction, Daniel Nettle (2008) found that in the United Kingdom, children of involved fathers had better cognitive development and social mobility, and that this effect was stronger among highly educated fathers. This implies that male reproductive strategies and their results vary with social background. The reason why "some dads get more involved than others" (Nettle, 2008, p. 416) may thus be that highly investing educated fathers see higher returns from their involvement in children.

Conflicts and Stepfamilies

Kin ties are on average quite harmonious for two reasons: Kin tend to help and support each other, and there is reduced sexual conflict between them. Close kin rarely subject each other to sexual aggression such as mate guarding, jealousy, harassment, or rape, which are common in couple relations. This can change if non-kin become part of the family household—for instance, in the form of step-parents or step-siblings.

Step-parenting has been the topic of much evolutionary theorizing. One can expect stepfamilies to be comparatively less stable and harmonious than families in which all members are genetically related (Hofferth & Anderson, 2003). As a lay saying gently captures it, "A new family is one in which not all family members have a love relation with each other." In some of the early sociobiological writings, stepfamilies were described in slightly alarming tones as "crucibles of conflict" that "profoundly disrupt both the social harmony and stability of the new family unit" (Emlen, 1997, p. 573). Stephen Emlen made four specific predictions, expecting step-parents to invest less in offspring, step-parents to more often have sexual relations with offspring, step-offspring to invest less in each other, and the stepfamily to be less stable compared to a family in which both parents are related to all offspring. Physical abuse, sexual abuse, and homicide are therefore predicted to be more likely to be conducted by step-parents than biological parents (Daly & Wilson, 1996). These predictions contrasted with the rosier view presented by some parts of non-evolutionary family sociology, which praised step-families as "brave new families" embodying the demise of patriarchy and the oppressive nuclear family (e.g. Stacey, 1990).

Emlen's four predictions have found support in empirical studies (Archer, 2013). For instance, a nationwide US study of child maltreatment reported higher rates of physical, emotional, and sexual abuse and of child neglect in families with a step-parent compared to families with two biological or adoptive parents (Finkelhor, Vanderminden, Turner, Hamby, & Shattuck, 2014). The presence of step-parents is also known to have other adverse outcomes on children, including worse cognitive and developmental outcomes from growing up in a blended family compared to growing up in a biological nuclear family or growing up with a single mother (Cherlin, 2008). A better understanding of the potential risks facing stepchildren has crucial implications for preventive social work.

However, several modifications and additions have also been made as stepfamilies have become more common and socially accepted, and our understanding of stepfamilies more nuanced. Three such modifications will be discussed, each related to the beneficial contributions of step-parents. First, as stressed previously, family relations are driven not by an abstract assumption of genetic relatedness but, rather, by psychological mechanisms that have evolved to favor individuals cued as close kin. The actual investment in a child by a parent figure who is not the biological parent will depend on length of co-residence and strength of attachment. Furthermore, step-parents can more easily "catch up" with the original parents in some areas of child development than in others. Regarding their importance for child cognitive and intellectual development, for example, investments from step-parents are often comparable to those of biological parents. By contrast, even very devoted step-parents may not always be able to compensate for emotional challenges facing children in recomposed families. Thus some studies found persistent differences in socioemotional development between stepchildren and biological children have in some studies found to persist and be larger for step-children, often due to the events preceding family recomposition (Lee & McLanahan, 2015).

Another modification to general stepfamily theory is the importance of social context. The drawbacks and benefits of having blended families and step-kin vary with the type of society and social class. Having too few providers in the family can in some cases be more fatal than being subjected to step-parents. For instance, in preindustrial Sweden, the presence of a step-parent often saved household members from starvation (Andersson, Högberg, & Åkerman, 1996). The benefits of stepfamilies may be why humans often choose to have new spouses. We are not psychologically averse to seeking replacement mates after widowhood or divorce, as should be the case if remarriage had repeatedly had detrimental effects on offspring over the course of evolution. Instead, humans have probably evolved in societies in which *de facto* serial monogamy and hence stepfamilies were not uncommon.

Surprisingly few studies have investigated the actual effects of repartnering on fertility and child well-being in the long term. One of these studies found that women who had many marital partners also had more children, suggesting a reproductive benefit to the mother of having several husbands (a benefit that need of course not translate to the first-born children of that mother, who may suffer from the drawbacks of remarriage) (Borgerhoff Mulder, 2009). A similar finding was reported from agrarian Finland, where remarriage following the death of a spouse led to an increased number of descendants surviving to adulthood for both men and women, again suggesting an evolutionary benefit of remarriage. However, this fertility benefit from remarriage among agrarian Finns disappeared when the number of grandchildren was considered: Twice-married men or women in Finland had as many grandchildren as did once-married men or women (Pettay, Rotkirch, Courtiol, Jokela, & Lummaa, 2013), indicating no genetic benefits but also no genetic penalty from remarriage.

A third modification to the general view of stepfamilies in evolutionary family studies concerns sibling relations. Individuals of the same family generation—usually siblings or cousins—compete for the same family resources from elder kin. As predicted by kin selection theory, empirical studies from contemporary societies show that full siblings are typically emotionally closer and more altruistic toward each other compared to half siblings or step-siblings. Half siblings also compete more than full siblings for the resources of the parent they both share, again fully in line with predictions based on genetic relatedness (Schlomer, Del Giudice, & Ellis, 2011). However, full siblings appear to have more conflicts overall than do half siblings. This unexpected finding can be explained as resulting from diluted sibling competition. The diluted sibling competition hypothesis suggests that because half siblings have no competition with the parts of their kin networks that do not overlap—for instance, the different fathers and paternal grandparents of two children who have the same mother—they compete less overall for parental resources (Tanskanen, Danielsbacka, Jokela, David-Barrett, & Rotkirch, 2016; Tanskanen, Danielsbacka, Jokela, & Rotkirch, 2017).

In sum, contemporary evolutionary family sociology approaches stepfamilies with less alarm compared to the early days of sociobiology, but with less ideological optimism than in feminist family sociology. By understanding the logic of interaction between close kin, less close kin, and non-kin, resources and services can be more effectively targeted in order to improve the wellbeing of all types of families.

Sex Ratios of Parents and Children

Within studies of mating and parenting, sex ratio research is an excellent illustration of a topic for which the research questions and methods of sociologists and evolutionists align quite smoothly. Demographic sex ratios, or the ratios of males to females in specific age groups, have consistently been found to affect marriages and family formation (South & Trent, 1988). On a general level, when an adult population has more members of one sex compared to the other, the more abundant sex experiences intensified competition for access to the scarcer sex, which, in turn, has a greater choice of heterosexual mating partners. To this undisputed sociological insight, evolutionary research has contributed the use of sexual selection theory to explain and predict sex ratio effects in different populations. For instance, how competition over the scarcer sex manifests will depend both on gender differences and on the social context. In most species including humans, male competition over females is likely to take more physically aggressive forms than female competition over males. Nevertheless, the content of male "competition" can vary dramatically. Depending on society, male competition may be expressed in many forms, such as higher risk-taking and use of violence among males; aggression toward females; or competition to please females, for instance, in signaling trustworthiness and willingness to invest in offspring (Kokko & Jennions, 2008). The demographic fact of "more males" does not necessarily mean "more violence" (Schacht, Rauch & Borgerhoff Mulder, 2014). This is why, in contemporary developed societies, a higher proportion of young adult men can also lead to a population with more stable marriages and a strong social position of women (Trent & South, 1988). A higher proportion of reproductive-age women compared to men is, in turn, related to intensified competition between women, higher male bargaining power within couples, later marriages, more divorces and more cohabitation (Chipman & Morrison, 2013; Durante, Griskevicius, Simpson, Cantú, & Tybur, 2012).

Evolutionary sociologists have also contributed to sex ratio studies by providing a new perspective on how families shape the sex ratio of children born. The so-called Trivers–Willard effect predicts that in societies with female hypergamy, or the tendency for women to marry men of higher social status than that of themselves, parents of high social status should invest more in sons, to help them attract the best women, while parents of low social status should invest more in their daughters, who can marry men of higher social status (Trivers, 1972; Trivers & Willard, 1973). This biased parental investment could be conscious or unconscious, and take place through physiological or social mechanisms. Thus, the Trivers–Willard effect predicts that high-status individuals should conceive more sons (a physiological process) as well as provide more parental investment for sons than daughters (a social behavior). The Trivers–Willard effect can explain why parental behavior overruns prescribed social norms, for instance, if poor parents invest more in daughters, who can be expected to marry socially upward, although their culture assigns more importance to sons (Cronk, 1995).

Within US sociology, the Trivers–Willard hypothesis was the subject of the first sociological dissertation explicitly testing evolutionary theories with contemporary data (the hypothesis was rejected; Freese & Powell, 1999). Perhaps due to this status as a "Does evolutionary theory work?" topic, the debate has continued ever since (Schnettler, 2013). Because many other factors also affect parental investment, and ecological sex ratio effects tend to be minor overall, large data are needed to detect any influence. Rosemary Hopcroft (2005) found that when measuring long-term parental investment in the United States, the Trivers–Willard hypothesis was supported. She also found that high-status men in the United States had more sons, and these sons attained more education than daughters, whereas daughters of low-status fathers received more education than sons (Hopcroft & Martin, 2016; for similar results from China, see Luo, Zhao, & Weng, 2016). Expanding this discussion to Europe, Kolk and Schnettler (2013) found that higher status Swedes did not have more sons than daughters, and neither was any psychological preference favoring either sons or daughters detected. Evidence for the Treivers-Willard effect remains mixed.

Grandparenting

The second research field in which evolutionary theory and mainstream sociology have been interacting lately is that of cross-generational family relations. Generational ties, especially parenting and grandparenting, have constituted a prominent field within sociology since the 1970s (Bengtson & Allen, 1993; Bengtson & Kuypers, 1971; Rossi & Rossi, 1991). During the past two decades, there has been a flourishing of studies on intergenerational transfers (Attias-Donfut, Ogg, & Wolf, 2005; Kohli, 1999; Lee, 2013), often in relation to family solidarity (Bengtson, 2001) and ambivalence (Luescher & Pillemer, 1998; Szydlik, 2016). Research on family generations has also been boosted by the emergence of large surveys on generations, grandparenting, and aging, such as the Longitudinal Study of Generations, the Gender and Generations Survey, and SHARE (Survey of Health, Ageing and Retirement in Europe), as well as new research methodologies and measures such as the National Transfer Accounts (Mason, Lee, Tung, Lai, & Miller, 2006).

Within this field, the Darwinian perspective has highlighted how genetic relatedness shapes behavior. Especially the importance of systematically paying attention to kin lineages is stressed by evolutionary approaches. On the other hand, sociological concepts and insights have helped specify in which cases predictions made by evolutionary theory appear to hold for humans and cases in need of elaboration and revision.

Generational Transfers

The "intergenerational stakes" hypothesis as developed within family sociology (Bengtson & Kuypers, 1971) originated from the observation that parents view ties to their children more favorably than vice versa. The hypothesis predicted more investment from elder family generations to the younger and explained this with values and lifestyle goals. Despite merits of this hypothesis, it is also characteristic of late 20th-century sociology through its lack of interest in why such "intergenerational stakes" and values would develop in the first place and whether they were unique to humans (Hopcroft, 2016). Nevertheless, the focus the intergenerational stakes hypothesis makes on the importance of extended family ties and helping among kin, as well as its main predictions, fit well with evolutionary theory, which also predicts a downward flow of investment from older to younger family members (Hughes, 1988).

In biology, "reproductive value" (Fisher, 1930) is measured as an individual's average expected contribution of genes to future offspring. The term "reproductive potential" refers to the same idea but further takes into account individual characteristics such as health (Hughes, 1983). Reproductive value is dependent on sex and age, and it is usually highest just before an individual reaches biological adulthood, or approximately age 16–18 years for women. Reproductive value then declines with age, and for women it reaches zero with menopause. The direction and amount of help between family members and kin are assumed to trace the recipient's genetic relatedness (see Table 21.1) as well as his or her reproductive value (Hughes, 1988, pp. 42–47). Here lies the ultimate, evolutionary explanation for why older generations help younger generations more often and more eagerly than vice versa. When combined, the amounts of lifetime parental and grandparental investments in offspring will not be equaled by reciprocal offspring investments in their parents or grandparents: Children do not usually "pay off."

The assumption of a mainly downward flow of kin assistance has been empirically confirmed in many studies throughout the world (Coall & Hertwig, 2010; Izuhara, 2010). Among childless individuals, the flow of help is typically to the genetically closest member of the next generations, such as nieces and nephews (Pollet, Kuppens, & Dunbar, 2006; Tanskanen & Danielsbacka, 2014). The flows of assistance between family generations in a particular society will also depend on the amount of public transfers available and on the complex interplay between family exchanges and public transfers. For instance, some public services can replace the help to family members that would otherwise be provided by kin—what in family sociology and social policy is known as the "crowding out" effect. However, public services may also stimulate cross-generational help by freeing up energy and time to interact more with family members— the so-called "crowding in" effect (Brandt, Haberkern, & Szydlik, 2009; Herlofson & Hagestad, 2012). For example, when social services provide regular home visits to dependent elderly, they may thereby substitute a task an adult child would otherwise have to perform for a parent ("crowding out"). However, use of a home care service to a grandfather may also mean that his spouse, a grandmother, is free to visit and take care of her grandchildren ("crowding in") (Arber & Attias-Donfut, 2002).

As a rule, in developed countries, professional providers tend to take over the education of children and the most demanding care of the sick, the disabled, and the elderly. Parents and other kin remain crucial for infant care and for providing less demanding forms of help to family members of various ages (Arber & Attias-Donfut, 2002). Crucially, kin continue to represent the most reliable support when public services are absent or fail or when life situations unexpectedly deteriorate. When people divorce or become unemployed, for instance, their parents are often the first to provide financial support and shelter. Another important finding from contemporary Europe is that elderly parents tend to help the child who is in the most acute need of help (Szydlik, 2016, p. 112). In this sense, kin relations constitute a well-timed and flexible complement to public services (Coall & Hertwig, 2010). It remains unknown, however, how parental kin help relates to the reproductive value of children. For instance, one could investigate to what extent help provided to adult children in need is also help with the highest return to investment with regard to future reproduction.

Although transfers often flow downward within families and kin lineages, they no longer necessarily do so for society as a whole. Using evolutionary life history theory, demographer and economist Ronald Lee first modeled the general effect of intergenerational transfers on mortality patterns and later applied these models to human societies (Lee, 2003, 2008; see also Gurven, Stieglitz, Hooper, Gomes, & Kaplan, 2012). Lee and colleagues developed the National Transfer Accounts measure to collect data on economic behavior and generational support flows in different types of societies. In today's wealthy and aging societies, the proportion of consumption taken up by the elderly has increased rapidly, mostly due to advances in health care and consequently health consumption. Currently in the United States, the largest deficit between consumption and production of different age groups is among those aged 65 years or older (Mason et al., 2006). For the first time, perhaps, in all human history, societal resources flow mostly from the younger to the older. The fact that private transfers continue to flow from the older to the younger family generations provides a much-needed if small equaling effect between generations.

Proximity to Related Offspring

The reproductive value of individuals in a population shapes household formation. According to Hughes (1988), genetic relatedness can be expected to constitute the "basis of residential group formation in all societies." (p. 75). Hughes expected individuals to live nearest to the dependent offspring to whom they are most closely related. He also suggested that fissures in household composition would follow genetic relatedness to the youngest household members. This gives us a loop effect between social rules and offspring clustering so that marriage systems affect who becomes related to whom, which then influences who lives close to whom.

Hughes' (1988) method of predicting adults' residence from the perspective of their offspring intuitively appears to hold, but to my knowledge it has been little investigated. It does appear to conform with geographical and sociological research on residential proximity over the life course. Thus, in line with Hughes' assumption, a meta-analysis of social network studies found family network size to be surprisingly stable across different life stages (Wrzus, Hänel, Wagner, & Neyer, 2013). Close kin tend to live near each other in adulthood. In a study using register data from Sweden, Martin Kolk (2015) found that after children had left the parental home, the geographical distances to both their parents and their grandparents remained quite stable. Most Swedes have at least some close adult kin living within both a 20 km and a 75 km distance throughout their lives.

Another interesting finding from sociological life course studies is that the proportion of kin in a person's social network increases with age. In the social contacts of the elderly, kin feature more prominently than do non-kin friends (Kalmijn, 2012). This may stem from intensified interest in the well-being of adult children and also grandchildren, in line with Hughes' (1988) predictions of reproductive value and spatial clustering; however, studies separating this hypothesis from other possible explanations are warranted.

Why Some Grandparents Invest More Than Others

Evolutionary theory introduced the concept of "grandparental investment" to studies of intergenerational exchange (Euler & Michalski, 2008). Grandparental investment is defined in a similar way as parental investment (Trivers, 1972), and it refers to all the resources (care, financial support, and practical support) a grandparent provides a certain grandchild (Coall & Hertwig, 2010). Such investment can benefit the recipients in many ways, including logistic help to working parents, enhanced fertility of parents, or improved cognitive development and well-being of the grandchild (Aassve, Meroni, & Pronzatio, 2012; Coall & Hertwig, 2010; Tanskanen & Rotkirch, 2014).

The notions of "matrilineal advantage" or "biased grandparental investment" capture a common pattern for grandparental investment in which maternal kin invest more in offspring than do paternal kin, and women invest more than men (Chan & Elder, 2000; Euler & Weitzel, 1996). Although observations of biased grandparental investment have been made by family researchers since the 1970s, evolutionary theory provided a larger theoretical framework accounting for differences in grandparenting by both gender and lineage and suggested some new research hypotheses (Euler, 2011; van den Berghe, 1979). Thus, grandparenting proved to be a fruitful study area for integration of evolutionary and sociological approaches (Kaptijn, Thomese, Liefbroer, & Silverstein, 2013; Pollet, Nettle, & Nelissen, 2006, 2007; for reviews, see Coall & Hertwig, 2010; Sear & Coall, 2011).

Why does grandparental investment vary? A first and obvious factor is gender roles. Care work is socially perceived as a feminine chore, and it can also be evolutionarily related to the greater investment women make in each offspring (for a full discussion, see Euler, 2011). However, gender differences cannot explain why the maternal grandfather typically invests more in grandchildren than does the paternal grandmother.

Another factor relates to paternity uncertainty, or the fact that biological paternity is rarely fully certain in mammals (Euler & Weitzel, 1996; Pashos, 2000; Smith, 1991). If the genetic father of a child is not the assumed social father due to extra-pair sexual relations, the social father and his kin can be expected to reduce investment in this child compared to what they would invest in a genetic offspring (Alvergne, Faurie, & Raymond, 2010; Pashos & McBurney, 2008). On the population level, even a small possible uncertainty about paternity may translate into a reduced likelihood of assisting kin. In grandparenting, a family constellation involving two generations, up to two fatherhood "links" can be uncertain. Only the maternal grandmother has no paternity uncertainty links to her daughter's daughter. Every maternal grandmother can therefore be fully certain that a grandchild is genetically related to her (except in cases of adoption and assisted reproduction). The maternal grandfather and paternal grandmother both have one potentially uncertain genetic link through a male relative, and the paternal grandfather has two potentially uncertain genetic links through two males (Euler, 2011).

In order to test the possible influence of paternity certainty on behavior, studies have compared investment in different grandchildren by the same grandparent. Maternal grandfathers and paternal grandmothers are in theory as genetically close to their grandchild, because both have one link of possible paternity uncertainty through male kin. Additionally, some individuals have grandchildren via both a daughter and a son, and thus have a role as both a paternal and a maternal grandparent. This allows studies to test how resources are channeled when both investment options are present for the same individual (Laham, Gonsalkorale, & von Hippel, 2005). It is crucial to note that the subtle influence of paternity certainty on grandparental behavior is here assumed to be unconscious, and not related to actual doubts about paternity. Results from contemporary Europe show that among individuals with investment options in both a daughters' and a son's child, mothers provided most child care to their daughter's children while men invested least childcare in their son's children. Interestingly, women provided exactly as much child care to their son's children as men provided to their daughter's children (Danielsbacka, Tanskanen, Jokela, & Rotkirch, 2011). This suggests that genetic relatedness and investment options affect grandparenting.

Other explanations, such as chromosomal relatedness effects, have also been proposed to explain biases in grandparental investment (Fox et al., 2010). It can also prove difficult to actually tease apart the explanatory strength of different sociological and evolutionary explanations for why grandparental investment varies with grandparental type.

Can Parental Investment Be Rejected?

One challenge in evolutionary theory as applied to humans is the assumption that investment is always welcomed by the recipient. In parent–offspring conflict theory, parental investment—and, by extension, grandparental investment—is per definition always smaller than what would be optimal from the offspring's point of view (Trivers, 1972). There is also an assumed life history trade-off faced by the provider of the investment: In principle, any investment in a child or grandchild diverts resources that the individual could have used for his or her own growth and development, for mating, or for investment in other children or grandchildren (Michalski, 2010).

Among most species, parental investment is indeed never rejected by the offspring. However, the complexity of the human mating and family system leads to situations in which a parent or grandparent would like to invest more in younger generations than what they can actually do (Sims & Rofail, 2013). The parents of a small child often act as "gatekeepers" and may hinder access to a grandchild (Robertson, 1975). Generational ruptures occur following divorce, migration, or illness (Drew & Silverstein, 2007) and are likely to affect grandchild relations especially between paternal kin. This dilemma is accentuated in modern society, in which children typically do not live with their grandparents and divorces and remarriages affect grandparenting (Tanskanen, Danielsbacka, & Rotkirch, 2014). Consequently, differences in grandparental investment are driven not only by willingness to invest but also by the preferences of the child's parents, who can encourage some grandparents to invest more and some to invest less in their grandchildren.

Emotional Closeness in the Extended Family

Kin contacts are to a large extent driven by liking each other—what psychologists call affectual ties or emotional closeness (Euler, Hoier, & Rohde, 2001; Rotkirch, 2017). As discussed previously, this psychological preference for interacting with each other is used as a basis for evolutionary definitions of the family. In general, people tend to be more willing to help those to whom they feel closer and to feel closer to those to whom they are genetically closely related (Daly, Salmon, & Wilson, 1997).

Within the extended family, genetically related individuals are predicted to feel closer to each other compared to in-laws. This prediction is based on both the gender difference and paternity uncertainty arguments. Between adult family generations, the closest relationship is likely to emerge between a mother and her adult daughter, and the weakest relationship is likely to emerge between a mother-in-law and a daughter-in-law (Euler, 2011). One study confirmed this assumption with Dutch kin data (Curry, Roberts, & Dunbar, 2013). However, this study on Dutch families also found that emotional closeness is not enough to explain differential investment in grandchildren. Genetically close kin help each other even more than the higher emotional closeness between them can account for. Human behavior provides a "kin premium": People help their close kin because they feel close to them but also because they are kin (Curry et al., 2013; Hackman, Danvers, & Hurschka, 2015). Among unrelated close friends and among affinal kin, by contrast, emotional closeness accounts for much more of one's willingness to help (Danielsbacka, Tanskanen, & Rotkirch, 2015; Rotkirch, Lyons, David-Barrett, & Jokela, 2014).

Notwithstanding the abundance of lay anecdotes and assumptions, affinal relations in contemporary societies have been little investigated. It is therefore currently unclear what drives the kin "premium" behavior: For instance, how much is attributable to social norms and obligations—a core topic in mainstream sociology—and how much is due to a more instinctive and unconscious behavior? We do know that a sense of family obligations promotes grandchild care provision in today's Europe and that this sense of obligation is stronger between biological compared to nonbiological kin (Coall et al., 2014). Further cross-cultural studies would be illuminating, but they are currently hampered by the lack of large data with detailed information on emotional relations between kin and affines.

CONCLUSION

Evolutionary family sociology builds on the neo-Darwinian synthesis and the past few decades of work in family sociology, as well as evolutionary ecology, primatology, anthropology, and psychology. Family is understood as a kin group in which social relations continue after offspring have reached adulthood. Family behavior and living arrangements are expected to be shaped by genetical relatedness and reproductive value of the individuals involved. The notion of humans as cooperative breeders has been crucial for evolutionary family sociologists, who investigate how the involvement of three or more family generations, and two or more kin lineages, varies with social and ecological context and across the life course.

A central advantage of evolutionary family studies is that results are extendable to several species. General biological theories, such as inclusive fitness theory, sexual selection theory, and life history theory, can and should also be applied to humans. For instance, knowledge of other species helps us to fully appreciate the importance of affinal kin. Few species have family ties extending beyond reproduction, and very few (if any) other animals besides humans have extensive involvement of paternal kin in raising offspring. The technological, linguistic, and institutional complexities of human behavior are often mentioned as factors that set us apart from the rest of nature. Relations between affines deserve to be added to this list of what makes us truly exceptional.

Sociological results should, in turn, also be integrated into general biological knowledge. Sociological studies have taught us, for instance, that grandparental investment may be refused by the recipient, unlike the assumption in classical parental investment theory.

A central contribution of the evolutionary perspective to family studies is that it placed genetic relatedness, and the wealth of psychological cues, behavioral dispositions and social regulations affecting genetic relatedness, on the research agenda. For instance, in contemporary wealthy societies, the likelihood of kin sharing the same household is strong at the level of genetic 50% of shared genes—the ties that represent parents, children, and siblings in the nuclear family—but diminishes quickly with lower relatedness. The nuclear family is also the by far most desired and widespread family form on the planet. This remains the case even in highly liberal and secularized societies, although a multitude of other living arrangements could be possible. More studies of helping behavior and resource competition among different types of kin are needed to explain this widespread preference for household arrangements with only one breeding parent (Emlen, 1995; Henrich, Boyd, & Richerson, 2012).

Family sociology is only in its first stages of alignment with evolutionary studies. I have here discussed two broad fields in which integration is underway or likely: mating and grandparenting. There are still books in family sociology that make no mention of evolutionary theory at all, refusing to acknowledge that sociological and evolutionary perspectives are mostly complementary (Schnettler & Steinbach, 2011). If and when they are at odds with each other but represent testable hypotheses, this should only advance our understanding of the human family in all its incarnations.

To further interdisciplinarity, human interaction is often the *sine qua non* and more fruitful than any amount of wishful thinking in print. While collecting background information for this chapter, it has struck me how often theoretical integration stems from collegial interaction between, for instance, ecologists and sociologists (the inspiration for Emlen, 1995) or economists and demographers with anthropologists (the inspiration for Lee, 2003).

Several new research areas can be envisaged for an evolutionary family sociology. The use of longitudinal sociological data has started a *rapprochement* between sociological life course studies and evolutionary life history studies. Although these two theoretical strains are currently mostly unaware of each other, their integration could represent a major theoretical step within evolutionary family sociology. The use of big data also promises not only to merge evolutionary and sociological studies but also to combine them with insights from physics and network research.

Acknowledgments

The author is grateful to David Coleman and Mirkka Danielsbacka for comments to the manuscript and to the Academy of Finland for financial support (project nr. 266898).

References

Aassve, A., Meroni, E., & Pronzato, C. (2012). Grandparenting and childbearing in the extended family. *European Journal of Population, 28*, 499–518.

Alvergne, A., Faurie, C., & Raymond, M. (2010). Are parents' perceptions of offspring facial resemblance consistent with actual resemblance? Effects on parental investment. *Evolution and Human Behavior, 31*(1), 7–15.

Andersson, T., Högberg, U., & Åkerman, S. (1996). Survival of orphans in 19th century Sweden—The importance of remarriages. *Acta Paediatrica, 85*, 981–985.

Antfolk, J., Karlsson, M., Bäckström, A., & Santtila, P. (2012). Disgust elicited by third-party incest: The roles of biological relatedness, co-residence, and family relationship. *Evolution and Human Behavior, 33*(3), 217–223.

Arber, S., & Attias-Donfut, C. (Eds.). (2002). *The myth of generational conflict: The family and state in ageing societies.* London, UK: Routledge.

Archer, J. (2013). Can evolutionary principles explain patterns of family violence? *Psychological Bulletin, 139*(2), 403.

Attias-Donfut, C., Ogg, J., & Wolf, F. C. (2005). European patterns of intergenerational financial and time transfers. *European Journal of Ageing, 2*, 161–173.

Bengtson, V. L. (2001). Beyond the nuclear family: The increasing importance of multigenerational bonds. *Journal of Marriage and Family, 63*, 1–16.

Bengtson, V. L, & Allen, K. R. (1993). The life course perspective applied to families over time. In P. G. Boss, W. G. Doherty, R. LaRossa, W. R. Schumm, & S. K. Steinmetz (Eds.), *Sourcebook of family theories and methods: A contextual approach* (pp. 469–504). New York, NY: Plenum.

Bengtson, V. L., & Kuypers, J. A. (1971). Generational difference and the developmental stake. *Aging & Human Development, 2*(4), 249–260.

Bentley, G., & Mace, R. (2012). *Substitute parents: Biological and social perspectives on alloparenting in human societies.* New York, NY: Berghahn.

Borgerhoff Mulder, M. (1987). On cultural and reproductive success: Kipsigis evidence. *American Anthropologist, 89*(3), 617–634.

Borgerhoff Mulder, M. (2009). Serial monogamy as polygyny or polyandry? *Human Nature, 20*(2), 130–150.

Brandt, M., Haberkern, K., & Szydlik, M. (2009). Intergenerational help and care in Europe. *European Sociological Review, 25*, 585–601.

Burton-Chellew, M. N., & Dunbar, R. I. M. (2011). Are affines treated as biological kin? A test of Hughes's hypothesis. *Current Anthropology, 52*, 741–746.

Buss, D. M. (2017). *Evolutionary psychology: The new science of the mind* (4th ed.). New York, NY: Taylor & Francis.

Chan, C. G., & Elder, G. H., Jr. (2000). Matrilineal advantage in grandchild–grandparent relations. *The Gerontologist, 40*, 179–190.

Chapais, B. (2013). Monogamy, strongly bonded groups, and the evolution of human social structure. *Evolutionary Anthropology, 22*, 52–65.

Cherlin, A. J. (2008). Multiple partnerships and children's wellbeing. *Family Matters, 80*, 33–36.

Chipman, A., & Morrison, E. (2013). The impact of sex ratio and economic status on local birth rates. *Biology Letters, 9*(2).

Coall, D. A., & Hertwig, R. (2010). Grandparental investment: Past, present, and future. *Behavioral and Brain Sciences, 33*, 1–59.

Coall, D. A., Hilbrand, S., & Hertwig, R. (2014). Predictors of grandparental investment decisions in contemporary Europe: Biological relatedness and beyond. *PLoS One, 9*(1), e84082.

Curry, O., Roberts, S. G. B., & Dunbar, R. I. M. (2013). Altruism in social networks: Evidence for a "kinship premium." *British Journal of Psychology, 104*, 283–295.

Daly, M., Salmon, C., & Wilson, M. (1997). Kinship: The conceptual hole in psychological studies of social cognition and close relationships. In D. T. Kenrick & J. A. Simpson (Eds.), *Evolutionary social psychology* (pp. 266–296). New York, NY: Taylor & Francis.

Daly, M., & Wilson, M. I. (1996). Violence against stepchildren. *Current Directions in Psychological Science, 5*(3), 77–80.

Danielsbacka, M., Tanskanen, A. O., Jokela, M., & Rotkirch, A. (2011). Grandparental child care in Europe: Evidence for preferential investment in more certain kin. *Evolutionary Psychology, 9*, 3–24.

Danielsbacka, M., Tanskanen, A. O., & Rotkirch, A. (2015). The impact of genetic relatedness and emotional closeness on intergenerational relations. *Journal of Marriage and Family, 77*(4), 889–907.

del Giudice, M. (2009). Sex, attachment, and the development of reproductive strategies. *Behavioral and Brain Sciences, 32*(1), 1–67.

Dunbar, R. I. M., & Barrett, L. (2007). *Oxford handbook of evolutionary psychology.* Oxford, UK: Oxford University Press.

Durante, K. M., Griskevicius, V., Simpson, J. A., Cantú, S. M., & Tybur, J. M. (2012). Sex ratio and women's career choice: Does a scarcity of men lead women to choose briefcase over baby? *Journal of Personality and Social Psychology, 103*(1), 121–34.

Drew, L. M., & Silverstein, M. (2007). Grandparents' psychological well-being after loss of contact with their grandchildren. *Journal of Family Psychology, 21*(3), 372.

Emlen, S. T. (1995). An evolutionary theory of the family. *Proceedings of the National Academy of Sciences of the USA, 92*(18), 8092–8099.

Emlen, S. T. (1997). The evolutionary study of human family systems. *Social Science Information, 36*(4), 563–589.

Euler, H. A. (2011). Grandparents and extended kin. In C. A. Salmon & T. K. Shackelford (Eds.), *The Oxford handbook of evolutionary family psychology* (pp. 181–210). New York, NY: Oxford University Press.

Euler, H. A., Hoier, S., & Rohde, P. A. (2001). Relationship-specific closeness of intergenerational family ties: Findings from evolutionary psychology and implications for models of cultural transmission. *Journal of Cross-Cultural Psychology*, 32(2), 147–158.

Euler, H. A., & Michalski, R. L. (2008). Grandparental and extended kin relationships. In C. A. Salmon & T. K. Shackelford (Eds.), *Family relationships: An evolutionary perspective* (pp. 230–256). New York, NY: Oxford University Press.

Euler, H. A., & Weitzel, B. (1996). Discriminative grandparental solicitude as reproductive strategy. *Human Nature*, 7, 39–59.

Fingerman, K. L., Hay, E. L., & Birditt, K. S. (2004). The best of ties, the worst of ties: Close, problematic, and ambivalent social relationships. *Journal of Marriage and Family*, 66, 792–808.

Finkelhor, D., Vanderminden, J., Turner, H., Hamby, S., & Shattuck, A. (2014). Child maltreatment rates assessed in a national household survey of caregivers and youth. *Child Abuse and Neglect*, 38(9), 1421–1435.

Fisher, R. A. (1930). *The genetical theory of natural selection: A complete variorum edition.* Oxford, UK: Oxford University Press.

Flinn, M. V., & England, B. G. (1995). Childhood stress and family environment. *Current Anthropology*, 36(5), 854–866.

Fortunato, L. (2012). The evolution of matrilineal kinship organization. *Proceedings of the Royal Society of London B: Biological Sciences*, 279(1749), 4939–4945.

Fortunato, L., & Archetti, M. (2010). Evolution of monogamous marriage by maximization of inclusive fitness. *Journal of Evolutionary Biology*, 23(1), 149–156.

Fox, J. R. (1962). Sibling incest. *British Journal of Sociology*, 13(2), 128–150.

Fox, M., Sear, R., Beise, J., Ragsdale, G., Voland, E., & Knapp, L. A. (2010). Grandma plays favourites: X-chromosome relatedness and sex-specific childhood mortality. *Proceedings of the Royal Society of London B: Biological Sciences*, 277(1681), 567–573.

Freese, J., & Powell, B. (1999). Sociobiology, status, and parental investment in sons and daughters: Testing the Trivers–Willard hypothesis. *American Journal of Sociology*, 104(6), 1704–1743.

Gangestad, S. W., & Simpson, J. A. (2000). The evolution of human mating: Trade-offs and strategic pluralism. *Behavioral and Brain Sciences*, 23, 573–644.

Gibson, M., & Lawson, D. (2014). *Applied evolutionary anthropology. Darwinian approaches to contemporary world issues.* London, UK: Springer.

Gillette, M. T., & Gudmunson, C. G. (2014, March). Utilizing evolutionary life history theories in family studies. *Journal of Family Theory & Review*, 6, 5–17.

Gorelik, G., Shackelford, T. K., & Salmon, C. A. (2010). New horizons in the evolutionary science of the human family. *Review of General Psychology*, 14(4), 330.

Gurven, M., Stieglitz, J., Hooper, P. L., Gomes, C., & Kaplan, H. (2012). From the womb to the tomb: The role of transfers in shaping the evolved human life history. *Experimental Gerontology*, 47(10), 807–813.

Hackman, J., Danvers, A., & Hruschka, D. J. (2015). Closeness is enough for friends, but not mates or kin: Mate and kinship premiums in India and U.S. *Evolution and Human Behavior*, 36(2), 137–145.

Hamilton, W. D. (1964). The genetical evolution of social behaviour (I and II). *Journal of Theoretical Biology*, 7, 1–52.

Henrich, J., Boyd, R., & Richerson, P. J. (2012). The puzzle of monogamous marriage. *Philosophical Transactions of the Royal Society of London B*, 367(1589), 657–669.

Herlofson, K., & Hagestad, G. H. (2012). Transformations in the role of grandparents across welfare states. In S. Arber & V. Timonen (Eds.), *Contemporary grandparenting: Changing family relationships in global contexts* (pp. 27–49). Chicago, IL: Policy Press.

Hofferth, S. L., & Anderson, K. G. (2003). Are all dads equal? Biology versus marriage as a basis for paternal investment. *Journal of Marriage and Family, 65*(1), 213–232.

Hopcroft, R. L. (2005). Parental status and differential investment in sons and daughters: Trivers–Willard revisited. *Social Forces, 83*(3), 1111–1136.

Hopcroft, R. L. (2010). *Sociology: A biosocial introduction*. Boulder, CO: Paradigm.

Hopcroft, R. L. (2016). Grand challenges in evolutionary sociology and biosociology. *Frontiers in Sociology, 1.* doi:10.3389/fsoc.2016.00002

Hopcroft, R. L., & Martin, D. O. (2016). Parental investments and educational outcomes: Trivers–Willard in the U.S. *Frontiers in Sociology, 1.* doi:10.3389/fsoc.2016.00003

Hrdy, S. B. (1999). *Mother nature. A history of mothers, infants, and natural selection.* New York, NY: Pantheon.

Hrdy, S. B. (2009). *Mothers and others. The evolutionary origins of mutual understanding.* Cambridge, MA: Belknap.

Hughes, A. L. (1983). Kin selection of complex behavioral strategies. *The American Naturalist, 122*(2), 181–190.

Hughes, A. L. (1988). *Evolution and human kinship.* New York, NY: Oxford University Press.

Izuhara, M. (2010). *Ageing and intergenerational relations: Family reciprocity from a global perspective.* Chicago, IL: Policy Press.

Kalmijn, M. (2012). Longitudinal analyses of the effects of age, marriage, and parenthood on social contacts and support. *Advances in Life Course Research, 17*(4), 177–190.

Kaplan, H. (1996). A theory of fertility and parental investment in traditional and modern human societies. *American Journal of Physical Anthropology, 101*(S23), 91–135.

Kaplan, H. S., & Lancaster, J. B. (2003). An evolutionary and ecological analysis of human fertility, mating patterns, and parental investment. In K. W. Wachter & R. A. Bulatao (Eds.), *Offspring: Human fertility behavior in biodemographic perspective* (pp. 170–223). Washington, DC: National Academies Press.

Kaptijn, R., Thomese, F., Liefbroer, A. C., & Silverstein, M. (2013). Testing evolutionary theories of discriminative grandparental investment. *Journal of Biosocial Science, 45,* 1–22.

Kohli, M. (1999). Private and public transfers between generations: Linking the family and the state. *European Societies, 1*(1), 81–104.

Kokko, H., & Jennions, M. D. (2008). Parental investment, sexual selection and sex ratios. *Journal of Evolutionary Biology, 21*(4), 919–948.

Kolk, M., & Schnettler, S. (2013). Parental status and gender preferences for children: Is differential fertility stopping consistent with the Trivers–Willard hypothesis? *Journal of Biosocial Science, 45*(5), 683–704.

Laham, S. M., Gonsalkorale, K., & von Hippel, W. (2005). Darwinian grandparenting: Preferential investment in more certain kin. *Personality and Social Psychology Bulletin, 31*(1), 63–72.

Lahdenperä, M., Lummaa, V., Helle, S., Tremblay, M., & Russell, A. F. (2004). Fitness benefits of prolonged post-reproductive lifespan in women. *Nature, 428*(6979), 178–181.

Lee, R. (2003). Rethinking the evolutionary theory of aging: Transfers, not births, shape senescence in social species. *Proceedings of the National Academy of Sciences of the USA, 100*(16), 9637–9642.

Lee, R. (2008). Sociality, selection, and survival: simulated evolution of mortality with inter-generational transfers and food sharing. *Proceedings of the National Academy of Sciences of the USA, 105*(20), 7124–7128.

Lee, R. (2013). Intergenerational transfers, the biological life cycle, and human society. *Population and Development Review, 38*(Suppl. 1), 23–35.

Lee, D., & McLanahan, S. (2015). Family structure transitions and child development: Instability, selection, and population heterogeneity. *American Sociological Review, 80*(4), 738–763.

Luescher, K., & Pillemer, K. (1998). Intergenerational ambivalence: A new approach to the study of parent–child relations in later life. *Journal of Marriage and the Family, 60*(2), 413–425.

Luo, L., Zhao, W., & Weng, T. (2016). Sex-biased parental investment among contemporary Chinese peasants: Testing the Trivers–Willard hypothesis. *Frontiers in Psychology, 7,* 1215. doi:10.3389/fpsyg.2016.01215

Mace, R. (2008). Reproducing in cities. *Science, 319*(5864), 764–766.

Marlowe, F. (2000). Paternal investment and the human mating system. *Behavioural Processes, 51*(1–3), 45–61.

Marlowe, F. (2012). The socioecology of human reproduction. In J. C. Mitani, J. Call, P. M. Kappeler, R. A. Palombit, & J. B. Silk (Eds.), *The evolution of primate societies* (pp. 467–486). Chicago, IL: University of Chicago Press.

Mason, A., Lee, R., Tung, A. C., Lai, M. S., & Miller, T. (2006). *Population aging and intergenerational transfers: Introducing age into national accounts.* Working paper 12770, National Bureau of Economic Research.

Michalski, R. L. (2010). Measures of grandparental investment as a limiting factor in theoretical and empirical advancement. *Behavioral and Brain Sciences, 33,* 32–33.

Nettle, D. (2008.) Why do some dads get more involved than others? Evidence from a large British cohort. *Evolution and Human Behavior, 29*(6), 416–423.

Pashos, A. (2000). Does paternity uncertainty explain discriminative grandparental solicitude? A cross-cultural study in Greece and Germany. *Evolution and Human Behavior, 21,* 97–109.

Pashos, A., & McBurney, D. H. (2008). Kin relationships and the caregiving biases of grandparents, aunts, and uncles. *Human Nature, 19,* 311–330.

Pettay, J. E., Rotkirch, A., Courtiol, A., Jokela, M., & Lummaa, V. (2013). Effects of remarriage after widowhood on long-term fitness in a monogamous historical human population. *Behavioral Ecology and Sociobiology, 68*(1), 135–143.

Pollet, T. V., Kuppens, T., & Dunbar, R. I. (2006). When nieces and nephews become important: Differences between childless women and mothers in relationships with nieces and nephews. *Journal of Cultural and Evolutionary Psychology, 4*(2), 83–93.

Pollet, T. V., Nettle, D., & Nelissen, M. (2006). Contact frequencies between grandparent and grandchildren in a modern society: Estimates of the impact of paternity uncertainty. *Journal of Cultural and Evolutionary Psychology, 4,* 203–213.

Pollet, T. V., Nettle, D., & Nelissen, M. (2007). Maternal grandmothers do go the extra mile: Factoring distance and lineage into differential contact with grandchildren. *Evolutionary Psychology, 5,* 832–843.

Quinlan, R. J., & Quinlan, M. B. (2007). Human lactation, pair-bonds, and alloparents. *Human Nature, 19*(1), 87–102.

Robertson, J. F. (1975). Interaction in three generation families, parents as mediators: Toward a theoretical perspective. *International Journal of Aging and Human Development, 6,* 103–110.

Roos, J. P. (2008). Emile Durkheim versus Edward Westermarck: An uneven match. In H.-J. Niedenzu, T. Meleghy & P. Meyer (Eds.), *The New Evolutionary Social Science. Human Nature, Social Behavior, and Social Change* (pp. 135–146). Boulder, CO: Paradigm Publishers.

Rossi, A. S., & Rossi, P. H. (1991). *Of human bonding: Parent–child relations over the life course.* New York, NY: Aldine de Gruyter.

Rotkirch, A. (2017). Emotional closeness predicted by relatedness. In T. Shackelford & W. A. Weekes-Shackelford (Eds.), *Encyclopedia of evolutionary psychological science.* London, UK: Springer.

Rotkirch, A., Lyons, M., David-Barrett, T., & Jokela, M. (2014). Gratitude for help among friends and siblings. *Evolutionary Psychology, 12*(4), 673–686.

Runciman, W. G. (2015). Evolutionary sociology. In J. H. Turner, R. Malachek, & A. Maryanski (Eds.), *Handbook on evolution and society: Toward an evolutionary social science* (pp. 194–214). Boulder, CO: Paradigm.

Salmon, C. A., & Shackelford, T. K. (Eds.). (2008). *Family relationships: An evolutionary perspective.* New York, NY: Oxford University Press.

Salmon, C. A., & Shackelford T. K. (Eds.). (2011). *The Oxford handbook of evolutionary family psychology.* New York, NY: Oxford University Press.

Sanderson, S. (2001). *The evolution of human sociality. A Darwinian conflict perspective.* New York, NY: Rowman & Littlefield.

Sanderson, S. (2014a). *Human nature and the evolution of society.* Boulder, CO: Westview Press.

Sanderson, S. (2014b). Family systems in comparative perspective. In M. Sasaki, J. Goldstone, E. Zimmermann, & S. Sanderson (Eds.), *Concise encyclopedia of comparative sociology* (pp. 190–198). Leiden, the Netherlands: Brill.

Scelza, B. A. (2011). Female choice and extra-pair paternity in a traditional human population. *Biology Letters, 7*(6), 889–891

Schlomer, G. L., Del Giudice, M., & Ellis, B. J. (2011). Parent–offspring conflict theory: An evolutionary framework for understanding conflict within human families. *Psychological Review, 118*(3), 496–521.

Schnettler, S. (2013). Revisiting a sample of U.S. billionaires: How sample selection and timing of maternal condition influence findings on the Trivers–Willard effect. *PLoS One, 8*(2), 8–13.

Schnettler, S., & Steinbach, A. (2011). How do biological and social kinship play out within families in the U.S.? An evolutionary perspective on perceived parental care and closeness. *Zeitschrift für Familienforschung, 23*(2), 173–195.

Sear, R., & Coall, D. (2011). How much does family matter? Cooperative breeding and the demographic transition. *Population and Development Review, 37*(Suppl. 1), 81–112.

Segerstråle, U. (2000). *Defenders of the truth: The battle for science in the sociobiology debate and beyond.* New York, NY: Oxford University Press.

Schacht, R., Rauch, K. L., & Borgerhoff Mulder, M. (2014). Too many men: The violence problem? *Trends in Ecology & Evolution, 29* (4), 214–222.

Silk, J. B. (1983). Local resource competition and facultative adjustment of sex ratios in relation to competitive abilities. *The American Naturalist, 121*(1), 56–66.

Sims, M., & Rofail, M. (2013). The experiences of grandparents who have limited or no contact with their grandchildren. *Journal of Aging Studies, 27*(4), 377–386.

Smith, M. S. (1991). An evolutionary perspective on grandparent–grandchild relationships. In P. K. Smith (Ed.), *The psychology of grandparenthood* (pp. 157–176). New York, NY: Routledge.

South, S. J., & Trent, K. (1988). Sex ratios and women's roles: A cross-national analysis. *American Journal of Sociology, 93*(5), 1096–1115.

Stacey, J. (1990). *Brave new families: Stories of domestic upheaval in late-twentieth-century America*. Berkeley, CA: University of California Press.

Strassmann, B. I. (1997). Polygyny as a risk factor for child mortality among the Dogon. *Current Anthropology*, *38*(4), 688–695.

Strassmann, B. I., & Kurapati, N. T. (2016). What explains patrilineal cooperation? *Current Anthropology*, *57*(13), S118-S130.

Strassmann, B. I., Kurapati, N. T., Hug, B. F., Burke, E. E., Gillespie, B. W., Karafet, T. M., & Hammer, M. F. (2012). Religion as a means to assure paternity. *Proceedings of the National Academy of Sciences of the USA*, *109*(25), 9781–9785.

Szydlik, M. (2016). *Sharing lives: Adult children and parents*. London, UK: Routledge.

Tanskanen, A. O., & Danielsbacka, M. (2014). Genetic relatedness predicts contact frequencies with siblings, nieces and nephews: Results from the Generational Transmissions in Finland Surveys. *Personality and Individual Differences*, *69*, 5–11.

Tanskanen, A. O., Danielsbacka, M., Jokela, M., David-Barrett, T., & Rotkirch, A. (2016). Diluted competition? Conflicts between full and half siblings in two adult generations. *Frontiers in Sociology*, *1*(6). doi:10.3389/fsoc.2016.00006

Tanskanen, A. O., Danielsbacka, M., Jokela, M., & Rotkirch, A. (2017). Sibling conflicts in full- and half-sibling households in the UK. *Journal of Biosocial Science*, *49*(1), 31–47.

Tanskanen, A. O., Danielsbacka, M., & Rotkirch, A. (2014). Multi-partner fertility is associated with lower grandparental investment from in-laws in Finland. *Advances in Life Course Research*, *22*, 41–48.

Tanskanen, A. O., Jokela, M., Danielsbacka, M., & Rotkirch, A. (2014). Grandparental effects on fertility vary by lineage in the United Kingdom. *Human Nature*, *25*, 269–284.

Tanskanen, A. O., & Rotkirch, A. (2014). The impact of grandparental investment on mothers' fertility intentions in four European countries. *Demographic Research*, *30*, 1–26.

Therborn, G. (2004). *Between sex and power: Family in the world 1900–2000*. London, UK: Routledge.

Trivers, R. L. (1972). Parental investment and sexual selection. In B. Campbell (Ed.), *Sexual selection and the descent of man* (pp. 52–97). Chicago, IL: Aldine.

Trivers, R. L., & Willard, D. E. (1973). Natural selection of parental ability to vary the sex ratio of offspring. *Science*, *179*, 90–92.

Turner, J., & Maryanski, A. (2005). *Incest: Origins of the taboo*. New York, NY: Paradigm.

Uhlenberg, P., & Hammill, B. G. (1998). Frequency of grandparent contact with grandchild sets: Six factors that make a difference. *The Gerontologist*, *38*, 276–285.

van den Berghe, P. (1979). *Human family systems: An evolutionary view*. New York, NY: Elsevier.

van Schaik, C., van Noordwijk, M., & Nunn, C. (1999). Sex and social evolution in primates. In P. C. Lee & Phyllis C. Lee (Eds.), *Comparative primate socioecology* (pp. 204–240). Cambridge: Cambridge University Press. 204–240.

Walsh, A. (2014). *Biosociology: Bridging the biology-sociology divide*. New Brunswick, NJ: Transaction Publishers.

Waynforth, D. (2013). Evolutionary perspectives on father involvement. In N. J. Cabrera & C. S. Tamis-LeMonda (Eds.), *Handbook of father involvement: Multidisciplinary perspectives* (pp. 23–36). London, UK: Routledge.

Westermarck, E. (1891). *The history of human marriage*. London, UK: Macmillan.

Wrzus, C., Hänel, M., Wagner, J., & Neyer, F. J. (2013). Social network changes and life events across the life span: A meta-analysis. *Psychological Bulletin, 139*(1), 53–80.

Xu, Q. (2014). Absent or ambivalent mothers and avoidant children—An evolutionary reading of Zhang Kangkang's motherhood stories. *Finnish Yearbook of Population Research, 48*, 147–168.

CHAPTER 22

EVOLUTION AND HUMAN REPRODUCTION

MARTIN FIEDER AND SUSANNE HUBER

THE most obvious point of an evolutionary view of human fertility is that those individuals who did not reproduce are not part of our ancestral line. We should therefore be strongly adapted toward reproduction. But what forces and constraints influence reproduction? Why do some individuals have many descendants and others remain childless? What makes some individuals more successful in biological terms? To analyze these questions, we start on the level of the individual. Then we explain how genetic information and newly arising mutations can influence mating and fertility.

SOCIAL STATUS, WEALTH, AND REPRODUCTION

Central for the understanding of reproduction is Bateman's principle, which states that the overall mean lifetime reproductive success of both sexes has to be equal but that the individual variance in lifetime reproductive success is different between the sexes (Bateman, 1948). Interestingly, Bateman developed his approach based on *Drosophila melanogaster*, the fruit fly. As Bateman's principle has been proven for many species, however, it is clearly fundamentally correct for most sexually reproducing species. According to that principle, the sex with the smaller variance of lifetime reproductive success and the higher investment in reproduction should choose mating partners more carefully and also benefit more in being choosier. Among individuals of the less investing sex, in contrast, the variance in reproductive success should be higher, and they should benefit less from being choosy. This does not mean that this sex is not choosy at all, but merely that choosing the "wrong mate"—in terms of, for instance, being less fertile, too old, or not caring for the offspring—is usually less costly for that sex (with the exception of choosing an unfaithful mate leading to high parental uncertainty and, hence, lower fitness). In humans, females are the higher investing sex even if considering only the physiological costs of reproduction (i.e., low-energy-consuming sperm production in males vs. the demanding costs for egg production, pregnancy, and lactation in females). Accordingly, wrong mate selection in terms of, for instance, offering no or only few resources or protection should have more detrimental effects on females than on males. We therefore can expect that in humans, females—who have the higher risk in reproduction—are the choosier sex (for a review, see Barrett, Dunbar, & Lycett, 2002).

This principle becomes strikingly apparent when analyzing the relationship between social status and reproduction in humans. If we assume that women are choosier than men for a trait such as socioeconomic status (advantageous for rearing the offspring), then high-status men but not high-status women should have higher mating and, hence, increased reproductive success. This is indeed the case for traditional (e.g., the Turkmen pastoralist [Irons, 1979], the Kipsigis [Borgerhoff Mulder, 1988] and the Yanomano [Chagnon, 1988]) and preindustrial societies (Mealy, 1985; Voland, 1990; Cronk, 1991). In contemporary modern societies, however, social status and wealth long appeared to be "inversely related" to the number of children, representing the "central theoretical problem of human socio-biology" (Vining, 1986).

More recent publications revealed that this view emerged due to methodological issues. Those studies based on representative data sets from modern societies clearly demonstrate that particularly personal income is positively associated with the number of children in men but not in women, where the association is mostly neutral or even negative (Fieder et al., 2005; Hopcroft, 2006, 2015; Weeden, Abrams, Green, & Sabini, 2006; Nettle & Pollet, 2008; Fieder, Huber, & Bookstein, 2011; Barthold, Myrskylä, & Jones, 2012; Fieder & Huber, 2012). The position in a social hierarchy is also positively associated with offspring number in men but not women (Fieder et al., 2005; Fieder & Huber, 2012). In most cases, this positive relationship between socioeconomic status indicators and offspring number was explained by the higher chance of low-status men to remain unmated and, thus, childless. In society subsets, however, not only does the risk of childlessness increase among men of low income but also the number of children increases in those who reproduce at all (Fieder et al., 2005). This is in line with the predictions of Mace (2000) that status may be a more important dimension for particular subsamples of modern society than for representative samples of entire societies. Accordingly, this association may differ between subsets of societies (Mueller & Mazur, 1998; Stulp & Barrett, 2016). This may be particularly important in societies at risk of disintegration into subsamples—for instance, in the case of high immigration. Although income provides a rather "universal status indicator" (Fieder, Huber, & Bookstein, 2011), in immigrants, some status indicators could have a different meaning because migrants may partially use the partially deviating status system of their home society.

What are the reasons for the different results regarding the association between status and reproduction in modern humans obtained by social scientists such as Vining (1986)? A first explanation is the use of unrepresentative and arbitrary samples; the second is indistinct status indicators (Stulp, Barrett, Tropf, & Mills, 2015). If personal income is used as a status indicator, then the association between status and reproductive output is clearly positive for men and null or negative for women (Fieder & Huber, 2007). The picture is less clear, however, if education is used as a status indicator. Here, the association ranges from slightly positive to null or even negative for men (interestingly, results differ between the United States, United Kingdom, and other European countries) (Hopcroft, 2006, 2015; Weeden, Abrams, Green, & Sabini, 2006; Fieder & Huber, 2007; Nettle & Pollet, 2008). In modern women, both education and personal income are generally negatively related to their number of offspring (Hopcroft, 2006, 2015; Weeden, Abrams, Green, & Sabini, 2006; Fieder & Huber, 2007; Nettle & Pollet, 2008).

We believe that education is not a status indicator per se but, rather, a prerequisite for social status (in the sense of *embodied capital*; see Kaplan, Lancaster, Tucker, & Anderson, 2002). Although better education increases the probability of earning a higher income, the correlation between education and income is not perfect (in the United States, in 2010, the correlation between education and income for both sexes was 0.362 [IPUMS USA, https://www.ipums.org]). Also, education leads to postponing of reproduction (first birth), which holds particularly true for women (Mills, Rindfuss, McDonald, & Te Velde, 2011). As soon as the fertility window closes for women, they may not reach their intended family size or may even end up childless. Men, in contrast, may compensate postponing because they are able to reproduce longer, albeit with potential consequences concerning mutation risk (discussed later).

Income is thus probably a better indicator of social status in modern societies: It is universally transferable in a society and usually provides the resources necessary for reproduction, such as dwelling and nutrition. Nonetheless, there are other indicators of social status in modern societies—for example, position in the social hierarchy (Fieder & Huber, 2012), as well as inherited wealth. By reviewing existing literature on longitudinal data, Stulp and Barrett (2016) indeed found that the relationship between wealth and fertility is more often positive than negative. Although data are difficult to obtain, we assume that particularly inherited property should have a strong pro-fertility effect in societies in which the costs for property are rising, because an inherited dwelling will provide material security, fostering fertility.

The question remains, why for modern women are most status indicators negatively associated with fertility even though data suggest that also in modern societies, resources are crucial for women's reproduction? This is apparent from the finding that a woman's probability to remain childless decreases with increasing income of her husband (Huber, Bookstein, & Fieder, 2010). Also, particularly highly educated women have more offspring if they are married to a high-income man (Huber, Bookstein, & Fieder, 2010). These data suggest that resources provided by the husband usually have a pro-fertile effect on women's reproduction. Today, however, women can obtain resources by themselves so that they are no longer dependent on those offered by their spouses. However, this reorienting to earlier strategies in which women could provide more of their own resources (in horticultural and hunting and gathering societies, for instance, women had a major role in subsistence production) is time-consuming and forces women to remain longer in a "status of economic insecurity" (Musick, England, Edgington, & Kangas, 2009). Moreover, women shifting in the direction of their own resources not only face a trade-off between resource acquisition and reproduction, including the danger of missing their fertility window, but also may face a marriage squeeze. The higher the social–economic status of a woman, the more difficult it is for that woman to find an equal or even higher status spouse. Particularly women of high own status prefer a partner of at least comparable status (Bereczkei, Voros, Gal, & Bernath, 1997; Buston & Emlen, 2003). Such women run a higher risk of ending up unpaired and childless (Gender & Generation Survey Austria 2008/2009, http://www.ggp-austria.at/fileadmin/ggp-austria/familienentwicklung.pdf).

In line with life history theory (Mace, 2000, 2007), however, couples may find it reasonable to limit the number of offspring in order to invest more in each individual child. This notion has been proposed by human capital theory (Becker, 1993) and further developed to the "embodied capital theory" by Kaplan (1996). Based on their high reproductive costs, this holds particularly true for women, with a trade-off between a woman's investment in her status and her fertility (reviewed in Shenk, Kaplan, & Hooper, 2016). Moreover, Hopcroft and Whitmeyer (2010) found that "background status" approximated by the occupational status of the father also has a negative effect on a woman's fertility. Theoretically, under certain conditions, reduced fertility coupled with higher investment into each single child would lead to a more "stable reproduction" over generations. Nonetheless, empirical evidence for a fitness advantage over generations by reducing the number of children and investing more in fewer children is minimal or absent. Evidence suggests that on the one hand, low fertility increases the progenies' socioeconomic position, but on the other hand, it reduces long-term fitness (Goodman, Koupil, & Lawson, 2012). In addition, different strategies of maximizing versus optimizing fertility may lead to a conflict between the sexes (Moya, Snopkowski, & Sear, 2016).

HOMOGAMY AND REPRODUCTION

One largely underestimated aspect of human reproduction that is important both on the level of the individual and on the level of genetics is homogamy. *Homogamy* or assortative mating refers to mating based on similarity of characteristics. In 1903, Pearson analyzed the correlation of height within married couples. Since then, assortative mating has been shown for a great variety of traits, including ethnicity, age, religious background, educational attainment, physical characteristics such as height or weight, personality traits, and psychiatric conditions (Merikangas, 1982; Mascie-Taylor, 1986; Susanne & Lepage, 1988; Qian, 1998; Bisin, Topa, & Verdier, 2004; Schwartz & Mare, 2005; Speakman, Djafarian, Stewart, & Jackson, 2007).

A particularly high degree of homogamy has been found for religion (Fieder & Huber, 2016), as well as education (Huber & Fieder, 2011). An analysis of census data from IPUMS International (https://international.ipums.org/international) reveals a worldwide mean in religious homogamy of 94.82%. The highest prevalence of religious homogamy is found in the Muslim world (usually >99%), in which the Quran ensures the rate of high homogamy (Quran, 2:221, 5:5, 60:10), and the lowest value is reported in the Caribbean (<70%). The prevalence of religious homogamy is also high in secular societies that do not enforce religious denomination or religious homogamy. In the state of Tennessee, for instance, there is a 66% prevalence of homogamous Catholic marriages even though Catholics represent only 4% of the population, and in Illinois, Jews exhibit a 91% prevalence of homogamy within a population consisting of less than 2% Jews (Bisin, Topa, & Verdier, 2004). On the proximate level, this high prevalence of religiously homogamous marriages may be explained by the fact that these marriages are more stable: Spouses agree more on essential questions regarding the institution of marriage and family (Call & Heaton, 1997; Myers, 2006). Marriage stability and satisfaction may in turn affect fertility decisions. Indeed, religiously homogamous couples have a significantly lower chance of remaining childless but a higher average number of children, even controlling for religious intensity (Krishnan, 1993; Fieder & Huber, 2016).

Homogamy based on education may also be important. This is because education concerns many areas of life, such as social status and income, along with lifestyle, tastes, and values (Kalmijn, 1991). Accordingly, this usually yields a high frequency of educational homogamy, even though studies differ with regard to the actual degree and ongoing trends of educational homogamy (Birkelund & Heldal, 2003; Halpin & Chan, 2003; Schwartz & Mare, 2005; Domański & Przybysz, 2007).

Only a few studies have examined the association between educational homogamy and fertility. By analyzing US census data, we found that educational homogamy reduced the odds of remaining childless but that there was no effect on the average number of children (Huber & Fieder, 2011). Bauer and Jacob (2010) also reported that educationally and occupationally homogamous couples have a higher chance of becoming parents. A pro-fertile effect of educational homogamy has been demonstrated by Mascie-Taylor (1986) as well.

The clear pro-fertile effect of religious (Fieder & Huber, 2016) and, to a lesser extent, educational homogamy (Huber & Fieder, 2011, 2016) indicates that there may also be evolutionary reasons for the high prevalence of homogamous mating. From an evolutionary standpoint, marriage along a cultural trait may represent an expanded "kinship system" that may have evolved during the aggregation to larger social units. In the case of religious homogamy, for instance, despite the fact that a certain proportion of religious homogamous marriages can be expected among kin, individuals may recognize other individuals of the same religion "as somehow closer," sharing at least some essential values. A comparable mechanism may also hold true for educational homogamy, albeit educational homogamy represents a much younger "mating system."

Even if a trait is only moderately inherited, homogamy may still have an effect on biological evolution, despite the fact that homogamy per se does not change allele frequencies. Nonetheless, if fertility is higher for homogenous couples, then the frequency of the alleles for which a couple is homogamous will increase in the population. Such an increase in the frequency of homozygous individuals in a population provides a basis on which selection may act—for instance, via selection against the recessive homozygote (Relethford, 2012)—which may lead to a shift in allele frequencies in a population. In addition, homogamy on a certain cultural trait may lead to the construction of "cultural niches" (O'Brien et al., 2012) associated with cultural reproductive barriers to group outsiders. This would result in smaller groups, which in turn would lead to accelerated evolution (e.g., genetic drift has a stronger impact if a population is smaller; Relethford, 2012).

Not surprisingly, homogamy can be detected at the level of genes. Only recently have some studies reported on genetic homogamy. Guo, Wang, Liu, and Randall (2014) found in married couples positive and—to a much lesser extent—also negative genomic assortment based on all available autosomal single nucleotide polymorphisms. The positive assortment was comparable to the range of genomic correlation among second cousins. Genetic similarity between spouses has also been reported by Domingue, Fletcher, Conley, and Boardman (2014). Such genetic assortment may be adaptive because it augments the number of shared genes (Thiessen & Gregg, 1980; Rushton, 1989). The potentially negative consequences of inbreeding, however, must also be kept in mind (Bittles, Grant, Sullivan, & Hussain, 2002), including an increase in the recessive homozygote. In case of harmful mutations, this eliminates buffering by a dominant, non-mutated allele. Another consequence due to the increase in the frequency of homozygous alleles is a lower heterozygote advantage in case of overdominance effects (for review, see Charlesworth & Willis, 2009). Both mechanisms may increase mortality. Indeed, children of first-order cousins have a 3.5% increased mortality rate (Bittles & Black, 2010). Bittles and Black state, however, that adequate control for confounding variables may be difficult.

Accordingly, sexual relationships between close kin, such as sister and brother, mother and son, or father and daughter, are strictly banned in nearly every culture (some exceptions exist for royal families in ancient Egypt and Persia; Frandsen, 2009). Marriages between cousins and particularly higher order cousins, however, are usually allowed (the legal regulations are remarkably different for first-order cousins even between the US states: https://en.wikipedia.org/wiki/Cousin_marriage_law_in_the_ United_States_by_state). Also, many religions, including Judaism and Islam, are permissive toward marriages between first-order cousins (Bittles & Black, 2010). It can be assumed that cousin marriages were very frequent in our evolutionary past because no other sexual partners may have existed (Fox, 2015). Today, although consanguineous marriages have been declining, approximately 10.4% of the global population is still engaged in them (Hamamy & Bittles, 2008; Bittles & Black, 2010).

Thus, it is probably not surprising that a certain degree of inbreeding may also be beneficial. By investigating 46 small-scale societies, Bailey, Hill, and Walker (2014) found that the association between spousal relatedness and fitness was positive for societies with a general high level of inbreeding but negative for societies with a general low level of inbreeding. In addition, on the basis of data from Iceland, Helgason, Pálsson, Guðbjartsson, and Stefánsson (2008) impressively demonstrated that the number of children (and, to a lesser degree, also grandchildren) increased with increasing levels of inbreeding up to the level of second cousins (but see also Postma, Martini, & Martini, 2010). This pro-fertile effect of kinship marriage may be partially explained by age at reproductive onset as well as socioeconomic advantages of keeping wealth within kinship boundaries. However, genetic factors may also play a role. In addition to the fact that close inbreeding carries genetic risks (discussed previously), this may also be the case for distant outbreeding, although the effects of outbreeding are far less clear (Edmands, 2007). Thus, overall, fertility patterns according to "inbreeding versus outbreeding" seem to be more complex, probably depending on the genetic makeup of individuals and populations, ecological factors, and also the speed of change in conditions. Unpublished data, for instance, indicate that the reproductive depression of outbreeding between ethnical borders could be overcome by religious homogamy (Huber & Fieder, 2017).

On the level of society, homogamy along certain characteristics has consequences as well. Particularly educational homogamy may be an undervalued risk factor, resulting in less permeability of social stratification and hence a stronger segregation of the social strata. This has negative consequences for "social cohesion," increasing the tensions within a society. However, as noted by Francois Nielsen in Chapter 15 of this volume, genetic inheritance plays a central role in most status-related outcomes. In addition, sexual reproduction leads to a recombination of genes in each generation, which shows a regression to the population mean. As a result, many offspring of high socioeconomic status parents are born with abilities lower than those of their parents, and many offspring of lower socioeconomic status parents are born with higher abilities. In meritocratic societies, this increases social mobility and hence attenuates the effects of educational homogamy.

In times of global mass migrations, the high prevalence of religious homogamy, together with its reproductive effects, may also have far-reaching implications because it may lead to the breakup of societies into "parallel societies," which is why efforts to integrate migrants will be demanding. From an "inclusive fitness perspective" (Hamilton, 1964), integration will be successful if religious and cultural groups mix—that is, reproduce across group boundaries. In the case of such mixed reproduction, cooperation is expected to be high regardless of the cultural group to which the relatives and those related by marriage belong: Via their offspring, their grand-offspring, and subsequent generations of descendants, they share genes in common. Therefore, if cultural groups mix, the very strong "biological ties" of cooperation ensure sustainable social cohesion. Accordingly, these newly arising "mixed groups" may form new minimal endogamous sets in subsequent generations (Whitmeyer, 1997) in which cooperation may be high. Genetic data suggest that this process may have often occurred during human evolution and migration (Patterson et al., 2012). However, albeit only little is known about our early history, recent archeological records suggest that migration and admixture have not always been a peaceful process (http://www.sciencemag.org/news/2016/03/ slaughter-bridge-uncovering-colossal-bronze-age-battle).

Age of Fathers, Mutation, and Reproduction

Our DNA consists of roughly 3.2 billion base pairs (i.e., 3.2 billion pairs of adenine–thymine and guanine–cytosine covering the genomic information of humans, most of whose functions we do not yet understand) that, together with epigenetic signature, make us different from each other. Currently, we have only a relatively limited understanding of the phenotypical outcomes of our genetic makeup (Jobling, Hurles, & Tyler-Smith, 2013). Clearly, human genetics is extraordinarily complex. Nevertheless, there is no doubt that these variations in the DNA make some of us better adapted than others to certain environments. Those better adapted individuals (in the respective environments) eventually end up with more descendants. Due to the reproductive benefits for those better adapted individuals, the genetic information associated with this beneficial phenotype will spread in a population. Adaptation, however, always refers to the current environment. If the environmental conditions change, then a successful adaptation to the original environment may have no or even negative consequences on fertility. Such a maladaptive condition decreases the reproductive success of its carrier or, in the worst-case scenario, causes that lineage to die out.

Most mutations are thought to be neutral—that is, exerting no or hardly detectable effects on the phenotype—and therefore have no immediate adaptive value. Other mutations are harmful, especially if they occur in protein-encoding DNA sequences leading to an altered protein. A small number of mutations, however, may ultimately lead to a phenotype better adapted than others to its current environment. Such a phenotype will be favored by selection. The actual rate of harmful, neutral, or positive mutations, however, remains difficult to estimate (Keightley, 2012), particularly the rate of mutations that are positively selected for. In two *Drosophila* populations, Schneider, Charlesworth, Eyre-Walker, and Keightley (2011) estimated the rate of positive selected mutations for amino acid coding sequences (i.e., non-synonymous mutations) to be between 1% and 2% of all occurring mutations.

Where do most of the mutations come from? The very recently discovered answer in humans is impressive—from the age of the father (Kong et al., 2012). According to Kong et al., the father's age explains nearly all newly occurring (i.e., de novo) mutations in a child. Correspondingly, detrimental parental age effects have been demonstrated for a variety of Mendelian and mental disorders and even for educational attainment (for a review, see D'Onofrio et al., 2014). The reason is that in contrast to women, in whom all cell divisions in the egg are completed before birth, men continue producing sperm throughout their reproductive lives. Consequently, the number of cell divisions and chromosome replications that a sperm cell has gone through increases with the age at which the sperm is produced. This increases the risk that "errors" occur in terms of mutations (Crow, 2000).

Because the mutations induced by male age occur randomly in the human genome, the probability that they directly affect reproductive functioning is relatively low because a detrimental mutation occurring somewhere in our genome does not necessarily affect reproductive functioning. In such cases, an individual could still reproduce normally even if he or she carries a potentially harmful mutation. It would pass those harmful mutations on to the next generation, which may then accumulate over generations. It is thus conceivable that a mechanism may exist that helps avoid excessive mutation loads in future generations. We suggest that mate selection may provide such a mechanism to prevent too high mutation load. This view is supported by our recent findings based on a US sample (Wisconsin Longitudinal Study), in which we demonstrated that children of older fathers are less attractive (Huber & Fieder, 2014). Moreover, offspring of older fathers face a higher risk of remaining unmarried and therefore remaining childless (Fieder & Huber, 2015). Marriage was obligatory in the previously mentioned sample, thereby providing a good indicator for mating success. Comparable findings based on large human data sets have confirmed our results (Hayward, Lummaa, & Bazykin, 2015; Arslan et al., 2016). Similar effects of paternal age have also been reported in animal species ranging from bulb mites (Prokop, Stuglik, Żabińska, & Radwan, 2007) to house sparrows (Schroeder, Nakagawa, Rees, Mannarelli, & Burke, 2015). We therefore suggest that this phenomenon is a more fundamental biological principle: An individual's mutation load could affect mate selection, thus helping to reduce the mutation load of the progeny.

This view is also in line with the mutation–selection balance theory, proposing that a balance of forces between constantly arising, mildly harmful mutations and selection causes variation in genetic quality and phenotypic condition (Miller, 2000; Keller, 2008). This makes it unlikely that the accumulation of new deleterious mutations leads to a detectable fitness decline in current human populations (Keightley, 2012). The mutation–selection balance is assumed to be particularly important in traits influenced by many genetic loci (multigenic, such as human reproduction), providing a large target size for mutations (Keller, 2008).

Although most of the mutations induced by the age of the father are considered neutral or may be harmful, a small proportion of them are advantageous and provide fitness benefits. This raises an interesting question: Are we able to detect potentially promising mutations in a mate that may be adaptive in the long term? Detecting mutations that in the future may lead to an adaptive phenotype is unlikely. We therefore assume that this is probably a random process. Nevertheless, one can speculate that individuals choose extraordinary traits in potential mates—that is, traits that may be associated with newly induced mutations. The numerous examples include the peacock's tail (Zahavi & Zahavi, 1999), bower birds (Uy & Borgia, 2000), as well as height (Stulp, Barrett, Tropf, & Mills, 2015) and social status in men (Fieder & Huber, 2007; Nettle & Pollet, 2008; Barthold, Myrskylä, & Jones, 2012; Hopcroft, 2015). If such traits carry adaptive benefits outweighing potentially negative impacts, then selection would favor both the carrier of those mutations and the carrier's mating partners. Accordingly, mutations induced by a father's age can also be viewed as a "driving force" of evolution. The reason is that without mutations, evolution would not have taken place at all, and without mutations introduced into the population by male age, evolution would at least have been much slower. The positive mutations induced by age might thus be considered an "engine of evolution," leading to new phenotypes that could potentially be selected for.

Together with the usually higher status of older men, this positive effect might partially explain women's preference for somewhat older men (Buss, 1989). Basically, this preference reflects a trade-off between benefits associated with higher status and possible detrimental mutations caused by higher paternal age that may be passed to the offspring. However, because some mutations may be adaptive, overall the benefits may outweigh the costs, at least if the age difference between spouses is not too large. Accordingly, women usually prefer men who are only moderately older than themselves (Buss, 1989; Buunk, Dijkstra, Fetchenhauer, & Kenrick, 2002; Schwarz & Hassebrauck, 2012).

Future studies may aim to measure the impact of mutations directly and not just indirectly via the age of fathers, examining, for instance, if there is any evidence for a potential link between father's age, mutation rate, marriage fertility, and social status. According to D'Onofrio et al. (2014), higher paternal age is associated with lower educational attainment in the offspring. This finding suggests a possible association between de novo mutation rate and educational attainment, leading to the question whether social status goes beyond being solely culturally determined to also contain an inherited component. At least for educational attainment, this has recently been shown (Rietveld et al., 2013).

Early Life Factor Effects and the Role of Epigenetics

The phenotype follows from both the genetic makeup and the prevailing environment. Since the pioneering work of Barker, however, it is increasingly recognized that phenotypical outcome is additionally affected by the maternal and environmental conditions experienced during pre- and early postnatal life. This organizational phenomenon is termed early life programming, and it may have long-term physiological effects (Lucas, 1991; Barker, 1995). Particularly well examined are the long-term effects of stress during early life on susceptibility to disease later in life. Adverse childhood experiences such as exposure to maltreatment, abuse, early parental loss, or household dysfunction predict worse physical and mental health during adulthood (Felitti et al., 1998; Krause, 1998; Springer, Sheridan, Kuo, & Carnes, 2007). In addition, socioeconomic status during childhood has been found to influence adult health, with better childhood conditions being associated with better adult health (Marmot, Shipley, Brunner, & Hemingway, 2001; Kestilä et al., 2005), independently of adult socioeconomic status (Braveman et al., 2005).

Also, reproduction can be affected by early life conditions, as became apparent by analyzing the association of birth season and later reproductive performance (Smits et al., 1997; Lummaa & Tremblay, 2003; Huber, Fieder, Wallner, Iber, & Moser, 2004; Huber, Fieder, Wallner, Moser, & Arnold, 2004; Huber, Didham, & Fieder, 2008). In a study of 500,000 Vietnamese women, we demonstrated that a significant association exists between a woman's birth month and her later number of children (Huber & Fieder, 2009). The peak number of children was found for women born during the rainy season, with the lowest number of children for women whose own early fetal life concurred with the rainy season. Because the rainy season is associated with inadequate food and seasonal infections such as malaria and diarrheal disease (Lawrence, Coward, Lawrence, Cole, & Whitehead, 1987; Bates, Prentice, & Paul, 1991; Panter-Brick, Lotstein, & Ellison, 1993; Dicko et al., 2003), these findings point to a detrimental effect of adverse maternal and environmental conditions during early fetal development on woman's later reproductive functioning. Although there is evidence that maternal undernutrition during pregnancy affects later fertility (Ibanez et al., 2002), the underlying mechanisms of how early life experiences become "embedded" in reproductive physiology remain elusive.

From the extensive work on the effects of prenatal stress, however, epigenetics has now emerged as an ideal candidate to mediate such programming effects of early experiences on later life functioning (Harper, 2005; Miller, Chen, & Parker, 2011), providing a mechanism to fine-tune phenotypic development in response to prevailing environmental conditions, thereby enabling the organism to adapt to the immediate environment (Meaney, 2010; Szyf, 2014). This makes excellent adaptive sense because it provides the genetic makeup with a higher level of flexibility in response to environmental demands. Hence, from an evolutionary standpoint, epigenetics represents a faster and more flexible mechanism to respond to environmental demands compared to the slower process of mutations and selection alone (LaFreniere & MacDonald, 2013).

Epigenetic markings are functional modifications to the DNA that regulate gene expression without altering DNA sequences (Zhang & Meaney, 2010). Importantly, epigenetic markings can be modified by internal and external influences, enabling long-lasting effects of environmental signals on gene expression. The main epigenetic modifications include DNA methylation as well as remodeling of the chromatin structure, both of which modulate accessibility of the DNA for the transcriptional apparatus and thus regulate gene transcription. DNA methylation is the addition of a methyl group usually on a cytosine of a CpG dinucleotide. Although CpGs are typically methylated, in promoter regions, methylation of CpGs is usually low and regulates gene expression. Methylation interferes with the binding of transcription factors, thus downregulating gene transcription. DNA methylation acts in concert with modifications to the protruding amino tails of the histone proteins around which the DNA is wrapped. This remodels the chromatin, thereby improving or confining accessibility of transcription factors to DNA sites. Acetylation of histone tails, for instance, relaxes the tight interaction with the DNA, opening the chromatin and thus activating gene expression. In addition, epigenetic control of gene activity includes a variety of other histone modifications, such as methylation, phosphorylation, and ubiquitination, as well as non-coding RNAs.

Studies on the effects of maternal care on the stress physiology of the offspring in rats elaborately demonstrate how epigenetic modifications mediate the effects of early life conditions (Weaver et al., 2004). Weaver et al. determined that natural variation in maternal care resulted in lifelong differences in behavioral and neuroendocrine responses to stress in the offspring. They demonstrated that epigenetic alterations within the promoter region of the glucocorticoid receptor gene in the hippocampus, affecting transcription factor binding and thus gene expression, explained these maternal care effects on offspring physiology and behavior. McGowan et al. (2009) extended these findings to humans. They showed that the methylation pattern of the human homolog of the hippocampal glucocorticoid receptor promoter region was altered in suicide victims with a history of childhood abuse. In addition, methylation differences at this locus caused by maternal mood during pregnancy have in turn been shown to affect the endocrine stress response in infants (Oberlander et al., 2008). Although largely unexplored, epigenetic modifications may also underlie effects of the early environment on later fertility in humans. Regarding the previously mentioned Vietnam data, it is thus conceivable that adverse environmental conditions during the prenatal period affect epigenetic signatures and hence gene expression patterns affecting reproduction and fertility.

Environmentally induced epigenetic modifications can even be transmitted over generations if these alterations occur in the germline. Anway, Cupp, Uzumcu, and Skinner (2005), for instance, demonstrated in their classic experiment that male rats prenatally exposed to an anti-androgenic fungicide experienced reduced sperm count and viability: This was stably transmitted over four generations by a permanently altered epigenome in the sperm. On a population level, epigenetics thus offers a more rapid mechanism of adaptation than changes in the DNA sequence, facilitating a much higher degree of sensitivity to changing environmental conditions (Skinner, 2011).

Conclusion

An evolutionary perspective helps explain reproductive patterns in modern humans and may make a valuable contribution in the assessment of contemporary problems caused by current mating and fertility trends. Fertility trends in modern societies, for instance, are characterized by a decreasing number of offspring, a higher proportion of single and childless individuals, as well as increasing age at reproductive onset. In particular, highly educated women in prestigious positions have a high risk of missing their intended family size. In addition, in men, increasing age at reproduction may increase de novo mutation rate. Along with a high prevalence of homogamy, these trends may have detrimental effects for societies in terms of increasing social inequality; increasing costs for the public health system; and increasing pressure on the health, social, and pension systems.

References

Anway, M. D., Cupp, A. S., Uzumcu, M., & Skinner, M. K. (2005). Epigenetic transgenerational actions of endocrine disruptors and male fertility. *Science, 308*, 1466–1469.
Arslan, R. C., Willführ, K. P., Frans, E., Verweij, K. J., Myrskylä, M., Voland, E., . . . Penke, L. (2016). Older fathers' children have lower evolutionary fitness across four centuries and in four populations. *bioRxiv*, 042788.
Bailey, D. H., Hill, K. R., & Walker, R. S. (2014). Fitness consequences of spousal relatedness in 46 small-scale societies. *Biology Letters, 10*, 20140160.

Barker, D. J. (1995). Fetal origins of coronary heart disease. *British Medical Journal, 311*, 171–174.

Barrett, L., Dunbar, R., & Lycett, J. (2002). *Human evolutionary psychology* (pp. 131–170). Princeton, NJ: Princeton University Press.

Barthold, J. A., Myrskylä, M., & Jones, O. R. (2012). Childlessness drives the sex difference in the association between income and reproductive success of modern Europeans. *Evolution and Human Behavior, 33*, 628–638.

Bateman, A. J. (1948). Intra-sexual selection in *Drosophila. Heredity, 2*, 349–368.

Bates, C. J., Prentice, A. M., & Paul, A. A. (1991). Seasonal variations in vitamins A, C, riboflavin and folate intakes and status of pregnant and lactating women in a rural Gambian community: Some possible implications. *European Journal of Clinical Nutrition, 29*, 1–12.

Bauer, G., & Jacob, M. (2010). Fertilitätsentscheidungen im Partnerschaftskontext. Eine Analyse der Bedeutung der Bildungskonstellation von Paaren für die Familiengründung anhand des Mikrozensus 1996–2004. *Kölner Zeitschrift für Soziologie, 62*, 31–60.

Becker, G. S. (1993). *Human capital*. Chicago, IL: University of Chicago Press.

Bereczkei, T., Voros, S., Gal, A., & Bernath, L. (1997). Resources, attractiveness, family commitment; Reproductive decisions in human mate choice. *Ethology, 103*, 681–699.

Birkelund, G. E., & Heldal, J. (2003). Who marries whom? Educational homogamy in Norway. *Demographic Research, 8*, 1–30.

Bisin, A., Topa, G., & Verdier, T. (2004). Religious intermarriage and socialization in the United States. *Journal of Political Economy, 112*, 615–664.

Bittles, A. H., & Black, M. L. (2010). Consanguinity, human evolution, and complex diseases. *Proceedings of the National Academy of Sciences of the USA, 107*(Suppl. 1), 1779–1786.

Bittles, A. H., Grant, J. C., Sullivan, S. G., & Hussain, R. (2002). Does inbreeding lead to decreased human fertility? *Annals of Human Biology, 29*, 111–130.

Borgerhoff Mulder, M. (1988). Reproductive success in three Kipsigis cohorts. In T. H. Clutton-Brock (Ed.), *Reproductive success* (pp. 419–438). Chicago, IL: University of Chicago Press.

Braveman, P. A., Cubbin, C., Egerter, S., Chideya, S., Marchi, K. S., Metzler, M., & Posner, S. (2005). Socioeconomic status in health research: One size does not fit all. *Journal of the American Medical Association, 294*, 2879–2888.

Buss, D. M. (1989). Sex differences in human mate preferences: Evolutionary hypotheses tested in 37 cultures. *Behavioral and Brain Sciences, 12*, 1–14.

Buston, P. M., & Emlen, S. T. (2003). Cognitive processes underlying human mate choice: The relationship between self-perception and mate preference in Western society. *Proceedings of the National Academy of Sciences of the USA, 100*, 8805–8810.

Buunk, B. P., Dijkstra, P., Fetchenhauer, D., & Kenrick, D. T. (2002). Age and gender differences in mate selection criteria for various involvement levels. *Personal Relationships, 9*, 271–278.

Call, V. R. A., & Heaton, T. B. (1997). Religious influence on marital stability. *Journal for the Scientific Study of Religion, 36*, 382–392.

Chagnon, N. A. (1988). Life history, blood revenge and warfare in a tribal population. *Science, 239*, 985–992.

Charlesworth, D., & Willis, J. H. (2009). The genetics of inbreeding depression. *Nature Reviews Genetics, 10*, 783–796.

Cronk, L. (1991). Low socioeconomic status and female biased parental investment: The Mukogodo example. *American Anthropologist, 91*, 414–429.

Crow, J. F. (2000). The origins, patterns and implications of human spontaneous mutation. *Nature Review Genetics, 1*, 40–47.

D'Onofrio, B. M., Rickert, M. E., Frans, E., Kuja-Halkola, R., Almqvist, C., Sjölander, A., . . . Lichtenstein, P. (2014). Paternal age at childbearing and offspring psychiatric and academic morbidity. *JAMA Psychiatry, 71*, 432–438.

Dicko, A., Mantel, C., Thera, M. A., Doumbia, S., Diallo, M., Diakite, M., . . . Doumbo, O. K. (2003). Risk factors for malaria infection and anemia for pregnant women in the Sahel area of Bandiagara, Mali. *Acta Tropica, 89*, 17–23.

Domański, H., & Przybysz, D. (2007). Educational homogamy in 22 European countries. *European Societies, 9*, 495–526.

Domingue, B. W., Fletcher, J., Conley, D., & Boardman, J. D. (2014). Genetic and educational assortative mating among US adults. *Proceedings of the National Academy of Science of the USA, 111*, 7996–8000.

Edmands, S. (2007). Between a rock and a hard place: Evaluating the relative risks of inbreeding and outbreeding for conservation and management. *Molecular Ecology, 16*, 463–475.

Felitti, V. J., Anda, R. F., Nordenberg, D., Williamson, D. F., Spitz, A. M., Edwards, V., . . . Marks, J. S. (1998). Relationship of childhood abuse and household dysfunction to many of the leading causes of death in adults: The Adverse Childhood Experiences (ACE) study. *American Journal of Preventive Medicine, 14*, 245–258.

Fieder, M., & Huber, S. (2007). The effects of sex and childlessness on the association between status and reproductive output in modern society. *Evolution and Human Behavior, 28*, 392–398.

Fieder, M., & Huber, S. (2012). An evolutionary account of status, power, and career in modern societies. *Human Nature, 23*, 191–207.

Fieder, M., & Huber, S. (2015). Paternal age predicts offspring chances of marriage and reproduction. *American Journal of Human Biology, 27*, 339–343.

Fieder, M., & Huber, S. (2016). The association between religious homogamy and reproduction. *Proceedings of the Royal Society B, 283*, 20160294.

Fieder, M., Huber, S., & Bookstein, F. L. (2011). Socioeconomic status, marital status and childlessness in men and women: An analysis of census data from six countries. *Journal of Biosocial Science, 43*, 619–635.

Fieder, M., Huber, S., Bookstein, F. L., Iber, K., Schäfer, K., Winckler, G., & Wallner, B. (2005). Status and reproduction in humans: New evidence for the validity of evolutionary explanations on the basis of a university sample. *Ethology, 111*, 940–950.

Fox, R. (2015). Marry in or die out: Optimal inbreeding and the meaning of mediogamy. In J. H. Turner, R. Machalek, & A. Maryanski (Eds.), *Handbook on evolution and society* (pp. 171–192). London, UK: Routledge.

Frandsen, P. J. (2009). *Incestuous and close-kin marriage in ancient Egypt and Persia: An examination of the evidence* (Vol. 34). Copenhagen, the Netherlands: Museum Tusculanum Press.

Goodman, A., Koupil, I., & Lawson, D. W. (2012). Low fertility increases descendant socioeconomic position but reduces long-term fitness in a modern post-industrial society. *Proceedings of the Royal Society of London B: Biological Sciences, 279*, 4342–4351.

Guo, G., Wang, L., Liu, H., & Randall, T. (2014). Genomic assortative mating in marriages in the United States. *PLoS One, 9*, e112322.

Halpin, B., & Chan, T. W. (2003). Educational homogamy in Ireland and Britain: Trends and patterns. *British Journal of Sociology, 54*, 473–495.

Hamamy, H., & Bittles, A. H. (2008). Genetic clinics in Arab communities: Meeting individual, family and community needs. *Public Health Genomics, 12*(1), 30–40.

Hamilton, W. D. (1964). The genetical evolution of social behaviour: I. *Journal of Theoretical Biology, 7*, 1–16.

Harper, L. V. (2005). Epigenetic inheritance and the intergenerational transfer of experience. *Psychological Bulletin, 131*, 340–360.

Hayward, A. D., Lummaa, V., & Bazykin, G. A. (2015). Fitness consequences of advanced ancestral age over three generations in humans. *PLoS One, 10*, e0128197.

Helgason, A., Pálsson, S., Guðbjartsson, D. F., & Stefánsson, K. (2008). An association between the kinship and fertility of human couples. *Science, 319*, 813–816.

Hopcroft, R. L. (2006). Sex, status, and reproductive success in the contemporary United States. *Evolution and Human Behavior, 27*, 104–120.

Hopcroft, R. L. (2015). Sex differences in the relationship between status and number of offspring in the contemporary US. *Evolution and Human Behavior, 36*, 146–151.

Hopcroft, R. L., & Whitmeyer, J. M. (2010). A choice model of occupational status and fertility. *Journal of Mathematical Sociology, 34*, 283–300.

Huber, S., Bookstein, F. L., & Fieder, M. (2010). Socioeconomic status, education, and reproduction in modern women: An evolutionary perspective. *American Journal of Human Biology, 22*, 578–587.

Huber, S., Didham, R., & Fieder, M. (2008). Month of birth and offspring count of women: Data from the Southern hemisphere. *Human Reproduction, 23*, 1187–1192.

Huber, S., & Fieder, M. (2009). Strong association between birth month and reproductive performance of Vietnamese women. *American Journal of Human Biology, 21*, 25–35.

Huber, S., & Fieder, M. (2011). Educational homogamy lowers the odds of reproductive failure. *PLoS One, 6*, e22330.

Huber, S., & Fieder, M. (2014). Advanced paternal age is associated with lower facial attractiveness. *Evolution and Human Behavior, 35*, 298–301.

Huber, S., & Fieder, M. (2016). Worldwide census data reveal prevalence of educational homogamy and its effect on childlessness. *Frontiers in Sociology, 1*, 10.

Huber S., & Fieder, M. (2017). Mutual compensation of the effects of religious and ethnic homogamy on reproduction. *American Journal of Human Biology*, in press.

Huber, S., Fieder, M., Wallner, B., Iber, K., & Moser, G. (2004). Brief communication: Season of birth effects on reproduction in contemporary humans. *Human Reproduction, 19*, 445–447.

Huber, S., Fieder, M., Wallner, B., Moser, G., & Arnold, W. (2004). Brief communication: Birth month influences reproductive performance in contemporary women. *Human Reproduction, 19*, 1081–1082.

Ibanez, L., Potau, N., Ferrer, A., Rodriguez-Hierro, F., Marcos, M. V., & de Zegher, F. (2002). Reduced ovulation rate in adolescent girls born small for gestational age. *Journal of Clinical Endocrinology & Metabolism, 87*, 3391–3393.

Irons, W. (1979). Natural selection, adaptation and human social behavior. In N. A. Chagnon & W. Irons (Eds.), *Evolutionary biology and human social behavior: An anthropological perspective* (pp. 213–237). North Scituate, MA: Duxbury.

Jobling, M., Hurles, M., & Tyler-Smith, C. (2013). *Human evolutionary genetics: Origins, peoples & disease.* New York, NY: Garland.

Kalmijn, M. (1991). Status homogamy in the United States. *American Journal of Sociology, 97*, 496–523.

Kaplan, H. (1996). A theory of fertility and parental investment in traditional and modern human societies. *American Journal of Physical Anthropology, 101*, 91–135.

Kaplan, H., Lancaster, J. B., Tucker, W. T., & Anderson, K. G. (2002). Evolutionary approach to below replacement fertility. *American Journal of Human Biology, 14,* 233–256.

Keightley, P. D. (2012). Rates and fitness consequences of new mutations in humans. *Genetics, 190,* 295–304.

Keller, M. C. (2008). The role of mutations in human mating. In G. Geher & G. Miller (Eds.), *Mating intelligence: Sex, relationships, and the mind's reproductive system* (pp. 173–193). New York, NY: Erlbaum.

Kestilä, L., Koskinen, S., Martelin, T., Rahkonen, O., Pensola, T., Aro, H., & Aromaa, A. (2005). Determinants of health in early adulthood: What is the role of parental education, childhood adversities and own education? *European Journal of Public Health, 16,* 305–314.

Kong, A., Frigge, M. L., Masson, G., Besenbacher, S., Sulem, P., Magnusson, G., . . . Stefansson, K. (2012). Rate of de novo mutations and the importance of father's age to disease risk. *Nature, 488,* 471–475.

Krause, N. (1998). Early parental loss, recent life events, and changes in health among older adults. *Journal of Aging and Health, 10,* 395–421.

Krishnan, V. (1993). Religious homogamy and voluntary childlessness in Canada. *Sociological Perspectives, 36,* 83–93.

LaFreniere, P., & MacDonald, K. (2013). A post-genomic view of behavioral development and adaptation to the environment. *Developmental Review, 33,* 89–109.

Lawrence, M., Coward, W. A., Lawrence, F., Cole, T. J., & Whitehead, R. G. (1987). Fat gain during pregnancy in rural African women: The effect of season and dietary status. *American Journal of Clinical Nutrition, 45,* 1442–1450.

Lucas, A. (1991). Programming by early nutrition in man. In G. R. Bock & J. Whelan (Eds.), *The childhood environment and adult disease* (pp. 38–55). Chichester, UK: Wiley.

Lummaa, V., & Tremblay, M. (2003). Month of birth predicted reproductive success and fitness in pre-modern Canadian women. *Proceedings of the Royal Society London B: Biological Sciences, 270,* 2355–2361.

Mace, R. (2000). Evolutionary ecology of human life history. *Animal Behaviour, 59,* 1–10.

Mace, R. (2007). The evolutionary ecology of human family size. In R. Dunbar & L. Barrett (Eds.), *The Oxford handbook of evolutionary psychology* (pp. 383–396). Oxford, UK: Oxford University Press.

Marmot, M., Shipley, M., Brunner, E., & Hemingway, H. (2001). Relative contribution of early life and adult socioeconomic factors to adult morbidity in the Whitehall II study. *Journal of Epidemiology and Community Health, 55,* 301–307.

Mascie-Taylor, C. G. (1986). Assortative mating and differential fertility. *Biology and Society, 3,* 167–170.

McGowan, P. O., Sasaki, A., D'Alessio, A. C., Dymov, S., Labonte, B., Szyf, M., . . . Meaney, M. J. (2009). Epigenetic regulation of the glucocorticoid receptor in human brain associates with childhood abuse. *Nature Neuroscience, 12,* 342–348.

Mealy, L. (1985). The relation between social status and biological success: A case study of the Mormon religious hierarchy. *Ethology and Sociobiology, 6,* 249–257.

Meaney, M. J. (2010). Epigenetics and the biological definition of gene × environment interactions. *Child Development, 81,* 41–79.

Merikangas, K. R. (1982). Assortative mating for psychiatric disorders and psychological traits. *Archives of General Psychiatry, 39,* 1173–1180.

Miller, G. (2000). Mental traits as fitness indicators: Expanding evolutionary psychology's adaptationism. *Annals of the New York Academy of Sciences, 907,* 62–74.

Miller, G. E., Chen, E., & Parker, K. J. (2011). Psychological stress in childhood and suscepti-bility to the chronic diseases of aging: Moving towards a model of behavioral and biological mechanisms. *Psychological Bulletin, 137*, 959–997.

Mills, M., Rindfuss, R. R., McDonald, P., & Te Velde, E. (2011). Why do people postpone par-enthood? Reasons and social policy incentives. *Human Reproduction Update, 17*, 848–860.

Moya, C., Snopkowski, K., & Sear, R. (2016). What do men want? Re-examining whether men benefit from higher fertility than is optimal for women. *Philosophical Transactions of the Royal Society B, 371*, 20150149.

Mueller, U., & Mazur, A. (1998). Reproductive constraints on dominance competition in male *Homo sapiens. Evolution and Human Behavior, 19*, 387–396.

Musick, K., England, P., Edgington, S., & Kangas, N. (2009). Education differences in intended and unintended fertility. *Social Forces, 88*, 543–572.

Myers, S. M. (2006). Religious homogamy and marital quality: Historical and generational patterns, 1980–1997. *Journal of Marriage and Family, 68*, 292–304.

Nettle, D., & Pollet, T. V. (2008). Natural selection on male wealth in humans. *The American Naturalist, 172*, 658–666.

O'Brien, M. J., Laland, K. N., Broughton, J. M., Cannon, M. D., Fuentes, A., Gerbault, P., . . . Pyne, L. (2012). Genes, culture, and agriculture: An example of human niche construction. *Current Anthropology, 53*, 434–470.

Oberlander, T. F., Weinberg, J., Papsdorf, M., Grunau, R., Misri, S., & Devlin, A. M. (2008). Prenatal exposure to maternal depression, neonatal methylation of human glucocorticoid receptor gene (*NR3C1*) and infant cortisol stress responses. *Epigenetics, 3*, 97–106.

Panter-Brick, C., Lotstein, D. S., & Ellison, P. T. (1993). Seasonality of reproductive function and weight loss in rural Nepali women. *Human Reproduction, 8*, 684–690.

Patterson, N., Moorjani, P., Luo, Y., Mallick, S., Rohland, N., Zhan, Y., . . . Reich, D. (2012). Ancient admixture in human history. *Genetics, 192*(3), 1065–1093.

Pearson, K. (1903). Assortative mating in man. *Biometrika, 2*, 481–489.

Postma, E., Martini, L., & Martini, P. (2010). Inbred women in a small and isolated Swiss village have fewer children. *Journal of Evolutionary Biology, 23*, 1468–1474.

Prokop, Z. M., Stuglik, M., Żabińska, I., & Radwan, J. (2007). Male age, mating probability, and progeny fitness in the bulb mite. *Behavioral Ecology, 18*, 597–601.

Qian, Z. (1998). Changes in assortative mating: The impact of age and education, 1970–1990. *Demography, 35*, 279–292.

Relethford, J. H. (2012). Genetic drift. In *Human population genetics* (pp. 101–138). Hoboken, NJ: Wiley.

Rietveld, C. A., Medland, S. E., Derringer, J., Yang, J., Esko, T., Martin, N.W., . . . Albrecht, E. (2013). GWAS of 126,559 individuals identifies genetic variants associated with educational attainment. *Science, 340*, 1467–1471.

Rushton, J. P. (1989). Genetic similarity theory, human altruism, and group selection. *Behavioral and Brain Sciences, 12*, 503–517.

Schneider, A., Charlesworth, B., Eyre-Walker, A., & Keightley, P. D. (2011). A method for infer-ring the rate of occurrence and fitness effects of advantageous mutations. *Genetics, 189*, 427–1437.

Schroeder, J., Nakagawa, S., Rees, M., Mannarelli, M.-E., & Burke, T. (2015). Reduced fitness in progeny from old parents in a natural population. *Proceedings of the National Academy of Sciences of the USA, 112*, 4021–4025.

Schwartz, C. R., & Mare, R. D. (2005). Trends in educational assortative marriages from 1940 to 2003. *Demography, 42,* 621–646.

Schwarz, S., & Hassebrauck, M. (2012). Sex and age differences in mate-selection preferences. *Human Nature, 23,* 447–466.

Shenk, M. K., Kaplan, H. S., & Hooper, P. L. (2016). Status competition, inequality, and fertility: Implications for the demographic transition. *Philosophical Transactions of the Royal Society B, 371,* 20150150.

Skinner, M. K. (2011). Role of epigenetics in developmental biology and transgenerational inheritance. *Birth Defects Research, 93,* 51–55.

Smits, L. J., Poppel, F. W. A., Verduin, J. A., Jongbloet, P. H., Straatman, H., & Zielhuis, G. A. (1997). Is fecundability associated with month of birth? An analysis of 19th and early 20th century family reconstruction data from The Netherlands. *Human Reproduction, 12,* 2572–2578.

Speakman, J. R., Djafarian, K., Stewart, J., & Jackson, D. M. (2007). Assortative mating for obesity. *American Journal of Clinical Nutrition, 86,* 316–323.

Springer, K. W., Sheridan, J., Kuo, D., & Carnes, M. (2007). Long-term physical and mental health consequences of childhood physical abuse: Results from a large population based sample of men and women. *Child Abuse & Neglect, 31,* 517–530.

Stulp, G., & Barrett, L. (2016). Wealth, fertility and adaptive behaviour in industrial populations. *Philosophical Transactions of the Royal Society B, 371,* 20150153.

Stulp, G., Barrett, L., Tropf, F. C., & Mills, M. (2015). Does natural selection favour taller stature among the tallest people on earth? *Proceedings of the Royal Society B, 282,* 20150211.

Susanne, C., & Lepage, Y. (1988). Assortative mating for anthropometric characters. In C. G. Mascie-Taylor & A. C. Boyce (Eds.), *Human mating patterns* (pp. 83–99). Cambridge, UK: Cambridge University Press.

Szyf, M. (2014). Lamarck revisited: Epigenetic inheritance of ancestral odor fear conditioning. *Nature Neuroscience, 17,* 2–4.

Thiessen, D., & Gregg, B. (1980). Human assortative mating and genetic equilibrium: An evolutionary perspective. *Ethology and Sociobiology, 1,* 111–140.

Uy, J. A. C., & Borgia, G. (2000). Sexual selection drives rapid divergence in bowerbird display traits. *Evolution, 54,* 273–278.

Vining, D. R. (1986). Social versus reproductive success: The central theoretical problem of human sociobiology. *Behavioral and Brain Sciences, 9,* 167–216.

Voland, E. (1990). Differential reproductive success in the Krummhorn population. *Behavioral Ecology and Sociobiology, 26,* 65–72.

Weaver, I. C. G., Cervoni, N., Champagne, F. A., D'Alessio, A. C., Sharma, S., Seckl, J. R., . . . Meaney, M. J. (2004). Epigenetic programming by maternal behavior. *Nature Neuroscience, 7,* 847–854.

Weeden, J., Abrams, M. J., Green, M. C., & Sabini, J. (2006). Do high-status people really have fewer children? *Human Nature, 17,* 377–392.

Whitmeyer, J. M. (1997). Endogamy as a basis for ethnic behavior. *Sociological Theory, 15*(2), 162–178.

Zahavi, A., & Zahavi, A. (1999). *The handicap principle: A missing piece of Darwin's puzzle.* Oxford, UK: Oxford University Press.

Zhang, T.-Y., & Meaney, M. J. (2010). Epigenetics and the environmental regulation of the genome and its function. *Annual Review of Psychology, 61,* 439–466.

CHAPTER 23

EVOLUTION, SOCIETAL SEXISM, AND UNIVERSAL AVERAGE SEX DIFFERENCES IN COGNITION AND BEHAVIOR

LEE ELLIS

THIS chapter focuses on better understanding numerous *average sex differences in cognition and behavior*. Because the phrase is used frequently, it is henceforth abbreviated with the acronym *ASDCBs*. This abbreviation refers to any and all average sex differences in how humans think and behave. For ASDCBs that appear to exist in all societies and time frames, the term *universal ASDCBs* is used.

There are five parts to this chapter. Part 1 documents that numerous universal ASDCBs now appear to exist. Part 2 reviews evidence of how ASDCBs seems to vary in strength over time and across countries. In Part 3, findings from cross-cultural research on the nature of ASDCBs are described. Part 4 describes three theories for explaining ASDCBs, one being strictly environmental and two being of an evolutionary/biological nature. Part 5 explores how well the three theories explain what current evidence suggests about ASDCBs, as revealed in Parts 1–3.

In today's fast-paced communications world, some readers may simply be interested in this chapter's bottom line. For them, a brief conclusion section provides an overview of all five parts of the entire chapter.

PART 1: UNIVERSAL ASDCBs

Social scientists have been searching for possible universal ASDCBs for many years, some with expectations that few, if any, would be found (Kessler & McKenna, 1978;

Mead, 1963). Doubts about the existence of universal ASDCBs began to change in the 1970s with the publication of a book by Maccoby and Jacklin (1974). It summarized findings from several thousand studies published up to the early 1970s. Their review led them to identify four ASDCBs that seemed to be present across all cultures: (a) superior verbal ability in females, (b) greater visual–spatial ability in males, (c) better mathematical ability in males, and (d) more physical aggression in males.

Two decades later, a meta-analysis of thousands of additional studies was published by Feingold (1994). It brought him to confirm conclusions reached by Maccoby and Jacklin (1974) and then to add five more universal ASDCBs. Females, he said, were more anxious, friendly/gregarious, trusting of others, and tender-minded, whereas males were more assertive.

A decade and a half after Feingold's (1994) meta-analysis was published, eight colleagues and I published a book in which findings from more than 18,000 studies pertaining to sex differences were summarized (Ellis et al., 2008). Citations to the studies were organized into hundreds of different tables, each one pertaining to a separate possible ASDCB. Many of the tables had to do with strictly biological traits and included information on nonhumans, neither of which are of concern here. The majority of tables, however, actually pertained to some aspect of human cognition or behavior. From these tables, evidence of 65 universal ASDCBs was obtained. Methodologically, we designated an ASDCB as being apparently universal if (a) at least 10 relevant studies had been conducted and (b) each study without exception reported the same sex difference to exist to a statistically significant degree. For those interested in the details, each ASDCB is described in Ellis (2011a). To save space, here I merely provide a brief sketch of the nature of these 65 ASDCBs under seven subject headings:

1. *Stratification and work*: Twelve behavioral traits were identified having to do with social stratification or work. They indicate that males work longer hours outside the home and are more likely to be employed in a variety of "male-typical occupations" such as jobs of a supervisory, scientific, and engineering nature. Females, on the other hand, when employed outside the home, are more likely to work in people-oriented and caregiving occupations.

2. *Drug consuming and illegal behavior*: Central to the five traits under this category is that males consume more alcohol and engage in more criminal behavior than do females.

3. *Social and play behavior*: The general pattern seen in this category of 12 traits indicates that females are more cooperative and helpful to others throughout life and even in their childhood play activities. Males, on the other hand, tend to be more competitive and more prone to interact with members of the opposite sex in explicitly sexual ways.

4. *Personality and general behavior*: Seven personality and general behavior traits were identified. They boiled down to males throughout life being more inclined to explore their environments, to take greater physical risks, and to behave in hostile/aggressive ways toward one another. Females were found to be friendlier. In all the countries sampled, females also expressed greater concern about being overweight.

5. *Attitudes and preferences*: Twelve universal sex differences in attitudes and prefer- ences were found. Males express greater interest in physical science and technol- ogy, and they want to watch and participate in sports more often than do females. Females have a greater preference for marriage partners who are taller and wealth- ier than themselves, whereas males want mates who are shorter and younger than themselves. Females have greater interest in school, whereas males have more interest in sex.

6. *Mental health*: Twelve universal sex differences involved mental health issues, broadly defined. In this regard, alcoholism, learning disabilities, attention defi- cit disorder with hyperactivity, psychoticism, and autism are all more common in males. The cognitive/mental health traits that females exhibit more often are anorexia, bulimia, and panic attacks. Females are also more likely than males to blame themselves for any shortcomings, and they ruminate over unpleasant social experiences more.

7. *Emotions and perceptions*: The last category of universal sex differences involves females perceiving greater hazards in their environment, reporting greater feel- ings of stress, and crying more as adults. Males report feeling bored more.

Regarding emotions, readers might suspect that there are other universal tendencies, such as the tendency for women to be more depressed than men. There is in fact con- siderable evidence supporting this particular conclusion (Hopcroft & Bradley, 2007). However, a few exceptions exist (Ellis et al., 2008, p. 373). To give one of the most recent examples, data obtained from China revealed that equal proportions of men and women self-reported feeling depressed (Hopcroft & McLaughlin, 2012, p. 510).

Overall, it now appears safe to say that many universal ASDCBs exist. If one uses the criteria we set for confident conclusions in this regard, the number stands at 65. But if somewhat more liberal criteria are used, the number could be in the hundreds.

Of course, the search for universal ASDCBs is not over. Findings from hundreds of new studies of sex differences are published every year. No matter what criteria one sets, it is possible that (a) more universal ASDCBs will be located in the future and (b) excep- tions to those already identified may be eventually unearthed. With these provisos in mind, some rather surprising evidence pertaining to ASDCBs is briefly described next. This evidence has to do with the types of cultures in which one finds the *greatest degree* of sex differences in cognition and behavior.

PART 2: ASDCBs OVER TIME
AND ACROSS CULTURES

Societal efforts have been made in Western cultures to treat the sexes more equitably for well over a century. One of the earliest landmarks in this regard occurred in 1893 when New Zealand became the first country in the world to grant women the right to vote, a right now afforded to all women living in democratic countries (Ramirez, Soysal, & Shanahan, 1997).

In many Western countries, particularly the United States, laws now guarantee women equal access to higher education (Klein et al., 2014), to sporting activities (Hargreaves, 2002; Milner & Braddock, 2016), and to employment opportunities (Rossilli, 2000). Women's rights activists continue to work toward even greater equality, but undisputed progress has been made. For example, in Western societies, most adult women are now in the paid labor force, a dramatic increase over the past century (Durand, 2015). Even more dramatic changes have occurred in terms of higher education. At the start of the 20th century, roughly 90% of college graduates in industrialized countries were men; by the early 1990s, well over half of all college degrees were being awarded to women (Averett & Burton, 1996; Buchmann & DiPrete, 2006; Cho, 2007).

Given these trends, it is worthwhile asking if they have been paralleled by any changes in ASDCBs. For example, Have people's attitudes toward sex equality shifted? Have sex stereotypes changed? Or, have people's self-perceptions of themselves in masculine/feminine terms diminished? Although much of the relevant data are limited to the United States, the results are quite interesting. The following is a summary:

> *US attitudes regarding sex equality*: One study sought to determine if people in the United States are becoming more sympathetic to the idea that men and women should be treated more equally. To address this question, it compared responses to various questions about sex equality that were first administered in the early 1960s and then again in the mid-1990s (Thornton & Young-DeMarco, 2001). Findings indicated that substantial shifts have occurred. In particular, over the three decades involved, greater proportions of people of both sexes believed that men and women should be treated equally in interpersonal relations and in employment opportunities. From this investigation, it appears safe to infer that US attitudes regarding the desirability of treating the sexes equally have become more favorable in recent decades.

> *US sex stereotypes*: If attitudes toward treating males and females more equally have become more favorable, one might be led to believe that sex stereotypes have diminished. Sex stereotypes, of course, refer to the extent to which people believe that males and females behave differently regarding a wide range of traits. To address this question, one study compared sex stereotypes expressed by US respondents first in 1974 to similar respondents in 1997 nearly a quarter of a century later (Lueptow, Garovich-Szabo, & Lueptow, 2001). In both cases, respondents were given a list of behavior traits and asked to rate them as being either more typical of males (masculine) or of females (feminine, or not different regarding sex). Overall, this study concluded that nearly all of the stereotypes have remained virtually unchanged. The only exception involved a slight decrease in the extent to which females were stereotyped as exhibiting certain feminine traits, but there were no significant changes in the extent to which males were stereotyped as possessing masculine traits (see also Lueptow, 2005).

US masculinity–femininity self-perceptions: Another investigation sought to assess trends in personality sex differences by meta-analyzing findings from studies that had all used a popular measure of masculinity–femininity, known as the Bem Sex Role Inventory (Twenge, 1997). All of the studies included in the meta-analysis were conducted in the United States predominantly among college students from the mid-1970s through the early 1990s. Analyses revealed no significant changes in the degree to which males considered themselves to be masculine or feminine over a wide variety of interests and preferences. Females had not changed their self-ratings in terms of possessing masculine interests and preferences, but women sampled in the 1990s did express somewhat *more* feminine interests and preferences than did women sampled in the 1970s. Thus, although serious validity issues have been raised regarding the Bem scale (Hoffman & Borders, 2001), Twenge's meta-analysis suggests that despite all the changes that have occurred both culturally and legislatively in terms of more equal treatment of men and women, the extent to which US college students perceive themselves regarding masculine or feminine traits has changed very little.

PART 3: ASDCBs ACROSS CULTURES

E-mail communications and computerized data management have made it possible for researchers throughout the world to conduct large-scale cross-cultural studies. One such study involved assembling responses from prior studies of more than 23,000 respondents residing on four different continents (i.e., Africa, Asia, Europe, and North America). The goal was to search for varied sex differences in personality traits (Costa, Terracciano, & McCrae, 2001). In particular, the meta-study sought to determine if people living in Western countries (i.e., those in Europe and North America) exhibited stronger or weaker sex differences in personality traits compared to people from predominantly non-Western countries. Results revealed that across all four continents, similar sex differences existed in nearly all of the personality traits measured. However, to the amazement of the researchers, the *degree* of sex differences in personality traits was more pronounced in the Western countries than in the predominantly non-Western countries (p. 322). Thus, despite all the social and legislative efforts made to promote sex equality in Western countries, sex differences in personality traits were *greater* in the Western countries than in countries in which few such efforts have yet to be undertaken.

Another research team investigated personality traits using measures from the Big Five Personality Inventory from more than 17,000 respondents in 55 countries (Schmitt, Realo, Voracek, & Allik, 2008). The team's work revealed that countries in which people's health, lifespan, years of education, and wealth were the highest (i.e., predominantly Western industrial societies) were the countries with the greatest degree of sex differences in personality traits. Figure 23.1 shows how the findings from Schmitt et al.'s

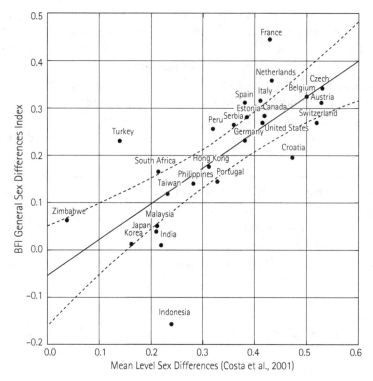

FIGURE 23.1 A scatterplot of the relationship between the mean sex differences in overall personality traits reported by Schmitt et al. (2008) and the mean sex differences reported by Costa et al. (2001) for the 25 countries sampled by both research teams. The dotted lines represent 95% confidence around the fitted linear regression line.

Source: Schmitt et al. (2008, p. 176).

study correlate with those from the study by Costa et al. (2001). Note in particular how both studies are in agreement that the greatest sex differences in personality are found predominantly in affluent Western countries, whereas less affluent non-Western countries have the fewest sex differences in personality.

Subsequent work by Schmitt (2015) involved measuring personality traits among respondents drawn from 26 different countries. It further reinforced the conclusion that the most extreme average sex differences were among respondents drawn from the most industrialized and affluent predominantly Western societies. Similar conclusions about affluent Western societies exhibiting the greatest sex differences have been reported not only for personality traits (McCrae & Terracciano, 2005; Schmitt et al., 2016) but also for depression, for which females typically surpass males (Hopcroft & Bradley, 2007; Hopcroft & McLaughlin, 2012).

In the case of academic achievement, most studies have found that females outperform males at least through adolescence (Ellis et al., 2008, pp. 278–279). A recent international study of more than 1 million adolescents was undertaken to determine if there were fewer tendencies for females to outperform males in predominantly Western egalitarian countries as opposed to countries in which equality of the sexes is generally discouraged. It found no significant differences in this regard (Stoet & Geary, 2015).

Overall, although Western attitudes toward sex equality have become more prevalent in recent decades, sex stereotypes and sex differences in ASDCBs (e.g., self-concepts and personality) have changed very little. Even more surprising, when Western industrial societies are compared to non-Western developing countries, sex differences in personality traits appear to be *more pronounced* in the former than in the latter. What in the world is going on? Perhaps theories of ASDCBs can shed light on these rather curious findings.

Part 4: Theories of ASDCBs

Ideas on why males and females seem to think and behave differently have been around for a long time. Proposals began to solidify enough to be identifiable as scientific theories much more recently. Basically, three theories with distinct properties can be identified.

Social Role Theory

The concept of *social roles* began to be used by social scientists in the 1940s. It refers to how human behavior often seems to be heavily influenced by the training and expectations one receives from others (e.g., parents, teachers, and other influential persons) within a particular culture as though people's behavior is being scripted by others (Merton, 1968; Parsons, 1942). This perspective began to take the form of a theory of sex differences in behavior in the 1960s (Rosenberg & Sutton-Smith, 1968; Tulkin, Muller, & Conn, 1969).

Social role theory (also sometimes called *sex role theory*) argues that all sex differences in behavior are learned through the socialization process. Basically, each individual learns what is culturally expected of men and women, and most then gradually conform to those particular norms depending on their own sex (Bussey & Bandura, 1999; Kessler & McKenna, 1978). To illustrate, one of the first things any expectant parent wants to know about his or her baby is whether it is a boy or a girl. As soon as one learns the answer, from birth onward, boys and girls are treated differently on average, and it is this differential treatment as well as a child's understanding of how he or she is *expected* to behave that cause average sex differences in behavior to develop throughout life (Eagly, 2013; Eagly & Wood, 1999; Eagly, Wood, & Diekman, 2000; Ridgeway & Correll, 2004).

Currently, among the most prominent proponents of social role theory are Eagly and Wood (1999; see also Eagly, 2013). They assert that were it not for learning and powerful socialization processes, males and females would be all but identical in their behavior. In their words, "extensive socialization is required to orient boys and girls to function differently" (Wood & Eagly, 2002, p. 705). Another proponent summarized social role theory as follows (Rogers, 2005): "Men are expected to be 'aggressive' and unemotional, women to be sensitive, intuitive, etc. From a very early age, they learn what is expected of them in terms of 'feminine' or 'masculine' personality, and this is heavily reinforced at puberty" (p. 11).

Social role theory reflects what has been termed a "blank slate" perspective because it assumes that males and females would behave the same if it were not for the societies in which they live having different expectations of what is "appropriate" behavior for males and females (Pinker, 2002, pp. 337–371). In other words, social role theorists "expect gender differences in personality to be smaller in cultures with more gender egalitarianism" (Schmitt et al., 2016, p. 1). It is worth keeping in mind that two surveys have both indicated that social role theory is by far the most popular theory for explaining sex differences in behavior, at least among sociologists (Horowitz, Yaworsky, & Kickham, 2014; Sanderson & Ellis, 1992).

Evolutionary Theory

Beginning in the 1970s, some social scientists began to move toward studying ASDCBs from an evolutionary perspective (Daly & Wilson, 1978; Simon, 1980). Since then, evolution-based proposals for explaining ASDCBs have expanded a great deal (Buss, 2012; Campbell, 2013; Geary, 2010; Hopcroft, 2016; Lippa, 2010; Mealey, 2000; Schmitt, 2015). Without denying the role of learning or culture, proponents of this perspective emphasize that biological and reproductive factors are even more important.

The main elements in all evolutionary explanations for ASDCBs can be summarized as follows: Biologically, the purpose of life is simply to produce more life, especially life resembling whatever organisms are currently living. In sexually reproducing species, two individuals are required to make new life: one male and one female. For males and females to attract one another, each must exhibit certain traits. In highly evolved species such as humans, the "right" combination of male and female traits for attracting the opposite sex includes behavior as well as physical characteristics.

To provide a simple illustration of the previously discussed line of reasoning, imagine that there are two groups of females in a human population. Group 1 prefers mating with males who control a continual supply of food and other resources and are willing to share them with their mates. Group 2 has no interest in males with resources, preferring instead males who appear to be young and attractive from a health standpoint. Which group of females will pass their genes on at the highest rate? Group 2 would have an advantage in the sense that young and health mates would be more likely to produce healthy offspring. However, Group 1 females would gravitate toward mates with resources to sustain them throughout each pregnancy. Especially given the lengthy gestation periods for each human pregnancy and the dependence that each offspring has on a stable supply of resources, under most circumstances, the females in Group 1 would probably out-reproduce those in Group 2.

Now pose the same question for two groups of males. Again assume that the males in Group 1 prefer females who control and share resources, whereas the males in Group 2 are primarily drawn to females who appear youthful and healthy. Keep in mind that because they do not gestate offspring, males have a much higher reproductive ceiling than do females. So which group of males would most likely have the most surviving offspring? By choosing females who control many resources, the Group 1 males would be drawn to women who are willing to spend considerable time working, which would probably limit the time these women would devote to gestating offspring. On the other hand, the Group 2 males who are most drawn to females who are relatively young and attractive would be able to pass their genes on at considerably higher rates, provided they (the males) are willing to devote time to resource provisioning.

The preceding evolutionary reasoning may seem almost too simple for its implications to be true in reality. However, notice how scenarios match evidence that males emphasize youthfulness and physical attractiveness more than females do when choosing mates, whereas most females are more interested in mating with males with the capacity to make a "decent living" (Conroy-Beam, Buss, Pham, & Shackelford, 2015; Zentner & Mitura, 2012). It is impossible to prove that these sex differences in human mate preferences are evolutionarily based, but the fact that there is virtually no society in which these mating patterns do not exist (Ellis et al., 2008, pp. 441–444; Shackelford, Schmitt, & Buss, 2005) is at least consistent with such an explanation.

Also, notice how the evolutionary arguments just presented can be extended to help explain some other well-documented sex differences:

1. Compared to females, males are more likely to choose jobs based on how much money they can earn (Ellis et al., 2008, pp. 462–463).
2. On average, among full-time workers, males work longer hours (Ellis et al., 2008, p. 782).
3. In every society ever studied, mothers spend more time caring for their children than do fathers (Ellis et al., 2008, pp. 651–652).
4. Throughout the world, males express stronger desires to have multiple sex partners than is the case for females (Ellis et al., 2008, pp. 435–437; Schmitt, 2003).

The overall point being made is that evolutionary reasoning can provide useful conceptual tools for making sense of quite a few apparently universal ASDCBs. Of course, social role theorists might explain these same sex differences by arguing that each one reflects a "cultural script" of what males and females should do. As discussed further in the following section, the main problem with the "cultural script" hypothesis is that it implies that very few, if any, universal ASDCBs should exist.

Evolutionary Neuroandrogenic Theory

It may be possible to strengthen conventional evolutionary theory, at least in terms of explaining ASDCBs, by combining it with evidence of how genes, hormones, and the brains of males and females differ. Biologically, the only things that survive indefinitely after an organism dies are the genes carried by its descendants. Within a given species, these genes come in two forms, one for males and the other for females. By and large, the collection of genes for males and for females are extremely similar. The main exception involves the so-called *sex chromosomes*, of which females carry two X chromosomes and males have just one X along with one Y chromosome.

In essence, female mammals (including humans) are the default sex, with males being just a variant on the female sex (Dennis, 2004; Woodson & Gorski, 2000). Genes on the Y chromosome serve to effectively switch the would-be female ovaries into becoming testes instead. Testes are special organs for producing a sex hormone known as *testosterone* along with other so-called *male sex hormones*, collectively known as *androgens*.

Hormones are biochemicals that are produced in one part of the body and then transferred to other parts of the body (usually via the blood system) where they have their primary effects. Although testosterone and other androgens are produced mainly in the male testes, small quantities are also produced in the female ovaries and in the adrenal glands of both sexes. Studies have shown that bodily exposure to androgens has many effects, including the promotion of muscle and bone tissue (Leonard et al., 2010), thereby explaining why males on average are stronger and taller than females (Ellis et al., 2008, pp. 15 and 30). However, it is the effects of androgens on the brain that are of greatest importance regarding ASDCBs.

Research has shown that androgens alter the brain in many ways, including the size of various parts of the brain, the biochemicals being released, and how the brain actually functions (Baron-Cohen, 2004; Kimura, 1992; McHenry, Carrier, Hull, & Kabbaj, 2014). These androgenic modifications occur both prenatally and postpubertally, with the prenatal effects of androgens being the most profound and irreversible (Auyeung, Lombardo, & Baron-Cohen, 2013; Baron-Cohen, 2004). As one would expect, many parts of male and female brains have been shown to differ on average, both structurally (Ellis et al., 2008, pp. 54–78) and functionally (Ellis et al., 2008, pp. 79–87).

To help explain universal ASDCBs, I have proposed a theory that can also be considered merely an extension of Darwinian evolutionary theory. Thus, it is called *evolutionary neuroandrogenic (ENA) theory* (Ellis, 2011a, 2011b). The theory stipulates that androgens have evolved as the main biochemicals responsible for masculinizing/defeminizing the brain of an otherwise female mammal. In other words, ENA theory asserts that androgens not only masculinized/defeminized the body as a whole (e.g., increased muscularity) but also masculinize/defeminize the brain specifically. Because the brain is the direct controller of both thought and behavior, ENA theory offers the following explanation for universal ASDCBs: By androgenizing the brain, natural selection has tailored male brains to exhibit thoughts and behavior that promote a *male reproductive strategy* and female brains to exhibit thoughts and behavior conducive to a *female reproductive strategy*. The nature of both strategies is the types of thinking and behavior that helps each sex pass on genes to future generations.

In more detailed terms, ENA theory asserts that androgens have evolved the ability to not only masculinize/defeminize the body as a whole (e.g., increased muscularity and bone density) but also masculinize/defeminize the brain, thereby impacting thought and behavior. The resulting sex differences in thought and behavior must serve both sexes' overall reproductive interests. More precisely, as a result of male brains being more heavily androgenized, they mainly produce masculine thoughts and behavior, most of which are part of an overall male reproductive strategy. Female brains, on the other hand, have evolved tendencies to retain feminine thoughts and behavior, which are part of a predominantly female reproductive strategy.

If the above reasoning is correct, one can make the following deductions: Most universal ASDCBs have evolved by natural selection and have been promoted by exposing the brains of males to high (male-typical) levels of androgens. This means that androgens are biochemicals naturally selected for modifying the "normal" female brain into a male brain.

It is worth adding that the nature of the evolved sex differences may not always be immediately apparent. For example, nearly all studies have found males on average to be more accurate than females when throwing objects such as balls or darts at targets (Ellis et al., 2008, p. 240). This ability may contribute little or nothing to male reproductive success in today's industrial societies. However, in the past, it is likely to have enhanced male hunting ability, which in turn allowed males to provide resources to mates who were gestating and breast-feeding their offspring. Of course, the average number of offspring they successfully rear would be the "reproductive payoff" for the better hunting ability of these males (and for the females who chose these males as mating partners).

ENA theory goes beyond conventional (Darwinian) evolutionary theory in the sense that it specifies *how* neurohormonal factors has been naturally selected so as to produce ASDCBs. This extra element in turn allows numerous testable hypotheses to be derived from ENA theory about ASDCBs that conventional evolutionary theory does not allow one to deduce.

To illustrate, consider the field of criminology. Many proposals have been made in recent years that evolutionary theory may help explain why males are more criminal than females, especially regarding serious property and violent offenses (Buss, 2012; Daly & Wilson, 1990; Duntley & Shackelford, 2008; Ellis, 2005; Roach & Pease, 2013). Most of these proposals hinge on the fact that males have a much higher reproductive ceiling than do females (i.e., a male can have many more offspring in a lifetime than can a female). Of course, for males to capitalize on their higher reproductive ceiling, they need to have numerous sex partners. But, as already noted, females generally prefer males with resource-procuring abilities. To meet expectations in this regard, males must usually compete with other males. Among the fastest ways to obtain resources and thereby to attract potential mates is for males to engage in thefts, burglaries, robberies, and embezzlements.

Additional criminal methods males can employ to acquire mating opportunities involves the use of physical force against prospective mates—that is, by committing rape or sexual assault (Ellis, 2005). Males can also effectively compete with rival males for resources and mating opportunities by assaulting or even murdering these rivals (Buss, 2012, Daly & Wilson, 1990).

The bottom line is that because males can reproduce much more prolifically than females, many males appear to have evolved several "dirty tricks" (that nearly all governments seek to suppress with the criminal justice system) to help pass their genes on to future generations. Of course, these evolutionary arguments are difficult to directly test. However, because ENA theory links its evolutionary arguments directly with arguments about the effects of androgens on the brain, it provides additional testable hypotheses about sex differences in offending. For example, if ENA theory is true, criminals should have brains that are more highly androgenized. In other words, although almost all males should have higher androgen levels than females, criminal males should have even higher androgen levels than males in general.

Recently, a colleague and I tested this line of reasoning using two separate samples, one from the United States (Hoskin & Ellis, 2015) and the other from both the United States and Malaysia (Ellis & Hoskin, 2015). In both studies, we provided respondents with a checklist of delinquent and criminal acts for them to self-report. To measure brain exposure to prenatal androgens, we used a measure known as the 2D:4D ratio. This measure simply involves the relative length of the second and fourth digits (usually on the right hand). Basically, the longer the fourth digit (ring finger) is compared to the second digit (pointing finger), the greater the exposure to prenatal testosterone and possibly other androgens (Manning, 2009).

Our findings were consistent with what ENA theory predicts: Respondents with the lowest 2D:4D ratios reported greater involvement in delinquency and crime than respondents with the highest ratios. We even tested the hypothesis separately by sex and found the same basic pattern: Both males and females with the lowest 2D:4D ratios self-reported more crime compared to their counterparts with relatively high 2D:4D ratios. This evidence, of course, does not by itself prove ENA theory because the theory basically makes the same predictions for all evolved traits that exhibit average differences between males and females (Ellis, 2011a, 2011b). Therefore, ENA theory provides a conceptual platform for theorizing about all manner of ASDCBs with more ways of being disproven than is true for conventional evolutionary theory.

PART 5: THEORETICALLY EXPLAINING SOCIETAL AND TEMPORAL VARIATIONS IN ASDCBs

The last issue to be covered in this chapter involves assessing each of the three theories just identified—social role theory, conventional evolutionary theory, and ENA theory—regarding their abilities to explain findings reviewed in Parts 1–3. In other words, which of these three theories can account for findings about the apparently universal ASDCBs documented so far?

Regarding Part 1, both of the evolutionary theories have an advantage over the social role theory. This is because social role theory assumes that cultural learning is largely responsible for ASDCBs. If this were true, one would not expect to find very many, if any, universal ASDCBs. To give just a few examples, why would alcoholism and interests in engineering be more common in men in all known societies if these sex differences are the result of culturally based learning? Similarly, one should be able to find societies in which boys express greater liking of school and seek to be more cooperative with others compared to females, but as of yet, such sex differences have failed to materialize in any empirical study (Ellis, 2011a).

In the case of the two evolutionary theories, both can explain the findings reviewed in Part 1 by simply noting that evolutionary forces have operated on human populations in essentially the same way for thousands of years. Therefore, if most ASDCBs are either directly or indirectly the result of natural selection, one would expect to find many universal ASDCBs. It is worth mentioning that ENA theory goes on to predict that the vast majority of universal ASDCBs will be associated with differential brain exposure to androgens, an implication that largely remains untested.

In the case of the findings reported in Part 2, the picture is more mixed in terms of judging the merits of the three theories. Recall that the main conclusions drawn from the studies reviewed in Part 2 pertained to trends in the United States. These trends were as follows:

1. Attitudes have become more accepting of equality between the sexes in recent decades.
2. Sex stereotypes have remained more or less stable during the past few decades.
3. Self-perceptions by men and women in terms of their being masculine, feminine, or somewhere in between have changed very little in recent decades.

Because social role theory considers culturally based learning to be responsible for all ASDCBs, it would probably explain attitudes toward sex equality also in terms of cultural learning. Thus, as anti-discrimination laws began to be passes in the United States especially in the 1960s, social role theorists would expect public opinion to shift away from sex discrimination, which it certainly has. Both of the evolutionary theories, however, are essentially silent to the possibility of attitudinal changes regarding sex equality, so they are weaker than social role theory in this regard.

Regarding the apparent stability of sex stereotypes and self-perceptions concerning people's feelings of masculinity/femininity, both evolutionary theories would probably have an edge over social role theory. This is because they envision most ASDCBs as having evolved over thousands of years, making them unlikely to change significantly over one or two generations.

Part 3 indicated that sex differences in personality traits were more pronounced in most Western industrial societies than in most non-Western developing countries. This poses a serious challenge to all three theories of ASDCBs. Social role theorists would be hard-pressed to explain why societies in which the greatest efforts have been made toward sex equality would end up exhibiting the most sex inequality, at least regarding personality. In the case of the two evolutionary theories, they are largely silent regarding any cross-country comparisons of sex differences in personality.

Because ENA theory has elements beyond what is found in conventional evolutionary theory, it might be possible for researchers to compare citizens from Western and non-Western societies in terms of average androgen levels. If sex differences in androgen levels are higher in countries with the greatest sex differences in personality, it could begin to provide a theoretical basis for explaining Western/non-Western patterns in this regard. Along these lines, a study by Manning, Fink, and Trivers (2014) compared countries in terms of their citizens' average prenatal androgen exposure and the percentage of elected officials who were females and the percentage of the paid workforce who were females. The study concluded that countries in which female exposure to prenatal testosterone (as indicated by 2D:4D ratios) was high and in which male exposure was low had the highest proportions of females in elective offices and in the labor force. This study seems relevant to ASDCB determination. However, notice that it implies that citizens of Western societies have *fewer* average sex differences in exposure to androgens than do citizens of non-Western societies. The studies summarized in Part 3 by Costa et al. (2001) and Schmitt et al. (2008), on the other hand, lead one to conclude that Western societies have *greater* average sex differences in personality than do non-Western societies. These seeming inconsistencies call for more empirical scrutiny.

Conclusion

This chapter was divided into five parts. Part 1 documented growing evidence of numerous universal ASDCBs (average sex differences in cognition and behavior). In particular, work by colleagues and myself led us to tentatively identify 65 such traits (Ellis, 2011a, 2011b; Ellis et al., 2008).

In Part 2, studies pertaining to three questions about ASDCBs were explored. First, have people's attitudes toward sex equality changed, and if so, in what direction? The answer is that these attitudes have changed. At least in the United States, acceptance of women being educated and allowed to work in jobs alongside men has grown considerably since the 1970s (Thornton & Young-DeMarco, 2001).

Second, have sex stereotypes changed, and if so, how? The answer appears to be that sex stereotypes have changed very little during the past few decades at least in the United States. Specifically, people's beliefs about how males and females differ in terms of basic interests, personality, and behaviors appear to have remained virtually the same in the 1990s as they were in the 1970s (Lueptow, 2005; Lueptow et al., 2001).

Third, have there been changes in men's and women's self-perceptions regarding their masculinity/femininity? In other words, do the sexes today think of themselves as just masculine, feminine, or somewhere in between, as was true in their parent's generation? The evidence suggests that the answer is that little has changed, with the possible exception of contemporary women having somewhat more feminine interests than those sampled in the 1970s (Twenge, 1997).

The issue addressed in Part 3 had to do with making cross-cultural comparisons regarding sex differences in personality. Surprisingly, the evidence suggests that *greater* sex differences exist in most Western industrialized societies than in most non-Western developing societies (Costa et al., 2001; Hopcroft & Bradley, 2007; Hopcroft & McLaughlin 2012; Schmitt et al., 2016). This finding seems counterintuitive because considerably more effort has been made in most Western societies to encourage sex equality than has been made in most non-Western societies.

Part 4 described the three theories that have been proposed for explaining ASDCBs. The oldest one to be proposed is social role theory (Eagly & Wood, 1999). This theory asserts that males and females would be virtually identical in how they think and behave if it were not for sex differences in sociocultural training and expectations (Eagly et al., 2000). Surveys among sociologists indicate that it remains the most popular theory among social scientists (Horowitz et al., 2014; Sanderson & Ellis, 1992).

Beginning in approximately the 1970s, Darwin's theory of evolution began to be specifically applied to the study of human ASDCBs (Hrdy, 1981; Wilson & Daly, 1978). Since then, numerous others have advocated an evolutionary approach to the study of ASDCBs (Archer, 1996; Geary, 2010; Hopcroft, 2016; Mealey, 2000). An evolutionary perspective explains why males and females think and behave differently based on how the sexes differ in their contributions to the reproductive process. In other words, the rate at which humans leave descendants (and therefore their genes) in future generations depends heavily on males and females thinking and behaving differently. Thus, whether operating through differential learning or some biological process, the most reproductively successful males will exhibit thought and behavior patterns than on average differ from those of the most reproductively successful females.

I have proposed a version of evolutionary theory that specifically incorporates brain and hormonal concepts (Ellis, 2006, 2011a, 2011b). This theory, called evolutionary neuroandrogenic (ENA) theory, is specifically designed to explain average sex differences in cognition and behavior. According to this theory, all mammals (including humans) are essentially females. However, a special chromosome has evolved that carries genes for making roughly half of these would-be females into males instead. In essence, these genes operate by causing the would-be female ovaries to develop into testes, special organs for producing large quantities of a masculinizing hormone called testosterone (along with other male hormones, called androgens). Androgens affect thought and behavior by infiltrating the brain both prenatally and following puberty. As a result of greater androgen exposure, males on average end up thinking and behaving in ways that serve their reproductive interests, whereas low androgen exposure in females causes them to think and behave in ways that generally contribute to their reproductive interests.

Finally, Part 5 addresses the question of how well the three theories described in Part 4 can shed light on the evidence summarized in Parts 1–3. Social role theory has difficulty explaining why there are numerous universal ASDCBs as discussed in Part 1. It also predicts that ASDCBs would weaken as societies become more sex egalitarian, which Parts 2 and 3 indicate have not happened.

Because evolutionary theory assumes that most ASDCBs have been naturally (or sexually) selected, it is able to account for why large numbers of ASDCBs exist, as indicated in Part 1. Furthermore, the evidence cited in Part 2 that people's stereotypes about sex differences and their self-concepts in terms of masculinity/femininity have changed very little in recent decades is also understandable in an evolutionary context. ENA theory, as an extended version of evolutionary theory, goes on to hypothesize that androgenic effects on the brain explain *how* ASDCBs have evolved. It remains to be seen if most ASDCBs are the result of neuroandrogenic factors, but at least one recent test of this hypothesis regarding sex differences in mate preferences provided moderate support (Ellis & Ratnasingam, 2015).

The evidence that sex differences in personality traits appear to be more pronounced in Western industrial societies than in most non-Western developing societies (Part 4) presents a conundrum for all three theories of ASDCBs. It is especially devastating to social role theory, which is based on the assumption that gender differences would be least prevalent in cultures that foster the greatest degree of "gender equality" (Schmitt et al., 2016). The fact that most sociologists subscribe to this theory more than any other (Horowitz et al., 2014; Sanderson & Ellis, 1992) suggests that a sea change is in the offering for how social scientists think about cognitive and behavioral sex differences.

There seems to be only a few ways to explain why the most sex egalitarian societies have the greatest degree of sex differences in terms of personality traits. One possibility is that more of the genes responsible for sex differences in cognitive and behavioral traits have accumulated in Western populations than in non-Western populations. If so, one would be likely to find that sex differences in physical traits would also be more prevalent in Western populations, a possibility for which I could find no evidence.

Another possibility is that by being more lenient in allowing its citizens to express themselves in sex-related terms, males in Western cultures may end up thinking and behaving in more male-typical ways, and females in more female-typical ways, than is typical of non-Western cultures. If this second line of reasoning is true, it would turn traditional sex-role theorizing on its head. In other words, social scientists who argue that one should not stereotype or try to influence people's behavior according to "conventional sex roles" because it contributes to sex inequality are mistaken. To the contrary, the effects of culturally prescribed sex roles would actually be *inhibiting* the expression of sex differences in thought and behavior. Thus, the more equitably males and females are treated by their sociocultural surroundings, the more different men and women will become.

In closing, I offer a proposal for social scientists to consider and test during the ensuing years. It is partly based on evidence that arranged marriages, particularly among close relatives (usually first cousins), are widespread both historically and even today in most developing countries (Desai & Andrist, 2010; Jurdi & Saxena, 2003). Contemporary developed countries appear to be among the only cultures in which arranged consanguineal marriages are rare (Hatfield, Rapson, & Martel, 2007).

I propose that one of the effects of freely marrying individuals from large pools of nonrelatives is that this cultural practice allows the expression of genes for traits to be maximized. This includes genes responsible for sexually dimorphic cognitive and behavioral traits. If so, it is in societies in which out-marrying is most common—that is, primarily Western industrial countries—that one will find the expression of genes for masculine traits in males and feminine traits in females to be the greatest.

Overall, it is clear that research is still needed to identify ASDCBs and to understand the factors responsible for them and for why they appear to be more pronounced in some cultures than in others. Nevertheless, the accumulation of ASDCB research so far is yielding tantalizing surprises that could fundamentally challenge some of sociology's more cherished assumptions.

ACKNOWLEDGMENTS

The comments provided by Rosemary L. Hopcroft, Anthony Hoskin, Malini Ratnasingam, and David P. Schmitt on drafts of this manuscript are greatly appreciated.

REFERENCES

Archer, J. (1996). Sex differences in social behavior: Are the social role and evolutionary explanations compatible? *American Psychologist*, 51, 909–917.

Auyeung, B., Lombardo, M. V., & Baron-Cohen, S. (2013). Prenatal and postnatal hormone effects on the human brain and cognition. *European Journal of Physiology*, 465, 557–571.

Averett, S. L., & Burton, M. L. (1996). College attendance and the college wage premium: Differences by gender. *Economics of Education Review*, 15, 37–49.

Baron-Cohen, S. (2004). *Essential difference: Male and female brains and the truth about autism*. New York, NY: Basic Books.

Buchmann, C., & DiPrete, T. A. (2006). The growing female advantage in college completion: The role of family background and academic achievement. *American Sociological Review*, 71(4), 515–541.

Buss, D. M. (2012). The evolutionary psychology of crime. *Journal of Theoretical and Philosophical Criminology*, 1, 90–98.

Bussey, K., & Bandura, A. (1999). Social cognitive theory of gender development and differentiation. *Psychological Review*, 106, 676–713.

Campbell, A. (2013). *A mind of her own: The evolutionary psychology of women*. New York, NY: Oxford University Press.

Cho, D. (2007). The role of high school performance in explaining women's rising college enrollment. *Economics of Education Review*, 26, 450–462.

Conroy-Beam, D., Buss, D. M., Pham, M. N., & Shackelford, T. K. (2015). How sexually dimorphic are human mate preferences? *Personality and Social Psychology Bulletin*, 41(8), 1082–1093.

Costa, P., Jr., Terracciano, A., & McCrae, R. R. (2001). Gender differences in personality traits across cultures: Robust and surprising findings. *Journal of Personality and Social Psychology*, 81, 322–331.

Daly, M., & Wilson, M. (1978). *Sex, evolution and behavior*. North Scituate, MA: Duxbury.

Daly, M., & Wilson, M. (1990). Killing the competition. *Human Nature*, 1, 81–107.

Dennis, C. (2004). Brain development: The most important sexual organ. *Nature, 427*, 390–392.

Desai, S., & Andrist, L. (2010). Gender scripts and age at marriage in India. *Demography, 47*, 667–687.

Duntley, J. D., & Shackelford, T. K. (2008). Darwinian foundations of crime and law. *Aggression and Violent Behavior, 13*, 373–382.

Durand, J. D. (2015). *The labor force in economic development: A comparison of international census data, 1946–1966*. Princeton, NJ: Princeton University Press.

Eagly, A. H. (2013). *Sex differences in social behavior: A social-role interpretation*. New York, NY: Psychology Press.

Eagly, A. H., & Wood, W. (1999). The origins of sex differences in human behavior: Evolved dispositions versus social roles. *American Psychologist, 54*, 408–423.

Eagly, A. H., Wood, W., & Diekman, A. B. (2000). Social role theory of sex differences and similarities: A current appraisal. In T. Eckes & H. M. Trautner (Eds.), *The developmental social psychology of gender* (pp. 123–174). Mahwah, NJ: Erlbaum.

Ellis, L. (2005). A theory explaining biological correlates of criminality. *European Journal of Criminology, 2*, 287–315.

Ellis, L. (2011a). Identifying and explaining apparent universal sex differences in cognition and behavior. *Personality and Individual Differences, 51*, 552–561.

Ellis, L. (2011b). Evolutionary neuroandrogenic theory and universal gender differences in cognition and behavior. *Sex Roles, 64*, 707–722.

Ellis, L., Hershberger, S. L., Field, E., Wersinger, S., Pellis, S., Geary, D. C., . . . Karadi, K. (2008). *Sex differences: Summarizing more than a century of scientific research*. New York, NY: Psychology Press.

Ellis, L., & Hoskin, A. W. (2015). The evolutionary neuroandrogenic theory of criminal behavior expanded. *Aggression and Violent Behavior, 24*, 61–74.

Ellis, L. & Ratnasingam, M. (2015). Naturally selected mate preferences appear to be androgen-influenced: Evidence from two cultures. *Evolutionary Psychological Science, 1*, 103–122.

Feingold, A. (1994). Gender differences in personality: A meta-analysis. *Psychological Bulletin, 116*, 429–456.

Geary, D. C. (2010). *Male, female: The evolution of human sex differences*. Washington, DC: American Psychological Association.

Hargreaves, J. (2002). *Sporting females: Critical issues in the history and sociology of women's sport*. New York, NY: Routledge.

Hatfield, E., Rapson, R. L., & Martel, L. D. (2007). Passionate love and sexual desire. In S. Kitayama & D. Cohen (Eds.), *Handbook of cultural psychology* (pp. 760–779). New York, NY: Guilford.

Hoffman, R. M., & Borders, L. D. (2001). Twenty-five years after the Bem Sex-Role Inventory: A reassessment and new issues regarding classification variability. *Measurement and Evaluation in Counseling and Development, 34*, 39–55.

Hopcroft, R. L. (2016). *Evolution and gender: Why it matters for contemporary life*. New York, NY: Routledge.

Hopcroft, R. L., & Bradley, D. B. (2007). The sex difference in depression across 29 countries. *Social Forces, 85*, 1483–1507.

Hopcroft, R. L., & McLaughlin, J. (2012). Why is the sex gap in feelings of depression wider in high gender equity countries? The effect of children on the psychological well-being of men and women. *Social Science Research, 41*, 501–513.

Horowitz, M., Yaworsky, W., & Kickham, K. (2014). Whither the blank slate? A report on the reception of evolutionary biological ideas among sociological theorists. *Sociological Spectrum*, 34, 489–509.

Hoskin, A. W., & Ellis, L. (2015). Fetal testosterone and criminality: Test of evolutionary neuroandrogenic theory. *Criminology*, 53, 54–73.

Hrdy, S. (1981). *The woman who never evolved*. Cambridge, MA: Harvard University Press.

Jurdi, R., & Saxena, P. C. (2003). The prevalence and correlates of consanguineous marriages in Yemen: Similarities and contrasts with other Arab countries. *Journal of Biosocial Science*, 35, 1–13.

Kessler, S. J., & McKenna, W. (1978). *Gender: An ethnomethodological approach*. Chicago, IL: University of Chicago Press.

Kimura, D. (1992). Sex differences in the brain. *Scientific American*, 267(3), 118–125.

Klein, S. S., Richardson, B., Grayson, D. A., Fox, L. H., Kramarae, C., Pollard, D. S., & Dwyer, C. A. (2014). *Handbook for achieving gender equity through education*. London, UK: Routledge.

Leonard, M. B., Elmi, A., Mostoufi-Moab, S., Shults, J., Burnham, J. M., Thayu, M., . . . Zemel, B. S. (2010). Effects of sex, race, and puberty on cortical bone and the functional muscle bone unit in children, adolescents, and young adults. *Journal of Clinical Endocrinology & Metabolism*, 95, 1681–1689.

Lippa, R. A. (2010). Gender differences in personality and interests: When, where, and why? *Social and Personality Psychology Compass*, 4, 1098–1110.

Lueptow, L. B. (2005). Increasing differentiation of women and men: Gender trait analysis: 1974–1997. *Psychological Reports*, 97, 277–287.

Lueptow, L. B., Garovich-Szabo, L., & Lueptow, M. B. (2001). Social change and the persistence of sex typing: 1974–1997. *Social Forces*, 80, 1–36.

Maccoby, E. E., & Jacklin, C. N. (1974). *The psychology of sex differences: Volume 1*. Stanford, CA: Stanford University Press.

Manning, J. T. (2009). *The finger ratio*. London, UK: Faber & Faber.

Manning, J. T., Fink, B., & Trivers, R. (2014). Digit ratio (2D:4D) and gender inequalities across nations. *Evolutionary Psychology*, 12(4), 757–768.

McCrae, R. R., & Terracciano, A. (2005). Personality profiles of cultures: Aggregate personality traits. *Journal of Personality and Social Psychology*, 89, 407–425.

McHenry, J., Carrier, N., Hull, E., & Kabbaj, M. (2014). Sex differences in anxiety and depression: Role of testosterone. *Frontiers in Neuroendocrinology*, 35, 42–57.

Mead, M. (1963). *Sex and temperament in three primitive societies*. New York, NY: Morrow.

Mealey, L. (2000). *Sex differences: Developmental and evolutionary strategies*. New York, NY: Academic Press.

Merton, R. K. (1968). Patterns of influence: Local and cosmopolitan influentials. In R. K. Merton (Ed.), *Social theory and social structure* (pp. 441–474). New York, NY: Free Press.

Milner, A. N., & Braddock, J. H., II. (2016). *Sex segregation in sports: Why separate is not equal*. New York, NY: ABC-CLIO.

Parsons, T. (1942). Age and sex in the social structure of the United States. *American Sociological Review*, 7, 604–616.

Pinker, S. (2002). *The blank slate: The modern denial of human nature*. New York, NY: Viking.

Ramirez, F. O., Soysal, Y., & Shanahan, S. (1997). The changing logic of political citizenship: Cross-national acquisition of women's suffrage rights, 1890 to 1990. *American Sociological Review*, 62, 735–745.

Ridgeway, C. L., & Correll, S. J. (2004). Unpacking the gender system: A theoretical perspective on gender beliefs and social relations. *Gender & Society, 18*, 510–531.

Roach, J., & Pease, K. (2013). *Evolution and crime.* London, UK: Routledge.

Rogers, B. (2005). *The domestication of women: Discrimination in developing societies.* London, UK: Routledge.

Rosenberg, B., & Sutton-Smith, B. (1968). Family interaction effects on masculinity–femininity. *Journal of Personality and Social Psychology, 8*, 117–120.

Rossilli, M. (2000). *Gender policies in the European Union.* New York, NY: Lang.

Sanderson, S. K., & Ellis, L. (1992). Theoretical and political perspectives of American sociologists in the 1990s. *American Sociologist, 23*, 26–42.

Schmitt, D. P. (2003). Universal sex differences in the desire for sexual variety: Tests from 52 nations, 6 continents, and 13 islands. *Journal of Personality and Social Psychology, 83*, 85–104.

Schmitt, D. P. (2015). The evolution of culturally-variable sex differences: Men and women are not always different, but when they are . . . it appears not to result from patriarchy or sex role socialization. In V. A. Weekes-Shackelford & T. K. Shackelford (Eds.), *The evolution of sexuality* (pp. 221–256). New York, NY: Springer.

Schmitt, D. P., Long, A. E., McPhearson, A., O'Brien, K., Remmert, B., & Shah, S. H. (2016). Personality and gender differences in global perspective. *International Journal of Psychology* [Epub ahead of print]. doi:10.1002/ijop.12265

Schmitt, D. P., Realo, A., Voracek, M., & Allik, J. (2008). Why can't a man be more like a woman? Sex differences in Big Five personality traits across 55 cultures. *Journal of Personality and Social Psychology, 94*, 168–182.

Shackelford, T. K., Schmitt, D. P., & Buss, D. M. (2005). Universal dimensions of human mate preferences. *Personality and Individual Differences, 39*, 447–458.

Simon, H. A. (1980). The behavioral and social sciences. *Science, 209*, 72–78.

Stoet, G., & Geary, D. C. (2015). Sex differences in academic achievement are not related to political, economic, or social equality. *Intelligence, 48*, 137–151.

Thornton, A., & Young-DeMarco, L. (2001). Four decades of trends in attitudes toward family issues in the United States: The 1960s through the 1990s. *Journal of Marriage and Family, 63*, 1009–1037.

Tulkin, S. R., Muller, J. P., & Conn, L. K. (1969). Need for approval and popularity: Sex differences in elementary school students. *Journal of Consulting and Clinical Psychology, 33*, 35–39.

Twenge, J. M. (1997). Changes in masculine and feminine traits over time: A meta-analysis. *Sex Roles, 36*, 305–325.

Wood, W., & Eagly, A. H. (2002). A cross-cultural analysis of the behavior of women and men: Implications for the origins of sex differences. *Psychological Bulletin, 128*, 699–727.

Woodson, J. C., & Gorski, R. A. (2000). Structural sex differences in the mammalian brain: Reconsidering the male/female dichotomy. In A. Malsumoto (Ed.), *Sexual differentiation of the brain* (pp. 229–239). Boca Raton, FL: CRC Press.

Zentner, M., & Mitura, K. (2012). Stepping out of the caveman's shadow: Nations' gender gap predicts degree of sex differentiation in mate preferences. *Psychological Science, 23*, 1176–1185.

CHAPTER 24

....

EVOLUTIONARY THEORY AND CRIMINOLOGY

....

ANTHONY WALSH AND CODY JORGENSEN

INTRODUCTION: CRIMINOLOGY NEEDS AN ORGANIZING PRINCIPLE

IN this chapter, we (a) demonstrate the relevance of evolutionary theory to criminology, (b) discuss the evolutionary origins of both prosocial and antisocial traits, and (c) show that evolutionary theory is invaluable to understanding two key issues that have been impervious to solution using the standard social science model—the sex ratio in criminal offending and the age–crime curve.

Evolutionary criminology is part of a broader biosocial approach to criminology that includes genetics and neurobiology in addition to evolutionary theory (Walsh & Beaver, 2009). Whereas genetic and neurobiological approaches are finding relatively widespread acceptance (Cooper, Walsh, & Ellis, 2010), with many books devoted to them, the evolutionary approach to criminology is barely acknowledged, currently with only two books devoted exclusively to it (Durrant & Ward, 2015; Roach & Pease, 2013). This is unfortunate because evolutionary theory can serve as a meta-theory for criminology and all other social sciences because of "its potential to tie together the forest of hypotheses about human behavior now out there" (de Waal, 2002, p. 187). Tooby and Cosmides (2005) agree, arguing that evolutionary psychology can coherently integrate all the human sciences:

> Evolutionary psychology is the long-forestalled scientific attempt to assemble out of the disjointed, fragmentary, and mutually contradictory human disciplines a single, logically integrated research framework for the psychological, social, and behavioral sciences—a framework that not only incorporates the evolutionary sciences on a full and equal basis, but that systematically works out all of the revisions in existing belief and research practice that such a synthesis requires. The long-term scientific goal

toward which evolutionary psychologists are working is the mapping of our universal human nature. (p. 5)

Criminology is certainly in need of an organizing principle to bundle its stew of contradictory theories into a relatively orderly package. Cooper and colleagues' (2010) study asking criminologists to identify the theory they believed accounted for the most variance in serious criminal behavior identified no less than 24 (and there are many others), with self-identified political ideology (conservative, moderate, liberal, and radical) being far the best predictor of the theories they chose. We do not claim that accepting an evolutionary approach (one not limited only to evolutionary psychology) will lead to an explosion of new criminological evidence as did, for example, the acceptance of atomic theory for chemistry in the 19th century (Knight, 1992). Rather, evolutionary analyses will add layers of new understanding to what we already know and will open up avenues to explore novel vistas.

Evolutionary criminology utilizes a Darwinian framework to animate its research agenda. Its vocabulary contains many biological terms, but it is "environmentally friendly" because it recognizes that pressures from the social environment formed a good part of the human genome. Evolutionary explanations of behavior differ from genetic explanations: Geneticists focus on differences among people and ask proximate-level "how" questions, whereas evolutionists focus on human similarities and ask ultimate-level "why" questions. For instance, a proximal explanation for sex difference in aggression may appeal to different testosterone levels, whereas evolutionary scientists would explore the adaptive rational for why sex differences in testosterone levels exist in the first place. Because evolved adaptations apply to all members of a species, unlike geneticists, evolutionary criminologists search for *environmental* sources of variation in criminal behavior. However, they readily acknowledge variation in human traits distributed around adaptive means, but their concern is central tendency rather than variation.

Many criminologists have an aversion to evolutionary thinking because it engages their naive fear of biology. Cooper et al. (2010) found that the modal number of biology classes taken by the 770 criminologists they surveyed was zero. This apparently reflects a belief that human behavior can be understood by appealing only to the environmental portion of the biosocial whole and that culture puts humans above biology. Such an attitude is scientifically indefensible. Humans are certainly unique in many ways, but so is every other animal species in one way or another. The attitude that humans are so special that they are set above nature and require a different set of ontological principles to understand their behavior delays progress in the human sciences. Human nature is the sum of human adaptations forged by the mechanisms of evolution—natural selection, sexual selection, mutation, genetic drift, and gene flow. An understanding of the adaptive significance of human nature's component parts forged by these processes should be fundamental to all branches of human science; models of human behavior without such information are incomplete.

Criminologists may also discount evolutionary theory because it is not shy about revealing the "dark" side of human nature, and in this sense it is "politically incorrect." It talks about reproductive success as the ultimate goal of all sexually reproducing animals and lays bare the aggression, deceptiveness, and egoism that have evolved as aids in pursuing it (mating effort). But other more positive human characteristics, such as altruism, nurturance, and empathy, have also evolved because they equipped us with parental skills (parenting effort) and valuable social skills as well. In *The Descent of Man*, Charles Darwin wrote about cooperation three times more often than he wrote about competition (Barrett, 2016; Levine, 2006). But it is negative traits that most interest criminologists, whose stock in trade is vice, not virtue.

EVOLUTION AND BEHAVIOR

We can think of the difference between mainstream criminology and evolutionary criminology as analogous to the difference between geography and geology. Geography *describes* the shape and location of the land (topography) as it presently exists, whereas geology looks beneath the surface to *explain* the processes that shaped it (plate tectonics and so forth). Evolution has likewise shaped the behavior and psychology of humans in adaptive (purpose-serving) ways, so biosocial criminologists hold it evident that it is crucial to look below the surface of behavior. Social scientists acknowledge that human anatomical and physiological features were selected over alternate designs because it best served some function that assisted the proliferation of genes underlying those features, and they are thus geologists of the body. However, most social scientists would probably dismiss the idea that behavior is also the product of the same evolutionary processes, and they are thus content to be geographers of the mind.

We are not disparaging geography while endorsing geology; there is much overlap in the two disciplines. Geology focuses on the physical features of the earth and is more closely aligned with physics. Geography has a broader perspective (What is the social, political, and economic impact of a specific environmental policy?), combines the natural and social sciences, and is more closely aligned with biology. Geography departments offer courses in evolutionary geography—how geography has shaped things such as human culture. In this sense, we would very much like to see criminologists become "geographers of the mind."

Commenting on mainstream social science's refusal to examine the adaptive significance of human behavior, Kenrick and Simpson (1997) state that "to study any animal species while refusing to consider the evolved adaptive significance of their behavior would be considered pure folly . . . unless the species in question is *Homo sapiens*" (p. 1). Alcock (2001) makes a similar point: "To say that human behavior and our other attributes cannot be analyzed in evolutionary terms requires the acceptance of a genuinely bizarre position, namely, that we alone among animal species have somehow managed to achieve independence from our evolutionary history" (p. 223). In addition, Plomin, DeFries, Craig, and McGuffin (2003) assert that "the behavioral genomic level of analysis may be the most appropriate level of understanding for evolution because the functioning of the whole organism drives evolution. That is, behavior is often the cutting edge of natural selection" (p. 533). Without an evolutionary under-standing, there is no scientific way to determine how a particular behavioral trait might have served the goal of enhancing survival and/or reproductive success over the course of time and how it can be coopted to serve other purposes, including criminal purposes (Durrant & Ward, 2012).

Some social scientists might take the position that although the human behavioral repertoire must have been designed by natural selection, evolved behaviors lost their relevance once we developed culture: "The beginning of mankind's psychosocial devel-opment represents the end of biological evolution" (Ruffie, 1986, p. 297). Ruffie does not specify what environmental pressures resulting from our "psychosocial development" might have led to the elimination of alleles underlying evolved behavioral traits that have supposedly been rendered irrelevant. Unless evolved traits become detrimental to survival and reproductive success, the genes underlying them will remain in the human gene pool. This does not mean that evolutionary criminologists consider culture unim-portant in explaining human behavior, although they do not view it as a realm decou-pled from biology. Evolutionists simply ask us to remember that "psychology underlies culture and society, and biological evolution underlies psychology" (Barkow, 1992, p. 635). It is true that the fine nuances of life are edited out as we move from proximate-level to ultimate-level explanations, but ultimate-level explanations complement proxi-mate explanations; they do not compete with them.

Contrary to Ruffie's (1986) puzzling contention that culture ended biological evo-lution, culture actually gave it a gigantic boost. Sophisticated gene technology has revealed that the rate of genomic change has been approximately 100 times greater dur-ing the past 40,000 years than it was during most of the Pleistocene due largely to the greater challenges posed by living in ever larger social groups: "The rapid cultural evo-lution during the Late Pleistocene created vastly more opportunities for further genetic changes, not fewer, as new avenues emerged for communication, social interaction, and creativity" (Hawks, Wang, Cochran, Harpending, & Moyzis, 2007, p. 20757).

Culture drives selection not only for psychological and behavioral traits but also for morphological changes. A number of studies of hominid crania dating as far back as 1.9 million years show more robust increases in cranial capacity in areas with greater population density and in colder and most northerly areas of the world in which food procurement was most problematic (Ash & Gallup, 2007; Kanazawa, 2008). Bailey and Geary (2009) found that latitude was strongly related to cranial capacity ($r = .61$), but population density was more strongly related ($r = .79$), and concluded that the burden of evolutionary selection has moved from "climactic and ecological to social" (p. 77). In many ways, the human brain is an artifact of culture because culturally created environ-ments have influenced both the anatomy and the physiology of the human brain above and beyond the influences posed by the challenges of the physical environment (Mithen & Parsons, 2008). Even today, new genetic variations affecting the brain's structure and function have been discovered as it continues to evolve in response to new ecological and social conditions (Evans et al., 2005; Mekel-Bobrove et al., 2005; Zhang, Landback, Vibranovski, & Long, 2011).

It must be stressed that we are adapted to seek the immediate means of achieving specific goals, not ultimate ends. As Daly and Wilson (1988) state, "Fitness consequences are invoked not as goals in themselves, but rather to explain why certain goals have come to control behavior at all, and why they are calibrated in one particular way rather than another" (p. 7). Humans are designed to satisfy proximate goals, which is why we use the phrase *adaptation executors* (acting in ways that would have maximized fitness in ancestral environments but not necessarily today) rather than *fitness maximizers* to refer to the evolved behavioral goals of modern humans.

When we have sex, for instance, we seek the pleasurable means by which reproductive success may be achieved, not reproductive success per se. In pre-contraceptive times, there was a tighter fit between means of satisfying proximate goals (sexual pleasure) and means of satisfying ultimate evolutionary goals (reproduction). Similarly, parents nurture and love their children because ancestral parents who did so saw more of them grow to reproductive age and pass on the genes underlying the traits than did parents practicing less solicitude. The neurohormonal substrates of nurturing behavior are adaptations because they solved a recurring adaptive problem—the survival of offspring. Parents who neglected or abused their children compromised their viability and thus the probability of their genes being represented in future generations. The love and nurturance of offspring increase the probability that parental genes will survive across the generations, but in no sense can this distal consequence be construed as parents' proximal motivation for lavishing love and care on their children.

THE EVOLUTION OF CRIMINAL TRAITS

The probability of survival and reproductive success of individuals increases in proportion to the degree to which they are able to harmoniously adjust themselves to their fellow humans and to their environment by developing appropriate approach–avoidance behaviors. But as the classic (and evolutionary) view of human nature has it, humans are designed to maximize their pleasure and to minimize their pain. This design feature of human nature can disrupt relationships with others when we place immediate concerns for gratification above the maintenance of social harmony and seek "money without work, sex without courtship, and revenge without court delays," to use Gottfredson and Hirschi's (1990, p. 89) words. Seeking needs and wants this way is what we call criminal. The traits that lead people down such dark roads are not traits that criminals possess and the rest of us lack; they are part of a universal human repertoire (wouldn't we all like "money without work," etc.?). We are all at risk for crossing the line from pro- to antisocial behavior given adequate provocation; it is simply that criminals routinely cross the threshold at lower levels of instigation. Criminals discount the delicate balance of the approach–avoidance imperative for a variety of reasons, such as being low on self-control, empathy, and fear and/or being high on aggression, callousness, and lust.

Criminal behavior is normal behavior engaged in by normal individuals. If this is so, the potential for it is in us all, and it must have conferred some evolutionary advantage. It is the traits underlying criminal behavior, not the specifics of criminal behavior (or of any other social behavior for that matter), that are the alleged adaptations. These traits are typically used illegitimately by individuals who, for whatever reason, cannot attain status and the resources that come with it legitimately. In other words, like all behavior linked to survival and reproductive success, the same traits can be used legitimately or illegitimately contingent upon many factors both internal and external to the actor.

Criminologists are increasingly finding that all traits associated with criminal behavior are substantially heritable (Barnes, Beaver, & Boutwell, 2011; Bentley et al., 2013) and are even zeroing in on specific genes associated with those traits (Beaver, Wright, & Walsh, 2008; Ferguson, 2010). Given this, we have to ask why genes promoting such traits exist. The human genome is the chemical archive of accumulated wisdom that has survived millions of years of ruthless selective retention and elimination of genes. Genes exist in the gene pool of any species because they somehow conferred an adaptive advantage on ancestral organisms, suggesting that genes underlying traits associated with criminal behavior have survived because they served some evolutionary purpose. Behaviors motivated by a particular trait may be morally repulsive, but the trait is nevertheless "natural" (the product of nature) rather than pathological.

These traits may lead to certain behavioral strategies that may be either pro- or antisocial depending on how they were shaped in the past by cues in an individual's environment (Wiebe, 2012). There is also considerable heritable variation in these traits that place individuals at risk for criminal behavior, which is likely preserved by balancing selection processes such as heterozygote advantage and negative frequency-dependent selection. Balancing processes maintain rare alleles in a population's gene pool when they have higher adaptive value than alternatives (Boutwell et al., 2015; Penke, Dennisen, & Miller, 2007). Heterozygote advantage occurs in situations in which the fitness value of a person with two different alleles (Aa) is greater than the fitness value of an individual with homozygous alleles (either AA or aa). This causes the retention of the alleles in the population regardless of differing fitness values of AA and aa alleles. In negative frequency-dependent selection, the fitness of a phenotype increases when it is rare and decreases when it becomes more common (Andrés et al., 2009).

Judith Harris (1998) speculates about the evolutionarily relevant advantages of certain traits in ancient hunter–gatherer leaders that are also useful for criminals:

> Almost all the characteristics of the "born criminal" would be, in watered-down form, useful to a male in a hunter–gatherer society and useful in his group. His lack of fear, desire for excitement, and impulsiveness made him a formidable weapon against rival groups. His aggressiveness, strength, and lack of compassion enable him to dominate his groupmates and give him first shot at hunter–gatherer perks. (pp. 299–300)

These perks were those most pertinent to survival and reproductive success—resources and women. Females would have been attracted to such men, not because they were sensitive "nice guys" but because they had high status and resources within the group and were good protectors and women who mated with such men would have enjoyed increased fitness (Buss, 2005). The traits described by Harris can overshoot their optimum and become liabilities, which is often the case when exercised too freely in modern evolutionarily novel societies.

These traits may also have been liabilities in small ancestral groups roaming the savanna if they led to exploitation because counteracting human competitive and status-striving motives is a powerful egalitarian instinct (Gavrilets, 2012; Rogers, Deshpande, & Feldman, 2011). When Hominids branched off from the ancestral primate line during the Plio-Pleistocene Epoch, they faced an ecology that exerted pressure for strong norms of reciprocal altruism. The nomadic lifestyle characterized by dangerous and uncertain prospects of obtaining survival resources probably kick-started the evolution of our species' powerful egalitarian instincts balancing out, but not eliminating, the evolutionarily more ancient primate behavioral patterns rooted in status competitions and dominance (Adkins & Guo, 2008; Charlton, 1997).

Foraging and hunting and gathering demanded strict group-wide cooperation, and scarce resources would have been distributed according to egalitarian principles lest the group fall into fractious disputes. In small hunter–gatherer groups, resource sharing would have taken place under the vigilant eyes of all in immediate time (as opposed to a delayed-time share of society's resources in agrarian and industrial societies). All band members would have demanded an equal share of the pie, leaving little, if any, room for exploitation, and perceptions of unequal distribution would have produced immediately adverse emotional reactions. It would still be the case that certain skills— hunter, speaker, fighter, peacemaker, strategist, and so on—would have conferred status on a person, and thus increased the person's fitness, but status would have been freely conferred based on meritocratic principles and subject to withdrawal if the person took what group members considered to be unfair advantage (Adkins & Guo, 2008).

Nevertheless, the traits Harris (1998) alludes to as advantageous in securing resources and mates legitimately can be put to illegitimate use. Even criminals are constrained to cooperate with their conspecifics most of the time, but due to other traits they may possess, such as low self-control, low empathy, and low fear, they may default on the norms of reciprocity when opportunities arise. Although there are far more opportunities to exploit fellow humans today, there have always been individuals we refer to as psychopaths, perhaps genetically maintained by one of the balancing selection processes referred to previously. Those who have commented on the trademark behavior of such people in classical, biblical, and medieval works recognized the same traits (impulsively self-serving and callous yet charming) in them as we do today (Hare, 1996). Aristotle wrote of men with a "brutish nature" arising from "reasons of injuries to the system, by reason of acquired habits, and by reason of originally bad nature" (as quoted in McKeon, 1947, p. 453). Even in cultures resembling ancient hunter–gatherer groups such as the Inuit that demand strong norms of cooperation, people recognize psychopathic individuals, whom the Inuit call *kunlangeta*, who repeatedly lie, steal, freeload, and "take advantage of many women" (Murphy, 1976, p. 1026).

ALTRUISM AND CRIMINALITY

Altruism is an active regard for the well-being of another and is the epitome of prosocial behavior. In many ways, it is the polar opposite of criminality—an active concern only for the self at the expense of others. Social life, as Plato and Freud as well as other lesser known luminaries have told us, is often a hedonic tug-of-war when the desire to expeditiously meet our wants and needs conflicts with the norms of cooperation. We desire both our pleasures and the good will of others, so most of us seek our pleasures in socially approved ways: "money from work, sex through courtship, and revenge delivered by the courts." Although criminal activity is not uncommon, *H. sapiens* is a species with "minds [that] are exquisitely crafted by evolution to form cooperative relationships built on trust and kindness" (Allman, 1994, p.14). These relationships lead to altruistic behavior, and from an evolutionary standpoint, we have to understand altruism in order to understand criminality.

A requisite condition for tit-for-tat reciprocity to be a stable strategy is frequent association and the ability to recognize reciprocators and non-reciprocators. Because of the mutual benefits of reciprocal altruism that accrue to all socially interacting species, altruism and cooperation have been strongly favored by natural selection. Although individual organisms are adapted to act in ways that tend to maximize their own fitness, not necessarily for the good of the group, their fitness goals are best realized by adhering to the rules of cooperation and altruism—by "being nice"—and that is for the good of the group. Altruists recoup the costs of extending benefits and cooperation to others many times over, so altruism is thus ultimately self-serving, but this observation does not diminish the value of altruism to its beneficiaries.

However, reciprocal altruism cannot explain situations in which individuals confer some benefit on strangers with no expectation of reciprocity. The phrase "psychological altruism" has been coined to distinguish this kind of altruism (Kruger, 2003). If reciprocal altruism is a gene-based adaptation, perhaps psychological altruism is an exaptation seized upon by natural selection to improve upon the operation of reciprocal altruism by infusing it with additional neurohormonal mediators. Psychological altruism is motivated by internal rewards such as guilt reduction or the joy experienced when beneficiaries express their gratitude for the benefactor's largesse (Brunero, 2002). Brain imaging studies consistently show that our pleasure centers "light up" when giving or receiving something valued, but brain areas associated with the pleasures of social attachments only fire when giving (Moll et al., 2006). We act altruistically because we tend to feel good when we do so and because such behavior confers social status on us by identifying us as persons who are kind, reliable, and trustworthy. In the ultimate sense, we do so because our distant ancestors who were altruistic and cooperative enjoyed greater reproductive success than those who were not. Possessing the neural architecture that produces rewarding feelings when we do good deeds for others is part and parcel of that adaptation (Barkow, 1997).

Selfishness in the evolutionary sense is morally neutral because biologists recognize that all sexually reproducing organisms have evolved to be concerned with their own survival and reproduction and will do what they must to realize those concerns (Tang, 2010). Selfishness as understood in the vernacular means a crabbed, spiteful, egoism stripped of any concern for the well-being of others. Such selfishness is ultimately maladaptive, which is hardly self-serving. Selfishness properly understood is the most adaptive of traits because it is precisely by cooperating and being actively concerned for others that we best serve our own interests. As Edward O. Wilson (1978) stated,

> Human beings appear to be sufficiently selfish and calculating to be capable of infinitely greater harmony and social homeostasis. This statement is not self-contradictory. True selfishness, if obedient to the other constraints of mammalian biology, is the key to a nearly perfect social contract. (p. 157)

If you help another person in need, it is altruism regardless of whether it lights up your pleasure center, gains you brownie points with God, puffs up your chest, or enhances your status in the group. If one insists that psychological altruism is not "real" altruism because it is not entirely selfless, one is unwittingly asserting that "real" behaviors are ineffable, biology-free, and cannot evolve.

All nontrivial behavior has to be animated by something, and altruistic acts are typically animated by experiencing empathy. Empathy channels altruism in social species without undue reliance being placed on cognitive ruminations about such things as reciprocity concerns. Empathy is the cognitive and emotional ability to understand the feelings and distress of others as if they were our own. The cognitive component allows us to understand the distress of others and why they are feeling it, and the emotional component allows us to "feel" that distress. To the extent that we feel empathy for others, we have an evolved visceral motivation to take some action to alleviate the distress of others if we are able. Altruism can thus be thought of as the co-evolved action component of empathy. The basis of empathy is the distress we feel personally when witnessing the distress of others, and if we can alleviate the distress of others, we thereby alleviate our own. Thus, empathy also has a selfish component, which is very good because if we were lacking in emotional connectedness to others, we would be callously indifferent to their needs and suffering.

Frans de Waal (2008) posits that empathy is an ancient phylogenetic capacity predating the emergence of H. sapiens and evolved rapidly in the context of parental care. Empathy is an integral component of the love and nurturing of offspring. Caregivers must quickly and automatically relate to the distress signals of their offspring. Parents who were not alerted to or who were unaffected by their offspring's distress signals or by their smiles and cooing are surely not among our ancestors. Like the diffusion of adaptive love and care of offspring to the non-adaptive love and care of the children of others and to pets, the capacity for empathetic responses, once locked into the human repertoire, diffused to a wider network of social relationships. It is the relative lack of empathy that allows criminals to exploit others for their own ends (Keysers & Gazzola, 2014; Walsh & Vaske, 2015).

Cooperation Creates Niches
for Cheats

Because cooperation occurs among groups of reciprocal altruists, it creates niches for cheats, who typically have low levels of empathy and altruism, to exploit (Durrant & Ward, 2015). It has been proposed that the stronger the selection for altruism in a species, the more vulnerable it becomes to "Machiavellian intelligence" (Runciman, 2005, p. 132). Cheats are individuals in a population of cooperators who signal cooperation but fail to reciprocate. If there are no deterrents against cheating, it is in an individual's fitness interests to obtain resources from others under the assumption of reciprocity and then to default, thus gaining resources at zero cost. "Social parasitism" of this sort has been observed among a variety of nonhuman animal species, and its ubiquity across species implies that it has had positive fitness consequences (Alcock, 2005). Cheating comes at a cost, however, so before deciding to default, the individual must weigh the costs and benefits of cooperating versus defaulting, as illustrated in the familiar prisoner's dilemma of game theory (Axelrod, 1984).

By cheating, each player in the game is behaving rationally—defined as a positive fit between ends and the means used to achieve them. However, cheating is only rational in circumstances of limited interaction and communication. In the prisoner's dilemma game, the participants were acquaintances who might never see each other again and thus need not fear any repercussions arising from their cheating. Had they been brothers, good friends, or members of a long-standing gang, they most likely would not have defaulted on their promise to cooperate, and each would have benefited rather than one benefitting at the expense of the other. Frequent interaction and communication breed trust among organisms with sufficient intelligence to recognize one another. Under such circumstances, cheating becomes less rational because cooperators remember and retaliate against those who have cheated them. Cheating ruins reputations, costs cheaters future cooperation, and can result in punishment, which is why most career street criminals either die early or end up destitute (Shover, 1985).

Cheats can only prosper in a population of unconditional altruists that game theorists call suckers. Suckers are individuals who continue to extend benefits to those who have cheated them. Any sucker genotype would soon be driven to extinction by cheats, leaving only cheats to interact with other cheats. Evolutionary logic predicts that a population of cheats could not thrive any more than could a population of suckers, and selection for cooperation would occur rapidly (Machalek, 1996). Pure suckers and cheats are thus unlikely to exist in large numbers in any social species. The vast majority of social animals, including human beings, are grudgers. Grudgers are susceptible to being cheated because they conform to the norms of mutual trust and cooperation and expect the same from others. But if cheated, they retaliate by not cooperating with perpetrator in the future, and perhaps repaying the cheat in kind. Cheaters interact with grudgers in a *repeated* game of prisoner's dilemma in which players adjust their strategies according to their experience with other players. Cooperation rather than cheating becomes the rational strategy under such circumstances because each player reaps in the future what he or she has sown in the past (Roach & Pease, 2013).

As predicted by evolutionary logic, in computer simulations of interactions between populations of cheats, suckers, and grudgers, cheats are always driven to extinction (Allman, 1994). Yet we continue to see cheating behavior despite threats of exposure and retaliation. The problem with computer simulations is that players are constrained to operate within the same environment in which their reputations quickly become known. Real-life strategies are not automated binary strategies (cheat/don't cheat) based on the behavior of a laboratory opponent. Although computer simulations are invaluable for fleshing out the basic logic of evolutionary processes, we should not form an overly simplistic view of cooperating and cheating from them (Raine, 1993). Cheats are not constrained to remain in one environment in the real world; they can move from location to location, meeting and cheating a series of grudgers who are unaware of their reputation. This is exactly what many career criminals do. They move from place to place, job to job, relationship to relationship, leaving a trail of misery behind them before their reputation catches up to them (Ellis, 2005). Cheats are much more likely to prosper in large cities in modern societies than in small traditional communities in which, as in evolutionary environments, the threat of exposure and retaliation is great (Ellis & Walsh, 1997; Sampson & Laub, 2005). However, factors such as the stability of the group and cultural dynamics must also be considered. For instance, criminologists know that there are communities in which a "badass" reputation is valued by males more than anything else, but even in these communities there must be a certain level of group cooperation (Anderson, 1999).

We have evolved psychological mechanisms that lead us to repay cooperation and defection in kind—any other strategy would be counterproductive. Among these mechanisms are the social emotions of empathy, guilt, shame, and the primary emotion of anger. Empathy moves us toward helping behavior, and shame and guilt preclude most of us from defecting in our social obligations and motivate us to engage in reparative behavior to restore our good name if we do so. Anger motivates us to retaliate if we are victimized by defection, and experiencing our anger may motivate the defector not to repeat. Punishing defectors is a valuable adaptive strategy as long as it does not exceed reasonable limits and is not imposed on unintentional defection because it is unlikely that cooperation would have evolved without it. As Buckholtz and Marois (2012) state, punishment "seems crucial for the evolutionary stability of cooperation and is the cornerstone of modern models of criminal justice" (p. 655).

THE SEX RATIO ISSUE: PARENTING VERSUS MATING EFFORT

Bernard, Snipes, and Gerould (2010) claim that the issue of why always and everywhere males commit more crime than females is the "single most important fact that criminology theories must be able to explain" (p. 299). Criminologists have been try-ing to come to grips with the issue armed only with the theoretical tools of sociology. Gottfredson and Hirschi (1990) have concluded that an explanation of sex differences in crime is "beyond the scope of any available set of empirical data" (p. 149). They mean, of course, any available data set from within the standard social science model, which attributes any behavioral or trait sex difference to socialization. The notion that the sex difference in criminal behavior is attributable to differential socialization is not even logically sustainable. If this were so, there would be *some* culture in *some* histori-cal period in which female rates equaled, or even exceeded, male rates, but there is no such culture to be found (for a book-length treatment, see Walsh and Vaske, 2015). We maintain that the concept of mating versus parenting effort provides the only scientifi-cally viable explanation at an ultimate level for sex differences in crime and that the only viable scientific explanation at a proximate level is sex differences in the neuroarchitec-ture and neurochemistry forged by sexual selection (de Vries & Sodersten, 2009; Del Giudice, 2009; Pezeshki Rad et al., 2014).

If everything in evolution, even survival, is subservient to reproductive success, we need to know how adaptive fitness traits are useful for either promoting or discouraging criminal activity. There are two ways that members of any animal species can maximize reproductive success: parenting effort and mating effort. Parenting effort is the propor-tion of reproductive effort invested in rearing offspring, and mating effort is that propor-tion allotted to acquiring sexual partners. Because acquiring sexual partners would have required overcoming the reticence of a careful female or vanquishing competitors vying for the same partner, traits such as aggression and a high need for status would be among those most useful. David Rowe (2002) provides a thumbnail sketch of some other traits useful to mating effort that can clearly be co-opted to support criminal behavior:

> A strong sexual drive and attraction to novelty of new sexual partners is clearly one component of mating effort. An ability to appear charming and superficially inter-ested in women while courting them would be useful. The emotional attachment, however, must be an insincere one, to prevent emotional bonding to a girlfriend or spouse. The cad may be aggressive, to coerce sex from partly willing partners and to deter rival men. He feels little remorse about lying or cheating. Impulsivity could be advantageous in a cad because mating decisions must be make quickly and without prolonged deliberation; the unconscious aim is many partners, not a high-quality partner. (pp. 62–63)

Probably almost all heterosexual males have falsely proclaimed love or used some other kind of mildly coercive/manipulative tactics in pursuit of sexual satisfaction, but most know to place limits on their behavior. Nevertheless, it is plain that high levels of the traits associated with mating effort coupled with the lack of constraint are serious risk factors for criminality.

The reverse is also true—traits that facilitate parenting effort underlie other forms of prosocial activity: "Crime can be identified with the behaviors that tend to promote mating effort and noncrime with those that tend to promote parenting effort" (Rowe,

1996, p. 270). Because female reproductive success hinges more on parenting effort than on mating effort, females have evolved higher levels of the traits that facilitate it (e.g., empathy and altruism) and lower levels of traits unfavorable to it (e.g., aggressiveness) compared to males. Of course, both sexes engage in mating and parenting strategies, and both follow a mixed mating strategy. It is only claimed that mating behavior is far more typical of males and parenting effort is far more typical of females and that the traits underlying those strategies have been forged by eons of sexual selection pressures (Campbell, 2009).

Because humans are born more dependent than any other animal, parenting effort is particularly important, and we have thus evolved to invest heavily in parenting. However, there is considerable variation within the species. Gender constitutes the largest division due to different levels of obligatory parental investment between the sexes. Female parental investment necessarily requires an enormous expenditure of time and energy, but the only *obligatory* investment of males is the time and energy spent copulating. Reproductive success for males increases in proportion to the number of females to whom they have sexual access, and thus males have an evolved propensity to seek multiple partners.

Reproductive success among our ancestral females rested primarily on their ability to secure mates to assist them in raising offspring in exchange for exclusive sexual access, and thus human females evolved a much more discriminating attitude about sexual behavior (Geary, 2000; Nedelec & Beaver, 2012). The inherent conflict between the reckless and indiscriminate male mating strategy and the careful and discriminating female mating strategy drove the evolution of traits such as aggressiveness in males and the lowering levels (relative to female levels) of empathy and constraint that help males overcome both male competitors and female reluctance. It is important to remember, however, that although these traits were designed by natural and sexual selection to facilitate mating effort, they are also useful in gaining nonsexual resources via illegitimate means (Quinsey, 2002; Walsh, 2006).

Empirical research supports the notion that an excessive concentration on mating effort is linked to criminal behavior. A review of 51 studies relating number of sex partners to criminal behavior found 50 of them to be positive, and in another review of 31 studies, it was found that age of onset of sexual behavior was negatively related to criminal behavior in all 31 (Ellis & Walsh, 2000). A British cohort study found that the most antisocial 10% of males in the cohort fathered 27% of the children (Jaffee, Moffitt, Caspi, & Taylor, 2003), and anthropologists tell us that there are striking differences in behavior between members of cultures that emphasize either parenting or mating strategies. Cultures emphasizing mating effort the world over exhibit behaviors (low-level parental care, hypermasculinity, and transient bonding) considered antisocial in Western societies (Ember & Ember, 1998).

Molecular genetic studies have also found significant relationships between sexual behavior and criminal behavior. Beaver et al. (2008) tested the evolutionary claim that the most antisocial males should have the most sex partners and found the same polymorphism of the dopamine transporter gene (*DAT1* 10-repeat) that was significantly related to both number of sexual partners and antisocial behavior. Another study found that males homozygous for the *DAT1* polymorphism had significantly more sex partners (an average of 5.66) compared to males who had only one or no copies (an average of 2.94), as well as significantly higher scores on delinquency and on other kinds of risky behaviors (Guo, Tong, & Cai, 2008). The 10-repeat allele of the *DAT1* gene is exceptionally efficient at clearing dopamine from the synaptic gap after it signals other neurons. Because dopamine gives us pleasure when we engage in activities such as sex, if it is cleared too fast, we are moved to seek more of the activity to get more pleasure (more dopamine). This constant seeking of activities to raise dopamine levels is the chemical basis of addiction to all sorts of things besides sex, such as drugs, smoking, food, gambling, and alcohol (Walsh, Johnson, & Bolen, 2012).

The fact that criminals are consistently found to have more sexual partners compared to members of the general population is at odds with historical data, which indicate that high-status males have always enjoyed greater reproductive success. Rosemary Hopcroft (2015a, 2015b) produces evidence from the National Longitudinal Study of Youth that greater reproductive success accrues to males who have achieved high status (defined in terms of personal rather than household income) legitimately. It is the opposite for women, however: "Annual personal income is negatively correlated with number of offspring for women, and positively correlated with number of offspring for men" (Hopcroft, 2015a, p. 148). She also provides evidence that high-status males today still enjoy greater copulatory opportunities, but in these times of effective birth control, this does not translate into the same high rate of reproductive success that it once did. Her findings, in conjunction with others from developed countries, suggest that "the demographic transition has attenuated, but not entirely broken, the link between social status and reproductive success in modern industrial societies" (2015a, p. 150). The same relationship between status and reproductive success obtains among criminals. "Badass" males in subcultures of violence are the big fish in that particular reproductive pool that attract women swimming in the same pool, even if they are low status in the legitimate pool.

"STAYING ALIVE": FEAR AND EMPATHY

Anne Campbell's (1999) *staying alive/low-fear hypothesis* is an evolutionary approach to the gender ratio issue, and it has been described as "perhaps the best attempt to account for gender differences in criminality" (Roach & Pease, 2013, p. 66). Campbell's hypothesis features the selection pressures faced by ancestral females with regard to parental investment and status striving. The obligatory parental investment of females is enormously greater than that of males. Only after months of gestation and months or years of lactation can a woman contemplate further children, which means that her reproductive success is far more tied to children she has than is that of a male. The greater dependence of the infant on its mother renders a mother's presence more critical to offspring survival, and hence to the mother's reproductive success, than the presence of a father. In ancestral environments, the care of nursing infants meant that females always kept them in close proximity, and this posed an elevated risk of injury to the child as well as the mother if the mother placed herself in risky situations. Because female survival is critical to infant survival, it is critical to female reproductive success. Campbell therefore avers that females have evolved a propensity to avoid engaging in behaviors that pose survival risks.

Campbell (2009) proposes that the evolved mechanism underlying this propensity is a physiology that responds to risky situations in ways that are subjectively experienced as fear. There are essentially no sex differences in fearfulness across a number of contexts *unless* a situation contains a significant risk of physical injury. Greater fear responses account for the greater tendency of females to avoid potentially violent situations and also to employ indirect and low-risk strategies in competition and dispute resolution relative to males. The most fearful ancestral females who avoided or removed themselves from situations containing a high risk of physical injury or death were those most likely to survive, and their survival increased the probability of the survival of their offspring and also the probability of the perpetuation of their genetic lineage.

The staying alive/low-fear hypothesis also has implications for sex differences in status seeking. Because males have greater variance in reproductive success compared to females but less parental certainty, they stand to gain greater fitness benefits by engaging in intrasexual competition for mating opportunities. High-status and dominant males always attract more females compared to low-status subservient males. Status and dominance striving is often risky business, and because attaining status is less reproductively consequential for females than for males, there has been less pressure for the selection of mechanisms useful in that endeavor for females. In evolutionary environments, a male's reproductive success often rested on involving himself in risky situations in which high fear would have been a definite handicap.

Campbell (1999) notes that there is female competition for mates, but it is mostly low key, low risk, and chronic as opposed to the high-key, high-risk, and acute nature of male competition. Females cannot compete for the assets most pertinent to attracting a committed mate, such as youth and beauty; a woman either possesses them or she does not. Male assets that attract females, unlike youth and beauty, can be achieved in competition with other males. Males are generally willing to incur risks to achieve status and dominance to gain the resources that come with it, and thus potentially gain access to more females.

Women do commit crimes, of course, but rarely do they involve risk of physical injury and are almost always committed for instrumental reasons. Campbell (1999) notes that although robbery and larceny/theft both involve expropriating resources from others, females constitute approximately 43% of arrests for larceny/theft and only approximately 7% of arrests for robbery, a crime carrying a relatively high risk for personal injury. Campbell notes that although women do aggress and do steal, "they rarely do both at the same time because the equation of resources and status reflects a particularly masculine logic" (p. 210). Robbery, and flaunting the material trappings signaling its successful pursuit, is seen ultimately as a campaign for respect and status in the street culture from which most robbers come (Jacobs & Wright, 1999). Studies of female robbers provide no mention that female robbers crave the additional payoffs of dominance that male robbers do, or seek reputations as "hard-asses" (Messerschmidt, 1993). A woman with a reputation as a "hard-ass" would be most unattractive as a long-term partner.

If pressed to boil down to a basic level the evolved traits that best account for the wide gender gap in criminal behavior, it would have to be the gender differences in empathy and fear fashioned by the respective reproductive roles of the sexes. Empathy and fear are the natural enemies of crime for the obvious reasons stated by Walsh and Vaske (2015):

> Empathy is other oriented and prevents one from committing acts injurious to others because one has an emotional and cognitive investment in the well-being of others. Fear is self-oriented and prevents one from committing acts injurious to others out of fear of the consequences to one's self. Many other prosocial tendencies flow from these two basic foundations, such as a strong conscience, altruism, self-control, and agreeableness. (p. 168)

MATING EFFORT AND
THE AGE–CRIME CURVE

The age–crime curve has been described as "the most important regularity in criminology" (Nagin & Land, 1993, p. 330). The age–crime curve is the statistical count of the number of known criminal/delinquent offenses committed in a population during a given period and mapped according to age categories. The curve shows a sharp increase in offending beginning in early adolescence, a peak in mid-adolescence, a steep decline in early adulthood, followed by a steady decline thereafter. The peak may be higher or lower at different periods, and the peak age may vary by a year or two, but the peak remains. This pattern has been noted in all cultures for which statistics are gathered and at all times. Charles Goring noted the constancy of the age–crime curve across times and culture and concluded that it was "a law of nature" (as quoted in Gottfredson & Hirschi, 1990, p. 124).

Laws of nature describe regularities of nature; they do not explain why the regularities occur. As with the gender ratio issue, the age–crime curve has long puzzled criminologists laboring under the illusion that biology is irrelevant for their discipline. Hirschi and Gottfredson (1983) have even stated that "the age distribution of crime cannot be accounted for by any variable or combination of variables currently available to criminology" (p. 554), and Shavit and Rattner (1988) write that the age peak in delinquency remains "unexplained by any known set of sociological variables" (p. 1457). To try to explain it, sociological criminologists often invoke peer influences, but they do not inform us *why* these peer influences become more salient during adolescence and why these influences are typically antisocial. To do so, Spear (2013) states that an evolutionary perspective may be what we need:

> Common behavioral proclivities seen in human adolescents and their counterparts in other species include elevations in peer-directed social interactions along with occasional increases in fighting with parents, increases in novelty seeking, sensation seeking, and risk taking. . . . These across-species similarities support the suggestion that certain neurobehavioral characteristics of adolescence may be tethered in part by biological roots embedded in the evolutionary past. (p. S8)

Mating effort entails a certain element of risk, and mating is particularly prevalent among adolescents and young adults (Ellis et al., 2012). Risky behavior among adolescents is frequently pathologized, which is understandable when we witness them engaging in reckless driving, binge drinking, and drug-taking. However, these things are all evolutionarily novel acts, and the costs of engaging in them heavily outweigh the benefits, but we rarely pause to consider what may be evolutionarily adaptive about risk-taking per se during adolescence (Ellis et al., 2012). Studies of a number of primate species have shown that their adolescents share with human adolescents the tendency to become very sensitive to rewards, risk-taking, sensation-seeking, and novelty. From an evolutionary perspective, the purpose of these tendencies is to compel the animal to leave the nest to find a mate from another troop. Mid-adolescence and early adulthood is a period of intense competition among males for dominance and status among many primate species, including *H. sapiens,* aimed ultimately at securing more mating opportunities than the next male. As Martin Daly (1996) states, "There are many reasons to think that we've been designed to be maximally competitive and conflictual in young adulthood" (p. 193).

Puberty is initiated with the activation of the hypothalamic–pituitary–gonadal axis, which dramatically increases the level of sex hormones signaling readiness for reproduction. At this time, many sex differences emerge or increase as the genes turned on by hormones activate brain areas organized along sexually dimorphic lines in utero. Ernst, Pine, and Hardin (2006) explain that at a proximal level, risk-taking is the result of the developmentally normal lack of balance between brain areas associated with approach/avoidance behaviors: "The propensity during adolescence for reward/novelty seeking in the face of uncertainly or potential harm might be explained by a strong reward system (nucleus accumbens), a weak harm-avoidance system (amygdala), and/or an inefficient supervisory system (medial/ventral prefrontal cortex)" (p. 299). Aaron White (2004) augments this with his summation of key messages from a New York Academy of Sciences neuroscience conference. The main points stressed are that much of adolescent behavior is rooted in the lack of synchrony between a physically mature body and a still maturing nervous system. One of the consequences of this is that adolescents have higher sensitivity to reward, meaning that they require higher levels of stimulation to obtain the same rewards as mature adults. This leads them to seek higher levels of novelty and stimulation to achieve the same feeling of pleasure. In short, biological changes in the body and brain, intermingling with environmental factors, result in adolescents being prone to risk-taking and experiencing wide emotional swings.

Adolescence can be an emotionally trying time when both sexes are experiencing many physical and social changes. Males are juiced up by the huge pubertal surge of testosterone while at the same time experiencing profound changes in their neurobiology. Functional magnetic resonance imaging studies show that adolescents have exaggerated nucleus accumbens (NAcc) activity relative to activity in regions of the prefrontal cortex (PFC) compared to children and adults (Eshel, Nelson, Blair, Pine, & Ernst, 2007; Galvan et al., 2006). Because the NAcc is implicated in reward-seeking behaviors and the PFC is an inhibitor of impulse, findings such as these reveal mechanisms behind the adolescent propensity to favor short-term hedonism over more reasoned long-term goals. This suggests that adolescence is accompanied by changes in the ratios of excitatory to inhibitory neurotransmitters, fiber architecture, and tissue composition; the excitatory transmitters dopamine and glutamate peak while the inhibitory transmitters γ-aminobutyric acid and serotonin are reduced (Bava & Tapert, 2010; Collins, 2004; Walker, 2002). The biological tools needed to increase novelty-seeking, sensation-seeking, status-seeking, and competitiveness are adaptations forged by natural selection in the service of reproductive success (Bava & Tapert, 2010; Spear, 2000; White, 2004).

In addition to the previously mentioned chemical changes, the adolescent brain is also going through an intense period of tissue resculpting. It shows a decrease in gray matter in prefrontal regions as unused synapses are pruned, increased myelination of the PFC, and changes in the density and distribution of dopamine receptors in pathways that connect the limbic system to the PFC (Steinberg, 2005). The pubertal hormonal surges prompt the increase of gene expression in the brain, and the genes then play their parts in slowly refining the neural circuitry to its adult form (Walker, 2002). Brain imaging studies reveal that the PFC (the modulator of emotions from the limbic system) undergoes a wave of synaptic overproduction just prior to puberty, which is followed by a period of pruning during adolescence and early adulthood (Giedd, 2004; Sowell, Thompson, & Toga, 2004). The selective retention and elimination of synapses relies crucially on experience-dependent input from the environment because the developing brain physically "captures" these inputs in somatic time the way that natural selection seizes on advantageous alleles in evolutionary time.

Because the adolescent PFC is also less completely myelinated than the adult PFC (Sowell et al., 2004), there is a larger "time lapse" between the onset of an emotional event in the limbic system and a person's rational judgment of it in the PFC. Diffusion tensor imaging studies demonstrate increasing fractional anisotropy (FA) and decreasing mean diffusivity (MD) as the brain matures from childhood to adulthood. FA is linked to increased axon myelination and is a scalar used to measure the integrity of white matter fiber (axons) tracts; the higher the FA, the greater the integrity of the connectivity between brain areas. MD is a measure reflecting water content and density throughout brain white matter. In short, increased FA and decreased MD indicate that the areas of the brain such as the "rational" PFC and the "emotional" limbic system are better able to communicate with each other as the brain matures (Lebel & Beaulieu, 2011).

These brain imaging studies show that there are physical reasons for the greater ratio of emotional to rational responses evidenced by teens. The physical immaturity of the adolescent brain combined with a "supercharged" physiology facilitates the tendency to assign faulty attributions to situations and the intentions of others, and this can lead to antisocial responses. In other words, "a brain on 'go slow' superimposed on a physiology on 'fast forward' explains why many teenagers find it difficult to accurately gauge the meanings and intentions of others and to experience more stimuli as aversive during adolescence than they did as children and will do so when they are adults" (Walsh, 2002, p. 143). As Richard Restak (2001) states, "The immaturity of the adolescent's behavior is perfectly mirrored by the immaturity of the adolescent's brain" (p. 76). Although parents may decry such behavior, it is how natural selection has designed human adolescents to be prepared to leave the nest and produce the next generation.

The human brain is evolution's masterpiece. It is the most complex and capable organ known. It is humanity's central processing unit and the great mediator to all human behavior. It processes the information we collect through our senses and makes sense of that information. Without such a complex brain, what it means to be human would be uninteresting; that is, the human condition would be nothing more than a monotonous routine in survival. Instead, our complex brains give us art, science, and morality (Pinker, 2002). Understanding the brain's structure, function, and evolutionary development is paramount to a more complete understanding of criminal behavior. As such, evolutionary theory and neurocriminology add significant explanatory power to the criminologist's toolkit. Understanding brain development can help explain the age–crime curve, but understanding abnormalities in brain structure and function can also help explain a variety of antisocial behaviors. Abnormalities in brain structures, such as the amygdala and PFC, and/or their functioning (e.g., metabolic activity) are routinely associated with violence, sex offenses, psychopathy, and addiction (Jorgensen & Barnes, 2016; Raine, 1993).

CONCLUSION

This chapter argues for nothing more nor less than the evolution of criminology through the integration of the theories, methods, and technological instruments gifted to it by the more robust sciences. In their disciplines' adolescence, chemistry borrowed shamelessly from physics, biology from chemistry, and psychology from biology, and all progressed by leaps and bounds when they did so. To insist on trying to explain human behavior without an evolutionary framework is akin to modern chemistry going about its business ignoring the very causal foundations of the discipline—atoms and the other basic forces governing the behavior of matter—as it was once urged to do by many of its leading luminaries (Walsh, 1997). This does not imply the colonization of criminology;

criminologists can go about their work in their areas of expertise just as do biologists in their numerous areas of research without invoking evolution. However, biologists realize that evolution draws all their sub-areas together because "nothing in biology makes sense except in the light of evolution," as the grandfather of the neo-Darwinian synthesis of genetics and evolution, Theodosius Dobzhansky (1973, p. 125), maintained long ago. Darwin himself (1859) predicted that one day, "psychology will be based on a new foundation, that of the necessary acquirement of each mental power and capacity by gradation. Much light will be thrown on the origin of man and his history" (p. 428). Much the same claim could be made of any behavioral discipline, including criminology.

An evolutionary approach can aid criminology in many ways in addition to providing the benefits outlined in this chapter. It can help explain why some people victimize others while simultaneously explaining why most of us do not. Another major benefit is that it can reconcile the tension between the two major criminological traditions whose assumptions about criminal behavior are radically at odds—social learning and social control theories (Pratt, Gau, & Franklin, 2011). The former views humans as naturally good (or at least a blank slate) until corrupted by bad neighborhoods, peers, families, and societies (how the sum of naturally good individuals equals bad groups is a question never asked), whereas the latter views individuals as naturally selfish and requiring social controls to get them to respect the rights of others. For the social learning tradition, crime is an aberration, so it asks, "What causes crime?" The control tradition views crime as the default option in the absence of controls, and it asks, "Since crime is a way to acquire valued resources immediately and at minimal costs, why don't we all commit it?" The problem with this tension is each tradition's strictly dichotomized assumptions about human nature: It is either naturally good or naturally selfish (the social learning tradition's assumption is implicit rather than explicit, whereas the assumption of the control tradition is explicit). However, viewed through an evolutionary lens, this is a false dichotomy.

Evolutionary criminology maintains that criminal behavior is normal and to be expected on a large scale when social cohesion breaks down, as the social control tradition (exemplified by Durkheimian anomie, social disorganization, social bond, self-control, and age-graded theories) avers. Evolutionary criminology also avers that the desire for peaceful coexistence by conforming to social norms and supporting their enforcement is also normal, as the social learning tradition maintains. Which of these features of human nature prevail—either at the social level or at the individual level—depends on the coalescence of a large number of contingent factors because, as Aristotle stated many centuries ago, we have both beast and angel in our nature. Humans have a set of evolved motivations and regulatory mechanisms that they can display in reckless ways or in adherence to social norms.

We have evolved to be reciprocal altruists who can realize our self-interests best by following rules than by not following them. The apparent paradox of social beings committing antisocial acts is resolved when we realize that our desire to cooperate with our fellows provides opportunities for non-cooperators to victimize us. The individuals most likely to do so are those who are disadvantaged in the competition for wealth, power, and status, which is what most mainstream criminological theories express. Adding evolutionary explanatory concepts to criminology theories would not only enrich and broaden their repertoire of concepts but also ground them in the one existing theory that has the potential to add unity and coherence across all disciplines that study the behavior of living things. Evolutionary theory highlights the types of environments in which the kinds of behaviors that trouble us most are likely to emerge, and it is the only extant meta-theory that is capable of uniting, integrating, and making sense of the disparate data on human behavior coming to us from many theories and many disciplines.

In summary, it is worth noting that less than 100 years ago, biology, like criminology today, was so fragmented that most biologists considered its unity "to be nearly an impossible task" (Smocovitis, 1992, p. 2). Biologists worried then about its autonomy as a science and about the intrusion of physics and chemistry into their discipline, just as many criminologists worry about the intrusion of biology today. Smocovitis quotes Joseph Woodger in his 1929 book *Biological Principles* on this fragmentation:

> If we make a general survey of biological science we find that it suffers from cleavages unknown [in unified sciences such as chemistry]. Long ago it [chemistry] has undergone that inevitable process of sub-division into special branches which we find in other sciences, but in biology this has been accompanied by a characteristic diversion of method and outlook between the exponents of the several branches which has tended to exaggerate their differences and has even led to certain traditional feuds between them . . . [instead of a unified science we have] a medley of ad hoc hypotheses. (pp. 4–5)

By substituting "criminology" for "biology" in the previous quotation, criminologists will recognize the present state of their disciple. Smocovitis (1992) concludes his history of the process from fragmentation to the paradigm shift inspired by the synthesis of Darwinian natural selection and Mendelian genetics (neo-Darwinism) by stating, "What the architects had worked to construct [the unity of biology], had by 1982 become a matter of fact" (p. 62). It will be a happy day when in the not too distant future another historian of science writes a similar conclusion with regard to the unity of criminology.

References

Adkins, D., & Guo, G. (2008). Societal development and the shifting influence of the genome on status attainment. *Research in Social Stratification and Mobility, 26,* 235–255.

Alcock, J. (2001). *The triumph of sociobiology.* New York, NY: Oxford University Press.

Alcock, J. (2005). *Animal behavior: An evolutionary approach.* Sunderland, MA: Sinauer.

Allman, W. (1994). *The stone age present.* New York, NY: Simon & Schuster.

Anderson, E. (1999). *Code of the street: Decency, violence, and the moral life of the inner city.* New York, NY: Norton.

Andrés, A., Hubisz, M., Indap, A., Torgerson, D., Degenhardt, J., Boyko, A., . . . Nielsen, R. (2009). Targets of balancing selection in the human genome. *Molecular Biology and Evolution, 26,* 2755–2764.

Ash, J., & Gallup, G. (2007). Paleoclimatic variation and brain expansion during human evolution. *Human Nature, 18,* 109–124.

Axelrod, R. (1984). *The evolution of cooperation.* New York, NY: Basic Books.

Bailey, D., & Geary, D. (2009). Hominid brain evolution: Testing climactic, ecological, and social competition models. *Human Nature, 20,* 67–79.

Barkow, J. (1992). Beneath new culture is an old psychology: Gossip and social stratification. In J. Barkow, L. Cosmides, & J. Tooby (Eds.), *The adapted mind: Evolutionary psychology and the generation of culture* (pp. 627–637). New York, NY: Oxford University Press.

Barkow, J. (1997). Happiness in evolutionary perspective. In N. Segal, G. Weisfeld, & C. Weisfeld (Eds.), *Uniting psychology and biology* (pp. 397–418). Washington, DC: American Psychological Association.

Barnes, J., Beaver, K., & Boutwell, B. (2011). Examining the genetic underpinnings to Moffitt's developmental taxonomy: A behavioral genetics analysis. *Criminology, 49,* 923–954.

Barrett, P. H. (2016). *The works of Charles Darwin: V. 22: Descent of man, and selection in relation to sex (with an essay by TH Huxley).* London: Routledge.

Bava, S., & Tapert, S. F. (2010). Adolescent brain development and the risk for alcohol and other drug problems. *Neuropsychology Review, 20,* 398–413.

Beaver, K., Wright, J., & Walsh, A. (2008). A gene-based evolutionary explanation for the association between criminal involvement and number of sex partners. *Biodemography and Social Biology, 54,* 47–55.

Bentley, M., Lin, H., Fernandez, T., Lee, M., Yrigollen, C., Pakstis, A. J., . . . Leckman, J. (2013). Gene variants associated with antisocial behavior: A latent variable approach. *Journal of Child Psychology and Psychiatry, 54,* 1074–1085.

Bernard, T., Snipes, J., & Gerould, A. (2010). *Vold's theoretical criminology.* New York, NY: Oxford University Press.

Boutwell, B., Barnes, J., Beaver, K., Haynes, R., Nedelec, J., & Gibson, C. (2015). A unified crime theory: The evolutionary taxonomy. *Aggression and Violent Behavior, 25,* 343–353. http://dx.doi.org/10.1016/j.avb.2015.09.003

Brunero, J. (2002). Evolution, altruism and internal reward explanations. *Philosophical Forum, 33,* 413–424.

Buckholtz, J., & Marois, R. (2012). The roots of modern justice: Cognitive and neural foundations of social norms and their enforcement. *Nature Neuroscience, 13,* 655–661.

Buss, D. (2005). *The murderer next door: Why the mind is designed to kill.* New York, NY: Penguin.

Campbell, A. (1999). Staying alive: Evolution, culture, and women's intrasexual aggression. *Behavioral and Brian Sciences, 22,* 203–214.

Campbell, A. (2009). Gender and crime: An evolutionary perspective. In A. Walsh & K. Beaver (Eds.), *Criminology and biology: New directions in theory and research* (pp. 117–136). New York, NY: Routledge.

Charlton, B. (1997). The inequity of inequality: Egalitarian instincts and evolutionary psychology. *Journal of Health Psychology, 2,* 413–425.

Collins, R. (2004). Onset and desistence in criminal careers: Neurobiology and the age–crime relationship. *Journal of Offender Rehabilitation, 39,* 1–19.

Cooper, J., Walsh, A., & Ellis, L. (2010). Is criminology ripe for a paradigm shift? Evidence from a survey of American criminologists. *Journal of Criminal Justice Education, 21,* 332–347.

Daly, M. (1996). Evolutionary adaptationism: Another biological approach to criminal and antisocial behavior. In G. Bock & J. Goode (Eds.), *Genetics of criminal and antisocial behaviour* (pp. 183–195). Chichester, UK. Wiley.

Daly, M., & Wilson, M. (1988). *Homicide*. New York, NY: Aldine de Gruyter.

Darwin, C. (1859). *On the origin of species by means of natural selection*. London, UK: Murray.

de Vries, G., & Sodersten, P. (2009). Sex differences in the brain: The relation between structure and function. *Hormones and Behavior, 55*, 589–596.

de Waal, F. (2002). Evolutionary psychology: The wheat and the chaff. *Current Directions in Psychological Science, 11*, 187–191.

de Waal, F. (2008). Putting the altruism back into altruism: The evolution of empathy. *Annual Review of Psychology, 59*, 279–300.

Del Giudice, M. (2009). On the real magnitude of psychological sex differences. *Evolutionary Psychology, 7*, 264–279.

Dobzhansky, T. (1973). Nothing in biology makes sense except in light of evolution. *The American Biology Teacher, 35*, 125–129.

Durrant, R., & Ward, T. (2012). The role of evolutionary explanations in criminology. *Journal of Theoretical and Philosophical Criminology, 4*, 1–37.

Durrant, R., & Ward, T. (2015). *Evolutionary criminology: Towards a comprehensive explanation of crime*. London, UK: Academic Press.

Ellis, B., Del Giudice, M., Dishion, T., Figueredo, A., Gray, P., Griskevicius, V., . . . Wilson, D. (2012). The evolutionary basis of risky adolescent behavior: Implications for science, policy, and practice. *Developmental Psychology, 48*, 598–623.

Ellis, L. (2005). A theory explaining biological correlates of criminality. *European Journal of Criminology, 2*, 287–315.

Ellis, L., & Walsh, A. (1997). Gene-based evolutionary theories in criminology. *Criminology, 35*, 229–276.

Ellis, L., & Walsh, A. (2000). *Criminology: A global perspective*. Boston, MA: Allyn & Bacon.

Ember, M., & Ember, C. (1998, October). Facts of violence. *Anthropology Newsletter*, 14–15.

Ernst, M., D. Pine, & M. Hardin (2006). Triadic model of the neurobiology of motivated behavior in adolescence. *Psychiatric Medicine, 36*, 299–312.

Eshel, N., Nelson, E., Blair, R., Pine, D., & Ernst, M. (2007). Neural substrates of choice selection in adults and adolescents: Development of the ventrolateral prefrontal and anterior cingulated cortices. *Neuropsychologia, 45*, 1270–1279.

Evans, P., Gilbert, S., Mekel-Bobrov, N., Vallender, E., Anderson, J., Vaez-Azizi, L., . . . Lahn, B. (2005). Microcephalin, a gene regulating brain size, continues to evolve adaptively in humans. *Science, 309*, 1717–1720.

Ferguson, C. (2010). Genetic contributions to antisocial personality and behavior: A meta-analytic review from an evolutionary perspective. *Journal of Social Psychology, 150*, 160–180.

Galvan, A., Hare, T., Parra, C., Penn, J., Voss, H., Glover, G., & Casey, B. (2006). Earlier development of the accumbens relative to orbitofrontal cortex might underlie risk-taking behavior in adolescents. *Journal of Neuroscience, 26*, 6885–6892.

Gavrilets, S. (2012). On the evolutionary origins of the egalitarian syndrome. *Proceedings of the National Academy of Sciences of the USA, 109*, 14069–14074.

Geary, D. (2000). Evolution and proximate expression of human paternal investment. *Psychological Bulletin, 126*, 55–77.

Giedd, J. (2004). Structural magnetic resonance imaging of the adolescent brain. *Annals of the New York Academy of Sciences, 1021*, 77–85.

Gottfredson, M., & Hirschi, T. (1990). *A general theory of crime*. Stanford, CA: Stanford University Press.

Guo, G., Tong, Y., & Cai, T. (2008). Gene by social context interactions for number of sexual partners among White male youths: Genetics-informed sociology. *American Journal of Sociology, 114*, S36–S66.

Hare, R. (1996). Psychopathy: A clinical construct whose time has come. *Criminal Justice and Behavior, 23*, 25–54.

Harris, J. (1998). *The nurture assumption: Why children turn out the way they do.* New York, NY: Free Press.

Hawks, J., Wang, E., Cochran, G., Harpending, H., & Moyzis, R. (2007). Recent acceleration of human adaptive evolution. *Proceedings of the National Academy of Sciences of the USA, 104*, 20753–20758.

Hirschi, T., & Gottfredson, M. (1983). Age and the explanation of crime. *American Journal of Sociology, 89*, 552–584.

Hopcroft, R. (2015a). Sex differences in the relationship between status and number of offspring in the contemporary US. *Evolution and Human Behavior, 36*, 146–151.

Hopcroft, R. (2015b). Sociobiology at work in modern populations. In J. H. Turner, R. Machalek, & A. Maryanski (Eds.), *Handbook on evolution and society: Toward an evolutionary social science* (pp. 122–135). Boulder, CO: Paradigm.

Jacobs, B., & Wright, R. (1999). Stick-up, street culture, and offender motivation. *Criminology, 37*, 149–173.

Jaffee, S., Moffitt, T., Caspi, A., & Taylor, A. (2003). Life with (or without) father: The benefits of living with two biological parents depend on the father's antisocial behavior. *Child Development, 74*, 109–126.

Jorgensen, C., & Barnes, J. (2016). Bad brains: Crime and drug abuse from a neurocriminological perspective. *American Journal of Criminal Justice, 41*(1), 47–69.

Kanazawa, S. (2008). Temperature and evolutionary novelty as forces behind the evolution of general intelligence. *Intelligence, 36*, 99–108.

Kenrick, D., & Simpson, J. (1997). Why social psychology and evolutionary psychology need one another. In J. Simpson & D. Kenrick (Eds.), *Evolutionary social psychology* (pp. 1–20). Mahwah, NJ: Erlbaum.

Keysers, C., & Gazzola, V. (2014). Dissociating the ability and propensity for empathy. *Trends in Cognitive Sciences, 18*, 163–166.

Knight, D. (1992). *Ideas in chemistry: A history of the science.* New Brunswick, NJ: Rutgers University Press.

Kruger, D. (2003). Evolution and altruism: Combining psychological mediators with naturally selected tendencies. *Evolution and Human Behavior, 24*, 118–125.

Lebel, C., & Beaulieu, C. (2011). Longitudinal development of human brain wiring continues from childhood into adulthood. *Journal of Neuroscience, 31*, 10937–10947.

Levine, D. (2006). Neural modeling of the dual motive theory of economics. *Journal of Socio-Economics, 35*, 613–625.

Machalek, R. (1996). The evolution of social exploitation. *Advances in Human Ecology, 5*, 1–32.

McKeon, R. (Ed.). (1947). *Introduction to Aristotle.* New York, NY: The Modern Library.

Mekel-Bobrov, N., Gilbert, S., Evans, P., Vallender, E., Anderson, J., Hudson, R., . . . Lahn, B. (2005). Ongoing adaptive evolution of *ASPM*, a brain size determinant in *Homo sapiens. Science, 309*, 1720–1722.

Messerschmidt, J. (1993). *Masculinities and crime.* Lanham, MD: Rowman & Littlefield.

Mithen, S., & Parsons, L. (2008). The brain as a cultural artifact. *Cambridge Archeological Journal, 18*, 415–422.

Moll, J., Krueger, F., Zahn, R., Pardini, M., de Oliveira-Souza, R., & Grafman, J. (2006). Human fronto-mesolimbic networks guide decisions about charitable donation. *Proceedings of the National Academy of Sciences of the USA, 103*, 15623–15628.

Murphy, J. (1976). Psychiatric labeling in cross-cultural perspective. *Science, 191*, 1019–1028.

Nagin, D., & Land, K. (1993). Age, criminal careers, and population heterogeneity: Specification and estimation of a nonparametric, mixed Poisson model. *Criminology, 31*, 327–362.

Nedelec, J., & Beaver, K. (2012). The association between sexual behavior and antisocial behavior: Insights from an evolutionary informed analysis. *Journal of Contemporary Criminal Justice, 28*, 329:345.

Penke, L., Denissen, J., & Miller, G. F. (2007). The evolutionary genetics of personality. *European Journal of Personality, 21*, 549–587.

Pezeshki Rad, M., Momennezhad, M., Naseri, S., Nahidi, M., Mahmoudzadeh, A., & Aminzadeh, B. (2014). Sexual differences of human brain. *Reviews in Clinical Medicine, 1*, 51–56.

Pinker, S. (2002). *The blank slate: The modern denial of human nature.* New York, NY: Penguin.

Plomin, R., DeFries, J., Craig, I., & McGuffin, P. (2003). Behavioral genomics. In R. Plomin, J. DeFries, I. Craig, & P. McGuffin (Eds.), *Behavioral genetics in the postgenomic era* (pp. 531–540). Washington, DC: American Psychological Association.

Pratt, T., Gau, J., & Franklin, T. (2011). *Key ideas in criminology and criminal justice.* Thousand Oaks, CA: Sage.

Quinsey, V. (2002). Evolutionary theory and criminal behavior. *Legal and Criminological Psychology, 7*, 1–14.

Raine, A. (1993). *The psychopathology of crime: Criminal behavior as a clinical disorder.* San Diego, CA: Academic Press.

Restak, R. (2001). *The secret life of the brain.* New York, NY: Dana Press/Joseph Henry Press.

Roach, J., & Pease, K. (2013). *Evolution and crime.* New York, NY: Routledge.

Rogers, D., Deshpande, O., & Feldman, M. (2011). The spread of inequality. *PLoS One, 6*, e24683. doi:10.1371/journal.pone.0024683

Rowe, D. (1996). An adaptive strategy theory of crime and delinquency. In J. Hawkins (Ed.), *Delinquency and crime: Current theories* (pp. 268–314). Cambridge, UK: Cambridge University Press.

Rowe, D. (2002). *Biology and crime.* Los Angeles, CA: Roxbury.

Ruffie, J. (1986). *The population alternative: A new look at competition and the species.* New York, NY: Random House.

Runciman, W. (2005). Stone Age sociology. *Journal of the Royal Anthropological Institute, 11*, 129–142.

Sampson, R., & Laub, J. (2005). A life-course view of the development of crime. *American Academy of Political & Social Sciences, 602*, 12–45.

Shavit, Y., & Rattner, A. (1988). Age, crime, and the early lifecourse. *American Journal of Sociology, 93*, 1457–1470.

Shover, N. (1985). *Aging criminals.* Beverly Hills, CA: Sage.

Smocovitis, V. (1992). Unifying biology: The evolutionary synthesis of evolutionary biology. *Journal of the History of Biology, 25*, 1–65.

Sowell, E., Thompson, P., & Toga, A. (2004). Mapping changes in the human cortex throughout the span of life. *Neuroscientist, 10*, 372–392.

Spear, L. (2000). Neurobehavioral changes in adolescence. *Current Directions in Psychological Science, 9*, 111–114.

Spear, L. (2013). Adolescent neurodevelopment. *Journal of Adolescent Health, 52*(Suppl.), S7–S13.

Steinberg, L. (2005). Cognitive and affective development in adolescence. *Trends in Cognitive Sciences, 9,* 69–74.

Tang, S. (2010). Foundational paradigms of social sciences. *Philosophy of the Social Science, 41,* 211–249.

Tooby, J., & Cosmides, L. (2005). Conceptual foundations of evolutionary psychology. In D. Buss (Ed.), *The handbook of evolutionary psychology* (pp. 5–67). Hoboken, NJ: Wiley.

Walker, E. (2002). Adolescent neurodevelopment and psychopathology. *Current Directions in Psychological Science, 11,* 24–28.

Walsh, A. (1997). Methodological individualism and vertical integration in the social sciences. *Behavior and Philosophy, 25,* 121–136.

Walsh, A. (2002). *Biosocial criminology: Introduction and integration.* Cincinnati, OH: Anderson.

Walsh, A. (2006). Evolutionary psychology and criminal behavior. In J. Barkow (Ed.), *Missing the revolution: Darwinism for social scientists* (pp. 225–268). Oxford, UK: Oxford University Press.

Walsh, A., & Beaver, K. (2009). *Biosocial criminology: New directions in theory and research* (pp. 154–175). New York, NY: Routledge.

Walsh, A., Johnson, H., & Bolen, J. (2012). Drugs, crime, and the epigenetics of hedonic allostasis. *Journal of Contemporary Criminal Justice, 28,* 314–328.

Walsh, A., & Vaske, J. (2015). *Feminist criminology through a biosocial lens* (2nd ed.). Durham, NC: Carolina Academic Press.

White, A. (2004). *Substance use and the adolescent brain: An overview with the focus on alcohol.* Durham, NC: Duke University Medical Center.

Wiebe, R. (2012). Integrating criminology through adaptive strategy and life history theory. *Journal of Contemporary Criminal Justice, 28,* 346–365.

Wilson, E. (1978). *On human nature.* Cambridge, MA: Harvard University Press.

Woodger, J. H. (1929). Biological *principles: A critical study.* London, UK: Routledge.

Zhang, Y., Landback, P., Vibranovski, M., & Long, M. (2011). Accelerated recruitment of new brain development genes into the human genome. PLoS Biology, 9, e1001179. doi:10.1371

CHAPTER 25

THE BIOSOCIAL STUDY OF ETHNICITY

FRANK SALTER

THIS chapter reviews biosocial studies of ethnic solidarity and conflict. Biological factors are important because they apply to the whole species and help explain the persistence of ethnicity as a major cause of social and political behavior. Although mainstream theorists, especially Marxists such as the late Eric Hobsbawm, thought that tribal behavior is vestigial and will eventually be eliminated by modernity, ethnic distinctions continue to be implicated in many of the bloody conflicts throughout the world, as they were throughout history (Hopcroft, 2010). Ethnic and national identities also bind societies, facilitating public goods (Collier, 2013, Chap. 11).

These practical implications are joined by the theoretical. Are the universals of ethnic behavior the outcome of selection among individuals or groups? Do the physiological, genetic, and psychological mechanisms cueing ethnocentrism mean that group conflict is inevitable?

The definition of an ethnic group (hereafter, "ethny") should attract the attention of biologically oriented social scientists. An *ethny* is a population with a collective proper name, a common myth of descent, a shared history, a distinctive shared culture, connection to a known territory, and some degree of solidarity (Smith, 1986, pp. 22–30; Weber, 1922/1946). *Ethnicity* is behavior contingent on membership of such a population. One branch or another of biology is concerned with ancestry, territory, culture, and solidarity.

Ancestry is the most important dimension of ethnicity and the most biological. All definitions of ethnicity agree that common descent, or belief in it, is the most important component. That makes race a component of ethnicity, not vice versa. The German sociologist Max Weber identified "notions of common descent" based on shared characteristics as central to ethnic identity and solidarity (Weber, 1922/1946, p. 173). Some late 20th-century scholars, such as Walker Connor, refer to a "sense of common ancestry" as the "pristine" meaning of ethnicity (Connor, 1994, p. 102). The historian Anthony D. Smith calls myths of origin and descent the essential element of ethnicity (Smith, 1986, p. 24).

Other research confirms a strong connection between linguistic and genetic phylogeny. Geneticist Cavalli-Sforza and others have shown that in Europe, divisions and subdivisions of languages correspond remarkably well with populations as defined by genetic distances and boundaries of steep genetic gradients (Barbujani & Sokal, 1990; Cavalli-Sforza, 1997). Because language is an ethnic marker, this is strong evidence that the ethnic myth of common descent usually has a basis in fact.

Despite the prominence of ancestry, biology has not been much used to study ethnicity, perhaps due to the social sciences' continuing separation from the life sciences (Degler, 1991). Nevertheless, biosocial ideas have a persistent role in research and, less so, teaching about ethnicity. Those ideas merit study because they are yielding important findings in such disciplines as ethology, sociobiology, evolutionary psychology, and genetics.

In ethnic studies, biosocial theories are often classified as types of primordialism because they focus on perennial human nature and social relations. There is truth in this, although primordialism need not be biological. The late Clifford Geertz (1973), the scholar who introduced the term, meant by it a psychological domain defined in vague and unbiological ways. Biology is not used by contemporary primordialists such as Steven Grosby (1995). Another primordialist, Walker Conner (1994), accepts the power of biological and kinship metaphors to bond populations and points to the emotional, irrational wellsprings of ethnic motivation. But Connor makes no use of genetics or behavioral biology.

Primordialism is opposed by modernism, since World War II the dominant theory in ethnicity and nationalism studies. Modernism emphasizes contingent factors affecting identity, solidarity, and conflict, including the state and its elites, the rise of print media and mass education, industrialization, and other aspects of the post-1789 world (Anderson, 1983). Instrumentalism is a type of modernism in which ethnic identity and solidarity are not values in themselves but, rather, pathways to or diversions from real values of resources and power (Hobsbawm, 1990). These theories are conducive to radical ideology because they represent ethnicity, nations, and nationalism as products of recent social and economic change, not the products of slow-to-change conservative qualities.

Connor (1994) notes that modernist theories generally ignore or fail to explain the irrationality and passion of ethnic and national solidarity and conflict, or their appearance in ancient times. Neither do they conceptualize ethnic behavior as the expression of evolved motivations. Because primordialism does attribute ethnicity to such qualities, it is conducive to conservative ideology. But again, this is not a neat fit.

Pierre van den Berghe (1981), a sociobiological theorist of ethnicity, explicitly rejects the primordial label and admits to being a modernist and a political progressive. He acknowledges that the kinship basis of ethnic and national solidarity need only be putative to have a binding effect. "Socially defined kinship" is a well-known concept in anthropology and is a staple of biopolitics. Evolutionary ideas allow for strong cultural and instrumental impacts on ethnic behavior, though within limits set by a slow-to-change human nature. This is another reason to reject the primordial–modernist distinction as presently formulated.

This chapter is organized by biosocial disciplines and theories of ethnicity. It begins with a historical overview, summarizes tests and heuristics of leading biosocial theories, and reports some novel research.

ETHOLOGY

Ethology—the biological study of behavior—was first applied to ethnicity by Austrian zoologist Irenäus Eibl-Eibesfeldt in the early 1970s. From cross-cultural observations of social behavior, he concluded that community identity and solidarity are based on the extension to larger communities of mechanisms originally adapted to bind families. In anonymous mass societies, citizens are roused to unity by rhetoric that calls them brothers and sisters. The country is referred to as the motherland. National festivals are modeled on family celebrations (Eibl-Eibesfeldt, 1970/1971, p. 219).

This was not a wholly new idea. It was well known by anthropologists that kinship sets the parameters of social organization in humans, as it does in other species (Fox, 1979). In 1947, anthropologist Arthur Keith (1947/1968) described the prejudice of family members in favoring one another. "When children graduate from parental control to take their place in the life of their group, the family feeling or spirit expands so as to embrace all the members of a group, as if the group had become their family" (p. 44). He attributed this idea to Darwin and others. The pioneer sociologist William G. Sumner (1906, pp. 12–13) emphasized bonds of kinship as a cause of "ethnocentrism," a term he invented. Another early sociologist, Vilfredo Pareto, thought that ethnicity develops generally from sentiments resulting from "persistence of relationships of family and kindred groups" (Pareto, 1916/1963, pp. 1016–1040, quoted in Lopreato & Crippen, 1999, pp. 252–253).

Eibl's innovation was to analyze ethnic behavior using the fourfold ethological research agenda described by Niko Tinbergen (1963). He studied immediate precursors (proximate causes), how these develop through childhood (ontogeny), survival value (function), and evolutionary history (phylogeny or ultimate causes). He drew on observations, made across cultures and across species, of family social signals and bonds. He studied the emergence of these behaviors through childhood and in communities, the adaptive functions of these behaviors in families and larger social groups, and how the behaviors evolved in the ancient human past (Eibl-Eibesfeldt, 1998/2001). All human bonds evolved, Eibl argued, from the maternal, including tribal ties. This and similar proposals have attracted the name ethnic nepotism theory, to date the most productive biosocial approach to ethnic studies.

Eibl described political behavior as being drawn from various primordial precursors, such as infantile appeals and parental care. These are deployed politically by being ritualized and performed according to culturally transmitted scripts. Visiting dignitaries are greeted with elaborations of spontaneous gestures. Politicians attract public support by addressing constituents as if they are family. They hold babies in public view.

Subsequent research on political behavior confirms that leaders often evoke national unity by using kinship terminology (Holper, 1996; Johnson, 1987).

Consistent with the good-of-the-species assumptions then prevalent in continental ethology, in the 1970s, Eibl (1975/1979) asserted that in principle symbolic identification could bring about universal unity because humans are preadapted to "regard humanity as a family" (p. 230). He quoted Darwin in support (p. 229; see Darwin, 1871/1913).

The notion that behavior can evolve to benefit the species is an extreme form of group selectionism. Neo-Darwinists such as Richard Dawkins (1976/1989, p. 2) criticized Eibl's original assumption that groups have been units of selection. This reflected a thorough-going criticism of group selectionism based on ideas about units of selection—genes, individuals, and groups—that emerged in the 1960s. The notion of species selection had been received wisdom among ethologists until the 1960s and as such poorly examined. The neo-Darwinian criticism was that an individual that reduces its own reproduction in favor of non-kin will have its genes replaced by "selfish" free-riders that do not limit their reproduction (Williams, 1966). In this view, altruism directed toward non-kin will be weeded out.

From the mid-1970s, Eibl-Eibesfeldt paid more attention to units of selection. He adopted neo-Darwinian theory but retained a limited version of group selection— that ethnic solidarity was adaptive at the level of foraging bands and tribes. By this, he meant that cohesive groups were more successful at spreading their genes by reproducing faster than other groups. He argued that individual sacrifice for the community can be adaptive because members are related genetically. The kinship bond ties individuals into solidary groups the members of which monitor each other to prevent free-riding (Eibl-Eibesfeldt, 1982). He argued that these groups then became units of selection. More successful groups fissioned and replaced others. Fissioning occurred along kinship boundaries (Chagnon, 1975). This group selection explanation for ethnic solidarity runs counter to early sociobiologists' insistence that genes are the sole units and individuals the only vehicles of selection (Eibl-Eibesfeldt, 1984/1989, pp. 90–103). Eibl-Eibesfeldt's position is an example of multilevel selection theory (Sober & Wilson, 1998), discussed later.

A related idea is advanced by Eibl concerning the function and evolution of indoctrinability, the predisposition to identify with groups larger than the family (Eibl-Eibesfeldt, 1998/2001). The concept originated with social psychologist D. T. Campbell (1972) and is compatible with psychological research on social identity mechanisms (Eibl-Eibesfeldt & Salter, 1998/2001). Eibl deployed the indoctrinability concept to explain anthropological observations of how culture and ritual shape concepts of "us" and "the other." An example is initiation ceremonies in traditional societies, which expand identity from the family and small group to the tribe. Small-group identities form spontaneously from kinship relationships, whereas identification with larger units is based on artifices, accumulated and passed down the generations in rituals. Cross-cultural comparison of these traditions indicates that group identity is constructed using myths of descent from common ancestors, embodied in stories, sacred objects, and monuments (Suetterlin, 2017).

SOCIOBIOLOGY

Sociobiology is a set of evolutionary theories developed by ethologists to explain social behavior. The theories are neo-Darwinian, based on the synthesis of Darwinian natural selection and Mendelian genetics pioneered by R. A. Fisher and others from the 1930s. The new approach took a gene-eyed view in which genetic variants coding for particular physiology or behavior become more or less numerous in a gene pool depending on whether they promote the reproduction of individuals.

The most consequential sociobiological theory also led to an important advance in ethnic nepotism theory. It was an attempt by a doctoral student, William D. Hamilton, to explain altruism within the neo-Darwinian frame (Hamilton, 1964). Hamilton was a gifted ethologist interested in social insects, which show extreme altruism. The worker castes of bees and wasps do not reproduce at all, meaning that their individual fitness is zero. The workers are genetically programmed to sacrifice for the hive. Hamilton tried to work out how the genes of social insects that program them to sacrifice themselves are *not* weeded out of the gene pool. The same problem attends altruism in other species. Darwin's original theory implies a solution for parental altruism because this is involved in individual reproduction. But ethnic nepotism goes beyond parents nurturing offspring.

Hamilton's solution was his theory of "inclusive fitness" or kin selection. He argued that an individual's fitness is affected not only by personal reproduction (individual fitness) but also by how well blood relatives reproduce (inclusive fitness), because they bear copies of some of the individual's gene variants. Hamilton showed formally that inclusive fitness allows a gene that codes for altruism toward kin to spread, even if that altruism reduces the actor's individual fitness. For example, worker bees propagate their genes by helping their mother, the queen, to reproduce. Altruism is adaptive to the actor if the resulting rise in inclusive fitness spreads more of the actor's genes than are lost through the resulting decline of her individual fitness. Hamilton specified the conditions, now known as "Hamilton's rule," under which altruism is adaptive, meaning that the genes coding for the altruism become more numerous. An act is adaptive when $c < br$, where c is the actor's loss of individual fitness, b is the sum of fitness gains to all individuals who benefit from the act, and r is the average relatedness of the beneficiaries to the actor. Hamilton (1963/1996) described it as follows: "An animal acting on this principle would be sacrificing its life adaptively if it could thereby save more than two brothers, but not for less" (p. 7).

Inclusive fitness theory was widely accepted in behavioral biology but was not generally taken up by those interested in ethnicity, even by many sociobiologists, partly because Hamilton had maintained in his 1964 paper that inclusive fitness could only work among close kin. This caveat was cited repeatedly even after Hamilton abandoned it in 1971. Richard Dawkins, a popular interpreter of Hamilton, thought that ethnic altruism was necessarily maladaptive because it benefited selfish free-riders

(Dawkins, 1981; Miele, 1995, p. 83). Another criticism of the adaptiveness of ethnic altruism came from Harvard geneticist Richard Lewontin, who dismissed genetic differences between populations as minor compared to differences between individuals within populations (Lewontin, 1972). It took three decades for a refutation of this influential argument, by Anthony Edwards (2003), to be widely accepted, although Hamilton (1971, 1975) had already provided the theoretical basis for refutation by arguing that ethnic altruism could be adaptive (Salter, 2008). Sociobiologists and scholars of ethnicity generally ignored Hamilton's extension of inclusive fitness theory to include ethnic solidarity.

Some social scientists found Hamilton's initial theory compelling. As noted previously, anthropologist Pierre van den Berghe used inclusive fitness theory to study ethnicity, with a paper in 1978 and a book-length treatment in 1981. As an established anthropologist, van den Berghe's work appeared in journals of social science (Salter, 2001). He became the leading representative of biosocial science in the field of ethnic studies, albeit often deployed as a counterpoint to mainstream theory. His core idea is a sociobiological elaboration of ethnic nepotism theory—that ethnic solidarity is kin selection on a large scale, nepotism extended beyond the family and clan. As a heuristic, he treated humans as evolved actors (Hopcroft, 2009, p. 399): We act as though protecting our genetic interests because our motivational system evolved in the recent past when ties with family, clan, and tribe had fitness consequences. Van den Berghe's theory recognized the centrality of common descent in ethnic identity. It was compatible with the passion of ethnic conflict, both self-sacrificial and aggressive, behavior unexplained by modernist theory (Connor, 1994; Stern, 1995).

Van den Berghe's analysis applies knowledge about kin recognition to ethnic identity, and it draws a distinction between cultural and racial markers. For most of human existence, neighboring populations were racially similar. Recognition of out-groups must have been largely based on culture, often slight differences in language, dress, and rituals. The rise of long-distance trade and empires after the Neolithic introduced racial differences to ethnic relations. Populations separated for tens of millennia and subjected to different climatic selection pressures can evolve visible racial differences that join culture as ethnic markers. This introduced a new dimension to ethnic differentiation, one that could not be erased through enculturation to language, religion, or material culture (van den Berghe, 1999).

Van den Berghe's theory proposed a positive function for ethnic identity and solidarity, a function that did not necessarily entail xenophobia. This implied that ethnic conflict was or could be a side effect of fitness-striving. Van den Berghe viewed ethnicity not as primarily aggressive in function but, rather, as a breeding system based on endogamy (van den Berghe, 1999, p. 30). This positivity also existed in Hamilton's (1964, 1971) original formulation and in sociological contributions to van den Berghe's theory (Whitmeyer, 1997).

Van den Berghe's theory of nepotistic signaling elaborated Eibl-Eibesfeldt's (1970/ 1971) observations, and it was empirically confirmed by studies of political rhetoric (Holper, 1996; Johnson, 1987). Patriotic speeches in literature and American politics were found to contain kinship terminology that portrayed the nation as a family and citizens as kin.

Paul R. Shaw and Yuwa Wong, foreign policy analysts, adopted a quantitative rational actor model of ethnic nepotism theory to test the conditions under which ethnic solidarity could be adaptive according to Hamilton's theory. Like van den Berghe, they identified recognition markers that can release cooperation: kinship, phenotypic similarity, language, religion, and territory (Shaw & Wong, 1989).

Biologist David S. Wilson and philosopher Elliott Sober proposed a multilevel selection model that supplemented inclusive fitness. Levels included individuals and social groups of various sizes, the small nested within the large. In the model, selfish strategists ("free-riders") are controlled by policing and punishment, facilitated in humans by cultural transmission of traditions (Wilson & Sober, 1994). Multilevel selection can result in adaptive units, such as bee colonies, that behave like "superorganisms" (Wilson & Sober, 1989). In humans, the process can work with related individuals, such as tribes, and with collections of unrelated individuals, as sometimes arises in religions. D. S. Wilson (2002) modeled organized religion, a common ethnic marker, as a superorganism evolved through multilevel selection, with cultural and genetic components.

Wilson and Sober's emphasis of group selection, as a domain of selection distinct from inclusive fitness, focused on seemingly maladaptive moral behavior (Sober & Wilson, 1998). They maintained that individual fitness cannot yield altruistic morality. However, inclusive fitness can produce altruistic behavior, including self-sacrifice and celibacy.

A problem for ethnic nepotism theories was that no one had put a figure on ethnic kinship. Hamilton's rule for adaptive altruism used knowledge about the relatedness of close family relatives. A high kinship coefficient, as between parent and child, eases the condition for altruism between those kin being adaptive, but a low coefficient, such as between cousins removed by various degrees, raises practical barriers. Ethnic nepotism theorists had failed to quantify their assumption that ethnic kinship existed, although they assumed that it must be very low. Lopreato and Crippen (1999) stated,

> Ethnic groups have a history of homogamy and assortative mating. Accordingly, the average coefficient of genetic relatedness by descent between two members of the same group may be expected to be larger, by however minute a fraction, than that found on the average between two members of different ethnic groups. (p. 270)

Population geneticist Doug Jones (2000) attempted a solution to this problem using a quantitative genetic selection model. He showed that nepotism jointly expressed by a group toward kin increases the effective kinship coefficient. Jones' model works for small groups and thus can apply to the evolutionary past. But in the past several thousand years, tribes and ethnies have grown to number in the thousands or millions. They occupy large territories. If the kinship of random pairs is low, many such kin must be aided for Hamilton's rule to be satisfied. Political scientist David Goetze (1998) argued that collective goods, such as homeland defense and other services to the community, provide vehicles through which individuals can invest in a large scattered population and thus in aggregate kinship. Group identity can be counted as a collective good, not least because it is a necessary condition for other collective goods.

Henry Harpending, a population geneticist, showed that ethnic kinship is often substantial. On a global scale, it typically approximates that of cousins in an outbred population and sometimes higher (Harpending, 1979, 2002). Political ethologist Frank Salter (2002b, 2003/2007) combined Harpending's analysis with global genetic assay data to apply Hamilton's rule to contemporary ethnic groups. The fitness lost through one population replacing part of another in its home territory is sufficiently high to make self-sacrificial defense adaptive, when free-riders are controlled. The finding is relevant to understanding the evolution of emotional attachment to territory (Eibl-Eibesfeldt, 1975/1979, pp. 60–77; Grosby, 1995; van den Berghe, 1977). This body of research indicates that ethnic solidarity is not merely a simulacrum of adaptive behavior as van den Berghe supposed but can actually improve inclusive fitness.

Monitoring and punishment of free-riders are necessary for ethnic nepotism to be adaptive but can themselves incur costs that reduce fitness. Anthropological studies find that forager groups punish free-riders collectively using low-cost techniques such as gossip. Collective management of reputation is a powerful means of exercising social control over cooperators and free-riders within groups. In hunter–gatherer and other small-scale societies, this control has been motivated by egalitarian norms (Boehm, 1999; Wiessner, 1998).

Ethnic nepotism theory's free-rider problem has received considerable attention. Free-riders are a problem because they capitalize on cooperation from other group members without reciprocating. When free-riders increase their fitness relative to cooperators, their rising numbers cause cooperation to decline. In that case, cooperation is "evolutionarily unstable." Thus, a key question in evolutionary thinking about ethnicity is whether ethnic altruism can ever be evolutionarily stable. Early sociobiologists answered "no" and therefore argued against the possibility of group selection (Williams, 1966). Subsequently, some theorists viewed humans as a special case, due to culture and domain-general intelligence (Wilson & Sober, 1994). Computer simulations have assisted research on the subject. An example is a simulation of competing strategies—selfish, humanitarian, and ethnocentric—using an agent-based evolutionary model (Hammond & Axelrod, 2006). Ethnocentrism was operationalized as behaviors that favor the in-group. The simulation indicated that such behaviors can become widespread under a range of conditions, even in one-move prisoner's dilemma games. Ethnocentrism can persist even when cooperation becomes costly to participants' individual fitness.

These findings were replicated by a computer simulation of strategies competing on the global scale—selfish, traitorous, humanitarian, and ethnocentric (Hartshorn, Kaznatcheev, & Shultz, 2013). Ethnocentrism dominated other strategies because ethnocentric actors cooperate with the in-group but not with out-groups. This led to the in-group colonizing other territories. The closest competitor to ethnocentrism was humanitarianism, which included reciprocity across borders. Ethnocentrism won by exploiting this aspect of humanitarianism. Immigration could delay but not prevent this outcome.

EVOLUTIONARY PSYCHOLOGY

The subdiscipline of evolutionary psychology is the most popular of the evolutionary social disciplines, originating in the United States but growing in Europe and elsewhere. It has resemblances to ethology, including acknowledging a universal human nature with innate elements produced by a long evolutionary process. Human innate psychology is thought to have evolved before some populations migrated out of Africa, the "environment of evolutionary adaptedness," approximately 50,000 years ago. The result is human universals or "species-typical characteristics" (although new genetic findings are undermining this dogma [Hawks, 2013; Hawks, Wang, Cochran, Harpending, & Moyzis, 2007]). Like ethology, evolutionary psychology draws on findings in anthropology and genetics, although concepts and methods are psychologically oriented.

Since the 1960s, the field has generated some findings on ethnic solidarity. At that early stage, some psychologists proposed that ethnic behavior evolved in ancestral environments, in which fitness was enhanced by affiliative, cooperative responses to the home group but xenophobic responses to out-groups. Hamilton's (1964) theory was already being noticed. Campbell (1965, 1972) noted that human self-sacrifice for tribe resembled insect eusociality. He assumed that genetic causality was insufficient to produce this behavior in humans and proposed additional cultural factors, social inventions such as methods of indoctrination and sanctioned rules found in organized religion.

Psychologist Marilynn Brewer (1968, 1981) presented her case study of tribal attitudes in East Africa as evidence for the primordial origins of ethnic identity, ethnocentrism, and ethnic conflict. Subsequent research, such as that by anthropologist Elizabeth Cashdan (2001), found that ethnic solidarity does not correlate with interethnic hostility, in agreement with van den Berghe's (1999) theory of ethnicity as an endogamous breeding pattern. Brewer (1999) subsequently reviewed the subject, emphasizing the leading causal role of in-group favoritism, not necessarily tied to xenophobia. To analyze discrimination and prejudice, she argued, it is necessary to understand "the functions that in-group formation and identification serve for human beings" (p. 429).

The prosocial origin of ethnic solidarity is indicated by the psychological cost of killing in intertribal conflict. Johan van der Dennen (1995, pp. 532–534) documents ritual absolution and purification made by tribal warriors after killing. Considerable time and effort are invested in these rituals, inconsistent with killing, even of enemy warriors, being an evolved competency. Further evidence of ethnocentrism's prosocial origin is the finding that blood levels of oxytocin, a hormone associated with maternal bonding, act to increase ethnocentrism in men. Double-blind tests indicate that oxytocin promotes a "tend and defend" response by increasing group trust and cooperation and defensive, but not aggressive, action directed at competing out-groups (de Dreu et al., 2010; de Dreu, Greer, Kleef, Shalvi, & Handgraaf, 2011).

Evolutionary psychologists were early to see that Hamilton's 1964 theory had relevance for ethnicity, although it seems many were deflected by political taboos and Dawkins's and others' erroneous interpretation that ethnic kinship is too weak to satisfy

Hamilton's rule for adaptive altruism. The misunderstanding of Hamilton's work on ethnicity has contributed to this subject receiving only fitful treatment by evolutionary psychologists (Salter, 2008). Elementary misconceptions are common. A high-profile example is Steven Pinker (2007), perhaps the best known evolutionary psychologist in the United States, who argued that co-ethnics are negligibly related genetically.

A small number of evolutionary psychologists attempted to apply Hamilton's theory directly to ethnicity without cultural factors. This developed from the study of assortative mating observed in many species. Del Thiessen and Barbara Gregg (1980) observed that in humans endogamous mating is pronounced along ethnic and racial lines. Moderate assortment that avoids inbreeding depression caused by incest correlates with more stable marriages, fecundity, higher parental kinship, and stronger communication and altruism. Anthropologist Robin Fox (2015) notes that cross-cousin marriage is the rule in hunter–gatherer societies and appears to maximize fertility. As Thiessen and Gregg thought, higher parental kinship results from endogamy (Harpending, 2002). That boosts inclusive fitness by increasing the efficiency of parental investment (Salter, 2002b). This analysis offers a directly biological explanation for endogamy and, by implication, ethnic solidarity, based on genetic similarity within ethnies. The argument elaborates van den Berghe's (1978, 1981) interpretation of ethnicity as an extended endogamous kinship system.

Sociologist Joseph Whitmeyer (1997) extended van den Berghe's theory to mathematically model a link between normative endogamy and ethnic ties. Endogamy is normal and expected behavior for all ethnic groups. Whitmeyer argued that this normativity itself was adaptive because it produced solidarity across the ethny. Individuals who follow the norm of marrying within the ethny promote the expectation of future ethnic kinship, an expectation that facilitates nepotism in the present among non-kin as well as kin in anticipation of future kinship. The model indicates how normative endogamy might reduce the fitness cost of lower parental kinship resulting from exogamy.

Assortment in human mate choice formed the basis of J. Philippe Rushton's (1989a) genetic similarity theory (GST), which he presented as a general theory of assortment within and between ethnic groups. Rushton also applied GST to ethnic nationalism, arguing that the binding effect of genetic similarity helps extend A. D. Smith's theory of ethnosymbolism (Rushton, 2005). Smith's theory of ethnic solidarity resembles that of van den Berghe by relying on shared cultural symbols, including shared religion, dress, and foundation myths, which work psychologically to build cooperation. To this, Rushton added inherited characteristics and a psychology adapted for nepotistic favoritism. He noted the robust levels of kinship that can be found within ethnies in multi-ethnic societies (Salter, 2003/2007). Indirect support for GST derives from the finding that genetic diversity—within and among ethnies—correlates with social conflict (Arbatli, Ashraf, & Galor, 2015).

Direct support for GST derives from evidence of assortment in choice of friends, mates, and business partners in ethnically mixed societies. In these societies, ethnic kinship can be substantial, such as immigrant societies drawing on populations evolved in different regions and continents. In that case, Rushton's theory is expected theoretically

(Salter & Harpending, 2013) and supported by numerous empirical studies (Arbatli et al., 2015; McPherson, Smith-Lovin, & Cook, 2001; Salter 2002a, 2004; Thiessen & Gregg, 1980). Disconfirmation of GST in ethnically mixed societies is rare (Curry & Dunbar, 2013).

Genetic models question the possibility of genetic similarity affecting behavior within ethnically homogeneous societies because phenotypic similarity in one or a few traits does not correlate with genome-wide similarity, a prerequisite for inclusive fitness processes to work (Grafen, 1990; Salter & Harpending, 2013). Nevertheless, multiple studies find some genetic similarity among friends within ethnic groups, extending to approximately 1% of their genomes, equivalent to the relatedness of cousins four times removed (Christakis & Fowler, 2014; Rushton, 1989b).

The motivations that direct investment toward kin and tribe are receiving more attention from evolutionary psychologists. A Swiss research group found cross-cultural evidence that ethnic favoritism conditions the moral emotions such that norm violations by fellow ethnics against an outsider are punished less severely than the reverse (Bernhard, Fischbacher, & Fehr, 2006). The authors point to ways in which multilevel selection and kin-selection theories could explain their results. A group's reputation for going out of its way to punish external aggression might have been a protective factor in intertribal relations.

Most psychological contributions to ethnic studies have not been evolutionary. Knowledge of assortment by similarity, social identity mechanisms, and individualism/collectivism, all bearing on group identity and solidarity, were developed without reference to natural selection, although they generally provide support for an evolutionary interpretation (MacDonald, 2001). The same applies to Lawrence Hirschfeld's (1996) theory of innate categorization of descent groups, including races. Despite rejecting the objective reality of race (p. 13), Hirschfeld's ingenious social psychological experiments indicate that uninstructed 3-year-old children distinguish inherited from acquired characteristics. Hirschfeld found that "even preschoolers see race as immutable, corporeal, differentiated, derived from family background, and at least consistent with biological principles of causality" (p. 98). He concluded that humans have an innate special-purpose competence for identifying and representing human descent groups.

Research has continued into innate mental competencies affecting ethnic behavior, which may have evolved from different selection pressures. This idea has been explored by MacDonald (2001) and developed by Cristina Moya and Robert Boyd (2015). Ethnic behavior appears to consist of several distinct adaptations: stereotyping, essentialism 1 (belief in the biological transmission of characteristics and stability of identity), essentialism 2 (mutual exclusivity of group identity), intentional ethnic markers, intragroup assortment, and intergroup competition and hostility. By interviewing people from different communities in the Peruvian Altiplano, Moya and Boyd find evidence that these types of ethnic behavior are not closely correlated. For example, stereotyping by language is weaker than stereotyping by economic function. Moya and Boyd find that even different types of essentialism, the belief that group characteristics are innate, do not co-vary. Language categories are not considered mutually exclusive, but religions generally are considered to be so.

Moya and Boyd's (2015) interpretation de-emphasizes genetic evolution as a cause of ethnic behaviors but emphasizes selection of cultural differences. This builds on earlier research by Boyd and Peter Richerson (1985) that developed a model of culture-led group selection. In the model, communities develop ways of life governed by rituals and rules that suppress free-riders and shape genetic evolution through group selection—one group replacing another. The effect on gene frequencies is an indirect effect of group selection acting on culturally transmitted traits. Like Eibl-Eibesfeldt, Boyd and Richerson (1992) argue that monitoring and punishing free-riders allow group selection to operate. The result is commitment to the tribe, culturally defined (Richerson & Boyd, 2001). These models extend the dual-inheritance model of evolution—involving the feedback between genes and culture—proposed by Charles Lumsden and Edward O. Wilson (1981). They also develop Campbell's ideas discussed previously—that social inventions can elicit eusociality and control free-riders—by proposing that cultural constructs such as religions and sanctioned rules act as powerful selective agencies between cultural groups. Their theory of cultural group selection resembles Arnold Gehlen's (1940/1958; cited in Lorenz, 1971/1950, pp. 172–173) idea that humans have domesticated themselves to become innately cultural beings by constructing environments that then, inadvertently, select for changes in human nature.

Cultural group selection theory has received some empirical support. A field study of New Guinean communities confirmed elements of the theory (Soltis, Boyd, & Richerson, 1995). Kevin MacDonald (1994) used the theory as a basis for a case study of Judaism, in which he argued that cultural traditions such as endogamy have operated to preserve and evolve the Jewish gene pool. MacDonald's case study formed part of D. S. Wilson's (2002) theory of religion as a selective unit. Wilson's theory is group selectionist, whereas MacDonald's combines group and individual theories. Culturally transmitted strategies define and discipline the behavior of ethnies, but in doing so they increase endogamy, tending to segregate the gene pool, which preserves or increases ethnic kinship. The fitness payoffs yielded by the cultural strategy operating on ethnic kin boost their inclusive fitness, as conceptualized by Hamilton, van den Berghe, and Rushton.

Boyd and Richerson have been careful to distinguish their hypothetical evolutionary band from descent groups. They maintain that cultural group selection could not have operated on extended kin groups because of gene flow between competing groups. Defeated groups are not exterminated but, rather, absorbed by others. Wife capture is a common motivation for intergroup raiding. As a result, lineages are distributed across bands (Richerson & Boyd, 1998/2001). This assumption sets up cultural group selection as contradicting ethnic nepotism theory, although as discussed previously, MacDonald argued that the two theories can be complementary in the case of Judaism. Further evidence works against Boyd and Richerson's assumption. Hamilton's (1975) genetic theory of tribal solidarity allowed for genetic differences between populations to remain despite permanent low-level migration between them. Also, gene assay data show that genetic differentiation exists among foraging groups (Bowles, 2007; Jones, 2000, p. 787). This is unsurprising considering that communities fission along kinship lines (Chagnon, 1975; Freedman, 1984).

By de-emphasizing nepotism, cultural group selection theory has some qualities of instrumentalism in ethnic theory, the idea that ethnic identity and solidarity are tactics for achieving non-ethnic goals such as individual status or resource acquisition. Like non-biosocial types of instrumentalism, this view is associated with the idea that ethnic identity and solidarity can be reduced or eliminated through cultural and economic interventions.

An early expression of biosocial instrumentalism derived from geneticist Richard Lewontin (1972), who concluded that race has no taxonomic or genetic significance because only approximately 15% of human genetic diversity exists among populations, whereas 85% exists among individuals within populations. Harpending (2002) observed that Lewontin's genetic data have been confirmed by subsequent assays. However, far from undermining the significance of ethnic nepotism, the figures cited by Lewontin mean that ethnic kinship is remarkably high in global comparison, comparable to that found between first cousins in outbred populations (Harpending, 2002).

Explicit biosocial arguments against van den Berghe's theory were advanced by primatologist Vernon Reynolds (1980). Like Boyd and Richerson, Reynolds doubted the existence of genetic differentiation between foraging bands. He asserted that humans construct their social realities and the way they view themselves and that humans also largely construct themselves, making language and cultural categories decisive in forming social relations, not the objective, unconstructed processes shaping other species. Reynolds correctly noted that radical social construction theory along these lines is common in sociology, social anthropology, and social psychology (p. 313), helping explain those disciplines' resistance to biosocial science. A difficulty for Reynold's argument is that social constructivism, if true, renders irrelevant all biosocial theories of human behavior based on genetics and evolution, including Reynold's own biosocial criticisms of ethnic nepotism theory (Salter, 2001).

Another biosocial instrumentalism was argued by psychologists Irwin Silverman and Danielle Case (1998/2001). They conducted psychological tests on Canadian students and found that willingness to favor own ethnies declined rapidly as attendant risks increased. The students adopted "pragmatic" options, which minimized individual risk. Silverman and Case concluded that strong ethnic solidarity did not evolve in humans because the greatest fitness payoff during hominid evolution would have come from flexibility in forming alliances that maximized individual benefit. As circumstances changed, so would the choice of alliance partners. This implies that when ethnic loyalty is shown, it is really an alliance of convenience meant to benefit the individual. Loyalty to ethny is an instrument for other purposes.

Self-sacrifice for tribe and the "orgies of passion" described by van den Berghe are problems for Silverman and Cases's model of humans as selfish pragmatists. However, an analysis by psychologists Robert Kurzban, John Tooby, and Leda Cosmides (2001) avoids this defect by questioning not ethnic commitment but, rather, categorization as a basis for social alliances. Their experimental study of White university students, average

age 19 years, found that participants in a coalition game minimized their use of racial classification when race did not correlate with team membership. The same was not true of sex, which remained a robust category however coalitional makeup was arranged. The authors concluded that ethnicity is a less salient category when it does not correspond with the coalitional terrain. This is Silverman and Case's thesis about pragmatism applied to identity.

Kurzban et al.'s (2001) experiment might be taken as evidence of the flexibility and culture dependency of ethnic behavior shown in response to changing circumstances. However, Kurzban et al. go further by asserting that their results disprove the assumption of innate ethnic behavior and are consistent with the genetic and phylogenetic marginality of ethnicity. This is Lewontin's argument. The study's hypotheses, method, and interpretation all rest on taking strong positions on that side of the debate—for example, that ethnicity has insignificant genetic correlates (p. 15387) and that the study's participants, mainly middle-class White teenagers, were raised to have prejudicial racial views in a society riven by racial alliances. Despite lifelong inculcation of prejudicial assumptions, Kurzban et al. argue, teenagers were cured of their prejudices in one brief experiment, indicating that ethnocentrism is not an evolved competence (p. 15389). They use the latter assumption to dismiss Hirschfeld's (1996) contradictory finding that 3-year-olds identify race but not occupation as heritable (p. 15388). Kurzban et al. conclude that racial discrimination can be "erased," echoing the view of critical race theorists that White people in the United States are unnaturally obsessed with race and that "whiteness" is an instrumentalism that can be abolished (Roediger, 1999). The radical instrumentalism claimed in the study has not been supported by two replication studies, which show substantially reduced effect sizes (Voorspoels, Bartlema, & Vanpaemel, 2014). Despite the elaborate experimental conditions being duplicated, participants continued to code coalition members by race.

Although the variability of ethnic commitment and, less so, that of identification are well-known phenomena, there is mounting evidence of nepotism being learned by innate processes situated in the family. Compatible with Hirschfeld's findings, studies of young children indicate that preference for own-race faces is evident by the age of 3 months but not at 1 month (Kelly et al., 2005). This preference is moderated by exposure to out-groups during childhood (Bar-Haim, Ziv, Lamy, & Hodes, 2006), indicating social learning of ethnic cues. Competency at recognizing faces narrows from 3 months, when infants can distinguish faces from several races, to 9 months, when they can distinguish only own-race faces (Kelly et al., 2007). This is interpreted to be due to learning from the appearance of caregivers. Other research finds that by age 11 months, infants notice and attend to faces different from their own race and pay more attention to some racial differences than others (Singarajah et al., 2016).

Also contradicting Kurzban et al.'s (2001) study is the finding that fear responses in adults conditioned on faces of different races did not extinguish when the images were shown without shocks, whereas fear responses did recede for own-race faces (Olsson, Ebert, Banaji, & Phelps, 2005). The results are consistent with other evolutionarily prepared responses, such as fear of heights. Subsequent research using the same methods found that conditioned fear responses to out-groups only failed to extinguish when the exemplars were men (Navarrete et al., 2009). This and related findings support an evolutionary hypothesis in which male tribal warriors were the agents of intergroup conflict (McDonald, Navarrete, & Van Vugt, 2012).

Brain imaging research that measures implicit (subconscious) responses to racial out-groups contradicts a tenet of critical race studies—that hostile ethnic sentiments originate solely in White majorities in Western cultural contexts (Roediger, 1999). For example, Lipp, Mallan, Martin, Terry, and Smith (2011) found that implicit race bias is shown by participants of any race in any cultural context.

The "implicit association test" was developed by social psychologists Mahzarin Banaji and Anthony Greenwald (2013/2016). The test found a broad trend in the United States of "White preference," meaning that White Americans take longer to sort together Black faces and pleasant words than to sort together White faces with the same words. Test-takers were often unaware of their bias, and they consciously repudiated it. Thus, the bias did not consist of conscious dislike, disrespect, or hatred.

Almost 75% of Americans who take the implicit association test show White preference. Further experimental research has found that White preference in sorting faces and words predicts discriminatory behavior independently of ideology. Even those who have egalitarian views but score high on White preference prefer Whites in practice, although the correlation is only 0.24, explaining just 6% of the variation in the behavior (Banaji & Greenwald, 2013/2016, p. 49).

Banaji and Greenwald (2013/2016) did not explore biosocial factors, which might explain their focus on White bias. They did not test for cross-ethnic universals. They report Barack Obama losing the White vote in the 2008 presidential election by 12% as evidence of White bias, without mentioning that Obama led the Black vote over John McCain by 91% (p. 186). This appears to be the same sort of minority ethnocentrism displayed by critical race theorists. Nevertheless, their research was valuable by drawing attention to the distinction between implicit and explicit ethnicity, which has proven fruitful in exploring this dimension of human nature.

The distinction between implicit and explicit ethnicity helps explain the impact of culture on ethnic behavior. Brain imaging of people with different political orientation and ethnicities shows similar implicit responses. MacDonald (2008) reviewed research indicating that when participants viewed pictures of other-race individuals for approximately 1/30th of a second, their brains showed a negative emotional response (in the amygdala). But when they viewed the picture for longer than half a second, the negative response was suppressed by executive processing (in the prefrontal cortex). MacDonald interprets this as evolved implicit processing being regulated by explicit processing by the conscious mind. Because the latter is the seat of social norms and general intelligence, this brain architecture allows humans to control their automatic impulses, although when ideology and impulses conflict, control takes time to process.

Explicit verbalized race bias emerges from age 3 years in the manner described by Hirschfeld (1996) but then begins to decline as the child learns to inhibit automatic responses to ethnic difference. However, there is evidence that implicit bias continues to influence behavior, because at the same time that explicit bias declines, schoolchildren self-segregate in choice of friends, avoiding cross-racial interactions (MacDonald, 2008, pp. 1022–1023).

MacDonald's (2008) distinction between implicit and explicit ethnicity could have political consequences because ideological appeals are aimed at the conscious mind, which can override or magnify implicit ethnocentrism. "Culture wars" over ethnicity might serve an evolutionary function of inhibiting or freeing individuals' investment in ethnic kin.

Tests and Heuristics: Diversity

This section reviews tests and applications of biosocial theories of ethnicity in the context of intrastate ethnocultural diversity. It identifies some of the issues that have stimulated research during the past two decades. Most of the studies have tested aspects of ethnic nepotism theory.

Political psychologist James Sidanius provides a biosocial theory for conceptualizing ethnic cultural contests in liberal democracies such as the United States (Sidanius & Pratto, 1999). He documents group dominance resulting from ethnic conflict in diverse societies. Sidanius also researches the psychological mechanisms underlying persistent discrimination (Navarrete et al., 2009). He posits a universal "will to group dominance" fed by a species-specific, evolved strategy for aiding the survival of "breeding populations" through evolutionary time. Ethnic hierarchy takes the form of hegemony or "consensual social dominance," the shaping of beliefs and norms via centralized organs of culture.

Biosocial concepts are also central to economist Janet Landa's (2002, 2009) study of trust and cooperation in ethnic middleman groups. Landa adopts D. S. Wilson's theory of superorganisms or adaptive units to explain how middleman minorities can achieve market dominance (Wilson & Sober, 1989; see also van den Berghe, 1981, pp. 137–156). Sociologist Eric Kaufmann, whose research and teaching include biological themes such as genetics, has examined cases of minorities achieving political dominance over majorities (Kaufmann, 2004).

Findings from several disciplines indicate that individuals of shared ethnicity can show increased trust (Salter, 2002a, 2007). As a result, ethnic networks are often implicated when risky business is transacted on a regular basis, in such settings as organized crime gangs, long-range exchange networks traders lacking the protection of contract law, certain US Supreme Court proceedings, dissenters from totalitarian societies, among nationalist freedom fighters, and even among tourists. Outside such risky transactions, ethnic solidarity is a pervasive weak tie sensitive to rituals and ideology. It is usually intermediate in strength between strong kinship bonds and interactions between non-ethnics.

Non-biosocial studies of diversity, most famously by political scientist Robert Putnam (2007; and see Healy, 2007), also find that shared ethnicity facilitates trust and other indicators of social capital. Putnam found that rising ethnolinguistic diversity correlated with falling trust and civic engagement. There have been some disconfirming observations at the national level (Portes & Vickstrom, 2011). However, Putnam's result is confirmed by studies conducted at the local community level (Dinesen & Soenerskov, 2015; Laurence & Bentley, 2015). A complementary finding is that individuals living among fellow ethnics are happier than individuals living as an ethnic minority (Kanazawa & Li, 2015).

Shared ethnicity also facilitates charitable giving and welfare. An observational study of street beggars in Moscow that was led by Marina Butovskaya found that beggars received the largest gifts from fellow ethnics, the next largest from a genetically similar ethnic group, and least from a relatively distant ethnic group (Butovskaya, Salter, Diakonov, & Smirnov, 2000).

More generally, ethnic heterogeneity depresses the willingness of citizens to contribute to public goods (Salter, 2004, 2007). Research contributing to this finding examines charitable giving in the United States (more homogeneous counties give more), a global comparison of welfare states (ethnic heterogeneity correlates negatively with welfare rights), and foreign aid (relatively homogeneous states give more).

Ethnic conflict has been found to increase with ethnic diversity. Wars among and within states are influenced by ethnic nepotism (Thayer, 2003). Sociologist Tatu Vanhanen (1991, 2012) tested ethnic nepotism theory cross-nationally in a series of studies, beginning with a case study of India. His global comparative study of 176 contemporary societies based on data gathered in 2010 examined ethnic conflict defined broadly to include discrimination, ethnic parties and interest groups, as well as ethnic violence and civil war. He tested the hypothesis that greater diversity would increase conflict due to reduced genetic similarity. Two-thirds of the variation in ethnic conflict was explained by ethnic diversity.

New Research: National Character and the State

Some biosocial research on ethnicity provides new perspectives on the old concept of national character.

Because ethnies are descent groups, they can also bear epigenetic information imprinted from common experiences. Methylation of DNA produced by stressors and diet can be passed onto offspring. For example, recent research finds that obese men pass on obesity to their children via alterations to sperm. The effect on sperm is reversed when the men return to normal weight (Donkin et al., 2016). One set of epigenetic studies on rats has found that stress and diet restriction have significant effects on reproductive and maternal behavior (Levay, Tammer, Penman, Kent, & Paolini, 2010). Based on this and related findings in primatology and human ethology, historian James Penman (2015) developed a theory of the rise and development of civilizations. The theory's key explanatory variable is temperament. The theory proposes that organized religions underpin the rise of civilizations by altering temperament to better serve work regimes and extended hierarchies. They do this using such interventions as restricting food and sexual behavior and regulating how children are reared. Penman's theory is a novel version of Campbell's (1972) argument that organized religion is a social invention for shaping the behavior of populations.

Another biosocial approach to ethnic temperament concerns the disposition to violence. States are sets of organizations that monopolize the use of legitimate violence within a territory. Early states are notorious for the high rate at which they executed felons. The rate was sufficiently high in the Roman Empire, Peter Frost and Henry Harpending argue, to genetically pacify the population by weeding out gene variants predisposing to violence (Frost, 2010; Frost & Harpending, 2015). This has had secondary effects, such as making civilizations vulnerable to incursions from more aggressive populations.

Economist Gregory Clark (2007) has proposed a different selective path to pacifism, established by the state imposing a rule of law that encompassed the aristocracy. Clarke's thesis is that denial of violence or theft as economic tactics gave hard-working individuals a fitness advantage, which led to evolutionary change. Clark studied English wills that were written from 1200 to 1800, and found that wealthy individuals had more surviving children. He attributes the rise in work ethic, which he characterizes as "genetic capitalism," to this evolutionary process, initiated by the proto-liberal state. Clark concludes that this has contributed to population differences in work behavior.

"Cultural neuroscience" is an evolutionary approach to studying national character (Chiao, Cheon, Pornpattananangkul, Mrazek, & Blizinsky, 2014). Evidence has been found that a population's placement on the collectivism–individualism spectrum is affected by ethnic-specific gene frequencies, perhaps produced by culture–gene co-evolution. Chiao and Blizinsky (2010) found that the frequency of alleles coding for the serotonin transporter functional polymorphism 5-HTTLPR may play a role in producing collectivistic cultures. Across 29 nations, the latter were more likely to include individuals carrying the short (S) allele of 5-HTTLPR. There is evidence that variation in collectivism–individualism has been differentially selected by pathogen prevalence (Fincher, Thornhill, Murray, & Schaller, 2008). This has implications for ethnic culture, including interethnic ideology, because collectivist cultures are more likely to be ethnocentric and conformist.

Conclusion

This chapter reviewed the history of biological analyses of ethnic solidarity and conflict. Biology is a likely factor in any social phenomenon affected by descent. The biosocial approach is unique in tracing causal chains back to adaptations, including brain functions, and the evolutionary process that selected for them. Treating humans as an evolved species has also been fruitful in suggesting new research.

The universality of ethnic behavior and its frequent altruism point to evolutionary origins. The genetic similarity of fellow ethnics is consistent with an adaptive function of group solidarity, although the finding of substantial ethnic genetic kinship has not yet been formally synthesized with group selection models. An influential school of thought has emerged among biosocial theorists that selection for ethnic solidarity occurred at multiple levels and was influenced by cultural group strategies.

Biological analysis is not widely accepted in the field of ethnic studies, despite the significant empirical and theoretical advances reviewed previously. Biosocial science continues to be largely excluded from the study of ethnicity, as it is from the sociological disciplines and the humanities. Currently, there is no dedicated undergraduate textbook suitable for teaching biosocial perspectives in ethnicity, although this subject is included in some broader biosocial texts (Hopcroft, 2010; Lopreato & Crippen, 1999; Sanderson, 2014).

It is unfortunate that ethnic studies remain largely isolated from biology because formulating and testing hypotheses about something as complex as ethnicity requires collaboration between disciplines in the social and life sciences. The same is true of policy analysis, including ethics. In this regard, the liberal cosmopolitanism taken for granted in the social sciences is not self-evidently normative because prosocial values are promoted by national identity and solidarity. It is not at all obvious that immigration policies that increase diversity are morally irreproachable when it is known that diversity is a major risk factor for social conflict (Vanhanen, 2012). Economist Paul Collier (2013) summarized research in the area when he noted, "From the perspective of cooperation between people, nations are not selfish impediments to global citizenship; they are virtually our only systems for providing public goods" (p. 236).

Banaji and Greenwald (2013/2016) refer to the "hidden biases of good people," which assumes that discrimination is not something good people do. However, from the perspective of ethnic nepotism theory, it is not at all obvious that common types of discrimination in favor of ethnic kin are necessarily bad, any more than discriminating in favor of one's children.

Policymakers need all the insights they can muster in a world in which nationalism remains influential and intrastate ethnic diversity, known to correlate with social breakdown, is on the rise.

REFERENCES

Anderson, B. R. O. G. (1983). *Imagined communities. Reflections on the origin and spread of nationalism.* London, UK: Verso.

Arbatli, C. E., Ashraf, Q., & Galor, O. (2015, April). *The nature of conflict.* National Bureau of Economic Research Working Paper No. 21079.

Banaji, M., & Greenwald, A. (2016). *Blindspot: Hidden biases of good people*. New York, NY: Bantam. (Original work published 2013)

Barbujani, G., & Sokal, R. R. (1990). Zones of sharp genetic change in Europe are also linguistic boundaries. *Proceedings of the National Academy of Sciences of the USA, 87*(5), 1816–1819.

Bar-Haim, Y., Ziv, T., Lamy, D., & Hodes, R. M. (2006). Nature and nurture in own-race face processing. *Psychological Science, 17,* 159–163.

Bernhard, H., Fischbacher, U., & Fehr, E. (2006). Parochial altruism in humans. *Nature, 442,* 912–915.

Boehm, C. (1999). *Hierarchy in the forest: The evolution of egalitarian behavior.* Cambridge, MA: Harvard University Press.

Bowles, S. (2007). *Genetic differentiation among hunter–gatherer groups.* Unpublished manuscript, Santa Fe Institute and Universitá di Siena.

Boyd, R., & Richerson, P. J. (1985). *Culture and the evolutionary process.* Chicago, IL: University of Chicago Press.

Boyd, R., & Richerson, P. J. (1992). Punishment allows the evolution of cooperation (or anything else) in sizable groups. *Ethology and Sociobiology, 13,* 171–195.

Brewer, M. B. (1968). Determinants of social distance among East African tribal groups. *Journal of Personality and Social Psychology, 10,* 279–289.

Brewer, M. B.. (1981). Ethnocentrism and its role in interpersonal trust. In M. B. Brewer & B. E. Collins (Eds.), *Scientific inquiry and the social sciences: A volume in honor of Donald T. Campbell* (pp. 345–360). San Francisco, CA: Jossey-Bass.

Brewer, M. B. (1999). The psychology of prejudice: Ingroup love and outgroup hate? *Journal of Social Issues, 55*(3), 429–444.

Butovskaya, M., Salter, F., Diakonov, I., & Smirnov, A. (2000). Urban begging and ethnic nepotism in Russia: An ethological pilot study. *Human Nature, 11*(2), 157–182.

Campbell, D. T. (1965). Ethnocentric and other altruistic motives. In D. Levine (Ed.), *Nebraska symposium on motivation: Vol. 13* (pp. 283–311). Lincoln, NE: University of Nebraska Press.

Campbell, D. T. (1972). On the genetics of altruism and the counter-hedonic components in human culture. *Journal of Social Issues, 28*(3), 21–37.

Cashdan, E. (2001). Ethnocentrism and xenophobia: A cross-cultural study. *Current Anthropology, 42*(5), 760–765.

Cavalli-Sforza, L. L. (1997). Genes, peoples, and languages. *Proceedings of the National Academy of Sciences of the USA, 94,* 7719–7724.

Chagnon, N. A. (1975). Genealogy, solidarity, and relatedness: Limits to local group size and patterns of fissioning in an expanding population. *Yearbook of Physical Anthropology, 19,* 95–110.

Chiao, J. Y., & Blizinsky, K. D. (2010). Culture–gene coevolution of individualism–collectivism and the serotonin transporter gene. *Proceedings of the Royal Society B: Biological Sciences, 277*(1681), 529–537.

Chiao, J. Y., Cheon, B. K., Pornpattananangkul, N., Mrazek, A. J., & Blizinsky, K. D. (2014). Cultural neuroscience: Understanding human diversity. In M. J. Gelfand, C.-Y. Chiu, & Y.-Y. Hong (Eds.), *Advances in culture psychology* (Vol. 4, pp. 1–77). Oxford, UK: Oxford University Press.

Christakis, N. A., & Fowler, J. H. (2014). Friendship and natural selection. *Proceedings of the National Academy of Sciences of the USA, 111*(Suppl. 3), 10796–10801 .

Clark, G. (2007). *A farewell to alms: A brief economic history of the world.* Princeton, NJ: Princeton University Press.

Collier, P. (2013). *Exodus: Immigration and multiculturalism in the 21st century.* London: Allen Lane.

Connor, W. (1994). *Ethnonationalism: The quest for understanding.* Princeton, NJ: Princeton University Press.

Curry, O., & Dunbar, R. I. M. (2013). Do birds of a feather flock together? The relationship between similarity and altruism in social networks. *Human Nature, 24,* 336–347.

Darwin, C. (1913). *The descent of man and selection in relation to sex* (1913 ed.). London: Murray. (Original work published 1871)

Dawkins, R. (1981). Selfish genes in race or politics. *Nature, 289*(5798), 528.

Dawkins, R. (1989). *The selfish gene* (2nd ed.). Oxford, UK: Oxford University Press. (Original work published 1976)

de Dreu, C. K. W., Greer, L. L., Handgraaf, M. J. J., Shalvi, S., Kleef, G. A. V., Baas, M.,. . . Feith, S. W. W. (2010). The neuropeptide oxytocin regulates parochial altruism in intergroup conflict among humans. *Science, 328,* 1408–1411.

de Dreu, C. K. W., Greer, L. L., Kleef, G. A. V., Shalvi, S., & Handgraaf, M. J. J. (2011). Oxytocin promotes human ethnocentrism. *Proceedings of the National Academy of Sciences of the USA, 108*(4), 1262–1266.

Degler, C. (1991). *In search of human nature: The decline and revival of Darwinism in American social thought.* Oxford, UK: Oxford University Press.

Dinesen, P. T., & Soenerskov, K. M. (2015). Ethnic diversity and social trust: Evidence from the micro-context. *American Sociological Review, 80*(3), 550–573. doi:10.1177/0003122415577989

Donkin, I., Versteyhe, S., Ingerslev, L. R., Qian, K., Mechta, M., Nordkap, L., . . . Barrés, R. (2016). Obesity and bariatric surgery drive epigenetic variation of spermatozoa in humans. *Cell Metabolism, 23*(2), 369–378.

Edwards, A. W. F. (2003). Human genetic diversity: Lewontin's fallacy. *BioEssays, 25*(8), 798–801.

Eibl-Eibesfeldt, I. (1971). *Love and hate: The natural history of behavior patterns* (G. Strachan, Trans.). London, UK: Methuen. (Original German edition published 1970)

Eibl-Eibesfeldt, I. (1979). *The biology of peace and war: Men, animals, and aggression* (E. Mosbacher, Trans.). London, UK: Thames & Hudson. (Original German edition published 1975)

Eibl-Eibesfeldt, I. (1982). Warfare, man's indoctrinability and group selection. *Ethology (Zeitschrift für Tierpsychologie), 60,* 177–198.

Eibl-Eibesfeldt, I. (1989). *Human ethology.* New York, NY: Aldine de Gruyter. (Original work published 1984)

Eibl-Eibesfeldt, I. (2001). Us and the others: The familial roots of ethnonationalism. In I. Eibl-Eibesfeldt & F. K. Salter (Eds.), *Ethnic conflict and indoctrination: Altruism and identity in evolutionary perspective* (pp. 21–53). Oxford, UK: Berghahn. (Original work published 1998)

Eibl-Eibesfeldt, I., & Salter, F. K. (Eds.). (2001). *Ethnic conflict and indoctrination: Altruism and identity in evolutionary perspective.* Oxford, UK: Berghahn. (Original work published 1998)

Fincher, C. L., Thornhill, R., Murray, D. R., & Schaller, M. (2008). Pathogen prevalence predicts human cross-cultural variability in individualism/collectivism. *Proceedings of the Royal Society B: Biological Sciences, 275*(1640), 1279–1285.

Fox, R. (1979). Kinship categories as natural categories. In N. A. Chagnon & W. Irons (Eds.), *Evolutionary biology and human social behavior. An anthropological perspective* (pp. 132–144). North Scituate, MA: Duxbury.

Fox, R. (2015). Marry in or die out. In J. H. Turner, R. Machalek & A. Maryanski (Eds.), *Handbook on evolution and society: Toward an evolutionary social science* (pp. 350–382). Boulder, CO: Paradigm.

Freedman, D. G. (1984). Village fissioning, human diversity, and ethnocentrism. *Political Psychology, 5*(4), 629–634.

Frost, P. (2010). The Roman state and genetic pacification. *Evolutionary Psychology, 8*(3), 376–389.

Frost, P., & Harpending, H. (2015). Executions cull gene linked to violence. *Evolutionary Psychology, 13*(1), 230–243.

Geertz, C. (1973). *The interpretation of cultures.* New York, NY: Basic Books.

Gehlen, A. (1958). *Der Mensch, seine Natur und seine Stellung in der Welt* [*Man, his nature and his place in the world*] (6th ed.). Berlin, Germany: Athenaum. (Original work published 1940)

Goetze, D. (1998). Evolution, mobility, and ethnic group formation. *Politics and the Life Sciences, 17*(1), 59–71.

Grafen, A. (1990). Do animals really recognize kin? *Animal Behaviour, 39*, 42–54.

Grosby, S. (1995). Territoriality: The transcendental, primordial feature of modern societies. *Nations and Nationalism, 1*(2), 143–162.

Hamilton, W. D. (1964). The genetic evolution of social behavior: Parts 1 and 2. *Journal of Theoretical Biology, 7*, 1–51.

Hamilton, W. D. (1971). Selection of selfish and altruistic behavior in some extreme models. In J. F. Eisenberg & W. S. Dillon (Eds.), *Man and beast: Comparative social behavior* (pp. 59–91). Washington, DC: Smithsonian Institute Press.

Hamilton, W. D. (1975). Innate social aptitudes of man: An approach from evolutionary genetics. In R. Fox (Ed.), *Biosocial anthropology* (pp. 133–155). London, UK: Malaby Press.

Hamilton, W. D. (1996). The evolution of altruistic behavior. In W. D. Hamilton (Ed.), *Narrow roads of gene land. Vol. 1: Evolution of social behaviour* (Vol. 97, pp. 6–8). Oxford: W. H. Freeman. (Original work published 1963)

Hammond, R. A., & Axelrod, R. (2006). The evolution of ethnocentrism. *Journal of Conflict Resolution, 50*(6), 926–936.

Harpending, H. (1979). The population genetics of interactions. *American Naturalist, 113*, 622–630.

Harpending, H. (2002). Kinship and population subdivision. *Population and Environment, 24*(2), 141–147.

Hartshorn, M., Kaznatcheev, A., & Shultz, T. (2013). The evolutionary dominance of ethnocentric cooperation. *Journal of Artificial Societies and Social Simulation, 16*(3).

Hawks, J. (2013). Significance of Neanderthal and Denisovan genomes in human evolution. *Annual Review of Anthropology, 42*, 433–449.

Hawks, J., Wang, E. T., Cochran, G. M., Harpending, H. C., & Moyzis, R. K. (2007). Recent acceleration of human adaptive evolution. *Proceedings of the National Academy of Sciences of the USA, 204*(52), 20753–20758.

Healy, E. (2007). Ethnic diversity and social cohesion in Melbourne. *People and Place, 15*(4), 49–64.

Hirschfeld, L. A. (1996). *Race in the making: Cognition, culture, and the child's construction of human kinds.* Cambridge, MA: MIT Press.

Hobsbawm, E. J. (1990). *Nations and nationalism since 1780: Programme, myth, reality.* Cambridge, UK: Cambridge University Press.

Holper, J. J. (1996). Kin term usage in *The Federalist*: Evolutionary foundations of Publius's rhetoric. *Politics and the Life Sciences, 15*(2), 265–272.

Hopcroft, R. L. (2009). The evolved actor in sociology. *Sociological Theory*, 27(4), 390–406.

Hopcroft, R. L. (2010). *Sociology: A biosocial introduction* (pp. 211–238). New York, NY: Routledge.

Johnson, G. R. (1987). In the name of the fatherland: An analysis of kin terms usage in patriotic speech and literature. *International Political Science Review*, 8, 165–174.

Jones, D. (2000). Group nepotism and human kinship. *Current Anthropology*, 41(5), 779–809.

Kanazawa, S., & Li, N. P. (2015). Happiness in modern society: Why intelligence and ethnic composition matter. *Journal of Research in Personality*, 59, 111–120.

Kaufmann, E. P. (Ed.). (2004). *Rethinking ethnicity: Majority groups and dominant minorities*. New York, NY: Routledge.

Keith, A. (1968). *A new theory of human evolution*. New York, NY: Philosophical Library. (Original work published 1947)

Kelly, D. J., Quinn, P. C., Slater, A. M., Lee, K., Ge, L., & Pascalis, O. (2007). The other-race effect develops during infancy: Evidence of perceptual narrowing. *Psychological Science*, 18(12), 1084–1089.

Kelly, D. J., Quinn, P. C., Slater, A. M., Lee, K., Gibson, A., Smith, M., . . . Pascalis, O. (2005). Three-month-olds, but not newborns, prefer own-race faces. *Developmental Science*, 8(6), F31–F36.

Kurzban, R., Tooby, J., & Cosmides, L. (2001). Can race be erased? Coalitional computation and social categorization. *Proceedings of the National Academy of Sciences of the USA*, 98, 15387–15392.

Landa, J. (2002). Cognitive and classificatory foundations of trust and informal institutions: A new and expanded theory of ethnic trading networks. In F. K. Salter (Ed.), *Risky transactions: Kinship, ethnicity, and trust* (pp. 129–142). Oxford, UK: Berghahn.

Landa, J. (2009). Homogeneous middleman groups as superorganisms, endogamous ethnic groups, and trust networks: Reply to comments on Janet Landa's target article, "The Bioeconomics of Homogeneous Middleman Groups as Adaptive Units." *Journal of Bioeconomics*, 11(2), 191–199.

Laurence, J., & Bentley, L. (2015). Does ethnic diversity have a negative effect on attitudes towards the community? A longitudinal analysis of the causal claims within the ethnic diversity and social cohesion debate. *European Sociological Review*, 32(1), 54–67.

Levay, A. E. A., Tammer, A. H., Penman, J., Kent, S., & Paolini, A. G. (2010). Calorie restriction at increasing levels leads to augmented concentrations of corticosterone and decreasing concentrations of testosterone in rats. *Nutrition Research*, 30(5), 366–367.

Lewontin, R. C. (1972). The apportionment of human diversity. In T. Dobzhansky, M. K. Hecht, & W. C. Steere (Eds.), *Evolutionary biology* (Vol. 6, pp. 381–398). New York, NY: Appleton-Century-Crofts.

Lipp, O. V., Mallan, K. M., Martin, F. H., Terry, D. J., & Smith, J. R. (2011). Electro-cortical implicit race bias does not vary with participants' race or sex. *Social Cognitive and Affective Neuroscience*, 6(5), 591–601.

Lopreato, J., & Crippen, T. (1999). *Crisis in sociology. The need for Darwin*. New Brunswick, NJ: Transaction Publishers.

Lorenz, K. (1971). Part and parcel in animal and human societies: A methodological discussion (R. Martin, Trans.). In K. Lorenz (Ed.), *Studies in animal and human behaviour* (Vol. 2, pp. 115–195). London, UK: Methuen. (Original German edition published 1950)

Lumsden, C. J., & Wilson, E. O. (1981). *Genes, mind, and culture*. Cambridge, MA: Harvard University Press.

MacDonald, K. B. (1994). *A people that shall dwell alone: Judaism as a group evolutionary strategy*. Westport, CT: Praeger.

MacDonald, K. B. (2001). An integrative evolutionary perspective on ethnicity. *Politics and the Life Sciences, 20*(1), 67–79.

MacDonald, K. B. (2008). Effortful control, explicit processing and the regulation of human evolved predispositions. *Psychological Review, 115*(4), 1012–1031.

McDonald, M. M., Navarrete, C. D., & Van Vugt, M. (2012). Evolution and the psychology of intergroup conflict: The male warrior hypothesis. *Philosophical Transactions of the Royal Society of London B: Biological Sciences, 367*(1589), 670–679.

McPherson, M., Smith-Lovin, L., & Cook, J. M. (2001). Birds of a feather: Homophily in social networks. *Annual Review of Sociology, 27*, 415–444.

Miele, F. (1995). Darwin's dangerous disciple: An interview with Richard Dawkins. *Skeptic, 3*(4), 80–85.

Moya, C., & Boyd, R. (2015). Different selection pressures give rise to distinct ethnic phenomena: A functionalist framework with illustrations from the Peruvian Altiplano. *Human Nature, 26*, 1–27.

Navarrete, C. D., Olsson, A., Ho, A. K., Mendes, W. B., Thomsen, L., & Sidanius, J. (2009). Fear extinction to an out-group face: The role of target gender. *Psychological Science, 20*(2), 155–158.

Olsson, A., Ebert, J. P., Banaji, M. R., & Phelps, E. A. (2005). The role of social groups in the persistence of learned fear. *Science, 309*, 785–787.

Pareto, V. (1963). *Treatise on general sociology*. New York, NY: Dover. (Original work published 1916)

Penman, J. (2015). *Biohistory*. Cambridge, UK: Cambridge Scholars.

Pinker, S. (2007). Strangled by roots. *New Republic*, August 6. https://newrepublic.com/article/77729/strangled-roots

Portes, A., & Vickstrom, E. (2011). Diversity, social capital, and cohesion. *Annual Review of Sociology, 37*, 461–479.

Putnam, R. D. (2007). E Pluribus Unum: Diversity and community in the twenty-first century. The 2006 Johan Skytte Prize lecture. *Scandinavian Political Studies, 30*, 137–174.

Reynolds, V. (1980). Sociobiology and the idea of primordial discrimination. *Ethnic and Racial Studies, 3*(3), 303–315.

Richerson, P. J., & Boyd, R. (2001). The evolution of human ultrasociality. In I. Eibl-Eibesfeldt & F. K. Salter (Eds.), *Indoctrinability, ideology, and warfare: Evolutionary perspectives* (pp. 71–95). Oxford, UK: Berghahn. (Original work published 1998)

Richerson, P. J., & Boyd, R. (2001). The evolution of subjective commitment to groups: A tribal instincts hypothesis. In R. M. Nesse (Ed.), *The evolution and the capacity for subjective commitment* (pp. 186–220). New York, NY: Russell Sage Foundation.

Roediger, D. R. (1999). *The wages of whiteness: Race and the making of the American working class*. New York, NY: Verso.

Rushton, J. P. (1989a). Genetic similarity, human altruism, and group selection. *Behavioral and Brain Sciences, 12*, 503–559.

Rushton, J. P. (1989b). Genetic similarity in male friends. *Ethology and Sociobiology, 10*, 361–373.

Rushton, J. P. (2005). Ethnic nationalism, evolutionary psychology, and genetic similarity theory. *Nations and Nationalism, 11*, 489–507.

Salter, F. K. (2001). A defense and an extension of Pierre van den Berghe's theory of ethnic nepotism. In P. James & D. Goetze (Eds.), *Evolutionary theory and ethnic conflict* (pp. 39–70). Westport, CT: Praeger.

Salter, F. K. (2002a). *Risky transactions: Trust, kinship, and ethnicity*. New York, NY: Berghahn.

Salter, F. K. (2002b). Estimating ethnic genetic interests: Is it adaptive to resist replacement migration? *Population and Environment, 24*(2), 111–140.

Salter, F. K. (Ed.). (2004). *Welfare, ethnicity, & altruism: New data & evolutionary theory*. London, UK: Cass.

Salter, F. K. (2007). Ethnic nepotism as heuristic: Risky transactions and public altruism. In R. I. M. Dunbar & L. Barrett (Eds.), *Handbook of evolutionary psychology* (pp. 541–551). Oxford, UK: Oxford University Press.

Salter, F. K. (2007). *On genetic interests: Family, ethnicity, and humanity in an age of mass migration*. New Brunswick, NJ: Transaction Publishers. (Original work published 2003)

Salter, F. K. (2008). Misunderstandings of kin selection and the delay in quantifying ethnic kinship, *Mankind Quarterly, 48*(3), 311–344.

Salter, F. K., & Harpending, H. (2013). J. P. Rushton's theory of ethnic nepotism. *Personality and Individual Differences, 55*, 256–260.

Sanderson, S. K. (2014). *Human nature and the evolution of society*. Boulder, CO: Westview.

Shaw, R. P., & Wong, Y. (1989). *Genetic seeds of warfare: Evolution, nationalism, and patriotism*. London, UK: Unwin Hyman.

Sidanius, J., & Pratto, F. (1999). *Social dominance: An intergroup theory of social hierarchy and oppression*. Cambridge, UK: Cambridge University Press.

Silverman, I., & Case, D. (2001). Ethnocentrism vs. pragmatism in the conduct of human affairs. In I. Eibl-Eibesfeldt & F. K. Salter (Eds.), *Ethnic conflict and indoctrination: Altruism and identity in evolutionary perspective* (pp. 389–406). Oxford, UK: Berghahn. (Original work published 1998)

Singarajah, A., Chanley, J., Gutierrez, Y., Cordon, Y., Nguyen, B., & Burakowski, L. (2016). Infant attention to same- and other-race faces. *Cognition, 159*, 76–84.

Smith, A. D. (1986). *The ethnic origins of nations*. Oxford, UK: Basil Blackwell.

Sober, E., & Wilson, D. S. (1998). *Unto others: The evolution and psychology of unselfish behavior*. Cambridge, MA: Harvard University Press.

Soltis, J., Boyd, R., & Richerson, P. J. (1995). Can group-functional behaviors evolve by cultural group selection? An empirical test [with peer commentary]. *Current Anthropology, 36*(3), 473–494.

Stern, P. C. (1995). Why do people sacrifice for their nations? In J. L. Comaroff & P. C. Stern (Eds.), *Perspectives on nationalism and war* (Vol. 7, pp. 99–121). Amsterdam, the Netherlands: Gordon & Breach.

Suetterlin, C. (2017). The construction of Neolithic corporate identities. In M. Benz, H. G. K. Gebel, & T. Watkins (Eds.), *Studies in early Near Eastern production, subsistence, and economy* (Vol. 20, pp. 35–52). Berlin: Ex Oriente.Sumner, W. G. (1906). *Folkways*. Boston, MA: Ginn.

Thayer, B. A. (2003). Ethnic conflict and state building. In A. Somit & S. A. Peterson (Eds.), *Human nature and public policy: An evolutionary approach* (pp. 225–242). New York, NY: Pelgrave Macmillan.

Thiessen, D., & Gregg, B. (1980). Human assortative mating and genetic equilibrium: An evolutionary perspective. *Ethology and Sociobiology, 1*, 111–140.

Tinbergen, N. (1963). On the aims and methods of ethology. *Zeitschrift für Tierpsychologie, 20*, 410–433.

van den Berghe, P. L. (1977). Territorial behavior in a natural human group. *Social Science Information, 16*(3–4), 419–430.

van den Berghe, P. L. (1978). Race and ethnicity: A sociobiological perspective. *Ethnic and Racial Studies, 1*(4), 401–411.

van den Berghe, P. L. (1981). *The ethnic phenomenon.* New York, NY: Elsevier.

van den Berghe, P. (1999). Racism, ethnocentrism and xenophobia: in Our genes or in our memes? In K. Thienpont & R. Cliquet (Eds.), *In-group/out-group behaviour in modern societies. An evolutionary perspective* (pp. 21–36). Brussels, Belgium: NIDI CBGS.

van der Dennen, J. M. G. (1995). *The origin of war: The evolution of a male-coalitional reproductive strategy* (Vol. 2). Groningen, the Netherlands: Origin.

Vanhanen, T. (1991). *Politics of ethnic nepotism: India as an example.* New Delhi, India: Sterling.

Vanhanen, T. (2012). *Ethnic conflicts: Their biological roots in ethnic nepotism.* London, UK: Ulster Institute for Social Research.

Voorspoels, W., Bartlema, A., & Vanpaemel, W. (2014). Can race really be erased? A pre-registered replication study. *Frontiers in Psychology, 5,* 1035. http://journal.frontiersin.org/article/10.3389/fpsyg.2014.01035/full

Weber, M. (1946). The nation. In H. H. Gerth & C. W. Mills (Eds.), *From Max Weber: Essays in sociology* (pp. 171–179). New York, NY: Oxford University Press. (Original work published 1922)

Whitmeyer, J. M. (1997). Endogamy as a basis for ethnic behavior. *Sociological Theory, 15*(2), 162–178.

Wiessner, P. (1998). Levelling the hunter: Constraints on the status quest in foraging societies. In P. Wiessner & W. Schiefenhövel (Eds.), *Food and the status quest: An inderdisciplinary perspective* (pp. 171–191). Oxford, UK: Berghahn.

Williams, G. C. (1966). *Adaptation and natural selection: A critique of some current evolutionary thought.* Princeton, NJ: Princeton University Press.

Wilson, D. S. (2002). *Darwin's cathedral: The organismic nature of religion.* Chicago, IL: University of Chicago Press.

Wilson, D. S., & Sober, E. (1989). Reviving the superorganism. *Journal of Theoretical Biology, 136,* 337–356.

Wilson, D. S., & Sober, E. (1994). Reintroducing group selection to the human behavioral sciences. *Behavioral and Brain Sciences, 17,* 585–654.

CHAPTER 26

···

HUMAN SOCIOSEXUAL
DOMINANCE THEORY

···

KRISTIN LIV RAUCH AND
ROSEMARY L. HOPCROFT

Through it all I discerned one clear and certain truth: In the core of the
heart of the American race problem the sex factor is rooted, rooted so
deeply that it is not always recognized when it shows to the surface. Other
factors are obvious and are the ones we dare deal with; but, regardless of
how we deal with these, the race situation will continue to be acute as long
as the sex factor persists. . . . It may be innate; I do not know. But I do know
it is strong and bitter.

—James Weldon Johnson (1933, p. 170)

IN this chapter, we present an evolutionary theory of race discrimination. Evolutionary
theories of race and ethnicity (van den Berghe, 1981; Whitmeyer, 1997) have been treated
as "primordial" theories that are no better explanations of the phenomenon than class
or economic interest theories (Newman, 1982). However, class-based theories of race
and ethnicity cannot account for gender differences in the experience of race discrimination or why African American lower class men attract both more and different types
of discrimination than do African American lower class women (Harnois & Ifatunji,
2011). We build on Sidanius and co-authors' *subordinate male target hypothesis*, which
describes the role of sexual selection in promoting predispositions toward discrimination by and against males within group-based hierarchies (Sidanius & Pratto, 1999;
Sidanius & Veniegas, 2000). We go beyond Sidanius and company by suggesting that
such discrimination continues to limit mating opportunities for minority group males.
We also highlight the ways that coalitions, culture, and social institutions can be used
in the quest for mating opportunities. In what follows, we outline this theory of human
sociosexual dominance and give historical and contemporary evidence in support of it.

Sexual Selection and Social Hierarchy

Male and female reproductive success is limited by different factors (Bateman, 1948; Trivers, 1972), especially for mammals. Because of the heavy costs of gestation and lactation, female reproductive success is limited by their access to the necessary resources to carry out successful pregnancies and infant care. Males, on the other hand, are not required to invest large quantities of resources to reproduce successfully (although they often do, especially in the case of humans). Therefore, the major limiting factor for male reproductive success is access to fertile females. Following from these observations, there are several potential strategies that males might employ to increase access. They might directly monopolize female mates by physically preventing contact between those females and other males, or they might indirectly control access to female mates by monopolizing the resources that are essential for reproduction (Emlen & Oring, 1977). Therefore, "it becomes crucial to understand the manner in which access to mates can be controlled" (Emlen & Oring, 1977, p. 215).

Social rank is an important component of competition over mates. Socially dominant individuals have multiple advantages in the pursuit of mating opportunities because high-ranking males are often found more attractive by females (intersexual selection) and can also use their status to dominate other male mate competitors (intrasexual selection). Among many group-living animals, dominant males are able to monopolize mating opportunities (Ellis, 1995). Research on a wide range of human populations in both premodern and modern societies indicates a positive relationship between resource acquisition (measured as personal income) and male reproductive success (for a review, see Hopcroft, 2006; see also Barthold, Myrskylä, & Jones, 2012; Pollet & Nettle, 2008), and many studies report female preferences for resource-accrual capacities in their mates (Borgerhoff Mulder, 1990; Buss, 1989; Feingold, 1992).

One theory that specifically draws connections between social hierarchies, dominance tactics, and the pursuit of mating opportunities is social dominance theory (SDT) developed by Sidanius and colleagues. Although SDT focuses primarily on the psychological bases of group-based discrimination and oppression, the subordinate male target hypothesis (SMTH) pertains specifically to the role of sexual selection in race discrimination (Sidanius & Pratto, 1999; Sidanius & Veniegas, 2000). Sexual selection refers to selection of traits over evolutionary time because they helped the bearers win mating competitions and be disproportionately chosen as mates. Thus, traits that promoted winning over other competitors in mate competitions increased in frequency relative to traits that did not promote winning. For males, their competitors in mate competitions are other males.

Sidanius et al.'s critical observation was that acts of aggression and discrimination were directed disproportionately toward subordinate-group males. The idea of "double jeopardy," that subordinate women were at a twofold disadvantage because of their status as subordinates *and* as women, was not supported by the overwhelming evidence that they present (Sidanius & Pratto, 1999). They conclude that because subordinate-group females are potential mates, whereas subordinate-group males are potential competitors for mates, dominant-group males stand to benefit more from destructive forms of discrimination directed against subordinate-group males compared to subordinate-group females. Discrimination directed at subordinate-group females is viewed as an attempt to control them rather than to debilitate them, whereas discrimination against subordinate-group males is interpreted as an attempt to incapacitate them. They suggest that traits promoting such discrimination were selected for over evolutionary time.

Later work (McDonald, Navarrete, & Sidanius, 2011) proposed a *theory of gendered prejudice* acknowledging that out-group targets of intergroup aggression need not be "subordinate," although in cases of large power imbalances between groups, members of subordinate groups will take the brunt of the aggression from members of dominant groups because the risks and costs involved are so much lower for the latter. Because power differentials between racial groups in the United States are substantial, application of the SMTH is still appropriate in the examples presented in this chapter, which are found to support the hypothesis.

In most nonhuman animals, dominance is maintained through physical aggression and is short-lived. Dominant males will eventually lose their status when they are no longer able to physically defend it from rivals. This is not the case with humans. Human social rank is rarely a matter of physical prowess but, rather, has more to do with political or economic power. Human dominance is sustained by *culture* and *institutions* that grant individuals *authority*—even if those individuals are physically weak, frail, or elderly. Human social dominance is also coalitional: It is not simply individual high-ranking males defending their personal access to a group of mates but also entire symbolically marked groups (races, ethnicities, religions, classes, etc.) defending their access to whole groups of similarly marked females against out-group incursions. We refer to these social, coalitional, and institutionalized forms of dominance that help certain males in contests over mates as *sociosexual* dominance. It is in attention to the ongoing use of social dominance in gaining sexual access that our work differs from previous work on SMTH.

Previous work (McDonald et al., 2011; McDonald, Navarrete, & Van Vugt, 2012; Navarrete, McDonald, Molina, & Sidanius, 2010; Van Vugt, De Cremer, & Janssen, 2007) characterizes the role of sexual selection in human social dominance as a force that operated in our evolutionary past, shaping male and female concerns and strategies in different ways such that males were under greater selective pressure than females to be preoccupied with dominance, hierarchy, and intergroup conflict. In other words, present-day men have higher levels of social dominance orientation (SDO) compared to present-day women because ancestral men who exhibited high SDO had greater reproductive success than their competitors (not necessarily the case for women), and thus the trait was adaptive and inherited by ensuing generations of men. The legacy of the effects of sexual selection in our evolutionary past can be observed in the contemporary sex differences in levels of SDO and functional motivations for out-group prejudice.

Sexual selection is portrayed as a force in our deep prehistory that shaped the traits of our ancestors in ways that were adaptive for them in their particular context, but this signature of evolutionary baggage is not necessarily adaptive in the modern context (McDonald et al., 2012, p. 677).

Our argument extends the reach of Sidanius and colleagues by being explicit about the sexual preoccupations in past and in modern-day intergroup relations, and we note that the psychological traits they highlight, such as SDO, continue to have adaptive consequences for majority group males. We take the gender asymmetry of racial discrimination demonstrated by Sidanius, McDonald, Navarrete, and colleagues for granted (as well as its sexually selected underpinnings) and add to this area of research by showing how racism directed at subordinate group men is a tool in ongoing mating competition, both in the recent past and in the present. We also emphasize the role of culture in creating and maintaining coalitions for sociosexual dominance, including the legitimizing myths described by Sidanius and colleagues. We further note how major features of the institutional structure of modern societies—notably the prison system—are effectively used to limit the mating opportunities of minority group males. In short, our work goes beyond previous work on the SMTH by incorporating contemporary operation of sexual selection and the institutionalized control over access to mates.

THE HUMAN SOCIOSEXUAL DOMINANCE FRAMEWORK

1. Mate competition is ubiquitous, particularly among males. Sexual preoccupations often surface unexpectedly around issues of social dominance that are not consciously construed as pertaining to sexual access.
2. Such contests are coalitional and asymmetrical. The competition takes place between symbolically marked groups. People in dominant groups will use their status to try to constrain the competitive strategies of subordinate group members, resulting in marked asymmetries in the rules of competition and the standards of assessment according to relative rank.
3. There are cultural supports that maintain the hierarchy. Human power is often symbolic, rather than physical, and dominance is codified through norms and culture.

This framework suggests that the ultimate cause of racial discrimination is the concern with reproductive success of dominant-group males and their allies. This concern may or may not be conscious, but it shapes social behavior and beliefs in ways that are frequently discriminatory. We argue that this human sociosexual dominance (HSD) framework can be fruitfully applied to a variety of contexts, including the earliest civilizations (Betzig, 1993), immigration law, the Indian Hindu caste system, and myriad colonial settings (Rauch, 2012). However, this chapter focuses specifically on examples pertaining to African American and European American relations in the United States both in the past and in the present: lynching, anti-miscegenation laws, White supremacy groups, and the war on drugs. We also show that this discrimination effectively reduces the mating opportunities of subordinate group males.

EXAMPLE 1: LYNCHING IN
THE UNITED STATES

Lynching is an act that can be usefully analyzed under the HSD framework. A widespread motivation for these violent acts was the perception of African American men as a sexual threat. The second leading justification for lynching African American men was the rape or attempted rape (real or, more often, imagined) of a White woman (National Association for the Advancement of Colored People [NAACP], 1919, p. 36). For example, in Mississippi in 1955, 14-year-old African American Emmett Till died a cruel death at the hands of White men seeking revenge because Emmett had supposedly whistled at a White woman. The sexual preoccupation of lynch mobs is made obvious by the commonplace practice of castration rituals (Harris, 1984, p. 22; Jordan, 1968, pp. 156–157). Lynching was also clearly coalitional. It was carried out by "mobs"—not just individual men protecting their own mates but, rather, groups of men defending an entire social category ("White women"), and indeed this was viewed as their chivalrous duty (Hall, 1993; Wells-Barnett, 2002). Lynching was also asymmetrical in several ways. Although it is commonly viewed as an expression of anti-Black racism, the violence was more specific than that and aimed almost exclusively at men: Ninety-eight percent of African American lynching victims were male (NAACP, 1919, p. 30).

Whereas any Black male sexual relations with White females (real or imagined) were subject to severe sanction, the sexual abuse of African American women by White men was not classified as rape (Stoler, 1989, p. 641). Indeed, during the early half of the 1900s (before capital punishment for rape was deemed unconstitutional), 405 of the 455 men to receive the death penalty for rape were African American (Mauer, 2006, p. 134), and there is no record of any White man being executed for raping an African American woman, although its occurrence is well documented (Radelet & Vandiver, 1986, p. 98). There is "an age-old conflict where men from dominant groups attempt to protect their sexual property from subordinate-group men, while simultaneously ignoring the victimization of subordinate-group women" (LaFree, 1982, pp. 325–326).

Cultural support for lynching is rooted in long-held beliefs regarding the supposedly savage sexuality of African American men (Jordan, 1968, pp. 32–43, 151–162, 398) and the accompanying myth of the Black Rapist. After the Civil War, propaganda spread by Southern politicians warned of "the sexual appetite of Black males for White women"

(Greene, 1996, p. 151), and a wave of hysteria arose surrounding the so-called "New Negro Crime" (Douglass, 1955, pp. 493, 498–499, 501–502; Johnston, 1910, p. 464; Jordan, 1968, p. 398; Miller, 1996, p. 188). Popular media fortified the Black Rapist myth through books such as Thomas Dixon's *The Clansman* (1905) and films such as D. W. Griffith's *The Birth of a Nation* (1915) (Ayton, 2011, pp. 54–55). Dixon associated voting rights for African Americans with the hazard of "barbaric violation" of Southern White women (Rose, 2007, p. 63).

However, the fear of interracial rape of White women was not founded in its actual occurrence. In his ethnography of a Depression-era Southern town, first published in 1937, John Dollard (1988) asks, "Whence comes this conviction of the lustful and violent desire of Negro men for White women? Why do the infrequent actual confirmations serve to keep it so brightly alive?" (p. 163). In American history, sexual aggression from White men toward Black women was much more common than that from Black men toward White women. For example, there are innumerable cases of slavemasters having coercive sexual relationships with their slave women (Roberts, 1997) and even forcing them into prostitution schemes serving White diplomats with a sexual appetite for "cuffy" (i.e., light-skinned mixed-race women) (Baptist, 2001).

However, whether based on truth or not, popular (mis)conceptions were often vigorously defended. In 1892, when African American journalist Ida B. Wells editorialized about the "thread bare lie that Negro men rape White women," her Memphis-based newspaper (ironically titled *Free Speech*) was forcefully shut down, as was the newspaper of J. C. Duke, a White man, for similar comments (Wells-Barnett, 2002, pp. 30–31).

EXAMPLE 2: ANTI-MISCEGENATION LAWS

Anti-miscegenation laws forbidding interracial marriage existed in 41 US states and were finally declared unconstitutional in the 1967 case *Loving v. Virginia* (Kennedy, 2000). The sexual preoccupation is obvious, as these laws were designed to prevent interracial unions. The laws were coalitional in the sense that all politics are coalitional. Perhaps most telling is the asymmetrical element: These laws only forbid a certain kind of race mixing (Pascoe, 1994). Consider the specific wording of some early statutes. A Pennsylvania law enacted in 1821 made it a "penal act for a Negro to marry a White man's daughter" (Turner, 1911), and a 1664 statute in Maryland forbid marriage between "freeborn English women" and "Negro slaves" (Pascoe, 1994, p. 100). African American author James Baldwin struck at the heart of this asymmetry when he told a White (male) segregationist, "You're not worried about me marrying *your* daughter. You're worried about me marrying your *wife's* daughter. I've been marrying your daughter ever since the days of slavery" (as quoted in Spickard, 1989, p. 268). The asymmetry reveals that it was not a fear of race mixing that motivated the enacting of these laws but, rather, a fear of African American men infringing upon the sexual entitlements of White men. Race mixing was only considered bad when it involved subordinate-group men.

This hypocrisy had numerous cultural and institutional supports, the most powerful being the laws themselves, but also a great deal of propaganda. A mid-19th-century pamphlet written by L. Seaman, LL.D., now housed in the Library of Congress, bears the heading "What Miscegenation Is!" above a drawing of a White woman and Black man embracing and kissing. The pamphlet is subtitled "And What We Are to Expect Now That Mr. Lincoln Is Re-elected." With this cover design, Mr. Seaman has subtly defined miscegenation as specifically the union of a White woman and a Black man. Contemporary opposition to race mixing is expressed in a recent poster depicting President Obama eating fried chicken, with the caption "Miscegenation Is a Crime Against American Values. Repeal *Loving v. Virginia*" (Avlon, 2010, p. 102). Remember, of course, that Barack Obama is the child of a White mother and a Black father—importantly, not the other way around.

Example 3: Contemporary White Supremacy Groups

White supremacy groups are a contemporary example of HSD at work in American race relations. The coalitional aspect is obvious—these are "groups" and are opposed to other symbolically marked groups. And although the concern of White supremacists is ostensibly with race in general, sex between White women and African American men is an enduring theme (Ferber, 1998). For example, a 1979 editorial in the White supremacist publication *National Vanguard* reads, "Civil rights for Black men do not really mean equal employment opportunities; they mean equal enjoyment opportunities with White women." Another example derives from the futuristic White supremacy novel *The Turner Diaries* (Macdonald, 1996), in which corpses of White women swing from the trees and lamp posts throughout the town—their punishment for race mixing. Again, we find a glaring asymmetry in patterns of punishment:

> There are many thousands of hanging female corpses like that in this city tonight, all wearing identical placards around their necks. They are the White women who were married to or living with Blacks, with Jews, or with other non-White males. There are also a number of men wearing the I-defiled-my-race placard, but the women easily outnumber them seven or eight to one. (p. 161)

Consider the case of White supremacist serial killer Joseph Paul Franklin, who killed or wounded at least 19 people for their involvement in African American male/White female interactions but tallied no White male victims for race mixing (Ayton, 2011; Blanco, 2012a). Some of his famous victims include African American civil rights leader Vernon Jordan, whom Franklin shot in Fort Wayne, Indiana, as Jordan was being dropped off at his hotel room by a White female co-worker. In an interview 16 years later, Franklin explained that he was not certain "if the man who exited the car near a corner room was Jordan, but he decided to shoot anyway, as he was enraged when he saw a Black man with a White woman" (Ayton, 2011, pp. 180–181). Another victim was Larry Flynt, publisher of *Hustler* magazine, whom Franklin shot and paralyzed for publishing a series of pornographic images of an African American man and a White woman titled "Butch and His Georgia Peach" (Ayton, 2011; Bell, 1997). Franklin reported that on his sniper missions he would conceal himself behind bushes or other cover in places with clear views of populated areas, waiting for an interracial couple to pass by so he could shoot them (Blanco, 2012b). It is improbable that Franklin never saw a White man with a non-White woman as he sat poised for murder in his sniper hideouts. It is also difficult to imagine that he had never seen a pornographic image featuring a White man and a non-White woman, yet it was the *Hustler* photos that incited his homicidal rage.

Franklin is not alone in the asymmetry of his violent reaction to race mixing. White supremacists employ numerous cultural supports in the form of ideologies, moralities, worldviews, and so on to successfully promote dominant-group male mate monopolies.

Example 4: Mass Incarceration and the War on Drugs

Perhaps the most glaring case of HSD at work in the contemporary United States is mass incarceration and the "war on drugs," which may be better named the "war on minority men." Housing large numbers of men in prison is, needless to say, an effective way of removing them from the mate competition arena. It is also an effective way of permanently reducing their attractiveness as mates because ex-convicts are severely compromised in terms of their ability to garner the resources necessary to provide for their mates and offspring. The United States has one of the highest per capita imprisonment rates in the world, and the inmates of its prisons are predominantly minority group males.

American drug policy is among the most punitive in the world, and it is the primary reason for the country's enormous and ever-expanding prison system. Almost three-fourths (72.1%) of federal drug prisoners have no history of violence (Sentencing Project, 2006), and a 2002 report by Congress's Sentencing Commission found that weapons were involved in only 2.3% of crack cases and only 1.2% of powder cocaine cases (Provine, 2007, p. 138). Thus, the justification often given for the aggressive tactics of the war on drugs—that drug crime is synonymous with violent crime—is spurious.

The disproportionate imprisonment of minority group males arises due to racial asymmetries in the enforcement of laws, especially drug laws. Perhaps the best way to illustrate these asymmetries is to compare drug use and sales to drug convictions. The majority of drug users in the United States are White. The percentage of individuals *within each race* who have used illegal drugs in the past month is fairly similar, if slightly higher for African Americans and slightly lower for Hispanics: 9.1% of Whites, 10.7%

of African Americans, and 8.1% of Hispanics (Substance Abuse and Mental Health Services Administration [SAMHSA], 2011, p. 21). However, because African Americans represent a much smaller proportion of the total US population, there are tens of millions more White drug users than Black users. For example, Fellner (2009) notes,

> SAMHSA estimates that 111,774,000 people in the United States age twelve or older have used illicit drugs during their lifetime, of whom 82,587,000 are White and 12,477,000 are Black. . . . If Black and White drug users are combined, Blacks account for 13% of the total who have ever used an illicit drug. (pp. 266–267)

Evidence on specific drugs also suggests that minorities are less likely to use many drugs. Data from 2008 show that 69% of people reporting ever using crack in their lifetime are White, whereas 18% are African American and 10% are Hispanic (SAMHSA, 2009, Table 1.34A). National data show that Black high school students use drugs at a lower rate than their White counterparts. A recent survey of 12th graders sponsored by the National Institute on Drug Abuse and the National Institutes of Health found that 5.9% of White students had used cocaine in their lifetime compared to 1.6% of Black students, 2.2% of White students compared to 0.9% of Black students had used crack, and 1.4% of White high school seniors had used heroin compared to 0.8% of Black high school seniors (Johnston, O'Malley, Bachman, & Schulenberg, 2011). Rates of marijuana use were almost equivalent (43.3% of White students and 41% of Black students). In fact, "for nearly *all drugs*, 12th-grade African American students reported lifetime, annual, 30-day, and daily prevalence rates that are lower—sometimes dramatically so—than those for White or Hispanic 12th graders" (Johnston et al., 2011, p. 99).

Although African Americans are more likely to sell drugs than are European Americans, the vast majority of drug sellers are White. Using data from the 1991 National Household Survey on Drug Abuse, Fellner (2009, p. 268) found that 0.7% of adult Whites reported selling drugs in the past year compared to 1.4% of adult Blacks. Yet in absolute numbers, White drug sellers far outnumber Black drug sellers: "Although the proportion of sellers was twice that among Blacks than among Whites, in absolute numbers far more Whites (939,345) reported drug selling than Blacks (268,170)" (p. 268). If all self-reported drug sellers are combined into one group, only 12% of them are Black (p. 268)—a proportion close to the percentage of African Americans in the overall US population. Research suggests that most drug users purchase their drugs from same-race/ethnicity dealers (Riley, 1997, pp. 1, 15–16), and because most drug users are White, this also indicates that most drug dealers are White.

Although African Americans and other minorities are not disproportionately likely to use drugs, they are disproportionately likely to be convicted for drug crimes. A study using data collected in Seattle between 1999 and 2002 found that between 36% and 69% of crack users were White, but only 26% of those arrested for crack possession were White; Blacks represented between 15% and 47% of crack users, but 63% of crack possession arrestees were Black (Beckett, Nyrop, Pfingst, & Bowen, 2005, p. 427, Table 2). As the drug war escalated between 1976 and 1996, the rate of White drug arrests increased by 86%, whereas the rate of Black drug arrests increased by 400% (Provine, 2007, p. 17). Another recent study found that African Americans were nearly four times as likely as Whites to be arrested on charges of marijuana possession in 2010, even though the two groups used the drug at similar rates (Urbina, 2013). Of all the people sent to US prisons for drug charges, 75% are Black or Latino (as many as 90% in some states) (Mauer & King, 2004, p. 3). There are more than a dozen states in which African American men go to prison for drug charges at a rate 20–57 times that of White men (Alexander, 2010, p. 96; Human Rights Watch, 2000, Table 14). In 1996, the federal government submitted a list of individuals who had received crack cocaine charges during a 3-year period for consideration in the case of *Armstrong v. the United States*. The list contained the names of more than 2,000 people. Only 11 of these people were *not* African American, and none of them were White (Alexander, 2010, p. 114).

How can we account for the huge disparity between drug use/selling patterns and drug conviction patterns? According to the Office of National Drug Control Policy, more than 1 in 10 Americans violate drug laws in a given year, and because the sheer volume of lawbreakers would overwhelm law enforcement capacities, "strategic choices must be made about whom to target and what tactics to employ" (Alexander, 2010, pp. 101–102). In 2006, 1 out of every 106 White men older than age 18 years was incarcerated compared to 1 out of every 15 African American men (Warren, 2008). Gender disparities in incarceration indicate targeting of subordinate-group men. The White male incarceration rate is approximately 8 times that of White females. But for both African Americans and Latinos, the male incarceration rate is more than 12 times higher than the female rate (Bureau of Justice Statistics, 2008).

Cultural Support for American Race-Based Sociosexual Dominance

The previously discussed biased drug enforcement tactics are sustained in part by cultural "racial scripts" and/or unconscious biases that help sustain discrimination against Black and Brown men.

For example, in one study, when subjects were asked to close their eyes and imagine a drug user, 95% of them pictured an African American person (Burston, Jones, & Roberson-Saunders, 1995). This is a curious result, considering the extent of highly publicized White celebrity drug use (e.g., Keith Richards, Kurt Cobain, Charlie Sheen, Chris Farley, John Belushi, River Phoenix, Jim Morrison, Gary Busey, Robert Downey Jr., Heath Ledger, Anna Nicole Smith, Amy Winehouse, Drew Barrymore, Courtney Love, Lindsey Lohan, and Marilyn Monroe). Why should nearly all of the study subjects imagine an African American drug user when there are so many ready examples of White drug users? In another study, in which news viewers were shown short clips from crime stories, a majority of subjects reported seeing a perpetrator when no image of a suspect was actually shown—and of these, 70% reported that the perpetrator they falsely remembered seeing was African American (Gilliam & Iyengar, 2000): "The crime script generates strong expectations about crime, allowing viewers to fill in gaps in the script. Lacking concrete evidence about the perpetrator, viewers infer what must have happened" (p. 564).

There is also evidence of race discrimination in beliefs about rapists. For instance, a study of college students in New England found that approximately 60% of White men and women believe the most likely victim of an African American rapist is a White woman (Donovan, 2007), when in reality less than 17% of rapes involve an African American male rapist and a White female victim (Bureau of Justice Statistics, 2006).

The labeling of White women is another piece of evidence that a great deal of racism boils down to sexual access. In the Old South, White women were placed on a pedestal and seen as pure and delicate. But the character of any White woman who entered into a relationship with a Black man was immediately shifted to that of a degenerate floozy (Hodes, 1993, pp. 67–69). Likewise, a very common contemporary stereotype of White women who are intimate with Black men is that they are overweight, ugly, and low-class. The content of Internet chat rooms and blogs on the topic of interracial relationships is revealing. This content often shows that when a White woman crosses the color line, she is immediately labeled as undesirable. It is as if some dominant-group men are consoling themselves by insisting that they would not want these particular women anyway.

In fact, evidence suggests that race mixing is most offensive when an African American man has an *attractive* White mate. In an experimental study, Wade (1991) found that an interracial couple featuring an attractive White woman was judged more harshly and treated worse than the same couple when the woman was made to look unattractive. "This suggests that it is okay for [male] Blacks to marry and reproduce with [female] Whites that are otherwise undesirable" (p. 418). Wade also found that White male subjects judged and treated interracial couples (featuring Black men) more harshly than did White female subjects, suggesting an element of intrasexual competition. Wade's results are consistent with the idea that many prejudiced and discriminatory feelings and actions are motivated (at least in large part) by the competitive struggle over access to females. Dominant males are comfortable with subordinate males mating with females whom the dominant males do not desire. But dominant males intend to have first choice.

None of these cultural supports for discrimination against minority group males are necessarily conscious (although they may be), nor are they necessarily confined only to certain segments of the population. The Harvard University implicit association tests (https://implicit.harvard.edu/implicit/education.html) show that most White people in the United States, including the study authors, have greater difficulty associating Black faces with positive words than associating White faces with positive words, suggesting a bias favoring White people (Banaji & Greenwald, 2013). The results of these tests suggest that much of our racial bias operates outside of our awareness, and even the most avowedly nondiscriminatory may still have unconscious racial biases. The operation of these biases in day-to-day life likely serves to promote discriminatory outcomes, regardless of the conscious intent of the discriminator.

GENETIC EVIDENCE OF SOCIOSEXUAL DOMINANCE

Do the previously discussed tactics to preserve the mating entitlements of dominant White men repress the mating behavior of subordinate African American men? One way we could investigate this question is to examine the available genetic evidence. Conveniently for our purposes, certain kinds of genetic material are only inherited from one's mother (mitochondrial DNA [mtDNA]) or one's father (Y chromosomes). By identifying certain markers, geneticists can measure the relative amount of European male or female contribution to admixed populations, such as African Americans. This is not to suggest that there are any major genetic differences between the so-called races. The human genome is composed of approximately 23,000 protein-coding genes (and many more whose function is unknown), and so these markers represent a trivial amount of genetic information that is nonetheless useful for identifying the geographic origins (i.e., Europe or Africa) of a particular tiny portion of human DNA.

Genetic studies show that the average European genetic contribution to the African American gene pool is more than three times as high for Y chromosomes as it is for mtDNA (Lind et al., 2007). These data show that the introduction of European genetic material into the African American population was mostly accomplished by White men, not White women. In other words, throughout US history, White men have been mating with African American women at a much higher rate than African American men have been mating with White women. Geneticists call this process "sex-biased gene flow," and numerous studies confirm this result for African American populations (Kayser et al., 2003; Parra et al., 1998, 2001; Stefflova et al., 2009). Studies showing sex-biased gene flow in many populations throughout the world support the hypothesis that men from socially dominant groups have reproduced at the expense of men from socially subordinate groups (Bamshad et al., 1998; Mesa et al., 2000; Moore, McEvoy, Cape, Simms, & Bradley, 2006; Xie et al., 2007; Zerjal et al., 2003).

SUMMARY AND DISCUSSION

Some will say that the examples of human sociosexual dominance in this chapter are simply various examples of racism and that there is really nothing else going on here. But the critical point is how often sex enters into these expressions of racism: African American men were lynched for alleged sexual attacks on White women, politicians feared that equal rights for African Americans would somehow lead to interracial sex between White women and African American men, and the myth of the Black Rapist is so powerful that even today many White people erroneously believe that White women are more likely than Black women to be raped by a Black man. Of course, these are examples of racism, but the consistency of the sexual preoccupation suggests an ultimate cause of such racism. We argue that the ultimate cause is a sexually selected concern with reproductive success on the part of dominant-group males.

Such concerns with reproductive success are universal among males, but dominant-group males are able to create coalitions and utilize cultural scripts and social institutions in ways that tilt the competition in their favor. Thus, White men could rape Black women in the Old South without punishment, but Black men who were so much as suspected of sexually assaulting White women were put to death; contemporary White supremacists lament race mixing but turn a blind eye on White men who cross the color line; and African American men are dealt with more harshly by the criminal justice system than are White men who commit similar offenses. Asymmetries such as these ensure that competition for mates is tilted in favor of the long-term success of dominant-group males.

We suggest that all these phenomena are the hallmarks of human sociosexual dominance: asymmetrical and coalitional mate competition facilitated by elements of culture. The end result is that these racist and otherwise discriminatory behaviors lead to greater sexual opportunities for dominant males, whether or not that was their primary or explicit objective. In short, American race-based inequality is ultimately both a *result* and a *tool* of sexual competition. We are certainly not the first to implicate male mate competition between White and African American men as a key force behind the tension between these two groups (Day, 1974; Dollard, 1988; Ferber, 1998, p. 60; Graves, 2004, ch. 4; Hernton, 1988; Sidanius & Pratto, 1999, ch. 10; Stember, 1976). But we hope our work (and the work of others such as Sidanius and colleagues) will convince scholars working in other disciplines that evolutionary theory can be a crucial ally to the numerous and important explanations for discrimination and oppression that have also been developed.

REFERENCES

Alexander, M. (2010). *The new Jim Crow: Mass incarceration in the age of colorblindness.* New York, NY: New Press.

Avlon, J. (2010). *Wingnuts: How the lunatic fringe is hijacking America.* New York, NY: Beast Books.

Ayton, M. (2011). *Dark soul of the South: The life and crimes of racist killer Joseph Paul Franklin.* Washington, DC: Potomac Books.

Bamshad, M. J., Watkins, W. S., Dixon, M. E., Jorde, L. B., Rao, B. B., Naidu, J. M., ... Hammer, M. F. (1998). Female gene flow stratifies Hindu castes. *Nature, 395*(6703), 651–652.

Banaji, M. R., & Greenwald, A. G. (2013). *Blindspot: Hidden biases of good people.* New York, NY: Delacorte.

Baptist, E. E. (2001). "Cuffy," "fancy maids," and "one-eyed men": Rape, commodification, and the domestic slave trade in the United States. *American Historical Review, 106*(5), 1619–1650.

Barthold, J. A., Myrskylä, M., & Jones, O. R. (2012). Childlessness drives the sex difference in the association between income and reproductive success of modern Europeans. *Evolution and Human Behavior, 33*(6), 628–638.

Bateman, A. J. (1948). Intrasexual selection in *Drosophila*. *Heredity*, 2, 349–368.

Beckett, K., Nyrop, K., Pfingst, L., & Bowen, M. (2005). Drug use, drug possession arrests, and the question of race: Lessons from Seattle. *Social Problems*, 52(3), 419–441.

Bell, K. (1997, February 2). Convicted killer, avowed racist tells of a life of rage, hatred. *St. Louis Post-Dispatch*. Retrieved from https://business.highbeam.com/435553/article-1G1-56509349/convicted-killer-avowed-racist-tells-life-rage-hatred

Betzig, L. (1993). Sex, succession, and stratification in the first six civilizations: How powerful men reproduced, passed power on to their sons, and used power to defend their wealth, women, and children. In L. Ellis (Ed.), *Social stratification and socioeconomic inequality* (Vol. 1, pp. 37–74). Westport, CT: Praeger.

Blanco, J. I. (2012a). Joseph Paul Franklin. *Murderpedia*. Retrieved from http://murderpedia.org/male.F/f/franklin-joseph.htm

Blanco, J. I. (2012b). Joseph Paul Franklin—Confession. *Murderpedia*. Retrieved from http://www.murderpedia.org/male.F/f/franklin-joseph-confession.htm

Borgerhoff Mulder, M. (1990). Kipsigis women's preferences for wealthy men: Evidence for female choice in mammals? *Behavioral Ecology and Sociobiology*, 27, 255–264.

Bureau of Justice Statistics. (2006). *Criminal victimization in the United States*. Washington, DC: US Department of Justice.

Bureau of Justice Statistics. (2008). *Prison inmates at midyear 2007*. Washington, DC: US Department of Justice.

Burston, B. W., Jones, D., & Roberson-Saunders, P. (1995). Drug use and African Americans: Myth versus reality. *Journal of Alcohol and Drug Education*, 40(2), 19–39.

Buss, D. M. (1989). Sex differences in human mate preferences: Evolutionary hypotheses tested in 37 cultures. *Behavioral and Brain Sciences*, 12, 1–49.

Day, B. (1974). *Sexual life between Blacks and Whites: The roots of racism*. New York, NY: Crowell.

Dollard, J. (1988). *Caste and class in a southern town*. Madison, WI: University of Wisconsin Press.

Donovan, R. A. (2007). To blame or not to blame: Influences of target race and observer sex on rape blame attribution. *Journal of Interpersonal Violence*, 22(6), 722–736.

Douglass, F. (1955). Why is the Negro lynched? In P. S. Foner (Ed.), *The life and writings of Frederick Douglass* (Vol. 4, pp. 491–523). New York, NY: International.

Ellis, L. (1995). Dominance and reproductive success among non-human animals: A cross-species comparison. *Ethology and Sociobiology*, 16, 257–333.

Emlen, S. T., & Oring, L. W. (1977). Ecology, sexual selection, and the evolution of mating systems. *Science*, 197(4300), 215–223.

Feingold, A. (1992). Gender differences in mate selection preferences: A test of the parental investment model. *Psychological Bulletin*, 112, 125–139.

Fellner, J. (2009). Race, drugs, and law enforcement in the United States. *Stanford Law and Policy Review*, 20(2), 257–292.

Ferber, A. L. (1998). *White man falling*. Lanham, MD: Rowman & Littlefield.

Gilliam, F. D., Jr., & Iyengar, S. (2000). Prime suspects: The influence of local television news on the viewing public. *American Journal of Political Science*, 44(3), 560–573.

Graves, J. L., Jr. (2004). *The race myth: Why we pretend race exists in America*. New York, NY: Plume.

Greene, M. F. (1996). *The temple bombing*. Cambridge, MA: Da Capo Press.

Hall, J. D. (1993). *Revolt against chivalry: Jessie Daniel Ames and the women's campaign against lynching*. New York, NY: Columbia University Press.

Harnois, C. E., & Ifatunji, M. (2011). Gendered measures, gendered models: Toward an inter-sectional analysis of interpersonal racial discrimination. *Ethnic and Racial Studies, 34*(6), 1006–1028.

Harris, T. (1984). *Exorcising blackness: Historical and literary lynching and burning rituals.* Bloomington, IN: Indiana University Press.

Hernton, C. C. (1988). *Sex and racism in America.* New York, NY: Anchor.

Hodes, M. (1993). The sexualization of reconstruction politics: White women and Black men in the South after the Civil War. In J. C. Fout & M. S. Tantillo (Eds.), *American sexual politics: Sex, gender, and race since the Civil War* (pp. 59–74). Chicago, IL: University of Chicago Press.

Hopcroft, R. L. (2006). Sex, status, and reproductive success in the contemporary United States. *Evolution and Human Behavior, 27,* 104–120.

Human Rights Watch. (2000). Punishment and prejudice: Racial disparities in the war on drugs. *HRW Reports, 12*(2). Retrieved from https://www.hrw.org/reports/2000/usa/Rcedrg00-04.htm#P289_60230

Johnson, J. W. (1933). *Along this way.* New York, NY: Viking.

Johnston, H. H. (1910). *The Negro in the new world.* London, UK: Methuen.

Johnston, L. D., O'Malley, P. M., Bachman, J. G., & Schulenberg, J. E. (2011). *Monitoring the Future: National survey results on drug use, 1975–2010. Volume I: Secondary school students.* Ann Arbor, MI: Institute for Social Research, University of Michigan.

Jordan, W. D. (1968). *White over Black: American attitudes toward the Negro, 1550–1812.* Chapel Hill, NC: University of North Carolina Press.

Kayser, M., Brauer, S., Schädlich, H., Prinz, M., Batzer, M. A., Zimmerman, P. A., . . . Stoneking, M. (2003). Y chromosome STR haplotypes and the genetic structure of U.S. populations of African, European, and Hispanic ancestry. *Genome Research, 13*(4), 624–634.

Kennedy, R. (2000). The enforcement of anti-miscegenation laws. In W. Sollors (Ed.), *Interracialism: Black–White intermarriage in American history, literature, and law* (pp. 140–162). New York, NY: Oxford University Press.

LaFree, G. D. (1982). Male power and female victimization: Toward a theory of interracial rape. *American Journal of Sociology, 88*(2), 311–328.

Lind, J. M., Hutcheson-Dilks, H. B., Williams, S. M., Moore, J. H., Essex, M., Ruiz-Pesini, E., . . . Smith, M. W. (2007). Elevated male European and female African contributions to the genomes of African American individuals. *Human Genetics, 120*(5), 713–722.

Macdonald, A. (1996). *The Turner diaries* (2nd ed.). New York, NY: Barricade Books.

Mauer, M. (2006). *Race to incarcerate.* New York, NY: New Press.

Mauer, M., & King, R. S. (2004). *Schools and prisons: Fifty years after Brown v. Board of Education.* Washington, DC: Sentencing Project.

McDonald, M. M., Navarrete, C. D., & Sidanius, J. (2011). Developing a theory of gendered prejudice: An evolutionary and social dominance perspective. In R. M. Kramer, G. J. Leonardelli, & R. W. Livingston (Eds.), *Social cognition, social identity, and intergroup relations: A festschrift in honor of Marilynn B. Brewer* (pp. 189–220). New York, NY: Taylor & Francis.

McDonald, M. M., Navarrete, C. D., & Van Vugt, M. (2012). Evolution and the psychology of intergroup conflict: The male warrior hypothesis. *Philosophical Transactions of the Royal Society B: Biological Sciences, 367,* 670–679.

Mesa, N. R., Mondragon, M. C., Soto, I. D., Parra, M. V., Duque, C., Ortiz-Barrientos, D., . . . Ruiz-Linares, A. (2000). Autosomal, mtDNA, and Y-chromosome diversity in Amerinds: Pre- and post-Columbian patterns of gene flow in South America. *American Journal of Human Genetics, 67,* 1277–1286.

Miller, J. G. (1996). *Search and destroy: African-American males in the criminal justice system.* Cambridge, UK: Cambridge University Press.

Moore, L. T., McEvoy, B., Cape, E., Simms, K., & Bradley, D. G. (2006). A Y-chromosome signature of hegemony in Gaelic Ireland. *American Journal of Human Genetics, 78*(2), 334–338.

National Association for the Advancement of Colored People. (1919). *Thirty years of lynching in the United States: 1889–1918.* New York, NY: Author.

Navarrete, C. D., McDonald, M. M., Molina, L. E., & Sidanius, J. (2010). Prejudice at the nexus of race and gender: An outgroup male target hypothesis. *Journal of Personality and Social Psychology, 98*(6), 933–945.

Newman, W. M. (1982). Review of *The Ethnic Phenomenon* by Pierre L. van den Berghe and *The Ethnic Myth* by Stephen Steinberg. *Social Forces, 61*(1), 291–293.

Parra, E. J., Kittles, R. A., Argyropoulos, G., Pfaff, C. L., Hiester, K., Bonilla, C., . . . Shriver, M. D. (2001). Ancestral proportions and admixture dynamics in geographically defined African Americans living in South Carolina. *American Journal of Physical Anthropology, 114*(1), 18–29.

Parra, E. J., Marcini, A., Akey, J., Martinson, J., Batzer, M. A., Cooper, R., . . . Shriver, M. D. (1998). Estimating African American admixture proportions by use of population-specific alleles. *American Journal of Human Genetics, 63*(6), 1839–1851.

Pascoe, P. (1994). *Race, gender, and the privileges of property: On the significance of miscegenation law in United States history.* Paper presented at the New Viewpoints in Women's History: Working Papers from the Schlesinger Library 50th Anniversary Conference, Cambridge, MA.

Pollet, T. V., & Nettle, D. (2008). Driving a hard bargain: Sex ratio and male marriage success in a historical U.S. population. *Biology Letters, 4*, 31–33.

Provine, D. M. (2007). *Unequal under law: Race in the war on drugs.* Chicago, IL: University of Chicago Press.

Radelet, M. L., & Vandiver, M. (1986). Race and capital punishment: An overview of the issues. *Crime and Social Justice, 25*, 94–113.

Rauch, K. (2012). *Evolutionary perspectives on human assortative mating.* Doctoral dissertation, University of California, Davis. Retrieved from ProQuest Dissertations and Theses database (UMI No. 3511961).

Riley, K. J. (1997). *Crack, powder cocaine, and heroin: Drug purchase and use patterns in six U.S. cities.* Washington, DC: National Institute of Justice and the Office of National Drug Control Policy.

Roberts, D. (1997). *Killing the Black body: Race, reproduction, and the meaning of liberty.* New York, NY: Vintage.

Rose, D. (2007). *Violation: Justice, race and serial murder in the Deep South.* London, UK: HarperCollins.

Sentencing Project. (2006). *The federal prison population: A statistical analysis.* Retrieved from https://static.prisonpolicy.org/scans/sp/federalprison.pdf

Sidanius, J., & Pratto, F. (1999). *Social dominance: An intergroup theory of social hierarchy and oppression.* Cambridge, UK: Cambridge University Press.

Sidanius, J., & Veniegas, R. C. (2000). Gender and race discrimination: The interactive nature of disadvantage. In S. Oskamp (Ed.), *Reducing prejudice and discrimination* (pp. 47–69). Mahwah, NJ: Erlbaum.

Spickard, P. R. (1989). *Mixed blood: Intermarriage and ethnic identity in twentieth-century America.* Madison, WI: University of Wisconsin Press.

Stefflova, K., Dulik, M. C., Pai, A. A., Walker, A. H., Zeigler-Johnson, C. M., Gueye, S. M., . . . Rebbeck, T. R. (2009). Evaluation of group genetic ancestry of populations from Philadelphia and Dakar in the context of sex-biased admixture in the Americas. *PLoS One*, 4(11), e7842.

Stember, C. H. (1976). *Sexual racism: The emotional barrier to an integrated society*. New York, NY: Elsevier.

Stoler, A. L. (1989). Making empire respectable: The politics of race and sexual morality in 20th-century colonial cultures. *American Ethnologist*, 16(4), 634–660.

Substance Abuse and Mental Health Services Administration. (2009). *Results from the 2008 National Survey on Drug Use and Health: National findings*. Rockville, MD.

Substance Abuse and Mental Health Services Administration. (2011). *Results from the 2010 National Survey on Drug Use and Health: Summary of national findings* (NSDUH Series H-41, HHS Publication No. SMA 11-4658). Rockville, MD.

Trivers, R. (1972). Parental investment and sexual selection. In B. Campbell (Ed.), *Sexual selection and the descent of man* (pp. 136–179). Chicago, IL: Aldine.

Turner, E. R. (1911). *The Negro in Pennsylvania*. Washington, DC: American Historical Association.

Urbina, I. (2013, June 3). Blacks are singled out for marijuana arrests, federal data suggests. *New York Times*.

van den Berghe, P. L. (1981). *The ethnic phenomenon*. Westport, CT: Praeger.

Van Vugt, M., De Cremer, D., & Janssen, D. P. (2007). Gender differences in cooperation and competition: The male-warrior hypothesis. *Psychological Science*, 18(1), 19–23.

Wade, T. J. (1991). Marketplace economy: The evaluation of interracial couples. *Basic and Applied Social Psychology*, 12(4), 405–422.

Warren, J. (2008). *One in 100: Behind bars in America 2008*. Washington, DC: Pew Research Center. Retrieved from http://www.pewtrusts.org/~/media/legacy/uploadedfiles/wwwpewtrustsorg/reports/sentencing_and_corrections/onein100pdf.pdf

Wells-Barnett, I. B. (2002). *On lynchings*. Amherst, NY: Humanity Books.

Whitmeyer, J. M. (1997). Endogamy as a basis for ethnic behavior. *Sociological Theory*, 15(2), 162–178.

Xie, C. Z., Li, C. X., Cui, Y. Q., Zhang, Q. C., Fu, Y. Q., Zhu, H., & Zhou, H. (2007). Evidence of ancient DNA reveals the first European lineage in Iron Age central China. *Proceedings: Biological Sciences*, 274(1618), 1597–1601.

Zerjal, T., Xue, Y., Bertorelle, G., Wells, R. S., Bao, W., Zhu, S., . . . Tyler-Smith, C. (2003). The genetic legacy of the Mongols. *American Journal of Human Genetics*, 72(3), 717–721.

PART V

SOCIOCULTURAL EVOLUTION

CHAPTER 27

FROM PAGANISM TO WORLD TRANSCENDENCE

Religious Attachment Theory and the Evolution of the World Religions

STEPHEN K. SANDERSON

During the past 10,000 years, there has been striking parallel social evolution all over the globe. Societies have grown larger, adopted more advanced technologies, become more status differentiated and stratified by wealth, and developed more complex political systems marked by the increasing concentration of power at the top of the political hierarchy. This remarkable parallel evolution has by now become well known to anthropologists (Sanderson, 1999, 2007; Carneiro, 2003).

But one of the most important dimensions of social life, religion, has received limited attention in terms of its long-term evolution.[1] This chapter seeks to redress this problem. The simplest societies, primarily hunter–gatherer bands, have mostly had religions in which shamans were the principal type of religious specialist. Later religious evolution produced communal rites performed by the whole society or by significant segments of it. By approximately 5,000 years ago, the pagan religions of antiquity, with their pantheons of anthropomorphic gods and priestly classes, arose and dominated state-level societies for several thousand years. Then there was a shift to the religions familiar to us today—the world religions that are still the dominant type of religion on earth. They all emerged in a strikingly short period on a prehistoric timescale, the period between approximately 600 BCE and 1 CE, usually known as the Axial Age. Transcendent gods replaced the earlier anthropomorphic gods, and people looked to these new gods for salvation, which is to say release from earthly suffering. In some cases, there was a single god that emerged, One True God. In other cases, there was no single God, although one god was more important than the rest. Here again, we seem to have another case of long-term parallel evolution.

The religious shift during the Axial Age constituted the most dramatic and important religious transformation in world history (Jaspers, 1953, 1962; Eisenstadt, 1986a, 1986b). This chapter seeks to understand this momentous transformation by drawing on ideas developed by cognitive and evolutionary psychologists. After discussing the leading arguments of these perspectives, I make use of one specific theory, so-called religious attachment theory, to make sense of the Axial Age transformations. The central argument is that there were major social, economic, and political upheavals during the period of the Axial Age that led to severe disruptions in people's sense of safety and well-being, and that it was people's resulting existential anxiety and insecurity that led to the social construction of a radically new kind of god and altered forms of interaction between humans and this type of god.

Pagan Predecessors

In complex chiefdoms and ancient states, pagan religions predominated.[2] Some of the best known pagan religions were those of the ancient Sumerians and Egyptians; the ancient Greeks and Romans; the Aryans of South Asia; and the Maya, Aztecs, and Incas of the New World. Pagan religions have polytheistic pantheons of specialized gods who are highly anthropomorphic. Like humans, pagan gods are finite and mortal. Some are considered good, others evil; some are highly competent at what they do, whereas others are regarded as incompetent fools; they usually eat and drink and often have great banquets; many of them like sex and have frequent orgies; they also fight and go to war. Each god is usually responsible for a specific sphere of life, such as love, war, the weather, or agriculture. Some of the gods take an interest in human affairs in a positive way, but many are threatening to humans and often try to deceive and trick them.

Yehezkel Kaufmann (1960) contends that the most important feature of pagan religions is not their anthropomorphic gods but, rather, that these gods are derived from a preexisting order. They do not exist outside the universe and thus are not the source of everything that exists. They are the product of whatever existed in some primordial realm before they came into being. This primordial realm is often considered to be chaos or certain types of waters.

Pagan religions also have classes of priests, some part-time and some full-time, who preside over and direct religious rituals of numerous types. These priests in many cases are quite different from the later priests of the world religions. For example, Sumerian priests were more like soothsayers, healers, and sorcerers than like the priests of later religions (Woolley, 1965). Priests in Roman society were also more like Sumerian priests than the priests of the world religions.

Another universal trait of pagan religions is their emphasis on animal (and sometimes human) sacrifice. Because the gods are like humans, they need to be fed, and thus are regularly offered food, especially meat. In Arabia and much of North Africa, for example, camels were commonly sacrificed; bulls were important objects of sacrifice throughout the Mediterranean world, and pastoralists in Central Asia were noted for sacrificing horses (Harris, 1977).

THE AXIAL AGE

The term *Axial Age* was coined by the philosopher Karl Jaspers (1953, 1962), who dated it from approximately 800 to approximately 200 BCE.[3] Jaspers called it "axial" because he viewed it as an "axis" of world history, a period during which fundamentally new ways of philosophical and religious thinking emerged in remarkably parallel fashion throughout much of the Old World. Among the individuals responsible for the new thinking, Jaspers specifically mentioned Confucius and Laozi in China; the Buddha in India; Zarathustra in Iran; the Hebrew prophets Elijah, Isaiah, and Jeremiah; and the Greek philosophers. Jesus and Christianity were viewed as a "late product" of this age.

For Jaspers, the Axial Age was in essence a revolution in consciousness in which "consciousness became conscious of itself" and in which humans began "thinking about thinking." Pre-Axial cultures were bogged down in mythical thinking and were "unawakened." This basic idea has been extended by later scholars, especially S. N. Eisenstadt (1986a, 1986b). For Eisenstadt, the Axial Age amounted to a great "breakthrough" involving the creation of a transcendental, supra-mundane, and higher metaphysical and moral order. In the pre-Axial civilizations, the religious world was structured in a way very similar to the mundane, everyday world. Eric Weil (1975) echoes this idea, suggesting that the pre-Axial civilizations were not on the way to anything new and were, in that sense, anti-historical. The Babylonians, for example, were caught up in a blind sense of fatality. The Egyptians were more optimistic, but they too failed to produce anything new.

The Axial Age is often over-intellectualized—viewed as largely the product of religious wisdom offered by sages—and as a result what was happening among the masses has often been given short shrift. In Robert Bellah's (2011) book on religious evolution, for example, the Axial Age is interpreted as a product of great intellectuals and the masses are nowhere to be found. The same kind of emphasis is found in Eisenstadt's writings on the Axial Age. In reality, the Axial Age was a two-part process: Ideas were proposed by sages or prophets, and some of them caught on and spread. To understand the Axial Age, we need to understand why the new religious ideas came to have such enormous appeal to very large numbers of people.

The main Axial Age religions were Judaism, Christianity, Hinduism, Buddhism, Confucianism, and Daoism. The most important characteristics of these religions are shown in Table 27.1. Two characteristics appear most crucial, the first being the *transcendent character of the supernatural*. The world religions had a completely new conception of the supernatural. Gone were the anthropomorphic gods of the pagan religions, who were replaced by a god or gods conceived as *transcendent*. What is implied by the notion of transcendence is basically a god who was little, if anything, like humans and who, although

Table 27.1 Predominant Features of the Axial Age Religions[a]

Feature	Judaism	Christianity	Hinduism	Buddhism	Confucianism	Daoism
Date and place of origin	In Palestine about 1300 BCE in original polytheistic form; shift to monotheism around 600 BCE	Shortly after 1 CE in Eastern Mediterranean	Earliest form (the Vedas) about 1500 BCE in North India, but classical version 500 BCE to CE 1	Late sixth century BCE in North India	Sixth century BCE in China	Sixth century BCE in China
Founders/prophets	Biblical version: early Hebrew prophets (e.g., Moses, Abraham, Isaac); revisionist version: later prophets and kings (e.g., Hosea, Hezekiah, Josiah)	Jesus Christ (as interpreted by Paul of Tarsus and the authors of the Gospels)	No known founder	Siddhartha Gautama (the Buddha)	Confucius	Laozi
Development and spread	Throughout Palestine after 600 BCE, with diaspora communities throughout eastern Mediterranean; limited spread and geographical range	Spread slowly but then more rapidly through cities of Roman Empire; adopted and promoted by Constantine around 312 CE	Spread throughout India in first few centuries BCE, eventually displacing Buddhism as principal Indian religion	Spread throughout India in early centuries BCE, but then died out in India in favor of Hinduism around 1200 CE; spread to China and Southeast Asia in early first millennium CE	Spread throughout China to become its principal religion, although folk religions remained important (often more important); linked closely to Chinese state	Replaced Confucianism during Han period and became main popular faith along with Chinese folk religions; underwent decline in seventh century CE
Conception of supernatural	Transcendent God (Yahweh) as One True God	Transcendent One True God; Jesus Christ as Son of God and personal savior, but equal with God the Father and unified with Him and the Holy Spirit (doctrine of the Trinity)	Powerful High God Vishnu–Shiva, conceived either as two gods or two dimensions of a single God; many other minor deities worshiped in local and regional traditions	Original Buddhist doctrine atheistic, but eventual deification of the Buddha; Mahayana Buddhism believed in bodhisattvas who delay their achievement of nirvana and descend to earth to help others attain salvation	Traditionally understood to have no concept of supernatural agents; largely a secular philosophy rather than a religion; but some contend that it did emphasize dependence on a supreme power, and Confucius himself deified and people pray to him at temples	The Dao eventually evolved into a personal God in the form of Laozi; he assumed an incarnate form and descended to earth as a savior; but not monotheistic; contained a complex pantheon of gods

Salvation doctrines	Elimination of wickedness from the world, restoration of Israel to its rightful place among nations, and resurrection of the righteous dead	Forgiveness of sins and entry into an eternal afterlife in a heavenly paradise	Release from earthly suffering and endless cycle of rebirths; attainment of nirvana; no heaven or paradise	For elite Buddhists, release from earthly suffering and endless cycle of rebirths; attainment of nirvana; Buddhist masses did not seek nirvana but salvation in a paradise by a loving god	None; doctrines emphasizing right living and good government	For elite Daoists, achievement of ecstasy and becoming one with the Dao; for ordinary Daoists, avoidance of death and eternity of the body; those who avoid death go straight to paradise
Means of achieving salvation	Adherence to the Law (e.g., dietary rules, circumcision, rest on the Sabbath)	Belief in Christ as personal savior; repentance of sin, etc.	Rejection of material world through ascetic discipline and mystical contemplation; performance of obligations and devotion to a personal god	Rejection of material world through ascetic discipline and mystical contemplation; following eightfold path	No concept of salvation, but five principles of correct behavior	Elite Daoists entered trances to achieve ecstasy; masses used various techniques to achieve salvation and immortality; avoid sin (or repent)
Imagistic depictions of God	God is beyond human comprehension and therefore incapable of depiction	God is beyond human comprehension and therefore incapable of depiction (Jesus as Son of God can be depicted)	Elaborate	Elaborate	Yes	Yes

Descriptions refer to the nature of these religions at their time of origin and in ensuing centuries. They do not necessarily apply in all respects to contemporary versions.

creating the world, stood outside it. A transcendent god does not eat, have sex, marry, go to war, or have foibles and weaknesses. He is the "uncaused cause" and the "unmoved mover." As noted previously, whereas in the pagan religions the gods are derived from a preexisting order, a transcendent god is by definition "underived" (Kaufmann, 1960). All of the world religions had a transcendent supreme deity, whether in the form of a personal god or an abstract essence, and whether or not there were other gods that were also worshiped. Because world transcendence is common to all the world religions, and strict monotheism only to the Near Eastern religions, it seems more appropriate to call the Axial Age religions *world transcendent* rather than monotheistic religions.[4]

The second crucial characteristic is an *emphasis on salvation from this world and on God's love and mercy*. It was Weber (1978) more than anyone who emphasized that the major world religions were salvation religions. Salvation could take a variety of forms but most often involved a desire for *release from earthly suffering*. That this was something new has also been recognized by McNeill, who points out that earlier religions

> viewed the afterworld as essentially a continuation of life as lived on earth, perhaps with some inescapable diminution of its fullness. The new religions of salvation, on the contrary, held that life beyond the grave involved radical change and improvement in society, so that only purged and purified spirits could share in life eternal. (1963:338n)

Although earlier types of religion conceived of an afterlife that the spirit entered upon death—that is, they postulated a concept of *soul*—the soul was not something that had to be "saved" from anything. Similarly, numerous scholars have suggested that the world religions were religions of love and mercy (Jaspers, 1962; Harris, 1977; Stark, 1996). This is closely related to the dimension of salvation in that it is a worldly form of release from suffering. We find this especially evident in Christianity, in which God's love provides comfort and a sense of peace.

Because of this emphasis on salvation, the world religions can also be called *world salvation* religions. But what is it that people wanted to be saved *from*, and why was an emphasis on love and mercy such a critical feature of these religions? What was happening during the second half of the first millennium BCE that would have led to the emergence of the Axial Age religions? These are the critical questions to be addressed in this chapter.

THE NEW COGNITIVE AND EVOLUTIONARY PSYCHOLOGICAL THEORIES OF RELIGION

Some of the most recent and interesting theoretical work on religion has come from scholars using ideas from cognitive and evolutionary psychology. Here, I begin by discussing the work influenced primarily by cognitive psychology, after which I turn to the evolutionary dimensions of this approach.

Cognitive By-Product Theory

Cognitive by-product theorists stress that religious beliefs are products of how the brain works. Religious beliefs must be *counterintuitive* beliefs, or beliefs that are contradicted by the information that people acquire through their ordinary experience of reality (Boyer, 2001; Atran, 2002; Pyysiäinen, 2003, 2009; Barrett, 2004). Counterintuitive beliefs violate our natural intuitions with respect to folk biology, folk physics, and folk psychology. A being who requires no food to live, who is born in some exceptional way, or who does not age or die violates our biological expectations. Beings who are invisible or who can walk on water violate intuitive physics. And a being who knows everything and can read minds violates folk psychology (Boyer, 1994, 2000; Barrett, 2000; Pyysiäinen, 2009).

Pascal Boyer (2001) argues that supernatural entities are for the most part structured by our natural intuitions concerning *agency*. Humans have cognitive adaptations for agency in the sense that they recognize that persons and animals have goals and pursue various means to reach them. They cause things to happen. However, humans have a very strong tendency to extend their natural intuitions about agency beyond persons and animals to many features of nature, such as the sun, moon, or wind. They have a bias to assume that if the wind blows, it is because there is some agent that is causing it to blow, and to blow for some reason or purpose.

Like Boyer, Scott Atran (2002) argues that religious beliefs emerge from agent-based interpretations of complex events. Human brains appear to be programmed to search for agents as the causes of complex and uncertain happenings. The agent-detection schema or module of the brain is built for detecting predators, prey, and protectors. The brain is "trip-wired" to spot lurkers and seek protectors everywhere. In social interaction, people manipulate this hypersensitive cognitive aptitude so as to create the agents who order and unite the culture and the cosmos. People in all religions believe that the world has been deliberately created by unseen agents, that humans have souls that live on after their bodies die, and that through rituals they can persuade gods or spirits to change the world for human betterment.

The cognitive theorists assume that the architecture of the brain imposes strong constraints on the kinds of counterintuitive ideas and thus the kinds of supernatural agents that can be imagined (Boyer, 1994, 2001). Certain kinds of religious concepts exist rather than others because they are "attention grabbing." They resonate with people and are relatively easy to transmit to others. Religious concepts are counterintuitive, but there are limits to how counterintuitive they can be. An omniscient and omnipotent god that exists only on Wednesdays or that forgets everything instantly or spirits that punish you if you follow their commands are so implausible that they would fail to get traction anywhere (Boyer, 2001). And religious concepts cannot be relevant to just anything but, rather, must activate inference systems for agency, predation, death, morality, and social exchange (Boyer, 2001). Thus, cartoon characters such as Mickey Mouse, although certainly counterintuitive, cannot be supernatural entities because they have no relevance for these things. The same is true of supernatural beings such as Santa Claus (Barrett, 2008).

Another major dimension of the cognitive by-product theories concerns the evolutionary status of religious cognitions. Cognitive theories of religion are evolutionary theories, but there are two main types of evolutionary theories—so-called by-product theories and adaptationist theories. *Adaptationist* theories assume that anatomical structures or behavioral traits were directly selected for in evolution because they promoted survival and reproductive success. Such theories are the most common type of evolutionary theory generally speaking. But it is *by-product* theories that have come to be dominant in the cognitive and evolutionary study of religion. In contrast to adaptationist theories, by-product theories of religion assume that its elements are secondary side effects of other cognitive structures. A by-product is just along for the ride; it emerges from something that was selected for, but it is not itself an adaptation. The cognitive psychological theories are by-product theories. They assume that in the evolution of the human brain, there was no specific evolutionary selection for religious concepts—that is, there is no special religious center in the brain. Religious concepts have piggybacked on the extremely adaptive cognitive structures that are involved in agency detection (Boyer, 2001). At the risk of oversimplification, religion is in essence some sort of "gigantic mental accident" (Norenzayan, 2013).

The cognitive by-product approach can tell us why some kinds of religious beliefs are too implausible to exist anywhere, and yet there are several problems, two of which are especially noteworthy. One is cognitive theory's rather impoverished concept of causation. Boyer says that religious "concepts are not around because they are good for people or for society or because of an inherent need or desire to have them. They are around because they are more likely to be acquired than other variants" (2000:211). Such a position might be called "possibilism": If something is possible, it will happen in one way or another or at some time or another. Religion exists simply because it is possible for it to exist. The cognitive analysis of religion is not interested, Boyer says, in the question of whether religious concepts form a coherent whole or represent or explain the world. He deems such questions irrelevant in any cognitive analysis. A reasonable conclusion would seem to be that although a useful starting point, the cognitive approach does not appear to be a very ambitious undertaking. By itself, it seems unable to answer questions that seem most central to the majority of students of religion.

The second problem, closely related to the first, is the cognitive approach's apparent lack of interest in the causal significance of socioecological context. Boyer (1994) states that he is interested only in the cognitive constraints acting on the acquisition and transmission of religious concepts and that ecological and economic conditions do not interest him. These are to be treated merely as contingent background factors. The cognitive theorists are entitled to delimit their subject matter in this way (although see previous discussion), but Boyer makes a more problematic statement: "There is no indication, however, that changes in the way subsistence and exchange are organized could be correlated to [*sic*] changes in, for example, the recurrent connections between religious and intuitive ontologies" (1994:295). If he means that religious concepts and practices are unrelated to the economic and ecological differences among societies, this is simply wrong (see, for example, Sanderson and Roberts, 2008). In any event, the question of the relationship between religious concepts and practices and "contingent background conditions" is crucial if one wants a good general theory of religious variation and religious evolution. This leads us to consider adaptationist theories.

Evolutionary Adaptationists

Adaptationist theories of religion assume that religious beliefs and rituals are evolutionary adaptations that evolved because of the benefits they provide in terms of survival and reproductive success. An adaptationist argument focusing mainly on religious ritual has been developed by Richard Sosis and Candace Alcorta (Sosis, 2003; Alcorta and Sosis, 2005). Following up on William Irons's (2001) suggestion that religious rituals are "hard-to-fake" indicators of commitment, Sosis and Alcorta use *costly signaling theory* to explain why religious rituals are so important in all religions. The Israeli evolutionary biologists Amotz and Avishag Zahavi (1997) have added a new wrinkle to Darwinian evolutionary theory, the notion of a *costly* or *honest signal*. Animals communicate information to others about their fitness by means of certain signals. But not just any signal will do, because signals can be faked. Therefore, a good signal of fitness is one that is difficult to fake and thus honest, and an honest signal is one that will impose some cost on the signaler. For example, peacocks fan out their beautiful and elaborate tails and strut in front of peahens in order to show them off. In their displays, peacocks are showing off their tails—signaling—in order to attract mates. These ritual displays are honest signals because it takes a large amount of energy to grow a beautiful tail, and thus the peacocks with the most beautiful tails will be the fittest (have the best genes). The cost to the peacocks takes the form of their tails' handicaps. The best tails are heavy, and heavy tails make it more difficult for peacocks to escape predators. Beautifully colored tails are also highly visible to predators.

So what is the connection to religious rituals? Sosis and Alcorta argue that human religious rituals are forms of costly signaling. This is especially true in religions whose ritual demands are very great. Consider, for example, the demands placed upon the Hutterites, a communal religious sect in western Canada (Sosis, 2003). Hutterites are expected to devote themselves to daily church worship, communal meals three times a day that are preceded and followed by prayer, and frequent fasting. There are also many restrictions on their behavior. They are prohibited from owning or playing musical instruments, wearing jewelry, smoking tobacco, dancing, and gambling. Adhering to these demands is therefore costly, and therein lies the key, Sosis claims. Following costly demands communicates to others that one is highly committed to the group. Continued participation in costly rituals actually serves to create or intensify religious belief. At the same time, strong believers come to evaluate ritual performances as less costly than do those whose beliefs are weaker. For strong believers, ritual performance is viewed as less of a burden, and, moreover, the opportunity costs of engaging in other behaviors are lower. Such believers therefore receive a large payoff in religious group membership, whereas those who cannot muster a sufficient level of belief and commitment tend to drop out. Thus, in enhancing belief and commitment, costly, hard-to-fake signals contribute to interpersonal trust and social cohesion.

Sosis and Alcorta conclude that the main evolutionary function of religion is to promote group cooperation. Although this appears to be very similar to Durkheim's classic social cohesion argument, there is an important difference. Even though religion tends to promote social cohesion, belonging to a group with highly committed members also confers individual benefits. Other group members can be trusted and can be counted on to provide aid and assistance when it is needed. Because the costs of commitment are so great, highly committed members are also unlikely to be "free-riders," or individuals who reap the benefits of membership while giving back little or nothing in return. Sosis and Alcorta also acknowledge that religion has other individual benefits, such as the reduction of individual anxiety and the promotion of health.

Alcorta and Sosis contend that religious beliefs seem to go well beyond cognitive modules for agency detection. The core aspect of the authors' adaptationism is ontogenetic. They contend that there is an innate predisposition to believe in supernatural agents that is rooted in the neural architecture of the brain, especially in the prefrontal cortex, the temporal lobes, and the limbic areas. This predisposition is activated during childhood and adolescence, and thus there is a "developmentally sensitive window" for learning supernatural concepts. The authors refer to cross-cultural research suggesting that children between the ages of 3 and 12 years have a sort of "natural theism." They go on to state,

> This developmental predisposition to believe in socially omniscient and declarative supernatural agents contrasts with evolved mental modules of folk-psychology for natural categories. It also goes far beyond natural agency-detection modules to encompass socially strategic agents with behaviorally motivating characteristics. ... If religious beliefs are merely by-products of mental modules evolved to deal with the "natural world," *why do such beliefs consistently violate the basic cognitive schema from which they are presumed to derive?* (2005:327, emphasis added)

Joseph Bulbulia (2005) agrees with the adaptationist position of Alcorta and Sosis, but he gives more emphasis to the contribution of religious commitments to physical and psychological well-being. Religion, he argues, is important in helping people cope with what he calls a "traumatic world": In all societies, people are subject to disease and disability and poor reproductive prospects. People experience grief, anxiety, and fear, which create stresses that often lead to poor physical and mental health. Religion helps shield people from the "slings and arrows of existence . . . by altering damaging assessments of the world" (2005:89). "Supernaturalisms," he says, "seem to help us to endure the foxholes of life" (2005:89).

Andrew Newberg and Eugene d'Aquili are neuroscientists with a special interest in human mystical states and their sources in the brain (d'Aquili and Newberg, 1999; Newberg, d'Aquili, and Rause, 2001). The authors also note that humans are myth-making creatures, and to understand the neurological foundations of religion, we need an understanding of myth. The mind has "cognitive operators" that work to reduce intolerable anxiety and help us make sense of the world. People have existential worries: Why do we die and what happens after we die? How do we fit into the universe? Why is there suffering in the world? What is the origin of the universe and of humans? Newberg et al. note that

> in every human culture, across the span of time, the same mythological motifs are constantly repeated: virgin births, world-cleansing floods, lands of the dead, expulsions from paradise, men swallowed down the bellies of whales and serpents, dead and resurrected heroes, the primeval theft of fire from the gods. (2001:74)

Newberg and d'Aquili contend that these myth-making and religious tendencies evolved because of their adaptive value in promoting survival and well-being. The power of religion is that it alleviates "existential stress"; it decreases anxiety and uncertainty and gives people a greater sense of control in a terrifying world.

Erica Harris and Patrick McNamara (2008) are adaptationists in this sense. They identify three criteria whereby a trait can be considered to be an adaptation: It is a cultural universal, is acquired effortlessly, and has an "associated biology" (i.e., a known set of genetic, anatomical, or physiological systems). They note that the first two criteria are easily met. Religion has been found everywhere at all times, and children acquire religious beliefs with extraordinary ease (Barrett, 2012). The third criterion is more difficult to meet, but Harris and McNamara point to research showing that religiosity appears to be moderately to highly heritable (they suggest a heritability coefficient of .28 to .72)[5]; to neuroimaging studies indicating that parts of the brain high in the frequency of dopamine receptors, especially the prefrontal cortex, seem to be associated with religious experience; and to pharmacological studies showing that the *DRD4* gene correlates positively with different measures of religiosity.

To Harris and McNamara's (2008) points can be added that religion promotes both health and reproductive success. In an extremely comprehensive survey of studies on religiosity and physical and mental health (Koenig, McCullough, and Larson, 2001), it was shown that the majority of studies found better physical health and greater longevity among the more religious. Most studies focusing on mental health have reported the same findings. Indeed, religiosity seems to promote better physical health by also promoting better mental health. It decreases anxiety and uncertainty and gives people a greater sense of control in a difficult world (Koenig et al., 2001; Seybold, 2007). Regarding religiosity and reproductive success, people in better health are more likely to find mates, and good mates, than are people in poor health, and thus they are more likely to leave more offspring. Moreover, there is empirical research linking individual religiosity to higher fertility. Numerous studies conducted in a variety of countries show that women who express stronger religious beliefs and who practice their religion more frequently leave more offspring than do the less religious (Frejka and Westoff, 2006; Kaufmann, 2006; Blume, 2009).

In conclusion, I take the adaptationist position that there really is some sort of "religion module"—a bundle of highly specialized neurons and neuronal connections built by a set of genes—in the brain. It may well be that religious beliefs and rituals originated as by-products of cognitive modules intended for some other purpose, but it is also likely that at some point they became decoupled from these modules and evolved their own independent structure—that is, they became adaptations.[6]

Religious Attachment Theory

One important theory developed within the new cognitive and evolutionary psychological framework is what can be called attachment theory, which has been developed by Lee Kirkpatrick (2005). Kirkpatrick is a vigorous defender of by-product theory, but I argue that his theory works better as an adaptationist theory. He would object, of course, but I will treat his theory as such.

Kirkpatrick roots his argument in John Bowlby's (1969) classic attachment theory. Bowlby contended that the human infant is primed to form a strong bond with its parents, its mother in particular, because parents were needed for nurturance and protection in an ancestral environment filled with a wide range of dangers. For Kirkpatrick, many religious notions are extensions or generalizations of the parent–child bond. Supernatural agents are viewed as protectors from harm in much the way that parents are viewed as protectors. God becomes a *haven of safety* and a *secure base*. Kirkpatrick points out that people in modern societies often turn to religion in times of psychological distress and crisis, such as personal catastrophes, serious illness or injury, and death and grieving. He notes that much of Christian scripture, for example, reveals the importance of God in providing "a shield" or "strength." He also reviews research showing that people who display strong attachments to God show better physical and mental health and report less loneliness and depression, fewer psychosomatic symptoms, and greater life satisfaction (cf. Sanderson, 2008).

Kirkpatrick stresses that God or gods are primarily *substitute attachment figures* for natural attachment figures—that is, for mothers, fathers, and other close kin. The feeling of a relationship with God or gods is most likely to be activated when an individual's sense of security, safety, and freedom from anxiety falls below a certain threshold as a result of natural attachments being inadequate to life's challenges. Thus, children who fail to develop adequate attachments to parents should be more likely than other children to develop an attachment to God. Kirkpatrick calls this the *compensation hypothesis*. This language is particularly revealing because it converges with some aspects of the comparative sociology of religion of Max Weber (1978), who argued that what disprivileged classes seek most from religion is some sort of compensation. Kirkpatrick points to research on religious converts (Ullman, 1982, 1989) showing that 80% of converts reported poor attachments to their fathers and 53% poor attachments to their mothers compared to, respectively, only 23% and 7% of a control group, as well as to other research supportive of the compensation hypothesis.

Some of the thinking of the sociological theorist Anthony Giddens (1990, 1991) converges with the attachment theory in that Giddens has argued that the need for *ontological security* is a fundamental human need. This involves a need to feel that one's life and the lives of kin are secure, safe, free from harm, stable, predictable, and so on. Giddens defines this concept as

> the confidence that most human beings have in the continuity of their self-identity and in the constancy of the surrounding social and material environments of action. A sense of the reliability of persons and things, so central to the notion of trust, is basic to feelings of ontological security. (1990:92)

In the human ancestral environment, the most important things that can diminish onto-logical security are danger from animal predators, natural forces, and manipulative and deceitful humans, and the types of religions found in this environment largely reflect these concerns. In more advanced societies, the sense of ontological security is most likely to be disrupted by rapid and massive social change, and in these societies we see very different kinds of religions that seem to reflect these new concerns. In such societies, the problems of cosmological order and meaning and the fear of death also seem to loom larger.

Giddens' notion of ontological security actually parallels even more closely the Bowlby/Kirkpatrick notion of attachment. Giddens notes that the first context of trust is the kinship system, "which in most premodern settings provides a relatively stable mode of organizing 'bundles' of social relations across time and space" (1990:101). In fact, he has virtually independently rediscovered attachment theory, as is evident in the following passage:

> The trust which the child, in normal circumstances, vests in its caretakers, I want to argue, can be seen as a sort of *emotional inoculation* against existential anxieties—a protection against future threats and dangers which allows the individual to sustain hope and courage in the face of whatever debilitating circumstances she or he might later confront. (1991:39–40, emphasis added)

Giddens identifies two other types of social relations that contribute importantly to onto-logical security—the local community and religion. "Religious cosmologies," he says, "provide moral and practical interpretations of personal and social life, as well as of the natural world, which represent an environment of security for the believer" (1990:103).

Kirkpatrick's attachment theory and Giddens' notion of ontological security provide us with a critical component for understanding some of the features of religion, espe-cially the evolution of the world salvation religions, to which I now apply it.

APPLYING ATTACHMENT THEORY: WAR, URBANIZATION, AND ONTOLOGICAL INSECURITY IN THE AXIAL AGE

My own theoretical interpretation of the transition to the world transcendent religions emphasizes that there were two major changes during the Axial Age period—a dramatic increase in the scale and scope of warfare and large-scale and rapid urbanization—that were disruptive of people's social attachments and sense of ontological security and made them receptive to religions emphasizing salvation and transcendence. Let's first discuss increases in the scale and scope of war.

Warfare

The principal form of polity during the Axial Age—and in fact long before—was the empire, and empires grew increasingly larger over time. The main reason empires form and grow larger is war: More war leads to larger empires and larger empires generate more war, in a classic case of a positive feedback loop. In the agrarian empires of the Axial Age, war was the principal means of acquiring wealth, in fact a kind of huge business (Snooks, 1996).

In China in the Spring and Autumn period (770–475 BCE), nobles rode chariots and used bows, and the infantry used lances. A major technological development during this period was the crossbow, which was used along with the sword. New iron technology, originally developed by the Hittites in the Near East around 1200 BCE, was used for the manufacture of new versions of weapons already used, such as swords, lances, and dagger axes (Lewis, 1999; Tanner, 2010). During the Warring States period (481–221 BCE), there was a dramatic increase in the scale of war. There were major changes in military technology and strategy. Chariots declined in importance, and there was a major shift toward large-scale infantries. Military campaigns lasted much longer, and there was greater military specialization, with experts in command emerging (Tanner, 2010). Siege warfare was also an important innovation, as was the increasing use of cavalry (soldiers on horseback), and cavalries accompanied infantries. In the previous period, armies numbered at most some 30,000 soldiers, but they became much larger during the Warring States. In the state of Qin, there were 1 million armored infantry, 1,000 chariots, and 10,000 horses. In Zhao, the state was able to field several hundred thousand armored men, 1,000 chariots, and 10,000 cavalry. In Chu, there were a million infantry, 1,000 chariots, and 10,000 cavalry (Lewis, 1999).

What was happening in China was happening in the Near East and South Asia. As in China, empire and war were aided dramatically by the development of iron weapons, which became widely disseminated after approximately 1200 BCE. The Assyrians had used a battering ram with an iron head, and Greek hoplite soldiers had bronze shields and helmets but iron swords and iron-tipped spears (Derry and Williams, 1960; Mann, 1986; Runciman, 1998). Gradually, iron weapons spread and helped intensify warfare and greatly increase the number of war casualties because iron weapons dramatically increased the killing power of combatants. The number of war deaths soared at the time the Axial Age was beginning. William Eckhardt (1992) has estimated that between the sixth and the fifth century BCE, the number of war deaths in Europe and the Near East multiplied some 18-fold, and that between the sixth and first centuries, or the entire extent of the Axial Age, war deaths increased far more dramatically, some 51-fold.

It was this dramatic increase in warfare, I contend, that was one of the crucial factors in the creation and spread of the world transcendent religions. Here is where Kirkpatrick's attachment theory and Giddens' notion of ontological security are highly relevant. As we know, war is tremendously socially disruptive and psychologically distressing. It is not difficult to see how a dramatic increase in the scale of war and the number of people being killed would create new needs for security and comfort. And not only do people die but many are uprooted and displaced from their homes, which reduces ontological security and creates a greater need for a substitute attachment figure. Recall that one of the major themes of the emerging Axial Age religions was love and mercy—God's compassion.

Consider in particular the situation of the Israelites. For centuries, the ancient Israelites were located at a crossroads between empires and, as a result, were often caught in the middle of wars between these empires (Eisenstadt, 1986b). They also suffered direct destruction from warfare. In 721 BCE, the Kingdom of Israel was overwhelmed by the Assyrians, and many leading Hebrew families were forced into exile (McNeill, 1963). In 586 BCE, King Nebuchadnezzar captured and destroyed Judah, sending much of its population into exile. These were massive social and political crises. William McNeill says that the Hebrews "had to wrestle with crushing national disaster and human suffering" (1963:157). Max Weber states that

> Syria became a theatre of hitherto unprecedented military events. Never before had the world experienced warfare of such frightfulness and magnitude as that practiced by the Assyrian kings. . . . The Israelite literature preserved from the period, above all, the oracles of classical prophecy, express the mad terror caused by these merciless conquerors. As impending gloom beclouded the political horizon, classical prophecy acquired its characteristic form. (1952:267)

Weber adds that the "popular fear of war surged up to them with the question as to the reasons of God's wrath, for means to win his favor, and the national hope for the future in general" (1952:300).

Norman Cohn (1993) contends that the so-called Yahweh-alone movement that marked the beginning of the transition of Judaism from its pagan origins to a monotheistic religion was a response to a situation of severe political insecurity. Jews were worried about a "final defeat" and a "humiliation." Yahweh as a great god, as the only god, was a response to this situation. Yahweh might be punishing the Israelites for failing to live up to moral demands. If they lived up to these demands, he would save them from disaster. Finkelstein and Silberman state that

> we now know that the Bible's epic saga first emerged as a response to the pressures, difficulties, challenges, and hopes faced by the people of the tiny kingdom of Judah in the decades before its destruction and by the even tinier Temple community in Jerusalem in the post-exilic period. (2001:318)

These pressures, difficulties, and challenges were primarily the result of massive warfare. Concerning Antioch, a major city with a large Jewish diaspora population and then later a center of Christianity, Stark tells us that

> during the course of about six hundred years of Roman rule, Antioch was taken by unfriendly forces eleven times and was plundered and sacked on five of these occasions. The city was also put to siege, but did not fall, two other times. In addition, Antioch burned entirely or in large part four times, three times by accident and once when the Persians carefully burned the city to the ground after picking it clean of valuables and taking the surviving population into captivity. (1996:159)

Consider once again the case of China. The situation Confucius faced was one of social anarchy, brought on mainly by increasing warfare. Between the eighth and third century, conditions were very similar to what was happening in Palestine at the same time. In China, warfare had become almost continual, indeed virtually interminable. In previous times, prisoners of war were often held for ransom, but now conquerors killed them in large-scale executions. Entire populations were beheaded, even women and children, or, worse still, thrown into boiling cauldrons. Mass slaughters of up to 400,000 people have been reported (Smith, 1991).

Urbanization

The shift from bronze to iron metals also affected the technology of subsistence because the new iron plows were much more efficient cultivating instruments. Iron plows permitted increases in economic productivity and in the size of economic surpluses, which in turn made possible another major change that can be observed in the historical record in the time period after 600 BCE: expanding urbanization. Tertius Chandler (1987) has attempted to estimate the size of cities of 30,000 or more inhabitants in all regions of the world from very ancient times to the present. In 2250 BCE, Chandler estimates that there were only 8 cities in the world with a population of approximately 30,000 (total population of those cities = 240,000). By 650 BCE, Chandler identifies 20 cities ranging in population from 30,000 to 120,000 (total population = approximately 1 million). That represents about a fourfold increase in 1,600 years. But in the 220 years between 650 and 430 BCE, the number of large cities (30,000–200,000) increased to 51 (total population = nearly 3 million), a threefold increase in a much shorter period of time; by 200 BCE, there were 55 cities of 30,000 or more (the largest being Changan, China, at 400,000) totaling almost 4 million people; and by 100 CE, the number of large cities (30,000–450,000) had reached 75 (total population = approximately 5 million). So in the centuries of the Axial Age, urbanization occurred on a far greater scale than in the previous two millennia: There were many more large cities, and the largest of these were much larger.

These increases in urbanization were largely facilitated by two conditions: increases in the size of economic surpluses and, more important, the expansion and deepening of world trade networks (Sanderson, 1999). The expansion of world trade networks and urbanization went hand in hand because cities were the primary foci of trade. Urbanization was also related to the growth of empires, and larger empires led, along with increased military might made possible by iron weapons, to the larger and more destructive wars discussed previously.

What were these cities and where were they located? All of the 20 largest world cities in 650 BCE were located precisely in those regions where the Axial Age proper was soon to begin: the Near East, India, and China. In 430 BCE, 50 of 51 of the largest cities were located in the very same regions. The corresponding figures for 200 BCE and 100 CE are 51 of 55 and 69 of 75, respectively. It is extremely noteworthy that 62% of the population of these cities in 650 BCE lived in or around the very small region that produced Judaism and Christianity; the figures for 430 BCE, 200 BCE, and 100 CE are 57%, 48%, and 48%, respectively. (See Tables A1–A4 in the Appendix for complete lists of the cities and their estimated sizes.)

George Modelski (2003) has made a concerted effort to improve on Chandler's city size data. (Modelski's figures for the Axial Age period are reported in Table A5 in the Appendix.) His methods and results differ in two important respects from Chandler's: He uses intervals of a single century and, for the time period we are considering, he sets a minimum city size of 100,000 instead of Chandler's 30,000 as the operational definition of a world city. Modelski tends to give higher estimates of city size compared to Chandler. For example, he considers Alexandria to have had 600,000 inhabitants in 200 BCE compared to Chandler's estimate of only 200,000, and, for the same period, Modelski estimates Loyang in China at 200,000 compared to an estimate of only 60,000 by Chandler. But sometimes Modelski's estimates are lower; for example, he estimates Changan in China in 200 BCE at only 100,000 compared to Chandler's much larger estimate of 400,000. Obviously, these are wide discrepancies.

Nevertheless, Modelski's data show the same overall pattern as Chandler's, which is a dramatic increase in the size of large cities during the Axial Age. As shown in Table A6 in the Appendix, Chandler shows a 276% increase in urban populations from the beginning of the Axial Age to 200 BCE, whereas Modelski shows a 352% increase. For the longer period between 650/600 BCE and 100 CE, Chandler shows a 386% increase, and Modelski shows an increase of 614%. The correspondence should actually be considered very close when we realize that both scholars are making estimates based on certain broad assumptions and inferences for a time period for which data are much more scanty and much less reliable than for more recent times. And the key point is that both Chandler's and Modelski's figures show very large increases in urban populations during the Axial Age.

It is not simply a matter of the number of cities and the size of their populations. The *density* of populations matters also. Densities in some cities in the Roman Empire were extremely high. Antioch had a population of some 100,000, but it covered a mere 2 square miles, thus giving it a density of 50,000 persons per square mile. And density in Rome was even greater, at approximately 150,000 per square mile. These are staggering figures for preindustrial cities without modern technology and modern conveniences (Stark, 2006).

But how, exactly, would an increase in urbanization create new religious needs? The answer, I think, is much the same as what was said regarding the huge increase in warfare: Rapid and large-scale urbanization was tremendously disruptive of people's lives. But what was it that was being disrupted? One thing was people's attachments to kin and other social intimates (Bellah, 2005; Marangukadis, 2006). People were increasingly living in a world of strangers. Given the enormous importance of kin relations to humans everywhere, this was a significant blow. And the strangers people were increasingly living among were not just non-kin, but members of alien ethnic groups. This brought with it increased ethnic conflict, which became another source of disruption. We return once again to Kirkpatrick and Giddens on the effects of the disruption of attachment bonds and the sense of ontological security. People turn to God, Kirkpatrick says, as a substitute attachment figure, especially when there has been some sort of disruption in their attachments to parents, and God functions psychologically as a safe haven and secure base. And, as noted previously, Giddens also specifically mentions religion as a major source of ontological security. This, I submit, is what was happening to encourage the formation of the Axial Age religions of compassion, love, and mercy. Life increasingly in a world of strangers led to a much higher level of insecurity and anxiety, and it was this (in conjunction with the massive intensification of warfare) that generated new religious needs. An all-powerful, loving God was an excellent prescription for people's new sense of threat and danger. Humans evolved to live in small groups of kin, which they did in hunter–gatherer, horticultural, and even most intensive agricultural societies. They did not evolve to live in densely packed cities in which most of their social relations were carried on with non-kin and strangers (Massey, 2005). The result was new psychological needs, and the world transcendent religions that offered love, mercy, and release from suffering evolved to assist people in adapting to their radically changed circumstances. McNeill puts it almost perfectly:

> Christianity, Hinduism, and Mahayana Buddhism provided perhaps the first really satisfactory adjustment of human life to the impersonality and human indifference that prevails in large urban agglomerates. Nature religions, personifying the forces of earth and sky, could meet the psychological needs of village farmers whose social ties to their fellows were personal and close. State religions were adequate for the early civilized peoples, whose cultural inheritance was nearly uniform and who maintained a close personal identification with the body social and politic. But when such uniformity and cohesion in civilized society broke down . . . such official, state religions could not satisfy *the growing number of deracinated individuals whose personal isolation from any larger community was barely tolerable at best. . . .*
>
> Something more than either nature religion or a religion of state was needed for peace of mind in a great city, where strangers had to be dealt with daily, where rich and poor lived in different cultural worlds, and where impersonal forces like official compulsion or market changes impinged painfully and quite unpredictably upon daily life. Knowledge of a savior, *who cared for and protected* each human atom adrift

in such mass communities . . . certainly offered men *a powerful help in the face of any hardship or disaster*. In addition the religious community itself, united in a common faith and in good works, *provided a vital substitute* for the sort of primary community where all relations were personal, from which humankind had sprung and to which, in all probability, human instinct remains fundamentally attuned. (1963:352– 353, emphasis added)

But urbanization was also very likely important in another way. In his major study of early Christianity, Stark (1996) notes that during the period when Christianity arose, urban life was a source of chaos, misery, and crisis everywhere. People were often packed together in crowded tenements, living only in tiny cubicles. Privacy was scarce, tenements did not have furnaces or fireplaces, and rooms were smoky in winter. Problems of sanitation loomed large, and huge burdens were placed on systems of sewerage, water provision, and the disposal of garbage. "Most people in Greco-Roman cities," Stark contends, "must have lived in filth beyond our imagining" (1996:153). Moreover, the average Greco-Roman city must have been pervaded by infectious disease; mortality rates were very high, and thus longevity was short. Most people must have suffered from the pain and disability of chronic health problems. In addition, crime and disorder were no doubt rampant. Ethnic divisions and ethnic conflicts were common, and riots were a frequent occurrence (Stark, 1996). Describing the city of Antioch in particular, Stark states that it was "a city filled with misery, danger, fear, despair, and hatred" (1996:160). He notes,

> People living in such circumstances must often have despaired. Surely it would not be strange for them to have concluded that the end of days drew near. And surely too they must often have longed for relief, for hope, indeed for salvation. (1996:161)

Continuing, he says that Christianity

> arose in response to the misery, chaos, fear, and brutality of life in the urban Greco-Roman world. Christianity revitalized life in Greco-Roman cities by providing new norms and new kinds of social relationships able to cope with many urgent urban problems. To cities filled with the homeless and impoverished, Christianity offered charity as well as hope. To cities filled with newcomers and strangers, Christianity offered *an immediate basis for attachments*. To cities filled with orphans and widows, Christianity provided *a new and expanded sense of family*. To cities torn by violent ethnic strife, Christianity offered a new basis for social solidarity. . . . And to cities faced with epidemics, fires, and earthquakes, Christianity offered effective nursing services. (1996:161; emphasis added)

Little wonder then that the Greco-Roman world in the first two centuries BCE witnessed an endless parade of messiahs coming to relieve people of their suffering (Harris, 1974).

Stark (1996) speaks only of Christianity, but there is no reason in principle why his argument does not apply to the other major world religions that arose during the same historical period. Indeed, because urban densities were even greater in India and China than in the Near East, the conditions of life may well have been even worse, and thus people may have had an even more critical need for salvation doctrines that offered them release from suffering.

CONCLUSION

This chapter's main aim has been to situate one major stage in the evolution of religion, world salvation and world transcendent religion, in its socioecological context and thereby explain why this new type of religion emerged when and where it did. The main argument has been that the enormously disruptive effects of the intensification of warfare and large-scale and rapid urbanization during the second half of the first millennium BCE—the Axial Age—created new human needs for ontological security, anxiety reduction, and release from suffering. People's existing social attachments were being threatened by the altered circumstances they faced. The old pagan religions of the ancient world were not up to the task of meeting these new challenges. As a result, religious sages and prophets began to formulate new religious ideas that resonated well with the masses and that began to spread far and wide and new religions were born.

In the Near East, these were monotheistic religions based on One True God—an omnipresent, omniscient, omnipotent, and compassionate deity to which people could form strong personal and heartfelt attachments. A new kind of God entered the world, one who could provide salvation in a heavenly afterlife for anyone who professed the faith and followed the commands that this God laid down. The new God was not like anything in nature, as many of the old gods were, and not at all like humans. He was a Transcendent God outside the mundane world and unlike anything with which people had previously been familiar.

In East and South Asia, something similar happened, as new transcendent religions developed there too. However, in these regions, a big god was usually not the only god, being accompanied by other, often preexisting gods. But the Near Eastern and East and South Asian religions were strikingly alike in being responsive to human suffering and the need for release from it. As Weber (1978) strongly emphasized, the non-Western religions were, like the Western ones, salvation religions. Because all were salvation religions with transcendent deities, and because all arose at a strikingly similar time in world history, an overall theory to explain their origin seems compelling.

ACKNOWLEDGMENTS

I am grateful to Rosemary Hopcroft for a valuable critique of the first draft of this chapter, which prompted a substantial revision and, I believe, a much improved chapter. I also thank Christopher Chase-Dunn for useful discussions of some of the issues of this chapter, especially ancient polytheistic religions and political structures. He also suggested that I include Modelski's data on world city sizes along with Chandler's data. Randall Collins provided a penetrating critique at an early stage.

APPENDIX

ANCIENT CITIES AND ESTIMATED CITY SIZES

Table A1 Twenty Largest World Cities, 650 BCE

Near East		South Asia		East Asia	
City	Population	City	Population	City	Population
Ninevah (Assyria)	120,000	Kausambi	55,000	Lintzu (China)	80,000
Memphis (Persia)	80,000	Ayodhya	35,000	Loyang (China)	70,000
Babylon (Persia)	60,000			Kingchow (China)	42,500
Miletus (Greece)	50,000			Hsintien (China)	40,000
Sais (Egypt)	48,000			Changan (China)	35,000
Marib (Arabia)	45,000			Pyongyang (Korea)	30,000
Jerusalem (Persia)	45,000				
Ecbatana (Persia)	42,500				
Napata (Nubia)	42,500				
Calah (Assyria)	40,000				
Van (Persia)	35,000				
Susa (Persia)	30,000				
Total	623,000		90,000		297,500
Grand total: 1,010,500					

Note: Names in parentheses refer to the state, empire, or geographical location in which the city existed at the given time period. Some Greek cities were in Greek colonies in Italy or elsewhere.

Source: Chandler (1987, p. 460).

Table A2 Fifty-one Largest World Cities, 430 BCE

Near East		South Asia		East Asia	
City	Population	City	Population	City	Population
Babylon (Persia)	200,000	Patna	100,000	Yenhsiatu (China)	180,000
Athens (Greece)	155,000	Benares	54,000	Loyang (China)	100,000
Syracuse (Syracuse)	125,000	Anuradhapura	47,000	Hsueh (China)	75,000
Memphis (Persia)	100,000	Sravasti	47,000	Soochow (China)	60,000
Ecbatana (Persia)	90,000	Vaisali	45,000	Lintzu (China)	60,000
Corinth (Greece)	70,000	Kausambi	39,000	Lucheng (China)	50,000
Susa (Persia)	70,000	Dantapura	37,000	Fenghsiang (China)	42,500
Persepolis (Persia)	50,000	Rajagriha	32,500	Changsha (China)	40,000
Carthage (Carthage)	50,000	Ayodhya	32,500	Champa (Vietnam)	37,000
Jerusalem (Persia)	49,000	Trichinopoly	32,500	Pyongyang (Korea)	32,500
Meroe (Nubia)	47,000			Taiyuan (China)	32,500
Marib (Arabia)	45,000				
Ephesus (Persia)	42,500				
Sparta (Greece)	40,000				
Agrigentum (Greece)	40,000				
Argos (Greece)	40,000				
Tarentum (Greece)	40,000				
Messina (Greece)	38,000				
Sidon (Phoenicia)	36,000				
Sardis (Anatolia)	35,000				
Croton (Greece)	35,000				
Tyre (Phoenicia)	35,000				

(continued)

Table A2 Continued

Near East		South Asia		East Asia	
City	Population	City	Population	City	Population
Cyrene (Phoenicia)	35,000				
Corcyra (Greece)	35,000				
Rome	35,000				
Gela (Greece)	35,000				
Kerch (Greece)	32,500				
Damascus (Syria)	30,000				
Elis (Greece)	30,000				
Total	1,665,000		466,500		709,500
Grand total: 2,841,000					

Note: Names in parentheses refer to the state, empire, or geographical location in which the city existed at the given time period. Some Greek cities were in Greek colonies in Italy or elsewhere. Only 50 of the 51 largest cities are listed here because the other is a New World city that is far removed from the centers of the Axial Age.

Source: Chandler (1987, p. 461).

Table A3 Fifty-five Largest World Cities, 200 BCE

Near East		South Asia		East Asia	
City	Population	City	Population	City	Population
Alexandria (Egypt)	200,000	Patna	350,000	Changan (China)	400,000
Seleucia (Syria)	200,000	Ujjain	87,500	Pingcheng (China)	87,500
Carthage (Carthage)	150,000	Anuradhapura	65,000	Soochow (China)	65,000
Rome	150,000	Paithan	60,000	Loyang (China)	60,000
Antioch (Syria)	120,000	Taxila	60,000	Nanking (China)	51,000
Syracuse (Rome)	100,000	Benares	51,000	Lucheng (China)	39,000
Rayy (Syria)	87,500	Aror	51,000	Changsha (China)	38,000

(continued)

Table A3 Continued

Near East		South Asia		East Asia	
City	Population	City	Population	City	Population
Athens (Greece)	75,000	Vaisali	51,000	Kaifeng (China)	32,500
Balkh (Bactria)	75,000	Tosali	51,000		
Corinth (Greece)	70,000	Kolkai	51,000		
Memphis (Egypt)	65,000	Broach	40,000		
Babylon (Syria)	65,000	Peshawar	39,000		
Ecbatana (Syria)	51,000	Kolhapur	36,500		
Jerusalem (Egypt)	51,000	Sopara	36,500		
Marib (Arabia)	51,000	Srinagar	32,500		
Rhodes (Greece)	42,000	Trichinopoly	32,500		
Ephesus (Persia)	40,000	Madurai	32,500		
Cirta (Algeria)	39,000				
Meroe (Nubia)	36,500				
Messina (Greece)	35,000				
Pergamum (Anatolia)	35,000				
Damascus (Syria)	32,500				
Amasia (Greece)	32,500				
Cyrene (Phoenicia)	30,000				
Sparta (Greece)	30,000				
Olbia (Sardinia)	30,000				
Total	1,893,000		1,127,000		773,000
Grand total: 3,793,000					

Note: Names in parentheses refer to the state, empire, or geographical location in which the city existed at the given time period. Only 51 of the 55 largest cities are listed here because the others are New World cities that are far removed from the centers of the Axial Age.

Source: Chandler (1987, p. 462).

Table A4 Seventy-five Largest World Cities, 100 CE

Near East		South Asia		East Asia	
City	Population	City	Population	City	Population
Rome	450,000	Anuradhapura	130,000	Loyang (China)	420,000
Seleucia (Persia)	250,000	Peshawar	120,000	Soochow (China)	95,000
Alexandria (Egypt)	250,000	Paithan	82,500	Changan (China)	82,500
Antioch (Syria)	150,000	Patala	72,500	Nanking (China)	82,500
Carthage (Carthage)	100,000	Patna	67,500	Chengdu (China)	70,000
Smyrna (Rome)	90,000	Dohad	62,500	Wuchang (China)	67,500
Ecbatana (Syria)	82,500	Kavery	55,500	Tonggoo (China)	55,000
Athens (Greece)	75,000	Broach	55,500	Kashiwara (Japan)	50,500
Edessa (Anatolia)	72,500	Madurai	50,000	Kanchow (China)	47,500
Nisibis (Anatolia)	67,500	Kolhapur	47,500	Taiyuan (China)	42,000
Zafar (Arabia)	60,000	Aror	47,500	Peking (China)	38,500
Rayy (Syria)	55,500	Srinigar	47,500	Pingchang (China)	38,500
Syracuse (Rome)	55,500	Benares	47,500	Canton (China)	38,500
Babylon	55,500	Ujjain	38,500	Kingchow (China)	38,500
Ephesus (Anatolia)	51,000	Junnar	36,500	Namhan (Korea)	36,500
Corinth (Greece)	50,000	Tosali	33,000	Keishu (Korea)	34,500
Memphis (Egypt)	47,500	Jullundur	33,000	Hangchow (China)	33,000
Leptis (Libya)	47,500	Ayodhya	33,000	Changsha (China)	33,000
Balkh (Anatolia)	47,500			Tunhuang (China)	32,000
Merv (Turkmenistan)	42,000				
Stakhr (Persia)	42,000				
Pergamum (Anatolia)	40,000				
Apamea (Syria)	37,000				
Capua (Rome)	36,000				
Byzantium (Anatolia)	36,000				

(continued)

Table A4 Continued

Near East		South Asia		East Asia	
City	Population	City	Population	City	Population
Thessalonica (Greece)	35,000				
Oxyrhyncus (Egypt)	34,000				
Angora (Greece)	34,000				
Milan (Rome)	30,000				
Petra (Jordan)	30,000				
Gortyn (Greece)	30,000				
Ostia (Rome)	30,000				
Total	2,513,500		1,060,000		1,336,000
Grand total: 4,909,500					

Note: Names in parentheses refer to the state, empire, or geographical location in which the city existed at the given time period. Only 69 of the 75 largest cities are listed here because the others are New World cities that are far removed from the centers of the Axial Age.

Source: Chandler (1987, p. 463).

Table A5 Number and Size of Cities 100,000 or Larger, 700 BCE to 100 CE

Century	Near East	South Asia	East Asia	Total
700 BCE	200,000 (2)		200,000 (2)	400,000 (4)
600 BCE	200,000 (2)		400,000 (3)	600,000 (5)
500 BCE	500,000 (5)	100,000 (1)	1,000,000 (8)	1,600,000 (14)
400 BCE	670,000 (5)	200,000 (2)	1,650,000 (12)	2,520,000 (19)
300 BCE	1,550,000 (7)	700,000 (3)	2,020,000 (11)	4,270,000 (21)
200 BCE	1,510,000 (7)	700,000 (4)	500,000 (4)	2,710,000 (15)
100 BCE	2,025,000 (8)	550,000 (4)	900,000 (5)	3,475,000 (17)
1 CE	2,160,000 (8)	600,000 (6)	1,860,000 (9)	4,620,000 (23)
100 CE	3,015,000 (11)	750,000 (6)	520,000 (2)	4,285,000 (19)

Note: Numbers in parentheses are the number of cities with 100,000 or more inhabitants.

Source: Modelski (2003, pp. 42, 44, 45, 49).

Table A6 Chandler's and Modelski's City Size Totals, 650 BCE to 100 CE

Century	Near East	South Asia	East Asia	Grand Total
650/600 BCE	623/200	90/0	298/400	1,010/600
430/400 BCE	1,665/670	467/200	710/1,650	2,841/2,520
200 BCE	1,893/1,510	1,127/700	773/500	3,793/2,710
100 CE	2,514/3,015	1,060/750	1,336/520	4,910/4,285

Total % increase 650/600 BCE to 200 BCE

Chandler, 276%; Modelski, 352%

Total % Increase 650/600 BCE to 100 CE

Chandler, 386%; Modelski, 614%

Note: The first number is Chandler's estimate (cities > 30,000), and the second is Modelski's estimate (cities > 100,000). Numbers are expressed in thousands (e.g., 200 = 200,000).

Sources: Chandler (1987, pp. 460–463) and Modelski (2003, pp. 42, 44, 45, 49).

NOTES

1. Exceptions include Stark (2007), Bellah (2011), Bulbulia et al. (2008), Wright (2009), and Wade (2009).
2. Some may question use of the term "pagan" because it has often been used pejoratively, especially in Christianity, to refer to those who adhere to traditional non-Christian or pre-Christian religions. Etymologically, pagan derives from the Latin *paganus*, meaning "rustic" or "country dweller." Yet the term continues to be used in a nonpejorative way by many students of religion, including highly respected historians (MacMullen, 1981, 1984; Stark, 1996, 2006, 2011; Athanassiadi and Frede, 1999; for further clarification, see Clark, 2004). Shorn of any pejorative implication, it is actually quite a good term.
3. These are the original dates used by Jaspers (1953, 1962), but they need not be sacrosanct. The end date leaves out Christianity, which I consider a crucial part of the Axial Age, and the start date is slightly early, as Judaism did not become a transcendent and monotheistic religion until approximately two centuries later. I prefer the dates 600 BCE to 1 CE.
4. It is not completely clear that the God or gods of the East and South Asian religions are genuinely transcendent inasmuch as they retain something of a human-like quality. Vishnu and Shiva, for example, are said to have relatives, consorts, or offspring, and thus to resemble pagan gods. But even if we were to concede that the Asian gods are not truly transcendent, they are certainly different from pagan gods. Common behavior among pagan gods is promiscuity, drunkenness, deception, adultery, and murder, among many other human-like things. The Asian gods do not behave in this way, not even remotely. Neither the Buddha nor the bodhisattvas get drunk, marry, have offspring, or commit murder. The same is true for Vishnu–Shiva, as well as for Confucius and Laozi. Such behavior would be unthinkable for them.

5. But see Saler and Ziegler (2006) and Koenig, McGue, Krueger, and Bouchard (2005) for discussions of research findings on the genetics of religiosity.
6. A much more extensive discussion of the adaptationist position, including a defense, can be found in Sanderson (2008).

REFERENCES

Alcorta, Candace S., and Richard Sosis. 2005. "Ritual, Emotion, and Sacred Symbols: The Evolution of Religion as an Adaptive Complex." *Human Nature* 16: 323–359.

Athanassiadi, Polymnia, and Michael Frede, eds. 1999. *Pagan Monotheism in Late Antiquity.* Oxford: Clarendon.

Atran, Scott. 2002. *In Gods We Trust: The Evolutionary Landscape of Religion.* New York: Oxford University Press.

Barrett, Justin L. 2000. "Exploring the Natural Foundations of Religion." *Trends in Cognitive Sciences* 4: 29–34.

Barrett, Justin L. 2004. *Why Would Anyone Believe in God?* Lanham, MD: AltaMira.

Barrett, Justin L. 2008. "Why Santa Claus Is Not a God." *Journal of Cognition and Culture* 8: 149–161.

Barrett, Justin L. 2012. *Born Believers: The Science of Children's Religious Belief.* New York: Free Press.

Bellah, Robert N. 2005. "What Is Axial About the Axial Age?" *European Journal of Sociology* 46: 69–89.

Bellah, Robert N. 2011. *Religion in Human Evolution: From the Paleolithic to the Axial Age.* Cambridge, MA: Harvard University Press.

Blume, Michael. 2009. "The Reproductive Benefits of Religious Affiliation." Pp. 117–126 in *The Biological Evolution of Religious Mind and Behavior*, edited by E. Voland and W. Schiefenhovel. Berlin: Springer-Verlag.

Bowlby, John. 1969. *Attachment and Loss.* Vol. 1. New York: Basic Books.

Boyer, Pascal. 1994. *The Naturalness of Religious Ideas: A Cognitive Theory of Religion.* Berkeley: University of California Press.

Boyer, Pascal. 2000. "Functional Origins of Religious Concepts: Ontological and Strategic Selection in Evolved Minds." *Journal of the Royal Anthropological Institute* 6: 195–214.

Boyer, Pascal. 2001. *Religion Explained: The Evolutionary Origins of Religious Thought.* New York: Basic Books.

Bulbulia, Joseph. 2005. "Are There Any Religions? An Evolutionary Exploration." *Method and Theory in the Study of Religion* 17: 71–100.

Bulbulia, Joseph, Richard Sosis, Erica Harris, Russell Genet, Cheryl Genet, and Karen Wyman, eds. 2008. *The Evolution of Religion: Studies, Theories, and Critiques.* Santa Margarita, CA: Collins Foundation Press.

Carneiro, Robert L. 2003. *Evolutionism in Cultural Anthropology: A Critical History.* Boulder, CO: Westview.

Chandler, Tertius. 1987. *Four Thousand Years of Urban Growth.* Lewiston, NY: St. David's University Press.

Clark, Gillian. 2004. *Christianity and Roman Society.* Cambridge, UK: Cambridge University Press.

Cohn, Norman. 1993. *Cosmos, Chaos, and the World to Come: The Ancient Roots of Apocalyptic Faith.* New Haven, CT: Yale University Press.

d'Aquili, Eugene, and Andrew B. Newberg. 1999. *The Mystical Mind: Probing the Biology of Religious Experience.* Minneapolis: Fortress Press.

Derry, T. K., and Trevor I. Williams. 1960. *A Short History of Technology: From the Earliest Times to A.D. 1900.* New York: Dover.

Eckhardt, William. 1992. *Civilizations, Empires, and Wars.* Jefferson, NC: McFarland.

Eisenstadt, S. N. 1986a. "Introduction: The Axial Age Breakthroughs—Their Characteristics and Origins." Pp. 1–25 in *The Origins and Diversity of Axial Age Civilizations*, edited by S. N. Eisenstadt. Albany: State University of New York Press.

Eisenstadt, S. N., ed. 1986b. *The Origins and Diversity of Axial Age Civilizations.* Albany: State University of New York Press.

Finkelstein, Israel, and Neil Asher Silberman. 2001. *The Bible Unearthed: Archaeology's New Vision of Ancient Israel and the Origin of Its Sacred Texts.* New York: Simon & Schuster.

Frejka, Tomas, and Charles F. Westoff. 2006. "Religion, Religiousness, and Fertility in the U.S. and Europe." Working paper WP 2006-013. Rostock, Germany: Max Planck Institute for Demographic Research.

Giddens, Anthony. 1990. *The Consequences of Modernity.* Stanford, CA: Stanford University Press.

Giddens, Anthony. 1991. *Modernity and Self-Identity: Self and Society in the Late Modern Age.* Stanford, CA: Stanford University Press.

Harris, Erica, and Patrick McNamara. 2008. "Is Religiousness a Biocultural Adaptation?" Pp. 79–85 in *The Evolution of Religion: Studies, Theories, and Critiques*, edited by Joseph Bulbulia, Richard Sosis, Russell Genet, Erica Harris, Karen Wyman, and Cheryl Genet. Santa Margarita, CA: Collins Foundation Press.

Harris, Marvin. 1974. *Cows, Pigs, Wars, and Witches: The Riddles of Culture.* New York: Random House.

Harris, Marvin. 1977. *Cannibals and Kings: The Origins of Cultures.* New York: Random House.

Irons, William. 2001. "Religion as a Hard-to-Fake Sign of Commitment." Pp. 292–309 in *Evolution and the Capacity for Commitment*, edited by Randolph Nesse. New York: Russell Sage Foundation.

Jaspers, Karl. 1953. *The Origin and Goal of History.* Translated by Michael Bullock. New Haven, CT: Yale University Press.

Jaspers, Karl. 1962. *Socrates, Buddha, Confucius, and Jesus: The Paradigmatic Individuals.* Translated by Ralph Manheim. New York: Harcourt Brace.

Kaufmann, Eric. 2006. "Breeding for God." *Prospect Magazine*, Issue 128, December.

Kaufmann, Yehezkel. 1960. *The Religion of Israel: From Its Beginnings to the Babylonian Exile.* Translated by Moshe Greenberg. Chicago: University of Chicago Press.

Kirkpatrick, Lee A. 2005. *Attachment, Evolution, and the Psychology of Religion.* New York: Guilford.

Koenig, Harold C., Michael E. McCullough, and David B. Larson, eds. 2001. *Handbook of Religion and Health.* New York: Oxford University Press.

Koenig, Laura B., Matt McGue, Robert F. Krueger, and Thomas J. Bouchard, Jr. 2005. "Genetic and Environmental Influences on Religiousness: Findings for Retrospective and Current Religiousness Ratings." *Journal of Personality* 73: 471–488.

Lewis, Mark Edward. 1999. "Warring States Political History." Pp. 587–650 in *The Cambridge History of Ancient China: From the Origins of Civilization to 221 BC*, edited by Michael Loewe and Edward L. Shaughnessy. New York: Cambridge University Press.

MacMullen, Ramsay. 1981. *Paganism in the Roman Empire.* New Haven, CT: Yale University Press.

MacMullen, Ramsay. 1984. *Christianizing the Roman Empire, A.D. 100–400*. New Haven, CT: Yale University Press.

Mann, Michael. 1986. *The Sources of Social Power: Vol. 1. From the Beginning to AD 1760*. New York: Cambridge University Press.

Marangukadis, Manussos. 2006. "The Social Sources and Environmental Consequences of Axial Thinking: Mesopotamia, China, and Greece in Comparative Perspective." *European Journal of Sociology* 47: 59–91.

Massey, Douglas S. 2005. *Strangers in a Strange Land: Humans in an Urbanizing World*. New York: Norton.

McNeill, William H. 1963. *The Rise of the West: A History of the Human Community*. Chicago: University of Chicago Press.

Modelski, George. 2003. *World Cities, –3000 to 2000*. Washington, DC: Faros 2000.

Newberg, Andrew, Eugene d'Aquili, and Vince Rause. 2001. *Why God Won't Go Away: Brain Science and the Biology of Belief*. New York: Ballantine.

Norenzayan, Ara. 2013. *Big Gods: How Religion Transformed Cooperation and Conflict*. Princeton, NJ: Princeton University Press.

Pyysiäinen, Ilkka. 2003. *How Religion Works*. Leiden, the Netherlands: Brill.

Pyysiäinen, Ilkka. 2009. *Supernatural Agents: Why We Believe in Souls, Gods, and Buddhas*. Oxford: Oxford University Press.

Runciman, W. G. 1998. "Greek Hoplites, Warrior Culture, and Indirect Bias." *Journal of the Royal Anthropological Institute* 4: 731–751.

Saler, Benson, and Charles A. Ziegler. 2006. "Atheism and the Apotheosis of Agency." *Temenos* 42(2): 7–41.

Sanderson, Stephen K. 1999. *Social Transformations: A General Theory of Historical Development*. Updated edn. Lanham, MD: Rowman & Littlefield.

Sanderson, Stephen K. 2007. *Evolutionism and Its Critics: Deconstructing and Reconstructing an Evolutionary Interpretation of Human Society*. Boulder, CO: Paradigm.

Sanderson, Stephen K. 2008. "Adaptation, Evolution, and Religion." *Religion* 38: 141–156.

Sanderson, Stephen K., and Wesley W. Roberts. 2008. "The Evolutionary Forms of the Religious Life: A Cross-Cultural Quantitative Study." *American Anthropologist* 110: 454–466.

Seybold, Kevin S. 2007. "Physiological Mechanisms Involved in Religiosity/Spirituality." *Journal of Behavioral Medicine* 30: 303–309.

Smith, Huston. 1991. *The World's Religions: Our Great Wisdom Traditions*. New York: HarperSanFrancisco.

Snooks, Graeme Donald. 1996. *The Dynamic Society: Exploring the Sources of Global Change*. London: Routledge.

Sosis, Richard. 2003. "Why Aren't We All Hutterites? Costly Signaling Theory and Religious Behavior." *Human Nature* 14: 91–127.

Stark, Rodney. 1996. *The Rise of Christianity: A Sociologist Reconsiders History*. Princeton, NJ: Princeton University Press.

Stark, Rodney. 2006. *Cities of God: The Real Story of How Christianity Became an Urban Movement and Conquered Rome*. New York: HarperSanFrancisco.

Stark, Rodney. 2007. *Discovering God: The Origins of the Great Religions and the Evolution of Belief*. New York: HarperOne.

Stark, Rodney. 2011. *The Triumph of Christianity: How the Jesus Movement Became the World's Largest Religion*. New York: HarperOne.

Tanner, Harold M. 2010. *China: A History. Vol. 1: From Neolithic Cultures Through the Great Qing Empire*. Indianapolis, IN: Hackett.

Ullman, C. 1982. "Change of Mind, Change of Heart: Some Cognitive and Emotional Antecedents of Religious Conversion." *Journal of Personality and Social Psychology* 42: 183–192.

Ullman, C. 1989. *The Transformed Self: The Psychology of Religious Conversion.* New York: Plenum.

Wade, Nicholas. 2009. *The Faith Instinct: How Religion Evolved and Why It Endures.* New York: Penguin.

Weber, Max. 1952 [1922]. *Ancient Judaism.* Translated by Hans H. Gerth and Don Martindale. Glencoe, IL: Free Press.

Weber, Max. 1978 [1923]. *Economy and Society.* Vol. 1. Translated by Guenther Roth and Claus Wittich. Berkeley: University of California Press.

Weil, Eric. 1975. "What Is a Breakthrough in History"? *Daedalus* 104(2): 21–36.

Woolley, C. Leonard. 1965. *The Sumerians.* Oxford: Clarendon.

Wright, Robert. 2009. *The Evolution of God.* New York: Little, Brown.

Zahavi, Amotz, and Avishag Zahavi. 1997. *The Handicap Principle: A Missing Piece of Darwin's Puzzle.* Oxford: Oxford University Press.

CHAPTER 28

....

THE EVOLUTIONARY
APPROACH TO HISTORY

Sociocultural Phylogenetics

....

MARION BLUTE AND FIONA M. JORDAN

THERE are three forms of modern Darwinian evolutionism in the social sciences and humanities: the gene-based biological, the social learning-based sociocultural, and gene–culture coevolution dealing with their interaction. This chapter focuses on the second—sociocultural evolution (for discussion on the general subject, see Cavalli-Sforza & Feldman, 1981; Boyd & Richerson, 1985; Basalla, 1988; Hull, 1988; Plotkin, 1994; Fog, 1999; Richerson & Boyd, 2005; Turner & Maryanski, 2008; Runciman, 2009; Blute, 2010; Hodgson & Knudsen, 2010; Distin, 2011; Mesoudi, 2012; Richerson & Christiansen, 2013). Some prefer to think of this process as analogous to biological evolution. Others view both biological and sociocultural evolution as tokens of the same general type (variously termed evolutionary epistemology, generalized Darwinism, universal Darwinism, selection processes, etc.). Some prefer to speak of cultural evolution, some of social evolution, and some of sociocultural evolution. The substantive focus also varies—linguistics, archeology, cultural anthropology, political science, economics, sociology, science and technology, or literary studies. Whatever such differences in terminology or substantive focus, as Donald T. Campbell (personal communication) was fond of pointing out, they have all descended from Darwinism. Such evolutionists generally agree that there are four basic kinds of evolutionary explanations for stability or change and diversity but sometimes differ in their emphasis: (1) constraints (e.g., the laws of physics and chemistry), (2) chance or "drift" (sampling error in finite populations in which random effects are propagated through time), (3) what Darwin called the "unity of types" (shared ancestry), and (4) what he called "the conditions of existence" (selection). This chapter focuses on the third, history—on the ways in which history or shared descent from common ancestors can structure diversity in social and cultural phenomena.

This chapter is outlined as follows: history, contemporary methods, language trees and networks, testing hypotheses about cultural evolution using phylogenetic comparative methods (including ancestral state, tracking history, models of transformation, correlated evolution, and patterns and processes of change), phylogenetic approaches to cultural artifacts (including material culture and folk tales), and conclusions.

History

There are two (not mutually exclusive) ways to study the effects of history on sociocultural diversity. One can study what has been called the "relics"—just as paleontologists study biological fossils, archeologists study the material remains of prehistoric human settlements and activities, and historians and other kinds of historically oriented social scientists study documents and other artifacts from the past. This approach gives direct insight into the behaviors and material culture of particular human populations at particular points in time, but the archeological and relic record is patchy and not comprehensive across time and space. The other way is to compare contemporary forms and use that information to draw historical inferences. Classically, sociology and anthropology took that approach (e.g., on kinship terminologies, see Morgan 1871), but it was recognized early on in the history of both disciplines that this approach was problematic. Their taxonomies were commonly only one layer deep based on geographic or cultural areas, and they lacked suitable methods for drawing historical inferences from present forms. The result was "developmentalism" or unilineal "evolutionism," as in the work of Herbert Spencer, for example—stage theories of historical "progress" that, as Lovejoy (1936) showed, had its roots in the pre-Darwinian medieval idea of "a great chain of being." Present forms were arranged in a sequence from simpler to more complex—for example, "savage" to "civilization" as in Morgan (1877)—and then placed on an escalator. True Darwinian evolutionary thinking is not sequential or ladder-like, whether singular or "multilineal" (Blute, 1979). In contrast to such sequences, Darwin represented his view of history by a tree (first on page 36 of his Notebook B on the transmutation of species). Darwin's "unity of types" was his historical interpretation of Linnaeus' "natural system" by which he viewed species in the same genus as literally more closely related historically than those in different genera, those in the same family as more closely related historically than those in different families, and so on through the natural taxonomic hierarchy of Linnaeus' groups within groups.

In the social sciences, cultural inheritance ranges from the most micro foundations (social learning by observation or by linguistically encoded instructions) to the most macro—for example, the anthropologists "way of life of a people." Transmission is not always accurate, and there are many modes of variation or innovation in evolution (Blute, 2015), but all are said to be "random." Random does *not* mean uncaused, necessarily unique, equiprobable, or the absence of the transmission of acquired characteristics. It means only that innovations are nonprescient, as Donald T. Campbell emphasized. There is much evidence that sociocultural innovations, like biological mutations, similarly are not statistically biased in the direction required for them to spread. In that sense, sociocultural evolution is Darwinian, not Lamarckian. In addition to transmission and variation, there is selection—that is, some variants are transmitted further, whereas others are not, and among those that are, some are transmitted at faster rates or for longer than others.

The dynamics of cultural transmission can differ from biological inheritance in particular ways, but the distinctions are not as straightforward as some commentators have claimed (Borgerhoff Mulder, Nunn, & Towner, 2006). According to some, cultural evolution–biological evolution analogies are simply useful tools with which to think (Gray, Greenhill, & Ross, 2007; Lewens, 2015; Pagel, 2017). Applying particular methodologies to particular data sets does not rely on isomorphic mapping of cultural and biological "units" such as genes or cultural traits. It relies instead on the Darwinian evolutionary criteria (variation, inheritance, differential survival, and reproduction) being justified for the particular case at hand. The relative ease by which ideas may be horizontally transmitted between individuals within a social group versus inherited vertically from parents depends on the sort of cultural feature one is modeling (e.g., grammar vs. words), as does the "borrowability" and subsequent transmission and survival of cultural and linguistic features between populations (Gray et al., 2007). In addition, a rich body of theory and modeling has emerged in recent years to describe the social learning biases that are at work to influence the rise and fall of cultural features in human populations (Boyd & Richerson, 1985; Henrich & Boyd, 1998; Richerson & Boyd, 2005). Mechanisms such as model bias (e.g., copying prestigious or successful individuals), frequency dependence (e.g., copying majority or rare behaviors), and content biases (e.g., preferences for socially relevant information in certain contexts) all constitute important forces of cultural evolution alongside drift, natural selection, and the other traditional biological "forces of evolution." These forces work primarily at the microevolutionary level on individual social learning and cultural transmission at the small scale, but they are not in themselves the generators of sociocultural variation. The innovation of cultural features is currently an undertheorized aspect of cultural evolution theory, intersecting work between anthropology and psychology (e.g., see Sperber's [1996] work on "cultural attractors"). There is little evidence that cultural evolution is Lamarckian—that we as a species are particularly successful at innovating behaviors or beliefs that are inherently "spreadable." Indeed, given the creative agency and imagination afforded by our large brains, dense social networks, and long lives, it is unclear just how much individuals add to the cultural pool on average.

Contemporary Methods

Although Darwin's tree metaphor for biological history was revolutionary, ambiguities remained for a long time. In the 1960s and 1970s, biological taxonomy was revolutionized beginning with Hennig's (1966) cladistics or phylogenetic systematics. He formulated his phylogenetic principle, making assumptions that classification should be strictly historical; that branching is bivariate; and that some changes are recent, some older, and some older still. Two groups A and B can be inferred to derive from the same unique path only if they share characters that are *not* shared with an out-group C. Hence, a phylogenetic or cladistic classification is a nested set of such *shared, derived* characters that he called "synapomorphies." In his *Science as a Process*, David Hull (1988) used a variety of historical and sociological methods to tell the story of the three schools of taxonomic thought that subsequently vied for dominance in the 1970s and 1980s and, to some extent, still do: Hennig's cladistics or phylogenetic systematics, evolutionary taxonomy, and phenetics. These can be distinguished by the groups recognized and the characters used (Ridley, 1996; see Table 28.1). Since then, many applications of various computational tree-building methods borrowed from biology have been used in the social sciences and humanities to answer basic historical questions concerning, for example, the origins and relationships among populations, languages or other sociocultural entities (including material culture), as well as the dynamics of cultural evolution.

The basic concepts of the four major classes of methods are well explained in Baum and Smith (2013) and Nunn (2011). The concepts are summarized as follows:

Distance: Distance-based methods have descended from phenetics. They calculate a measure of feature distance between all pairs of taxa (e.g., shared vocabulary). A tree is generated from these distances that is most consistent with the distance matrix. Neighbor-joining is the most common instantiation of this approach. The other methods are "character-based" and work on the "raw" data—that is, they do not calculate distances between taxa but, rather, have an underlying set of assumptions about the model of evolutionary change. They are more computationally intensive.

Parsimony: Parsimony has descended from Hennig's cladistics. It selects the tree that can account for the data with the fewest evolutionary changes. Although intuitive, parsimony does not deal efficiently with variations in the rate of evolution.

Maximum likelihood: Given explicit modeling assumptions, it searches for the tree that has the highest probability of giving rise to the observed data.

Table 28.1 Differences Among Cladistic, Evolutionary, and Phenetic Systematics

Systematic	Groups Recognized			Characters Used		
	Monophyletic	Paraphyletic	Polyphyletic	Derived	Ancestral	Analogies
Cladistic	Yes	No	No	Yes	No	No
Evolutionary	Yes	Yes	No	Yes	Yes	No
Phenetic	Yes	Yes	Yes	Yes	Yes	Yes

Bayesian methods: Given explicit prior beliefs ("subjective probabilities") as well as an explicit model and the data, it yields a range of trees in proportion to their probability.

The topic of phylogenetic inference is quite complex because not only are there four different classes of methods (Felsenstein, 2004) but also there are a number of algorithms for each and sometimes many computer programs for each algorithm. Wikipedia (2016) provides a list of more than 50 programs, and Felsenstein's (2016) website, "Phylogeny Programs," currently includes 392 programs.

To infer phylogenies from linguistic and cultural data, researchers are increasingly adopting Bayesian inference methods for three reasons. First, they build on the strengths of maximum likelihood in that they force researchers to think carefully about an explicit model of cultural change and use models that allow for sources of variation such as rate heterogeneity (Greenhill & Gray, 2009). Second, prior knowledge, such as known dates of linguistic splits, or evidential inference from archeology or human genetics may be incorporated alongside reasoned models of evolutionary change. Finally, they produce a posterior sample of phylogenetic trees that represent aspects such as branching patterns and branch lengths in proportion to their probability. This allows the researcher to incorporate uncertainty by drawing conclusions based on a range of phylogenetic hypotheses. Newcomers can be guided by the ever-increasing cultural phylogenetic literature to appropriate methods; Bayesian tree-inference software such as BEAST and RevBayes have appropriate models for nongenetic data; and good introductions to theory and methods are given in Felsenstein (2004), Lemey, Salemi, and Vandamme (2009), and Drummond and Bouckaert (2015). The remainder of this chapter provides empirical examples to give readers a sense of the kinds of possibilities that exist.

LANGUAGE TREES AND NETWORKS

Darwin used the then known Indo-European language family as an analogy to explain his biological evolutionary theory. Over generations, historical linguists have constructed approximately 200 language families in each of which the languages have descended with modification from a common ancestral language (Crowley and Bowern, 2010). The evolutionary biologist Maynard-Smith (personal communication) once expressed amazement at how this had been accomplished without the use of quantitative methods. However, in recent years, various computational tree-building methods borrowed from biology have been applied to languages to answer various kinds of questions.

For example, Gray and Jordan (2000) used parsimony methods to infer a phylogeny of 77 languages of the Austronesian family, testing a hypothesis of the sequence of population movements that spread from Taiwan all the way to eastern Polynesia. Gray, Drummond, and Greenhill (2009) improved on this with Bayesian methods and an extended vocabulary data set (Greenhill, Blust, & Gray, 2008) to show that this expansion took place in a "pulse–pause" pattern. Four major expansion pulses and two pauses took place—the pauses being before the settlement of the Philippines approximately 3,800–4,500 years BP and after the settlement of western Polynesia by 2,800 years BP.

Stimulated by a long-standing archeological debate, "the most intensively studied, yet still the most recalcitrant problem of historical linguistics" (Diamond & Bellwood, 2003, p. 601) was tackled with Bayesian methods by Gray and Atkinson (2003). They tested two theories of the origin of the Indo-European language family: the Kurgan hypothesis (from the Pontic steppes north of the Caspian Sea by semi-nomadic horsemen approximately 6,000 years ago) and the Anatolian hypothesis (from Turkey by farmers approximately 8,000–9,000 years ago). Results supported the latter date (7,899–9,500 years ago). Bouckaert et al. (2012) improved on this with a Bayesian phylogeographic inference framework developed to study viral outbreaks using improved data that also supported the Anatolian origin. However, Chang, Cathcart, Hall, and Garrett (2015) employed the same model and data as those used by Bouckaert et al. but incorporated ancestry constraints from ancient and medieval languages. Their results inferred an older age for the root of the tree, supporting the steppe hypothesis. Recent genetic work suggests both steppe and Anatolian origins can be integrated in an emerging multiphase Indo-European story (Haak et al., 2015).

Large language families associated with Neolithic or agricultural dispersals of speakers have been a popular object of enquiry for phylolinguistic analysis. In addition to Austronesian and Indo-European, the family relationships of the Bantu languages of sub-Saharan Africa (Holden, 2002; Grollemund et al., 2015) and the Uto-Aztecan languages of Mesoamerica (Dunn, Greenhill, Levinson, & Gray, 2011) have been inferred, offering opportunities to test hypotheses about homelands, migration routes, timing and dating of roots and splits, and the social and ecological triggers for population movements. For example, Grollemund et al. used a time-calibrated tree of approximately 400 Bantu languages and mapped onto it the probable geographical location of each of the internal nodes of the tree. They showed that the Bantu expansion (beginning approximately 5,000 years ago) spread preferentially along emerging savannah corridors, avoiding rainforest habitats. When the latter did take place, expansion was slowed by an average of 300 years relative to the former. The list of language families to which computational phylogenetic methods have been applied has expanded greatly in the past decade and includes Aslian (Dunn, Kruspe, & Burenhult, 2013), Alor-Pantar (Robinson & Holton, 2012), Arawak (Walker & Ribero, 2011), Chapacuran (Birchall, Dunn, & Greenhill, 2016), Japonic (Lee & Hasegawa, 2011), Pama-Nyungan (Bowern & Atkinson, 2012), Semitic (Kitchen, Ehret, Assefa, & Mulligan, 2009), Tupi-Guarani (Michael et al., 2015), and Uralic (Honkola et al., 2013). Many of these studies have used cognate-coded basic vocabulary as their data. Two notable exceptions are studies on Dene-Yenesian (Sicoli & Holton, 2014) and Papuan languages (Dunn, Terrill, Reesink, Foley, & Levinson, 2005), both of which use typological features as their data, incorporating structural aspects of language such as word order and the presence of tense marking.

Finally on phylolinguistics, although many scholars are skeptical of the ability of both traditional and computational methods to infer deeper phylogenies (Campbell & Poser, 2008), some recent works have attempted to infer larger scale trees of human languages. From a database of reconstructed vocabulary, Pagel, Atkinson, Calude, and Meade (2013) inferred a "superfamily" that linked seven families across the Eurasian continent to a root of approximately 14,400 years ago. Their results suggested "ultraconserved" word meanings. At the global scale, Jaeger and Wichmann (2016) applied weighted sequence alignment and distance-based phylogenetic methods to word lists in phonetic transcription from more than 6,000 languages and dialects to infer a global tree of languages. The results not only recaptured established language families and their subgroupings but also revealed large-scale patterns that they interpreted as a statistical signal from deep time.

One common critique of phylolinguistics is the observation that aspects of language are not tree-like—that is, words, sounds, morphosyntax, and even grammatical structures can be transmitted horizontally between languages by borrowing and contact, thus adding conflicting signals to phylogenetic inference (Moore, 1994). This point is an empirical one at bottom, and the extent and likelihood of borrowing can differ for kinds of vocabulary; as a trivial example, compare pronouns versus words that name trade items (Gray et al., 2007; Gray, Bryant, & Greenhill, 2010). Simulations of feature borrowing have shown that phylogenetic inference can perform well under conditions of moderate realistic borrowing—that is, between sister populations (Greenhill, Currie, & Gray, 2009). Operationally, biologists deal with horizontal or lateral gene transfer in microbial populations as a matter of course, and measures such as the delta score (Holland, Huber, Dress, & Moulton, 2002) can give comparable measures of how reticulate or tree-like a data set is (for examples, see Gray et al., 2010; Wichmann, Walker, Rama, & Holman, 2011). Phylogenetic networks (Huson & Bryant, 2006) can be inferred in programs such as NeighbourNet and Network and allow for graphical representation of the conflicting or reticulate signal in a data set. Walker and Ribiero (2011) use NeighbourNet to show that Arawak languages have both well-formed subgroupings and evidence of reticulation among early splitting lineages.

LANGUAGE TREES AS POPULATION HISTORIES: TESTING HYPOTHESES ABOUT CULTURAL EVOLUTION USING PHYLOGENETIC COMPARATIVE METHODS

As discussed previously, inferring a phylogeny from language data affords investigators ways to answer questions such as the following: What are the relationships among languages? When and where did they originate? What is the rate of language change? and how reticulate or tree-like is linguistic evolution? The answers to a host of other questions are made possible by using language phylogenies as a scaffold for the history of speaker populations. Mapping social, cultural, political, and economic organization or other geographic, ethnographic, or biocultural data onto the tips of a (usually) language tree allows investigators to use phylogenetic comparative methods (PCMs) to examine the dynamics of cultural change. PCMs all employ a phylogeny, a set of "tip data," and a model of change for the feature under study, and they were developed in evolutionary biology to avert the problem of statistical non-independence between species (Felsenstein, 1985). Mace and Pagel (1994) then introduced them to anthropologists and linguists as a formal answer to Galton's Problem—the similar objection for comparative cross-cultural analyses that societies may share traits not due to any functional correspondences or universality of human cognition but, rather, simply due to inheritance from a common parental population.

Beyond rectifying statistical properties, PCMs allow new kinds of questions to be asked about cultural and linguistic evolution because the diachronic (timed) nature of a phylogeny gives insight into process as well as pattern. Answers to questions such as the following are possible (combined, modified, and added to from Currie [2013] and Jordan [2013]). What was the ancestral state of a feature? Does a trait track historical ancestor–descendant relationships or some other process such as cultural contact? If two traits change together, does one follow the other? Have trait changes followed a particular order? Is there an overall trend in the direction in which traits change? Are patterns of change gradual or punctuational and do rates of change differ? Next, we describe some empirical examples from this growing body of literature.

Ancestral State

Many features of human social and cultural life leave no material trace. Archeologists may sometimes infer social norms and behaviors from remains, but PCMs provide another window into the past. Jordan, Gray, Greenhill, and Mace (2009) mapped postmarital residence norms of 135 Austronesian-speaking populations onto the language phylogeny and inferred that matrilocal residence in which the husband moves to live with the wife's kin was likely the ancestral state approximately 5,000 years ago. The inferred model of cultural change showed that marriage systems had unequal likelihoods of change such that shifts to patrilocality became more common over time. This work was extended to other language families (Fortunato & Jordan, 2010; Fortunato, 2011a) showing similarities in the models of change but differences in the ancestral states. Fortunato (2011b) inferred ancestral marriage payment strategies in Indo-European populations, and Jordan (2013) inferred ancestral sibling term systems in Bantu and Austronesian languages. Linguists have also used PCMs to infer ancestral states of typological features. Calude and Verkerk (2016) investigated the ways in which Indo-European languages combine base numerals to form higher numeral terms. For example, English *eighty-nine* is $(8 \times 10 + 9)$, whereas French *quatre-vingt neuf* is $(4 \times 20 + $

9). Across a range of numeral features, they inferred all ancestral nodes including Proto-Indo-European, demonstrating, for instance, that "teen" numerals were formed as atom + 10 like English *eighteen*, with subsequent changes in different subgroups. Finally, other studies have used ancestral state inference beyond the time depth of a single language family. Using a global "supertree" derived from a combination of genetic and linguistic data from 133 published studies, Peoples, Duda, and Marlowe (2016) mapped seven different religious traits of 33 worldwide hunter–gather societies and inferred that one trait, animism, was ancestral in the most recent common ancestor.

Track History

PCMs allow investigators to measure phylogenetic signals—that is, the extent to which variation in a cultural trait is predicted by the phylogeny. These measures are a good indication of the importance of shared ancestry in structuring cultural diversity. Kushnick, Gray, and Jordan (2014) mapped land tenure (resource ownership) norms from 97 Austronesian societies onto language phylogenies to infer ancestral states and test sequential models from behavioral ecology about resource and risk management. The historical signals in four different kinds of tenure norms (none, versus ownership by village, kin-group, or individuals) were tracked for their degree of "clumping" through shared ancestry, on the one hand, and random distribution on the phylogeny, on the other hand. Norms of no tenure and kin-group ownership displayed moderate and strong signals. This study also tested phylogenetic versus geographical/spatial clustering and found that for all four norms, history was more important in structuring diversity. Bentz, Verkerk, Kiela, Hill, and Buttery (2015) used measures of phylogenetic signal in their study relating lexical diversity (the number of word forms in a language that convey the same information) to the proportion of non-native speakers in a language. Lexical diversity showed a "deep" phylogenetic signal across three large language families and multiple measures, indicating this property of lexicons to be strongly subject to inheritance.

Models of Transformation

Embedded in the statistical machinery of PCMs for inferring ancestral states is a flexible method for simultaneously estimating the model of change between traits, and this property can be used to both infer and test particular models for their fit. Currie, Greenhill, Gray, Hasegawa, and Mace (2010) examined how norms of Austronesian political complexity (acephalous societies, simple chiefdom, complex chiefdom, and state) evolved on language phylogenies, testing long-standing assertions in archeology and anthropology about "unilinear" cultural evolution in this trait. They showed that the model of political complexity that best fit Austronesian societies arises in a sequence of small steps but can fall by larger jumps. Kushnick et al. (2014) showed similarly that a sequential model of land-tenure norms applied to Austronesian societies but that the best supported model was one in which group and kin-group ownership evolved from individual tenure rather than individual ownership being the "endpoint." Peoples et al. (2016), in the study cited previously, modeled the ways in which hunter–gatherer religious beliefs changed on the phylogeny. From an animistic state, belief in an afterlife, then shamanism, and then ancestor worship emerged subsequently, whereas a belief in high gods stood apart and could emerge regardless of other properties. Returning to typological studies of language, Zhou and Bowern (2015) used Bayesian methods to investigate number terms in the Pama-Nyungan family (containing approximately 70% of Australian languages). They found that upper limits on number extent commonly vary between three and five, and beyond these as lower limits, languages can lose as well as gain numerals. Above the limits, Pama-Nyungan languages tend to add numerals by combining (e.g., 4 is 2 + 2) rather than inventing new words. A similar approach was taken by Haynie and Bowern (2016) to model the evolution of color term systems in Pama-Nyungan languages. Some languages have minimal basic colors as low as 3 terms (e.g., dark–light–red), whereas others have up to 12, and influential models of sequential development have been long established. Here, the authors tested the sequential model, showing both support for and departures from (i.e., that languages could lose terms) in these Australian languages.

Correlated Evolution

The "original" reason for introducing phylogenetic comparative methods to anthropology was the robust testing of functional relationships (adaptation and/or correlated evolution) while controlling for autocorrelation due to shared descent (Mace & Pagel, 1994). Pagel's (1994) "discrete" method is widely used in cultural phylogenetics because it not only allows the testing of correlations between categorical features (a "dependent" model) but also outputs the rates of trait changes, enabling directional models to be specified. Holden and Mace (2003, 2005) mapped mode of subsistence and descent system onto the language tree of Bantu societies to test the hypothesis that matrilineal descent did not persist when societies acquired cattle, because men acquired defensible resources that could be passed on to sons and thus increase reproductive success. In Bantu societies, the acquisition of pastoralism across the tree was associated with and led to patriliny, supporting the idea that "the cow is the enemy of matriliny." Again in Bantu societies, Opie, Shultz, Atkinson, Currie, and Mace (2014) used PCMs to test for correlated evolution between modes of post-marital residence and descent, challenging a broadly held notion that residence changes act as a precursor to changes in descent and other forms of kinship social organization. Their results supported correlated evolution throughout the course of the Bantu expansion, but in opposite trajectories to those proposed by Murdock (1969) and described by Jordan and Mace (2007) for Austronesian societies.

Linguists have used phylogenetic correlations across multiple language families to test for putative universal dependencies in typological features. Dunn et al. (2011)

examined the functional links between a suite of different features of word order (e.g., the positions of subjects, verbs, and adpositions) to explore the extent to which dependencies could be explained by either cognitive constraints (universals) or shared historical paths. Across four large language families (Austronesian, Bantu, Uto-Aztec, and Indo-European), they found lineage-specific correlations, and when correlations were shared, the directionality differed between families. Finally, driving factors in the evolution of religious beliefs and behaviors (Watts et al., 2015; Peoples et al., 2016; Watts, Sheehan, Atkinson, Bulbulia, & Gray, 2016) have been investigated with these methods. Watts et al. (2015) examined how moralizing high gods and broad threats of supernatural punishment interacted in the evolution of political complexity in Austronesian societies. Counter to influential theories positing that moralizing high gods drove societies toward political complexity (e.g., Norenzayan, 2013), Watts and colleagues showed that high gods followed complex societies, whereas supernatural punishment norms appeared to be the preceding factor.

Patterns and Processes of Change

Mace and Jordan (2011) measured how well the phylogenetic versus geographic nearest neighbors of Austronesian societies predicted what cultural features they shared. Although both historical and spatial associations were important in structuring diversity, phylogenetic nearest neighbors better predicted traits associated with kinship and heritable social and material resources, such as slavery or domesticated animals. Walker, Wichmann, Mailund, and Atkisson (2012) created a distance-based phylogeny of the Tupi language family of lowland South America that supported a homeland in west central Brazil. Onto this, they mapped 11 locally varying cultural features, such as shamanism, residence patterns, and paternity beliefs. By estimating the gains and losses of these features across the language family and the transition rates per 10,000 years, they showed that variety has decreased with time, associated not only with European contact but also with the independent emergence of nomadic hunter–gatherer societies.

Currie and Mace (2014), using the same set of traits as used by Mace and Jordan (2011), compared cultural trait evolution in (a) island Southeast Asian and the Pacific and (b) sub-Saharan Africa. They found similar rates of evolution across both regions and also found that features of social organization such as kinship evolved more rapidly than ecological features such as the mode of subsistence.

Atkinson, Meade, Venditti, Greenhill, and Pagel (2008) found that across three major language families (Bantu, Indo-European, and Austronesian), languages tend to evolve in punctuational bursts—that is, word replacement rates increase just after splits rather than along branches. Similar "burst" dynamics were found by Valverde and Solé (2015) in their study of programming language diversification, and Bromham, Hua, Fitzpatrick, and Greenhill (2015) demonstrated that in Polynesian languages, those with small populations lose words faster, whereas larger populations gain new words at higher rates.

PHYLOGENETIC APPROACHES
TO CULTURAL ARTIFACTS

A third category of cultural phylogenetic studies draws on both tree-building and PCM techniques and applies to these aspects of material culture and cultural artifacts. Archeologists in particular were quick to recognize the possibilities of these methods. Buchanan and Collard (2007) provide a recent example of phylogenetic analyses of Paleo-Indian projectile tools that provide insights into the peopling of North America. They used landmark measurements of projectile points across the continent as data in cladistic analyses and tested their trees against expectations from models of population migrations. Schillinger, Mesoudi, and Lycett (2016) used a novel approach to draw on data produced in cultural transmission studies in which participants were instructed to replicate a form model of a stone tool, an Acheulean hand-axe, down a transmission chain. They showed experimentally that phylogenetic reconstruction is more accurate in artifactual lineages in which copying error is lower. For further work on archeological artifacts, readers are directed to the collected papers in Lipo, O'Brien, Collard, and Shennan (2006).

Material Culture Craft and Design

Tehrani and Collard (2002) studied the characteristics of preparation and fabrication (flat-weave designs and pile-weave designs) of Turkmen tribal textiles from Iran. Permutation tests for phylogenetic signal and parsimony methods for inferring the best tree from these data were used to conclude that branching processes played a significant role over blending in the five populations under study. Matthews, Tehrani, Jordan, Collard, and Nunn (2011) extended this work using Bayesian tree-inference methods to show that pile-weave designs have a different phylogenetic history compared to other textile characteristics. These different histories could be reconciled with ethnographic information on the socioeconomic histories of the groups. Rogers, Feldman, and Ehrlich (2009) applied distance-based methods to a data set of traditional Polynesian canoes that similarly represented both design motifs and construction techniques. In their study, they inferred a Fijian ancestry for canoe forms and a sequence of cultural origins throughout Polynesia. They observed a serial founder effect and indicated that population history was more strongly reflected by functional than by stylistic traits. Subsequent analyses of the Polynesian canoe data set show that more accurate inferences about population history overall can be made by using PCMs and language trees as a scaffold for the canoe traits. Both functional and design traits display limited phylogenetic signal, with stylistic design features tracking history marginally more closely (Gray et al., 2010), perhaps as a symbol of cultural group identity.

Buckley (2012) used Bayesian and neighbor net techniques to study 36 characteristics of Southeast Asian Warp Ikat weaving. He showed that they have a common ancestry and one much older than had been thought—associated with Neolithic pottery motifs from the Asian mainland rather than with Bronze Age drums of the Dong-Son culture in coastal Vietnam between 500 BC and 100 AC.

Narrative Artifacts and Folk Tales

Tehrani (2013) drew on data from comparative folklore to study global variants of the stories "Little Red Riding Hood" and "The Wolf and the Kids" in an attempt to discover if they were different lineages of the same story or independent narratives. With a range of phylogenetic inference methods, Tehrani used the plot variations and tale motifs in 58 variants of the tales across 33 global populations. Results showed that although related, the two stories could be distinguished as distinct international tale types but that the East Asian "tiger grandmother' variant was a probable hybrid of the two. Da Silva and Tehrani (2016) extended this approach to uncover the ancient roots of the Indo-European folktale "Tales of Magic" and used ancestral state inference methods that plotted different tale types on the Indo-European language phylogeny. They found evidence that these oral traditions antedate written records and that over 75% showed a phylogenetic signal correlated with the language tree. Four tales were likely present in Proto-Indo-European, and one tale—"The Smith and the Devil"—likely dates back to the early Bronze Age. Similar phylogenetic approaches to folk tales have been taken by Ross, Greenhill, and Atkinson (2013), who used a phylogenetic control to characterize the strong geographic structuring of a set of variants of one folk tale throughout Europe, and by Ross and Atkinson (2016), who found that both spatial distance and historical shared ancestry structure the diversity of folk tales in 18 Arctic hunter–gatherer populations.

CONCLUSION

Do not only living things but also culture and social organization "descend with modification"? The examples described previously from the burgeoning field of cultural phylogenetics suggest a resounding "yes." The Darwinian principles of descent, innovation, and differential survival and transmission are present in the business of science as well. Yong (2013) published a "family tree" of more than 300 of the student descendants (i.e., students, grand students, and great-grand students) of the ecologist R. T. Paine. Paine invented the concept of a "keystone species," one whose removal yields drastic change in ecosystems. The 300 individuals on that tree did not include the peers he influenced horizontally and the students of peers he influenced obliquely. Although influenced by him in "attitudes, philosophies, and technical skills," he encouraged freedom and individuality in his students, so not surprisingly, this example of cultural descent included innovations. Some cultural descendants moved on from small-scale field experiments to large multilab collaborations studying hundreds of miles of coastline, for example. Of course, some students gave rise to many more grand and great-grand students compared to others.

Cultural or sociocultural evolutionary theory can reconcile many of the dilemmas in cultural and social theory—the relationships between history and science, conflict and cooperation, the ideal and the material, and also the problems of agency, subjectivity, and the nature of social structure (Blute, 2010). This is a young field, however, and much remains to be done. It is well known that Darwin did not solve the problem of the *origin* of species. Nor does sociocultural evolutionary theory obviously solve the problem of the origin of sociocultural entities. Although many definitions of species have been proposed, the most widely accepted remains that of Ernst Mayr that members of a species are actual or potential interbreeders—that is, recombination among members is possible. Setting aside the issue of defining cultural populations, it is true that in the sociocultural as in the biological realm, new variants commonly arise by recombination—as has been shown for technology by Arthur (2009). It is commonly thought that recombination is more promiscuous and multiple cultural parents are more common socioculturally than they are biologically, but this is an empirical issue of scale and boundaries. Blute (1979, p. 55) stated that "one may get an idea for a handle shape for a pot from a basket, but when was the last time characteristics among tables and curtains or staplers and rugs, say, were recombined." Although it now seems likely that barriers to recombination can originate by any geographical, ecological, or social means, what is most common remains unclear. For example, see Shennan, Crema, and Kerig (2015) on the archeological "population structure" of pottery and personal ornaments from Neolithic central Europe.

On the scientific selectionist "with modification" side of Darwin's theory, it seems likely that some general principles similar to the biological apply socioculturally—principles pertaining to density, scale, patchiness, uncertainty (with or without reliable cues), and so on. However, many problems here, too, remain unresolved. What exactly is the relationship between somatic and reproductive functions (in the social sciences, between individual and social learning)? How do new levels of selection arise? Biologically, how does evolution go from prokaryotic to eukaryotic cells, from the single-celled to the multi-celled, and from the multi-celled to eusocial colonies? Similarly, socioculturally, how does evolution go from individual norms and values to aggregates of these in social roles or statuses and then to aggregates of those in turn in organizations and institutions?

Returning to the historical "descent" side of Darwin's theory of "descent with modification," one aspect about sociocultural evolution is clear: As the examples summarized in this chapter (and others that could have been) illustrate, many of the computational tree-building methods developed in systematic biology can be utilized in the social sciences to answer a host of the kinds of questions about history that we could not answer in any other way. Many of these methods can also be used to examine other cultural phenomena in the future. For example, What about variants of Abrahamic religions, financial occupations, or rap music? We are limited only by our imaginations and sources of data.

NOTE

The authors contributed equally to this paper.

REFERENCES

Arthur, W. B. (2009). *The evolution of technology: What it is and how it evolves*. New York, NY: Free Press.

Atkinson, Q. D., Meade, A., Venditti, C., Greenhill, S. J., & Pagel, M. (2008). Languages evolve in punctuational bursts. *Science, 319*, 588.

Basalla, G. (1988). *The evolution of technology*. Cambridge, UK: Cambridge University Press.

Baum, D. A., & Smith, S. D. (2013). *Tree thinking: An introduction to phylogenetic biology*. Greenwood Village, CO: Roberts.

Bentz, C., Verkerk, A., Kiela, D., Hill, F., & Buttery, P. (2015). Adaptive communication: Languages with more non-native speakers tend to have fewer word forms. *PLoS One, 10*(6), e0128254.

Birchall, J., Dunn, M., & Greenhill, S. (2016). A combined comparative and phylogenetic analysis of the Chapacuran language family. *International Journal of American Linguistics, 82*, 255–284.

Blute, M. (1979). Sociocultural evolutionism: An untried theory. *Behavioral Science, 16*, 46–59.

Blute, M. (2010). *Darwinian sociocultural evolution: Solutions to dilemmas in cultural and social theory*. Cambridge, UK: Cambridge University Press.

Blute, M. (2015). Modes of variation and their implications for an extended evolutionary synthesis. In J. H. Turner, R. Machalek, & A. Maryanski (Eds.), *Handbook on evolution and society: Toward an evolutionary social science* (pp. 59–75). Boulder, CO: Paradigm.

Borgerhoff Mulder, M., Nunn, C. L., & Towner, M. C. (2006). Cultural macroevolution and the transmission of traits. *Evolutionary Anthropology: Issues, News, and Reviews, 5*(2), 52–64.

Bouckaert, R., Lemey, P., Dunn, M., Greenhill, S. J., Alekseyenko, A. V., Drummond, A. J., . . . Atkinson, Q. D. (2012). Mapping the origins and expansion of the Indo-European language family. *Science, 337*, 957–960.

Bowern, C., & Atkinson, Q. (2012). Computational phylogenetics and the internal structure of Pama-Nyungan. *Language, 88*(4), 817–845.

Boyd, R., & Richerson, P. J. (1985). *Culture and the evolutionary process*. Chicago, Chicago, IL: University of Chicago Press.

Bromham, L., Hua, X., Fitzpatrick, T. G., & Greenhill, S. J. (2015). Rate of language evolution is affected by population size. *Proceedings of the National Academy of Sciences of the USA, 112*(7), 2097–2102.

Buchanan, B., & Collard, M. (2007). Investigating the peopling of North America through cladistic analyses of Early Paleoindian projectile points. *Journal of Anthropological Archaeology, 26*(3), 366–393.

Buckley, C. D. (2012). Investigating cultural evolution using phylogenetic analysis: The origins and descent of the Southeast Asian tradition of Warp Ikat weaving. *PLoS One, 7*, 1–20.

Calude, A. S., & Verkerk, A. (2016). The typology and diachrony of higher numerals in Indo-European: A phylogenetic comparative study. *Journal of Language Evolution, 1*(2), 91–108.

Campbell, L., & Poser, W. J. (2008). *Language classification: History and method.* Cambridge, UK: Cambridge University Press.

Cavalli-Sforza, L. L., & Feldman, M. W. (1981). *Cultural transmission and evolution: A quantitative approach.* Princeton, NJ: Princeton University Press.

Chang, W., Cathcart, C., Hall, D., & Garrett, A. (2015). Ancestry-constrained phylogenetic analysis supports the Indo-European steppe hypothesis. *Language, 91,* 194–244.

Crowley, T., & Bowern, C. (2010). *An introduction to historical linguistics.* Oxford, UK: Oxford University Press.

Currie, T. E. (2013). Cultural evolution branches out: The phylogenetic approach in cross-cultural research. *Cross-Cultural Research, 47,* 102–130.

Currie, T. E., Greenhill, S. J., Gray, R. D., Hasegawa, T., & Mace, R. (2010). Rise and fall of political complexity in island South-East Asia and the Pacific. *Nature, 467,* 801–804.

Currie, T. E., & Mace, R. (2014). Evolution of cultural traits occurs at similar relative rates in different world regions. *Proceedings of the Royal Society B: Biological Sciences, 281,* 1622–1629.

da Silva, S. G., & Tehrani, J. J. (2016). Comparative phylogenetic analyses uncover the ancient roots of Indo-European folktales. *Royal Society Open Science.* doi:10.1098/sos.150645

Diamond, J., & Bellwood, P. (2003). Farmers and their languages: The first expansions. *Science, 300*(5619), 597–603.

Distin, K. (2011). *Cultural evolution.* Cambridge, UK: Cambridge University Press.

Drummond, A. J., & Bouckaert, R. R. (2015). *Bayesian evolutionary analysis with BEAST.* Cambridge, UK: Cambridge University Press.

Dunn, M., Greenhill, S. J., Levinson, S. C., & Gray, R. D. (2011). Evolved structure of language shows lineage-specific trends in word-order universals. *Nature, 473*(7345), 79–82.

Dunn, M., Kruspe, N., & Burenhult, N. (2013). Time and place in the prehistory of the Aslian languages. *Human Biology, 85*(3), 383–400.

Dunn, M., Terrill, A., Reesink, G., Foley, R. A., & Levinson, S. C. (2005). Structural phylogenetics and the reconstruction of ancient language history. *Science, 309*(5743), 2072–2075.

Felsenstein, J. (1985). Phylogenies and the comparative method. *American Naturalist, 125,* 1–15.

Felsenstein, J. (2004). *Inferring phylogenies.* Sunderland, MA: Sinauer.

Felsenstein, J. (2016). *Phylogeny programs.* Retrieved from http://evolution.genetics.washington.edu/phylip/software.html

Fog, A. (1999). *Cultural selection.* Dordrecht, the Netherlands: Kluwer.

Fortunato, L. (2011a). Reconstructing the history of residence strategies in Indo-European-speaking societies: Neo-, uxori-, and virilocalitry. *Human Biology, 83,* 107–128.

Fortunato, L. (2011b). Reconstructing the history of marriage strategies in Indo-European-speaking societies: Monogamy and polygamy. *Human Biology, 83,* 87–105.

Fortunato, L., & Jordan, F. (2010). Your place or mine? A phylogenetic comparative analysis of marital residence in Indo-European and Austronesian societies. *Philosophical Transactions of the Royal Society B, 365,* 3913–3922.

Gray, R. D., & Atkinson, Q. D. (2003). Language-tree divergence times support the Anatolian theory of Indo-European origin. *Nature, 426,* 435–439.

Gray, R. D., Bryant, D., & Greenhill, S. J. (2010). On the shape and fabric of human history. *Philosophical Transactions of the Royal Society B: Biological Sciences, 365*(1559), 3923–3933.

Gray, R. D., Drummond, A. J., & Greenhill, S. J. (2009). Language phylogenies reveal expansion pulses and pauses in Pacific settlement. *Science, 323,* 479–483.

Gray, R. D., Greenhill, S. J., & Ross, R. M. (2007). The pleasures and perils of Darwinizing culture (with phylogenies). *Biological Theory, 2*(4), 360–375.

Gray, R. D., & Jordan, F. M. (2000). Language trees support the express-train sequence of Austronesian expansion. *Nature, 405,* 1052–1055.

Greenhill, S. J., Blust, R., & Gray, R. D. (2008). The Austronesian basic vocabulary database: From bioinformatics to lexomics. *Evolutionary Bioinformatics, 4,* 271–283.

Greenhill, S. J., Currie, T. E., & Gray, R. D. (2009). Does horizontal transmission invalidate cultural phylogenies? *Proceedings of the Royal Society B: Biological Sciences, 276*(1665), 2299–2306.

Greenhill, S. J., & Gray, R. D. (2009). Austronesian language phylogenies: Myths and misconceptions about Bayesian computational methods. In A. Adelaar & A. Pawley (Eds.), *Austronesian Historical Linguistics and culture history: a festschrift for Robert Blust* (pp. 375–397). Canberra, Australia: Pacific Linguistics.

Grollemund, R., Branford, S., Bostoen, K., Meade, A., Venditti, C. & Pagel, M. (2015). Bantu expansion shows that habitat alters the route and pace of human dispersals. *Proceedings of the National Academy of Sciences of the USA, 112,* 13296–13301.

Haak, W., Lazaridis, I., Patterson, N., Rohland, N., Mallick, S., Llamas, B., & Fu, Q. (2015). Massive migration from the steppe was a source for Indo-European languages in Europe. *Nature, 522*(7555), 207–211.

Haynie, H. J., & Bowern, C. (2016). Phylogenetic approach to the evolution of color term systems. *Proceedings of the National Academy of Sciences of the USA, 113*(48), 13666–13671.

Hennig, W. (1966). *Phylogenetic systematics.* Urbana, IL: University of Illinois Press.

Henrich, J., & Boyd, R. (1998). The evolution of conformist transmission and the emergence of between-group differences. *Evolution and Human Behavior, 19*(4), 215–241.

Hodgson, G. M., & Knudsen, T. (2010). *Darwin's conjecture: The search for general principles of social and economic evolution.* Chicago, IL: University of Chicago Press.

Holden, C. J. (2002). Bantu language trees reflect the spread of farming across sub-Saharan Africa: A maximum-parsimony analysis. *Proceedings of the Royal Society B: Biological Sciences, 269*(1493), 793–799.

Holden, C. J., & Mace, R. (2003). Spread of cattle led to the loss of matrilineal descent in Africa: A coevolutionary hypothesis. *Proceedings of the Royal Society of London B: Biological Sciences, 270,* 2425–2433.

Holden, C. J., & Mace, R. (2005). The cow is the enemy of matriliny: Using phylogenetic methods to investigate cultural evolution in Africa. In R. Mace, C. J. Holden & S. Shennan (Eds.), *The evolution of cultural diversity: A phylogenetic approach* (pp. 217–234). London, UK: UCL Press.

Holland, B. R., Huber, K. T., Dress, A., & Moulton, V. (2002). δ plots: A tool for analyzing phylogenetic distance data. *Molecular Biology and Evolution, 19*(12), 2051–2059.

Honkola, T., Vesakoski, O., Korhonen, K., Lehtinen, J., Syrjänen, K., & Wahlberg, N. (2013). Cultural and climatic changes shape the evolutionary history of the Uralic languages. *Journal of Evolutionary Biology, 26*(6), 1244–1253.

Hull, D. L. (1988). *Science as a process: An evolutionary account of the social and conceptual development of science.* Chicago, IL: University of Chicago Press.

Huson, D. H., & Bryant, D. (2006). Application of phylogenetic networks in evolutionary studies. *Molecular Biology & Evolution, 23*(2), 254–267.

Jaeger, G., & Wichmann, S. (2016). Inferring the world tree of languages from word lists. In S. G. Roberts, C. Cuskley, L. McCrohon, L. Barceló-Coblijn, O. Feher, & T. Verhoef (Eds.),

The evolution of language: Proceedings of the 11th international conference (EVOLANG11). Retrieved from http://evolang.org/neworleans/papers/147.html

Jordan, F. M. (2013). Comparative phylogenetic methods and the study of pattern and process in kinship. In P. McConvell, I. Keen, & R. Hendery (Eds.), *Kinship systems: Change and reconstruction* (pp. 43–58). Salt Lake City, UT: University of Utah Press.

Jordan, F. M., Gray, R. D., Greenhill, S. J., & Mace, R. (2009). Matrilocal residence is ancestral in Austronesian societies. *Proceedings of the Royal Society B: Biological Sciences, 276,* 1957–1964.

Jordan, F. M., & Mace, R. (2007). *Changes in post-marital residence precede changes in descent systems in Austronesian societies.* Paper presented at the European Human Behaviour and Evolution Conference (EHBE 2007), London School of Economics, London, UK.

Kitchen, A., Ehret, C., Assefa, S., & Mulligan, C. J. (2009). Bayesian phylogenetic analysis of Semitic languages identifies an Early Bronze Age origin of Semitic in the Near East. *Proceedings of the Royal Society B: Biological Sciences, 276*(1668), 2703–2710.

Kushnick, G., Gray, R. D., & Jordan, F. M. (2014). The sequential evolution of land tenure norms. *Evolution & Human Behavior, 35,* 309–318.

Lee, S., & Hasegawa, T. (2011). Bayesian phylogenetic analysis supports an agricultural origin of Japonic languages. *Proceedings of the Royal Society B: Biological Sciences, 278,* 3662–3669.

Lemey, P., Salemi, M., & Vandamme, A. M. (2009). *The phylogenetic handbook: A practical approach to phylogenetic analysis and hypothesis testing.* Cambridge, UK: Cambridge University Press.

Lewens, T. (2015). *Cultural evolution: Conceptual challenges.* Oxford, UK: Oxford University Press.

Lipo, C. P., O'Brien, M. J., Collard, M., & Shennan, S. J. (2006). *Mapping our ancestors.* New Brunswick, NJ: Aldine Transactions.

Lovejoy, A. O. (1936). *The great chain of being: A study of the history of an idea.* Boston, MA: Harvard University Press.

Mace, R., & Jordan, F. M. (2011). Macro-evolutionary studies of cultural diversity: A review of empirical studies of cultural transmission and cultural adaptation. *Philosophical Transactions of the Royal Society of London B: Biological Sciences, 366*(1563), 402–411.

Mace, R., & Pagel, M. (1994). The comparative method in anthropology. *Current Anthropology, 35*(5), 549–564.

Matthews, L. J., Tahran, J. J., Jordan, F. M., Collard, M., & Nunn, C. L. (2011). Testing for divergent transmission histories among cultural characters: A study using Bayesian phylogenetic methods and Iranian tribal textile data. *PLoS One, 6*(4), e14810.

Mesoudi, A. (2012). *Cultural evolution: How Darwinian theory can explain human culture and synthesize the social sciences.* Chicago, IL: University of Chicago Press.

Michael, L., Chousou-Polydouri, N., Keith, B., Donnelly, E., Meira, S., Wauters, V., & O'Hagan, Z. (2015). A Bayesian phylogenetic classification of Tupí-Guaraní. *LIAMES—Línguas Indígenas Americanas, 15*(2), 193–221.

Moore, J. H. (1994). Putting anthropology back together again: The ethnogenetic critique of cladistic theory. *American Anthropologist, 96,* 925–948.

Morgan, L. H. (1871). *Systems of consanguinity and affinity of the human family* (Vol. 218). Washington, DC: Smithsonian Institution.

Morgan, L. H. (1877). *Ancient society; Or, researches in the lines of human progress from savagery, through barbarism to civilization.* New York, NY: Holt.

Murdock, G. P. (1969). *Outline of world cultures.* New Haven, CT: HRAF Press.

Norenzayan, A. (2013). *Big gods: How religion transformed cooperation and conflict.* Princeton, NJ: Princeton University Press.

Nunn, C. L. (2011). *The comparative approach in evolutionary anthropology and biology.* Chicago, IL: University of Chicago Press.

Opie, C., Shultz, S., Atkinson, Q. D., Currie, T., & Mace, R. (2014). Phylogenetic reconstruction of Bantu kinship challenges main sequence theory of human social evolution. *Proceedings of the National Academy of Sciences of the USA, 111*(49), 17414–17419.

Pagel, M. (1994). Detecting correlated evolution on phylogenies: A general method for the comparative analysis of discrete characters. *Proceedings of the Royal Society B: Biological Sciences, 255*(1342), 37–45.

Pagel, M. (2017). Darwinian perspectives on the evolution of human languages. *Psychonomic Bulletin & Review, 24,* 151–157.

Pagel, M., Atkinson, Q., Calude, A., & Meade, A. (2013). Ultra-conserved words point to deep language relationships across Eurasia. *Proceedings of the National Academy of Sciences of the USA, 110*(21), 8471–8476.

Peoples, H. C., Duda, P., & Marlowe, F. W. (2016). Hunter–gatherers and the origins of religion. *Human Nature, 27,* 261–282.

Plotkin, H. (1994). *Darwin machines and the nature of knowledge.* Cambridge, MA: Harvard University Press.

Richerson, P. J., & Boyd, R. (2005). *Not by genes alone: How culture transformed human evolution.* Chicago, IL: University of Chicago Press.

Richerson, P. J., & Christiansen, M. (2013). *Cultural evolution: Society, technology, language and religion.* Cambridge, MA: MIT Press.

Ridley, M. (1996). *Evolution* (2nd ed.). Hoboken, NJ: Blackwell.

Robinson, L. C., & Holton, G. (2012). Internal classification of the Alor-Pantar language family using computational methods applied to the lexicon. *Language Dynamics and Change, 2*(2), 123–149.

Rogers, D. S., Feldman, M. W., & Ehrlich, P. R. (2009). Inferring population histories using cultural data. *Proceedings of the Royal Society B: Biological Sciences, 276,* 3835–3843.

Ross, R. M., & Atkinson, Q. D. (2016). Folktale transmission in the Arctic provides evidence for high bandwidth social learning among hunter–gatherer groups. *Evolution and Human Behavior, 37*(1), 47–53.

Ross, R. M., Greenhill, S. J., & Atkinson, Q. D. (2013). Population structure and cultural geography of a folktale in Europe. *Proceedings of the Royal Society B: Biological Sciences, 280*(1756), 20123065.

Runciman, W. (2009). *The theory of cultural and social selection.* Cambridge, UK: Cambridge University Press.

Schillinger, K., Mesoudi, A., & Lycett, S. J. (2016). Copying error, evolution, and phylogenetic signal in artifactual traditions: An experimental approach using "model artifacts." *Journal of Archaeological Science, 70,* 23–34.

Shennan, S. J., Crema, E. R., & Kerig, T. (2015). Isolation-by-distance, homophily, and "core" vs. "package" cultural evolution models in Neolithic Europe. *Evolution and Human Behavior, 36,* 103–109.

Sicoli, M. A., & Holton, G. (2014). Linguistic phylogenies support back-migration from Beringia to Asia. *PLoS One, 9*(3), e91722.

Sperber, D. (1996). *Explaining culture: A naturalistic approach.* Oxford, UK: Blackwell.

Tehrani, J. (2013). The phylogeny of Little Red Riding Hood. *PLoS One, 8,* 1–11.

Tehrani, J., & Collard, M. (2002). Investigating cultural evolution through a phylogenetic analysis of Turkmen textiles. *Journal of Anthropological Archaeology, 21,* 443–463.

Turner, J. H., & Maryanski, A. (2008). *On the origin of societies by natural selection.* Boulder, CO: Paradigm.

Valverde, S., & Solé, R. V. (2015). Punctuated equilibrium in the large-scale evolution of programming languages. *Journal of the Royal Society Interface, 12*(107), 20150249.

Walker, R. S., & Ribeiro, L. A. (2011). Bayesian phylogeography of the Arawak expansion in lowland South America. *Proceedings of the Royal Society B: Biological Sciences, 278*(1718), 2562–2567.

Walker, R. S., Wichmann, S., Mailund, T., & Atkisson, C. J. (2012). Cultural phylogenetics of the Tupi language family in lowland south America. *PLoS One, 7,* 1–9.

Watts, J., Greenhill, S. J., Atkinson, Q. D., Currie, T. E., Bulbulia, J., & Gray, R. D. (2015). Broad supernatural punishment but not moralizing high gods precede the evolution of political complexity in Austronesia. *Proceedings of the. Royal Society B: Biological Sciences, 282*(1804), 20142556.

Watts, J., Sheehan, O., Atkinson, Q. D., Bulbulia, J., & Gray, R. D. (2016). Ritual human sacrifice promoted and sustained the evolution of stratified societies. *Nature, 532,* 228–231.

Wichmann, S., Walker, R., Rama, T., & Holman, E. W. (2011). Correlates of reticulation in linguistic phylogenies. *Language Dynamics and Change, 1*(2), 205–240.

Wikipedia. (2016). *Outline of evolution; Taxonomy, systematics and phylogeny; List of phylogenetics software.* Retrieved from http://en.wikipedia.org

Yong, E. (2013). Dynasty: Bob Paine fathered an idea—and an academic family—that changed ecology. *Nature, 493,* 286–289.

Zhou, K., & Bowern, C. (2015). Quantifying uncertainty in the phylogenetics of Australian numeral systems. *Proceedings of the Royal Society B: Biological Sciences, 282,* 1278–1283.

PART VI

CONCLUSION

CHAPTER 29

WHY SOCIOLOGY SHOULD INCORPORATE BIOLOGY

ROSEMARY L. HOPCROFT

In this volume, we have seen the variety of ways that scholars have used theory and methods from biology and evolutionary biology to illuminate sociological issues. A number of the chapters show how theory from evolutionary biology complements sociological theories by providing ultimate reasons for why sociological phenomena such as social solidarity, racial and ethnic behavior, family behavior, or religious behavior occur as they do. Whereas traditional sociological theories give the "what" and "how" of sociological phenomena and help us understand the myriad social and material factors influencing the social facts we see, evolutionary theories give the "why"— Why is it that those factors have the effects they do? Evolutionary theories thus do not compete with sociological theories, in the sense that if the former is correct, the latter must be incorrect. Instead, many sociological theories are entirely compatible with theory from evolutionary biology. Indeed, in many respects they have to be because there is no alternative to the fact that all life, including humans, evolved. If our sociological theories are not compatible with what has been learned about our evolutionary history and evolved human nature, then such theories need to be discarded.

Other chapters in this volume demonstrate how using the methods of biology—for example, methods for finding genetic correlates of social behaviors or the proportion of the variation in a social behavior that can be attributed to genetic factors—can further illuminate social processes of interest to sociologists, such as social mobility, educational achievement, crime, and delinquency. Some of the chapters show the long-term biochemical effects of stress and dominance competitions on individuals and suggest that these effects should be incorporated into sociological models of status competition, poverty, and mental illness in order to fully explain these phenomena.

This work is just beginning in sociology, but there are many reasons why sociologists should be doing more of it. First, although focusing on proximate causes of sociological issues in the environment and society may have served sociologists well in the past, not incorporating biological factors appears increasingly awkward as evidence accumulates

that personality, attitudes, intelligence, and many social behaviors have a genetic component (see Part III). This evidence is discussed in the mainstream media, so many people in the general public are aware of it. People are also very much aware of the roles of
biochemicals such as steroids and serotonin reuptake inhibitors (found in many anti-
depressants) in social behavior. Hence, political support for research programs that do
not take these factors into account is likely to waiver in the future, and sociologists who
insist on strict environmental determinism—whether it be the environment in the family, schools, or society as a whole—in explaining social phenomena are likely not to be
taken seriously.

Furthermore, although genes and biology play a role in social behavior, they are
not destiny for anyone, as McDermott and Hatemi illustrate so well in Chapter 12. It
is incumbent on sociologists to show how genes interact with environments to produce outcomes. The role of social and contextual factors in behavior must continue to
be studied by sociologists. Sociologists are best aware of the nature of these social and
contextual factors, and they have large reservoirs of empirical research on the family,
education, crime and delinquency, race and ethnicity, stratification and inequality, and
so forth to draw on that scholars in other disciplines often lack.

As many sociologists have long insisted, the importance of social context and environment is central to understanding all sorts of behavior, even behavior that is not
explicitly sociological. Think of the phenomena of handedness. Most people understand that handedness (the propensity to use one hand or the other) is in part a biological phenomenon or an innate tendency. Most people have an innate tendency to
favor their right hand, but some, for genetic and other reasons, have a tendency to favor
their left hand. This does not necessarily mean that "natural" left-handers grow up to
use their left hand for behaviors such as writing. Not so long ago, a whole generation
of natural left-handers were forced in schools to learn to write with their right hand, so
they became right-handed writers, although they would often continue to use their left
hand for other activities. The reasons for such policies were sociological and ideological, including prevailing ideas that left-handedness was undesirable and could easily be
done away with by training. These attitudes were not just a quirk of Western societies in
the early 20th century; in many societies, use of the left hand is frowned upon. The point
is that any behavior, social or otherwise, including handedness, is a result of this interaction between the environment, including the social environment, and the biological
potentials of the individual. Sociologists are best placed to study that interaction and are
more informed about the social environment compared to other scholars; as such, sociologists are more necessary than ever.

As illustrated by some of the chapters in this volume, evolutionary theory also can
help us understand how some cultural and contextual factors are themselves likely
shaped by evolved predispositions. Cultures that promote the promulgation of laws that
deprive minorities of rights and race discrimination are likely influenced by evolved
factors predisposing individuals to favor the in-group (see essays by Salter, Rauch, and
Hopcroft in Chapters 25 and 26). Similar arguments can be made about patriarchal cultures and unconscious gender biases (Hopcroft, 2009, 2016). In this case, it is likely that

evolved factors predispose men to sexual jealousy and preferences for the control of female sexuality. These in turn promote the formation of informal and formal societal practices that control and constrain the behavior of women.

Sociology has had moral concerns since its inception as an independent discipline as the science of human social behavior, and these should never be dismissed. The need to treat all people with respect and dignity, and concerns regarding the moral aspects of poverty and inequality, should not be taken lightly. There were mistakes made in early biological and medical research because they ignored basic human morality—the Tuskegee study of syphilis springs to mind. Obviously, such horrors are to be avoided at all costs. As I have argued elsewhere, the use of evolutionary theory in sociology is entirely consistent with most religious and secular moral codes because evolutionary theory implies a universal, evolved, human actor, albeit with minor differences from individual to individual (Hopcroft, 2012). Ultimately, the cause of morality is best served by being as accurate and truthful as possible in our analyses of social behavior.

Last, sociology has an abiding interest in social problems such as ethnic and racial discrimination, gender discrimination, crime, poverty, and mental illness. Our advice for solving those problems can only be as good as our explanations of them. If our explanations overlook crucial factors responsible for a phenomenon, and we overlook dealing with those factors in our proposed solutions to ameliorate the problem, then those solutions will likely prove inadequate. For example, the knowledge that male predispositions promote the creation of social rules that guarantee male paternity certainty is important to understanding patriarchal societies and cultural practices that discriminate against women and why they commonly occur across human societies. Building on this knowledge can help sociologists and others propose more effective ways of dealing with these problems.

Although the chapters in this volume reveal that the area holds much promise for sociology, they also show that like all healthy scholarly areas, it has many areas of debate. Why humans are more social than most primates, particularly compared to their closest relatives the apes, is a long-standing area of debate within evolutionary biology and is addressed by Turner and Maryanski in Chapters 5 and 6.

Another area of debate within evolutionary biology concerns the importance of selection at the group versus the individual level. Although for many years the consensus was that group selection was a relatively unimportant process, if it occurred at all, recent scholarship has challenged this view, as reflected in essays by Turner, Maryanski, Crippen, and Salter in Chapters 5, 6, 20, and 25.

Debates about whether techniques from evolutionary biology, developed to model the process of biological evolution, can be successfully used to model sociocultural evolution are also featured in this volume (see essays by Blute, Sanderson, and Crippen in Chapters 20, 27, and 28). In what sense is the process of sociocultural evolution analogous to biological evolution? How different or how similar are changes in gene frequencies compared to changes in cultural ideas?

Although all evolutionists agree with the evolutionary basis of human behavior, there is another debate on the extent to which evolved behaviors are adaptive in contemporary environments. Some of the chapters in this volume point to the extent to which current behaviors such as ethnic or religious behavior, educational and religious homogamy, and the pursuit of status by men, and even racial discrimination, are currently adaptive for individuals in terms of maximizing relative gene frequencies in subsequent generations (see essays by Fieder, Huber, Salter, Rauch, and Hopcroft in Chapters 22, 25, and 26).

Debates surrounding particular issues in evolutionary biology are not a reason for sociology to avoid using biology's repository of theory and method for its own uses. Some points are sufficiently well accepted for sociology to use. For example, although the precise role of biology and environment is always difficult to disentangle because of the complex interaction effects between the two, the fact that there is an interaction is indisputable, and sociologists will do well do incorporate that understanding into their scholarship.

A common theme in some of the chapters presented here is pessimism about the future of evolutionary thinking in sociology (e.g., see essays by Crippen and Sanderson in Chapters 20 and 27). It is true that a distaste for any use of ideas or methods from biology, as described by Machalek and Marshall in Chapters 2 and 3, has been dominant among sociologists. However, there is reason to believe that this will change and, in fact, is already changing. This book is proof that sociology as a discipline has changed, because 30 years ago this book would not have been written. The fact that it has been written, and was able to garner so many high-quality essays from sociologists (most of whom are employed by sociology departments), is a reason for optimism.

From my perspective, it is an exciting time in sociology, perhaps more so than in any other science. Sociology has long been dominated by descriptive studies of social phenomenon, and theory in sociology has been characterized by myriad small theories of limited scope (see essays by Lockyer, Hatemi, Walsh, and Jorgensen in Chapters 14 and 24). Incorporation of method and theory from biology can change that. As Wilson (1975) suggested more than 30 years ago, theory from evolutionary biology has the potential to unify much sociological theory and become the central paradigm of sociology, much as it has unified biology, and to unify all the disparate threads of the current discipline of sociology into a fully fledged science. If that happens, the prospects for sociology are tremendous.

References

Hopcroft, Rosemary L. 2009. "Gender Inequality in Interaction: An Evolutionary Account." *Social Forces* 87, 4: 1845–1872.

Hopcroft, Rosemary L. 2012. "Evolution, Biology and Society." In *The Handbook of Sociology and Human Rights*, edited by David L. Brunsma, Keri E. Iyall Smith and Brian Gran. Paradigm University Press.

Hopcroft, Rosemary L. 2016. *Evolution and Gender: Why It Matters for Contemporary Life.* New York, NY: Routledge.

Wilson, Edward O. 1975. *Sociobiology: The New Synthesis.* Cambridge, MA: Belknap Press of Harvard University Press.

INDEX

Page references for figures are indicated by *f*, for tables by *t*, and for boxes by *b*.